Macmillan
Encyclopedia of
Architects

Editorial board

Macmillan
Encyclopedia of

Architects

ADOLF K. PLACZEK, *editor in chief*

Volume 1

THE FREE PRESS

a division of Macmillan Publishing Co., Inc.
New York

COLLIER MACMILLAN PUBLISHERS
LONDON

THE FREE PRESS
A Division of Macmillan Publishing Co., Inc.
866 Third Avenue, New York, N. Y. 10022

Collier Macmillan Canada, Inc.

Library of Congress Catalog Card Number: 82-17256

Printed in the United States of America

printing number

2 3 4 5 6 7 8 9 10

Library of Congress Cataloging in Publication Data
Main entry under title:

Macmillan encyclopedia of architects.

    Includes bibliographies and indexes.
    1. Architects—Biography.   I. Placzek, Adolf K.
II. Title: Encyclopedia of architects.
NA40.M25   1982   720′.92′2 [B]   82-17256
ISBN 0-02-925000-5 (set)

Contents

The editors would like to thank the following individuals, from whose advice they benefited during the preparation of the *Macmillan Encyclopedia of Architects*.

List of Advisers

Nicholas Adams
Lehigh University

Anders Åman
*Konstvetenskapliga Institutionen
(Uppsala, Sweden)*

Wayne Andrews
Wayne State University

Renate Banik-Schweitzer
Vienna

Juan Bassegoda Nonell
*Institut d'Investigacio d'Historia de
l'Arquitectura i Restauracio de
Monuments (Barcelona, Spain)*

Fredric Bedoire
Enskede, Sweden

Barry Bergdoll
Columbia University

Catherine W. Bishir
*Architects and Builders in North
Carolina (Raleigh)*

Milka T. Bliznakov
*Virginia Polytechnic Institute and State
University*

B. M. Boyle
Arizona State University

Mosette Glaser Broderick
New York University

Jay Chewning
University of Massachusetts

David Chipman
Columbia University

Giorgio Ciucci
*Istituto Universitario de Architettura
(Venice, Italy)*

Michael R. Corbett
*Charles Hall Page and Associates,
Incorporated (San Francisco)*

Howard Crane
Ohio State University

Dora P. Crouch
*Art and Architecture Thesaurus (Troy,
New York)*

Maurice Culot
*Archives d'Architecture Moderne
(Brussels)*

Walter B. Denny
University of Massachusetts

Marc Dilet
Chicago

Dennis Doordan
San Francisco

Charling C. Fagan
Columbia University

Wilma Fairbank
Cambridge, Massachusetts

Carlos Flores Lopez
Madrid

Margaret Henderson Floyd
Tufts University

Kenneth Frampton
*Institute for Architecture and Urban
Studies (New York)*

Dennis Steadman Francis
New York City

Suzanne Frank
New York City

Diane Ghirardo
Stanford University

Andor Gomme
University of Keele

Elizabeth D. Harris
Rio de Janeiro, Brazil

John Harris
*Royal Institute of British Architects
    (London)*

Robert G. Hill
*Biographical Dictionary of
    Architects in Canada: 1800–1950
    (Toronto)*

Donald Leslie Johnson
*Flinders University of South
    Australia*

Lech Kłosiewicz
Warsaw

Bunji Kobayashi
Nihon University

Phyllis Lambert
*Canadian Centre for Architecture
    (Montreal)*

Barbara Miller Lane
Bryn Mawr College

Portia Legget
*Canadian Centre for Architecture
    (Montreal)*

Donald J. Lehman
Philadelphia

Douglas Lewis
*National Gallery of Art (Washington,
    D.C.)*

William L. MacDonald
Northampton, Massachusetts

David Mackay
Barcelona, Spain

Constantin Marin Marinescu
Rego Park, New York

John McAslan
London

R. D. Middleton
University of Cambridge

Herbert Mitchell
Columbia University

Stanislaus von Moos
Technische Hogeschool Delft

Victoria Newhouse
*Architectural History Foundation (New
    York City)*

Manfredi Nicoletti
Rome

James F. O'Gorman
Wellesley College

Christian F. Otto
Cornell University

Jo Anne Paschall
Atlanta College of Art

Chiara Passanti
Turin, Italy

Francesco Passanti
Paris

Charles E. Peterson
*Carpenters Company of the City and
    County of Philadelphia*

Elisabeth Walton Potter
*Oregon State Office of Historic
    Preservation (Salem)*

Ellie Reichlin
*Society for the Preservation of New
    England Antiquities (Boston)*

Douglas Richardson
University of Toronto

Marion Dean Ross
University of Oregon

Andrew Saint
London

Dennis Sharp
Architectural Association (London)

Earle G. Shettleworth, Jr.
*Maine Historical Preservation Commission
    (Augusta)*

Vladimír Šlapeta
Prague

Gavin Stamp
London

Gwen W. Steege
Williamstown, Massachusetts

Dorothy Stroud
*Sir John Soane's Museum
    (London)*

David T. Van Zanten
Northwestern University

H. H. Waechter
Creswell, Oregon

Marina Waisman
Córdoba, Argentina

David M. Walker
Edinburgh

J. Scott Weaver
Columbia University

Ron Wiedenhoeft
Colorado School of Mines

Wim de Wit
*Nederlands Documentatie-
    centrum voor de Bouwkunst
    (Amsterdam)*

Christine Yelavich
New York City

Charles E. Smith, *Publisher*

Barbara A. Chernow, *Senior Project Editor*

Toni Ann Scaramuzzo, *Picture Editor and Senior Editorial Assistant*
Susan Davis, *Senior Editorial Assistant*
Edward J. Mason, *Senior Editorial Assistant*

COPY DEPARTMENT

Elly Dickason, *Senior Editor*
Eugene K. Waering, *Senior Proofreader*
Kathleen Babkow, *Proofreader*
Dana Biberman, *Proofreader*
Antoinette M. Boone, *Editorial Assistant*
Machanda Gary Payton, *Editorial Assistant*

BIBLIOGRAPHY DEPARTMENT

Richard Cleary, *Senior Bibliographer*
Penny Jones, *Senior Bibliographer*
Steven McLeod Bedford
Sally Bender
Barry Bergdoll
Richard Berman
Gary Bertchune
David Boyle
Susan Copeland
Juanita M. Ellias
Barry Slinker
Paula Spilner

INDEXING DEPARTMENT

Barbara Lea, *Senior Indexer*
Judith E. Meighan, *Senior Indexer*
Joyce Alaya
Helen De Mott
Arthur I. Ellenbogen
Sherryl Ann Feinstein
Joseph Garvey
Marjorie B. Garvey
Penny Jones
Robert Karwowski
Erik Lauer
Marjorie Mahle
Dennis Southers

Morton I. Rosenberg, *Production Manager*

Linda Biondo, *Assistant Picture Editor*

Frederic J. Grevin, *Photographer, Rare Books and Prints*

Joan Greenfield, *Designer*

Editorial and Production Staff

ix

The very root of the word architecture—*archi,* the first or principal and *techne,* art or craft— connotes its early and central place among man's civilizing activities. After *homo faber*—man the toolmaker—lost his place in the animal garden of Eden and began his ascent to civilization, he built himself a shelter; and indeed, Adam's fabled hut recurs in literature and inconography. Unfortunately, on Adam the architect no data has been transmitted, and he therefore must remain unrecorded in the *Macmillan Encyclopedia of Architects,* much as we would have liked to include him in this, the most comprehensive assemblage of architectural biography ever attempted. From Adam's unrecorded shelter to the enormous skyscrapers of our cities runs the story of men and women in the great act of designing and building, often leading heroic lives, often having their precious works interrupted by war, destroyed by fire, ruined by economic disaster, or unrealized because of society's or a client's incomprehension. Still, together, they created the settings for man on earth, settings of the most varied forms and structures, with ever new materials and techniques, encompassing the whole range of human purpose: settings in which to dwell, to meet, to worship, to represent, to rejoice, to die, and in which to be buried. Since Adam's hut no civilized human being has been unaffected by architecture in its many forms— minimal and glorious, confining and enhancing, solemn and workaday, good and bad, but always the framework for settled existence. Except for the anonymous labor of agriculture, no work of man has shaped the face of the planet more than has architecture. The men and women who did the shaping, their lives, their personalities, their social and intellectual contexts, their traditions and innovations, their ideas, their styles and techniques, and above all the structures they created make up this encyclopedia. There are a great many architects to record: the encyclopedia includes more than twenty-four hundred spanning forty-six centuries. Some may have been overlooked; many more were obliterated by time or history's destructive hand. We could not rescue from oblivion all the names undeservedly forgotten. This is particularly true of the Middle Ages when the individual architect rarely stood out in sharp profile from the vast collective effort that built the incomparable cathedrals, however clearly individual genius seems imprinted on their towers and naves. The names of many architects of the ancient world have also been lost, not by reason of humble anonymity, as with the Gothic builders, but because of the collapse of Roman civilization which also wiped out so much of Greek civilization. Every effort has been made to recover as many of these ancient builders as possible. In some instances, a single architect was given extensive coverage not only on the strength of his own greatness but also as the protagonist of a time, place, and architecture that should be fully represented but

Foreword

lacked other major names; the long article on the Egyptian master builder Imhotep is the main example. Many more Greek than Egyptian names have survived, but even here long articles, such as the one on Iktinos, introduce the reader not only to the genius of this one architect but also to the glories and problems involved in building the paradigmatic Parthenon. We regret that particularly for China, Japan, and India such representative articles are lacking; no historic, aesthetic, or regional value judgment is implied. The veil of anonymity that hangs over many of the greatest architects of the ancient East is denser even than that enshrouding the master builders of the ancient and medieval West.

With the advent of the Renaissance, the "name-architect" came into his own in the West, as indeed did the "name-artist." The proliferation of entries in the encyclopedia from the fifteenth to the twentieth century vividly reflects the rise of individualism in European society. It also reflects the vast increase of domestic, public, and industrial architecture as compared with religious architecture and the enormous diversity of building types and building needs faced by the new name-architect. In this mighty development not everybody who built a house or signed the drawings for it can be called an architect, and even some of those who were may have been eminently forgettable. No wonder the encyclopedia's editorial board faced countless dilemmas as to whom to include and whom to leave out. Wherever possible we came down in favor of inclusion; the vernacular builder, the modest but masterly craftsman, the fantastic maverick, the accomplished amateur, and most importantly, the woman architect whose contribution has frequently been suppressed or concealed. There are omissions, some inadvertent, some for lack of adequate information, some by circumstance. No listing can ever be complete. But for all that, a greater and more varied array of architectural biographies has never been published.

The question of the cut-off date for contemporary architects was given the most careful consideration. Clearly, there had to be one, and it had to be applied across the board, impartially, without singling out some already prominent young architects. The editorial board therefore decided to include in the encyclopedia only those architects who were born by December 31, 1930. Unlike so many of the great poets and musicians, great architects are a peculiarly long-lived lot. They are tough. Dealing with material, structure, and society's demands, they have always had to be. Among the encyclopedia's twenty most outstanding architects, only two—Raphael and H. H. Richardson—died before they were fifty, and several did some of their finest work after they were seventy. Thus, for the young architects not included in the encyclopedia, a long and successful future may be anticipated and with it the assured inclusion in any new edition.

The articles range from fifty to ten thousand words.

Hard decisions as to the length of individual entries had to be made, and some will undoubtedly be found arguable. The historic importance of the architect, the availability of information, the nature and quality of the surviving buildings, the influence exerted—all these and many other considerations went into the allotments. The long articles constitute an unusual and valuable feature of the encyclopedia, representing some of the most eminent and detailed scholarship. Almost the entire international community of scholars—the Germans used to call it the *Gelehrtenrepublik*—has contributed to these major pieces. Among these major entries there are not only those on architects whose very names are household words at least in the Western world—Andrea Palladio, Michelangelo, Christopher Wren, Frank Lloyd Wright—but also those who were of decisive importance within their own context, as, for instance, the great Ottoman architect Sinan, heretofore so frequently omitted from architectural dictionaries, or Alexander Jackson Davis, prominent in the American development. And then there were those who, like Imhotep, almost alone represent an entire country or civilization.

What is an architect and what is expected of him? An architect, according to the Oxford English Dictionary, is "a skilled professor of the art of building, whose business it is to prepare the plans of edifices, and exercise a general superintendence over the course of their erection." This definition could already have been used by the Greeks. The Roman Vitruvius, in the first century A.D., demands from an architect that his work combine firmness (a building must not collapse!), beauty, and utility. It is always the combination of the aesthetic and the practical that distinguishes the architect. He not only designs but also builds. Yet, again and again, we have to widen our view of architecture. There is so much that goes into it: who would want to exclude the architectural visionaries, the utopians, the dreamers from among the great throng of actual builders gathered together in the following pages? Without their fantasies of form and their visions of utopia, Claude Nicolas Ledoux and Etienne Louis Boullée would get a few lines at best and Antonio Sant'Elia might be missing entirely. Architects, besides being tough are also frequently very articulate: through the centuries writing by architects has played a great role in what was eventually built. Nobody knows exactly what the ancient Greeks wrote on architecture since it was all lost; but according to Vitruvius they did write a great deal. And from then on architects like Sebastiano Serlio, Andrea Palladio, Gottfried Semper, Frank Lloyd Wright, Le Corbusier, and now Robert Venturi seemed eager to explain what they were doing and what ought to be done, evidently more so than musicians, painters or sculptors. Why? Perhaps because in architecture the theoretical and the practical are so interwoven; perhaps because so many of them were moved by the belief that perfect architecture could actually perfect human society. The writer–architect or the architect–writer is thus included in this encyclopedia even when he was not a "practicing" architect (Vitruvius, the first architectural writer whose books have survived, was; John Ruskin, for instance, was not).

As for the engineers, as designers of great structures they are certainly included—Gustave Eiffel being almost a household word. Bridge builders have always been part of the architectural scene, Bartolomeo Ammannati of the Ponte Santa Trinità in Florence and the Roeblings of the Brooklyn Bridge being two examples. Speaking of the architectural scene, what would that scene be without landscape architects, the great "Capability" Brown, for instance? Or America's Frederick Law Olmsted? And finally, the town planners who helped to change the fabric of our cities: they too are included (although, in this area, those whose influence was only through their writings are not included). The demarkation lines are thus drawn; but they cannot be drawn sharply because architecture reaches into and recruits its masters from many areas.

For so monumental an undertaking as this encyclopedia, thanks go to many people: to the distinguished members of the editorial board—Professors George R. Collins, Oleg Grabar, H. R. Hitchcock, Henry A. Millon, William H. Pierson, Jr., Damie Stillman, and Whitney S. Stoddard—who developed and supervised the project as a whole and in their respective areas; to the consultants from many countries who were of the most substantial help; and to the contributors of the great articles as well as to those who contributed the many hundreds of smaller entries which, having to be so condensed, were often most difficult to write. Thanks go also to the able support staff—editors, proofreaders, bibliographers, translators, and photographers. A particular note of thanks must go to Charles E. Smith, vice president of Macmillan Publishing Company, Inc., who first suggested the idea of the encyclopedia and gave the work his full personal support; to the fine project staff who labored devotedly for three years; and—finally—thanks to Barbara A. Chernow, the senior project editor, who was the focus, catalyst, organizer, and perfector of this exhaustive and exhausting enterprise. It will, I hope, prove not only an invaluable reference and research tool but also a source of enjoyment of the master art of architecture and of a deepened appreciation of its creators.

Adolf K. Placzek

Introduction

The *Macmillan Encyclopedia of Architects* is a completely new reference work that presents the history of civilization through the lives of its designers and builders. Begun in 1979, the encyclopedia includes more than twenty-four hundred biographies of architects from ancient times to the present and from all geographical regions.

For the purposes of the encyclopedia, architecture was viewed in its broadcast context—as a social art that reflects the needs of society; the influence of scientific innovation; the spirit, style, and aspirations of each historical era; and the individual creativity of each architect. As such, the biographies are more than life histories. Rather, they serve as settings for discussions of how each architect's artistic, technical, and historical perspectives contributed to the development of his or her ideas and approach to design, and the extent to which each architect furthered existing styles or developed new techniques.

Invariably, these ambitious goals had to be adapted to the special problems presented by architects about whom little is known, either because of the lack of adequate records or the destruction of executed plans. Since one of the main goals was to make the encyclopedia as comprehensive as possible, the editors decided to include several hundred briefer biographies that would provide whatever limited information was available on these architects. The effect is to rescue many architects from obscurity and to gather in one work information from scattered and often inaccessible sources.

SELECTION OF ARCHITECTS

In an encyclopedia, the selection of the subjects for inclusion is the most difficult phase of the work. The editors of the *Macmillan Encyclopedia of Architects* had to balance their own preferences, knowledge of the material, and judgment concerning the relative importance of each architect with the realities of time and space as well as the strong suggestions offered by regional advisers and local architectural historians for inclusive representation of their own areas.

When the editorial board reviewed the first draft of a table of contents, which had been compiled from established reference books and indexes to monograph series, the need for certain policy decisions became apparent. The first and major decision was the imposition of an age criterion—to be included an architect had to be born by December 31, 1930, or be deceased. Without this rule, the encyclopedia would have become a roster of contemporary architects and limitations of space would have forced the exclusion of many lesser known architects whose biographies are among the most useful feature of the work. Simultaneously, the board enlarged the scope of the encyclopedia to include engineers, bridge builders, landscape architects, town planners, a few patrons, and a handful of writers, if their contributions were so influential as to have changed the face of the human environment. At the request of the editors, specialized advisers throughout the world reviewed the new table of contents, suggesting additions and deletions.

In the final list, architects were divided into five categories: those whose work was of major importance to their own and future generations, those who developed or significantly expanded a particular style, those whose work left a mark on the thought of their generations or the appearances of specific localities, those about whom little is known but whose extant body of work is significant, and those whose work represents continuing developments and trends. All architects in the first four categories are included in the encyclopedia. In the last category, the encyclopedia includes a representative selection of architects, who provide an overview of each generation's work throughout the world. In some cases other choices might have served the purpose equally well.

On the basis of these five categories, the editors assigned lengths ranging from fifty words to ten thousand words to each biography. An even more subjective task than the selection of the architects themselves, the allotments were based on the editorial board's knowledge of each architect's significance, the availability of research materials, the condition of extant works, and an attempt fairly to represent each historical period and geographical region. Frequently, adjustments in length were made as the contributor writing a particular biography argued convincingly for additional space or confessed, infrequently, that fewer words would suffice.

SELECTION OF CONTRIBUTORS

The selection of contributors was based on the invited author's knowledge of the architect's work and reputation for scholarship, and on an effort to recruit scholars with diverse geographical and institutional affiliations. The encyclopedia has more than six hundred contributors from twenty-six countries, and the participants include almost the entire community of scholars from the most widely recognized to the emerging generation of researchers.

The editors owe a special debt to all who participated; the encyclopedia is, after all, their creation. But, a special note is due to those who submitted their articles on schedule and to those who prepared essential biographies when the original contributor failed to deliver.

EDITORIAL PROCEDURE

All of the biographies in the encyclopedia are original and are signed. Contributors received guidelines for the preparation of the manuscript and were cooperative in conforming to the stylistic policies established by the editors and in adhering to the strictly enforced word limits. The editors' aim was a writing style sophisticated enough for a professional audience, yet comprehensible to the general reader. Although the staff imposed a consistent style on all articles, contributors were allowed a certain flexibility in organization and tone. The former creates a usable, cohesive work; the latter gives its articles a distinctive character that will enable some of the longer biographies to stand as classic essays.

Each article was reviewed for clarity, content, and style by the editor in chief, the appropriate member of the editorial board or an area adviser, the senior project editor, and the copy editor before being returned to the contributor for final reading. The final manuscript was read again by a member of the editorial staff and by one of the proofreaders.

The biographies in the encyclopedia are presented in alphabetical sequence, with Mac and Mc treated separately. Where alternative spellings or listings of architect's names are possible, those alternatives are given with a cross-reference to the name as listed in the encyclopedia. The first line in the text of each biography gives the architect's full name along with dates of birth and death or years or century of active work. If an architect mentioned in the text of an article has his or her own biography in the encyclopedia, the name appears in capital and small capital letters.

LISTS OF WORKS

All articles include a selective list of works, except for briefer biographies of architects whose known body of work is small enough to have been mentioned in the text. The lists, prepared by the contributors, include only works actually built, although plans and unexecuted structures are often discussed in the texts.

Each entry gives the most specific dates available for the design and construction of the work, the name of the structure, and the location. The dates given indicate only the years the architect actually worked on a structure. If it was completed with other architects, after the architect's death, or if the architect built only part of the work, that information is provided in a parenthetical note following the name of the structure. An asterisk before the date indicates a work that is no longer extant and the symbol (A) indicates an attributed work. Finally, if works listed in succession are located in the same place, the works are separated by a semicolon instead of the usual period and the location is given only once at the end of the sequence. Although the name of the country generally forms part of the location, familiarly known cities and capitals of countries stand without further identification.

BIBLIOGRAPHIES

The most useful tools in reference works are often the bibliographies, which refer the interested reader to additional sources for further study. The bibliographies in the encyclopedia are selective and were prepared by the contributors. All articles have bibliographies except for those where the only printed source is one of the publications listed in the encyclopedia's general bibliography. This procedure avoids the repetition of the same readily available standard reference works in the bibliographies of several hundred articles.

A team of bibliographers verified all the bibliographies. Each reference includes the first date of publication and full publishing information. If a later or reprint edition is available, the original date of publication is followed by the most recent, with publishing information given only for the latter. This preserves the reader's historical perspective while supplying the data necessary to locate the newer and probably more accessible edition.

PICTURES

The encyclopedia has approximately fifteen hundred pictures, drawings, engravings, and woodcuts of buildings, plans, models, and elevations. Depending on the length of each biography, the significance of specific structures in the history of architecture, and the availability of pictures, contributors recommended specific illustrations to accompany their articles. Although the picture research staff tried to follow these recommendations, adjustments were made to insure inclusion of all buildings considered essential for the general reader, to overcome the failure of certain archives to respond to requests for illustrations or to provide necessary reprint rights, and to replace illustrations that were photographically but not architecturally acceptable. The editors made special arrangements with private photographic archives* and photographers, and employed a photographer to take pictures of works in rare books and reprints that were not available elsewhere. The editors wish to thank all contributors who supplied their own prints for use in the encyclopedia. Finally, some sources proved more cooperative than others and our choices reflect that reality.

GLOSSARY

As work on the encyclopedia progressed, the editors agreed that a glossary would enhance the reader's understanding of the material presented. At the same time, they judged the encyclopedia an inappropriate place for a complete glossary of architectural terms. Thus, the glossary includes definitions of architectural styles and elements that are not adequately explained in the texts of the biographies in which they appear. The glossary does not include military, artistic, and historical terms; academies; prizes; or most common building materials. When necessary, entries in the glossary have cross-references to other relevant definitions.

INDEXES

The encyclopedia has two computer-generated indexes—one of names of individuals and one of architectural works. Names printed in capital and small capital letters in the first index are subjects of biographies in the encyclopedia. To assist less experienced researchers, who might not always be familiar with the location of an architectural work, the index of works is alphabetized by the names of structures.

ACKNOWLEDGMENTS

The *Macmillan Encyclopedia of Architects,* first suggested by Jeremiah Kaplan, president of Macmillan Publishing Company, Inc., is the work of many individuals during the past three years. The support staff worked tirelessly and enthusiastically in organizing, editing, and illustrating the encyclopedia. A note of thanks is due to the members of the editorial board, who cooperated fully in developing and editing the biographies within an extremely demanding schedule, and to the area advisers, who sharpened our focus, insuring appropriate representation to all geographical regions. Above all, Adolf K. Placzek must be especially thanked for his patience, keen editorial eye, sense of diplomacy, and unflagging attention to every phase of the preparation of the encyclopedia.

Barbara A. Chernow

*Editorial Photocolor Archives (EPA) of New York, headed by Dr. Theodore Feder, was especially helpful in supplying photographs of the majority of Italian and French works which appear in these volumes. EPA made available the resources of its own archives as well as of its affiliate companies, Alinari of Italy and Giraudon of France, for this purpose.

List of Biographies

Directory of Contributors

Adams, Nicholas
Lehigh University
AGOSTINO DI DUCCIO; BENTLEY, JOHN FRANCIS; BINAGO, LORENZO; BOITO, CAMILLO; BREGNO, ANDREA; CATANEO, PIETRO; COLONNA, FRANCESCO; COZZARELLI, GIACOMO; IL CRONACA; FEDERIGHI, ANTONIO; FRIGMELICA, GIOVANNI; GHAMBARELLI FAMILY; GIULIO, ROMANO; GIOCONDO, GIOVANNI; GIORGIO DA SEBENICO; GRIMALDI, GIOVANNI FRANCESCO; LIPPI, ANNIBALE; MAIANO, GIULIANO DA; MANGONE FAMILY; NIGETTI, MATTEO; PELLI, CESAR; PICCHIATI, FRANCESCO ANTONIO; POGGI, GIUSEPPE; PONTELLI, BACCIO; POSI, PAOLO; PRIMATICCIO, FRANCESCO; ROBBIA, LUCA DELLA; RUSCONI, GIOVANNI ANTONIO; SPECCHI, ALESSANDRO; TEMANZA, TOMMASO; TRAMELLO, ALESSIO; VITONI, VENTURA; VITTORIA, ALESSANDRO

Albright, Priscilla
San Jose State University
ALGHISI, GALASSO; PALEARO FAMILY; PIERFRANCESCO DA VITERBO

Alexander, Robert L.
University of Iowa
GODEFROY, MAXIMILIAN; MILLS, ROBERT; PARRIS, ALEXANDER

Allan, Juliet E.
Department of the Environment (London)
FLITCROFT, HENRY

Allentuck, Marcia
Graduate Center, City University of New York
PRICE, UVEDALE

Allibone, Jill
London
BLORE, EDWARD; HARRIS, E. VINCENT; IVORY, THOMAS OF NORWICH; SAVAGE, JAMES; VULLIAMY, LEWIS; WHEELER, GERVASE; WOOD, SANCTON

Alofsin, Anthony
Columbia University
BOGNER, WALTER FRANCIS; COMEY, ARTHUR COLEMAN; (T)HE (A)RCHITECTS (C)OLLABORATIVE

Åman, Anders
Konstvetenskapliga Institutionen (Uppsala, Sweden)
KUMLIEN, AXEL, AND KUMLIEN, HJALMAR; ÖSTBERG, RAGNAR; SCHOLANDER, FREDRIK WILHELM; ZETTERVALL, HELGO

Amezqueta, Adolfo G.
Escuela de Arquitectura de Madrid
FERNÁNDEZ-SHAW E ITURRALDE, CASTRO; PALACIOS Y RAMILO, ANTONIO

Anderson, Stanford
Massachusetts Institute of Technology
BEHRENS, PETER

Andrews, Wayne
Wayne State University
HARRIS, HARWELL HAMILTON

Applewhite, E. J.
Washington, D.C.
FULLER, R. BUCKMINSTER

Arana, Mariano
Grupo de Estudios Urbanos (Montevideo)
PAYSSÉ REYES, MARIO

Archer, John
University of Minnesota
LUGAR, ROBERT; PLAW, JOHN; ROBINSON, P. F.

Armstrong, Frederick H.
University of Western Ontario
HAY, WILLIAM

Arthur, Kathleen Giles
James Madison University
MAITANI, LORENZO; ORCAGNA; PISANO FAMILY;
TALENTI FAMILY

Avgikos, Jan
Atlanta College of Art
BACON, HENRY; CAUDILL, ROWLETT, AND
SCOTT

Bacon, Mardges E.
Trinity College
FLAGG, ERNEST

Badawy, Alexander
University of California, Los Angeles
AMENHOTEP; IMHOTEP; SENMUT

Baker, Paul R.
New York University
HUNT, RICHARD MORRIS

Baldellou, Miguel Angel
Escuela de Arquitectura de Madrid
CORRALES, JOSÉ ANTONIO, AND VAZQUES
MOLEZUN, RAMON; FISAC SERNA, MIGUEL;
GARCIA DE PAREDES, JOSÉ MARIA; HIGUERAS
DIAZ, FERNANDO; SOTA MARTINEZ, ALEJANDRO
DE LA; VASQUEZ DE CASTRO, ANTONIO

Ball, Susan
University of Delaware
OZENFANT, AMÉDÉE

Ballantine, Anthony
Polytechnic of North London
TOWNSEND, CHARLES HARRISON

Ballon, Hilary
Massachusetts Institute of Technology

BACHELIER, NICOLAS; CHAMBIGES FAMILY;
DAMMARTIN FAMILY; GRAPPIN FAMILY;
PERRÉAL, JEAN

Banik-Schweitzer, Renate
Vienna
FERSTEL, HEINRICH VON; HASENAUER, CARL;
MAYREDER BROTHERS

Barnes, Carl F. Jr.
Oakland University
ERWIN VON STEINBACH; JEAN DES CHAMPS; JEAN
D'ORBAIS; LIBERGIER, HUGUES; MONTREUIL,
PIERRE DE, AND MONTREUIL, EUDES DE; ROBERT
DE LUZARCHES; WILLIAM OF SENS, AND WILLIAM
THE ENGLISHMAN

Bassegoda Nonell, Juan
*Institut d'Investigacio d'Historia de l'Arquitectura i
Restauracio de Monuments (Barcelona, Spain)*
BOHIGAS, MARTORELL, AND MACKAY; BONET
GARÍ, LUIS; FOLGUERA GRASSI, FRANCISCO;
FONTANA, GIOVANNI; FONT GUMA, JOSÉ;
FONTSERÈ MESTRÈS, JOSÉ; ILLESCAS MIROSA,
SIXTO; PUIG BOADA, ISIDRO; SOLER Y MARCH,
ALEJANDRO; ZUAZO UGALDE, SECUNDINO

Bassett, Sarah E.
Bryn Mawr College
CONTINI FAMILY; FALCONETTO, GIOVANNI
MARIA; GENGA, GIROLAMO; LURAGO, ROCCO;
MASCHERINO, OTTAVIANO

Bates, Ülkü U.
Hunter College, City University of New York
DAVUD, AGHA

Bayley, John
Newport, Rhode Island
ADLER, DAVID

Becherer, Richard
Auburn University
RUDOLPH, PAUL MARVIN

Beddall, Thomas G.
Cambridge, Massachusetts
DE LA TOUR D'AUVERGNE, BERNARD; ERICKSON,
ARTHUR; GUTBROD, ROLF; KALLMAN AND
McKINNELL; LEO, LUDWIG; LUMSDEN,
ANTHONY; MORGAN, WILLIAM; REVELL, VILJO;
SASAKI, HIDEO; WIENER, PAUL LESTER; WILSON,
COLIN ST. JOHN

Bedford, Steven McLeod
Columbia University
AYRES, LOUIS; BOSWORTH, WILLIAM WELLES;
BRUNNER, ARNOLD WILLIAM; COOK, WALTER;
DELANO AND ALDRICH; EGGERS AND HIGGINS;
FREEDLANDER, JOSEPH HENRY; HORNBOSTEL,
HENRY; LEWIS, SCHELL; SMITH, JAMES KELLUM;
SWARTWOUT, EGERTON; VAN ALEN, WILLIAM

Bedoire, Fredric
Enskede, Sweden
ADELCRANTZ FAMILY; AHLSÉN, ERIK, AND
AHLSÉN, TORE; CELSING, PETER; CLASON, ISAK
GUSTAF; DE LA VALLÉE, JEAN; ERSKINE, RALPH;
NYRÉN, CARL; PIPER, FREDRIK MAGNUS;
STENHAMMAR, ERNST; SUNDAHL, ESKIL;
WALLANDER, SVEN; WICKMAN, GUSTAF

Begley, W. E.
University of Iowa
'ABD AL-KARIM; AHMAD, USTAD; ᶜATA, ALLAH;
GHIYAS, MIRAK MIRZA

Benoit-Lévy, Georges (*fils*)
Paris
BENOIT-LÉVY, GEORGES

Bergdoll, Barry
Columbia University
BILLING, HERMANN; BÜRKLEIN, FRIEDRICH;
CHÂTEAUNEUF, ALEXIS DE; DEMMLER, GEORG
ADOLPH; DUTHOIT, EDMOND; GENTZ,
HEINRICH; GILLY, FRIEDRICH; HASE, CONRAD
WILHELM; HEIDELOFF, KARL ALEXANDER VON;
HESSE, LUDWIG FERDINAND; HITZIG,
FRIEDRICH; JUSSOW, HEINRICH CHRISTOPH;
KNOBLAUCH, EDUARD; LANGHANS, CARL
GOTTHARD; LANGHANS, KARL; LASSUS, JEAN-
BAPTISTE-ANTOINE; MOLLER, GEORG; PERSIUS,
LUDWIG; QUAGLIO FAMILY; RASCHDORFF,
JULIUS; SCHINKEL, KARL FRIEDRICH;
SCHUMACHER, FRITZ; SPEETH, PETER; STRACK,
JOHANN HEINRICH; STÜLER, FRIEDRICH AUGUST;
STÜRZENACKER, AUGUST; UNGEWITTER, G. G.;
VAUDREMER, EMILE; VOIT, AUGUST VON;
WIMMEL AND FORSMANN; ZIEBLAND, GEORG
FRIEDRICH; ZWIRNER, ERNST FRIEDRICH

Berger, Robert W.
Brookline, Massachusetts
D'ORBAY, FRANÇOIS; LE PAUTRE, ANTOINE; LE
VAU, FRANÇOIS; LE VAU, LOUIS

Betts, Richard J.
University of Illinois at Chicago Circle
FRANCESCO DI GIORGIO MARTINI

Billington, David P.
Princeton University
FREYSSINET, EUGÈNE; HENNEBIQUE, FRANÇOIS;
MAILLART, ROBERT

Binney, Marcus
Country Life (London)
TAYLOR, ROBERT

Birch, Eugenie L.
Hunter College, City University of New York
BAUER, CATHERINE K.; COIT, ELISABETH;
GOODMAN, PERCIVAL; MANNING, ELEANOR;

SMITH, CHLOETHIEL WOODARD; STEIN,
CLARENCE S.; WOOD, EDITH ELMER; WRIGHT,
HENRY; WURSTER, WILLIAM WILSON

Bishir, Catherine W.
Architects and Builders in North Carolina (Raleigh)
HAWKS, JOHN

Biver, Marie-Louise
Paris
PERCIER AND FONTAINE

Bizzarro, Tina Waldeier
Bryn Mawr College
ANTELAMI, BENEDETTO; BÄHR, GEORG;
BORELLA, CARLO; BRISEUX, CHARLES ETIENNE;
CALAMECH, ANDREA; CALDERARI, OTTONE;
CANONICA, LUIGI; GHIBERTI, LORENZO

Blair, Sheila S.
Fogg Museum, Harvard University
MUHAMMAD B. AL-HUSAYN AND HĀJJĪ B. AL-
HUSAYN AL-DĀMGHĀNĪ; SHUJĀᶜ B. QĀSIM AL-
IṢFĀHANĪ

Blake, Channing
Pawling, New York
CARRÈRE AND HASTINGS

Bland, John
McGill University
FOOTNER, WILLIAM; JONES, HUGH;
MACDONALD, ROBERT HENRY; PERRAULT
FAMILY

Blau, Eve M.
Wesleyan University
DEANE, THOMAS; DEANE AND WOODWARD;
O'SHEA BROTHERS; WOODWARD, BENJAMIN

Bletter, Rosemarie Haag
Columbia University
FISCHER, THEODOR; SCHEERBART, PAUL; SEMPER,
GOTTFRIED

Bliznakov, Milka T.
Virginia Polytechnic Institute and State University
BELKOVSKI AND DANCHOV; DAMIANOV, ANGEL;
FOMIN, IVAN A.; IOFAN, BORIS M.; LADOVSKY,
NIKOLAI A.; SHCHUKO, VLADIMIR A.; SHCHUSEV,
ALEKSEI V.; VASIL'OV AND TSOLOV; ZHOLTOVSKY,
IVAN V.

Bloom, Jonathan M.
Harvard University
AL-MUNĪF FAMILY

Bloomfield, Anne
San Francisco
CLEAVELAND, HENRY W.; CUMMINGS, G. P.;
FARQUHARSON, DAVID; LAVER, AUGUSTUS;
PORTOIS, PETER

Blumenthal, Arthur R.
Dartmouth College
PARIGI, GIULIO, AND PARIGI, ALFONSO

Blundell-Jones, Peter
University of Cambridge
SEGAL, WALTER

Bock, Thomas Alexander
Chicago
GÜNTHER, IGNAZ; GÜNTHER, MATTHÄUS;
LUCAE, RICHARD

Boekraad, Cees L.
Delft, Netherlands
HABRAKEN, N. J.; LOGHEM, J. B. VAN; TIJEN,
WILLEM VAN

Bohan, Peter J.
State University of New York, New Paltz
BURTON, DECIMUS; BURTON, JAMES

Bohigas, Oriol
Universidad Politécnica de Barcelona
DOMÈNECH I MONTANER, LLUÍS

Bold, John
*Royal Commission on Historical Monuments, England
(London)*
ALDRICH, HENRY; ARCHER, THOMAS; BELL,
HENRY; CLARKE, GEORGE; DICKINSON,
WILLIAM; GERBIER, BALTHAZAR; JAMES, JOHN;
PEACOCK, JAMES; SAMWELL, WILLIAM;
THORNHILL, JAMES; VARDY, JOHN

Boles, Daralice Donkervoet
New York City
KAHN, ALBERT; MUTHESIUS, HERMANN

Boucher, C. T. G.
Cheshire, England
RENNIE, JOHN

Bourgeois, Jean-Louis
New York City
HARDENBERGH, HENRY JANEWAY

Boutelle, Sara Holmes
Julia Morgan Association (Santa Cruz, California)
COLTER, MARY; MORGAN, JULIA

Boyarsky, Nicholas
Architectural Association Graduate School (London)
GIBBERD, FREDERICK

Boyle, B. M.
Arizona State University
ANDRONIKOS OF KYRRHOS; ANTISTATES;
CHARES OF LINDOS; CHERSIPHRON OF KNOSSOS;
COCCEIUS AUCTUS, LUCIUS; DAPHNIS OF
MILETOS; DECRIANUS; DEINOKRATES; EULALUIS;
EUPOLEMOS OF ARGOS; FAVENTINUS; HERON;
HIPPODAMUS; KALLIMACHOS; LIBON OF ELIS;

PAIONIOS OF EPHESOS; PALLADIUS; PAPPOS;
PHEIDIAS; PHILOKLES; PHILON OF ELEUSIS;
POLYKLEITOS THE YOUNGER; PYTHEOS; RHOIKOS
OF SAMOS; SOSTRATOS OF KNODOS; THEODORUS
OF SAMOS; THEODOTOS

Brill, Hans
Royal College of Art
LEOPARDI, ALESSANDRO

Broderick, Mosette Glaser
New York University
BABB, COOK, AND WILLARD; GIBSON, ROBERT
WILLIAMS; GILBERT, C. P. H.; HATCH, STEPHEN
D.; LUCE, CLARENCE SUMNER; MOFFATT,
WILLIAM B.; SCOTT, GEORGE GILBERT; SCOTT,
JOHN OLDRID; THOMAS, THOMAS, AND THOMAS,
GRIFFITH; WALKER, C. HOWARD

Brown, Elizabeth Mills
Guilford, Connecticut
HOADLEY, DAVID; SPRATS, WILLIAM

Brown, Frank E.
American Academy in Rome and
VITRUVIUS (BIOGRAPHY)

Brown, Theodore M.
Cornell University
RIETVELD, GERRIT; VAN DOESBURG, THEO

Brownlee, David B.
University of Pennsylvania
STREET, GEORGE EDMUND; WATERHOUSE,
ALFRED

Brown-Manrique, Gerardo
Miami University
UNGERS, O. M.

Bucher, François
Florida State University, Tallahassee
PARLER FAMILY; RORICZER FAMILY; VILLARD DE
HONNECOURT

Bullock, N. O. A.
King's College (Cambridge)
EBERSTADT, RUDOLF; GURLITT, CORNELIUS

Bush, Edward F.
Parks Canada (Ottawa)
BY, JOHN

Cameron, Christina
Canadian Inventory of Historic Buildings (Ottawa)
BAILLAIRGÉ, CHARLES

Campo, Mark à
Atelier Gettit Oorthuys (Amsterdam)
SCHELLING, H. G. J.; WILS, JAN

Caplow, Harriet McNeal
Indiana State University
MICHELOZZO DI BARTOLOMEO

Cardwell, Kenneth H.
University of California, Berkeley
MAYBECK, BERNARD R.

Carolan, Jane
Eagle Valley Research (Sloatsburg, New York)
DAVIS, BRODY, AND ASSOCIATES; FRANZEN,
ULRICH

Carr, Gerald L.
Southern Methodist University
BEDFORD, FRANCIS O.; LEE, THOMAS; LEWIS,
JAMES; MONEYPENNY, GEORGE; PINCH, JOHN;
RICKMAN, THOMAS

Carter, Rand
Hamilton College
DURAND, J. N. L.

Cast, David
Bryn Mawr College
GUILLAIN FAMILY; JARDIN, NICOLAS; LE
LORRAIN, LOUIS; SAULNIER, JULES; SHEPHERD,
EDWARD; VIGARANI, GASPARE

Catalano, Eduardo
*Eduardo Catalano Architects and Engineers,
Incorporated (Cambridge, Massachusetts)*
HARDOY, JORGE FERRARI

Cataldi, Giancarlo
Università degli Studi (Florence)
MURATORI, SAVERIO; VAGNETTI, LUIGI

Chafee, Richard
Providence, Rhode Island
BERG, CHARLES I.; LEFUEL, HECTOR; POPE, JOHN
RUSSELL; SPIERS, RICHARD PHENÉ

Chappell, Sally
De Paul University
BYRNE, BARRY; GRAHAM, ANDERSON, PROBST,
AND WHITE

Chase, David
Baltimore, Maryland
MASON, GEORGE C. SR.; MASON, GEORGE C. JR.;
NEWTON, DUDLEY

Chewning, J. A.
University of Massachusetts
ROOT, JOHN WELLBORN

Childs, Frances S.
Brooklyn College, City University of New York
HEINS AND LA FARGE

Chilvers, Ian
London
ABEL, JOHN; CAIUS, JOHN; DE CAUS, ISAAC; DE
KEYSER, HENDRICK; HOOKE, ROBERT; JACKSON,
JOHN; JANSSEN, BERNARD; LYMINGE, ROBERT;
MARSHALL, JOSHUA; MOLTON, JOHN; NEDEHAM,

JAMES; REDMAN, HENRY; SHUTE, JOHN; SIMONS,
RALPH; SMYTHSON, ROBERT; STONE, NICHOLAS;
THORPE, JOHN; WOOD, THOMAS

Christian, Karen
New York City
ARNOLFO DI CAMBIO; GIOTTO DI BONDONE

Clark, Robert Judson
Princeton University
MULLGARDT, LOUIS CHRISTIAN; OLBRICH,
JOSEPH MARIA

Cleary, Richard
Columbia University
ALAVOINE, JEAN ANTOINE; BEAUSIRE FAMILY;
BRUAND, LIBÉRAL; CELLÉRIER, JACQUES;
CHALGRIN, JEAN FRANÇOIS THÉRÈSE; CHERPITEL,
MATHURIN; DELAMONCE, FERDINAND;
DUFOURNY, LÉON; GISORS FAMILY; HÉLIN,
PIERRE LOUIS; HÉRÉ DE CORNY, EMMANUEL; LA
GUÊPIÈRE, PIERRE LOUIS PHILIPPE DE; LEROUX,
JEAN BAPTISTE; MAILLIER, NICOLAS; MOLINOS,
AUGUSTE ISIDORE; PIGAGE, NICOLAS DE; POYET,
BERNARD; TANNEVOT, MICHEL; THÉVENIN,
JACQUES JEAN; 'T KIND, DAVID; VESTIER,
NICOLAS

Cocke, T. H.
London
ESSEX, JAMES

Coffin, David R.
Princeton University
LIGORIO, PIRRO

Cohen, David
*Canadian Centre for Occupational Health and Safety
(Hamilton, Ontario)*
LENNOX, E. J.

Cohen, Judith
Metropolitan Museum of Art (New York)
MALLET-STEVENS, ROBERT; POMPEI,
ALESSANDRO; WILLIAM OF WYKEHAM

Coles, William A.
University of Michigan
VAN BRUNT, HENRY; WARE, WILLIAM R.; WARE
AND VAN BRUNT

Collins, Christiane C.
Parsons School of Design
HEGEMANN, WERNER; MIGGE, LEBERECHT;
SITTE, CAMILLO

Collins, George R.
Columbia University
GAUDÍ Y CORNET, ANTONIO; GUASTAVINO Y
MORENO, RAFAEL, AND GUASTAVINO Y
ESPOSITO, RAFAEL; PINGUSSON, GEORGES HENRI;
SORIA Y MATA, ARTURO

Collins, Nicolas B.
New York City
HARRIS, CYRIL M.; SABINE, WALLACE CLEMENT

Collins, Peter
McGill University
PERRET, AUGUSTE

Colvin, H. M.
St. John's College (Oxford)
BASTARD, WILLIAM, AND BASTARD, AND JOHN;
SMITH, JAMES

Condit, Carl W.
Northwestern University
BEMAN, SOLON S.; BOGARDUS, JAMES; HOLABIRD
AND ROCHE; JENNEY, WILLIAM LE BARON;
ROEBLING, JOHN AUGUSTUS, AND ROEBLING,
WASHINGTON AUGUSTUS

Connor, T. P.
Eton, England
BENSON, WILLIAM

Connors, Joseph
Columbia University
BORROMINI, FRANCESCO; CORTONA, PIETRO
BERRETTINI DA; MARUSCELLI, PAOLO;
MONTANO, GIOVANNI BATTISTA; SPADA,
VIRGILIO

Cooledge, Harold N. Jr.
Clemson University
SLOAN, SAMUEL

Coope, Rosalys
Epperstone, Nottingham, England
DE BROSSE, SALOMON; LEMERCIER, JACQUES

Copeland, Lee
University of Pennsylvania
MITCHELL/GIURGOLA

Corbett, Michael R.
Charles Hall Page and Associates, Incorporated (San Francisco)
PERCY, GEORGE WASHINGTON; PISSIS, ALBERT

Corden, Carol L.
Neighborhood Reinvestment Corporation (New York)
PERRIAND, CHARLOTTE

Coulton, J. J.
University of Oxford
HERMOGENES; KALLIKRATES

Craig, Maurice
Dublin
BURGH, THOMAS; IVORY, THOMAS; PEARCE,
EDWARD LOVETT; ROBINSON, WILLIAM

Cramer, Max
Hilversum, Netherlands
DUDOK, W. M.

Crane, Howard
Ohio State University
AḤMAD B. ABĪ BAKR AL-MARANDĪ; ʿIWAD

Crawford, Alan
Birmingham, England
ASHBEE, C. R.; BIDLAKE, W. H.; DAVIS, ARTHUR
JOSEPH; MACARTNEY, MERVYN

Crook, J. Mordaunt
Bedford College
BASEVI, GEORGE; BURGES, WILLIAM; DOBSON,
JOHN; HARRISON, THOMAS; SMIRKE, ROBERT;
SMIRKE, SYDNEY

Culot, Maurice
Archives d'Architecture Moderne (Brussels)
BALAT, ALPHONSE; BOURGEOIS, VICTOR; DE
KONINCK, LOUIS HERMAN; DEWEZ, LAURENT-
BENOIT; JACQMAIN, ANDRÉ; RENARD, BRUNO;
VANDENHOVE, CHARLES; VAN DER SWAELMEN,
LOUIS

Cummings, Abbott Lowell
*Society for the Preservation of New England
Antiquities (Boston)*
BENJAMIN, ASHER

Curl, James Stevens
Winchester, England
BUNNING, JAMES BUNSTONE; GEARY, STEPHEN;
MULHOLLAND, ROGER; WALTERS, EDWARD

Davies, Jane B.
New York City
DAVIS, ALEXANDER JACKSON; TOWN, ITHIEL;
TOWN AND DAVIS

Dee, Elaine Evans
Cooper-Hewitt Museum (New York)
BERAIN, JEAN I; LE PAUTRE, PIERRE;
MEISSONNIER, JUSTE-AURELE; OPPENORD,
GILLES-MARIE; PINEAU, NICOLAS

De Gary, Marie-Noële
Union Centrale des Arts Décoratifs (Paris)
DUGOURC, JEAN DEMOSTHÈNE

De la Croix, Horst
San Jose State University
VAUBAN, SÉBASTIAN LE PRESTRE DE

De Long, David G.
Columbia University
GOFF, BRUCE; RAPSON, RALPH

Dendy, William
Toronto
DARLING, FRANK

Denny, Walter B.
University of Massachusetts, Amherst
KALŪK IBN ʿABD ʿALLĀH; KALŪYĀN

De Paula, Alberto S. J.
Universidad Nacional de Lomas de Zamora
CHRISTOPHERSEN, ALEJANDRO; TAMBURINI,
FRANCISCO; THAYS, CARLOS

De' Seta, Cesare
University of Naples
BANFI, BELGIOJOSO, PERESSUTTI, AND ROGERS;
FIGINI, LUIGI, AND POLLINI, GINO; PAGANO,
GIUSEPPE; RIDOLFI, MARIO

Detwiller, Frederic C.
*Society for the Preservation of New England
Antiquities (Boston)*
ANDREWS, ROBERT DAY; BLACKALL, CLARENCE
H.; BRADLEE, NATHANIEL J.; DAWES, THOMAS;
ESTEY, ALEXANDER R.

Dilet, Marc
Chicago
BAKER, HERBERT; BÉLANGER, FRANÇOIS JOSEPH;
CARLONE FAMILY; CASTIGLIONE, ENRICO;
CASTIGLIONI, ACHILLE, and CASTIGLIONI, PIER
GIACOMO; CHAREAU, PIERRE; DERISET,
ANTOINE; D'IXNARD, MICHEL; FRANQUE,
FRANÇOIS; FRANQUE, JEAN-BAPTISTE; GEDDES,
ROBERT; GIRAL FAMILY; GODDE, ETIENNE
HYPPOLITE; JERMAN, EDWARD; LE BRETON,
GILLES; MILLS, PETER; PARKER, BARRY;
PRANDTAUER, JACOB; SÉGUIN, MARC; THUMB
FAMILY

Dimitriou, Sokratis
*Institut für Kunstgeschichte Technische
Universität Graz*
BAUER, LEOPOLD; FABIANI, MAX; FELLNER,
FERDINAND; LUNTZ, VIKTOR; OHMANN,
FRIEDRICH; POPP, ALEXANDER; SCHÖNTHAL,
OTTO

DiStefano, Lynne Delehanty
University of Western Ontario
DURAND, GEORGE

Dixon, Roger
Polytechnic of the South Bank (London)
BROOKS, JAMES; I'ANSON, EDWARD JR.;
LOCKWOOD, HENRY FRANCIS; ORDISH,
ROWLAND M.; PENNETHORNE, JAMES;
PRICHARD, JOHN; RICHARDSON, CHARLES J.;
ROBERTS, HENRY; RUSKIN, JOHN; TEULON,
SAMUEL SANDERS; WHITE, WILLIAM

Dodds, Jerrilynn D.
Columbia University
AḤMAD IBN BĀSO

Dolkart, Andrew Scott
New York Landmarks Preservation Commission
CADY, J. C.

Donhauser, Peter L.
New York City

ANDRÉ, EMIL; AZÉMA, LÉON; CARLU, JACQUES;
EIGTVED, NIKOLAJ; FISKER, KAY; GIRAULT,
CHARLES-LOUIS; GOUJON, JEAN; HERBÉ, PAUL;
HOLZMEISTER, CLEMENS; JAUSSELY, LÉON;
LABRO, GEORGES; PHILANDER, GUILLAUME;
RAINER, ROLAND; ROCHE AND DINKELOO;
SAMBIN, HUGUES; SHEPLEY, RUTAN, AND
COOLIDGE; SOHIER, HECTOR

Doordan, Dennis
San Francisco
ALOISIO, OTTORINO; ARATA, GIULIO ULISSE;
ASCHIERI, PIETRO; BALDESSARI, LUCIANO;
CALZA-BINI, ALBERTO; D'ARONCO, RAIMONDO;
DE FINETTI, GIUSEPPE; FALUDI, EUGENIO
GIACOMO; GRIFFINI, ENRICO AGOSTINO; LEVI-
MONTALCINI, GINO; MATTE-TRUCCO, GIACOMO;
MINNUCCI, GAETANNO; PALADINI, VINICIO;
PICCINATO, LUIGI; SARTORIS, ALBERTO; SAVIOLI,
LEONARDO; SOMMARUGA, GIUSEPPE

Downes, Kerry
University of Reading
HAWKSMOOR, NICHOLAS; VANBRUGH, JOHN;
WREN, CHRISTOPHER

Downing, Antoinette F.
*Rhode Island Historical Preservation Commission
(Providence)*
BROWN, JOSEPH; BUCKLIN, JAMES C.; GREENE,
JOHN HOLDEN; HARRISON, PETER; MUNDAY,
RICHARD; WARREN, RUSSELL

Draper, Joan E.
University of Illinois
BENNETT, EDWARD H.; HOWARD, JOHN GALEN

Drüeke, Eberhard
Technische Universität Braunschweig
ERDSMANNSDORFF, FRIEDRICH WILHELM VON;
GÄRTNER, FRIEDRICH VON; HÜBSCH, HEINRICH;
KLENZE, LEO VON; WEINBRENNER, FRIEDRICH

Duboy, Philippe
Nantes, France
SCARPA, CARLO

Dunbar, John G.
*Royal Commission on the Ancient and Historical
Monuments of Scotland (Edinburgh)*
BRUCE, WILLIAM; WALLACE, WILLIAM

Dunlap, Joseph R.
City College, City University of New York
COLE, HENRY; MORRIS, WILLIAM

Du Prey, Pierre de la Ruffinière
*Queens University and Canadian Centre for
Architecture (Montreal)*
BLACKBURN, WILLIAM; BRETTINGHAM, ROBERT;
HARDWICK, THOMAS; LEVERTON, THOMAS;
MITCHELL, ROBERT

Dwyer, Donald Harris
Huntington, New York
ATTERBURY, GROSVENOR

Edwards, Mary D.
Columbia University
BRUBAKER, CHARLES WILLIAM; CHURCH, THOMAS D.; KILEY, DANIEL URBAN; PERKINS, LAWRENCE B.; THIRY, PAUL; WILL, PHILIP JR.

Eidelberg, Martin P.
Rutgers University
COLONNA, EDWARD

Einarson, Neil
Winnipeg, Manitoba
THOMAS, WILLIAM

Ellias, Juanita M.
Columbia University
ABEILLE, JOSEPH; BETTO FAMILY; DE LA FOSSE, LOUIS RÉMY; JADOT, JEAN NICOLAS; LAINÉE, THOMAS

Elzea, Betty
Wilmington, Delaware
BLOMFIELD, REGINALD; CHAMPNEYS, BASIL; CRANE, WALTER; DRESSER, CHRISTOPHER; FOWKE, FRANCIS; LUBETKIN, BERTHOLD; ROBSON, EDWARD ROBERT; SEDDING, JOHN D.; STEVENSON, JOHN JAMES

Ennis, Robert B.
Athenaeum of Philadelphia
WALTER, THOMAS U.

Erouart, Gilbert
Ambassade de la Republique Française en Italie (Rome)
LEGEAY, JEAN-LAURENT

Esau, Erika
Bryn Mawr College
SCHWITTERS, KURT

Etlin, Richard A.
University of Maryland
BOULLÉE, ETIENNE LOUIS; MAZZONI, ANGIOLO

Ezequelle, Betty J.
Brooklyn, New York
THOMPSON, MARTIN E.

Fairbank, Wilma
Cambridge, Massachusetts
LIANG SSU-CH'ENG

Faison, S. Lane Jr.
Williams College
ASAM, COSMAS DAMIAN, and ASAM, EGID QUIRIN; CUVILLIÉS, FRANÇOIS THE ELDER; FISCHER, JOHANN MICHAEL; ZIMMERMANN BROTHERS

Farhad, Massumeh
Harvard University
AḤMAD IBN MOḤAMMAD AṬ-ṬABRIZI; AJAMĪ; MUHAMMAD B. ATSIZ; MUHAMMAD B. MAHMUD AL-ISFAHANI

Fawcett, Christopher
Architectural Association (London)
GOLLINS, MELVIN, WARD; LYNN, JACK; SMITH, IVOR; WEEKS, JOHN

Feaver, Jane G.
Villanova, Pennsylvania
HOWELLS, JOHN MEAD

Feeney, Alan
Thebarton, South Australia
WRIGHT, EDMUND WILLIAM

Fergusson, Frances D.
University of Massachusetts
FOSTER, JOHN; WYATT, JAMES

Field, Cynthia R.
Smithsonian Institution (Washington, D.C.) and George Washington University
MEIGS, MONTGOMERY C.

Flores Lopez, Carlos
Madrid
BERGAMÍN GUTIERREZ, RAFAEL; CODERCH Y DE SENTMENAT, JOSÉ ANTONIO; GARCÍA MERCADAL, FERNANDO; RODRIGUEZ AYUSO, EMILIO

Floyd, Margaret Henderson
Tufts University
BRIGHAM, CHARLES; CABOT, EDWARD CLARK; COLLING, JAMES KELLAWAY; GILMAN, ARTHUR DELAVEN; PEABODY AND STEARNS; STURGIS, JOHN HUBBARD

Frampton, Kenneth
Institute for Architecture and Urban Studies (New York)
GINSBURG, MOISEI YAKOVLEVICH; GOLOSOV, ILYA, and GOLOSOV, PANTELEMON; LEONIDOV, IVAN IVANOVICH; LISSITSKY, ELEAZAR M.; MILIUTIN, NIKOLAI ALEKSANDROVICH; VESNIN FAMILY

Francis, Dennis Steadman
New York City
DUDLEY, HENRY; GILBERT, C. P. H.; HATCH, STEPHEN D.; MOULD, JACOB WREY; THOMAS, THOMAS, AND THOMAS, GRIFFITH; VAUX, CALVERT

Frank, Suzanne
New York City
DE GROOT, J. H.; DUIKER, JOHANNES; GRANPRÉ-MOLIÈRE, M. J.; KRAMER, PIETER LODEWIJK; KROPHOLLER, MARGARET;

LAUWERICKS, J. L. M.; VAN DEN BROEK AND
BAKEMA; VAN EYCK, ALDO; WIJDEVELD, H. T.

Franklin, Jill
London
DEVEY, GEORGE; PARKER, CHARLES; PARNELL,
CHARLES OCTAVIUS

Franko, Ivan S.
Columbia University
BAUMEISTER, REINHARD; BÖHM, GOTTFRIED;
VAN DER NÜLL AND SICCARDSBURG

Friedman, Terry F.
Temple Newsam House (Leeds, England)
BURROUGH, JAMES; GIBBS, JAMES

Frommel, Christoph Luitpold
Bibliotheca Hertziana (Rome)
BORGO, FRANCESCO DEL

Frykenstedt, Holger
Stockholm
EHRENSVAERD, CARL AUGUST

Gallet, Michel
Paris
LEDOUX, CLAUDE NICOLAS

Garmey, Stephen S.
New York City
EIDLITZ, LEOPOLD; MELNIKOV, KONSTANTIN

Garms, Jörg
Historisches Institut beim Österreichischen Kulturinstitut in Roma.
BOFFRAND, GERMAIN

Garza, M. Elizabeth
Harvard University
GHERARDI, ANTONIO

Gayle, Margot
New York City
BADGER, DANIEL D.; CARSTENSEN, GEORG;
DARBY, ABRAHAM III; GAYNOR, JOHN P.;
KELLUM, JOHN; SLADE, J. MORGAN; VAN OSDEL,
JOHN MILLS

Gebhard, David
University of California, Santa Barbara
NEWSOM, SAMUEL, AND NEWSOM, JOSEPH
CATHER; PURCELL AND ELMSLIE; SMITH, GEORGE
WASHINGTON; VOYSEY, CHARLES F. A.; WEBB,
PHILIP S.; WRIGHT, JOHN LLOYD; WRIGHT,
LLOYD

George, Mary Hollers Jutson
San Antonio College
FORD, O'NEIL; GILES, ALFRED

Gersovitz, Julia
Montreal
AFFLECK, RAYMOND; BROWNE, JOHN JAMES;

HUTCHISON, ALEXANDER COWPER; OSTELL,
JOHN; TAYLOR, ANDREW; THOMAS, WILLIAM
TUTIN

Gerstein, Linda
Haverford College
SHEKHTEL, FEDOR

Ghirardo, Diane
Stanford University
PIACENTINI, MARCELLO; SANT'ELIA, ANTONIO;
TERRAGNI, GIUSEPPE

Gibberd, Frederick
London
JELLICOE, GEOFFREY

Gilbert, Sandra E.
American Federation of Arts (New York)
SNOOK, JOHN BUTLER

Gilbertson, Elsa
Starksboro, Vermont
SILSBEE, J. LYMAN; WEESE, HARRY MOHR

Gill, Brendan
The New Yorker
WHITE, STANFORD

Giurgola, Romaldo
Mitchell/Giurgola Architects (New York)
KAHN, LOUIS I.

Glaeser, Ludwig
New York City
MIES VAN DER ROHE, LUDWIG

Glahn, Else
International House (Philadelphia)
LI CHIEH

Gobran, Sophie
Columbia University
CUBITT, THOMAS; LUNDY, VICTOR; LYNCH,
KEVIN

Goethert, Reinhard
Massachusetts Institute of Technology
FATHY, HASSAN

Gomme, Andor
University of Keele
ALEXANDER, DANIEL ASHER; HARVEY, JOHN;
HIORNE, WILLIAM, AND HIORNE, DAVID; PATY,
THOMAS; ROBINSON, THOMAS; SANDERSON,
JOHN; SANDYS, FRANCIS; SMITH, FRANCIS

Goodman, Percival
New York City
CHOISY, AUGUSTE

Gordon, Alden Rand
Trinity College
MARIGNY, MARQUIS DE

Gow, Ian
Royal Commission on the Ancient and Historical Monuments of Scotland (Edinburgh)
MYLNE, ROBERT AND FAMILY

Grainger, Hilary J.
North Staffordshire Polytechnic
BRYDON, J. M.; CROWE, SYLVIA; LLEWELLYN-DAVIES, RICHARD

Graves, Linda L.
Chicago
MALCOLMSON, REGINALD FRANCIS

Gray, Christopher S.
Office for Metropolitan History (New York)
CARPENTER, J. E. R.; CROSS AND CROSS; HERTS AND TALLANT; MCKENZIE, VORHEES, AND GMELIN; ROTH, EMERY; SHREVE, LAMB, AND HARMON

Greenberg, Lynda
Columbia University
GRUEN, VICTOR; JOHNSON, RICHARD NORMAN; LYONS, ERIC; NOWICKI, MATTHEW; PORTMAN, JOHN; SYRKUS, HELENA, and SYRKUS, SZYMON

Greene, Elizabeth
Columbia University
CETTO, MAX; PIERMARINI, GIUSEPPE; SELVA, GIOVANNI ANTONIO

Greiff, Constance M.
Heritage Studies (Princeton, New Jersey)
LEBRUN, NAPOLEON; NOTMAN, JOHN

Grieken, Hans van
Hilversum, Netherlands
DUDOK, W. M.

Groningen, Catherina L. van
Rijksdienst voor de Monumentenzorg (Zeist, Netherlands)
POST, PIETER; VAN CAMPEN, JACOB

Grossman, Elizabeth Greenwell
Rhode Island School of Design
CRET, PAUL PHILIPPE

Gruber, Alain
Abegg-Stiftung Bern
PARIS, PIERRE ADRIEN

Güell Guix, Xavier
Barcelona, Spain
BALCELLS BUIGAS, EDUARDO MARÍA; FONT I CARRERAS, AUGUST; MESTRES I ESPLUGAS, JOSEP ORIOL; OLIVERAS GENSANA, CAMIL

Gutíerrez, Ramón
Universidad Nacional del Nordeste
BLANQUI, ANDRÉS; FOSSATI, PEDRO; PRIMOLI, JUAN BAUTISTA

Hager, Hellmut
Pennsylvania State University
DE ROSSI, GIOVANNI ANTONIO; DE ROSSI, MARCANTONIO; DE ROSSI, MATTIA; FONTANA, CARLO; MARCHIONNI, CARLO

Hall, Ivan
University of Hull
LIGHTOLER, TIMOTHY; PRITCHETT, JAMES PIGOTT

Hanson, Brian
London
HOWARD, EBENEZER; PARKER AND UNWIN; POWELL AND MOYA; ROBERTSON, HOWARD MORLEY; ROSENBERG, EUGENE; SHEPHEARD, PETER FAULKNER; TECTON; UNWIN, RAYMOND; WILLIAMS, OWEN; WOODHOUSE, CORBETT, AND DEAN

Harrington, Kevin
Chicago
BLONDEL, JACQUES FRANÇOIS; BLONDEL, JEAN FRANÇOIS; PATTE, PIERRE

Harris, Elizabeth D.
Rio de Janeiro, Brazil
ALEIJADINHO; BARRAGÁN, LUIS; BAYARDO, NELSON; BERNARDES, SERGIO; BONET, ANTONIO; BRATKE, OSWALDO; BURLE MARX, ROBERTO; CANDELA, FELIX; COSTA, LÚCIO; CUÉLLAR, SERRANO, AND GOMEZ; DIESTE, ELADIO; DUHART, EMILIO; GARCIA NUÑEZ, JULIÁN; GRANDJEAN DE MONTIGNY, AUGUSTE-HENRI-VICTOR; KLUMB, HENRY; LEVI, RINO; MOREIRA, JORGE; NIEMEYER, OSCAR; PANI, MARIO; REIDY, AFFONSO EDUARDO; ROBERTO BROTHERS; SALMONA, ROGELIO; TESTA, CLORINDO; TORO AND FERRER; VAUTHIER, LUIS; VEGAS AND GALIA; VIECO SANCHEZ, HERNAN; VILAMAJÓ, JULIO; VILLAGRAN GARCIA, JOSÉ; WARCHAVCHIK, GREGORI

Harris, John
Royal Institute of British Architects (London)
CARTER, JOHN; CHAMBERS, WILLIAM; CRUNDEN, JOHN; GWYNN, JOHN; HALFPENNY, WILLIAM; JONES, INIGO; KENT, WILLIAM; LANGLEY, BATTY; LEADBETTER, STIFF; MORRIS, ROBERT; MORRIS, ROGER; PEMBROKE, EARL OF; PRATT, ROGER; PRITCHARD, THOMAS; RIPLEY, THOMAS; SWAN, ABRAHAM; TALMAN, JOHN; TALMAN, WILLIAM; WARE, ISAAC; WEBB, JOHN; WRIGHT, STEPHEN; WRIGHT, THOMAS

Hasegawa, Takashi
Musashino College of Arts
KATAYAMA, TŌKUMA; MURANO, TŌGO; SAKAKURA, JUNZŌ; SATŌ, TAKEO; SHINOHARA, KAZUO; SHIRAI, SEIICHI; TSUMAKI, YORINAKA; YOSHIDA, ISOYA

Hauck, Alice H. R.
Providence College
GARBETT, EDWARD LACY; PUGIN, EDWARD
WELBY

Hawkins, William J. III
Allen, McMath, Hawkins (Portland, Oregon)
WILLIAMS, WARREN HAYWOOD

Haynes, Wesley
New York City
HAUGAARD, WILLIAM E.; PERRY, ISAAC G.;
PILCHER, LEWIS F.

Hazlehurst, F. Hamilton
Vanderbilt University
LE NOSTRE, ANDRÉ

Head, Raymond
London
SMITH, ROBERT

Heisner, Beverly
University of South Carolina
FISCHER VON ERLACH, JOHANN BERNHARD;
HILDEBRANDT, JOHANN LUCAS VON; IRWIN,
HARRIET MORRISON; LONGUELUNE, ZACHARIAS;
SCHMUZER FAMILY

Henneberg, Josephine von
Boston College
PORTA, GIACOMO DELLA

Herrmann, Wolfgang
London
BLONDEL, FRANÇOIS; DESGODETZ, ANTOINE;
LAUGIER, MARC-ANTOINE; PERRAULT, CLAUDE

Hersey, G. L.
Yale University
VANVITELLI, LUIGI

Heseltine, J. E.
London
MACKMURDO, A. H.; SEDDON, J. P.

Hibbard, Howard
Columbia University
BERNINI, GIOVANNI LORENZO; MADERNO,
CARLO; MICHELANGELO

Hill, Robert
*Biographical Dictionary of Architects in Canada,
1800–1950 (Toronto)*
CHAUSSE, JOSEPH ALCIDE; CUMBERLAND,
FREDERIC WILLIAM; FULLER, THOMAS;
MARCHAND, JEAN OMER; OUELLET, JOSEPH-
PIERRE; PEARSON, JOHN ANDREW; ROSS, GEORGE
ALLEN; SPROAT AND ROLPH; STORM, WILLIAM
GEORGE

Hilligos, Francine
Boulogne, France
BENOIT-LÉVY, GEORGES

Hines, Thomas S.
University of California, Los Angeles
BURNHAM, DANIEL H.; NEUTRA, RICHARD

Hoag, John Douglas
University of Colorado
ARCINIEGA, CLAUDIO DE; ARRIETA, PEDRO DE;
BECERRA, FRANCISCO; CHURRIGUERRA FAMILY;
COLONIA FAMILY; COVARRUBIAS, ALONSO DE;
GUAS, JUAN; HONTAÑON, JUAN GIL DE;
HONTAÑON, RODRIGO GIL DE

Holden, Wheaton
Northeastern University
PEABODY AND STEARNS

Hollander, Michael
Pratt Institute
CATALANO, EDUARDO; HUBBARD, ELBERT;
JOHANSEN, JOHN M.; MAYER, ALBERT; MCHARG,
IAN; NOYES, ELIOT

Holmes, Mary Patricia
Booneville, Missouri
LINK, THEODORE C.

Hořejší, Jořina
Prague
RIED, BENEDIKT

Howarth, Thomas
University of Toronto
MACKINTOSH, CHARLES RENNIE; MORRIS,
ROBERT SCHOFIELD

Howell, Peter
Oxford
JACKSON, THOMAS GRAHAM

Howie, Robert L. Jr.
*Society for the Preservation of New England
Antiquities (Boston)*
CODMAN, OGDEN JR.

Hughes, Jeffrey
Terre Haute, Indiana
BANDINELLI, BACCIO; BRAMANTINO; LE MUET,
PIERRE; MÉTEZEAU FAMILY; RICCHINO,
FRANCESCO MARIA; SANFELICE, FERDINANDO

Hull, Judith S.
Columbia University
AHLBERG, HAKON; ÅHRÉN, UNO; ALMQVIST,
OSVALD; ASPLUND, ERIK GUNNAR; BACKSTROM,
SVEN; BERGSTEN, CARL; BJERKE, ARVID;
ERICSON, SIGFRID; FENGER, LUDVIG; GALLEN-
KALLELA, AKSELI; KNUTSEN, KNUT;
LALLERSTEDT, ERIK; LEWERENTZ, SIGURD;
MALMSTEN, CARL; PEI, I. M.; SIRÉN, HEIKKI,
AND SIRÉN, KAIJA; SIRÉN, JOHAN; SONCK, LARS
ELIEL; SØRENSON, CARL THEODORE; UPJOHN,
RICHARD MICHELL

Iglesias, Helena
Escuela de Arquitectura de Madrid
DE CUBAS Y GONZALEZ-MONTES, FRANCISCO;
PALACIO Y ELISSAGUE, ALBERTO DEL

Ind, Rosemary
The Open University
EMBERTON, JOSEPH; TAIT, T. S.

Isaacs, Reginald R.
Harvard University
ABERCROMBIE, PATRICK; ALBERS, JOSEF;
BARTNING, OTTO; BAYER, HERBERT; BEHRENDT,
WALTER CURT; BREUER, MARCEL; GROPIUS,
WALTER; HORIGUCHI, SUTEMI; HUDNUT, JOSEPH
FAIRMAN; MARKELIUS, SVEN GOTTFRID;
MARTIN, LESLIE; MAY, ERNST; MEYER, ADOLF;
MEYER, HANNES; POELZIG, HANS; SERT, JOSEP
LLUIS; STAM, MART; VAN DE VELDE, HENRY;
WAGNER, MARTIN

Jackson, Anthony
Technical University of Nova Scotia
MORIYAMA, RAYMOND

Jackson-Stops, Gervase
*National Trust for Places of Historic Interest or
Natural Beauty (London)*
MAROT, DANIEL; STANTON, WILLIAM; STRONG,
EDWARD; STRONG, THOMAS THE YOUNGER

Jacobus, John
Dartmouth College
BAUDOT, JOSEPH EUGÈNE ANATOLE DE; BOILEAU,
LOUIS AUGUSTE; DUTERT, CHARLES LOUIS
FERDINAND; EIFFEL, GUSTAVE; JOHNSON, PHILIP

James, Martin S.
Brooklyn College, City University of New York
GIEDION, SIEGFRIED

Jenkins, Frank
University of Manchester
FOULSTON, JOHN

Johns, Christopher
Newark, Delaware
BERTOTTI-SCAMOZZI, OTTAVIO

Johnson, Donald Leslie
Flinders University of South Australia
ARCHER, JOHN LEE; GREENWAY, FRANCIS;
McGRATH, RAYMOND; SEIDLER, HARRY;
WARDELL, WILLIAM WILKINSON; WILKINSON,
LESLIE

Johnson, Eugene J.
Williams College
ALBERTI, LEON BATTISTA

Johnsson, Ulf G.
Nationalmuseum (Stockholm)
HÅRLEMAN FAMILY; TESSIN FAMILY

Jørgensen, Lisbet Balslev
Kunstakademiets Bibliotek (Copenhagen)
BAUMANN, POVL; HAGEN, G. B.; HOLM, HANS
JØRGEN; JACOBSEN, ARNE; JACOBSEN, HOLGER;
JACOBSEN, VIGGO; JENSEN-KLINT, PEDER
VILHELM; KLINT, KAARE; KRISTENSEN, SVENN
ESKE; MØLLER, C. F.; ROSEN, ANTON S.;
STEGMANN, POVL

Kalman, Harold
Ottawa
SORBY, THOMAS CHARLES

Kambartel, Walter
University of Bielefeld
BOSSE, ABRAHAM; DAVILER, CHARLES; FÉLIBIEN
DES AVAUX, ANDRÉ

Kaplan, Janet
Moore College of Art
BROWN, DAVID; BURNS, FRED; FORESTIERE,
BALDASARE; KIESLER, FREDERICK; LAFFERTY,
JAMES V.; PLUMB, GEORGE; PRISBREY, TRESSA;
RODIA, SIMON; SCHMIDT, CLARENCE; STENMAN,
ELIS; TIGERMAN, STANLEY; WERNERUS,
MATTHIAS

Kaufman, E. N.
New Haven
FERREY, BENJAMIN; SALVIN, ANTHONY

Kaufman, Thomas DaCosta
Princeton University
SANTINI AICHEL, JAN BLAŽEJ

Kaufmann, Edgar jr.
New York City
COLLECINI, FRANCESCO; HORTA, VICTOR;
LODOLI, CARLO; SANTOS DE CARVALHO,
EUGÉNIO DOS; WRIGHT, FRANK LLOYD

Keebler, Patricia Heintzelman
Downingtown, Pennsylvania
DAY, FRANK MILES; KLAUDER, CHARLES Z.

Kelder, Diane M.
College of Staten Island, City University of New York
GALLI BIBIENA FAMILY

Kellam, Shelley Smith
Columbia University
HUBACHER, CARL; PRUTSCHER, OTTO;
SCHWECHTEN, FRANZ

Keller, Fritz-Eugen
Freie Universität Berlin
BROEBES, JEAN BAPTISTE; CAPRIANO DA
VOLTERRA, FRANCESCO; CORNARO, ALVISE; DE
BODT, JEAN; DU RY FAMILY; GERLACH, PHILIPP;
GONTARD, KARL VON; KNOBELSDORFF, GEORGE
WENCESLAUS VON; MEMHARDT, JOHANN
GREGOR; NERING, JOHANN ARNOLD; SCHLÜTER,
ANDREAS

Keller, Ina Maria
Berlin
GONTARD, KARL VON; KNOBELSDORFF, GEORGE
WENCESLAUS VON

Kelly, Cathie C.
University of Nevada
CHIAVERI, GAETANO; FANZAGO, COSIMO; POZZO,
ANDREA; RUSCONI SASSI, LUDOVICO

Kelly, Charlotte A.
Henry Francis du Pont Winterthur Museum
(Delaware)
STURGIS, RUSSELL

Kelsall, Frank
Greater London Council
BARBON, NICHOLAS; SPILLER, JAMES

Kemp, Emory
West Virginia University
TURNER, C. A. P.

Kent, Douglas R.
Friends of Hyde Hall, Incorporated (Jordan, New
York)
HOOKER, PHILIP

Kestenbaum, Joy M.
Institute of Fine Arts, New York University
BELTRAMI, LUCA; CALDERINI, GUGLIELMO;
DUDLEY, HENRY; FABRIS, EMILIO DE; FERNBACH,
HENRY; HATCH, STEPHEN D.; MENGONI,
GIUSEPPE; MOULD, JACOB WREY; SCHULZE,
PAUL; THOMAS, THOMAS, AND THOMAS,
GRIFFITH; VAUX, CALVERT; ZUCKER, ALFRED

Kieven, Elisabeth
Bibliotheca Hertziana (Rome)
ANTINORI, GIOVANNI; GALILEI, ALESSANDRO

Kihlstedt, Folke T.
Franklin and Marshall College
KECK AND KECK; KOCHER AND FREY

Kilham, Walter H. Jr.
Kent, Connecticut
HOOD, RAYMOND M.

Kinchin, Juliet
Glasgow Museums and Art Galleries (Scotland)
COLLCUTT, T. E.

Kirby, John B. Jr.
Branford, Connecticut
AUSTIN, HENRY

Kirker, Harold
University of California, Santa Barbara
BULFINCH, CHARLES

Klingensmith, Samuel J.
Cornell University
EFFNER, JOSEPH; WELSCH, MAXIMILIAN VON;
ZUCCALLI FAMILY

Kłosiewicz, Lech
Warsaw
BIEGANSKI, PIOTR; BRUKALSKA, BARBARA, AND
BRUKALSKI, STANISLAW; CHMIELEWSKI, JAN
OLAF; GUTT, ROMUALD; HRYNIEWIECKI, JERZY;
KARPÍNSKI, ZBIGNIEW; LACHERT, BOHDAN;
OSTROWSKI, WACLAW; SWIERCZYŃSKI, RUDOLF

Koch, Robert
Southern Connecticut State College
TIFFANY, LOUIS C.

Kohler, Sue
United States Commission of Fine Arts (Washington,
D.C.)
BROWN, GLENN

Koós, Judith
Budapest.
FESZL, FRIGYES; GIERGL, KÁLMÁN; KOZMA,
LAJOS; LECHNER, ÖDÖN; MOHOLY-NAGY,
LÁSZLÓ; SCHOFFER, NICOLAS

Kopp, Anatole
Université de Paris VIII (Vincennes, St.-Denis,
France)
BARCHTCH, M.; KAZAKOV, MATVEI F.;
OKHITOVITCH, M.; PASTERNAK, A.; ROSSI, KARL
I.; SABSOVICH, L. M.

Kornwolf, James D.
College of William and Mary
BAILLIE SCOTT, M. H.

Kowsky, Francis R.
State University College at Buffalo
WITHERS, FREDERICK CLARKE

Kramer, Ellen
Scarsdale, New York
LIENAU, DETLEF

Krause, Walter
Institut für Kunstgeschichte der Universität Wien
WIELEMANS, ALEXANDER

Krinsky, Carol Herselle
New York University
CESARIANO, CESARE DI LORENZO; FOUILHOUX,
JACQUES ANDRÉ; REINHARD AND HOFMEISTER;
URBAN, JOSEPH

Krotzer, Henry W. Jr.
Koch and Wilson (New Orleans, Louisiana)
GALLIER, JAMES JR.; HOWARD, HENRY

Kuban, Doğan
Istanbul Teknik Üniversitesi
ELDEM, SEDAT HAKKI; SINAN

Lacaze, Charlotte
American College in Paris
BALTARD, LOUIS PIERRE; BRONGNIART,
ALEXANDRE THÉODORE; LEROY, JULIEN DAVID;

VALLIN DE LA MOTHE, JEAN BAPTISTE MICHEL;
VASSÉ, FRANÇOIS ANTOINE; VIGNON,
ALEXANDRE PIERRE

Laing, Alan K.
University of Illinois at Urbana-Champaign
RICKER, N. C.

Lamberini, Daniela
Florence
BELLUZZI, GIOVANNI BATTISTA

Lambert, Phyllis
Canadian Centre for Architecture (Montreal)
CORMIER, ERNEST; ROHAULT DE FLEURY
FAMILY

Lancaster, Clay
Salvisa, Kentucky
SHRYOCK, GIDEON

Landau, Royston
*Architectural Association School of Architecture
(London)*
DREW, JANE B.; FRY, EDWIN MAXWELL

Landau, Sarah Bradford
New York University
CONGDON, HENRY M.; POTTER, EDWARD T.;
POTTER, WILLIAM A.; ROBERTSON, R. H.;
WIGHT, PETER B.

Landy, Jacob
City College, City University of New York
LAFEVER, MINARD

Lane, Barbara Miller
Bryn Mawr College
BESTELMEYER, GERMAN; BOBERG, FERDINAND;
BONATZ, PAUL; CANEVARI, RAFFAELE; CARIMINI,
LUCA; CARNEVALE, PIETRO; CHEDANNE,
GEORGES; DE ANGELIS, GIULIO; DÜLFER,
MARTIN; FAHRENKAMP, EMIL; HAESLER, OTTO;
HARTUNG, HUGO; HAUBERRISSER, GEORG VON;
KAUFMANN, OSKAR; KÖRNER, EDMUND; KREIS,
WILHELM; LICHT, HUGO; MARCH, OTTO; MEBES,
PAUL; NYROP, MARTIN; PIACENTINI, PIO;
SACCONI, GIUSEPPE; SCHMITTHENNER, PAUL;
SEIDL, GABRIEL VON; SPEER, ALBERT;
SÜSSENGUTH, GEORG; TENGBOM, IVAR;
THIERSCH, FRIEDRICH VON; TODT, FRITZ;
TROOST, PAUL LUDWIG; WAHLMAN, LARS;
WALLOT, PAUL; WESTMAN, CARL

Langmead, Donald
South Australian Institute of Technology
KINGSTON, GEORGE S.; LAYBOURNE-SMITH,
LOUIS

Lanmon, Lorraine Welling
Corning, New York
LESCAZE, WILLIAM; SOISSONS, LOUIS DE

Lassner, Jacob
Wayne State University
AL-MANSŪR

Laurie, Michael
University of California, Berkeley
HALPRIN, LAWRENCE

Leach, Peter
Skipton, England
COUSE, KENTON; GARRETT, DANIEL; PAINE,
JAMES; PLATT FAMILY

Lee, Antoinette J.
Arlington, Virginia
BUTTON, S. D.

Lehman, Donald J.
Philadelphia (Philadelphia)
MULLETT, ALFRED B.

Lehmann, Phyllis Williams
*Smith College and Institute of Fine Arts, New York
University*
IKTINOS; SKOPAS

Lehrman, Sara
Bryn Mawr College
ABACCO, ANTONIO DALL'; ABBONDI, ANTONIO
DI PIETRO; ALBERTI, ALBERTO; ALBERTI,
MATTEO; AVANZINI, BARTOLOMEO

Lemire, Robert
Canadian Centre for Architecture (Montreal)
ARCHIBALD, JOHN SMITH; MAXWELL, EDWARD,
AND MAXWELL, W. S.; TURNER, PHILIP JOHN

Lenain, Pierre
Archives d'Architecture Moderne (Brussels)
BRUYN, WILLEM DE; COBERGHER, WENZEL;
FAYDHERBE, LUCAS; FRANCQUART, JACQUES;
VAN BAURSCHEIT, JAN PIETER; VANDELVIRA,
ANDRES DE; VAN OBBERGEN, ANTON; VAN
PEDE, HENRI; VREDEMAN DE VRIES, HANS;
WILDE, BERNARD DE

Leopold, Ellen
University College (London)
LEWIS, WHITFIELD

Lerski, Hanna
Georgia State University
CONDER, JOSIAH

Lever, Jill
Royal Institute of British Architects (London)
HAGUE, THOMAS; HAKEWILL FAMILY; HANSOM,
JOSEPH A.; HARDWICK, PHILIP; HUNT, THOMAS
FREDERICK

Levin, Steven
Kansas City University
RAPP AND RAPP

Lewcock, Ronald
University of Cambridge
ANREITH, ANTON; GUEDES, AMANCIO;
THIBAULT, LOUIS MICHEL

Lewis, Douglas
National Gallery of Art (Washington, D.C.)
BON, GIOVANNI; BON, BARTOLOMEO; AND BON,
BARTOLOMEO (BERGAMASCO); CODUCCI, MAURO;
GASPARI, ANTONIO; LONGHENA, BALDASSARE;
MUTTONI, FRANCESCO; PALLADIO, ANDREA;
ROSSI, DOMENICO; SANMICHELI, MICHELE;
SANSOVINO, JACOPO; SARDI, GIUSEPPE;
SCAMOZZI, VINCENZO

Lewis, Lesley
Society of Antiquaries of London
NEWTON, WILLIAM; REVETT, NICHOLAS;
STUART, JAMES

Lewis, Miles
University of Melbourne
BLACKBURN, JAMES; KNIGHT, J. G.; LEWIS,
MORTIMER; RUSSELL, ROBERT

Limouze, Dorothy
Princeton University
AVOSTALIS DE SOLA, ULRICO; BERRECCI,
BARTOLOMMEO; FRISONI, DONATO GIUSEPPE

Linstrum, Derek
University of York
AMBLER, THOMAS; CHANTRELL, ROBERT DENNIS;
WYATT, BENJAMIN; WYATT, THOMAS HENRY,
AND WYATT, THOMAS HENRY; WYATVILLE,
JEFFRY

Lipstadt, Hélène
Cambridge, Massachusetts
DALY, CÉSAR

Liscombe, R. Windsor
University of British Columbia
ABRAHAM, ROBERT; AIKIN, EDMUND; BRITTON,
JOHN; CHAWNER, THOMAS; CLAYTON, A. B.;
CLUSKEY, CHARLES B.; CUNDY FAMILY; ELMES,
HARVEY LONSDALE; FERGUSSON, JAMES;
GANDY-DEERING, JOHN PETER; GWILT, JOSEPH;
HOPPER, THOMAS; INWOOD, WILLIAM, AND
INWOOD, HENRY W.; KERR, ROBERT; LEEDS,
WILLIAM HENRY; PILKINGTON, WILLIAM; POPE,
RICHARD SHACKLETON; PORDEN, WILLIAM;
RATTENBURY, F. M.; REPTON AND REPTON;
ROPER, DAVID RIDALL; SMITH, GEORGE; STARK,
WILLIAM; WEBSTER, GEORGE; WILKINS,
WILLIAM

Lloyd, David W.
Harlow, England
THOMPSON, FRANCIS; TITE, WILLIAM

Longstreth, Richard W.
Kansas State University
BROWN, A. PAGE; COXHEAD, ERNEST; HUTTON,
ADDISON; POLK, WILLIS; RAPP AND RAPP;
SCHWEINFURTH, A. C.

Lorch, Richard
Darwin College (Cambridge)
BRETTINGHAM, MATTHEW; CHAMBERLIN,
POWELL, AND BON; COLVIN, BRENDA;
DANNATT, TREVOR; EVELEIGH, JOHN;
RICHARDSON, GEORGE; SEARLES, MICHAEL

Louhenjoki, Pirkko-Liisa
Yale University
BLOMSTEDT, AULIS; ERVI, AARNE; GESELLIUS,
HERMAN; HANSSON, OLOF; LAPPO, OSMO;
LINDEGREN, YRJÖ; LINDGREN, ARMAS;
LINDQVIST, SELIM A.; NYSTRÖM, CARL GUSTAF;
PIETILÄ, REIMA; RUUSUVUORI, AARNO;
SUOMALAINEN, TIMO

Loyer, François
Archives d'Architecture Moderne (Brussels)
HANKAR, PAUL

Luchs, Alison
*Center for Advanced Study, National Gallery of Art
(Washington, D.C.)*
APPIANI, GIUSEPPE; ARNOLD VON WESTPHALEN;
FRANCKE, PAUL; GUMPP FAMILY; HÜLTZ,
JOHANNES; KUEN, JOHANN GEORG

Lukacher, Brian
University of Delaware
ATKINSON, THOMAS; ATKINSON, WILLIAM;
BEAZLEY, SAMUEL; GANDY, J. M.; JAY, WILLIAM;
PALMER, JOHN; SHAW, JOHN I; SHAW, JOHN II;
SIMPSON, ARCHIBALD; STEPHENSON, DAVID

Maass, John
Office of the City Representative (Philadelphia)
MCARTHUR, JOHN JR.; SCHWARZMANN,
HERMANN J.

Macaulay, James
Glasgow, Scotland
GRAHAM, JAMES GILLESPIE; HIORNE, FRANCIS;
PLAYFAIR, JAMES, AND PLAYFAIR, W. H.

MacDonald, William L.
Northampton, Massachusetts
ANTHEMIOS; APOLLODORUS; BRASINI,
ARMANDO; COSSUTIUS; FRONTINUS, SEXTUS
JULIUS; HADRIAN; HARDOUIN MANSART, JULES;
ISIDOROS; MANSART, FRANÇOIS; RABIRIUS;
SEVERUS AND CELER; VIGNOLA, GIACOMO
BAROZZI DA

Mack, Caroline M.
University Park, Maryland
HAIGHT, CHARLES C.

Mack, Charles Randall
University of South Carolina
BAGLIONI FAMILY; MEDICI, GIOVANNI DE';
ROSSELLINO, BERNARDO; SANTI DI TITO;
SEREGNI, VINCENZO; SILVANI, GHERARDO;
VALERIANO, GIUSEPPE; VESPIGNANI, VERGILIO

Mackay, David
Martorell, Bohigas, and Mackay (Barcelona, Spain)
GANCHEGUI, LUIS PEÑA; SOSTRES, JOSEP MARIA

MacKay, Robert B.
*Society for the Preservation of Long Island Antiquities
(Setauket, New York)*
BRYANT, GRIDLEY J. F.

Mainstone, Rowland
St. Albans, England
BOULTON AND WATT; BRUNEL, ISAMBARD K.;
FAIRBAIRN, WILLIAM; RANSOME, ERNEST LESLIE;
SMEATON, JOHN; STEPHENSON, GEORGE, AND
STEPHENSON, ROBERT; TELFORD, THOMAS

Makinson, Randell L.
University of Southern California, Pasadena
GREENE, HENRY MATHER, AND GREENE,
CHARLES SUMNER

Malcolmson, Reginald
University of Michigan
HILBERSEIMER, LUDWIG KARL; MALEVICH,
KASIMIR; NELSON, PAUL; VANTONGERLOO,
GEORGES; WACHSMANN, KONRAD; WEININGER,
ANDREW; WILLIAMS, AMANCIO

Mallory, Nina A.
State University of New York, Stony Brook
BIZZACHERI, CARLO; DE SANCTIS, FRANCESCO;
GREGORINI, DOMENICO; VALVASSORI, GABRIELE

Mancoff, Debra N.
Northwestern University
TALLMADGE, THOMAS EDDY

Marder, Tod A.
Rutgers University
FONTANA, DOMENICO; VALADIER, GIUSEPPE

Mariani, Riccardo
University of Florence
LIBERA, ADALBERTO; MUZIO, GIOVANNI;
PERSICO, EDOARDO

Marinescu, Constantin Marin
Rego Park, New York
ANTONESCU, PETRE; CANTACUZINO, GHEORGHE
MATEI; CREANGA, HORIA; DAMIAN, ASCANIO;
DELAVRANCEA-GIBORY, HENRIETTE; DOICESCU,
OCTAV; GHICA-BUDESTI, NICOLAE; IONESCU,
GRIGORE; LAZARESCU, CEZAR; MARCU, DUILIU;
NENCIULESCU, NICOLAE; PORUMBESCU, NICOLAE;
RICCI, TIBERIU; SMARANDESCU, PAUL;
SOCOLESCU, TOMA T.

Markowitz, Arnold L.
New York University
ZUCKER, PAUL

Martínez i Matamala, Adolf
Barcelona, Spain
BASSEGODA FAMILY; BERENGUER I MESTRES,
FRANCESCO; JUJOL I GIBERT, JOSEP MARIA; MASÓ
I VALENTI, RAFAEL; PUIG I CADAFALCH,
JOSEPH

Martorell, Josep
Barcelona, Spain
CANO LASSO, JULIO

Maxtone-Graham, John
New York City
GUIMARD, HÉCTOR; MEWÈS, CHARLES

Maycock, Susan E.
Cambridge Historical Commission (Massachusetts)
HARTWELL AND RICHARDSON

McAslan, John
London
BURNET, J. J.; CAMPBELL, JOHN ARCHIBALD;
MACLAREN, JAMES M.; REID, ROBERT; SALMON
AND GILLESPIE; THOMSON, ALEXANDER

McCarthy, Michael
University of Toronto
BECKFORD, WILLIAM; BLONDEL, GEORGES
FRANÇOIS; CHUTE, JOHN; KEENE, HENRY;
MILLER, SANDERSON; MÜNTZ, JOHANN
HENRICH; WALPOLE, HORACE

McCleary, Peter
University of Pennsylvania
LE RICOLAIS, ROBERT

McCormick, Thomas J.
Wheaton College
CLÉRISSEAU, CHARLES-LOUIS; MONTFERRAND,
AUGUSTE RICARD DE; STASOV, VASILI
PETROVICH; THOMON, THOMAS DE;
VORONIKHIN, A. N.; ZAKHAROV, ADRIAN
DMITRIEVICH

McCoy, Esther
Santa Monica, California
AIN, GREGORY; DAVIDSON, J. R.; GILL, IRVING;
JONES, A. QUINCY; SCHINDLER, R. M.

McCue, George
Kirkwood, Missouri
COPE AND STEWARDSON; EADS, JAMES
BUCHANAN

McFadden, Dennis
New York City
BORING, WILLIAM A.; CLINTON, CHARLES W.;
HAMLIN, A. D. F.; HAMLIN, TALBOT F.; LAMB,
THOMAS W.; LAMB AND RICH; LORD, AUSTIN

W.; LORD, JAMES B.; REED AND STEM; WARREN AND WETMORE

McHardy, George
Royal Institute of British Architects (London)
PAPWORTH, JOHN B.

McLane, Elizabeth
Horsham, England
AUBERTIN, JACQUES MARCEL; DEGLANE, HENRY; GRÉBER, JACQUES; LAPRADE, ALBERT; LAVIROTTE, JULES AIMÉ; MAGNE, AUGUSTE; MAGNE, LUCIEN; PLUMET, CHARLES; PROST, HENRI; SAUVAGE, HENRI

McLaughlin, Charles C.
American University
OLMSTED, FREDERICK LAW

McMath, George A.
Allen, McMath, Hawkins (Portland, Oregon)
DOYLE, ALBERT E.; WHIDDEN AND LEWIS

McParland, Edward
Trinity College (Dublin)
COOLEY, THOMAS; GANDON, JAMES; JOHNSTON, FRANCIS

Mead, Christopher
University of New Mexico
ABADIE, PAUL; GARNIER, CHARLES; GUADET, JULIEN

Metcalf, Priscilla
London
KNOWLES, J. T. SR.; KNOWLES, J. T. JR.

Meyer, Edina
Ramot Shavin, Israel
BAERWALD, ALEXANDER; KAUFFMANN, RICHARD YITZCHAK

Michels, Eileen Manning
College of St. Thomas
ELLIS, HARVEY

Middleton, R. D.
University of Cambridge
CESSART, LOUIS ALEXANDRE DE; CONTANT D'IVRY, PIERRE; CORDEMOY, JEAN LOUIS DE; COUTURE, GUILLAUME MARTIN; DESTAILLEUR, HIPPOLYTE-ALEXANDRE-GABRIEL; DIET, ARTHUR STANISLAS; DOMMEY, ETIENNE THÉODORE; DUBAN, FÉLIX; ESPÉRANDIEU, JACQUES HENRY; FÉLIBIEN DES AVAUX, JEAN FRANÇOIS; FRÉZIER, AMÉDÉE FRANÇOIS; GAUTHEY, EMILAND MARIE; HOREAU, HECTOR; LALOUX, VICTOR ALEXANDRE FRÉDÉRIC; LUSSON, ADRIEN LOUIS; MOREY, MATHIEU PROSPER; NAISSANT, CLAUDE; NICOLE, NICOLAS; PASCAL, JEAN LOUIS; PERRONET, JEAN RODOLPHE; QUATREMÈRE DE QUINCY, ANTOINE CHRYSOSTHÔME; QUESTEL, CHARLES AUGUSTE; RONDELET, JEAN BAPTISTE; SEDILLE, PAUL;

SEHEULT, FRANÇOIS LEONARD; SERVANDONI, GIOVANNI NICOLANO GERONIMO; VAUDOYER, ANTOINE LAURENT THOMAS, AND VAUDOYER, LÉON; VIOLLET-LE-DUC, EUGÈNE EMMANUEL

Miller, Naomi
Boston University
BULLANT, JEAN; DELORME, PHILIBERT; DU CERCEAU FAMILY; DUPÉRAC, ETIENNE; LESCOT, PIERRE

Miller, R. Craig
Metropolitan Museum of Art (New York)
EAMES, CHARLES O.; SAARINEN, ELIEL, AND SAARINEN, EERO

Millon, Henry A.
Center for Advanced Study, National Gallery of Art (Washington, D.C.)
ANTONELLI, ALESSANDRO; BARBERIS, LUIGI MICHELE; BARONCELLO, GIOVANNI FRANCESCO; BERTOLA, ANTONIO; BETTINO, ANTONIO; BIGIO, NANNI DI BACCIO; BOETTO, GROVENALE; BONSIGNORE, FERDINANDO; BONVICINI, PIETRO; BORRA, GIOVANNI BATTISTA; CAPRINO, MEO DA; CASTELLAMONTE, AMEDEO DI; CASTELLI, FILLIPO; CEPPI, CARLO; COSTAGUTA, ANDREA; DE CARLO, GIANCARLO; FEROGGIO, GIOVANNI BATTISTA; GALLO, FRANCESCO; GAROVE, MICHELANGELO; GUARINI, GUARINO; JUVARRA, FILIPPO; LANFRANCHI, CARLO EMANUELE; MAGNOCAVALLO, FRANCESCO OTTAVIO; MARTINEZ, FRANCESCO; MAZZUCHETTI, ALESSANDRO; NEGRO DI SANFRONT, ERCOLE; PACIOTTI, FRANCESCO; PALAGI, PELAGIO; PASSANTI, MARIO; PLANTERY, GIAN GIACOMO; PROMIS, CARLO; RANA, CARLO AMEDEO; RENACCO, NELLO; RIGOTTI, ANNIBALE; ROBILANT, FILIPPO NICOLIS DI; SACCHETTI, GIOVANNI BATTISTA; SCAPITTA, GIOVANNI BATTISTA; TALUCCHI, GIUSEPPE; VASCONI, FILIPPO; VITTONE, BERNARDO ANTONIO

Moneo, José Rafael
Madrid
SAENZ DE OIZA, FRANCISCO JAVIER

Moogk, Peter N.
University of British Columbia
MAILLOU, JEAN BAPTISTE

Moore, Katherine C.
Rye, New York
TROWBRIDGE AND LIVINGSTON

Moos, Stanislaus von
Technische Hogeschool Delft
BILL, MAX; MOSER, KARL; MOSER, WERNER M.; ROTH, ALFRED; SALVISBERG, OTTO R.; VENTURI, ROBERT

Morgan, William
University of Louisville
MURPHY, D. X.; VAUGHAN, HENRY

Morrison, Andrew Craig
Philadelphia
FURNESS, FRANK; MCELFATRICK, J. B.

Morrow, E. Joyce
Calgary, Alberta
MAWSON, THOMAS HAYTON

Morton, James P.
Cathedral of St. John the Divine (New York)
HEINS AND LA FARGE

Morton, W. Brown III
Waterford, Virginia
FEILDEN, BERNARD

Mosser, Monique
Groupe Histoire Architecture Mentalités Urbaines (Paris)
ANTOINE, JACQUES-DENIS

Murphy, Robert T.
Columbia Magazine (New Haven)
KEELY, PATRICK CHARLES

Murray, Peter
Birkbeck College
BRAMANTE, DONATO

Muthesius, Stefan
University of East Anglia
BUTTERFIELD, WILLIAM

Myer, John R.
Arrowstreet, Incorporated (Cambridge, Massachusetts)
VALLE, GINO

Myers, Denys Peter
Historic American Buildings Survey (Washington, D.C.)
ROGERS, ISAIAH

Navaretti, Peter
Burwood, Australia
DODS, ROBIN; IRWIN, LEIGHTON; PITT, WILLIAM

Ness, Leah
Columbia University
ECKBO, GARRETT; FITCH, JAMES MARSTON

Neuman, Robert
Florida State University
AUBERT, JEAN; BULLET DE CHAMBLAIN, JEAN BAPTISTE; COURTONNE, JEAN; DE COTTE, ROBERT; DELAMAIR, PIERRE ALEXIS; LASSURANCE, PIERRE

Nevins, Deborah
New York City
GRAY, EILEEN

Newhall, Amy W.
Harvard University
AḤMAD B. AḤMAD B. MUḤAMMAD AṬ-ṬŪLŪNĪ AND FAMILY; ḤASAN B. ḤUSAYN AṬ ṬŪLŪNĪ

Newhouse, Victoria
Architectural History Foundation (New York)
FATIO, MAURICE; HARRISON AND ABRAMOVITZ; VOLK, JOHN; WYETH, MARION SIMS

Nichols, Frederick D.
University of Virginia
JEFFERSON, THOMAS

Nicoletti, Manfredi G.
Rome
BASILE, ERNESTO; BASILE, GIOVANNI BATTISTA FILIPPO; CAMPANINI, ALFREDO; MORETTI, GAETANO; ROCCO, EMMANUELE

Nicolini, Alberto
Universidad Nacionalde Tucuma
BENOIT, PEDRO; GUIDO, ANGEL; NOEL, MARTIN; SACRISTE, EDUARDO

Niebling, Howard V.
Gannon University
BÖHM, DOMINIKUS; SCHWARZ, RUDOLF

Niroumand-Rad, Farhad
Chicago
CRAIG, JAMES; MARCONI FAMILY; SHEPPARD AND ROBSON; STERN, RAFFAELLO; TOLEDO, JUAN BATISTA DE

Norberg-Schulz, Christian
Oslo
DIENTZENHOFER, KILIAN IGNAZ; DIENTZENHOFER BROTHERS

Norton, Paul F.
University of Massachusetts at Amherst
COCKERELL, SAMUEL PEPYS; MCINTIRE, SAMUEL; RAMÉE, DANIEL; RAMÉE, JOSEPH JACQUES; STEUART, GEORGE

Oberlander, Judith
New York City
BACON, EDMUND; BALDWIN, BENJAMIN; BASSETT, FLORENCE KNOLL

O'Callaghan, John
London
GODWIN, EDWARD WILLIAM; PHIPPS, CHARLES JAMES

O'Dea, Shane
Memorial University of Newfoundland
BUTLER, WILLIAM F.; GREENE, WILLIAM H.; GREY, WILLIAM; KEOUGH, PATRICK; PURCELL, JAMES; SOUTHCOTT, JOHN T.

O'Donnell, Roderick
Magdalen College (Cambridge)

DONTHORN, W. J.; KEELING, E. BASSETT;
PILKINGTON, F. T.; SCOTT, MICHAEL; SELLERS,
J. H.; WILSON, HENRY

Oechslin, Werner
Universität Bonn
ALGAROTTI, FRANCESCO; BARABINO, CARLO
FRANCESCO; BUONAMICI, GIANFRANCESCO;
CANINA, LUIGI; CARAMUEL DE LOBKOWITZ,
JUAN; D'AGINCOURT, JEAN BAPTISTE SEROUX;
MILIZIA, FRANCESCO; MOOSBRUGGER, CASPAR;
SOUFFLOT, JACQUES-GABRIEL

O'Gorman, James F.
Wellesley College
BILLINGS, HAMMATT

Ohmi, Saka-e
Nihon University
ASHIWARA, YOSHINOBU; HAYASHI, SHŌJI;
MAEKAWA, KUNIO; OKADA, SHIN-ICHIRŌ;
TAKEDA, GOICHI; YOSHIDA, TETSURŌ;
YOSHIZAKA, TAKAMASA

Oliver, Richard
New York City
GOODHUE, BERTRAM GROSVENOR

Orth, Myra Dickman
American College in Paris
BLÈVE, JEAN LOUIS; BONNARD, JACQUES
CHARLES; BRÉBION, MAXIMILIEN; BULLET,
PIERRE; LENOIR LE ROMAIN, SAMSON NICOLAS;
LHÔTE, FRANÇOIS; LOUIS, VICTOR; NEUFFORGE,
JEAN FRANÇOIS DE; PIÈTRE, HENRI

Ortiz, Federico F.
University of Buenos Aires
ACOSTA, WLADIMIRO; AUSTRAL; BULLRICH,
FRANCISCO; VILAR, ANTONIO UBALDO;
VIRASORO, ALEJANDRO

Otto, Christian F.
Cornell University
NEUMANN, JOHANN BALTHASAR; PÖPPELMANN,
MATTHÄUS DANIEL

Otto, Stephen A.
*Ontario Ministry of Citizenship and Culture
(Toronto)*
BURKE, EDMUND; DICK, DAVID BRASH; LANE,
HENRY BOWYER

Overby, Osmund
University of Missouri—Columbia
YOUNG, AMMI B.

Pagliara, Pier Nicola
Rome
RAPHAEL, 1483–1520

Paine, Judith C.
Connecticut State Historic Preservation Office

(Hartford, Connecticut)
RIDDLE, THEODATE POPE

Pariset, François-Georges
*Académie Nationale des Sciences, Belles-Lettres et Arts
de Bordeaux (France)*
BARREAU DE CHEFDEVILLE, FRANÇOIS; COMBES,
LOUIS

Parks, Janet
Columbia University
HELLMUTH, OBATA, AND KASSABAUM

Paschall, Jo Anne
Atlanta College of Art
BECKET, WELTON; ESHERICK, JOSEPH; FRANK,
JOSEF; HÖGER, FRITZ; YAMASAKI, MINORU

Passanti, Chiara
Turin, Italy
ALFIERI, BENEDETTO

Patetta, Luciano
Milan
CERUTI, GIOVANNI; MORETTI, LUIGI

Pearlman, Jonathan
Austin, Texas
DEXTER, GEORGE MINOT

Pearson, Cliff
Columbia University
OTTO, FREI; SCHULTZE-NAUMBURG, PAUL

Pearson, Marjorie
New York Landmarks Preservation Commission
EDBROOKE, W. J.; GILBERT, BRADFORD L.;
KIMBALL, FRANCIS H.; LOWELL, GUY

Pearson, Paul David
City College, City University of New York
AALTO, ALVAR

Peatross, C. Ford
Library of Congress (Washington, D.C.)
NICHOLS, WILLIAM; SMITHMEYER AND PELZ

Peckham, Nicholas
Peckham and Wright (Columbia, Missouri)
GORES, LANDES

Pedio, Renato
Rome
MUSMECI, SERGIO; NICOLETTI, MANFREDI G.;
PELLEGRIN, LUIGI

Pedretti, Carlo
University of California, Los Angeles
LEONARDO DA VINCI

Peisch, Mark Lyons
Tenafly, New Jersey
GRIFFIN, MARION MAHONY; GRIFFIN, WALTER
BURLEY

Pellegri, Marco
Parma, Italy
PETITOT DI LIONE, ENNEMONDO ALESSANDRO

Pérez i Sànchez, Miguel
Barcelona, Spain
MARTORELL, JOAN; RASPALL, MANUEL J.

Peterson, Charles E.
Carpenters' Company of the City and County of Philadelphia
SMITH, ROBERT

Petruccioli, Attilio
Rome
ASTENGO, GIOVANNI

Petsas, Vassilia Ph.
Columbia University
KONSTANTINIDIS, ARIS; PIKIONIS, D. A.

Phillips, Patricia C.
SITE (New York)
BARBER, DONN; BARNES, EDWARD LARABEE; BAYLEY, JOHN B.; CIAMPI, MARIO; DOXIADIS, CONSTANTINOS A.; GOLDBERG, BERTRAND; GUGLER, ERIC; LAPIDUS, MORRIS; MUJICA, FRANCISCO; O'NEILL, GERARD; PRICE, WILLIAM; SOLERI, PAOLO; STACY-JUDD, ROBERT; TYNG, ANNE GRISWOLD; WARD, JASPER D.; WEIDLINGER ASSOCIATES; WELLS, MALCOLM

Pierson, William H. Jr.
Williams College
RICHARDSON, H. H.

Pinkney, David H.
University of Washington
HAUSSMANN, GEORGES-EUGÈNE

Pinocelly, Salvador
Dirreción de Arquitectura y Conservación del Patrimonio Artístico Nacional (Mexico City)
DEL MORAL, ENRIQUE; PÉREZ PALACIOS, AUGUSTO; SORDO MADALENO, JUAN

Pinto, John
Smith College
FUGA, FERDINANDO; MICHETTI, NICOLA; NOLLI, GIOVANNI BATTISTA; RAGUZZINI, FILIPPO; RASTRELLI, BARTOLOMMEO; SALVI, NICOLA; TEODOLI, GIROLAMO

Placzek, Adolf K.
Columbia University
DIETTERLIN, WENDEL

Plunz, Richard A.
Columbia University
CANDILIS JOSIC WOODS; CHERMAYEFF, SERGE IVAN

Pollak, Martha
Massachusetts Institute of Technology
ASPRUCCI, ANTONIO; BARBERI, GIUSEPPE; BELLI, PASQUALE; CAMPORESE FAMILY; CASTELLAMONTE, CARLO; CORTINI, PUBLIO; DEL DUCA, GIACOMO; DOLCEBUONO, GIOVANNI GIACOMO; DOTTI, CARLO FRANCESCO; GUERRA FAMILY; LANFRANCHI, FRANCESCO; MICHELA, COSTANZO; PALMA, ANDREA; QUARINI, MARIO LUDOVICO; SIMONETTI, MICHELANGELO; VALPERGA, MAURIZIO; VITOZZI, ASCANIO

Popova, Maria
Columbia University
ANGELOVA-VINAROVA, VICTORIA; DIMCHEV, EMIL; IORDANOV AND OVCHAROV; KANTARDZHIEV, PETUR; MILANOV, IORDAN; MOMCHILOV, PETKO; OVCHAROV, GEORGI RADEV; POPOV, IVAN

Poppeliers, John
United States Department of the Interior (Washington, D.C.)
WINDRIM, JAMES H.

Port, M. H.
Queen Mary College
GOODWIN, FRANCIS

Posener, Julius
Akademie der Künste (Berlin)
BERG, MAX

Potter, Elisabeth Walton
Oregon State Office of Historic Preservation (Salem)
BEBB, CHARLES H.; CUTTER, KIRTLAND K.; GOULD, CARL F.; HEIDE, AUGUST F.; LEWIS, DAVID C.; STOREY, ELLSWORTH P.; TOURTELLOTTE, JOHN E.; WHITEHOUSE, MORRIS H.

Powers, Alan
London
COOPER, EDWIN; GOODHARD-RENDEL, H. S.; HOLDEN, CHARLES; SMITHSON, ALISON, AND SMITHSON, PETER; SPENCE, BASIL; STIRLING AND GOWAN; TREHEARNE AND NORMAN; WEBB, ASTON; YORKE, FRANCIS

Prelovšek, Damjan
Slovenska akademija znanosti in umetnosti (Ljubljana, Yugoslavia)
PLEČNIK, JOŽE

Puppin, Carla
Bryn Mawr College
MASSARI, GIORGIO; RIZZO, ANTONIO

Quinan, Jack
State University of New York, Buffalo
GREEN, E. B.; NICHOLSON, PETER; PAIN, WILLIAM; WILLARD, SOLOMON

Quiney, A. P.
London
BARLOW, W. H.; BRODERICK, CUTHBERT; PEARSON, J. L.

Rabreau, Daniel
Groupe Histoire Architecture Mentalités Urbaines (Paris)
CEINERAY, JEAN BAPTISTE; CRUCY, MATHURIN; DAMESNE, LOUIS EMMANUEL AIMÉ; DE WAILLY, CHARLES; HUVÉ, JEAN-JACQUES-MARIE; PEYRE FAMILY

Radke, Gary M.
Syracuse University
ALESSI, GALEAZZO; ARRIGONI, ATTILIO; CACCINI, GIOVANNI BATTISTA; CAGNOLA, LUIGI; MAGNANI FAMILY; ORSOLINO FAMILY; PACCHIONI FAMILY; PACIOLI, LUCA; SOAVE, FELICE; TERZI, FILIPPO

Rasmussen, William M. S.
Virginia Museum of Fine Arts
ARISS, JOHN; BUCKLAND, WILLIAM

Rattner, Selma
Victorian Society in America (New York)
ASPINWALL, JAMES L.; RENWICK, JAMES

Reed, Henry Hope
Classical America (New York)
BAKEWELL AND BROWN; PLATT, CHARLES ADAMS; SHUTZE, PHILIP TRAMMELL; TRUMBAUER, HORACE; YORK AND SAWYER

Reiff, Daniel D.
State University of New York College, Fredonia
HADFIELD, GEORGE; HALLET, ETIENNE SULPICE; HOBAN, JAMES; L'ENFANT, PIERRE CHARLES; THORNTON, WILLIAM

Reiss, Sheryl E.
Princeton University
AMADEO, GIOVANNI ANTONIO; BASSI, MARTINO; DOMENICO DA CORTONA; FANCELLI, LUCA

Reitzes, Lisa B.
University of Delaware
BLOUET, G. ABEL; FAMIN, AUGUSTE; GARLING, HENRY B.; HUYOT, JEAN NICOLAS; LAVES, GEORGES LUDWIG FRIEDRICH; LEBAS, LOUIS HIPPOLYTE; LECLÈRE, ACHILLE; LEFRANC, PIERRE BERNARD; PAXTON, JOSEPH; PENCHAUD, MICHEL ROBERT; RENIÉ, ANDRÉ MARIE

Reuther, Hans
Technische Universität Berlin
DECKER, PAUL THE ELDER; HOCHEDER, KARL; NEUMANN, F. I. M.

Reynolds, Donald Martin
New York City
ABBEY, EDWIN A.; ALMIRALL, RAYMOND F.; ALSCHULER, ALFRED S.; ALSTON, JOHN M.; ANDREWS, FRANK M.; ANGELL, FRANK W.; ANGELL, TRUMAN OSBORN; BRADLEY, LUCAS; BUNSHAFT, GORDON; FRAZEE, JOHN; FROST, CHARLES S.; FROST, HARRY T.

Richards, J. M.
London
BRYGGMAN, ERIK; COATES, WELLS; ENGEL, CARL LUDWIG

Richardson, Douglas
University of Toronto
MEDLEY, EDWARD; ZEIDLER, E. H.

Richardson, Margaret
Royal Institute of British Architects (London)
AITCHISON, GEORGE; BRANDON, DAVID; DONALDSON, THOMAS LEVERTON; FLETCHER, BANISTER FLIGHT; GIBSON, JOHN; GINGELL, WILLIAM BRUCE; GODWIN, GEORGE; GREEN, WILLIAM CURTIS; JEKYLL, GERTRUDE; MAUFE, EDWARD BRANTWOOD; SCOTT, CHESTERTON, AND SHEPHERD

Riches, Anne
Edinburgh
BRETTINGHAM, MATTHEW; LEONI, GIACOMO

Riopelle, Christopher
Institute of Fine Arts, New York University
GUTTON, HENRI B.; LENORMAND, LOUIS; LETAROUILLY, PAUL MARIE

Robins, Anthony W.
New York City Landmarks Preservation Commission
BAUM, DWIGHT J.

Robinson, John Martin
London
WYATT, LEWIS; WYATT, SAMUEL

Rogers, James G. III
Butler Rogers Baskett Associates, Incorporated (New York)
ROGERS, JAMES GAMBLE

Rogerson, Robert W. K. C.
Glasgow, Scotland
COIA, JACK

Rohatgi, Pauline
India Office Library (London)
AGG, JAMES; ANBURY, THOMAS; COLEMAN, G. D.; COWPER, T. A.; DANIELL, THOMAS; FORBES, W. N.; GARSTIN, JOHN; GOLDINGHAM, JOHN; HAVILLAND, T. F. DE; WYATT, CHARLES

Roman, Gail Harrison
Vassar College
TATLIN, VLADIMIR EVGRAFOVICH

Ronchi, Lisa
Rome
ZEVI, BRUNO

Rosenfeld, M. N.
Musée des Beaux-Arts de Montréal
SERLIO, SEBASTIANO

Rosenthal, Earl E.
University of Chicago
MACHUCHA, PEDRO

Ross, Marion Dean
University of Oregon
BELLUSCHI, PIETRO; KRUMBEIN, JUSTUS; LAWRENCE, ELLIS FULLER; LAZARUS, EDGAR M.; PARKER, JAMIESON KIRKWOOD; PIPER, WILLIAM W.; ROSENBERG, LOUIS CONRAD; SCHACT, EMIL; WILLCOX, WALTER ROSS BAUMES; YEON, JOHN B.

Roth, Leland M.
University of Oregon
BIGELOW, HENRY FORBES; MCKIM, MEAD, AND WHITE

Rousset-Charny, Gérard
Paris
BARRÉ, JEAN BENOÎT VINCENT; BERTRAND, CLAUDE; DELAFOSSE, JEAN CHARLES; DESMAISONS, PIERRE; GONDOUIN, JACQUES; LE CAMUS DE MEZIÈRES, NICOLAS; LE CARPENTIER, ANTOINE MATHIEU; LEGRAND, JACQUES GUILLAUME; LE MASSON, LOUIS; LEMOINE, PAUL GUILLAUME; MIQUE, RICHARD; MOLINOS, JACQUES; MOREAU-DESPROUX, PIERRE-LOUIS; PETIT-RADEL, LOUIS-FRANÇOIS; POTAIN, NICOLAS MARIE; RAYMOND, JEAN ARNAUD; ROUSSEAU, PIERRE; ROUSSET, PIERRE NOËL; SOUFFLOT LE ROMAIN, FRANÇOIS; TARAVAL, LOUIS GUSTAVE; TROUARD, LOUIS FRANÇOIS; VIGNY, PIERRE DE

Rowan, Alistair
University College (Dublin)
BRYCE, DAVID; KNIGHT, R. P.

Rub, Timothy F.
Institute of Fine Arts, New York University
PRICE, BRUCE

Rubens, Godfrey
London
GEORGE, ERNEST; KNOTT, RALPH N.; LETHABY, W. R.; MAY, EDWARD JOHN; NEWTON, ERNEST; PITE, ARTHUR BERESFORD

Russell, James
New York City
KOUZMANOFF, ALEXANDER

Russo, Kathleen
Florida Atlantic University
CARTAUD, JEAN; DULIN, NICOLAS; LE BLOND, JEAN; MANSART DE SAGONNE, JACQUES HARDOUIN

Rutherford, J. M.
The Royal Pavilion, Art Gallery and Museums (Brighton, England)
BUSBY, CHARLES AUGUSTUS

Saalman, Howard
Carnegie-Mellon University
BRUNELLESCHI, FILIPPO; MANETTI CIACCHERI, ANTONIO DI

Saint, Andrew
London
ADAMS, MAURICE B.; CRESWELL, H. B.; DOYLE, J. F.; EDIS, R. W.; FLORENCE, H. L.; GARNER, THOMAS; NESFIELD, W. EDEN; SHAW, R. NORMAN

Salvadori, Mario G.
Columbia University
NERVI, PIER LUIGI

Sanders, John L.
University of North Carolina
PATON, DAVID

Santomasso, Eugene A.
Brooklyn College, City University of New York
ENDELL, AUGUST; HABLIK, WENZEL; KOHTZ, OTTO; OBRIST, HERMANN; STEINER, RUDOLF

Satkowski, Leon
Syracuse University
AMMANNATI, BARTOLOMEO; BUONTALENTI, BERNARDO; VASARI, GIORGIO

Savage, Peter
University of Edinburgh
LORIMER, ROBERT S.

Schall, Jan
Atlanta College of Art Library
SIBOUR, JULES HENRI DE; STONOROV, OSCAR; VILLANUEVA, CARLOS RAÚL

Schneider, Donald D.
Scarsdale, New York
LECOINTE, J.-F.-J.; LEPÈRE, JEAN-BAPTISTE

Schorske, Carl E.
Princeton University
WAGNER, OTTO

Schumacher, Thomas L.
University of Virginia
ALBINI, FRANCO; BENEVOLO, LEONARDO; CAPPONI, GIUSEPPE; CATTANEO, CESARE; COSENZA, LUIGI; DANERI, LUIGI CARLO; LINGERI, PIETRO; NIZZOLI, MARCELLO; VIGANÓ, VITTORIANO

Schwartzbaum, Elizabeth
Rome
ARNOULT DE BINCHE; BOULOGNE, JEAN AMEL DE; KELDERMANS FAMILY; MATHIEU DE LAYENS; VAN BOGHEM, LOUIS; VAN HENEGOUWEN, JAN; VAN RUYSBROECK, JAN; VAN THIENEN, JAKOB; WAGHEMAKERE FAMILY

Scully, Arthur Jr.
Tulane University
DAKIN, JAMES

Searing, Helen
Smith College

BERLAGE, H. P.; DE KLERK, MICHEL; OUD,
J. J. P.; VAN DER VLUGT AND BRINKMAN

Segger, Martin
University of Victoria
MACLURE, SAMUEL

Sekler, Eduard F.
Harvard University
HOFFMANN, JOSEF; LE CORBUSIER; MOSER,
KOLOMAN

Sekler, Mary Patricia May
Harvard University
JEANNERET, PIERRE; LE CORBUSIER

Severini, Lois
Institute of Fine Arts, New York University
SAELTZER, ALEXANDER

Sexton, Mehrangiz Nikou
Nyack, New York
CHADIRJI, RIFAT; MANSFELD, ALFRED; ROA,
YVES; SHARON, ARYEH

Shank, Wesley I.
Iowa State University
COCHRANE AND PIQUENARD; ECKEL, E. J.; MIX,
EDWARD T.; RAGUE, JOHN FRANCIS

Shapiro, Ellen R.
Yale University
BAZZANI, CESARE; BROGGI, LUIGI; CHIATTONE,
MARIO; GIOVANNONI, GUSTAVO; LA PADULA,
ERNESTO BRUNO; MEDUNA, GIOVANNI
BATTISTA; QUARONI, LUDOVICO; SAMONÀ,
GIUSEPPE

Sharp, Dennis
Architectural Association (London)
ATKINSON, GEORGE; CONNELL, WARD, AND
LUCAS; FINSTERLIN, HERMANN

Sheaff, Nicholas
National Trust Archive (Dublin)
CASTLE, RICHARD; STAPLETON, MICHAEL

Shubert, Howard
University of Toronto
CAPORALI, GIOVAN BATTISTA; CAPRAROLA,
COLA DA; CIVITALI, MATTEO DI GIOVANNI AND
FAMILY; FRANCIONE; LUCANO, GIOVANNI
BATTISTA DA; PIETRASANTA, JACOPO DA;
PUGLIANE, COSIMO

Shutlak, Garry D.
Public Archives of Nova Scotia (Halifax)
HILDRITH, ISSAC; STIRLING, DAVID

Siegel, Stuart N.
New York City
HOPPIN, FRANCIS L. V.

Silk, Gerald D.
Columbia University

BALLA, GIACOMO; MARCHI, VIRGILIO;
PRAMPOLINI, ENRICO

Silverman, Debora
University of California, Los Angeles
JOURDAIN, FRANTZ

Singelenberg, Pieter
University of Nijmegen
CUYPERS, EDUARD; CUYPERS, P. J. H.; VAN
EESTEREN, CORNELIS

Singer, Harry
Tamarac, Florida
CHAMBLESS, EDGAR

Šlachta, Štefan
Bratislava, Czechoslovakia
JURKOVIČ, DUŠAN; KARFÍK, VLADIMÍR

Šlapeta, Vladimír
Prague
BENŠ, ADOLF; ČERNÝ, FRANTIŠEK M.; CHOCHOL,
JOSEF; EISLER, OTTO; FEUERSTEIN, BEDŘICH;
FRAGNER, JAROSLAV; FUCHS, BOHUSLAV; GOČÁR,
JOSEF; HAVLÍČEK, JOSEF; HONZÍK, KAREL;
JANÁK, PAVEL; KOTĚRA, JAN; KRÁLÍK, EMIL;
KRANZ, JOSEF; KREJCAR, JAROMÍR; KROHA, JIŘÍ;
KYSELA, LUDVÍK; LINHART, EVŽEN; NOVOTNÝ,
OTAKAR; ROŠKOT, KAMIL; ROZEHNAL,
BEDŘICH; STARÝ, OLDŘICH; TYL, OLDŘICH; ŽÁK,
LADISLAV

Sloan, Thomas L.
University of Virginia
BOYINGTON, WILLIAM W.

Smith, Charles Saumarez
Christ College (Cambridge)
CAMPBELL, COLEN

Smith, Christine
Rosary College
ANGELO DA ORVIETO; BONANNO;
BONAVENTURA; BUSCHETO; D'ANGICOURT,
PIERRE; GADDI, TADDEO; LANFRANCO; MATAS,
NICCOLO; RAINALDO; RISTORO, FRA, AND SISTO,
FRA; TEDESCO, JACOPO

Smith, Elizabeth A. T.
New York City
ARTIGAS, FRANCISCO; CABRERO, FRANCISCO;
REPULLES I VARGAS, ENRIQUE; RODRÍGUEZ
TIZÓN, VENTURA; TORROJA MINET, EDUARDO;
VILLANUEVA, JUAN DE

Smith, Elizabeth A. T.
Columbia University
HURTADO IZQUIERDO, FRANCISCO

Smith, Elizabeth A. T.
Columbia University
GALLISSÀ SOQUÉ, ANTONIO

Solà-Morales, Ignasi de
Barcelona, Spain
GONZALES Y ALVARE-OSSORIO, ANIBAL;
MARTINELL BRUNET, CÉSAR; RUBÍO I BELLVER,
JOAN

Soria y Puig, Arturo
Madrid
CERDÁ, ILDEFONSO

Sowell, Joanne E.
Florida State University
BUCHSBAUM, HANNS; GANGHOFER, JÖRG;
HEINZELMANN, KONRAD; WOLFF, JACOB THE
ELDER, AND WOLFF, JACOB THE YOUNGER

Spence, T. Rory
London
STOKES, LEONARD

Spencer, John R.
Duke University
IL FILARETE

Spiro, Anna Lee
Columbia University
GOODWIN, PHILIP L.; RICCI, LEONARDO

Sprague, Paul E.
University of Wisconsin
ADLER AND SULLIVAN; BAUMANN, FREDERICK;
SULLIVAN, LOUIS H.

Squarzina, Silvia Danesi
Rome
DE RENZI, MARIO; LABO, MARIO; PONTI, GIO

St. Laurent, Beatrice
Harvard University
KEMALETTIN; MEHMET TAHIR AĞA

Stacpoole, John
Auckland, New Zealand
CLERE, F. DE J.; GUMMER, W. H.; LAWSON,
R. A.; MAHONEY, EDWARD AND MAHONEY,
THOMAS; MASON, WILLIAM; MOUNTFORT,
B. W.; PETRE, F. W.; SCOTT, JOHN; THATCHER,
FREDERICK; WARREN, MILES; WOOD, CECIL

Stage, Jeanine Clements
Florida State University
BÖBLINGER, MATTHÄUS, AND BÖBLINGER, HANS;
ENSINGEN, ULRICH VON; ENSINGER, MATTHÄUS;
EOSANDER, JOHANN FRIEDRICH; SCHOCH, HANS

Stamp, Gavin
London
ADAMS, HOLDEN, AND PEARSON; BEGG, JOHN;
CHISHOLM, ROBERT F.; GEORGE, WALTER;
GRANVILLE, WALTER; HOLDEN, CHARLES; LAMB,
E. B.; LEITH, GORDON; LUTYENS, EDWIN;
MEDD, H. A. N.; MOORE, TEMPLE; REILLY,
CHARLES HERBERT; RICHARDSON, ALBERT E.;

RUSSELL, ROBERT TOR; SCHULTZ, ROBERT WEIR;
SCOTT, ADRIAN GILBERT; SCOTT, GILES GILBERT;
SCOTT, GEORGE GILBERT JR.; SHOOSMITH, A. G.;
STEVENS, FREDERICK WILLIAM; WITTET,
GEORGE

Stanton, Phoebe B.
The Johns Hopkins University
LONG, ROBERT CAREY; PUGIN, AUGUSTUS
CHARLES; PUGIN, AUGUSTUS WELBY
NORTHMORE; UPJOHN, RICHARD; WILLS, FRANK

Stargard, William B.
Columbia University
ALEOTTI, GIOVANNI BATTISTA

Steege, Gwen W.
Williamstown, Massachusetts
ALLEN, ZACHARIAH; BABCOCK, CHARLES; BELL,
WILLIAM E.; BRADY, JOSIAH R.; CLINTON AND
RUSSELL; COSTIGAN, FRANCIS; EAMES, WILLIAM
S.; EDBROOKE, FRANK E.; EIDLITZ, CYRUS;
EISENMANN, JOHN; HAMILTON, ANDREW;
HIGGINSON, AUGUSTUS BARKER; HOPKINS,
JOHN HENRY; KIMBALL, THOMAS ROGERS;
KLETTING, RICHARD; LEE, FRANCIS D.; LITTLE,
ARTHUR; MASON, GEORGE DEWITT; OTIS,
ELISHA GRAVES; REID, JAMES WILLIAM;
SCHWEINFURTH, CHARLES FREDERICK; STOKES,
I. N. PHELPS; WHEELWRIGHT, EDMUND M.

Steinmann, Martin
Archithese (Zurich)
ARTARIA, PAUL; BERNOULLI, HANS; HAEFELI,
MAX ERNST; SCHMIDT, HANS; STEIGER, RUDOLF

Stern, Robert A. M.
Columbia University
HOWE, GEORGE

Stewart, J. Douglas
Queens University
BROWNE, GEORGE

Stillman, Damie
University of Delaware
ADAM, JAMES; ADAM, JOHN; ADAM, ROBERT;
ADAM FAMILY; BAXTER, JOHN; BONOMI, JOSEPH;
HUBERT, AUGUSTE; JOHNSON, JOHN; MANGIN,
JOSEPH FRANÇOIS; MCCOMB, JOHN JR.

Stoddard, Whitney S.
Williams College
THOMPSON, BENJAMIN

Strauss, Susan
New York City
BADOVICI, JEAN; BRAGDON, CLAUDE F.;
FRIEDMAN, YONA; GRAHAM, BRUCE JOHN;
HEJDUK, JOHN; KIKUTAKE, KIYONORI;
MAYMONT, PAUL; MOORE, CHARLES W.;
PARENT, CLAUDE; POLSHEK, JAMES STEWART;

SCHAROUN, HANS; SKIDMORE, OWINGS, AND
MERRILL; STEVENS, JOHN CALVIN; STONE,
EDWARD DURELL; STUBBINS, HUGH ASHER JR.;
TANGE, KENZO; UTZON, JØRN

Stroud, Dorothy
Sir John Soane's Museum (London)
BROWN, CAPABILITY; DANCE, GEORGE THE
ELDER; DANCE, GEORGE THE YOUNGER;
HOLLAND, HENRY; REPTON, HUMPHRY; SOANE,
JOHN

Summerson, John
Sir John Soane's Museum (London)
AUDSLEY, G. A.; CLARKE, G. SOMERS; EMMETT,
JOHN T.; NASH, JOHN

Swain, Richard O.
Rider College
BOYCEAU, JACQUES; LONDON, GEORGE; MOLLET
FAMILY; SHENSTONE, WILLIAM; SWITZER,
STEPHEN; WISE, HENRY

Symondson, Anthony
London
CARPENTER, R. C.; COMPER, JOHN NINIAN;
DARBISHIRE, H. A.; MICKLETHWAITE, J. T.

Tadgell, Christopher
London
CHEVOTET, JEAN-MICHEL; GABRIEL, ANGE
JACQUES; GABRIEL, JACQUES

Tait, A. A.
University of Glasgow
ADAM, WILLIAM; CAMERON, CHARLES; MAY,
HUGH

Tarán, Marina E. L.
Córdoba, Argentina
KRONFUSS, JUAN

Tarn, J. N.
University of Liverpool
ELLIS, PETER

Tarragó Cid, Salvador
Barcelona, Spain
TORRES CLAVÉ, JOSEP

Tatum, George B.
University of Delaware
DOWNING, A. J.; HAVILAND, JOHN; JOHNSTON,
WILLIAM L.; STRICKLAND, WILLIAM

Taylor, Jennifer
University of Sydney
DALTON, JOHN

Taylor, Jeremy
University of York
FOWLER, CHARLES

Tegethoff, Wolf
Bonn
HÄRING, HUGO

Teitelman, Edward
Camden, New Jersey
EYRE, WILSON

Terranova, Antonino
Rome
BURBA, GARIBALDI; DEL DEBBIO, ENRICO;
FIORENTINO, MARIO; FOSCHINI, ARNALDO;
GORIO, FEDERICO; MORANDI, RICCARDO;
PALANTI, GIANCARLO

Thorpe, F. J.
National Museum of Man (Ottawa)
VERRIER, ETIENNE

Tobriner, Stephen
University of California, Berkeley
AMATO, GIACOMO; AMATO, PAOLO; AMICO,
GIOVANNI BIAGIO; BATTAGLIA, FRANCESCO;
CARNELIVARI, MATTEO; GAGLIARDI, ROSARIO;
ITALIA, ANGELO; ITTAR, STEFANO; LABISI,
PAOLO; MARVUGLIA, GIUSEPPE VENANZIO;
SINATRA, VINCENZO; VACCARINI, GIOVANNI
BAPTISTA; VERMEXIO FAMILY

Toker, Franklin
University of Pittsburgh
BOURGEAU, VICTOR; O'DONNELL, JAMES

Tooley, M. J.
University of Durham
MELLOR, TOM

Torbert, Donald R.
University of Minnesota
BUFFINGTON, LEROY SUNDERLUND

Tucci, Douglass Shand
Harvard University
ALLEN AND COLLENS; CRAM, RALPH ADAMS

Tuck, Robert C.
Prince Edward Island
HARRIS, WILLIAM CRITCHLOW

Turak, Theodore
Germantown, Maryland
EDELMANN, JOHN

Tuttle, Richard J.
Tulane University
BORROMEO, CARLO; DANTI FAMILY;
FIORAVANTI, ARISTOTELE; ROSSETTI, BIAGIO;
SANGALLO FAMILY; TIBALDI, PELLEGRINO

Tyrwhitt, Jaqueline
Ekistics (Athens)
GEDDES, PATRICK

Vago, Pierre
Paris
ECOCHARD, MICHEL

Vancsa, Eckart
Institut für Österreichsche Kunstforschung des Bundesdenkmalamtes (Vienna)
FÖRSTER, EMIL VON; FÖRSTER, LUDWIG VON; KORNHÄUSEL, JOSEF; MOREAU, KARL VON

Van Ingen, Anne H.
New York City
HARRISON, HENRY G.

Van Zanten, Ann Lorenz
Chicago Historical Society
ATWOOD, CHARLES B.; BAILLY, ANTOINE-NICOLAS; BALLU, THEODORE; BALTARD, VICTOR; CENDRIER, FRANÇOIS-ALEXIS; DAVIOUD, GABRIEL; DUC, LOUIS

Van Zanten, David T.
Northwestern University
BINDESBØLL, GOTTLIEB; BOSSAN, PIERRE; GARNIER, CHARLES; GAU, FRANZ CHRISTIAN; HITTORFF, JACQUES IGNACE; JONES, OWEN; LABROUSTE, HENRI; LABROUSTE, THÉODORE; VISCONTI, LUDOVICO

Varnedoe, Kirk
Institute of Fine Arts, New York University
CHEVAL, FERDINAND

Varriano, John
Mt. Holyoke College
CASTELLI, DOMENICO; LONGHI FAMILY; MARTINELLI, DOMENICO; MORELLI, COSIMO; PONZIO, FLAMINIO; RAINALDI, GIROLAMO; VASANZIO, GIOVANNI

Verey, David
Cirencester, England
BODLEY, GEORGE F.

Verheyen, Egon
The Johns Hopkins University
BEER, MICHAEL; FISCHER, KARL VON; FURTTENBACH, JOSEPH; HOLL, ELIAS; LEUTHNER VON GRUND, ABRAHAM; PILGRAM, ANTON; STURM, L. C.

Villadsen, Villads
Randers Kunstmuseum (Denmark)
HANSEN, CHRISTIAN FREDERIK; HANSEN, HANS CHRISTIAN; HANSEN, THEOPHILUS; HERHOLDT, J. D.; HETSCH, G. F.; JENSEN, ALBERT; JØRGENSEN, EMIL; JØRGENSEN, THORVALD; KAMPMANN, HACK; NEBELONG, J. H.; PETERSEN, CARL; PETERSEN, VILHELM; THOMSEN, EDVARD; TUSCHER, MARCUS; TVEDE, GOTFRED

Viñuales, Graciela M.
Universidad Nacional del Nordeste las Heras
ROCA, FRANCISCO

Von Eckardt, Wolf
Washington, D.C.
MENDELSOHN, ERIC

Waddy, Patricia
Syracuse University
ARRIGUCCI, LUIGI; SORIA, GIOVANNI BATTISTA

Waechter, H. H.
Creswell, Oregon
KLEIN, ALEXANDER; TAUT, BRUNO; TAUT, MAX

Wagg, Susan
Montreal
NOBBS, PERCY ERSKINE

Waisman, Marina
Córdoba, Argentina
ALVAREZ, MARIO ROBERTO; TEDESCHI, ENRICO

Walker, Bruce
Duncan of Jordanstone College of Art and University of Dundee
ANDERSON, R. ROWAND; CLARKE AND BELL; HAMILTON, THOMAS; HONEYMAN AND KEPPIE; KEMP, GEORGE; RHIND, DAVID

Walker, David M.
Edinburgh
BURN, WILLIAM; HAMILTON, DAVID; SELLARS, JAMES; THOMSON, JAMES

Walton, Hannah
London
WALTON, GEORGE

Ward, James
Institute of Fine Arts, New York University
NÉNOT, HENRI-PAUL; PAUL, BRUNO; SCHOLER, FRIEDRICH; SELMERSHEIM, TONY; TESSENOW, HEINRICH

Watkin, David
University of Cambridge
COCKERELL, C. R.; HOPE, THOMAS; TATHAM, CHARLES H.

Weakley, Joan C.
New York City
DIAPER, FREDERIC

Weisman, Winston
Pennsylvania State University
GILBERT, CASS; POST, GEORGE BROWNE

Weitze, Karen J.
Elk Grove, California
BEASLEY, CHARLES

Welch, Anthony
University of Victoria
'ABBAS; AKBAR

Westfall, Carroll William
University of Illinois at Chicago Circle
ANTOLINI, GIOVANNI ANTONIO; BALDI,
BERNARDINO; LAURANA, LUCIANO

Whiffen, Marcus
Arizona State University
BARRY, CHARLES; BARRY, EDWARD M.; WHITE,
THOMAS

White, C. Stuart Jr.
Banwell, White, and Arnold, Incorporated (Hanover,
New Hampshire)
STEIN, RICHARD G.; STEPHENSON, ROBERT
STORER

White, Janet R.
Helmuth, Obata, and Kassabaum (Alton, Illinois)
HERRON, RON

White, John
University of Western Australia
JEWELL, RICHARD ROACH; POOLE, GEORGE
TEMPLE; REVELEY, HENRY WILLEY

Wiebenson, Dora
University of Virginia
BARBIER, FRANÇOIS; CARMONTELLE, LOUIS
CARROGIS; GARNIER, TONY; GIRARDIN, RENÉ
LOUIS; MOREL, JEAN-MARIE; ROBERT, HUBERT;
VITRUVIUS (WRITINGS) WATELET, CLAUDE-
HENRI

Wiedenhoeft, Ron
Colorado School of Mines
BLUNTSCHLI, A. F.; DÖCKER, RICHARD;
EIERMANN, EGON; EISENLOHR, LUDWIG;
ELSAESSER, MARTIN; FORBAT, FRED; GENZMER,
FELIX; GROPIUS, MARTIN; HEBEBRAND, WERNER;
HENRICI, KARL; HENTRICH, HELMUT; HÖGG,
EMIL; KRAEMER, FRIEDRICH WILHELM;
LUCKHARDT, HANS, AND LUCKHARDT, WASSILI;
MARCH, WERNER; MÖHRING, BRUNO; OTZEN,
JOHANNES; SCHWEITZER, HEINRICH;
SCHWEITZER, O. E.; STRAUMER, HEINRICH;
WOLF, PAUL

Wietek, Gerhard
Der Landesmuseumsdirektor des Landes Schleswig-
Holstein (Gottorp, Germany)
ARENS, JOHANN AUGUST

Wileman, Jane Anne
New York City
WOOD FAMILY

Wilk, Christopher
New York City
RIEMERSCHMID, RICHARD

Wilkinson, Catherine
Brown University
CANO, ALONSO; EGAS, ENRIQUE; HERRERA, JUAN
DE; SILOE, DIEGO DE

Williamson, Roxanne
University of Texas
CLAYTON, NICHOLAS J.; COOK, ABNER H.;
GORDON, J. RIELY; MYERS, ELIJAH E.; STAUB,
JOHN F.; TROST, HENRY CHARLES

Willinge, Mariet J. H.
Nederlands Documentatiecentrum voor de Bouwkunst
(Amsterdam)
BILHAMER, JOOST JANSZOON; DE KEY, LIEVEN;
DORTSMANN, ADRIAEN; FLORIS, CORNELIS II;
ROMEIN, THOMAS; SWART, PIETER DE; VAN
HERENGRAVE, HERMAN; VAN 'S GRAVESANDE,
ARENT; VENNECOOL, STEVEN; VINGBOONS,
PHILIPS

Willis, Alfred
New York City
BASCOURT, JOSEPH; BEYAERT, HENRI; BLÉROT,
ERNEST; BRAEM, RENAAT; CAUCHIE, PAUL;
CHAMBON, ALBAN; CLOQUET, LOUIS;
CLUYSENAAR, J. P.; DOW, ALDEN B.; EGGERICX,
JEAN J.; HÉBRARD, ERNEST; HOSTE, HUIB;
KROLL, LUCIEN; LURÇAT, ANDRÉ; O'GORMAN,
JUAN; POMPE, ANTOINE; PROUVÉ, JEAN;
SAINTENOY, PAUL; SERRURIER-BOVY, GUSTAVE;
SNEYERS, LÉON; STRAUVEN, GUSTAVE; VAN
RIJSSELBERGHE, OCTAVE

Willis, Carol
New York City
CORBETT, HARVEY WILEY; FERRISS, HUGH;
GEDDES, NORMAN BEL; KAHN, ELY JACQUES;
LAMB, CHARLES ROLLINSON; WALKER, RALPH
THOMAS

Willis, Peter
University of Newcastle upon Tyne
BRIDGEMAN, CHARLES; WOMERSLEY, PETER

Wilson, John H.
Institute of Fine Arts, New York University
BOARI, ADAMO; HARRIS, THOMAS; JAPPELLI,
GIUSEPPE; KOCH, GAETANO; PEACOCK, JOSEPH;
POELAERT, JOSEPH; TRESGUERRAS, FRANCISCO
EDUARDO DE

Wilson, Samuel Jr.
Koch and Wilson (New Orleans, Louisiana)
GALLIER, JAMES SR.; LATROBE, BENJAMIN H.

Wilton-Ely, John
University of Hull
PIRANESI, FRANCESCO; PIRANESI, GIOVANNI
BATTISTA

Wiseman, Carter
New York City
Loos, Adolf

Wit, Wim de
Nederlands Documentatiecentrum voor de Bouwkunst (Amsterdam)
Bauer, W. C.; Bazel, K. F. C. de; Gendt, A. L. van; Husly, J. Otten; Kromhout, Willem; Merkelbach, Ben; Outshoorn, Cornelis; Peters, C. H.; Posthumus Meyjes, C. B.; Roosenburg, Dirk; Staal, J. F.; Van der Mey, J. M.; Van 't Hoff, Robert

Wittkower, Margot
New York City
Burlington, Earl of

Wolf, Peter
New York City
Hénard, Eugène

Woods, Mary N.
Columbia University
Avery, Henry O.; Maginnis, Charles D.; Ware, William Rotch

Wragg, R. B.
University of Sheffield
Carr, John

Wright, Janet
Parks Canada (Ottawa)
Scott, Thomas Seaton

Wriston, Barbara
New York City
Tefft, Thomas Alexander

Wurm, Heinrich
Göttingen, Germany
Peruzzi, Baldassarre

Wyatt, Graham S.
New York City
Mizner, Addison

Yamaguchi, Hiroshi
Nihon University
Maki, Fumihiko; Ohe, Hiroshi; Ohtaka, Masato; Raymond, Antonin; Shimizu, Kisuke; Taniguchi, Yoshirō; Tatsuno, Kingo; Urabe, Shizutarō; Yoshimura, Junzō

Yegül, Fikret K.
University of California, Santa Barbara
Mnesikles

Yelavich, Christine
New York City
Labatut, Jean

Zaitzevsky, Cynthia
Brookline, Massachusetts
Cummings and Sears; Emerson, William Ralph

Zanella, Vanni
Bergamo, Italy
Quarenghi, Giacomo

Zukowsky, John
Art Institute of Chicago
Schmidt, Garden, and Martin

AALTO, ALVAR

Hugo Alvar Henrik Aalto (1898–1976), after being prepared for practice in provincial classicism and National Romanticism, became one of the prime developers of the early International style in the second decade of the twentieth century. The unique style which he derived within that development and into which he ultimately incorporated vernacular classicism and rustic romanticism, led to his establishment as Finland's most renowned architect.

Aalto was born in the small village of Kuortane in Ostro-Bothnia. His father was a land surveyor, and Alvar spent the first nine years of his life in that rustic area of Finland. In 1907, the family moved to the town of Jyväskylä in central Finland. As a young boy, Alvar demonstrated a reasonable skill in drawing, and he remembered being impressed by the published work of ELIEL SAARINEN and his partners. His rambunctious country enthusiasm and his determined devotion to architecture led him to become involved in the design and construction of his parents' summer house in Alajärvi only two years after his graduation from secondary school.

Jyväskylä, the emerging governmental and distribution center for the densely forested lake region surrounding it, provided a stimulating background for Alvar's development. In Jyväskylä, he served in the local militia during the struggle for independence following the Russian Revolution and became imbued with the national pride and patriotism so characteristic of the natives of that region. During this period, too, he often found himself in the company of architects. It was, moreover, to Jyväskylä that Aalto returned after graduation from Helsinki Technical University in 1921 and established himself as a qualified architect.

In Helsinki, Aalto had no difficulty adapting to the cultural life of the capital city. He made friends in theatrical circles and enjoyed to the fullest the life of an architectural student. At the Technical University, he was a protégé of ARMAS ELIEL LINDGREN who was a partner of Eliel Saarinen and a significant figure in the National Romantic movement in Helsinki. That movement, led primarily by Saarinen and LARS SONCK, was the embodiment of the aesthetic values found in Finland's medieval stone churches and Karelian loghouses. It yielded a stern, rough-hewn stone architectural style appropriate for cathedrals, museums, banks, and commercial buildings. At that time, Finland was a country of architectural richness combining the romantic heritage of a northern land, which for centuries had been dominated by either the Swedes or the Russians, with the

freshness of a classic style demanded by the new political independence.

Perhaps the most significant influences on the young Aalto during his student days were CARL GUSTAF NYSTROM, an architectural historian, and Yrjö Hirn, an aesthetician. Nystrom, who died early in Aalto's student career, was one of Finland's chief boosters of Greek architecture. Hirn, one of the early investigators into the link between psychology and aesthetic values, certainly provided guidance for Aalto's work well into his mature years. This philosophical enrichment at the feet of his professors carried a meaning of practical relevance rarely available to emerging architects, for at that very time in Finland's history the search for an architectural style or styles appropriate for the new democratic state was widely debated in the profession. Not only was it discussed in the architectural journal *Arkkitehti* but members of the profession also deliberated at length over the form and nature of the required style. Classical design, both Greek and Italianate in spirit, was put forward as filling the needs of a young democracy. There was, moreover, a developing neoclassical mood throughout northern Europe during Aalto's first years as a professional.

His early professional years involved him primarily in the designing of buildings and facilities for exhibitions and fairs. In 1920, while still a student, he worked for Carolus Lindberg on the Tivoli area for the Finnish National Fair, and for his diploma project he chose the design and planning of a fairground near the center of Helsinki. In 1921, he traveled to Stockholm and then worked for ARVID BJERKE on the design of the Congress Hall for the Göteborg World's Fair held in 1923. The first project he executed as an independent professional—the complex of exhibition pavilions at the Tampere Industrial Exposition (1922)—not only demonstrated his developed interest in classicism but also revealed his continuing concern with forms found in nature and those derived from engineering techniques.

In 1923, Aalto established his practice in his adopted home town of Jyväskylä. There, he followed the normal development of architectural practice in Finland, which included participating in competitions to secure commissions. He was not successful at first—receiving only an honorable mention for his entry in the Finnish Houses of Parliament Competition in 1923, and nothing for his entry in the World Headquarters Competition for the League of Nations in 1926. But in 1927, he won second place and was awarded the commission for the Jyväskylä Civil Guard House (1927–1929) and first place in the competition for the Agricultural Cooperative of Southwestern Finland (1927–1929) in Turku. In the same year, he failed to place in any of three church competitions: the Töölö Church of Helsinki, the Viinika Church in Tampere, and the Taulumäki Church in Jyväskylä.

The impression Aalto made on the architectural scene in that remote section of Finland at this time, however, was not due to his ability to compete so much as his ability to secure commissions and build. Earliest of his notable works was the Railway Employees Housing (1923–1924), a bravely Spartan version of a neoclassical garden apartment block. More ornamentally robust were those projects that followed the arrival of Aino Marsio in his firm. She became both his partner and his wife in the spring of 1924. In the previous year, Aalto had traveled to Vienna, and for their honeymoon the Aaltos traveled to Greece and Italy. The lessons of the Wagnerschule and, more important at that time, the classical spirit of the Mediterranean, provided the foundation for their first entry into the realm of the new classical environment then being created for Finland's new image.

The Workers Club (1924–1925) in Jyväskylä combined a carefully contrived Germanic version of a classically adorned and proportioned exterior with an adventurously planned circular interior arrangement on both the lower restaurant and upper theater floors. The inventiveness of ornamental motif closely parallels that found on the Stockholm Town Hall by RAGNAR ÖSTBERG. The careful attention to detail, so often identified with Aalto's work for the greater part of his career, is significantly embodied in the design. The inventiveness exhibited by the Aaltos was clearly in evidence in their entry in a furniture competition sponsored by the Finnish journal *Käsiteollisuus* (1925).

By comparison, however, the nature of Aalto's Civil Guard House (1925) in Seinäjoki is more refined and more completely classical in organization and detail than any other building he had previously attempted. Although it is somewhat rustic due to its cladding of board and batten, the care-

Aalto.
Workers Club.
Jyväskylä, Finland.
1924–1925

fully proportioned pilasters on the Corinthian-ordered façade extending from a heavy base to support a highly stylized and attenuated mock pediment at the edge of a hip roof, give a clear impression of the devotion of the Aalto partnership to the spirit of the times. There is also, however, an air of distinction and freshness. The buildings which follow this development such as the Villa Väinölä (1926) built for his brother in Alajärvi and the Municipal Hospital (1927) also in that village, indicate a comparatively waning interest in richness or ornament. His preparation was by this time sufficient to win the major competition for the Civil Guard House (1927–1929) in Jyväskylä. More casual in composition and more urbane in setting, the design contains allusions to Italianate influences. The Muurame Parish Church (1927–1929) is essentially a stripped-down version of a rural Italian Renaissance basilica complete with tripartite massing arrangement including a campanile. This formula in various transformations was employed in 1927 for the three church competitions previously mentioned.

Since the proposed site of the Agricultural Cooperative of Southwestern Finland was in Turku, and since correspondence between that city and Jyväskylä was somewhat limited, Aalto chose to relocate his office in Turku, Finland's oldest city and former capital. In Turku, he was to accelerate his development culturally and socially as a participant in that city's more polished and metropolitan environment. He came into contact with architects and their works that otherwise would have remained unfamiliar. Although by nature he might not seem to have much in common with Turku and its citizenry, his persistent boyish charm brought him first into friendship and then partnership with one of Finland's most revered and quietly sophisticated architects, ERIK BRYGGMAN, who was considered an architect's architect by many throughout Finland.

Having won out over his two seniors, Bryggman and Hilding Ekelund, in the Co-op competition, Aalto was awarded the commission to prepare construction drawings and supervise what was to be the first large building of his career. By virtue of his adroit execution of this large multipurpose building, housing a theater, offices, a hotel, restaurant, and shops in a single structure, and his comprehensive design approach, Aalto was established as an architect of major rank. In its original appearance, the exterior possessed the sharp clarity and boldness of the work of the Wagnerschule; the actual building demonstrated a greater degree of simplification and less ornament, yet it was more delicate and freer in spirit.

Turning his attention to domestic architecture,

Aalto.
Southwestern Agricultural
Cooperative.
Turku, Finland.
1927–1929

he designed and executed the six-story, concrete-frame, precast-floor Tapani apartment block (1928–1929) while the Co-op building was under construction. This building represented a major turn in his career because it was the first one he built that was not dependent on historical prototypes for inspiration. More closely, it shows the influence of the Swedish modernists who were practicing in nearby Stockholm where he often visited during these years. Less known and more important in terms of his development as a modernist are his entries in the vacation house competition sponsored by *Aitta* magazine, which he produced shortly after his arrival in Turku. His designs for a small three-room summer vacation house were entered under two separate mottos. One, entitled *Kumeli,* was a rustic sod-roof stucco house, which was a take-off of the Villa Flora (1926), a summer house designed and built by Aino for a family in Alajärvi. The other, entitled *Konsoli,* used the same plan and fenestration arrangement but was designed in such a manner that all surfaces were flat, all edges crisp, the roof flattened, and the composite fascia/gable an inverted L-shape. The result, though never realized in an actual building, was the first totally modern functionalist building in Finland's history. The design won first prize and was published in a special color rendering on the cover of the book listing the results of the competition.

The Turun Sanomat Newspaper Plant and Offices (1928–1930) in Turku, often hailed as Finland's first International style building, employed the five points of LE CORBUSIER's famous plan. It was actually inspired by two unexecuted office buildings designed by Erik Bryggman. The Sanomat Building, moreover, was the first example of modern architecture to be widely known outside Finland, and it was the building that Aalto showed to his colleagues attending the Congrès Internationaux d'Architecture Moderne (CIAM) in 1929. The organization of the façade employed strip windows on the office floors and originally employed a blowup of a daily newspaper page behind a giant window not unlike that proposed by

the Vesnin brothers (see VESNIN FAMILY) for the Leningrad Pravda Headquarters (1924). Important for Aalto, the design development during the project resulted in a superbly resolved example of commercial architecture and, in spite of alterations to the famous press room columns (except one), the building seems as much ahead of its surroundings today as it did when just completed.

As the major projects from the first two years at Turku were drawing toward completion, Aalto entered and won the first prize in the competition for the Tuberculosis Sanatorium at Paimio (1929–1933). This commission for the most important building of his entire career was won over the competition of all the major architects in Finland and it was not a popular result. His travels to the Netherlands in 1928, where he had observed at first hand JOHANNES DUIKER's Zonnestraal Sanatorium (1926–1928) near Hilversum, provided him not only with the working knowledge of an efficient layout for such a facility but also exposed him to a series of construction details that enabled him to assemble a design with an articulated armature, each leg or wing of which faced its own rationalized orientation. The bond between detail and concert has led scholars and enthusiasts to characterize this building as belonging to the heroic age of modern architecture. In Paimio's development, Aalto brought modern architecture to a higher level of concern for its users than had been previously attempted by designing a total environment for the convalescing patient: furniture, lavatories, beds, lighting fixtures, color schemes, ventilating systems, view, privacy, convenience. Integrating all these elements into a singular aesthetic expression brought Aalto to the forefront of the world architectural scene. His status even surpassed that of Eliel Saarinen. It did not, however, make him popular among his colleagues at home. Nevertheless, nearly every subsequent competition was studded with imitations and take-offs. Aalto ultimately obtained the commission to design residences for doctors, staff, and administrators, thus completing the self-sufficient colony in the north woods that became a major stop in the pilgrimage to modern Scandinavia and the Baltic region of every young architectural graduate.

During development and construction of the Paimio Sanatorium, Aalto teamed with Erik Bryggman to design the site and exhibition buildings for Turku's Seven Hundredth Anniversary Fair (1929). The results were strongly reminiscent of the designs of the Russian Constructivists. Light-weight frame and canvas-covered rectangular forms were painted with bright geometric propagandistic graphics topped by soaring pylons guyed down tightly to give an unbalanced effect.

Aalto continued, as did nearly every important architect, to participate in the competitions for major public building commissions, but his prizes during this period were not usually the top award. He did win a competition for the new Municipal Library at Viipuri (Vyborg) in 1927, the same year as the Co-op competition, but due to political wrangling this first design never went into construction. Aalto's first-place entry was a neoclassical reorganization of ERIK GUNNAR ASPLUND's Stockholm Municipal Library (1921–1928), but by the time the second phase was reached in 1930 Aalto had undergone such a radical change that a seemingly functionalist design was produced by merely stripping the ornament from the competition entry and adding modern-looking square-mullioned fenestration. Because of still more political disagreement, another site was chosen, and in 1933 Aalto took that opportunity to turn out his third and final version, which was now fully committed to modernity in a substantive manner. The

scheme was essentially two sealed environments joined in echelon along a common side. By that time Aalto's work in southwestern Finland had been mostly completed and he relocated to the capital city of Helsinki to be nearer his newly emerging masterpiece at Viipuri.

Following the year of Aalto's arrival in Helsinki, his style, which until then had been dedicated more or less to the aesthetic and social values of the International style and CIAM, began to undergo a development in the direction of romantic humanistic considerations. Less rigid and more relaxed visual effects were achieved through the use of exposed curvilinear forms, wood textures, and playful spatial arrangements. The application of a scientific basis for the creation of skylights, acoustical surfaces, and concealed natural-gravity ventilation, gives the Viipuri Library Building (1933–1935) a technical prominence in Aalto's work not held by any other project. The actual building, though not restored to its original splendor and furnishing, remains as evidence of the most advanced fusion of aesthetic and technological considerations of any example of modern architecture of its time. The Viipuri Library, the Turun Sanomat Building, and the Paimio Sanatorium represent the most significant and best-known of Aalto's work during the first half of his career.

The technical experiments which Aalto incorporated into his ever widening definition of modern architecture—evidenced in his use of light-

Aalto.
Pulp Mill.
Sunila, Finland.
1934–1935

reflecting baffles, acoustically shaped ceilings, and expressed skeletal structural elements for competition projects and buildings during this period, along with such free-form elements as found in the Paimio and Viipuri buildings—pointed the way for the emergence of a more diverse and environmentally personal style. With this command of the comprehensive nature of architecture well in hand, Aalto entered nearly every major competition for public buildings in the period following his move to Helsinki—railway stations, stadia, exhibition halls. Yet, he failed to even attract a mention in the results.

At that point in Aalto's career, when he was known and respected to a far greater degree in the world than in his homeland, he was discovered by Harry and Maire Gullichsen, industrialists and patrons, who transformed him into a financially secure designer with a renowned reputation. The first major monument of the Gullichsen years, the Sunila Pulp Mill (1934–1935)—based to a certain degree on earlier industrial prototypes by Väinö Vähäkallio—became Aalto's best-known work of this period. The planar delineation of the contrasting brick cubic forms of the manufacturing buildings set off by white painted concrete storage sheds, gives the composition a lighter and more unified effect than its predecessors. The innovative aspect of Sunila, however, is the bold manner in which Aalto retained the natural environment and visually buried the building foundations into the rough Baltic granite outcropping, an effect much imitated in the following decades. It was this observance of nature in the execution of architecture that was to play a significant role in Aalto's progression toward a mature style on the international scene.

The Workers' Village at Sunila (1934–1954), on the shore opposite the peninsula-sited mill complex, ranks as the earliest successful attempt at a comprehensively planned multiple-dwelling housing estate in the modern idiom in Finland.

Vaguely reminiscent of the Weissenhof housing development in Stuttgart of 1927 and adhering quite closely to the values adopted by CIAM, the building arrangement of this unique housing complex was organized in combinations of irregularly spaced fan-shape relationships. Most notable of the buildings within the complex are the radially planned executive rowhouses (1935) with their splayed garden-wall layout and rustic-pole trellis patio enclosures, as well as the stepped apartments of the workers' housing (1938) featuring opposite-side arrangements for the entrances to upper maisonnette and lower efficiency units.

Aalto, who participated in CIAM's Frankfurt Conference in 1929 and contributed to its publication, *Die Wohnung für das Existenzminimum,* for the 1930 conference in Brussels, had prepared and held a Model Apartment Exhibition in Helsinki (1930) in collaboration with Erik Bryggman, Pauli Blomstedt, and others, which closely reflected the pared-down modernity of that organization. Also aligned with the ideas set forth in CIAM publications were his entries in housing competitions as well as the design for his own residence (1934–1936), which reveal a commitment to open planning and crisp rectangular forms articulated with large expanses of glass and which contain the same bold inclusion of the natural habitat as that seen on the rocky base of Sunila.

From the earliest days of his practice in Jyväskylä, Aalto and his partner Aino had been involved in designing furniture and furnishings. In 1929, they executed designs for a stacking chair, which was ultimately used in the Civil Guard House at Jyväskylä and in many other Aalto buildings throughout the years. Moreover, it sold widely around the world along with other Aalto designs for forty years or more. His first bent plywood chairs, developed and built with Turku manufacturer Otto Korhonen and reaching their climax in the Paimio Chair (1930–1933), were inspired by the earlier molded plywood furniture of the A. M. Luther Company of Tallinn, Estonia. Aalto's technique for bending structural supports made of laminated wood plies eventually gave rise to the cantilevered spring leaf supported chair of 1935. This was developed on the idea of MARCEL BREUER's chrome-leg dining chair but executed totally in wood and technically more adventurous and sophisticated. From 1933 on, Aalto's furniture was shown at exhibitions internationally and continued to be as well known as his architecture. The involvement of the Aaltos in the design of fabrics, glassware, and lighting fixtures as well as furniture led to the formation of Artek, a partnership with Maire Gullichsen chartered to produce well-designed home furnishings for Finland's increasing numbers of modern design enthusiasts. This included the exclusive domestic dealership of the Aalto furniture.

Aalto's own residence was in the International style in volumetric solution, but the varied treatment of natural-finished wood cladding and rough-hewn railings, which contrasted with white painted brick walls, was a prelude to one of the most unusual departures, philosophically, to be experienced within the general development of the international Modern movement. Aalto's rejection of a perceived harshness and inappropriate rigidity as far as Finland was concerned, plus his interest in a return to a more romantic use of natural materials and even forms, brought him to the threshold of the mature style that was to characterize his work throughout the remainder of his career.

Being imbued with a new spirit and a fully developed sense of confidence, Aalto entered the competition for the Finnish Pavilion at the Paris World's Fair in 1937. He won first and second prizes, secured the commission, and executed the first-prize design for the pavilion (1937). Constructed entirely of wood—comprising a wealth of surface textures and displaying virtually every aspect of the Finnish wood and wood product industries—the building complex was organized around an open courtyard enclosed by a series of differentially proportioned rectangular volumes each individually detailed in a different cladding of varying textures of timber. Assisting Aalto on both entries and listed as participants on the second-place scheme were his two most prominent employees, AARNI ERVI and VILJO REVELL. Following this success in the same international arena in which Eliel Saarinen had achieved recognition for himself and his homeland, Aalto proceeded to translate this new spirit of romantic rationalism into designs for housing as well as for institutional uses. Having little success in the competitive cycle of Finland's architectural practice, he nevertheless secured commissions for and built the Savoy Restaurant in Helsinki (1937), the land-hugging stepped apartments in Kauttua (1938–1940), and the masterpiece of his domestic architecture career, the Villa Maires (1937–1938), the summer house for the Gullichsens on the Ahlström family estate in Noormarkku.

Basically incorporating every aspect of his newly developed desire for enrichment of form, texture, tonality of material, and completeness of detail, Aalto brought about a design of such quality and agreement as is rarely achieved in architecture. An L-shaped, two-story house with bedrooms on the upper floors, the composition—essentially a series of articulated rectangular volumes—is augmented and accented with the free-form shape of the entrance shed, the kidney-shaped pool, and the crowning form of the finely battened irregular volume of Maire's painting studio. The detailing of natural wood poles included at various points on the exterior—sometimes bound together with lashings in woodsman style—was done to achieve a sympathetic interaction with the woods surrounding the villa. In each aspect of the house, Aalto employed materials of polished grains and natural roughness to set the tone of a refined dwelling in the natural setting of the countryside. In addition to the decided romanticism of this house and its vast array of natural stone and wood details, the technical schemes for environmental comfort are striking and totally integrated visually into the scheme. Although incorporating giant removable sashes of double-glazed plate glass, the building is a sealed entity with a natural-gravity ventilation system concealed between the floors and vented through the natural wood ceilings. Sunlight is controlled on the exterior of the large windows by means of an external venetian-blind system while the smaller windows of the bedrooms are actually slanted away from the rising sun to achieve the effect of a longer night during the extended midsummer days of the northern latitudes. Spatially, the main living spaces on the lower floor constitute a free-flowing plan with aspects of a classic pinwheel arrangement. The overall effect of the house, with its sod-roof covered walkway stretching to sauna and dressing room at the rear, is not unlike that of the Prairie houses of FRANK LLOYD WRIGHT, relating a different quadrant of the site to different areas of the interior. The innovative combinations of spatial and textural effects attracted the attention of designers of domestic architecture throughout the world, especially in

Aalto. Villa Maires. Noormarkku, Finland. 1937–1938

the United States where watered-down versions of Aalto's effects were incorporated into the tracts of builder and architect-designed housing for the postwar building boom. Separate floor textures denote subfunctions within the interior volumes.

The Villa Maires, shown internationally for the first time (though still unfinished) at New York's Museum of Modern Art's retrospective exhibition of Aalto's work in 1938, became the best-known example of his house designs and remained the best example of his humanistic version of the International style then emerging to a wider public.

Following the close of the Paris World's Fair and during the height of construction of the Villa Maires, Aalto entered the competition for the design of the Finnish Pavilion for the New York World's Fair to be held in 1939. He won all three prizes and was awarded the commission to undertake the design of the interior space as well as program, design, and install the exhibition that would represent modern Finland to the West. Aino Marsio Aalto was actually credited as the author of the third-place entry, but it is certain that both of them worked on all prize-winning schemes. The experience and reputation accorded to the Aaltos as a result of the Paris Pavilion the previous year undoubtedly played a role in determining their total control of the content and make-up of the New York exhibition and its architectural environment.

More a lavish wooden showcase of undulating walls and textures than a backdrop, the New York World's Fair Pavilion (1938–1940) was an aesthetically unified two-level scheme displaying the same story of wood and wood products as in Paris but in a tighter confined interior space with a more sophisticated montage of manufactured elements, photographs, movies, and even native food. The Pavilion, destroyed when the fair buildings were razed after its closing in 1940, featured a triple-tiered molded plywood curtain stretching the entire length of the interior and decorated with vertical battens and photomurals laminated directly on the curving surface. Among the fair's hodgepodge of predominantly streamlined modern and weirdly eclectic amalgamations of architectural styles, Aalto's pavilion stood as a positive assertion of his and Finland's commitment to a progressive world in which modern ideals, design excellence, and the observance of nature are inseparable from life. For modern architects, it remains the best remembered example of design at the fair.

Coordinating the opening of his retrospective at the Museum of Modern Art with his initial visit to inspect the Fair site, Aalto traveled to the United States for the first time in the spring of 1938. He was invited to lecture at New York University's Morgan Atelier and at Yale University's School of Architecture. He made a trip to visit Eliel Saarinen at the Cranbrook Academy in Bloomfield Hills, Michigan, before returning home to resume his practice. The following spring he returned to the United States to inspect the work underway on the Pavilion, and this time he seriously investigated the possibility of relocating his practice in America as Saarinen had done in the mid-1920s following his success as second-place winner in the Chicago Tribune Competition. In his travels on both East and West Coasts, Aalto sought to establish a basis for an architectural practice in America. He inquired about teaching positions and even looked into the possibility of establishing an architectural research institute with his friend WILLIAM WILSON WURSTER. Ultimately, he was hired to teach under Wurster at the Massachusetts Institute of Technology's School of Architecture, and he arrived in Cambridge in the autumn of 1940 to begin his duties. But a month later, he departed due to increasing concern about Finland's future as a German ally in the war and an unprecedented chance to participate in a competition for a large housing estate outside Helsinki—in which he failed to receive a mention.

During the war years, Aalto not only competed for the commissions available via that route but also produced a series of planning projects and designs for industrial buildings for the Gullichsen-controlled Ahlström company. Many of these projects, however, did not see realization until after the war's conclusion. Best known of the Ahlström work, the Sawmill Extension at Varkaus (1944–1945), which was demolished in 1977, demonstrated his continuing interest in the creation of accents from free-form geometries, and the uses of stryated surfaces, which appeared in his prewar architecture. The most significant of Aalto's postwar planning projects was the town plan for the redevelopment of Rovaniemi (1944–1945), much of which was used to guide the expansion of that Arctic-circle city.

Having survived the spare days of the war, Aalto planned to return to M.I.T. and eventually relocate his family in America. During December 1945, he visited FRANK LLOYD WRIGHT at Spring Green, Wisconsin, and was enthused enough to enroll his own son as an apprentice at Taliesin. Neither the relocation of his family to America nor his son's apprenticeship at Taliesin came to pass. Aalto, however, continued to visit M.I.T., and in 1946 he was given the commission to design a dormitory for the senior students. The resulting Baker House (1946–1949), designed by Aalto initially at Helsinki and later worked out in a series of visits to Cambridge, was the product of

collaboration with the Boston firm of Perry, Dean, and Shaw. Originally conceived as a series of linked pavilions, the well-known undulating well was derived from an interim proposal that utilized a Z-shaped configuration to maximize the number of student windows that command a view of the Charles River. In his use of red irregular-faced brick and ivy-covered trellis work, Aalto hoped to recall the vernacular of older American campus buildings and their weathered qualities. Although somewhat Spartan in the detailing of materials and finishes, the Baker dormitory with its unusual cantilevered twin straight-run stairways stretching the length of its rear or main entrance façade, remains the most impressive example of Aalto's design talent in North America.

In January 1949, Aino Marsio Aalto died after an extended illness and left Alvar at the midpoint of his career a widower and without a partner. The previous year, the Aaltos had won the top prize in the National Pension Bank competition. Alone, he went on to win the competition for the Master Plan and Main Building Complex for the relocation to Otaniemi of the Technical Institute (1949) and proceeded with the design for the Town Hall at Säynätsalo (1950–1952). He suffered from the loss of Aino until he was remarried to Elsa Mäkiniemi in 1952. Elissa, as she was called by Alvar, was an architect in his employ and his assistant on the Säynätsalo Town Hall before their marriage, at which time she became his full partner and shared credit as Aino had for their work. Aino and Alvar's partnership can be described as an enthusiastic earthy search for new ideas and appropriate solutions for architectural problems, complicated by Finland's relationship with the outside

world and its own environment. That of Elissa and Alvar could be characterized as a more soundly run practice dealing with a burgeoning architectural office of international reputation and constantly in demand. Despite this new devotion to professional development in a busy office, there was no poverty of new ideas in Aalto's work.

The Town Hall at Säynätsalo, the nucleus of a village plan evolving from a war-time scheme that featured two rows of housing blocks (never built), was finally given the organization of an open courtyard arrangement similar to courtyards found in large Roman residences. Aalto's courtyard is even complete with a pool where the cistern would have been. The building is elevated to set it off from the surrounding buildings with the grassy courtyard at the second-floor level connected to the encompassing ground level by a series of monumental irregular-shaped sodded terrace stairways. The crowning feature of this small complex of various village services is the cubically proportioned council chamber, its sloping roof supported by a unique arrangement of exposed wooden fan-shaped trusses.

During the early 1950s, Aalto more and more concerned himself with building opportunities and projects for Finnish industrial interests, producing paper and pulp mills, office buildings, workers' housing complexes, and even club houses for employees. Altogether, in the two decades from 1950 to 1970, Aalto secured more commissions and constructed more buildings than he had during the rest of his entire fifty-four years of productivity.

Following the competition prize in 1948 and its follow-up schematic development later that

Aalto.
Finnish Pavilion.
World's Fair.
New York.
1938–1940

Aalto.
Baker House.
Massachusetts Institute of
*   Technology.*
Cambridge, Massachusetts.
1946–1949

year, the Helsinki site for the National Pension Bank (1952–1956) was changed to a larger parcel, more regular in shape though essentially a triangle and perhaps more challenging. Housing the operations for a large number of employees in discretely different volumes and locations on the site, the overall unity of technique bonds the building into a cohesively visual statement—an office building in harmony with its residential surroundings. The use of red brick, a little-employed building material in Helsinki, sets the building chromatically apart and adds warmth to the cold winter days. Aalto became an advocate of brick as a basic material after visiting Frank Lloyd Wright and hearing him lecture on the universality of the masonry unit as building tool.

Following the business success of the early 1950s, Aalto received his first commission for a commercial building in Helsinki. The Rautatalo Office Building (1953–1955)—or "the House of Iron," a reference to the business of its principal tenants—is an eight-story office structure organized around a triple-storied lobby on the second floor, which is accessible from the main ground-level entrance by escalator. The tiered space with its two balconies is skylighted by a grid of the same large conical portholes used in Viipuri in 1935 and many subsequent buildings. During the same period, he designed and built his own summer house near Säynätsalo in a thickly forested section of shoreline called Muuratsalo (1953–1955), undertook the master planning and began construction on the first stage of the Teachers College Campus at Jyväskylä (1953–1956), and relocated to a new studio (1953–1956) in the Helsinki suburb of Munkkiniemi three blocks from his residence. The studio, by far the most interesting building of this group, is a white brick building surrounding a courtyard on three sides, of which the main feature is an informal, modestly stepped amphitheater formed by a series of terraces. The building, a variant of the scheme employed at Säynätsalo and one of the more misunderstood examples of Aalto's work, is quite simply a two-story structure, the upper level of which is intended for use by architects and principals; the lower level contains the entrance, secretarial offices, lavatories, staff dining room, kitchen, and caretaker's quarters. The most striking features of the building are the semicircular amphitheater and the south wall of the master's studio, which is concavely curved to parallel the terraced steps of the amphitheater. If Aalto intended this outdoor space to become the setting for a forum led by the "Maestro," as he was affectionately called by his associates and employees, he never found the opportunity to employ it extensively. The studio wall which is curved not only in plan but also in profile, yields a trumpet-shaped interior volume curving outward to a high end wall containing a large L-shaped window with vertical mullions. The grandly proportioned space, with its sculptural effect and wide array of Aalto details and motifs, reveals its greater suitability as a conference room than an architect's atelier.

The most significant group of buildings created from the mid-1950s on include the main building of the Finnish Technical Institute (1955–1964) in Helsinki, the Vuoksenniska Church in Imatra (1956–1958), and the Maison Carre (1956–1959) in the Paris suburb of Bazoches sur Guyonne.

The soaring wedge of the great lecture hall in the main building at the Finnish Technical Institute, one of the elements not present in the 1949 scheme for the competition entry, identifies the purpose of the building as educational more than any other aspect of its design. The classroom wings and school of architecture at the southern extremity of this complex is based on several of Aalto's earlier trials at staggered parallel blocks to yield a fanning or wedge shape to the resultant open space toward the south. Aalto's adherence to the red brick of several of his earlier projects gives a unified effect rarely found in complexes covering such a large area.

The Vuoksenniska Church was designed to stand out in its chaotic industrial environment and achieve a significant degree of visual identity. The horizontal wedge-shaped profile of the auditorium, balanced by the tall campanile, recalls the Italianate nature of Aalto's earlier churches. In this case, however, he simplified the complex nature of the church's forms through the simple use of contrasting stucco walls and copper roofs. The forms, which are asymmetrical in balance and aspect, are an outgrowth of the liturgy of the worship services and a desire for flexibility in the church's seating capacity. Three large circular forms reflecting a twin system of rolling acoustical partitions make the building decidedly expressive when viewed from the rear. In free-form geometrical terms, the Vuoksenniska Church is Aalto's most complex and clearly resolved spatial concept—being asymmetrical and irregular from any view and any position.

The Maison Carre, built for a famous art dealer, is among the least visited of Aalto's buildings and perhaps for that reason the least understood spatially. The dwelling, based primarily on the notion of a formal central gallery for the display of paintings surrounded by all the elements of a lavish country house, fails to provide the degree of domestic privacy found in the Villa Maires. The massing of the exterior, a series of triangular solids joined in echelon, and the concealed curvilinear cross-sections of the centralized gallery space recall the combination of forms used in the Vuoksenniska Church.

The exterior, with its thin fascia and acute angles executed in white brick on a travertine base, gives a simplified effect uncharacteristic of an Aalto building. This is perhaps due to the fact that this house was Elissa's first project executed by herself and her lack of total familiarity with the Aalto detail system.

Near the end of the 1950s, Aalto produced the Parish Church at Seinäjoki (1958–1960), the Cultural Center at Wolfsburg, Germany (1958–1962), and won first prize for the Opera House in Essen, Germany (1959), which remains ready for construction but is not yet built.

The Wolfsburg Cultural Center, intended originally to be only one element of a central urban scheme, was to assume the role of an open-air gathering space for the townspeople on market days and at other times. This—the most complete and high-quality of a series of multifunction cultural-governmental buildings he undertook during the last years of his productivity—combines virtually every spatial technique, textural motif, volumetric expression, and technical-environmental innovation that is identified with the work of Aalto. In both library and roof terrace, this building expresses his strong preference for sunken forms or double-height spaces open to the sky or skylighted. His inclusion of a series of five irregular polygonally planned volumes expresses the size and functional nature of the meeting room complex. Built with the Volkswagen World Headquarters as patron and client, the richness of textural motifs such as the undulating wood ceilings, striated columns and walls executed in white and blue tile units, and the trellis poles surrounding the open stairwells recall the playful collection of elements in the World's Fair pavilions nearly twenty years earlier. The Wolfsburg building is a finely polished urban cultural center in every sense of the word. The inclusion of the recessed skylight trough and the conical skylights not only control the library light naturally, but they also do not permit any direct light or glare to reach the reading tables. The range of the aesthetic-technical palette which Aalto employed encompasses the broadest definition of environmental design and points up the truly universal appeal of his personal version of the international Modern movement.

During the period between 1959 and 1962, Aalto designed and executed the Central Finnish Museum in Jyväskylä and the headquarters of the Enso-Gutzeit Company on the Helsinki waterfront. While working on these major commis-

Aalto.
Cultural Center.
Wolfsburg, Germany.
1958–1962

sions, he also involved himself in the planning and design study for the redevelopment of a large portion of Helsinki's Töölö Bay area. Called "The City Center Plan," the proposal (illustrated by a giant white cardboard and wood model which was shown around the world) provided for the assembly of cultural functions in a series of new buildings stretching down the western shore of the bay. Along the opposite shore, an elevated expressway system with three attenuated plazas stretched from a newly renovated business district to the narrow southern end of the bay (now actually a lake). Although much heralded by city planning and urban design enthusiasts in the 1960s, the scheme would have significantly changed the use of, and even eliminated, parkland and would have introduced needless vehicular access to the modest-sized capital city. A principal cultural facility associated with this plan, and perhaps the real reason for the study's undertaking, is the concert hall and conference center located in the park at the southwestern corner of the bay. Finlandia Hall (1962–1975), as it was eventually named, was originally designed in 1962 and constructed in two stages: the concert hall complex and its dependencies between 1967 and 1971, the conference center between 1973 and 1975. Executed in white marble, a material Aalto reserved for certain cultural buildings in his later years, the concert hall–conference center is a series of expressed volumes denoting the assembly nature of the interior spaces, which rise from a multilevel base housing lobbies, restaurants, lounges, and administration offices. The wedge-shaped volume of the concert hall, with its rear wall articulated in three separate seating banks, recalls the Constructivist form of the Moscow Tram Workers Club (1927) by KONSTANTIN S. MELNIKOV, a possible source of inspiration for other designs by Aalto, especially those featuring divisible partitions to create a flexibility of capacity.

Aalto's experience and reputation as a designer of civic buildings led to an ever increasing number of commissions during the 1960s. He designed and developed cultural centers, civic centers, and re-

Aalto.
Seinajöki Civic Center.
Finland.
1952–1966

lated religious and commercial facilities in over a dozen Finnish towns and cities. The most complete of these is the Seinajöki Civic Center, consisting of a church (1952–1960), parish hall (1964–1966), town hall (1961–1965), and the library (1963–1965). It was, in fact, Aalto's own favorite complex and, in later years, he urged visitors to see it firsthand. Developed with a clear separation of vehicular and pedestrian circulation, the overall scheme is unified by an armature of paved esplanade stretching from the heart of the civic-cultural complex to the edge of the square formed by the church and its parish center. Although each building is executed in a clearly differentiating formal makeup, color, and siting disposition, a sense of cohesiveness is created by the contrasting of Aalto's signature motifs featuring a wide range of details from his extensive design vocabulary. The church, earliest of the buildings, is a long narrow version of Aalto's famous fan-shaped plan with high imposing walls capped with a pyramidal roof of metallic cladding. The bold massing and the high bell tower easily remind one that Aalto began his career in the 1920s attempting to secure commissions for parish churches with designs which while eclectically Italianate, seem to have a spiritual tie to this church complex. Centerpiece of the civic group at the opposite end of the axial arrangement is the town hall clad in dark blue tile units arranged in a vertical ribbed pattern. The main floor of the two-story town hall is actually at the second-floor level, with the council chamber on pilotis completely free from the ground. The council chamber volume, the main end of a very simple double-loaded corridor office wing, is crowned by an unusually high skylighted monitor, shaped like half of a gambrel roof. The main entrance is by way of a stair located at the side of the council chamber pavilion. This staircase is integrated with a pyramid of sodded terraces splayed in a regular fashion to give the illusion of monumental stairs. The library opposite the town hall attests to the simplicity appropriate for a small town. In

fact, the main accent of the irregular fan-shaped main reading room affirms Aalto's interest in the modest and small as well as the grand and vast. The high-ceilinged fan-shaped floor plan contains the characteristic sunken space in the center, which is radially aligned with the control desk. Lacking the extensive skylight system of his larger libraries, natural illumination is introduced into the building through a high, full-length louvered window along the southern face of the room. Further lighting control is provided by a coordinated undulation of the free-form ceiling to insure that no direct light interferes with the reader.

Working with the series of signature motifs that were restated and tailored to each of the designs of his mature years, Aalto continued to achieve an effect of richness of texture, form, and color, as well as a control of light and sound, that seemed endless in its permutations. Aalto believed that the main business of the architect was the absolute devotion of his creative talents in both technical and aesthetic areas of design.

Contrary to usual practice in Finland, where many of the buildings are erected without the architect's full control, Aalto continually refused to have his designs prepared for construction by anyone outside his office. Sadly, however, this was not always true of buildings he built abroad. Sometimes only the sketches were translated by a deputy in the field into an Aalto-style building, and if time permitted, the Maestro would occasionally visit and pass judgment.

Aalto, who had so enthusiastically received visitors traveling to remote Finland to see his works—sometimes even personally conducting tours of Paimio, Viipuri, and other buildings in southern Finland—became more and more reclusive and finally inaccessible to all but a small number of old friends. Embittered by what he perceived as America's lack of concern for Finland's plight during the war and the devastation following it, he grew to regard with contempt the land which had once so impressed him with its openness and excitement that he entertained the idea of relocating there. Following the completion of the Baker dormitory at M.I.T., he found it difficult to meet his commitment for teaching duties, and in 1951 he resigned his adjunct position. Having reached a position of acclaim in his own country, he received large numbers of commissions at home and abroad. In 1957, he was awarded the Royal Gold Medal of Architecture in Britain, and in 1963, the Gold Medal of the American Institute of Architects.

Aalto's interest in CIAM waned early on and, despite his occasional attendance, he contributed nothing to the collection of documents after the

Athens conference in 1933. In the last years of his professional activity, he played a role of decreasing dominance in the design of projects, and the buildings arising from that period reflect a reduced richness of form and detail. The debilitating effect of a life of heavy drinking combined with diseases common to the elderly brought Aalto's creative genius to a standstill several years before his death.

Throughout Aalto's fifty-four years of practice, he designed scores of projects and, exclusive of single-family dwellings, produced over two hundred buildings, making him, after Frank Lloyd Wright, the most productive, prominent architect of the twentieth century.

PAUL DAVID PEARSON

WORKS

1922, Industrial Exposition, Tampere, Finland. 1923–1924, Railway Employees Housing; 1924–1925, Workers Club; Jyväskylä, Finland. 1925, Civil Guard House, Seinäjoki, Finland. 1926, Villa Väinölä; 1927, Municipal Hospital; Alajärvi, Finland. 1927–1929, Civil Guard House, Jyväskylä, Finland. 1927–1929, Parish Church, Muurame, Finland. 1927–1929, Southwestern Agricultural Cooperative; 1928–1929, Standard Apartment for Tapani; 1928–1930, Newspaper Plant and Offices for Turun Sanomat; 1929, Seven Hundredth Anniversary Fair (with Erik Bryggman); Turku, Finland. 1929–1933, Tuberculosis Sanatorium, Paimio, Finland. 1933–1935, Municipal Library, Viipuri, Finland. 1934–1935, Pulp Mill, Sunila, Finland. 1934–1936, Alvar Aalto House, Helsinki. 1934–1954, Workers' Village, Sunila, Finland. *1937, Finnish Pavilion, World's Fair, Paris. 1937, Savoy Restaurant, Helsinki. 1937–1938, Villa Maires, Noormarkku, Finland. *1938–1940, Finnish Pavilion, World's Fair, New York. 1938–1940, Terraced Housing, Kauttua, Finland. 1941, Kokemäki River Valley Master Plan, Finland. *1944–1945, Sawmill Extension, Varkaus, Finland. 1944–1945, Rovaniemi Town Plan, Finland. 1946–1949, Baker House, Massachusetts Institute of Technology, Cambridge, Mass. 1950–1952, Town Hall, Säynätsalo, Finland. 1952–1956, National Pension Bank, Helsinki. 1952–1966, Seinäjoki Civic Center, Finland. 1953–1955, Alvar Aalto House, Muuratsalo, Finland. 1953–1955, Rautatalo Office Building; 1953–1956, Alvar Aalto Studio, Munkkiniemi; 1955–1964, Finnish Institute of Technology (main building), Otaniemi; Helsinki. 1956–1958, Vuoksenniska Church, Imatra, Finland. 1956–1959, Maison Louis Carre, Bazoches sur Guyonne, France. 1958–1960, Parish Church, Seinäjoki, Finland. 1958–1962, Cultural Center, Wolfsburg, Germany. 1959–1962, Central Finnish Museum, Jyväskylä, Finland. 1959–1962, Enso-Gutzeit Company Headquarters; 1962–1975, Finlandia Hall Concert and Convention Center; Helsinki. 1963–1968, Library, Rovaniemi, Finland. 1965–1970, Library, Mount Angel Benedictine College, Mount Angel, Ore. 1969–1973, Art Museum, Aalborg, Denmark. 1972–1976, Riola Parish Center (not completed until 1978), Bologna, Italy. 1972–1976, Theater (not completed until 1978), Rovaniemi, Finland.

BIBLIOGRAPHY

BURCHARD, JOHN E. 1959 "Finland and Architect Aalto." *Architectural Record* 125:126.
FLEIG, KARL 1963 Volume 1 in *Alvar Aalto: 1922–1962*. Zurich: Verlag für Architekur Artemis.
GOLDSTONE, HARMON HENDRICKS 1939 "Alvar Aalto." *Magazine of Art* 32:208–221.
GUTHEIM, FREDERICK A. 1960 *Alvar Aalto*. New York: Braziller.
LABÒ, GIORGIO 1948 *Alvar Aalto*. Milan: Balcone.
MOSSO, LEONARDO 1965 *L'Opera di Alvar Aalto*. Milan: Edizioni di Comunità. Exhibition catalogue.
NEUENSCHWANDER, EDOUARD, and NEUENSCHWANDER, CLAUDIA 1954 *Finnish Buildings: Atelier Alvar Aalto, 1950–1951*. Zurich: Verlag für Architektur.
PEARSON, PAUL DAVID 1978 *Alvar Aalto and the International Style*. New York: Whitney Library of Design.
SALOKORPI, ASKO 1970 *Modern Architecture in Finland*. London: Weidenfeld & Nicolson; New York: Praeger.
SHAND, P. MORTON 1936 "Viipuri Library, Finland." *Architectural Review* 79:107–114.
WICKBERG, NILS ERIK 1962 *Finnish Architecture*. Helsinki: Otava.

ABACCO, ANTONIO DALL'

Born in Vercelli, Antonio dall'Abacco (1495–1567?) (also known as d'Abacco, dall'Abaco, Labbacco, Labacco) is best known in his architectural endeavors as a student and assistant of Antonio da Sangallo the Younger (see SANGALLO FAMILY). Abacco's work, moreover, reveals the influence of studies of DONATO BRAMANTE's creations. Though details of Abacco's arrival in Rome are sparse, it is believed that he came to the city around 1507 with his father, architect Giovanni Maria dall'Abacco. Once in the city, Antonio dall'Abacco joined the Sangallo workshop. From 1526 Abacco was active under his master on construction of fortifications in Parma and Piacenza.

Returning to Rome, Abacco together with Bartolomeo Baronino, prepared the decoration for the Conclave of Pope Julius III, which took place in 1550. In 1559 Abacco collaborated with GIACOMO BAROZZI DA VIGNOLA and two other architects for the Conclave of Pope Pius IV. Continuing his work in this city, Abacco then participated in constructions on the church and baptistery of the Lateran, for which an extant document records a payment of 500 scudi to Abacco in 1567. Abacco is said, as well, to have designed and built the travertine marble entrance of the Palazzo Colonna-Sciarra in Rome.

In spite of his association with so eminent an architect as Sangallo, Abacco was not particularly prolific in this profession and is, consequently, better known today as an engraver. In 1538, Sangallo was appointed director of work on St. Peter's by Pope Pius III, and was entrusted with the creation of a definitive model and grand plan of the basilica. Abacco is said to have made the engravings of this plan of St. Peter's. No prints of the ground plan are in existence today. In 1558, Abacco published his major work, *Libro d'Antonio d'Abacco appartenante à l'architectura*, which was embellished by numerous engravings by Abacco himself and his son, Maria dall'Abacco. He was also active in the restoration of ancient Roman monuments and in 1522 published the results of his work. A second edition of this popular book appeared as early as 1559, and a third in 1576 in Venice.

SARA LEHRMAN

WORKS

1515?, Palazzo Farnese (with Giuliano Sangallo), Rome. 1526, Fortifications (with Sangallo), Parma, Italy. 1526, Fortifications (with Sangallo), Piacenza, Italy. 1550, Conclave Decoration (for Julius III; with Bartolomeo Baronino); 1559, Conclave Decoration (for Pius IV; with Giacomo Barozzi da Vignola and others); 1567, Lateran (church and baptistery); n.d., Palazzo Sciarra-Colonna; *n.d., St. Peter's (models); Rome.

BIBLIOGRAPHY

BENEZIT E.   (1911–1923)1976 Volume 1, page 3 in *Dictionnaire des peintres, sculpteurs, dessinateurs, et graveurs.* New ed. Paris: Grund.

BERTOLOTTI, F.   1884 *Artisti subalpini in Roma nei secolo XVL Ricerche e studi negli archivi romani.* Mantua, Italy.

BOTTARI, G. G.   (1754–1768)1822–1825 *Raccolta di lettere sulla pittura, scultura ed architetture scritte da'piu celebri personaggi dei secoli XV, XVI, e XVII.* Reprint. Milan: Silvestri.

FACICO, CESARE   (1558)1894 *Di Antonio Labacco architetti Vercellese nel sec. XV.* Vercelli, Italy.

GORI GANDELLI, GIOVANNI   (1771)1808–1816 *Notizie istoriche degli intagliatori di Siena.* Turin, Italy: d'O. porri.

PEPE, MARIO 1963 "I Labacco architetti e incisori." *Capitolium* 38:25–27.

TITI, F. 1763 *Descrizione delle pitture, sculture e architecture esposte in Roma.* Rome.

Abadie.
Basilica of Sacré Coeur.
Paris.
1874–1884 (not completed until 1919).

ABADIE, PAUL

Paul Abadie (1812–1884) was born in Paris where he entered the Ecole des Beaux-Arts in 1835 as a student of ACHILLE LECLÈRE. A mediocre student there, Abadie was better suited to his appointment in 1845 as *inspecteur des travaux* for the restoration of the Gothic Cathedral of Notre Dame, Paris, by EUGÈNE EMMANUEL VIOLLET-LE-DUC and JEAN-BAPTISTE-ANTOINE LASSUS. Abadie succeeded Viollet-le-Duc as *architecte diocésain* of Paris in 1874. He succeeded Emile Gilbert at the Académie des Beaux-Arts in 1875. Abadie's principal restoration projects were the Romanesque cathedrals of Saint Front in Périgueux (1852–1884) and Saint Pierre in Angoulême (1854–1882), where he depended as much upon his imagination as upon archeology in rebuilding the churches. His major original design was for the basilica of Sacré-Coeur (1874–1884) in Paris; Abadie's project was chosen on July 28, 1874, and construction proceeded under his direction from 1876 to 1884. Abadie was succeeded as chief architect by Honoré Daumet, Charles Laisné, Henri Rauline, and LUCIEN MAGNE, yet despite modifications the church is consistent with Abadie's design in which Romanesque and Byzantine elements reflect the influence of Saint Front at Périgueux. These two works exemplify the nineteenth-century interpretation of history with its symbiotic correspondence between past and present: Saint Front explains the Sacré-Coeur's medieval references and the Sacré-Coeur justifies the restoration of Saint Front.

CHRISTOPHER MEAD

WORKS

1852–1853, Church of Saint Martial, Angoulême, France. 1852–1884, Cathedral of Saint Front (restoration; not completed until 1901), Périgueux, France. 1854–1882, Cathedral of Saint Pierre (restoration), Angoulême, France. 1855–1856, Church of Notre Dame, Bergerac, France. 1858–1867, Hôtel de Ville, Angoulême, France. 1859–1865, Church of Saint Croix (restoration), Bordeaux, France. 1864–1876, Lycée of Angoulême (additions); 1868–1869, Church of Saint Ausome; Angoulême, France. 1874–1884, Basilica of Sacré-Coeur (not completed until 1919), Paris. n.d., Church of Saint Barthelemy, Faux; n.d., Church of Saint Bernard, Mussidan; Dordogne, France. n.d., Church of Saint Ferdinand, Bordeaux, France. n.d., Church of Saint Georges, Périgueux, France. n.d., Church of Saint Marie de la Bastide, Bordeaux, France. n.d., Hôtel de Ville, Jarnac, France.

BIBLIOGRAPHY

BAUCHAL, CHARLES 1887 *Nouveau dictionnaire biographique et critique des architectes français.* Paris: André, Daly.

BERTHELÉ, JOSEPH 1884 "M. Paul Abadie, note nécrologique." In *Extrait de la Revue poitevine et saintongeaise.* Melle, France: Lacuve.

HAUTECOEUR, LOUIS 1957 *La fin de l'architecture classique.* Volume 7 in *Histoire de l'architecture classique en France.* Paris: Picard.

LÉON, PAUL 1951 *La vie des monuments français. Destruction. Restauration.* Paris: Picard.

SAINT-PAUL, ANTHYME 1874 "L'Eglise du Voeu National." *Bulletin Monumental* 40:618–632.

'ABBAS

Ruler of Iran from 1587 to 1629, 'Abbas acceded to the throne at the age of sixteen as the fifth shah of the Shi'a Muslim Safavi dynasty (1501–1722). As nominal governor of Herat from 1573 to 1587, he had grown up in the midst of an impressive heritage of historic architecture and distinguished patronage, particularly during Timurid rule (1380–1506). Since none of his dynastic predecessors had functioned as a significant patron of building, the corpus of Safavi buildings before Shah 'Abbas is small, and although his first decade of rule from the old capital of Qazvin was too turbulent to be architecturally productive, it was 'Abbas who emerged at the end of the sixteenth century as the great patron behind the creation of Safavi architecture. Dynamic and ruthless, he had a keen sense for architecture as the expression of social, religious, political, and aesthetic convictions.

In 1598, after a series of military victories and administrative reforms had stabilized his position, 'Abbas established a new capital in the ancient city of Isfahan in central Iran and launched a building program that was to last well beyond his reign and made Isfahan the showpiece of Safavi architecture. Its focus was his *maydan-i shah* (royal quadrangle), measuring 510 by 165 meters and situated on a north–south axis between the old city and New Julfa, a Christian Armenian quarter through which much of Iran's international trade passed. Connecting the *maydan* and the king's personal gardens to the south was the 1500-meter-long Chahar Bagh, a broad avenue lined with trees and water-courses and flanked by gardens laid out in geometric patterns.

The open *maydan* was enclosed by two-storied, pointed-arched arcades, the lower level serving as shops, the upper as temporary residences for visiting merchants. Active with caravans, parades, businesses, and entertainments, the *maydan* was the social and commercial center of the royal city. On its north side, a recessed, arched entrance led into the Royal Bazaar that extended nearly two kilometers to link old and new Isfahan and housed many of the state monopolies in textiles and ceramics that were essential to Iran's prosperity. Three other structures, all located in the *maydan*'s southern half, interrupted the arcade.

On the west side, the 'Ali Qapu (High Gate) led into the monarch's private palace and garden, the Chehel Sotun, and served as his administrative center. Its second-story *talar* (pillared porch) provided an unrestricted view over the entire *maydan*.

On the east side is a small kiosk mosque, most frequently called the Mosque of Shaykh Lotfallah, erected between 1601 and 1628. Its prayer chamber, built over a crypt, is covered by a single-shell dome nearly thirteen meters in diameter. Most of the mosque's exterior and interior is clothed in a multicolored skin of ceramic tile or mosaic and provides the shimmering surface and dazzling color variations most characteristic of Safavi architecture.

The Royal Mosque (1612–1638) on the south side is an enormous complex, using the classic Iranian four-*eyvan* plan and clearly derived from the fifteenth-century mosque of Gawhar Shad in Mashhad. Flanked by twin minarets, its gateway dominates the *maydan* and projects monumental epigraphs proclaiming Shi'a belief and the Shah's name as founder. The Royal Mosque's surface is almost entirely covered in seven-colored tiles whose arabesques and geometric patterns reveal both the technical abilities and the Timurid models typical of most Safavi architecture.

'Abbas was also active in promoting the construction of gardens, forts, bridges, caravansaries, and city walls, and substantial restoration projects were undertaken at Shi'a shrines in Mashhad and elsewhere.

'Abbas's role as architectural patron is comparable to that of some of his baroque contemporaries in India and Europe. Although neither the *maydan* nor his particular building types were new to Islamic history, they were dramatic restatements of traditional forms. It is not yet clear how much 'Abbas himself had to do with this grandiose architectural composition, but contemporary texts (chiefly the *Tarikh-i 'Alam-Ara-yi 'Abbasi*) and the evidence of arts like painting and calligraphy indicate that he was a highly involved patron. It seems hardly possible, therefore, that he would not have been actively engaged in the planning of a project of the *maydan*'s magnitude. In Safavi history, there is no actual architect of stature similar to the Ottoman empire's SINAN who created a classic idiom that pervaded visual culture for more than two centuries. Safavi architecture is neither a new creation nor a renascence; instead, it is a revival of traditional types, though decked out in more fulsome ceramic adornment. This historicizing rather than highly original architectural style was as dependent upon lavish surface as it was upon space and form, and its dissemination through Iran in the seventeenth century was due to an enterprising and gifted patron rather than to an architectural genius.

ANTHONY WELCH

WORKS

1590, Masjid-i jami' (southwest chamber); 1598, 'Ali Qapu Palace; 1598-c.1612, Maydan-i Shah and Chahar Bagh Avenue; c.1600, Chehel Sotun Palace and Gardens (much altered by later rebuilding); 1601–1628, Mosque of Shaykh Lotfallah; 1612–1638, Royal Mosque; Isfahan, Iraq.

BIBLIOGRAPHY

ARDALAN, NADER 1974 "Color in Safavid Architecture: The Poetic Diffusion of Light." Pages 164–178 in Renata Holod (editor), *Studies on Isfahan*. Boston: Society for Iranian Societies.

BAKHTIAR, ALI 1974 "The Royal Bazaar of Isfahan." Pages 320–347 in Renata Holod (editor), *Studies on Isfahan*. Boston: Society for Iranian Studies.

CARSWELL, JOHN 1968 *New Julfa: The Armenian Churches and Other Buildings*. Oxford University Press.

GALDIERI, EUGENIO 1974 "Les Palais d'Isfahan." Pages 380–405 in Renata Holod (editor), *Studies on Isfahan*. Boston: Society for Iranian Studies.

GODARD, ANDRÉ 1937 "Isfahan." *Arthar-e Iran* 2:6–176.

HUNAFAR, LUTF ALLAH 1969 *Ganjina-yi asar-i Tarikhi-yi Isfahan*. Isfahan, Iraq: Saghafi.

ISKANDAR BEG MUNSHI 1978 *History of the Shah 'Abbas the Great*. Translated by Roger M. Savory. Boulder, Colo.: Westview.

POPE, ARTHUR UPHAM 1938–1939 "The Safavid Period." Pages 1165–1225 in Arthur Upham Pope and Phyllis Ackerman (editors), *A Survey of Persian Art*. Oxford University Press.

POPE, ARTHUR UPHAM 1965 *Persian Architecture*. New York: Braziller.

SAVORY, ROGER M. 1980 *Iran Under the Safavids*. Cambridge University Press.

WELCH, ANTHONY 1973 *Shah 'Abbas and the Arts of Isfahan*. New York: Asia Society.

WILBER, DONALD 1962 *Persian Gardens and Garden Pavilions*. Rutland, Vt.: Tuttle.

WILBER, DONALD 1974 "Aspects of the Safavid Ensemble at Isfahan." Pages 406–415 in Renata Holod (editor), *Studies on Isfahan*. Boston: Society for Iranian Studies.

ZANDER, GIUSEPPE 1974 "Observations sur l'architecture civile d'Ispahan." Pages 294–319 in Renata Holod (editor), *Studies on Isfahan*. Boston: Society for Iranian Studies.

ABBEY, EDWIN A.

Edwin Austin Abbey (1852–1911), illustrator and mural painter, was born in Philadelphia and died in London. He studied briefly at the Pennsylvania Academy with Christian Schussele. His supremacy as a draftsman can be recognized in illustrations for *Harper's* of Shakespeare, Goldsmith, and Herrick works. He settled in London in the late 1870s, where he enjoyed success as a Royal Academician. His major murals include historical and allegorical decorations for the Pennsylvania State Capitol (completed posthumously, supervised by John Singer Sargent) and the Quest of the Holy Grail series for the Boston Public Library (installed 1901).

DONALD MARTIN REYNOLDS

BIBLIOGRAPHY

Edwin Austin Abbey, 1852–1911. 1973 New Haven: Yale University Art Gallery. Catalogue of an exhibition.

LUCAS, E. V. 1921 *Edwin Austin Abbey: Royal Academician.* 2 vols. London: Methuen; New York: Scribner.

MATHER, FRANK JEWETT, JR. 1943 Volume 1, pages 3–8 in *Dictionary of American Biography*. New York: Scribner.

ABBONDI, ANTONIO DI PIETRO

Of Milanese origins and active in Venice, Italy, Antonio di Pietro Abbondi (?–1549), also called Scarpagnino, constructed the German Fondaco after designs by Girolamo Tedesco. He then worked on the reconstruction of several bridges and buildings destroyed by the fire of 1514. From 1523, Abbondi worked on the Doge's Palace and Venetian churches.

SARA LEHRMAN

WORKS

1508, German Fondaco; 1514–1522, Fabbriche Vecchie di Rialto; 1514–1523, Rialto Bridge; c.1536–1549, San Sebastiano (façade); 1545–1549, Doge's Palace (courtyard); Venice, Italy.

BIBLIOGRAPHY

FORLATI, F. 1940 "Il Fondaco dei Tedeschi." *Palladio* 4:275–286.

LORENZI, G. B. 1868 Volume 1 in *Monumenti per servire alla storia del Palazzo Ducale di Venezia*. Venice, Italy.

LORENZETTI, G. (1936) 1956 *Venezia e il suo estuario*. 2d ed. Rome.

MARIACHER, G. 1960 "Abbondi." *Dizionario Biografio degli Italiani*. Rome: Giovanni Treccami.

PAOLETTI, P. 1893 *L'architettura e la scultura del Rinascimento in Venezia*. Venice, Italy.

SELVATICO, P. 1847 Pages 208–213 in *Sulla architettura e sulla scultura in Venezia*. Venice, Italy.

TEMANZA, TOMMASO 1778 *Vite dei più celebri architetti e scultori Veneziani*. Venice, Italy.

'ABD AL-KARIM

'Abd al-Karim, called Ma'muri (1570?–1648), served as chief architect of the Mogul Emperor Jahangir and later was appointed by Emperor Shah

Jahan to the administrative post of superintendent of buildings (*Darogha-i-'Imarat*) at Agra, India. Though few in number, his surviving buildings mark an important stage in the evolution of Mogul architecture from the complicated eclecticism of the period of Akbar to the harmonious refinement of the reign of Shah Jahan.

His earliest documented independent project involved remodeling work and construction of new royal palaces at Mandu (1615–1617). As reward for these, Jahangir promoted the architect to noble rank and gave him the title of Ma'mur Khan. One year later (1618), 'Abd al-Karim brought to completion some imposing new palaces in the Lahore fort, which formed part of an extensive renovation project that had been started some six years earlier (under the charge of the trusted noble Khwaja Jahan). The architect's most ambitious undertaking in the Lahore fort was the vast white marble Royal Tower (*Shah Burj*), which was begun in 1623 but not completed until 1631, during the fourth regnal year of Shah Jahan.

Thereafter, 'Abd al-Karim seems to have designed no more buildings. From 1631 until his death in 1648, he functioned as a ranking official in the Mogul bureaucracy, first as a minister (*diwan*) in the Punjab, then as overseer of buildings at Agra. For some unknown reason, his title Ma'mur Khan was dropped and he became known as Mir ("noble lord") 'Abd al-Karim instead. It was during his tenure as superintendent of buildings that the Taj Mahal was built, but the actual designer was almost certainly the great Mogul architect USTAD AHMAD, a slightly younger contemporary of 'Abd al-Karim, who may possibly have collaborated with him at Lahore during the 1620s. Of 'Abd al-Karim's own buildings, the Shah Burj in the Lahore fort most clearly reveals the transitional character of his architectural style and its probable influence upon the mature work of Ustad Ahmad.

W. E. BEGLEY

WORKS

1613–1618, Royal Palace (*Daulat Khana*) and other Jahangiri Buildings, Lahore Fort, Pakistan. 1615–1617, Jahangiri Palaces, Mandu, India. 1623–1631, Royal Tower (*Shah Burj*) and Gateway, Lahore Fort, Pakistan.

BIBLIOGRAPHY

JAHANGIR (1829)1968 In H. Beveridge (editor), *The Tūzuk-i-Jahāngīrī; or Memoirs of Jahāngīr*. Translated by A. Rogers. 2 vols. Reprint, Delhi, India: Munshiram Manoharlal.
NUR BAKHSH 1902–1903 "Historical Notes on the Lahore Fort and its Buildings." *Archaeological Survey of India: Annual Report* 1902–1903:218–224.
VOGEL, J. PH. 1914 "The Master Builder of the Lahore Palace." *Journal of the Punjab Historical Society* 3:67–69.

ABEILLE, JOSEPH

Joseph Abeille (1669?–1752?), engineer and architect, served as *ingénieur du roi* from 1693–1705. Between 1706 and 1720, he designed especially lavish hotels (i.e. townhouses) for notable Swiss families. Returning to France and to engineering after 1720, he worked with ANGE-JACQUES GABRIEL on rebuilding the city of Rennes which had been ravaged by fire. He developed a visionary proposal for crisscrossing France with canals.

JUANITA M. ELLIAS

WORKS

1707–1712, Hôtel Saussure, 24 rue de la Cité, Geneva. 1711, Château de Thunstetten, Berne. 1711, Fountain du Molard, Geneva.

BIBLIOGRAPHY

ABEILLE, JOSEPH 1699 "Méthode pour trouver des Courbes, le long desquelles un corps tombant, s'approche ou s'éloigne de l'Horizon en telle raison des tems qu'on voudra." *Mémoires de l'Academie Royale des Sciences* 1:90–93.
ABEILLE, JOSEPH 1740 *Etat des avantages que produira le canal de Cosne tant pour Paris que pour les provinces, en descendant les rivières d'Yonne et de Loire*. Paris: Lameste.
BARNES, HELEN 1978 "La Maison de Saussure: Restoring the Elegance of a Sumptuous Past in Geneva." *Architectural Digest* 35–36:36–43.
HAUTECOEUR, LOUIS 1950 *Première moitié du XVIIIe siècle: Le style Louis XV*. Volume 3 in *Histoire de l'architecture classique en France*. Paris: Picard.

ABEL, JOHN

John Abel (c.1578–1675) was a master carpenter, active mainly in Herefordshire, England. He was given the title of King's Carpenter for constructing a mill for the Royalist forces during the siege of Hereford in 1645. His local celebrity is attested by the numerous timber-framed buildings attributed to him, but little surviving work is securely documented as his.

IAN CHILVERS

WORKS

*(A)c.1600, Old Market Hall, Hereford, Herefordshire, England. *1624, Market Hall, Brecon, Brecknockshire, Wales. 1625, Grammar School, Kington; 1633, Market Hall (rebuilt as Grange Court), Leominster; 1633, Saint Mary's Church (restoration of ceilings, and (A)screen), Abbey Dore; *1654, Market Hall, Kington; Herefordshire, England.

BIBLIOGRAPHY

FORD R. A. 1963 "John Abel, a 17th Century Architect." *Transactions of the Woolhope Naturalists' Field Club* 68:107–109.
PEVSNER, NIKOLAUS 1963 *The Buildings of England: Herefordshire*. Harmondsworth, England: Penguin.

ABERCROMBIE, PATRICK

Leslie Patrick Abercrombie (1879–1957) was born at Ashton-upon-Mersey, England. Following formal education at Uppingham, he worked for six years in architectural offices in Manchester and in Liverpool where in 1907 he joined the staff of the University's school of architecture. In 1913, with Sydney Kelly, he won an international competition for Dublin's city plan and two years later became the Lever Professor of Civic Design in the school of architecture at the University of Liverpool, where he, as editor, had launched *Town Planning Review* in 1910. In 1935, he became professor of town planning at the Bartlett School of Architecture of the University College of the University of London, retiring in 1946.

Abercrombie developed plans for English regions and cities following his principle "to retain the old structure, where discernible, and make it workable under modern conditions." He called for limiting London's size by directing all new growth for fifty years into ten satellite towns and into existing towns separated from London by a green belt.

Honors included knighthood in 1945, the Royal Gold Medal for Architecture in 1946, the Gold Medal of the American Institute of Architects in 1949, and the Gold Medal of the Town Planning Institute in 1955. He was a founder and chairman of the Council for the Preservation of Rural England, a member of the Royal Fine Arts Commission, and president of the International Union of Architects and of the Franco-British Union of Architects.

REGINALD R. ISAACS

WORKS

TOWN AND REGIONAL PLANS

1922, Doncaster, England. 1922, Dublin (with Sydney Kelly and Arthur Kelly). 1923, Deeside (with Sydney Kelly and Theodore Fyfe), England. 1923, Stratford-upon-Avon (with Lascelles Abercrombie); England. 1924, Sheffield (with R. H. Mattocks), England. 1925, East Kent (with John Archibald), England. 1929, Thames Valley (with Walter Mayo), England. 1930, Bristol and Bath (with Bertrand Brueton), England. 1931, Oxfordshire (with Mayo), England. 1932, Cumbria, England. 1935, East Suffolk (with Sydney Kelly); 1941, Dublin (with Sydney Kelly). 1943, County of London (with J. H. Forshaw). 1943, Plymouth, England. 1943, West Midlands (with Herbert Jackson), England. 1944, Greater London. 1945, Kingston-upon-Hull (with EDWIN LUTYENS), England. 1945, Sheffield (with John Owens et al.), England. 1946, Bournemouth, Poole, and Christchurch (with Richard Nickson), England. 1946, Clyde Valley (with Robert Matthew), England. 1949, Edinburgh (with Derek Plumstead). 1949, Warwick (with Nickson), England. 1956, Addis Ababa (with Gerald Dix), Ethiopia.

OTHER WORKS

n.d., Camps and Homes for English Miners; n.d., Hostel, Leningrad. n.d., Town Hall, Haifa, Israel. n.d., University of Ceylon (with A. C. Holliday), Peradenuja, Ceylon.

BIBLIOGRAPHY

ABERCROMBIE, PATRICK 1924 "The Preliminary Survey of a Region." *International Town Planning Conference: Papers* 1:36–50.
ABERCROMBIE, PATRICK 1926 *The Preservation of Rural England.* Liverpool (England) University Press.
ABERCROMBIE, PATRICK (1933)1959 *Town and Country Planning.* Edited by D. Rigby Child. 3d rev. ed. London: Oxford University Press.
ABERCROMBIE, PATRICK 1934 *Country Planning and Landscape Design: The Stevenson Lecture for 1933.* Liverpool (England) University Press.
ABERCROMBIE, PATRICK 1937a In *Planning in Town and Country.* London: Hodder & Stoughton.
ABERCROMBIE, PATRICK 1937b "National and Regional Planning in Great Britain." Pages 42–50 in *National and Regional Planning.* Letchworth, England: Garden City Press.
ABERCROMBIE, PATRICK (editor) 1939 *The Book of the Modern House.* London: Hodder & Stoughton.
MUMFORD, LEWIS 1945 "The Plan of London (Abercrombie and Forshaw architects)." In *City Development.* New York: Harcourt.
STEPHENSON, FLORA, and POOL, PHOEBE 1944 *A Plan for Town and Country.* London: Pilot Press.

ABRAHAM, ROBERT

Trained as a surveyor, Robert Abraham (1774–1850) developed a successful architectural practice, beginning with the County Fire Office, Regent Street, London (1819). A competent, eclectic designer, he was patronized by various Catholic noblemen, notably the twelfth duke of Norfolk, some of whose residences he altered. His pupils included his son, H. R. Abraham.

R. WINDSOR LISCOMBE

WORKS

*1819, County Fire Office, Regent Street; *1819–1820, Norfolk House (remodeling, with addition of portico and balcony in 1842), Saint James's Square; *1820, 176–186 Regent Street; 1821–1822, Craven Chapel, Foubert's Place; London. 1823–1824, Mildenhall School, Wiltshire, England. Before 1827, Alton Towers (conservatories and garden buildings), Staffordshire, England. *1827–1828, Western Synagogue, Saint Alban's Place; *1830–1834, Westminster Bridewell, Tothill Fields; London. (A)1836, Town Hall, Arundel, England.

BIBLIOGRAPHY

"Survey of London." 1963 Volume 31, pages 200–201
    in F. H. W. Sheppard, *Parish of St. James, Westminster:
    Part II, North of Piccadilly.* London: Athlone.
WILLIAMSON, ROSS 1940 "Staffordshire's Wonder-
    land." *Architectural Review* 87:157–164.

ABRAMOVITZ, MAX

See HARRISON and ABRAMOVITZ.

ACOSTA, WLADIMIRO

Wladimiro Acosta (1900–1967) was born in
Odessa, Russia, and settled in Argentina in 1928.
A convinced functionalist, he designed typical
skeleton structures with meticulously plastered
white walls. In his designs for smaller buildings,
however, his ground plans are not as flexible as
those of his European counterparts.

One of Acosta's main concerns was the relation
of architecture to climate. His Helios principle is
an ingenious system of heat control by placing a
sunshade slab over and above the main body of a
building. In the midst of a decidedly eclectic architectural environment, Acosta designed much but
built little.

FEDERICO F. ORTIZ

WORKS

n.d., Apartment Building, Avenida Figueroa Alcorta,
Buenos Aires; n.d., Helios Houses, Bahía Blanca, Ar-
gentina. Villa del Parque, Buenos Aires. n.d., Helios
Houses, La Falda, Córdoba, Argentina. n.d., Helios
Houses, Ramos Mejía, Argentina. n.d., Helios
Rosario, Santa Fé, Argentina. n.d., Helios Houses,
Punta del Este, Uruguay. n.d., Polytechnic Institute,
Caracas. n.d., Psychiatric Hospital, Oliveros, Santa Fé,
Argentina.

BIBLIOGRAPHY

ACOSTA, WLADIMIRO (1936)1947 *Vivienda y ciudad.*
    2d ed. Buenos Aires: Ediciones Anaconda.
ACOSTA, WLADIMIRO 1976 *Vivienda y clima.* 2d ed.
    Buenos Aires: Ediciones Nueva Visión.

ADAM, JAMES

The third son of WILLIAM ADAM, James Adam
(1732–1794) is best known as the partner and principal assistant of his older brother ROBERT ADAM.
In the 1750s, he was a partner in the family architectural firm in Scotland with his brothers JOHN
ADAM and Robert. From 1760 to 1763, he was in
Italy, accompanied by GEORGE RICHARDSON and

CHARLES-LOUIS CLERISSEAU. Joining Robert in
London in 1763 after the latter's basic style had
been set, he played an important if subsidiary role
in the firm's total activity and output, as well as
producing a few independent designs. From 1769
to 1782, he was joint architect of the king's works,
succeeding Robert on the latter's election to Parliament.

DAMIE STILLMAN

WORKS

*For his work in the 1750s in Scotland, as part of the family
partnership, see the list of works under John Adam. Much of
his subsequent work was in partnership with Robert Adam
and is listed under that name.*

1767–1771, Shire Hall, Hertford, Hertfordshire, England. c.1770–1775, Lowther Village, Westmoreland,
England. 1776, Portland Place (façades), London.
1792–1794, Saint George's Episcopal Church and
Manse, Edinburgh. 1793, College Houses, 169–173,
179–183 High Street; c.1793–1796, Assembly Rooms;
1794, Tron Church; *1798, Barony Church: Glasgow,
Scotland.

BIBLIOGRAPHY

ADAM, JAMES 1789 *Practical Essays on Agriculture.*
    2 vols. London: Cadell.
ADAM, ROBERT, and ADAM, JAMES 1773–1778 *The
    Works in Architecture of Robert and James Adams.* 2
    vols. London: The authors. A third volume was pub-
    lished posthumously in 1822 in London by Priest-
    ley & Weale. A one-volume reprint of all three vol-
    umes, edited by Robert Oresko, was published in
    1975 in London by Academy Editions.
BOLTON, ARTHUR T. 1918 "The Shire Hall, Hert-
    ford." *Architectural Review* 43:68–73.
BOLTON, ARTHUR T. 1922 *The Architecture of Robert
    and James Adam (1758–1794).* 2 vols. London: Coun-
    try Life.
FLEMING, JOHN 1962 *Robert Adam and His Circle.*
    London: Murray.
ROWAN, ALISTAIR 1973–1974 "After the Adelphi:
    Forgotten Years in the Adam Brothers' Practice."
    Journal of the Royal Society of Arts 122:659–678.

ADAM, JOHN

The eldest son of WILLIAM ADAM, John Adam
(1721–1792) succeeded on his father's death in
1748 to his architectural, contracting, and other
business activities, as well as to his position as Master Mason to the Board of Ordnance for North
Britain and to the estate of Blair Adam, Kinross-
shire. Taking his brothers, ROBERT ADAM, and,
subsequently, JAMES ADAM, into partnership, John
continued his father's works and began a number
of new ones. They continued also as contractors,
especially at Fort William, Inverness-shire. The

partnership with Robert was dissolved in 1758 and that with James in 1760. John practiced alone in Scotland in the 1760s, but thereafter, most of his activity was outside the architectural field, though he remained interested in his brothers' affairs in London.

DAMIE STILLMAN

WORKS
ROBERT ADAM, JAMES ADAM, AND
JOHN ADAM

1750–1760, Hopetoun House (completion of house, offices, and interiors), West Lothian, Scotland. *1751, Buchanan House (alterations), Stirlingshire, Scotland. 1753–1755, Adam Family Mausoleum (Greyfriars Cemetery), Edinburgh. 1753–1756, Castle Grant (additions), Morayshire, Scotland. 1753–1758, Arniston, (west wing interiors), Midlothian, Scotland. 1753–1759, Dumfries House, Ayrshire, Scotland. 1753–1761, Exchange (executed by others; now the City Chambers), Edinburgh. 1755–1757, Town House, Inveraray, Argyllshire, Scotland. *1757, Hawkhill Villa, South Leith, Edinburgh. *1757–1761, Douglas Castle, Lanarkshire, Scotland. c.1758–1761, Gothic Bridge and various outbuildings, Inveraray, Argyllshire, Scotland. c.1758–1761, Yester House (saloon interior), East Lothian, Scotland.

JOHN ADAM

c.1760, Ballochmyle House (since remodeled), Ayrshire, Scotland. 1761, Moffat House, Dumfriesshire, Scotland. 1763–1765, Moy House (alterations), Morayshire, Scotland. *1766–1771, Broomall, Fifeshire, Scotland.

BIBLIOGRAPHY
ADAM, WILLIAM (1812)1980 *Vitruvius Scoticus.* Reprint. Edinburgh: Pane Harris; New York: AMS.
FLEMING, JOHN 1962 *Robert Adam and His Circle.* London: Murray.
LINDSAY, IAN G., and COSH, MARY 1973 *Inveraray and the Dukes of Argyll.* Edinburgh University Press.

ADAM, ROBERT

Born in Scotland and trained there and in Italy, Robert Adam (1728–1792) settled in London at the end of the 1750s, establishing a career as one of the two leading British architects of the last half of the eighteenth century. He was, at the same time, a central figure in the international neoclassicism that dominated those years throughout Europe. His work, and especially the decorative side of it, set the standard for one aspect of that style, an elegant and refined adaptation of classical antiquity very much attune to the tenor of sophisticated life in the Age of Enlightenment.

With unstinting praise, but also with a sub-stantial amount of accuracy, he and his brother JAMES ADAM readily identified the contributions of their partnership, of which Robert was the principal designer and dominating figure, in the two lavish folio volumes of *The Works in Architecture of Robert and James Adam,* which they published in 1773 and 1778. Taking credit for "a remarkable improvement in the form, convenience, arrangement, and relief of apartments; a greater movement and variety, in the outside composition, and in the decoration of the inside, an almost total change" (vol. 1, part 1, p. 3), they claimed "in some measure to have brought about, in this country; a kind of revolution in the whole system of this useful and elegant art" (ibid.).

If we leave aside the hyperbole, those statements do indicate both the nature of Adam's accomplishments and the degree of his success. Part of the reason for the publication of the *Works in Architecture* was the great popularity of the Adam style by the 1770s and the fairly widespread "imitation of other artists" (*Works,* vol. 1, part 1, p. 3). Ultimately, his influence, not only in the British Isles, but on the Continent and as far afield as Russia and the United States, was enormous. This was indicated in 1792, the year of Adam's death, by Thomas Malton, when he wrote that

To their researches among the vestiges of antiquity, we are indebted for many improvements in ornamental architecture; and for the introduction of a style of decoration, unrivalled for elegance and gaiety; which, in spite of the innovations of fashion, will prevail so long as good taste exists in the nation [1792, vol. 1, p. 40].

Born in Kirkcaldy, Fifeshire, the second son of WILLIAM ADAM, the leading Scottish architect of the second quarter of the eighteenth century, Robert grew up and matured in an intellectual circle in Edinburgh where he was exposed to the activities of architecture and building. In 1743, after attending the High School in Edinburgh, he entered Edinburgh University, though it seems that he did not graduate. Instead, he joined his father's architectural office, where, together with his older brother JOHN ADAM, he assisted in the various projects at hand. On their father's death in 1748, the two older Adam brothers formed a partnership, later joined by James, continuing their father's architectural works and his building commissions for the Board of Ordnance. Of the latter, the most important—and most lucrative—was Fort George, Inverness-shire, begun in 1748; but there were both other architectural and contracting operations and various business enterprises of William Adam's that occupied the sons and provided the wealth that made possible Robert's and James's trips to Italy. The Adam brothers began to attract new commissions as well.

In these commissions, three of the most significant of which were the completion of Hopetoun House, West Lothian (c.1750–1760); an addition to Arniston, Midlothian (1753–1758); and Dumfries House, Ayrshire (1753–1759), the Adams, with Robert playing perhaps the most significant role in design, demonstrated their awareness of current English tastes. Taking only the sense of movement from his father's robust style with its Vanbrughian (see JOHN VANBRUGH) and Gibbsian (see JAMES GIBBS) character, he introduced aspects of Burlingtonian Palladianism (see LORD BURLINGTON and ANDREA PALLADIO) and rococo decorative details, some of which had begun to appear in the father's later works. Any acquaintance with these tendencies acquired through this means was heightened by books and engravings and by a trip to England in 1749–1750 on which he recorded his impressions in a sketchbook. Also seen here and in other drawings of these years is an enjoyment of landscape and of the playful, unarcheological type of Gothic popular at the time.

These tastes were, in turn, overlaid by the influence of classical antiquity and the theories, spirit, and character of neoclassicism then beginning to flower in Rome, as Robert Adam began a Grand Tour to Italy which was to change not only his architectural style but his whole future development. Leaving Edinburgh in October 1754, he paused briefly in London before pushing on for Brussels, where he was to meet his traveling companion, Charles Hope, younger brother of one of the Adams' principal clients, the earl of Hopetoun. With Hope sharing the expenses and providing an aristocratic introduction for Adam, the two men traveled through Paris, the south of France, Genoa, and Pisa to Florence. There, Adam made the most important acquaintance of his Grand Tour (and perhaps of his whole career), CHARLES LOUIS CLÉRISSEAU, a French architect and delineator of ruins, who had been a *pensionnaire* at the French Academy in Rome, was abreast of the latest ideas, and, as Adam wrote eight months later, "has all these Knacks, so necessary to us Architects" (letter to James Adam, October 19, 1755).

From Clérisseau, whom Adam persuaded to accompany him to Rome and to stay with him there, Adam learned how to draw in a free manner, but he also learned about antiquities, ornaments, and neoclassicism. During his two-year sojourn in Rome, from February 1755 to May 1757, Adam, after his early separation from Hope, studied and drew the ancient, Renaissance, and baroque monuments; learned drawing with Clérisseau and Laurent Pecheux; met various traveling Englishmen, some of whom would stand him in good stead on his return; and became immersed in the aesthetic milieu, which included especially GIOVANNI BATTISTA PIRANESI.

From Piranesi, whom Adam considered the only Italian at the time "to breath the Antient Air," Adam learned even more of the incredible wonder and variety of antiquity, but also of the excitement of archeology and the sense of megalomaniacal scale. Despite occasional differences, largely the result of national temperaments, they remained friendly colleagues over the years, with Piranesi citing Adam in later works and dedicating to him his *Campo Marzio* of 1762.

All of this activity in Rome, and his progress in his study, convinced Adam that he should set his sights on London rather than Edinburgh, and from then on he set about ensuring his success in that endeavor. One means of doing this, it seemed to him, was to publish a book that would indicate his deep familiarity with the antiquities, and he contemplated a number of projects along this line. Most of them, including a corrected version of ANTOINE DESGODETZ's *Les edifices antiques de Rome* of 1682, with the latter's mistakes to be shown "by a red line, which lets them see the error" (letter to James Adam, July 4, 1755), came to naught. But one, the *Ruins of the Palace of the Emperor Diocletian at Spalatro in Dalmatia,* did in fact appear, though by the date of its publication, Adam no longer really needed the publicity it gave him.

Chosen probably for such pragmatic reasons as its relative accessibility from Venice and the fact that it had not been previously investigated, Spalato, or Split, in what is now Yugoslavia, did provide a significant example of Roman domestic architecture, despite the relatively late date (C.A.D. 300) of the palace. During his five weeks there, Adam examined the ruins, sketched, and supervised, while Clérisseau, who was still with him, made perspective views and two draftsmen he had been using in Rome did measured drawings. Engraved by a variety of Italian and English engravers, after drawings by Clérisseau and the two draftsmen, and with a foreword and historical description ghost-written by Adam's cousin, William Robertson, principal of Edinburgh University, the sumptuous volume, bearing only Adam's name and, under the plates, that of the engraver, was published in 1764.

Having provided himself with the material for a dramatic demonstration to the British public of his knowledge of antiquities and of his taste and having acquired membership in the Accademia di San Luca in Rome and the academies of Florence and Bologna, Adam, accompanied by the two draftsmen, but not Clérisseau, who remained in Italy to guide and teach James Adam on his Grand

Tour, left Italy, traveled through Germany and the Low Countries, and reached London on January 17, 1758.

From his arrival there, he lost no time in establishing himself as an architect of distinction. In that, he was before too long extremely successful. Within eight days, he was proposed for membership in the Society of Arts, and a week later he was elected. Just as quickly, he set about meeting prospective clients. Before the first year was out, he was already embarked on several commissions; and by the early 1760s, the nobility and gentry were clamoring for his work. In March 1763, he could write, without exaggeration, to Lord Kames of "having business all over England, which I am with difficulty able to get managed with Honour to myself & Satisfaction to my Employers" (Abercairny Papers, CD 24/1/564, Register House, Edinburgh). Two years earlier, he had been made a Fellow of the Royal Society and had been appointed, together with his archrival, WILLIAM CHAMBERS, joint Architect of the King's Works. For the next decade and a half, the two of them were to dominate English architecture almost completely.

Other architects, beginning with JAMES WYATT, arose in the 1770s and 1780s to challenge the hegemony that he had earlier shared only with Chambers, but Adam remained an important and influential architect, and his total output was both very large and of high quality. Although the early and mid-1780s were marked by a significant lessening of Adam's architectural activity, due both to the economic situation following the American War of Independence and increased competition from a new generation of architects, he was again extremely active with commissions, primarily, however, in Scotland, in the few years before his death in 1792. In fact, as his obituary notice stated, "in the space of one year preceding his death, he designed 8 great public works, beside 25 private buildings, so various in their style, and so beautiful in their composition, that they have been allowed, by the best judges, sufficient of themselves to establish his fame unrivaled as an artist" (Gentleman's Magazine 62: 282–283). At his burial in Westminster Abbey, his pallbearers included one duke, two earls, a viscount, a baron, and a distinguished commoner.

In addition to the honors he had achieved at the beginning of his career, he was elected subsequently to both the Royal Society of Edinburgh and the Society of Antiquaries there. He was, however, never a member of the Royal Academy, due, undoubtedly, to the opposition of Chambers, the treasurer and one of the most powerful figures in that institution. In 1769, Adam was elected Member of Parliament for Kinross-shire, at which time he resigned from his position as Architect of the King's Works, to be succeeded in that post by his brother James, who held it until the position itself was abolished in 1782, with the reorganization of the Office of Works. Robert did retain until his death the Surveyorship of Chelsea Hospital, which he had held since 1765.

Adam's architectural production during the thirty-four years of his London career was enormous, and there is no doubt that, despite the help of a great many individuals, he was the principal designer and guiding spirit of the whole enterprise. In this, he was assisted by his brother James, who from 1760 to 1763 had likewise been in Italy under Clérisseau's tutelage; their younger brother William, whose principal responsibility was finance; a number of draftsmen; and scores of craftsmen. While still in Italy, Robert had begun to assemble an office staff, so to speak, and he brought back with him two draftsmen, Agostino Brunias and a Liègois, almost certainly LAURENT-BENOÎT DEWEZ, who soon returned to his native Belgium, where he became a leading neoclassical architect. James came back with other draftsmen, and both Italian and Scottish names which appear in the Adam bank account can be identified as office assistants. The Italians include Giuseppe Manocchi, JOSEPH BONOMI, and Antonio Zucchi, although the latter was employed primarily as a decorative painter, with GEORGE RICHARDSON, who had worked for the Adams in Scotland and accompanied James on his Italian tour, being among the Britishers employed.

It was they, and their successors, who were responsible for the finished renderings that still indicate, after two centuries, the nature and quality of Adam's designs. The executed works owe a great deal to the "regiment of artificers," as Mrs. Montagu called Adam's craftsmen in 1779 (letter to the duchess of Portland, July 20, 1779), for they transferred his conception from paper to stucco, paint, marble, ormolu, and a variety of other materials. The most consistently employed was the firm of Joseph Rose, led first by an uncle and then by his nephew of the same name, who, together, were responsible for the decorative plasterwork in a whole succession of Adam buildings, beginning with Shardeloes in the early 1760s. Faithfully following the Adam designs, their stucco decorations give to these buildings what is perhaps their most distinctive character. Also extremely important were the decorative painters, chief among whom was Antonio Zucchi. Others included Giovanni Battista Cipriani, Michael Angelo Pergolesi, Biagio Rebecca, and William Hamilton. Carvers in both stone and wood, metalsmiths, braziers, cabinetmakers, and carpet manufacturers, to say nothing about glaziers, slaters, bricklayers, and carpenters, contributed to the complement of skilled artists and artisans whom Adam employed. Without any of them, the end result would not have been the same; but the creation and development of Adam's architectural oeuvre was due, above all else, to his genius and his drive.

As he and James described it, "if we have any claim to approbation, we found it on this alone: That, we flatter ourselves, we have been able to seize, with some degree of success, the beautiful spirit of antiquity, and to tranfuse it, with novelty and variety, through all our numerous works" (Adam, *Works,* vol. 1, part 1, p. 6). And, indeed, classical antiquity was perhaps the most important source for the Adam style, though, as they indicated, most of what Robert took was modified and combined in such a way as to stamp it with his own imprint. Of ancient sources of inspiration, those from monuments in and around Rome were, as might be expected, the most important, with grotesque or arabesque decoration and the plans of Roman baths being especially influential. Antiquities that he had seen further afield, such as those in Pompeii, Herculaneum, and neighboring sites on the one hand and Spalato on the other, also provided elements to emulate, though neither of these areas was actually that influential. Other Roman monuments were suggested to him by books, of which Robert Wood's *Ruins of Palmyra* of 1753 was perhaps the most significant in this respect; and his relatively limited use of Greek elements depended on similar means.

Ancient sources were only one factor in the creation of the Adam style. Another was the Renaissance, which served not only to confirm but to modify the antique examples. This was especially true for grotesque decoration, where such examples as those in the Vatican *logge* or the Palazzo Madama contributed to his conception of this form of ornament. Other Renaissance, mannerist, and baroque buildings, too, left their imprint, with, for example, the ceilings of the Villa Pamphilj (now Doria-Pamphilj) serving as important models for his earliest decorative work in England. Piranesi, who was a strong formative influence on Adam, continued to be a source of inspiration long after Adam had left Italy; his *Diverse maniere d'adornare i cammini* of 1769 provided suggestions for two of the relatively few new features of Adam's style after about the mid-1760s—his Etruscan rooms and his more complex chimneypieces. Eighteenth-century French influence was to be seen in the form of planning, with suites of rooms and enfilades providing ideas; colonnaded entrance screens seem also to be derived from this

source. Though there may have been some inspiration of contemporary French decoration on Adam, the reverse is also in part true; on the whole, although the two are related, they are not so close as to suggest specific influence of the one on the other.

The one significant additional source upon which Adam drew was the architecture of his Burlingtonian Palladian predecessors in England. For despite his criticism of this architecture, singling out for special attack the massive entablature, ponderous compartmented ceiling, and tabernacle frame, he was indebted to it far more than he cared to admit. Though he rejected its heaviness, its proportions, and a good deal else and often radically altered that which he borrowed, he continued to employ all through his career such distinctive aspects of the manner of Burlington, WILLIAM KENT, and their followers as the staccato rhythm, the Palladian motif within relieving arch, and a variety of decorative patterns and motifs from modillion cornices to caryatid chimneypieces.

In his earliest work in England, one is especially cognizant of many of these sources, for the total ensemble reflects the multitude of influences rather than a synthesis of them. The relief, too, is still pronounced, due partially, Adam felt, to his inability "to get English workmen who will leave their angly Stiff Sharp manner" (letter to James Adam, probably November or December 1758).

Soon, however, he began to synthesize the various elements in his repertoire, creating unified and elegant compositions; and by the middle of the 1760s, he had arrived at a characteristic manner. From then on, he primarily refined his style, attenuating it even further. There were innovations, such as the Etruscan decoration and more complex chimneypieces derived from Piranesi and the picturesque castle style that became especially important in the last fifteen years of his life. But, essentially, the Adam style was formed within a few short years of his return from Italy.

During this early period, and even in general throughout his career, much of Adam's work was concerned with the decorative aspect of architecture. This was the result, in part, of the very large amount of country house building that had occurred in the second quarter of the century, but it also reflects, to some extent, his own predilections. As Robert's brother-in-law and would-be biographer noted, the Adam brothers felt:

that their art must ever remain extremely deficient, untill they should be able to supply some new & undiscovered resources for the internal decoration of private apartments, by introducing elegance, gayity, & variety, instead of that dull & elaborate floridity, which universally prevailed in the buildings of this Island, till the time of Mr. Adam's return from abroad [John Clerk of Eldin, draft notes for a life of Robert Adam].

This is not to say that there are not a great many Adam designs for new buildings, as well as a significant number of executed examples, but his redecoration of older houses and his completion of houses which had already been begun were very common. His finest achievements—as at Syon House, Osterley Park, Kedleston Hall, or the library at Kenwood, for example—are of this type, and he tackled with relish the problems they posed.

Although decoration and interior conception were the aspects of architecture in which both he and his contemporaries felt his greatest contributions lay, he yearned for grand opportunities and made some not inconsiderable efforts in exterior compositions. In most of these, he emphasized the quality of movement, which he defined as

the rise and fall, the advance and recess, with other diversity of form, in the different parts of a building, so as to add greatly to the picturesque of the composition . . . they serve to produce an agreeable and diversified contour, that groups and contrasts like a picture, and creates a variety of light and shade, which gives great spirit, beauty and effect to the composition [*Works*, vol. 1, part 1, p. 3].

Related to the staccatolike emphasis on center and ends that had characterized such Burlingtonian buildings as Holkham or the Horse Guards, this concept appears in the earliest Adam exteriors—the Admiralty Screen in London (1759–1760) and the projected south front of Kedleston, Derbyshire (c.1760–1761)—and continues to the end of his career.

At Kedleston, the domed central block was to have been joined to two projecting wings by lower curved quadrants, creating exactly the kind of movement Adam later described. The design was characterized by other Burlingtonian inheritances, too—the rusticated ground floor, emphasized *piano nobile* with pedimented windows in the main block, and the Palladian motif within relieving arch, here used in groups of three, as Burlington himself had done on the garden façade of Chiswick. Aside from attenuating the proportions and making the composition more elegant, Adam combined these influences from the architecture of his English predecessors with two antique motifs—the organizational pattern of the Arch of Constantine and the saucer dome of the Pantheon—thereby demonstrating both his use of antiquity and his transforming of it. This is beautifully adumbrated in the executed center section, for the late Roman richness of the famous triumphal arch has been pruned in a manner exactly analogous to his draftsmen's alterations of the equally late antique decoration at Spalato.

For the next thirty years, Adam retained his compositional formula and the facets of it, though, as with other aspects of his art, they became more elongated, more refined, more two-dimensional. This can be seen a decade after Kedleston in his façade for the Society of Arts, London (1772–1776), where he adapted antiquity even more freely in order to suit his purposes. In this case, he juxtaposed Ionic capitals with a Doric triglyph-and-metope frieze, a practice which he and James defend in the *Works*:

We can see no reason for assigning to each order its

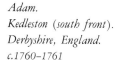

Adam.
Kedleston (south front).
Derbyshire, England.
c.1760–1761

precise entablature, fixed down unalterably both in figure and dimension. Different circumstances of situation and propriety ought to vary the form, and also the proportion, of all entablatures. A latitude in this respect, under the hand of an ingenious and able artist, is often productive of great novelty, variety, and beauty [vol. 1, part 2, p. 7].

The Society of Arts façade also illustrates the attenuation and refinement increasingly characteristic of Adam's style, as well as the combination of both classical motifs and Burlingtonian Palladian ones into an elegant and flat ensemble. These tendencies are equally evident in the years just before his death, as, far example, at Gosford House, East Lothian, begun in 1790, where the staccato rhythm and many of the same ingredients as at both the contemplated Kedleston composition and the Society of Arts are again present, though, as always, in a somewhat different arrangement.

The possibilities for variation were endless, and Adam exploited them to the full. Various orders of columns or pilasters, from the familiar to the unusual, could be employed; the shafts could be fluted or left plain or even replaced by panels filled with anthemia, bell flowers, or arabesque scrolls. These columned or pilastered units, which, in larger buildings, were generally answered by equal emphasis on the ends of the façades, could be pedimented or not; they could be lowered to the ground floor instead of raised; or they could be opened as a screen, as Adam did masterfully in the remodeling of Osterley Park, Middlesex, beginning about 1765. The decorative motifs could be altered in a host of ways. The material might be different—stone, brick, or Liardet's cement, this last a patented invention whose purchase and use by the Adams embroiled them in a nasty lawsuit, decided in their favor by the presiding judge, Lord Mansfield, who happened also to be a client and supporter of the brothers. Regardless of the actual composition or details, the basic principles were generally not significantly different.

This is even true of Adam's castle style, where the spirit employed is not at all the same. Here, battlements and turrets are the distinctive features; yet, the compositional patterns are not that different from the more obviously neoclassical buildings. Wedderburn Castle, Berwickshire (1771–1775), for example, has a rusticated ground floor and pronounced emphasis on center and ends. And such later castellar designs as Culzean, Ayrshire (1777–1792), or Mauldsley, Lanarkshire (1791–1796), have not only the symmetry but also the staccato rhythm and the "movement," including the "picturesque" quality and the "variety of light and shade," that the Adams advocated for and employed in their classical designs.

Adam.
Society of Arts (engraving of façade).
London.
1772–1776

Like those, too, Adam's castles, especially the later ones, combine a variety of influences—from ROGER MORRIS's Inveraray Castle, upon which the Adam brothers were working as contractors in the 1750s, and Roman, Early Christian, and Renaissance structures in Italy which Robert drew during his Grand Tour, to Tudor Syon, whose interior Adam completely redid in the 1760s, and the turreted Scottish buildings that he knew from his youth. The classical interiors of all his castles suggest that he did not intend to reproduce medieval designs. Rather, as with all of his work, he was creating out of a multitude of sources a design that conveyed an effect appropriate to the lives of his clients and the setting of their houses. Synthesis and refinement were his tools; movement and originality, as he understood them, or novelty and variety, as he often called them, were his creeds.

Even more significant than Adam's exterior designs were his planning and his decoration. His

Adam.
Culzean Castle.
Ayrshire, Scotland.
1777–1792

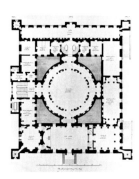

Adam.
Syon House Plan.
Middlesex, England.
c.1760–1769

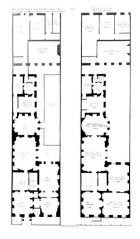

Adam.
Derby House Plan.
London.
1773–1774

fascination with the problems of planning, of creating arrangements of rooms of various forms and dispositions, was evident from the beginning of his career and that of his brother James. Seen in James's sketches of the mid-1750s and in Robert's voluminous group of sketch plans drawn in Rome, this tendency was characteristic of Robert's early work in England and throughout his life. Influenced by the varied room shapes and juxtapositions of Roman thermae, tempered by an appreciation of the French enfilade, he produced liveliness and infinite variety in his interior arrangements. Such spatial manipulations were not limited to new construction; on the contrary, one of the most dramatic demonstrations of his abilities along this line was within the sixteenth-century shell of Syon House, Middlesex, where, near the start of his career, he was called upon by the earl and countess of Northumberland to fashion a modern environment out of an old house.

Beginning with a quadrangular house with varying floor levels, Adam created at Syon a series of unusual and felicitous room shapes, transforming awkward spaces by means of apses, ovals, and columned screens. From the two-story entrance hall, with a coffered apse at one end and a screen of columns at the other, one moves through the columned screen and up a short flight of curving stairs to the anteroom, which Adam converted from a rectangle to a square by inserting a screen of columns parallel to but away from one wall. Next comes a long dining room, with a screened apse at each end, followed by the drawing room, which sports a coved ceiling but no internal spatial tricks. This, in turn, gives way to the long gallery, a heritage of the early seventeenth-century habit of providing space for walking during inclement weather. Again, Adam's talents were put to a severe test, but his manipulation of this space was effected mainly through decorative devices rather than spatial ones. In sharp contrast to this space are the two small closets at either end of it, one circular, the other square.

Only this much of Adam's remodeling of Syon was carried out, but his original plan envisioned these spatial sleights-of-hand complemented by a good many others. Not executed were a proposed oval anteroom on the other side of the hall from the rectangular-cum-square one, a staircase in the form of a horizontal oval flanked by two transversely oriented oval dressing rooms, and a great circular saloon, inspired by the Pantheon, occupying the center of the quadrangle. Although this last remained unbuilt, a temporary version of it, comfortably holding more than 300 people, was installed in 1768 for a reception for the king of Denmark.

The more restricted space of a London townhouse could provide a similarly challenging commission, as is evident in the plan for Derby House, Grosvenor Square, of 1773. Here, again, he was dealing with an existing house, one of five bays in width, to which he made an addition to the rear wing. But within this shell, he adroitly combined rooms with one and two apsed ends, others with alcoves separated by column screens, and squares, circles, and octagons into a lively succession of different spatial experiences.

In new houses planned and built by Adam, the enjoyment of varied and unusual room shapes is also present, though the delight in sleight-of-hand manipulations is perhaps less evident because it was unnecessary. At Luton Hoo, Bedfordshire (1766–1774), for example, the plan was completely symmetrical, yet it featured many of the same shapes as those employed in the remodeling of Derby House. But Adam also envisioned here a wealth of ovals, a saloon with two screened ends and a bow projecting from the central space between them, and a great circular tribune, though not all of these were actually carried out. At Gosford, East Lothian, conceived in 1790, near the end of his life, there is a circular saloon, a drawing room with two apsed ends and projecting columns at the junction of the main part and the apses, and an octagonal billiard room and kitchen.

Even more lively juxtapositions, employed within such general exterior shapes as triangles, octagons, and semicircles, appear in a whole group of relatively late villa designs, some preserved only on paper though others actually executed. Of the paper variety, there is a design of 1779 for Great Saxham, Suffolk, which presents the house as a semicircle and includes a circle, a flattened circle, and a trefoiled trapezoid, along with two rectangles with one apsed end, behind the curved entrance front.

There are other, equally ingenious, plans among Adam's unexecuted designs, but some were also built. At Walkinshaw, Renfrewshire (1791), a triangular plan featured octagonal towers—and rooms—at the three angles, a semicircular entrance-stairhall in the center of one façade, and a double-apsed room in the center of the other two fronts. A variation on this is to be found at Airthrey, Stirlingshire (1790–1791), where the shape is semicircular and the two front angle rooms are square; in this case, the entrance hall is circular, and the saloon in the center of the garden façade has a bowed exedra projecting out from that square.

Within these various imaginative spaces, and the conventionally shaped ones as well, Adam created an amazing series of refined and elegant interiors, which are, as he himself realized, perhaps his greatest accomplishment. For it is, indeed, his decorative work that is conjured up by the label "Adam style," and it is in that realm that he and James claimed to have wrought "a kind of revolution" and "an almost total change" (*Works*, vol. 1, part 1, p. 3). Here, Adam's wide diversity of sources was most obviously synthesized into a highly original style that, despite the general similarities between numerous designs, consists of an enormous number of variations adroitly conceived on a relatively few themes. Except for such speculative projects as the Adelphi of 1768–1772 and Portland Place of 1776–1780, there is incredibly little duplication, and even in these cases variation is far more common than repetition.

In his early decorative work in England—and that aspect was the predominant one in his commissions of the late 1750s and early 1760s—the various sources of the Adam style are not yet completely integrated, and the relief is, for Adam, relatively high. At Hatchlands, Surrey, upon which Adam was engaged before his first year in London (1758) was out, he was asked to design the interiors for a newly erected house. Immediately, he demonstrated the fruits of his Italian sojourn through such motifs as anthemia, guilloche, and Greek keys; a ceiling derived in part from one in the Villa Pamphilj; and the unexecuted design for the walls of the dining room with grotesque panels, a classical overmantel subject, and a large ruin scene. But together with these insignia of his Grand Tour there are still a number of remembrances of his earlier Scottish manner—from modillioned cornices and tabernacle frames to door cornices on brackets and a caryatid chimneypiece.

Though neither the grotesques and ruin scenes here, nor similar Italian-inspired motifs of other drawings of these first years in London—screens of column under arches, niches, and long classical panels—were carried out, they became increasingly important in Adam's decorative style, assuming precedence over the more conservative elements, though those certainly lingered on for a while. Very shortly, the style was refined, the relief reduced, and his interiors were suffused by elegance. This can be seen at Shardeloes, Buckinghamshire (1761–1764), where rather delicate grotesque panels with sphinxes, an urn, and a classical plaque adorn the dining room; and it is also characteristic of a whole succession of major country houses begun in the first half of the 1760s.

Thus, in the earlier interiors of Syon House, Middlesex; Kedleston, Derbyshire; Croome Court, Worcestershire; and Bowood, Wiltshire, all begun in the first year or two of the new decade,

Adam.
Syon House (entrance hall).
Middlesex, England.
c.1760–1769

can be found a panoply of antique elements, those already noted being joined by the orders, coffering, trophies, and an assortment of other classical motifs. But they are still rendered in a slightly pronounced relief and are accompanied by such Burlingtonian Palladian inheritances as modillioned cornices and relatively heavy overmantels.

By the mid-1760s, however, the antique inspiration is even more evident, and so is the synthesis. Refinement and elegance are the keywords; the three-dimensionality has been suppressed. The later rooms at Bowood and Kedleston demonstrate this, as do the early rooms at Osterley Park, Middlesex; Harewood House, Nostell Priory, and Newby Park, Yorkshire; and Kenwood, now part of London but originally outside it, all of these interiors having been commenced about 1765–1767. The interiors of his earlier London townhouses, such as Lansdowne House, begun in 1761 or 1762, but with the main interiors dating from the middle of the decade, and Coventry House, of 1764–1766, illustrate this same tendency.

Typical is the hall at Osterley, designed 1767–1768, where Adam employed such antique themes as pilasters, apsed alcoves with coffered half-domes, panels with Roman trophies or arabesques, and Greek key friezes. A number of these motifs, or related ones, had appeared a half-decade or so earlier in the hall at Syon, and the trophy panels, derived from the trophies of Octavianus Augustus atop the Campidoglio in Rome, were employed in the anteroom there; but at Osterley the scale and relief are substantially reduced, and the whole is infinitely more refined. Adam's free use of antiquity is seen not only in his transformation of the trophies, but, even more, in his combination of an

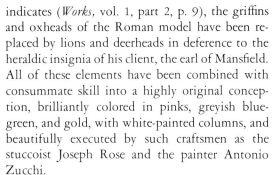

unusual Roman capital, discovered in the peristyle at Spalato, with an entablature composed only of a narrow Greek key frieze. His unification of the total composition is emphasized by the way in which the basic format of the paved floor echoes that of the ceiling, without in any way duplicating the actual pattern or motifs, a tendency foreshadowed in the hall and anteroom at Syon. The muted color scheme of pale blue, medium blue, and white and the somewhat martial air of the room are also characteristic, for Adam preferred those qualities for his entrance halls, as can be seen at Newby, Harewood, and Mersham-le-Hatch.

Rooms for entertaining, on the other hand, would normally be richer and gayer, and the various houses cited here all furnish dramatic examples of this kind of treatment. Perhaps the finest of these is the library at Kenwood (1767–1769), where Adam used a grand barrel-vaulted ceiling and two screened apses, both indicative of the influence of Roman antiquity. This is also evident in the multipaneled treatment of the ceiling, the inset paintings, the arabesque stucco panels, and the friezes. In the main frieze, one sees Adam's delight in modifying classical precedents, for, as he himself

indicates (*Works,* vol. 1, part 2, p. 9), the griffins and oxheads of the Roman model have been replaced by lions and deerheads in deference to the heraldic insignia of his client, the earl of Mansfield. All of these elements have been combined with consummate skill into a highly original conception, brilliantly colored in pinks, greyish blue-green, and gold, with white-painted columns, and beautifully executed by such craftsmen as the stuccoist Joseph Rose and the painter Antonio Zucchi.

In the 1770s, Adam's decorative style became flatter and even more refined, almost brittle, with the various components blended in a synthesis that is, above all, linear and extremely elegant. To HORACE WALPOLE, it was "all gingerbread, filigrane, and fan-painting" (letter to Sir Horace Mann, April 22, 1775), and the work of this decade is certainly marked by delicacy and even overelaboration. Yet, the effect is characterized, too, by an elegant refinement that is the essence of Adam's brand of neoclassicism.

Although especially associated with a series of London townhouses, of which the finest are perhaps Wynn House (20 Saint James's Square), Derby House (23 Grosvenor Square), and Home House (20 Portman Square), all executed between 1772 and 1776, this most paradigmatic Adam manner can be seen, as well, in the later rooms at Osterley Park and Nostell Priory and in new country house commissions. These include Headfort House, County Meath, Ireland (1771–1775); Wormelybury, Hertfordshire (1777–1779); and the early rooms at Culzean Castle, Ayrshire, begun in 1777. Equally evocative of this spirit are the temporary fête pavilion erected at The Oaks, Surrey, in 1774 and the interior of the Theatre Royal, Drury Lane, of 1775–1776, both of which were resplendent manifestations of the Adam manner at its height.

In all of these spaces, small-scale detailing, delicate linear elegance, and extreme attenuation are the most persistent characteristics. Increasingly complex ceiling patterns, often in a tripartite arrangement, are also typical, as are broader, flatter, and more complex chimneypieces, the latter suggested by Piranesi's *Diverse maniere* of 1769.

Piranesi's volume was also the source for another significant innovation of this decade, the Etruscan rooms, such as that at Osterley, of 1775–1777. Inspired by both the theoretical justification and the actual examples of wall decoration given in the Piranesi volume, Adam employed the motifs and coloring of classical vases, probably actually Greek though generally thought in the eighteenth century to be Etruscan, to create this very special type of decorative treatment for at least eight different commissions. As was typical, he refined his source, making it more elegant, more attenuated, more rarefied—and very much akin to his other interiors of this date.

Many of the tendencies of his mature style of the 1770s were continued by Adam into the next decade and until his death in 1792. This can be seen in major commissions for nobility and even royalty, as in his redecoration of Cumberland House, Pall Mall, London (c.1780–1782 and further in 1785–1788); but it is equally true of Archerfield, East Lothian (1789–1791), where his client was a commoner and the setting was outside Edinburgh. At times, as at Newliston, West Lothian, of those same years, delicate and complex sections were combined with a relatively sparser section; yet, the characteristic elegance, refinement, and elaboration are still present.

Aside from his work in the classical vein, which comprised the vast majority of his projects and designs, Adam occasionally produced designs in the Gothic manner. Although some interpreters of his casteller mode have seen this as primarily a medieval manifestation, in many ways, as noted earlier, its roots and spirit are quite different from the image conjured up by the words Gothic Revival. Indeed, the interiors of almost all those castles are classical. When the occasion—or the client—demanded, Adam could create interiors in the playful, rather unarcheological form of Gothic that enjoyed a vogue in the mid- and later eighteenth century. Robert himself had indulged in this taste in some of his early pre-Grand Tour drawings, and for the leading champion of the Gothic Revival, Horace Walpole, he produced designs for a ceiling and chimneypiece in the Round Tower at Strawberry Hill in 1766–1768. A few years later, presumably on the urging of the duchess of Northumberland, he began to transform the interior of Alnwick Castle, Northumberland, in a similar vein. Begun at the end of the 1760s and continued during most of the 1770s, these Gothic decorations have mostly been obliterated in subsequent remodelings. But some, of 1778, do survive in Hulne Abbey, on the Alnwick estate. Like the extant work at Strawberry Hill and the Adam drawings for Alnwick, they demonstrate that Adam's response to Gothic was fanciful and light-hearted, resulting in delicate and elegant interiors that are, in a way, closer to his classical work than to their medieval sources, despite the fact that Walpole even provided Adam with appropriate models.

In addition to the individual country and townhouses that formed the bulk of his practice, Adam also engaged in a number of larger-scale urban planning schemes and speculative develop-

ments. Most of the former, from a youthful scheme to rebuild Lisbon after the earthquake of 1755 to plans for the extension of Bath beyond the Avon (1777–1782) and for substantial civic improvements in Edinburgh, including South Bridge Street (c.1785), came to naught. Smaller ones and speculative developments were carried out in both Edinburgh and London. Of these, the grandest and most financially disastrous was the Adelphi, London (1768–1772). Combining the embankment of the Thames with an expected lease by the government of warehouses under the street level, this enterprise, which severely strained the Adam finances, was saved only by an Act of Parliament, a lottery, and help from individual friends. As an urban planning project, however, it was quite successful, for it created a terrace of elegant townhouses overlooking the Thames and more restrained but nevertheless desirable residences arranged in a modified H-plan of streets between the terrace and the Strand.

Despite the financial difficulties caused by this speculative development, or perhaps because of

Adam.
Etruscan Room.
Osterley Park.
Middlesex, England.
1775–1777

Adam.
Adelphi (view from river).
London.
1768–1772

*Adam.
Charlotte Square.
Edinburgh.
1791-1792 (not completed
until 1807).*

them and other unsuccessful business ventures, the Adam brothers undertook a number of other, less grandiose, development schemes. These included Mansfield Street (1770–1775), Portland Place (1776–c.1780), and Fitzroy Square (1790–1794) in London; and Charlotte Square in Edinburgh (1791–1807), together with various smaller projects.

In some ways, the larger schemes of this kind came closest to "the grand," that ambitious theme about which Robert often wrote in letters home from Rome, for he had few commissions for major public buildings. There were two in Edinburgh, the Register House (1774–1792) and the University, begun 1789–1793, though the latter was completed only in the nineteenth century and not to his designs. Among his grand unexecuted schemes for important projects are those for Lincoln's Inn, London (1771–1772) and for King's College and a University Library at Cambridge (c. 1784–1789), both imposing conceptions that would have satisfied his yearning for "the grand."

Adam built a few churches, including Croome, Worcestershire (1763), in a Gothic mode, and Gunton, Norfolk, completed in 1769, in the form of a classical temple, and he made a number of interesting designs for others; the only major one executed to his designs was that at Mistley, Essex, of 1776, where he dramatically altered a church of 1735, though only the towers now survive.

On a smaller scale, Adam designed a number of mausolea, some of which were carried out. Among the latter are one for the countess of Shelburne at Bowood, Wiltshire (1761–1764); that of David Hume in Old Calton Burying Ground, Edinburgh, designed in 1777 and completed the next year; and Arthur Upton's at Castle Upton, County Antrim, Ireland, of 1789. In a related realm, Adam was also responsible for the design of a group of church monuments executed by various sculptors. These range from the Townshend Monument in Westminster Abbey, raised in memory of an officer killed at Fort Ticonderoga in

1759, to that of the duchess of Montagu of 1775 at Warkton Church, Northamptonshire.

Adam's designing interests not only extended from buildings to church monuments; they also included a whole range of furnishings for domestic interiors. At one time or another, he designed furniture, carpets, silver vessels, stove grates, door furniture, candlesticks, ink wells, and a great deal more. He did not do this for every commission, and, in fact, more than a few such objects for any one client was relatively unusual. But for many, he produced designs for one or two mirrors or tables, escutcheons and door knobs, or an occasional other decorative object. For a few projects, Osterley being perhaps the most obvious, he designed a substantial number and variety of such elements, with the result being a remarkably unified whole. In the Etruscan Room there, for example, the chairs and the firescreen employ both the same motifs and the coloring as the walls. But even at Osterley, he did not by any means design everything, his client, Robert Child, employing, for example, the distinguished cabinetmaker John Linnell to provide a substantial amount of furniture of his own design. The same is, of course, true of other leading cabinetmakers, such as Thomas Chippendale, who only occasionally executed furniture to Adam's design, though a good deal of his furniture was made for Adam clients, with Adam often approving the bills for payment.

Despite the fact that, unlike Chambers, he had no pupils, Adam exerted, through his buildings and his published designs, a very strong influence on British architecture during the last forty years of the eighteenth century. Older architects like JAMES PAINE succumbed to his style, and many of the major architects of the next generation, including James Wyatt, GEORGE DANCE THE YOUNGER, HENRY HOLLAND, and the young JOHN SOANE, were, at least in their early works, deeply influenced by his manner. This was even more true of lesser figures, local builders, and pattern book authors, a good example of this last group being WILLIAM PAIN, whose stylistic allegiances changed abruptly to the Adam manner with his third book, *The Practical Builder* of 1774. Adam's influence was by no means limited to Britain. The Adamesque style was extremely popular in the United States in the last decade and a half of the eighteenth century and first decade or two of the nineteenth, and examples can be found all along the Atlantic seaboard from the Salem, Massachusetts, houses of SAMUEL MCINTIRE and the Boston buildings of CHARLES BULFINCH to such Charleston, South Carolina, houses as those built for Joseph Manigault or Nathaniel Russell. Through CHARLES CAMERON, it penetrated Russia, with

Tsarskoe Selo providing a major example of this.

Adam and his architecture can be studied not only in his buildings and his publications, but also through his drawings, of which almost 9,000 are preserved at Sir John Soane's Museum, London, along with smaller groups elsewhere. His early letters, deposited with the Clerk of Penicuik Papers in the Register House, Edinburgh, and his bank records at Drummond's Branch of the Royal Bank of Scotland, London, are invaluable documents, as are those papers scattered in a variety of private and public repositories throughout Great Britain.

DAMIE STILLMAN

WORKS

All the works listed below were by the firm of Robert and James Adam. For Robert's work in the 1750s in partnership with his brothers, see under John Adam.

1758–1761, Hatchlands (interiors), Surrey, England. 1759–1760, Admiralty Screen, London. 1759–1771, Harewood House (interiors; modifications of exterior designs), Yorkshire, England. 1760–1767 and later, Croome Court (interiors and garden buildings), Worcestershire, England. c.1760–1767, Compton Verney (additions and alterations), Warwickshire, England. 1760–1769, Syon House (interior remodeling), Middlesex, England. c.1760–1771, Kedleston Hall (south front, interiors, and garden buildings), Derbyshire, England. 1761–1764, Shardeloes (interiors and portico), Buckinghamshire, England. *1761–1764, Bowood House (portico, interiors, and offices); 1764, Bowood Mausoleum; Wiltshire, England. *1761/1762–1768, Lansdowne House (façade re-erected; two rooms dismantled and reinstalled, one in the Metropolitan Museum of Art in New York, the other in the Philadelphia Museum of Art), Berkeley Square, London. 1762–1766, Mersham-le-Hatch, Kent, England. 1762–1771, Ugbrooke Park, Devon, England. 1763, Croome Church, Worcestershire, England. *1763–1766, 19 Arlington Street (alterations), London. 1763–1766, Audley End (interiors), Essex, England. 1764–1766, Coventry House (interiors), Piccadilly, London. 1765–1780, Osterley Park (remodeling), Middlesex, England. 1765–1785, Nostell Priory (interiors and north wing), Yorkshire, England. 1766–1767, Auchencruive House (interiors), Ayrshire, Scotland. 1766–1767, Strawberry Hill (round room interior), Middlesex, England. 1766–1774, Luton Hoo (interiors later rebuilt), Bedfordshire, England. 1767–1769, Kenwood House (remodeling and additions), Hampstead, London. 1767–1771, Shire Hall, Hertford, Hertfordshire, England. 1767–c.1780, Newby Hall (additions and remodeling), Yorkshire, England. *1768–1771, Clerk House (remodeling; also in 1771–1774 and 1779), Duchess Street; *1768–1772, The Adelphi; London. 1768–1779, Saltram (interiors), Devon, England. ?–1769, Gunton Church, Norfolk, England. 1769–1774, Pulteney Bridge, Bath, Somerset, England. c.1769–1775, Mamhead (alterations), Devon, England. *c.1770, British Coffee House; 1770–1774, Chandos House; London. c.1770–1775, Lowther Village, West-

moreland, England. 1770–1775, Mansfield Street; *1770–1775, Northumberland House, The Strand; London. c.1770–1778, Mellerstain, Berwickshire, Scotland. *c.1770–1780, Alnwick Castle (interiors and outbuildings), Northumberland, England. 1771–1775, Headfort House (interiors), County Meath, Ireland. 1771–1775, Wedderburn Castle, Berwickshire, Scotland. 1771/1772–1777, Stowe (south front design; altered when executed), Buckinghamshire, England. c.1771–1778, Apsley House (later remodeled), Piccadilly; 1772–1774, Royal Society of Arts, Adelphi; 1772–1776, Wynn House, 20 Saint James's Square; *1773–1774, Derby House, 23 Grosvenor Square; 1773–1776, Home House, 20 Portman Square; London. ?–1774, Assembly Rooms (interiors), Derby, England. *1774, Fête Pavilion, The Oaks, Surrey, England. 1774–1792, Register House, Edinburgh. *1775–1776, Theatre Royal (remodeling and new façade), Drury Lane, London. 1775–1777, Etruscan Rooms, Osterley, England. *1776, Mistley Church, Essex, England. 1776–c.1780 and later, Portland Place; *1777–1778, Roxburghe House (remodeling), Hanover Square; London. 1777–1779, Wormleybury (interiors), Hertfordshire, England. 1777–1792, Culzean Castle, Ayrshire, Scotland. 1778, Auchencruive House (tower), Ayrshire, Scotland. 1778, David Hume Monument, Old Calton Burying Ground, Edinburgh. *1780–1782, 1785–1788, Cumberland House, 86 Pall Mall, London. 1780–1782, Oxenfoord Castle, Midlothian, Scotland. 1784–1785, Brasted Place, Kent, England. 1789, Mausoleum, Castle Upton, County Antrim, Ireland. 1789–1791, Newliston, West Lothian, Scotland. 1789–1791, Seton Castle, East Lothian, Scotland. 1789–1793, University of Edinburgh (completed later in modified fashion). 1790–1791, Airthrey Castle, Stirlingshire, Scotland. *1790–1791, Archerfield House (interiors); 1790–1792, Dunbar Castle; East Lothian, Scotland. 1790–1794, Fitzroy Square, London. 1790–1796, Belleville House (also known as Balavil House), Inverness-shire, Scotland. 1790–c.1800, Gosford House, East Lothian, Scotland. *1791, Walkinshaw House, Renfrewshire, Scotland. c.1791–1793, Balbardie House, West Lothian, Scotland. 1791–1793, Dalkeith Bridge, Midlothian, Scotland. 1791–1794, Trades House; *1791–1795, Royal Infirmary; Glasgow, Scotland. *1791–1796, Mauldsley Castle, Lanarkshire, Scotland. 1791–1807, Charlotte Square; 1792–1794, Saint George's Episcopal Chapel; Edinburgh. 1793–1794, Tron Church; *1796–1798, Assembly Rooms (construction; designed earlier), Glasgow, Scotland.

BIBLIOGRAPHY

ADAM, ROBERT 1764 *Ruins of the Palace of the Emperor Diocletian at Spalatro in Dalmatia.* London: The author.

ADAM, ROBERT, and ADAM, JAMES 1773–1778 *The Works in Architecture of Robert and James Adam.* 2 vols. London: The authors. A third volume was published posthumously in 1822 in London by Priestley & Weale. A one-volume reprint of all three volumes, edited by Robert Oresko, was published in 1975 in London by Academy Editions.

BEARD, GEOFFREY 1958 "Robert Adam's Craftsmen." *Connoisseur Year Book* 1958:26–32.

BEARD, GEOFFREY   1962   "New Light on Adam's Craftsmen." *Country Life* 131:1098–1100.

BEARD, GEOFFREY   1966   *Georgian Craftsmen and Their Work*. London: Country Life.

BEARD, GEOFFREY   1975   *Decorative Plasterwork in Great Britain*. London: Phaidon.

BEARD, GEOFFREY   1978   *The Work of Robert Adam*. New York: Arco.

BOLTON, ARTHUR T.   1922   *The Architecture of Robert & James Adam (1758–1794)*. 2 vols. London: Country Life.

CROFT-MURRAY, EDWARD   1962–1971   *Decorative Painting in England: 1537–1837*. 2 vols. London: Country Life.

FLEMING, JOHN   1955   "Robert Adam the Grand-Tourist." *The Cornhill* 168, no. 1004:118–137.

FLEMING, JOHN   1962   *Robert Adam and His Circle*. London: Murray. A new edition is in preparation.

FLEMING, JOHN   1968a   "'Retrospective View' by John Clerk of Eldin with Some Comments on Adam's Castle Style." Pages 75–84 in John Summerson (editor), *Concerning Architecture: Essays Presented to Nikolaus Pevsner*. London: Allen Lane.

FLEMING, JOHN   1968b   "Robert Adam's Castle Style." *Country Life* 143:1356–1359, 1443–1447.

HARRIS, EILEEN   1962   "Robert Adam and the Gobelins." *Apollo* 76:100–106.

HARRIS, EILEEN   1963   *The Furniture of Robert Adam*. London: Tiranti.

HUCHON, RENÉ   1906   *Mrs. Montagu, 1720–1820: An Essay*. London: John Murray.

HUSSEY, CHRISTOPHER   1956   *English Country Houses: Mid-Georgian, 1760–1800*. London: Country Life.

LEES-MILNE, JAMES   1947   *The Age of Adam*. London.

MALTON, THOMAS   1792   *A Picturesque Tour Through the Cities of London and Westminster*. 2 vols. London: The author.

"Obituary."   1792   *Gentleman's Magazine* 62:282–283.

ROWAN, ALISTAIR J.   1974   "After the Adelphi: Forgotten Years in the Adam Brothers' Practice." *Journal of the Royal Society of Arts* 122:659–710.

STILLMAN, DAMIE   1961   "The Genesis of the Adam Style." 2 vols. Unpublished Ph.D. dissertation, Columbia University, New York.

STILLMAN, DAMIE   1966   *The Decorative Work of Robert Adam*. London: Tiranti.

STILLMAN, DAMIE   1967   "Robert Adam and Piranesi." Pages 197–206 in Douglas Fraser, Howard Hibbard, and Milton J. Lewine (editors), *Essays in the History of Architecture Presented to Rudolf Wittkower*. London: Phaidon.

SUMMERSON, JOHN   (1953)1977   *Architecture in Britain: 1530–1830*. 6th ed., rev. Harmondsworth, England: Penguin.

SWARBRICK, JOHN   1915   *Robert Adam & His Brothers*. London: Batsford.

TOMLIN, MAURICE   1972   *Catalogue of Adam Period Furniture*. London: Victoria and Albert Museum.

WALPOLE, HORACE   1903–1905   *The Letters of Horace Walpole*. Edited by Paget Toynbee. Oxford: Clarendon.

ADAM, WILLIAM

Perhaps unfairly William Adam (1689–1748) is best known as the father of ROBERT ADAM and JAMES ADAM. He deserves better, for the course of eighteenth-century architecture in Scotland was decisively shaped by his career and his attitudes to classicism, the Gothic, and the baroque.

Like many self-made men, Adam was evasive about his beginnings. He came from Fife and had some practical experience either as a mason or a stone merchant. Though he was later a professional man and minor landowner, he retained his interests in trade, especially in all forms of mining and land development. It was a trait inherited by his sons though without William Adam's success. As an architect he was also more or less self-educated, and in his early career he was dependent on his patron, Sir John Clerk of Penicuik, and particularly on his architectural library. The relations between the two were happy, and this was true of his association with most of his clients. The first earl of Fife was the outstanding exception.

Stylistically as well as professionally, Adam succeeded Sir WILLIAM BRUCE, and his talents as a designer extended over all aspects of architecture. As mason to the Board of Ordnance he worked on the Highland forts. He designed the University Library at Glasgow (1732–1745) and the Royal Infirmary (1738–1748) in Edinburgh, developed the mining town at Grangemouth, and directed a large country house practice. Of the last, his two grandest commissions were Hopetoun House (1723–1748; where he succeeded Bruce) and Duff House at Bamff (1735–1739). Both reflected his capacity to design big and in the grand manner. Whereas Hopetoun was perhaps rather conventional in its classicism, Duff House was a stupendous, though unfinished, essay in the Scottish baroque. At the other end of the architectural scale was his pioneering of the villa form in Scotland which he introduced in his collaborative design with Sir John Clerk for Mavisbank (1723–1727). In this and in a series of smaller country houses, such as Arniston (1726–1732), Adam offered a fair interpretation of the Palladian (see ANDREA PALLADIO) villa which would combine, as at The Drum (1726–1730), a baroque richness both within and outside.

As much part of this Anglophile taste was his interest in the informal gardens of Alexander Pope and WILLIAM KENT. This led him to write in 1746 that "the risings and fallings of ground are to be humoured and generally make the greatest beautys in Gardens." William Adam never built outside Scotland though he was always keen to have a British rather than Scottish reputation. To this end, he engraved several of his designs to form a book along the lines of COLEN CAMPBELL's *Vitruvius Britannicus* (1716–1725). After many vicissitudes, it appeared in the early nineteenth century as *Vitruvius Scoticus* (1810). Though Adam was associated with ROGER MORRIS at Inveraray Castle (1745–1748) and possibly with JAMES GIBBS at Balvenie, he remained his own master, creating a style sufficiently eclectic to be both modern and pleasing to a conservative Scottish patronage.

A. A. TAIT

WORKS

1721–1726, Floors Castle, Roxburghshire, Scotland. 1723–1727, Mavisbank (with John Clerk), Midlothian, Scotland. 1723–1748, Hopetoun House, West Lothian, Scotland. 1724–1726, Lawers, Perthshire, Scotland. 1725–1726, Mellerstain, Berwickshire, Scotland. 1726–1730, The Drum; 1726–1732, Arniston; Midlothian, Scotland. c.1730, Yester, East Lothian, Scotland. 1730–1732, Robert Gordon's Hospital, Aberdeen, Scotland. 1731, Cumbernauld House; 1731–1743, Chatelherault; Lanarkshire, Scotland. 1732–1735, Haddo House, Aberdeenshire, Scotland. 1732–1745, University Library, Glasgow. 1733, Hamilton Church, Scotland. 1735–1739, Duff House, Bamff, Scotland. 1738–1748, Royal Infirmary, Edinburgh. 1745–1748, Inveraray Castle (after Roger Morris), Argyllshire, Scotland.

BIBLIOGRAPHY

ADAM, WILLIAM (1810)1980 *Vitruvius Scoticus.* With an introduction by James Simpson. Reprint. Edinburgh: Harris; New York: AMS.
FLEMING, JOHN 1962 Pages 1–75 in *Robert Adam and His Circle.* London: Murray.
TAIT, A. A. 1980 *The Landscape Garden in Scotland.* Edinburgh University Press.

ADAM DE REIMS

See JEAN D'ORBAIS.

ADAM FAMILY

A leading family of architects in Scotland and later in England, the Adams first achieved significance in this field through WILLIAM ADAM, the major architect in Scotland between 1721 and his death in 1748. Three of his sons followed him in the architectural profession: JOHN ADAM and ROBERT ADAM taking over the father's work, joined in the 1750s by JAMES ADAM. John remained in Scotland, devoting much of his time to other activities, but the other two moved to London, where Robert, beginning in 1758 and assisted by James from 1763 on, became one of the most important and influential architects of the last half of the eighteenth century.

DAMIE STILLMAN

WORKS

See under John Adam, Robert Adam, and William Adam.

BIBLIOGRAPHY

See under Robert Adam and William Adam.

ADAMS, HOLDEN, and PEARSON

Harry Percy Adams (1865–1930) was an accomplished English designer of hospitals who in 1899 took as assistant CHARLES HENRY HOLDEN, who was largely responsible for all the notable work of the firm. Holden worked out the massing and elevations for Adams's efficient plans. Holden became Adams's partner in 1907; in 1913, they were joined by Lionel Pearson (1879–1953), who was responsible for the Royal Artillery Memorial, Hyde Park Corner, London (1925), with sculpture by Charles Sargeant Jagger.

GAVIN STAMP

WORK

1925, Royal Artillery Memorial (with sculpture by Charles Sargeant Jagger), Hyde Park Corner, London.

ADAMS, MAURICE B.

For fifty years architect and art editor of the *Building News,* Maurice Bingham Adams (1849–1933) was a charming and fluent pen draftsman and an important propagandist for the English domestic revival in architecture. His own buildings followed the lead of R. NORMAN SHAW, whom he knew well, but they counted for less than his journalism.

ANDREW SAINT

WORKS

*1880–1881, Chiswick School of Art; 1881, Houses, Bedford Park; 1893, Public Library, Haggerston; 1895–1896, Public Library, Hammersmith; 1896–1897, Public Library, Edmonton; 1896–1898, Camberwell School of Art and South London Art Gallery; 1897–1898, Public Library, Stepney; 1898–1899, Public Library, Acton; 1899, London School of Economics; 1902, Public Library, Camberwell; 1907, Public Library, Woolwich; London.

BIBLIOGRAPHY

ADAMS, MAURICE B. 1883 *Artists' Homes.* London: Batsford.
ADAMS, MAURICE B. 1904 *Modern Cottage Architecture.* London: Batsford.
GREEVES, T. AFFLECK 1975 *Bedford Park.* London: Ann Bingley.
"Obituary" 1933 *The Builder* 145, Aug. 25:295.

ADELCRANTZ FAMILY

Göran Josuae Adelcrantz (1668–1739) was the most elaborate Swedish architect working in the late high baroque, a pupil of the more classically oriented architect Nicodemus Tessin the Younger (see TESSIN FAMILY). After studies in Germany, Italy, and France in 1704–1706, he was appointed royal architect in 1707; in 1715, he was put in charge of the construction of the royal palace. Göran showed the more sculptural late baroque in the completion of two churches in Stockholm, Katarina and Hedvig Eleonora, both originally designed by JEAN DE LA VALLÉE. His career was ended in 1727 because of political reasons.

Against the father's will, his son, Carl Fredrik Adelcrantz (1716–1796), also became an architect, making a journey to Germany, Italy, France, and Holland in 1739–1743. Like his father, Carl was in charge of the royal palace, and the building was completed under his supervision. From 1757, he was the superintendent of all building activity of the state.

The architecture of Carl Fredrik Adelcrantz clearly illustrates the changes in attitudes from the late baroque and rococo to the abstract neoclassicism of the late eighteenth century. A very fine example of Adelcrantz's first period is the Chinese Pavilion at Drottningholm Palace outside Stockholm (1763–1769), an elegant, French-inspired, palacelike group of buildings with exotic, slightly Chinese features. At Drottningholm, he also designed the theater (1764–1766), with its machinery the best preserved theater of the world. Very much interested in theater and music, he also designed an opera house for King Gustav III at Gustav Adolfs Torg in Stockholm (1777–1782; destroyed in 1892, its identical counterpart on the other side of the square, designed by ERIK PALMSTEDT, still preserved). French classicism characterizes also the Adolf Fredrik Church in Stockholm (1768–1783), and the neoclassicism is first totally developed in the Doric portico of the Royal Mint in Stockholm (1783–1790). As the leader of Swedish artistic life during the decades up to the 1780s Carl Fredrik Adelcrantz had a great influence on his contemporaries. His works are distinguished by refinement and high quality, both in plans and in exteriors.

FREDRIC BEDOIRE

WORKS
GÖRAN JOSUAE ADELCRANTZ
1704–1739, Royal Palace (completed by Carl Fredrik Adelcrantz); n.d., Saint Katarina (completion; design by Jean de Vallée); n.d., Saint Hedvig Eleonora (completion; design by Jean de Vallée); Stockholm.

CARL FREDRIK ADELCRANTZ
1763–1769, Chinese Pavilion; 1764–1766, Theater; Drottningholm Palace, near Stockholm. 1772, Johannishus Manor House, Blekinge Province, Sweden. 1772–1776, Fredrikshov Palace, Stockholm. 1776, Court of Appeal, Old Wasa (Korsholm), Finland. *1777–1782, Opera House, Gustav Adolfs Torg, Stockholm. 1781, Sturehov Palace, near Stockholm. 1783–1790, Royal Mint, Stockholm.

BIBLIOGRAPHY
FOGELMARCK, STIG 1957 *Carl Fredrik Adelcrantz, arkitekt.* With a summary in French. Stockholm: Almqvist & Wiksell.

ADLER, DAVID

David Adler (1888–1949) was the house architect for the Chicago establishment. He built nothing but houses, town and country, mainly from 1912 to 1934. His work falls entirely within the bounds of architecture as outlined by Edith Wharton and OGDEN CODMAN, JR., in their *The Decoration of Houses* (1897). It is the architecture of the classical tradition.

JOHN BAYLEY

BIBLIOGRAPHY
WHARTON, EDITH, and CODMAN, OGDEN, JR. (1897)1978 *The Decoration of Houses.* Classical America Reprint. New York: Norton.

ADLER and SULLIVAN

In *The Autobiography of an Idea* written in 1924, LOUIS H. SULLIVAN states unequivocally, yet incorrectly, that he and Dankmar Adler (1844–1900) founded the famous Chicago firm of Adler and Sullivan on May 1, 1881. In fact, the partnership was not formed until two years later, on May 1, 1883. Why Sullivan erred so significantly in this regard is not known, but the new dating raises

Adelcrantz.
Chinese Pavilion.
Drottningholm Palace.
Near Stockholm.
1763–1769

questions about the extent of Sullivan's role in the design of a number of important early buildings underway before May 1, 1882 when Sullivan and Adler first became associated partners in D. Adler & Co. These are the Borden Block (1880), Rothschild Building (1881), Borden House (1881), Rosenfeld Buildings (1881, 1882), and the Jewelers (1881) and Revell Buildings (1881). To what extent Sullivan's friend JOHN EDELMANN and even Adler himself may have participated in these designs remains a matter of speculation.

There is no question, however, that after the formation of Adler and Sullivan, Adler left matters of design substantially in Sullivan's hands (despite recent assertions to the contrary; see Menocal, 1981), while he concentrated on the business and engineering aspects of architecture. This does not mean that Adler had no hand at all in the buildings produced by the firm. His concern for the utilitarian part of architecture, as revealed by his published writings on foundations, structural systems, vertical transportation, adequate illumination and ventilation, acoustics, and so on, meant that Adler had to play a role in the design process. Sullivan's art thus was continually conditioned by Adler's functionalism, a fact to which the admirably integrated and unified architectural edifices built by the two men bear testimony.

Nonetheless, it was Sullivan who gave to their buildings the aesthetic quality for which the work of Adler and Sullivan is justly famous. Although Adler was trained as an architect, he never developed into a strong designer. Much more important to Adler was architectural engineering, the study of which he began while in the Topographical Engineer's office during the Civil War.

Adler and Sullivan did not achieve prominence until late in 1886 when they secured the monumental commission for the Chicago Auditorium Building, consisting of a hotel, office building, and theater for grand opera. After that, their business soared with commissions coming in for a variety of high-rise office buildings, and for hotels and theaters, all of which were built in Sullivan's early modern style of architecture and ornament.

In July 1895, the effects of the severe depression that had begun in 1893 left Adler and Sullivan almost without commissions. Adler left Sullivan to shift for himself with no commissions to speak of except for the completion of the Guaranty Building in Buffalo. Various reasons have been advanced to explain Sullivan's refusal to renew the partnership early in 1896 when Adler decided to return to practice. Whatever Sullivan's real reasons, the decision to remain alone did not affect the outcome of his career in architecture;

Adler died prematurely in 1900, several years before Sullivan's practice began its steady and irreversible decline.

PAUL E. SPRAGUE

WORKS

*1884, Ryerson Building; *1884, Troescher Building; 1886–1890, Auditorium Building; 1887–1888, Ryerson Tomb; *1888–1889, Walker Warehouse, Chicago. *1888–1891, Pueblo Opera House, Colo. 1890, Getty Tomb; 1890–1891, Kehilath Anshe Ma'ariv Synagogue; *1890–1891, McVicker's Theater; Chicago. 1890–1891, Wainwright Building, St. Louis, Mo. *1891–1892, Schiller Building, Chicago. 1891–1892, Wainwright Tomb, St. Louis, Mo. *1891–1893, Transportation Building, Chicago. 1892–1893, Union Trust Building, St. Louis, Mo. 1892–1894, Chicago Stock Exchange Building. *1892–1894, Saint Nicholas Hotel, St. Louis, Mo. 1894–1896, Guaranty Building, Buffalo, N.Y.

BIBLIOGRAPHY

SALTZSTEIN, JOAN 1967 "Dankmar Adler: The Man, The Architect, The Author." *Wisconsin Architect* 38, no. 6–7:15–19; no. 8:10–14; no. 11:16–19.
SCHUYLER, MONTGOMERY (1896)1961 "A Critique of the Works of Adler & Sullivan." Volume 2, pages 377–404 in William Jordy and Ralph Coe (editors), *American Architecture and Other Writings by Montgomery Schuyler.* Cambridge, Mass.: Harvard University Press.
SULLIVAN, LOUIS (1924)1956 *The Autobiography of an Idea.* Reprint. New York: Dover.
WRIGHT, FRANK LLOYD (1947)1971 *Genius and the Mobocracy.* New York: Norton.

AFFLECK, RAYMOND

Raymond Tait Affleck (1922–) was born in Penticton, British Columbia, Canada, and raised in Montreal, where in 1947 he received his architectural degree from McGill University. In 1955, he became a founding partner in the firm of Affleck, Desbarats, Dimakopoulos, Lebensold, and Sise. The practice was reorganized in 1970 under the name of Arcop Associates, Architects and Planners. Both partnerships have produced a variety of large-scale projects in Canada and abroad that are notable for their design, use of innovative construction technology, and clarity of structural system.

Affleck's particular contribution is evident in such complex buildings as The Stephen Leacock Building (1961–1965) and Place Bonaventure (1964–1967), both in Montreal, in which he uses the pedestrian circulation system as the structuring device of his design. The movement spine, sometimes passage, sometimes bridge, often naturally lit, is articulated like a public street. The urban parallel is strengthened by the exterior materials that are brought inside to act as interior finishes in the public spaces.

JULIA GERSOVITZ

WORKS

1958–1963, Place Ville Marie (with I. M. PEI and Partners); 1961–1965, Stephen Leacock Building, McGill University; Montreal. 1964–1967, Arts and Culture Center, Saint John's, Newfoundland. 1964–1967, Place Bonaventure, Montreal. 1967–1970, Life Sciences Complex, Dalhousie University, Halifax, Nova Scotia. 1975–1978, Mughal Hotel (with Ramesh Khosla), Agra, India. 1975–1978, Les Terrasses de la Chaudière, Hull, Quebec. 1975–1978, Winnipeg Square, Manitoba. 1976–1977, Fisheries Heritage, Charlottetown, Prince Edward Island. 1978–1983, Maison Alcan; 1980–1983, Place Beaver Hall; Montreal. 1981–1984, Bankers' Hall (with Cohos, Evamy, and Partners), Calgary, Alberta.

AGG, JAMES

Captain James Agg (1746/1747–1827), the son of a Gloucestershire stonemason, served with the Bengal Engineers (1777–1797). As assistant in Calcutta to the chief engineer, Colonel Henry Watson, Agg's only known work is St. John's Church (1784–1786), built in the style of JAMES GIBBS. Although altered several times during the nineteenth century, the building survives with much of its original character.

PAULINE ROHATGI

BIBLIOGRAPHY

ROHATGI, PAULINE 1978 "Colonial Architecture in India: St. John's Church, Calcutta." *Roopa-Lekha* 44:68–72.

AGOSTINO DI DUCCIO

The son of a Florentine textile worker Agostino di Duccio (1418–1481) became one of the best-known sculptors in Renaissance Italy. Fleeing his native town in 1446 due to an accusation for theft, he went to Venice and then to Rimini where he received the commission for the sculptural decoration of the Tempio Malatestiano. As an architect, Agostino di Duccio built only two works, both in Perugia and both so highly decorated that it might be said that the building is little more than a frame for carving.

Agostino's early career is something of a mystery. He unexpectedly appeared in Rimini, where the lord of Rimini, Sigismondo Malatesta, had commissioned LEON BATTISTA ALBERTI as the architect and Matteo de' Pasti as assistant to trans-

form the Gothic church of San Francesco into a classical funerary temple for himself and his mistress. Agostino's contribution was a series of chapels on classical themes. Using low relief carving for the most part, he created scenes of great freshness and beauty, based, in some instances, on Greek models provided by Malatesta's advisers.

In 1457, Agostino di Duccio transferred to Perugia where he was commissioned to build a façade for the Oratory of San Bernardino (1457–1462). The façade recalls the Tempio Malatestiano in design but in place of the restrained classicism of the Rimini façade there is a riot sculpture: scenes from the life of San Bernardino, of the Virgin, and, in the center, San Bernardino in Glory attended by four flying angels. Without the careful direction he received in Rimini, Agostino's work here is much less controlled. Nonetheless the façade has a vivacity in its juxtaposed relief levels that, although quite unclassical in tone, is pleasurably witty.

In 1463, Agostino moved to Bologna where he prepared a model for the façade of the church of San Petronio. In 1473, he returned to Perugia to direct the construction of a portal for the city, the Porta delle Due Porte (1473–1481), also known as the Porta San Pietro. This three-arched rusticated entryway depends for its decorative inspiration on the Etruscan Gate, also in Perugia. Although it was left unfinished, Agostino's reinterpretation of Perugia's pre-Roman heritage is one of his most interesting works, the sophistication of his response to the preclassical past being quite unexpected.

NICHOLAS ADAMS

WORKS

1457–1462, Oratory of San Bernardino; 1473–1481, Porta delle Due Porte; Perugia, Italy.

BIBLIOGRAPHY

GASSER, MANUEL 1974 "Das Oratorium S. Bernardino von Agostino di Duccio in Perugia." *Du* 34, Nov.:54–63.
MODE, ROBERT L. 1973 "San Bernardino in Glory." *Art Bulletin* 55, Mar.:58–76.
POPE-HENNESSY, JOHN 1958 *Italian Renaissance Sculpture.* London: Phaidon.

AHLBERG, HAKON

Hakon Ahlberg (1891–), born in Laholm, Sweden, completed studies in architecture at the Tekniska Högskolan and at the Royal Academy in Stockholm in 1917. In addition to his architectural work, Ahlberg was very active in professional organizations as well as in teaching and writing. His importance for Scandinavian architecture was recognized in 1974 when Finland awarded him the ALVAR AALTO medal.

JUDITH S. HULL

WORKS

1923, Arts and Crafts Pavilion, Jubilee Exhibition, Göteborg, Sweden. c.1946, Church, Malmberget, Sweden. 1946–1949, University Hospital, Maracaibo, Venezuela. c.1949, Lower Court of Appeals for Western Sweden, Göteborg.

BIBLIOGRAPHY

AHLBERG, HAKON 1925 *Swedish Architecture of the Twentieth Century.* London: Benn. Originally published in Swedish.
"Alvar Aalto-medaljen til Hakon Ahlberg." 1974 *Arkitekten* 76, no. 3:67.

AHLSÉN, ERIK, and AHLSÉN, TORE

Erik Ahlsén (1901–) and Tore Ahlsén (1906–) were originally trained as engineers and were educated as architects at the Royal Institute of Technology in Stockholm (1933 and 1934). For a decade, they were employed at the architects' office of the Swedish Cooperative Union and Wholesale Society. Starting their own practice in 1936, they showed the strong influence of their teacher ERIK GUNNAR ASPLUND, especially in their early works. In the 1940s, the Ahlsén brothers represented a new trend in architecture, called the New Empiricism, with works such as the artistically decorated and irregularly shaped brick buildings for the Årsta Community Center near Stockholm (1947–1953). Characteristic of their conceptions is a remarkable care for materials and colors and an unusual feeling for volumes. Many of their clients were Swedish townships, and many of their commissions concerned public buildings.

FREDRIC BEDOIRE

WORKS

1936–1940, Town Hall (extension), Kristianstad, Sweden. 1945–1946, Terrace Houses, Torsvik, Lidingö; 1947–1953, Årsta Community Center; Stockholm. 1953–1960, Housing Areas, North and South Biskopsgården; 1953–1960, Kortedala (including nursery and center); Göteborg, Sweden. 1953–1960, Krämaren Housing and Commercial Blocks, Örebro, Sweden. 1957, Folksam Insurance Office, Göteborg, Sweden. 1960, PUB Department Store (extension), Stockholm. 1962–1964, Municipal Offices, Uppsala, Sweden. 1965, Assembly Halls; 1965, Community Center; 1965, Theater; Örebro, Sweden. 1967–1971, Henriksdalsberget Housing Area, Stockholm. 1969–1972, City Hall, Uppsala, Sweden.

BIBLIOGRAPHY

"The Ahlsén Brothers." 1980 *Arkitektur* 80, no. 6:special issue.

AHMAD B. ABĪ BAKR AL-MARANDĪ

Ahmad B. Abī Bakr al-Marandī was a Seljuk architect active in Anatolia in the first quarter of the thirteenth century. The more important of his two known buildings is the great *ṣifaiye* (hospital) (1217–1220) of the Seljuk Sultan ʿIzz al-Dīn Kaykāʾūs I at Sivas. The largest and most elaborate of Anatolian Seljuk hospitals, it is laid out on a four-*iwān* plan, with dormitory rooms arranged around a rectangular central court, and the faïence-decorated tomb of its founder on the south. Ahmad was also the builder of a brick tomb tower, known today as the Kırk Kızlar Türbesi (c.1220) at Niksar in northern Anatolia. The Iranian character of both structures as well as Ahmad's name (*nisba*) al-Marandī suggests that he was of Iranian origin, from the town of Marand in Adharbāydjān.

HOWARD CRANE

WORKS

1217–1220, Şifaiye of Sultan ʿIzz al-Dīn Kaykāʾūs I, Sivas, Turkey. c.1220, Kırk Kızlar Türbesi, Niksar, Turkey.

BIBLIOGRAPHY

GABRIEL, ALBERT 1934 Pages 126–127, 146–150 in *Monuments turcs d'Anatolie.* Paris: Boccard.

AHMAD B. AHMAD B. MUHAMMAD AT-TŪLŪNĪ and FAMILY

For six generations members of the Ahmad b. Ahmad b. Muhammad at-Tūlūnī family were described as master architects and master engineers, under the Mamlūk sultans of Egypt. Shihāb ad-Dīn Ahmad b. Muhammad at-Tūlūnī, third in the line, received a robe of honor for his part in the construction of the Madrasa of Sultan Barqūq in Cairo (completed 1386). However, his name does not appear on the building, and a different person is named as superintendent in charge of construction. The title chief surveyor might better describe his position. Accounts mention that he also was responsible for repairs on the Masjid al-Harām in Mecca. He was to have built resthouses along the pilgrimage route to Mecca, but he died en route there in 1399. The dynasty continued with his son,

Nāṣir ad-Dīn Muḥammad, grandson, BADR AD-DĪN HAṢAN, and ended with his great-grandson Aḥmad.

AMY W. NEWHALL

BIBLIOGRAPHY

ʿABD AL-WAHHĀB, HASAN 1946 *Tarikh al-Masājid al-Athāriyya.* Cairo: Dar al-Kutub Misrīyya.

Ibn Taghribirdi: An-nujûm az-Zâhira. 1909–1950 Edited by William Popper. Berkeley: University of California Press.

MAYER, LEO A. 1956 *Islamic Architects and Their Works.* Geneva: Kundig.

ROGERS, MICHAEL 1976 "The Stones of Barqūq: Building Materials and Architectural Decoration in the Late Fourteenth Century." *Apollo* 103:307–313.

AL-SAKHAWI, MUHAMMAD IBN ʿABD AL-RAHMĀN 1935–1938 *al-Dawʿ al-lāmiʿ l-ahl al-qarn al-tāsiʿ.* Cairo: Mektāb al-Quds.

AHMAD IBN BĀSO

A native of Seville, Spain, Aḥmad ibn Bāso (12th century) executed for his Almohad patrons a number of important works, of which unfortunately only one survives. Lost to us through neglect and rebuilding after the reconquest of Spain by Christians are military and civil constructions in Gibraltar (1160) and Córdoba (1160s?) and the Buhaira Palace (1171?) which graced a suburb of his native Seville at the height of Almohad rule. We can appreciate the architectural style of Aḥmad ibn Bāso, only through vestiges that remain of the Great Mosque of Seville (1172–1185) and its elegant minaret, called *La Giralda* (1183?–1198?) today.

Only portions of the sahn of Seville's largest mosque survive today. Building was begun in 1172, when Abu Ya'qub Yusuf (1163–1184) brought ibn Bāso together with a number of master masons called from North Africa and all corners of *Al Andalus.* Just how much of the design of the Great Mosque can be attributed to Aḥmad ibn Bāso is difficult to determine; the participation of the patron seems to have been great. Abu Ya'qub Yusuf is said to have laid out the site for the mosque, marking off its limits himself. He further visited the construction site most days until its completion on April 30, 1182. In plan, the T-type hypostyle mosque continued a conservative style fostered by the reformist Almohads at Tinmal, and at the Kutubiya Mosque in Marrakesh. The pointed horseshoe arches, formed of carefully laid courses of baked brick, create a stern and austere articulation of thin planes that seems both formally and philosophically in keeping with Almohad taste in Spain and North Africa. Differences from the North African monuments remind us of ibn Bāso's Spanish formation, in particular the size of the sahn, which evokes the grandeur of Córdoba's Great Mosque.

Of the minaret, we can be certain only that the lowest portion was actually executed under the direction of Aḥmad ibn Bāso. It shows great attention to solid geometric form and to the same simplicity and refinement of decoration that distinguishes the mosque. It is possible that the upper portions of the minaret, which were actually completed by the architects 'Ali al Ghumari and Abu al Laith as Siqilli, might have followed the original plans of Aḥmad ibn Bāso. Panels of interlace display a delicacy and complexity that foreshadow the extraordinary developments of Nasrid and Mudejar decoration.

The date of the death of Aḥmad ibn Bāso is not known, though texts suggest that he lived to see the dedication of *La Giralda* (1198) despite the fact that he was not able to complete work there himself.

JERRILYNN D. DODDS

WORKS

*1160, Military Works, Gibraltar, Spain. *After 1160?, Fortress restoration, Córdoba, Spain. 1171?, Buhaira Palace; 1172–1185, Great Mosque; 1183?–1198?, Minaret (La Giralda); Seville, Spain.

BIBLIOGRAPHY

ANTUÑA, MELCHOR MARTINEZ 1930 "Sevilla y sus monumentos árabes." *Religión y Cultura* 9, no. 25:38–55.

GARCÍA GÓMEZ, EMILIO 1947 "Algunas preciciones sobre la runia de la Córdoba omeya." *Al-Andalus* 12:267–293.

RENAUD, H. P. J. 1937 "Les Ibn Bâso." *Hesperis* 24:1–12.

TORRES BALBÁS, LEOPOLDO 1946 "Arquitectos andaluces de las épocas almorávide y almohade." *Al-Andalus* 11:214–224.

TORRES BALBÁS, LEOPOLDO 1949 "Arte Hispanoalmohade." Volume 4, pages 17–29 in *Ars Hispaniae.* Madrid: Plus Ultra.

AHMAD IBN MOHAMMAD AT-TABRIZI

Aḥmad ibn Shams ad-dīn Moḥammad aṭ-Ṭabrizi completed the Masjid-i Shāh at Mashhad, Iran, in 1451. This Timurid structure has been known as a Sunni mosque, but it was originally commissioned by Shāh Rūkh as a mausoleum. It houses the tomb of one of his governors, and three others in the crypt. The building was also used as a *kānaqāh.* It has been proposed that Aḥmad ibn Moḥammad aṭ-Ṭabrizi was also responsible for the Blue Mosque (1465) in Tabriz, Iran, but this still lacks conclusive evidence.

MASSUMEH FARHAD

WORK

1451, Masjid-i Shāh, Mashhad, Iran.

BIBLIOGRAPHY

Diez, Ernst 1918 Pages 77–78 in *Churasanische Baudenkmäler*. Berlin: Reimer.
Mawlavi, Abdul-Hamid 1968 "Masjid-i Shāh ya Maqbara-i Amir Ghiyās al-dīn Malik Shāh." *Hunar va Mardum* 74–75, Nov.–Dec.:75–92.
Mayer, Leo A. 1956 *Islamic Architects and Their Works*. Geneva: Kundig.

AHMAD, USTAD

Ustad Ahmad Lahori (Master Ahmad of Lahore) (1580?–1649) was one of the great architects of the seventeenth century. Though he referred to himself simply as Ahmad Mi'mar (Ahmad the Architect), he was at once a skilled engineer and learned scholar in the sciences of astronomy, geometry, and mathematics. Ultimately, he rose to become the chief architect of the Mogul emperor Shah Jahan (c.1628–1658), who is supposed to have awarded him the honorary title of *Nadir al-'Asr*, or "Wonder of the Age," in recognition of his artistic accomplishments.

The exact date of his birth is unknown, but by 1629 Ustad Ahmad had already achieved a distinguished reputation as a scholar, since in that same year his expertise was gratefully acknowledged in the preface to the new astronomical tables *Zich-i-Shahjahani*, which were presented to the emperor by the royal astronomer Mulla Farid. In the official court history of Shah Jahan's reign, the *Padshah Nama*, Ustad Ahmad is credited along with a colleague named Ustad Hamid (possibly his brother), with being the skillful designer of the vast palace complex in the Red Fort at Delhi (1639–1648), the crowning glory of the emperor's new capital of Shahjahanabad. Moreover, literary evidence discovered only in the 1930s strongly suggests that Ustad Ahmad was also the architect of the world-famous Taj Mahal, which Shah Jahan ordered to be built as a tomb for his wife Mumtaz Mahal after her death in 1631.

Before this evidence came to light, the identity of the Taj's architect was unknown, since the *Padshah Nama* lists only the names of the two government officials placed in charge of the project. Consequently much speculation ensued, and during the nineteenth century, certain Western writers advanced the chauvinistic theory that the Taj Mahal had been designed by a European, either the itinerant Italian craftsman Geronimo Veroneo (d.1640), or perhaps the French goldsmith Augustin de Bordeaux (d.1632), who was known to have been in the employ of Shah Jahan's father, the emperor Jahangir (c.1605–1627). However, although European influences were strong on Mogul painting, this was not the case with architecture. The Taj Mahal complex clearly stands as the logical culmination of the earlier Mogul architectural tradition, combining bold engineering and massive scale with formal elegance and a totally coordinated design of flawless visual symmetry.

The evidence linking Ustad Ahmad with the Taj Mahal was discovered in a manuscript called *Diwan-i-Muhandis*, containing a collection of poems written by the architect's son Lutf Allah, in which he mentions that he and his two brothers 'Ata Allah and Nur Allah had all followed their father's profession and had become architects as well as scholars and engineers. This claim is amply corroborated by numerous surviving mathematical treatises authored by two of the brothers. Along with this information, Lutf Allah also includes several verses eulogizing his father's accomplishments, both as a scholar and as an architect. In these, he claims that Shah Jahan commanded his father to build the Taj Mahal as well as the Red Fort, and that these two magnificent edifices "represent only one aspect of his many-sided genius and constitute a single pearl out of his mine of pearls" (translated in Chaghtai, 1937, p. 202).

Since Lutf Allah also mentions that his father died in 1649, we now have a fairly good idea of his various architectural commissions during the last twenty years of his life. However, his earlier life and training are still uncertain. We know that Ustad Ahmad's father was named Yusuf and that the family may have been settled in Herat before shifting to Lahore. After growing up in Lahore, Ustad Ahmad may have worked in the atelier of 'Abd al-Karim, who was the emperor Jahangir's chief architect and who was subsequently appointed by Shah Jahan to be his superintendent of buildings at Agra. In the official histories, 'Abd al-Karim is listed as one of the two supervisors of the construction of the Taj, the other being the noble Mukramat Khan, who held the post of minister of public works. Thus, Ustad Ahmad obviously worked closely with these two men during the period 1632–1643 when the Taj complex was under construction. Although the architect was of lesser rank than Mukramat Khan, we know that the two were close friends and associates. According to one source, Mukramat Khan was also a scholar and consented to be the tutor of 'Ata Allah, Ustad Ahmad's eldest son.

When the Taj Mahal was in the planning stage, three enormous Mogul garden tombs were already built or in progress: the tombs of the emperors Humayun, Akbar, and Jahangir. Though based on

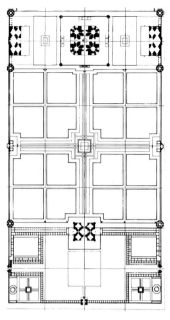

Ahmad.
Taj Mahal Complex.
Agra, India.
1632–1643 and later

Ahmad.
Plan of the Taj Mahal.
Agra, India.
1632–1643 and later

Ahmad.
Gateway.
Taj Mahal Complex.
Agra, India.
1632–1643 and later

the first of these, the Taj is much larger in scale and at the same time more balanced in its proportions and more sensitive in the articulation of its vast white marble surfaces. Moreover, the controlled placement of the mausoleum and its subsidiary structures within a garden setting reflects a sophisticated concern for total planning and an interest in visual unity and dramatic vistas comparable to the aesthetic ideals of European baroque architecture.

The engineering aspects of the tomb are no less amazing. The dome rises to a total height of 280 feet above the ground, while the terrace, supporting the mausoleum and its adjacent structures at the northern end of the garden, consists of a solid block of masonry some 983 feet long, 367 feet wide, and more than 50 feet thick. Since the river

Jumna flows along the northern face of this terrace, the architect ingeniously incorporated numerous cylindrical wells into the foundation, thus allowing it to withstand the encroaching effects of annual flooding.

Surprisingly, this vast foundation platform and the mausoleum proper were completed within only about four years after excavation was started in January 1632, although the inlay work on the interior was not completed until around December 1638. By February 1643, the remainder of the tomb complex was also complete, including the garden, the enormous entrance gateway, and the marketplace and caravansaries lying to the south of the entrance forecourt. In some respects, the inlay work on the gateway is even more impressive than that on the mausoleum, since the bold contrast between the red sandstone and bands of white marble allow us to perceive more clearly the innovative dramatic character of its geometric design.

The plan of the Taj is innovative in its placement of the marble mausoleum at one end of the quadripartite garden (*chahar-bagh*) rather than in the exact center as had been the practice previously. By adopting this unusual layout, the architect seems to have been inspired by a then well-known Islamic cosmological diagram depicting the gardens of Paradise on the Day of Resurrection, in an apparent attempt to make each part of the tomb complex correspond allegorically to a celestial architectural model (Begley, 1979, pp. 11ff). Paradise imagery was widespread in both literature and art in the Mogul period, and since Ustad Ahmad was a distinguished scholar and intellectual, as well as architect and engineer, he may have helped conceive the Taj's symbolic program in addition to implementing it structurally. Although Ustad Ahmad's role as architect and engineer was probably crucial, it is also likely that Shah Jahan himself contributed to the design of the tomb. According to the official histories, the emperor was directly involved in all of his building projects, not only by inspecting and approving plans, but also by frequently ordering alterations during the course of construction.

Ustad Ahmad's next major commission was the design and construction of the Red Fort in Shah Jahan's new capital at Delhi, the foundations of which were laid at an astrologically auspicious moment on May 12, 1639. By this time, the main structures of the Taj complex had already been completed, so Ustad Ahmad was free to devote all his energies to the new assignment, again under the supervision of Mukramat Khan, now promoted to governor of Delhi. The Red Fort was intended to serve as the great ceremonial center of Shah Jahan's vast empire, and European travelers in the mid-seventeenth century described it as one of the largest and most magnificent palace complexes in the world at that time. Like the Taj, the Fort's original conception was rigidly symmetrical, although its northern extension is slightly irregular in order to accommodate it to the pre-existing Salimgarh Fort which lies adjacent. Within the fortification walls, an imposing array of courtyards, gardens, and palaces were laid out on either side of a central axis passing through the Lahore Gate on the west. The largest of these courtyards lay in front of the Hall of Public Audience, where the emperor daily held court when he was in residence.

Although many of the structures inside the Fort were demolished following the Indian Mutiny of 1857, the Hall of Private Audience survives relatively intact and gives a good idea of the sumptuous elegance of the imperial living quarters. In its design and ornamental details, this building reflects several changes in architectural style since the Taj. Cusped arches have replaced the simple curves on the Taj, and ornament—particularly the foliate motif—has become much more elaborate and three-dimensional, though without sacrificing the continuity of the planar surfaces. On April 18, 1648, Shah Jahan made his first state entry into the recently completed fort, and as a sign of his royal approval, he ordered the following couplet to be inscribed on the interior of the Hall of Private Audience:

> If there be a Paradise on earth,
> It is here, it is here, it is here!

In addition to serving as imperial architect, Ustad Ahmad designed buildings for other patrons, including the fabulous, but now destroyed palace at Lahore which had been commissioned by Asaf Khan, the Vakeel of Shah Jahan and the father of the deceased queen Mumtaz Mahal. The date of this palace is uncertain, but it was probably constructed around 1636–1638, after the Taj mausoleum was substantially complete, but before the commencement of the Red Fort at Delhi. Even during the period 1639–1648, when the Red Fort was in progress, the architectural services of Ustad Ahmad were occasionally sought in connection with state projects outside Delhi. Thus, sometime around 1645, the then Mogul governor of the Punjab was requested to have Ustad Ahmad summoned from Delhi, in order to complete the construction of the Shamshirgarh and Hasan Abdal Forts, and also the now sadly damaged garden complex at Wah.

In 1649, just one year after the completion of the Red Fort, Ustad Ahmad died, leaving his three sons to carry on the family profession. Although there is no documentary evidence, it is possible that before his death, Ustad Ahmad, in conjunction with his colleague Ustad Hamid, had already prepared the plans for the Jami' Masjid at Delhi (1650–1656), the vast congregational mosque that was Shah Jahan's last great architectural project in his new capital. There are marked similarities be-

Ahmad.
Red Fort.
Delhi, India.
1639–1648

Ahmad.
Hall of Private Audience.
Red Fort.
Delhi, India.
1639–1648

tween the façade of this mosque and the Taj gateway, although the later stylistic characteristics of Ustad Ahmad are also evident. While preserving order and symmetry, the architect has heightened the rhythmic intensity of the façade through the boldly attached minarets and the undulating sequence of cusped arches. Above each of the ten smaller arches are rectangular white marble panels with calligraphy designed by Ustad Ahmad's youngest son Nur Allah, who may also have assumed some of his father's responsibilities as imperial architect, in conjunction with Ustad Hamid.

In sum, it appears that the architect Ustad Ahmad played a major role in the formulation and development of Mogul architecture during the reign of Shah Jahan. At once opulent, awe-inspiring, and rigorously formal, his buildings served as perfect expressions of the emperor's exalted image of himself and his empire. They also influenced the course of Indian architecture for the next two centuries.

W. E. BEGLEY

WORKS

1632–1638, Tomb of Mumtaz Mahal; 1632–1643 and later, Mosque, Gateway, and other structures, Taj Mahal Complex; Agra, India. *1636?–1638?, Palace of Asaf Khan, Lahore, Pakistan. 1639–1648, Hall of Public Audience (with Ustad Hamid), Hall of Private Audience, and other structures, Red Fort, Delhi, India. 1645–1647?, Shamshirgarh and Hasan Abdal Forts; 1645–1647?, Wah Garden; Punjab, Pakistan.

BIBLIOGRAPHY

AHMAD, NAZIR 1956–1957 "'Imam-ud-Din Husain Riadi, the Grandson of Nadir-ul-'Asr Ahmad, the Architect of the Taj Mahal, and his *Tadhkira-i-Baghistan.*" *Islamic Culture* 30:330–350; 31:61–87.
BEGLEY, W. E. 1979 "The Myth of the Taj Mahal and a New Theory of Its Symbolic Meaning." *Art Bulletin* 61:7–37.
BEGLEY, W. E. 1980 "The Symbolic Role of Calligraphy on Three Imperial Mosques of Shah Jahan." In J. Williams (editor), *Kaladarsana: American Studies in the Art of India.* New Delhi: American Institute of Indian Studies.
CHAGHTAI, M. A. 1937 "A Family of Great Mughal Architects." *Islamic Culture* 11:200–209.
CHAGHTAI, M. A. 1938 *Le Tadj Mahal d'Agra.* Brussels: Editions de la Connaissance.
CHAGHTAI, M. A. 1957 *Ahmad Ki'mar Lahori and His Family.* Lahore, Pakistan: Kitab Khana Nauras. Published in Urdu.
KANWAR, H. I. S. 1974 "Ustad Ahmad Lahori." *Islamic Culture* 48:11–32.
MAHMUD BANGALORI 1951 *Taj.* Lahore, Pakistan: Cosha Adab. Published in Urdu.
NADVI, S. SULAIMAN 1948 "The Family of the Engineers Who Built the Taj Mahal and the Delhi Fort." *Journal of the Bihar Research Society* 34:75–110.

ÅHRÉN, UNO

The Swedish architect, city planner, and theorist Uno Åhrén (1897–1977), who is perhaps best known for his role in introducing modern architecture and theory in Sweden, studied at the Royal Technical Institute, Stockholm (1915–1919). He began architectural practice with Ragnar Hjorth in 1919 and two years later practiced with ERIK GUNNAR ASPLUND (1921–1923). Åhrén concentrated at first on furniture and interior design, which he exhibited at major national and international exhibitions and which he continued to design until the early 1930s. Among the earliest examples of modern architecture in Sweden are Åhrén's Villa Dahl (1928–1929), Sigtuna; the Ford Motor Company (1930–1931), Frihamnen, Stockholm; and the Cinema Flamman (1929–1930), Stockholm. His Student Club at the Royal Technical Institute (1929–1930), Stockholm (with SVEN GOTTFRID MARKELIUS) and his contributions to the 1930 Stockholm Exhibition as co-director with Gunnar Sundbarg of the Home Section demonstrate how conspicuously he participated in winning acceptance for modern architecture. Toward this end, he, along with Asplund, Wolter Gahn, Markelius, Gregor Paulsson, and Eskil Sundahl, published *acceptera* in 1933, the theoretical manifesto of modern architecture in Sweden.

Having shaped modern Swedish architectural theory and design, Åhrén turned to city planning. He collaborated with the social economist Gunnar Myrdal in publishing *Bostadsfrågan som socialt planläggningsproblem* (1934) and was thereby instrumental in founding the state housing commission which created the basis of modern Swedish housing policy between 1933 and 1947. During the rest of his life, Åhrén held important planning positions, including head of city planning, Göteborg (1935–1943); member of the State Committee for Building Research (1942–1949); chief, Swedish National Building Department (1943–1945); chair professor, City Planning, Royal Technical Institute, Stockholm (1947–1963); and member of the Swedish City Planning Commission. Throughout his career, Åhrén was concerned not only with traffic problems, sanitary conditions, parks, and housing, but also with the need for large-scale urban planning, the role of community planning, and the problems of long-term development. In addition to many publications, Åhrén edited *Byggmästaren* (1929–1932) and founded both *Plan* (1947) and the publication series of the Swedish National Building Committee (1944).

JUDITH S. HULL

WORKS

1917, Liljevalchs's Exhibition (interiors), Stockholm. c.1920, Solsidan Villa, Sigtuna, Sweden. 1923, Göteborg Exhibition (interiors), Sweden. 1923, Paris (interiors), Exposition. 1925, Bakery (with Eskil Sundahl), Stockholm. 1926, Cinema; 1928–1929, Dahl Villa; Sigtuna, Sweden. 1929–1930, Flamman Cinema; 1929–1930, Royal Technical Institute (student clubhouse; with Sven Markelius); 1930, Stockholm Exhibitions (villa and interiors). 1930–1949, Ford Motor Company (exhibition rooms and factory), Frihamnen, Stockholm. 1937, General Plan, Lundby, Sweden. 1943–1954, Plan of Center, Årsta, Sweden. 1948–1949, General Plan, Botkyrka, Sweden. 1949, General Plan, Skelleftea, Sweden. 1952, General Plan, Kramfors, Sweden. 1954, General Plan, Skelleftea landskommun, Sweden. 1955–1956, General Plan, Sandviken, Sweden. 1957, Regional Plan, Kalmar-Nybro, Sweden. 1957–1966, General Plan, Solleftea, Sweden. 1959, General Plan, Fagersta, Sweden.

BIBLIOGRAPHY

AHLBERG, C. F.; ERIXON, S.; FRIBERGER, E.; HASSLOF, SO.; LINDSTROM, S.; and ÅHRÉN, UNO 1943 *Bygg bättre samhällen.* Stockholm.
AHLBERG, C. F. 1977 "Uno Åhrén, 6/8 1897–8/10 1977." *Plan* 1977:362.
ÅHRÉN, UNO 1942 *Arkitektur och demokrati.* Stockholm: Norstedts.
ÅHRÉN, UNO 1959 *Försöksenkät beträffande stadsplanekostnader för bostadsområden.* Stockholm: För Bostadskommitten inom ECE.
ÅHRÉN, UNO, and ÅKESSON, TORVALD 1944 *Bostadsförsörjning och samhäl•lsplanering.* Stockholm.
ÅHRÉN, UNO, and MYRDAL, GUNNAR 1933 *Bostadsfrågen såsom socialt planläggningsproblem.* Stockholm.
ÅHRÉN, UNO, and OLSSON, I. 1941 *Amatörbyggeri eller yrkesmässig småtugeproduktion?* Göteborg, Sweden.
ASPLUND, ERIK GUNNAR; GAHN, WOLTER; MARKELIUS, SVEN; PAULSSON, GREGOR; SUNDAHL, ESKIL; and ÅHRÉN, UNO 1931 *Acceptera.* Stockholm: Bokförlagsktiebolaget Tiden.

AICHEL, JAN BLAZEJ SANTINI

See SANTINI AICHEL, JAN BLAZEJ.

AIKIN, EDMUND

Edmund Aikin (1780–1820) was born in Lancashire, England. He was articled to JOHN CARR, entered Royal Academy Schools in 1801, and practiced as a Greek Revivalist. His publications include *Designs for Villas* (1808)—in the Picturesque mode—and the scholarly *Essay on the Doric Order* (1810). Aikin assisted Sir Samuel Bentham in designing various naval dockyards (1810–1813).

R. WINDSOR LISCOMBE

WORKS

*1808–1809, Presbyterian Chapel, Jewin Street, London. 1815–1816, Wellington Assembly Rooms (now the Irish Center); *1817, Royal Institution; Liverpool, England.

BIBLIOGRAPHY

AIKIN, EDMUND 1808 *Designs for Villas and Other Buildings.* London: J. Taylor.
AIKIN, EDMUND 1810 *An Essay on the Doric Order of Architecture.* London: Architectural Society.
AIKIN, LUCY 1823 Volume 1, pages 267–272 in *Memoir of John Aikin, M.D.* London: Baldwin.
MCMORDIE, MICHAEL 1975 "Picturesque Pattern Books and Pre-Victorian Designers." *Architectural History* 18:43–59.

AIN, GREGORY

Gregory Ain (1908–) was born in Pittsburgh, Pennsylvania. He attended the school of architecture and fine arts at the University of Southern California, Los Angeles (1926–1927). Before opening his office in 1936, he worked for RICHARD NEUTRA (1931–1935), who, with R. M. SCHINDLER, was a major influence. His interest in low-cost social housing was furthered by exploration of panel systems on a Guggenheim Fellowship (1940). Collaborating with landscape planner GARRETT ECKBO, he produced staggered units in garden settings for various tracts (Park Planned Homes, Altadena, California, 1946, and the 1948 Mar Vista Housing and Avenel Cooperative, Los Angeles). Ain, Joseph Johnson, and Alfred Day designed an exhibition house for the garden of the Museum of Modern Art, New York, 1950. Ain was dean of the School of Architecture, Pennsylvania State University, from 1963 to 1967.

ESTHER MCCOY

AITCHISON, GEORGE

George Aitchison (1825–1910) was an architect of pioneer commercial buildings and master of interior decoration. He was born in London and was articled to his father, George Aitchison. He traveled in Italy, from 1853 to 1855, where he met Frederic, Lord Leighton, for whom he designed Leighton House (1865) with its Arab Hall (1877), his major work. In 1898, he received the Gold Medal of the Royal Institute of British Architects.

MARGARET RICHARDSON

WORKS

1864, 59–61, Mark Lane; *1864, 1–2 Hammond Court; 1865, Leighton House, 12 Holland Park Road; *1869, 44 Belgrave Square (interior decoration); *1873, 15

Berkeley Square (interior decoration); 1877, Arab Hall; 1877, 52 Princes' Gate (interior decoration; partially extant); 1877, Founders' Hall; *1879, G. F. Watts's Studio (picture gallery), 6 Melbury Road; *1883, 9 Chesterfield Gardens (interior decoration); *1885, Royal Exchange Assurance Offices, 29 Pall Mall; 1886, 29 Chesham Place (music room and conservatory); London. 1888, Lythe Hill (interior decoration), Haslemere, Surrey, England. 1892, Goldsmith's Company Livery Hall (interior decoration), London.

BIBLIOGRAPHY

"The Late Professor Aitchison, R.A." 1910 *Journal of the Royal Institute of British Architects.* Series 3 17:581–583.
"Obituary." 1910 *Building News* 93:683–684.
ORMOND, RICHARD, and ORMOND, LEONÉE 1975 *Lord Leighton.* New Haven and London: Yale University Press.
"Professor Aitchison." *The Builder* 98:592.
RICHARDSON, MARGARET 1980 "George Aitchison: Lord Leighton's Architect." *Journal of the Royal Institute of British Architects* 39:37–40.

AJAMĪ

Ajamī b. Abī Bakr al-bannā' an-Nakhjiwānī constructed the Gunbad-i Atā Bābā (1161–1162) and the Tower of Atabeks (1186–1187), the mausoleum of Mu 'minah Khātūn at Nakhichevan (Azerbaijan). The former consists of an octagonal brick tower with simple geometric decoration, while the more elaborate decagonal Tower of Atabeks combines burnt and glazed brick. Both tomb towers follow the type prevalent in northwestern Iran.

MASSUMEH FARHAD

WORKS

1161–1162, Gunbad-i Atā-Bābā (mausoleum of Yusuf b. Kathīr), 1186–1187, Tower of Atabeks (mausoleum of Mu 'minah Khātūn); Nakhichevan, Azerbaijan.

BIBLIOGRAPHY

BRETANITŠKĬJ, L. S. 1966 *Zodchestvo Azerbaĭjana XII–XV vv.* Moscow.
HILL, DEREK 1964 *Islamic Architecture and Its Decoration A.D. 800–1500.* A Photographic Survey by Derek Hill, with an Introductory Text by Oleg Grabar. University of Chicago Press.
MAYER, LEO A. 1956 *Islamic Architects and Their Work.* Geneva: Kundig.

AKBAR

In 1556, at the age of fourteen, Akbar became emperor of an initially small Muslim state in northern India. He reigned until 1605 and expanded the Mogul empire in almost annual military campaigns so that by the early seventeenth century it encompassed the northern two-thirds of the Indian subcontinent. An administrative genius, he created a centralized state with the emperor firmly controlling an extensive bureaucracy that placed the provinces under the direct control of the capital. Through a policy of conciliation and official tolerance he brought into his government the Hindus who composed the vast majority of India's population, but he failed in his attempt to create a syncretic pan-Indian faith—the *Din Ilahi*—that would eliminate India's religious diversity, unify Mogul society, and firmly establish the supremacy of the imperial autocrat.

Akbar was a brilliant, energetic patron of the arts. In painting, he oversaw the production of a variety of manuscripts—traditional Persian literary classics, Persian translations of Hindu religious texts, dynastic histories designed to support the Mogul right to rule—that testify to a broad interest in Islam and in non-Muslim India as well as to a very evident sense of purpose as a patron. His taste was essentially eclectic, and his court painters turned to diverse traditions—Indian, Iranian, and European—to develop around 1590 a classic Mogul style of painting. Some aspects of his activities as a patron may have been affected by his close association with Abu'l-Fazl, a learned courtier who was his boon companion and chief adviser and who was the author of the *Akbarnamah* and the *'A'in-i Akbari,* two of our most valuable sources for knowledge of the emperor and his reign.

Akbar's achievements should not be seen in isolation, for they had a historical foundation in nearly 400 years of the Muslim Delhi sultanate, established in 1191. Although the Tughluq dynasty (1320–1398) can be correctly viewed as a precursor of the Mogul in many of its policies and achievements, it was only with the Moguls that a stable, long-enduring Muslim state with vast resources was created, essential for the creation of a classic architectural style that could be disseminated throughout the empire.

Akbar's architectural patronage reflects a wide-ranging mind that was innovative and flexible. Chronologically, there are three phases in his activity as a patron. The major structures of the first phase are the 1566 West Gate of the Agra Fort and the massive mausoleum built in Delhi for his father, Humayun. Begun in 1568–1569 under the direction of an Iranian architect, MIRZA GHIYASH, the tomb is located in the middle of an immense walled garden laid out in a geometrically symmetric grid pattern. Adjacent to the religious complex founded by the Chistiya sufi saint Nizam al-Din Awliya, the tomb associated the deceased emperor

Akbar.
Humayun's Tomb.
Delhi, India.
1564–c.1568

with holiness so that more than a hundred later members of the Mogul family and its adherents were buried at the site, and for many years a madrasah (seminary) offered instruction at the tomb. In Iran, these kinds of honors were generally reserved for religious figures, and royal tombs of this period were not conspicuous. In the Mogul state under Akbar, a definite imperial cult was initiated which made the ruler's tomb a quasi-religious monument and center for pilgrimage.

Humayun's tomb is faced with red sandstone articulated with white marble and is crowned by a white marble dome, a subdued but highly effective use of materials dating from the early fourteenth century. Raised on a plinth 6.7 meters high and 95 meters on a side, the tomb presents nearly identical faces on its four sides: high pointed arches with octagonal wings at the corners that project in front of the arches. The central tomb chamber, with the king's cenotaph in the middle of the room, is covered by an immense double dome on a high drum. Windows on the west side contain *mihrab* (prayer niche) forms, indicating the direction of prayer and reinforcing the structure's religious function. Despite the often cited Iranian characteristics of this building, Humayun's tomb establishes basic principles of the classic Mogul architecture of the seventeenth century: both garden and mausoleum reflect a passion for geometrical symmetry, regularity, and logical predictability. This architectural mathematics is a calculated metaphor of the divine order, and celebrated Mogul buildings such as the Taj Mahal have their structural and compositional origins in this first building produced under Akbar's aegis.

The second phase of his patronage began in 1570 at the city of Fathpur Sikri, 37 kilometers to the southeast of Agra, along with Delhi and Lahore one of the three great urban centers of the Mogul empire. Largely completed by 1572 and essentially abandoned in 1586 due to a failing water supply, much of the city (which functioned as Akbar's capital during this period) is in an excellent state of preservation. Its many buildings, almost entirely of red sandstone, can be classified in three basic divisions on an east–west axis.

1. Administration centered on the *Daulat-khanah* (government quarters), a complex of walled rectangles, arcades, and buildings serving a variety of functions and located in the eastern part of the royal city. The *Diwan-i 'Amm* (public audience hall) was an open, rectangular court with cloisters on four sides and a large, peristyled pavilion on the west side where the emperor received ambassadors and petitioners and conducted much of the empire's official business. A door led from the pavilion west into the royal garden and on into a more sequestered governmental area, another large rectangle divided into subsidiary spaces by walls and arcades. At the south end was a square pool with four causeways leading to a square platform, presumably restricted for the emperor, while at the north end was a square building, perhaps the *Diwan-i Khass* (private audience hall). Its interior chamber contains only a single pillar supporting an elaborately bracketed capital and circular platform, linked by four diagonal bridges to a narrow walkway constituting the building's second-story. Derived directly from Buddhist-Hindu sculpture, the pillar was there the seat of a god, and Akbar was fully conscious of its symbolism. Both the *Diwan-i Khass* and the pool to its south were calcu-

Ahmad.
Hall of Private Audience.
Red Fort.
Delhi, India.
1639–1648

Akbar.
Jami' Mosque.
City of Fathpur Sikri.
India.
1570–1572

lated architectural statements, designed to illuminate and enhance the emperor's role as autocrat of Indian life. Further to the south were administrative offices, where records were kept and documents written, and to the northeast of the administrative quarters was the *Karkhanah,* the workshops where precious manuscripts and other goods were produced for imperial use.

2. To the west of the *Daulatkhanah,* the *Haram Saray* was the residential area of the emperor and his extended family. Among its several buildings, the largest (usually termed Jodh Bai's Palace) is a two-storied structure, built around a large open court: it must have served as the residence for most of the emperor's harem. Two small palaces to the east and west ("Raja Birbal's House" and "Maryam's House") were apparently reserved for specially favored wives. Near the northeastern end of the *Haram Saray* is a five-storied, open-arcaded wind tower (*Panj Mahal*) that provided relief from heat and also gave an unrestricted view into the *Daulatkhanah.* With the exception of some decorative motifs, these structures have little in common with Muslim regal architecture to the west but are based instead on Hindu palace types.

3. Religious life was diverse at the Mogul court, but architecturally it focused on the jami' mosque at the western end of the complex. Based on traditional mosque design, a central open court (110.8 × 135 meters) was enclosed by arcades. The Royal Gate was on the east side, appropriately opposite the *qiblah* (prayer wall) on the west, but in 1573, Akbar returned from crucial victories in Gujarat and apparently constructed then the larger and more elegant *Buland Darwaza* (High Gate) on the south side. The mosque's *qiblah* is marked by a deeper arcade and by three domes on high drums, the central dome larger than its neighbors. Though later mosques have gates of roughly equal size on the south, east, and north sides, the Fathpur Sikri jami' establishes the classic Mogul mosque type.

The city also functioned as a major center for the sufi Chistiya order, initially closely associated with the emperor. The tomb of Salim Chisti is a white-marble pavilion on the north side of the mosque's courtyard; adjoining it on the east is a *jama'atkhanah* (meeting hall) where the sufis gathered for special worship. To the west, outside the confines of the mosque, are a large number of other Chisti buildings.

About sixty meters to the northeast of the east entrance to the mosque was apparently located a unique structure, the *'Ibadatkhanah* (house of worship), which served Akbar's idiosyncratic interest in world religions, and wide-ranging religious discussions for the emperor's edification took place there between orthodox Muslims, less orthodox sufis, Parsees, Christians of various persuasions, Jains, and others. It was probably here that Akbar developed many of the ideas he tried to promulgate in his heretical *Din Ilahi,* the mark of his final apostasy from Islam. After his death, the building was demolished, and neither literary nor archeological evidence presents us with a plausible impression of its appearance.

Built almost entirely in two years between 1570 and 1572 from Akbar's thirty-second to thirty-fourth year, when he was also active as a patron of painting, the city represents his mature architectural aesthetic, almost perfectly preserved, as his palace-citadels at Lahore and Agra were not. It is clear that what appears to be eclecticism is rather the function of imperial needs and ideology. It is a formative period and it therefore lacks the architectural cohesion of his grandson Shah Jahan's equally impressive building program (see under USTAD AHMAD). Whereas the jami' mosque, except for decorative details, adheres to the basic canons of Islamic religious building to the west, the palaces and the imperio-centric *Diwan-i Khass* show a very conscious and selective use of India's Buddhist-Hindu traditions, particularly as a means of establishing the Mogul monarch as a ruler exercising semidivine authority over the empire's racial and religious heterogeneity.

Akbar's construction of central urban citadels and palace complexes at Agra and Lahore were, except for walls and main gates, all extensively reworked and altered by Shah Jahan. The single structure of major significance that can be assigned to Akbar's reign is the Jahangiri Mahal in Agra fort: both in plan and detail it is derived from a Hindu model like the early sixteenth-century Fort of Man Singh at Gwalior. The great number of utilitarian structures—forts, caravansaries, wells, baths, milestones, and other buildings—indicates that he had established a very extensive, well-funded, and efficient ministry of building.

The third and final phase of his architectural activities is less clear-cut. His tomb at Sikandra outside Agra was probably begun in the last years of the sixteenth century, but it was finished under his son Jahangir (1605–1628) who recorded in his *Memoirs* that he was dissatisfied with what the architects had done and ordered portions of the building substantially reworked. Despite the fact that it is a problematic structure, the Sikandra mausoleum reflects Akbar's taste and approach in several fundamental ways. As at Humayun's tomb, massive gates lead into a completely enclosed, geometrically patterned garden, a landscape metaphor of paradise with the mausoleum as an imperial shrine at the center. Formally, it combines diverse architectural elements, such as "Iranian" pointed arches and "Hindu" bracketing, that testify to Akbar's abiding eclecticism. Outwardly more sophisticated and better educated, Jahangir and Shah Jahan synthesized these elements from Akbar's search for expressive models and set both architecture and the other arts in a stylistically more uniform and consistent aesthetic.

The creator of the Mogul state, Akbar was a patron of genius whose vigorous eclecticism was a measure of his originality and not of his lack of aesthetic direction. His political and social ambition to incorporate India's diverse elements into a pan-Indian unity under Mogul autocracy first faltered and then failed under his successors. In the arts, there was a greater measure of success: in painting, a classic Mogul style emerged by the late sixteenth century; in architecture, it was achieved under Shah Jahan in the middle of the seventeenth century. These styles were abiding and spread throughout later Indian visual culture in the service of political and religious ideals strikingly different from those of the Moguls. A vital part of the Mogul ideal of kingship, architectural patronage was most strikingly expressed under Akbar whose practical knowledge and vital personality made him an active, rather than a passive, patron who knew what he wanted and whose changing architectural tastes reflected his shifting ideological inclinations. If his most idiosyncratic buildings, like the *Diwan-i Khass* in Fathpur Sikri, left no descendants, structures like Humayun's tomb and the jami' masjid of Fathpur Sikri established types that were the foundation for later Mogul architectural achievement.

ANTHONY WELCH

WORKS

1564–c.1568, Humayun's Tomb, Delhi, India. 1566, Agra Fort (west gate and probably the south gate), India. 1568–c.1570, Humayun's Tomb, Delhi, India. c.1570, Ajmer Fort, India. c.1570, Jahangiri Mahal, Agra Fort, India. c.1570, Lahore Fort, Pakistan. 1570–1572, City of Fathpur Sikri, India. 1581, Atak Fort, Pakistan. 1583, Allahabad Fort, India. c.1600–c.1610, Akbar's Tomb, Sikandra, India.

BIBLIOGRAPHY

BROWN, PERCY (1942–1943)n.d. *Indian Architecture.* 3d ed. Bombay: Taraporevala.
NAQVI, S.A.A. 1937 *Delhi Humayun's Tomb and Adjacent Buildings.* Delhi: Archaeological Survey of India.
RIZVI, SAIYID ATHAR ABBAS, and FLYNN, VINCENT JOHN A. 1975 *Fathpur-Sīkrī.* Bombay: Taraporevala.
SMITH, EDMUND W. 1894–1898 *The Moghul Architecture of Fathpur-Sikri.* 4 vols. Allahabad: Archaeological Survey of India.
SMITH, EDMUND W. 1909 *Akbar's Tomb: Sikandarah near Agra.* Allahabad: Archaeological Survey of India.

ALAVOINE, JEAN ANTOINE

Born in Paris, Jean Antoine Alavoine (1777–1834) was the son of a master sculptor. He studied architecture at the Ecole des Beaux-Arts under Jean Thomas Thibault, interrupting his training from 1798 to 1801 for military service that took him to Italy. By the age of thirty he had found employment with the *Bâtiments Civils,* and he held government positions for the rest of his career. Alavoine was never elected to the Institut de France, but in 1831 he served on the commission appointed by the Count of Montalivet, minister of the interior, to make recommendations for the reorganization of the Ecole des Beaux-Arts.

In 1811, Alavoine was appointed site architect under the direction of JACQUES CÉLLÉRIER for the Napoleonic monument in the form of an elephant planned for the Place de la Bastille. The following year, he took charge of the project but was able to realize only the foundations and the full-scale plaster model of the elephant before political events halted work. Alavoine designed several projects of his own for the site. With the sculptor Pierre Charles Bridan, he proposed in 1817 a fountain surrounded by a colonnade, and in 1830 the state commissioned him to design a colossal column honoring the dead of the revolutions of 1789 and 1830. The Colonne du Juillet, however, was built to the designs of his assistant, JOSEPH LOUIS DUC.

Alavoine was a proponent of the use of cast iron as a building material. In his restoration of the Cathedral of Sées (1817–1823), he experimented with cast-iron replacements for stone colonnettes. When the spire of the Cathedral of Rouen burned in 1822, he prepared the damage report and in 1823 presented plans calling for a new spire to be built entirely of cast iron. Despite its novelty, the project soon received approval, but its construction proceeded very slowly, and Alavoine did not live to see it completed.

RICHARD CLEARY

WORKS

*1810, Bains Montesquieu, Paris. 1817–1823, Cathedral of Sees (restoration), France. Begun 1823, Cathedral of Rouen (spire and restoration; not completed until after his death), France.

BIBLIOGRAPHY

CHIROL, PIERRE 1920 *Jean-Antoine Alavoine.* Rouen, France: Lainé.
DESPORTES, JEAN PHILIPPE 1971 "Alavoine et la flèche de la cathédrale de Rouen." *Revue de l'art* 13:48–62.

ALBERS, JOSEF

Josef Albers (1888–1976) spent five years as an elementary school teacher near his birthplace, Bottrop, Westphalia, before study at the Royal School of Art in Berlin beginning in 1913. He was a pupil of Max Doerner and of Franz Stuck at Munich's Academy of Art from 1919 to 1920 after which he went to the Weimar Bauhaus. Promoted in 1923 to "young master," he taught the preliminary course which he organized systematically following the loose expressionist and mystical beginning under Johannes Itten's direction. He moved with the Bauhaus to Dessau in 1925 where he was named master. From 1928 to 1930, he was also in charge of the furniture workshop. In 1932, Albers moved with the Bauhaus to Berlin. After the closing of that school in 1933, Albers taught at Black Mountain College in North Carolina until 1949 and at Yale (1948–1950) where he became professor and head of the department of design. Albers was much sought as a guest lecturer and accepted invitations throughout the western hemisphere.

WALTER GROPIUS described Albers:

He is absolutely a born teacher, knew it himself and made himself indispensable. . . . I consider him the best art teacher I have ever met, particularly on account of his subtle psychological talent, treating every student in a different way [Statement, February 9, 1966].

Albers is remembered not only for his roles as teacher and painter but also as art theorist, typographer, designer, and experimental photographer. Albers's work related to that of Piet Mondrian, THEO VAN DOESBURG, and *de Stijl* and, particularly in architecture, to that of LUDWIG MIES VAN DER ROHE. The perfection of his work, its proportions and rectilinearity, and its harmony of color inspired not only artists and graphic designers but obviously also architects, many of whom acknowledge him as the source of their own ideas.

REGINALD R. ISAACS

BIBLIOGRAPHY

ALBERS, JOSEF (1936)1975 *Interactions of Color.* Rev. ed. New Haven: Yale University Press.
ALBERS, JOSEF 1944 "The Educational Value of Manual Work and Handicraft in Relation to Architecture." Pages 688–694 in Paul Zucker (editor), *New Architecture and City Planning.* New York: Philosophical Library.
ALBERS, JOSEF 1958 *Poems and Drawings.* New Haven: Readymade Press.
ALBERS, JOSEF 1962 *Homage to the Square.* New Haven: Ives-Stillman.
ALBERS, JOSEF 1969 *Search versus Re-Search: Three Lectures, Trinity College.* Hartford, Conn.: Trinity College Press.
ALBERS, JOSEF 1971 *Paintings and Graphics: 1917–1970.* Edited by Sam Hunter. N.J.: Princeton University Press.
ALBRECHT, HANS 1974 *Farbe als Sprache: Robert Delaunay, Josef Albers, Richard Paul Lohge.* Cologne, Germany: Dumont.
BUCHER, FRANÇOIS (1961)1977 *Josef Albers: Despite Straight Lines: An Analysis of His Graphic Constructions.* Rev. ed. Cambridge, Mass.: M.I.T. Press.
GOMRINGER, EUGEN 1968 *Josef Albers.* New York: Wittenborn.
SPIES, WERNER 1970 *Josef Albers.* New York: Abrams.

ALBERTI, ALBERTO

Born in Borgo San Sepolcro, Italy, Alberto Alberti (1525/1526–1599?) was an architect, military engineer, sculptor, and engraver. Alberti was active until 1563 as chief of the Medici Florentine fortifications. From 1563 to 1586, he worked in Rome on several churches and further Medici commissions. He died in Rome, leaving his workshop to Antonio Cantagallina.

SARA LEHRMAN

WORKS

1554–1564, Medici Fortifications, Livorno, Italy. 1561–1565, Medici Fortifications, San Sepolcro, Italy. 1563, Medici Fortifications, Ancona, Italy. 1563–1586, Villa Medici, Monte Pincio; 1584–1589, Choir and Convent of San Bartolomeo; 1587, Santa Chiara (cloister); 1591–1595, Palazzo delle Laudi (loggia); 1594, San Lorenzo; Rome.

BIBLIOGRAPHY

BELLI, BARSOLI, I. 1960 "Alberti, A." *Dizionario Biografico degli Italiani.* Rome: Giovanni Treccami.
DEGLI AZZI, G. 1914 *Inventario degli Archivi di San Sepolcro.* Rocca San Casciano, Italy.

ALBERTI, LEON BATTISTA

Leon Battista Alberti (1404–1472) was one of the greatest architects of the fifteenth century, and the first and most important theoretician of Italian

Renaissance architecture. Born in 1404 in Genoa, Alberti was the illegitimate son of a member of a great Florentine mercantile family that had been exiled from its native city in 1387 by political rivals. He was educated in Latin and Greek in Padua, and in law at Bologna, where he also studied mathematics and physics on his own. Deprived of any inheritance, he supported himself as an *abbreviatore* at the papal court. In addition, from 1432 until his death in 1472 he held the living of the priory of San Martino in Gangalandi, west of Florence. Alberti was a considerable stylist in Latin and Italian. He wrote treatises on moral and social subjects, as well as on cartography, painting, sculpture, and, the most substantial of all his writings on the arts, ten books on architecture, *de re aedificatoria* (c.1450). To all these projects Alberti brought prodigious knowledge, indefatigable curiosity, and intellectual powers seldom matched and probably never exceeded by any other architect.

Alberti did not come to architecture through an apprenticeship to an established master, from whom he learned the craft of building. Instead, he approached all the arts as intellectual disciplines, the only possible route for him, given his interests, education and birth. Painting was the first of the arts to which he addressed himself, in *della Pittura* of 1436. This book grew out of his acquaintance with the leading practitioners of the new art that had developed in Florence around 1420. The book, in its Italian version, is dedicated to the architect FILIPPO BRUNELLESCHI. In *della Pittura,* Alberti codified the principles of one point perspective, which Brunelleschi had invented some fifteen years earlier.

We know that during the 1420s and 1430s Alberti tried his hand at painting, sculpture, and perspectival devices. Of these works, only one seems to have survived: a profile self portrait on a bronze plaque (Kress Collection, National Gallery of Art, Washington), that shows Alberti at a relatively young age. (Another profile portrait, on a medal by Matteo de' Pasti, shows him in his forties, and he may also appear, in his sixties, in Andrea Mantegna's frescoes in the Camera degli Sposi, Palazzo Ducale, Mantua, Italy.) Probably his first architectural work was the new apse added to the medieval church at San Martino in Gangalandi of the 1430s or early 1440s. This semicircular apse, covered in white stucco, is articulated by six channeled, grey stone pilasters, four on the curve and two at the corners. The pilasters support an entablature, with an inscribed frieze, from which the white stucco curve of a half dome rises. In this work Alberti clearly took up the approach to architecture first established by Brunelleschi in the Old Sacristy of San Lorenzo, Florence, around 1420.

de re aedificatoria. The importance of *de re aedificatoria* for the subsequent history of architecture is incalculable. In it Alberti succeeded simultaneously in turning the fragmented knowledge of architecture that had come down from antiquity into a coherent whole; in establishing architecture as an intellectual discipline, rather than a craft; in wedding history to theory, and joining both to practice; and in setting down a flexible approach to architectural design, and to the architecture of antiquity that could guide other architects and their clients, even in other times and other lands.

Begun in the 1440's, the work was presented by Alberti to Pope Nicholas V in 1452, according to the 15th century chronicler Mattia Palmieri. Written in Latin, so that it was accessible to princes and humanists, but not to craftsmen or most artists, *de re aedificatoria* is a synthesis of Alberti's vast knowledge of ancient authors; of his painstaking investigation of any ancient building from which he thought he could learn; of building practices and technical knowledge gleaned from countless sources.

In imitation of the Roman architect VITRUVIUS, whose treatise, *de architectura,* is the only work on architecture to come down from antiquity, Alberti divided his work, the first modern treatment of the subject, into ten books. But, as Richard Krautheimer (1963) has pointed out, Alberti organized the material in a far more consistent way than that employed by his Roman predecessor. Vitruvius said that good architecture consists of three parts, *Utilitas, Firmitas,* and *Venustas* (function, structure, and design, in modern parlance). Alberti used these categories as the three concepts around which he organized his whole work. Book one is an introduction. Books two and three deal with *Firmitas,* books four and five with *Utilitas,* and books six through nine with *Venustas.* Book ten then takes up questions of water supply and the restoration of buildings.

In book one, Alberti defines the architect as "him who with sure and perfect method knows how to project rationally and to realize practically, by means of moving weights and joining bodies, works that are adapted in the most beautiful way to the most dignified uses of man. To this end he needs a knowledge of the best and most learned disciplines." In book nine, Alberti returns to describe the architect:

Architecture is a great thing, which cannot be undertaken by all. One must have intelligence, and persevering zeal, the best knowledge and long practice, and above all grave and severe judgment and counsel to succeed in the profession of architect. For in matters of building the first glory of all is to judge well that which is fitting. To build, in fact, is a necessity. To build conveniently responds to necessity and utility, but to build so that one is praised by men of glory and not criticized by the frugal, can only come from the ability of a learned, wise and judicious artist.

The disciplines in which the architect *must* be learned are two, painting and mathematics. Architecture for Alberti is a social art of enormous importance and utility to the individual, the family and the state, whatever the political system.

A central theme of *de re aedificatoria* is the vast variety of building types, which for Alberti derives from the diverse needs of humanity. According to Alberti, architecture should be based on nature, which has developed forms to suit individual organisms. Buildings are divided into two types, public and private. Of the public, temples take pride of place. The temple should be the chief ornament of the city, raised up on a podium in a prominent place. It should have a central plan, preferably a circle, the most perfect form, therefore most appropriate for a house of the gods. (By temple Alberti also means church, but there is some overlap in his discussion between pagan and Christian buildings.) The porticos of temples should be trabeated, and their interior spaces vaulted.

To the temple Alberti opposes the basilica, a public building in which justice is dispensed. Because justice comes from a divine source, the basilica has religious connotations, but it is, according to Alberti's rather strict sense of hierarchy, to be slightly less elevated in treatment—literally, in that the basilica is placed on a lower podium, and figuratively, in that its parts are less noble. The basilica is not vaulted, but covered by an open timber roof.

Although he laments the passing of public entertainments in theaters, amphitheaters and circuses, Alberti gives them as much attention as he gives temples and basilicas. Buildings for public performance formed a major part of the repertoire of ancient architects. He knew about theater design from Vitruvius, and he had before his very eyes the Colosseum and the Circus Maximus. The section on public buildings closes with a discussion of ancient baths, for Alberti a hybrid type, utilizing features of public and private buildings.

Alberti describes building types by analogy. Thus, a house is like a small city. The house is the focus of the section on private buildings. The house of the king rises in the middle of the city and appears open. That of the tyrant is a fortress connected to the city walls, because the tyrant must defend himself, even against his own subjects. "The *rocca* (tyrant's fortress) should be menacing, hard, savage and seem invincible," Alberti writes in a passage that shows his understanding of the psychological power of architectural form.

The house for the private citizen plays a special role in *de re aedificatoria*. Alberti felt a deep affection for the family life he never had, a life he celebrated in his treatise *della famiglia* (c.1441), written a decade or more before *de re aedificatoria*. His concerns in the design of the private house are for convenience, and for the well being of the family and of each individual member. In the town house sobriety is necessary, particularly in the public parts. The family should also have a villa not too far from town. There, architecturally speaking, almost anything goes, as long as it is not obscene.

Alberti begins his discussion of private houses with an invocation to thrift and moderation. Ornament does not depend on expense, but on ingenuity. But lest he be misunderstood, Alberti immediately modifies his statement on thrift: "Because it is good to pass on a fame for wisdom and also for power, we build big buildings to seem big to posterity. . . . we are used to ornamenting our houses, for the honor of country and family, and for love of magnificence, which no one will deny to be the duty of every good man." Alberti, of course, means that magnificence can be achieved, through ingenuity, in concord with thrift and moderation. Indeed, moderation in all things is Alberti's constant advice to his readers.

One can even say that Alberti's whole argument is unified by a sense of proportion. Proportion, of course, is always relative. In *de re aedificatoria* there are no absolutes, rather a constant urging to do that which is fitting and well considered. In *della pittura* (1436), Alberti laid down the rules for constructing pictures according to the principles of one point perspective. The system depends on a simple proportional observation—that things look smaller, the farther they are away from the viewer. Thus two objects that are side by side on the flat surface of the picture can appear to rest at different points in space by manipulating the size of one relative to the other. This sense of proportional relationship is developed in more complex ways in Alberti's discussion of beauty in architecture.

Because architecture serves many needs, and therefore takes many forms, Alberti felt he could give no absolute rule for beauty. In book six, taking inspiration from Socrates, he says that "beauty is the harmony of all the members, so that nothing can be taken away or added or changed, except for the worse." In book nine he gives more specific advice. Beauty in a building depends on three things, number (*numero*), proportion (*finitio*), and location (*collocatio*). By *numero* Alberti means quite simply, how many of each part. By *finitio* he means proportion, "the reciprocal correspondence between the lines that define the dimensions—

length, width, height." In discussing *finitio,* Alberti states unequivocally: "The numbers that have the power to give consonance to sounds are the same that can fill with joy our eyes and spirits." In other words, the harmonic ratios that have been established for music are equally valid for architecture. *Collocatio* Alberti handles briefly, because, he says, it is easier to tell when it is badly done than to describe how to do it right. By *collocatio* he means the location of the various parts of the building in relation to each other, and the inclusion in a building of only those parts appropriate to it.

These three components produce a total greater than the sum of their parts. That total Alberti calls *concinnitas,* by which he means the ordering of all parts in a building so that they are subservient to the whole: "By natural instinct we aspire to the best. *Concinnitas* I call companion of the soul and mind. Everything that manifests itself in nature is regulated by the laws of *concinnitas,* and nature has no stronger tendency than to make her products perfect." "For that," he adds, "one also wants symmetry."

Concinnitas is not reached effortlessly, at least by Alberti himself. Rather plaintively he wrote: "I have to say that very frequently a conception of a work has come to mind in forms that at first appeared most praiseworthy, but instead, once drawn, they revealed the gravest errors, precisely in those parts that had pleased me most. Returning then afresh and meditating over what I had designed, and measuring the proportions, I recognized and deplored my mistakes."

Beauty, for Alberti, is intrinsic in the work itself, whereas ornament is added. "In all architecture," he writes, "the fundamental ornament is undoubtedly the column." A good part of book six of *de re aedificatoria* is devoted to the rules governing the design of the ancient orders. Proper proportions are essential to the designing of the orders. Indeed, so concerned is Alberti that his numbers in this section be transmitted correctly that twice he enjoins copyists of his manuscript to spell out the numbers, rather than write them in Roman numerals, which are subject to error in transcription.

The section on the orders is the one part of *de re aedificatoria* that deals pedantically with ancient architecture, but Alberti was not a slavish student of the past. He was, as Krautheimer aptly put it, a counselor at antiquity; at the same time he knew the limits of antiquity's usefulness for his own time. We do not, he wrote, "have to hold ourselves strictly to [the ancients'] schemes and take up each and every one in our works, as if they were unquestionable laws; rather, having their lessons as points of departure, we will seek to find new solutions,

and to arrive at a glory equal to theirs, if not greater."

Alberti's only preserved architectural drawing, save for a notation in a letter about the Tempio Malatestiano, has been published by Howard Burns (1979). A plan for a bath building, it consists of some thin ink lines drawn, not completely accurately, with the aid of a straight edge. The drawing bears out Alberti's advice in *de re aedificatoria* that architectural drawings should be nude and simple, so that one admires the mind rather than the hand of the designer. Burns believes that the drawing demonstrates that Alberti made use of numerous interrelated proportional systems within the same building. For whom the drawing was made, and for what purpose we do not know.

The Rome of Nicholas V. When Alberti wrote *de re aedificatoria,* he had had little experience as an architect. During the years of the pontificate of Nicholas V (1447–1455) he was active in Rome, probably helping to direct parts of Nicholas's ambitious scheme to reconstruct many of the city's churches. Alberti was probably involved in the refurbishing of the Aqua Vergine, the only ancient aqueduct that still functioned, and he may have had a hand in designing its modest terminal fountain, with arms of Nicholas V, that was replaced in the eighteenth century by the stupendous Fontana di Trevi. Alberti may also have taken part in the remodeling of the little, domed, circular church of San Teodoro on the slopes of the Palatine Hill. Certainly the round arched portico, topped by a triangular gable and bearing the arms of Nicholas V, prefigures ideas developed in Alberti's later documented church façades. We know, from book ten of *de re aedificatoria,* that he had a project for restoring the clerestory walls of Old St. Peter's that had leaned dangerously out of plumb. For Nicholas he designed a roof, supported on columns, to cover the Ponte Sant'Angelo; GIORGIO VASARI owned a drawing for this unexpected project.

Nicholas V, a man of extraordinary abilities, began a far reaching scheme for the renewal and reconstruction of Rome that set a pattern carried out by subsequent popes and culminated, two hundred years later, in the great urbanistic plans of Alexander VII. The restoration of decaying churches and aqueducts was important to Nicholas only as part of a far more comprehensive scheme for the entire city. Nicholas V's plan for Rome is the first systematic scheme for reorganizing a city in post-medieval times. The originality and grandeur of the conception have led scholars to suggest that Alberti's mind was behind the plans, even though his name is never mentioned in such a context in contemporary documents. The most recent writer on the subject, Carroll William

Westfall (1974), argues vigorously that the conceptions must have been Alberti's. Given that conceptually the Nicholas V plan is strongly Albertian, the actual buildings erected by Nicholas show little, if any, evidence of Alberti's hand.

Alberti's architectural career in Rome under subsequent popes is unknown. Certain parts of buildings seem to bear Albertian character, particularly the coffered barrel vault of the entrance hall to Palazzo Venezia, begun in 1455 by Cardinal Pietro Barbo, who enlarged the palace after he became Pope Paul II in 1464.

Tempio Malatestiano in Rimini. Sigismondo Malatesta, lord of Rimini, gave Alberti his first major commission. (Alberti may have had a hand in the designing of the Arco del Cavallo in Ferrara in the 1440s, but the attribution is far from certain.) In 1447 Sigismondo began to construct a chapel at the southwest corner of the Gothic church of San Francesco in Rimini, in which the Malatesta had long been buried. In 1450, however, Sigismondo decided to remodel the entire interior. At the same time, or perhaps a year later, Sigismondo called on Alberti to design a new shell to encase the old church. Work plunged ahead in 1451, but ten years later the building was abandoned by Sigismondo, as his political fortunes crumbled.

Alberti's project survives in a medal struck by Matteo de'Pasti, the architect in charge of the interior remodeling. The medal shows the elevation of the west façade on which four engaged columns, raised on a tall stylobate, flank two niches and a central portal. Above, two pilasters frame a large window and support a round arch capped by foliate ornament. Segmental curves mark the west

ends of the side roofs. Behind the façade a hemispherical, ribbed dome rises from a presumably circular drum.

As the church now stands, the façade is incomplete, and the domed east end unbuilt. There were changes in the design during construction. The niches, intended to hold sarcophagi, were walled up for structural reasons, while the curved side roofs were replaced by sloping, straight roofs. This latter change Alberti had made by the fall of 1454, when he sketched the right roof, capped by a volute, in a letter (Morgan Library, New York) to Matteo de'Pasti.

Under each arch on the south flank was placed the sarcophagus of a distinguished humanist of Sigismondo's court. The corner pier carries an inscription, in Greek, that declares the church Sigismondo's gift to God and his city in thanksgiving for his victories. The notion of triumph, of course, is conveyed in the façade itself, which is based closely on the triumphal arch of Augustus that stands a few blocks away. The flanks are derived from the lower story of the Mausoleum of Theodoric in nearby Ravenna, where sarcophagi still stood under the arches in the fifteenth century. The temple is Alberti's most archeologically correct design. He deliberately let his sources show, to make the parallels between ancient and modern triumphs, and ancient and modern rulers clear. The façade and flanks of the Tempio, with their robust relief, their strong play of light and shade, of mass and void, mark the first recreation of the spirit, as well as the detail of Roman architecture since antiquity.

The question of the nature of the rotunda is still very much open. From the medal we cannot be sure of its size, nor can we tell the exact plan or placement of the dome in relation to the nave. There must be some connection between the rotunda and the one Michelozzo designed in 1444 for the Santissima Annunziata in Florence—a building on which Alberti himself worked in the last years of his life. Clearly, the triumphal arch façade and the domed rotunda were intended to form one structure that memorialized the Malatesta family. That purpose sings out in the beautiful inscription, in Roman capitals surely designed by Alberti himself, that runs across the frieze of the façade, the first of many such dynastic celebrations inscribed on the façades of churches in the fifteenth and subsequent centuries.

The Tomb of Leonardo Bruni. Alberti's name has, from time to time, been associated with the architectural setting of the tomb of the great humanist and statesman, Leonardo Bruni (d.1444), in the church of Santa Croce in Florence. The sculpture of the tomb is clearly the work of

Alberti.
San Francesco (Tempio Malatestiano; never completed).
Rimini, Italy.
1450?–1461

BERNARDO ROSSELLINO and his workshop, and the tomb would seem to date between 1446 and 1451.

Nothing in Rossellino's known architectural work prepares us for the clarity, simplicity of proportional relations and unity of parts in the Bruni tomb, which is ultimately related to the portal of the Pantheon, a source that Alberti tapped for the main portal of Santa Maria Novella (1458–1471) and the central arch of Sant'Andrea in Mantua (1470–1481). Like the tomb, the façade of the Tempio Malatestiano (designed c.1450), was to have contained sarcophagi in the round arched niches flanking the main portal. Finally, there is the crucial question of the inscription on the Bruni tomb. In earlier fifteenth century Florentine tombs, such as the Coscia monument in the Florentine Baptistry by Donatello and MICHELOZZO DI BARTOLOMEO, the inscription is raised high above the viewer, whereas in the Bruni tomb it lies squarely at eye level. In de re aedificatoria, written while the Bruni tomb was being erected, Alberti states: "We are disposed to accept any site for a sepulchre, as long as the name of the dead is placed in a preeminent place." Even if Alberti himself were not consulted about the tomb (I would tend to see him as a consultant laying out the general disposition and proportions), whoever did conceive the remarkable new architectural scheme of the Bruni tomb must have been acquainted with Alberti's thinking while he was writing de re aedificatoria.

Palazzo Rucellai. For the Palazzo Rucellai in Florence (1452?–1470?), Alberti was the architect only of the façade. Giovanni Rucellai acquired the site of the palace between 1428 and 1466, starting from the house in which he was born at the corner of Via della Vigna and Via del Palchetto. By 1446 he had acquired all of the houses located behind the first five bays of the façade, counting from his birthplace at the left, and by 1452 he seems to have completed extensive interior remodeling. The façade was a separate project, conceived after the completion of the interior. Scholars do not agree on the date of the façade design. Brenda Preyer (1981) argues for a date of c.1455 for a first façade project, five bays wide, that was completed by 1458, the year in which Giovanni Rucellai acquired the house that is covered by bays six and seven. Preyer dates the actual construction of these bays, and the partly executed eighth bay, between 1465 and 1470. Preyer demonstrates convincingly that the quality of execution in bays six and seven is greatly inferior to the work in the first five bays, except for the decorated frieze of the lowest order. That frieze, of high quality, is continuous across the whole of the completed façade.

Others argue, because of the alternating emblems of three feathers and two feathers projecting from a diamond ring carved in this frieze, that the façade design must postdate 1461, the year in which Giovanni's son became engaged to a granddaughter of Cosimo de'Medici. The feather and ring emblems can be seen as Medicean, but Preyer has shown that other Italian families used the same *imprese.* Actually, the archeological evidence suggests that the ground floor frieze was finally carved only after the façade had been brought to its present state of completion.

Rucellai also built, across the street from the palace, a three-bay loggia, attributed to Alberti by Vasari, who has been followed by some modern scholars. The loggia violates a rule laid down in *de re aedificatoria* and never transgressed in any building surely by Alberti—that is, arches should be supported by piers, not by columns, as they are in the Rucellai loggia. For this reason, the Vasari attribution seems dubious.

A new type of palace for Florentine aristocrats had been established by Michelozzo in the house he designed for Cosimo de' Medici in the 1440s. From the Medici palace Alberti borrowed the heavy stone capping cornice and the two part windows (*bifore*) placed under round arches. The Rucellai design, however, uses a constantly flat ashlar surface, in contrast to the widely varied depths of relief employed by Michelozzo. In addition, and more importantly for the future history of domestic architecture, Alberti applied the ancient orders to his design, thus claiming them for the private house, as well as for public buildings.

The source for Alberti's design is generally assumed to be Roman—the arched orders of the Colosseum are frequently cited. It is not typical of Alberti, however, to take an idea devised for an amphitheater and transfer it to the house of a Florentine banker. One wonders if Alberti may not rather have been inspired by an Etruscan funerary urn in the form of a private house. One such urn, preserved in the Museo Archeologico in Florence, shows, on its short side, an arrangement of pilasters, smooth surfaced ashlar blocks separated by grooves, and a round arched opening that suggest the Rucellai façade. The rectangular field on the long side contains a kind of abstracted *opus reticulatum* like that of the ground floor of the Rucellai palace. We do not know if Alberti ever came in contact with such an urn, but Etruscan objects, unearthed in the fifteenth century, were the cause of widespread interest. Alberti discussed Etruscan architecture, as he knew it from Vitruvius, in *de re aedificatoria,* and he cited it as a precedent in his letter of 1470 concerning Sant'Andrea in Mantua.

In Alberti's façade, each change in depth acts to clarify the design, as do the textural shifts from smooth pilasters to beveled joints. The stone blocks that separate the windows and pilasters read horizontally as part of the over-all wall surface, yet, ambiguously, the same blocks form piers that support the round arches of the windows. The actual blocks of stone that make up the revetment are much larger than they appear. Each large stone has been carved, probably *in situ,* into the small blocks we see. Here the border between relief sculpture and architecture is blurred. Indeed, Alberti's façade is the closest architectural equivalent we have to Donatello's *rilievo schiacciato.* It may also be related to the painted palace façades found in Florence from c.1450.

Santa Maria Novella, Florence. The façade of Santa Maria Novella (1458–1471) was Alberti's second commission from Giovanni Rucellai. Probably, Alberti's design dates from 1458. The upper entablature bears a date of 1470, by which time the façade was complete, save for the marble encrustation of the right volute, added in modern times.

Alberti was confronted with a partly completed façade (the church was begun c.1300) that included three doors and six tombs that were part of an over-all decorative scheme of green and white marble that rose up at least as far as the capitals of the thin pilasters, clearly fourteenth century. To this lower part of the façade Alberti engaged four tall green marble half columns. He widened the façade by adding striped corner piers that rise outside the columns from a common socle. In the center, he filled the splayed main portal to create

the rectangular, arched door that derives directly from the portal of the Pantheon.

Across the lower part of the façade runs an entablature, with the Rucellai sail in the frieze. Above this entablature Alberti built a high attic story, decorated with green marble squares and capped by its own cornice. The rose window of the upper façade is framed by a temple front motif flanked by volutes that conceal the lines of the aisle roofs.

Alberti advocated simple proportions for buildings. Thus he widened the façade and built the attic to arrive at a ground floor relationship of 1 to 2, if one measures across the façade from outer corner to outer corner, and from ground to cornice over attic. The temple front, from attic cornice to gable, can be inscribed in a square equal to one half of the lower façade. Thus Alberti gave the old structure the kinds of proportions that pleased him, but he had to resort to unusually tall, almost Gothic proportions for his columns and pilasters. These thin members accord better with the old pilasters of the lower story, however, in a way that helps to tie old and new together, a procedure that Alberti consistently championed.

The design is closely related to the twelfth-century façade of San Miniato al Monte, Alberti's self-confessed favorite building. The polychromed marble encrustation, the engaged green marble half columns on the lower story, the column and pier on a common socle at each corner, the four pilaster temple front of the upper story—all derive from this jewel of the Florentine Romanesque. For Alberti, Florentine medieval architecture reflected the architecture of Florence in antiquity, and so it was a doubly resonant source. Alberti fused Florentine medieval traditions, as transmitted through the façade of San Miniato, with the classical vocabulary he had learned from antiquity. He created, at the same time, an archetypal classicized church façade that would become the most widespread type used in the Renaissance and Baroque periods.

The Rucellai Chapel in San Pancrazio, Florence. The Rucellai chapel in San Pancrazio (1460–1467) belongs to that select group of family mausolea constructed by important Florentines in the new style of the fifteenth century—the Old Sacristy at San Lorenzo (Medici) and the Pazzi Chapel at Santa Croce. Alberti reused a rectangular room attached to the northwest corner of the old church; he raised the walls slightly and covered the whole with a barrel vault. The two free-standing Corinthian columns that originally separated the chapel from the nave have now been moved to the façade of the church.

The gray and white chapel contains a jewellike building within a building, a "reconstruction" of

the Holy Sepulchre in Jerusalem, as that famous shrine could be "copied" by a man of the fifteenth century who had never seen it. (The oft cited letter of Giovanni Rucellai to his mother, in which he says that he has sent someone to Jerusalem to bring back measurements, has been demonstrated to be a forgery). A rectangular block terminated by a semicircular eastern apse, the shrine is encrusted with a rich, polychromed marble revetment of extraordinarily refined craftsmanship. Once again Alberti revived this Tuscan medieval practice.

Although the designs for Sigismondo Malatesta and Giovanni Rucellai are all based on ancient prototypes, there is a striking difference between the prototypes chosen. At Rimini and Florence, Alberti used *local* sources, demonstrating that very appropriateness he had advocated eloquently in *de re aedificatoria.*

An inscription over the low door that leads into the interior of the shrine gives the date of 1467 for its completion. The inception of the design probably falls, therefore, between those of the two Mantuan churches, San Sebastiano and Sant'Andrea.

Alberti.
Santa Maria Novella
  (façade).
Florence.
1458–1471

Alberti.
Rucellai Chapel.
San Pancrazio.
Florence.
1460–1467

San Sebastiano in Mantua. San Sebastiano (1460–1472) was the first commission Alberti realized from the Gonzagas, whose favor he had courted since the 1430s, when he dedicated the Latin text of *De Pictura* to Gianfrancesco Gonzaga, first marquess of Mantua. Gianfrancesco's son, Lodovico, however, became Alberti's close friend and patron. As early as 1459, while Alberti was part of the papal entourage at the Council of Mantua, Lodovico may have been planning to build San Sebastiano, which was begun in great haste in the spring of 1460, apparently after a dream had galvanized Lodovico into action.

Alberti's original plan for the church has probably come down to us in three sixteenth-century drawings, the most useful of which is by Antonio Labacco (Uffizi 1779A). This plan shows a building with a square central space, from which radiate four rectangular arms. Three of these terminate in semicircular apses, while the fourth or west arm opens through three doors into a transversely poised portico. A sketch below the plan shows the building from the exterior, with the central square covered by a hemispherical dome capped by a lantern. To the left of this sketch Labacco recorded the major dimensions of the space, which in almost all cases accord very well with the building as it stands. Richard Lamoureux (1979) has demonstrated that the measurements show that Alberti used very simple ratios in the design.

As constructed, the building differs from the Labacco drawing in several respects. The whole church is raised up on a crypt, created by a forest of thirty-six square piers. The doors at the north and south ends of the porch were suppressed and replaced by two additional openings in the west wall, and two square, domed chambers were constructed north and south of the west arm of the church. Lamoureux believes that the Labacco drawing shows a first stage in the design; the church as built probably resulted from the intervention of Lodovico Gonzaga in the design process.

Since the restoration of the church in the 1920s, two sets of steps have led to the outer openings. Earlier, access to the upper church was gained through a staircase to the left of the façade, that was not part of the original construction. How Alberti would have arranged steps to the upper church, or doors to the crypt, remains a matter of conjecture. Lamoureux has suggested three possibilities. The third, two flights moving toward the outer façade openings, then turning ninety degrees to reach a landing in front of the central opening, may be preferable, because it most happily accommodates a central crypt portal. This solution may be reflected in the staircases designed by Giuliano da Sangallo (see SANGALLO FAMILY) for the villa of Lorenzo de' Medici at Poggio a Cajano.

San Sebastiano is the first of the long line of freestanding, domed churches on Greek cross plans. In it, Alberti fused two Roman mausolea types (square with radiating arms, usually cross vaulted, and circular, with dome and often with crypt) with the Roman porticoed temple set on a podium. All this he put to contemporary Christian and dynastic purposes. Placed on the largely uninhabited southern edge of Mantua, San Sebastiano recalled in its isolation Roman mausolea along, say, the Via Appia, while its dome was intended as a monumental statement, of the ambitions of Lodovico Gonzaga as a ruler and patron of the arts. It seems likely that Lodovico planned one of the small domed rooms off the west arm of the church as his burial chamber.

The Tribuna of the Santissima Annunziata, Florence. In 1444, Piero de' Medici, son of Cosimo de' Medici, the "political boss" of Florence, initiated an elaborate project to reconstruct the Gothic church of the Santissima Annunziata. This design, by Michelozzo, included the addition of a large rotunda, partly surrounded by seven semicircular chapels, to the west wall of the old rectangular apse. In 1449, Lodovico Gonzaga, who had been named captain of the Florentine armies two years earlier, agreed to spend two thousand of his five

thousand ducat salary as captain on the tribuna, an act motivated by political reasons. Lodovico needed the friendship of Florence to help maintain his independence from his voracious neighbors, Milan and Venice. By 1455, the walls of the rotunda had reached a height of roughly eight meters, and the chapels had been vaulted, when work came to an almost complete halt for fifteen years.

Alberti entered the picture probably in 1470, when Lodovico agreed to spend his entire five thousand ducats on the rotunda. Michelozzo's rotunda would scarcely have been visible from the rest of the church. Alberti opened up a grand triumphal arch between tribune and apse, eliminating not only the old west apse wall, but also the two chapels that flanked it. To replace these chapels, Alberti added two semicircular chapels to either side of the triumphal arch. The arch allowed Alberti to fuse the two parts of the building as best he could. The height of the arch, however, forced the raising of the roof of the old church. Alberti's other major contribution to the tribuna seems to have been the hemispherical dome without a lantern, Alberti's plan became the object of some very complicated and heated political maneuvering, as well as some legitimate functional objections. Only a serious threat by Lodovico Gonzaga to withdraw his support for the project stilled criticism and allowed the tribuna to be finished. At the end of the sixteenth century the sculptor Giovanni da Bologna rebuilt the eastern chapel of the rotunda in rectangular form, and in the seventeenth century a giant order of pilasters was inserted between the openings of the side chapels.

Sant'Andrea in Mantua.   Sant'Andrea in Mantua (1470–1472), Alberti's last major architectural design, is his masterpiece. Lodovico Gonzaga planned work at the eleventh-century church of Sant'Andrea as early as 1460. Alberti's involvement dates from October 1470, when he sent an unsolicited design for the new church to Lodovico. Alberti's drawings are lost, but the remarkable letter that accompanied them is preserved. He wrote:

Also I understood in these days that your Highness and these your citizens were thinking of building here at Sant'Andrea. And that your principal intention was to have a great space where many people would be able to see the Blood of Christ. I saw that model of Manetti's. I liked it. But to me it does not seem apt to your intentions. I have thought and conjectured about that which I send you. This will be more capacious, more lasting, more worthy, and happier. It will cost much less. This type of temple was called by the ancients the Etruscan. If it should please you, I will draw it up in proportion.

This letter sums up diplomatically Alberti's acute understanding of the problem to be solved.

Alberti.
Sant'Andrea (*interior*).
Mantua, Italy.
1470–1472 (*not completed until 1481*)

Sant'Andrea shelters two vases said to contain blood shed by the crucified Christ, mixed with earth from Calvary. In 1401 Francesco Gonzaga instituted the practice of displaying the vases annually on Ascension Day, an event that swiftly began to attract hordes of pilgrims. The new church had to accommodate throngs of pilgrims in a large space with good sight lines, and Alberti's plan accomplished precisely these ends. Sant'Andrea has a Latin-cross plan, measuring, on the interior, 99.66 meters from portal to apse and 18.6 meters across the nave. The nave is flanked to either side by three large, barrel vaulted chapels separated by large masonry piers. The piers are hollowed out to form small, square, domed chapels that communicate with the nave through rectangular portals. The wide nave offered ample space for the faithful who came to view the relics, while the domed crossing provided a fitting space for their display. The plan breaks conclusively with the traditional Christian basilical form of nave flanked by aisles that persisted from the fourth century through the fifteenth. While at least one earlier *quattrocento* church, the Badia in Fiesole (begun 1461) has a similar plan, Sant'Andrea was the building that really established a new type of Christian church with vaulted nave flanked by vaulted side chapels, rather than aisles.

The building history of Sant'Andrea is long and complex. What we see today was erected over a 300 year period, from 1472, when the foundations of the nave and west porch were laid, to 1781, when the dome, designed in 1732 by FILIPPO JUVARRA, was brought to completion. The façade, which abuts a late Gothic tower, represents a fusion of two classical prototypes: the triumphal arch and the pedimented temple front. The width

Alberti.
Sant'Andrea.
Mantua, Italy.
1470–1472 (not completed
until 1481)

of the façade is equal to its height, so that the whole design can be inscribed in a square. Above the pediment rises a peculiar vaulted structure, called the "big umbrella," because it acts as a parasol over the large round window that lights the nave from the west.

The structure of Sant'Andrea is entirely of brick—brick piers that support brick vaults, and brick walls that separate inside from out. This structural system is expressed metonymically—a typical Albertian device—in the articulation of the nave walls. The pilasters are applied to the inner ends of the supporting piers, and visually stand for those piers, while the round arches are applied to the chapel vaults, and stand for the vaults. The points of intersection between the vertical and horizontal systems are expressed by the cherub heads in the frieze of the entablature.

The structural system of Sant'Andrea is derived from that of the Pantheon. The brick faced drum that supports the Pantheon's immense dome appears solid, but actually the structure is a honeycomb of piers and vaults that transforms a point support system into a continuous ring of masonry under the dome. No light passes through the Pantheon walls into its interior. Alberti used his structural voids, however, to light his nave, by placing windows high up in the exterior walls of the large chapels, and by allowing light to pass through the piers, above the domes of the small chapels. The interior of Sant'Andrea is richly decorated by frescoes dating from the sixteenth and eighteenth centuries. It is possible that Alberti, in response to

strong local tradition, intended such decorations from the outset. It is notable that the decorations do not obscure the clear architectural system.

At Sant'Andrea Alberti succeeded, to a greater degree than in any of his other buildings, in achieving his purposes as an architect. He erected a building that satisfied his patron's passion to build, to pass on a monument to posterity, and to embellish his city with the noblest form of architecture, the temple. In his design, Alberti reused elements of the past, ancient and even medieval, in the service of the present; he produced beauty economically (Sant'Andrea, for its size, was cheap to build); and he conceived a building that served both its function and its site well. Alberti's skillful manipulation of proportions and details on the west façade, the inspired visual continuity between exterior and interior, the breath stopping sense of spatial expansion entering the nave from the west, and the beautifully modulated, silvery light inside combine to make Sant'Andrea one of the noblest buildings in western architecture.

EUGENE J. JOHNSON

WORKS

1430?–1440?, San Martino Priory (apse), Gangalandi, Italy. 1450?–1461, San Francesco (Tempio Malatestiano; never completed), Rimini, Italy. 1452?–1470?, Palazzo Rucellai (façade); 1458–1471, Santa Maria Novella (façade); 1460–1467, Rucellai Chapel, San Pancrazio; Florence. 1460–1472, San Sebastiano (not completed until 1529?); 1470–1472, Sant'Andrea (not completed until 1481); Mantua, Italy. 1470–1472, Santissima Annunziata (tribuna; not completed until 1481), Florence.

BIBLIOGRAPHY

ACCADEMIA NAZIONALE DEI LINCEI, ROME   1974 *Convegno internazionale indetto nel V centenario di Leon Battista Alberti (Rome-Mantova-Firenze, 25–29 aprile 1972).* Rome: Bardi.

ALBERTI, LEON BATTISTA   1972   *On Painting and Sculpture.* Edited and translated by Cecil Grayson. London: Phaidon.

ALBERTI, LEON BATTISTA   (c.1441)1971   *The Albertis of Florence: Leon Battista Alberti's Della famiglia.* Translation, introduction, and notes by Guido A. Guarino. Lewisburg, Penn.: Bucknell University Press.

ALBERTI, LEON BATTISTA   (1485)1966   *Alberti's Ten Books on Architecture.* Edited by John Rykwert. Translated by James Leoni. Reprint. New York: Transatlantic Arts. Originally published with the title *de re aedificatoria.*

BORSI, FRANCO   (1975)1977   *Leon Battista Alberti.* Translated by Rudolf Carpanini. Oxford: Phaidon; New York: Harper.

BROWN, BEVERLY LOUISE   1978   "The Tribuna of SS. Annunziata in Florence." Unpublished Ph.D. dissertation, Northwestern University, Evanston, Ill.

BURNS, HOWARD 1979 "A Drawing by L. B. Alberti." *Architectural Design* 49, nos. 5-6:45-56.

CHAMBERS, DAVID SANDERSON 1977 "Sant'Andrea at Mantua and Gonzaga Patronage: 1460-1472." *Journal of the Warburg and Courtauld Institutes* 40:99-127.

DEZZI BARDESCHI, MARCO 1966 "Il complesso monumentale di San Pancrazio a Firenze e il suo restauro." *Quaderni dell' Istituto di Storia dell' Architettura* 13, nos. 73-78:1-66.

DEZZI BARDESCHI, MARCO 1970 *La Facciata di Santa Maria Novella.* Pisa, Italy: Nistri Lischi.

FACOLTA DI ARCHITETTURA, FLORENCE UNIVERSITY 1972 *Omaggio ad Alberti.* Vol. 1 in *Studi e Documenti di Architettura.* Florence: Teorema.

FORSTER, KURT W. 1976 "The Palazzo Rucellai and Questions of Typology in the Development of Renaissance Buildings." *Art Bulletin* 58:109-113.

GADOL, JOAN 1969 *Leon Battista Alberti: Universal Man of the Early Renaissance.* University of Chicago Press.

GRAYSON, CECIL 1960 "The Composition of L. B. Alberti's *Decem libri de re aedificatoria.*" *Münchner Jahrbuch der Bildenden Kunst* 11:152-161.

GRAYSON, CECIL 1979 "Leon Battista Alberti: Architect" *Architectural Design* 49, nos. 5-6:7-17.

HORSTER, MARITA 1973 "Brunelleschi und Alberti in ihrer Stellung zur Römischen Antike." *Mitteilungen des Kunthistorischen Institutes in Florenz* 17:29-64.

JOHNSON, EUGENE J. 1975a "A Portrait of Leon Battista Alberti in the Camera degli sposi?" *Arte Lombarda* 42-43:67-69.

JOHNSON, EUGENE J. 1975b *S. Andrea in Mantua: The Building History.* London and University Park: Pennsylvania State University Press.

KENT, F. W. 1974 "The Letters Genuine and Spurious of Giovanni Rucellai." *Journal of the Warburg and Courtauld Institutes* 37:342-349.

KLOTZ, HEINRICH 1969 "L. B. Alberti's 'De re aedificatoria' in Theorie und Praxis." *Zeitschrift für Kunstgeschichte* 32:93-103.

KRAUTHEIMER, RICHARD (1961)1969 "Alberti's Templum Etruscum." Pages 62-72 in *Studies in Early Christian, Medieval, and Renaissance Art.* Reprint. New York University Press.

KRAUTHEIMER, RICHARD (1963)1969 "Alberti and Vitruvius." Pages 42-52 in *Studies in Early Christian, Medieval, and Renaissance Art.* Reprint. New York University Press.

LAMOUREUX, RICHARD E. 1979 *Alberti's Church of San Sebastiano in Mantua.* London and New York: Garland.

LORENZ, HELMUT 1976 "Zur Architektur L. B. Albertis: Die Kirchenfassaden." *Wiener Jahrbuch für Kunstgeschichte* 29:65-100.

MACK, CHARLES RANDALL 1974 "The Rucellai Palace: Some New Proposals." *Art Bulletin* 56:517-529.

MANCINI, GIROLAMO (1911)1967 *Vita di Leon Battista Alberti.* Reprint 2d ed. Rome: Bardi.

MARANI, ERCOLANI (editor) 1974 *Il Sant' Andrea di Mantova e Leon Battista Alberti.* Mantua, Italy: Biblioteca Communale di Mantova.

MITCHELL, CHARLES 1973 "An Early Christian Model for the Tempio Malatestiano." In Peter Block (editor), *Intuition und Kunstwissenschaft: Festschrift für Hanns Swarzenski.* Berlin: Mann.

NAREDI-RAINER, PAUL VON 1976 "Bemerkungen zur Säule bei L. B. Alberti." *Jahrbuch des Kunsthistorischen Institutes der Universität Graz* 11:51-61.

PARRONCHI, ALESSANDRO 1972 "Otto piccoli documenti per la biografia dell' Alberti." *Rinascimento* 12:229-235.

PREYER, BRENDA 1977 "The Rucellai Loggia." *Mitteilungen des Kunsthistorischen Institutes in Florenz* 21:183-198.

PREYER, BRENDA 1981 "The Rucellai Palace." Pages 155-225 in *Giovanni Rucellai ed il suo Zibaldone II: A Florentine Patrician and His Palace.* London: Warburg and Courtauld Institutes.

RICCI, CORRADO 1925 *Il Tempio Malatestiano.* Milan and Rome: Bestetti & Tumminelli.

RIMINI, CITTA DI 1970 *Sigismondo Pandolfo Malatesta e il suo Tempo.* Vicenza, Italy: Neri Pozza.

RITSCHER, ERNST 1899 "Die Kirche S. Andrea in Mantua." *Zeitschrift für Bauwesen* 49:1-20, 181-200.

SCHULZ, ANNE MARKHAM 1977 *The Sculpture of Bernardo Rossellino and His Workshop.* N.J.: Princeton University Press.

TEUBNER, HANS 1978 "Das Langhaus der SS. Annunziata in Florenz." *Mitteilungen des Kunsthistoristchen Institutes in Florenz* 22:27-60.

VAGNETTI, LUIGI 1973 "Concinnitas; riflessioni sul significato di un termine albertiano." *Studi e documenti di architettura* 2:137-161.

VERGA, CORRADO 1977 *Un altro malatestiano.* Crema, Italy: Donarini e Locatelli.

WESTFALL, CARROLL WILLIAM 1974 *In This Most Perfect Paradise: Alberti, Nicholas V, and the Invention of Conscious Urban Planning in Rome, 1447-55.* London and University Park: Pennsylvania State University Press.

WITTKOWER, RUDOLF (1949)1971 *Architectural Principles in the Age of Humanism.* Reprint. New York: Norton.

ALBERTI, MATTEO

Born in Venice, Italy, Matteo Alberti (1660?-1716), engraver as well as architect, studied initially in Paris. He then became a hydraulic engineer in Venice, where he supervised the maintenance of canals and seawalls. From 1691 to 1716, he was superintendent of fortifications and civil construction for the German Elector. Alberti died in Düsseldorf, Germany.

SARA LEHRMAN

WORKS

1700-1716, Bensberg Castle, Mülheim-am-Rhein, Germany. 1709-1712, Ursuline Church (façade), Cologne, Germany.

BIBLIOGRAPHY

DOBISCH, W. 1938 "Das neue Schloss zu Bensberg." *Rheinischer Verein für Denkmalpflege und Heimatschutz* 31:15ff.

HERMANIN, F. 1934 "L'Opera del genio italiano all'estero." Volume 1 in *Gli artisti italiani in Germania.* Rome.

HESPE, R., and FERRARI, G. E. 1960 "Alberti, M." *Dizionario Biografico degli Italiani.* Rome: Giovanni Treccami.

MARZOLO, FRANCESCO, and GHETTI, A. 1949 *Fiumi, lagune e boni-fiche Veneteane: Guida bibliografica.* Padua, Italy: ACEDAM.

ALBINI, FRANCO

Franco Albini (1905–1977) was one of the more influential Italian architects of the post-World War II era. Born in Robbiate, near Como, he received his diploma from the Milan Politecnico in 1929 and designed some important buildings and exhibits during the 1930s. Albini emerged in the postwar period as a leader of Italian architecture with a series of renovations of Renaissance palaces and the celebrated museum of the Tesoro di San Lorenzo (1952) in Genoa. These works, along with the larger and more ambitious Rinascente Store (1957–1961) in Rome and the Milan Metro Stations (1962–1963), all display Albini's attention to simple detail and absolute elegance of line.

THOMAS L. SCHUMACHER

WORKS

1936, Fabio Filzi Quarter Project (with R. Camus and G. PALANTI); 1936, Room for One Person, Milan Triennale Exhibit. 1937, Palace of Italian Civilization Project, EUR, Rome, 1938, Milano Verde Urban Project (with G. Pagano, Camus, Palanti, and G. Mazzoleni), Milan. 1950, Palazzo Bianco (renovations); 1952, Tesoro di San Lorenzo (renovations); 1952–1961, Palazzo Rosso (renovations); Genoa, Italy. 1957–1961, La Rinascente Department Store, Rome. 1962–1963, Stations (with Franca Heig), Milan Metro.

BIBLIOGRAPHY

GREGOTTI, VITTORIO 1968 *New Directions in Italian Architecture.* New York: Braziller.

MOSCHINI, F. 1979 *Franco Albini.* London: Academy Editions.

SAMONÀ, GIUSEPPE 1958 "Franco Albini e la Cultura Architettonica in Italia." *Zodiac* 3:83–115.

SETA, CESARE DE' 1972 *La Cultura Architettonica in Italia tra le due Guerre.* Bari, Italy: Laterza.

ALDRICH, CHESTER

See DELANO and ALDRICH.

ALDRICH, HENRY

Henry Aldrich (1648–1710), dean of Christ Church, Oxford, had a considerable reputation for learning, being skilled in music and architecture as well as in mathematics and the classics. Two volumes of his drawings survive and show him to have been a skilled draftsman. His personal papers were, however, destroyed in accordance with his will and therefore our knowledge of his architectural activities is limited. His one authenticated work, the Peckwater Quadrangle (1707–1714), is extraordinary in the context of eighteenth-century baroque Oxford in being a conscious piece of early Palladianism (see ANDREA PALLADIO). Aldrich's unfinished scholarly treatise, drawing heavily on VITRUVIUS and Palladio, was published as *Elementa Architecturae Civilis* in 1789.

JOHN BOLD

WORKS

(A)1701–1710, All Saints Church; 1707–1714, Peckwater Quadrangle, Christ Church; Oxford.

BIBLIOGRAPHY

SHERWOOD, JENNIFER, and PEVSNER, NIKOLAUS 1974 *Oxfordshire.* Harmondsworth, England: Penguin.

ALEIJADINHO

Antonio Francisco Lisboa (1738–1814), known as O Aleijadinho (the little cripple), created a uniquely decorative form of baroque architecture in the gold-mining towns of colonial Brazil. The illegitimate son of a Portuguese stonemason and an African slave, Aleijadinho was born near Ouro Prêto in 1738 and became free when baptized. He was struck with a debilitating disease at age thirty-nine, often described as venereal disease or scurvy aggravated by leprosy or possibly zamparna, an epidemic scourge which left its victims partially paralyzed or as in Aleijadinho's case horribly deformed. He lost his toes compelling him to walk on his knees, and later the disease atrophied his fingers which led to the account that his carving tools had to be strapped to his hands.

Little is known about his youth, but his biographer Rodrigo José Ferreira Brêtas referred to him as an energetic figure who as a boy learned to read and write and maintained a special fervor for Biblical scripture giving him inspiration for his many religious sculptures and interior church decorations.

In 1766, Aleijadinho was registered in Brazil as a craftsman and presumably learned his trade as an apprentice to his father. Architecture was not a recognized profession; instead, stonemasons were responsible for church designs and subsequently hired carpenters, craftsmen, and scholars to elaborate on the basic plan. In the same year, Aleijadinho's father died while working on São Francisco de Assis Church in Ouro Prêto and left his son to finish the job. Soapstone, a soft, durable stone which when carved resembles stucco, was Aleijadinho's favorite material and first appeared at this church. The exterior decoration is indicative of Aleijadinho's fine craftsmanship which turned stone into billowing wreaths outlining the main entrance and framing the two upper story windows. In addition, he transformed the façade from a flat cap on the box plan into a sinuous concave-convex form abutted by rounded towers. A few years later at São Francisco de Assis in São João del Rei, he discarded the traditional interior hall plan for the more intimate space of an elliptical nave. Aleijadinho initiated the enhancement of these hall-like churches, which pervaded Brazil during the first part of the gold rush from 1690 until 1800.

As a true baroque artist, he was a master of sculpture as well as architecture, creating a synthesis of forms in his dramatic staircase lined with emotive sculptures of the twelve apostles at the Church of Nosso Senhor do Bom Jesus de Matosinhos in Congonhas do Campo. The deep relief of his applied decoration, the emotional power of his sculptures, and his sensuous architectural designs specifically defined his style.

ELIZABETH D. HARRIS

WORKS

1766–1776, São Francisco de Assis Church (completion); 1767–1780, Nossa Senhora do Carmo Church; Ouro Prêto, Brazil. 1769–1771, Nossa Senhora do Carmo Church, Sabara, Brazil. 1774–1820?, São Francisco de Assis Church, São João del Rei, Brazil. 1777–1805, Nosso Senhor do Bom Jesus de Matosinhos Church (sanctuary, courtyard, and statuary), Congonhas do Campo, Brazil. 1778, Nosso Senhor do Bom Jesus Church (façade decoration), Ouro Prêto, Brazil.

BIBLIOGRAPHY

BAZIN, GERMAIN 1963 *Aleijadinho et la sculpture baroque au Brésil.* Paris: Le Temps.
BRÊTAS, RODRIGO JOSÉ FERREIRA 1951 *Antônio Francisco Lisboa—O Aleijadinho.* Rio de Janeiro: Publicações da Directoria do Património Histórico e Artistico Nacional.
BURY, JOHN B. 1952 "Estilo Aleijadinho and the Churches of Eighteenth Century Brazil." *Architectural Review* 111, Feb.:92–100.
MARIANNO FILHO, JOSÉ 1942 "Da participação de Antonio Francisco Lisboa na arquitetura sacra Mineira." *Estudos de Arte Brasileira* 1942:45–53.
SMITH, ROBERT C., JR. 1939 "The Colonial Architecture of Minas Gerais in Brazil." *Art Bulletin* 21, June:110–159.

Aleijadinho.
Nosso Senhor do Bom Jesus de Matosinhos Church (sanctuary, courtyard, and statuary).
Congonhas do Campo, Brazil.
1777–1805

ALEOTTI, GIOVANNI BATTISTA

Giovanni Battista Aleotti (1546–1636), called L'Argenta after his birthplace, is known not only for his architecture but also for his work as a military and hydraulic engineer, a writer of technical and theoretical treatises, and a stage designer. He served Duke Alfonso II d'Este in Ferrara (1575–1597), where he eventually became city architect in 1598. Aleotti traveled to Rome (1591 and 1601) as well as to other cities such as Modena, Piacenza, and Venice where his technical expertise was in demand. At the turn of the seventeenth century, Aleotti began to receive more prestigious architectural commissions, such as that with Giovanni Battista Magnani for the Church of Santa Maria del Quartiere in Parma (1604). The Church of San Carlo in Ferrara (1613–1623), whose façade is characterized by a dramatic inward and outward thrusting of forms, stands as one of his most striking mature works.

Aleotti's most famous and significant work, however, is the Teatro Farnese in Parma (1618–1628). Originally commissioned in 1617–1618 by Ranuccio I Farnese in anticipation of a visit from Cosimo II de' Medici, it was not completely finished until 1628 and then as part of a marriage celebration between these two families. Aleotti converted the armory in the Pilotta, Palazzo Nuova, into a theater with a U-shaped arrangement of tiered seating opening up onto a stage placed at one end of the rectangular hall, thereby forming a large, open, central space that could accommodate the actors and props of a performance. Although the U-shaped arrangement recalls antique prototypes and is important for later theater design, the position of the stage and the large, open space resembles a tournament theater such as that of BERNARDO BUONTALENTI's in the Uffizi Palace of 1585. Aleotti adopted the double-tiered arcade motif of ANDREA PALLADIO's Basilica to serve as the backdrop for the audience, and this was to be an important source for the galleries of later theaters; an earlier, unexecuted design reveals that Aleotti considered placing seats in between the arches and on top of the cornice. The rectangular proscenium arch defining the stage departs significantly from both the scenae frons of Palladio's Teatro Olimpico and the proscenium of VINCENZO SCAMOZZI's Teatro in Sabbioneta in its size and panoramic scope. It is generally accepted that Aleotti was the first fully to employ stage wings, namely, wooden frames on wheeled undercarriages allowing for several changes of scenery. Aleotti's break with local tradition and style in the sources he chose helped create what many consider to be the model for the modern theater.

WILLIAM B. STARGARD

WORKS

(A)1570s, Palazzo Avogli-Trotti, Ferrara, Italy. 1579, Fortress of Mont-Alfonso (designed by Marcantonio Pase, called Il Montagnana), Garafagnana, Italy. 1579–1583, Castello (designed by Pase), Mesolo, Italy. 1579–1594, Cathedral (campanile; with Alessandro Balbi); 1582, San Pietro (ramparts); 1583–1585, Palazzo Bentivoglio (redesigned façade); 1589–1597, San Giacomo (wall; designed by Bentivoglio); 1590s, Palazzo Pareschi; *1597, Santa Maria della Rotondo; 1599, Chapel of Santa Giustina; Ferrara, Italy. 1603, Turret, Arengo, Italy. 1604, Santa Maria del Quartiere (with G. B. Magnani), Parma, Italy. 1604, University Tower; *1606, Accademia degli Intrepedi Theater; Ferrara, Italy. 1606–1607, Clocktower, Faenza, Italy. 1606–1609, San Francesco (campanile), Ferrara, Italy. 1608, Waterworks, Po River, Italy. 1610, University (façade); 1610–1612, Ariosto Tomb (now in the Biblioteca Comunale), San Benedetto; 1611–1612, Porta Paola (now the Porta Rena); 1612, San Apollinare; 1613–1623, San Carlo; Ferrara, Italy. *1617–1618, Teatro Farnese (opened 1628), Parma, Italy. 1618, Fortress; 1618–1622, San Francesco Romana; 1621–1636, San Benedetto (campanile; not completed until 1646); *1627, Chapel of Santissimo Sacramento, Sant' Andrea (decoration destroyed in 1867; extant remains moved to the Church of Celletta, near Argenta, Italy); Ferrara, Italy.

BIBLIOGRAPHY

ADORNI, BRUNO 1974 L'Architettura Farnesiana a Parma: 1546–1630. Parma, Italy: Battei.
ALEOTTI, GIOVANNI BATTISTA 1589 Gli Artifitiosi Et Curiosi Moti Spiritali di Herrone. Tradotti Da M. Gio, Battista Aleotti D'Argenta. Aggiontoui dal medesimo Quattro Theoremi non mentelli, & curiosi de'gli altrj. Et il modo con che si fà artificiosamente salir un Canale d'Acqua viva, ò morta in cima d'ogn'alta Torre. . . . Ferrara, Italy: Baldini.
ALEOTTI, GIOVANNI BATTISTA 1601 Difesa per riparare alla sommersione del polesine di s. Giorgio, et all rovina dello stato di Ferrara etc. Ferrara, Italy: Baldini.
ALEOTTI, GIOVANNI BATTISTA 1612 Relazione intorno alla Bonifazione Bentivoglio. Ferrara, Italy: Baldini.
BANDI, D. 1871 Memorie bigrafiche di G.B. Aleotti. Argenta, Italy.
BAUR-HEINHOLD, MARGARETE 1967 The Baroque Theatre. New York: McGraw-Hill.
BJURSTRÖM, PER 1961 Giacomo Torelli and Baroque Stage Design. Stockholm: Almqvist & Wiksell.
COFFIN, DAVID R. 1962 "Some Architectural Drawings of Giov Battista Aleotti." Journal of the Society of Architectural Historians 21, no. 3:116–128.
MAGAGNATO, LICISCO 1954 Teatri italian del Cinquecento. Venice, Italy: Pozza.
MAINPRICE, J. L. 1967 "Aleotti's Idrologia." British Museum Quarterly 32:2–3.
PADOVANI, GIORGIO 1955 "Architetti ferraresi." Deputazione (Provinciale) Ferraresedi Storia Patria 15:115–132.
RAPP, F. 1930 "Ein Theater-Bauplan des Giovanni Battista Aleotti." Schriften der Gesellschaft für Theatergeschichte 41:79–125.
STROCCHI, G. 1926 Cenni sul codice autografo cinquecentesco inedito di G. B. Aleotti. Faenza, Italy: Lega.

ALESSI, GALEAZZO

Born in Perugia, Galeazzo Alessi (1512–1572) became the leading architect of the mid-sixteenth century in Genoa and Milan. His style permeated the residences of the Genoese aristocracy on their Strada Nuova (planned c.1555), and his lavish decoration of the Palazzo Marino (1557) in Milan revived the ornate Lombard tradition which had been suppressed earlier in the century by DONATO BRAMANTE and his followers. Though Alessi's works can be divided into three stylistic groups which correspond to his activities in and around Perugia, Genoa, and Milan respectively, his works are all characterized by a refined coordination of the architectural members and by a reduction of the basic architectural units into essential, geometric forms. His precisely and sometimes novelly articulated vaults often paralleled the movement of his distinct structural units. Even when Alessi designed his Milanese buildings with dense ornament, the structural elements remained clearly visible. He favored the use of paired columns or pilasters set on pedestals, and he usually varied his aediculated windows by crowning them alternately with arched and triangular pediments. His later works demonstrate a fascination with a geometricized, tapering order which derives from the support of a classical herm. Round arches set on architraved columns also recur in his work.

Alessi's earliest works were erected in his native Perugia after he had spent a number of years in the service of Cardinal Ascanio Parisani in Rome. Alessi, son of the patrician Bevignate di ser Lodovico Alessi, is said to have studied first with the Perugian architect GIOVAN BATTISTA CAPORALI and then to have become friends with MICHELANGELO in Rome, but the example of Antonio da Sangallo the younger (see SANGALLO FAMILY) and BALDASSARE PERUZZI seems to have been most important for the development of his personal style. Indeed, his first commission in Perugia was for the Rocca Paolina (1542–1544), where Sangallo is documented to have been active in 1540. Alessi's earliest surviving structure, a loggia (1546) soon converted to serve as the oratory of Sant'Angelo della Pace, shows him working in the sober manner of Sangallo. The loggia probably marked the terminus of a new street laid out for Cardinal Tiberio Crispo, who also engaged Alessi in the construction of the Via Nuova (1547), an essential training ground for Alessi's later urbanistic projects in Genoa.

While working in Perugia on yet other projects such as the Church of Santa Maria del Popolo (1547) and a loggia for the Palazzo dei Priori (c.1547), Alessi probably met Bartolomeo Sauli, a Genoese banker and Apostolic Treasurer of Perugia and Umbria between the years 1546 and 1548. Sauli may have encouraged Alessi's move to Genoa, where Alessi designed the family's centralized memorial church, Santa Maria di Carignano. The construction had been provided for in the 1481 testament of Bendinello Sauli but was commissioned only in 1549. Work began in 1552 and continued haltingly for the rest of the century. In 1565, Alessi agreed to a seven-month-a-year contract, but the dome was not completed until 1603. The plan, a Greek cross inscribed within a square from which the apse slightly protrudes, is rooted in Michelangelo's and Sangallo's plans for St. Peter's in Rome. In Alessi's design, however, the piers are so extraordinarily large that they diminish the effect of the five domes that dominate the plan. The narrow width of the central dome fails to unite the interior, which consists of a series of separate spatial units, but the four cross arms are tied together by an undulating architrave which projects over the giant pilasters and recedes over the wall areas. In turn, the vaulting also rises and lowers. The effect of separate shifting plates of vaulting is increased by the varied sizes and shapes of Alessi's coffers, which move from large to small and from perfectly square to thinly rectangular. The vaulting culminates in the diamond-shaped,

basket-woven coffers of the apse's half-dome. On the exterior, the church's exceedingly high central dome was to have been balanced by four towers at the corners. Only two were erected. The façades are marked by pediments, each of which is pierced by a large lunette. Alessi was particularly fond of Santa Maria di Carignano. His design for the cupola of Santa Maria degli Angeli in Assisi (1568) derived from it, as may his designs for El Escorial (c.1562–1569). Alessi's cordial relationship with the Sauli family also led to his work on the renovation of Genoa Cathedral after Girolamo Sauli became archbishop in 1550. A model was ordered in 1556. In the Church of San Matteo, Alessi provided a design for the tomb of Giovanni Paolo Pinelli (1557–1559).

Meanwhile, Alessi had been developing a more decorative style appropriate to Luca Giustiniani's suburban villa (now the Villa Cambiaso, begun 1548). The plan, with its two slightly projecting wings flanking a central core, is generally similar to Peruzzi's Villa Farnesina in Rome, but Alessi subjected the interior to a perfectly symmetrical, axial arrangement. Similar insistent logic lies behind the articulation of the façade, where paired Doric columns on pedestals support paired Corinthian pilasters which support paired segments of solid parapet above each projecting wing. In reverse order, an open balustrade corresponds to the pierced, fenestrated wall below. The effect is gracefully rich. In the loggia on the second floor, Alessi first demonstrated his new taste for applied herms, dense vegetal friezes, and decorative vault and niche patterns.

The style and spirit of the Villa Giustiniani set a new standard for Genoese aristocratic residences. It is best illustrated in the Strada Nuova, where the Genoese built the first organized street of independent, blocklike palaces in their history. Each palace is unique, but each is related to its neighbor by similar height and by the placement of major entrances opposite one another. The basic design of the street is generally credited to Alessi himself (c.1555), but the palaces are by other architects working in his manner.

A growth of elaboration in Alessi's architecture was evident in the Villa Grimaldi (later Sauli, c.1555?), whose fountains and gardens were highly praised by GIORGIO VASARI. Only a few fragments of richly carved decorations survive from the villa, but their lavishness was continued and reached a climax in the Palazzo Marino (1557), built for a Genoese client in Milan who began to acquire the necessary property in 1553. Construction on the gargantuan palace halted around 1565, and the west façade on the Piazza della Scala was completed only between 1888 and 1892 by LUCA

BELTRAMI. For the courtyard Alessi intensified the decorative vocabulary of his suburban villas, while on the façade he combined Tuscan and Ionic orders with a new geometricized and tapering order. Large heads wedged between the paired brackets above each tapering pilaster attest to their derivation from antique herms. On the ground story, Alessi framed his windows with the same brusque columns, partially encased in large blocks of stone, which he had employed for his Porta del Molo (1551–1553) in Genoa. Inside the courtyard the façade's density relaxes for a moment in an airy arcade supported on paired, architraved columns. Alessi had already employed this motif in the courtyard of the Villa Grimaldi, but now he crowned it with a second story of unprecedented bombast. The entire second story became an indissoluble, sculptural mass of voluptuous herms, scrolls, strapwork reliefs, festoons, and masks.

Even the centers and edges of the balustrades sprouted leafy volutes.

In a sense, the façade of Santa Maria presso San Celso (1568) was to have been the ecclesiastical equivalent of the Palazzo Marino. According to a design preserved in the Biblioteca Ambrosiana, the upper stories were to have been fully sculptural. In the façade as executed after 1575, MARTINO BASSI relegated the sculpture to isolated patches and reduced the height of the obelisks, which had been an integral part of Alessi's design. The splendid choir stalls inside the church, executed according to Alessi's designs (1570), give a more accurate sense of his decorative sensibilities. His work on a smaller scale consisted of a wooden tabernacle for the Church of San Pietro in Perugia (1567) and a bronze tabernacle for the high altar of San Francesco, Assisi (1570, now in the Treasury).

In the Church of San Barnaba (1561) for the newly founded Barnabite order, Alessi leashed his exuberance and directed his habit of recessing and projecting vaults and piers to express clearly the functional divisions of nave, presbytery, and choir. The rise of three steps from the nave to the presbytery, two from the nave to the side aisles, and three more to the altar are located at the divisions determined by distinct vaults and triumphal arches. This type of church, also favored by his follower VINCENZO SEREGNI, was later codified by San Carlo Borromeo in his *Instructiones* of 1573. Alessi's other ties to church reforms are documented by his participation in the project for the Sacro Monte di Varallo (c.1562–1566) and the so-called *Libro dei Misteri* of this giant religious theme park. In the 1560s, Alessi was also engaged on unspecified work in Milan Cathedral.

Alessi's last years were spent in Perugia. His major works of this period, the Chiostro delle Stelle (1571) of San Pietro, Perugia, and the renovation of the Cathedral of San Rufino (1571) in Assisi show him largely chastened of his northern decorativeness, but the handsome southern doorway of the cathedral in Perugia is more in keeping with his Milanese work. A triumphal arch erected for the arrival of Cardinal Alessandrino (Michele Bonelli) in 1570 may have been designed similarly. In 1571, Alessi was granted admission to the Arte della Mercanzia, and in 1572 he served as a prior of the government.

The plans and elevations of many of Alessi's buildings achieved an international reputation as a result of their publication by Peter Paul Rubens in his *Palazzi di Genova* of 1622 and 1652.

GARY M. RADKE

WORKS

*1542–1544, Rocca Paolina (loggia and Stanze); 1546,

Sant'Angelo della Pace (loggia, later oratory); 1547, Palazzo dei Priori (loggia); c.1547, Santa Maria del Popolo (now Camera di Commercio); 1547, Via Nuova; Perugia, Italy. 1548, Villa Giustiniani (later Cambiaso); 1549–1572, Santa Maria di Carignano (not completed until 1603); 1551–1553, Porta del Molo; *c.1555?, Villa Grimaldi (later Sauli); Genoa, Italy. 1557, Palazzo Marino; 1561, San Barnaba, Milan. c.1562–1566, Sancro Monte di Varallo (porta maggiore and chapel of Adam and Eve), Varallo, Italy. *1564, Auditorio delle Scuole Canobiane, Milan. *1567, Church of San Pietro (wooden tabernacle); 1567–1568, Duomo (southern portal); Perugia, Italy. 1568, Santa Maria degli Angeli, Assisi, Italy. 1568, Santa Maria presso San Celso, Milan. 1570, San Francesco (bronze tabernacle), Assisi, Italy. 1570–1572, Palazzo dei Priori (renovation); 1571, San Pietro (Chiostro delle Stelle); Perugia, Italy. 1571, San Rufino (renovation), Assisi, Italy.

BIBLIOGRAPHY

ALESSI, GALEAZZO 1974 *Libro dei misteri: Progetto di pianificazione urbanistica, architettonica e figurativa del Sacro Monte di Varallo in Valsesia (1565–1569).* Preface by Anna Maria Brizio. Critical commentary by Stefania Stefani Perrone. 2 vols. Bologna, Italy: Forni.

BRIGGS, MARTIN SHAW 1915 "Architects of the Later Renaissance in Italy. II: Galeazzo Alessi." *Architectural Review* 38, Aug.:26–31.

BROWN, NANCY A. 1964–1965 "The Church of San Barnaba in Milan." *Arte Lombarda* 9, no. 2:62–93; 10, no. 1:65–98.

BROWN, NANCY A. HOUGHTON 1980 *The Milanese Architecture of Galeazzo Alessi.* New York: Garland.

Galeazzo Alessi, Genova, Palazzo Bianco, 16 aprile–12 maggio 1974, Mostra di fotografie, rilieve, disegni. 1974 Genoa, Italy: SAGEP.

Galeazzo Alessi e l'architettura del Cinquecento, Atti del convegno internazionale di studi, Genova, 16–20 aprile 1974. 1975 Genoa, Italy: SAGEP.

HEYDENREICH, LUDWIG H., and LOTZ, WOLFGANG 1974 *Architecture in Italy: 1400–1600.* Harmondsworth, England: Penguin.

LABÒ, M. 1960 "Galeazzo Alessi." Volume 2, pages 238–242 in *Dizionario Biografico degli Italiani.* Rome: Istituto della Enciclopedia Italian.

VENTURI, ADOLFO 1940 Pages 589–673 in *Storia dell'arte italiana.* Volume 11, part 3 in *Architettura del Cinquecento.* Milan: Hoepli.

ALEXANDER, DANIEL ASHER

Daniel Asher Alexander (1768–1846) was a Londoner, whose early career as surveyor to the London Dock Company involved him in the design of large warehouses whose dramatic simplicity owed much to his admiration for GIOVANNI BATTISTA PIRANESI. This manner he later found well-adapted to prison architecture, though it lends a somewhat forbidding air to his only known country house. As surveyor to Trinity House he designed numerous lighthouses.

ANDOR GOMME

WORKS

*1790, Scott's Warehouses, Bankside, London. 1793–1801, Mote Park, Maidstone, Kent, England. 1796–1820, Warehouses, London Dock Company, Wapping, London. 1806–1809, Dartmoor Prison of War, Princetown, Devon, England. 1807–1810, Queen's House (colonnades and pavilions), Greenwich, London. *1810–1812, Baptist College, Bristol, England. 1811–1819, County Jail, Maidstone, Kent, England.

BIBLIOGRAPHY

GOMME, ANDOR; JENNER, MICHAEL; and LITTLE, BRYAN 1979 Pages 232, 360 in *Bristol: an Architectural History.* London: Lund Humphries.

NEWMAN, JOHN 1969 Pages 388, 397–398 in *The Buildings of England: West Kent and the Weald.* Harmondsworth, England: Penguin.

PEVSNER, NIKOLAUS 1952 Pages 249–250 *The Buildings of England: South Devon.* Harmondsworth, England: Penguin.

ALFIERI, BENEDETTO

Not much is known about the formative years of Benedetto Innocente Alfieri (1699–1767) and his early architectural career in the small centers of Piedmont until the beginning of his government career in Turin. He was born in Rome into a noble family from Asti, Piedmont; he returned to Asti in 1714, then entered the Collegio Reale (royal preparatory school) in Turin and studied law at the university there. During the following years, he may have practiced law. Beginning in 1726, he held administrative positions in Asti, first as councilman, then (in 1730) as mayor. As such, he had to deal with issues of building maintenance and administration. He also designed a church tower in 1724, a bridge in 1729, and probably a few other items in Asti between 1725 and 1732. All this suggests that Alfieri must have benefited from some sort of architectural education (either self-taught or formal) as early as 1724; in any case, these works are rather provincial. The palace for Marchese Ghilini in Alessandria (1732) marks a significant jump, both because of the size and status of the commission—a large city palace for a prominent patron—and because of the formal and distributional sophistication of Alfieri's design. This is the first building exhibiting traits typical of his later mature approach, as seen in a very personal way of controlling quotations from other buildings or architects, including much of FILIPPO JUVARRA. At the same time, there are abrupt transitions and hesitant details in this design, and it is possible that Alfieri based it on an earlier Juvarra project of unknown import. We have no firm knowledge of commissions, travels, or architectural studies during the following years until 1738, when he moved to Turin to preside over the construction of the Teatro Regio. Thus, much remains unexplained about the beginning of his governmental career, sanctioned in 1739 by his appointment to the post of royal architect by King Carlo Emanuele III. The post had been vacant since Juvarra's death in 1736. The king preferred Alfieri over another possible candidate, the Piedmontese architect BERNARDO ANTONIO VITTONE, whose style was then developing in a more personal, less official, and less representational direction. The choice of Alfieri suggests that Carlo Emanuele III valued, in a royal architect, qualities of governmental administrator besides the more specific ones of architect. During the following twenty years, while holding the post of first architect, Alfieri also had several other posts in the city administration of Turin, where he was mayor in 1742. He traveled to Rome in 1739, and to Rome and Naples in 1743.

Alfieri's principal architectural works after 1739 were royal commissions, but there was also a large group of designs for nonroyal patrons; both groups include several interior designs. To the group of royal commissions belongs first of all a series of buildings in the military-governmental center of Turin to replace or complete existing ones: the Teatro Regio (royal theater, 1738–1740); the Segreterie di Stato (state offices, 1738–1757); the Cavallerizza (riding school, partially built, 1740–1741); works at Palazzo Reale (1739–1767); the remodeling of Palazzo Chiablese (1753–1767); unbuilt designs for Palazzo Madama (1761) and for the Duomo Nuovo (before 1753). Still in Turin, Alfieri remodeled Via and Piazza delle Erbe (1756) and designed the Palazzo del Senato (1740). Outside Turin, there were partially executed designs for the royal residences of Stupinigi and Venaria Reale (1739–1767) and an unexecuted design for the castle of Chambéry. To the group of nonroyal commissions belong the façade of the Cathedral of Saint Pierre in Geneva (1752–1756); the Teatro Carignano in Turin (1752–1753); the bell tower of San Gaudenzio in Novara (1753–1773); the parish church of Carignano (1756–1764); the façade of Palazzo Sormani in Milan (1756); the remodeling of Palazzo Caraglio in Turin (1753–1776) and of other palaces in Turin and Asti; the façade of Saint Eusebio in Vercelli (1758–1761); and the Seminary in Asti (1763–1767).

When designing for the king, Alfieri almost always had to deal with pre-existing designs by Juvarra, either built or on paper. These commissions therefore entailed continuity with the under-takings of the previous king, Vittorio Amedeo II. Yet, Alfieri's answer is different from Juvarra's, and a different idea of royal architecture is embodied in his—and Carlo Emanuele III's—buildings. Thus, Juvarra's church in Venaria, airily scenographic and open-structured, is strait-jacketed on the outside by Alfieri's disciplined system of façade and adjoining transitional elements; in place of the "open control" over the surrounding landscape by Juvarra's buildings we find the "closed control" of Alfieri's (compare, for example, their respective projects for Stupinigi and Palazzo Madama); instead of Juvarra's freer handling of the Turinese urban fabric, we find a stiffer conformity to it by Alfieri. Juvarra's style is regal; Alfieri's could better be described as governmental.

Alfieri's architecture is partly rooted in baroque classicism as it was understood in mid-eighteenth century-Rome—from MICHELANGELO to ALESSANDRO GALILEI, through GIOVANNI LORENZO BERNINI and CARLO FONTANA. Even more, it is rooted in a Piedmontese tradition going from CARLO CASTELLAMONTE and AMEDEO DI CASTELLAMONTE to FRANCESCO GALLO, leaving out GUARINO GUARINI and interpreting Juvarra as explained above. Alfieri's is a sort of Italian version of Piedmontese, not in the least provincial. French influence, handled with independence, can be found in his interior decoration.

It is hard to discern a single style or a clear evolution of style in Alfieri's oeuvre. The heavy academic manner of certain designs contrasts with the rigorous and rational purism of others, which we perceive today as tantalizingly modern (for example, the Seminary at Asti). Within the same building, classicizing and almost neoclassical elements coexist with baroque ones in utter harmony and mutual restraint (for instance, the façade of Palazzo Sormani and, on an almost giant scale, the façade of Saint Pierre, Geneva). By the same token, Piedmontese "military" sobriety is sometimes closely coupled with Roman baroque influence mediated through Juvarra as in the base and the upper part of the bell tower of San Gaudenzio; or it is coupled with free and lively rococo decoration, as on the outside and inside of Palazzo Chiablese. In this ambiguity is rooted one of the most fascinating aspects of Alfieri, his ability to stay perfectly poised between so many different tendencies, with assurance, clarity, and great elegance.

A possible unifying factor, and one certainly characteristic of Alfieri and well in tune with his royal patron, is a tendency toward "control." For example, the church of Carignano exhibits an odd ring-shaped plan, probably based on ideas by Juvarra: now, one of its charms is precisely the way in which the idea of this plan has been carried out. Granted, the space is odd and unusual for a church; yet, it is kept in check by controlled views, it has clear boundaries, and it is articulated through clear and rational structures. In Turin, the ensemble of Via and Piazza delle Erbe is held together by strict proportional ratios and, again, by controlled views: the façade of City Hall, which should be the focus of the whole, is integrated in the system of wall articulation which tightly binds together all façades through the use of repetitive elements—arcades below, fields of tightly fitted and sharply framed windows above, and strips of flat rustication to reinforce the boundaries of the fields. It is a "closed system," yet at the same time it shapes an important urban mode.

Alfieri handled issues of structure, technique, and distribution in the same rational way; they seem to have commanded much of his attention. In the Teatro Regio, the various access routes are perfectly defined and controlled, and the careful handling of technical problems such as acoustics elicited contemporary praise. The vault of the Cavallerizza is a daring and "economical" structure. The porticoed façade of Saint Pierre, iconographically modeled after the Pantheon, cleverly solves the problem of buttressing the Gothic structure behind it. It also displays a remarkable empiricism rather than allegiance to abstract "principles." The dome of the Roman model is here shrunk and laterally squeezed; it is manifestly fake and is used to hide the upper part of the Gothic nave behind it.

Among the interiors, one should single out those of Palazzo Chiablese and especially those of Palazzo Caraglio, outstanding achievements on a par with the best European examples. Alfieri's use of models—such as French rococo interiors of the early eighteenth century and Juvarra's interiors in Turin—is here entirely personal. The jewel among these interiors, the octagonal drawing room at Palazzo Caraglio, dervives its unique compositional unity from the way in which mirrors and decoration are used and related to each other: the mirrors are no longer panels but matter which defines space while multiplying it; the decoration becomes a sort of continuous architectural structure, giving rise in turn to its own decorations and achieving extraordinary finesse, grace, and liveliness. This is an imaginary world in which delicately harmonious lights, colors, and gilding are multiplied ad infinitum.

Alfieri had strong influence in Piedmont, where most architects of the second half of the century used a correct architectural language derived from his own and operated competently within and around the state organization. In Piedmontese as well as European terms, Alfieri contributed to the transformation of contemporary architecture in a classicizing and neoclassical as well as "rational" direction. Thus, the façade of Saint Pierre was an immediate precedent for JACQUES GERMAIN SOUFFLOT's Church of Sainte-Geneviève in Paris, while in Lombardy the façade of Palazzo Sormani left its mark on GIUSEPPE PIERMARINI's façades of a few decades later.

CHIARA PASSANTI

WORKS

1732, Palazzo Ghilini, Alessandria, Italy. *1738–1740, Teatro Regio; 1738–1757, Segreterie di Stato; Turin, Italy. 1739–1767, Castle of Venaria Reale (works), Italy. 1739–1767, Palazzo Reale (works), Turin, Italy. 1739–1767, Palazzina of Stupinigi (works), Italy. 1740, Palazzo del Senato (unfinished), Turin, Italy. 1740–1741, Basilica del Sacro Monte (altar and tribune), Varallo, Italy. 1749–1767, Parish Church (not completed until 1770), Piovà Massaia, Italy. 1751, Palazzo Mazzetti di Frinco; After 1751, Palazzo Ottolenghi; Asti, Italy. 1752–1753, Teatro Carignano (destroyed and rebuilt), Turin, Italy. 1752–1756, Cathedral of Saint Pierre (façade), Geneva. 1753–1767, Palazzo Isnardi di Caraglio (not completed until 1776); 1753–1767, Palazzo Chiablese; Turin, Italy. 1753–1767, San Gaudenzio (bell tower; not completed until 1773), Novara, Italy. 1753, 1764, Piazza San Carlo (works), Turin, Italy. 1756, Palazzo Sormani (façade), Milan. 1756, Via and Piazza delle Erbe, Turin, Italy. 1756–1764, Parish Church, Carignano, Italy. 1758–1761, Cathedral (façade), Vercelli, Italy. 1763–1767, Seminary, Asti, Italy. 1764–1767, Chapel of San Evasio, Cathedral, Casale, Italy.

BIBLIOGRAPHY

ALFIERI, BENEDETTO 1761 *Il nuovo teatro regio di Torino apertosi nell'anno 1740.* Turin, Italy.
ARGAN, G. C. 1964 "Lo zio di Vittorio." *Il Messaggero* Feb. 8.
BELLINI, A. 1978 *Benedetto Alfieri.* Milan.
CARBONERI, NINO 1963 *Architettura: Catalogo della mostra del barocco piemontese.* Turin, Italy.
CAVALLARI MURAT, A. 1968 "Attualità ed inattualità di Benedetto Alfieri a duecent'anni dalla morte." *Bollettino della Società Piemontese di Archeologia e Belle Arti* 1968:7–43.
CHEVALLEY, G. 1916 *Un avvocato architetto: Il conte Benedetto Alfieri.* Turin, Italy.
PAROLETTI, M. 1824 *Vita e ritratti di sessanta piemontesi illustri.* Turin, Italy.
PASSANTI, CHIARA 1968 "Benedetto Alfieri architetto." Unpublished B.A. thesis, University of Turin, Italy.
POMMER, RICHARD 1967 *Eighteenth-Century Architecture in Piedmont.* New York University Press.
ROSCI, MARCO 1953 "Benedetto Alfieri e l'architettura del '700 in Piemonte." *Palladio* New Series 3:91–100.
VALLE, G. DELLA 1794 *Prefazione al tomo XI delle "Vite" del Vasari.* Siena, Italy.

ALGAROTTI, FRANCESCO

Francesco Algarotti (1712–1764) is one of the most remarkable personalities of the cultural and intellectual life in the Europe of the Englightenment. Coming from a Venetian milieu that traditionally cultivated contacts with England as with France, Algarotti quickly became the figurehead of Illuminist internationalism in Italy, maintaining contacts with all of Europe. As a poet and writer, as a cultural and art critic, as a dilettante and disseminator of new theoretical positions in science (Newton) and art (CARLO LODOLI), he contributed substantially to the salon culture of the mid-eighteenth century, inclined as it was to modernistic and Enlightenment themes. He established his fame with his *Newtonianismo per le Dame* (1737) which, together with Voltaire's *Elémens de la Philosophie de Neuton, mis à la portée de tout le monde* (1738), belonged to the decisive precursors of so-called Newtonianism. His fame was perpetuated by Frederick the Great of Prussia, to whom Algarotti acted as artistic adviser.

Blamed for his superficiality and accused of plagiarism in connection with Lodoli's theses on architectural theory, he was also early praised by his biographer, Michelessi (1770, p. 17), as the first Italian to set himself the task of making the language of the philosophers comprehensible to everyone.

Born into aristocratic surroundings in Venice, Algarotti studied in Rome and Bologna where he attended the famous Istituto delle Scienze, made the acquaintance of Eustachio Manfredi and Francesco Maria Zanotti, and studied philosophy and natural science. His training, as well as his contact with Antonio Conti (who had tried to mediate between Leibnitz and Newton) and the publication of Giovanni Rizzetti's *De luminis affectionibus* (1727) inspired him to his *Newtonianismo per le Dame* which was seen as a manifesto of Italian Newtonianism and a classic of popularized scientific literature. The work, which uses the dialogue form and is influenced by Fontenelle's *Entretiens sur la pluralité des mondes* (1686), opened a European career to Algarotti and secured for him the acknowledgment of such people as Voltaire and Maupertuis.

Algarotti became an agent of Italian art and culture, both for King August III of Saxony for whose Dresden gallery he undertook the purchase of a number of Italian masters in 1743–1745, and above all for Frederick the Great. Through Algarotti, Palladianism (see ANDREA PALLADIO) took hold in Potsdam: he prompted Frederick to have copies of the most famous of Palladio's palaces built by, among others, Johann Gottfried Buring. Later, Algarotti returned to Bologna, became a member of the Accademia Clementia, founded his own Accademia degl'Indomiti, and retired to Pisa. On his tomb Frederick the Great ordered the inscription: "Algarotto Ovidii aemulo, Newtoni discipulo, Fredericus rex" (To Algarotti, rival of Ovid, disciple of Newton, King Frederick).

Algarotti's relation to art is that of the connoisseur, the agent, and the collector. He championed Italy as the Greece of his time and recommended to the French that they send their new generation of artists to be trained in the Italian academies. It was he who suggested to Canaletto the "capriccio palladiano" in which Palladian buildings and projects appear together in an idealized *veduta* and which became a manifesto of Palladianism. Algarotti was in tune with English-Venetian Palladianism not only by virtue of his aristocratic background, his eager collecting, and his status as a dilettante and member of the *repubblica dei letterati;* his love of travel and his rich literary production, by preference in the form of essays and letters, were added bonds. No theme fashionable in the Enlightenment—the influence of climate on culture, the question why geniuses emerge by the dozen at one and the same time—was left untouched.

Algarotti's *Lettere sopra la pittura* and his *Lettere sopra l'architettura* were concerned with art history questions and problems of artistic taste. For instance, with TOMMASO TEMANZA he discusses the use of double columns, and with his friend Mauro Tesi, the projects for the completion of San Petronio in Bologna. The *Saggio sopra l'architettura* dated 1756 (first published in his *Opere varie*, 1757) was of considerable significance for the architectural theory of his time. Although later accused of plagiarism, Algarotti deserves credit for having been the first—together with Girolamo Zanetti—to promulgate the doctrines of Lodoli. In this he did not so much follow the anti-Vitruvian (see VITRUVIUS) utterances of Lodoli regarding material, function, representation, and ornament in architecture, but rather was more generally interested in the possibility of a theoretical ("philosophical") discussion of architecture as propagated in his *Saggio*. Algarotti's role was that of a mediator rather than an independent creative thinker in architectural theory. Hence, his influence as a catalyst is all the more highly to be valued.

WERNER OECHSLIN
*Translated from German by
Beverley R. Placzek*

BIBLIOGRAPHY

ALGAROTTI, FRANCESCO   1737   *Il Newtonianismo per le Dame ovvero Dialoghi sopra la Luce e i Colori.* Naples, Italy.

ALGAROTTI, FRANCESCO   1791–1794   *Opere del Conte Algarotti.* 17 vols. Venice, Italy.

GABRIELLI, A.   1938   "L'Algarotti e la critica d'arte in Italia nel Settecento." *Critica d'Arte* 3, no. 3:155–169; 4, no. 1:24–31.

HASKELL, F.   1963   Pages 347–360ff. in *Patrons and Painters.* London.

KAUFMANN, EDGAR, JR.   1944   "At an Eighteenth Century Crossroad: Algarotti vs. Lodoli." *Journal of the Society of Architectural Historians* 4, no. 2:23–29.

MATTIOLI ROSSI, L.   1980   "Collezionismo e mercato dei verdutisti nella Venezia del Settecento." *Richerche di Storia dell'Arte* 11:79–92.

OECHSLIN, WERNER   1970   "Aspetti dell'internazionalismo nell'architettura italiana del primo Settecento." Pages 141–155 in *Barocco europeo, barocco italiano, barocco salentino.* Lecce, Italy.

RAGGHIANTI, C. L.   1936   "L'Architettura 'in funzione' e Francesco Algarotti." *Casabella* 105.

RYKWERT, J.   1980   *The First Moderns: Architects of the Eighteenth Century.* Cambridge, Mass.: M.I.T. Press.

ALGHISI, GALASSO

Galasso (Galeazzo) Alghisi da Carpi (?–1573) was a well-known military engineer and civic architect active in Italy in the middle of the sixteenth century. First records of him seem to indicate that he was the disciple and assistant of Antonio da Sangallo the Younger (see SANGALLO FAMILY) in Rome during the pontificate of Paul III and may have worked on the Palazzo Farnese. He was invited to participate in two rounds of conferences of outstanding soldiers and military architects which were called by Paul III in 1534–1535 and 1542–1545 to discuss fortifications for Rome. These meetings were an important source of ideas for almost all work in this field in Italy in the second half of the sixteenth century.

Alghisi was one of the last major architects to be trained both as a civil architect and as a military engineer. In 1549, he was recorded in Loreto, where he worked on the construction of the sanctuary, and in the following year, he designed Santa Maria delle Virgini near Macerata, a centrally planned church in the tradition of Donato Bramante. In 1558, he presented a plan for the municipal tower at Macerata. After this, he settled in Ferrara and completed for Ercole II and Alfonso II d'Este various projects, including hydraulic works and a theater in the palace.

Alghisi wrote a treatise on military architecture entitled *Delle fortificazione libri tre* (Venice, 1570 and 1575), which reveals the conservative character of his thought. Whereas increasing numbers of military architects at this time were specialists who came from the ranks of professional soldiers and who concentrated on the practical problems of fortifications, Alghisi was critical of these men and remained loyal to the humanistic tradition by stressing the importance of theory—mathematics, geometry, and perspective—in military design. His ideal plans present eighteen versions of stellated polygons with bastionated points, of which he claimed, incorrectly, to be the inventor. These fortification rings appear to be elegant patterns conceived by a geometrician rather than solutions to specific problems of irregular terrain and city plan.

Alghisi's theories influenced the Dutch school of fortification in the seventeenth century through his student Marcaurelio da Pasino.

PRISCILLA ALBRIGHT

WORKS

1550, Santa Maria delle Virgini, Macerata, Italy. After 1558, Loggiato de'Camerini; after 1558, Palazzo Communale (parts); Ferrara, Italy.

BIBLIOGRAPHY

CITTADELLA, LUÍGI NAPOLEONE   1868   *Notizie amministrative, storiche, artistiche relative a Ferrara.* Ferrara, Italy: Taddei.

DE LA CROIX, HORST   1960   "Military Architecture and the Radial City Plan in Sixteenth Century Italy." *Art Bulletin* 42, no. 4:263–290.

DE LA CROIX, HORST   1963   "The Literature on Fortification in Renaissance Italy." *Technology and Culture* 4, no. 1:30–50.

HALE, JOHN R.   1964   "The Argument of Some Military Title Pages of the Renaissance." *Newberry Library Bulletin* 6, no. 4:91–102.

HALE, JOHN R.   1977   *Renaissance Fortification: Art or Engineering.* London: Thames & Hudson.

NATALE, G.   1907   "Un tempio bramantesco poco noto (S. Maria delle Vergini a Macerata)." In *Raccolta di scritti storici in onore del prof. Giacinto Romano.* Pavia, Italy: Fusi.

PROMIS, CARLO   1874   "Biografie di ingegneri militari italiani dal seccolo XIV alla meta del secolo XVIII." *Miscellanea di storia italiana.* 14:186–189.

QUINTAVALLE, A. O.   1960   "Galasso Alghisi." Volume 2, pages 361–362 in *Dizionario biografico degli italiani.* Rome: Societa Grafica Romana.

VASARI, GIORGIO   (1568)1973   *Le opere di Giorgio Vasari, con nuove annotazioni e commenti.* 9 vols. Edited by G. Milanesi. Reprint. Florence: Sansoni. Originally published in 1550 with the title *Le vite de piv eccelenti architetti.* There are many English translations and selections from Vasari's *Lives,* the standard one by G. du C. de Vere was published in ten volumes in London by the Medici Society in 1912–1915.

ALLEN, ZACHARIAH

Zachariah Allen (1795–1882) was an early and influential industrial designer from Providence, Rhode Island. His Allendale Mill (1822, 1839), a masonry building with central tower, typifies the nineteenth-century American factory and demonstrates a fire-resistant technique known as slow-burning construction, as well as Allen's innovative fire control methods.

GWEN W. STEEGE

WORKS

1822, 1839, Allendale Mill, North Providence, R.I.
1853, Bernon Mill, Georgiaville, R.I.

BIBLIOGRAPHY

ALLEN, ZACHARIAH 1829 *The Science of Mechanics, as Applied to the Present Improvements in the Useful Arts.* Providence: Hutchens & Cory.
HUXTABLE, ADA LOUISE 1956 "Allendale Mill—1822." *Progressive Architecture* 37:123–124.
PIERSON, WILLIAM H., JR. 1978 *American Buildings and Their Architects: Technology and the Picturesque, The Corporate and the Early Gothic Styles.* Garden City, N.Y.: Doubleday.

ALLEN and COLLENS

Allen and Collens (later Allen, Collens, and Willis), a Boston firm formed by Frederick R. Allen (1843–1931) and Charles Collens (1873?–1956), though little studied subsequently, was in the early twentieth century among the leading American neo-Gothic architects of the RALPH ADAMS CRAM school. They designed several important churches and collegiate buildings, including the Brown Tower, the James Tower and the Memorial Chapel at Union Theological Seminary in New York (1908–1910). The firm often worked with distinguished artist-collaborators, such as Johannes Kirchmayer (at the Second Church, Newton, Massachusetts, 1909–1916) and Frank Koralewski (at the Lindsey Chapel, Emmanuel Church, Boston, 1920–1924), and on at least one occasion with JOHN NINIAN COMPER, who designed the Lindsey Chapel altar and glass. Hammond Castle, Gloucester, Massachusetts (1928), and the Cloisters in New York (1938) are examples of their neo-Gothic work integrated with original medieval work. They scandalized Cram by compromising structural integrity, as at the Riverside Church, New York (1930), built with Henry C. Pelton and Burnham Hoyt, the oversized tower of which is actually a steel-framed neo-Gothic office building. They also designed Colonial Revival churches, such as the United Church, Bridgeport, Connecticut (c.1928).

DOUGLASS SHAND TUCCI

AL-MANṢŪR

Al-Manṣūr, Abū Jaᶜfar ᶜAbdallāh b. Muḥammad (?–775), the second caliph of the ᶜAbbāsid dynasty, was responsible for establishing the great ᶜAbbāsid capital at Baghdad in 762. The centerpiece of the urban setting was the magnificent palace complex that served as his administrative center. The structure, which was perfectly circular, consisted of several major elements: outer fortifications, a residential area for the administrative personnel, a series of arcades originally intended for security personnel, a zone which contained the agencies of the government, the residences of the caliph's younger children and the apartments of several key personnel, and a great inner court that contained the caliph's residence and an adjoining mosque.

There does not seem to be any architectural prototype for the structure as a whole, but it is clear that certain elements were borrowed directly from the caliph's Umayyad predecessors. The relationship between the Umayyad palace-mosque at Wāsiṭ and the Round City at Baghdad are not accidental. Al-Manṣūr who had been a remarkably inconspicuous figure in his youth, seemingly compensated for his lack of distinction by creating government structures of incredible complexity and breadth. He encased himself within walls of monumental architecture and surrounded himself with a highly centralized bureaucracy of staggering dimensions. His actions stemmed from a keen awareness of the desirability of integrating image with function in conducting the affairs of imperial government.

The extent of the caliph's personal involvement in the design of the city is not entirely clear, but there is reason to believe that he monitored its development from the conception of the city plan to the completion of its last elements four years later. The caliph also built several other provincial administrative centers. The most significant of these was probably the complex at al-Rāfiqah, which was reportedly modeled after the plan in Baghdad.

JACOB LASSNER

BIBLIOGRAPHY

LASSNER, JACOB 1970 *The Topography of Baghdad in the Early Middle Ages: Text and Studies.* Detroit, Mich.: Wayne State University Press.
LASSNER, JACOB 1980 *The Shaping of Abbasid Rule.* N.J.: Princeton University Press.

ALMIRALL, RAYMOND F.

Born in Brooklyn, New York, Raymond Francis Almirall (1869–1939) earned a degree in architecture at Cornell University in 1891. He studied under VICTOR LALOUX at the Ecole des Beaux-Arts, Paris, 1892–1896. In independent practice in New York from around 1900, he designed many churches, houses, and public buildings. He was an aide in restoration of the palaces of Versailles, Fontainebleau, and the Cathedral of Rheims (1924), for which he was made a member of the Legion of Honor (1928).

DONALD MARTIN REYNOLDS

BIBLIOGRAPHY

"Almirall Dies: Architectural Firm Head, 70." 1939 *New York Herald Tribune* May 19.

"Almirall, Raymond Francis." 1941 Volume 29, pages 321–322 in *The National Cyclopedia of American Biography.* New York: White.

LANIER, HENRY W. (editor) 1928 *The Players' Book: A Half Century of Fact, Feeling, Fun, and Folklore.* New York: The Players.

"Obituary." 1939 *New York Times* May 19.

"Raymond F. Almirall." 1924 Volume 21, page 361 in *American Art Annual.* Washington: American Federation of Arts.

ALMQVIST, OSVALD

Osvald Almqvist (1884–1950), whose stature in Swedish architecture is indicated by his colleagues' designation of him as the conscience of the Swedish architectural profession (Linn, 1967, p. 121), was trained at the Royal Institute of Technology and the Royal Academy of Arts, Stockholm. In 1910, he and six other architectural students, including SIGURD LEWERENTZ and ERIK GUNNAR ASPLUND, left the Academy to found an independent architectural school, the Klara school, where RAGNAR ÖSTBERG, CARL WESTMANN, IVAR TENGBOM, and CARL BERGSTEN taught and offered an alternative to the classicism of the Academy.

Almqvist has been called the first Swedish functionalist (Ahlberg, 1950, p. 48) because of post-World War I designs such as the Bergslagsbyn village for workers (1916–1920) and the Forshuvudforsen Power Station (1917–1921), the latter building completely without historical reference. During the 1920s, Almqvist built three more power stations of functionalist design, collaborating with the Stockholm engineering firm Vattenbyggnadsbyran; these are considered his masterpieces.

Interested in standardization, he was appointed in 1921 to a committee to determine requirements of workmen's housing and wrote an important appendix to the committee's report. This appendix on town planning codified ideas which he had expressed in building Bergslagsbyn. The next year, he undertook an investigation of kitchen equipment, and in 1934 he published *Köket och Ekonomiavdelningen,* the first Swedish kitchen standards. For the Stockholm Exhibition of 1930, in addition to a house, Almqvist designed three standardized objects: the concrete lamppost for the Exhibition, a conical flowerpot that is used today in Stockholm parks, and a prefabricated cast-iron spiral staircase.

Almqvist also contributed to functionalist theory with his definition of sanitary aesthetics in "Gatubelysningsarmatur. Några reflexioner i anledning av lyktstolpstävlingen" (*Byggmästaren,* 1924). This article preceded what has been hailed as the first theoretical presentation of functionalism in Sweden, UNO ÅHRÉN's 1925 review championing LE CORBUSIER over traditional design at the 1925 Paris Exposition.

Almqvist's work in city planning took him to the United States in 1921. As head of the Stockholm Park Department, 1936–1938, he formulated the park system which his successors built. He also designed the Stockholm suburb of Årsta.

JUDITH S. HULL

WORKS

1911–1913, Apartment Building (with Gustaf Linden), Stockholm. 1911–1913, Hotel, Nyköping, Sweden. 1916–1920, Industrial Village, Bergslagsbyn, Sweden. 1916–1920, Domnarvet Iron Works, Dalcercalia, Sweden. 1917–1921, Forshuvudforsen Power Station (with Vattenbyggnadsbyran), Domnarvet, Sweden. 1924, Folkskola, Sundsvall, Sweden. 1926–1927, Power Station (with Vattenbyggnadsbyran), Krangforsen, Sweden. 1926–1930, Chenderoh Power Station (with Vattenbyggnadsbyran), Perak River, Malay. 1928, Hammarforsen Power Station (with Vattenbyggnadsbyran), Sweden. 1930, Terrace House, Stockholm Exhibition. 1939–1940, Årsta Suburb Plan (with Albert Lilienthal), Stockholm.

BIBLIOGRAPHY

AHLBERG, HAKON 1943 *Gunnar Asplund, Arkitekt, 1885–1940: Ritningar, Skisser, och Fotografier.* Stockholm: Byggmästarens Forlag.

ALMQVIST, OSVALD 1913 "Täflan angående ny folkskola i Kalmar." *Arkitektur* 29.

ALMQVIST, OSVALD 1921 *Byggnadsplaner för bostadsområden: Några allmänna synpunkter.* Stockholm. Appendix to *Praktiska och Hygieniska bostäder.*

ALMQVIST, OSVALD 1922a "Forshuvudforsens kraftverk." *Byggmästaren* issue 81.

ALMQVIST, OSVALD 1922b "Köksinredningarne på 'Bygge och Bo.'" *Svenska Slöjdföreningens tidskrift* 62.

ALMQVIST, OSVALD 1923*a* "Internationella stads-byggnadsutställningen ISBU." *Byggmästaren* issue 213.

ALMQVIST, OSVALD 1923*b* "Stadsplanefrågor och bostadsområdens planläggning." *Byggmästaren* issues 247, 259, 275.

ALMQVIST, OSVALD 1924 "Gatubelysningsarmatur: Några reflexioner i anledning av lykstolpstävlingen. *Byggmästaren* issue 52.

ALMQVIST, OSVALD 1925 "Sjätte våningen." *Byggmästaren* issue 48.

ALMQVIST, OSVALD 1927 "Omputsning." *Byggmästaren* issue 105.

ALMQVIST, OSVALD 1928 "Kökets standardisering: Några synpunkter vid pågående utredningsarbete. *Byggmästaren* issue 105.

ALMQVIST, OSVALD 1929 "Nyare kraftverksanläggningar: Synpunkter på deras arkitektoniska utformning." *Byggmästaren* issue 79. Also published as Svenska Vattenkraftföreningens Publications, No. 217.

ALMQVIST, OSVALD 1933 *Domnarvets industriskolas nybyggnad.* Stockholm.

ALMQVIST, OSVALD 1934*a* Köket och ekonomiavdelningen i mindre bostadslägenheter. Stockholm: Committee for Building Standardization.

ALMQVIST, OSVALD 1934*b* "Den Statsunderstodda egnahemsverksamheten m. m." *Byggmästaren* issue 2.

LINN, BJÖRN 1967 *Osvald Almqvist: Ein Arkitekti och hans Arbete.* Stockholm: Byggmästaren.

ALOISIO, OTTORINO

Ottorino Aloisio (1902–) was born in Udine, Italy, in 1902. He graduated from the Scuola Superiore di Architettura of Rome in 1925. He established his practice in Turin, Italy, and in 1932 joined the faculty of the Politecnico of Turin. He was active in both the Futurist and Rationalist movements in Italy.

DENNIS DOORDAN

WORKS

1934, Casa Littoria, Asti, Italy. 1959–1963, Palazzo SIPRA, Turin, Italy.

BIBLIOGRAPHY

CENNAMO, MICHELE 1973 *La Prima Esposizione Italiana di Architettura Razionale.* Naples: Fausto Fiorentino.

POZZETTO, MARCO 1977 *Vita ed opere dell'architetto udinese Ottorino Aloisio.* Florence: Centro Di.

POZZETTO, MARCO 1978 "Ottorino Aloisio: A Futurist Architect?" *Lotus* 20:96–103.

ALSCHULER, ALFRED S.

Born in Chicago, Alfred S. Alschuler (1876–1940) graduated from Armour Institute of Technology (1899) and studied at the Art Institute in 1899. That year he joined the office of Samuel A. Treat in Chicago, and the firm became Treat and Alschuler (1904–1907). In 1908, he established Alfred S. Alschuler, Incorporated. A pioneer in reinforced concrete, he built many commercial, industrial, and religious buildings in Chicago, New York, and New Jersey. His major achievement was the London Guarantee and Accident Building, Chicago (1922–1923).

DONALD MARTIN REYNOLDS

BIBLIOGRAPHY

"Alfred S. Alschuler." 1924 Volume 21, page 362 in *American Art Annual.* Washington: American Federation of Arts.

"Alschuler, Alfred S." 1932 Volume 17 in *Who's Who in America.* Chicago: Marquis.

CONDIT, CARL W. (1973)1976 *Chicago 1910–1929: Building, Planning, and Urban Technology.* University of Chicago Press.

"Obituary." 1940 *Chicago Tribune* November 7.

"Obituary." 1940 *New York Times* November 7.

ALSTON, JOHN M.

John M. Alston or Allston (1823/1824–1910) was born in Scotland and died in Pittsburgh. He settled in Pittsburgh around 1830, where he attended elementary school. He pursued the stonecutting trade before studying architecture and drafting with Joseph W. Kerr, his patron, who pioneered the revival styles in Pittsburgh.

DONALD MARTIN REYNOLDS

BIBLIOGRAPHY

"Obituary of John Alston." 1910 *American Institute of Architects Quarterly Bulletin* 11, no.1:16.

VAN TRUMP, JAMES D., and ZIEGLER, ARTHUR P., JR. 1967 *Landmark Architecture of Allegheny County, Pennsylvania.* Pittsburgh History and Landmarks Foundation.

ALVAREZ, MARIO ROBERTO

Mario Roberto Alvarez (1913–) is the quintessential modern architect of Argentina, known by the high technical quality and careful design of his buildings and the great volume of work done.

Born in Buenos Aires, he received Gold Medals both at high school and at the University of Buenos Aires, from which he graduated as an architect in 1937. His main activity has been that of a designer, but at the beginning of his career he worked in public offices: Public Works Agency (1937–1942), director of the Architectural Department in the municipal government of Avellaneda (1942–1947), and in recent years as adviser to government agencies. His firm, Mario Roberto Alvarez y Asociados, has produced a great number (nearly 400) and variety of buildings for industry, commerce, residences, health care, education, theater, and hydraulic and road works. This has been successfully achieved through a disciplined organization of the office—a quality not very common in Argentina.

Some qualities are ever present in its buildings: the searching for clear and simplified solutions, from the general layout to the last detail; the use of permanent materials such as steel, glass, and marble; the careful detailing; the restriction of expressiveness; the attention paid to mechanical equipment and technical elements; the ease of maintenance achieved. The language and the general typologies derive from LUDWIG MIES VAN DER ROHE, with necessary changes due to function, site, and other requirements. The firm also designed several huge hydraulic projects such as a river tunnel (Santa Fe, Paraná, 1965) and a Hydro-electric Dam and International Highway (Salto Grande, 1975).

Alvarez has received many awards, including the main National Prize for the Arts in Argentina. In 1976 he became an honorary fellow of the American Institute of Architects.

MARINA WAISMAN

WORKS

1937, San Martin Sanatorium, Gral San Martin, Buenos Aires. 1948, Six Health Centers at Salta, Santiago del Estero, Corrientes, Catamarca, Tucmán, and Jujuy, Brazil. 1953, General San Martín Municipal Theater (with M. O. Ruiz); 1953–1954, City Cultural Center; 1958, Banco Popular Main Office; 1960, Grain Exchange Building; 1965, Bank of America Headquarters (with Aslan y Ezcurra); Buenos Aires. 1965, Santa Fe-Paraná River Tunnel, Entre Ríos, Brazil. 1968, INTA Animal Virus Laboratories (with Ralph Parsons Company), Castelar, Brazil. 1970, Club Alemán; 1971, Galería Jardín Shopping Center; 1978–1980, Chacofi Office Tower; 1978–1980, Güemes Sanatorium; 1981, International Business Machines Headquarters for Argentina; Buenos Aires.

BIBLIOGRAPHY

ALVAREZ, MARIO ROBERTO, and RUIZ, M. OSCAR 1959 *Teatro Municipal General San Martín.* Buenos Aires: Ediciones Infinito.
TRABUCCO, MARCELO A. 1965 *Mario Roberto Alvarez.* Buenos Aires: Instituto de Arte Americano e Investigaciones Estéticas.
WAISMAN, MARINA 1974 *SUMMA* Sept.:special issue.

AMADEO, GIOVANNI ANTONIO

A prolific sculptor as well as an architect and engineer, Giovanni Antonio Amadeo (1447–1522) was a native of Pavia, Italy. Throughout his long and productive career, Amadeo worked primarily in Pavia and Milan and in other Lombard centers including Bergamo, Lodi, and Saronno. Amadeo was the son-in-law of Guinforte Solari (see SOLARI FAMILY) and thus was closely tied to the artistic dynasty that dominated Quattrocento Lombardy. Amadeo was the most important native Lombard architect active in the region during DONATO BRAMANTE's years in Milan and on occasion collaborated with him.

Amadeo's training remains unknown, but recent scholarship has tended to deny the possibility of a visit to Tuscany during his youth (Middeldorf, 1956, p. 140; Seymour, 1966, p. 190). Amadeo's first documented artistic activity was in 1466 when he received payments for work at the Certosa of Pavia, the great Carthusian monastery begun in 1396 during the reign of Giangaleazzo Visconti, where he was to be active throughout his life. His first work there was on the cloisters, and his portal of the Piccolo Chiostro dates from about 1470.

Amadeo's first important architectural undertaking was the Colleoni Funerary Chapel which was added to the Church of Santa Maria Maggiore in Bergamo. The structure itself dates from 1470 to 1473; the sculptural decoration, including the tomb of the geat *condottiere* Bartolommeo Colleoni who died in 1475, seems to have occupied Amadeo through most of the decade. The Colleoni Chapel was a monument of landmark importance for the history of architecture in Lombardy. The centrally planned building, with its high octagonal drum and dome, reflects central Italian developments, and its more immediate prototype is to be found in the Portinari Chapel at Sant' Eustorgio in Milan. The facade of the Colleoni Chapel juxtaposes a wealth of classicizing ornament (including *all'antica* candelabra, rinceaux pilasters, putti heads, and roundels with busts of Julius Caesar and Trajan) with a richly polychromed geometric ground. Amadeo's classical vocabulary may have been derived through contact with IL FILARETE. This fantastic synthesis of native love of rich decoration with antique motifs also characterizes Amadeo's work on the façade of the Certosa of Pavia. Amadeo was first associated with the façade in 1474 when he was allotted half of the sculpture (the other half being given to the Mantegazza brothers, Cristoforo and Antonio), and in 1491 he was placed in charge of the entire project.

In 1481, Amadeo was named *architect* of the Duomo of Milan for the first time and from that year until 1495 he was also *architect* of the Ospedale Maggiore in the city. In 1486, he was asked to execute Bramante's façade design for the Milanese Church of Santa Maria presso San Satiro, a project which was not completed. In 1488, Amadeo was named principal engineer to the new Cathedral of Pavia which had been under Cristoforo de Rocchi. In 1490, Bramante was called in and the wooden model, carved by Giovanni Pietro Fugazza, reflects Bramante's input as well as that of Amadeo and Gian Giacomo Dolcebuono, another local architect. Dolcebuono was also Amadeo's collaborator on the *tiburio* or crossing tower of the Milanese Duomo, a project allotted to the Lombard architects in 1490 after the *opere* rejected the solutions of Bramante, LEONARDO DA VINCI, and others. The *tiburio* as realized (with alterations suggested by FRANCESCO DI GIORGIO MARTINI) reflects Bramante's opinion that the structure had to conform to the Gothic fabric of the building.

Amadeo's other important architectural works include the Bramantesque Palazzo Bottigella in Pavia (documented between 1492 and 1494) of which only the courtyard survives; the cupola of the Shrine at Saronno which was undertaken in 1505; and the completion of the Incornata at Lodi, where he was called in 1513. Amadeo was also consulted as a hydraulic engineer, preparing plans in 1492 to divert the Adda river from its course. Amadeo was for over forty years a key figure in Lombard architecture, contributing to nearly every significant project of the late fifteenth and early sixteenth centuries.

SHERYL E. REISS

WORKS

c.1466–1470, Cloisters of Certosa (various works), Padua, Italy. Begun 1470, Colleoni Chapel, Santa Maria Maggiore, Bergamo, Italy. Begun 1474, Certosa (façade; with the Mantegazza brothers), Padua, Italy. 1481–1495, Ospedale Maggiore, Milan. 1488, Cathedral (with others), Padua, Italy. 1490, Duomo (tiburio, with Gian Giacomo Dolcebuono), Milan. 1492–1494, Palazzo Bottigella, Padua, Italy. 1505, Shrine at Saronno (cupola), Italy. 1513, Incornata at Lodi (completion of upper portions), Italy.

BIBLIOGRAPHY

ARSLAN, EDOARDO 1956 Pages 634–637, 670–678, and 713–724 in *Storia di Milano*. Volume 7 in *L'Eta Sforzesca dal 1450 al 1500*. Milan: Treccani degli Alfieri.

BERNSTEIN, JO ANNE GITLIN 1968 "A Reconsideration of Amadeo's Style in the 1470s and 1480s and Two New Attributions." *Arte lombarda* 13:33–42.

BERNSTEIN, JO ANNE GITLIN 1972 "The Architectural Sculpture of the Cloisters of the Certosa of

Padua." Unpublished Ph.D. dissertation, New York University.

FERRARI DA PASSANO, CARLO, and BRIVIO, ERNESTO 1967 "Contributo allo studio del tiburio del Duomo di Milano." *Arte lombarda* 12:3–36.

MAGENTA, CARLO 1897 *La Certosa di pavia*. Milan: Fratelli Bocci.

MAIOCCHI, RODOLFO 1903 "Giovanni Antonio Amadeo . . . secondo i documenti negli archivi pavesi." *Bollettino della Società pavese di Storia Patria* 3:39–80.

MALAGUZZI-VALERI, FRANCESCO 1904 *Gio. Antonio Amadeo, scultore e architetto lombardo (1447–1522)*. Bergamo, Italy: Istituto italiano d'arti grafiche.

MIDDELDORF, ULRICH 1956 "Ein Jugendwerk des Amadeo." Pages 136–142 in *Kunstgeschichtliche Studien für Hans Kauffmann*. Berlin: Mann.

SEYMOUR, CHARLES, JR. 1966 *Sculpture in Italy 1400 to 1500*. Harmondsworth, England: Penguin.

AMATO, GIACOMO

Giacomo Amato (1643–1732), a member of the Padri Ministri degli Infermi, became active as an architect in Palermo after his return from a twelve-year stay in Rome, where he supervised the construction of the Convent of the Maddalena. His most notable works in Palermo, the Churches of the Pietà (1678–1723) and Santa Teresa alla Kalsa (1686–1706), are modeled on Carlo Rainaldi's Santa Maria in Campitelli in Rome, but they lack the proportional graciousness, plasticity, and complexity of their model. Unlike most Sicilian architects' drawings, Amato's survived and are a unique resource for Sicilian architectural history.

STEPHEN TOBRINER

WORKS

1678–1723, Church of the Pietà; 1686–1706, Santa Teresa alla Kalsa; 1686, San Mattia Apostolo; *1700–1709, Santa Rosalia; Palermo, Italy.

BIBLIOGRAPHY

BIAGI, LUIGI 1939 "Giacomo Amato e la sua posizione nell'architettura Palermitana." *L'Arte* 42:29–48.

CALANDRA, ENRICO 1938 *Breve storia dell'architettura in Sicilia*. Bari, Italy: Laterza & Figli.

CARONIA ROBERTI, S. 1935 *Il Barocco in Palermo*. Palermo, Italy: Ciuni.

MELI, FILIPPO 1938–1939 "Degli architetti del Senato di Palermo nei secoli XVII e XVIII." *Archivio Storico per la Sicilia* 4–5:307–352.

AMATO, PAOLO

Paolo Amato (1634–1714), born in Ciminna, Sicily, went to Palermo as a child and later became a member of the order of the Padri Ministri degli

Infermi known as the "Crociferi." Although he worked with GIACOMO AMATO, who was also a member of the same order, the two architects were not related. As a *sacerdote,* Paolo Amato designed buildings in the Palermo area and collected material for a treatise on perspective, *La nuova pratica di prospettiva,* which was published posthumously by Don Giuseppe Di Miceli in 1736. Amato was granted Palermo citizenship in 1687, and in the same year he became architect of the Senate, a post he held until his death.

STEPHEN TOBRINER

WORKS

1672, Sepulchre of Don Giuseppe Lozano, Cathedral; *1679, New Church of the Monastery of San Giuliano (façade); *1681, Theater of Music, near Porta Felice; 1682, Chapel of the Madonna di Libera Infermi, Cathedral; 1697, Church of the Hospital of the Sacerdoti al Papireto; 1698, Fountain of Garraffo; Palermo, Italy.

BIBLIOGRAPHY

AMATO, PAOLO, and DI MICELI, GIUSEPPE 1736 *La nuova pratica di prospettiva.* Palermo, Italy: Toscano and Gramignani.
CARONIA, ROBERTI SALVATORE 1935 Pages 53–64 in *Il Barocco in Palermo.* Palermo, Italy: Ciuni.
COMOLLI, ANGELO (1791)1964–1965 Volume 3, pages 177–180 in *Bibliografia storico-critica dell'architettura civile ed arti subalterne.* Reprint. Milan: Labor riproduzioni e documentazini.
MELI, FILIPPO 1938–1939 "Degli architetti del Senato di Palermo nei secoli XVII e XVIII." *Archivio Storico per la Sicilia* 4–5:305–470.

AMBLER, THOMAS

The son of a Leeds engineer, Thomas Ambler (1838–1920) worked almost exclusively in his native city in Yorkshire, England. His practice was varied and his style eclectic. Much of his work was of a routine commercial nature, but the patronage of the Leeds clothing manufacturer Sir John Barran offered Ambler unusual opportunities. The monumental Second Empire Trevelyan Temperance Hotel (c.1866–1870), the Hispano-Moorish warehouse, Saint Paul's House (1878), and the half-timbered house Parcmont (1883) all were commissioned by Barran. The second of these buildings is Ambler's best-known, a bravura essay in brick, terra cotta, and faïence with corner minarets—a rare example of this architectural style.

DEREK LINSTRUM

WORKS

*1861, Working Class Housing, Beeston Hill; c.1863, Warehouse, 30 Park Place; c.1866–1870, Trevelyan Temperance Hotel (later Chambers), Boar Lane; Leeds, England. *1871, Woodbank, Ilkley, West Yorkshire, England. *c.1873, Warehouse, 46 Basinghall Street; 1878, Saint Paul's House, Park Square; 1883, Parcmont, Roundhay; *1897, Victoria Arcade; Leeds, England.

BIBLIOGRAPHY

LINSTRUM, DEREK 1978 *West Yorkshire Architects and Architecture.* London: Lund Humphries.

AMENHOTEP

Amenhotep (c.1450–1370 B.C.), called Huy, was the son of Hapu and his wife Itu of Athribis. He was an Egyptian "scribe of recruits" under Amenhotep III, was called to the court in 1400 B.C., and as "master-builder" erected the two colossi (21 meters in height) in front of the mortuary temple of that pharaoh in Western Thebes, and others at Karnak. His devotion to Amenhotep III, "searching for monuments; caring about all his problems, and those of his statues," was acknowledged: the king allowed his colossi to stand in the proximity of his own, his mortuary temple behind the royal one, named him as his representative during the jubilee festival, and later allowed him to figure in the consecration of and be portrayed in the temple at Soleb in the Sudan; he also appointed him controller of the estates of princess Sitamun. The Twenty-first dynasty version of the royal decree of endowment for the mortuary temple of Amenhotep in recognition of his "perfection" shows the popular devotion to Amenhotep and his rise to a healing god, together with IMHOTEP, both appearing on opposed doorjambs in temples, or together on stelae. Prayers were recited before his colossal statues in Thebes.

The mortuary temple of Amenhotep was the only private one in the row of royal temples in Western Thebes, next to that of Thutmose II–III. Built in brick with sandstone revetment, it stands out on account of its size and originality: square court with twenty trees around a huge basin cut from the bedrock, a massive pylon fronting a court flanked by two porticoes and four contiguous vaulted rooms, a transverse vestibule and three sanctuaries forming the rear surrounded by long rooms. Wall scenes in relief on the court and paintings on stucco in the contiguous rooms denote a refined art. In this temple, as well as in the mortuary temple of the king, and that at Soleb (Badawy, 1968, pp. 279–280, fig. 154) described as an "excellent fortress, surrounded with a great wall, whose battlements shine" both size and massiveness express, as in the colossal statuary, the "personal style" of Amenhotep, perhaps reminiscent of his early military connection. Originality marks his portraits as "wise man": a long-haired, long-robed

Amenhotep.
Mortuary Temple of
Amenhotep.
Western Thebes, Egypt.

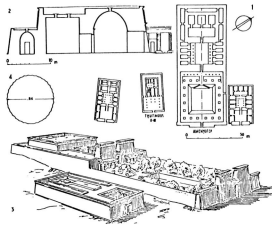

scribe Huy, appearing alone on an ostracon, or in the company of royalty as in the tomb of Inherkhawy.

ALEXANDER BADAWY

BIBLIOGRAPHY

BADAWY, ALEXANDER 1968 *A History of Egyptian Architecture: The Empire.* Berkeley and Los Angeles: University of California Press.
HELCK, HANS WOLFGANG 1972 "Amenophis; Sohn des Hapu." Volume 1, pages 219–221 in Hans Wolfgang Helck and Eberhard Otto (editors), *Lexikon der Ägyptologie.* Wiesbaden, Germany: Harrassowitz.
ROBICHON, CLÉMENT, and VARILLE, ALEXANDRE 1936 *Le temple du scribe royal Amenhotep: Fils de Hapou.* Cairo: Institut français d'archéologie orientale.
VARILLE, ALEXANDRE 1968 *Inscriptions concernant l'architecte Amenhotep: Fils de Hapou.* Cairo: Institut français d'archéologie orientale.
WILDUNG, DIETRICH 1977 Pages 251–297 in *Imhotep und Amenhotep.* Munich: Deutscher Kunstverlag.

AMICO, GIOVANNI BIAGIO

Born in the city of Trapani, Italy, Giovanni Biagio Amico (1684–1754) became a priest in 1705 and began to design buildings in his native city less than ten years later. In 1725, he was accorded the title of royal architect and moved to Palermo where he repaired many buildings which had suffered earthquake damage. It was Amico who in the 1730s designed the façade of Sant'Anna in Palermo, one of the first Sicilian façades to incorporate convex walls. Around 1740, he returned to Trapani which he used as a base for designing buildings throughout western Sicily. He wrote the only complete architectural treatise to be published in eighteenth-century Sicily, *L'Architetto practtico* (Palermo, 1726 and 1750), which gives invaluable information about the architect himself and the practice of architecture on the island.

STEPHEN TOBRINER

WORKS

1712–1714, Church of the Purgatorio (façade), Trapani, Italy. 1720, Church of the Catena, Salemi, Italy. 1721, Santa Caterina, Calatafimi, Italy. 1723, Santa Oliva, Alcamo, Italy. 1726, Immacolata (column); c.1736, Sant'Anna (façade); Palermo, Italy. 1740, San Lorenzo, Trapani, Italy. 1742, San Pietro, Alcamo, Italy. 1744, Seminary (loggia), Mazara, Italy. 1745, Church of the Crocifisso, Calatafimi, Italy. 1748, Church of the Carmine (façade), Licata, Italy.

BIBLIOGRAPHY

AMICO, GIOVANNI BIAGIO (1726)1750 *L'Architetto prattico.* Palermo, Italy: Felicella.
BLUNT, ANTHONY 1968 *Sicilian Baroque.* London: Weidenfeld & Nicolson.
COMANDÈ, GIOVAN BATTISTA 1965 "Architettura Practica di Giovanni d'Amico." *Quaderni dell'Istituto di Storia dell'Architettura, Roma* 12:33–58, 67–70.
SCUDERI, VINCENZO 1961 "L'opera architettonica di Giovan Biagio Amico (1684–1754)." *Palladio* 11, nos. 51–52:56–65.

AMMANNATI, BARTOLOMEO

Bartolomeo Ammannati (1511–1592) designed some of the most striking buildings in sixteenth-century Italy. Drawing freely from contemporaries like JACOPO SANSOVINO, MICHELANGELO, and GIACOMO BAROZZI DA VIGNOLA, he synthesized their individual styles into one. His good-natured personality and his capacity for hard work and swift execution made him the ideal court artist for the princely patrons whom he served throughout his long career. Unlike ANDREA PALLADIO, he published no theoretical treatise, but he left an unusual collection of plans for the major building types found in an ideal city. While Ammannati's influence was limited to Tuscany, the vigorous, three-dimensional qualities of his forms contrast remarkably with the planarity that characterizes Florentine architecture.

Born in Settignano in 1511, Ammannati began as a sculptor and later turned to architecture without any formal training. After an orthodox education in the studio of Baccio Bandinelli, he sculpted in several Italian cities—among them Padua, Urbino, and Naples—before returning to Florence in search of work. Unsuccessful, he left shortly for Venice where he helped Sansovino carve the architectural decoration of the Library of Saint Mark (1536–1553).

Sculpture and architecture were inseparable in Ammannati's earliest work. A triumphal arch (1544–1546) in Padua honoring Marco Benavides employs a robust Doric order framing the central opening and its flanking niches, and the details recall Sansovino's buildings in Venice. The

Benavides tomb (1545) in the Eremitani, Padua, attempted to fuse architecture and sculpture into an aesthetic unity by using the forms of Michelangelo's Medici chapel in San Lorenzo (begun 1520). While its tripartite architectural background for the sarcophagus and allegorical sculpture was openly derived from the Florentine model, Ammannati avoids Michelangelo's dynamism by balancing the entire composition and leaving weights fully supported. The great height of the project was inspired by earlier Venetian wall tombs.

Ammannati soon shed his reliance on monumental sculpture for architectural inspiration. In 1550 he moved to Rome where he executed several commissions for the new pontiff, Julius III. The first project—a family chapel in San Pietro in Montorio (1550–1553)—may owe more to GIORGIO VASARI, who collaborated on its design, and to Michelangelo, who criticized it. Ammannati also completed a palace, for the Pope's brother Balduino, now known as the Palazzo di Firenze (1553). In this case, Ammannati's design was limited by existing construction, but he solved these problems by completing one arm of the courtyard in the forms of the other two sides. Yet the final side presented additional difficulties. Since the site was trapezoidal, the remaining façade required an altogether unique solution. Each elevation was differentiated according to its location; the palace side was executed in an elegant shallow relief derived from Vignola while the garden loggia was boldly articulated with a superimposed Roman order similar to the Theater of Marcellus (23–13 B.C.).

Ammannati's most impressive work in the Roman style was on the Villa Giulia (1551–1555), the papal retreat designed for Julius III. Its complex design develops along a single axis punctuated by a casino, a loggia, and a nymphæum. The chronology and attribution of the entire project are uncertain, but the villa was the result of an elaborate collaboration among Vasari, the overall supervisor, Michelangelo, and Vignola. Ammannati's impressive contributions—the enclosing walls, the loggia, and the nymphæum—thus heightened the design begun by others. The most arresting quality of the project is the two-level drop from the loggia to the nymphæum. A pair of curved stairs leads down to the first level, but the true focus of the complex—a grotto framed by four caryatids—is accessible only through a hidden passageway.

In 1555, after the death of Pope Julius, Ammannati returned to Florence. Duke Cosimo I de Medici gave him the opportunity to design his masterpiece—the additions to the Palazzo Pitti (begun 1560). Part palace and part villa, its two wings flank a *quattrocento* suite of rooms, thus creating a courtyard which was axilly linked to a hippodrome-shaped garden on the hillside above. While its scale and magnificence competed with other Italian ducal residences, the Pitti's planning solved the complex requirements of Cosimo's household. The two new wings respectively contained family apartments with their own entrance and housing for guests; the older central block housed ceremonial rooms. Although the connection between palace and garden was by then common, the choice of a hippodrome-shaped garden to be seen from the Pitti's loggia may have been suggested by Pliny's description of his ancient villa in Tuscany, which employed similar forms. If this is true, then the result is an appropriate metaphor between antiquity and Cosimo's new Tuscan state.

The three-story rusticated courtyard is the Pitti's most distinctive feature. Rustication was a common element in Renaissance palace façades and city gates, but it appears infrequently in courtyard design. Ammannati's motivation for this decision was twofold. Since the cortile faced the garden, rustication was an appropriate expression of the design's pastoral (if not primitive) character. At the same time, it shows Ammannati's sympathy for the Pitti's *quattrocento* façade with his translation of its massive blocks and pilasters within window jambs into *bugnati* and herms. With a fascinating contrast between inventive grammar and a respect for tradition, the Pitti combines both anti-classical and classical sentiments within a single design.

The gravity of the Pitti's courtyard also contrasts with the tense elegance of the Ponte Santa Trinita (1567–1569), which spans the Arno River with three elliptical arches. This bold conception may have been due to Michelangelo, who had discussed the project with Vasari and sent drawings to Florence for it. In any case, the execution was totally in Ammannati's hands, for the same billowy plastic moldings used at the Pitti are employed here on a monumental scale.

The somber, repetitive effect of Ammannati's other Florentine palaces is due to external circumstances. Almost all were limited by existing construction. Patrons were usually courtiers to the duke, hence their residences had to be less elaborate than those of the older nobility. Exterior façades, however, were free of constraints, and Ammannati's designs emphasized elaborate arched entries and rusticated window frames placed in façades that were sometimes covered with sgraffito decoration. Both the façade system and its individual elements date back to fourteenth- and fifteenth-century prototypes, but in spirit and form they were one with the Pitti. This system was flexible enough to be varied for each commission. Among them, the Palazzo Grifoni (1557–1574) is notable for its location on the Piazza Santissima Annunziata and the Palazzo Giugni (1570s) for its compact plan with four individual courtyard loggias.

Ammannati's profound religiosity affected his ecclesiastical projects. Toward the end of his career, he embraced the Counter-Reformation philosophy of the Jesuits. In painting and sculpture he denounced nude figures as lustful, and in his churches he employed the aisleless plans favored by contemporary architects and churchmen. For San Giovannino (1579–1585), the Jesuit church in Florence, Ammannati's broad, vaulted nave recalls Vignola's Gesù (begun 1568) in Rome with its series of confessionals located between side chapels. A similar arrangement was used for the church of Santa Maria in Gradi (1592) in Arezzo, his last project. Yet these schemes cannot be properly called Jesuit: there are no domes and the clerestory-lit naves continue beyond the stunted transepts, creating ascetic interiors similar to earlier Franciscan examples like IL CRONACA's San Salvatore al Monte (1480–1504) in Florence. San Giovannino's façade, executed after Ammannati's death, turned to Florentine secular models for inspiration by using both niches from Vasari's Uffizi Palace

(begun 1560) and Michelangelo's famous recessed columns from the Laurentian Library (begun 1524). A measure of Ammannati's fondness for this small structure is that he was buried within it after his death in 1592.

LEON SATKOWSKI

WORKS

1544–1546, Triumphal Archway, Palazzo Benavides; 1545, Benavides Tomb; Padua, Italy. 1550–1553, San Pietro in Montorio (Del Monte Chapel); 1551–1555, Villa Giulia (with Giorgio Vasari, Giacomo Barozzi da Vignola, and Michelangelo); 1553, Palazzo Firenze; Rome. 1557–1574, Palazzo Grifoni; 1558–1559, Laurentian Library (execution of Michelangelo's model for the staircase); begun 1560, Palazzo Pitti; (A)1564–1569, Santo Spirito (second cloister); 1567–1569, Ponte Santa Trinita; 1568, Palazzo Mondragone; 1568, Palazzo Ramirez-Montalvo; 1570s, Palazzo Giugni; 1575, Houses for the Arte della Lana; Florence. 1575, Madonna del Umilità (restoration of cupola), Pistoia, Italy. (A)1576, Villa Medici, Rome. 1577, Palazzo della Signoria, Lucca, Italy. 1579–1585, Jesuit College and Church of San Giovannino, Florence. 1580, Palazzo Bernardi-Micheletti, Lucca, Italy. (A)1581, Collegio Romano, Rome. 1592, Church of Santa Maria in Gradi, Arezzo, Italy.

BIBLIOGRAPHY

AMMANNATI, BARTOLOMEO 1970 *La città*. Edited by Mazzino Fossi. Rome: Officina Edizioni.

Ammannati.
Palazzo Pitti (courtyard).
Florence.
Begun 1560

ANDRES, GLENN M. 1976 *The Villa Medici in Rome.* 2 vols. New York: Garland.

BELLI BARSALI, ISA 1960 "Bartolomeo Ammannati." Volume 2, pages 798–801 in *Dizionario biografico degli Italiani.* Rome: Istituto della Enciclopedia Italiana.

FOSSI, MAZZINO 1967 *Bartolomeo Ammannati: Architetto.* Naples: Morano Editore.

KINNEY, PETER 1976 *The Early Sculpture of Bartolomeo Ammannati.* New York: Garland.

VENTURI, ADOLFO 1939 "Bartolomeo Ammannati." Volume 11, part 2, pages 212–350 in *Storia dell arte italiana.* Milan: Hoepli.

VODOZ, E. 1941 "Studien zum architektonischen Werk des Bartolomeo Ammannati." *Mitteilungen des Kunsthistorischen Instituts in Florenz* 6:1–141.

ANBURY, THOMAS

Major-General Sir Thomas Anbury (c.1760–1840) served with the Bengal Engineers in various posts, including as Superintendent of Buildings at Barrackpore near Calcutta (1815–1816). Although no building can definitely be ascribed to him, he probably designed Barrackpore House (completed c.1815), the country residence of the governor-general of India.

PAULINE ROHATGI

BIBLIOGRAPHY

ANBURY, THOMAS 1798 *Hindoostan Scenery Consisting of Twelve Select Views in India Drawn on the Spot . . . During the Campaign of . . . the Marquis Cornwallis.* London.

ANDERSON, R. ROWAND

Robert Rowand Anderson (1834–1921) was a leading Scottish architect and educator. Born in Forres, Scotland, he trained in law and served in the Corps of Royal Engineers studying construction and design. Despite drafting deficiencies, he set up an architectural practice in Edinburgh about 1865. He had a large output in a wide range of styles including restoration work. He was instrumental in setting up formal architectural education in Scotland; he organized the incorporation of regional societies into the Institute of Scottish Architects, becoming its first President; and he inaugurated the National Art Survey. Anderson was knighted in 1902 and received the Gold Medal of the Royal Institute of British Architects in 1916.

BRUCE WALKER

WORKS

1878–1888, Medical School, Edinburgh. 1879, Mount Stuart, Bute, Scotland. 1881–1884, Central Station Hotel, Glasgow. 1882, Saint George's West Church (campanile); 1882–1884, Conservative Club; Edin-

burgh. 1884–1888, Old Parish Church, Govan, Scotland. 1885–1890, National Portrait Gallery and National Museum of Antiquities of Scotland, Edinburgh. 1889–1897, McEwan Hall, Edinburgh University. 1903–1905, William Pearce Memorial Institute, Govan, Scotland.

BIBLIOGRAPHY

ANDERSON, R. ROWAND 1870–1875 *Examples of the Municipal, Commercial and Street Architecture of France and Italy from the 12th to the 15th Century.* London, Edinburgh, and Glasgow: W. Mackenzie.

ANDERSON, R. ROWAND, and NEWTON, ERNEST 1916 "The Royal Gold Medal Presentation." *Journal of the Royal Institute of British Architects* Series 3, 23:265–273.

ANDERSON, R. ROWAND; ROSS, THOMAS; and OLDRIEVE, W. T. (editors) 1921 *National Art Survey of Scotland: Examples of Scottish Architecture From the Twelfth to the Seventeenth Century.* Edinburgh and London: G. Waterson.

"Obituary of Sir R. Rowand Anderson, LL.D., FRIBA." 1921 *Journal of the Royal Institute of British Architects* Series 3, 28:457–458.

PATERSON, A. N. 1921 "Sir Robert Rowand Anderson: An Appreciation." *Journal of the Royal Institute of British Architects* Series 3, 28:511–513.

ANDRE, EMILE

As a member of the Ecole de Nancy, Emile André (1871–?) became a major figure in the French Art Noveau movement at the turn of the twentieth century. Born in Nancy, the son of an architect, André, like most aspiring architects of the period, studied in Paris, where he was first apprenticed as a draftsman to Jacques de Morgan. By 1901, he had settled back in Nancy and undertook several projects in both the civic and private realms. These included the planning scheme for the Parc de Saurupt and a department store design, both in Nancy and both executed with the firm of Waxelaire and Pignot.

The design credo espoused by André and his colleagues of the Nancy School stressed natural and organic forms as an essential element in the ultimate aspiration of artistic unity (*l'unité de l'art*). Ideally, a variety of material—everything from ceramics and wood to cast iron—also was necessary in fulfilling this goal. For André, these notions were most significantly manifested in the decorative elements of his architecture such as balusters, window ornament, and particularly iron grillwork.

PETER L. DONHAUSER

WORKS

1901, Department Store (with Waxelaire and Pignot); 1901, Urban Plan, Parc de Saurupt *quartier* (with

Waxelaire and Pignot); Nancy, France. *1902, Ecole de Nancy pavilion, Exposition Internationale des Arts Décoratifs Modernes, Turin, Italy. 1903, House, 30 rue du Sergent-Blandon; 1904, House, 71 Avenue Foch; *1909, Ecole de Nancy Pavilion (with Gaston Munier), Exposition Internationale de l'Est de la France; 1910, Bank, 9 rue Chanzy; Nancy, France.

BIBLIOGRAPHY

CHARPENTIER, THÉRÈSE 1977 "Nancy Architecture, 1900." *Monuments Historiques* 4:65–68.

ANDREWS, FRANK M.

Born in Des Moines, Iowa, Frank Mills Andrews (1867–1948) studied civil engineering at Iowa State College and earned a B.S. degree in architecture from Cornell University (1888). He practiced in Chicago (1893–1898) until he established F. M. Andrews and Company in New York. Andrews designed state capitols, hotels, industrial plants, and commercial buildings in New York, Chicago, Kentucky, Montana, Ohio, Massachusetts, Connecticut, and Washington.

DONALD MARTIN REYNOLDS

BIBLIOGRAPHY

"Andrews, Frank Mills." 1916 Volume 9, in *Who's Who in America.* Chicago: Marquis.
"Obituary." 1948 *New York Herald Tribune* September 3.
"Obituary." 1948 *New York Times* September 3.

ANDREWS, ROBERT DAY

Robert Day Andrews (1857–1928) studied in Europe, at the Massachusetts Institute of Technology, and with H. H. RICHARDSON. In 1885, he became a partner of Andrews, Jacques, and Rantoul, and later of Andrews, Jones, Biscoe, and Whitmore. His work is in the Beaux-Arts, Romanesque, and classical styles.

FREDERIC C. DETWILLER

WORKS

1887–1888, Emmanuel Church, Dublin, N.H. 1889, House, 448 Beacon Street, Boston. c.1892, Boston Building, Denver, Colo. c.1892, Colorado College Buildings, Colorado Springs. c.1892, Equitable Life Insurance Company Building, Denver, Colo. c.1892, Equitable Life Insurance Company Building, Des Moines, Iowa. 1897–1898, Worcester County Courthouse, Mass. 1898, Jamaica Plain High School; 1900, Appleton (Muller) Building; 1902, State Mutual Insurance Building; 1907–1908, Hornblower and Weeks Building; 1913, Dexter Building; Boston. 1913–1917, Connecticut School for the Blind; 1913–1917, Connecticut State Capitol (restoration); Hartford. 1914–1917, Massachusetts State Capitol (east and west wings; with William Chapman and R. Clipston Sturgis), Boston. 1915, Brookline High School, Mass.

BIBLIOGRAPHY

BUNTING, BAINBRIDGE (1965)1975 *Houses of Boston's Back Bay: An Architectural History.* Cambridge, Mass: Harvard University Press.
FOX, PAMELA, and KOCH, MICKAIL 1980 *Central Business District Inventory.* Boston Landmarks Commission.
"Obituary." 1929 *American Art Annual* 26:383.

ANDRONIKOS OF KYRRHOS

Andronikos of Kyrrhos (1st century B.C.) was the designer of the so-called Tower of the Winds (a horologion), in Athens (c.50–37 B.C.). A small octagonal building, it contained a waterclock inside and sundials on two exterior faces; upon its summit a bronze triton turned to point to the winds, personified by reliefs on the walls below. As the only surviving example of the type, the building is interesting not only for the information it contains about mechanical technology in antiquity, but also for the eclectic originality of its details, Corinthian on the exterior, and a diminutive but variant Doric order internally.

B. M. BOYLE

WORK

c.50–37 B.C., Tower of the Winds (Horologion), Athens.

BIBLIOGRAPHY

English translations of the ancient texts can be found in the volumes of the Loeb Classical Library series, published by Harvard University Press and Heinemann.
DINSMOOR, WILLIAM B. (1950)1973 *The Architecture of Ancient Greece.* Reprint. New York: Biblo & Tannen.
LAWRENCE, ARNOLD W. (1957)1975 *Greek Architecture.* Harmondsworth, England: Penguin.
PRICE, EREK DE SOLLA, and NOBLE, JOSEPH V. 1968 "The Water-Clock in the Tower of the Winds." *American Journal of Archaeology* 72:345–355.
VARRO, *De re rustica,* Book 3.5.17.
VITRUVIUS, *De architectura,* Book 1.6.4.

ANGELL, FRANK W.

Frank W. Angell (1851–1943) was born in Providence, Rhode Island, where he began the study of architecture in the office of William R. Walker. Angell began to design houses independently in 1880. He retired around 1933.

DONALD MARTIN REYNOLDS

WORKS

1876, Narragansett Pier Railroad Stations, R.I. 1883, Narragansett Boat Club Clubhouse, R.I. 1886, Auburn Baptist Church, R.I. 1886, Murray Universalist Church, Attleboro, Mass. 1891, Hazard Memorial Building, Peace Dale, R.I. 1891, Wilson Hall, Brown University, Providence, R.I.

BIBLIOGRAPHY

Additional material on Frank W. Angell is in the Rhode Island Historical Preservation Commission Archives and the Rhode Island Historical Society Graphics Department, both in Providence, R.I.

CADY, JOHN HUTCHINS 1957 *The Civic and Architectural Development of Providence; 1636-1950.* Providence, R.I.: Book Shop.

"Design for a Roller Skating Rink." 1885 *Carpentry and Building* 7, no. 4:69-72.

HAZARD, CAROLINE 1929 *A Precious Heritage.* Boston: Merrymount Press.

ANGELL, TRUMAN OSBORN

Truman Osborn Angell (1810-1887) was born in North Providence, Rhode Island, where he trained as a carpenter and joiner beginning around 1827. By 1833, he was working at his trade in upstate New York. He worked on several Mormon temples in Ohio and Illinois. In the temple at Nauvoo, Illinois (1841-1845), he introduced Mormon orders and forms (moonstone bases and sunstone capitals, for example). As Brigham Young's architect of public works, to which position he was appointed around 1850, and subsequently as church architect, he became the most important architect of the period in Utah Territory.

DONALD MARTIN REYNOLDS

WORKS

1841-1845, Mormon Temple, Nauvoo, Ill. 1853-1855, Beehive House; 1853-1887, Salt Lake City Temple (not completed until 1893); 1855-1856, Lion House; 1868-1870, Salt Lake Tabernacle (gallery); 1870-1877, Saint George Temple; 1877-1884, Logan Temple; n.d., Territorial Capitol Building (unfinished); Salt Lake City, Utah.

BIBLIOGRAPHY

Truman O. Angell's journals are in the Church Historian's Office, Salt Lake City, Utah.

ANDERSON, PAUL 1980 Review of Laurel B. Andrew, *The Early Temples of the Mormons: The Architecture of the Millennial Kingdom in the American West. Journal of the Society of Architectural Historians* 39:337-338.

ANDREW, DAVID S., and BLANK, LAUREL B. 1971 "The Four Mormon Temples in Utah." *Journal of the Society of Architectural Historians* 30:51-65.

ANDREW, LAUREL B. 1978 *The Early Temples of the Mormons: The Architecture of the Millennial Kingdom in*
the American West. Albany: State University of New York Press.

CHURCHILL, STEPHANIE D. 1972 *Utah: A Guide to Eleven Tours of Historic Sites.* Salt Lake City: Utah Heritage Foundation.

"The First Mormon Temple." 1876 *American Architect and Building News* 1:52.

GOELDNER, PAUL 1969 *Utah Catalog: Historic American Buildings Survey.* Salt Lake City: Utah Heritage Foundation.

JENSON, ANDREW (1901-1936)1971 *Latter-Day Saint Biographical Encyclopedia.* 4 vols. Reprint. Salt Lake City: Western Epics.

ANGELO DA ORVIETO

First documented (in 1317 or 1319) together with LORENZO MAITANI in connection with work on the hydraulic system of the Fontana Maggiore in Perugia, Italy, Angelo da Orvieto (14th century) is best known for his designs for communal palaces in Umbria. Although there is no agreement regarding the precise dates for, or extent of, his participation in most of the major projects attributed to him, the Palace of the Consuls in Gubbio (1332-1337) and the Communal Palace in Città di Castello (1334-1352) are generally accepted as his work. In these, Angelo elaborated a type of urban palace influenced by the Palazzo del Capitano in Orvieto (c.1250) and the Palazzo Vecchio in Florence (early 1300s), but distinguished from them by a greater sophistication in the construction of monumental barrel-vaulted interior spaces.

CHRISTINE SMITH

BIBLIOGRAPHY

GUERIERI, OTTORINO 1959 *Angelo da Orvieto, Matteo Giovanello Gattaponi e i palazzi pubblici di Gubbio e di Città di Castello.* Perugia, Italy: Grafica.

SIMSON, OTTO VON 1972 *Propyläen Kunstgeschichte: Das Mittelalter, II.* Berlin: Propyläen.

WHITE, JOHN 1966 *Art and Architecture in Italy: 1250-1400.* Harmondsworth, England: Penguin.

ANGELOVA-VINAROVA, VICTORIA

Victoria Angelova-Vinarova (1902-1947) was one of the first eminent women architects in Bulgaria. Born in Turnovo, Bulgaria, she obtained an architecture degree in Dresden, Germany, in 1925. After establishing her practice in Sofia, she specialized in the design of hospitals and health centers. Most notable are her Psychiatric Clinic and Venereal Diseases Clinic of the Alexandrov's Hospital (1934-1935), Sofia, and the Sanatorium (1939-1942) in Raduntsi, Bulgaria.

Angelova-Vinarova created clear functional compositions applying the Bauhaus approach to science, technology, and art in architecture, as, for example, in the Second Surgery Clinic (1935–1936) and the Higher Medical Institute (1938–1939), both in Sofia.

MARIA POPOVA

WORKS

1926, Ministry of Civic Buildings, Roads and Urbanization, Sofia. 1930–1931, Resort Hotel, Black Sea Shore, Varna, Bulgaria. 1934–1935, Psychiatric Clinic and Venereal Diseases Clinic, Alexandrov's Hospital; 1935–1936, Second Surgery Clinic (with T. Harbov and B. Kapitanov); 1937, Natural History Museum; 1938–1939, Higher Medical Institute (with Harbov and Kapitanov); Sofia. 1939–1942, Sanatorium, Raduntsi, Bulgaria, 1947–1949, Kindergarten, Sofia.

BIBLIOGRAPHY

BŬLGARSKA AKADEMIĬA NA NAUKITE 1965 *Kratka Istoriiā na Bŭlgarskata Arkhitektura*. Sofia: The academy.
BŬLGARSKA AKADEMIĬA NA NAUKITE 1963–1969 in *Kratka Bŭlgarska Entsiklopediiā*. Sofia: The academy.
"Sanitoriumut v Raduntsi" 1959 *Arkhitektura* 1959:4.

ANREITH, ANTON

Anton Anreith (1754–1822) was born in Riegel, Baden, Germany and died in Cape Town, South Africa. After training in Germany, he enrolled as an ordinary soldier in the service of the Dutch East India Company in Amsterdam in 1777. Sent to the Cape, he was soon employed as a sculptor, and by 1768 was master sculptor to the company. Henceforth, he worked closely with the architect LOUIS M. THIBAULT. Besides a large volume of sculpture, often of impressive quality, Anreith was commissioned by church congregations and private patrons to design and execute pulpits, furniture, and buildings, and by the company and other patrons to design in collaboration with Thibault. His architectural works are generally in a polished South German, late rococo style; an essay in neoclassicism in the façade of the Lutheran church proved less satisfactory.

RONALD LEWCOCK

WORKS

1768, Cape Town Castle (Kat Balcony; with Louis Michael Thibault); *(A)c.1791, Dutch Reformed Church Sexton's House (façade); c.1781–1782, Lutheran Parsonage (façade); 1791, Groot Constantia Wine Cellar (pediment; with Thibault); 1792, Lutheran Church (façade); (A)1798, Rust en Vreugd (façade); Cape Town.

BIBLIOGRAPHY

BOSDARI, D. DE 1954 *Anton Anreith, Africa's First Sculptor*. Cape Town: Balkema.
MEINTJES, JOHANNES 1951 *Anton Anreith, Sculptor, 1754–1822*. Cape Town: Juta.

ANTELAMI, BENEDETTO

Justly considered by many the greatest sculptor of the Italian Romanesque style, Benedetto Antelami (1150?–1230?) bequeathed an architectural legacy matched in individuality and artistic scope by no other Italian of his day. Both his sculptural and his architectural works look, like the double-faced Janus of Roman mythology, to the past as well as to the future for artistic inspiration. Born during a period that witnessed the slow rebirth of the artistic personality after centuries of anonymous medieval creation, Antelami emerges as an artist eminently aware of his classical Roman heritage and carefully alert to the nascent French Gothic style.

Unfortunately for architectural history, there is a paucity of documentary evidence to ascertain Antelami's imputed architectural activity; however, some records and epigraphs coupled with the analysis of stylistic affinities and historical events militate for the hypothesis that Antelami, while engaged in multifarious sculptural programs such as the episcopal cathedra at Parma (1180) and the sculptural program of the Parma Baptistery (1196–1216), never abandoned his architectural proclivity. Also, his surname links him to the *magistri Antelami* or civil builder's guild of the Lake Como area in Italy where Benedetto was probably born.

Benedetto's sculptural apprenticeship may have been served at Saint Trophîme at Arles (largely twelfth century) where a colony of Lombard masons worked on the decoration of the choir. Throughout the duration of his artistic career, Antelami demonstrated an appreciation for contemporary French developments, visiting France probably three times.

Intermittently between 1188 and 1218, Benedetto worked on the nave, façade, crypt, and choir of the Cathedral of Borgo San Donnino (now Fidenza), slightly northwest of Parma in the Emilia-Romagna region of Italy. The unfinished façade of the church is composed of a squarish mass gabled at the top, penetrated by three portals, the largest being in the center, and flanked by two undecorated belfry towers. Despite its unhomogeneous character, the church demonstrates Antelami's attempts to reconcile the architectural styles of northern Italian Romanesque and the Romanesque of Provençal France. This is evident, for example, in the linking of such features as the square belfry towers and gables of Italian liking with Provençal elements such as the columns flanking the central portal, the strong horizontal accent of the lower part of the façade and sculptural motifs such as fleshy acanthus scrolls. These elements occur at the Cluniac church of Saint-Gilles-du-Gard (1116?–1170) in France.

While working at Borgo San Donnino, Antelami was called upon in 1196 to execute the construction and sculptural program of the Baptistery of Parma which dragged on chronically until 1270, the year the building was consecrated. The sacrament of baptism was first administered in 1216 in the incomplete edifice whose function of initiation of large numbers of unbaptized into the faith is almost anachronistic in twelfth-century Italy.

Set diagonally across the piazza from the Cathedral, the six-storied octagonal edifice boasts a magnificent exterior shell of stone and brick, abundant in this rich, alluvial area. The façade is pierced by four stories of colonnaded galleries separated by a series of trabeations, comprising about one-half the height of the building. The lacy insubstantiality of the central zone is held in check by the massive corner pilasters and the display of thick masonry of the portal and is capped by an arched corbel table over a decorative arcade at its summit.

This layered architectural façade acts like a protective shell and masks the interior ribbed ogival cupola whose apex is coterminal with the top of the exterior façade. Effectively, the onlooker moves from the solid, imposing exterior into a surprisingly uplifting and vertically oriented interior space. In a technically audacious and sound manner, the octagonal plan translates into a sixteen-sided polygon on the interior where sixteen engaged columns on the ground floor lead into the sixteen ribs of the cupola.

Stylistically, the Baptistery bespeaks at least a dual origin: that of the incipient Gothic style as exemplified in Saint Denis (1135–1144) and Chartres Cathedral (1135–1180) and evidenced in the pointed arch system of the Baptistery's top story and interior as well as in its sculptural program, and a classical tradition, probably filtered through the Romanesque style of French Provence, an area where the legacy of the Greco-Roman world smoldered far longer than in other parts of the country. The Baptistery is classicizing in its proportions and use of the language and syntax of classical architecture, for example, the horizontal definition of the façade through trabeation over free-standing columns.

One must not overlook, in assessing Antelami's stylistic origins, the immediate and perva-

Antelami. Baptistery. Parma, Italy. 1196–1216 (not completed until 1270).

sive influence that the Tuscan Romanesque must have exerted, exemplified by such buildings as the Cathedral at Pisa (1063, 1089–1272). A glance at Antelami's colonnaded galleries calls quickly to mind the four-storied arcading of the façade of the Cathedral at Pisa which was for the most part completed at about the same time as the Baptistery.

The balance between the gravity and horizontality of Romanesque elements and the pointed, vertical impulse of the Gothic is tipped in favor of the Gothic in Antelami's last architectural work, the Abbey and Church of Sant'Andrea at Vercelli, about equidistant from Milan and Turin. Commissioned by Cardinal Guala, the church was begun in 1219 and finished in about 1225–1226. Antelami was superintendent of construction.

A voyage to France in about 1218 where Antelami certainly saw the Gothic churches at Laon, Vauxelles, and Braisne explain away the style of the ecclesiastical complex at Vercelli. While remnants of the Tuscan Romanesque linger on in the two-storied arcade of the church façade and

Antelami.
Abbey and Church of
Sant'Andrea.
Vercelli, Italy.
1219–1225/1226

decorative arcading of the nave and numerous towers, the predominance of Gothic characteristics is overriding: flying buttresses, rose windows, a longing for height in exterior as well as interior proportions, an intense interest in structural clarity and organization, a desire for interior light, ribbed vaulting, and a steady movement from one bay to the next marking the slow rhythm of the buildings.

Benedetto Antelami showed himself at Sant'Andrea to have perceived and grasped the changing taste of the day for the Gothic style, a style which never took firm hold in his native Italy. He probably died shortly after completing Sant'Andrea at Vercelli.

He was surrounded throughout his life by numerous disciples and collaborators, witness to his great talent. The sculptural work of Oldrado da Tresseno (thirteenth century) demonstrates Benedetto's influence, and his artistic style had repercussions in many areas such as Umbria, the Marches, and central Italy.

TINA WALDEIER BIZZARRO

WORKS

1188–1218, Cathedral of Borgo San Donnino (now Fidenza), Italy. 1196–1216, Baptistery (not completed until 1270), Parma, Italy. 1219–1225/1226, Abbey and Church of Sant'Andrea at Vercelli, Italy.

BIBLIOGRAPHY

ARGAN, GIULIO CARLO (1938)1978 *L'Architettura italiana del Duecento e Trecento.* Bari, Italy: Dedalo.
CONANT, KENNETH JOHN (1959)1978 *Carolingian and Romanesque Architecture 800 to 1200.* 2d ed., rev. Harmondsworth, England: Penguin.
DE FRANCOVICH, GEZA 1952 *Benedetto Antelami: Architetto e Scultore e l'Arte del suo Tempo.* 2 vols. Milan: Stucchi; Florence: Electa Editrice.
JACKSON, THOMAS GRAHAM (1913)1920 *Byzantine and Romanesque Architecture.* 2d ed. Cambridge University Press.
KUBACH, HANS ERICH 1975 *Romanesque Architecture.* New York: Abrams.
PORTER, ARTHUR KINGSLEY 1909 *Medieval Architec-ture: Its Origins and Development.* New York: Baker & Taylor.
PORTER, ARTHUR KINGSLEY 1915–1917 *Lombard Architecture.* New Haven: Yale University Press.
ROSATI, GOFFREDO 1959 "Antelami, Benedetto." Volume 1, pages 466–473 in *Encyclopedia of World Art.* New York: McGraw-Hill.

ANTHEMIOS

Anthemios (first half of the sixth century) was born in Tralles (now Aydin) in Asia Minor (Turkey), one of five gifted brothers, all eminent professionals. He was "by profession an engineer or architect, one of those people who apply geometrical speculation to material objects and make models or imitations of the natural world" (Agathias, 5.6). He may have been educated, in part, in Alexandria, still in his day the hallowed center of scholarship and teaching. His genius and many interests are lauded by several contemporary writers—historians, poets, and scientists—whose lively appreciation of him comes clearly through the overladen style of the period and the all but obligatory deference to the pre-eminent abilities of the emperor, Justinian.

The picture of Anthemios gained from the texts is that of an experimental scientist, a thinker, a solver of problems both theoretical and practical, to whom the mastery of the technical aspects of architecture would come quite naturally. But he was also a splendid artist, as the Hagia Sophia records and as Agathias proclaims, saying that he had exhibited signal proof of his own excellence "by designing the most wonderful artistic creations in the capital and in many other places, indeed so wonderful that as long as they were standing their sheer beauty would suffice, without a single word being spoken about them, to perpetuate the glory of his memory" (5.6). Paul, a court poet, refers to him as a man "of many crafts" (verse 550), and modern scholars rank his studies in advanced geometry and physics highly:

Anthemios was one of the last great geometers of antiquity . . . the Arab estimate of (him) as the peer of Archimedes in the study of mirrors was not based upon a misconception of his originality. In his building and in his writings, and in the work of his contemporaries, there is proof that the age of Justinian witnessed a late flowering of creative mathematical thinking. We recognize that Anthemios was a distinguished follower of the great Hellenistic geometers (Huxley, p. 30).

Some of his scientific treatises survive, somewhat mutilated, and there are glimpses of him in other texts as a writer on paradoxes and as a designer and constructor of elaborate mechanical devices. It was a many-sided, highly creative man, then, that Justinian chose to be the designer of the Hagia Sophia (532–537), by any standard a building of great artistic significance and astonishing originality.

The previous church to the Holy Wisdom that had stood where Anthemios was to build in Constantinople had been burned down by rioters early in 532. Nearby were the patriarchate, the imperial palace, the senate house, and other major public buildings. The earlier church had been of basilican plan, its focus and space governed by an elongated horizontal axis leading from the centered entranceway to the apsidal sanctuary. The speed with which Anthemios and his associate ISIDOROS got the new building up has led some to think that Justinian may have quietly put the whole project in train before the riots. And it has also been suggested, perhaps with good reason, that a small church Justinian and his wife Theodora had commissioned a few years earlier, Saints Sergius and Bacchus, was a kind of trial exercise, on a small scale, for the Hagia Sophia. Sergius and Bacchus does have quite a lot in common with the conception behind the Hagia Sophia, and it is possible that the earlier building was one of the "creations in the capital" spoken of by Agathias.

There is a famous lengthy and engrossing description of the construction of the Hagia Sophia in a work entitled *On the Buildings* (of Justinian) by the court historian Procopius. Treading softly before the autocrat, Procopius gives him a fair amount of spurious credit for the successful conclusion of construction. Yet Anthemios's creativity shines through, as a few sentences will show:

The emperor, disregarding all considerations of expense, hastened to begin construction and raised craftsmen from the whole world. It was Anthemios of Tralles, the most learned man in the discipline called engineering, not only of all his contemporaries, but also as compared to those who had lived long before him, that ministered to the emperor's zeal by regulating the work of the builders and preparing designs in advance . . . (the) enormous spherical dome . . . seems not to be founded on solid masonry, but to be suspended from heaven by that golden chain [of the *Iliad,* 8.19] . . . in mid-air (1.1. 23–50).

At another point, in order that Justinian not feel left out, Procopius spins a tale about "the piers on top of which the structure was being built (being) unable to bear the mass that was pressing down on them . . . (so the terrified staff) referred the matter to the Emperor . . ." who solved the problem, although, as Procopius says, "he is not an engineer." He adds that the story would seem to be incredible, just flattery, if there weren't so many witnesses available (1.1. 68–72).

Anthemios. Hagia Sophia (with Isidoros). Constantinople (Istanbul), Turkey. 532–537

Anthemios. Hagia Sophia (interior; with Isidoros). Constantinople (Istanbul), Turkey. 532–537

Referral to past architecture is not very useful in assessing the Hagia Sophia. It is correct to say that the domical and basilican systems of Roman and early Christian architecture are combined in the building, but neither one gives it its essential quality. The way in which Anthemios so creatively managed their fusion amounted to a new architectural creation, a stylistic and structural quantum leap rarely seen in historical architecture. At ground level he in effect produced a basilicalike plan complete with flanking arcades and an apse. But the space is toed-in at the corners by angled, vaulted exedras, and the longitudinal volume continues up and beyond the place where the relatively low horizontal roof of a basilica would be, to terminate in a lofty, centered dome. Since a dome cannot be smoothly fitted directly onto a basilica, Anthemios supported his on monumental pendentives which in turn rest on four massive stone arches and piers standing at the ends of the parallel basilican arcades. Two facing sides of the resulting square plan of piers are open to the apsidal and entrance ends of the basilican scheme by way of hovering semidomes above and the angled exedras below. The whole, save the sanctuary, is wrapped by ground-floor aisles with superposed galleries, the structure of which assists in bringing the thrusts from the great brick dome and its supporting mechanism properly to the ground. The result is a huge unobstructed main space some 265 feet long and 180 feet high, presided over by a (reconstructed) dome whose base is pierced by forty windows and whose encompassing form flows downward, as it were, by way of the pendentives, semidomes, exedrae and other vaults, and a number of arches large and small. Structural solids are withheld from view, curve meets curve delicately and tangentially, and the whole interior reads as a precisely fitted assembly of thin, perforated surfaces.

The dematerialization of the building's structural reality is carried out in almost every detail of the design. Capitals and cornices are lacy, compacted descendants of the ancient, formulaic systems of the classical Orders; deep drilling into the marbles creates a staccato play of light and dark emphasized by the acre or so of splintery, gold-ground mosaic that once covered the vaults, and by the many-hued, thin sheets of marble that sheath the brick and stone walls and piers. Later rulers commissioned figural mosaics for the build-

ing, but in Anthemios's day the mosaics were abstract and symbolic in nature. Even now, with most of the mosaic lost and with rather discordant Turkish stencils as substitutes, the eye glides from part to part and discovers that harmony of large and small, of light and dark, that Anthemios created. In a sense the building consists of a space composed of billowing volumes enclosed by apparently insubstantial shells of color. There is, surprisingly, no fragility in all this, even though there is little that expresses the load-support relationship except in the lowest zone, the one most apprehensible to the observer. The binding ingredient is light. Huge beams pry through the building on sunny days, made material by the dust that sifts through the grand volume of the nave. This light comes in directly from the outside to the nave only through the superstructure windows and those of the sanctuary. Elsewhere the aisles and galleries intervene, darkening, relatively, the lower zone and emphasizing the awesome, airy and expanding void overhead. For night ceremonies, hundreds of lamps flickered along the cornices and bloomed not far above the worshippers' heads from dozens of broad, wheel-shaped chandeliers suspended from the arches vaults.

The exterior is by contrast more familiarly architectonic; there the surfaces of the interior are revealed as being part of powerful, three-dimensional solids. Four massive buttresses stand out from the main piers and the pendentives, and structural thickness and strength become palpable. The Turkish minarets add graceful vertical accents, and domed tombs of Ottoman sultans echo the form of Anthemios's domed octagonal baptistery standing hard by the imperial entranceway to the main building. The great dome one sees today is an elevated reconstruction of the original, which came down in an earthquake in the spring of 558. Some twenty feet were added then to its height; perhaps Anthemios's design had been too audacious or perhaps the earthquake would have brought down a far less daring design. But it is certain that the original profile of the dome was quite shallow; even the present, higher one, completed in 563 well after Anthemios's death by Isidoros the Younger, subtends about 18 degrees less than a semicircle. The building was made into a mosque at the time of the conquest of the city by the Turks in 1453, and it has been a museum since 1934.

Some authorities avoid calling Anthemios an architect in the traditional sense of the word. Perhaps, like MICHELANGELO, he considered his architectural work secondary to his other creations. But what else, in view of the Hagia Sophia, can Anthemios be called but an architect? In one

Anthemios.
Ground Floor Plan, Hagia
Sophia (with Isidoros).
Constantinople (Istanbul),
Turkey.
532–537

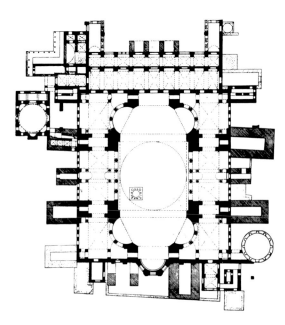

stroke he created the major monument of Byzantine architecture. He drew heavily on Roman imperial, late antique, and early Christian concepts, but the Hagia Sophia belongs in none of those categories. All the traditional churches of the Byzantine, Slavic, and Orthodox worlds, built over 1400 years' time, are to some degree its descendants.

WILLIAM L. MACDONALD

WORKS

532–537, Hagia Sophia (with ISIDOROS); *540s–550s, Church of the Holy Apostles (with Isidoros); Constantinople (Istanbul), Turkey.

BIBLIOGRAPHY

Contemporary writing about Anthemios and the Hagia Sophia can be found in English in Cyril A. Mango, THE ART OF THE BYZANTINE EMPIRE, 312–1453. *Englewood Cliffs, N.J.: Prentice-Hall, 1972.*

AGATHIAS, *The Histories,* Book 5. Quotations in the text are from the translation by J. F. Frendo, published in Berlin and New York by de Gruyter in 1975.

DOWNEY, GLANVILLE 1946–1948 "Byzantine Architects, Their Training and Methods." *Byzantion* 18:99–118.

HUXLEY, G. L. 1959 *Anthemius of Tralles: A Study in Later Greek Geometry.* Cambridge, Mass.: Harvard University Press.

KRAUTHEIMER, RICHARD (1965)1975 Chapter 9 in *Early Christian and Byzantine Architecture.* Rev. ed. Harmondsworth, England: Penguin.

MACDONALD, WILLIAM L. 1957 "Design and Technology in Hagia Sophia." *Perspecta* 4:20–27.

MATHEWS, THOMAS F. 1976 Pages 242–259, 262–312 in *The Byzantine Churches of Istanbul: A Photographic Survey.* University Park: Pennsylvania State University Press.

PROCOPIUS, *On the Buildings,* Book 1, chapter 1.

VAN NICE, ROBERT L. 1965 Volume 1 in *St. Sophia in Istanbul: An Architectural Survey.* Dumbarton Oaks Center for Byzantine Studies. Locust Valley, N.Y.: Augustin.

ANTINORI, GIOVANNI

Giovanni Antinori (1734–1792) was more prominent as an engineer than as an architect. He was born in the small village of Camerino (Marche), Italy, but nothing is known about his family background and his early youth. At the latest around 1750, he must have come to Rome, where he enrolled in the Accademia di San Luca to study architecture under GIROLAMO TEODOLI. In 1754, he won a second prize for the design of a "villa for a person of rank." The drawings are preserved in the archives of the Academy. A further design for a

villa, presumably done at the same time, he dedicated to Cardinal Neri Corsini. Both designs show Antinori influenced by the somewhat dry style of PAOLO POSI; the groundplans certainly reveal some imagination, but in the organization of the façades, a degree of uncertainty in the disposition of order, decor, and distribution of stories is apparent.

In 1755, Antinori went to Lisbon where he was introduced to the king by a countryman, the Apostolic Nuncio Monsignore Innocenzio Conti who was also born in Camerino. He was to participate in the rebuilding of Lisbon, which had been destroyed by an earthquake. He was appointed court architect and developed plans for the royal palace in Campolide and for buildings on the Piazza del Comercio. For unexplained reasons—either because of intrigues of envious colleagues or because of political disfavor at court—he was arrested shortly thereafter and held in prison for two years. He was able to return to Rome in 1756 after his Portuguese wife had bought him free.

Almost nothing is known about the following years. Possibly as compensation for the imprisonment he had suffered, Antinori was appointed professor of architecture at the Portuguese Academy in Rome. In the 1760s, he worked as architect for the Pamphilj family, but he appears to have worked mainly as an engineer. For the reception of Emperor Joseph II and his brother Pietro Leopoldo, grand duke of Tuscany, which took place in April 1769, he collaborated with Francesco Nicoletti on remodeling the interior court of the Palazzo Doria Pamphilj at the Corso into a ballroom. On this occasion, he may also have produced the design of a villa for the Tuscan grand duke, the existence of which is known only through literature.

Around 1767–1769 at the Villa Doria Pamphilj, he expanded the old canal constructed in the seventeenth century, created three cascades along its course and enlarged the lake. In 1772, the monastery church of Monte Oliveto Maggiore near Siena was remodeled after his plans in the simple, more serene forms of the Roman late baroque.

Antinori's best known work is the setting up of the three obelisks in Rome. In 1781, the obelisk of the mausoleum of Augustus was discovered and excavated. Pius VI ordered its erection on the Piazza del Quirinale where it was to be added to the group of the Dioscuri. Antinori proposed three variants in which he was above all concerned with the urbanistic context. As against a "dry lining up next to each other," he offered the better perspective effect of a slightly diagonal composition. Thus the group became not only the center point of the square, but also the visual end point of a long

Antinori.
Obelisk, Trinità dei Monti.
Rome.
1786–1789

street axis toward the Porta Pia; a masterful scenic arrangement which reveals an outstanding sense of city planning contexts. His contemporaries particularly admired the technical perfection with which he succeeded in moving the Dioscuri without damage and the smooth transportation and erection of the obelisk in 1783.

In 1786, Antinori faced similar problems in the erection of the Sallustian obelisk originally designated for the Lateran. It was to be incorporated into a complicated axial system of various vanishing lines of a church (Trinità dei Monti), the Spanish Steps, and the lines of the two streets that converge on the square in front of the church. Again, with the skillful turn of the pedestal, Antinori incorporated the obelisk into the relational network, thus achieving a solution satisfactory from every viewpoint. The work was completed in 1789. In 1790–1792, there followed the erection of the last obelisk which had been excavated in 1748 behind the Palazzo Ludovisi. Antinori proposed the Piazza di Spagna to establish an axial relation between the obelisk on the Piazza del Popolo and that in front of Trinità dei Monti; but the pope chose the square in front of the former Palazzo Ludovisi in Piazza di Montecitorio which was closest to the place where the obelisk had been found. The archeological point of view prevailed over the urbanistic one.

Shortly after the completion of this work, Antinori died in Rome. As an architect he had scarcely any opportunities for self-expression. The style shown in the few designs of his youth is still immature and tradition formed. The erection of the obelisks revealed in him a predilection for scenic effects and a baroque imagination coupled with great technical skill and mathematical mastery. Thus, Antinori in his own way demonstrated the strangely indecisive attitude of Roman architecture in the second half of the eighteenth century.

ELISABETH KIEVEN
Translated from German by
Beverley R. Placzek

WORKS

1767–1769? Villa Doria Pamphilj (expansion of cascade and lake); Rome. 1772–1778, Church of Monte San Oliveto (remodeling), near Siena, Tuscany, Italy. 1781–1783, Obelisks, Palazzo del Quirinale; 1786–1789, Obelisk, Trinità dei Monti; 1790–1792, Obelisk, Piazza di Montecitorio; Rome.

BIBLIOGRAPHY

BIANCHI, LIDIA 1955 *Disegni di Ferdinando Fuga e di altri architetti del Settecento.* Rome: Gabinetto Nazionale delle Stampe.
CARANDENTE, GIOVANNI 1975 *Il Palazzo Doria Pamphilj.* Milan: Electra.
CORBO, ANNA MARIA 1972 "L'attivita romana e il testamento di Giovanni Antinori, architetto di Pio VI." *L'Arte* no. 17:133–146.
D'ONOFRIO, CESARE 1967 *Gli obelischi di Roma.* 2nd ed. rev. Rome: Bulzoni.
LAVAGNINO, EMILIO 1940 *Gli artisti in Portogallo.* Rome: Libreria dello Stato.
PEREGO, LUIGI MARIA 1903 *Guida illustrata di Monte Oliveto Maggiore.* Monte Oliveto Maggiore, Italy: Edizione San Bernardino.
PIETRANGELI, CARLO 1942 "L'obelisco del Quirinale." *Roma* 11:411–442.
SCHIAVO, ARMANDO 1942 *Villa Doria Pamphilj.* Milan: Alfieri & Lacroix.

ANTISTATES

Antistates (flourished c.520–500 B.C.) was one of four architects who together laid the foundations and platform of the temple of Olympian Zeus in Athens. Modeled on the colossal Ionic temple plans of Asia Minor, it would have been the largest Doric temple ever built, had it been carried out as planned. However, the project was abandoned in 510 B.C., and when work was resumed more than three centuries later the order was changed to Corinthian. The base alone survives of the original project.

B. M. BOYLE

BIBLIOGRAPHY

DINSMOOR, WILLIAM B. (1950)1973 *The Architecture of Ancient Greece.* Reprint. New York: Biblo & Tannen.
LAWRENCE, ARNOLD WALTER (1957)1975 *Greek Architecture.* Rev. ed. Harmondsworth, England: Penguin.
VITRUVIUS, *De architectura,* Book 7, Praef., 15.

ANTOINE, JACQUES-DENIS

Jacques-Denis Antoine (1733–1801) occupies a unique position in French neoclassical architecture as the creator of a style drawing on French classicism and the Roman baroque rather than on the antiquarian formulas then in vogue. Born in Paris, he did not have a formal architectural education in the schools of the Académie Royale d'Architecture or of JACQUES-FRANÇOIS BLONDEL, but instead received his training in the building trades, learning construction techniques from his family. At a young age, he became a mason. At twenty, he was a contractor, and, in course, he obtained the position of *expert-entrepreneur.* Throughout his life, Antoine was highly regarded for his technical skills. He perfected a method of vaulting with fireproof bricks and was entrusted with completing the construction of the Barrières des Fermiers Généraux after the dismissal of CLAUDE NICOLAS LEDOUX in 1787. This autodidact did not ignore the theoretical foundations of his art, however, and being a great admirer of ANDREA PALLADIO, MICHELE SANMICHELI, and MICHELANGELO, he traveled to Italy (1777–1778).

The beginnings of Antoine's career are not well-known, but he soon won recognition for a highly original project for a theater for the Comédie-Française (1760) featuring a semicircular façade that echoes the shape of the auditorium. Following this, he designed several other theater projects, but none of these was ever realized. He also applied himself to ecclesiastical architecture, including a simple country church in Charny (1766–1768) and a curious façade with a pyramidal bell tower for Saint-Nicholas-du-Chardonnet in Paris (1765).

His government career began when he was charged with the construction of the new mint (1768–1775) behind the façade built by ANGE-JACQUES GABRIEL in the Place Louis XV (today the Place de la Concorde). Due to political intrigues, it was along the quai Conti, on the bank of the Seine opposite the Louvre, that Antoine was finally allowed to erect the foremost financial institution of the realm. For this building, emblematic of royal power, at once palace and factory, he conceived an expressive structure that unites the massive monumentality of the riverside façade with an ingenious arrangement of areas intended for the minting of coins.

After this success, Antoine, unanimously admired, was named a member of the Académie Royale d'Architecture (1776). He held two official positions, as *contrôleur des hôtels des monnaies du royaume* and as architect of the *Révérends Pères de la Charité* for whom he built several hospitals. Much in demand, Antoine served a large clientele of wealthy patrons designing for them inventive and well-built residences in a severe style, such as the Hôtel Brochet de Saint-Prest (1768–1774), the Hôtel de Jaucourt (1770?), the Château de Herces in Berchères-sur-Vesgre (1770–1772), and the

Château du Buisson-du-Mai in Saint-Aquilin-de-Pacy (1782). He also remodeled many châteaux from the planning of the gardens to details of the interior decoration.

Antoine remained greatly interested in large-scale programs of public utility. He prepared projects, along with the most celebrated architects of the time, for works such as the Corn Exchange, Discount Bank, the National Assembly, and the restoration of the Pantheon. He also made extensive plans for the redevelopment of the Ile-de-la-Cité (including a Place Louis XVI, reconstruction of the Palais de Justice, new churches, and improvements to the parvis of Notre Dame) and for the joining of the Louvre to the Tuileries.

Called to Bern, Switzerland, Antoine built the mint (1790–1792) but had to forego the construction of other projects. He also worked for prominent foreigners: the duke of Alba (stairway, interior decoration, and gardens of the Berwick Palace in Madrid [1773]) and the prince of Salm (Château and gardens of Kirn at Kyrbourg in the Palatinate [1782?]). Antoine's election to the Institute in 1799 filling the vacancy left by the death of ETIENNE LOUIS BOULLÉE crowned the impressive career of an artist whose discreet, occasionally austere character merits more than a supporting role.

MONIQUE MOSSER
Translated from French by
Richard Cleary

WORKS

1760, Theater for the Comédie Française; 1765, Saint-Nicolas-du-Chardonnet (façade); Paris. 1766–1768, Church, Charny, Seine-et-Marne, France. 1768?–1774, Hôtel Brochet-de-Saint-Prest (now the Ecole des Ponts-et-Chaussées); 1768–1775, The Mint, quai Conti; 1770?, Hôtel de Jaucourt; Paris. 1770–1772, Château de Herces a Berchère-sur-Vesgre, Eure-et-Loire, France. 1772–1775, Chapel of the Communion, Saint-Nicholas-des-Champs, Paris. *1773, Berwick Palace (stairway, interior decorations, and gardens), Madrid. 1776, Rochefoucauld Asylum; *1780?, Hospital of Charity; Paris. 1782, Château du Buisson-du-Mai a Saint Aquilin-de-Pacy, Eure, France. 1782?, Château a Kirn-Kyrbourg (château and gardens), Palatinate, Germany. 1782–1784, Chapel of the Visitation to Nancy, Meurthe-et-Moselle, France. *1782–1785, Palais de Justice (stairway, waiting hall, and archives), Paris. 1790–1792, The Mint, Bern.

BIBLIOGRAPHY

HAUTECOEUR, LOUIS 1952 *Pages 247–260 in Seconde moitié du XVIIIᵉ siècle: Le style Louis XVI, 1750–1792.* Volume 4 in *Histoire de l'architecture classique en France.* Paris: Picard.

LE BRETON, JOACHIM 1803 "Notice sur la vie et les travaux de J. D. Antoine." *Magazine encyclopédique* (de Millin) 22.

LUSSAULT, N. 1801 *Notice historique sur défunt J. D.*

Antoine. Paris: Journal des bâtimens civils, des monumens et des arts.

MAZEROLLE, FERNAND 1897 "Jacques-Denis Antoine: Architecte de la Monnaie, 1733–1801." *Réunion des Sociétés des Beaux-Arts des départements* 1897:1038–1050.

MAZEROLLE, FERNAND 1907 *L'hôtel des Monnaies, les bâtiments, le musée, les ateliers.* Paris: Laurens.

MOSSER, MONIQUE 1971 "L'hôtel des Monnaies de Paris: Oeuvre de J.-D. Antoine." *L'information d'histoire de l'art* 6, no. 2:94–99.

ANTOLINI, GIOVANNI ANTONIO

Born in Castelbolognese, Italy, Giovanni Antonio Antolini (1756–1841) was an accomplished hydraulic engineer and architectural author, who built little. Associated by 1775 with Roman neoclassicists, including FRANCESCO MILIZIA, he is best known for his Foro Bonaparte (1800–1802) in Milan. Its grandiose circuit of public buildings, residences, and workshops surrounding the Castello Sforzesco celebrated Napoleon's founding of a new republic. Officially undertaken in January 1801, it was scuttled by the successor government the next year. Rewarded in 1804 with posts, including the chair of architecture at the Bologna Academy, the Austrians ousted him in 1815.

CARROLL WILLIAM WESTFALL

WORK

*1800–1802, Foro Bonaparte, Milan.

BIBLIOGRAPHY

ANTOLINI, GIOVANNI ANTONIO 1801a *Piano economico-politico del Foro Bonaparte.* Milan: Federico Agnelli.

ANTOLINI, GIOVANNI ANTONIO 1801b *Progetto sul Foro che doveva eseguirisi in Milano dell' architetto. . . .* Milan: Bettalli.

ANTOLINI, GIOVANNI ANTONIO 1806 *Descrizione del Foro Bonaparte.* Milan and Parma, Italy: Tipi Bodoniani.

GIORDANI, PIETRO 1854–1862 "Descrizione del Foro Bonaparte." Volume 8, pages 113–135 in Antonio Gussalli (editor), *Opere di Pietro Giordani.* Milan: Borroni & Scotti.

MEZZANOTTE, GIANNI 1966 *Architettura neoclassica in Lombardia.* Naples: Edizioni Scientifiche Italiane.

WESTFALL, CARROLL WILLIAM 1969 "Antolini's Foro Bonaparte in Milan." *Journal of the Warburg and Courtauld Institutes* 32:366–385.

ANTONELLI, ALESSANDRO

Alessandro Antonelli (1798–1888), who hailed from the Piedmont region in Italy, studied in Milan, Turin, and Rome. From 1836 to 1857, he taught at the Accademia Albertina in Turin and served in the Piedmontese parliament. Antonelli began his architectural practice in the 1830s. In the 1840s, he added a dome and spire to the seventeenth-century crossing of San Guadenzio in Novara (1841–1888), demonstrating in his first major work his structural ingenuity. The construction, which reached a height of 121 meters, was built of masonry alone, as was his masterpiece in Turin, the Mole Antonelliana (1863–1884). Begun as a synagogue with an extremely tall central space, it became a municipal museum for the *Risorgimento.* Antonelli achieved a height of 167.5 meters in this unusual structure by superimposing, on the exterior, many layers of orders of different sizes, attics, a tall four-sided cloister vault dome, and a layered spire.

HENRY A. MILLON

WORKS

1830–?, Sanctuary (unfinished), Boca, Italy. 1841–1888, San Gaudenzio (cupola); 1854–1869, Cathedral (rebuilding); Novara, Italy. 1863–1884, Mole Antonelliana, Turin, Italy.

BIBLIOGRAPHY

CAVALLARI MURAT, AUGUSTO 1961 "Progetto di Antonelli per il palazzo del Parlemento (1860)." Volume 3, pages 447–456 in *Scritti di Storia dell'arte in onore di Mario Salmi.* Rome: De Luca.

GABETTI, ROBERTO 1960 "Due opere di Antonelli a Soliva e Castagnola." *Atti E Memorie del Terzo Congresso Piemontese di Antichità ed Arte: Congresso di Varallo Sesia* Sept.:175–182.

GABETTI, ROBERTO 1962 "Problematica antonelliana." *Atti e Rassegna tecnica della Società degli ingegneri e degli architetti* 16, no. 6:159–194.

MEEKS, CARROLL L. V. 1966 *Italian Architecture: 1750–1914.* New Haven: Yale University Press.

ANTONESCU, PETRE

Petre Antonescu (1873–1965), a Rumanian architect, graduated from the Ecole des Beaux-Arts in Paris in 1899. He taught history of architecture at the School of Architecture in Bucharest from 1900 to 1938. He was a promoter of the neo-Rumanian style; the original and suggestive forms of his works responded to the architectural demand of the rising spirit and economic growth of Rumania. His compositional imagination gave his buildings a special equilibrium, and the details and decorative elements give them a special refinement.

CONSTANTIN MARIN MARINESCU

WORKS

1910, Municipal Building, Bucharest. 1913, Casino

(now the House of Culture), Sinaia, Rumania. 1915, Building (now the UNESCO European Center for Higher Education); 1923, Marmorosch Bank (now the Bank of Investment); 1928, Apartment Building (now the State Guest House), 12 Soseaua Kiseleff; Bucharest. 1931, Rumanian Academy, Valle Giulia, Rome. 1935, Triumphal Arch; 1935, Law School, University of Bucharest; 1939, Institute of History; Bucharest.

BIBLIOGRAPHY

CANTACUZÈNE, GEORGE 1927 "L'architecture roumaine d'aujourd'hui." *L'Architecture* 40, no. 10:351–357.

IONESCU, GRIGORE 1965 Volume 2 in *Istoria Arhitecturii in Romania.* Bucharest: Editura Academiei Republicii Romañe.

IONESCU, GRIGORE 1969 *Arhitectura in Romania: Perioda anilor 1944–1969.* Bucharest: Editura Academiei Republicii Socialiste Româñia.

IONESCU, GRIGORE 1972 "Saptezeci si cinci de ani de la infiintarea invatamintului de arhitectura din Romania." *Arhitectura* 20:35–42.

IONESCU, GRIGORE 1973 "Petre Antonescu: 100 de ani de la nasterea sa." *Arhitectura* 21, no. 1:38–40.

LUPU, MIRCEA 1970 "Arhitectura în România în sec. XIX şi Inceptui sec. XX: Şcoala Românească de Arhitectură." *Arhitectura* 18, no. 4:54–67.

MAMBRIANI, ALBERTO 1969 *L'Architettura Moderna nei Paesi Balcanici.* Bologna, Italy: Capelli.

MARCU, ANGHEL 1979 "Vechi preocupari pentru o arhitectura româneasča noua." *Arhitectura* 3:67.

PATRULIUS, RADU 1973–1974 "Contributii Romanesti i Arhitectura Anilor '30." *Arhitectura* 21, no. 6:44–52; 22, no. 1:53–59.

SASARMAN, GHEORGHE 1972 "Incepturile gindirii teoretice in arhitectura româneasča (1860–1916)." *Arhitectura* 20, no. 6:44–46.

APOLLODORUS

Apollodorus (first third of the second century), said to have come from Damascus, was the chief architect of the Roman emperor Trajan. The author of technical treatises now lost, he was also a master engineer and bridge-builder and may have been a major sculptor as well. He and some of his buildings are mentioned by several authors of the imperial period, an unusual degree of recognition in an age whose vast building and engineering programs remain largely anonymous. Dio Cassius says that he designed Trajan's Forum, Odeion (concert hall), and Baths, all in Rome, and adds that Emperor HADRIAN, Trajan's successor, had him executed out of jealousy, an unlikely tale. He worked on at least one project with Hadrian, and when the emperor–architect sent him his plans for the Temple of Venus and Rome, Apollodorus replied constructively if somewhat tartly. His relative prominence in the ancient texts, together with the importance of his work in Rome (enough survives for architectural analysis), has generated a considerable modern literature about him in which his name has sometimes been gratuitously attached to buildings other than those specifically mentioned in the written sources. It is possible that more attention has been paid to him than to any other architect who lived during the long period between VITRUVIUS and FILIPPO BRUNELLESCHI.

Trajan's Forum (dedicated in 112) and its dependencies—the famous sculptured Column (symmetrically flanked by two libraries), the huge Basilica Ulpia, and the terraced Markets spread across the steep shoulder of the Esquiline Hill—covered an area of at least forty thousand square meters in the center of Rome. The Ulpia alone, turned at right angles to the major axis of the open Forum proper, was nearly 170 meters long. All of the elements of the ensemble except the upper stories of the Markets were placed on a common level created by excavation and fill. The whole was on an almost Egyptian scale, its nearest Roman relatives being the grand sanctuary of Fortune at Palestrina, of about 100–80 B.C., and the Forum of Augustus in Rome, consecrated in 2 B.C. The preparation of the ground, including the cutting and terracing of the Esquiline for the Markets, the erection of the Column, and the now-lost roofs of the Ulpia certify Apollodorus's engineering skills. More important, however, is his artistic breadth, for the remains show that he was the master of both the traditional, largely rectilinear architecture of the Orders—albeit in a full-blooded, High Empire fashion—as well as of the much newer vaulted style, the style of interior spaces of both simple and complex shapes that had evolved from the work of architects such as SEVERUS AND CELER in the previous century. Some have thought that he was also responsible for the design and carving of the Column's spiral frieze, with its twenty-five hundred figures in 114 scenes.

Only fragments of the Forum and the Ulpia are preserved; they have not been much studied. The

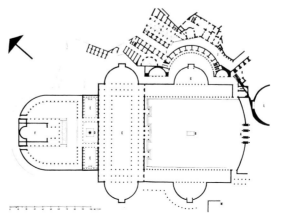

Apollodorus. Plan of Forum, Basilica, and Markets, Trajan's Forum. Rome. 112

Markets, built in the first decade of the second century of concrete with brick facing, are much better preserved. Approximately 170 rooms, most with their vaults intact, can still be seen. Arranged in tiers, symmetrically at Forum level but ever more casually up the hillside, most of the rooms are tabernas or shops, a familiar Roman design element of simple rectangular plan with a wide doorway and a barrel-vaulted ceiling running fore and aft. Ramps and stairs pass up and down through the fabric at convenient locations, and three paved access roads, with drains and sidewalks, run transversely through the whole at different levels.

Apollodorus's originality can best be seen in the covered market street and its dependencies that lie at the high northern portion of the remains, the aula Traiana. It consists of a main floor 40 by 120 Roman feet flanked by files of shops. On the down side there is another, basement file of shops opening onto one of the transverse streets. Above the shops of the main floor level are galleries and more shops, and above those, on the eastern, uphill side, more still. The main space was covered by a six-bay groin vault, still in place, supported on fourteen plain, unobtrusive piers. Because the transverse ends of the groin-bays are open to the galleries, the whole is airy and well lit. Circulation and function are also efficiently accommodated, the structure is fire resistant, and the complex mediates successfully between the Esquiline heights and the imperial, dynastic colonnaded structures below. The Orders are conspicuously absent, and it is the ingenious agglomeration of vaulted shops that chiefly gives the Markets their architectonic character. As socially responsive architecture the design is first rate.

The Baths, opened in 109, are not as well preserved as the Markets but are just as important. The remaining fragments, which record the meticulousness of Apollodorus's workmen, are now being carefully studied. They suggest not only the maturity of the new vaulted style but its adroit marriage with traditional, trabeated architecture. Peristyles existed there in artistic harmony with vaulted interiors, colonnades with semidomed exedras. Perhaps the neighboring but now lost Baths of Titus (opened in 80) were to a degree Apollodorus's inspiration, but it seems likely that it was he who gave final definition to the imperial bath building, a type which subsequently proliferated in Rome and in the capitals of the provinces with few major changes in the governing scheme.

That scheme consisted of a basically rectangular walled enclosure (which in the case of Trajan's Baths covered an area of approximately 110 by 150 meters), expanded symmetrically by curved or rectilinear extensions for lecture halls and libraries. The huge freestanding bath building proper, separated from the enclosure wall by gardens, sports facilities, and colonnades, contained grand halls,

Apollodorus.
Markets, Trajan's
*   Forum.*
Rome.
112

internal peristyles, and duplicate sets of the numerous vaulted spaces of various sizes and shapes required by the traditional bathing ritual. Not a few seeds of Beaux Arts planning can be found in this formidable social creation, one of the chief Roman contributions to Western architecture.

Dio Cassius says that the bridge over the Danube, of which a few fragments can still be seen,

had twenty piers of squared stone one hundred and fifty feet in height above the foundations and sixty feet in width, and these, standing at a distance of one hundred and seventy feet from one another, are connected by arches. . . . Yet the very fact that the river in its descent is contracted here from a great flood to such a narrow channel, after which it again expands into a greater flood, makes it all the more violent and deep, and this must be considered in estimating the difficulty of constructing the bridge (68.13).

The arches were of timber. A partial view of the bridge appears on the Column of Trajan (Scene LXXIV, which shows five of the timber arches and two abutment arches of masonry).

It is possible, but perhaps not likely, that Apollodorus designed Hadrian's Pantheon in Rome (begun in 118). There has been some enthusiasm for giving him credit for the excavation and construction of the huge new ports built on the west coast of Italy in Trajan's time, at Porto, by the Tiber mouth, and at Centumcellae (Civitavecchia), but this rests only on his reputation as a master builder and engineer and, however likely, cannot be proven. A half-dozen other major structures, such as the monumental arches honoring Trajan still standing at Ancona and Benevento, have also been attributed to him but also without proof. Still, such suggestions are attractive, given his reputation and his apparent position as architect in chief.

The fact that one of the texts refers to him as Apollodorus of Damascus has spawned profitless speculation about his influence on architectural style. The discussion has centered on the gratuitous inference that because he was from the Hellenistic east he would have brought mature Hellenistic architecture to Rome; in this way his name was dragged into the fierce debate that once raged over the question of what was western and what was of eastern origin in the art of the Roman Empire. But Hellenistic architecture had long been established in Rome before Apollodorus appeared there, and by that time any architect worth his salt had to be able to provide sophisticated designs that incorporated those Hellenistic elements and motifs routinely expected by clients both public and private. The debate continues, subdued and more sensible, but Apollodorus's presumed role as the bringer of Hellenistic style to the benighted Romans has evaporated. It has been aptly said that if he had been from Tivoli instead of Damascus, the question would not have arisen, so thoroughly Roman is his work.

Apollodorus's prestige as a professional comes through clearly in the texts. Vitruvius, and Cicero as well, say that architecture was a major profession. The former gives quite an elaborate list of the disciplines the architect should be familiar with, a list sometimes dismissed by modern writers. But what is known about Apollodorus makes it clear that he lived up to Vitruvius's prescription. And Dio gives us one of the two existing accounts of the direct association of a Roman master architect with the head of state. Having said that Trajan's Forum, Odeion, and Baths in Rome were Apollodorus' work, he goes on to say that ". . . once when Trajan was consulting (Apollodorus) on some point about the buildings he . . . said to Hadrian, who had interrupted with some remark, 'Be off, and draw your pumpkins. You don't understand any of these matters' (Book 69). Apollodorus was so secure in his position that he could speak sharply to the emperor's knowledgeable kinsman and probable heir, who had nettled him (the reference may be to pumpkin-shaped vault surfaces of the kind found in Hadrianic buildings at several sites, rather than to actual vegetables).

It is difficult to say whether Apollodorus was as creative as Severus and Celer. But judging from the remains of his Forum, Basilica, and Baths, and especially from his Markets, it is clear that he was a gifted and innovative designer. The covered, bazaarlike market hall may perhaps have been derived in part from the central groin-vaulted hall of the lost Baths of Titus, but the over-all design of the Markets would seem to secure Apollodorus a high reputation. And then there is the probability that he gave the grand, symmetrical imperial bath building its definitive form. What is beyond doubt, however, is that his work embodied the central principles, the full maturity, of one of the main sources of subsequent architecture, the Roman imperial style.

WILLIAM L. MACDONALD

WORKS

*c.105, Bridge across the Danube at Drobeta (Turnu-Severin), Romania. 109 (date of opening), Trajan's Baths; 112 (date of consecration), Trajan's Forum (including the Basilica Ulpia, the two libraries, the Markets, the construction of the helical Column, and perhaps the sculpture); n.d., Odeion of Trajan; Rome.

BIBLIOGRAPHY

English translations of the ancient texts can be found in the volumes of the Loeb Classical Library series, published by Harvard University Press and Heinemann.

AUGUSTAN HISTORY (*Scriptores Historiae Augustae*), biography of Hadrian, chapter 19.

BLANCKENHAGEN, PETER H. VON 1954 "The Imperial Fora." *Journal of the Society of Architectural Historians* 13, no. 4:21–26.

DE FINE LICHT, KJELD 1974 *Untersuchungen an den Trajansthermen zu Rom.* Hafniae, Denmark: Munksgaard.

DIO CASSIUS, *Roman History,* Books 68 and 69.

HEILMEYER, WOLF-DIETER 1975 "Apollodoros von Damaskus, der Architekt des Pantheon." *Jahrbuch des deutschen archäologischen Instituts* 90:316–347.

MACDONALD, WILLIAM L. 1965 Volume 1, chapter 6 in *The Architecture of the Roman Empire.* New Haven: Yale University Press.

PROCOPIUS, *On the Buildings,* Book 4, chapter 6.

APPIANI, GIUSEPPE

The painter Giuseppe Appiani (c.1701–1786), born in Porto near Milan, decorated numerous palaces and churches in southern Germany and Switzerland. Working in a style influenced by G. B. Tiepolo, he served as court painter to the elector of Mainz. His projects include the series of frescoes and altarpieces in JOHANN BALTHASAR NEUMANN's Church of Vierzehnheiligen (1764–1769).

ALISON LUCHS

WORKS

*1749, Parish Church, Lindau, Germany. 1750–1751, Prämonstratenser Abbey (refectory), Obermarchtal, Germany. 1751–1752, Schloss Seehof (scenes on ceilings), near Bamberg, Germany. 1755–1756, Saint Peter (frescoes; mostly destroyed in World War II), Mainz, Germany. *1758, Jesuitenkirche, Saarbrücken, Germany. 1759–1761, Cathedral (frescoes), Arlesheim, Germany. 1760, Church of Deutschordenschloss (frescoes), Althausen, Germany. 1760–1761, Neues Schloss and Seminary Chapel (frescoes), Meersburg, Germany. 1764–1769, Vierzehnheiligen (frescoes and altarpieces), Germany. 1773, Michaelskirche (frescoes), Würzburg, Germany. c.1774, Michaelskirche, Mainz, Germany. 1780–1783, Church (murals), Camberg, Germany. n.d., Saint Ignatius, Mainz, Germany.

BIBLIOGRAPHY

"Giuseppe Appiani." 1972 Volume 1, page 215 in *Dizionario Enciclopedico Bolaffi dei Pittori e degli Incisori Italiani dall' XI al XX Secolo.* Turin, Italy: Bolaffi.

HEMPEL, EBERHARD (1965)1977 *Baroque Art and Architecture in Central Europe.* 2d ed., rev. Baltimore: Penguin.

HEYER, HANS RUDOLF 1969 "Giuseppe Appianis Fresko im Treppenhaus des neuen Schlosses zu Meersburg." *Unsere Kunstdenkmäler* 20:337–346.

VOSS, HERMANN 1963 "Giuseppe Appiani—Versuch einer Würdigung." *Pantheon* 21:339–353. Key article with color illustration, English summary, and list of dated works.

ZUBEK, PAUL 1969 "Vier neuentdeckte Zeichnungen Giuseppe Appianis." *Pantheon* 27:480–485.

ARATA, GIULIO ULISSE

Giulio Ulisse Arata (1881–1962), who was born in Piacenza, Italy, studied architecture at the Brera Academy and the Milan Politecnico. Active in Naples and Milan, his *stile liberty* designs reflected the influence of GIUSEPPE SOMMARUGA. He participated in the *Nuove Tendenze* movement. He also contributed important reviews and articles to various art periodicals.

DENNIS DOORDAN

WORKS

1908, Carugati-Felisari House, Milan. 1909, La Pensione; 1911, Palazzo Mannajuolo; Naples. 1911, Terme, Agnano, Italy. 1911–1914, Berri Meregalli House, Milan. 1924–1931, Galleria Ricci-Oddi, Piacenza, Italy.

BIBLIOGRAPHY

ARATA, GIULIO ULISSE 1942a *Costruzioni e progetti.* Milan: Hoepli.

ARATA, GIULIO ULISSE 1942b *Ricostruzioni e restauri.* Milan: Hoepli.

MELANI, ALFREDO 1913 *L'Architettura di G.U. Arata.* Milan: Destetti & Tumminelli.

NICOLETTI, MANFREDI 1978 *L'Architettura Liberty in Italia.* Bari, Italy: Laterza.

THEA, PAOLO (editor) 1980 *Nuove Tendenze: Milano e l'altro Futurismo.* Milan: Electa Editrice.

ARCHER, JOHN LEE

Irish-born and London-trained (by JOHN RENNIE), John Lee Archer (1791–1852) was architect and engineer to the Colony of Van Dieman's Land (Tasmania). His architecture was Georgian, plain, yet proportionately refined and complete with architectonic clarity. His many works included churches, schools, jails, civil and harbor works, and bridges.

DONALD LESLIE JOHNSON

WORKS

*1828, Saint David's Church, Hobart; 1830–1835, (King's) Orphan School and Saint John's Church, New Town; 1831, Penitentiary Chapel (Old Trinity Church), Hobart; 1835–1841, Customs House, Hobart; 1836, Ross Bridge; 1836–1852, Saint George's Church (not completed until 1888), Battery Point, Hobart; Tasmania, Australia.

BIBLIOGRAPHY

ROBERTSON, E. GRAEME 1970 *Early Buildings of Southern Tasmania.* 2 vols. Melbourne: Georgian House.

SMITH, ROY S. 1962 *John Lee Archer: Tasmanian Architect and Engineer.* Hobart, Australia: Tasmanian Historical Research Association.

SMITH, ROY S. 1966 "John Lee Archer." Volume 1, pages 23–24, in A. G. L. Shaw and C. M. H. Clark (editors), *Australian Dictionary of Biography.* Melbourne University Press.

ARCHER, THOMAS

Thomas Archer (1668–1743), son of a Warwickshire, England, country gentleman, was an amateur architect of considerable distinction. He did not hold any architectural posts under the Crown, failing to secure the comptrollership of the works in 1713 when JOHN VANBRUGH was dismissed, but through his connections at court (he was appointed groom porter to Queen Anne in 1705), he was able to build up a substantial country house practice. As one of the Commissioners for Building Fifty New Churches under the Act of 1711, he was also able to demonstrate his expertise in ecclesiastical works.

The nature of Archer's training is unknown as are the reasons why he turned to architecture in his middle thirties. Unlike his contemporaries, NICHOLAS HAWKSMOOR and Vanbrugh, he probably had first-hand experience of continental baroque architecture. He traveled abroad between 1691 and 1695, and from his recorded presence in Padua in 1691 it might be presumed that he visited Rome. His architecture is unique in England in its employment of features of the mature Roman baroque style: the giant order, broken pediments, eared architraves and curved surfaces. Following the publication of DOMENICO ROSSI's *Studio d'architettura civile* in 1702, the motifs of the Italian baroque were readily available in England, and Archer probably used the engravings as patterns for his own work, reinforcing a preference developed during his travels. However, it is not only his often literal translation of motifs that sets him apart from his contemporaries in England, but also his manipulation of space. In his two London churches built under the Act of 1711, Saint Paul, Deptford (1713–1730) and Saint John, Westminster (1713–1728), he investigated the possibilities of contrasting axes in the centrally planned building with admirable results. His houses are generally less spatially adventurous, although baroque motifs abound. Chettle House (after 1711), Dorset, a firmly attributed house, is the striking exception to this, having convex curves instead of right angles at both the corners of the building and in the projecting entrance hall.

Archer's baroque is never as thorough-going as that of FRANCESCO BORROMINI because Archer tended to apply its most readily identifiable features as a dressing rather than treat the entire structure organically. It is for this reason that even his most successful buildings, despite their accomplishment, never achieve the heights scaled by their continental equivalents.

JOHN BOLD

WORKS

1702, Chatsworth House (Cascade House); 1704–1705, Chatsworth House (north front), Derbyshire, England. 1705, Cliveden House, Buckinghamshire, England. 1707–1710, Heythrop House, Oxfordshire, England. 1709–1711, Garden Pavilion, Wrest Park, Bedfordshire, England. 1710–1712, Roehampton House, Wandsworth, Surrey, England. 1710–1715, Saint Philip's Church, Birmingham, England. (A)1711?–?, Chettle House, Dorset, England. 1713–1728, Saint John's Church, Smith Square, Westminster; 1713–1730, Saint Paul's Church and *Rectory, Deptford; London. 1715?, Hale House, Hampshire, England. (A)1716–1717, Russell House, 43 King Street, Covent Garden; (A)*1717–1718, Monmouth House, Soho Square; London. (A)1720?, Marlow Place, Buckinghamshire, England. *1725?, Harcourt House, 1 Cavendish Square, London.

BIBLIOGRAPHY

DOWNES, KERRY 1966 *English Baroque Architecture.* London: Zwemmer.

LEES-MILNE, JAMES 1970 *English Country Houses: Baroque.* London: Country Life.

WHIFFEN, MARCUS 1973 *Thomas Archer: Architect of the English Baroque.* Los Angeles: Hennessey.

ARCHIBALD, JOHN SMITH

John Smith Archibald (1872–1934), a native of Inverness, Scotland, went to Montreal in 1893 to work as a draftsman and assistant to EDWARD MAXWELL. In 1897, he began practice with Charles Jewett Saxe, a fellow draftsman in Maxwell's office. Saxe and Archibald dissolved partnership in 1915, each continuing under his own name.

Emmanuel Congregational Church (1907), Montreal; the George Rabinovitch House (1913), Westmount, Quebec; and the Masonic Memorial Temple (1928), Montreal, all convey Archibald's ideal of formal classicism. In contrast, his large picturesque hotels are contributions to the style which has been dubbed "châteauesque."

ROBERT LEMIRE

WORKS

1898, C. Manhire House, Westmount, Quebec. *1901, Belleview Apartments, Montreal. 1904, F. H. Anson House, Westmount, Quebec. 1904, Bishop Court Apartments; 1907, Emmanuel Congregational Church;

1907, Montefiore Club; Montreal. 1908, A. Falconer House, Westmount, Quebec. 1909, G. W. Badgley House; Technical School (with Maurice Perrault); 1909, A. Woods House; 1910, J. M. Wilson House; 1912, E. G. M. Cape House; 1913, C. I. Desola House; Montreal. 1913, George Rabinovitch House, Westmount, Quebec. 1914, Church of Saint James the Apostle (additions and alterations); 1914, La Sauvegarde Insurance Building; Montreal. 1915, J. S. Archibald House; 1919, Arena Garage; Westmount, Quebec. 1921, Elizabeth Ballantyne School; 1922, J. F. McLean House; 1922, Windsor Hotel (alterations); Montreal. 1923, Heroes Memorial School, Cowansville, Quebec. *1924, Forum Building (original building); 1925, Terminal Building for Montreal Tramways Company; 1925, Williams Thomas Building; *1927, Baseball Stadium and Exhibition Building; Montreal. 1927–1929, Château Laurier Hotel (additions and alterations), Ottawa. 1928, General Brock Hotel, Brockville, Ontario. 1928, Halifax Hotel and Station, Nova Scotia. 1928, Manior Richelieu Hotel, Murray Bay, Quebec. 1928, Masonic Memorial Temple, Montreal. 1928, Queen's University Memorial Gymnasium, Kingston, Ontario. 1929, Dominion Engineering Building, Lachine, Quebec. 1929, Hotel Saskatoon, Saskatchewan. 1929, N. A. Timmins House, Westmount, Quebec. 1930–1932, Bessborough Hotel, Saskatoon, Saskatchewan.

BIBLIOGRAPHY

ARCHIBALD, JOHN S. 1906 "A Statutory Qualification for Architects." *Canadian Architect and Builder* 19:138–140.

"The Forum Building, Montreal." 1925 *Construction* 18, no. 3:82–86.

KALMAN, HAROLD D. 1968 *The Railway Hotels and the Developments of the Château Style in Canada.* University of Victoria, Maltwood Museum.

LAMBERT, PHYLLIS, and LEMIRE, ROBERT 1977 *Dossier 25: Inventaire des bâtiments du vieux Montréal.* Quebec: Ministère des Affaires Culturelles.

LEMIRE, ROBERT, and TREPANIER, MONIQUE 1981 *Inventaire des bâtiments construits entre 1919 et 1959 dans le vieux Montréal et les quartiers Saint-Georges et Saint-André.* Ottawa: Parcs Canada.

MAXWELL, W. S. 1934 "John S. Archibald." *Journal of the Royal Architectural Institute of Canada* 11, no. 3:44.

SINAITICUS 1930 "The Masonic Memorial Temple, Montreal." *Construction* 23, no. 12:387–391.

ARCINIEGA, CLAUDIO DE

Claudio de Arciniega (c.1520–1593) arrived in Mexico in 1554, after having worked in Madrid on the Alcazar and, intermittently, between 1542 and 1548 as a sculptor for RODRIGO GIL DE HONTAÑON at Alcala de Henares. He designed the monument for the obsequies of Charles V in 1559 and in 1560 was appointed master of the works of New Spain. Because his drawings of the Cathedral of Mexico, begun in 1563, were in 1567 sent to Spain for approval, he was almost certainly master of the works from their beginning. About 1584, a model of the building was made, probably connected with a change from an original rib-vaulted hall church scheme to the present centralizing, double-clearstory, basilican elevation. Since Mexico's sister cathedral, Puebla, was begun new in 1575, this building, too, may safely be attributed to Arciniega.

JOHN DOUGLAS HOAG

WORKS

1559, Monument for the Obsequies of Charles V; 1563–1593, Cathedral of Mexico (not completed until 1667); Mexico City. (A)1575–1593, Cathedral of Puebla (not completed until 1649), Mexico.

BIBLIOGRAPHY

ANGULO INIGUEZ, DIEGO 1945 Volume 1 in *Historia del Arte Hispano-americano.* Barcelona, Spain: Salvat.

KUBLER, GEORGE, and SORIA, MARTIN 1959 *Art and Architecture in Spain and Portugal and Their American Dominions.* Baltimore: Penguin.

MARCO DORTA, ENRIQUE 1951 Volume 1 in *Fuentes para la Historia del Arte Hispano-americano.* Sevilla, Spain: Instituto "Diego Velazquez," Seccion de Sevilla.

ARENS, JOHANN AUGUST

Born and educated in Hamburg, Johann August Arens (1757–1806) studied first at the University of Göttingen and then at the Academy in Copenhagen, where his teacher was Caspar Frederik Harsdorff. In 1783, he received the great Gold Medal and then started on several years of travel: he worked under CHARLES DE WAILLY in Paris, studied landscape architecture in England, and spent two years in Italy (1786–1788). While in Italy, he met Goethe who, a year later, called him to Weimar to rebuild the Schloss (1789–1792) and to build the so-called Roman House (1790–1792). Most of his work, however, was carried on in his native city of Hamburg, where he and his Danish colleague CHRISTIAN FREDERIK HANSEN, became the leading architects of mature classicism. Almost all of his numerous country houses, town houses, monuments, chapels, and churches were destroyed by fires and by wars. However, his pupils and successors contributed to the continuity of the rational and restrained classicist architecture of which Arens was the major representative in Hamburg and northern Germany.

GERHARD WIETEK
Translated from German by Beverley R. Placzek

WORKS

1789–1792, Schloss Weimar (rebuilding), Germany. *1789–1794, Arens House; *1789–1794, Flor House; *1789–1794, Matsen House; *1789–1794, Rücker House; *1789–1794, Siemsen House; Hamburg, Germany. 1790–1792, Roman House; 1790–1792, Schlosspark; Weimar, Germany. *1793–1794, Voght House and Park, Flottbeck, Germany. 1794–1796, Friehof Chapel, Hamburg, Germany. 1795–1800, Church, Wandsbek, Germany. 1795–1800, School- and Workhouse; 1800–1803, Büsch Monument; 1800–1803, Hagedorn Monument; Hamburg, Germany.

BIBLIOGRAPHY

DOEBBER, ADOLF 1911 Das Schloss in Weimar. Jena, Germany: Fischer.

GRUNDMANN, GÜNTHER 1957 Jenischpark und Jenischhaus. Hamburg, Germany: Hans Christian.

WIETEK, GERHARD 1951 "Goethes Verhältnis zur Architektur." Unpublished Ph.D. dissertation, University of Kiel, Germany.

WIETEK, GERHARD 1972 J. A. Arens: Ein Hamburger Architekt des Klassizismus. Hamburg, Germany: Altonaer Museum. Exhibition catalogue.

ARISS, JOHN

A notice placed in the *Maryland Gazette* in 1751 by John Ariss (c.1725–1799) of Virginia ("lately [returned] from GREAT BRITAIN") announced his interest in undertaking "Buildings of all Sorts" and in preparing "Plans" and "Bills." Documents indicate that Ariss was primarily involved with designs, estimates, and inspections of small church buildings in northern Virginia.

WILLIAM M. S. RASMUSSEN

WORKS

*1766, Payne's Church, Fairfax County, Va. *1772, Church (possibly never built), Clarke County, Va.

BIBLIOGRAPHY

CHAMBERS, B. DUVALL 1932 Old Chapel and The Parish in Clarke County, Virginia. Washington: Roberts.

SLAUGHTER, PHILIP 1907 The History of Truro Parish in Virginia. Philadelphia: Jacobs.

WATERMAN, THOMAS TILESTON 1945 The Mansions of Virginia, 1706–1776. Chapel Hill: University of North Carolina Press.

ARNOLD VON WESTPHALEN

Arnold von Westphalen (15th century) ranks among the most important late Gothic architects of central Germany. Called to the Wettiner court at Meissen in 1470, he began working under Hugold von Schleinitz and went on to become supervisor of all construction in Saxony. In the service of Elector Ernst and Duke Albrecht of Saxony, he developed a highly personal late Gothic style represented in his principal work, the Albrechtsburg (1471–?), with its rich and fantastic vaulting. The "curtain arch" became a characteristic decorative form of his school. His pupils carried his style into eastern Europe, especially Lusatia.

ALISON LUCHS

WORKS

(A)1460–1470, Schloss Hinterglauchau, Germany. 1470–1475, Burghaus (renovation), Rochsburg, Germany. 1471–?, Albrechtsburg, Meissen, Germany. 1471–?, Burg Kriebstein, Germany. 1471–?, Residenzschloss (west wing), Dresden, Germany. 1471–1476, Sankt Maria (vaulting of choir), Mittweida, Germany. c.1472, Castle (east gatehouse), Rochlitz, Germany. c.1472, Unser Liebe Frau auf dem Berge, Penig, Germany. 1472–?, Rathaus, Meissen, Germany. 1472–1476, Meissen Cathedral, Germany. (A)1476, Sankt Kunigunde, Rochlitz, Germany. 1476, Schloss, Tharandt, Germany. 1478–1480, Schloss, Leipzig.

BIBLIOGRAPHY

BIALOSTOCKI, JAN 1972 Spätmittelalter und beginnende Neuzeit. Berlin: Propyläen.

BRAUNFELS, WOLFGANG 1978 "Meissen." Pages 41–58 in Erich Hubala and Gunter Schweikhart (editors), Festschrift Herbert Siebenhüner. Würzburg, Germany: Kommissionsverlag Ferdinand Schöningh.

HAMMER, ERICH 1970 "Rochlitz: Die Baugeschichte des Schlosses und die Anfänge der Stadtentwicklung." Unpublished dissertation, Rheinische-Westfälische Technische Hochschule, Aachen, Germany.

LEMPER, ERNST-HEINZ 1972 "Arnold von Westfalen: Berufs- und Lebensbild eines deutschen Werkmeisters der Spätgotik." Pages 41–55 in Hans-Joachim Mrusek, Die Albrechtsburg zu Meissen. Leipzig: Seemann.

RADOVÁ-ŠTIKOVA, MILADA 1971 "Architektura Arnolda Vestfálského." Architektura ČSR 31:422–425.

RADOVÁ-ŠTIKOVA, MILADA 1974 "Zdroje architektonické tvorby Arnolda Vestfálského." Umění 22:138–146.

ARNOLFO DI CAMBIO

In a document of 1300 from Florence, Arnolfo di Cambio (c.1245–c.1310) is described as "more famous and skilled in the building of churches than anyone else in the region." The same document identifies Arnolfo as the architect of the cathedral there. Despite his obvious importance during his lifetime, little is known today about the life of Arnolfo di Cambio or the extent of his work as an architect. He was born in the small Tuscan town of Colle di Valdelsa, probably between 1240 and 1250. He died in Florence between 1301 and 1310. The cathedral there is the only building to which Arnolfo's name is connected by documents or continuous tradition. Beginning however with GIORGIO VASARI in the sixteenth century, other buildings have been attributed to him. The most important and widely accepted of these are the Badia, Santa Croce, and the Palazzo della Signoria, all in Florence.

Like several of the most exceptional Italian masters of his era, such as Giovanni Pisano (see PISANO FAMILY) and GIOTTO DI BONDONE, Arnolfo was renowned for skills in more than one field: he was one of the most significant Italian sculptors of his time as well as an important architect. The earliest record of him is a *discipulus* in the sculptural workshop of Nicola Pisano in Siena, Italy, between 1265 and 1268, yet Arnolfo's sculptural style suggests that he worked with Nicola from an even earlier time. Where and with whom Arnolfo trained as an architect remains controversial. One can only speculate about whether Arnolfo assisted Nicola on architectural projects during his early years.

The few contemporary documents and inscriptions concerning Arnolfo as an independent master show that his work took him beyond his native Tuscany to Umbria, to Rome for at least ten years, and possibly to Naples. These travels seem to have been predominantly connected with sculptural projects, most of which, tombs and large altar ciboria for example, used architectural elements on a small scale. Arnolfo was gaining ideas that would later be used in his architectural designs, however. Certainly, the long Roman sojourn provided him

with a knowledge of its ancient monuments which is reflected in his architecture.

The earliest of the buildings attributed to Arnolfo is the Badia (1284–1310), a Benedictine church whose interior was remodeled in the seventeenth century. The choir façade shows the influence of Romanesque churches in Umbria, while the subtle harmony of its geometric order looks forward to the later designs for Santa Croce and the Florentine Cathedral façade.

Arnolfo's ambitious project for Santa Maria del Fiore, the cathedral in Florence, was begun between 1294 and 1296, but work was interrupted at his death. The design was changed and greatly enlarged in the mid-fourteenth century under Francesco Talenti (see TALENTI FAMILY). Only a partial idea of Arnolfo's plan can be derived from surviving evidence, but recent excavations of the foundations have demonstrated that Arnolfo intended a timber-roofed basilica with a large dome on an octagonal base. (Nothing further has been proved about Arnolfo's intentions for the eastern end of the church.) Arnolfo's incomplete façade decoration was dismantled in 1587, but a drawing attributed to Bernardino Poccetti records the state of the façade shortly before its destruction. Up to the broad topmost cornice in the drawing, most of the architectural conception seems attributable to Arnolfo.

The document that associates Arnolfo's name with the design of the cathedral also expresses the hope that the church will be the most beautiful in all Tuscany. His intended plan shows a general conformity to the long tradition of Tuscan domed cathedrals, such as those at Pisa (begun 1063; construction continued into the thirteenth century) and Siena (dome completed 1264; nave 1264–1284); however, Arnolfo's plan called for a greater nave width and a larger dome. The sculpturally profuse façade, an idea new to Florence, may have received impetus from Giovanni Pisano's façade for the cathedral in the rival city of Siena (1284–1314/1320). Arnolfo's arrangement also owes ideas to earlier thirteenth-century Gothic façades north of the Alps, to both medieval and ancient Roman art, and to the Romanesque tradition. The plastic rectilinear organization and the geometric designs of the green and white marble revetment of Arnolfo's work on the façade and flanks of the cathedral are a particular link to Romanesque Florentine architecture, most notably to its supreme monument, the Baptistery (c.1060–1150) with which the cathedral shared the ecclesiastical center of the city. Significantly, the Baptistery was considered at that time to be a converted Roman temple.

Santa Croce (begun 1294/1295; consecrated

Arnolfo di Cambio.
Santa Maria del Fiore
(drawing of façade).
Florence.
1294/1296–1310

1442) is the main Franciscan church in Florence. The transept with its multiple chapels and the openness of space in the timber-roofed nave are some of the characteristics shared with earlier Italian mendicant churches. Instead of the usual barnlike nave of these churches, however, the nave and aisles of Santa Croce are of basilican form. The immense nave (95.5 meters long; 19.5 meters wide; 34 meters high) is one of the largest in Europe. Indeed, its size closely approximates the old St. Peter's in Rome. The representation of the Franciscan ethos of poverty and humility in a church of such beauty, complexity, and scale make Santa Croce one of the most significant examples of mendicant architecture in Europe.

The Palazzo della Signoria, or Palazzo Vecchio (1299–1323), was built as the home of the dominant governing body, the Priors. This imposing building with its soaring tower rose in what was to be the political center of the city. Supporting the attribution to Arnolfo is the respect for the past shown in its design: the plan and the articulation

and military character of the originally freestanding block reflect earlier Italian communal palaces, particularly the Bargello in Florence (begun 1255). Furthermore, the striking use of heavily rusticated stone on the exterior seems to derive from the Forum of Augustus in Rome.

Santa Croce and the Palazzo della Signoria were, along with the cathedral, the most important buildings begun in Florence around 1300, a time of rapid growth and great ambition there. These buildings share a deep respect for their appropriate traditional types, yet each transcends its models through sophisticated organization and clarity of design, exalted scale, and masterful synthesis of eclectic ideas. Outstanding among these ideas is the intended reference in design and detail to Roman or early Christian architecture, an important aspect of Romanesque architecture in Florence, but one of lesser significance in the Gothic buildings there before the 1290s. The buildings associated with Arnolfo that were begun in this decade gave architectural form to the popular idea

Arnolfo di Cambio.
Santa Croce.
Florence.
1294/1295–1310 (not
completed until 1442).

that Florence had been an important Roman city and was heir of the greatness of ancient Rome. Yet, the buildings are decidedly Gothic. Although the links with Gothic architecture outside Italy are for the most part of a broad stylistic nature, Santa Croce and the Palazzo della Signoria (which, unlike the cathedral, were largely completed according to their original plans) demonstrate a level of excellence and ambition equal to that anywhere in Europe around 1300.

Arnolfo died without leaving any important follower. His influence came from his work. His cathedral design influenced the later parts of the building as well as the third and last member of the cathedral group, the Campanile (1334–1360), particularly its first project by Giotto. The design of Santa Croce is reflected in the Franciscan churches in Siena and Pisa from the early fourteenth century, and the influence of the Palazzo della Signoria extended into the fifteenth century. More important than the dissemination of particular design ideas, Arnolfo's buildings in Florence set a standard of quality and provided fourteenth-century architects there with buildings that successfully expressed Florentine aspirations while integrating Florentine traditions into the Gothic style.

KAREN CHRISTIAN

WORKS

(A)1284–1310, Badia; (A)1294/1295–1310, Santa Croce (not completed until 1442); 1294/1296–1310, Santa Maria del Fiore; (A)1299–1310, Palazzo della Signoria (not completed until 1323); Florence.

BIBLIOGRAPHY

PAATZ, WALTER 1937 *Werden und Wesen der Trecento-Architektur in Toskana: Die grossen Meister als Schöpfer einer neuen Baukunst: Die Meister von Santa Maria Novella; Niccolò Pisano; Giovanni Pisano; Arnolfo di Cambio und Giotto.* Burg bei Main, Germany: Hopfer.

PAATZ, WALTER, and PAATZ, ELISABETH 1940–1954 *Die Kirchen von Florenz: Ein kunstgeschichtliches Handbuch.* 6 vols. Frankfurt: Klostermann.

ROMANINI, ANGIOLA MARIA 1969 *Arnolfo di Cambio e lo stil novo del gotico italiano.* Milan: Ceschina.

TOKER, FRANKLIN 1978 "Florence Cathedral: The Design Stage." *Art Bulletin* 60:214–231.

TRACHTENBERG, MARVIN 1971 *The Campanile of Florence Cathedral: "Giotto's Tower."* New York University Press.

VASARI, GIORGIO (1568)1966–1967 Volume 1, pages 47–57 and volume 2, pages 111–193 in *Le vite de più eccelenti pittori scultori, e architettori nelle redazioni del 1550 e 1568.* Florence: Sansoni. Volume 1, entitled Testo, is edited by Rosanna Bettarini; volume 2, entitled Commento, is edited by Paola Barocchi. Originally published in 1550 with the title *Le vite piv eccelenti architetti.* There are many English translations and selection from Vasari's *Lives;* the standard one by G. du C. de Vere was published in ten volumes in London by the Medici Society in 1912–1915.

WHITE, JOHN 1966 *Art and Architecture in Italy: 1250–1400.* Baltimore: Penguin.

Arnolfo di Cambio. Santa Croce. Florence. 1294/1295–1310 (not completed until 1442).

ARNOULT DE BINCHE

Arnoult de Binche (13th century) has long been recognized as the architect of Our Lady of Pamele in Oudenaarde, Belgium, through an inscription on a stone set into the outer wall of the ambulatory:

ANNO D(OM)NI M.CC.XXX.IIII:IIII
ID.MARTII:INCEPTA FUIT
ECCL(ESI)A:ISTA:A MAG(IST)RO
ARNULPHO:DE BINCHO.

Begun in 1234, construction of this important example of Scaldian Gothic proceeded throughout the thirteenth century in three identifiable campaigns, which nevertheless produced a building of visual and structural homogeneity.

ELIZABETH SCHWARTZBAUM

WORK

1234–c.1300, Our Lady of Pamele, Oudenaarde, Belgium.

BIBLIOGRAPHY

BORCHGRAVE D'ALTENA, JOSEPH DE 1962 "L'église Notre-Dame-de-Pamele à Audenarde." *Congrès Archeologique de France* 120:143–152.
DEVOS, PATRICK 1978 *De Onze-Lieve-Vrouwkerk van Pamele te Oudenaarde. 1: Architektuur.* Ghent, Belgium: Provinciale Raad van Oost-Vlaanderen.
VAN ASSCHE, AUGUSTE 1881 *Monographie de l'église de Notre-Dame-de-Pamele à Audenarde.* Bruges, Belgium: Société de Saint-Augustin.

ARRIETA, PEDRO DE

Pedro de Arrieta (?–1738) arrived in Mexico before 1690, having received his training perhaps in Aragon or Catalonia. In 1695, he was master of the architects' guild and of the Inquisition. In 1720, he became master of the works of the cathedral of Mexico City and of the vice-regal palaces in Mexico City. His sober, angular style follows seventeenth-century Spanish practice.

JOHN DOUGLAS HOAG

WORKS

1690–1714, Church of San Miguel, Mexico City; 1695–1709, Basilica of Guadalupe, Mexico. 1714–1720, Church of La Professa; 1723–1737, Palace of the Inquisition; Mexico City.

BIBLIOGRAPHY

BERLIN, HEINRICH 1945 "El arquitecto Pedro de Arrieta." *Boletin del Archivo General de la Nacion* 16:73–94.
BERLIN, HEINRICH 1947 "Three Master Architects in New Spain." *Hispanic American Historical Review* 27:375–383.
KUBLER, GEORGE, and SORIA, MARTIN 1959 *Art and Architecture in Spain and Portugal and Their American Dominions.* Baltimore: Penguin.
TOUSSAINT, MANUEL (1962)1967 *Colonial Art in Mexico.* Austin: University of Texas Press. Originally published in Spanish.

ARRIGONI, ATTILIO

Serving as chief engineer of the Ospedale Maggiore in Milan, Attilio Arrigoni (17th century) designed a notable graveyard, originally consisting of a Greek-cross plan church (San Michele de' Nuovi Sepulcri) surrounded by a simple square courtyard. Dedicated on September 25, 1700, the church, crowned by a cupola, was intended to serve as a covered burial place. The undulating octagonal portico now surrounding the building was added by Francesco Croce in 1731.

GARY M. RADKE

WORK

1698–1700, San Michele de' Nuovi Sepulcri, Milan.

BIBLIOGRAPHY

CAMERINO, U.; LENA, M.; and MARTINONI, G. 1963 "La Rotonda di San Michele, a Milano." *L'Architettura* 8:840–849.
LATUADA, SERVILIANO 1737 Volume I, pages 265–273 in *Descrizione di Milano.* Milan: Cairoli.

ARRIGUCCI, LUIGI

Born in Florence, Luigi Arrigucci (1575–?) was called to Rome by his countryman Pope Urban VIII and named *architetto camerale* (succeeding CARLO MADERNO) in 1630. His work for the pope included a number of renovations, characterized by restraint, careful composition, and a linear quality unlike the more plastic and vigorous designs of his Roman contemporaries.

PATRICIA WADDY

WORKS

1624, Convent of Santa Maria Maddalena dei Pazzi (renovation and enlargement), Florence. 1630, San Sebastiano al Palatino (renovation and façade); 1632, Santi Cosma e Damiano (renovation); 1636, Sant'Antastasia (façade); 1641, San Giacomo alla Lungara (façade); Rome. 1644, Cathedral (renovation), Spoleto, Italy.

BIBLIOGRAPHY

BAGLIONE, GIOVANNI (1642)1935 *Le vite de' pittori, scultori ed architetti.* Facsimile ed. Rome: Calzone.
BATTAGLIA, ROBERTO 1942 "Luigi Arrigucci

architetto camerale d'Urbano VIII." *Palladio* 6:174–183.

POLLAK, OSKAR 1928–1931 *Die Kunsttätigkeit unter Urban VIII.* 2 vols. Vienna: Filser.

ARTARIA, PAUL

Paul Artaria (1892–1959), of Basel, was important for a renewal of wood construction in terms of modern architecture. Trained as a draftsman, he worked with HANS BERNOULLI from 1912 to 1920. He had his own office from 1925 to 1930 together with HANS SCHMIDT, to whom the austere *Sachlichkeit* of their architecture is due. Artaria defended his ideas as a writer and as a teacher at the Gewerbeschule in Basel.

MARTIN STEINMANN

WORKS

1920, Vacation House, Prêle, Bern. 1924–1925, Habermatten Estate, Riehen; Basel-Stadt. 1928, Schorenmatten Estate, Basel. 1933, Painter's House, Saignelégier, Jura, Switzerland. 1935, Painter's House, Riehen, Basel-Stadt. 1935, Vacation House, Beinwil, Aargau, Switzerland. 1936, House for a Childless Couple, Reinach, Basel-Land. 1952–1953, Museum fur Volkskunde, Basel.

BIBLIOGRAPHY

ARTARIA, PAUL 1933 *Fragen des neuen Bauens.* Basel: Wepf.
ARTARIA, PAUL 1936 *Schweizer Holzhäuser.* Basel: Wepf.
ARTARIA, PAUL 1938 *Ernst Egeler, Giovanni Panozzo: 6 neue schweizer Holzhäuser.* Basel: Wepf.
ARTARIA, PAUL (1939)1948 *Vom Bauen und Wohnen.* 3d ed. Basel: Wepf.
ARTARIA, PAUL 1943 *Gut Wohnen.* Basel: Wepf.
ARTARIA, PAUL 1947 *Ferien- und Landhäuser.* Zurich: Verlag für Architektur.

ARTIGAS, FRANCISCO

Francisco Artigas (1916–) was born in Mexico City and studied at the Universidad Nacional de México. His work, consisting of residences, apartment buildings, and offices, typifies mid-century modern architectural tendencies in Mexico. He is most noted for his houses built in the 1950s in Jardines del Pedregal, a residential section of Mexico City. Reminiscent of LUDWIG MIES VAN DER ROHE's "court" house projects in their light, pavilionlike quality, Artigas's buildings are structuralist works characterized by accentuation of vertical and horizontal elements and interpenetration of interior and exterior space. Within a predominantly International style vocabulary, Artigas

makes use of materials such as stone and exposed concrete.

ELIZABETH A. T. SMITH

WORKS

1951, Residence, 265 Farallon (with Santiago Greenham); 1952, Federico Gómez Residence, calle del Risco, Jardines del Pedregal, Mexico. 1953, Señora Carmen del Olmo de Artigas Residence, San Ángel, Mexico. 1956, Fernández Residence, 421 Paseo del Pedregal, Mexico City. Completed 1961?, Residence near Apple Valley, California. Completed 1963?, Artigas Residence and Office, Mexico City. Completed 1963?, Gueugnier Residence, Jardines del Pedregal, Mexico.

BIBLIOGRAPHY

ARTIGAS, FRANCISCO 1963 "Gueugnier Residence, Jardines del Pedregal, Mexico." *Architectural Design* 33, Sept.:433.
CETTO, MAX L. 1961 *Modern Architecture in Mexico.* Translated by D. Q. Stephenson. London: Tiranti.
"Desert House by Francisco Artigas, Architect." 1961 *Arts and Architecture* 78, Feb.:24–25.
"Habitation et agence de l'architecte Francisco Artigas dans un quartier résidentiel de Mexico." *L'Architecture d'Aujourd'hui* 1963 34, Sept.:82–83.
HITCHCOCK, H. R. 1955 *Latin American Architecture Since 1945.* New York: Museum of Modern Art.
KATZMAN, ISRAEL 1964 *La arquitectura contemporánea mexicana: Precedentes y desarrollo.* Mexico City: Instituto Nacional de Anthropología e Historia.
MYERS, I. E. 1952 *Mexico's Modern Architecture.* New York: Architectural Book Publishing Company.

ASAM, COSMAS DAMIAN, and ASAM, EGID QUIRIN

Cosmas Damian Asam (1686–1739) and Egid Quirin Asam (1692–1750), who formed a lifelong partnership, were the leading exponents of Bavarian baroque architecture—Rome-inspired but locally inflected and developed. Although both brothers were highly inventive architects, neither was trained to that end. Cosmas Damian studied painting at the Accademia di San Luca in Rome, where he won a first prize in 1713. Egid Quirin trained in Munich with the sculptor Andreas Faistenberger from about 1714 to 1716. Both Asams received early instruction under their father, Hans Georg Asam, a fresco painter known for his work at the venerable Bavarian abbeys of Benediktbeuern and Tegernsee and also at the pilgrimage church of Freystadt in the Oberpfalz (1708), where the sons assisted him in what must have been minor capacities.

Cosmas Damian Asam was born at Benediktbeuern, Egid Quirin Asam at Tegernsee. Cosmas Damian died in Munich, Egid Quirin at Mann-

Asam Brothers.
Benedictine Abbey.
Weltenburg, Germany.
1716–1735

heim, Germany. It is known that Cosmas Damian went to Rome in or about 1711 and returned in 1713 or 1714. That Egid Quirin accompanied him is not documented, but the assumption that he did so can hardly be avoided. Only a profound exposure to baroque Rome, especially to the monumental sculpture of GIOVANNI LORENZO BERNINI, can satisfactorily account for his development, already at full tide by 1720. Egid's training in Munich under the old-fashioned wood sculptor Faistenberger, seems to have had about the same insignificance creatively, as MICHELANGELO's training in painting under Domenico Ghirlandaio. Furthermore, virtually all of Egid's sculpture is in stucco, unlike that of his master.

No document explains the sudden emergence of both brothers as architects. In 1716, Cosmas Damian provided the plan for the Benedictine abbey church of Weltenburg, on the Danube between Ingolstadt and Regensburg; and in the following year Egid Quirin designed the Augustinian Priory Church of Rohr, a few miles south of Weltenburg. Before 1716, Cosmas Damian had painted frescoes in the abbey church of Ensdorf, north of Regensburg, and in the Trinity Church in Munich; but in 1717, Egid Quirin was only twenty-five and had completed his training in Munich only the year before. It is hardly surprising that Rohr was apparently the first commission that came to him. The whole design must be ascribed

to Egid—plan, structure, stucco decor, and the masterful high altar of the Assumption of the Virgin. The possibly anticipated nave fresco by Cosmas Damian did not eventuate, no doubt because of his many activities elsewhere. Egid's work in Rohr was completed by 1723, yet during these years he also carried out the enormous task of stucco decor and altar sculpture in his brother's church at Weltenburg. Work by both brothers continued intermittently there until 1735.

Because Weltenburg is a major example, despite its early date, of the collaborative work of the two brothers, I will discuss it in some detail as an innovative and highly influential Bavarian transformation of Roman baroque church design. Nothing of the sort had appeared in southern Germany before, not even Agostino Barelli's Theatine church in Munich, a rather clumsy variation on the Roman Church of Sant' Andrea della Valle. Weltenburg's oval plan, initiating a new development in German churches, reversed that of Bernini's Sant' Andrea in Quirinale in placing the entrance on the short end, thus preserving something of the effect of the long basilican plan, traditional in the North. H. R. Hitchcock has convincingly suggested that the Roman source of this plan came from such small chapels as that of Saint Cecilia in the church of San Carlo ai Catiniari by ANTONIO GHERARDI. Here, the coved drum beneath an oval cupola is roughly similar to the crown of the

Weltenburg nave, but it is transverse and supported on pendentives, whereas the Weltenburg cupola rests directly on the oval-shaped walls of the interior. Furthermore, the Saint Cecilia chapel has no extension, as at Weltenburg, to provide for a great high altar, where Egid Quirin's majestic image of Saint George holds sway under a Bernini-like triumphal arch, brilliantly lit from behind by invisible side windows. (The Saint George surprisingly resembles Rubens's equestrian Marie de' Medici's in the Louvre series. Overhead in the nave, Cosmas Damian's frescoed cupola, painted on a flat surface but creating a heavenly illusion in the manner of ANDREA POZZO's Roman ceiling designs, is also lit by concealed windows (visible, however, from the outside). The result of these arrangements is an interior unified by effects of changing light: a dark entrance hall, a mysterious half-light in the nave with a burst of golden light above, a darkened altar space, and a final burst of light in the far end. Cornices, pilasters, and col-

Asam Brothers.
Benedictine Abbey (interior
toward high altar).
Weltenburg, Germany.
1716–1735

umns have a Roman grandeur, especially the colossal serpentine Berninesque ones enframing the high altar. Colors attain the dark opulence of Roman polychromy, heightened by a liberal use of gold. But the two explosions of light dramatize what Bernhard Rupprecht has aptly called *Das Grosse Bild*—the Big Picture. Working together—on Cosmas Damian's plan—the Asams, untrained as architects, announced themselves as organizers of *interior space.* Frankly, the exterior of Weltenburg is ungainly, even crude, and the dull façade is not their work, but that of a later architect.

All this baroque splendor does not preclude touches of lively humor. Among the stucco putti and billowy clouds that physically support a golden ring or crown under Cosmas Damian's cupola—seemingly like a balcony railing—is Egid's half-length stucco portrait of Cosmas Damian himself, who returned the compliment by including his brother among other portraits in his heavenly fresco. At the base of Egid's grandiose figure of Saint Martin of Tours—the secondary patron of the church—standing to the left of Saint George in the high altar, a putto comically apes the saint's gesture from beneath his massive robes. A goose, symbolic of the saint because its cackling revealed his hiding place when he modestly tried to refuse the Tourangeaux's invitation to become their bishop, shrieks in terror at the adjacent dragon, under attack by Saint George. Finally, much of the profuse ornament that animates the whole interior echoes, as Hitchcock has pointed out, the turn-of-the-century *Régence* trend introduced by JOSEF EFFNER on his return to Munich from a period of training in Paris.

A much later collaborative work of the Asams, the Church of Saint John Nepomuk in Munich, shows significant differences from Weltenburg. The chief dates are: building, 1733–1734; ceiling fresco, 1735; and stucco decor and sculpture, from 1735 into the mid-1740s (carried out by Egid Quirin after Cosmas Damian's death in 1739). On this project, it was Egid Quirin who took the lead. Beginning in 1729, the year of the saint's canonization, Egid bought four houses on the Sendlingerstrasse (facing east) and planned the church to occupy the two central lots. He built his own three-story house to the left of the church and another of the same height for the priest on the right (unfortunately this was extended to four stories in the 1770s and thus interferes with the interior lighting of the church on that side). The dictates of site precluded any consideration of the church's exterior shape and allowed only for an imposing façade, here conceived by Egid as if it were made up of three superposed high altar constructions gaining in size from bottom to top, but pressed into the same plane. Within, Egid transformed an inpropitious narrow rectangle (the plan measures only 9 meters in width by 28 meters deep) by manipulating concave and convex walls, broken cornices, and a fantastic array of stucco decor and sculptures into an illusory, undulating oval space. The relatively great height of the interior lifts the eye upward. Above the massive base story is a very narrow projecting gallery, and high above that is Cosmas Damian's enormous fresco. Shallow wall arcades at both floor and gallery levels recede illusionistically into wall paintings by Cosmas Damian that further extend the space laterally. Egid's high altar is two-tiered, corresponding to the main horizontal division of the nave; but it is further crowned by the *Gnadenstuhl,* gilded and silvered: the image of the crucified Christ surmounted by God the Father and, yet higher, the dove of the Holy Spirit. Higher still is the iconographical culmination of Cosmas Damian's vast fresco: a personification of the Institution of the Roman Church, presided over by another figure of God, wearing the triple tiara as in the *Gnadenstuhl* below. The profound piety here manifested—an aspect of both German baroque and German rococo that cannot be overemphasized—has an unbroken continuity stretching back through the Renaissance to the Middle Ages. This no doubt explains the similarity of the *Gnadenstuhl* group to Albrecht Dürer's *Trinity* (oil or woodcut version).

Light in the Nepomukkirche is dim at floor level, but floods in higher up through large windows in the façade, smaller ones over the lateral gallery, on the north side toward the apse (beyond the point where the priest's house blocks side lighting), and—to an extent still being hotly debated—at the altar end. Egid's image of the patron saint, presumably in adoration of the Virgin, was so badly deteriorated by moisture that in 1820 it was taken down and replaced by an oil painting by Andreas Seidl. This survived until the bombings of World War II. In 1960 it was replaced by an equally large stucco relief (the work of the Munich sculptor Lorch) representing the saint in ecstasy; but adverse criticism resulted in its being replaced after 1975 by a free-standing colossal statue of the saint, lit from behind by a huge window. The oil painting of 1820, however, and the stucco relief of 1960 that replaced it were lit only from side windows. Controversy was again sparked by the discovery of a document of 1795 indicating that Egid's upper high altar was a silvered stucco relief (*Altarblatt*) representing Saint John Nepomuk kneeling before the Virgin Mary. This could likewise have been lit only from side windows. On the basis of this evidence (see Bauer et al., 1977) a new

reconstruction of the apse—totally destroyed in World War II bombings—proceeds as of this writing. Controversy resurfaced in 1981 in letters to the *Münchener Stadtanzeiger* (especially the issues of September 25 and October 9) concerning the "large round window" (*ein gross rundes Fenster*), mentioned in the document of 1795 as existing in the end wall of the apse and as having caused the excessive moisture that ruined Egid Quirin's altarpiece. R. Bauer, in reply, appears to have established the authenticity of the current reproduction of the original arrangements. The large round window would refer to the window under the apse vault—rectangular but with a rounded top—that afforded back lighting to the suspended Gnadenstuhl.

The church is familiarly known as the Asamkirche, for it was conceived, executed, and adorned by the brothers at their own expense. Egid Quirin had a private entrance to the lateral gallery from his house. He never married, but Cosmas Damian

Asam Brothers. Cathedral (decoration). Freising, Germany. 1723–1724

maintained a fine country residence for his family outside Munich at Thalheim. There, with the help of Egid, he built a private chapel in gratitude for the important commission to decorate the enormous Swiss pilgrimage church of Einsiedeln (1724–1726).

That the Asams were primarily designers of interior space is further supported by the fact that most of their work consisted in "baroquizing" already existing buildings, whether medieval ones such as the Cathedral of Freising and the abbey of Saint Emmeram at Regensburg (1731–1733) or churches just completed by other architects, such as the Premonstratensian abbey of Osterhofen (built 1726–1728 by JOHANN MICHAEL FISCHER, decorated 1729–1735) and the Swiss abbey of Einsiedeln, referred to above. From an architectural point of view, the Asams' contribution at Freising is perhaps the most important of these and many other challenging commissions. Windows in the grim twelfth-century fabric were enlarged to admit much more light at the gallery and especially the clearstory level—the floor area remains dark by contrast. Giant pilasters lead the eye rapidly up to Cosmas Damian's extensive ceiling frescoes. Surfaces are enlivened by stucco decor and such masterly figure sculptures as Egid Quirin's Mater Dolorosa on the north side of the nave. On the high altar, Rubens's flamboyant *Apocalyptic Woman* (modern copy, original now in Munich) does not seem out of place, although the Asams' art had already moved, since Weltenburg, in a blonder, more sprightly direction. Their vast undertaking, begun in 1723, was finished in time for Freising's millennium celebration in 1724 of the establishment of the church.

I perforce omit Cosmas Damian's many individual fresco commissions, as at the great Benedictine abbey of Weingarten (1718–1720), and others as far afield as Bohemia and Silesia, as well as Egid Quirin's separate sculptural works, such as his harmonious matching of Erasmus Grasser's image of Saint Peter (c.1490) with statues of the four church fathers in the high altar of the Church of Saint Peter in Munich (1733). In this instance, Egid also matched the material, wood—one of his few departures from stucco.

In 1740, the year after his brother's death, Egid Quirin designed an exceptionally sumptuous high altar for the Pilgrimage Church of Maria-Dorfen, east of Erding (destroyed in or before 1868, but the drawing preserved in Munich). In 1747–1748, he executed the Saint Peter high altar and adjacent window sculptures at Sandizell, east of Augsburg, and accepted an invitation to the Rhenish city of Mannheim to paint the ceiling frescoes of the Jesuit church (destroyed in World War II, a drawing

preserved in the National Gallery of Art, Washington). The invitation to paint at Mannheim, where Egid died in 1750, probably resulted from the great success of his brother's fresco in the Schlosskapelle, completed as early as 1730.

The brothers' last collaborative work was the Ursuline Convent Church at Straubing, on the Danube below Regensburg. Built in 1736–1738 and decorated in the two following years, it is once again primarily the work of Egid Quirin, but Cosmas Damian lived long enough to paint the ceiling fresco and three superb altarpieces. The narrow street façade, rising between the conventual buildings, presented the same restriction as at the Nepomukkirche; indeed, it is only a simplified and much flattened version of that design. But Egid's plan represents a new departure for the Asams, as its 20-by-26 meter interior dimensions quickly indicate. A circular cupola on pendentives surmounts an irregular Greek cross structure with curved arms, the transept areas greatly reduced, but the altar space more extended than the vestibule entrance opposite. A huge street window and important subsidiary ones over the side and altar arms flood the whole compact interior with a nearly even light. No longer the spotlighted drama of Weltenburg and the Asamkirche! Here, the influence of centrally planned churches by Fischer is apparent—and along with it the fast-developing rococo spirit of the architecture of the times. In that spirit, too, Egid's high altar figures have a new lilt and more elegant forms, noticeably different from the intensely physical ones at Weltenburg and Rohr. If, at Rohr, the Apostles below the Berninesque Virgin—angel-propelled toward heaven—are unexpectedly emaciated, it is clearly in a spirit that can only be called dramatic-Expressionist. Such an attitude reaches back to violent German Gothic sculpture and forward to Kokoschka and the modern German painters of *Die Brücke*.

Between 1735 and 1738, the brothers returned to Freising to decorate the Johanniskapelle, off the south transept of the cathedral. A large circular window lights this small chamber with much the same effect as that at Straubing. Below it three saints John—Baptist, Nepomuk, and Evangelist—gesticulate gently from their high pedestals. Their pure whiteness and their suavely elongated proportions again echo the new rococo temper, that is, within the limits of Egid Quirin's vocabulary. Cosmas Damian's small fresco, like the larger one at Straubing, has more open space, a total absence of heavily baroque architectural elements, and blonder colors than before. A chronological study, not appropriate here, of Cosmas Damian's fresco art and the sculptural career of Egid Quirin would show a gradual departure from their Roman-oriented premise toward the rococo age. From the standpoint, however, of contemporary and even earlier buildings and their décor by FRANÇOIS CUVILLIÉS or the ZIMMERMANN BROTHERS, the Asams' sense of the rococo seems hesitant indeed.

S. LANE FAISON, JR.

WORKS

COSMAS DAMIAN ASAM

1714–1716, Benedictine Abbey (frescoes), Ensdorf, Germany. 1715, Trinity Church (frescoes), Munich. 1716–1721, Benedictine Abbey (frescoes), Michelfeld, Germany. 1718–1720, Benedictine Abbey (frescoes), Weingarten, Germany. 1726–1728, Benedictine Abbey (frescoes), Březnov, Czechoslovakia. *1728, Schlosskapelle (frescoes), Mannheim, Germany. 1730, Schloss (frescoes), Alteglofsheim, Germany. 1732, Schlosskapelle (frescoes), Ettlingen, Germany. (A)1732–1734, Santa Maria de Victoria (frescoes), Ingolstadt, Germany. 1733, Benedictine Priory Church (frescoes), Wahlstatt, Silesia, Germany. 1734, Landhaus (frescoes), Innsbruck, Austria.

EGID QUIRIN ASAM

1717–1723, Augustinian Priory Church, Rohr, Germany. 1733, Saint Peter (Four Fathers of the Church); *1738, Saint Anna am Lehel (side altars); Munich. *1740, Pilgrimage Church (high altar), Maria Dorfen, Germany. 1747–1748, Church (altar sculptures), Sandizell, Germany. *1747–1750, Jesuit Church (ceiling frescoes), Mannheim, Germany.

COSMAS DAMIAN ASAM AND EGID QUIRIN ASAM

1716–1735, Benedictine Abbey, Weltenburg, Germany. c.1720, Cistercian Abbey (frescoes and stuccoes), Aldersbach, Germany. 1722, Saint Jakobi Parish Church (frescoes and stuccoes), Innsbruck, Austria. 1722–1737, Cistercian Abbey (decoration), Fürstenfeldbruck, Germany. 1723–1724, Cathedral (decoration), Freising, Germany. 1724–1726, Benedictine Abbey (decoration), Einsiedeln, Switzerland. 1727, Heilig-Geistkirche (frescoes); *1729, Saint Anna am Lehel (decoration); Munich. 1729–1735, Premonstratensian Abbey (decoration), Osterhofen, Germany. 1731–1733, Saint Emmeram Benedictine Abbey, Regensburg, Germany. 1733–1740s, Saint John Nepomuk, Munich. 1735–1738, Freising Cathedral, Johanniskapelle, Germany. 1736–1740, Ursuline Convent Church, Straubing, Germany.

BIBLIOGRAPHY

BAUER, RICHARD ET AL. 1977 *St. Johann Nepomuk im Licht der Quellen.* Munich: Bauer.

BAUER, RICHARD, and DISCHINGER, GABRIELE 1981 *Die Asamkirchen in München.* Munich: Schnekl & Steiner.

BAUER, RICHARD ET AL. 1977 *St. Johann Nepomuk im Licht der Quellen.* Munich: mz-Verlagsdruckerei GmbH.

FEULNER, ADOLF 1923 *Bayerisches Rokoko.* Munich: Kurt Wolff.

HANFSTAENGL, ERIKA 1939 *Cosmas Damian Asam.* Munich: Neuer Filserverlag.

HANFSTAENGL, ERIKA 1955 *Die Brüder Cosmas Damian und Egid Quirin Asam.* Munich and Berlin: Deutscher Kunstverlag.

HITCHCOCK, H. R. 1968 *Rococo Architecture in Southern Germany.* London: Phaidon.

LIEB, NORBERT (1953)1976 *Barockkirchen zwischen Donau und Alpen.* 4th ed., rev. Munich: Hirmer.

LIEB, NORBERT, and SAUERMOST, HEINZ JÜRGEN 1973 *Münchens Kirchen.* Munich: Süddeutscher.

RUPPRECHT, BERNHARD, and MULBE, WOLF VON DER 1980 *Die Brüder Asam: Sinn und Sinnlichkeit im Bayerischen Barock.* Regensburg: Pustet.

TINTELNOT, HANS 1951 *Die Barocke Freskomalerei in Deutschland: Ihre Entwicklung und europäische Wirkung.* Munich: Bruckmann.

TROTTMAN, HELENE 1980 "Die Zeichungen Cosmas Damian Asams für den Concorso Clementino der

ASCHIERI, PIETRO

Pietro Aschieri (1889–1952) was born in Rome in 1889. He graduated from the Facolta di Ingegneria in Rome in 1913. Aschieri was a member of the Movimento Italiano per l'Architettura Razionale. He was also active in set design for state and cinema during the 1930s.

DENNIS DOORDAN

WORKS

1930, Casa De Salvi; 1931, Casa di Lavoro dei Ciechi di Guerra; 1933, Facolta di Chimica, University of Rome; 1939, E'42 Exhibition Building; Rome.

Asam Brothers. Johanniskapelle, Freising Cathedral. Germany. 1735–1738

BIBLIOGRAPHY

ACCASTO, GIANNI; FRATICELLI, VANNA; and NICOLINI, RENATO 1971 *L'Architettura di Roma Capitale: 1870-1970.* Rome: Edizioni Golem.

GIACOMELLI, ANNA 1977 *Pietro Aschieri architetto.* Rome: Bulzoni.

ASHBEE, C. R.

Charles Robert Ashbee (1863–1942) is best known as a designer of metalwork and as the founder of the Guild of Handicraft, one of the most experimental workshops in the English Arts and Crafts movement. But he also designed and executed some sixty buildings, mostly houses, the best of them being concentrated in Cheyne Walk, Chelsea, on London's riverfront, and in Chipping Campden in Gloucestershire.

In Chelsea, Ashbee's attention focused on façades and streetscape. The loosely composed and faintly Queen Anne brick elevation of 37 Cheyne Walk (1893–1894) incorporated a three-story oriel modeled on the seventeenth-century wooden front of Sir Paul Pindar's House in Bishopsgate, London. The house at 72–73 Cheyne Walk (1897) was plainer, with vernacular detail—unmolded brickwork, wooden casements, and roughcast on the

Ashbee.
72–74 Cheyne Walk.
London.
1897–1898

oriels—and more artful: the windows were disposed with careful and deceptive irregularity to look "functional." The roughcast projection on the front of 74 Cheyne Walk (1898) made it look like the back of a townhouse, as if Ashbee had turned the old saw about Queen Anne fronts and Mary-Ann backs on its head. And 38 and 39 Cheyne Walk (1898?–1899) presented flat façades of brick below and roughcast above, in the style of Old London. Though they were designed and built together, Ashbee was at pains to make the openings and roof details as different as possible for picturesque effect. The contrived variety of elevation, the vernacular details and the antiquarian allusions were all designed to foster the sense of a village in the city.

In 1902, Ashbee moved the Guild of Handicraft from London to Chipping Campden in Gloucestershire. During the next five years, he was responsible for restorations, additions and new buildings in this idyllic Cotswold town. His conservative aim was to fit in with Campden's stone-built vernacular; the old work was carefully repaired, and the new was kept modest and unpretentious. His most remarkable building was the Norman Chapel (1906?–1907) at Broad Campden, just outside the town. He found a ruined chapel of around 1100 with late medieval additions and adapted it sympathetically as a dwelling, adding an understated service wing to his own design.

Ashbee is often seen as one of those turn-of-the-century architects whose simple and apparently functional work looked forward to the innovations of the twentieth century. He was, for instance, one of the first European architects to admire the work of FRANK LLOYD WRIGHT; and the plainness of his own work suggested a rejection of past styles. But it was a plainness rich in ambiguity. It had vernacular associations and so became a vehicle for a quite unmodernist traditionalism and for Ashbee's highly developed sense of place. It was in this plain style that he enhanced the architectural traditions of Chipping Campden and evoked the cultural traditions of Chelsea. These were the peculiar functions of Ashbee's best buildings.

ALAN CRAWFORD

WORKS

*1893–1894, 37 Cheyne Walk, London. 1895–1897, The Wodehouse (additions), Wombourne, Staffordshire, England. *1897, 72–73 Cheyne Walk; *1898, 74 Cheyne Walk; 1898?–1899, 38 and 39 Cheyne Walk; *1902–1903?, 75 Cheyne Walk; London. 1903, The High House, Sheep Street; 1904, Woodroffe House (additions), Westington; Chipping Campden, Gloucestershire, England. *1905, House, Stefania District, Budapest. 1906?–1907, Norman Chapel (restoration and additions), Broad Campden, Gloucestershire, England. 1907, Byways, Yarnton, Oxfordshire, England. 1908–1909, Villa San Giorgio, Taormina, Italy. *1913, 71 Cheyne Walk, London.

BIBLIOGRAPHY

ASHBEE, C. R.   1906   *A Book of Cottages and Little Houses.* Chipping Campden, England, and London: Essex House & Batsford.

ASHBEE, C. R.   1907   "The 'Norman Chapel' Buildings at Broad Campden in Gloucestershire." *The Studio* 41:289–296.

ASHBEE, C. R.   (1911)1968   "Frank Lloyd Wright: A Study and An Appreciation." In *Frank Lloyd Wright: The Early Work.* New York: Horizon. Originally published in *Frank Lloyd Wright: Ausgeführte Bauten.*

BURY, SHIRLEY   1967   "An Arts and Crafts Experiment: The Silverwork of C. R. Ashbee." *Victoria and Albert Museum Bulletin* 3:18–25.

CHELTENHAM MUSEUM AND ART GALLERY   1981   *C. R. Ashbee and the Guild of Handicraft.* Cheltenham, England: The museum. Catalogue of an exhibition.

CRAWFORD, ALAN   1970   "Ten Letters from Frank Lloyd Wright to Charles Robert Ashbee." *Architectural History* 13:64–76.

CRAWFORD, ALAN   1978   *A Tour of Broadway and Chipping Campden.* London: The Victorian Society.

Neubauten in London.   1900   Berlin: Wasmuth. Volume 3 in the Moderne Städtebilder series.

SERVICE, ALASTAIR   (1977)1978   *Edwardian Architecture.* London: Thames.

ASHIWARA, YOSHINOBU

Born in Tokyo, Japan, Yoshinobu Ashiwara (1918–) graduated from Tokyo University in 1942 and took a master's degree from Harvard University in 1953. He worked in the office of MARCEL BREUER for several years, after which he returned to Japan where he opened his own office in 1956. He was awarded a prize from the Architectural Institute of Japan for his Chūoh-kōron Building in 1960 and another special prize from the same institution for the National Komazawa Gymnasium (1964) for the Olympic Games. He was a professor of architecture at Tokyo Univeristy from 1970 to 1979.

SAKA-E OHMI
Translated from Japanese by
Bunji Kobayashi

WORKS

1956, Chūoh-kōron Building; 1964, National Komazawa Gymnasium, Olympic Games; 1966, Sony Building; 1969, Fuji Film Main Office; 1981, Daiichi-kangin Bank; Tokyo.

BIBLIOGRAPHY

ASHIWARA, YOSHINOBU   1962   *Gaibukūkan no Kōsei.* Tokyo: Shokokusha.

Ashiwara.
Daiichi-kangin Bank.
Tokyo.
1981

ASHIWARA, YOSHINOBU   1979a   *Kenchikukūkan no Miryoku.* Tokyo.

ASHIWARA, YOSHINOBU   1979b   *Machinami no Bigakü.* Tokyo.

Gendainihon Kenchikuka Zenshū.   1971   Volume 15. *Tokyo.*

ASPINWALL, JAMES L.

James Lawrence Aspinwall (1854–1936), the son of wealthy New York socialites, was educated by private tutors and is reputed to have studied with L. Colian (sometimes spelled Collain or Collan), a French architect and engineer residing in New York. In 1875, he was employed as a draftsman by JAMES RENWICK whose wife was the young architect's distant cousin, and in 1883, he was promoted to partnership. Following Renwick's death in 1895, Aspinwall became the senior partner, the firm name being changed to Renwick, Aspinwall, and Owen. Aspinwall retired from active practice in 1925, the firm continuing as Renwick, Aspinwall, and Guard.

SELMA RATTNER

WORKS

*1896?, George Bullock House, Oyster Bay, N.Y. 1899, Adam Lanfear Norrie House (extensively altered in 1925), New York. 1899?–1900, H. W. Garrett House, Baltimore. 1906–1907, Grace Church Neighborhood House; 1908, Provident Loan Society Main Building;

1916–1917, American Express Company Building; *1919, Pictorial Review Company Building, New York. 1920–1921, McCullough Memorial Public Library, Bennington, Vt. *1921–1922, Lawyers' Mortgage Company Building, New York.

BIBLIOGRAPHY

"J. Lawrence Aspinwall." 1924 *American Art Annual* 21:363.

"J. L. Aspinwall, 82, Architect, is Dead." 1936 *New York Times* May 16, section 2, page 9, column 1.

ASPLUND, ERIK GUNNAR

Erik Gunnar Asplund (1885–1940) was born in Stockholm and became the outstanding modern architect in Sweden and, after ALVAR AALTO and ELIEL SAARINEN, in the other Nordic countries. He studied at the Royal Institute of Technology, Stockholm, between 1905 and 1909 and was awarded the Institute's Travel Scholarship which he spent in Germany. Upon his return, he rejected the neoclassical training of the Royal Academy of Art, and with six other architectural students, SIGURD LEWERENTZ, OSVALD ALMQVIST, Melchior Wernstedt, Erik Karlstrand, and Josef Östlin, founded an independent school where CARL BERGSTEN, RAGNAR ÖSTBERG, IVAR TENGBOM, and CARL WESTMAN taught. Instruction at the Klara School stressed the appropriateness of indigenous Scandinavian architecture for contemporary design and thus encouraged National Romanticism rather than imported classical styles.

Although he rejected the teaching at the Royal Academy, Asplund's early work show that elements of both neoclassicism and Scandinavian romanticism affected him. His earliest work, for example, the early villas, shows the influence of Östberg's and Westman's National Romanticism. The impact of the classicism of the second decade of the twentieth century becomes evident in the 1916 design (he had won first prize in the 1913 competition) for the Göteborg Law Courts; this may have been the result of his studying in Germany. Asplund's ability to fuse the informal and emotional effects of National Romanticism with classical details becomes apparent in the Woodland Cemetery (1915), an area of the Stockholm South Cemetery. He and Sigurd Lewerentz entered the competition and drew up an informal, romantic plan that was suitable for the rugged terrain. The chapel, which was Asplund's design, shows the steeply pitched roof characteristic of indigenous Swedish architecture, a Doric portico, and circular interior. The austerity of the interior is relieved by simple lighting fixtures and fluted Doric columns. The juxtaposition of vernacular and clas-

sical elements and the overall simplicity promote a rustic effect that is appropriate to the setting. The sympathetic position of the chapel within the cemetery, where trees mark the graves, shows a feeling for the relationship between architecture and environment which marks Asplund's architecture even in his interpretation of the modern.

The designs for the Stockholm Public Library (1920–1928) show Asplund combining motifs once again. Modernistic in its use of simplified classical forms but Swedish in the sweetness and delicacy of the details, the Public Library may have been influenced by PETER BEHRENS and twentieth-century German classicism. Even more striking is the specific reference to CLAUDE NICOLAS LEDOUX's Barrière de la Villette (1784–1789). Asplund makes Ledoux's design highly abstract by enlarging the base upon which the central drum is placed, by reducing the sculptural qualities of the surface to a mere skin, and by regularizing and limiting classical details. Although some critics have viewed this classicism and the delicate realism of the decoration as retardataire elements which made Asplund's purely functionalist work of the Stockholm Exhibition all the more remarkable, others have regarded the building as a successful compromise between the best of traditional and modern architecture.

Although there were examples of purely modern, functional architecture before 1930 in Sweden, they were isolated and unknown except to the avant-garde. Thus, the 1930 exhibition gave Asplund the distinction of introducing the modern to the Swedish public. Originally planned as a large, prestigious display of Swedish industrial design and handicrafts, the exposition became renowned not only for Asplund's architecture and planning but also for the housing section, directed by Gunnar Sonderberg and UNO ÅHRÉN, with small homes designed by various architects. Although displays of traditional crafts and luxury goods were included in the exhibition, the modern design of the buildings and their furnishings were what attracted attention. In drawing attention to the new style, the exposition created controversy; one historian called it "the principal and physically greatest propaganda effort of early Swedish functionalism." What was shocking was the thorough-going application of the machine aesthetic to domestic architecture and furnishings which had been dominated not only by historical style, but by handcrafted goods in the Swedish tradition. It is thus not surprising that one very outspoken critic was CARL MALMSTEN who based his furniture on traditional Swedish designs. It was against Malmsten and other critics that a group of six architects, Asplund, Walter Gohn, SVEN GOTTFRID

MARKELIUS, Gregor Paulsen, Eskil Sundahl, and Uno Ahrén directed their manifesto, *accaptera*, published in 1931.

The 1930 Exhibition, which was the first planned by a single architect, was in some ways a résumé of modern architectural ideas. The main building, which had long strip windows set flush to the exterior wall surface and bold displays of steel and glass, might be called International style. Bauhaus-inspired sansserif lettering, designed by Lewerentz, was used on the signs. The influence of Russian Constructivism was visible in the decorative flags hoisted on poles and on light, open metal frames. The glass and actual openness of many parts of the main building made it suggest temporary pavilions, and along with the flags, it gave a festive, inviting air. The over-all effect, including the lightness which SIEGFRIED GIEDION particularly praised and called typical Swedish, was in no way derivative.

Indeed, many elements made the design of the Exhibition more than a wholesale importation of foreign ideas. Representing a departure from the usual materials of modern architecture, wood, abundant in Scandinavia and a common building material there, was used in furnishings and interior fittings. Wood was in fact the basis of the structural system of the small, temporary pavilions where glued wooden trusses were used. Furthermore, Asplund's planning

was an important departure from the radical urbanism of the Modern Movement. Instead of dispersing his buildings in the parklike setting, he used an essentially traditional urban scheme, with esplanades, cul-de-sacs, and buildings arranged to form streets. . . . Asplund was seriously addressing a problem that Le Corbusier, Mies and Gropius ignored because they did not see its solution as important, and that was the problem of how to create a unified and vital urbanism along traditional lines with the new style [Wrede, 1980, p. 129].

Despite the fervor with which Asplund and his colleagues espoused functionalism, in the early 1930s, there was soon a classicizing reaction. His speech before the Swedish Architectural Association in 1936 shows his re-evaluation of functionalism and a move away from the machine aesthetic: "One should not conceive of utility as an end in itself, but merely as a means to increase choice and well being for people in this life. Technology does not suffice to achieve this; what I would call art must also be an ingredient" (Wrede, 1980, p. 153). Asplund's last two buildings, the Göteborg Law Courts (1934–1937) and the Woodland Cemetery (1935–1940), show the development of this thinking.

Having won the original competition for an annex to the Göteborg Law Courts in 1913, Asplund made many changes before the design was finalized and built (1935–1936). In the use of a simplified classical block that extends the older Law Courts on one side, the annex is regarded as an outstanding example of the union of modern and traditional design as well as of contextualism. The interior, although not classical, can in no way be called functionalist, due to the use of wood in the paneling and furnishings and the delicacy of the freestanding staircase.

This contextualism and assertion of classicism as a means of design is evident also in the Woodland Crematorium, a project which he began in 1915 with Sigurd Lewerentz. By the mid-1930s, Asplund had developed the naturalistic landscaping and design for one large and two small chapels. The classical references are evident in the posts and lintels of the white marble loggie and the interior of the large chapel with its columns and large painted mural. Typically modern characteristics appear in the clean, smooth exterior surfaces, almost devoid of decoration; the materials and juxtaposed masses provide visual interest in the building complex. Yet, the composition of the masses is complex and rich by functionalist requirements. What is superlative about the Crematorium is the way in which the buildings and landscape are integrated. The chapels and the long driveway define the rise of the slope while the main chapel and the large freestanding cross provide a focal point on the horizon. Asplund's genius for blending the traditional and modern in architecture and the natural and artificial in the landscape is dramatically summarized.

JUDITH S. HULL

WORKS

1912–1918, Secondary School, Karlshamn, Sweden. 1913, Villa Selander, Örnsköldsvik, Sweden. 1914, Ruth Villa, Kuusankoski, Finland. 1915, Woodland Cemetery (with Sigurd Lewerentz), Stockholm South Burial Ground. 1917–1918, Snellman Villa, Djursholm, Sweden. 1917–1921, Lister County Courthouse, Sölvesborg, Sweden. 1918–1920, Woodland Chapel, Stockholm South Burial Ground. 1920–1928, Stockholm Public Library. 1922–1923, Skandia Cinema; 1922–1924, Woodland Cemetery Offices, Stockholm South Burial Ground; 1931, Swedish Society of Arts and Crafts (reconstruction, interior, and furnishings); 1933–1937, State Bacteriological Laboratory; Stockholm. 1934–1937, Göteborg Law Courts Annex, Sweden. 1935–1940, Woodland Crematorium and Chapels, Stockholm South Burial Ground. 1936–1940, Asplund's Villa, Stennäs, Sweden.

BIBLIOGRAPHY

AHLBERG, HAKON 1943 *Gunnar Asplund Arkitekt, 1885–1940. Ritringer, Skisser, och Fotografier.* Stockholm: Byggmästaren.

ÅHRÉN, UNO 1928 "Reflexioner i Stadsbiblioteket. *Byggmästaren*.

ASPLUND, ERIK GUNNAR; GAHN, WOLTER; MARKELIUS, SVEN; PAULSSON, GREGOR; SUNDAHL, ESKIL; and ÅHRÉN, UNO 1931 *Acceptera*. Stockholm: Bokförlagsaktiebolaget Tiden.

BLOMBERG, ERIK 1928 "Stadsbiblioteket i Stockholm." *Svenska Slöjdforeningnens Arsbok*.

DE MARÉ, ERIC 1955 *Gunnar Asplund: A Great Modern Architect*. London: Art & Technics.

GRAVES, MICHAEL 1975 "The Swedish Connection." *Journal of Architectural Education*.

NAGY, ELEMÉR 1974 *Erik Gunnar Asplund*. Budapest.

WREDE, STUART 1980 *The Architecture of Erik Gunnar Asplund*. Cambridge, Mass.: M.I.T. Press.

ASPRUCCI, ANTONIO

Son of an architect, Antonio Asprucci (1723–1808) studied with NICOLA SALVI and first worked with his father. He was a member of the Accademia di San Luca and architect of the grand duke of Tuscany in Rome. His major patron was Marcantonio Borghese, for whom he directed the work of decorating the casino and the park of Villa Borghese (1782–1802).

Asprucci contrasted eighteenth-century sumptuousness with neoclassical austerity in the sculpture gallery of the Casino Borghese. His Temple of Esculapius (1783) was much copied, and in the Piazza di Siena Temple he revived a pure Doric order.

MARTHA POLLAK

WORKS

1782–1802, Villa Borghese; 1783, Temple of Esculapius; n.d., Piazza di Siena Temple; Rome.

BIBLIOGRAPHY

LAVAGNINO, EMILIO 1961 Volume I in *L'arte moderna dai neoclassici ai contemporanei*. Turin: Unione Tipografico-Editrice Torinese.

MEEKS, C. L. V. 1966 *Italian Architecture, 1750–1914*. New Haven: Yale University Press.

ASTENGO, GIOVANNI

Giovanni Astengo (1915–), Italian architect and planner, began his career after World War II as head of the group responsible for the master plans of Turin and Piedmont. He designed the "organic" Falchera residential quarter in Turin (1951) and devised master plans for Assisi (1957), Chiesaquart (1959), and Gubbio (1960). In the 1960s, he made a substantial contribution to the formulation of new urban planning laws. Later, he was responsible for the revision of master plans for Genoa (1963), Assisi (1964–1966), and Bergamo (1966).

His activity as administrator of the Piedmont Region from 1975 to 1980 is summed up in his *Rapporto sulla pianificazione e gestione urbanistica in Piemonte*. He has taught urban planning at the University of Venice since 1949.

His writings underline the necessity of updating the legal structures as they relate to urban planning. Between 1952 and 1975, he was editor of the journal *Urbanistica*.

ATTILIO PETRUCCIOLI

WORKS

1951, Falchera, Residential Quarter, Turin, Italy. 1957, Assisi Master Plan, Italy. 1959, Chiesaquart Master Plan, Italy. 1960, Gubbio Master Plan, Italy. 1963, Genoa Master Plan (revision), Italy. 1964–1966, Assisi Master Plan (revision), Italy. 1966, Bergamo Master Plan (revision), Italy.

BIBLIOGRAPHY

ZEVI, BRUNO 1961 *Storia dell'Architettura moderna*. Turin, Italy: Einaudi.

ᵓATA ALLAH

ᵓAta Allah, called Rushdi (?–1665?), was the eldest son of the great seventeenth-century Mogul architect USTAD AHMAD, the builder of the Taj Mahal and the Red Fort at Delhi. Along with his two brothers, Lutf Allah, called Muhandis ("the engineer"), and Nur Allah, ᵓAta Allah followed in his illustrious father's footsteps and became an architect and scholar of mathematics and geometry. Numerous manuscripts of his treatises on arithmetic and algebra survive, including one translated from Sanskrit in 1634–1635 and dedicated to Emperor Shah Jahan.

ᵓAta Allah must have collaborated with his father on numerous projects, and only one major monument can be ascribed to him alone. This is the Bibi-ka-Maqbara at Aurangabad, or tomb of Rabi'a Daurani, the wife of Emperor Aurangzeb, who died in 1657. According to its gateway inscription, the tomb was completed in 1660–1661, about four years after the queen's death. The inscription identifies ᵓAta Allah as the architect, Haspat Rai as engineer, and Aqa Abuᵓl-Qasim Beg as official superintendent of construction.

Though frequently criticized as an inferior, mannered imitation of the Taj Mahal, the Bibi-ka-Maqbara is in many respects a highly original and innovative building. If ᵓAta Allah's design seems cramped and idiosyncratic beside the work of his father, his unusual handling of spatial tension and florid surface ornament nonetheless exerted a strong influence on the development of Mogul architecture in the eighteenth century.

W. E. BEGLEY

WORK

1657–1661, Bibi-ka-Maqbara (tomb of Rabi'a Daurani), Aurangabad, India.

BIBLIOGRAPHY

AHMAD, NAZIR 1956–1957 "Imam-ud-Din Husain Riadi, the Grandson of Nadir-ul°Asr Ustad Ahmad, the Architect of the Taj Mahal, and his *Tadhkira-i-Baghistan.*" *Islamic Culture* 30:330–350; 31:60–87.
CHAGHTAI, M. ABDULLAH 1937 "A Family of Great Mughal Architects." *Islamic Culture* 11:200–209.
IDRISULLAH, M. 1951–1952 "Two Persian Inscriptions Carved on the Gate of Bibi ka Maqbara, Aurangabad." *Epigraphia Indica—Arabic and Persian Supplement* 1951–1952:34–35.

?Ata Allah.
Bibi-ka-Maqbara (Tomb of Rabi'a Daurani).
Aurangabad, India.
1657–1661

ATKINSON, GEORGE

Born in Suffolk, England, George Atkinson (1915–) studied architecture and town planning at the Bartlett School, University College, London. During World War II, he became involved in civil engineering and the Cement and Concrete Association. In 1947, he joined the Building Research Station in Watford, and in 1948 he became the first head of the then Colonial Liaison Section (later Overseas Division). He became head of the Architects' Division of the Building Research Station in 1961. Still actively involved in architectural affairs, Atkinson is also a member of the CIB Working Commission on Information and technical correspondent on research and development to *Building* magazine. He is the author of numerous articles in international publications on the subject of building design in the tropics.

DENNIS SHARP

ATKINSON, THOMAS

Thomas Witlam Atkinson (1799–1861) began his career as a bricklayer and quarryman in a Yorkshire village. A self-taught sculptor and draftsman, Atkinson studied and copied Gothic sculpture and architectural ornament in Lincolnshire, England, resulting in a set of lithographs published in 1829. Working in London and Manchester, Atkinson designed in the Gothic style, executing commissions for banks and churches. He later abandoned architecture and became an explorer and topographic artist, publishing records of his travels to Siberia, India, and China.

BRIAN LUKACHER

WORKS

1831, Hyde Church, Cheshire, England. 1834, Manchester and Liverpool District Bank; 1836–1839, Saint Luke's Church; Manchester, England.

ATKINSON, WILLIAM

William Atkinson (c.1773–1839) was a prolific designer of picturesque country houses and villas in early nineteenth-century England. Trained in the Royal Academy School, he studied with JAMES WYATT. Atkinson's trademark was profuse Gothic detail applied to irregularly planned houses with little regard for archeological accuracy. He published numerous pattern books and had an active interest in geology and botany. With this background, Atkinson's aesthetic epitomized the picturesque fascination with creating the natural artifice.

BRIAN LUKACHER

WORKS

1807–1815, Rossie Priory, Perthshire, Scotland. 1816–1823, Abbotsford, Roxburghshire, Scotland. 1818, Grove End; 1824, Dudley House; London. 1830, Silvermore, Cobham, England.

ATTERBURY, GROSVENOR

Although he had a long and successful career as a designer of conservative, large-scale residential architecture for the rich, Grosvenor Atterbury (1869–1956), a New York-based, Beaux-Arts trained contemporary of FRANK LLOYD WRIGHT, is of especial note as the architect of Forest Hills Gardens (begun 1909), Queens, New York, the archetypal American middle-class community of the early twentieth century, and as the designer of America's first practical prefabricated concrete houses. Both achievements are the direct result of philanthropic ideals concerning the amelioration of the working man's environment held by influential friends of Atterbury's family such as Henry Phipps and Robert W. de Forest. De Forest, as president of the Russell Sage Foundation, was responsible for the Forest Hills Gardens commission. Frederick Law Olmsted, Jr., developed the flowing street plan and the lavish plantings, while Atterbury was in charge of all architecture, establishing a picturesque unity of solidly built, beautifully textured Germano-Tudor structures. He designed the major buildings around Station Square and many of the row, grouped, and single houses. It was here, also, that Atterbury had the backing to try, on a fairly large scale both in 1913 and 1918, his system for the building of houses from a very few precast concrete sections. He had been working on the scheme since 1904 as a way of simultaneously lowering housing costs and upgrading the structure. Two earlier demonstrations, in 1907 and 1910, were inconclusive. At Forest Hills, Atterbury was able to erect an entire precasting plant and work out the problems in minute detail. Unfortunately, the system never proved to be economically feasible, and when the Russell Sage Foundation withdrew its support in 1922, Atterbury was forced to continue his experiments at his own expense, which he did until his death. In effect, his designs for rich men's houses paid for poor men's construction.

DONALD HARRIS DWYER

WORKS

1897, Houses for H. O. Havemeyer, Islip, N.Y. 1898, Robert W. de Forest House, Cold Springs Harbor, N.Y. 1907, First Phipps Model Tenement, New York. Begun 1909, Forest Hills Gardens, Queens, N.Y. 1915, Russell Sage Foundation Building, New York. 1915–1916, Indian Hill Community, Worcester, Mass. 1916, Community at Erwin, Tenn. 1921–1923, Aldus C. Higgins House, Worcester, Mass. 1922–1924, American Wing, Metropolitan Museum of Art, New York. 1936, Florence L. Pond House, Tucson, Ariz.

BIBLIOGRAPHY

ATTERBURY, GROSVENOR 1930 *The Economic Production of Workingmen's Homes.* n.p.: Privately printed.
ATTERBURY, GROSVENOR 1936 "Bricks Without Brains: A Challenge to Science and the Factory-made House." *Architecture* 73, no. 4:193–196.
BURCHARD, JOHN ELY, and BUSH-BROWN, ALBERT 1966 *The Architecture of America: A Social and Cultural History.* Boston: Little, Brown.
DWYER, DONALD 1980 "Grosvenor Atterbury." Supplement 6, pages 25–27 of *Dictionary of American Biography.* New York: Scribner.
SQUIRES, FREDERICK 1915 "Houses at Forest Hills Gardens." *Concrete-Cement Age* 6, Jan.:3–8, 53–54.

ATWOOD, CHARLES B.

Although Charles Bowler Atwood (1849–1895) obtained and executed few commissions in his own right during his brief career, he is acknowledged as designer of one of the most famous of early skyscrapers, the Reliance Building in Chicago. Atwood was one of a class of architects created by the growth of large architectural offices in late nineteenth-century America: brilliant designers but erratic individuals who achieved success and stability only in working for other men. Like HARVEY ELLIS, another such shadow designer, Atwood was attractive but unstable; whereas Ellis was an alcoholic, Atwood turned to drugs when personal tragedy and professional failure entered his life. But as a designer, he won the admiration of giants like DANIEL H. BURNHAM and Charles McKim (see McKIM, MEAD, AND WHITE), and he left his mark on the style of Burnham's architecture long after his brief tenure in the office.

Atwood was born in Charlestown, Massachusetts. In 1865, he joined the office of Elbridge Boyden in Worcester as a draftsman, working on Boyden's project for the New York State Capitol competition. The next year, he joined the Boston firm of WARE AND VAN BRUNT, staying for three years before going to Lawrence Scientific School for formal architectural study. He then returned to Ware and Van Brunt before setting up independently in 1872. In that year, he designed a small commercial building in Worcester on his own. In 1872, he was also an invited competitor for the commission to design the Connecticut State Capitol at Hartford. Though neither of the two projects he submitted won, he was able to adapt one of them, a High Victorian Gothic scheme, to win the competition for the Holyoke, Massachusetts, City Hall in 1874. Dismissed from that commission when the building was nearly complete, Atwood moved to New York, where he worked for Herter Brothers, a firm of decorators. He was their architect (with J. B. SNOOK) for the W. H. Vanderbilt Houses in New York (1879–1881), among the most admired houses of the period, and in 1884 he received independent commissions from Mrs. Vanderbilt to design houses for two of her daughters and their husbands. That same year, Atwood won first prize in the abortive competition for the Boston Public Library with a design that looked forward two decades to the Edwardian baroque. In 1886, he moved to Great Barrington, Massachusetts, where he worked for two years on the completion of Mrs. Mark Hopkins's House. In 1888, he won a competition for an addition to New York City Hall, but his hastily prepared drawings were disqualified on a technicality.

Frustrated by being denied commissions that he had won in competition and apparently nearly crazed with grief over the death of his five-year-old son, Atwood was ready for a radical change in his life by 1891. In the spring of that year, on the recommendation of Ware, Daniel Burnham of Chicago hired Atwood to replace his design partner, JOHN WELLBORN ROOT, who had just died. Atwood was almost immediately made chief architect of the World's Columbian Exposition of 1893 in Chicago, designing approximately sixty structures for the complex in Jackson Park. The most celebrated, the Fine Arts Building, brought Atwood wide praise in the architectural press but was also criticized for drawing directly on Emile Bernard's 1866 Grand Prix design from the Ecole des Beaux-Arts. Whatever its source, Atwood's Greco-Roman design epitomized the classicizing goals of the "White City" planners and was the only building retained from the Fair, to be reincarnated in 1929–1940 as the Museum of Science and Industry.

On completing his exposition duties, Atwood became chief designer and a partner in D. H. Burnham and Company. In that capacity he was architect of the Reliance Building (1894–1895; erected on a first story designed by John Root in 1890), a remarkably light and open fifteen-story structure of steel clad in glazed white terra cotta and large areas of glass. Rejecting the Romanesque bulk and darkness of the firm's work under Root, Atwood turned toward a clean, sparkling, and almost delicate image of the tall building which coincided with the urban ideals expressed in the Columbian Exposition. He followed the Reliance with the Gothic Fisher Building (1895), clad in highly decorated salmon-colored terra cotta and designed with an even purer vertical emphasis than its predecessor. At the same time, Atwood helped establish the robust, plastic, Renaissance classicism which characterized D. H. Burnham and Company's work well into the 1910s with his Marshall Field Annex in Chicago (1892–1893) and Ellicott Square Building in Buffalo, New York (1894–1895). He also helped Burnham design a new lakefront development for Chicago which was the forerunner of the celebrated Chicago Plan of 1909. But despite his genius for giving form to Burnham's monumental urban visions, Atwood began to lose his grip on day-to-day existence in 1895,

Atwood.
Fine Arts Building (now
*   the Museum of Sciences*
*   and Industry).*
Chicago.
1893 (rebuilt 1929–1940).

missing sixty days at the office in the last seven months of that year and often staying for only an hour or two when he did come in. On December 10, his resignation was requested. Nine days later, he was dead at the age of forty-six.

ANN LORENZ VAN ZANTEN

WORKS

1872, State Mutual Assurance Company Building, Worcester, Mass. 1874, City Hall, Holyoke, Mass. *1879–1881, W. H. Vanderbilt Houses (with Herter Brothers and John B. Snook); *1884, W. Seward Webb and H. McK. Twombly Houses; New York. 1886–1888, Mrs. Mark Hopkins House (completion), Great Barrington, Mass. 1892–1893, Marshall Field Retail Store Annex; 1893, Fine Arts Building (rebuilt in 1929–1940 as the Museum of Science and Industry), *Terminal, *Peristyle, etc., World's Columbian Exposition; Chicago. 1894–1895, Ellicott Square Building, Buffalo, N.Y. 1894–1895, Reliance Building (later altered); 1895, Fisher Building (not completed until 1896; later altered); Chicago.

BIBLIOGRAPHY

BURNHAM, DANIEL H.   1896   "Charles Bowler Atwood." *Inland Architect and News Record* 26, no.6:56–57.
JENKINS, CHARLES E.   1895   "A White Enameled Building." *Architectural Record* 4:299–306.
WOLTERSDORF, ARTHUR   1924   "A Portrait Gallery of Chicago Architects: III. Charles B. Atwood." *Western Architect* 33, no.8:89–94.

AUBERT, JEAN

Jean Aubert (?–1741), member of a Parisian family of architects, was a draftsman under JULES HARDOUIN MANSART in the Service des Bâtiments du Roi from 1702 to 1708. Although he left Mansart's employ to become the architect of the Bourbon-Condé, his work represents a development of Mansart's style. For Louis-Henri, duc de Bourbon, Aubert supervised the remodeling of the Château de Chantilly in the Île-de-France. The stables (1721–1735) constitute the most impressive element in the scheme. Their huge size and the organization down a single axis linked with the château imply a deliberate reference to Mansart's stables of the Palace of Versailles (1679–1686), whereas the delicately layered wall surface, with its channeled rustication, is closer to the contemporary work of PIERRE LASSURANCE and ROBERT DE COTTE. In his redecoration of the apartments of the Petit Château (1718–1733), Aubert emerged as one of the leading designers of the rococo interior. His designs are distinguished by the dissolving of tectonic boundaries through the intrusion of curvilinear and asymmetrical motifs and by the application of an unprecedented profusion of decorative elements in relief, such as medallions, tendrils, and ribbons.

In 1724, Aubert took over the commission for the Hôtel de Lassay, Paris, and the project for the Palais Bourbon, Paris, from the recently deceased Lassurance. Aubert made major contributions to both, although the precise extent is unknown. In collaboration with JACQUES V. GABRIEL, Aubert built the Hôtel Peyrenc de Moras (1727–1730), Paris. Its free-standing block of simple proportions and restrained decoration is a highpoint in the history of the *hôtel* (urban mansion).

ROBERT NEUMAN

WORKS

*1709–1710, Château de Saint-Maur (remodeling), France. 1718–1733, Petit Château de Chantilly (decoration); 1721–1735, Stables; Chantilly, France. 1724–1726, Hôtel de Lassay; *1724–1729, Palais Bourbon; 1727–1730, Hôtel de Peyrenc de Moras (now Rodin Museum); Paris. 1736–1741, Château abbatial de Châalis (not completed until 1741); France.

BIBLIOGRAPHY

HAUTECOEUR, LOUIS 1950 *Première moitié du XVIIIᵉ siècle: Le style Louis XV.* Volume 3 in *Histoire de l'architecture classique en France.* Paris: Picard.
KALNEIN, WEND GRAF, and LEVEY, MICHAEL 1972 *Art and Architecture of the Eighteenth Century in France.* Baltimore: Penguin.
MACON, GUSTAV 1903 *Les Arts dans la maison de Condé.* Paris: Librairie de l'Art ancien et moderne.
SOUCHAL, FRANÇOIS 1969 "Jean Aubert, architecte des Bourbon-Condé." *Revue de l'Art* 6:29–38.

AUBERTIN, JACQUES MARCEL

Son of Paris city architect Alexandre Emile Aubertin, Jacques Marcel Aubertin (1872–1926) began his career as a model Beaux-Arts architect of the *belle époque*. He broadened his interests by founding the Société Française des Urbanistes in 1910 and publishing two of the guidelines for reconstructing French cities following World War I.

ELIZABETH MCLANE

WORKS

*1900, Palace of Land and Sea Armies (with Gustav Umbdenstock), Exposition Universelle; n.d., Ecole Alsacienne; n.d., Restaurant Bal Tabarin; Paris.

BIBLIOGRAPHY

AUBERTIN, JACQUES MARCEL; AGATHE, M.; and REDOUT, M. 1915 *Comment Reconstruire Nos Cités Détruites: Notions d'Urbanisme s'appliquant aux Villes, Bourgs et Villages.* Paris: Colin.
AUBERTIN, JACQUES MARCEL, and BLANCHARD, HENRI 1917 *La Cité de demain dans les régions dévastés.* Paris.
DELAIRE, EDMOND A. 1907 *Les Architectes-Elèves de l'Ecole des Beaux-Arts.* Paris: Librairie de la construction moderne.

AUDSLEY, G. A.

The reputation of George Ashdown Audsley (1838–1925) rests chiefly on his twenty-five books, dealing mainly with popular aspects of craftsmanship and decorative art. In his later years he achieved some fame as a designer of organs. Born in Scotland, he practiced as an architect in Liverpool where, with his younger brother, William, he built three churches and a synagogue between 1865 and 1875 in a polychromatic style, influenced by JOHN RUSKIN. He moved to London and in 1892 left England for New York, where he spent the rest of his life. His most important work in the United States was the Milwaukee Art Gallery (1888). His books include *Guide to the Art of Illuminating* (1861); *Handbook of Christian Symbolism* (1865); *Outlines of Ornament in the Leading Styles* (1881); *The Ornamental Arts of Japan* (1882–1885), his most substantial work; and *The Organ of the 20th Century* (1919). The organ in the Festival Hall at the Saint Louis Exposition (1904) was built to his specification.

JOHN SUMMERSON

BIBLIOGRAPHY

AUDSLEY, G. A. (1861)1864 *Guide to the Art of Illuminating.* 6th ed. London: Rowney.
AUDSLEY, G. A. 1865 *Handbook of Christian Symbolism.* London: Day.
AUDSLEY, G. A. (1881)1968 *Designs and Patterns from Historic Ornament.* Reprint. New York: Dover. Originally published as *Outlines of Ornament in the Leading Styles.*

AUDSLEY, G. A. 1882–1885 *The Ornamental Arts of Japan.* 2 vols. London: Sampson.

AUDSLEY, G. A. (1919)1970 *The Organ of the 20th Century.* Reprint. New York: Dover.

HAMLIN, T. F. (1928)1943 "George Ashdown Audsley." Volume 1, pages 422–423 in *Dictionary of American Biography.* New York: Scribner.

PEVSNER, NIKOLAUS 1969 *Lancashire.* 2 vols. Harmondsworth, England: Penguin.

AUSTIN, HENRY

Henry Austin's (1804–1891) architectural practice spanned fifty-four years, during which he produced a large volume of work in varied popular styles in Connecticut and beyond.

Austin was born in Hamden, Connecticut just north of New Haven, and was apprenticed to a carpenter at a young age. In the 1820s, he worked for architect ITHIEL TOWN. In the early 1830s, Austin started his own building business but soon went bankrupt. He opened an architectural office in New Haven on January 7, 1837, and in 1840, Austin opened a temporary office in Hartford, Connecticut, where he was probably handling projects for Town. He returned to New Haven in 1841 and maintained an office there for the rest of his life.

Austin's earliest designs were small Greek Revival homes with a two storied central section with portico flanked by one story wings, but his first building to win acclaim was the Yale College Library (1842–1845). This stone Gothic structure is related in design to King's College Chapel, Cambridge, and was similar to Gore Hall, the Harvard College Library of 1838–1841 by Richard Bond. Austin was probably aided in this project by the English draftsman Henry Flockton, who was in New Haven during the 1840s. Austin's library was remodeled in 1931 and is now Dwight Memorial Chapel.

Austin's most enduring work is the Egyptian Revival sandstone gate at the entrance to New Haven's Grove Street Cemetery. The design for the pylon gate with its two bundled papyrus columns, torus moldings, and cavetto cornice was created as early as 1839, but it was not constructed until 1845–1848.

In 1848, Austin won the commission for the first New Haven Railroad Station; it ranks among the most incredibly fanciful buildings ever erected in New England. The three-hundred-foot long building had arcaded windows and was called Italianate, but its central section was topped by a Chinese style tower resembling a pagoda. At each end were imposing towers: one of these towers resembled an Indian stupa; the other had elements of the Indian chaitya hall. Most of this fantastic structure was destroyed by fire on the Fourth of July 1894.

Austin's interest in Asian architectural forms continued into the late 1840s. The James Dwight Dana House (1848–1849) in New Haven was then called an oriental villa. It was originally cubical in shape with flaring eaves and a central cupola. The four columns of the porch were derived from the Buddhist and Hindu rock-cut caves of India.

Austin's most distinguished use of oriental elements was in the house built for New York *Sun* publisher Moses Yale Beach in Wallingford, Connecticut (1850). Thirty-seven Indian columns lined the porch, and wide flaring eaves provided a series of exciting planes topped by a soaring cupola. The house was demolished in 1960, but some of the columns were incorporated in the bank that replaced it.

Austin is recognized primarily for his mastery of the Italian Villa style. Of the few examples that survive, the Morse-Libby House (1859–1863) in Portland, Maine, is the most important. Its lavishly decorated interior, which remains intact with much of the original furnishings, is one of the finest examples of nineteenth-century eclecticism to survive in the United States. Now called the Victoria Mansion, it is operated as a summer museum by the Victoria Society of Maine Women.

In 1861, Austin designed the New Haven City Hall. It was one of the first High Victorian Gothic buildings in the country and was considered spectacular when it opened in 1862. The design was derived from a drawing for a hotel by Ernest George (see Ernest GEORGE AND Harold A. PETO) which was exhibited at London's Royal Academy. The clock tower has been reconstructed, and the main body of the building has been razed, but the stone façade stands proudly overlooking the New Haven Green. A noted feature of the building was a large staircase hall with a central cast iron stairs leading up to the second floor; a large skylight illuminated the frescoed hall.

Austin's practice peaked in the 1850s. His works were not limited to residences, and he designed banks, public halls, hotels, and commercial structures throughout the state. He also designed and renovated many churches. DAVID R. BROWN, Austin's chief draftsman, became his partner for a few months during the winter of 1855–1856, but there were conflicts, and Brown departed only to return to work for Austin a few years later

In addition to David R. Brown, RUFUS G. RUSSELL, and Leoni Robinson, who had also worked for Austin in the 1850s and early 1860s, opened their own offices after the Civil War. This competition from former associates led to a marked decline in Austin's commissions.

His last creative buildings were towered wooden structures along the Connecticut shore. The W. J. Clark House (1879–1880) in the Stony Creek section of Branford, Connecticut, is a superb example of the stick style. On a hill overlooking the sea, the front is surrounded on three sides by a porch which is decorated by numerous turned and patterned wooden elements. To the rear of the house is a great steeply pitched tower which can be seen for miles around.

By 1880, Henry Austin's finances were failing, and his popularity was declining. He died on December 4, 1891; his exceptionally creative works over a long span of time have given him the reputation of being the most outstanding of New Haven's notable architects.

JOHN B. KIRBY, JR.

WORKS

1842–1845, Yale College Library; 1845–1848, Grove Street Cemetery Gate; 1848–1849, James Dwight Dana House; New Haven. *1848–1849, New Haven Railroad Station. *1850, Moses Yale Beach House, Wallingford, Conn. 1859–1863, Morse-Libby House (now the Victoria Mansion), Portland, Maine. 1861–1862, New Haven City Hall. 1879–1880, W. J. Clark House, Branford, Conn.

BIBLIOGRAPHY

The papers of Henry Austin are in the Manuscript and Archives Department at Yale University Library, New Haven.

BROWN, ELIZABETH MILLS 1976 *New Haven: A Guide to Architecture and Urban Design.* New Haven and London: Yale University Press.
DANA, ARNOLD G. (editor) n.d. "New Haven, Old and New, 1641–1974." 152 vols. New Haven Colony Historical Society. Collection of scrapbooks.
KELLEY, BROOKS MATHER 1974 *New Haven Heritage: An Area of Historic Houses on Hillhouse Avenue and Trumbull Street.* The New Haven Preservation Trust.
New Haven Architecture. 1970 Washington: Historic American Buildings Survey.
SEYMOUR, GEORGE DUDLEY 1942 *New Haven.* New Haven: Tuttle.

Austin.
Moses Yale Beach House.
Wallingford, Connecticut.
1850

AUSTRAL

In 1939, a group of young Buenos Aires architects founded the *Grupo Austral* to rescue modern architecture, which, they said, had lost the spirit of its founders. The promoters were ANTONIO BONET, JORGE FERRARI HARDOY, and Juan Kurchan. Austral's first public document appeared as a manifesto in the June 1939 issue of *Nuestra Arquitectura.*

Ideological differences within the group, which also included other architects, were evident from the beginning. Some adhered strictly to the ideals of functionalism, while others believed that it was this attitude that had stifled creativity.

FEDERICO F. ORTIZ

WORKS

1939, Apartment Building with ground floor shops; 1941–1942, Apartment Building; 1942, Apartment Building; Buenos Aires. 1942–1944, Four Houses, Martínez, Greater Buenos Aires. 1944, House, Chapadmalal, Province of Buenos Aires. 1945–1947, Five Houses, one Hotel, and one Restaurant, Portezuelo and Punta Ballena, Uruguay. 1945–1947, Portezuelo, Punta Ballena, and Laguna de Sauce (urban planning; only the first phase was completed), Uruguay.

BIBLIOGRAPHY

BALDELLOU, MIGUEL ANGEL, and ORTIZ, FEDERICO 1978 *La Obra de Antonio Bonet.* Buenos Aires: Summa.
Bauen und Wohnen 1953 no. 8:12–14. Includes an apartment building by Ferrari Hardoy and Kurchan, 2446 calle Virrey del Pino, Buenos Aires.
BULLRICH, FRANCISCO 1963 *Arquitectura Argentina Contemporánea.* Buenos Aires: Nueva Visión.
GUTÍERREZ, RAMON, and ORTIZ, FEDERICO 1972 *La Arquitectura Argentina: 1930–1970.* Madrid: Editorial Obra Sindical del Hogar.
Neustra Arquitectura 1939, 1944, 1946, 1953 Includes documents and designs by Austral group.
Tecne 1942 Includes apartments by Ferrari Hardoy and Kurchan in Buenos Aires.

AVANCINI, BARTOLOMEO

Bartolomeo Avancini (1600?–1658) began his career in Rome, city of his birth, where he fell under the influence of GIOVANNI LORENZO BERNINI. In 1634, Duke Francesco I called Avancini to Modena, where Avancini took charge of the reconstruction of the Palazzo Ducale. He completed only the façade of the palace; the actual execution was entrusted to Avancini's student, Antonio Luraghi. From around 1634, Avancini continued to be employed in Modena by the Este family, among others. At this time, he was also involved in Modena as official architect and assistant to the ducal secretary. He died there, leaving his workshop to Antonio Luraghi.

SARA LEHRMAN

WORKS

1634, Sanctuary of Madonna di Fiorra; 1634, San Vicenzo; 1634–1688, Palazzo Ducale; 1645, Rocca di Sassuolo, Modena, Italy.

BIBLIOGRAPHY

CAMPORI, G. 1855 *Gli artisti italiani e stranieri negli stati Estensi.* Modena, Italy.
GHIDIGLIA QUINTAVALLA, A. 1962 "Avanzini, Bartolomeo Luigi." *Dizionario Biografico degli Italiani.* Rome: Treccami.
MESSORI RONCAGLIA, G. 1878 *Il Santuario de Fiorano ed il suo architetto Bartolomeo Avanzini.* Modena, Italy.
ZANUGG, L. 1942 "Il palazzo ducale di Modena e il problema della sua costruzione." *Rivista del Istoria di Archeologia e Storia dell'Arte* 9:212–252.

AVERLINO, ANTONIO

See IL FILARETE.

AVERY, HENRY O.

Henry Ogden Avery (1852–1890) is best remembered as the young architect in whose memory the Avery Architectural Library at Columbia University was founded. Samuel P. Avery, a New York art dealer, apprenticed his son in 1871 to RUSSELL STURGIS, a family friend. At Sturgis's suggestion, Avery went to the Ecole des Beaux-Arts in Paris in 1872 and enrolled in Jules André's atelier. Returning to New York in 1879, he worked as a draftsman for RICHARD MORRIS HUNT. Avery established his own practice in 1883. He was one of the founders of the Architectural League.

MARY N. WOODS

WORKS

1883, Monument to Victims of the Newhall House Fire, Milwaukee, Wis. 1885, Monument to Confederate War Dead, Nashville, Tenn. 1885, Stewart L. Woodford House, Brooklyn, N.Y. 1886–1887, Ambrose Burnside Monument, Providence, R.I. 1887, Ortigies Galleries and Samuel P. Avery Galleries, New York. 1888, J. W. Ellswort House (picture gallery), Chicago. 1889, C. C. Buel House, New Rochelle, N.Y. 1889, Chicago Art Institute (five galleries).

BIBLIOGRAPHY

The drawings, sketchbooks, and scrapbooks of Henry O. Avery are among the Henry O. Avery Papers, in the Avery Architectural Library, Columbia University, New York.

"Avery Architectural Library." 1890 *Architecture and Building* 13, 26 July:46.
BAKER, GEORGE H. 1894 "Special Collections in Columbia College Library, II: The Avery Memorial Library." *Columbia Literary Monthly* 2:158–170.
DELAIRE, E. 1907 Page 165 in *Les Architectes élèves de l'Ecole des Beaux-Arts.* 2d ed. Paris: Librairie de la Construction Moderne.
"Henry O. Avery." (1898)1967 *National Cyclopedia of American Biography.* Reprint. Ann Arbor: University of Michigan Microfilms.
"Henry O. Avery." 1890 *American Architect and Building News* 28:77, 91. *In Memoriam Henry Ogden Avery.* 1890 New York.
"Nécrologie." 1890 *La Construction Moderne* 5:479.
STURGIS, RUSSELL; DE PEYSTER, FREDERIC J.; and ANDREWS, WILLIAM L. 1890 "In Memoriam—Henry Ogden Avery." *Architecture and Building* 12, June 7: 274–275.

AVOSTALIS DE SOLA, ULRICO

Born in Savosa, near Lugano, Switzerland, Ulrico Avostalis de Sola (?–1597) worked in Bohemia during the late Renaissance. After apprenticeship under Bonifaz Wohlmut and Gian Battista Avostalis, Ulrico became imperial architect in 1575, serving Maximilian II and Rudolf II. His best known work is the Castle at Litomyšl (1568–1575) where fortification walls enclose a palace with an arcaded courtyard designed after Genoese models as was then fashionable in central Europe. Innovations in the courtyard include the application of rusticated, Doric, and Ionic orders to the three stories and the open arcading of the uppermost loggia, creating an interplay between interior and exterior space.

Avostalis was also important in the development of the ornate gable in Bohemia. Voluted gables of his invention are found, together with elegant sgraffito decoration, at Litomyšl, and gables were built after his designs at Lysá nad Labem and Karlštejn Castle.

DOROTHY LIMOUZE

WORKS

1557–1563, Belvedere Palace (mason on upper story); 1562–1564, Archepiscopal Palace (after plans by Bonifaz Wohlmut); Prague. 1568–1575, Litomyšl Castle; 1571–1573, Pardubice Castle; Bohemia, 1573–1574, Rožmberk Palace (garden); 1575–1576, Chapel of Saint Adalbert on the Hradschin (possibly after plans by Wohlmut); Prague. 1578–1579, Bubeneč (rebuilding of pleasure palace), near Prague. 1583–1584, Prague Imperial Garden (lion house); 1588, Italian Chapel on the Hradschin; Prague. 1589–1590, Bubeneč (garden building and water basin; with Giovanni Antonio de Pambio), near Prague. 1595–1597, Jindřichův Hradec (supervision of construction), Bohemia.

BIBLIOGRAPHY

BIAŁOSTOCKI, JAN 1976 *The Art of the Renaissance in*

Eastern Europe. Ithaca, N.Y.: Cornell University Press.

FREJKOVÁ, OLGA 1941 *Palladianismus v české renensanci.* Prague: České Akademie věd a Umění.

KRČÁLOVÁ, JARMILA 1964 "Il palladianesimo in Cecoslovacchia e l'influenza del Veneto sull'Architettura Ceca." *Bolletino del Centro Internationale di Studi sull architetto Andrea Palladio* 6:89–110.

KRČÁLOVÁ, JARMILA 1970 "Palác Pánů z Rožmberka." *Umění* 18:469–485.

KRČÁLOVÁ, JARMILA (1974)1976 *Centrální stavby české renesance.* 2d ed. Prague: Academia.

KRČÁLOVÁ, JARMILA et al. 1979 *Die Kunst der Renaissance und des Manierismus in Böhmen.* Hanau, Germany: Dausien.

NEUMANN, JAROMÍR 1970 *Das böhmische Barock.* Vienna: Forum.

ŠAMÁNKOVÁ, EVA 1961 *Architektura české renesance.* Prague: Státní Nakladatelstvi Krásné Literatury a Umění.

AYRES, LOUIS

Born in Bergen Point, New Jersey, Louis Ayres (1874–1947) entered Rutgers College in 1891. In 1896, he received a B.S. degree in electrical engineering. Deciding to pursue a career in architecture, he joined the firm of McKim, Mead, and White in 1897. Following three years of study there, Ayres joined the office of York and Sawyer, becoming a partner in 1910, and remaining there until his death.

Ayres became prominent in New York professional circles as a designer of monumental commercial buildings in a variety of historical styles. He collaborated on many important buildings in New York, including the neoclassical Guaranty Trust Building (1911), for which the firm received the 1915 Architectural League Gold Medal, the neo-Renaissance Federal Reserve Bank (1920–1924), and the Byzantine/Lombardian New York Academy of Medicine (1926). Outside of New York he assisted in the design of the Department of Commerce Building (1912–1932) in Washington and buildings at Rutgers College (1908–1932) in New Brunswick, New Jersey.

In recognition of his contributions to his profession, Ayres received an L.H.D. from Rutgers in 1926 and the Medal of Honor from the New York Chapter of the American Institute of Architects in 1932. He was appointed a member of the U.S. Fine Arts Commission under President Wilson and served on the Smithsonian Fine Arts Commission from 1939 to 1947.

STEVEN MCLEOD BEDFORD

WORKS

1903, Riggs National Bank, Washington. 1906, Broadway Savings Bank, New York. 1908, Rutgers College Chemical Laboratory, New Brunswick, N.J. 1911, Guaranty Trust Building, New York. 1912–1932, Department of Commerce Building, Washington. 1920, Federal Building, Honolulu, Hawaii. 1920–1924, Federal Reserve Bank, New York. 1921, First National Bank of Boston. 1923, Bowery Savings Bank, New York. 1924–1932, Rutgers College Gymnasium and Dormitories, New Brunswick, N.J. 1926, New York Academy of Medicine. 1928, Royal Bank of Canada, Montreal. 1931, Guggenheim Dental Clinic, New York. 1932, World War I Memorial Chapel, Meuse Argonne, France. 1944, Brick Presbyterian Church, New York.

BIBLIOGRAPHY

MOORE, CHARLES (1929)1969 *The Life and Times of Charles Follen McKim.* Reprint. New York: Da Capo.

SAWYER, PHILLIP 1951 *Edward Palmer York.* Stonington, Conn.: Privately printed.

YORK AND SAWYER, NEW YORK 1948 *York & Sawyer: A Brief History.* New York: Privately printed.

AZEMA, LEON

Born in France, Léon Azéma (1898–) began to design in Paris in the 1920s. His principal works were completed in the 1930s and include the Palais de Chaillot in Paris (1937), designed with Louis Hyppolite Boileau and Jacques Carlu, and the Church of Saint-Antoine de Padoue, also in Paris (1936). Built of plain brick material, the church conveys an earthiness and simplicity of form resembling vernacular architecture, but it is also derived from earlier expressionistic design.

PETER L. DONHAUSER

WORKS

1933, Post Office, Paris. 1935, Post Office, Vichy, France. 1936, Church of Saint-Antoine de Padoue, Paris. 1936, Hospital, Bobigny, France. 1936, Terrains de Sport de l'A.S.P.S.; 1937, Palais de Chaillot (with Jacques Carlu and Louis H. Boileau); Paris.

BIBLIOGRAPHY

AZÉMA, LÉON 1927 *Documents d'architecture contemporaine.* Paris: Vincent.

AZÉMA, LÉON 1936a "Hôtel des Postes de Vichy." *L'Architecture d'Aujourd'hui* 7:20, 27.

AZÉMA, LÉON 1936b "Eglise Saint-Antoine de Padoue." *L'Architecture d'Aujourd'hui* 7:30, 33.

AZÉMA, LÉON, and CARLU, JACQUES 1938 "New State Theater, Paris." *Architect's Journal* 88:370–372.

BOURQUIN, LOUIS 1936 "Eglise Saint-Antoine de Padoue à Paris: Terrains de Sport de l'A.S.P.S." *Construction Moderne* 51:893–902.

FAVIER, JEAN 1936 "L'Hopital Franco-Musulman de Bobigny." *Construction Moderne* 51:502–508.

GOBILLOT, RENÉ 1936 "L'Eglise Saint-Antoine de Padoue." *L'Architecture d'Aujourd'hui* 49:73–80.

BABB, COOK, and WILLARD

George Fletcher Babb (1836–1915), the elder of the three partners of Babb, Cook, and Willard, was born in New York City. Babb's family moved to New Jersey early in his childhood, and Babb designed four houses there in 1858–1859 while working in the New York office of T. R. Jackson. In 1859, Babb joined with Nathaniel G. Foster in a partnership that ran to 1865. By 1868, Babb was a senior draftsman in the office of RUSSELL STURGIS where he met Charles Follen McKim and William Rutherford Mead (see MCKIM, MEAD, AND WHITE).

In 1877, Babb went into partnership with Walter Cook (1846–1916). Cook had graduated from Harvard in 1869, studied in Munich in 1871–1873, and in Paris in the atelier of JOSEPH AUGUSTE EMILE VAUDREMER in 1873–1876. It is difficult to sort out who was the major designer of the firm's greatest building—the De Vinne Press Building of 1885–1886—Babb or Cook, but by the 1890s, Cook was clearly the principal designing partner. In 1884, Daniel W. Willard joined the firm as a partner.

MOSETTE GLASER BRODERICK

WORKS

GEORGE F. BABB

1858–1859, D. C. Otis Villa, Lakewood, N.J. 1858–1859, Swiss Cottages, Orange, N.J. 1870, First Presbyterian Church, Englewood, N.J. 1874–1876, Battell Chapel (interior; exterior by Russell Sturgis), Yale University, New Haven. 1876, Mechanics' National Bank (with Sturgis), Albany, N.Y.

BABB AND COOK

1877–1880, Loft Building, 173–175 Duane Street; 1880, Mrs. F. R. Brown House, 104th Street; *1881, Cast-iron Office Building, 55 Broadway; New York.

BABB, COOK, AND WILLARD

1884, McKim House, 5 Westridge Road, Cooperstown, N.Y. *1884, Teaneck Grange (alteration and enlargement), Englewood, N.J. *1885, Hanan Building, White and Centre Street, New York. *1885, Turner Building, Newburgh, N.Y. 1885–1886, De Vinne Press Building, 393–399 Lafayette Place (now Street); 1886, Rosewell Smith House (alteration and addition; now part of the Villard Houses), 24 East 51st Street; New York. 1887, Lincoln Hall, Berea College, Ky. *1888–1889, Theodore De Vinne House, 76th Street on the southwest corner of West End Avenue, New York. *1888–1889, New York Life Insurance Company, 395 Minnesota Avenue, Saint Paul, Minn. *1888–1890, New York Life Insurance Company, 5th Street and 2nd Avenue South, Minneapolis, Minn. 1890–1891, Atwater House, 321 Whitney Avenue, New Haven. 1890, 47 Montgomery Place, Brooklyn, N.Y. *1895, James

Otis Hoyt House, 310 West 75th Street; *1895, J. D. Smillie Studio, 156 East 36th Street; *1896, Paul Cravath House, 107 East 39th Street; *1896, F. J. Stimson House, 312 West 75th Street; New York. 1897–1898, Frederick B. Pratt House, 229 Clinton Avenue, Brooklyn, N.Y. 1898, Alfred Corning Clark Neighborhood House, Rivington and Cannon Streets; 1899–1901, Andrew Carnegie House (now Cooper Hewitt Museum), 2 East 91st Street; New York. *1903, Winslow Pierce House, Bayville, N.Y. 1903, Augustus Saint Gaudens Studio, Cornish, N.H. *1905 and later, Paul Cravath House, Locust Valley, N.Y. 1905, Mott Haven Branch Library, East 140th Street; 1905, New York Public Library, 328 East 67th Street; New York. *1905–1916. H. I. Pratt House, Muttontown Road, Syosset, N.Y. 1909, Seward Park Branch Library, 192 East Broadway, New York.

BIBLIOGRAPHY

COOK, CLARENCE 1884 "Seed in Stony Places." *Studio* Sept. 13:25–28.

DAVIES, JANE B. 1975 "Llewellyn Park in West Orange, New Jersey." *Antiques* 107, Jan.:142–158.

LANDAU, SARAH B. 1982 "The Tall Office Building Artistically Reconsidered: Arcaded Buildings of the New York School c.1870–90." This article will be included in a *Festschrift* to be published in honor of H. R. Hitchcock in New York by the Architectural History Foundation Press.

The New York Sketch Book of Architecture. 1874 1, Jan.:2, plate III.

SCHULL, DIANTHA DOW 1980 *Landmarks of Otsego County.* N.Y.: Syracuse University Press.

SCULLY, VINCENT, JR., 1971 *The Shingle Style and the Stick Style.* New Haven: Yale University Press.

BABCOCK, CHARLES

Charles Babcock (1829–1913), a founding member of the American Institute of Architects, worked with RICHARD UPJOHN from 1853 to 1858, first as apprentice, then as member of the firm. From 1871 to 1897, he taught at Cornell University's newly established architectural school and designed several buildings for the university, including the president's Gothic villa (1871).

GWEN W. STEEGE

WORKS

c.1858, Chapel of the Holy Innocents, Germantown, N.Y. 1871, Andrew D. White Villa (with George Hathorne and W. H. Miller); 1873–1874, Sage College; 1874, Sage Chapel; 1881, Franklin Hall; Cornell University, Ithaca, N.Y.

BIBLIOGRAPHY

PARSONS, KERMIT C. 1963 "The Quad on the Hill: An Account of the First Buildings at Cornell." *Journal of the Society of Architectural Historians* 22:199–216.

SCHUYLER, MONTGOMERY 1868 "Architecture of American Colleges: Cornell University (1868)." *Architectural Record* 30:565–573.

WODEHOUSE, LAWRENCE 1976 *American Architects from the Civil War to the First World War.* Detroit, Mich.: Gale.

WRITERS' PROGRAM. WORK PROJECTS ADMINISTRATION 1940 *New York: A Guide to the Empire State.* New York: Oxford University Press.

BACHELIER, NICOLAS

Nicolas Bachelier (?–1556) was born in Arras (Picardy), France, but his architectural work was concentrated in Toulouse. A leading practitioner of the Renaissance style, he established himself first as a master mason but is referred to as the directing architect in contracts from 1538 on. He also worked as an engineer on municipal improvement projects and a sculptor for local churches. The lively sculptural treatment of his windows and doors with their herms and classical orders characterizes his work.

HILARY BALLON

WORKS

*1534, Cathedral of Saint-Etienne (altar and retable); 1538–1546, Hôtel de Bagis; Toulouse, France. 1539–1546, Château, Castelnau d'Estrètefons, France. c.1540, Château, Pibrac, France. 1540, 1544–1545, Hôtel Buet; 1542–1543, 1546, Hôtel de Nolet; 1543–1544, Pont Neuf; Toulouse, France. 1545–1547, Château, Saint-Jory, France. 1545–1550, Church, Montgiscard, France. *1553–1555, Cour Présidiale, Toulouse, France. 1555–1556, Château, Lasserre-les-Montastruc, France.

BIBLIOGRAPHY

BLUNT, ANTHONY (1953)1973 *Art and Architecture in France 1500 to 1700.* 2d ed., rev. New York: Penguin.

CORRAZE, RAYMOND 1945 "Les origines de Nicolas Bachelier." *Bulletin monumental* 103:107–111.

DUPRAT, CLEMENCE-PAUL 1954a "Les sources d'inspiration du milieu plastique dans lequel apparait vers 1535 l'art de Nicolas Bachelier." *Mémoires de la Société archéologique du Midi de la France* 12:57–78.

DUPRAT, CLEMENCE-PAUL 1954b "L'influence espagnole sur le décor sculpté des hôtels toulousains de la Renaissance." *Annales du Midi* 66:129–142.

GRAILLOT, HENRI 1914 *Nicolas Bachelier, Imagier et maçon de Toulouse au XVIe siècle.* Toulouse, France: Edouard Privat.

HAUTECOEUR, LOUIS (1943)1963–1965 Volume 1, parts 1 and 2 in *Histoire de l'architecture classique en France.* 2d ed., rev. Paris: Picard.

LAVEDAN, PIERRE 1929 "Anciennes maisons." (Toulouse) *Congrès archéologique de France* 92:134–160.

LOIRETTE, M. G. 1921–1925 "Une oeuvre disparue de Nicolas Bachelier, le rétable du grand autel de la Dalbade." *Bulletin de la Société archéologique du Midi de la France* Series 2 47:400–427.

RACHOU, HENRI 1937 "Musée de Toulouse." *Bulletin des Musées de France* 9:59–62.

REY, RAYMOND 1929 *La Cathédrale de Toulouse.* Paris: Laurens.

SZAPIRO, E. 1963 "Nicolas Bachelier et le château de Castelnau d'Estrètefons." *Annales du Midi* 75:241–282.

VITRY, PAUL 1929 "Le château de Pibrac." *Congrès archéologique de France* 92:161–164.

BACKSTROM, SVEN

Sven Backstrom (1903–) graduated from the Royal Institute of Technology (1929) and studied with LE CORBUSIER (1932–1933); he engaged in further studies abroad in 1935 and 1937. He opened an office in Stockholm in 1936 with Leif Reinius, with whom he almost always collaborates. Known for their commercial architecture and housing schemes, they followed plans developed by the Stockholm City Planning Commission and were responsible for the centers of two planned suburbs: Vällingby (1956–1957) and Farsta (completed 1960).

JUDITH S. HULL

WORKS

1939, Olle Engvist House (with Leif Reinius); 1939–1940, Elfingsgardan Apartments (with Reinius); 1944–1947, Grondal Apartments (with Reinius); Stockholm. 1956–1957, Public Buildings (with Reinius), Vällingby, Sweden. Completed 1960, Public Buildings (with Reinius), Farsta, Sweden.

BACON, EDMUND

As an architect, city planner, and author, Edmund Bacon (1910–) is an important figure in the planning field most noted for his work in Philadelphia. He was educated as an architect at Cornell University and at the Cranbrook Academy, where he studied city planning under ELIEL SAARINEN. Following work in Shanghai, China, and in Michigan, Bacon returned to Philadelphia in 1940 to work for the City Housing Association and later the City Planning Commission, for which he served as executive director from 1949 to 1970. Since then, he has been in private practice as vice president of design for Mondev International, a development company based in Montreal. Bacon has also taught at the University of Pennsylvania since 1950 and has served on numerous professional committees, including the Task Force on the Potomac River Basin, the Citizen's Advisory Committee on Recreation and Natural Beauty, the Urban Transportation Advisory Council, the Franklin Institute Board, and the Urban Design Jury for the 1981 Progressive Architecture Awards.

Bacon's work in Philadelphia, his plans for its future growth, and his extensive writings on planning and urban design issues have made him an outstanding planner of his generation. Under his direction, a series of plans, designed to restructure Philadelphia, renew its historic core, preserve landmarks, and provide housing, neighborhood parks, and transportation systems, were implemented during the 1950s and 1960s. In recognition of his contributions, Bacon has received numerous awards.

JUDITH OBERLANDER

WORKS

1934, Residences (with Henry Killam Murphy), Shanghai, China. 1941, Phillips Residence, Torresdale, Pa.

BIBLIOGRAPHY

BACON, EDMUND 1960 "A Case Study in Urban Design." *Journal of the American Institute of Planners* 26:224–235.

BACON, EDMUND 1961 "Downtown Philadelphia: A Lesson in Design for Urban Growth." *Architectural Record* 129:131–146.

BACON, EDMUND 1963a "Pei in the Sky and Other Aspects of the Philadelphia Story." *Architectural Association Journal* 79:103–112.

BACON, EDMUND 1963b "Urban Design as a Force in Comprehensive Planning." *Journal of the American Institute of Planners* 29:2–8.

BACON, EDMUND 1968 "American Homes and Neighborhoods, City and Country." *Annals of the American Academy of Political and Social Science.*

BACON, EDMUND 1971 "Seven Principles for an Urban Land Policy." *Urban Land* 30:3–8.

BACON, EDMUND 1973 "Energy: Shaper of Future Living Patterns." *Journal of the American Institute of Architects* 60:39–41.

BACON, EDMUND 1974 *Design of Cities.* Rev. ed. New York: Viking.

BACON, EDMUND 1976 "Time, Turf, Architects and Planners." *Architectural Record* 159:97–102.

DAVERN, JEANNE M. 1977 "Four U.S. Projects Under Development by Mondev International." *Architectural Record* 162:96–107.

"Five Noted Thinkers Explore the Future." 1976 *National Geographic* 150:68–75.

MORRIS, A. E. J. 1975 "Philadelphia: Idea Powered Planning." *Built Environment Quarterly* 1:148–152.

"Philadelphia Story." 1976 *Progressive Architecture* 57, no. 4:entire issue.

BACON, HENRY

The reputation of Henry Bacon (1866–1924) rests upon the best known and most important achievement of his distinguished career, the Lincoln

Memorial (1911–1922) in Washington for which he received the Gold Medal of the American Institute of Architects in 1923. Executed in the spirit of the French academic tradition which characterized Bacon's many buildings and monuments, the Lincoln Memorial gave evidence of Bacon's scholasticism in its simplified peripteral Greek Doric temple style with its refined attention to detail. Dedicated less than a year before his death, the Memorial marked a peak in the wave of the classical revival of the late nineteenth and early twentieth centuries in America.

Bacon was born in Watseka, Illinois, and received his early education in Boston. In 1884, he attended the University of Illinois for one year before embarking upon his architectural career. He first served as a draftsman with the firm of Chamberlin and Whidden in Boston before joining the New York firm of McKim, Mead, and White, a leading proponent of the imported Beaux-Arts theory of design in the United States and one of the most influential architectural firms in the country. It was there that Bacon developed his academic stylistic vocabulary, augmented by the award of the prized Rotch Traveling Scholarship in 1889 which afforded him two years of European travel. In 1891, he returned to McKim, Mead, and White where he worked for the next six years. In 1897, he established a partnership with James Brite; the firm received numerous and varied commissions, including their award-winning Public Library (1898) in Jersey City, New Jersey, and the Hall of History at the American University (1891) in Washington. In 1902, Bacon began working independently; throughout a long and successful practice, he completed commercial, public, and residential buildings which included banks, hospitals, churches, libraries and homes. Exhibiting an early interest in monumental work, Bacon came to specialize in commemorative buildings and public monuments. He collaborated with several leading sculptors—among them Augustus St. Gaudens and Daniel Chester French—in designing pedestals and architectural settings.

JAN AVGIKOS

WORKS

1891, Hall of History, American University, Washington. 1898, Public Library, Jersey City, N.J. 1906, Danforth Memorial Library, Paterson, N.J. 1908, Eclectic Society Building, Middletown, Conn. 1915, Court of the Seasons, Pan-Pacific Exposition, San Francisco. 1911–1922, Lincoln Memorial, Washington.

BIBLIOGRAPHY

FLETCHER, BANISTER (1961)1977 *A History of Architecture.* 4th ed. New York: Scribner's.
HITCHCOCK, H. R. (1958)1977 *Architecture: Nineteenth and Twentieth Centuries.* Baltimore: Penguin.
KIDNEY, WALTER C. 1974 *The Architecture of Choice: Eclecticism in America, 1880–1930.* New York: Braziller.
SCULLY, VINCENT 1969 *American Architecture and Urbanism.* New York: Praeger.
TALLMADGE, THOMAS E. (1927)1936 *The Story of Architecture in America.* 3d ed., rev. New York: Norton.

BADGER, DANIEL D.

Daniel D. Badger (1806–1884) was a leader in the production of cast iron and established in New York one of America's greatest foundries producing architectural ironwork.

Born into a shipbuilding family on Badger's Island in the harbor of Portsmouth, New Hampshire, he was apprenticed to a blacksmith after a few years of schooling. Moving to Boston, he advertised himself as a blacksmith and also as a whitesmith making decorative ironwork. In 1842, he prevailed on a Boston client to let him build a storefront of iron columns and beams.

In 1843, Badger bought a patent for rolling iron shutters from inventor Arthur L. Johnson and became the leading producer of shutters which rolled up and down in the grooves of the iron columns of a storefront providing a security system. Known as "Badger fronts," they were a boon to stores and warehouses. Badger moved to New York City in 1846, setting up a small foundry at 42 Duane Street and winning a gold medal for his iron shutters at the 1847 American Institute Fair.

Badger fronts gained prominence when architect JOHN B. SNOOK installed them on the entire ground floor of the trend-setting marble department store of A. T. Stewart in New York City on which construction began in 1846. James Bogardus, too, contracted for Badger fronts to be installed in the big iron front building that he was erecting in Baltimore for the *Sun* newspaper in 1851. Bogardus, a New York inventor and manufacturer, in 1848 had introduced his concept of iron-walled buildings. Its warm reception inspired many foundry operators who had been casting stoves, utensils, safes, and pipes to enter the new market for cast-iron architecture. The iron-fronted commercial building became a favored building type, especially in urban areas under pressure to provide commercial space. It offered strength and lightness of structure, durability and incombustibility, style and varied design at economical prices, while a coat of paint refurbished it. Wide window expanses, more so than possible in masonry structures, improved interior lighting. Devising innovative methods of producing shapes in cast iron that traditionally had been executed in wood and stone, the iron foundries mass-produced a wide range of interchangeable building elements and launched prefabrication in the construction industry.

To iron storefronts Badger added production of iron fronts for buildings up to six stories, his first consequential example being the six-story Gilsey office block in New York City (1853) with two iron façades, according to William J. Fryer, chronicler of iron construction, writing in 1898 in the *History of Real Estate Building and Architecture in New York City,* who added "No man connected with the business ever did so much as Mr. Badger to popularize the use of cast iron fronts."

By 1854, Badger had moved uptown to a vastly enlarged foundry on East 14th Street, his outgrown downtown foundry converted to offices and showroom with modish iron front added by architect Snook.

In 1852, Badger employed an English architect, George H. Johnson, who designed for him such architectural elements as panels, balustrades, columns, brackets, cornices, and, most important for the production of iron fronts, entire modules composed of scores of separate castings bolted together that could be assembled in various combinations to form ornamental façades. Johnson was succeeded by Neils Poulson, Danish architect-engineer who later established the Hecla Iron Works.

In 1856, Badger incorporated his firm as the Architectural Iron Works of New York and built some of his best-known buildings: the Haughwout Store, often called the parthenon of iron buildings, and the Cary Building. He also shipped tons of iron buildings to Chicago.

During the next decade, the Architectural Iron Works built the unique all-iron Watervliet Arsenal (1859) for the United States Army, on the Hudson River near Troy, iron fronts in New York and other cities, as well as ferry houses and grain storage bins. All were depicted as completed works in his famous catalogue of 1865 in hard cover with splendid wood engravings, replicated twice in recent years. Several huge commissions came to the Architectural Iron Works following its publication, including the Powers Building in Rochester, New York (1869), the eight-story Gilsey Hotel in New York City (1869); the wide-span Manhattan Market (1872), gutted by fire soon after it was built; and most important, the soaring train-shed of Cornelius Vanderbilt's Grand Central Depot (1869–1871), 200 feet wide and 100 feet high. The lengthy, arched iron-and-glass roof carried on ornamental trusses of great elegance was a prime tourist attraction.

Due to ill health, perhaps augmented by the financial panic of 1873, Badger retired from active business in that year. The Architectural Iron Works closed three years later.

MARGOT GAYLE

WORKS

1846–1850, Stewart Department Store (iron store fronts with iron shutters), 280 Broadway; *1853, Gilsey Building, Broadway at Cortlandt Street; 1853–1859, Cooper Union (store fronts and interior cast iron work), Third Avenue and Eighth Street; 1856, Cary Building, 105 Chambers Street; New York. *1856, Halsey Building, Fulton Street, Brooklyn, N.Y. 1856, Haughwout Store, 490 Broadway, New York. *1856, Link Building, Lake and LaSalle Streets; *1856, Robbins Building, 205 South Waters Street; Chicago. 1857, 620 Broadway, New York. *1857, Lloyd and Jones Buildings, Randolph and Wells Streets, Chicago. 1857, 93 Reade Street, New York. *1857, Tuttle Buildings, Lake and State Streets, Chicago. *1859, Grover and Baker Sewing Machine Company, 495 Broadway, New York. 1859, Watervliet Arsenal, Hudson River, near Troy, N.Y. 1860, Brisk and Jacobson Store, 51 Dauphin Street, Mobile, Ala. 1861, Condict Building, 55 White Street, New York. 1861, The Ironblock, 205 East Wisconsin Avenue, Milwaukee, Wisc. 1861, Kidd Building, 51 North Pearl Street, Albany, N.Y. *1862, King's County Courthouse, Joralemon Street, Brooklyn, N.Y. *1863, Fulton Ferry Terminal, Fulton Street, New York. 1863, Howard Building, 7 Liberty Street, Bath, N.Y. 1863, Magnesia Springs Pavilion, Sharon, N.Y. *1864, South Ferry Terminal; *before 1865, Bulkley–Dunton Paper Company, 75 Duane Street; *before 1865, Singer Sewing Machine Company, Mott Street; New York. *Before 1865, Tulane Building, 211 Camp Street, New Orleans, La. Before 1865, 50 Warren Street; 1869, Gilsey Hotel, 1200 Broadway; New York. 1869, Powers Building, Rochester, N.Y. *1869–1871, Grand Central Depot, 42nd Street; 1872, 90 Maiden Lane; *1872, Manhattan Market, 34th Street at Eleventh Avenue; New York. 1872, Page Building, Lake and State Streets, Chicago. 1873, Boston Post Building, 17 Milk Street, Boston.

BIBLIOGRAPHY

A History of Real Estate, Building, and Architecture in New York City. (1898)1967 Reprint. New York: Arno.
BADGER, JOHN COGSWELL 1909 *Giles Badger and His Descendants.* Manchester, N.H.: Clarke.
GAYLE, MARGOT, and GILLON, EDMUND V. 1974 *Cast Iron Architecture in New York: A Photographic Survey.* New York: Dover.
GAYLE, MARGOT 1982 Introduction to *Badger's Illustrated Catalogue of Cast Iron Architecture.* Reprint. New York: Dover.
HUXTABLE, ADA LOUISE 1957 "Store for E. V. Haughwout & Co.—1857." *Progressive Architecture* 39, no. 2:133–136.
"Obituary." 1884 *New York Times* Nov. 19, p. 2.

STURGES, W. K. (1865)1970 Introduction to *The Origins of Cast Iron Architecture in America.* Reprint. New York: Da Capo. Originally published with the title *Illustrations of Iron Architecture Made by the Architectural Ironworks of the City of New York.*

BADOVICI, JEAN

Notwithstanding a traditional Beaux-Arts education in Paris, the reputation of Rumanian-born Jean Badovici (1893–1956) rests primarily on his literary accomplishments as an editor and architectural critic. Of his three works of architecture, *E-1027,* a seaside retreat at Roquebrune-Cap-Martin (1926–1929), on which he and EILEEN GRAY collaborated, is the best known. Following their commitment to liberate all aspects of design from tradition, Gray designed the furnishings and Badovici invented (and later patented) a "mechanical folding screen type window" for the house. LE CORBUSIER, a friend of Badovici, painted murals in various locations in the house in 1929 and in 1938 projected the final drawing for a painting of three nude women on one wall. Houses for himself at Vézelay (1924) and near the Pont de Sèvres in Paris (1934) constitute the remainder of Badovici's architectural *oeuvre.*

A student in the atelier of JULIEN GUADET and Edmond Jean Baptiste Paulin, Badovici was graduated first in his class from the Ecole Speciale d'Architecture; he also earned degrees from the Institut d'Urbanisme, the Ecole des Hautes Etudes Sociales and the Ecole des Hautes Etudes Internationales in Paris.

L'Architecture Vivante, an avant-garde revue founded by Badovici in 1922 and published by Albert Morancé, was the vehicle for Badovici's rise as one of the foremost apologists of modern art and architecture in Paris in the 1920s and 1930s. The periodical contained descriptive texts, drawings, and photographs of executed buildings embodying the principles of modernism, as well as polemical statements, manifestoes, and critiques. Badovici published a special issue entitled *E-1027: Maison en bord de mer.*

As one of a select group of poets, painters, and art historians including Fernand Leger and LÁSZLÓ MOHOLY-NAGY, Badovici attended the fourth Congrès Internationaux des Architectes in 1933 at which the principles of the Athens Charter were formalized. Following World War II, Badovici was appointed assistant to the chief architect for reconstruction in France.

SUSAN STRAUSS

WORKS

1924, Badovici House, Vézelay, France. 1926–1929, E-1027 (with Eileen Gray), Roquebrune-Cap-Martin, France. 1934, Badovici House, near the Pont de Sèvres, Paris.

BIBLIOGRAPHY

BADOVICI, JEAN 1923 *Maisons de Rapport de Charles Plumet.* Paris: Morancé.
BADOVICI, JEAN (editor) (1923–1933)1975 *L'Architecture vivante, 1923–33.* Reprint edition in 5 volumes of periodical originally published in France. New York: Da Capo.
BADOVICI, JEAN 1924 *Intérieurs de Süe et Mare.* Paris: Morancé.
BADOVICI, JEAN 1925 *Intérieurs Français.* Paris: Morancé.
BADOVICI, JEAN 1926 "La Maison d'aujourd'hui." *Cahiers d'Art* 1:12–13.
BADOVICI, JEAN 1926–1930 *L'Architecture Russe en URSS.* 2 vols. Paris: Morancé.
BADOVICI, JEAN 1931 *Grandes Constructions.* Paris: Morancé.
BADOVICI, JEAN 1937a *Architecture de Fêtes: Arts et Techniques.* Paris: Morancé.
BADOVICI, JEAN 1937b "Peinture Murale ou Peinture Spatiale." *L'Architecture d'aujourd'hui.* 8, Mar.:75–78.
BADOVICI, JEAN, and GRAY, EILEEN n.d. *E-1027: Maison en Bord de Mer.* Paris: Morancé.
BLUMENTHAL, MAX 1956 "Jean Badovici—1893–1956." *Techniques et Architecture* Nov.:24.
JOHNSON, J. STEWART 1980 *Eileen Gray—Designer.* London: Debrett's Peerage.
RYKWERT, JOSEPH 1972 "Eileen Gray: Pioneer of Design." *Architectural Review* 152:357–361.
VON MOOS, STANISLAUS 1979 *Le Corbusier: Elements of a Synthesis.* Cambridge, Mass.: M.I.T. Press.

BAERWALD, ALEXANDER

Alexander Baerwald (1877–1930) was a seminal figure in modern Palestinian (Israeli) architecture. He was born in Berlin and received his architectural education there. He first worked in the Prussian civil service and was involved in the planning of many public buildings. A prolific writer, he published numerous professional articles about his work.

In 1909, Baerwald was asked by a group of German Jews to plan a technical institute in Haifa, Palestine. The imposing structure which he designed, the Technion, was the first technical institute in the Middle East. One of the main works of Baerwald, this building combines European technology with Islamic and Persian architectural elements. This effort to define a local style suitable to both the landscape and the lifestyle of Palestine may also be seen in many of the private houses he designed primarily in Haifa. Among the more prominent examples is the house of the German-

Jewish artist Hermann Struck (1924). The chief components of Baerwald's style are pointed arches, flat roofs, and rustic stone façades. In planning large functional structures, such as the hospital in Afula (1929), Baerwald built in the simpler International style.

From 1925 until his death in 1930 in Jerusalem, Baerwald served as a professor of architecture at the Technion where he was responsible for educating the first generation of architects for the Jewish settlement in Palestine.

EDINA MEYER

WORKS

1910–1914, Technion; 1924, Hermann Struck House; 1925, Anglo-Palestine Bank; Haifa, Israel. 1926, Dr. Soskin House, Tel Aviv. 1929, Hospital, Afula, Israel.

BAGLIONI FAMILY

This prominent Florentine family of woodworkers and architects included Bartolomeo (1462–1543), better known as Baccio d'Agnolo, and his three sons. Unfortunately, Baccio is best remembered through MICHELANGELO's disparagement of the section of gallery he attached (1508–1516) to the dome of the cathedral in Florence, Italy. His architectural projects reveal a debt to such earlier masters as Giuliano da Maiano (see MAIANO FAMILY) and IL CRONACA as well as an awareness of the innovations of DONATO BRAMANTE, RAPHAEL, and Michelangelo. Among the several Florentine palaces attributed to Baccio, the Palazzo Bartolini-Salimbeni (1520–1529) is the most notable. Its well-proportioned façade is accented by an aedicula portal and niches that alternate with the three cross windows of the *piano nobile*. Baccio's most significant ecclesiastical works were his Bramantesque bell tower (1503–1543) at Santo Spirito, Florence, and his Church of San Giuseppe (1519–?) in Florence with its barrel-vaulted nave and domical side chapels.

Baccio's High Renaissance architectural style was continued in a number of palaces and religious buildings by his sons Giuliano (1491–1555), like his father the *capomaestro* of Florence Cathedral, Domenico (1511–?), and Filippo (n.d.).

CHARLES RANDALL MACK

WORKS

BACCIO D'AGNOLO BAGLIONI

c.1500, San Lorenzo (blind arcades on exterior flanks); 1503–1504, Palazzo Taddei; 1503–1543, Santo Spirito (bell tower not completed until 1571); 1508–1515, Cathedral (gallery section for dome); 1512–1515, San Vincenzo Ferreri (little cloister); c.1515–?, Palazzo Borgherini; c.1515–1525, Palazzo Ridolfi; 1516–1525, Confraternita dei Servi (portico with Antonio da Sangallo the Elder); 1517–?, San Michele Bertelde (bell tower); 1518–?, Villa Borgherini, on Bellosguardo; 1518–1527, San Miniato ai Monti (bell tower); 1519–?, San Giuseppe; 1520–1529, Palazzo Bartolini-Salimbeni; c.1540, Palazzo Bartolini-Giuntini; c.1540, Palazzo Bartolini-Torrigiani; c.1540, Palazzo Cocchi-Serristori; c.1540, Palazzo Gagliano; c.1540, Palazzo Lanfredini; c.1540, Palazzo Nasi (completed after 1547 by Domenico Baglioni); c.1540, Palazzo Ricascoli; c.1540, Santi Apostoli (bell tower); Florence. c.1540, Villa Bartolini, Rovezzano, Italy.

DOMENICO BAGLIONI

1547–?, Palazzo Nasi (completion); 1548–?, Palazzo Montauto (Niccolini-Bourturlin); 1548–?, Palazzo Niccolini; 1548–?, Villa Ginori; Florence.

FILIPPO BAGLIONI

n.d., Palazzo Nasi in Borgo San Niccolo; n.d., Palazzo Martellini; Florence.

GIULIANO BAGLIONI

1532–?, Palazzo Campana, Colle Valdelsa, Italy. 1539, Palazzo Conti, Florence. 1539, Palazzo Grifoni, San Miniato al Tedesco, Italy. 1539, San Martini, Montughi, Italy. 1539, Turini Chapel, Cathedral, Pescia, Italy. 1539, Villa Campana, Montighi, Italy.

BIBLIOGRAPHY

BERTI, LUCIANO 1963 "Baglioni." Volume 5, pages 202–205 in *Dizionario Biografico degli Italiani*. Rome: Istituto della Enciclopedia.
BUCCI, MARIO 1971–1973 *Palazzi di Firenze*. 4 vols. Florence: Vallecchi.
PAATZ, WALTER, and PAATZ, ELISABETH 1940–1954 *Die Kirchen von Florenz*. 6 vols. Frankfurt: Klostermann.
VASARI, GIORGIO (1550)1973 *Le opere di Giòrgio Vasari, con nuove annotazioni e commenti*. Edited by G. Milanesi. Reprint. Florence: Sansoni. Originally published with the title *Le vite de' più eccelenti pittori, scultori, et architetti*. There are many English translations and selections from Vasari's *Lives;* the standard one by G. du C. de Vere was published in London by the Medici Society (1912–1915).
VENTURI, ADOLFO (1939)1967 Volume 11, part 2, pages 552–556 in *Storia dell'arte italiana. Architettura del Cinquecento*. Reprint. Nendeln, Germany: Kraus.

BÄHR, GEORG

Born almost twenty years before his compatriots Bach and Handel, Georg Bähr (1666–1738) illustrates the Saxon baroque style in architecture. Bähr grew up in Fürstenwalde in the Erzgebirge (or Ore Mountains, so-called because of the plethora of metal deposits found there) in Germany, by then

Bähr.
Frauenkirche.
Dresden, Germany.
1722–1738 (not completed
*   until 1743 by Schmidt).*

religiously divided and depleted after the Thirty Years War (1618–1648).

Bähr's artistic career was marked by its genesis within the guild system, a path common to baroque artists in many central European countries, as contrasted, for example, with contemporary France and Italy where the academic tradition had prevailed over the medieval guild system. At a very young age, Georg was an apprenticed carpenter and is known through official records to have dabbled also in the mechanics of musical instruments and the *camera obscura,* a popular interest in the seventeenth century. This mixing of media is a hallmark of the baroque period; the fame of GIOVANNI LORENZO BERNINI draws equally from his sculpture and architecture.

At thirty-nine, Bähr is recorded as *Ratszimmermeister* or master carpenter in the city of Dresden, the baroque royal capital in Upper Saxony and home of the splendorous and unique *Kunstkammer* of the Elector Augustus (1553–1586) as well as of Bähr's chef d'oeuvre, the Protestant Frauenkirche.

Commissioned by the city council, the architecturally exemplary Frauenkirche underwent many changes in plan before the establishment of its final square ground plan between 1722 and 1726. The foundation was laid in 1726, and though most of the building was erected by 1738, the year of Bähr's death, it was completed posthumously after Bähr's plans by his cousin and stylistic successor, Johann Georg Schmidt, between 1740 and 1743.

The undulating rhythm of the four equally balanced façades of the ill-fated church (it was destroyed during the 1945 bombing of Dresden), whose curves grow into an imaginatively wrought concave roof before disappearing under the massive and dominating dome topped by a lantern, is made static through the uniformity and heaviness of the stone masonry. Bähr's church looks to the influential Italian baroque in plan and decorative scheme but to the future in terms of articulation. It would not be far-fetched to point to the organic movement of Bähr's roofline and façade as formally heralding, for example, the Art Nouveau architectural forms of ANTONIO GAUDÍ I CORNET.

The church's profile punctuates the landscape in such a picturesque way that it has often been represented by painters, most notably in the panoramic and detailed cityscape, "Dresden from the Right Bank of the Elbe" (1748), by the Italian Bernardo Bellotto called Canaletto.

Along with Johann G. Schmidt, Andreas Hüningen and Christian Friedrich Exner helped disseminate Bähr's architectural legacy.

TINA WALDEIER BIZZARRO

WORKS

1705–1708, Church, Loschwitz, Germany. 1713–1716, Church, Schmiedeberg, Germany. 1719–1726, Church, Forchheim, Germany. 1722–1738, Frauenkirche (not completed until 1743 by Johann Georg Schmidt), Dresden, Germany.

BIBLIOGRAPHY

HEMPEL, EBERHARD 1965 *Baroque Art and Architecture in Central Europe.* Harmondsworth, England: Penguin.
POPP, HERMANN (1913)1924 *Die Architektur der Barock- und Rokokozeit in Deutschland und der Schweiz.* Stuttgart, Germany: Hoffmann.
The Splendor of Dresden: Five Centuries of Art Collecting. 1978 New York: Metropolitan Museum of Art. An exhibition from the State Art Collections of Dresden, German Democratic Republic, held at the National Gallery of Art in Washington from June 1– September 4, 1978.

BAILLAIRGE, CHARLES

Charles Philippe Ferdinand Baillairgé (1826–1906), architect, civil engineer, and surveyor, belonged to the fourth generation of Baillairgés active in Quebec City. Apprenticed in architecture to his father's cousin Thomas, he practiced during Quebec's economic boom in the 1850s, winning major religious and civic contracts. He introduced Gothic and Greek Revival styles and contemporary materials into residential and commercial structures. While supervising construction of the Quebec Prison (1860–1863), Baillairgé was called to Ottawa in 1863 to oversee completion of the Parliament Buildings. Unjustly dismissed in 1865, he returned to Quebec, where he worked as city engineer from 1866 to 1898 and wrote extensively on architecture, engineering, language, and mathematics.

CHRISTINA CAMERON

WORKS

*1846–1857, Eglise Saint-Jean-Baptiste, Quebec. 1848–1849, Clermont, Sillery, Quebec. *1849–1850, Bilodeau Store; 1849–1850, De Blois Store; Quebec. *1849–1850, Eglise de Beauport, Quebec. 1850–1851, DeFoy Store, Quebec. 1850–1854, Asylum and Chapel of the Sisters of Charity; *1851–1853, Quebec Music Hall; Quebec. 1852–1853, Manor House, Saint-Roch-des-Aulnaies, Quebec. 1852–1854, Têtu House; 1853–1854, Bilodeau House; 1853–1854, Ursulines Convent (Notre-Dame-de-Grace Wing); *1853–1854, Têtu Warehouse; Quebec. 1853–1857, Eglise de l'Isle-Verte, Quebec. 1854–1856, Eglise de Saint-Romuald, Quebec. 1854–1857, Central Pavilion, Laval University, Quebec. 1854–1860, Eglise de Sainte-Marie de Beauce, Quebec. 1855–1857, Eglise Saint-Patrice, Rivière-du-Loup, Quebec. 1855–1857, Pensionnat, Laval University; 1855–1860, Monument aux Braves; 1856, DeFoy House; 1856–1857, Morin–Hamel House; 1857–1858, Caisse d'économie Notre-Dame de Québec Bank; 1857–1858, Leaycraft House; 1857–1862, Venner Tomb; 1858–1859, Desbarats Block; Quebec. *1860, Cap-Rouge Pottery Factory, Quebec. 1860–1863, New Quebec Prison; 1863–1864, Elm Grove; Quebec. 1863–1865, Departmental Buildings, Ottawa, Ontario. *1866–1867, Berthelot Market Hall; *1866–1867, Jacques Cartier Market Hall; *1866–1867, Saint John Gate; 1866–1868, Chapel of the Sisters of the Good Shepherd; 1878–1879, Dufferin Terrace; Quebec.

BIBLIOGRAPHY

BAILLAIRGÉ, CHARLES 1899 *Bilan de M. Baillairgé, comme Architecte, Ingénieur, Arpenteur-Géomètre, durant les 21 ans avant d'entrer au service de la Cité, ésqualité d'Ingénieur des Ponts et Chaussées, ou de 1845 à 1866. Puis-entre heures-de 1866–1899.* Quebec.

BAILLAIRGÉ, CHARLES 1900 *Rapport de l'ex'Ingénieur de la Cité, des travaux faits sous le Maire, Hon. S. N. Parent et le Conseil-de-Ville actuels et sous leurs prédécesseurs durant le dernier tiers de Siècle: 1866 à 1899.* Quebec: Darveau.

"Bibliography of C. Baillairgé." 1895 *Proceedings and Transactions of the Royal Society of Canada for the Year 1894* 12:6–8.

CAMERON, CHRISTINA n.d. "Charles Baillairgé: Profile of an Architect." In preparation.

CARON, ROBERT 1980 *Un couvent du XIXe siècle: La maison des Soeurs de la Charité de Québec.* Quebec: Libre Expression.

C. Baillairgé. Arct. Ing. dessins architecturaux. 1979 Quebec: Ministère des affaires culturelles.

NOPPEN, LUC; PAULETTE, CLAUDE; and TREMBLAY, MICHEL 1979 *Québec: Trois siècles d'architecture.* Quebec: Libre Expression.

BAILLIE SCOTT, M. H.

Mackay Hugh Baillie Scott (1865–1945), one of Britain's most important architects from 1890 to 1914, and a vociferous exponent of the Arts and Crafts movement, together with C. F. A. VOYSEY, C. R. MACKINTOSH, C. R. ASHBEE, BARRY PARKER, and RAYMOND UNWIN, altered the history of domestic architecture, the decorative arts, and town planning internationally. Born near Ramsgate, Kent, Baillie Scott graduated from the Royal Agricultural College at Cirencester in 1885 and was articled to Charles E. Davis, city architect of Bath, learning little before leaving in 1889. Influence came instead from the burgeoning Arts and Crafts movement and related architecture of R. NORMAN SHAW, ERNEST GEORGE, Voysey, and publications of American Shingle style architects. He began his practice at Douglas, Isle of Man. His earliest known design, the unexecuted Bates Bungalow (1889), is derived from American sources and is quite similar to FRANK LLOYD WRIGHT's earliest work. By 1901, when he relocated at Bedford, his illustrated articles in *The Studio* and other publications won him international attention. Commissions came from Europe and America; articles also appeared. His interiors (1897–1898) for the Duke of Hesse were a catalyst for the Darmstadt Artists' Colony (1898), principal source for the *Werkstätten* to follow. In America, his work helped make 1901 a seminal year for the Arts and Crafts movement: Gustave Stickley began *The Craftsman*, Arts and Crafts societies were founded, and Wright joined the Chicago Arts and Crafts Society.

Architectural voice of *The Studio* from 1895 to 1914, Baillie Scott fused the vernacular characteristics of EDWIN LUTYENS's earliest architecture with GERTRUDE JEKYLL's landscape design. In *Houses and Gardens* (1906), he advanced new planning concepts, integrating and subordinating other rooms in the house to the "living" room. In placing living areas toward the garden away from the road, he reversed existing practices. Staunchly Arts and Crafts, he thought furniture ought to be built in when possible, and the architect ought to design uniformly for *all* people and to design all objects, from dinner fork to village community. Repeatedly he castigated the view of architecture as the decoration of construction; for him, they were interchangeable. Unlike Wright he saw "organic" architecture as a passive, even negative, element in the landscape. Bringing architecture and landscape into a new, antirevivalist, interpenetrating, balanced whole, he was like Wright and Paul Cézanne who brought their art to an ultimate point of liberation from revival associations without rejecting traditional imagery and materials. Maturing in theory and design before ADOLF LOOS and Wright, and publishing regularly, he greatly influenced them and their generation.

His design is characterized by its unassuming vernacular domesticity, its generalization of a specifically British indigenous idiom. Germans saw this as producing liveability (*Wohnlichkeit*), however, not by imitation of the British manner, but by using its principles to draw from their own tradition. In this way Wright's Prairie school assumes international dimensions. Some of his best designs from 1901 to 1906 appear in *Houses and Gardens,* though many were not built or remain unlocated. By 1906 he was involved with the garden city as PARKER AND UNWIN were developing it at Letchworth and Hampstead. His houses there widely influenced English, German, Scandinavian, and American garden city planning. Waldbühl (1907–1914) in Uzwil, Switzerland, his best preserved work, marks the culmination of his country houses. Yet his housing for the garden city, nonminimal but economical houses for average people, is most important historically.

Baillie Scott's architecture, like Wright's, underwent a crisis around 1914 closely related to the demise of the Arts and Crafts movement. Unlike Wright or OTTO BARTNING who chose to express defunct Arts and Crafts ideals after the war, Baillie Scott, ever reticent, designed muted Tudor or Georgian houses when not pursuing his earlier idiom. A fire in his Bedford office in 1911 destroyed most records and drawings, and just before World War I he moved his practice to London. In 1939, World War II and the death of his wife conspired to end the practice. In 1941 bombs destroyed his London office. During the war and until his death in Brighton in 1945 he painted landscapes. The epitaph on the simple cubic stele marking his grave reads "Nature he loved and next to Nature, Art."

Nikolaus Pevsner saw Baillie Scott, Voysey, and other Arts and Crafts exponents as "pioneers" of Modernist design developed from 1919 to 1933 by WALTER GROPIUS and the Bauhaus architects. However, in 1933, Baillie Scott with his partner A. Edgar Beresford published a second version of *Houses and Gardens* defending what the Arts and Crafts movement, once radical ethically and a near *tabula rasa* aesthetically, had devolved into—"Traditional" architecture, ethically enfeebled and aesthetically reactionary. This they facetiously pitted against Modernist, flat-roofed, antivernacular architecture associated with the Bauhaus. Baillie Scott, like Voysey, denied influencing this school, yet early Modernist work affirms Arts and Crafts influence in planning by area and level rather than by room and floor, in retaining simple, white, unadorned walls with flush-set windows, in advocating "total" design, and, in Gropius's case, emphasizing housing for ordinary people. Engineering and Cubism surely account for what is different about Modernist architecture; but not for what is the same. Before 1922, apart from engineering and historicist architecture, there was precious little else for Modernists to draw from except the Arts and Crafts–garden city movement, which is why LE CORBUSIER praised Baillie Scott in 1912 as one of "les plus grands artistes" and Gropius included art and craft in the Bauhaus curriculum. Because Baillie Scott is both a pioneer of Modernist theory and design and a Romantic respecting indigenous, vernacular traditions and preservation of the landscape, he and the Arts and Crafts both paved the way for Modernism between the world wars and have stimulated the a-Modernist ambivalence of today.

JAMES D. KORNWOLF

WORKS

1894–1896, Bexton Croft, Knutsford, Cheshire, England. 1896–1897, Semidetached houses, Onchan, Isle of Man, England. *1897–1898, Ducal Palace (interiors), Darmstadt, Germany. 1898–1899, The White Lodge, Wantage, Berkshire, England. 1899–1900, The Garth, Cobham, Surrey, England. 1908, Multiple houses, Hampstead Garden Suburb, London. 1907–1914, Waldbühl, Uzwil, Switzerland. 1909, Walterlow Court, Hampstead Garden Suburb, London. 1912–1914, Binsse House, Short Hills, N.J. 1928–1929, Ashwood, Woking, Surrey, England.

BIBLIOGRAPHY

BAILLIE SCOTT, M. H. 1906 *Houses and Gardens.* London: Newnes.
BAILLIE SCOTT, M. H., and BERESFORD, A. E. 1933

Baillie Scott.
Plans for Multiple Houses.
Hampstead Garden
    Suburb, London.
1908

Baillie Scott.
Multiple Houses.
Hampstead Garden
    Suburb, London.
1908

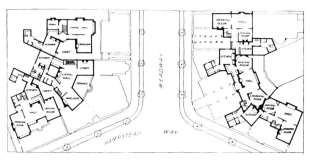

Houses and Gardens. London: Architecture Illustrated.

BAILLIE SCOTT, M. H.; UNWIN, R.; ET AL. 1909 *Town Planning and Modern Architecture at the Hampstead Garden Suburb.* London: Unwin.

BAILLIE SCOTT, M. H. ET AL. 1910 *Garden Suburbs, Town Planning, and Modern Architecture.* London: Unwin.

BETJEMAN, JOHN 1938 "Baillie Scott and the 'Architecture of Escape.'" *The Studio* 16, Oct.:177–180.

BETJEMAN, JOHN 1965 "M. H. Baillie Scott on the Isle of Man." *The Weekend Telegraph* Oct. 29.

BETJEMAN, JOHN 1968 "M. H. Baillie Scott." *Journal of the Manx Museum* 7:77–80.

CREESE, WALTER L. 1966 *The Search for Environment: The Garden City Before and After.* New Haven and London: Yale University Press.

FISKER, KAY 1947 "Tre Pionerer fra Aarhundredskiftet." *Byggmästaren* 26:221–232.

FRED, W. 1905 "Der Architekt M. H. Baillie Scott." *Kunst und Kunsthandwerk* 4:53–73.

KOCH, ALEX. (editor) 1902 *Meister der Innenkunst: Haus eines Kunstfreundes des M. H. Baillie Scott.* Darmstadt, Germany: Zeitschrift für Innendekoration.

KORNWOLF, JAMES D. 1972 *M. H. Baillie Scott and the Arts and Crafts Movement: Pioneers of Modern Design.* Baltimore: Johns Hopkins University Press.

MEDICI-MALL, KATHARINA 1979 *Das Landhaus Waldbühl von M. H. Baillie Scott.* Bern, Switzerland: Gesellschaft für Schweizerische Kunstgeschichte.

MEIER-GRAEFE, JULIUS 1905 "M. H. Baillie Scott." *Moderne Bauformen* 4:34ff.

MEYER, PETER 1937 "Baillie Scott's Waldbühl." *Das Werk* 24:140–153.

MUTHESIUS, HERMANN 1900 "M. H. Baillie Scott." *Dekorative Kunst* 5:5–7, 40–48.

MUTHESIUS, HERMANN 1904–1905 *Das englische Haus.* Berlin: Wasmuth.

PEVSNER, NIKOLAUS (1949)1974 *Pioneers of Modern Design from William Morris to Walter Gropius.* Middlesex, England: Penguin.

TAYLOR, NICHOLAS 1965 "Baillie Scott's Waldbühl." *Architectural Review* 138:456–458.

VON BERLEPSCH-VALENDAS, H. E. 1909 "Hampstead—Eine Studie über Stadtebau in England." *Kunst und Kunsthandwerk* 12:241–284.

WHITE, J. P. 1901 *Furniture Made at the Pyghtle Works, Bedford, by John P. White Designed by M. H. Baillie Scott.* London.

BAILLY, ANTOINE-NICOLAS

As a student of F. L. J. DUBAN and François Debret and a draftsman for PAUL M. LETAROUILLY, Antoine-Nicolas Bailly (1810–1892) became a skilled designer in the French Renaissance mode. His Tribunal de Commerce (1860–1866) was compromised by specific demands of style and form made on it by Napoleon III and GEORGE EUGÈNE HAUSSMANN. But his Mairie of the fourth *arron-*

dissement (1862–1867) is a vigorous and original design.

ANN LORENZ VAN ZANTEN

WORKS

1857, Grandstand, Longchamps, France. Late 1850s, Lycée Saint-Louis (façade); 1860–1866, Tribunal de Commerce; 1862–1867, Mairie of the Fourth Arrondissement; Paris.

BIBLIOGRAPHY

HAUTECOEUR, LOUIS 1957 *La fin de l'architecture classique, 1848–1900.* Volume 7 in *Histoire de l'architecture classique en France.* Paris: Picard.

BAKEMA, J. B.

See VAN DEN BROEK and BAKEMA.

BAKER, HERBERT

Born in Cobham, Kent, England, Herbert Baker (1862–1946) was educated at Tonbridge School and trained at the Royal Academy School in London under R. NORMAN SHAW and GEORGE F. BODLEY from 1879 to 1881.

He started his own practice in 1890. In 1892, he moved to Cape Town, South Africa, where he, along with several others, was appointed architect to Cecil Rhodes. In 1902, he established a practice in Johannesburg, South Africa, designing a number of churches, private houses, schools, public housing, and government buildings. The Union Buildings in Pretoria show his use of traditional European neoclassical forms with a serious concern to adapt to local technology and materials. He introduced a new formal vocabulary that influenced the architecture of neighboring countries.

In 1913, he returned to London and established a practice both in London and in New Delhi, where he was associated with EDWIN LUTYENS in the design of secretariats, legislative buildings, and the Circular Council Chamber.

As principal architect to the War Graves Commission from 1918 until 1928, he built a number of war memorials, cemeteries, and churches. He wrote several books and was awarded with the Royal Gold Medal for Architecture in 1927, and several honorary doctorates. He was knighted in 1930 and named Royal Academician in 1937.

MARC DILET

WORKS

1882–1887, Redroofs, Streatham Common, London. 1882–1887, Waterside House, Westgate-on-Sea, Kent, England. 1892–1902, Housing, Sommerset West, Cape

Town, South Africa. 1894, Saint Andrew's, Newlands Cape, South Africa. 1898, Wilson and Miller Building; 1900, Juta Building; 1902, Rhodes Building; Cape Town, South Africa. 1905, Saint Alban's Cathedral; 1907, Government House; Pretoria. 1908, Rhodes Memorial, Cape Town, South Africa. 1909, Pretoria Railway Station. 1911, Rhodes University College, Cape Town, South Africa. 1912, South African Institute for Medical Research, Johannesburg, South Africa. 1913–1928, Secretariat, Legislative and Staff Building, New Delhi. 1928, India House, Aldwych, London. 1928–1930, Government House, Nairobi. 1934–1935, South Africa House, Trafalgar Square; 1935–1941, Royal Empire Society, Northumberland Avenue; London.

BIBLIOGRAPHY

BAKER, HERBERT 1888 *Plas Mawr, Conway, North Wales.* London: Farmer.
BAKER, HERBERT 1934 *Cecil Rhodes by His Architect.* London: Oxford University Press.
BAKER, HERBERT 1944 *Architecture and Personalities.* London: Country Life.
TROTTER, ALYS FANE 1900 "The Origin of Old Cape Architecture." Pages 1–7 in *Old Colonial Houses of the Cape of Good Hope.* London: Batsford.

BAKEWELL and BROWN

John Bakewell, Jr. (1872–1963), born in Topeka, Kansas, and Arthur Brown, Jr. (1874–1957), born in Oakland, California, obtained degrees at the University of California, Berkeley, and, on the advice of BERNARD R. MAYBECK, went to the Ecole des Beaux-Arts in Paris. Bakewell was in the Ateliers of JULIEN GUADET and Edmond Paulin and obtained his diploma in 1900, Brown in the Atelier of VICTOR A. F. LALOUX, getting diplomas in 1901 and 1903. They formed a partnership in 1906 which lasted to 1928. Brown, the designer of the firm, was a leading classical architect produced by the West in the American Renaissance, responsible for the city hall of San Francisco (1912–1915).

HENRY HOPE REED

WORKS

1909, Berkeley City Hall, Calif. 1910, Burlingame Country Club, Calif. 1912–1915, San Francisco City Hall. 1915, Santa Fe Railroad Station, San Diego, Calif. 1919, Stanford University Library, Calif. 1922–1932, San Francisco Opera House (with G. Albert Lansburgh). 1922–1932, San Francisco Veterans Building. 1925, Pacific Gas and Electric Building; 1926, San Francisco Art Institute; 1926, Temple Emanu-El (with Sylvain Schnaittacher); San Francisco. 1927, Pasadena City Hall, Calif. 1933, Coit Tower; 1936, Federal Office Building; San Francisco. 1941, Hoover Tower, Stanford University, Calif. 1942, Sproul Hall; 1950, Library Annex; University of California, Berkeley,

BIBLIOGRAPHY

JENSEN, ROLLIN 1960*a* Building List and Fact Sheet on Arthur Brown, Jr." Unpublished manuscript.
JENSEN, ROLLIN 1960*b* "Some Notes on Classical Architecture in San Francisco." Unpublished manuscript.
REED, HENRY HOPE (1959)1970 *The Golden City.* 2d ed. New York: Norton.

BALAT, ALPHONSE

The original personality of Alphonse Hubert François Balat (1818–1895) stands apart from the chaos of eclecticism as the purist survivor of the classical tradition.

Originally directed toward sculpture by his father, a master quarrier, he studied architecture at the academies of Namur and Antwerp (1834–1838). A trip to Italy, study in Paris (1839), and the theories of French classicism had a great influence on him. In 1851, he became the architectural consultant to King Leopold II of Belgium.

His monumental projects, informed by his increasing desire for formal purity, wedded the classical ideal (Palais des Beaux-Arts, 1875) to modern engineering (greenhouses of Laeken, 1883–1887). A detractor of the compilation of styles and architectural plagiarism, Balat advocated rational design and the principle of simplicity. These ideas influenced the young VICTOR HORTA, who worked in Balat's atelier in 1884.

MAURICE CULOT
Translated from French by Shara Wasserman

WORKS

1850–1860, Château Mirwart (restoration), Belgium. 1850–1860, Château Seilles (restoration), Belgium. 1858–1860, Assache Palace; 1875, Palace of Fine Arts (now the Museum of Ancient Art); Brussels. 1883–1889, Laeken Palace (greenhouses, pavilions, and galleries), Belgium. 1885–1889, Place du Trône (remodeling); 1885–1889, Royal Palace (grand staircase, state rooms, and façades); Brussels. 1889, Church of Iron, Royal Palace, Laeken, Belgium. n.d., Castaigne Bookstore; n.d., Jonghe Mansion; n.d., Liedekerke-Beaufort Mansion; Brussels.

BALCELLS BUIGAS, EDUARDO MARÍA

Eduardo María Balcells Buigas (1877–1965) undertook his studies at the Superior Technical School for Architecture in Barcelona and obtained his degree in 1905. His first buildings—Enrique Calado House, Sant Cugat (1905); Tosquella

House, Calle Ballester, Barcelona (1906); and the Lluch House, Sant Cugat (1906)—were eclectic in their search for novelty and absence of traditional precepts. Balcells then appeared to follow the path of nineteenth-century brutalism as established by the English architect WILLIAM BUTTERFIELD and the American FRANK FURNESS. Influenced by the contemporary style in Spain, he evolved toward an evaluation of vernacular architecture, examples of which are the Miguel Brugarolas House, Cerdanyola (1906); the Jaime Boleda House, La Torrasa, Hospitalet (1907); the Manuel Mestres House, Cerdanyola (1907); and the Reotoral House, Cerdanyola (1908).

Beginning in 1910, Balcells experimented with a subtle but very significant change of style, in which the brutal composition became more refined and vaguely recalled the Expressionist movement, an evolution which is reflected in the Masachs House, Cerdanyola (1910). The 1913 design for a house for his brother Carlos in Cerdanyola breaks definitively with Art Nouveau and carries to the extreme the new Expressionist trend begun in the Masachs House. Balcell substituted vernacular architecture for a more international one without renouncing his traditional aesthetic criteria and his sensibility toward local architecture.

Together with the architects Rafael Valenti Masó and Pericas, Balcell created the link, by means of Expressionism, between the death of Art Nouveau and the rationalist architecture of the postwar years.

XAVIER GUËLL GUIX
Translated from Spanish by
Tomlyn Barns

WORKS
1905, Enrique Calado House, Sant Cugat, Spain. 1906, Miguel Brugaryolas House, Cerdanyola, Spain. 1906, Lluch House, Sant Cugat, Spain. 1906, Tosquella House, Calle Ballester, Barcelona, Spain. 1907, Jaime Boleda House, La Torrasa, Hospitalet, Spain. 1907, Manuel Mestres Houses; 1908, Reotoral House; 1910, Masachs House; 1913, Carlos Balcells Buigas House; Cerdanyola, Spain.

BALDESSARI, LUCIANO

Luciano Baldessari (1896–) was born in Rovereto, Italy, then part of the Hapsburg Empire. As a young man, he participated in the Futurist activities of Fortunato Depero in Rovereto. Conscripted into the Austrian army during World War I, Baldessari served on the Eastern front. Returning to Italy in 1919, he enrolled in the Milan Politecnico. He received his architecture degree in 1922. Baldessari then moved to Berlin where he

became acquainted with many of the leading German artists and architects. After traveling in Germany and France, he returned to Italy in 1926. He established an office in Milan and quickly emerged as one of the leading designers of his generation. After eight years in New York City (1940–1948), Baldessari returned to Milan. During the 1950s, he designed an important series of temporary exhibition pavilions in Milan. He was the only Italian architect invited to participate in the international project for the Hansaviertel development in Berlin, designing an apartment building in 1957. Working with ideas drawn from Futurism, rationalism, and German Expressionism, Baldessari created a highly personal, lyrical style. An active set designer as well as architect, he lives in Milan.

DENNIS DOORDAN

WORKS
*1930, Bar Craja (with Figini and Pollini); *1933, Press Pavilion, Fifth Triennale; 1934–1936, Italcima Factory; *1951, Breda Pavilion, International Trade Fair; *1952, Breda Pavilion, International Trade Fair; *1953, Breda Pavilion, International Trade Fair; *1954, Breda Pavilion, International Trade Fair; Milan. 1957–1958, Apartment Building, Hansaviertel, Berlin. 1961–1973, Fratelli Fontana Technical Institute, Rovereto, Italy.

BIBLIOGRAPHY
Controspazio 1978 10, nos. 2–3: special issue.
DE'SETA, CESARE 1972 *La cultura architettonica in Italia tra le due guerre.* Bari, Italy: Laterza.
VERONESI, GIULIA 1957 *Luciano Baldessari Architetto.* Trent, Italy: Collana di Artisti Trentini.

BALDI, BERNARDINO

Bernardino Baldi (1553–1617) included works about his native Urbino in his extensive literary output. His description of its palace and the life of its builder remain useful. Both conspicuously evoke the courtly atmosphere delineated earlier by Baldasare Castiglione. His studies of VITRUVIUS were sufficiently valuable to be restudied and reissued into the nineteenth century.

CARROLL WILLIAM WESTFALL

BIBLIOGRAPHY
BALDI, BERNARDINO (1590)1859 "Descrittione del Palazzo ducale d'Urbino." In Filippo Ugolini and Filippo-Luigi Polidori (editors), *Versi e prose scelti di Bernardino Baldi.* Florence: Felice le Monnier. Originally published in *Versi e prose.* Venice, Italy: Sanese.
BALDI, BERNARDINO (1824)1826 *Vita e fatti di Federigo di Montefeltro, Duca di Urbino istoria.* Edited by Francesco Zuccardi. 3 vols. Bologna and Turin, Italy: Veroli. Written in 1602–1603.
BALDI, BERNARDINO 1612 *De verborum Vitrvvianorvm significatione Siue, Perpetuus in M. Vitruuium Pollionem*

commentarius. Augsburg, Germany. Reprinted in 1649 with *Scamilla impares* (1612) in Vitruvius, *de Architectura.* Edited by John de Laet. Amsterdam: Ludovicum Elzivirium.

BALDI, BERNARDINO 1612 *M. Vitruviani Pollionis architecti vita.* Augsburg, Germany.

BALDI, BERNARDINO 1612 *Scamilla impares Vitruviani . . . nova ratione explicate: Refutatis priorum interpretum Gvlielmi Philandri Danielis Barbari, Baptistae Bertani, sententijs.* Augsburg, Germany. Reprinted in 1649 with *De verborum* (1612) in Vitruvius, *de Architectura.* Edited by John de Laet. Amsterdam: Ludovicum Elzivirium.

BILIŃSKI, BRONISŁAW 1973 *La vita di Copernico di Bernardino Baldi.* Wrocław, Poland: Accademia Polacca della scienza, biblioteca e centro di studi a Roma.

PROMIS, CARLO 1875 *Vocaboli latini di architettura posteriori a Vitruvio oppure a lui sconosciuti raccolti da . . . a complemento del Lessico Vitruviano di Bernardino Baldi.* Turin, Italy: Reale.

BALDWIN, BENJAMIN

Both an architect and interior designer, Benjamin Baldwin (1913–) studied painting with Hans Hoffman, and architecture at Princeton University and at the Cranbrook Academy of Art with EERO SAARINEN AND ELIEL SAARINEN. Following a partnership with HARRY WEESE, with whom he won several furniture design awards, Baldwin moved to New York. His interiors, notably the Yale Center for British Art (1974–1977) in New Haven and the Tandy Corporation Offices (1979) in Fort Worth, Texas, combine attention to detail with sumptuous materials in order to create refined spaces in harmony with each building.

JUDITH OBERLANDER

WORKS

1939, Fountains (with M. Labatut), New York World's Fair. 1953, John Danziger Ladies' Shop, Montgomery, Ala. 1959, Townhouse (conversion), Chicago. 1966, Benjamin Baldwin Apartment, New York. 1968, Ritz-Carlton Hotel Bar, Boston. 1969–1970, Benjamin Baldwin Residence, East Hampton, N.Y. 1970–1972, Phillips Academy Library and Dining Hall (interior), Exeter, N.H. 1974–1977, Yale Center for British Art (interior), New Haven. 1976, Benjamin Baldwin House, Sarasota, Fla. 1979, Tandy Corporation Executive Offices (interior), Fort Worth, Tex.

BIBLIOGRAPHY

ABERCROMBIE, STANLEY 1977 "Yale Center for British Art." *Contract Interiors* 136:52–59.

"The Americana, Fort Worth." 1981 *Interior Design* 52, no. 9:320–331.

"80 Year-Old Chicago Townhouse: Baldwin's Off Beat, Prize-Winning Conversion." 1960 *Interiors* 119:158–163.

"Finesse in Chicago: A Facile Design Team." 1956 *Interiors* 116:140–143.

"An Intuition for Space." 1976 *Architectural Digest* 32:108–113.

SMITH, C. R. 1979 "Spatial Harmony: A Center of Peace in the Middle of the City." *Architectural Digest* 36:140–145.

"Tandy Corporation: Executive Office Interiors." 1979 *Interior Design* 50:190–197.

"Three Architects Speak Their Minds." 1970 *House and Garden* 137:124.

"Three Houses Built for Summer." 1970 *House and Garden* 137:86–95.

BALLA, GIACOMO

Giacomo Balla (1871–1958), the Italian Futurist artist, was not an architect, but the designs he produced throughout his career greatly influenced the Futurist architectural movement. His first major project was murals in a Düsseldorf, Germany, home in 1912. Balla published manifestoes, including the 1914 "Antineutral Clothing," which urged the tailoring of "aggressive, energetic, luminous" apparel, appropriate to the Futurist's dynamic vision of the world. His most ambitious proposal, the 1915 "Futurist Reconstruction of the Universe" (coauthored with Fortunato Depero), prescribed the recreation of objects based on forms discovered through the analysis of speed and motion. Among these were kinetic, multimedia sculpture (called plastic complexes), furniture, wooden flowers, metal animals, and stage sets. Balla also collaborated on and wrote Futurist plays and films.

GERALD D. SILK

BIBLIOGRAPHY

BARRICELLI, ANNA 1966 *Balla.* Rome: De Luca.

DE MARCHIS, GIORGIO 1977 *Giacomo Balla: L'Aura Futurista.* Turin: Giulio Einaudi.

DORAZIO, VIRGINIA DORTCH 1970 *Giacomo Balla: An Album of His Life and Work.* New York: Wittenborn.

FAGIOLO DELL'ARCO, MAURIZIO 1970 *Futur Balla.* Rome: Mario Bulzoni.

GAMBILLO, MARIA DRUDI, and FIORI, TERESA 1958–1962 *Archivi del Futurismo.* Rome: De Luca.

KIRBY, MICHAEL 1971 *Futurist Performance.* New York: Dutton.

BALLU, THEODORE

A student of LOUIS H. LEBAS and winner of the Grand Prix de Rome in 1840, Théodore Ballu (1817–1885) was a highly successful conservative French architect during the Second Empire. After carrying out the Gothic designs of FRANZ CHRISTIAN GAU for Sainte-Clotilde (1853–1857), he produced his own eclectic, theatrical church of La Trinité (1861–1867) in Paris. His career closed with his rebuilding of the Hôtel de Ville (1874–1882) in Paris in a rich French Renaissance style.

ANN LORENZ VAN ZANTEN

WORKS

1853–1857, Sainte-Clotilde (completion; begun by Franz Christian Gau); 1858–1863, Tower of Saint-Germain l'Auxerrois; 1861–1867, La Trinité; 1862, Protestant Church of Saint-Esprit; 1863–1865, Saint-Ambroise; 1867–1874, Saint-Joseph; 1874–1882, Hôtel de Ville (rebuilding; with P. J. E. Deperthes); Paris.

BIBLIOGRAPHY

BALLU, THÉODORE 1868 *Monographie de l'église de la Sainte Trinité construite par la ville de Paris.* Paris: Dupuis.

DELABORDE, HENRI 1887 *Institut de France: Notice sur la vie et les ouvrages de M. Théodore Ballu, . . .* Paris: Firmin-Didot.

HAUTECOEUR, LOUIS 1957 *La fin de l'architecture classique.* Volume 7 in *Histoire de l'architecture classique en France.* Paris: Picard.

SEDILLE, PAUL 1886 *Théodore Ballu, architecte (1817–1885), notice lue dans la séance solennelle du congrès, des architectes français à l'Ecole nationale des beaux-arts, le 12 juin 1886.* Paris: Chaix.

BALTARD, LOUIS PIERRE

Louis Pierre Baltard (1764–1846) was an architect, painter, and engraver. During the French Revolution, he helped JULIEN DAVID LEROY save the School of Architecture. Later he taught at the Ecole des Beaux-Arts where one of his pupils was his son, Victor Baltard. His activities included stage design and engineering.

CHARLOTTE LACAZE

WORKS

1815–1818, Prisons of Saint Lazare and Saint Pelagie (chapels), Paris. 1828, Salt Storage House; 1830–1836, Prison of Saint Joseph in Perrache; 1836–1842, Palais de Justice (Courthouse); 1840–1846, Arsenal for the Artillery; Lyons, France.

BIBLIOGRAPHY

BALTARD, LOUIS-PIERRE 1818 *Grands Prix d'architecture, projets couronnés par l'Académie royale des beaux-arts de France, gravés et publiés par A. L. T. Vaudoyer et L. P. Baltard.* Paris.

BALTARD, LOUIS-PIERRE 1875 *Arc de triomphe du Carroussel édifié par Percier et Fontaine, gravés d'après leurs dessins, par Louis-Pierre Baltard, précédé d'un aperçu sur les monuments triomphaux, rédigé par Fontaine, et d'une notice sur l'arc du Carroussel tirée presque entièrement de ses mémoires manuscrits.* Paris: Claye.

EGBERT, DONALD DREW 1980 *The Beaux-Arts Tradition in French Architecture.* N.J.: Princeton University Press.

HAUTECOEUR, LOUIS 1952–1955 Volumes 4–6 in *Histoire de l'architecture classique en France.* Paris: Picard.

HITCHCOCK, H. R. (1958)1977 *Architecture: 19th and 20th Centuries.* 3d ed. Baltimore: Penguin.

KAUFMANN, EMIL (1955)1968 *Architecture in the Age of Reason.* Reprint. New York: Dover.

PÉROUSE DE MONTCLOS, JEAN-MARIE 1969 *Etienne-Louis Boullée.* Paris: Arts et Métiers Graphiques.

BALTARD, VICTOR

Victor Baltard (1805–1874) was the son of the purist neoclassical architect and professor of theory at the Ecole des Beaux-Arts LOUIS-PIERRE BALTARD. He attended the Ecole as a student of his father, winning the Grand Prix de Rome in 1833 with a severe design for a military academy. In Rome, he became a protégé of the painter J. A. D. Ingres and executed the *néo-grec* polychrome background of his *Antiochus and Stratonice.* Baltard's first great opportunity as a designer came in 1845, when he and Félix Callet were appointed architects of the proposed Halles Centrales for Paris. After extensive study of existing market buildings, the two submitted a project for a complex of eight massive stone pavilions which was approved in 1848. One of these pavilions was built between September 1851 and June 1853, but it was so derided by the vendors who used it that Napoleon III himself ordered construction halted. The emperor's desire for a "vast umbrella" to house the market was translated by his prefect, GEORGES-EUGÈNE HAUSSMANN, into a demand for an iron-and-glass structure similar to projects offered by other architects and engineers. Baltard finally acquiesced with a design for fourteen iron-and-glass pavilions connected by roofed streets and covering 87,790 square meters. Six of these were completed by 1858 and four more by 1870, while two were added in the 1930s. Baltard, a conservative by birth, education, and avowed inclination, was distressed by the lack of dignity of the materials he was forced to use, and his solution was clearly a result of a sense of duty rather than of conviction. Yet, he brought to the project an academic sense of axial organization and concern for circulation that ultimately contributed to the functional success of the complex. The Halles Centrales provided a model for numerous other market structures, but their own vast scale and location in the center of Paris doomed them to eventual demolition during urban renewal in 1973.

Baltard's friendship, dating from his youth, with Haussmann brought him the position of chief architect of the city of Paris under the Second Empire. In this capacity, he completed the Timbre National begun by Paul Lelong (1846–1850) and executed a complex for the archives, tax authority, and public works department of the city of Paris (with Félix Roguet; 1857–1858). Baltard particularly concerned himself with restorations and additions to a number of Parisian churches, continuing an interest established before the Second Empire. Saint-Germain-des-Prés, Saint-Germain l'Auxerrois, Saint-Eustache, and Saint-Leu incorporate the most original work by him. In 1862, Baltard commenced his one independent church commission, that for Saint-Augustin. Occupying a wedge-shaped site dramatically placed at the intersection of two boulevards, the church both monumentally marks a vista and provides a theatrical enclosure for bourgeois worship. Its stone exterior, an eclectic combination of Byzantine, Gothic, and baroque elements composed to adapt to the odd site, is reinforced by an armature of iron which is exposed and decoratively wrought on the interior. Criticized by classicists for being too radical in its forms and by rationalists for inappropriately combining materials, the church appears to the modern eye as a showy architectural hybrid, richly evocative of the society that created it. It also reflects more accurately than the Halles Centrales the agonies of a classicist's confrontation with new materials, changing historical sources, and an era of fickle taste.

ANN LORENZ VAN ZANTEN

WORKS

*1845–1870, Halles Centrales (with others); 1846–1850, Timbre National (completion); *1857–1858, Government Building Complex (with Félix Roguet); 1862–1868, Sainte-Augustin; Paris.

BIBLIOGRAPHY

BALTARD VICTOR, and CALLET, FÉLIX 1863 *Monographie des halles centrales de Paris construites sous le règne de Napoléon III.* Paris: Morel.

DECONCHY, M. F. 1875 *Victor Baltard, sa vie, ses oeuvres.* Paris: Ducher.

GARNIER, CHARLES 1874 *Notice sur Victor Baltard.* Paris: Didot.

HAUSSMANN, GEORGES-EUGÈNE 1890–1893 *Mémoires de Baron Haussmann.* 3 vols. Paris: Victor-Havard.

SÉDILLE, PAUL 1874 "Victor Baltard, architecte." *Gazette des Beaux-Arts* 9:485–496.

VAN ZANTEN, DAVID 1978 "Victor Baltard." In *The Second Empire: Art in France Under Napoleon III.* Philadelphia Museum of Art.

Baltard.
Halles Centrales.
Paris.
1845–1870 (with others).

BANDINELLI, BACCIO

Baccio Bandinelli (1493–1560) or, more fully, Bartolommeo di Michelangelo de'Bandi, was born in Florence, Italy, in 1493. His father deduced an early talent and apprenticed his son to the sculptor Francesco Rustici. His tenure with Rustici was spent copying the works of Donatello and Verochio. GIORGIO VASARI believed that he was associated with the return of the de' Medici to Florence in 1512. Bandinelli was under the protection of the de' Medici and their patronage afforded him the opportunity to execute several large-scale sculptural works. He received a very important commission in 1540 from Duke Cosimo to sculpt the monument to Giovanni delle Bande Nere, and was extremely jealous of MICHELANGELO, whom he constantly wished to surpass. The architectural elements for a new choir of the Cathedral of Florence were begun in 1547. Bandinelli was responsible for many of the reliefs decorating the new choir; particularly noteworthy was a series of prophet figures on the low wall of the central enclosure.

JEFFREY HUGHES

BIBLIOGRAPHY

AVERY, CHARLES 1970 *Florentine Renaissance Sculpture.* New York: Harper.

BANFI, BELGIOJOSO, PERESSUTTI, and ROGERS

Gian Luigi Banfi (1910–1945), Ludovico Belgiojoso (1900–), Enrico Peressutti (1908–1976), and Ernesto Nathan Rogers (1909–1969) formed a group with the initials BBPR in 1932, and they proposed to follow the direction of European Rationalism in their architecture. Rogers played a special role in the group with his activities as critic, newspaper contributor, lecturer, and promoter of international initiatives. Their interests were homogeneous and were distributed over a broad range of subjects, including urban studies and industrial design, not to mention their shared didactic interests; all of this helped consolidate their association. BBPR was one of the rare teams of Italian architects to make a substantial contribution to an international debate: during the prewar years, by sustaining and spreading the Rationalist message, and after the war, by showing how the crisis of Rationalism could be overcome by reference to history, from which would spring a relationship with the architecture of earlier times which was absolutely original in the panorama of Italian culture.

While they studied architecture at the Milan Polytechnic Institute, the four students, in contrast with the tendencies of the school, demonstrated a great interest in international developments in architecture. This interest emerged in their thesis projects (1932), where, along with some eclectic weaknesses, there were also some motifs that were to be better developed later. In the first projects from the BBPR studio, their faithfulness to the assumptions of the Modern movement was evident in particular references to the work of the "masters" of the Modern movement. Their solutions to developing a typical Casa del Fascio (in the lictoral competitions of 1932) present traces of monumentalism, although in the language of Rationalism; the Casa del Sabato for newlyweds (1933) referred to the work of WALTER GROPIUS as well as to that of LUDWIG MIES VAN DER ROHE and LE CORBUSIER; finally, in the project for the Palazzo del Littorio (1934), even EDOARDO PERSICO, although quite positive in his judgment, discerned a "wavering between the style of Gropius and that of Le Corbusier." In the Master Plan for Pavia (1932), the thesis of "corporative urbanism," derived from the Fascist theory of corporativism, was wedded to the principles of functionalist urbanism and in particular to the theories of Le Corbusier, from whom they acquired the idea of demolishing and "sanitizing" old urban centers. Although BBPR ignored the relationship between urban environment and monument in their proposal to isolate monuments along archeological walkways, the theme of the "museumification" of the city, or rather the attention to the architecture of earlier times which characterized BBPR's subsequent activities, had already begun to flower, BBPR ingenuously understood corporative urbanism to be an alternative to the uncontrolled growth of the city, and this also surfaced in their writings for the magazine *Quadrante,* on

which they collaborated beginning in 1933. They had bypassed the idea of corporative urbanism, after their collaboration with an enlightened patron, Adriano Olivetti (1936), in their work with other Italian architects on the master plan for Val d'Aosta. In the Feltrinelli House (1935), they affirmed the validity of the theme of the relationship between the individual and the environment, which was also to be a constant in their work: The motif of an "adherence to circumstances." With the restoration and enlargment of the Villa Venosta (1936), BBPR confronted for the first time a design problem upon which much of their subsequent interest turned, that of the rapport between the new and the old in a particular location. In the Colonia Elioterapica (1938), even though the architectural language clearly referred to European Rationalism, there is evidence of greater freedom of interpretation. The contemporaneous Post Office at EUR (1940), instead, is a work for the regime; the effort to overcome a certain monumentalism is more apparent in the competition for the Palazzo della Civiltà Italiana (1937). In the competition for Piazza Fiume (1937), the motif of the reticulum, already present in two earlier works, is interpreted in a more complex and free manner.

BBPR was interested from the beginning in the field of furnishings and exhibitions, because it responded to two profoundly felt needs: that of experimenting and obtaining immediate verification of results, and the integration of figurative arts and architecture. In this field as in that of architecture, we can discern the evolution of their poetic conception, which began with a rigorous attachment to Rationalism (Grillo Bar, 1932) and arrived at a greater experimentation with new languages (Marine Pavilion at the Paris International Exposition in 1937; scenography section of the Villa Olmi Exhibit, 1937; the Spiga and Corrente Galleries in Milan, 1940.

Toward the end of the 1930s, parallel with the ideological and political crisis which led the group to oppose Fascism (a turn which can also be seen in their architecture), they were also influenced by the work of ALVAR AALTO, and they began their experiments in an alternative language. Noteworthy in this respect are the Belsana Paper Mills (1940), the villa at Desenzano (1940); and the "ideal houses" (1942).

The war and their active participation in the Resistance were sorrowful experiences for the group: Peressutti went to the Russian front; Rogers was exiled to Switzerland; Belgiojoso and Banfi were deported to Mauthausen, Austria (1944), where Banfi died in 1945. Once the dramatic parenthesis of the war had closed, the studio began again in 1945 to resume their professional and cultural activities. Among other things, they helped draft the Master Plan for Milan(1945), picked up their contacts with the Congre's Internationaux d'Architecture Moderne (CIAM) again, to which they had belonged since 1935, and led in the formation of the MSA (Movimento Studi Architettura). After he had taught in London and at Harvard, Rogers was called to the Polytechnic Institute in Milan (1952); Peressutti taught courses at the most prestigious foreign universities until 1973; and Belgiojoso taught first in Venice (1954) and then in Milan (since 1963).

Among the first works of the postwar period, the memorial to those who died in German concentration camps should be noted (1946): the thin tubular trusses in iron are linked with prewar production and represent an acknowledgment of a moral and cultural debt to the tradition of Rationalism. This did not impede BBPR from surpassing the primitive positions of the modern movement with their resolution of the problem of the relationship of new works with older works of architecture, which they began to think of as "complementary moments" in the process of the historical formation of the city. In an editorial for the reborn *Casabella* in January 1954, Rogers clarified the group's attitude: continuity both with the Modern tradition as well as with the tradition of the built city which must be reworked. This turn to history did not entail a rejection of the Modern movement, but instead addressed the need to return to its origins through a recovery of the work of the "masters of the masters." Thus, the apparent abandonment of Rationalist orthodoxy (which can be seen in the USA pavilion at the Ninth Triennial in 1951, or in the pavilion in the royal park of the Royal Palace of Stupinigi) is justified precisely by the critical intention of returning to the sources of Rationalism and the recovery of such pioneers as AUGUSTE PERRET, HENRY VAN DE VELDE, ADOLF LOOS, VICTOR HORTA, and others. In New York in 1954, BBPR realized a store for Olivetti which summarizes many aspects of their creative tradition: continuity with memories of the rural tradition and current technological perfection; the integration of architecture and the figurative arts; and interest in design problems in general. The 1950s, in fact, marked a particular moment in the career of BBPR both for the quality of their work and for the interest and polemics which they provoked, especially with the restoration and systematization of the Castello Sforzesco (1956) and the well-known Torre Velasca (1956–1958). The former, despite their intention to have the museum fulfill its didactic function by making it accessible to the masses, excited huge polemical battles, with BBPR being accused of having been

incautious and intrusive and of having created a work which did violence to the objects on exhibit. The Torre Velasca is absolutely one of the group's most felicitous works; in it, the dialogue between the tradition of the new and the tradition of the city produces original results.

Toward the end of the 1950s, the group alternated between periods of great success and times of uncertainty and crisis. In general, they revealed an attitude of agnosticism and a yielding to the logic of Italy's dawning capitalism, which is especially apparent in the Milan Master Plan of 1958 and is confirmed by the interest in themes such as residential tourism (Capo Stella, 1960; Santa Margherita Ligure, 1960) and by the professional routine evident in the projects for low-cost housing (the housing quarters C.E.C.A. in Sesto San Giovanni and Loggetta in Naples, 1957, and Moriggia in Gallarate, 1957).

The early 1960s were characterized by a particular interest in design. After designing the Spanish headquarters for Olivetti in Barcelona (1965), it was not until 1969 that a work of particular vigor appeared. In the building in Piazzale Meda (1969), Milan, BBPR addressed the problem of the preexisting structures, and although their resolution lacked the conviction of the Torre Velasca, they managed to achieve forms that evoked ancient architecture with the typical materials of modern technology. This is the last work of the old BBPR group, of which only Belgiojoso remained after the deaths of Rogers and Peressutti. Belgiojoso now works with a large team and has dedicated himself to large international competitions and commissions, and in particular to planning in the Middle East, in addition to an involvement in the traditional areas of restoration and interior decoration. BBPR's unanimously recognized virtue is that of having created a language to serve as an alternative to the tired formulas of the Modern movement, but without denying its lessons and those of its masters, and indeed, linking up with them by means of the continuity of history.

CESARE DE' SETA
Translated from Italian by
Diane Ghirardo

WORKS

*1932, Grillo Bar (interior); *1933, Casa del Sabato (for newlyweds; with Piero Portaluppi); 1935, Casa Feltrinelli (with Alberico Belgiojoso); 1936, Villa Venosta (enlargement), Gornate Olona, Varese, Italy. *1937, Marine Pavilion, Paris International Exposition. *1937, Cinemagraphic Scenography Section, Exhibit of Italian Theater, Villa Olmi, Como, Italy. *1938, Colonia Elioterapica, Legnano, Italy. 1940, Belsana Paper Mills, Lera, Genoa, Italy. 1940, Post Office, E'42, Rome. *1940, Spiga and Corrente Galleries (interiors); 1945,

Milan Master Plan (with others); 1946, Memorial to the Dead in German Concentration Camps; *1951, United States of America Pavilion, IX Triennal; *1953, Stupinigi Palace (pavilion in the park), International Exposition of Fabrics and Fashion; Milan. 1954, Olivetti Exposition Store, New York. 1956, Castello Sforzesco (restoration and systematization); 1956–1958, Torre Velasca; Milan. 1957, Housing Quarter (Moriggia; for IACP), Varese, Italy. 1965, Offices (for Hispano Olivetti), Barcelona, Spain. 1969, Building, Piazza Meda, Milan.

BIBLIOGRAPHY

BELGIOJOSO, LUDOVICO 1979 *Intervista sul mestiere di architetto.* Edited by Cesare de'Seta. Rome: Laterza.
BONFANTI, EZIO, and PORTA, MARCO 1973 *Città museo e architettura: Il gruppo BBPR nella cultura architettonica italiana, 1932–1970.* Florence: Vallechi.
PACI, ENZO 1959 "Continuità e coerenza dei BBPR." *Zodiac* 4:82–115.
PONTI, GIO 1942 "Stile di BBPR." *Lo Stile* 22:11–18.
SINISGALLI, LEONARDO 1950 "Gli architetti BBPR." *Comunità* 8:12–18.

BARABINO, CARLO FRANCESCO

Carlo Francesco Barabino (1768–1835) was one of the Italian architects of the Napoleonic and post-Napoleonic era who owed their training to the pro-French milieu in the circle of the Accademia della Pace in Rome. As one of the most successful of these, he contributed substantially to the classicistic reshaping of the Italian cities between Naples and Venice. His training took place in various stages: from the Accademia ligustica in Genoa (1785) he moved on to the Accademia di San Luca in Rome (1788), where GIUSEPPE BARBARI introduced him to the full range of ideal architecture and architectural drawing and where he became acquainted with the world of antiquity, studied the architecture of the Thermae, and was drilled in academic subjects; finally came his participation in the competition of the Academy in Parma (1792). In his "Molo di Genova"—a pier intended as a monument to Christopher Columbus—for the Roman Accademia della Pace, he displayed a heroic style which he resumed in his early designs for ideal projects and in the competition project for the Madeleine in Paris (1807), in which the Pantheon and the Mausoleum of Halicarnassos are boldly merged into a supermonument. In 1797, in the *Repubblica Ligure Democratica* set up by the French Directoire Barabino took over as leading architect of the building committee, but he was replaced shortly thereafter, falling to second rank behind Gaetano Cantoni and Andrea E. Tagliafichi. During the Napoleonic years, he was occu-

pied with ideal designs, festival architecture (a triumphal arch for the reception of Napoleon in 1805), and with teaching in Genoa. In addition, under the auspices of the *Repubblica Cisalpina,* he was called on to contribute to the development of the Foro Bonaparte in Milan with his own projects and expert opinions. Only after the Restoration was Barabino given an opportunity to develop his talents fully. In 1818, he became architect of the city of Genoa. In this capacity, he put through architectural and urbanistic plans that were fitted to the needs of a modern city: regulating the traffic patterns, forming city squares, and setting up establishments for public needs from theaters to cemeteries and prisons. In all these works and in his involvements in secular and sacred architecture (Santo Siro, portico of the Nunziata), Barabino realized the classicist ideals to which he had been exposed during his training. This applies not only to his mastery of modern building types, such as the theater, but also, in equal measure, to his eclectic understanding of style. In addition to a correct command of the principles of ancient architecture, this grasp permitted the use of a great number of artistic motifs and means (aediculae, niches, friezes, rustication) to achieve an enrichment of the forms. Barabino's ability to deal with difficult urbanistic situations is documented by his main work, the Teatro Carlo Felice (1825–1832). Artistically, this building is linked to the Odeon of CHARLES DE WAILLY in Paris; however, the arrangement of its temple façade and portico have been adjusted to suit the actual orientation of the fronting plaza and to achieve integration into a complex urbanistic situation.

WERNER OECHSLIN
*Translated from German by
Beverley R. Placzek*

WORKS

1818–1821, Senarega Chapel, San Lorenzo; 1918, San Giro (façade); 1824–1826, Oratory of the Rosary; 1825–1832, Teatro Carlo Felice; Genoa, Italy.

BIBLIOGRAPHY

DeNEGRI, E. 1971 "Carlo Barbarino e il concurso per la Madeleine." *Quaderni dell'Istitutoedi Elementi di Architettura* 5:27ff.
DeNEGRI, E. 1977 *Ottocento e rinnovamento urbano: Carlo Barabino.* Genova, Italy: Saged.
MEZZANOTTE G. 1966 *Architettura neoclassica in Lombardia.* Naples, Italy: Scientifiche.

BARBER, DONN

Born in Washington, Donn Barber (1871–1925) spent his professional life in New York. He studied at Yale University, Columbia University, and the Ecole des Beaux-Arts in Paris. Barber helped develop the atelier concept in the United States and formed the Atelier Donn Barber in New York. He was president of the Society of Beaux-Arts Architects (1909–1910), and editor of *The Architectural Yearbook* (1912) and of *The New York Architect* for four years.

PATRICIA C. PHILLIPS

WORKS

1900, Connecticut State Supreme Court, Hartford. 1910, Institute of Musical Art of the City of New York. ?–1917, Central Branch, Young Men's Christian Association, New York. 1923, New York Cotton Exchange. n.d., Department of Justice Building, Washington.

BIBLIOGRAPHY

BARBER, DONN (editor) 1912 Volume 1 in *The Architectural Yearbook*. New York: Baker.
"Obituary." 1925 *New York Times* May 30.
SKY, ALISON, and STONE, MICHELLE 1976 *Unbuilt America*. New York: McGraw.

BARBERI, GIUSEPPE

Painter and architect, Giuseppe Barberi (1749–1809), became a member of the Accademia di San Lucca in 1787. His project for Palazzo Braschi, with forty-two shops at the ground level, was criticized as inappropriate by the press. Beside the four ceremonial apartments of the family, the palace also contained eight apartments for rent.

While the grandeur and ornamentation of his buildings and the large dimensions of his urban designs showed acquaintance with the work of GIOVANNI ANTONIO ANTOLINI and of Giani, he also reminded contemporaries of the work of FRANCESCO BORROMINI. The drawings in his 1796 manuscript are annotated with his self-criticism.

MARTHA POLLAK

WORKS

1777, Villa Altieri (works), Rome. 1783, San Giorgio, Oriolo Romano, Italy.

BIBLIOGRAPHY

BARBERI, GIUSEPPE 1796 "Pal. Reale in stile borrominiano fatto in questo anno 1796." Unpublished manuscript, Bibliotheca Archaeologia e storia d'arte, Rome.
BERLINER, RUDOLF 1965 "Zeichnungen der römischen Architekten Giuseppe Barberi." *Münchner Jahrbuch der Bildenden Kunst* 16:165–216.
FASOLO, F. 1962 "Contributo alla conoscenza dell'opera dell'architetto Giuseppe Barberi: La chiesa di S. Giorgio in Oriolo Romano." *Quaderni ISAR* 52–53:24–40.

FISCHER, MANFRED K. 1969 "Studien zur Planungs- und Baugeschichte des Palazzo Braschi in Rom." *Römisches Jahrbuch für Kunstgeschichte* 12:95–104, 132–135.

BARBERIS, LUIGI MICHELE

Luigi Michele Barberis (1725–1798) was born and died in Turin, Italy, where he was a student and assistant of BENEDETTO ALFIERI. Among his many commissions are the Chapel of Sant' Eusebio in the Cathedral of Vercelli (1763–1783); the Villa Viarana at San Maurizio Canavese (1769); San Giuseppe at Vercelli (1769); and the Palazzo Vallesa in Turin (1783). There are echoes of BERNARDO ANTONIO VITTONE as well as of Alfieri in his work.

HENRY A. MILLON

WORKS

1763–1783, Chapel of San Eusebio, Cathedral; 1769, San Giuseppe; Vercelli, Italy. 1769, Villa Viarana, San Maurizio Canavese, Italy. 1783, Palazzo Vallesa, Turin, Italy.

BIBLIOGRAPHY

BERNARDI, MARZIANO 1950 *Il Palazzo Vallesa*. Turin, Italy: Editrice Torinese.
BRAYDA, CARLO; COLI, LAURA; and SESIA, DARIO 1963 *Ingegneri e architetturi del sei e settecento in piemonte*. Turin, Italy: Società Ingegneri e Architetti.
CARBONERI, NINO 1963 Volume I, pages 83–85 in *Architettura, Mostra del Barocco Piemontese*. Turin, Italy: Catalogo a cura di Vittorio Viale.
CHICCO, GIUSEPPE 1943 *Memorie del Vecchio duomo di Vercelli, sua Demolizione e Successiva Ricostruzione*. Vercelli, Italy: Gallardi.
MILLON, HENRY A. 1967 "Michelangelo Garove and the Chapel of the Beato Amedeo of Savoy in the Cathedral of Vercelli." Pages 134–142 in *Essays in the History of Architecture presented to Rudolf Wittkower*. London: Phaidon.
OLIVERO, EUGENIO 1937 *Miscellanea di architettura Piemontese del settecento*. Turin, Italy: Bouis.

BARBIER, FRANÇOIS

François Barbier studied at the French Academy from 1764 to 1765. An architect and technical consultant on gardens and individual structures in gardens, which he designed in the fantastic and theatrical manner of LOUIS CARROGIS CARMONTELLE, he is best known for his work at the Désert de Retz (1774) for François-Nicolas-Henri Racine de Monville.

DORA WIEBENSON

WORKS

1774, Désert de Retz (garden structures, including the Chinese pavilion, according to owner's design), near

Marly, France. n.d., Hôtel de la Rochefoucauld Garden; n.d., Hôtel de Thélusson Gardens; Paris.

BIBLIOGRAPHY

CHOPPIN DE JANVRY, OLIVIER 1970 "Le Désert de Retz." *Bulletin de la Société de l'Histoire de l'Art Français* 1970:125–148.
GALLET, MICHEL 1964 Pages 44, 98, 172 in *Demeures Parisiennes à l'époque de Louis XVI*. Paris: Le Temps.

BARBON, NICHOLAS

Nicholas Barbon (1638?–1698) was a speculator, chiefly in urban development in London but also in associated schemes of fire insurance, banking, and market building. He rebuilt some thirty sites after the Great Fire of 1666, then expanded into the suburbs, refining the technique of development by building lease and standardizing the house plan and its details. Early speculations in London were profitable, but overambitious site acquisition in the 1680s, particularly in Holborn (more than fifty acres taken from five different landowners) brought financial difficulties in the 1690s. Building at his own house of Osterley (1690) was his only nonspeculative venture.

FRANK KELSALL

WORKS

1669, 5 and 6 Crane Court; 1675–1676, Essex House Estate; 1675–1682, Devonshire House Estate; 1675–1685, New Court, Essex Court, Vine Court, Elm Court, Pump Court, and Cloisters, Middle Temple; 1676–1679, Exeter House Estate and Exeter Exchange; 1677–1685, Military Ground, Newport House Estate, and Newport Market; 1685–?, Red Lion Fields, Conduit Shott, Lambs Conduit Fields, and Saint Clement Danes Charity Estate, Holborn; London. 1690, Osterley Park (alterations), Middlesex, England. 1691–1694, New Square, Lincoln's Inn, London.

BIBLIOGRAPHY

BARBON, NICHOLAS (1685)1976 *An Apology for the Builder.* Reprint. New York: Scholarly.
BRETT-JAMES, NORMAN G. 1935 *The Growth of Stuart London.* London: Allen and Unwin.
JONES, P. E., and REDDAWAY, T. F. 1967 *The Survey of Building Sites in the City of London after the Great Fire of 1666.* London Topographical Society Publications, vol. 1.
KELSALL, A. F. 1974 "The London House Plan in the Later 17th Century." *Post-medieval Archaeology* 8:80–91.
LETWIN, WILLIAM (1963)1975 *The Origins of Scientific Economics.* London: Methuen.
SIMS, J. M. 1972 "The Trust Lands of the Fire Office." *The Guildhall Miscellany* 4:88–113.
SUMMERSON, JOHN (1945)1978 *Georgian London.* 3d ed. London: Barrie and Jenkins.

BARCHTCH, M.

M. Barchtch (1904–1976) was born and lived in the Soviet Union. He belonged to the Union of Contemporary Architects, the Constructivists who fought for the principles of modern architecture which they thought to be one of the elements of the "Reconstruction of the Way of Life," one of the major goals of Soviet social planning in the 1920s. This "reconstruction" meant the collectivization of most functions until then performed within the family cell: meal preparation, laundry, child rearing, and so on. For Barchtch as for all the members of the Constructivist movement, architecture was one of the tools of this reconstruction. He was one of the rare Soviet architects whose allegiance to the modern movement did not mean the end of all activities under the Stalin regime as it developed in the early 1930s. Thus, he projected model schools for Moscow in 1939–1940. After World War II, Barchtch was a member of the team in charge of the reconstruction of the center of Minsk designed in the new Stalinist "classical" style. But he went back to modern forms when the Stalinist "classical revival" was condemned by Nikita Khrushchev in 1953. The Museum of Cosmonautics in Kaluga (1967) is characteristic of this new turn in Barchtch's career and reminds one of his first major work, the Moscow Planetarium (1927).

ANATOLE KOPP

WORKS

1927, Moscow Planetarium (with N. Siniavski); 1929–1930, Communal House, Gogol Boulevard; Moscow. 1967, Museum of Cosmonautics, Kaluga, Russia.

BIBLIOGRAPHY

KOPP, ANATOLE (1967)1970 *Town and Revolution.* Translated by Thomas Burton. New York: Braziller.

BARLOW, W. H.

William Henry Barlow (1812–1902) was a civil engineer associated with the Railway Age. Born in Charlton in southeast London, he trained in the nearby Woolwich dockyard and then at London Docks. After six years in Turkey, he returned in 1838 to become assistant engineer to the Manchester and Birmingham Railway. In 1842, he joined the future Midland Railway, building in 1862–1869 the southern portion of their line to London, including the terminus at Saint Pancras (with Roland Mason Ordish, 1863–1865, opened 1868). An immense, pointed, iron-and-glass tunnel vault, 100-feet high, it remained, at 243 feet, the widest span for twenty-five years and was much copied. Barlow also advised on cathedral restoration and published much on structural problems. He was president of the Institution of Civil Engineers and a Fellow of the Royal Society.

A. P. QUINEY

WORKS

1860–1864, Clifton Suspension Bridge (completion; with John Hawkshaw), Bristol, England. 1863–1865, Train Shed (with Roland Mason Ordish), Saint Pancras Station, London. 1882–1887, Tay Bridge, Scotland.

BIBLIOGRAPHY

"Obituary of W. H. Barlow." 1902–1903 *Minutes of the Proceedings of the Institution of Civil Engineers* 151:388–400.

BARNES, EDWARD LARABEE

Edward Larabee Barnes (1915–) established his architectural office in New York in 1949. Born in Chicago, he studied architecture at Harvard University (1938–1942). He has designed a broad range of buildings and projects including museums, commercial, religious, office, and academic buildings, housing complexes, and master and campus plans. In addition to his design work, he has taught at Pratt Institute in Brooklyn (1954–1959) and Yale University (1957–1964) and served as vice-president of the American Academy in Rome (1972). Barnes's work is admired for its restraint and its sensitivity to site and materials.

PATRICIA C. PHILLIPS

WORKS

1960, El Monte Housing Complex, San Juan. 1963, Neiman–Marcus Shopping Center, Fort Worth, Texas. 1971, Walker Art Center, Minneapolis, Minn. 1979–?, International Business Machines Building, New York.

BIBLIOGRAPHY

This article is based in part on materials owned by and conversations with Susan H. Harris of Edward Larabee Barnes Associates.

"The Architecture of Edward Larabee Barnes." 1979 *Journal* June:9–29. Available in Edward Larabee Barnes's office.

SKY, ALISON, and STONE, MICHELLE 1976 *Unbuilt America.* New York: McGraw.

BARONCELLO, GIOVANNI FRANCESCO

Giovanni Francesco Baroncello (?–1694) was an assistant to AMEDEO DI CASTELLAMONTE from 1673 to 1683. At Castellamonte's death, he assumed direction of much of Castellamonte's work. In 1684, he began to work for the prince of Carignano on the Castello of Racconigi and the Palace in Turin. In 1683, the Palazzo Graneri was begun, perhaps on Baroncello's designs. He was the supervisor of construction, but it is also attributed to Castellamonte and to MICHELANGELO GAROVE. In 1692, Baroncello began work on the entrance, stair, and grand salon of the Palazzo di Druent. Baroncello's work, like that of his contemporaries, shows the influence of both GUARINO GUARINI and Castellamonte.

HENRY A. MILLON

WORKS

(A)1683–1694, Palazzo Graneri (not completed until 1702), Turin, Italy. 1684, Sanctuary of Santa Maria del Pilone, Moretta, Italy. 1692–1693, Palazzo di Druent (Palazzo Barolo; atrium, stair, and grand salon), Turin, Italy.

BIBLIOGRAPHY

BRAYDA, CARLO; COLI, LAURA; and SESIA, DARIO 1963 *Ingegneri e architetti del sei e settecento in piemonte.* Turin, Italy: Società Ingegneri e Architetti.

CARBONERI, NINO 1963 Volume 1, pages 36–37 in *Architettura: Mostra del Barocco Piemontese.* Turin, Italy: Catalogo a cura di Vittorio Viale.

MILLON, HENRY A. 1967 "Michaelangelo Garove and the Chapel of the Beato Amedeo of Savoy." Pages 134–142 in D. Fraser; Howard Hibbard; and M. Lewine (editors), *Essays in the History of Architecture presented to Rudolf Wittkower.* London: Phaidon.

BARRAGÁN, LUIS

Born and raised on a ranch near Guadalajara, Mexico, Luis Barragán (1901–) has tried to recreate the serenity and beauty of his childhood surroundings through a romantic approach to landscape architecture. After graduating in civil engineering from the University of Guadalajara, he turned his interest toward architecture and traveled to Europe attending lectures by LE CORBUSIER and talking with the French intellectual, painter, and landscape architect Ferdinand Bac. Unlike his contemporaries, he discarded Le Corbusier's theories and those of the International school for Bac's which focused upon the garden as a magical elusive environment. Before returning to Mexico, he visited Greece where he became enamored with the simplicity of common village dwellings, and in Spain he found his ideal, the Alhambra, a walled-in Moorish garden with fountains of running water.

He resumed his familial responsibilities on the ranch until 1936 when he moved to Mexico City to devote himself to the creation of peaceful environments. Determined to follow his own aspirations rather than adapting to the whims of his clients, he purchased 865 acres of lava desert in 1944 and built the subdivision El Pedregal (1945–1950) in Mexico City, predicated on a love of privacy and respect for nature. Each house occupied no more than ten percent of walled-in plots, and lava was the main building material. The addition of waterfalls and landscaping enhanced the inherent beauty of the site.

Sensitive to cultural traditions and modern aesthetics, he has employed adobe, stucco, unfinished wood, and cobblestones for his many gardens and homes, which reflect the starkness of village architecture highlighted by intense colors. At his San Cristobal residence (1967–1968) in Mexico City, modular slabs surrounded by pools of shallow water conjure up images of Mexico's open-air churches of the seventeenth and eighteenth centuries, the aqueducts of his youth, or possibly twentieth-century minimalist sculpture.

Barragán's uncanny ability to create quietude through landscaping and architecture while exploiting the beauties of Mexico has brought him international recognition, the most recent being the 1979 International Pritzker Architectural Prize.

ELIZABETH D. HARRIS

WORKS

1928, Enrique Aguilar House; 1929, Playground, Parque de la Revolucion; Guadalajara, Mexico. 1936–1940, Apartment Building, Plaza Melchor O Campo; 1945–1950, El Pedregal (landscaping and residential plan); Mexico City. 1947, Barragán House, Tacubaya, Mexico. 1957, Towers of Satellite City (with Mathias Goeritz), Queretaro Highway; 1958–1961, *Las Arboledas* Residential Subdivision; 1967–1968, San Cristobal (stable, horse pool, swimming pool, and house; with Andréas Casillas); Mexico City. 1976, Gilardi House, Tacubaya, Mexico.

BIBLIOGRAPHY

AMBASZ, EMILIO 1976 *The Architecture of Luis Barragán.* New York: Museum of Modern Art.
BAKER, A. T. 1980 "Mexico's Master of Serenity." *Time* 115, May:12, 50.

BARRE, JEAN BENOÎT VINCENT

Jean Benoît Vincent Barré (c.1732–1824), after having attended the school of the French Académie d'Architecture, inherited the clientele of AN-TOINE MATHIEU LE CARPENTIER and worked in particular for financiers. The *hôtel* he built for Grimod de La Reynière at the entrance to the Champs Elysées (1769) was demolished to make room for the United States Embassy. The house remains known through Barré's beautiful renderings. Such is the case of the *hôtels* d'Aubeterre and d'Harvelay, also demolished, which apparently were built by Barré at the expense of J. J. de La Borde in the district of the rue de la Chaussée d'Antin.

A kinder fate saved the châteaux. That of Montgeoffroy in Anjou (1771–1776) was built according to Barré's plans by a local architect named Simier for the elderly Maréchal de Contades and his friend, Madame Hérault. The beautiful arrangement of the ground floor of Montgeoffroy is the result of four individuals, each possessing a difficult personality, who managed to overcome their discord. In the Loire valley, Barré completed the château du Lude for Madame de La Vieuville in a spirit evocative of the Renaissance. In his parc de Méréville, Monsieur de La Borde entrusted Barré with the construction of a round Corinthian temple, which has since been moved to the parc de Jeurre. For Monsieur d'Ivry, Barré remodeled the château d'Hénonville, near Beauvais. Above all, he built for Monsieur le Maître the sumptuous château du Marais in the Remarde valley south of Paris. Called to Brussels, Barré there constructed the French legation and later submitted plans for the Place Royale and the church of Saint Jacques de Coudenberg which were interpreted by the architects Barnabé Guimard and Fisco.

Barré presented himself but never obtained membership in the Académie d'Architecture. Rich and well-executed, his work is that of a skilled architect, at the same time eclectic and traditional. However, it offers worthy evidence of the domestic planning and decoration favored by the French aristocracy at the end of the *ancien régime*.

GÉRARD ROUSSET-CHARNY
Translated from French by
Richard Cleary

WORKS

*1769, Hôtel Grimod de La Reynière, Champs Elysées, Paris. 1771–1776, Château Montgeoffroy (Barré's design executed by Simier), Anjou, France. n.d., Château d'Hénonville (remodeling), near Beauvais, France. n.d., Château de Lude, Loire Valley, France. n.d., Château du Marais, Remarde Valley, France. n.d., French Legation, Brussels. *n.d., Hôtel d'Aubeterre; *n.d., Hôtel d'Harvelay; Rue de la Chaussée d'Antin, Paris.

BIBLIOGRAPHY

LETELLIER, DOMINIQUE 1979 "Montgeoffroy: Un château angevin du début du règne de Louis XVI." *Arts de l'Ouest* 6:1–36.

BARREAU DE CHEFDEVILLE, FRANÇOIS

François Barreau de Chefdeville (1725–1765), a Parisian by birth, took first place in the *Prix de Rome* in 1749 and sojourned in Italy from 1752 to 1756. He was a subscriber to the ideas of Sir WILLIAM CHAMBERS's *Treatise on the Decorative Part of Civil Architecture* (1759) and a founder of the early French neoclassical revival.

In Paris, he designed a private chamber, later destroyed, for the house of the nobleman La Live de Jully, which was furnished by Joseph Le Lorrain. The La Live Cabinet, as it is called, was the origin of the Greek Revival in France.

He worked on the Palais Bourbon (1762), which was completed by ANTOINE MATHIEU LE CARPENTIER: a palace that is huge beyond measure, noble, unembellished. Today the building is occupied by the French National Assembly.

For the Intendant of Guienne, he designed a number of projects, some of them megalomaniacal, none of them accomplished: among them, the architectural setting for the Intendancy, in what would later be a Louis XVI style. He began the Church of Saint Nicolas of Nérac (1762), which would be completed under Napoleon III: four colossal pilasters supporting a frieze between two bell towers—a successful pseudo-Palladian building, unique in the France of its time. The new style rapidly penetrated to the provinces.

FRANÇOIS-GEORGES PARISET
Translated from French by Richard Koffler

WORKS

1762, Palais Bourbon, Paris. 1762, Saint Nicolas, Nérac, France.

BIBLIOGRAPHY

ERIKSEN, SVEND 1974 *Early Neo-classicism in France.* London: Faber.
PARISET, FRANÇOIS-GEORGES 1962 "L'architecte Barreau de Chefdeville." *Bulletin de la Société de l'Histoire de l'Art français* 1962:77–99.
PARISET, FRANÇOIS-GEORGES (editor) 1968 *Bordeaux au XVIII. siècle.* Volume 5 in *Histoire de Bordeaux.* Bordeaux, France: Fédération historique de Sud-Ouest.
PARISET, FRANÇOIS-GEORGES 1969 "L'église Saint Nicolas de Nérac." *Congrès archéologique de France: Agenais* 127:120–124.

BARRY, CHARLES

Charles Barry (1795–1860), knighted in 1852, was born in Westminster within a stone's throw of the site of his masterpiece, the Houses of Parliament.

At the age of fifteen he was articled to Middleton and Bailey, architects and surveyors, of Lambeth. In his six years with them, Barry received a sound training in professional practice, while finding time for drawings that were exhibited at the Royal Academy.

In June 1817, Barry set out on a continental tour, financed by a legacy from his father, that took him to France, Italy, Greece, and Turkey. In August 1818, he was about to return home when a traveler he had met in Athens, David Baillie, offered him £200 a year and expenses for his company and sketches on a tour of Egypt and Syria. Barry thus became the first English architect to visit Egypt, and this distinction brought him important contacts when he returned to Rome in January 1820, among them the third marquess of Lansdowne, who advanced his career by introducing him to the Holland House circle of Whig aristocrats. He also met John Lewis Wolfe, who became a close friend. It was with Wolfe, and in large measure thanks to him, that Barry made a careful study of Renaissance buildings in Rome, Florence, and northern Italy, which proved infinitely more important for his (and English) architecture than the Egyptian experience.

Barry owed his first two public commissions, for the Gothic churches of Saint Matthew, Campfield, Manchester (1822–1825) and All Saints, Stand, Lancashire (1822–1826), to Sir JOHN SOANE's recommendations. The churches were built under the so-called "Million Act" of 1818, by which Parliament had voted a million pounds for building churches as prophylactics against revolution. The commissioners who administered the act favored Gothic over Greek on the ground of cost. Plaster-vaulted, galleried boxes of practically identical design except that the west tower at Campfield was surmounted by a spire, they were better than most of the "Commissioners' Churches," but hardly outstanding. Of the seven other Gothic churches built to Barry's designs in the 1820s, Saint Peter's, Brighton, Sussex (1823–1828), was the most original.

In 1824 Barry won a limited competition for the design of the Royal Institution of Fine Arts in Manchester. Completed in 1835, the Manchester City Art Gallery (as it is now known) is one of the finest Greek Revival buildings in England. Although the order is Ionic, it has a weightiness and plasticity which make it Doric or perhaps even Egyptian in spirit. Admiration for it led Thomas Potter (later the first Mayor of Manchester) to commission Barry to design a Greek villa at Pendleton, Lancashire. Buile Hill (1825–1827; now much altered as the Salford Natural History Museum) was Barry's last Greek Revival building.

Before its completion he had already initiated the Renaissance Revival in England with a small church in a *quattrocento* manner, the Brunswick Chapel at Hove, Sussex (1827–1828). In 1829–1830, he followed this with a villa at Brighton, Sussex, for a solicitor, Thomas Attree, which was distinguished from earlier "Italian villas" by its symmetry and its terraced garden. He also won the competition for a London clubhouse with what was to prove one of the most influential designs of the century.

The Travellers' Club (1829–1832, completed with the addition of the smoking tower in 1843) was the first English imitation of an astylar *palazzo* of the High Renaissance. No one building served as a model; surviving drawings show that such resemblance as the street front may have to the Palazzo Pandolfini (c. 1520–1527) in Florence appeared late in the development of the design and that the garden front was originally to have been strongly Venetian. The Travellers' Club was greatly admired from the first and in 1839 W. H. Leeds made it the subject of a monograph, which was soon pirated in France. By then Barry had employed the *palazzo* formula in two more clubhouses, the Athenaeum in Manchester (1836–1839, now the annex to the City Art Gallery), and the Reform Club (1837–1841) next to the Travellers' in London. The Reform Club is a reduced version of the Palazzo Farnese (begun in 1517) in Rome, less MICHELANGELO's top story. Its great novelty was the central hall with its partly glazed roof. Barry's competition design showed a *cortile* open to the sky; he took the idea of roofing it over with glass and iron from C. R. COCKERELL, since the successful competitor was allowed to adopt features from the others' designs.

In 1836 Barry won the greatest architectural competition of the nineteenth century—that for the new Houses of Parliament at Westminster to replace those destroyed by fire in 1834. According to the terms of the competition, published in June 1835, designs had to be Gothic or Elizabethan. A select committee of Parliament chose four designs from the ninety-seven submitted and passed them on to William IV for his final choice. In the preparation of the competition design (and again in 1844–1852) Barry had the inestimable advantage of the paid assistance of A. W. N. PUGIN, who had already worked for him on King Edward VI's Grammar School at Birmingham (1833–1837), with his unrivaled facility in the production of Gothic detail. The plan of the Houses of Parliament, however, was Barry's, and the form and distribution of Pugin's ornament were controlled by Barry following principles of his own. For more than twenty years Barry supervised the work, bat-

*Barry.
Travellers' Club.
London.
1829–1832*

tling for his design and his integrity as an architect with committees and commissions and consultants as well as for reasonable remuneration, which he never got, with the Treasury. The foundation stone was laid in 1840, and in 1847, the Lords moved into their new chamber. After the Commons moved into theirs in 1852, Queen Victoria made her first state entry through the Victoria Tower. The building was at last completed by the architect's son, Edward Middleton Barry, in 1870.

On the architectural character of the Houses of Parliament there is an often quoted remark by Pugin: "All Grecian, sir! Tudor details on a classic body." Pugin was passing in his boat at the time, and it is true that the river front, with its symmetry and terminal emphases, is thoroughly classical in composition. But, as H. R. Hitchcock has pointed out, it is rarely seen from a viewpoint that makes its symmetry noticeable. Even then, the over-all symmetry is destroyed by the two asymmetrically placed towers, the Victoria Tower and the Clock Tower (which alone of all the major features of the building owes its form to Pugin). Besides being a functional masterpiece, the Houses of Parliament are the culminating work of the Picturesque movement, a building for all seasons, all lights, and all distances, while they have, in T. S. R. Boase's happy phrase, "the symbol-making greatness."

From the mid-1830s the remodeling and enlargement of existing buildings formed a large part of Barry's practice. His first work of the kind was an Italianization of GEORGE DANCE THE YOUNGER's Royal College of Surgeons, London (1833–1837); its *cinquecento* austerity is in strong contrast to the baroque richness of his transformation of Soane's Board of Trade (1844–1846). "Richness" and "grandeur" were the qualities sought in his many country house "conversions," as his biographer–son termed them. Most of these, including Bowood House, Wiltshire (1834–1838), Trentham Hall, Staffordshire (1834–1849), Walton House, Walton-on-Thames, Surrey

(1835–1839), and Shrubland Park, Suffolk (1849–1854), were Italianate; Highclere Castle, Hampshire (1842–1850), which was Barry's favorite, is Elizabethan; Canford Manor, Dorset (1848–1852) is in the Tudor Gothic of the house by EDWARD BLORE that Barry was called upon to enlarge, and Cliveden, Buckinghamshire (1850–1851), is in the style of its burned seventeenth-century predecessor on the same site.

Barry rarely remodeled a country house without giving it a new setting of the kind he had first designed for the Attree villa. Inspired by the formal gardens of Italy and France—Versailles in particular—these "architectural gardens," as he called them, earned Barry a prominent place in the history of landscape design. Trafalgar Square, London, which Barry laid out in 1840, is an urban counterpart that would be an even closer one if he had achieved his ambition of enlarging the National Gallery.

Of the relatively few works built from the ground up to Barry's design during the last twenty years of his life, the church at Hurstpierpoint, Sussex (1841–1843), was the one church in which he followed the prescription of the High Church liturgical reformers who called themselves ecclesiologists, with a cruciform plan, a deep chancel, and fourteenth-century Gothic detail. In Bridgewater House, London (1845–1850), in plan an enlarged Reform Club, he demonstrated how far the contemporary taste for richness could be indulged without abandoning the astylar *palazzo* formula. Barry was a great lover of towers—they are features of most of his country house conversions—and his last building, the Town Hall at Halifax, Yorkshire (1859–1860), has a tower and spire of extraordinary originality. Except for the spire, Halifax Town Hall is strictly Renaissance in detail; in its proportions and the emphasis on verticality it recalls Flemish town halls of the late Gothic period, while its controlled exuberance makes it one of the finest buildings of High Victorian classicism.

Barry does not stand in the very front rank of English architects with INIGO JONES, CHRISTOPHER WREN, JOHN VANBRUGH, and Soane, but he was one of the great English architects of the generation that came to artistic maturity around 1830. His chief rival, Cockerell, did not have his mastery of plan or his feeling for what the French eighteenth-century theorists called *caractère*, the style for the job, as his design for the Reform Club shows with its plethora of staircases and overgrand Berninesque façade. Barry's reputation suffered for several decades because of the silly controversy, started by Pugin's son, EDWARD W. PUGIN, in 1878, about the identity of the "art architect" of the Houses of Parliament. More recently he has been criticized for lack of taste, largely because of his country house conversions. Certainly it was sometimes regrettable, but other architects were doing equally regrettable things to Gothic churches in the name of restoration. At least Barry's criteria were aesthetic, not archeological; he never ceased to be an architect. Affable yet shrewd, he liked to please his clients when he could; when he could not, he usually managed to get his own way—even, though the effort probably shortened his life, when the client was the British government. Two of his sons, Charles and EDWARD MIDDLETON BARRY, became architects, and JOHN GIBSON and G. SOMERS CLARKE achieved prominence in the profession after being trained in his office.

MARCUS WHIFFEN

WORKS

*1822–1825, Church of Saint Matthew's, Campfield, Manchester, England. 1822–1826, Church of All Saints', Stand, Lancashire, England. 1823–1828, Saint Peter's, Brighton, England. 1824–1835, Royal Institution of Fine Arts (now the City Art Gallery), Manchester, England. 1825–1827, Buile Hill, Pendleton, Lancashire, England. 1827–1828, Brunswick Chapel, Hove, Sussex, England. 1829–1830, Thomas Attree Villa, Brighton, England. 1829–1832, Travellers' Club, London. *1833–1837, King Edward VI's Grammar School, Birmingham, England. 1833–1837, Royal College of Surgeons (alterations), London. *1834–1838, Bowood House (alterations, additions, and gardens), Wiltshire, England. *1834–1849, Trentham Hall (additions and gardens), Staffordshire, England. *1835–1839, Walton House (additions), Walton-on-Thames, Surrey, England. 1835–1860, Houses of Parliament, London (completed by his son Edward Middleton Barry in 1870). 1836–1839, Athenaeum, Manchester, England. 1837–1841, Reform Club; 1840, Trafalgar Square, London. 1841–1843, Hurstpierpoint Church, Sussex, England. 1842–1848, British Embassy, Istanbul, Turkey. 1842–c.1850, Highclere Castle, Hampshire, England. 1843–1850, Harewood House (alterations and gardens), Yorkshire, England. 1844–1846, Board of Trade (enlargement and remodeling), London. 1844–1848, Dunrobin Castle (reconstruction with W. Leslie), Sutherland, England. 1845–1847, 12, 18–19, and 20, Kensington Palace Gardens; 1845–1850, Bridgewater House; London. 1848–1852, Canford Manor (additions), Dorset, England. 1849–1854, Shrubland Park (additions, alterations, and gardens), Suffolk, England. 1850–1851, Cliveden House and Gardens, Buckinghamshire, England. 1859–1860, Town Hall, Halifax, Yorkshire, England (not completed until 1862 with an interior by Edward Middleton Barry).

BIBLIOGRAPHY

BARRY, ALFRED (1867)1970 Memoir of the Life and Works of the Late Sir Charles Barry. 2d ed. London: John Murray.
BINNEY, MARCUS 1969 "The Travels of Sir Charles Barry." Country Life (London) 146:494–498, 550–552, 622–624.
BOASE, THOMAS SHERRER ROSS 1959 English Art 1800–1870. Oxford: Clarendon.
FLEETWOOD-HESKETH, PETER 1964 "Sir Charles Barry." In Peter Ferriday (editor), Victorian Architecture. Philadelphia and New York: Lippincott.
HITCHCOCK, H. R. (1954)1972 Early Victorian Architecture in Britain. 2 vols. Reprint. New York: Da Capo.
LEEDS, WILLIAM HENRY 1839 The Travellers' Club House. London: Weale.
PORT, MICHAEL HARRY 1973 "The New Houses of Parliament." In volume 6 in H. M. Colvin (editor), The History of the King's Works. London: Her Majesty's Stationery Office.
PORT, MICHAEL HARRY (editor) 1976 The Houses of Parliament. New Haven and London: Yale University Press.
WHIFFEN, MARCUS 1950 The Architecture of Sir Charles Barry in Manchester and Neighbourhood. Manchester, England: Royal Manchester Institution.

BARRY, EDWARD M.

Edward Middleton Barry (1830–1880) was born in London in 1830, the third son of CHARLES BARRY. While still in his twenties he achieved prominence with the Royal Opera House, Covent Garden (1857), and the adjacent Floral Hall (1857–1858). Succeeding to his father's practice in 1860, he completed Halifax Town Hall and the Houses of Parliament. Like his father, he was an eclectic who preferred the classical styles; though able, he was no innovator.

MARCUS WHIFFEN

WORKS

1855–1856, Saint Saviour, Hampstead; 1857, Royal Opera House, Covent Garden; 1857–1858, Floral Hall, Covent Garden; 1859–1860, National Schools, Endell Street; 1863–1865, Charing Cross Hotel; London. 1866–1871, Crewe Hall, Cheshire, England. 1871–1874, Fitzwilliam Museum (staircase), Cambridge. 1871–1874, Wykehurst Park, Sussex, England. 1878–1879, Temple Gardens Building, London.

BIBLIOGRAPHY

DIXON, ROGER, and MUTHESIUS, STEFAN 1978 Victorian Architecture. New York and Toronto: Oxford University Press.
GIROUARD, MARK (1971)1979 The Victorian Country House. Rev. & enl. ed. New Haven: Yale University Press.
SUMMERSON, JOHN 1970 Victorian Architecture: Four Studies in Evaluation. New York: Columbia University Press.

BARTNING, OTTO

Otto Bartning (1883–1959) began his architectural studies in 1904 at the Berlin-Charlottenburg Technische Hochschule, continuing thereafter at Karlsruhe's Hochschule. In 1906, while a student, he designed his first church; in the following ten years, he built twenty-five churches and church-connected structures, many of which were destroyed in World War I.

Bartning, idealistic and radical, took part in the ferment of postwar Germany as a member of the Novembergruppe, the Arbeitsrat für Kunst, and, a few years later, of the Ring. When the Bauhaus moved to Dessau in 1925, he was appointed director of the successor school, the Bauhochschule, where he remained for four years, being supplanted by the Nazi-appointed PAUL SCHULTZE-NAUMBURG. In 1926, Bartning became a cofounder of the Reichsforschungsgesellschaft. From that time to the end of World War II, he built or reconstructed thirty church structures. Not a member of the Nazi Party, he moved in 1943 to Neckarsteinach. In 1946, he became chairman of the re-established Werkbund.

His interest in the building of churches continued; between 1948 and 1951, he was involved in a hundred more. Though Bartning's church building tends to obscure his other works, these are at least equal in number, and some are notable for their design and innovation.

From 1951 to 1959, he was president of the Bund Deutscher Architekten in which role he fought to improve the status of the profession.

REGINALD R. ISAACS

WORKS

1906, Evangelical Church, Peggau, Steiermark, Austria. 1926–1928, Housing Development (forty-eight thousand units); 1927, Factory Administration Building; Berlin. 1928, Pressa Steel Church, Cologne, Germany. 1929, Heating Plant and Laundry, Berlin. 1929–1930, Round Church, Essen, Germany. 1929–1931, Housing, Siemensstadt, Berlin. 1930, Church of the Resurrection, Essen, Germany. 1930–1932, Clinic, Wilmersdorf, Berlin. 1932, Gustav Adolf Church, Charlottenburg, Berlin. 1932–1933, Haselhorst District Housing Development (three hundred units) and Laundry, Berlin. 1933–1936, Clinic, Luxemburg. 1936–1937, Goethearchiv, Leipzig. 1946, Prefabricated timber churches, Germany. 1948–1950, Forty-eight Churches (with associated architects). 1950–1951, Daneskirche, Wedding, Berlin. 1950–1951, Women's Clinic, Darmstadt, Germany.

BIBLIOGRAPHY

BARTNING, OTTO 1947 *Erdball.* Leipzig: Insel.
BARTNING, OTTO (editor) 1952 *Mensch und Raum.* Darmstadt, Germany: Neue Darmstädter.
BARTNING, OTTO 1955 *Erde, Geliebte.* Hamburg, Germany: Classen.
BARTNING, OTTO 1958 *Entzückte Meerfahrt.* Hamburg, Germany: Rowohlt.
BARTNING, OTTO 1959 *Kirchen: Handbuch für den Kirchenbau: Book 2.* Munich: Callwey. Book 1 by Willy Weyres.
MAYER, HANS (1951)1958 *Der Baumeister Otto Bart-ning und die Wiederentdeckung des Raumes.* Heidelberg, Germany: Lambert Schneider.
POLLAK, ERNST 1926 *Der Baumeister Otto Bartning: Unser Lebensgefühl gestaltet in seinem Werk.* Berlin: Pollak.
SIEMON, ALFRED (editor) 1958 *Otto Bartning.* Bramsche bei Osnabrück, Germany: Rasch.

BASCOURT, JOSEPH

The Belgian Joseph Bascourt (1863–1927), trained at the Antwerp Academy, achieved while still a young man recognition as one of the leading architects of Antwerp. An exuberant eclectic, he was a proficient designer in a number of revived styles, notably the Flemish Baroque, and also in an original Art Nouveau manner. Most of his work was for residential commissions.

ALFRED WILLIS

WORKS

1895, Villas, 55, 57, and 59 Cogelslei; c. 1903, House, 16 Sint-Vincentiusstraat; Antwerp, Belgium. 1904, Nottebohm Hospital, Berchem, Belgium.

BIBLIOGRAPHY

BRAEM, RENAAT 1963 "De 'Libre Esthètique' te Antwerpen." *Bouwkundig Weekblad* 81:477–483.
L'Emulation 1890, 1897, 1898, 1903, 1904, 1913 15:10–13; 22:43–45; 23:56–57; 28:48–50; 29:13–14; 38:26.
PUTTEMANS, PIERRE 1976 *Modern Architecture in Belgium.* Translated by Mette Willert. Brussels: Vokaer.
RUSSELL, FRANK (editor) 1979 *Art Nouveau Architecture.* New York: Rizzoli.

BASEVI, GEORGE

George Basevi (1794–1845)—JOHN SOANE's most successful pupil—was an architect of Jewish birth, related to the D'Israeli and Ricardo families. As a young man, he traveled extensively in Italy, Greece, and Turkey. From Soane he inherited a passion for the antique; the Ricardo connection gave him several country house commissions; and his links with a future prime minister hardly hindered his success in two competitions for London's Carlton and Conservative Clubs. Basevi's own talents as architect and town planner were considerable. His Fitzwilliam Museum, Cambridge (1836–1845), dramatically marks the transition from Regency to Victorian, from neoclassicism to neobaroque. His London squares and terraces—notably Belgrave Square (1825–1840), Thurloe Square (1839–1845), Pelham Place and Alexander Square (1833 onward)—made him the JOHN NASH of

Kensington and Belgravia. It was as surveyor to
the Thurloe and Alexander estates, to the Smith's
Charity estate and to the financiers W. and
G. Haldimand that Basevi achieved these later successes. And had it not been for his sudden death—
he fell from the belfry of Ely Cathedral—he might
well have emerged as the leading classical architect
of mid-Victorian London. There are collections of
Basevi's drawings at Sir John Soane's Museum and
in the Drawings Collection of the Royal Institute
of British Architects.

J. MORDAUNT CROOK

WORKS

c.1820, Gatcombe Park, Gloucestershire, England.
1825–1840, Belgrave Square; 1827–1830, Alexander
Square; London. 1827–1832, Painswick House,
Gloucestershire, England. 1833 and later, Pelham Crescent and Place, Brompton (now Egerton) Crescent and
Walton Place, London. 1836–1845, Fitzwilliam Museum (completed by C. R. COCKERELL and E. M. BARRY
from 1845–1848 and 1870–1875), Cambridge. c.1839–
1845, Thurloe Square; 1843–1844, Conservative Club
(with SYDNEY SMIRKE), Saint James's Street; London.

BIBLIOGRAPHY

BOLTON, A. T. 1925 *Architectural Education a Century
Ago.* London: Sir John Soane's Museum.
HOBHOUSE, HERMIONE 1969 "The Building of Belgravia." *Country Life* 145:1154–1157, 1312–1314.
SMIRKE, SYDNEY 1852 In W. Papworth (editor), *Dictionary of Architecture.* London: Architectural Publication Society.

BASILE, ERNESTO

Ernesto Basile (1857–1932) was one of the leading
personalities of Italian Modern architecture. Born
in Palermo, Italy, where he graduated in 1878,
Basile started his career assisting his father, GIO-
VANNI BATTISTA FILIPPO BASILE, in the competition designs for the Monument to Victor Emanuel, the Palace of Justice (1884), and the
Parliament House (1889) in Rome. In 1890, he
replaced his father in the works of the Teatro
Massimo and in the chair of architecture at the
University of Palermo. After the National Exhibition (1891–1892) and the Bordonaro Palace
(1893–1896) in Palermo, his vocabulary turned
from a sophisticated classical eclecticism to a personalized modernistic "Liberty" style. The small
Ribaudo's kiosk (1894), in spite of its composite
vocabulary, can be considered the beginning of
this new creative trend and the first example of
"Liberty" architecture in Italy. Other works in this
style were the elaborate Villino Florio (1899), the
Hotel Villa Igiea (1899–1900), and the Utveggio

House (1901), all in Palermo.

Among his finest Modern works are the Villini
Fassini (1903) and Basile (1903) in Palermo, the
Municipal Palace of Licata (1904), the Belmonte
Palace in Spaccaforno (1906), and a vast production of interior designs, an area in which he excelled internationally. Later, he returned to a classicism animated by *floreale* decorations, as in the
Assicurazioni Generali (1912) and the Santa
Rosalia Church (1928), both in Palermo. His
major work, restrained by stylistic traditions, was
the extension of GIOVANNI LORENZO BERNINI's
Montecitorio Palace in Rome (1902–1927) which
was converted into the House of Parliament.

MANFREDI G. NICOLETTI

WORKS

*1891–1892, Pavilions, National Exhibition; 1893–
1896, Bordonaro Palace; 1894, Ribaudo's Kiosk, Piazza
Teatro Massimo; 1899, Villino Vincenzo Florio; 1899–
1900, Grand Hotel Villa Igiea; 1901, Utveggio House;
Palermo, Italy. 1902, Palazzina Vanoni; 1902–1927,
Montecitorio Palace (extension; now the House of Par-
liament); Rome. 1903, Villino Basile; *1903, Villino
Fassini; Palermo, Italy. 1904, Municipal Palace, Licata,
Italy. 1906, Palace of Bruno di Belmonte, Spaccaforno,
Italy. 1907, Electric Power Station, Caltagirone, Italy.
1907–1912, Cassa di Risparmio Vittorio Emanuele;
1912, Assicurazioni Generali Venezia; Palermo, Italy.
1914, Municipal Palace, Reggio Calabria, Italy. 1915,
Ribaudo's Kiosk, Piazza Castelnuovo, Palermo, Italy.
1924, Villino Gregorietti, Mondello, Italy. 1926–1927,
Casa di Risparmio Vittorio Emanuele, Messina, Italy.
1928, Santa Rosalia Church, Palermo, Italy.

BIBLIOGRAPHY

A.W.R.S. 1903 "Sicily." *The Studio* 30, no. 127:
BASILE, ERNESTO 1981 *Architettura, dei suoi principi e
del suo rinnovamento, 1882.* Palermo, Italy: Nove-
cento.
BORSI, FRANCO 1966 *L'architettura dell'Unità d'Italia.*
Florence: Le Monnier.
CARONIA ROBERTI, SALVATORE 1935 *Ernesto Basile e
cinquant' anni di architettura in Sicilia.* Palermo, Italy:
Ciuni.
DAMIGELLA, ANNA MARIA 1976 *Il liberty nella Sicilia
Orientale.* Palermo, Italy.
MEEKS, CARROLL L. V. 1966 *Italian Architecture:
1750–1914.* New Haven: Yale University Press.
NICOLETTI, MANFREDI 1973 "Art Nouveau in
Italy." Pages 32–62 in J. M. Richards and Nikolaus
Pevsner (editors), *The Anti-Rationalists.* London:
Architectural Press.
NICOLETTI, MANFREDI 1978 *L'Architettura Liberty in
Italia.* Rome and Bari, Italy: Laterza.
PIACENTINI, MARCELLO 1932 "Ernesto Basile."
Architettura e arti decorative 11:507.
PIRRONE, GIANNI 1971 *Palermo Liberty.* Rome: Scias-
cia.
PIRRONE, GIANNI 1976 *Studi e schizzi di E. Basile.*

Palermo, Italy: Sellerio.

SESSA, ETTORE 1980 *Mobile e arredi di Ernesto Basile nella produzione Ducrot.* Palermo, Italy: Novecento.

ZEVI, BRUNO (1950)1973 *Storia dell'Architettura Moderna.* Turin, Italy: Einaudi.

ZIINO, VITTORIO 1959 "La cultura architettonica in Sicilia, dall'Unità alla prima guerra mondiale." *La Cassa* 6:96–119.

BASILE, GIOVANNI BATTISTA FILIPPO

Giovanni Battista Filippo Basile (1825–1891) studied in Palermo, Italy, where he was born, and later in Rome at the Sapienza and the Accademia di San Luca. A revolutionary in 1848 and a follower of Garibaldi in 1860, he acquired the chair of architecture at the University of Palermo in 1863. In 1864, an international jury headed by GOTTFRIED SEMPER awarded him first prize in the competition design for the Teatro Massimo in Palermo, his most important work. Among the many public and private buildings that he realized, the Villa Favaloro (1889) in Palermo, designed at the end of his life, shows definite modernistic premonitions.

MANFREDI G. NICOLETTI

WORKS

1863–1870, Palermo Master Plan, Italy. 1864, Teatro Massimo (not completed until 1897 by ERNESTO BASILE), Palermo, Italy. 1865, Cemetery of Monreale, Italy. 1878, Italian Pavilion, Exposition Universelle, Paris. 1889, Villa Favaloro, Palermo, Italy.

BIBLIOGRAPHY

MEEKS, CARROLL L. V. 1966 *Italian Architecture: 1750–1914.* New Haven: Yale University Press.

PIRRONE, GIANNI 1965 "Palermo e il suo 'verde'." *Quaderno* 5–7.

ZIINO, VITTORIO 1959 "La cultura architettonica in Sicilia, dall'Unità d'Italia alla prima guerra mondiale." *La Casa* 6:96–119.

BASSEGODA FAMILY

The Bassegoda are a Catalan family of architects residing in Barcelona since the beginning of the nineteenth century. To the first generation belongs Pere Bassegoda i Mateu (1817–1908), master builder. Of his three sons, two became architects: Joaquim Bassegoda i Amigó (1854–1938), professor and director of the School of Architecture of Barcelona, and Bonaventura Bassegoda i Amigó (1862–1940), author of various works, some in collaboration with his brother and his father. He was also an outstanding writer, contributing to the magazine *La Renaixensa,* a central organ of the movement with the same name that would promote the renaissance of Catalonia and within whose ambit *Modernisme* would attain its plenitude. A militant of the League of Catalonia Party—like the modernist architects LLUÍS DOMÈNECH I MONTANER and JOSEP PUIG I CADAFALCH—Bonaventura Bassegoda participated in the Exhibit of Industrial Art of 1892.

Like the previous five exhibits organized since 1822, this last was arranged with the purpose to revitalize Catalan crafts, which had achieved such a high level of development in the Middle Ages. This series of exhibits culminated in the International Exhibit of 1888, of which Bassegoda was assistant director for Architecture and which marked the entry of a new modernist spirit into the problems of art and industry. However, this historical evocation in line with the tenets of the Arts and Crafts movement would lead, in the case of the more conservative architects, to an archeological nostalgia. Unable to accept the route of modernity suggested by the new style in its moments of greater maturity, such architects preferred a revivalist eclecticism, not exempt from modernist references. Eclecticism of this sort characterizes the production of Bonaventura Bassegoda i Amigó.

Bonaventura's sons, Pere Jordi and Bonaventura, represent the third generation of the family. Pere Jordi Bassegoda i Musté (1891–) was a poet and specialist in legal architecture, and Bonaventura Bassegoda i Musté (1896–) was a professor at the School of Architecture of Barcelona and the author of several technological monographs on themes central to construction. The latter's sons constitute the fourth generation of this architectural dynasty: Bonaventura Bassegoda i Nonell (1926–) and his brother Juán Bassegoda i Nonell (1930–), professor at the School of Architecture of Barcelona and author of a great number of monographs and promoter of studies on ANTONIO GAUDÍ Y CORNET.

ADOLF MARTÍNEZ I MATAMALA
Translated from Spanish by
Florette Rechnitz Koffler

WORKS

BONAVENTURA BASSEGODA I AMIGÓ

1891–1892, Bosch i Alsina (with Pere Bassegoda and Joaquim Bassegoda), 8 Catalonia Square; 1891–1892, House, 88 Catalonia Avenue; 1906, County College, 6 Amadeo Vives Street, 1907–1909, Berenguer House, 246 Diputacion Street; 1910, Pares de Plet House, 231 Muntaner Street; 1918, Rocamora Houses, 6–14 Avenue de Gracia; n.d., Alba Foundation, San Cipriano

Street; n.d., Casino of Masnou; Barcelona, Spain.

BIBLIOGRAPHY

BOHIGAS, ORIOL (1968)1973 *Arquitectura modernista.* Barcelona, Spain: Lumen.

BASSETT, FLORENCE KNOLL

A protégée of EERO SAARINEN and ELIEL SAARINEN, Florence Knoll Bassett (1917–) was educated at the Cranbrook Academy of Art, the Architectural Association in London, and the Illinois Institute of Technology, where she studied architecture under LUDWIG MIES VAN DER ROHE. Together with her husband, Hans Knoll, she established the Knoll design firm in 1946 and directed its planning unit until 1965. As an innovative designer, her interiors with furniture designed by Mies, MARCEL BREUER, and EERO SAARINEN as well as herself, have significantly influenced contemporary architecture.

JUDITH OBERLANDER

WORKS

1949, Hewitt-Robins Company Offices (interior); 1951, Knoll Showroom; New York. 1952, Student Union Building (interior), Ohio State College, Columbus. 1954, Alcoa Building (interior), Pittsburgh. 1954, Center for the Advanced Study of the Behavioral Sciences, Palo Alto, Calif. 1954, Columbia Broadcasting System Executive Offices, New York. 1955, M. D. Anderson Hospital for Cancer Research; 1955, Demoustier Residence; Houston, Tex. 1956, Dining Hall, University of Rochester, N.Y. 1956, Student Center (interior), Southern Methodist University, Dallas, Tex. 1957, Connecticut General Life Insurance Company (interiors), Hartford. 1960, Knoll Showroom, Rome. 1960, First National Bank, Miami, Fla. 1964–1966, Columbia Broadcasting System Building (interiors), New York.

BIBLIOGRAPHY

"All That Glitters: Knoll's Recent Exhibition." 1972 *Industrial Design* 19, Apr.:62–67.
"CBS Offices." 1955 *Architectural Forum* 102, Jan.:134–139.
CLIFF, U. 1961 "Gallery 4: Florence Knoll." *Industrial Design* 8, Apr.:66–71.
"Distinguished Interior Architecture for CBS." 1966 *Architectural Record* 139, June:129–134.
"Furniture Preview: Knoll's Spare Parallel Bar System." 1957 *Interiors* 115, Jan.:106–107.
GUEFT, O. 1957 "Florence Knoll and the Avant Garde." *Interiors* 116, July:58–66.
"Human Campus for the Study of Man." 1955 *Architectural Forum* 102, Jan.: 130–133.
RAE, C. 1971 *Knoll au Louvre.* New York: Chanticleer.
"Vingt-cinq ans de dessin à l'avant-garde." 1972 *Oeil* 206–207, Feb.–Mar.:64–67.

BASSI, MARTINO

Martino Bassi (1542–1591), one of the most important architects active in Milan in the latter part of the sixteenth century, was born in Soregno, Italy, in 1542. According to his eighteenth-century biographer Francesco Bernardino Ferrari, Bassi was drawn to civil architecture as a youth. His style is indebted to those of Lombardy's other major architects, GALEAZZO ALESSI and PELLEGRINO TIBALDI. Bassi is first documented in lists of Milanese engineers dating from the late 1560s. His early architectural activities include the direction of the project for the unfinished Milanese Church of San Vittore al Corpo, which he took over in 1567, and the designing of a façade for Santa Maria presso San Celso, also in Milan, about 1570.

Martino Bassi is perhaps best known for his virulent opposition to Pellegrino Tibaldi's projects for the Cathedral of Milan. In 1569, Bassi submitted a group of objections to Tibaldi's methods and ideas to the *Fabbrica* of the Duomo, but after an inquiry his charges were dropped as unfounded. Bassi, however, was unwilling to let the issue die, and in 1572 he published a small book attacking Tibaldi entitled *Dispareri in materia di architettura et perspettiva con parei di eccelenti et famosi architetti che li risolvono.* The *Dispareri* were directed in particular against Tibaldi's inaccurate perspectival rendering of an Annunciation group which was to be placed above one of the Duomo's portals. In addition to Bassi's criticisms, the book collected negative opinions of Tibaldi's work solicited from the major architects of the day, including ANDREA PALLADIO, GIORGIO VASARI, GIACOMO DA VIGNOLA, and Giovanni Battista Bertani.

In 1574, Bassi began work on his greatest realized project, the rebuilding of the fourth-century Church of San Lorenzo in Milan, the Romanesque dome of which had collapsed in 1573. Bassi's challenge was to span the vast centrally planned space of the early Christian structure, and his designs raised great controversy among Milan's architects. The dome as completed in the seventeenth century follows Bassi's plans which included a high drum.

Despite continuing criticism, Tibaldi remained architect of the Duomo for nearly a decade after the publication of Bassi's *Dispareri,* not resigning the office until 1585 following the death of his primary supporter, CARLO BORROMEO. In November 1587, Bassi himself became architect of the Duomo, and his foremost concern was with the planning of its façade. Bassi prepared several designs which he presented to the Deputies of the *Fabbrica* and which were subsequently sent to Pope Gregory XIV. Bassi's major extant projects, like those of his predecessor, use a classical or

"Roman" vocabulary and do not attempt to harmonize with the Gothic fabric of the Cathedral. Bassi's façade designs are particularly richly ornamented and are characterized by obelisks at the corners. It has been suggested that a drawing in the Ambrosiana, Milan, records Bassi's ideas for a Gothic façade (Bascapè, 1967, p. 42). This "historicizing" approach, which sought to maintain visual unity throughout the building, had been advocated before Bassi's time by LEONARDO DA VINCI and DONATO BRAMANTE and was ultimately followed in the nineteenth century when the façade of the Duomo was completed.

Other Milanese works by Martino Bassi include the choir and tribunes of San Fedele della Compagnia di Gesù, a church begun by Tibaldi in 1569, and the alteration of Santa Maria della Passione into a Latin-cross plan, a project undertaken about 1573. Among Bassi's works elsewhere in Lombardy were the Sacro Monte at Varallo, where Gatti Perer (1964a) places the architect as early as 1570; contributions to the choir of the Certosa of Pavia which he commenced in 1578; and restorations at the Duomo at Lodi (1586) where he also worked on several secular commissions.

SHERYL E. REISS

WORKS

1567, San Vittore al Corpo (supervision), Milan. 1570, Sacro Monte, Varallo, Italy. 1570, Santa Maria presso San Celso (façade); 1573–1591, Santa Maria della Passione; 1574–1591, San Lorenzo (rebuilding); Milan.

1578, Certosa (choir), Pavia, Italy. 1586, Duomo at Lodi (restoration), Italy.

BIBLIOGRAPHY

BARONI, COSTANTINO 1940–1968 *Documenti per la storia dell'architettura a Milano nel Rinascimento e nel Barocco.* 2 vols. Florence: Sansoni.
BASCAPÈ, MARIAROSA 1967 "I disegni di Martino Bassi nella raccolta Ferrari: Catalogo." *Arte Lombarda* 12:33–64.
BASSI, MARTINO 1572 *Dispareri in materia d'architettura et perspectiva con pareri di eccellenti e famosi architetti che li risolvono.* Brescia, Italy.
FERRARI, FRANCESCO BERNARDINO (1771)1964 "Vita di Martino Bassi, architetto Milanese." *Arte Lombarda* 9, no. 2:57–61.
GATTI PERER, MARIA LOUISA 1964 "Martino Bassi, il Sacro Monte di Varallo e Sta Maria presso San Celso a Milano." *Arte Lombarda* 9, no. 2:21–57.
KRÜGER, GIUSEPPE STRUFFOLINO 1971 "Disegni inediti d'architettura relativi alla collezione di Venanzio de Pagave." *Arte Lombarda* 16:277–290.
WITTKOWER, RUDOLF 1974 *Gothic vs. Classic: Architectural Projects in Seventeenth Century Italy.* New York: Braziller.

BASTARD, JOHN, and BASTARD, WILLIAM

The brothers John (c.1688–1770) and William (c.1689–1766) Bastard were the leading members of a family of architects and master builders established at Blandford in Dorset, England. They were the sons of Thomas Bastard, a joiner by trade, and were themselves practicing joiners as well as architects. In the former capacity they were responsible for decorative woodwork of high quality, often rococo in style, in the latter for a number of buildings in a vernacular baroque style of considerable merit. A favorite motif that recurs often in their work is a capital with inturning volutes derived from FRANCESCO BORROMINI. Although this was illustrated in books such as DOMENICO ROSSI's *Studio d'architettura civile* (1702), it is likely that the Bastards derived this and other features of their baroque repertoire from personal contact with the gentleman architect THOMAS ARCHER, who lived only twenty miles from Blandford.

A fire which destroyed much of Blandford in 1731 gave the Bastard brothers an opportunity to rebuild the center of this small country town to their own designs. They built a new church (1735–1739) somewhat in the style of the "Fifty New Churches" in London, a town hall (1734) with a front of Palladian character, and two inns (1734–1735) with characteristic baroque façades. In 1760 John Bastard, as "a considerable sharer in the general calamity," erected a Doric pumphouse

John and William Bastard.
Parish Church.
Blandford, England.
1735–1739

near the church "in Remembrance of God's dreadful visitation by Fire . . . And to prevent, by a timely supply of water (with God's Blessing) the fatal Consequences of FIRE hereafter." An obelisk in the churchyard commemorates the brothers' "skill in Architecture and Liberal Benefactions to this Town." Outside Blandford, a house at Poole (1746–1749) and a monument in Gillingham Church (c.1725) appear to be their only surviving architectural works, but the interior of Lulworth Castle (1740–1758) was largely their work.

H. M. COLVIN

WORKS

c.1725, John Dirdoe Monument in Gillingham Church, Dorset, England. 1734, Town Hall; 1734–1735, Greyhound and Red Lion Inns; c.1735, 75 East Street; 1735–1739, Parish Church; Blandford, England. *1740–1758, Lulworth Castle (interiors), Dorset, England. 1746–1749, House on Market Street, Poole, England.

BIBLIOGRAPHY

ADAMS, JOHN 1968 "The Bastards of Blandford." *Architectural Review* 43:445–450.
COLVIN, H. M. 1977 "The Bastards of Blandford: Architects and Master-Builders." *Archaeological Journal* 104:178–195.

BATTAGLIA, FRANCESCO

Francesco Battaglia (1710–1788), a native of Catania, Italy, was a builder and an architect who, while incorporating into his architecture the exuberant ornamentation which characterized the style of early eighteenth-century Catania, also designed more classically baroque façades and cosmopolitan rococo interiors. Undoubtedly influenced by GIOVANNI BATTISTA VACCARINI, who in 1730 brought to Catania news of the recent developments in Rome, Battaglia developed a classicizing style which became more severe as the century progressed. In addition to designing new buildings, he worked extensively on the repair and reconstruction of churches damaged by the tremors which periodically shook Sicily.

STEPHEN TOBRINER

WORKS

c.1742 Benedictine Monastery (portions); 1747–1755, Church (portions), Benedictine Monastery; 1757, Church of the Crociferi Fathers (completion); Catania, Italy. 1759–1784, Chiesa Madre (reconstruction), Aci San Filippo, Italy. 1762, Collegio Cutelli, Catania, Italy. 1763, San Giuseppe (reconstruction of façade), Aci Catena, Italy. 1764, Palazzo Biscari, Catania, Italy. 1765, Chiesa Madre (belltower), Militello, Italy. 1766, Santa Chiara (portal); 1771–1777, Benedictine Monas-tery (southern dormitory and eastern façade); 1771–1782, Crociferi Fathers' House (completion); 1771–1787, San Michele; 1776, Palazzo Reburdone (interior and enlargement); Catania, Italy.

BIBLIOGRAPHY

FICHERA, FRANCESCO 1934 *G. B. Vaccarini e l'architettura del Settecento in Sicilia.* 2 vols. Rome: Reale Accademia D'Italia.
LIBRANDO, VITO 1963 "Francesco Battaglia: Architetto del XVIII Secolo." Volume 2, pages 129–154 in *Cronache di archeologia e di storia dell'arte.* Catania, Italy: Universitàdi.

BAUDOT, JOSEPH EUGENE ANATOLE DE

Joseph Eugène Anatole de Baudot (1834–1915) was born in Sarrebourg, France. He began his architectural studies in the atelier of HENRI LABROUSTE, but when the latter decided to give up teaching in 1856, de Baudot was one of several students who persuaded EUGÈNE EMMANUEL VIOLLET-LE-DUC to open a studio. Over the next half-century, de Baudot would prove to be the most capable of this controversial medievalist's disciples, continuing to support rationalist and structuralist doctrines in his buildings, teachings, and writings until the end of his life. His long career links the Gothic Revival of the mid-nineteenth century with the new developments in reinforced concrete construction that appeared just before and after 1900. In this quest, he was measurably assisted by the views of his mentor concerning the development of new materials and techniques in construction.

De Baudot's earliest achievements both as a restorer of medieval monuments and as an original architect came while he was an associate of Viollet-Le-Duc. His Gothicizing designs for the Church of Saint-Lubin, Rambouillet (1865–1869), provoked criticism largely because he had employed visible iron columns flanking the nave of an otherwise masonry-vaulted edifice. After Viollet-Le-Duc's death in 1879, the tentative character of his work slowly gave way to designs that more fully realized the older architect's largely unfulfilled hopes of developing a rational and structurally expressive modern style in architecture. However, a decade and a half would pass before the design of his masterpiece, the concrete-ribbed church of Saint-Jean-de-Montmartre, Paris (1894). Even then, the construction of this building was delayed by conflicts with the authorities, and it was completed only in 1904. By this date, the novelty of a concrete skeleton or frame had been blunted by the appearance the previous year of AUGUSTE PERRET's block of flats at 25 bis Rue Franklin, Paris.

De Baudot's unique church is an audacious outgrowth of certain of Viollet-Le-Duc's designs contained in the *Entretiens sur l'Architecture* (1863–1872) and hence ultimately of medieval prototypes, whereas Perret's concrete forms are derived from the familiar French academic classic tradition as reinterpreted by Perret's master, JULIEN GUADET. The latter was a professed rationalist who nonetheless was, throughout his career, an antagonist of Viollet-Le-Duc and his followers. On the exterior, Saint-Jean-de-Montmartre clearly reveals its concrete skeleton frame which contrasts with the non-load-bearing walls of brick. The simplified tracery of the windows continues and underscores the basic structural motif. On the interior, the rational ordering of the building's components is even clearer. The piers and ribs of brick and concrete form a continuous linear skeletal network which itself is also the church's decorative system. In this respect, de Baudot's interior offers analogies if not real similarities of style to the more sinuously designed interiors of such contemporary masters of the Art Nouveau as HECTOR GUIMARD and VICTOR HORTA.

De Baudot was seventy years old when Saint-Jean was completed. The remaining decade of his life saw the creation of a number of unexecuted projects for monumental interiors of varying function. In appearance, these grew out of the design of his revolutionary church, and in their forms they anticipate certain creations of mid-twentieth-century engineers, notably PIER LUIGI NERVI. Many of these were illustrated in his posthumous book, *L'Architecture, le Passé, le Présent* (1916) which provides a resumé of the rationalist doctrine to which he adhered throughout his career in the face of persistent academic opposition.

JOHN JACOBUS

WORKS

1865–1869, Saint-Lubin, Rambouillet, France. 1882–1888, Lycée Lakanal, Sceaux, France. 1894–1896, Lycée Victor Hugo; 1894–1904, Saint-Jean de Montmartre, Paris.

BIBLIOGRAPHY

BAUDOT, ANATOLE DE 1905 *L'Architecture et le Béton Armé.* Paris.
BAUDOT, ANATOLE DE 1916 *L'Architecture, le Passé, le Présent.* Paris: H. Laurens.
BERCÉ, F. 1965 "Anatole de Baudot." *Les Monuments Historiques de France* 3.
BOUDON, F. 1973 "Recherche sur la Pensée et l'Oeuvre d'Anatole de Baudot." *Architecture, Mouvement, Continuité* 28, Mar.

BAUER, CATHERINE K.

Catherine Krouse Bauer (1905–1964) was born in Elizabeth, New Jersey, and educated at Vassar College. Her youthful association with architectural critic Lewis Mumford led to her career in housing which encompassed promoting reform through writing, lobbying, public administration, and teaching. She was noted for her advocacy of human-scale public housing which she first articulated in her 1934 book *Modern Housing*.

EUGENIE L. BIRCH

BIBLIOGRAPHY

BAUER, CATHERINE K. 1934 *Modern Housing.* Boston: Houghton-Mifflin.
BAUER, CATHERINE K. 1957 "The Dreary Deadlock of Public Housing." *Architectural Forum* 106, no. 5:140–143.
COLE, SUSAN 1980 "Catherine Krouse Bauer." In Barbara Sicherman (editor), *Notable American Women: The Modern Period.* Cambridge, Mass.: Belknap.
"Woman Hiker Dead: Aided Three Presidents on City Planning." 1964 *New York Times,* Nov. 24, p. 40.

BAUER, LEOPOLD

Leopold Bauer (1872–1938) was a pupil of CARL HASENAUER and of OTTO WAGNER at the Academy of Fine Arts in Vienna. He was both an architect and an arts and crafts designer, as well as a writer on these subjects. He took a mediating position between Historicism and Secession, thereby meeting the taste of most of his contemporaries. In his early villa buildings, he followed the example of JOSEPH MARIA OLBRICH; showing discernment in his treatment of ornamentation and color, his interior designs were distinctly appealing. Later, he turned to the new *Biedermeier* style, distancing himself from the *Jugendstil*. Though there was some protest, he became Otto Wagner's successor at the Vienna Academy (1913–1918). In his later buildings he was an eclectic. Though his taste was sure, he failed to keep pace with the developments of his time.

SOKRATIS DIMITRIOU
*Translated from German by
Beverley R. Placzek*

WORKS

1901, Dr. R. House, Brno, Czechoslovakia. 1902, Villa Kurz, Jägerndorf, Czechoslovakia. 1908, Villa Hecht Brno, Czechoslovakia. 1913–1918, Printing press of the Austrian-Hungarian Bank, Vienna.

BIBLIOGRAPHY

BAUER, LEOPOLD 1899 *Verschiedene Skizzen, Entwürfe und Studien.* Vienna: Schroll.

BAUER, LEOPOLD 1931 *Leopold Bauer: Seine Anschauung in Wort and Werk.* Vienna and Leipzig: Elbemühl.
POZZETTO, MARCO 1979 *La scuola di Wagner: 1894–1912.* Trieste, Italy: Commune di Trieste.
WAGNER-RIEGER, RENATE 1970 *Wiens Architektur im 19. Jahrhundert.* Vienna: Österreichischer Bundesverlag.

BAUER, W. C.

Willem Cornelis Bauer (1862–1904) was born in The Hague, where he also went to school. In 1888, he settled in Amsterdam. Due to lack of commissions, Bauer restricted himself to making competition designs which never won because of the willfullness of his designs. Only in 1898 and after did he get some commissions from the poet Frederik van Eeden for his agricultural colony *Walden* in Bussum, Holland, and from the circle of friends of his brother, the painter Marius Bauer.

WIM DE WIT

WORKS

1898, Walden Cottages; 1899, De Lelie Villa for Frederik van Eeden; Bussum, Netherlands. 1902, Villa for George Breitner; *1902, Villa Stamboel for Marius Bauer; Aerdenhout, Netherlands.

BIBLIOGRAPHY

BECKER, FRANS, and FRIESWIJK, JOHAN 1976 *Bedrijven in Eigen Beheer: Kolonies en produktieve associaties in Nederland tussen 1901 en 1958.* Netherlands: Socialistiese Uitgeverij Nijmegen, Sunschrift No. 101.
Nederlandse Architectuur, 1893–1918: Architectura. 1975 Amsterdam: Stichting Architectuurmuseum.
Nooit Gebouwd Nederland. 1980 Amsterdam: Koninklijk Verbond van Grafische Ondernemingen.

BAUM, DWIGHT J.

Dwight James Baum (1886–1939) was a highly respected practitioner of the eclectic residential styles popular in the United States during the 1920s and 1930s. Born in Little Falls, New York, Baum graduated from Syracuse University in 1909, and opened a New York City office in 1915. Among his earliest works was his own house, Sunnybank (1915), in Riverdale, New York, a section of the Bronx then being developed. The elegant, asymmetrical Colonial Revival framehouse was greatly admired, and it led to scores of other Riverdale commissions. Baum designed houses in a number of eclectic styles including the Colonial, Georgian, Italian Villa, English, and Dutch Colonial types. His scholarly adaptations owed a great deal to the extensive architectural library main-tained in his office. Although best known for and represented by his Riverdale work, Baum designed houses throughout the country, notably John Ringling's Venetian-style palace in Sarasota, Florida (1922–1926). He also designed university buildings and civic structures, including the West Side YMCA in Manhattan (1930). Baum was awarded a gold medal, sponsored by the American Institute of Architects, for the best designed small house built in America between 1926 and 1930.

ANTHONY W. ROBINS

WORKS

1915, Sunnybank (Dwight James Baum Residence); *1920, Riverdale Country Club; 1922, Anthony Campagna Residence; 1922, William P. Hoffman Residence; Riverdale, Bronx, N.Y. 1922–1926, Ca' d'Zan (John Ringling Residence), Sarasota, Fla. 1924, Lawridge (Robert Law, Jr., Estate), Port Chester, N.Y. *1924, Ben Riley's Arrowhead Inn, Riverdale, Bronx, N.Y. 1928, Armour Hall (addition to Wave Hill Estate), Riverdale, Bronx, N.Y. 1930, West Side Young Men's Christian Association Building, New York.

BIBLIOGRAPHY

BAUM, DWIGHT JAMES 1927 *The Work of Dwight James Baum: Architect.* With a commentary text by Charles M. Price. New York: Helburn.
BINNEY, MARCUS 1976 "Ca' d'Zan, Sarasota, Florida." *Country Life* 160:1202–1205.
Dwight James Baum, Architect, New York City: Architectural Catalog, May 1922. 1922 New York: Baum.
"Dwight James Baum, 1886–1939." 1940 *Pencil Points* 21:57.

BAUMANN, FREDERICK

Although an architect, Frederick Baumann (1826–1921) is remembered primarily for his improvement in the technology of erecting buildings on isolated piers which made possible the construction of tall buildings on the compressible soil of Chicago where piles were neither feasible nor desired. His methodology was eventually superseded by caisson foundations, first used in Chicago in 1893. According to Baumann's theory, published in 1873, each footing was to be sized according to the weight it would carry with the result that settlements everywhere in a tall building would be nearly equal.

As an architect, Baumann was responsible for many now largely forgotten buildings in Chicago, where he practiced for over half a century. Following a technical education in Berlin, he emigrated to Chicago in 1851. Except for eleven years from 1858 to 1868 when Bauman worked as contractor and as carpenter and architect, he practiced architecture primarily in partnership with several others.

PAUL E. SPRAGUE

WORKS

*1854, Marine Bank; *1872, Ashland Block; *1872, Bryant Block; *1872, Metropolitan Block; *1886, Union Bank; Chicago.

BIBLIOGRAPHY

BAUMANN, FREDERICK (1873)1892 *The Art of Preparing Foundations for All Kinds of Buildings, with Particular Illustration of the "Method of Isolated Piers" as Followed in Chicago.* Reprint. Chicago: Wing.
BAUMANN, FREDERICK 1884 *Improvements in the Construction of Tall Buildings.* Chicago.
ERICSSON, HENRY 1942 *Sixty Years a Builder.* Chicago: Kroch.
RANDALL, FRANK 1949 *History of the Development of Building Construction in Chicago.* Urbana: University of Illinois Press.
SULLIVAN, LOUIS (1924)1956 *The Autobiography of an Idea.* Reprint. New York: Dover.
TALLMADGE, THOMAS 1941 *Architecture in Old Chicago.* University of Chicago Press.

BAUMANN, POVL

Povl Baumann (1878–1963) left the Royal Academy in Copenhagen to become a student of P. V. JENSEN-KLINT. In his search for a "natural architecture," Baumann at first adopted Jensen-Klint's vernacular in brick and tile. Later, he joined with CARL PETERSEN in a revival of neoclassicism that they developed into Expressionism. Inspired by Ivar Bentsen, he gave up the historic style and from the 1930s built in a Danish "functional tradition."

LISBET BALSLEV JØRGENSEN

WORKS

1916, Aage Lunn House, Hellerup, Denmark. 1917, Non-profit Housing (with Ivar Bentsen), Borups allé; 1920, Non-profit Housing, Struensegade; 1930, Non-profit Housing (with Aage Müller), Klokkergården and Storgården; 1930–1932, Vesterport Office Building (with Ole Falkentorp); 1946, Ellebjerg School (with Müller); Copenhagen.

BIBLIOGRAPHY

FISKER, KAY 1958 "Povl Baumann fylder 80 år." *Arkitekten* 60:373–382.
JØRGENSEN, LISBET BALSLEV 1979 Pages 99–128, 179 in *Danmarks arkitektur, Enfamiliehuset.* Copenhagen: Gyldendal.
HARTMANN, SYS 1979 Pages 160–165, 177 in *Danmarks arkitektur, Byens huse, Byens plan.* Copenhagen: Gyldendal.
LUND, HAKON 1980 Page 109 in *Danmarks arkitektur, Magtens bolig.* Copenhagen: Gyldendal.

BAUMEISTER, REINHARD

Reinhard Baumeister (1833–1917) was one of the leaders of progressive city planning in Germany during the latter part of the nineteenth century. His ideas anticipated many of the planning principles publicized by his younger contemporaries, CAMILLO SITTE and Joseph Stübben.

Baumeister's comprehensive book, *Stadt-Erweiterungen,* published in 1876, appeared at a time of rapid urban expansion and dealt with the problems of housing, transportation, parks, sanitation, building codes, and financing. This book is considered to be the first in which city planning is conceived to be dependent on vehicular traffic and is precocious in its adamancy on zoning. Baumeister also criticized the dominant use of grid-iron systems, and advocated a choice of gridiron, radial, triangular, and picturesque designs, to be selected in accordance with a city's topographical and historical layout.

Baumeister stressed artistic city planning, and his own preference was for the aesthetic effect of curved streets. His many lectures and publications form an extensive dialogue with Camillo Sitte.

IVAN S. FRANKO

BIBLIOGRAPHY

BAUMEISTER, REINHARD 1876 *Stadt-Erweiterungen in technischer, baupolizeilicher und wirtschaftlicher Beziehung.* Berlin: Ernst & Korn.
BAUMEISTER, REINHARD 1902 *Stadtbaupläne in alter und neuer Zeit.* Volume 27, book 6 in *Zeitfragen des christlichen Volkslebens.* Stuttgart, Germany: Belser.
BAUMEISTER, REINHARD 1914 "Städtebau." Volume 3, pages 1519–1532 in S. Körte (editor), *Deutschland unter Kaiser Wilhelm II.* Berlin: Hobbing.
COLLINS, GEORGE R., and COLLINS, CHRISTIANE C. 1965 *Camillo Sitte and the Birth of Modern City Planning.* New York: Random House.

BAXTER, JOHN

Son of an Edinburgh master builder of the same name, John Baxter (?–1798) was in Italy from 1761 to 1767, during which time he entered at least one architectural competition and became a member of the Accademia di San Luca in Rome. Succeeding his father on his return to Scotland, he designed and built a number of country houses and other buildings.

DAMIE STILLMAN

WORKS

*c.1769, Mortonhall House, Midlothian, Scotland. *1769–1782, Gordon Castle (remodeling), Morayshire, England. *c.1770–1778, Penicuik House (alterations),

Midlothian, Scotland. *1771–1773, Callander Church, Perthshire, Scotland. 1775–1790, Fochabers New Town, Morayshire, Scotland. 1779–1780, Gartmore House (alterations; since remodeled), Perthshire, Scotland. *1781–1787, Ellon Castle, Aberdeenshire, Scotland. 1788, Merchant's Hall (ground floor altered), Edinburgh. 1788, Town Hall, Peterhead, Aberdeenshire, Scotland. *1792–1794, Avontoun House, West Lothian, Scotland. 1795–1797, Bellie Church, Fochabers, Morayshire, Scotland. *1798, Glenfiddich Lodge (alterations), Banffshire, Scotland.

BIBLIOGRAPHY

SIMPSON, ANN M. 1971 "The Architectural Work of the Baxter Family in Scotland, 1722–1798." Unpublished M.A. Thesis, Edinburgh University.
SIMPSON, ANN M., and SIMPSON, JAMES 1973 "John Baxter, Architect, and the Patronage of the Fourth Duke of Gordon." *Bulletin of the Scottish Georgian Society* 2.
STILLMAN, DAMIE 1973 "British Architects and Italian Architectural Competitions, 1758–1780." *Journal of the Society of Architectural Historians* 32:43–66.
STILLMAN, DAMIE 1977 "Chimney-Pieces for the English Market: A Thriving Business in Late Eighteenth-Century Rome." *Art Bulletin* 59:85–94.

BAYARDO, NELSON

Uruguayan architect Nelson Bayardo (1922–) has distinguished his career by evolving a new teaching methodology based on a special student–professor relationship and the development of intellectual factors as opposed to learning techniques aided by convention criticism. Since 1953, he has been a professor at the University of Montevideo, where he was given a permanent chair in 1969. In 1975, he began disseminating his didactic philosophy at major Latin American universities in Venezuela, Brazil, and Paraguay. Bayardo's Columbarium (1961–1962) displays his intellectual approach to architecture by integrating complex solids and voids into a straightforward monumental structure.

ELIZABETH D. HARRIS

WORKS

1949, Pan de Azucar Savings Bank, Maldonade, Uruguay. 1954, Municipal Cooperative Market; 1961, Buceo Apartment Complex Neighborhood Center; 1961–1962, Columbarium (Northern Cemetery); 1965, Plaza Union Cultural Center; 1975, Banco Republica Club; 1980, Biarritz Park Infant Playground; Montevideo.

BIBLIOGRAPHY

BULLRICH, FRANCISCO 1969 *New Directions in Latin American Architecture.* New York: Braziller.
ZEVI, BRUNO 1950 *Storia dell' architettura moderna.* Turin, Italy: Editorial Einaudi.

BAYER, HERBERT

Following school in Linz, Austria, and military service, Herbert Bayer (1900–) in 1920 became apprentice to Emanuel Margold, in Darmstadt, Germany. Thereafter, he studied mural painting with Wassily Kandinsky at the Weimar Bauhaus, where, other than travel in Italy in 1923–1924, he remained as a "young master" until 1928. Subsequently, he augmented his teaching in typography and graphic design with photography and exhibition design as director of the Dorland Studio and of Berlin Vogue. Bayer-designed typefaces, including his sans serif Universal type, were directly responsible for the revolution in typography in the 1920s, and his experiments in photomontage were pioneering.

In 1938, Bayer came to New York and designed books, exhibitions, posters, and other work for industries and magazines like *Fortune* and *Harper's Bazaar.* Bayer became art director and vice-president of Dorland International.

In 1946, Bayer moved to Aspen, Colorado, to participate in it's development as a ski resort and cultural center. While in Aspen, he served as chairman of the design department to Container Corporation of America, consulting on questions of design such as communication design, interiors, and architecture. He was also consultant for the Aspen Institute of Humanistic Studies for its architecture and total environmental development. His civic responsibilities have included chairmanship of the county–city zoning board, membership on the city building commission, historic conservation, and urban renewal. His more recent work for the Atlantic Richfield Company is equally broad in its scope.

Though Bauhaus masters guided the development of Bayer's skills, it was WALTER GROPIUS who encouraged his sense of interrelatedness which has distinguished his work and has made him one of the most comprehensive artists of the century. An example of his total view is his 1953 "Geo-graphic World Atlas" which relates demography, geography, history, natural ecology, agriculture, mineral resources, industry, commerce, and climate.

In 1968, he designed the definitive Bauhaus exposition which began its worldwide tour in Stuttgart. That same year, an exhibition of his work was held at the Marlborough Gallery in London that re-emphasized his versatility as a painter, photographer, designer, typographer, sculptor, architect, interior architect, and all-purpose ideas man. In 1977, an exhibition "from type to landscape," at Hanover, New Hampshire, demonstrated his comprehensiveness.

The impact of this modest Bauhausler has been quietly and anonymously influential on architecture and design—on all design—everywhere.

REGINALD R. ISAACS

WORKS

1950, Opera House (restoration), Aspen, Colo. 1950, Orchestra Hall (remodeling), Chicago. 1953, Seminar Building, Aspen Institute for Humanistic Studies, Colo. 1958–1959, Research Center, Container Corporation of America, Valley Forge, Pa. 1961, Walter Paepcke Memorial Building, Aspen Institute for Humanistic Studies; 1963, Music Festival Tent and Facilities, Music Associates of Aspen; 1973–1974, Anderson Park, Aspen Institute for Humanistic Studies; Colo.

BIBLIOGRAPHY

BAYER, HERBERT 1953 *World Geo-graphic Atlas: A Composite of Man's Environment.* Chicago: Container Corporation of America.
BAYER, HERBERT 1961 *Book of Drawings.* Chicago: Theobald.
BAYER, HERBERT 1967 *Herbert Bayer: Painter/Designer/Architect.* New York: Reinhold.
BAYER, HERBERT 1971 *"Typography and Design" in Concepts of the Bauhaus.* Cambridge, Mass.: Busch-reisinger Museum.
DORNER, ALEXANDER (1947)1958 *The Way Beyond Art: The Work of Herbert Bayer.* Rev. ed. New York University Press.
NEUMANN, ECKHARD (editor) 1970 *Bauhaus and Bauhaus People.* Translated from the German by Eva Richter and Alba Lorman. New York: Van Nostrand.
RODRIGUEZ PRAMPOLINI, IDA 1975 *Herbert Bayer: Un Concepto Total.* Mexico City: Instituto de Investigaciones Estheticas, University of Mexico.

BAYLEY, JOHN B.

The projects and proposals of John Barrington Bayley (1914–) reflect a strong classical orientation. He studied architecture at Harvard Graduate School of Design (1939–1942, 1970) and spent three years in Rome at the American Academy (1947–1950). Bayley's belief that classical architecture confers a human dimension, scale, and sense of permanence absent in modern architecture has been his guiding philosophy. He practices in New York.

PATRICIA C. PHILLIPS

WORKS

1959–1961, General Services Administration Building (with EGGERS AND HIGGINS, Kahn and Jacobs, and Alfred Easton Poor); 1967, Fraunces Tavern Block (renovation; with H. H. Goldstone); 1973–1975, Frick Collection (addition; with Harry van Dyke); New York.

BIBLIOGRAPHY

BAYLEY, JOHN BARRINGTON 1958–1959 "In the Roman Style." *Landscape* 8, Winter: 23–25.
SKY, ALISON and STONE, MICHELLE 1976 *Unbuilt America.* New York: McGraw.

BAZEL, K. P. C. DE

Karel Petrus Cornelis de Bazel (1896–1923), born in Den Helder, Netherlands, very early received recognition for his architectural skills when P. J. H. CUYPERS appointed him first as surveyor for a church in Hilversum, Netherlands (1890–1891), and later as manager at his office in Amsterdam (1892–1895).

At Cuypers's office, De Bazel got to know Cuypers's ideas about the amalgamation of all arts under the direction of architecture, ideas he adhered to for the rest of his life. He also met J. L. M. LAUWERIKS there and became a close friend of his. Both De Bazel and Lauweriks became very interested in a new trend in architecture which produced designs based on a modular system. Rejecting Cuypers's neo-Gothic, they turned instead to the ancient arts of Assyria and Egypt, in which they found a similar modular system.

When De Bazel and Lauweriks both joined the theosophical movement, the Roman Catholic Cuypers forced them to leave his office. In 1895, they started a studio for architecture and applied arts, which was the beginning of a fruitful period of ideas and initiatives, but without many commissions. In order to propagate their theory of design and their theosophical philosophy, they started teaching a course, the so-called Vahâna course, in 1897. At the same time, they published the magazine *Bouw- en Sierkunst* (1897–1899). In 1900, their collaboration came to an end.

De Bazel settled into a large practice in Bussum. A great part of his work are villas and housing. His last work was also his largest: the office of the Nederlandse Handelsmaatschappij in Amsterdam (1919–1923).

WIM DE WIT

WORKS

1902–1905, Model Farm Oud-Bussum, Bussum, Netherlands. 1904, House, Koningslaan, Netherlands. 1906–1907, Villa (De Maerle), Bussum, Netherlands. 1912–1913, Heide Maatschappij Office Building, Arnhem, Netherlands. 1914–1918, Workers Housing, Van Beuningenplein; 1919–1923, Nederlandse Handelsmaatschappij Office Building (not completed until 1926), Vijzelstraat; Amsterdam.

BIBLIOGRAPHY

BERLAGE, H. P. 1906 "K. P. C. de Bazel." *Elsevier's Geïllustreerd Maandblad* 32:73–87.

FANELLI, GIOVANNI (1968)1978 *Moderne architectuur in Nederland: 1900–1940.* Translated from Italian by Wim de Wit. The Hague: Staatsuitgeverij.

LAUWERIKS, J. L. M. (1925)1935 *De houtsneden van K. P. C. de Bazel.* Amsterdam: Van Looij.

Nederland bouwt in baksteen: 1800–1940. 1941 Rotterdam, Netherlands: Museum Boymans van Beuningen.

Nederlandse architectuur 1893–1918: Architectura. 1975 Amsterdam: Van Gennep.

REININK, A. W. 1965 *K. P. C. de Bazel, Architect.* Leiden (Netherlands) University Press.

BAZZANI, CESARE

Cesare Bazzani (1873–1939) was an eclectic deeply tied to the classical tradition of his native Rome. A member of the prestigious Accademia d'Italia, he received innumerable commissions from the Fascist regime in the 1930s for government buildings all over Italy. Among Bazzani's most successful works are the Biblioteca Nazionale in Florence (1907–1935) and the Palazzo delle Belle Arti (now Galleria Nazionale di Arte Moderna) in Rome (1908–1911).

ELLEN R. SHAPIRO

WORKS

1907, Altar of San Gaetano, Church of San Andrea della Valle; Rome. 1907–1935, Biblioteca Nazionale, Florence. 1908–1911, Palazzo delle Belle Arti (now the Galleria Nazionale di Arte Moderna), Rome. 1911, Alterocca Printing Company Building, Terni, Italy. 1913–1928, Ministry of Public Education, Rome. 1929, Government Palace, Foggia, Italy. 1930–1935, Church of the Gran Madre di Dio; 1930–1935, Fatebenefratelli Hospital; Rome. 1930–1935, Government Palace, Terni, Italy. 1934–1936, National Institute of Social Welfare, Aquila, Italy. 1934–1936, Social Welfare Headquarters, Terni, Italy.

BIBLIOGRAPHY

ACCASTO, GIANNI; FRATICELLI, VANNA; and NICOLINI, RENATO 1970 *L'Architettura di Roma Capitale: 1870–1970.* Rome: Golem.

BORSI, FRANCO 1966 *L'Architettura dell'Unità d'Italia.* Florence: Le Monnier.

INSOLERA, ITALO 1971 *Roma Moderna.* Torino, Italy: Einaudi.

MEEKS, CARROLL L. V. 1961 "The Real Liberty of Italy." *Art Bulletin* 93:113–130.

PIACENTINI, MARCELLO 1939 "Cesare Bazzani." *L'Architettura* 18:331–338.

PORTOGHESI, PAOLO 1959 "La Vicenda Romana." *La Casa* 6:42–95.

RACHELI, ALBERTO M. 1980 "La Galleria Nazionale d'Arte Moderna di Cesare Bazzani e le vicende della sua costruzione: Primi risultati di indagini documentarie." In Gianna Piantoni (editor), *Roma 1911.* Rome: De Luca.

BBPR

See BANFI, BELGIOJOSO, PERESUTTI, and ROGERS.

BEASLEY, CHARLES

Charles Beasley (1827–1913) was born in Missouri and practiced carpentry in the Mississippi river town of Louisiana City. By 1860, he had migrated to California, and, by 1871, was established as a builder-architect in Stockton. As a designer, Beasley displayed a passion for juxtaposing rich and varied building materials.

Like his peers, Beasley designed many small houses and often accepted renovation work, reusing earlier designs on occasion. Employing his sons Thomas and William, his firm was briefly known as Beasley and Sons, before evolving into the partnership of Charles and William Beasley. Like other Stockton architects, he worked mainly in the San Joaquin Valley. Beasley's forte was large, corner commercial blocks.

Beasley, however, was also a man with progressive notions. In 1880, he remodeled Stockton's African Methodist Episcopal Church. Seven years later, he designed the San Joaquin County Agricultural Pavilion with an Oriental motif. The pavilion fronted Stockton's Chinatown. During the 1890s, Beasley accepted commissions from the Italian communities in Stockton and San Francisco and employed Italian designs. Finally, following the 1906 earthquake, Beasley immersed himself in the redesign of San Francisco's Chinatown. It was the architect's ethnic design work that placed him outside the mainstream of nineteenth-century California.

KAREN J. WEITZE

WORKS

*1872, Franklin School; 1873, Weber School; *1880, African Methodist Episcopal Church (remodeled); 1882, Avon Theater; *1886, Farmers' Cooperative Union Warehouse; *1887, California Steam Navigation Company Warehouse; *1887, San Joaquin County Agricultural Pavilion; *1888, Stewart Memorial Library; *1889, Fremont School; 1890, Hall of the Pioneers; *1890, Union Block; *1891, A. Alberti Block (Southern Hotel); *1891, McMullin Block; 1891, Sperry Flour Mills Office; *1895, Imperial Hotel; 1896, Poulterer Block; 1897, W. R. Clark Business Block; 1897, Clark and Hennery Block; 1898, Fair Oaks School; 1899, Farmers' Union and Milling Company Warehouse; 1899, Handball Court and Bowling Alley, Terminal City Wheelman; 1899, Tracy City Hall and Jail; 1900, John Cornazzani Building; 1900, Foresters' Building; 1900, M. McAllen Hotel; 1901, S. L. Magee Block; 1901, Red Men's Building; 1906, East Side Fire Engine House, Stockton, Calif. 1906–?, Chinatown buildings; 1906, St. Peter's Episcopal Church; San Francisco.

BIBLIOGRAPHY

WEITZE, KAREN J.   1980   "Charles Beasley, Architect (1827–1913): Issues and Images." *Journal of the Society of Architectural Historians* 39:187–207.

BEAUSIRE FAMILY

The first generation of the Beausire Family of French architects included Simon (1648–?), who settled in Rome and changed his name to Busiri; Pierre; and Jean (1651–1743), who entered royal service, was chief architect for the city of Paris, and became a member of the Académie d'Architecture in 1716. Jean passed his official positions to his eldest son, Jean-Baptiste Augustin, known as Beausire le Fils, who entered the Académie in 1732 and bequeathed his titles to his son in law, Laurent Destouches, in 1751. Another son of Jean Beausire, Jérôme (1708?–1761), known as Beausire le Jeune, also served as *architecte des bâtiments du roi* and assumed his father's chair in the Académie in 1740.

RICHARD CLEARY

WORKS

JEAN BEAUSIRE

*1719, Petit Pont (reconstruction), Paris.

JEAN BAPTISTE AUGUSTIN BEAUSIRE

1734, Hôtel d'Ecquevilly, Paris. 1735, Château d'Avron, near Villemomble, France. *1737–1743, Storm Drain, Quartier du Temple, Paris.

JÉRÔME BEAUSIRE

*1745, Cathedral (decoration of choir), Beauvais, France.

BIBLIOGRAPHY

GALLET, MICHEL   1972   *Stately Mansions: Eighteenth Century Paris Architecture.* New York: Praeger.
LABARRE DE RAILLICOURT, DOMINIQUE   1958   "Les Beausire; Architectes du roi." *Bulletin de la Société de l'Histoire de l'Art Français* 1958:83–87.
LEMONNIER, HENRY (editor)   1911–1929   *Procès-verbaux de l'Académie Royale d'Architecture: 1671–1793.* 10 vols. Paris: Champion.

BEAZLEY, SAMUEL

Samuel Beazley (1786–1851) was the most prominent theater architect of early nineteenth-century England. Also a playwright and novelist, Beazley often staged and directed his own works. As an architect, Beazley worked in several idioms, demonstrating his flexibility as a designer in the neoclassical and Gothic revival styles. Attentive not only to the splendor and elegance of the theater interiors, Beazley was equally concerned with the efficiency of stage operations and acoustics. He also designed hotels, cottages, castles, and railway stations, apparently mastering each building type with considerable ease.

BRIAN LUKACHER

WORKS

1816, Royal Lyceum Theatre, London. 1820, Theatre Royal, Birmingham, England. 1834, Royal Soho Theatre; 1835, St. James's Theatre; London.

BIBLIOGRAPHY

HARBRON, DUDLEY   1936   "Samuel Beazley—A Victorian Vanbrugh." *Architectural Review* 79:131–134.

BEBB, CHARLES H.

Charles H. Bebb (1856–1942), born in Surrey, England, was educated at King's College, London, and the University of Lausanne, Switzerland, where he studied engineering. He emigrated to the United States in 1880 and spent ten years in Chicago, during which time he became supervisor of construction for ADLER AND SULLIVAN. Representing the Chicago firm on an unrealized theater and hotel project, he arrived in Seattle, Washington, in 1890. In 1901, he formed a partnership with Louis L. Mendel. Bebb and Mendel were awarded gold medals for their Washington State and Good Roads Buildings and a silver medal for their King County Building for the Alaska-Yukon-Pacific Exposition in Seattle in 1909. In 1911, Bebb was named supervising architect for the State Capitol Group in Olympia, which was constructed from designs by the New York firm of Wilder and White between 1912 and 1926. He worked with CARL F. GOULD from 1914 until Gould's death in 1939, and over the years, the firm produced noteworthy buildings in both traditional and modernistic styles. Bebb and Gould were appointed architects of the University of Washington campus plan in 1915 and subsequently designed numerous buildings on the campus in Seattle. Bebb was associated with John Paul Jones at the end of his career.

ELISABETH WALTON POTTER

WORKS

1889–1891, Bailey Block, Seattle, Wash. 1901, Everett Theater, Wash. 1903, Oriental Building (Corona Hotel); 1908, Frye Hotel; *1909, Good Roads Building, Alaska-Yukon-Pacific Exposition; *1909, King County Building, Alaska-Yukon-Pacific Exposition; *1909, Washington State Building, Alaska-Yukon-Pacific Exposition; 1910, First Church of Christ Scientist; 1910, Fred S. Stimson House; 1911, Hoge Building; 1914–1915, Administration Building, United States Government Locks (with Carl Gould); 1915, Seattle Times Building (with Gould); 1915–1937, University of Washington Campus Plan (with Gould); 1924–1929, Olympic Hotel (with GEORGE B. POST and Company); 1926, Suzzallo Library (with Gould), University of Washington; 1927, Henry Art Gallery (with Gould), University of Washington; 1932, Seattle Art Museum (with Gould), Volunteer Park; 1934, United States Marine Hospital (United States Public Service Hospital; with Gould and John Graham, Sr.); Seattle, Wash.

BIBLIOGRAPHY

"Chas. H. Bebb, F.A.I.A. (Elect)." 1910 *Pacific Builder and Engineer* 10, no. 22:204–205.
"Obituary." 1942 *New York Times* June 22, p. 15, col. 2.
WOODBRIDGE, SALLY BYRNE, and MONTGOMERY, ROGER 1980 *A Guide to Architecture in Washington State.* Seattle: University of Washington Press.

BECERRA, FRANCISCO

Born in Trujillo, Spain, Francisco Becerra (c.1545–1605) was trained by his father in the rib-vaulted brick-and-stone architecture of the school of Alonso Berruguete. Becerra arrived in Mexico in 1573, where he was appointed by Viceroy Don Martin Enriquez as master of the works of the Cathedral of Puebla in 1575. He laid the foundations probably from the designs of CLAUDIO DE ARCINIEGA. By 1581, he was in Quito, Ecuador, where he is said to have designed monastic churches for the Augustinians and the Dominicans. As with his many claimed interventions in Mexico, nothing remains of his work there. In 1582, he was summoned to Lima by Don Martin Enriquez, then viceroy of Peru, to design the cathedrals of Lima and Cuzco. Work on these buildings was delayed until after 1598 when he redrew the projects. Both buildings have been much transformed, but their basic hall church design with rib vaults springing from compound piers, Ionic in Lima and Doric at Cuzco, capped by segments of entablature can be attributed to Becerra. Nothing remains of his houses, palaces, and bridges in Lima cited in numerous documents.

JOHN DOUGLAS HOAG

WORKS

1582–1605, Cathedral of Cuzco (not completed until 1654), Peru. 1582–1605, Cathedral of Lima (not completed until 1613/1632; vaults rebuilt after 1746).

BIBLIOGRAPHY

KUBLER, GEORGE, and SORIA, MARTIN 1959 *Art and Architecture in Spain and Portugal and Their American Dominions.* Baltimore: Penguin.
MARCO DORTA, ENRIQUE 1951 Volume 1 in *Fuentes para la historia del Arte Hispano-Americano.* Seville, Spain: Instituto Diego Velázquez, Sección de Sevilla.

BECKET, WELTON

At once the chief designer and sole owner of what was and, following his death, continues to be one of the United States' largest architectural firms, Welton Davis Becket (1902–1969) was dedicated to the philosophy of "total design." This philosophy embraces all requirements demanded of an architectural problem: preliminary research, site selection, economic analysis, traffic surveys, and the actual design of the building or complex of buildings, for which Becket employed his own team of architects, mechanical and electrical engineers, landscape architects, and interior designers. True to its name, "total design" attempts to control every detail of a commission that concerns design. The firm of Welton Becket and Associates is the embodiment of this architectural philosophy.

Born in Seattle, Washington, Becket studied at the University of Washington and did a year of graduate study at the Ecole des Beaux-Arts in Paris. Upon his return to the United States, Becket began a partnership in Los Angeles with fellow classmate Walter Wurdeman and an older architect, Charles Plummer. This partnership designed residences primarily in the Los Angeles area. Following Plummer's death in 1939, the partnership continued under the name of Wurdeman and Becket. The total design concept was beginning to become integral to the firm by this time, and it prospered during the 1940s. After Wurdeman's untimely death in 1949, the firm became known as Welton Becket and Associates.

The versatile designs of this firm are not identified with a particular style but attempt instead to articulate each client's character and needs. After Becket's death, the firm continued under the same name, directed by his son, Welton Becket, Jr.

JO ANNE PASCHALL

WORKS

1934, Pan Pacific Auditorium (with Walter Wurdeman), Los Angeles. 1947, Bullock's Department Store (with Wurdeman), Pasadena, Calif. 1948, Prudential Square (with Wurdeman), Los Angeles. 1955, Beverly Hilton Hotel, Beverly Hills, Calif. 1960, Kaiser Center, Oakland, Calif. 1964, Dorothy Chandler Pavilion, Los Angeles Music Center. 1967, Gulf Life Tower (with Kemp, Bunche, and Jackson), Jacksonville, Fla. 1968, Xerox Square, Rochester, N.Y. 1969, Aetna Life and Casualty Building; 1969, Mutual Benefit Life Building, San Francisco.

BIBLIOGRAPHY

HUNT, WILLIAM DUDLEY, JR. 1972 *Total Design:*

Architecture of Welton Becket and Associates. New York: McGraw-Hill.

SHEEHAN, ROBERT 1967 "Portrait of the Artist as a Businessman." *Fortune* 75:144–148, 178, 183–184, 188.

"Welton Becket and Associates." 1959 *Interiors* 119:110–131, 202–204.

BECKFORD, WILLIAM

William Beckford (1760–1844) claimed to have been instructed in architecture by WILLIAM CHAMBERS, and at least one plan for a house survives in his hand. But he is principally remembered as the rich, learned, and eccentric patron who commissioned JAMES WYATT to design for him the vast neo-Gothic Fonthill Abbey in Wiltshire, England, which was still not quite complete at the death of Wyatt in 1813. Until its sale in 1822, Fonthill Abbey was renowned also as the repository of Beckford's fine collection of paintings, books, manuscripts, and *objets de vertu.* Two monographs of 1823, *Delineations of Fonthill and Its Abbey* by J. Rutter, and *Graphical and Literary Illustrations of Fonthill Abbey* by J. Britton, spread the fame of the building, which was frequently the subject of picturesque watercolors and etchings. Beckford settled in Bath, Somerset, England, after 1822 and employed the architect Henry E. Goodridge in alterations to the houses he bought at 19 and 20 Lansdown Crescent to house his continuously growing collections. For the same purpose he had, by 1827, erected the Lansdown Tower, an Italianate house with a tower 154 feet in height crowned by a variation on the Choragic Monument of Lysicrates. Many of the fittings of Fonthill and Lansdown Tower were designed by Beckford himself, and his houses were influential not only for their eccentricity and picturesqueness of design but also because they were the residence of the author of the widely popular romance *Vathek,* first published in 1786.

MICHAEL MCCARTHY

BIBLIOGRAPHY

BOYD, ALEXANDER 1962 *England's Wealthiest Son: A Study of William Beckford.* London: Centaur.

FOTHERGILL, BRIAN 1979 *Beckford of Fonthill.* London: Faber.

LEES-MILNE, JAMES 1976 *William Beckford.* Tisbury, England: C. Russell.

BEDFORD, FRANCIS O.

The designer of ten late Georgian churches, Francis Octavius Bedford (1784–1858) was among the more important architects to work for the Church Building Commission of 1818.

Although nothing is known about his upbringing, Bedford did have the rare fortune to study firsthand the remains of ancient Greece when, in 1811–1813, he participated in important surveys in Asia Minor for the Society of Dilettanti. The results, published in 1817 and 1840 (and belatedly in 1912), were well-received by contemporaries. More fateful for his career was a second-place competition finish for the prestigious church of Saint Pancras, London, in 1818. Within three years his winning designs for four large south London churches, all of them based on his Grecian-style Saint Pancras project and all sited near his Camberwell home, assured him professional prominence. Their low construction costs also soon gained him supervision of six Gothic-style churches in London and the provinces.

His paranoid personality and doubtful technical competence, poor critical reception of his buildings, and his employers' desire to minimize expenses, cut short his career. As an archeologist he irritated his companions; as an architect he proved much more difficult. Construction stability problems and Bedford's shrill responses to them ostracized him from the profession by 1838.

GERALD L. CARR

WORKS

1822–1824, Saint George, Camberwell; 1822–1825, Saint John, Waterloo Road, Lambeth; 1822–1825, Saint Luke, West Norwood; 1823–1825, Holy Trinity, Newington; London. 1827–1828, Saint George, Newcastle-Under-Lyme, England. *1827–1828, Saint Mary the Less, Lambeth, London. 1830–1831, Saint James, Riddings, Derbyshire, England.

BIBLIOGRAPHY

CARR, GERALD L. 1976 "The Commissioners' Churches of London: 1818–1837." Unpublished Ph.D. dissertation, University of Michigan, Ann Arbor.

CLARKE, BASIL F. L. 1966 *Parish Churches of London.* London: Batsford.

SUMMERSON, JOHN (1945)1978 *Georgian London.* 3rd ed., rev. Cambridge, Mass.: M.I.T. Press.

YOUNG, ELIZABETH, and YOUNG, WAYLAND 1956 *Old London Churches.* London: Faber.

BEER, MICHAEL

The importance of Michael Beer (?–1666) for seventeenth-century German architecture rests primarily on his designs for the Residence and the Church of Saint Lawrence in Kempten in south Germany and on his being the first master of the so-called *Auer Zunft* (guild of Au) which he founded in Au near Bregenz, Austria, in 1657. This guild was part of the *Vorarlberger Bauschule,* which for a long time had been considered to emphasize traditional elements, but which recently underwent a re-evaluation (see Oechslin, 1973). The guild provided structured practical architectural training as well as theoretical instructions, emphasizing a system of family-oriented workshops. Competition among the members of the guild was not permitted. Further, there was the obligation that the family workshop continue a project left unfinished at the time of the death of the planner, thereby assuring continuity of the plan. Frequent intermarriages of the leading families, especially the Beers, the THUMB FAMILY, and the Moosbruggers (see CASPAR MOOSBRUGGER) make it difficult at times to establish exact genealogies.

The precise date of Michael Beer's birth is not known. Church records in Au begin only with the year 1611 and do not mention his birth or baptism. Therefore, this year must be considered the *terminus ante quem* for his birth, which generally is assumed to have occurred around 1605. Knowledge about his early career is based on a document of January 29, 1651, which states that Beer was born in Au and had been apprenticed to a certain Hans Garttner in Poysdorf (Lower Austria, approximately thirty-five miles north of Vienna). His apprenticeship was completed in 1625. Since it usually lasted three years, it may be assumed that Beer had joined Garttner's workshop in 1622. Since the document containing this information was issued in Poysdorf in 1651, it is likely that Beer had remained there until he was commissioned to design the Residence in Kempten (1651–1653). He left Kempten in 1653, seeking employment in Friedrichshafen in 1654 (Benedictine Priory in Buchhorn) and in Isny in 1656 (Benedictine Monastery). On January 25, 1654, he married Maria Metzler, who died on April 1, 1660, the day of the birth of Franz II Beer, known as Franz Beer II von Bleichten (1660–1726), a leading architect of the *Vorarlberger Bauschule*. Beer died in 1666 when he drowned in the Au river.

Michael Beer's known career as an architect begins with his plans for Kempten. From 1651 to 1653, he worked in the large complex of the residence, commissioned by Abbot Roman Giel von Gielsberg, for which he signed a contract on May 25, 1651. This project was the first monumental work of ecclesiastical architecture after the Thirty-Years' War (1618–1648). The residence is built on a rectangular ground plan with two internal courtyards. Only a small part was executed by Beer (north wing of the western court), the rest by Johann Serro, who succeeded Beer in 1654. Apart from the monastic complex of the residence, Beer designed in 1652 the Church of Saint Lawrence,

Beer.
Church of Saint Lawrence.
Kempten, Germany.
1652–1653

which had to fulfill two functions: to serve as church of the monastery and as parish church; the latter had been destroyed in 1632. As with the residence, Saint Lawrence Church was completed by Johann Serro. At that time, the nave had been constructed. Since Serro changed Beer's design by heightening the walls of the nave and enlarging its windows, it may be assumed that criticism of his plan was the reason for Beer's departure. Saint Lawrence Church is characterized on the outside by the combination of the nave and its integrated towers with the octagonal choir and its dome, while, inside, the choir for the monks and the nave for the parishioners are clearly separated. In fact, the dome is not even visible from the nave. The nave consists of a barrel-vaulted hall with dominating wall piers which separate rather than integrate the side aisles, as do the low galleries in them. Beer's design for the nave, which derived from buildings such as the Jesuit churches in Munich, Vienna, and Innsbruck, was influential in the formulation of the so-called *Vorarlberger Münsterschema* which is best expressed in Michael Thumb's churches in Ellwangen (1682) and Obermarchthal (1686). It was used again by Beer in his Saint Mary's Chapel in Fischen, begun in 1664. As in other religious and secular buildings—the colleges built for the Jesuits in Rottenburg (1662–1665), Landshut (1665–1666), and Ebersberg (1666–1666)—, the chapel's architecture emphasizes simple cubic forms with a minimum of decorative elements added to the outside.

EGON VERHEYEN

WORKS

1650–1651, Church, Bludesch, Austria. 1651–1653, Residence (completed by Johann Serro); 1652–1653, Church of Saint Lawrence (completed by Serro); Kempten, Germany. 1654, Benedictine Priory, Buchhorn, Germany. 1656–1657, Benedictine Monastery,

Isny, Germany. 1662–1665, Jesuit College, Rottenburg, Germany. 1664–1666, Saint Mary's Chapel, Fischen, Germany. 1665–1666, Jesuit College (not completed until 1670), Landshut, Germany. 1666, Jesuit Monastery (not completed until 1668), Ebersberg, Germany.

BIBLIOGRAPHY

GENZMER, WALTER 1952 "Das Lebenswerk des Vorarlberger Baumeisters Michael Beer." *Das Münster* 5:72–84.
GENZMER, WALTER 1966 "Der Einfluss der Bauweise Michael Beers auf die Bregenzerwälder Barockbaumeister." *Montfort* 18:362–372.
LIEB, NORBERT, and DIETH, FRANZ (1960)1976 *Die Vorarlberger Barockbaumeister.* Munich and Zurich: Schnell & Steiner.
OECHSLIN, WERNER (editor) 1973 *Die Vorarlberger Barockbaumeister: Ausstellung in Einsiedeln und Bregenz zum 250. Todestag von Caspar Moosbrugger.* Einsiedeln, Switzerland: Benziger.
PETZET, MICHAEL 1964 "Die Fischener Frauenkapelle: Der letzte Kirchenbau Michael Beers." *Das Münster* 17:311–313.
ROEDINGER, MARTHA 1938 *Die Stiftskirche St. Lorenz in Kempten.* Burg bei Magdeburg, Germany: Hopfer.

BEGG, JOHN

John Begg (1866–1937) was the most accomplished British architect yet to be given an official appointment in India. In his work he adapted the sophisticated classicism current in early twentieth-century Britain to meet Indian conditions and occasionally employed native styles of architecture. Begg was a Scot who had been articled to Hippolyte J. Blanc. He won several prizes and worked for ALFRED WATERHOUSE and R. W. EDIS before going out to South Africa in 1896 as architect to the Real Estate Corporation. In 1902, he was appointed consulting architect to the government of Bombay and, in 1908, succeeded James Ransome as consulting architect to the government of India. Begg left government service in 1921. In 1922, he became head of the architectural school of the Edinburgh School of Art.

GAVIN STAMP

WORKS

1903–1909, General Post Office, Bombay. 1909, Council House Street Secretariat (with James Ransome); Calcutta. 1912, Post Office, Agra, India. 1912, Stationary Office; Calcutta. 1913–1919, Lardy Hardinge Medical Hospital and College, Delhi, India. 1917, Central Provinces Council Chamber, Nagpur, India.

BIBLIOGRAPHY

BEGG, JOHN 1920 "Architecture in India." *Journal of the Royal Institute of British Architects* Series 3 27:333–349.
"Obituary: John Begg, F.R.I.B.A." 1937 *The Builder* 157:534.

BEHRENDT, WALTER CURT

Walter Curt Behrendt (1885–1945) studied architecture in Berlin and earned his doctorate of engineering in architecture at the Munich Technische Hochschule. Dissatisfied with private practice, he entered public service. From 1912 on, he was an administrator in the Prussian Ministry of Public Buildings and that of Public Health. Between 1919 and 1926, he was in the Department of Housing and City Planning, and from 1927 to 1933 he served as technical adviser to the Ministry of Finance, responsible for review of all public building projects in Prussia. He was concerned with public policy in respect to housing and city development as well as regional projects for greater Hamburg, the Ruhr, and middle Germany.

In 1920, Behrendt wrote about the controversy over styles in the arts and in 1927 about the victory of contemporary design; his *Modern Building,* published in 1937, was then one of the best books in English on the subject. Earlier, in 1925, he was the editor of *Form,* the journal of the Deutscher Werkbund.

In 1933, he was ousted by the Third Reich and a year later he migrated to the United States where he became visiting lecturer in city planning and housing at Dartmouth College. In 1937, Behrendt became professor of city planning at the University of Buffalo and technical director of the Buffalo City Planning Association. He returned to Dartmouth as full professor in 1942. An exacting teacher, he was as critical of the work of his students and colleagues as he was of his own lectures. Among the first of the refugees of the 1930s whose intellectual qualities enriched the United States, he broadened the understanding and appreciation of contemporary architecture of all who listened.

REGINALD R. ISAACS

BIBLIOGRAPHY

BEHRENDT, WALTER CURT 1911 *Die einheitliche Blockfront als Raumelement im Stadtbau, ein Beitrag zur Stadtbaukunst der Gegenwart.* Berlin: Cassirer.
BEHRENDT, WALTER CURT 1920 *Der Kampf um den Stil in Kunstgewerbe und in der Architektur.* Stuttgart, Germany: Deutscher Verlag.
BEHRENDT, WALTER CURT (1926)1927 *Städtebau und Wohnungswesen in den Vereinigten Staaten.* Berlin: Hackebeil.
BEHRENDT, WALTER CURT 1927 *Der Sieg des neuen Baustils.* Stuttgart, Germany: Akademischer Verlag Wedekind.
BEHRENDT, WALTER CURT 1928 *Die Holländische Stadt.* Berlin: Cassirer.

BEHRENDT, WALTER CURT 1934 "Post-War Housing in Germany." Pages 37–40 in Carol Aronovici (editor), *America Can't Have Housing.* New York: Museum of Modern Art.

BEHRENDT, WALTER CURT 1937a "A City Planner Looks at Buffalo." (Buffalo) *City Planning* 13: entire issue.

BEHRENDT, WALTER CURT 1937b *Modern Building.* New York: Harcourt.

MUMFORD, LEWIS (editor) (1952)1972 *Roots of Contemporary American Architecture.* Reprint. New York: Dover.

BEHRENS, PETER

Peter Behrens (1868–1940), born in Hamburg, Germany, was highly influential in the origins of modern architecture. Although his productive career spanned from the late nineteenth century until near his death, the distinctiveness and strength of his work is to be noted particularly in the decade prior to World War I when he made important contributions to both architecture and industrial design. It was also during this period (1908 to 1912) that three of the most renowned architects of the succeeding generation, WALTER GROPIUS, LUDWIG MIES VAN DER ROHE, and Charles-Edouard Jeanneret (LE CORBUSIER), worked in Behrens's atelier. Favorable critical and historical commentary was enjoyed by Behrens throughout his career and continues to the present; however, since the 1930s these judgments often reveal a projection of quite alien polemical concerns upon Behrens's thoughtful production.

Trained as an artist at the Kunstschule in Karlsruhe and privately in Düsseldorf and Munich (1886–1891), Behrens was a member of the progressive artists' groups in Munich in the 1890s and received remarkable attention for a quite modest production in painting and the graphic arts. An autodidact in architecture, Behrens saw the true architect as an artist, a leader in a cultural elite charged with providing the correct form for a historically determined society. Behrens's formally diverse work over the length of his career is united by this difficult and ambiguous quest for the realization of the artist's will in harmony with and yet necessarily superior to the historical necessity of the material world. Inversely stated, changes in Behrens's assessment both of the correct artistic form and of historical reality account for the diversity of his production.

Behrens's most enthusiastic endorsement of the artist as prophet came in the heady environment of the Artists' Colony in Darmstadt from 1899 to 1903. The group of artists invited by Ernst Ludwig, prince of Hessen, to form a colony near

his seat were specifically charged in the realization of their homes and working environment to create a "Document of German Art"; it opened to the public as an exhibition in May 1901. In collaboration with his friend Richard Dehmel and his poet-colleague at the Colony, Georg Fuchs, Behrens conceived a formalized, lyrical "relief-theater" where uplifting poetry was eurythmically declaimed on a shallow stage which enforced movements conducive to viewing the performers as in an antique relief. The audience itself would arrive in processions to the classicizing semicircular auditorium, close to the priestlike actors in the ceremonial theater building, the highest cultural symbol of emergent, modern, secular society. Although these ideas received only partial fulfillment later and elsewhere, Behrens and Fuchs did conceive and realize the inaugural ceremony for the Colony in which the artist-priest appeared bearing a crystal as the symbol of form transcending matter, art transforming life.

Behrens was the only artist at the Colony to insist on claiming the design of his own house for himself rather than entrusting it to the architect invited to the colony, JOSEPH M. OLBRICH. The Behrens House (1900–1901) is an honorable if not exceptional first work in architecture. The use of molded bricks in ogival form shows a deference to the medieval architecture of Behrens's native northern Germany, but the linear, graphic quality of these brick moldings against white stucco planes, as well as the interiors, may be seen in relation to contemporary *Jugendstil* design. What is most remarkable and at the same time characteristic for Behrens is that the house, within the limits of domestic building, produces a microcosm of Behrens's cultural hierarchy: from the ordinariness of the kitchen to the ceremonial music room complete with its image of artists, priestesses, and repeated use of the motif of the crystal.

The pretensions of the Artists' Colony were readily vulnerable to both caricature and criticism, facilitated also by the then increasingly ready dis-

Behrens.
Behrens House, Kunstler-
Kolonie,
Darmstadt, Germany.
1900–1901

missal of Art Nouveau programs throughout Europe. Yet, Behrens was sufficiently idiosyncratic in his works and so new to architecture that he could leave the Artists' Colony and take over the direction of the Kunstgewerbeschule in Düsseldorf (1903) accompanied by the praise and enthusiastic hopes of one of Germany's most noted international art critics, Julius Meier-Graefe.

Behrens's Düsseldorf years (1903–1907) provided an important period of self-education and retrenchment. He brought into his school young teachers familiar with artistic and architectural developments in Vienna and Amsterdam as well as a historian trained under August Schmarsow. Behrens concentrated his attention on what might be termed internal issues both of architecture and of the history of art. Endorsing Schmarsow's theory, Behrens conceived architecture as essentially the art of the definition of space; sculpture as the occupation of space. In appreciative reading of the Viennese theoretician Alois Riegl, Behrens confirmed his belief in the will of the artist, but also heightened his conviction in the collective wills (*Kunstwollen, Volksgeist, Zeitgeist*) manifested in artistic development: autonomous developments within the potentials of art forms and their emergence and service under the spirit of a people and a time. Relatively slight and ephemeral projects such as exhibition rooms (Mannheim, 1907) and pavilions (Oldenburg, 1905) allowed Behrens to explore autonomous spatial forms. The Crematorium at Hagen (1905–1907), simultaneously weighted by the universal force of death and engaging the contemporary polemic of cremations, brought these autonomous explorations into the context of monumental building with complex social and symbolic implications. The Obenauer House in Saarbrücken (1905–1906), an impressive formal exercise that ingeniously meets a difficult

site and a domestic program, is perhaps one of Behrens's best works, certainly of this period.

During the Düsseldorf years, Behrens came in contact with industrialists, such as Karl Ernst Osthaus and others, and received his first commissions from the Allgemeine Elektricitäts Gesellschaft (AEG). In the same year (1907) that both Behrens and the AEG participated in the founding of the Deutscher Werkbund (an unprecedented organization linking artists, craftsmen, and producers in a broad polemical program for innovative, sound design and production), Behrens moved to Berlin-Neubabelsberg to open his design and architectural atelier from which he could fulfill his new responsibilities as artistic consultant to the AEG. In this position, he was responsible for virtually the whole of the visual character of a large, modern corporate enterprise: the letterheads, advertising graphics, trade exhibitions, the entire building program, and much of the product design of the AEG. Although the frequent claim that Behrens was the first industrial designer must be debated according to differing views about design for industry, there is an important, influential, and characteristic sense in which he did initiate modern industrial design. The directors and staff of the AEG, including the founder Emil Rathenau, and his noted son Walther were well aware of, and ambitious for, the deep implication of their distinctively modern industry in the economic, political, and eventually social and cultural life of imperial Germany. Behrens, with the full encouragement of his patrons, made it his task not to solve each highly diverse design problem according to its own proximate set of conditions but rather to achieve a corporate style that would evidence the solidarity, effectiveness, and power of this corporation, this prime example of the driving force behind not only economic but also political

Behrens.
A. E. G. Turbine Factory.
Berlin.
1908–1909

Behrens.
German Embassy.
Leningrad (St. Petersburg).
1911–1912

and cultural change. Behrens thus took up industrial design (his arc lamps, 1907, are a particularly noted example) in the service of a total corporate image, much as IBM, Olivetti, and Braun later were to do.

Behrens's first major architectural commission from the AEG was the Turbine Factory at the most prominent corner of a large factory complex in Berlin-Moabit. The temple façade of this building is the single image that means "Peter Behrens" in the established history of architecture. It is also the building on which the advocacy of later commentators has been projected. It has been cited for its originality in the use of concrete, iron, and glass although, in any straightforward sense, the Turbine Factory has no such priority. It has been seen as "frank industrial architecture" in which engineering principles, material conditions, and functional purpose have won out over traditional forms and ornament. It has been seen as an instance of pure, formal architecture. It has been seen as a dignified place of work as if the social and intellectual welfare of the workers had motivated the designer. But an examination of the building or of Behrens's career and advocacy will readily convince one that none of these claims is true. Behrens had escaped the arbitrary fantasies of the Artists' Colony and the abstractness of his learning period in Düsseldorf; but the very tangibility of power and the direct association of the AEG and himself with the imperial seat and the cultural world of Berlin only intensified his will to provide the symbols of a new order. Perhaps only a contemporary advocate of Behrens can voice what has been distanced from us by time and historiography

As Behrens sets out to achieve compelling symbols for electricity, he feels more strongly than ever that sacred will which would erect a festival house on the high mountain of which Behrens himself, as a world-priest of beauty said: "Here above we are filled with the impression of a higher purpose which can only be translated into that which is sensible; it is our spiritual need, the gratification of our metaphysical sense" [R. Breuer, *Werkkunst*, III, 1908, pp. 145–149].

Behrens was not interested in moving architecture to some new, mundane, empirical realm under the rubric of the factory but rather to bring the factory under the rubric of architecture—architecture in its highest form which for Behrens, now as always, stems from and represents the ultimate source of power.

This last point may be reinforced in looking to Behrens's contemporary work under more traditional commissions. For a villa (for example, the Wiegand House, Berlin-Dahlem, 1911–1912) or an office building (the Mannesmannrohren-Werke, Düsseldorf, 1911–1912), or an embassy (the German Embassy, St. Petersburg, now Leningrad, 1911–1912), Behrens worked innovatively within the classical tradition. He could plausibly argue that his designs responded to new conditions of their moment, but in no way were they intended to nor do they move toward a radical modernism, formally or functionally. The factory joined these building types, not the other way around.

Nonetheless, in Behrens's hierarchical world, the built environment reflects that hierarchy. Not every factory carries the symbolic load of the Turbine Factory. Other AEG factories grade off from the still monumental Small Motors Factory (1910–1913) through the Large Machine Factory (1911–1912) and High Tension Factory (1909–1910; all three on the AEG factory site at the Humboldthain, Berlin) to the simple, small suburban factories in Hennigsdorf near Berlin (1910–1919). Similarly, AEG workers' housing in Hennigsdorf is of a lesser social and architectural order than the contemporary villas.

The AEG factories are very large, often joined continuously, so that a single impression of the whole is difficult to achieve. Despite their diversity all the major AEG factories evidence a willingness to adjust not only the detail but even the entire concept of a building as one turns a corner or moves from a street façade to an operational factory elevation. The gas works of the Frankfurter Gasgesellschaft are differently conceived. Here Behrens deployed a few, relatively small, typical building units, to form a functional complex around the central coal storage. The Gas Work constructions employ a brick technology and forms that again go back to German medieval usage, but now it is a robust, fully plastic construction that does justice not only to the medieval precedents but also to the revived interest in these works by the early nineteenth century classicists whom Behrens admired: FRIEDRICH GILLY and KARL FRIEDRICH SCHINKEL. The exploration of types additively set out on a grid reveals an obvious debt to neoclassicism and undercuts the claims that Behrens's Gas Works is an early Expressionist building.

Although World War I caused only temporary irregularities in the industrialization of Germany, it did radically alter the political and cultural hierarchies that had been central to Behrens's thought and work. Behrens's practice and the significance of his work would never again approximate that of the prewar years. Behrens was caught up in Expressionist work of the 1920s, often derivative, occasionally managing something of his old forcefulness as in the administration building for I. G.

Farben in Frankfurt-Hoechst (1920–1924).

In the late 1920s, Behrens was pulled along toward what was subsequently called the International style, as when Mies van der Rohe included Behrens as the only member of the older generation in the justly famous Weissenhof Siedlung in Stuttgart (1927). Behrens's contribution was atypical for the exhibition and interesting in type if not brilliant in execution: a series of stepped blocks forming an apartment building with terraces.

Two major works of the early 1930s, continuing in the International mode, were two office buildings on the Alexanderplatz in Berlin (1929–1931) and a factory for the State Tobacco Factory in Linz, Austria (1932–1934; with ALEXANDER POPP).

Behrens taught at the academies of Vienna (1922–1927) and Berlin (1936–1940). Under the National Socialist regime, he designed a German embassy for Washington (unexecuted).

STANFORD ANDERSON

WORKS

1900–1901, Behrens House, Künstler-Kolonie, Darmstadt, Germany. *1902, Hamburg Vestibule, First International Exhibition of Decorative Arts, Turin, Italy. *1905, Pavilions and Garden, Northwest German Art Exhibition, Oldenburg, Germany. 1905–1906, Obenauer House, Saarbrücken, Germany. *1905–1906, Pavilion and Garden, Garden and Art Exhibition, Düsseldorf, Germany, 1905–1907, Crematorium (marble sheathing replaced with stucco in 1910), Hagen, Germany. *1906, Ankermarke Linoleum Works Pavilion and Exhibition rooms, Third German Exhibition of Arts and Crafts, Dresden, Germany. *1907, International Art Exhibition (interior with exhibit), Mannheim, Germany. *1908, AEG Pavilion, Germany Shipbuilding Exhibitio;, 1908–1909, AEG Turbine Factory; Berlin. 1908–1909, Schroeder House, Hagen, Germany. 1908–1910, Catholic Lodging House, Neuss, Germany. 1909–1910, AEG High Tension Factory, Berlin. 1909–1910, Cuno House, Hagen, Germany. *1910, AEG Salesrooms, Berlin. *1910, Hall of Machines and other elements of German section, International Exposition, Brussels. 1910–1912, Goedecke House, Hagen, Germany. 1910–1913, AEG Small Motors Factory, Berlin. 1910–1915, 1918–1919, AEG Factories and Rental Housing for Workers, Hennigsdorf Germany. 1911–1912, AEG Factory for Large Machines; 1911–1912, AEG New Factory for Electric Railway Equipment; 1911–1912, AEG Rowing Club Elektra; Berlin. 1911–1912, German Embassy, Leningrad (St. Petersburg). 1911–1912, Mannesmann Office Building, Düsseldorf, Germany. 1911–1912, Wiegand House, Berlin. 1911–1913, Frankfurter Gas Works. 1911–1920, Continental Rubber Company Office Building, Hannover, Germany. *1914, Festhalle, Deutscher Werkbund Exhibition; 1914, Frank and Lehmann Commercial Building; Cologne, Germany. 1915–1917, AEG Housing and Factory, Nationale Automobil AG, Berlin *1917–1919,

Behrens.
I. G. Farben Office Building.
Hoechst, Germany.
1920–1924

Hannoversche Waggonfabrik Factory, Germany. 1920–1921, Deutsche Werft Housing, Altona, Germany. 1920–1924, I. G. Farben Office Building, Hoechst, Germany. 1921–1925, Gutehoffnungshütte Offices and Warehouse, Oberhausen, Germany. *1922, Dombauhütte, Craft Exhibition, Munich. 1923–1926, Bassett-Lowke House, Northampton, England. 1924–1925, St. Peter's Monastery (monastery building and revisions to the church), Salzburg, Austria. 1924–1929, Three Low-income Housing Blocks, Vienna. *1925, Winter Garden Pavilion, Exposition des Arts Décoratifs, Paris. 1926–1927, Terrace House Apartments, Stuttgart, Germany. 1929–1930, Kurt Lewin House; 1929–1931, Office Buildings, Alexanderplatz; Berlin. 1930, Apartment Building in Bolivarallée, Westend, Berlin. 1931–1932, Clara Ganz Villa, Kronberg im Taunus, Germany. 1932–1934, Austrian State Tobacco Factory (with Alexander Popp), Linz.

BIBLIOGRAPHY

ANDERSON, STANFORD 1968 "Peter Behrens and the New Architecture of Germany: 1900–1917." Unpublished Ph.D. dissertation, Columbia University, New York. Published in part in *Architectural Design* 39, no. 2, and in *Oppositions* nos. 11, 21 & 23.

BEHRENS, PETER 1900 *Feste des Lebens und der Kunst: Eine Betrachtung des Theaters als höchsten Kultursymbols.* Leipzig: Diederichs.

BEHRENS, PETER 1901 *Ein Dokument deutscher Kunst: Die Ausstellung der Künstler-Kolonie in Darmstadt 1901.* Munich: Bruckmann.

BEHRENS, PETER 1914a "Einfluss von Zeit- und Raumausnutzung auf moderne Formentwicklung." *Der Verkehr* 1914:7–10.

BEHRENS, PETER 1914b "Über den Zusammenhang des baukünstlerischen Schaffens mit der Technik." Pages 251–265 in *Berlin, Kongress für Ästhetik und allgemeine Kunstwissenschaft: Bericht.* Stuttgart, Germany: The congress.

BEHRENS, PETER 1919 "Reform der künstlerischen Erziehung." Pages 93–106 in Berlin, Zentrale für Heimatdienst, *Der Geist der neuen Volksgemeinschaft: Denkschrift für das deutsche Volk.* Berlin: S. Fisher.

BEHRENS, PETER 1919–1920 "Die Gruppenbauweise." *Wasmuths Monatschefte für Baukunst* 4:122–127.

BEHRENS, PETER 1920 "Über die Beziehungen der künstlerischen und technischen Probleme." *Wendingen* 3:4–20.

BEHRENS, PETER 1925a "Administration Buildings for Industrial Plants." *American Architect* 128:167–174. Translation of part of Behrens's address at the dedication of the Mannesmann Building in 1912.

BEHRENS, PETER 1925b "Seeking Aesthetic Worth in Industrial Buildings." *American Architect* 128:475–479.

BEHRENS, PETER, and FRIES, HEINRICH DE 1918 *Vom sparsamen Bauen: Ein Beitrag zur Siedlungsfrage.* Berlin: Bauwelt.

BUDDENSIEG, TILMANN, and ROGGE, HENNING 1976 "Peter Behrens and the AEG Architecture." *Lotus* 12:90–127.

BUDDENSEIG, TILMANN; ROGGE, HENNING; ET AL. 1979 *Industrielkultur: Peter Behrens und die AEG, 1907–14.* Berlin: G. Mann.

CREMERS, PAUL JOSEPH 1928 *Peter Behrens: Sein Werk von 1909 bis zur Gegenwart.* Essen, Germany: Baedeker.

GRIMME, KARL MARIA 1930 *Peter Behrens und seine Wiener akademische Meisterschule.* Vienna: Luser.

HOEBER, FRITZ 1913 *Peter Behrens.* Munich: Müller & Rentsch.

HOEPFNER, WOLFRAM; NEUMEYER, FRITZ; ET AL. 1979 *Das Haus Wiegand.* Mainz, Germany: Zabern.

MEYER-SCHÖNBRUNN, F. 1913 *Peter Behrens.* Dortmund, Germany: Ruhfuss.

NÜRNBERG, GERMANISCHES NATIONALMUSEUM 1980 *Peter Behrens und Nürnberg.* Munich: Prestel.

ROGERS, ERNESTO ET AL. 1960 "Peter Behrens." *Casabella continuità* 240:entire issue.

SHAND, P. MORTON 1959 "The Machine: Peter Behrens." *Architectural Association Journal* 75:173–178.

WEBER, WILHELM (editor) 1966 *Peter Behrens (1868–1940).* Kaiserslautern, Germany: Pfalzgalerie.

BELANGER, FRANÇOIS JOSEPH

François Joseph Bélanger (1744–1818), a French architect, studied physics under the Abbot Nollet and architecture (1764–1765) at the Académie Royale d'Architecture under JULIEN DAVID LEROY and PIERRE CONTANT D'IVRY. Bélanger never went to Italy but he did travel in England observing the architecture and the landscape. He was later considered to have "dissolved the Italian Renaissance into French architecture." In 1767, he was *dessinateur des menus* in Versailles under C. M. A. Challe and designed a jewelry cupboard for Marie Antoinette. After meeting Sophie d'Arnould, the opera prima donna, in 1769, he was introduced to wealthy clients such as the comte de Lauragais who commissioned him to build the Hôtel de Brancas which he designed as a *pavillon à l'antique*. In 1770, Bélanger redesigned the Château de Baudour and landscaped the Hôtel de Beloeil, both in Belgium. In 1777, he bought the position of *premier architecte* to the comte d'Artois (younger brother of Louis XVI). The comte, an indiscriminate spender, commissioned numerous projects, among them the Pavillon de Bagatelle (1777) built in sixty-four days, and the remodeling of the Château de Maison (1777–1779). For Claude Saint James, he designed the Folie Saint James in Neuilly (c.1780) and its gardens, done in the picturesque style. Bélanger's interiors were influential for their inventive style, colors, and use of materials. For his future wife, Mademoiselle Delvieux, he built in 1786 three houses on the rue Saint Georges in

Paris. A project for the Hôtel de Mirepoix demonstrated his admiration for antiquity in its proportions, columns, and classical allegories.

Imprisoned for a year as a royalist during the revolution, Bélanger was named Commissaire de la Commune in 1795 and Architecte du Conservatoire in 1796.

In 1808–1813, he replaced the dome of the Halle au Blé, which had burned in 1802, with a masterpiece of engineering, realizing the first cast-iron dome in history. Bélanger worked on his own estate in Santeny (1800–1815), experimenting with new designs. He left numerous drawn projects which complement his built oeuvre.

MARC DILET

WORKS

1770, Château de Baudour (remodeling); 1770, Hôtel de Beloeil (landscaping); Belgium. 1770, Hôtel de Brancas, Paris. 1773, Hôtel des Gardes, Versailles, France. 1777, Pavillon de Bagatelle, Bois de Boulogne, Paris. 1777–1779, Château de Maison (remodeling); c.1780, Folie Saint James and garden; Neuilly-sur-Seine, France. 1786–1788, three houses, rue Saint Georges; 1796, Hôtel des Menus Plaisirs (restoration); 1799, Bibliothèque Nationale (extension); Paris. 1800–1815, Bélanger House, Santeny, France. 1808–1813, Halle au Blé (dome), Paris.

BIBLIOGRAPHY

"Eloge de Brongiart." 1813 *Journal des Arts et Sciences et de la Litterature.* June.
"Lettres sur les Arts par un ami des artistes." 1777 *Journal de Paris.*

BELKOVSKI and DANCHOV

The firm of Belkovski and Danchov (1928–1939), leading promoters of modern architecture in Bulgaria, created not only admirable models of Modernism, such as the Bulgaria Hotel and Concert Hall Complex (1930–1935) and the Balkan Apartments Hotel and Cinema-Theater Complex (1932–1936) in Sofia, but also a school of followers. Stancho Iliev Belkovski (1891–1962) and Ivan Petkov Danchov (1893–1972) were both born in Sofia, Bulgaria; both participated in the Balkan war (1912–1913) and World War I (1914–1918); and both graduated from the Berlin Polytechnic Institute at Charlottenburg, Germany, Belkovski in 1920, Danchov in 1922.

Belkovski practiced alone from 1920 to 1922 and from 1925 to 1927 and briefly joined Ivan Vasil'ov (see VASIL'OV AND TSOLOV), but he created his best works in partnership with Danchov. Belkovski organized the design program at the foundation in 1943 of an architecture department at the Sofia Polytechnic Institute. He directed the Institute of Urbanism and Architecture of the Bulgarian Academy of Sciences from 1961 to 1962.

Danchov, a leading designer of industrial complexes, began his career heading the design and construction office of the Bulgarian State Railroads (1923–1925), worked alone (1925–1927), and joined Belkovski for a most successful and wide-ranging practice. Returning from the front in 1945, Danchov organized the department of industrial plants design at Sofia Polytechnic Institute (1945–1948) and at Varna State University (1948–1951) in Varna, Bulgaria. From 1951 on, he taught at the Sofia Polytechnic Institute, while also practicing as head of Studio Eight of the Central Architectural Design Organization in Sofia. For participating (with GEORGI RADEV OVCHAROV and Racho Ribarov) in the speedy realization of Georgi Dimitrov's Mausoleum (1949) in Sofia, Danchov received the Dimitrov's Award in 1951.

As educators, Belkovski and Danchov formed the views and design philosophy of the first generation of architects educated in Bulgaria by sharing their expertise and demonstrating in their executed works the principles of functionalism.

MILKA T. BLIZNAKOV

WORKS

STANCHO ILIEV BELKOVSKI

1922–1923, Institute for Foreign Languages, Slaveikov Square; 1925–1926, Housing Cooperative, 120 Rakovski Street; 1938–1939, Stock Exchange (now Ministry of Commerce); 1939–1940, Office Building (now United States Embassy), Stamboliiski Street; 1942–1946, Central Telephone Exchange; Sofia.

IVAN PETKOV DANCHOV

1923–1925, Custom House, Sofia Railroad Terminal. 1923–1925, Locomotive Shop, Triavana, Bulgaria. 1925–1927, Railroad Freightcar Factory, Drianovo, Bulgaria. 1925–1927, Slaughter House and Meat Plant, Gabrovo, Bulgaria. 1931–1933, Textile Factory (Semerdziev), Sofia. 1931–1933, Textile Factory, Gorna Bania, Bulgaria. 1933–1935, Jewish Memorial Hospital; 1940–1941, Office Building, 26 Denkoglu Street; 1949, Georgi Dimitrov's Mausoleum (with Georgi Ovcharov and Racho Ribarov); 1955–1957, Ministry of Electrification (with others); Sofia.

BELKOVSKI AND DANCHOV

1925–1930, Miners' Housing Complex (Tvurdi livadi), Pernik, Bulgaria. 1926, Popular Bank and Hotel, Kazanluk, Bulgaria. 1930, Central Telephone Exchange, Turnovo, Bulgaria. 1930–1931, Apartment Cooperative, 17 Ruski Street; 1930–1935, Hotel and Concert Hall Complex; 1931–1932, German College (now State Conservatory); 1932–1933, Students' Dormitory Club, Narodno Subranie Square; 1932–1936, Apartments Hotel and Cinema Theater (now National Youth Theater); 1933, Semerszhiev Residence (now

Vietnam's Embassy), 12 Oborische Street; Sofia. 1933–1934, German College, Burgas, Bulgaria. 1935, Kuiumdzhiev Residence (now housing for United States Embassy), Sofia. 1938–1940, Balabanov Country Mansion, Boiana, near Sofia.

BIBLIOGRAPHY

BELKOVSKI, STANCHO 1952 "Industrialno-montazhno Stroitelśtvo na sgradi." *Arkhitektura i Stroitelśtvo* 2:1–6.

BELKOVSKI, STANCHO 1954 "Obshchestvenite sgradi v natsionalnata arkhitekturna izlozhba." Arkhitektura 5–6:1–14.

BELKOVSKI, STANCHO 1960 "Tipovo masovo industrialno zhilishchno Stroitelśtvo s ednorazmerni elementi." *Arkhitektura* 10:1–6.

BELKOVSKI, STANCHO; DRAGANOV, S.; and APOSTOLOV, G. 1960 *Problemi na tipovoto proektirane i masovoto Stroitelśtvo na chitalishchni sgradi.* Sofia.

BŬLGARSKA AKADEMIĬA NA NAUKITE 1954 *Arkhitektura v Bulgariĭa Sled 9 Septemvri 1944.* Sofia: The academy.

BŬLGARSKA AKADEMIĬA NA NAUKITE 1965 *Kratka istoriĭa na Bŭlgarskata arkhitektura.* Sofia: The academy.

DANCHOV, T., AND MARKOVSKI, P. 1955 *Promishleni sgradi.* Sofia.

MAMBRIANI, ALBERTO 1969 *L'architettura moderna nei paesi Balcanici.* Bologna, Italy: Cappelli.

NENKOV, BORIS 1952 "Bulgarskata arkhitektura sled Purvata svetovna voina." *Arkhitektura i Stroitelśtvo* 4:9–14.

"Profesor arkhitekt Ivan P. Danchov." 1968 *Arkhitektura* 3–4:34–37.

STOICHEV, LIUBEN 1968 "25 godini visshe tekhnichesko obrazovanie v Bulgaria." *Arkhitektura* 5:38–40.

TANGUROV, JORDAN, and DRAGANOV, STEFAN 1962 "Arkhitekt Stancho Belkovski." *Arkhitektura* 3:21–27.

BELL, HENRY

Henry Bell (1647–1711), merchant, alderman, and mayor of Kings Lynn, Norfolk, England, was an educated and traveled gentleman who practiced architecture as a pastime. He worked in a style that owed something to Holland and much to CHRISTOPHER WREN. He was involved in the rebuilding of Northampton after the fire of 1675. Although works elsewhere have been attributed to him on stylistic grounds, all his other documented works are in the Kings Lynn area. Bell's manuscript, *An Historical Essay on the Original of Painting,* was published posthumously in 1728.

JOHN BOLD

WORKS

1677–1680, All Saints Church, Northampton, England.

Bell.
Customs House.
Kings Lynn, England.
1683

1683, Customs House; 1684, Dukes Head Inn; Kings Lynn, England. 1703–1713, North Runcton Church, Norfolk, England. *1707–1710, Market Cross, Kings Lynn, England.

BIBLIOGRAPHY

ARCHDALE, M. 1966 "Henry Bell as a Country House Architect." *Country Life* Sept. 15 & 29:614–616, 756–758.

COLVIN, H. M., and WODEHOUSE, L. M. 1961 "Henry Bell of Kings Lynn." *Architectural History* 4:41–62.

BELL, WILLIAM E.

William E. Bell (19th century), architect and builder, wrote *Carpentry Made Easy* (1858), the first comprehensive description of an important innovation in building technique, developed in the Midwest in the 1830s and known as the balloon frame. A cagelike wood frame constructed of rather closely spaced, mechanically produced lightweight framing members, fastened together by factory-made nails, replaced the traditional heavy timbers joined by mortise and tenon. Spurred by the building boom in Chicago and a shortage of skilled labor, this simple, rapid technique grew in popularity nationwide as its strength, versatility, and economy became apparent. It remains a common framing technique.

GWEN W. STEEGE

BIBLIOGRAPHY

BELL, WILLIAM E. (1894)1904 *Carpentry Made Easy; or, The Science and Art of Framing on a New and Improved System. With Specific Instructions for Building Balloon Frames, Barn Frames, Mill Frames, Winehouses,*

Church Spires, etc., Comprising Also a System of Bridge Building. 4th ed., rev. Philadelphia: Ferguson.

FIELD, WALKER 1942 "A Reexamination into the Invention of the Balloon Frame." *Journal of the Society of Architectural Historians* 2:3–29.

HITCHCOCK, H. R. (1938–1939)1976 *American Architectural Books.* Reprint of 1962 edition. Minneapolis: University of Minnesota Press.

JENSEN, ROBERT 1971 "Board and Batten Siding and the Balloon Frame: Their Incompatibility in the Nineteenth Century." *Journal of the Society of Architectural Historians* 30:40–50.

BELLI, PASQUALE

Pasquale Belli (1752–1833) studied with Pietro Camporese (see CAMPORESE FAMILY), whom he helped in his last commissions. He worked also with RAFFAELLO STERN, finishing the Braccio Nuovo at the Vatican, one of the great neoclassical musea, after the latter's death in 1821. Through his work at San Paolo fuori le Mura (1825–1833) he helped establish a purist, frigid, and anonymous architectural language, emphasized by the ostentatiously "new" construction on the fifth-century plan.

He completed the façades of Santa Maria della Consolazione (1800) and San Andrea delle Fratte (1826), and designed the crypt of the lower church of San Francesco in Assisi to house the remains of the saint (1818).

MARTHA POLLAK

WORKS

1800, Santa Maria della Consolazione (façade), Rome. 1818, San Francesco (lower church and crypt), Assisi, Italy. 1821, Braccio Nuovo, Vatican; 1825–1833, San Paolo fuori le Mura; 1826, San Andrea delle Fratte (façade); Rome.

BIBLIOGRAPHY

LAVAGNINO, EMILIO 1961 Volume I in *L'arte moderna dai neoclassici ai contemporanei.* Turin: Unione Tipografico-Editrice Torinese.

MEEKS, C. L. V. 1966 *Italian Architecture, 1750–1914.* New Haven: Yale University Press.

BELLUSCHI, PIETRO

Pietro Belluschi, born in Ancona, Italy, on August 18, 1899, entered the Italian army in March 1917, became an officer, and served until 1920. He graduated in engineering from the University of Rome in 1922, and then went to Cornell University on an exchange fellowship, receiving the degree of civil engineer in 1924. Dissatisfied as a mining engineer in Idaho, he went to Portland, Oregon, in April 1925, with a letter of introduction to Albert E. Doyle, one of the leading architects in the northwest, and incidentally rather an Italophile. Employed in the office, he soon became one of the principal designers. In 1928 the firm was reorganized as A. E. Doyle and associate, continuing under this name until 1943 when it was again reorganized under the name of Pietro Belluschi. Throughout these years Belluschi was the chief designer and since 1933 a partner. When Belluschi left Oregon to become dean of architecture and planning at the Massachusetts Institute of Technology in 1951, he sold his practice to SKIDMORE, OWINGS, AND MERRILL.

During his Oregon years, Belluschi made his reputation as an architect, particularly in commercial, domestic, and religious buildings. His first important work was the Portland Art Museum (1931–1932, 1937–1938). It was modern without being either Bauhaus or Modernistic. With the contemporary Finley Mortuary, Portland (1936–1937), it brought him national acclaim.

Commercial buildings were a major concern of the firm, and Belluschi designed many offices, shops, and shopping centers. A growing relation to the International style was evident in an addition to the Salem branch of the United States National Bank of Oregon (1940–1941), and in projects of the war years. These designs led to his masterpiece, the Equitable Building (1945–1948), Portland. Significant for technological developments as well as design, it was the first of the taut-skinned grid structures which became so popular in the 1950s.

The domestic and religious buildings were quite different in character. In the late 1930s, Belluschi, together with JOHN YEON, who also worked in the Doyle office, may be said to have invented a regional style of domestic architecture. It appeared fully developed in the Sutor House (1937–1938), Portland, and was followed by many others in the 1940s. These wooden houses with their forms inspired by vernacular barns and sheds, and an occasional hint of the Japanese; with their natural materials; and their sensitive siting formed the basis for a true regional style. The churches were related in form and material to the houses and like the houses led to a regional development. From Saint Thomas More (1939–1941), Portland, to the First Presbyterian Church (1949–1951), Cottage Grove, they show the "simplicity and restraint" that Belluschi has frequently said are the essence of good architecture. By the time he left Oregon, Belluschi was one of the foremost church architects in the country.

Acceptance of academic status was not the end of his career as a practicing architect; in fact, he became even more active in his years at M.I.T. and after retirement in 1965. His system of working

Belluschi.
First Presbyterian Church.
Cottage Grove, Oregon.
1949–1951

changed. Always a believer in the necessity of teamwork in twentieth century architecture, he chose to collaborate with other firms rather than establish a large office of his own. In effect this permitted him to design a far greater number of buildings in more locations than would otherwise have been possible. Churches and other religious buildings continued to be a large part of his work, ranging from small parish churches, Saint Joseph's (1964–1968), Roseburg, Oregon, to metropolitan cathedrals, Saint Mary's (1963–1973), San Francisco. The earlier churches are longitudinal, the later ones generally centralized. He has been responsible for the design of many office, educational, and cultural buildings. In his long career he has designed more than a thousand buildings.

In an active career of more than fifty years Pietro Belluschi has received many distinctions, awards for design, honorary degrees, and decorations. In 1972 he received the Gold Medal of the American Institute of Architects, the highest distinction in the profession.

MARION DEAN ROSS

WORKS

1931–1932, 1937–1938, Portland Art Museum; 1936–1937, Finley Mortuary; 1937–1938, Sutor House; 1939–1941, Saint Thomas More Church; 1940–1941, Platt House; Portland, Ore. *1940–1941, United States National Bank of Oregon, Salem Branch (addition); 1942,

Bagley Downs Shopping Center and McLoughlin Heights Shopping Center, Vancouver, Wash. 1944–1947, Burkes House; 1945–1948, Equitable Building; 1945–1948, Federal Reserve Bank of San Francisco, Portland Branch; 1945–1948, Oregonian Building; Portland, Ore. 1946, First National Bank of Oregon, Salem Branch. 1946, Wilson Houses, Warm Springs, Ore. 1948–1951, Zion Lutheran Church; 1949–1951, Central Lutheran Church; Portland, Ore. 1949–1951, First Presbyterian Church, Cottage Grove, Ore. 1955–1970, Julliard School of Music (with EDUARDO CATALANO, Helge Westermann, and Associated Architects), New York. 1956, Temple Israel (with Carl Koch and Associates), Swampscott, Mass. 1957, First Lutheran Church, Boston. 1958–1959, Bennington College Library (with Carl Koch and Associates), Vt. 1962, Pan American Building (consultant with WALTER GROPIUS to EMERY ROTH and Sons), New York. 1963–1973, Saint Mary's Cathedral (with McSweeney, Ryan, and Lee Associates, and PIER LUIGI NERVI), San Francisco. 1964–1968, Saint Joseph's Church (with Wolff, Zimmer, Gunsul, and Frasca), Roseburg, Ore. 1964–1968, Temple B'nai Jeshurun (with Grunzen and Partners), Short Hills, N.J. 1965–1972, John M. Tobin Elementary School (with Sasaki, Dawson, De May, and Associates), Cambridge, Mass. 1966–1970, Undergraduate Dormitory, Massachusetts Institute of Technology (with The Architects Collaborative), Cambridge. 1970–1973, Dormitory, Phillips Exeter Academy (with Jung/Brannen Associates), Andover, Mass. 1970–1975, International Business Machines Center (with Emery Roth and Sons), Baltimore. 1975–1980, Symphony Hall (with Skidmore, Owings, and Merrill), San Francisco. 1976–1980, Emmanuel Lutheran Church (with Belluschi/Daskalakis Inc.), Silverton, Ore.

BIBLIOGRAPHY

The Pietro Belluschi Collection is in the George Arents Manuscript Library, Syracuse University, Syracuse, New York.

FARR, LIBBY DAWSON 1977 "The Architecture of Pietro Belluschi." Unpublished M.A. thesis, Reed College, Portland, Ore.

GORDON, WALTER 1958 "The Architecture of Pietro Belluschi." *Northwest Review* Fall–Winter: facing page 32.

GUBITOSI, CAMILLO and IZZO, ALBERTO (editors) 1974 *Pietro Belluschi: Edifici e progetti 1932–1973.* Rome: Officina Edizioni.

HEYER, PAUL (1966)1978 *Architects on Architecture: New Directions in America.* 2d ed., rev. New York: Walker.

HOSFIELD, JOHN D. 1960 "A Study of the Architecture of Pietro Belluschi: Oregon 1925–1950." Unpublished M.A. thesis, University of Oregon, Eugene.

ROSS, MARION DEAN 1966–1967 "The Museum Building as a Work of Art." In *Notes on the Collections,* Portland Art Association Reports, No. 7. Portland (Ore.) Art Museum.

ROSS, MARION DEAN 1972 "The 'Attainment and Restraint' of Pietro Belluschi." *Journal of the American Institute of Architects* 58:17–24.

STUBBLEBINE, JO (editor) 1953 *The Northwest Architecture of Pietro Belluschi.* New York: Dodge.

BELLUZZI, GIOVANNI BATTISTA

Giovanni Battista Belluzzi or Bellucci (1506–1554), called Sanmarino, was the military architect of Cosimo I, grand duke of Tuscany. Born in the Republic of San Marino, he became an architect at the age of thirty, when he married the daughter of GIROLAMO GENGA, architect of the Della Rovere, from whom he learned the rudiments of architectural design, directing his interests particularly toward military architecture according to the new canons of the Venetian school.

Arriving in Florence in 1542 as ambassador for San Marino, he was taken into employment by the de' Medici and promoted to chief military engineer by the young duke Cosimo in his ambitious campaign to renew the defenses of Tuscany. In his ten years in Cosimo's service, Belluzzi was concerned with adapting medieval circuits of walls to the new exigencies of modern artillery, using bastions and temporary earth defenses. In Florence itself, Pistoia, Montepulciano, Barga, Castrocaro, Borgo San Sepolcro, and numerous other minor centers, he designed new defenses around old circuits. In 1548, he received the prestigious commission to plan a new city, Cosmopolis (Portoferrai) on the island of Elba.

Early on, he wrote for Cosimo a never completed general treatise on fortifications. Another treatise on earth fortifications codified for the first time this important aspect of military defenses. His treatises circulated in manuscript for many years in Italy and throughout Europe; publication of the general treatise in a poor edition in 1598 under the mangled name of Belici created confusion about the identity of this ultimately forgotten personality famous in his own day. He was partially rediscovered in the nineteenth century, and the treatise on earth fortifications has been published recently.

Given their originally provisional character and their subsequent transformations, few of his fortifications remain. Apart from his writings, a series of autograph drawings of fortified circuits of central and north Italian cities survive in Florence.

DANIELA LAMBERINI

WORKS

*1537–1538, Fortifications; *1537–1538, Villa Imperiale; Pesaro, Italy. *1544–1545, Fortifications, Borgo San Sepolcro, Italy. *1544–1545, Fortifications, Castrocaro, Italy. *1544–1545, Fortifications, Florence. *1544–1545, Fortifications, Livorno, Italy. *1544–1545, Fortifications, Montepulciano, Italy. *1544–1545, Fortifications, Pisa, Italy. *1544–1545, Fortifications, Pistoia, Italy. *1548, Foundation of Cosmopolis, Portoferraio, Elba, Italy. *1549–1550, Fortifications, Barga, Italy. *1551, Fortifications, San Miniato al Monte and San Piero Gattolini, Florence. *1552, Fortifications, Empoli, Italy. *1552, Fortifications, Piombino, Italy. *1552, Fortifications, San Casciano, Italy. *1553–1554, Fortifications, Siena, Italy.

BIBLIOGRAPHY

BELLUZZI, GIOVANNI BATTISTA 1907 *Diario autobiografico (1535–41).* Edited by Pietro Egidi. Naples: Ricciardi.

BELLUZZI, GIOVANNI BATTISTA 1980 "Il trattato delle fortificazioni di terra." Edited by Daniela Lamberini. Pages 375–401 in Franco Borsi et al., *Il disegno interrotto: Trattati medicei d'architettura.* Florence: Gonnelli.

LAMBERINI, DANIELA 1981 "Giovanni Battista Belluzzi: Ingegnere militare e la fondazione di Portoferraio." In *Cosmopolis Portoferraio Medicea secoli XVI–XVII: Mostra documentaria.* Pisa, Italy: Pacini.

BELTRAMI, LUCA

Luca Beltrami (1854–1933), a student of CAMILLO BOITO, studied at the Polytechnic Institute and Academy of his native city of Milan. In 1876, he continued his education in Paris at the Ecole des

Beaux-Arts, attending the atelier of JEAN LOUIS PASCAL, and, at this time, assisting with the restoration of the Hôtel-de-Ville. After his return to Milan in 1880, Beltrami began a distinguished and varied career as an architect, teacher, restorer, art historian, and critic. From 1891, he served as the first director of monuments of Lombardy. His successful effort to preserve the fifteenth-century Castello Sforzesca in Milan resulted in its considerable and rather fanciful reconstruction (1893–1905) after his design. For his numerous public and commercial works, Beltrami favored a classicism derived principally from the Cinquecento. In 1920, he moved to Rome. As architect of the Vatican under Pope Pius XI, he designed the Pinacoteca Vaticana (1932).

JOY M. KESTENBAUM

WORKS

1883–1885, Palazzo per L'Esposizione Permanente di Belle Arti; 1886–1892, Palazzo Marino (completion); 1890–1892, Tempio Israelitico (with Luigi Tenenti); 1893–1905, Castello Sforzesca (reconstruction); 1897–1899, Palazzo Venezia delle Assicurazioni Generali di Milano (with Luigi Tenenti); 1898, Casa Alesina, "Via Cappuccio (with Luigi Tenenti); 1900–1902, Casa Dario-Biandra (now Banco di Napoli; with Luigi Repossi); 1903–1904, Corriere della Sera (with Luigi Repossi); 1905–1911, Banca Commerciale; 1910, Casa Bernasconi (with Luigi Repossi); 1918–1927, Banca Commerciale; Milan. 1932, Pinacoteca Vaticana, Vatican City, Rome.

BIBLIOGRAPHY

ANNONI, AMBROGIO 1950 "Tre Architetti dell' Ottocento. 3. Luca Beltrami." *Metron* 37:45–46.
ARMATO, MARIA MICHELE 1952 *Luca Beltrami, 1854–1933; l'Uomo sulla Scorta di Documenti Inediti.* Florence: Carnesecchi.
BELTRAMI, LUCA, and MORETTI, GAETANO. 1898 *Resoconto dei Lavori di Restauro Eseguiti al Castello di Milano.* Milan: Allegretti.
BESSONE-AURELJ, ANTONIETTA MARIA 1947 *Dizionario degli Scultori ed Architetti Italiani.* Genoa, Italy: Società Anonima Editrice Dante Alighieri.
GRANDI, MAURIZIO, and PRACCHI, ATTILO 1980 *Milano. Guida all'Architettura Moderna* Bologna, Italy: Zanichelli.
"Luca Beltrami." 1933 *Architettura* 12:586.
MEEKS, CARROLL L. V. 1966 *Italian Architecture: 1750–1914.* New Haven: Yale University Press.

BEMAN, SOLON S.

A Chicago architect chiefly known for the design of the company-built town of Pullman, Illinois, Solon Spencer Beman (1853–1914) was born in Brooklyn, New York, on October 1, 1853. After completing an elementary and secondary educa-

tion in various public and private schools, he entered the office of RICHARD UPJOHN in 1870, where he remained as apprentice, draftsman, and designing associate until 1877. In the latter year he founded an independent office in New York, and in 1879, through a combination of his own abilities, a vigorous and engaging personality, and the connections he formed in association with the influential Upjohn and his clients, Beman was awarded one of the largest and most enviable architectural commissions of the time.

George M. Pullman, already moving toward the establishment of a virtual monopoly in the manufacture and operation of railroad sleeping cars, needed expanded manufacturing facilities for his rapidly growing enterprise. He engaged the young architect, who had previously designed his Chicago mansion, along with the New York landscape architect Nathan F. Barrett, to design all the buildings and the landscaping work and to prepare the site plan for an entire town, to be built on open land along Lake Calumet, some miles south of Chicago. This most celebrated—indeed, notorious—of company towns included complete manufacturing facilities, rail and water access, housing, a shopping center, churches, parks, and other recreational spaces. Construction and planning were inaugurated almost simultaneously in 1879, when Beman moved his office to Chicago, and by 1884 the new community was largely completed.

The Pullman commission brought Beman national attention, and when the original factory of the Procter and Gamble Company in Cincinnati burned in 1884, he received the commission for what was at first conceived as another complete company-built town, named Ivorydale. Construction began in 1884, on a spacious tract between railroad lines in Saint Bernard, Ohio, and was completed in 1889 (according to the dates of the final drawings). The plan for housing was abandoned, and Beman's designs were limited to manufacturing, storage, and administrative buildings, all sturdily constructed of fireproof brick and stone masonry.

Among the numerous commissions that Beman secured in Chicago, the Middle West, New York State, and Portland, Oregon, five in Chicago are perhaps the most distinguished. The Pullman Building (1884), designed to house the company's inner-city offices, and the First Studebaker (later the Fine Arts) Building (1886) were freehanded adaptations of the popular Romanesque style. Grand Central Station (1889–1890), opened to service for the Chicago and Northern Pacific Railway in 1890, was a masterpiece of rail terminal design, a unified composition of prismatic and blocklike masses done in a severe Nor-

Beman.
Pullman Building.
Chicago.
1884

man Romanesque. The interior, by contrast, was open and flooded with light because of the extensive glass curtains along the inner side and front of the balloon train shed. The Mines and Mining Building (1893) of the World's Columbian Exposition represented the ruling classicism of the fair. The façade of the Second Studebaker (now the Brunswick) Building (1894–1895) provides a remarkably transparent, delicately articulated work in the dominant mode of the Chicago school.

In addition to his architectural works, Beman acted as a consultant to the Pullman Company for the interior design of cars, in which capacity his most prominent achievement was the interior decor of Pullman's exhibition train at the Columbian Exposition. After a flourishing career of thirty-seven years, he died in Chicago on April 24, 1914. His position in American architecture rests to a great degree on the projects for the Pullman and the Procter and Gamble companies, which reveal a mastery of the planning of towns and industrial parks.

CARL W. CONDIT

WORKS

1879–1884, Pullman Company Industrial Park and Town, Pullman (now Chicago). *1884, Pullman Building, Chicago. 1884–1889, Procter and Gamble Company Industrial Park (Ivorydale), Saint Bernard, Ohio. 1886, First Studebaker (now Fine Arts) Building; *1889–1890, Grand Central Station; *1893, Mines and Mining Building; 1894–1895, Second Studebaker (now Brunswick) Building; Chicago. 1895, Chicago and Alton (now Illinois Central Gulf) Station, Springfield, Ill. 1906, Berger Building, Pittsburgh.

BIBLIOGRAPHY

Original source material on Beman is in the Procter and Gamble Company archives in Cincinnati, Ohio.

BACH, IRA J. (1969)1977 *Chicago on Foot: Walking Tours of Chicago's Architecture.* 3d ed., rev. Chicago: Rand McNally.

"Beman, Solon Spencer." 1910 Volume 14, pages 304–305 in *National Cyclopaedia of American Biography.* New York: James T. White.

BUDER, STANLEY 1967 *Pullman: An Experiment in Industrial Order and Community Planning, 1880–1930.* New York: Oxford University Press.

CONDUIT, CARL W. 1964 *The Chicago School of Architecture: A History of Commercial and Public Building in the Chicago Area, 1875–1925.* University of Chicago Press.

RANDALL, FRANK A. 1949 *History of the Development of Building Construction in Chicago.* Urbana: University of Illinois Press.

BENEVOLO, LEONARDO

Leonardo Benevolo (1923–), born in Orta, near Novarra, Italy, is one of the premier architectural historians of the post–World War II era. Benevolo graduated from the University of Rome in 1946 and has taught in Italy at the universities of Rome, Florence, and Venice. He has also taught abroad, including Columbia University, New York.

Benevolo's contribution resides primarily in his interweaving of social movements and architectural production. His *Origins of Modern Town Planning* (1963) remains the most concise and most influential of his works. He has also pursued an architectural practice with Carlo Melograni and T. G. Longo.

THOMAS L. SCHUMACHER

BIBLIOGRAPHY

BENEVOLO, LEONARDO (1960a)1971 *History of Modern Architecture.* 2 vols. Rev. ed. Cambridge, Mass.: M.I.T. Press.

BENEVOLO, LEONARDO (1960b)1966 *Una Introduzione all'Architettura.* Rome, and Bari, Italy: Laterza.

BENEVOLO, LEONARDO (1963)1967 *Origins of Modern Town Planning.* Cambridge, Mass.: M.I.T. Press.

BENEVOLO, LEONARDO 1969 *La Città Italiana del Rinascimento.* Milan: Polifilo.

BENEVOLO, LEONARDO 1977 *Roma Oggi.* Rome, and Bari, Italy: Laterza.

BENEVOLO, LEONARDO 1978 *The Architecture of the Renaissance.* Boulder, Colo.: Westview.

BENEVOLO, LEONARDO 1980 *History of the City.* Cambridge, Mass.: M.I.T. Press.

BENEVOLO, LEONARDO, and LONGO, T. G. 1977 *La Progettazione della Città.* Rome and Bari, Italy: Laterza.

BENJAMIN, ASHER

Asher Benjamin (1773–1845) published the first American builders' guide. His seven architectural books played a major role in disseminating late Georgian designs by ROBERT ADAM'S popularist, WILLIAM PAIN, the Federal style of the Boston architect CHARLES BULFINCH, and later the new language of the Greek Revival. Born in Hartland,

Connecticut, in 1773, Benjamin was probably apprenticed in nearby Suffield, Connecticut, where he was paid by Oliver Phelps in 1795 "for two Ionic Capitals" (Oliver Phelps Cashbook, Phelps–Gorham Papers, New York State Library, Albany). Between 1795 and 1802, he designed several buildings throughout the upper Connecticut River valley, the earliest surviving of which, the William Coleman House, Greenfield, Massachusetts (1797), contains one of the first elliptical staircases in New England, inspired by PETER NICHOLSON's *Carpenter's New Guide* (1792).

Benjamin's first architectural book was the *Country Builder's Assistant* (1797). He had come to realize, he wrote later, that the American mechanic is, "in purchasing European publications, under the necessity of paying two thirds the value . . . for what is of no real use to him" (1806, p.v.). His chief influence in this first work was WILLIAM PAIN's *Practical House Carpenter* (1789). The American author borrows directly with only minor simplifications, but he increases the proportions of the orders as an accommodation to the provincial New England experience.

The most important design in the *Country Builder's Assistant* is the meetinghouse modeled apparently on those designed by Bulfinch in Taunton, Massachusetts (1790–1792), and Lavius Fillmore in East Haddam, Connecticut (1791–1794). This plate had a far-reaching impact upon early nineteenth-century ecclesiastical building throughout New England and as far west as Ohio.

Benjamin moved to Boston in 1802, where he is described in the directories as housewright. He quickly made the transition from country builder to urban architect, as characterized in the title page of his second and more highly polished publication, the *American Builder's Companion* (1806). In the first edition, which was coauthored by Daniel Raynard, a Boston stucco-worker, he continued to borrow extensively from William Pain and added material on staircase construction from the second London edition of Peter Nicholson's *Carpenter's and Joiner's Assistant* (1797). Benjamin's Yankee background is again apparent in such frank departures from canonical practice as his design for a Doric mutule block "represented with holes bored in it, instead of bells, which will save one half the labour of making them; and, at a distance of fifteen or twenty feet, look as well if not better" (1806, p. 13).

Charles Bulfinch, however, represented the major new influence upon Benjamin which led him to proclaim his second work as "A New System of Architecture." Of his important ecclesiastical commissions during this period, the West Church (1806) and Charles Street Meetinghouse (1807) in Boston are inspired by Bulfinch's Holy Cross Church (1800–1803) and New North Church (1803–1804) in Boston.

Benjamin's access to some fifty-five publications catalogued by the Social Architectural Library of Boston in 1809 helps to explain the growing diversity of English sources in his own works. The second, 1811 edition of the *American Builder's Companion* was his most thorough revision and draws heavily on Sir WILLIAM CHAMBERS's *Treatise on Civil Architecture* (1759). Chambers is responsible for the metamorphosis by which Benjamin's manuals cease to be merely pattern books and are henceforward architectural handbooks, mingling theory with practice and formal knowledge with technical advice.

In his fourth work, the *Practical House Carpenter* (1830) Benjamin, then aged fifty-six, revealed an increasing preoccupation with the new Greek Revival style which culminated in his fifth and sixth works, the *Practice of Architecture* (1833) and the *Builder's Guide* (1838). He was never entirely at ease with this later shift in classical emphasis, however, as observed also in his private work, for example, the Thatcher Magoun House in Medford, Massachusetts (1834), in which a modified Greek Ionic peristyle envelopes a traditional five-bay New England house. The *Practical House Carpenter*, nevertheless, was Benjamin's most popular book, and its twenty-one recorded reprintings rendered it the most popular American architectural handbook of the nineteenth century. This success can best be explained by the adroit juxtaposition of Roman and Greek detail, which spoke to a wide-ranging audience, and the author's continued appeal to New England common sense.

Benjamin operated a paint store in Boston between 1810 and 1824, during much of which period he acted also as agent for Ward Nicholas Boylston's extensive real estate in Boston. In 1825, he was appointed agent for the Nashua (New Hampshire) Manufacturing Company and lived there until 1828, designing the Olive Street Congregational Church (1825) and playing a major supervisory (and design) role in the construction of canal locks, laying out of streets, and erection of mill buildings for the company.

His seventh and last work, the *Elements of Architecture* (1843) is concerned almost entirely with building technology, including the structural uses of cast iron and pioneer tests for stress and strain on American timbers, carried out under his direction. In the contract and specifications for *Belmont,* home of John Perkins Cushing in Belmont, Massachusetts (1840), and the most imposing of Benjamin's later commissions, are found provision for furnaces, boilers, hot-air ducts to warm bathrooms, and funnels for ventilation.

Having earlier been a founder and first trustee of the Associated Housewrights of the Town of Boston in 1804, Benjamin was also a founding member of the American Institute of Architects in 1836. He remained active until the end, the *Elements of Architecture* being published only two years before his death in 1845.

Asher Benjamin was essentially an instructor. With frequent reprintings, his seven works reached an estimated volume of thirty to forty thousand copies. Because of his country builder's background, he could address his audience in a simple, unaffected, and knowing manner. If his designs were not highly creative or startlingly progressive, they did at least establish a level of competence in style and execution which helped two if not three generations of American rural builders throughout the North, South, and Midwest to achieve a measurable degree of sophistication.

ABBOTT LOWELL CUMMINGS

WORKS

*c.1796, Luke Baldwin House, Brookfield, Mass. *c.1796, Samuel Hinckley House, Northampton, Mass. 1797, William Coleman House; 1797, Leavitt–Hovey House; Greenfield, Mass. 1797–1798, First Deerfield Academy Building (Memorial Hall), Mass. *c.1799, Hubbard House; 1799–1800, Old South Meetinghouse; c.1800, Fullerton House (rebuilt in New Canaan, Conn.); *c.1800, Harriet Lane House; Windsor, Vt. *1802, United States Marine Hospital, Charlestown, Mass. 1806, West Church; *1806–1809, Exchange Coffee House; 1807, Charles Street Meetinghouse; 1808, James Smith Colburn Houses; *1808, Fourth Meetinghouse, First Church; Boston. *1811–1812, First Parish Church, Northampton, Mass. 1813–1814, Center Church, New Haven. *1817, Rhode Island Union Bank, Newport. 1818, Ward Nicholas Boylston House, Princeton, Mass. *1825, Olive Street Congregational Church, Nashua, N.H. 1830, Isaac Munson House, South Wallingford, Vt. *1832, Cambridgeport Town Hall, Cambridge, Mass. 1833–1834, Asher Benjamin Houses, 7–9 West Cedar Street, Boston. *1834, Thatcher Magoun House, Medford, Mass. 1835, Lexington–Concord Battle Monument, Peabody, Mass. 1836, William Ellery Channing House, Boston. 1836, George Shattuck Monument, Mount Auburn Cemetery, Cambridge, Mass. *1836, F. O. J. Smith House, Westbrook, Maine. 1838, Fifth Universalist Church, Boston. *1840, John Perkins Cushing House, Belmont, Mass. *1840, Unitarian Meetinghouse (Third Religious Society), Dorchester, Mass. *1841–1842, Edmund Hastings House, Medford, Mass.

BIBLIOGRAPHY

ALLEN, HARRIS 1920 "Architecture in the United States One Hundred Years Ago." *Building Review* 19, Feb.:21–27, 30.

BACH, RICHARD F. 1917 "Asher Benjamin Revived." *American Architect* 112:449–450.

BENJAMIN, ASHER (1797)1972 *The Country Builder's Assistant.* Reprint. New York: Da Capo. Introduction by Everard Upjohn.

BENJAMIN, ASHER (1806)1972 *The American Builder's Companion.* Reprint. New York: Da Capo. Introduction by William Morgan.

BENJAMIN, ASHER (1814)1976 *The Rudiments of Architecture.* Reprint. New York: Da Capo.

BENJAMIN, ASHER (1830)1976 *The Practical House Carpenter.* Reprint. New York: Da Capo.

BENJAMIN, ASHER (1833)1976 *The Practice of Architecture.* Reprint. New York: Da Capo.

BENJAMIN, ASHER (1838)1854 *The Builder's Guide.* Boston. Subsequent editions undated.

BENJAMIN, ASHER (1843)1976 *The Elements of Architecture.* Reprint. Boston: Mussey.

BISHER, CATHERINE W. 1979 "Asher Benjamin's *Practical House Carpenter* in North Carolina." *Carolina Comments* 27, May 3:66–74.

CANDEE, RICHARD M. 1971 "Three Architects of Early New Hampshire Mill Towns." *Journal of the Society of Architectural Historians* 30:155–163.

CHAMBERS, WILLIAM (1759)1968 *Treatise on Civil Architecture.* Reprint. New York: Blom.

COMSTOCK, HELEN 1950 "Windsor House at New Canaan, Connecticut." *Antiques* 58:462–467.

CONGDON, HERBERT WHEATON 1950 "Our First Architectural School?" *Journal of the American Institute of Architects* 13:139–140.

CROCKER, MARY WALLACE 1979 "Asher Benjamin: The Influence of His Handbooks on Mississippi Buildings." *Journal of the Society of Architectural Historians* 38:266–270.

CUMMINGS, ABBOTT LOWELL 1950 "An Investigation of the Sources, Stylistic Evolution, and Influence of Asher Benjamin's Builder's Guides." Unpublished Ph.D. dissertation, Ohio State University, Columbus.

DEAN, NANCY REISTER 1963 "Asher Benjamin's Nashua Years." Unpublished M.A. thesis, Brown University, Providence, R.I.

EMBURY, AYMAR, II (editor) 1917 *Asher Benjamin.* New York: Architectural Book Publishing.

GREENE, JOHN GARDNER 1940 "The Charles Street Meeting-house, Boston." *Old-Time New England* 30, Jan.:86–93.

HALL, LOUISE 1950 "First Architectural School? No! But . . . ." *Journal of the American Institute of Architects* 14:79–82.

HAMLIN, TALBOT F. 1929 "Asher Benjamin." Volume 2, pages 179–180, in *Dictionary of American Biography.* New York: Scribner.

HOWE, FLORENCE THOMPSON 1941 "Asher Benjamin: Country Builder's Assistant." *Antiques* 40:364–366.

HOWE, FLORENCE THOMPSON 1954 "More About Asher Benjamin." *Journal of the Society of Architectural Historians* 13, Oct.:16–19.

KIRKER, HAROLD 1961 "The Boston Exchange Coffee House." *Old-Time New England* 52, Summer:11–13.

MINOT, WILLIAM, JR.   1841   "'The Builder's Guide . . .' by Asher Benjamin, Architect . . . ." *North American Review* 52:301–320.

NICHOLSON, PETER   (1792)1871   *Carpenter's New Guide.* 16th ed., rev. Philadelphia: Lippincott.

NICHOLSON, PETER   (1797)1815   *Carpenter's and Joiner's Assistant.* 4th ed., rev. London: Taylor.

O'DONNELL, THOMAS E.   1926   "Asher Benjamin: A Pioneer Writer of Architectural Books." *Architecture* 54:375–378.

PAIN, WILLIAM   (1789)1815   *Practical House Carpenter.* 8th ed. London: Taylor.

PRATT, RICHARD H.   1927   "From Georgian to Victorian." *House and Garden* 51, Apr.:120–121, 142, 146, 196.

QUINAN, JACK   1973   "The Architectural Style of Asher Benjamin." Unpublished Ph.D. dissertation, Brown University, Providence, R.I.

QUINAN, JACK   1974   "Asher Benjamin as an Architect in Windsor, Vermont." *Vermont History* 62:181–194.

QUINAN, JACK   1979*a*   "Asher Benjamin and American Architecture." *Journal of the Society of Architectural Historians* 38:244–256.

QUINAN, JACK   1979*b*   "The Boston Exchange Coffee House." *Journal of the Society of Architectural Historians* 38:256–262.

RALEY, ROBERT L.   1972   "Daniel Pratt: Architect and Builder in Georgia." *Antiques* 102:425–433.

REINHARDT, ELIZABETH W., and GRADY, ANNE A.   1977   "Asher Benjamin in East Lexington, Massachusetts." *Old-Time New England* 67, Winter-Spring:23–35.

STURGES, WALTER KNIGHT   1954   "The Black House, Ellsworth—An Asher Benjamin House in Maine." *Antiques* 65:398–400.

TOMLINSON, JULIETTE   1954   "Asher Benjamin—Connecticut Architect." *Connecticut Antiquarian* 6, Nov.:26–29.

VAN METER, MARY   1979   "A New Benjamin Church in Boston." *Journal of the Society of Architectural Historians* 38:262–266.

VOYE, NANCY S.   1976   "Asher Benjamin's West Church: A Model for Change." *Old-Time New England* 67, Summer-Fall:7–15.

BENNETT, EDWARD H.

Edward H. Bennett (1874–1954), an Englishman trained at the Ecole des Beaux-Arts in Paris, became a prominent American architect and planner. He assisted DANIEL H. BURNHAM with plans for San Francisco (1904–1905) and Chicago (1906–1909). Bennett was a consultant to the Chicago Plan Commission (1910–1930) and the designer of more than forty urban schemes in the United States and Canada, many based on the ideals of the City Beautiful movement.

JOAN E. DRAPER

WORKS

1909–1915, Recreation Buildings, Fuller Park; 1914–1927, Grant Park; 1924–1927, Buckingham Fountain; *1929–1933, Century of Progress Exposition, Administration Building (with Daniel Burnham, Jr., and John A. Holabird [see HOLABIRD AND ROCHE]), Agriculture Building (with Arthur Brown, Jr.), Travel and Transportation Building (with Daniel Burnham, Jr. and John Holabird); Chicago. 1931–1934, Botanic Garden; 1931–1936, Capitol Grounds Enlargement; 1931–1937, Apex Building; Washington.

BIBLIOGRAPHY

AMERICAN INSTITUTE OF ARCHITECTS, COMMITTEE ON EDUCATION   1923   *The Significance of the Fine Arts.* Boston: Marshall Jones.

BENNETT, EDWARD H.   1917   *Plan of Minneapolis.* Edited by Andrew Wright Crawford. Minneapolis, Minn.: Civic Commission.

BENNETT, EDWARD H., and FROST, HARRY T.   1929   *The Axis of Chicago.* Chicago: Bennett, Parsons and Frost.

BURNHAM, DANIEL H., and BENNETT, EDWARD H.   (1906)1972   *Report on a Plan for San Francisco.* Reprint. Berkeley: Urban Books.

BURNHAM, DANIEL H., and BENNETT, EDWARD H.   (1909)1970   *Plan of Chicago.* Reprint. New York: Da Capo.

"Master Draftsmen; XIV. Edward H. Bennett."   1925   *Pencil Points* 6, Aug.:42–56.

NOLEN, JOHN (editor)   (1916)1929   *City Planning.* 2d ed. New York and London: Appleton.

BENOIT, PEDRO

Pedro Benoit (1836–1897) was born in Buenos Aires, Argentina. From the age of fourteen, he trained as a designer working with his father at the Departamento Topográfico. Later he studied at the University of Buenos Aires and graduated as an architect in 1879.

He produced more than 1800 projects, including town-planning designs, fortifications, bridges, drainages, churches, hospitals, town halls, and private houses, all of them conceived in the eclectic languages of the 1880s. His major work was built in the new city of La Plata, where he supervised, designed, or directed all the public buildings between 1883 and 1890. He died at Mar del Plata when he was building the neo-Gothic parish of Saint Peter.

ALBERTO NICOLINI

WORKS

1871, Orphan Asylum; 1879, City Hall (renovation); 1883, Engineers' Department, La Plata; 1883, Melchor Romero Hospital, La Plata; 1883, Ministry of the Government, La Plata; 1883, Ministry of the Treasury, La Plata; 1883, Police Station and Jail, La Plata; 1883, Saint

Ponciano Church, La Plata; 1885, Cathedral, La Plata; 1893, Saint Peter Church, Mar del Plata; Buenos Aires.

BIBLIOGRAPHY

Cutolo, Vincente Osvaldo 1968 *Nuevo Diccionario Biográfico Argentino: 1750–1930.* Buenos Aires: Editorial Elche.
Etchichury, Luis M. 1914 *La Plata: Estudio Histórico-Estadístico-Demográfico.* La Plata, Argentina: Imprenta Municipal.
Orfila, Alfredo 1897 "Pedro Benoit." *Anales de la Sociedad Científica Argentina* 43:259–262.

BENOIT-LEVY, GEORGES

Born in Paris, Georges Benoit-Lévy (1880–1971) specialized in studies of garden cities. He was active in the Association of Garden Cities of France, founded in 1903, developing extension programs for the cities of Paris, Lyons, and Marseilles. He also designed entire industrial villages. In 1923, he became involved in the International Association of Linear Garden Cities, a development begun in 1888 by Arturo Soria y Mata.

GEORGES BENOIT-LÉVY (*fils*) and
FRANCINE HILLIGOS

BIBLIOGRAPHY

Benoit-Lévy, Georges (1904)1911 *La Cité-Jardin.* 3 vols. 2d ed. Paris: Cités jardins de France.
Benoit-Lévy, Georges 1906 *Le Roman des Cités-Jardins.* Paris: Cités-Jardins de France.
Benoit-Lévy, Georges 1910 *La Ville et Son Image.* Paris: Cités-Jardins de France.
Benoit-Lévy, Georges 1920 *Extrême Urgence.* Paris: Associations des Cités-Jardins.
Benoit-Lévy, Georges 1921 *La Maison Heureuse.* Paris: Cités-Jardins de France.
Benoit-Lévy, Georges 1927 *Paris s'étend.* Paris: The author.
Benoit-Lévy, Georges 1931 *Londres . . . Demain.* Nice, France: The author.
Benoit-Lévy, Georges 1932 *Cités-Jardins 1932.* Nice, France: The author.
Benoit-Lévy, Georges n.d. *La Cité Linéaire.* n.p.: Madrilena de Urbanizacion.
Feather, William 1928 *100% Américain.* Edited by Georges Benoit-Lévy. Nice, France: The editor.

BENŠ, ADOLF

Adolf Benš (1894–) attended the Technical University in Prague, Czechoslovakia, and received his practical training in the atelier of JOSEF GOČÁR. From 1945 to 1970, Benš was professor of architecture at the School of Industrial Arts in Prague. His

works from the functionalistic era in his career display pure volumes and elegant details.

VLADIMÍR ŠLAPETA

WORKS

1927–1935, Electric Transport Administration House (with Josef Kříž), Holešovice District; 1928, Villa, Troja; Prague. 1931, Czechoslovak State Pavilion, Liège, Belgium. 1931–1935, Airport, Ruzyně; 1937, Adolf Benš Residence, Baba District; Prague. 1965, Prague Castle (reconstruction of gardens; with R. F. Podzemný).

BIBLIOGRAPHY

Krise, Jindřich 1969 "Adolph Benš & 18.5.1894." *Architektura ČSSR* 28, nos. 9–10: 566–568.

BENSON, WILLIAM

William Benson (1682–1754) was an English amateur architect. In 1709, he built his own house, Wilbury, on the model of JOHN WEBB'S Amesbury, Wiltshire, where he then lived. Wilbury is a significant indication of the revival of interest in Jonesian (see INIGO JONES) classicism in early eighteenth-century England.

Successful intrigue among Whig politicians led to his appointment to replace no one less than CHRISTOPHER WREN as Surveyor of the Royal Works in 1718, with COLEN CAMPBELL as his deputy. After only fifteen months he was dismissed both for incompetence and because of opposition to his scheme to demolish the Houses of Parliament in order to rebuild them in a more modern style.

T. P. CONNOR

WORKS

1709, Wilbury, Wiltshire, England. 1721, Saint Michael's Church (east window), Quarley, Hampshire, England.

BENTLEY, JOHN FRANCIS

John Francis Bentley (1839–1902) was an English architect and designer whose career spanned the High Victorian and early Edwardian periods. Although he is generally considered a mediocre talent, he was the most important Roman Catholic architect in England in the late nineteenth century and a key figure in the evolution of an English Roman Catholic architectural style. Born in Doncaster, England, in 1839, he was apprenticed, against his will, to a firm of mechanical engineers in Manchester. In 1857, he joined the office of the Gothic Revival architect HENRY CLUTTON (1819–1893), a Roman Catholic convert. In 1862,

Bentley himself converted to Roman Catholicism.

Although trained initially in the Gothic by Clutton and inclined toward it by disposition, Bentley commanded a remarkable variety of architectural styles: Italian, French, Dutch, and English Renaissance as well as the various Gothic styles. A peculiar mixture of Italian Renaissance and Gothic may be seen in an early work, the house for Nathaniel Westlake (1863). Another work, Saint John's Beaumont (1887–1888), a Roman Catholic boys' school, combines Dutch and French Renaissance in a way that recalls the work of R. NORMAN SHAW.

Of Bentley's works, his contemporaries most admired the Church of the Holy Rood, Watford (1883–1890). Sited on a corner, its asymmetrical tower and Bath stone banding suggest a jagged Butterfieldian (see WILLIAM BUTTERFIELD) Gothic building, but the surface of flint stones and the modest perpendicular tracery modify the effect, giving a softer tone.

Undoubtedly Bentley's major work is Westminster Cathedral, London, begun in 1895 and left incomplete on his death in 1902. In fact, the interior is still unfinished and decorative tesserae for the upper levels of the nave remain piled in the triforium area. The history of the cathedral begins with the Reform Act of 1829, which gave English Roman Catholics their civil rights. In 1850, the decision to create a new diocese of Westminster in central London provoked anti-Catholic riots. When the second archbishop of Westminster, Cardinal H. E. Manning, finally purchased some land, Clutton was selected to design the new cathedral, and he produced, in 1875, a creditable if somewhat bland Gothic design. In 1883, the site was changed, and Manning's successor, Cardinal Herbert Vaughan, deciding that a new design and a new architect were needed, selected Bentley. Vaughan determined the style of the new cathedral, which combined the styles of the cathedrals of Sant' Ambrogio in Milan, San Vitale in Ravenna, and San Marco in Venice. The cathedral also reflects elements of Byzantine architecture, as well as English and French Renaissance decorative elements.

In a sense, more important than the style adopted—clearly a heterogeneous mixture of eastern and western styles—is the style that was *not* selected. It was considered essential that the cathedral not compete with the Gothic of Westminster Abbey or the Gothic Revival of the Houses of Parliament just down the road. Originally hidden behind the stores along Victoria Street, the cathedral has recently been exposed by the creation of a small piazza in front.

Bentley was a nervous and somewhat insecure

man. His death in 1902 was hastened, so it was said, by anxiety over the stability of the vaults of the Cathedral.

NICHOLAS ADAMS

Bentley.
Westminster Cathedral.
London.
1895–1902

WORKS

1861, Church of St. Francis of Assisi (begun by Henry Clutton); 1863, Nathaniel Westlake House; 1871, Distillery, Finsbury; 1875–1888, Convent of the Sacred Heart, Hammersmith; London. 1883–1890, Church of the Holy Rood, Watford, England. 1887–1888, Saint John's School, Beaumont, Old Windsor, England. 1891–1893, Redemptorist Monastery; 1895–1902, Westminster Cathedral; London.

BIBLIOGRAPHY

LETHABY, W. R., and SWAINSON, HAROLD 1894 *The Church of Sancta Sophia Constantinople: A Study of Byzantine Building.* London: Macmillan. The source for much of the description of the Byzantine ornament of Westminster Cathedral.

L'HOPITAL, WINEFRIDE DE 1919 *Westminster Cathedral and Its Architect.* London: Hutchinson.

VAUGHAN, HERBERT A. 1942 *Letters of Herbert Cardinal Vaughan to Lady Herbert of Lea, 1867 to 1903.* Edited by Shane Leslie. London: Burns.

VICTORIA AND ALBERT MUSEUM 1971 *Victorian Church Art.* London: The Museum. Catalogue for an exhibit held at the Museum between November 1971 and January 1972.

BERAIN, JEAN I

Jean I Berain (1640–1711) was born in Saint Mihiel in Lorraine, the son of a master gunsmith who four years later moved his family to Paris. Having learned to etch metal in his father's workshop, Berain applied the technique to the similar process of making engravings and etchings on paper, publishing the first of many prints, a series of designs for gun mounts, in 1659. His graphic skills did not go unnoticed, for he was employed by Louis XIV as engraver from 1670 to 1674. At the end of 1674, Berain was appointed to the extremely important position of *dessinateur du chambre et du cabinet du roi* in the office of *menus-plaisirs,* where the decorations for all festivities, celebrations, and funerals for the court were produced. For thirty-odd years, Berain designed costumes and stage sets for the academy of music as well. Except for a few interiors, furniture, and decorative object designs, known through engravings, most of Berain's efforts were directed at planning structures that were by nature ephemeral. Were it not for a wealth of engravings and some drawings, the power of his influence would be little understood.

The three-dimensional structures, such as stage sets, machines for fireworks, and chimneypieces that are recorded in the engravings are massive and follow conventional academic rules of symmetry and proportion. Although Berain continued the line of mannerist French tradition in decoration, in his capable, facile hand the flat interlacing bandwork of the School of Fontainebleau is enlivened with graceful, crisply swirling arabesques on walls, furniture, fabrics, and tapestries. It is a surface pattern, the origins of which were antique Roman wall decoration, gloriously reinvented by RAPHAEL in the Vatican Loggia, and reinterpreted, flattened, and embellished by Berain.

ELAINE EVANS DEE

WORKS

1682–1684, Versailles (Cabinet des Medailles and Petite Galerie), France. 1687–1688, Hôtel de Mailly-Nesles (ceilings), Paris. 1688–1689, Grand Trianon (interior), Versailles, France. 1697, Collegiale de Saint Quentin (organ), France. 1699, Chateau de Meudon (interiors), France.

BIBLIOGRAPHY

HAUTECOEUR, LOUIS 1948 Volume 2 in *Histoire de l'architecture classique en France.* Paris: Picard.

KIMBALL, FISKE (1943)1980 *The Creation of the Rococo.* Reprint. New York: Dover.

WEIGERT, ROGER-ARMAND 1936–1937 *Jean I Berain.* 2 vols. Paris: Editions d'art et histoire.

BERENGUER I MESTRES, FRANCESCO

Francesco Berenguer i Mestres (1866–1914) was the closest assistant to the architect ANTONIO GAUDÍ I CORNET. Born in Reus, like the latter, Berenguer was fourteen years younger than his teacher. At the age of fifteen, he moved with his family to Barcelona, where he began his studies of fine arts and architecture, abandoning them at twenty-one in order to work with Gaudí.

Although it is nearly impossible to analyze the mutual influence, it is possible to show, as a central characteristic of Berenguer's contribution to the work of Gaudí, the intent formally to reduce those ornamental elements that belonged to the free expression of *Modernismo* by way of its rigid geometrizing and its reductive assimilation to cubic variations. This type of treatment, without parallel in Gaudí himself, is detectable in the interior façade of the Nativity Doorway of the Church of the Holy Family, Barcelona, where Berenguer's direct intervention seems evident. In the same fashion, this idea appears as a constant of his own work, and it is transformed into the central subject of the most ambitious of his works: the Güell de Garraf Warehouses, Barcelona (1888–1890), a building conceived as a triangular, leaning prism, in which there is no distinction between wall and roof and which appears as one continuous stony volume. One must point to a certain parallel between this work and Gaudí's Bellesguard, in whose execution Berenguer had intervened directly, though in the latter the attempted unity of volume is limited to uniformity of the external reshaping applied to its previous volume, a product of its own spatial complexity.

The same attitude of geometric schematization inspired his works in forged iron. In this fashion, the railing for Gaudí's Vicens House is composed of the reiteration of a palm leaf, and the railing of the Güell Warehouses relies on the mobility of a group of heavy chains.

During twenty-seven years of collaboration with Gaudí, in addition to the works already cited, his contributions to the Ranch of Güell de Pedralbes, to the Crypt of the Colonis Güell, and to the Schools of the Holy Family also seem possible.

At Berenguer's death, Gaudí would praise his collaborator and friend with these words: "With Berenguer I lost my right arm!"

ADOLF MARTÍNEZ I MATAMALA
Translated from Spanish by
Florette Rechnitz Koffler

WORKS

1888–1890?, Güell Warehouse, Garraf; 1893, Market of Freedom, Freedom Square; Barcelona, Spain. 1900, The Poal (Count Güell House), Lérida, Spain. 1900, Saint John of Grace House, Square of the Vice Queen; 1904, House, Güell Park; 1905, House, 77 Calle Mayor de Gràcia; 1905, Mayoral Office (de Gràcia; façade), Rius i Taulet Square; 1906, Mateu House (pavilion and gates), Llinars del Vallés; 1908, Francesco Berenguer i Mestres House, Rubio; 1909, Center Moral de Gràcia, 9 Ros de Olano Street; 1910–1914, Saint Joseph of the Mountain Sanctuary, Avenida Sanctuari; 1914, House of the Master (cooperative and decoration of the Masía Güell Complex), Santa Coloma de Cervelló; n.d., Houses, 15, 50–52, 196 and 237 Calle Mayor de Grácia; Barcelona, Spain.

BIBLIOGRAPHY

BOHIGAS, ORIOL (1968)1973 *Arquitectura modernista.* Barcelona, Spain: Lumen.
INFIESTA, MANUEL 1954 "Francisco Berenguer." *Cuadernos de Arquitectura* 18:8–13.
MACKAY, DAVID 1964 "Berenguer." *Cuadernos de Arquitectura* 136:410–416.

BERG, CHARLES I.

Born in Philadelphia, Charles I. Berg (1856–1926) studied architecture at the Ecole des Beaux-Arts in Paris (1877–1879) and in offices in London. He practiced in New York City from 1880 on. His buildings there are in a somewhat florid classicism like that of his contemporaries, CARRÈRE AND HASTINGS.

RICHARD CHAFEE

WORKS

*1897, Gillender Building; Completed by 1903, Hotel Touraine; Completed by 1903, Kaskel Building; Completed by 1903, Windsow Arcade; New York.

BIBLIOGRAPHY

"Obituary." 1926 *American Architect* 130, no. 2507:324.
"Obituary." 1926 *Journal of the American Institute of Architects* 14, no. 11:504.
SILVER, NATHAN (1967)1971 *Lost New York.* Reprint. New York: Schocken.

BERG, MAX

Born in Stettin, Poland, Max Berg (1870–1947) studied architecture at the Technical University at Berlin-Charlottenburg under Karl Schäfer, who also taught his contemporary HANS POELZIG. Schäfer was convinced that the essence of the Gothic style was the true expression of construction. In Berg's architecture, the true expression of construction was to be an essential feature.

It is not easy to assemble biographical material concerning Max Berg. Unlike Hans Poelzig and his other contemporary, PETER BEHRENS, Berg has only recently been recognized as one of the leading architects of the period just before and after World War I.

In the years preceding the war, the city of Breslau had achieved a special position in the cultural life of Germany. In 1903, Poelzig was called to Breslau as head of the art school which, from 1911 onward, was known as the Breslau Academy of Fine Arts. Poelzig immediately developed an active practice as an architect in Breslau and other places in Silesia, and he proved equally active as a teacher. By introducing workshop practice into the study of architecture, he moved in the direction which WALTER GROPIUS, in 1919, took up in the Bauhaus at Weimar. Poelzig considered Gropius a fitting successor when he left Breslau in 1916.

For the centenary of the war of liberation of 1813, a large exhibition space was to be created in a public park near Breslau. The project included gardens, a restaurant with terraces, a large exhibition hall, a group of smaller exhibition buildings linked by passages and pergolas (to be built by Poelzig), and, dominating this vast ensemble, the great memorial hall known as the Jahrhunderthalle. With the exception of the group of buildings de-

Berenguer i Mestres.
Güell Warehouse.
Garraf, Barcelona, Spain.
1888–1890.?

Berg.
Jahrhunderthalle Plan and
    Section (with Richard
    Konwiartz).
Breslau, Germany.
1912–1913

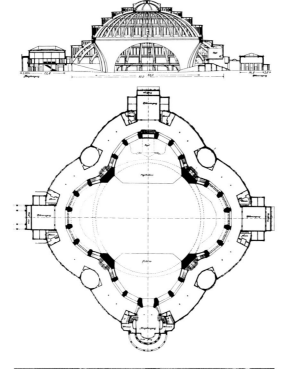

Berg.
Jahrhunderthalle Plan and
    Section (with Richard
    Konwiartz).
Breslau, Germany.
1912–1913

Berg.
Jahrhunderthalle (with
    Richard Konwiartz).
Breslau, Germany.
1912–1913

signed by Poelzig, Max Berg was the architect and planner of this ambitious scheme. Its construction was taken up again after the interruption caused by the war and was finished only in 1925, when Max Berg left Breslau. The ambitious centerpiece—the Jahrhunderthalle—however, was ready for the memorial of 1913. It is doubtless Berg's crowning achievement. The cruciform building consists of a cylindrical central space crowned with a cupola, which is surrounded by large apses on four sides. The dimensions were unheard of in 1913: the cupola was erected over a diameter of 67 meters, that is, it measured 23 meters more than the cupola of

Saint Peter's in Rome; the distance from apse to apse measured 95 meters, and the cupola rose to a height of 40 meters inside. It was, in fact, the largest building covering a continuous space without any intermediary supports then known.

Berg abandoned steel as his material of construction and decided in favor of reinforced concrete for the hall. This decision was taken not only for reasons of economy and fire-proofing, but also "because concrete leant itself to a more significant shape both structurally and as a work of architecture." Considering that reinforced concrete as a material for architecture was still in its infancy, Berg's decision was significant. As a work of engineering, the Jahrhunderthalle surpassed everything Behrens or Poelzig had achieved at that time; not even the buildings of Walter Gropius achieved an equal degree of expressive purity.

The Jahrhunderthalle was not Berg's only contribution in the domain of engineering. Twelve years later, on an adjacent site, Berg produced the exhibition hall, whose roof, made of timber beams supported by a series of light segmental arches of the same material, is another example of his fine handling of this kind of building. Among his numerous buildings for Breslau—schools, hospitals, housing developments—the two hydroelectric plants on the river Oder (1921, 1924) stand out as buildings of a telling simplicity.

Berg produced a plan for the extension of Breslau and a number of studies investigating the introduction of high-rise office buildings to the city of Breslau and other German cities. Berg spoke of high-rise office buildings because he did not wish those structures to be labeled skyscrapers. Berg admired the American skyscraper as a planning and an engineering achievement, but he did not approve of the way in which they were crowded together in a place like Manhattan. Berg produced a number of schemes placing a high-rise building right next door to the venerable town hall.

Information about the later years of Berg's life is scanty. After 1925, he lived in Berlin. We know nothing of his attitude toward the Nazi government, but it is difficult to imagine him on good terms with the regime. Berg's architecture places him in a unique position. His work is less rich than that of his more famous contemporaries, but its daring construction and lasting value make him their equal.

JULIUS POSENER

WORKS

1912–1913, Jahrhunderthalle (with Richard Konwiartz); 1912–1925, Centenary Exhibition Buildings (Exhibition Hall with Ludwig Moshamer); 1921, Electrical Plant; 1924, Electrical Plant; n.d., Hospitals; n.d., Housing Developments; n.d., Schools; Breslau, Germany.

BIBLIOGRAPHY

BERG, MAX 1913 "Die Jahrhunderthalle und das neue Ausstellungsgelände der Stadt Breslau." *Deutsche Bauzeitung* 47, no. 50:462–466.
DRYSSEN, AND AVERHOFF 1926 "Kölner Hochhaus-Carneval." *Wasmuths Monatshefte für Baukunst* 10:90–124.
"Hochhäuser im Stadtbild." 1921–1922 *Wasmuths Monatshefte für Baukunst* 6:101–120.
KONWIARZ, RICHARD 1925 "Neue Baukunst in Breslau." *Wasmuths Monatshefte für Baukunst* 9:152–164.
KONWIARZ, RICHARD 1926 *Die Baukunst Breslau.* Breslau, Germany: Grass, Barth.

BERGAMÍN GUTIERREZ, RAFAEL

Rafael Bergamín Gutierrez (1891–1970), by training an architect and a forestry engineer, together with FERNANDO GARCÍA MERCADAL and CASTO FERNÁNDEZ SHAW introduced into Spain an architecture akin to the European Modern movement. The house he built for the Marquis of Villora (Madrid, 1926–1927) represents the first avant-garde construction in Spain. Also prominent in the vast body of work completed by Bergamín are the complex of the Park-Residence (1931–1933) and the colony of El Viso (1933–1936), both located in Madrid. The colony of El Viso, with its 242 dwellings, not only presupposes the arrival within Spain of the Modern movement on a grand scale, but also a certain conception, going beyond conventional ones, of the city garden, approaching ARTURO SORIA's theories about "lineal cities," since this complex has its backbone along an avenue of rapid traffic, the Calle Serrano.

CARLOS FLORES LOPEZ
Translated from Spanish by
Florette Rechnitz Koffler

WORKS

1926–1927, Marquis de Villora House; 1931–1933, Park-Residence Complex; 1933–1936, El Viso Colony; Madrid.

BIBLIOGRAPHY

FLORES LOPEZ, CARLOS 1961 *Arquitectura Española Contemporanea.* Madrid.

BERGSTEN, CARL

Carl Gustav Bergsten (1879–1935), born in Norrköping, Sweden, architect and interior designer, studied in Stockholm at the Royal Institute of Technology (1897–1901) and at the Royal Academy (1901–1903). Subsequently, Bergsten traveled extensively in Europe, especially in Germany and Austria. Noted for works of National Romanticism and for bringing the ideas of the German Werkbund to Sweden, Bergsten was well known as a teacher and writer.

JUDITH S. HULL

WORKS

*1906, Arts and Crafts Exhibition (with G. Merssing), Nörrkoping, Sweden. 1913, Church, Enskede, Sweden. 1914–1917, Liljevalch Art Exhibition Hall, Stockholm. *1925, Swedish Pavilion, Paris Exposition. 1928, *Kungsholm* Swedish American liner (interior decoration). 1934, City Theater, Göteborg, Sweden.

BIBLIOGRAPHY

JOHANSSON, B. O. H. 1965 *Carl Bergsten och svensk arkitekturpolitik.* Sweden: Uppsala University Press.
KAIN, ROBERT 1929 "Deutsche Werkkunst auf dem Schwedendampfer 'Kungsholm'." *Die Kunst* 62, no. 2:65–72.
LINDAHL, GÖRAN 1958 "En ensam radikal—Carl Bergsten." *Paletten* 1, March:10–17.

BERLAGE, H. P.

Hendrik Petrus Berlage (1856–1934) was the major pioneer of modern architecture in the Netherlands, devoting his prodigious energies to creating a modern style characterized by directness, geometric order, and repose. A socialist, Berlage considered architecture and society inextricably linked and his artistic credo, "Unity in Multiplicity" ("*Eenheid in Veelheid*"), had political as well as aesthetic connotations. He rejected historicism not only as false and extravagant, but also as a manifestation of bourgeois individualism.

Born in Amsterdam into a middle-class family, Berlage initially planned to be a painter. After studying briefly at the Academy of Fine Arts in Amsterdam, he decided his talents were more suited to architecture. In 1875 he enrolled in the Bauschule of the Eidgenössische Technische Hochschule in Zürich.

In 1878, after receiving his diploma, Berlage commenced a three-year journey to Germany and Italy, making sketches that later provided formal inspiration at the beginning of his career. He returned to Holland in 1881 and took a position with the engineer Theodorus Sanders. One of their first efforts was the competition design (1884–1885) for the Amsterdam Beurs. With its complicated massing, mansard roofs, and florid ornament, the rather bombastic project would be equally at home in Second Empire France or Victorian England, although it was given a native flavor through Dutch Renaissance details. They won fourth prize but the program was shelved until 1896, when Berlage alone received the commission and completely reworked the design.

The only member of his generation to sign the 1928 foundation manifesto of the Congrès Internationaux d'Architecture Moderne, Berlage insisted that architecture was first and foremost a spatial art and that one must design from within outward. He propagated the concept of *Sachlichkeit,* a functionalist doctrine stressing sobriety of form and economy of means. Also seminal was his use of geometry as the chief ordering element of design. However, like his near contemporaries PETER BEHRENS and OTTO WAGNER, Berlage was a prophet rather than a practitioner of the modern architecture identified with the International style developed by WALTER GROPIUS, LUDWIG MIES VAN DER ROHE, and J. J. P. OUD. He sought a monumentality that the younger generation would condemn, while he himself abjured the dematerialization of architecture considered desirable and viable by the avant-garde after World War I. His was for the most part a mural architecture, and the space that he celebrated was firmly contained by heavy masses. While the brick bearing walls of his buildings are smooth and taut, they give an impression of weightiness that runs counter to modern taste. His embrace of *Sachlichkeit* did not mean that he omitted ornament, although it is invariably integrated with the structural materials. Berlage never denied that architecture belonged with the fine arts, and he denounced as materialistic and uninspiring the *neue Sachlichkeit* of the 1920s and 1930s. He believed in composing with a few basic units but never took standardization to monotonous extremes.

For Berlage, no part of the environment was too small or too large to be shaped by the architect. He was involved with arts and crafts and the furniture, books, textiles, posters, and lighting fixtures he produced belong to the finest examples of *Nieuwe Kunst,* the austere and rectilinear Dutch version of Art Nouveau. Berlage was given opportunities for large-scale urban projects enjoyed by few of his colleagues. He was commissioned to make extension plans for a number of major Dutch cities, and designed new areas of Amsterdam, Utrecht, and Rotterdam. His first attempts were picturesque and medievalizing (Amsterdam South I, 1903) but he came to understand that the nature of twentieth-century traffic demanded broader, more baroque schemes. His definitive plan for Amsterdam South (1914–1915; realized in slightly altered form 1919–1930) superimposed wide, sweeping arteries over a denser, more com-

plex pattern of intimate streets and squares virtually created by perimeter blocks containing dwellings. Here he achieved his urbanistic goal: monumental in over-all layout, picturesque in details. Berlage also designed several garden suburbs, whose curving streets reveal a study of English models; among these are Vreewijk (1914) in Rotterdam and Oog in Al (1918–1920) in Utrecht.

Two nineteenth-century titans, GOTTFRIED SEMPER and EUGÈNE EMMANUEL VIOLLET-LE-DUC, profoundly influenced Berlage. Semper headed the Bauschule since it opened in 1855 and although he ended his professorship in 1871, his ideas continued to guide the course of study. From Semper he acquired a profound respect for the nature of materials, an interest in applied arts (he conceived of furniture as architecture in miniature), and an obsession with style. From Viollet-Le-Duc he imbibed a belief in structural rationalism and the notion that the exterior massing must reflect the interior disposition of spaces, which should be organized logically but not necessarily symmetrically. Both authors also had explored the role of geometry in design. Semper noted that all the variety perceived in nature is based on a few simple geometric forms, while the French theorist analyzed the use of proportional systems in the great buildings of the past. Berlage's ornamental motifs were mathematical stylizations of vegetal and geometric forms and from the Amsterdam Bourse's definitive design of 1897 to the Municipal Museum in The Hague (1927–1935), grids of squares and isosceles triangles determined, respectively, his ground plans and his elevations. Proportional systems were a means to achieve order, which for Berlage was one of the first ingredients of style.

Berlage's work often shows astounding formal affinities with American architecture. Once he had outgrown revivalism, his career went through three phases that recapitulate successively the styles of H. H. RICHARDSON, LOUIS H. SULLIVAN, and FRANK LLOYD WRIGHT. Berlage traveled to the United States in 1911 and later published *Amerikaansche Reisherinneringen* (1913), illustrated with work by Sullivan and Wright. He also lectured extensively and was instrumental in introducing Wright's architecture to the Netherlands, where his impact was greater than in any other European country.

Before his definitive project for the Bourse, Berlage's style underwent a rapid evolution. His first executed work, De Hoop (1883–1884), a working-man's coffeehouse in Amsterdam, displayed a polychromatic Dutch Renaissance vocabulary. Strikingly different was the next building by Berlage and Sanders, the Focke and Meltzer store

Berlage.
Bourse.
Amsterdam.
1897–1903

(1884–1886), on the Kalverstraat in Amsterdam, in the Italian Renaissance mode favored by Semper. It makes a noteworthy contrast with the offices for De Algemeene Insurance Company (1892–1894) also in Amsterdam and Berlage's first important commission after he left Sanders in 1889. Both buildings are monochromatic and have similarly organized façades: large shop windows on the ground story, two identically fenestrated floors above, and an attic story where the rhythm of the windows has quickened. But in the later work, the vocabulary derives from the Middle Ages rather than the sixteenth century, suggesting Viollet-Le-Duc's influence.

In two subsequent insurance offices—for De Nederlanden van 1845—one in Amsterdam (1894–1895; enlarged 1911) and one in The Hague (1895–1896; enlarged 1901, 1909), Berlage reaches for a more personal manner. Romanesque breadth and severity are achieved with local materials of brick dressed with stone. Berlage's comments about Richardson's Trinity Church are apposite here. He wrote that it was understandable that an architect would turn to the Romanesque after rejecting the neo-Gothic and neo-Renaissance because this style corresponds best to "our primary modern concern for simplicity and massiveness in the total conception, structurally as well as ornamentally" (1913, pp. 20–21). But he found the church itself too imitative and restless,

whereas in his own work he strove for *Sachlichkeit* and repose. All unnecessary ornamental details have been pared away and those that remain are kept flush with the wall plane. Projections in plan and massing are restrained and all are sanctioned by changes in interior function.

These two buildings were rehearsals for Berlage's first masterpiece, the Amsterdam Beurs. The initial designs were made in 1896; the third project of 1897–1898 was executed and completed in 1903 (some structural alterations were made in 1909). The sober, rather monastic building is enormous—143 meters in length, 55 meters in breadth at its widest point—and houses produce, grain, and stock exchanges, postal and telegraph facilities, numerous offices and meeting rooms, a cafe, and a boiler house. As is the case with all of Berlage's designs, the variety of spaces within has been expressed on the exterior through the silhouette and the fenestration.

The Beurs (Stock Exchange) is the first modern building to be executed according to a geometric system. The dimensions of the plan are based on the square, while the elevations were drawn over a guiding grid of isosceles triangles with a ratio of base to height of 8:5 (the so-called Egyptian triangle). Here Berlage was indebted to three younger Dutch designers who put into practice Viollet-le-Duc's researches into proportional systems—JAN H. DE GROOT, J. L. M. LAUWERIKS, and K. P. C. DE BAZEL. All three had employed simple geometric figures as a basis for two-dimensional design, as Berlage would do in his ornament for the Beurs. Even more important, however, was de Bazel's extension of proportional systems to the third dimension, in two competition projects (1895; 1896). Significantly, Berlage was a member of both juries. De Bazel's entries, in a neo-Romanesque mode with massive walls kept taut and planar, must have influenced Berlage in several respects in his final designs for the Bourse.

While the Beurs was considered sober and rationalistic by many of Berlage's contemporaries, sensual touches are not lacking. Berlage engaged sculptors and painters to carry out a comprehensive decorative program that elucidates the purpose of the building through a symbolic narration of Amsterdam's history. The architectural elements themselves also provide aesthetic satisfaction. Although they are frankly exposed, the iron trusses supporting the skylit roofs of the exchanges are elegantly profiled and merge gracefully with the supporting masonry piers. The detailing of the beautifully laid brick walls lends further visual interest, and lively polychromatic patterns animate the predominately yellow interior surfaces.

Having at last created a calm and monumental personal style, Berlage employed it for each and every program. In the Henny House (1898) in The Hague and the headquarters of the ANDB (Diamond Workers' Union, 1899–1901) in Amsterdam, *Sachlichkeit* and geometric order prevail and, just as in the Beurs, the naked brick wall is employed both inside and out. The culmination of this first phase of Berlage's career is the magnificent hunting lodge, Sint Hubertus (1915–1919), in Otterlo, for the Kröller–Müller family, which

had commissioned projects from Behrens and Mies van der Rohe, and would later employ HENRY VAN DE VELDE. From 1913 to 1919 they monopolized Berlage, who moved to The Hague to be nearer their firm, the William H. Müller Company.

In Holland House (1914–1916), the Müller premises in London, Berlage substituted a steel frame for the bearing wall, but his treatment masks its skeletal qualities. Thick, gray-green tiles clad the frame, and the cofferlike spandrels and projecting vertical piers (suggesting the influence of Sullivan) maintain a sense of massiveness. The building's weightiness is also emphasized by the blunt and chamfered main corner, covered with blocks of polished black granite. The corner's base is carved to resemble a ship's prow cleaving the waves, a dynamic touch which demonstrates that Berlage was not entirely immune to Expressionist currents then developing in Amsterdam among young architects like MICHEL DE KLERK. Berlage employed the standardized frame only for commercial buildings and he never abandoned his preference for solidity in architecture. This approach can be seen in two works in The Hague—the premises for Meddens (1914) and the offices for De Nederlanden van 1845 (1924–1927, enlarged after Berlage's designs, 1954).

During the last decade of his life, Berlage returned to the brick wall as the formative element in the creation of architectural space. At the same time the influence of Wright appears, especially in the relative looseness of the massing and in the uncompromising geometry of the building's forms. These tendencies are exhibited in the two masterworks of his late style, the First Church of Christ, Scientist (1925–1926), and the Gemeentemuseum (Municipal Museum, [designed 1927–1929; completed posthumously 1935]), both in The Hague. While Berlage had consistently expressed interior dispositions in the massing, his earlier works were compact in plan; in the final period spaces seem flung outward centrifugally and each reads clearly as a separate volume, resulting in compositions of tremendous complexity. The rise and fall and projection and recession of the distinctly articulated parts serve not only to clarify the spatial organization but also to humanize the scale of the huge museum. Its concrete frame is concealed behind the relatively unbroken polytonal brick surfaces.

When Berlage, long recognized as the most famous Dutch architect of the twentieth century, died in The Hague at age seventy-eight, he had to his credit more than sixty executed buildings as well as extension plans, furniture, and many ideal projects. He had seen great changes in the architec-

Berlage.
Gemeentemuseum.
The Hague.
1927–1934 (not completed until 1935).

tural world, some of which he helped set in motion, and others which he came to deplore. His theories and buildings provided inspiration for younger Dutch architects of diametrically antithetical viewpoints. His belief in the ordering power of geometry survived among those associated with *De Stijl,* like Oud and GERRIT RIETVELD, while his championship of the brick wall as the ideal definer of architectural space was continued by members of the Amsterdam school. His thoughtful practice of theories formulated early in his career did not hinder personal stylistic development, and a comparison of the Beurs and the Gemeentemuseum provides a convincing demonstration of the range of formal nuances that could be achieved by faithful adherence to proportional systems, and to the goals of *Sachlichkeit* and unity in multiplicity.

HELEN SEARING

WORKS

*1883-1884, De Hoop Coffeehouse (with Theodorus Sanders); 1884-1886, Focke and Meltzer Store (with Sanders); 1891-1892, E. D. Pijzel House; *1892-1894, De Algemeene General Life Insurance Building; Amsterdam. 1894, G. Heymans House, Groningen, Netherlands. 1894-1895, De Nederlanden van 1845 Insurance Company Building, Amsterdam. 1895-1896, De Nederlanden van 1845 Insurance Company Building, The Hague. 1897-1903, Beurs, Amsterdam. 1898, Carel Henny House, The Hague. 1899-1901, General Dutch Diamond Workers' Union Building; *1900, Villa Parkwijk; Amsterdam. 1902, De Algemeene, Leipzig. 1906, Voorwaarts Workers' Cooperative Building; *1910, De Nederlanden van 1845 Insurance Company Building; Rotterdam, Netherlands. 1910-1913, Workers' Housing, Tolstraat; 1911-1913, Workers' Housing for Algemeene Woningbouwvereeniging, Transvaalbuurt; 1912-1915, Workers' Housing, Javaplein; Amsterdam. 1913, Berlage Family House; 1914, Meddens and Son (shops and offices); The Hague. 1914-1916, Holland House (offices of W. H. Müller Company), London. 1915-1919, Sint Hubertus Hunting Lodge, Otterlo, Netherlands. 1924-1927, De Nederlanden van 1845 Insurance Company Building (with A. D. N. van Gendt and W. N. van Vliet); 1925-1926, First Church of Christ, Scientist; The Hague.1925-1932, Amsterdamse Bank, Rembrandtplein; 1926, Berlage Bridge; Amsterdam. 1927-1934, Gemeentemuseum (not completed until 1935), The Hague. 1929, Town Hall, Usquert, Netherlands.

BIBLIOGRAPHY

BANHAM, REYNER 1960 *Theory and Design in the First Machine Age.* New York: Praeger.
BERLAGE, H. P. 1905 *Gedanken über Stil in der Baukunst.* Leipzig: Zeitler.
BERLAGE, H. P. 1908 *Grundlagen und Entwicklung der Architektur.* Berlin: Bard.
BERLAGE, H. P. 1913 *Amerikaansche Reisherinneringen.* Rotterdam, Netherlands: Brusse.
FANELLI, GIOVANNI 1968 *Architettura moderna in Olanda 1900-1940.* Florence: Marchi & Bertolli.
GRINBERG, DONALD 1977 *Housing in the Netherlands 1900-1940.* Netherlands: Delft University Press.
REININK, ADRIAAN WESSEL 1975 *Amsterdam en de Beurs van Berlage: Reacties van tijdgenoten.* The Hague: Staatsuitgeverij.
SEARING, HELEN 1974 "Berlage and Housing, 'the most significant modern building type.'" *Nederlands Kunsthistorisch Jaarboek* 25:133-179.
SINGELENBERG, PIETER 1972 *H. P. Berlage: Idea and Style, The Quest for Modern Architecture.* Utrecht: Haentjens.
SINGELENBERG, PIETER, and BOCK, MANFRED 1975 *H. P. Berlage, Bouwmeester 1856-1934.* The Hague: Gemeentemuseum.

BERNARD DE SOISSONS

See JEAN D'ORBAIS.

BERNARDES, SERGIO

Born in Rio de Janeiro, Sergio Bernardes (1919–) already had projects constructed before he graduated from the Federal University's department of architecture in 1948. One project after the next received awards or commendations. In 1953 he won a grand prize at the Venice Triennial for the Helio Cabral House (1951-1953); in 1958, he received a gold star for the Brazilian Pavilion (1957-1958) at the International Fair in Brussels.

Bernardes's most audacious designs include his former home (1970) perched on a rocky incline in Rio de Janeiro overlooking the ocean, a Cultural Center (1972-1980) in Brasília whose structural integrity was based upon suspension bridge engineering, and the Schering Pharmaceutical Plant (1974) in Barra da Tijuca, whose special microclimate was produced by exploiting the tensile strength of steel with a tubular metal roof spanning 350 by 150 meters.

Architecture for Bernardes has been only a starting point for his lifetime pursuits. Designer of airplanes, cars, furniture, as well as some of Brazil's most technologically daring structures, Bernardes considers architecture to be a finite art, thus inadequate for expanding urban centers. Since the late 1950s, he has devoted himself to conceptual studies that go beyond architecture and city planning to universal ordering in order to improve the quality of everyday life. In 1978, he built the *Laboratório de Investigações Conceptuais* in Barra da Tijuca, a conceptual think tank that houses a large architectural workshop, offices, and a library devoted to expanding the dimensions of architectural endeavors.

ELIZABETH D. HARRIS

WORKS

1947, Country Club, Petropolis, Brazil. 1951–1953, Helio Cabral House, Rio de Janeiro. 1953, Paulo Sampaio Country House, Petropolis, Brazil. *1957–1958, Brazilian Pavilion, International Fair, Brussels. 1969, Hotel Tropical, Manaus, Brazil. 1970, Sergio Bernardes House, Rio de Janeiro. 1972–1980, Cultural Center, Brasília. 1974, Schering Pharmaceutical Manufacturing Plant; 1978, Laboratório de Investigações Conceptuais; Barra da Tijuca, Brazil.

BIBLIOGRAPHY

DELONG, JAMES 1970 "Flying Down to Rio." *House Beautiful* 112, June:72–77.
Inquérito Nacional de Arquitectura. 1963 Belo Horizonte, Brazil: Escola de Arquitectura da Universidade de Minas Gerais.
WERNECK DE CASTRO, MOACIR 1980 "Sergio Bernardes: A Descoberta de um Novo Brasil." *Brasil 21* 3, March:82–87.

BERNINI, GIOVANNI LORENZO

Giovanni Lorenzo Bernini (1598–1680) was the last of the universal artists who were so typical of the Italian Renaissance. His father Pietro was a Florentine mannerist sculptor of some distinction who worked in Naples, where he married and where Gianlorenzo (as he is usually called) was born. The family settled in Rome around 1606 when Pietro was called to work for Pope Paul V Borghese (1605–1621). Bernini learned the craft of sculpture from his father and at an early age showed such talent that he was already famous in the second decade of the seventeenth century. His chief early patron was the papal nephew, Cardinal Scipione Borghese, for whom Bernini carved famous groups still to be seen in the Galleria Borghese in Rome. Bernini's genius soon came to the attention of Cardinal Maffeo Barberini, who became his close friend. When Barberini became Pope Urban VIII (1623–1644), Bernini's fortune was settled and he became in every sense the leading artist of Rome. One of Urban's objectives was to make Bernini a new MICHELANGELO, dominant in all of the arts. Although his efforts to have Bernini paint large-scale decorations failed, Bernini got his first architectural commissions almost immediately. With the help of the papal architectural experts, including CARLO MADERNO and his brilliant assistant, FRANCESCO BORROMINI, Bernini was able to achieve designs that would other-

wise have been beyond his powers, notably the baldachin in St. Peter's, built under his supervision and at least in part after his designs. Bernini's activity as an architect remained a sideline during most of this period although he designed and began bell towers on the façade of St. Peter's that had to be abandoned. After Urban's death, Bernini was in temporary disfavor and worked more and more for private patrons, notably in the Cornaro Chapel in Santa Maria della Vittoria. Bernini's emergence as an architect of world significance, rooted in such commissions, was confirmed under Pope Alexander VII (1655–1667), who used Bernini's services in preference to all others. Alexander was determined to rebuild Rome, and it is under him that Bernini designed and built the Piazza before St. Peter's, his single most important architectural design. In addition, he built one of the most perfect baroque churches, Sant'Andrea al Quirinale, and many other works. Bernini, unique as a sculptor, had gifted rivals in architecture: PIETRO BERRETTINI DA CORTONA and Francesco Borromini were in their own right of equal importance and significance. Nevertheless, it was Bernini whose reputation carried beyond the confines of the Papal States and even of Italy, and it was he whom Louis XIV commanded to come to Paris in 1665 to rebuild the Louvre.

Bernini was constantly engaged in works of decoration for festivals and canonizations; he excelled in the design of fountains, which transformed Rome's piazzas into a kind of fairyland: Bernini's significance as an architect transcends traditional definitions of architecture. His most important innovation was the fusion of all the visual arts—painting, sculpture, architecture—into a beautiful whole. The most famous example is the Cornaro Chapel but similar achievements are found in his churches. His later works are not so much sculptural or even architectural as religious, incorporating all of his ingenuity in the service of the Church to which he was passionately devoted.

Bernini's earliest architectural designs may have been frames for his own sculptural portraits, but we have no secure information and in one case we have a reliable report that the architecture was designed by someone else. Under Urban VIII, Bernini emerged as an architect. In the summer of 1624, after the discovery of the remains of an early Christian martyr, the small church of Santa Bibiana was entrusted to Bernini for rebuilding. He also carved a statue of the saint as the altarpiece, all being completed in 1626. Bernini's design has two outstanding features: the exterior façade and the altar area. The façade incorporates a narthex and is divided into three arched bays on the ground floor. The salient center bay is framed by clusters of Ionic pilasters. Above, a prominent central aedicula with a broken pediment rises above palacelike bays to the sides, which are crowned by a balustrade. The central motif uses a modified colossal order, giving the church a focus that is also found in his later façades.

The apse of Santa Bibiana contains the statue of the martyr, who seems to look upward, where we find a painted image of God the Father and a choir of angels in two of the coffers of the barrel vault. One of the coffers is opened to the sky, allowing light to fall onto the statue, a primitive attempt at the kind of unification of the arts with natural light that culminated in the Cornaro Chapel.

Bernini's chief commission of this period was for the decoration of the crossing of new St. Peter's. In June 1624, he was made responsible for erecting a gigantic decoration of gilt bronze over the high altar, which was perhaps already designed in some sense by the papal architect Carlo Maderno. The altar was over the grave of the Apostle, and since Peter was considered to have been the first pope, the significance of the site is obvious. The baldachin uses gigantic bronze versions of twisted marble columns from Old St. Peter's that had supposedly come from the Temple of Solomon in Jerusalem. Their forms link the new church with the old and with the Temple of the Old Testament.

Bernini had to organize all the available resources of the papal works (*Fabbrica di San Pietro*) and employed his entire family as well as many others in order to make the molds and cast the huge sections of the bronze columns, which were erected by June 1627. An engraving of 1626 shows that Bernini's project was to have been crowned by a statue of the Resurrected Christ. During the next years, the plans changed; eventually, a more novel, stable, and architectonic design was chosen that incorporates volute-scrolls joined above to support a symbolic ball and cross. The entire work was finished and dedicated in June 1633.

The baldachin is the first unquestionably baroque monument. Neither sculpture nor architecture, it incorporates architectonic elements decorated with sculpture to produce something new. Its antecedents are the domed ciborium and the temporary baldachin, which customarily took the form of a cloth canopy supported by staves. Above the columns of the baldachin stand four bronze angels with bronze swags that purportedly hold the bronze lappets of the canopy in order not to have columns support even a fictive cloth. The volutes seem to spring from the corners of the canopy. The unprecedented height of the structure, 28.5 meters, seems normal in the gargantuan space of St. Peter's. Bernini decorated the baldachin

Bernini.
St. Peter's (altar
*   decoration).*
Rome.
1624

Bernini.
St. Peter's (baldachin).
Rome.
1624–1633

with heraldry referring to the papacy and specifically to the Barberini.

Borromini, still technically an assistant in the papal works, was Bernini's chief architectural consultant. It was he who determined the proportional heights of the members, so that the structure would blend with the more traditional architecture of St. Peter's. He also designed some of the decorations and was possibly partially responsible for the magnificent crowning structure. Nevertheless, the only conceptual drawings that have survived for that part of the baldachin are by Bernini.

In the baldachin, Bernini created what his enemies, for good reason, called a "chimera." It combines hitherto disparate genres into a new whole that echoes the form of early Christian monuments while creating a new form and a new style. Irving Lavin has stated that "it is as though Bernini joined words from different languages to form a complete sentence, the subject of which is a divine mystery that knows no boundaries, namely, the process whereby at the tomb of the apostles the sacrifice of Christ is celebrated and the salvation of mankind is achieved (Lavin, 1980, I, p. 20).

While the baldachin was underway, Bernini also designed and began other decorations for the crossing of St. Peter's. He began a tomb for Urban VIII to be placed to the right of the main (western) apse, flanked by a remodeled tomb of Paul III Farnese—popes whose reigns bracketed the Counter Reformation. These monuments are set into niches that seem to have been designed by Borromini: Bernini was still dependent on the masters of the *Fabbrica*. He left details of draftsmanship and technical matters to assistants, whom he used creatively throughout his career, inspiring mere workmen to perform like artists.

St. Peter's possesses relics of four saints that were brought to the crossing for display. Four giant marble statues of these saints were planned for niches in the crossing piers, facing the altar. These niches are surmounted by balconies framed by the antique "Solomonic" marble columns from Old St. Peter's. Within, putti and angels displaying symbols of the relics float on stucco and marble clouds. Thus, in his earliest works associated with architecture, Bernini proved himself to be an imaginative decorator, using ideas and materials in the service of a higher idea, or *concetto*, a principle that informs all of his works.

Bernini's architecture of the 1620s and early 1630s encompasses temporary decorations for beatifications, an architectural catafalque for the funeral of Carlo Barberini (1630; drawings by Borromini), and the high altar design for San Paolo in Bologna (1634)—a surprising commission because the tabernacle was to contain a statuary group by his most talented rival, the Bolognese Alessandro Algardi. It is a large, free-standing columnar structure with a half-dome at the center supported by free-standing columns, providing a semicircular "theater" for the statuary. These columns seem inspired by ANDREA PALLADIO's Redentore and have echoes in Bernini's later designs for sculptural settings.

Carlo Maderno, the architect of St. Peter's, died early in 1629 and Bernini was immediately appointed to that position, signaling the end of the DOMENICO FONTANA-Maderno dynasty. St. Peter's was now in a new, essentially decorative phase, for it was architecturally complete apart from the façade companili. As architect, Bernini inherited the group that had worked with Maderno, including Borromini, who remained an assistant in the *Fabbrica* until September 1632. But Bernini also brought in new assistants, often Florentines.

The most important architectural project of these transitional years was the Palazzo Barberini on the Quirinal, which had been designed under Maderno with drawings by Borromini, but with ideas brought in from all sides—including, quite probably, Bernini's. He was the pope's favorite, had already superseded Maderno in the crossing of St. Peter's, and is often given credit for the entire palace in the old sources. He was not the designer, but his ideas may have affected its appearance, particularly the garden façade and the interior.

The building was just underway when Maderno died; Bernini became the nominal architect, assisted by Borromini and others. Old reports that give Bernini credit for the rectangular stairway and Borromini for the oval one are wrong, although they may have modified them in execution. They depend on earlier plans and resemble works by Maderno. The oval *sala* toward the garden on the main floor, with its doors on the short axis, is a form found repeatedly in Bernini's later designs, including an unexecuted casino for the Barberini at Mompecchio, near Castel Gandolfo, of 1633, and the chapel for the Palazzo di Propaganda Fide of 1634. The *sala ovale* of the Palazzo Barberini appears in Borromini's drawings done under Maderno but its completion seems to date from the period after Borromini left the papal works. Here and elsewhere, Bernini's chief contribution was decorative: doors and windows were modified from the Maderno-Borromini plans. The interaction of Bernini and Borromini in these designs can be followed through drawings that indicate Bernini's thoughts to have been essentially sculptural, Borromini's architectonic. Between them they evolved a heightened architectural language of traditional forms that we label baroque:

decorative moldings that had formerly been parallel to the wall now move outward, "ears" develop around frames, and volutelike forms project at an oblique angle. Previously linear elements dissolve into sculptural fluidity. The most famous example are the attic windows of the main façade in the transitional bays between the arched frontispiece and the projecting wings, traditionally given to Borromini, which may be the result of collaboration. A chief inspiration for these innovations was Michelangelo, bolstered by the example of late antique decoration. Bernini seems to have been inspired by Michelangelo throughout his career. His importance must have been reinforced by Bernini's friendship with Urban VIII, who prized Michelangelo's architecture above all other.

Bernini's Cappella dei Re Magi in the Palazzo di Propaganda Fide was begun in May 1634. The chapel was later replaced by a larger one by Borromini; what we know of Bernini's building transpires from Borromini's site drawings and from the documents. The building, inserted into an older structure, had a façade with its central portal framed by pairs of Tuscan pilasters, presumably supporting a pediment. The chapel was oval with its long axis parallel to the façade, bringing the high altar close to the entrance. Bernini also had chapels on the ends of the long axis, which could have created a conflict of focus (a feature he corrected at Saint'Andrea, some twenty-five years later.) Bernini was also called on to design the small façade of the old palace, toward the Piazza di Spagna (1644). His simple brick facing uses decorative vertical buttressing. Bernini has been incorrectly credited with the campanili for the Pantheon (destroyed), built by Maderno and Borromini. His responsibility for the façade of Saint'Anastasia by the Palatine is also unlikely; the façade, with two high campanili, was built by Luigi Arrigucci in 1636–1640.

Maderno's original façade of St. Peter's was designed without bell towers. While construction was underway, flanking campanili were ordered by the *Fabbrica,* and Maderno built their foundations to the height of the main façade, halting because of danger to the structure caused by an underground stream that had been discovered on the site of the left (south) campanile when foundations were excavated. In the mid-1630s, the *Fabbrica* determined to resume the building of the campanili; Bernini's design was presented in a wooden model in November 1636. It was more massive and elaborate than Maderno's and would have cost more than twice as much. Bernini's towers are recorded in drawings, engravings, and painted views. The lower story, open in the center, was supported by heavy piers at the corners with flanking columns.

The same scheme was repeated on a smaller scale above and, according to one design, by a third story with an elaborate crown and coat of arms. Work began in 1638; the south campanile was essentially finished in mid-1641 but the top story was taken down soon for aesthetic reasons: it looked too small. Later designs incorporated the top element into the second story. The north tower was also begun late in 1641 but work did not proceed very far. The vicissitudes of Bernini's designs are not wholly clear, but work continued into 1644, when Urban VIII died and was succeeded by a pope hostile to both the Barberini and Bernini, Innocent X Pamphilj (1644–1655).

In 1645–1646, inquiries were held concerning cracks that appeared in Maderno's substructures for the south campanile. Various new projects and criticisms were entertained, including one by Borromini. Bernini took part in the polemics, which drew most of the architects of Rome. Bernini had always been dissatisfied with Maderno's façade and over the years proposed many modifications, including isolation of the campanili and elimination of the pediment over the center of the façade. All of this was for naught. On February 23, 1646, a decree was issued ordering destruction of the campanili, and Bernini's income was partially sequestered. For the time being, he was in disgrace and his old Barberini connections made his position worse. But he never lost his position as architect of St. Peter's and soon he was also reinstated in papal favor—even Innocent X could not do without him.

Bernini's interior designs took an important step ahead with the Raimondi Chapel in San Pietro in Montorio, built 1640–1647. There he first unified all of the elements of design, incorporating the framework of the altar tabernacle, the tombs, and the chapel itself into one architectural system. The visitor is first aware of monochromatic coolness, for the chapel is essentially of white marble, with painted scenes only on the vault. The effect is classicizing but the method of integration is novel. The sculptured altarpiece is set back from its framework in a space that seems mystically lighted by hidden windows to left and right. The illusionistic vault paintings and the altarpiece seem to break down the traditional framework of the chapel walls, which have unusual, delicate relief carvings. The decorative scheme erupts into three dimensions in the two sculptured tombs at left and right and in the altar framework.

The Raimondi Chapel was preceded by designs for the choir of Santa Maria in Via Lata (1636–1643) and is coeval with the Confessio of Santa Francesca Romana in Santa Maria Nova (1641–1649), neither of which is preserved as Bernini built them. In 1643, he used the system of the Raimondi Chapel in the shallow, semicircular Pio Chapel in Sant'Agostino, a more modest design. The vault decoration here is of special importance; Bernini created a mixture of fresco with modeled and painted stucco that seems to show a heavenly glory of clouds and angels floating in front of the vault architecture, which is a ribbed half-dome. Below, the chapel is monochromatic, and the tabernacle is integrated into the design rather than being a separate piece of architectural furniture. These features also appear in his later works, most particularly at the Cornaro Chapel. Bernini allowed the altar tabernacles to follow the curves of the apses (in the Raimondi Chapel, the relief of the altarpiece is also concave). These decisions produced three-dimensional curves in the projecting gables, which were then broken back to create additional complication.

The Cornaro Chapel is in the left transept of a church built by Maderno for the Barefoot Carmelites. The patron of the chapel, Cardinal Federico Cornaro of Venice, obtained the transept for his own use in January 1647; it was finished in 1651. The chapel is dedicated to Saint Teresa of Avila, a great Carmelite reformer who was canonized in 1622. Bernini carved his most famous marble group for the altar, representing the "transverberation" of the saint, according to the account in her *Autobiography,* which was the central miracle cited in her process of canonization.

Bernini found the church relatively unadorned. He added rich pilasters on either side of the arch leading to the chapel. The architecture is richly colored marble, breaking dramatically with the monochrome designs we have discussed; but he had used colored marbles in the *confessio* of Santa Maria Nova and in the contemporary decorations for the nave of St. Peter's—his use of color in architecture was partially governed by the available funds.

In the Cornaro Chapel, Bernini followed the principles he had evolved in the Raimondi and Pio Chapels, uniting the altar tabernacle with the overall architectural scheme. Here, the tabernacle is convex to make room for an oval space in which he set the sculptural group on a carved marble cloud. Outside the chapel, Bernini built a kind of chimney containing a window, allowing daylight to fall into the space of the sculptural group in order to give the effect of heavenly light illuminating the mystical scene. The marble angel with Teresa appears to have descended from the vault of the chapel, where Bernini again covered the architectural revetment with stucco clouds and painted angels, achieving a spiritual unity that works independently of the architectural framework.

The altar tabernacle is essentially convex but the paired columns at either side, set on concave bases, support broken pieces of concave gable; behind them rises the convex triangle of the main pediment. The columns are greenish *breccia africana* set against yellow *giallo antico;* the adjacent pilasters framing the opening are *verde antico;* many other marbles are used as incrustation, all framed with white Carrara marble. The sculpture is also white: Bernini never imitated the colors of nature in his figures.

At either side of the chapel, Bernini conceived shallow spaces decorated with perspective reliefs, before which we see marble busts of members of the Cornaro family, chiefly deceased: cardinals and a doge as well as the patron; all seem to be discussing or contemplating the vision of Saint Teresa. This chapel, with its painted vault, colored marbles, integrated architecture, and conceptual unity, made Bernini's son Domenico exclaim that here his father had surpassed himself and conquered art.

Even before Bernini designed the Cornaro Chapel, he had the task of decorating the nave of St. Peter's for the Jubilee of 1650. In 1645, he began covering the piers, pilasters, arches, and spandrels with a three-dimensional decoration that included putti holding reliefs of the popes and papal insignia, together with the Pamphilj heraldry. This marble incrustation breaks decisively with the low-relief work of around 1600 that can be seen in the adjacent Clementine Chapel. Most of the sculptors of Rome were pressed into service to work on this project, which included stucco Virtues set above the arches of the nave.

Bernini's fountains are not precisely architecture yet not wholly sculptural. Like so many of his creations, they occupy a new position in the history of the genre. Perhaps his first was the Barcaccia in the Piazza di Spagna (1627–1629). It seems to be a sunken ship that spouts water from holes like gun mounts. The attribution has often been discussed because the aging Pietro Bernini, Gianlorenzo's father, was nominally architect of the Acqua Vergine, the aqueduct furnishing the water, and some sources attribute the fountain to him. The design is so novel that Gianlorenzo surely provided it, transforming the traditional ship fountain into a quasi-organic form, set low in order to accommodate the lack of water pressure. The fountain, decorated with papal insignia, was the subject of a distich by the learned Urban VIII. Since the site had supposedly been occupied by a naumachia in antiquity, Bernini may have made reference to it. He was also alluding to the ship of the Church, the *navicella* of Peter, and there may be overtones of actual warfare (the pope's poem refers to a warship), for in these years Urban was plotting with

France and Spain to invade Great Britain. This example of Bernini's *concettismo* may suffice, but each fountain has its own unique form and meaning.

Bernini made plans for the Trevi Fountain (1640), which was given its actual form in the next century by NICOLA SALVI. His most evocative fountain is perhaps the Triton in Piazza Tritone (Barberini), of 1642, which transforms the traditional geometric piazza fountain of Rome into a fairytale from Ovid: instead of a jet of water rising from an architectural element and falling into a geometric basin, Bernini made it organic. The sea-creature holding a shell spouts water that falls into a huge opened conch supported by dolphins. Below is an elaborate geometric pool. The papal arms again invite us to interpret the image as an emblematic message.

The Four Rivers Fountain in Piazza Navona is the most grandiose, erected as part of a papal program to turn the piazza into a Pamphilj showcase. In 1645, Borromini had begun the work of bringing in a large supply of water; he also projected a fountain employing an obelisk found outside of Rome in the Circus of Maxentius. Earlier projects were scrapped when Bernini's project came to the pope's attention. Bernini envisioned a great perforated rock supporting the obelisk. At the corners he placed marble statues of rivers, symbolizing the four known continents. Surmounted by a Pamphilj dove and decorated with papal arms below, the fountain became a personal as well as a papal symbol of Roman Catholic power. Above all it is a showy monument with splashing water, a seemingly precarious balance of heavy obelisk over a void that evokes our wonder. Of all Bernini's permanent creations it is closest to his festival decorations and gives an idea of the temporary works of architecture and sculpture that were a feature of baroque Rome. Bernini also remodeled one of the side fountains in the piazza, creating a larger pool and designing a central sculpture of a Moor holding a fish as the main figure while using older sculptural elements around the rim. The Four Rivers Fountain was completed in 1651, the Moor Fountain in 1654. Together with the remodeled Pamphilj Palace flanked by the new Church of Sant'Agnese, built by the Rainaldi (see GIROLAMO RAINALDI and CARLO RAINALDI) and Borromini, the Piazza Navona is the most spectacular ensemble of Roman baroque art.

In 1653, Bernini was commissioned by Niccolò Ludovisi, who was related to the papal family by marriage, to remodel a palace near Piazza Colonna. Bernini's project was not finished according to his plans; it was completed by CARLO FONTANA and is now the Palazzo di Montecitorio, the Chamber of Deputies of the Italian government. Bernini's design displays the triptych façade that he often used. Because of the site, the central section stands as a plane with wings angling back. He articulated the center with colossal pilasters and gave the portal and its large window sculptural embellishment. The linking bays are without orders or framing motifs; projecting bays on each end are framed by a colossal order. On the ground level, the bases of these pilasters are rusticated, contrasting the sophistication of the orders with rough nature.

Beginning in 1652, Bernini was employed by Cardinal Fabio Chigi to finish decorating the family chapel in Santa Maria del Popolo, a work by RAPHAEL. When Chigi became Pope Alexander VII (1655–1667), Bernini enlarged his operations and in 1656–1658 restored the façade of the church and crowned the adjacent Porta del Popolo with an architectural decoration that features the Chigi arms. Bernini also began to remodel the entire Quattrocento church. He enlarged the arcuated entablature over the bays of the nave, setting stucco figures of saints on it with relief elements extending up to the new windows he put in the clearstory. New altars and organs changed the appearance of the transept. Polychrome stuccoes, now removed, covered the entablature frieze and columns of the nave, giving the effect of marble. The dome was newly frescoed. Together with Bernini's sculptural additions to the Chigi Chapel, the church took on a new character.

Bernini was also occupied with projects for a large Chigi Chapel in the Cathedral of Siena (1658–1664). It was set into what had been the external corner of the right transept and corresponds to an older chapel in the left transept. It is an almost circular oval with columns set into the walls. The dome, decorated with both coffers and ribs, follows Bernini's preferred scheme that unites two separate traditions. Construction and execution was in the hands of Bernini's studio.

Bernini designed smaller chapels, including the De Silva Chapel in Sant'Isidoro (1660–1663) and the Fonseca Chapel in San Lorenzo in Lucina (1660–1666), which again show his attempts to unify architecture through an iconographic program using the other arts. Bernini worked on an endless series of mundane works of extension, repair, and remodeling, including the continuation of the Quirinal Palace toward the east (1656–1659).

Bernini's greatest works of independent architecture date from the pontificate of Alexander VII, one of the most ambitious of all papal builders. First place is taken by the great Piazza di San Pietro, Bernini's solution to the organization of space before Saint Peter's and the papal palace. Many projects were submitted in 1656–1657 by

Bernini.
Piazza di San Pietro,
*   St. Peter's.*
Rome.
1656–1667

various architects; but the final plan for a trans-verse oval, consonant with so many of Bernini's other projects, may have come from the pope. The problems of the site were manifold and a number of valuable buildings eventually were demolished, including Raphael's Palazzo dell'Aquila. The piazza had to have as its center the obelisk which had been moved under Sixtus V to a site at a considerable distance from the façade of the church, roughly on axis. Bernini had to deal with the sharply sloping site and to consider the multiple functions served by the piazza. Normal papal blessings were given from the Vatican palace to the north and Bernini needed to create room for pilgrims to see

this in addition to making a space for the throngs who gather for the Easter blessing given from the Benediction Loggia of St. Peter's. The chief entrance to the Vatican was to the right of St. Peter's, ennobled by a clock tower built under Paul V. Bernini had to tear this structure down and still retain a monumental entrance to the palace. His solution created a trapezoidal area leading down from Saint Peter's, bordered by covered walkways, and eventually he was forced to rebuild the stairway to the upper floors, the Scala Regia. Thus, the piazza design created new entrances both to St. Peter's and to the Vatican Palace.

Bernini's choice of a simple Tuscan colonnade

Bernini.
Piazza di San Pietro,
*   St. Peter's.*
Rome.
1656–1667

with an unbroken Ionic frieze for the main wings of the piazza shows that he wanted to make the enclosure as self-effacing as possible while creating a noble space. The sources of the oval have been debated: Bernini may have been influenced by ancient harbors and temple precincts, Palladio, and new theories of oval architecture promulgated by Juan Caramuel Lobkowitz, who was in Rome at this time and later published a book on the subject.

Bernini began by making the entrance to the Vatican a continuation of a straight street, the Borgo Novo (via Alessandrina). He had to center the widest portion of the oval on the obelisk, which also allowed maximum view of the window of the pope in his palace. In order to see over the colonnade the visitors had to stand away from the closer edge, near the obelisk and beyond. Thus some kind of bulge in that area was needed. The choice of these oval colonnades was not based on the viewpoint of the visitor who wanted to see the Benediction Loggia, for in the curves it is invisible. Bernini made the colonnades segments of circles, which are pulled apart (so to speak) to create an oval space. Both sides are equal and, in the same spirit, both sides of the trapezoid are the same. By making it lower than the church but abutting it, he made a visual adjustment to the façade that he had longed to achieve in more direct ways, for the façade was considered to be too long. When the new campanili were abandoned and pulled down, the old flaws of Maderno's façade with the additions of bases for the campanili became permanent aspects of the church. Bernini made an optical adjustment by pinching it inward by the low, oblique walls, making the façade appear higher and narrower.

Maderno's beautifully remodeled fountain before St. Peter's was off-center and unrelated to the new piazza. Bernini moved it, setting it up with an enlarged pool on the north axis of the obelisk-oval and built a twin fountain on the south. Thus the two magnificent fountains and the obelisk that make so great an impression were legacies that Bernini transformed creatively into a new design.

Bernini's colonnades comprise two sets of parallel columns with a road in the middle, vaulted to make the arms a covered passageway for pedestrians and coaches. In plan, each is composed of four rows of columns and piers laid out on radial lines converging on the axis of the fountains. Bernini's colonnades recall ancient porticoes, which were mentioned in discussions of the time; they were intended to provide protection from the sun and the rain for those going to church and palace. But the space within the oval is of even greater importance, forming the people who gather there into a

little world to receive the papal blessing, which is given *urbi et orbi:* to the city and to the world. Although considerable symbolism is attached to the piazza, Bernini's own explanation of its meaning is basic: he saw it as the embracing arms of the Mother Church.

The Scala Regia (1663–1666) created a grand stairway to the Vatican palace, replacing the old narrow and dangerous steps by which the pope had to be carried down to St. Peter's and up to the palace. The passage is between the Sistine Chapel and St. Peter's, an irregular space that did not allow a grand and wide passageway. Again, Bernini solved the problem (to the degree that it could be solved) by optical means: he made the vaulted entrance grand and wide, with columns set apart from the walls on either side. The viewer, seeing this, assumes that the ascending columns of the stairway are of the same height and distance from the wall. The stairway actually narrows and decreases in height; the columns ultimately abut the walls and their height is much reduced. In order to avoid too much telescoping, Bernini broke the stair with a lighted landing half way up and also put a window at the end. But the second flight, doubling back, is narrow.

Because the Scala Regia links the Vatican with St. Peter's, Bernini made a sculptural decoration at its entrance, opposite the portico of the church. This grand work, a colossal equestrian statue of the Emperor Constantine in the act of converting to Christianity, is both a useful transition for those coming from the church, who have to turn left to go up to the palace, and a significant iconographical

Bernini.
Scala Regia, Vatican
*   Palace.*
Rome.
1663–1666

Bernini.
Sant'Andrea al Quirinale.
Rome.
1658–1670

symbol, reinforcing papal claims to legitimacy.

These symbols are stressed within St. Peter's where Bernini built a throne of St. Peter suspended in the apse, blessed by a throng of sculptured angels and bathed in the light of the afternoon sun, which floods through a novel stained-glass window imprinted with the image of the Holy Spirit. This great work of sculpture (1657–1666) is essentially coeval with the piazza and, together with the Scala Regia and the baldachin, makes Bernini's transformation of the church and its precinct almost complete. He also restored and decorated the bridge leading to the Vatican, the Ponte Sant'Angelo (1667–1669), which was given sculptured statues of angels bearing instruments of the passion. Within St. Peter's, he constructed two great papal tombs, that of Urban VIII (1628–1647) and of Alexander VII (1671–1678). He also remodeled the Chapel of the Holy Sacrament with a new altar and tabernacle (1673–1674), a bronze tempietto adored by two bronze angels.

Bernini's three churches also date from the period of Alexander's pontificate. The most important and the richest is Sant'Andrea al Quirinale (1658–1670), the church of the Jesuit novitiate. It is built on a shallow site, and at first Bernini planned a polygonal building. He soon changed to a transverse oval like those he had planned in the 1630s and like the piazza at Saint Peter's. Unlike his chapel for the Propaganda Fide, Bernini closed the long ends of the oval, setting the side chapels off axis. He thus created a more powerful, undivided main axis from the portal to the high altar, which he treated as a kind of religious theater. The sanctuary is lighted from an invisible source and over the altar sculptured angels seem to deposit the heavy frame of a painted altarpiece depicting the crucifixion of Saint Andrew. As we enter the church we immediately focus on this "event," thanks to richly colored pairs of marble columns framing the sanctuary. Above, hovering in the gable, we see a white stucco statue of Saint Andrew, seemingly rising into the "dome of heaven," where the dove of the Holy Spirit awaits him in the light of the lantern. In order to make the symbolism work, the side chapels are dark; light comes in from windows at the base of the dome, contrasting the dark purgatory of life with the brilliance of heaven. The large oval dome is decorated with Bernini's favored coffers and ribs, and the cornice supports symbolic stucco sculptures. The church, richly endowed by Prince Camillo Pamphilj, is sumptuously revetted with colored marble.

The façade of Sant'Andrea breaks with the traditional two-story façades of the sixteenth and early seventeenth centuries. It appears as a huge pedimented portal framed by colossal Corinthian pilasters. Within this framework the door is protected by a segmental porch roof that seems to have swung down to open an arched window; the roof is supported by two free-standing Ionic columns that stand on a semicircular entranceway that was originally reached by three stairs. These have now been multiplied because of a change in the street level.

The oval dome is supported by ornamental volute-buttresses on the flanks, and the exterior is partially shielded by low quadrant walls coming out from the portico. The convex center set against these concave wings creates a formula that was to have echoes in Bernini's first Louvre designs. Monumental and grand in itself, the façade is a symbolic entranceway that draws the visitor into the church for what should be an overwhelming religious experience. Bernini's architecture is usually at the service of a higher goal; here, as at the Cornaro Chapel, he used the other arts to achieve it.

Bernini's second church, San Tommaso Villanova at Castel Gandolfo (1658–1661), is a high Greek-cross structure with conventional features that make it resemble a High Renaissance structure. The interior is classicizing, the dome is again coffered and ribbed, and once more there is an iconographic program that unifies the design. The façade, of two unequal stories, is articulated with pilasters, the central element crowned by a pediment.

Bernini's third church, dedicated to the Assumption of the Virgin, is opposite a palace of the Chigi family at Ariccia near Castel Gandolfo. The town had been purchased by the Chigi in 1661, and the pope immediately set about improving the area. Construction of the church entailed the destruction of buildings on the site, which was precipitous. Bernini designed a Pantheon-like structure with a low dome; a pedimented entrance portico of three arches is set between pilasters. At either side of the façade he built flanking structures that carry on the pilaster order of the portico. These low buildings make the small church seem more imposing. Around the church on both sides new curving streets lead down to the hill town. Within, the circular structure is divided into shallow chapels by arches and Corinthian pilasters. The dome is Bernini's familiar type with iconographic references to the Assumption, which is depicted behind the altar in paint, but without hidden lighting.

The church is roughly contemporary with Bernini's studies of the Pantheon and with abortive efforts to clear the area in front and beside the ancient monument in order to make it more suitable, but nothing came of these plans. The pope's efforts were everywhere concerned with regularizing Rome and making the piazzas large and monumental. In 1660, Bernini also seems to have made a design for what are now called the Spanish Steps, leading to the Trinità dei Monti. His drawing incorporates curving ramps, a central fountain, and an equestrian statue. The project was not begun and the present stairs date from the next century.

The normal entrance to Rome from the north was through the Porta del Popolo, which Bernini rebuilt. The adjoining Piazza del Popolo had been ornamented with an obelisk and fountain under Sixtus V, but the space remained inchoate. The obelisk marked the convergence of three streets that penetrate to the heart of Rome. The Corso in the center leads to the Piazza Venezia, the left street (now via del Babuino) leads to the Piazza di Spagna, and the via di Ripetta on the right goes to the Ponte Sant'Angelo and so to the Vatican. It was typical of Alexander VII to want to make a monumental entrance display, and in 1662 he determined to erect twin churches on the points of property dividing the three avenues. The architect was Carlo Rainaldi, but one of the churches (Santa

Maria di Monte Santo, toward the left) was soon put into Bernini's hands. Carlo Fontana, who worked closely with both Rainaldi and Bernini, completed the church by 1675. The façades seem not to be Rainaldi's design but Fontana's under the influence of Bernini. They employ free-standing temple porticoes for the first time in Rome, using columns from the dismantled campanili of St. Peter's. We do not know the full extent of Bernini's activity here but since he was in constant friendly contact with the pope it seems possible that the entire project was in some sense his. Thus one of the most scenographic features of baroque Rome is to some extent Bernini's work. Such projects, built and unbuilt, served to make Rome into a grand city of pilgrimage and tourism, which is reflected in the books of engravings by Giovanni Battista Falda celebrating the new constructions of Alexander VII.

In March 1664, Bernini received a letter from Louis XIV's first minister, Jean Baptiste Colbert, asking him to submit plans for completing the Louvre palace. Pietro da Cortona and Carlo Rainaldi also submitted designs. Bernini's first plans were bold and of great future significance, but they did not please. He conceived a concave frontispiece framing a large convex center section with an attic rising above the rest of the palace. The centerpiece was articulated with a colossal order of pilasters alternating with two stories of arches. The flanking wings were less unusual, with a pilaster order and traditional windows. Bernini then sent a second facade project from Rome, with a long concave center section and concave wings joining onto standard side pavilions. This design was also unacceptable but in April 1665 the aging Bernini set off for Paris together with his architectural executant Mattia de' Rossi and others. After a triumphant voyage, Bernini arrived outside Paris on June 2, where he was met by Paul Fréart, sieur de Chantelou, the friend and patron of Nicolas Poussin, who was Bernini's companion during his stay. Chantelou's diary of Bernini's visit not only gives a picture of Bernini and of his conversation but also a glimpse into the life and manners of the time that is unrivaled in the history of art.

Bernini now designed a final Louvre project, which was more traditional, planar, and Italian. Although foundations were begun and work continued for some time, Bernini's design lacked the internal comforts and conveniences that French architects had begun to offer. Bernini put the king's apartment in the noisy center of the complex for the sake of decorum; but as Colbert finally said, Bernini's palace, for all its grand stairs, halls, and rooms, left the king as cramped and uncomfortable as before. Work was abandoned soon after

Bernini.
Palazzo Chigi (Odescalachi;
reconstruction).
Rome.
1664–1666

Bernini left, late in 1665, and the palace was eventually built according to French plans.

Bernini's Louvre façade is related to plans that Bernini had evolved for a new Chigi Palace on the Piazza Santi Apostoli. This building, which had been partially rebuilt by Maderno, was now refurbished and given a grand façade (1664–1666) as well as an expanded courtyard. Now vastly enlarged again, it can best be appreciated in old engravings, which show Bernini's emergence as a master designer of traditional palace architecture. Always sensitive to proportions, he divided the façade into a projecting center section with wings. The seven-bay frontispiece was given a colossal order on the *piano nobile* that supports a balustrade with statuary. A columnar portal surmounted by a window decorated with Chigi arms accents the center. The side blocks were given horizontal grooving but no order and the windows are plainer. Bernini combined architectural features designed by DONATO BRAMANTE and Raphael, Michelangelo, GIACOMO BAROZZI DA VIGNOLA, and Palladio to culminate some 150 years of Renaissance thought about palace façades. Perhaps more than any other work, it shows the secular mastery that Bernini could achieve, solving problems of aesthetic design that had been posed by his great predecessors.

Bernini's last important project, for the tribune of Santa Maria Maggiore, was never built. He conceived a columnar portico surmounted by an attic (one drawing shows a dome), which takes up the rejected first version of his Louvre design. The façade would have connected with two chapels on either side built by Sixtus V and Paul V. Because the church is on the crest of the Esquiline hill, a steep flight of steps led down to the piazza toward the city. Although favored by Bernini's friend Clement IX Rospigliosi (1667–1669), the design was abandoned for lack of funds and replaced by a cheaper one by Carlo Rainaldi. In the 1650s and 1660s, there were increasing cries of discontent from the populace, which saw the popes lavish hundreds of thousands of *scudi* on projects like the Piazza di San Pietro while they were starving. The impoverished papacy soon had to curtail such building; the great age of baroque construction came to an end before Bernini's death.

Bernini's last important chapel, in San Francesco a Ripa (1671–1675), honors the newly beatified Ludovica Albertoni, whose statue he carved. Unlike the sumptuous Cornaro Chapel, this was an inexpensive remodeling: Bernini opened a rear wall to allow space for the statue and a painted altarpiece, with hidden windows at either side.

Bernini's influence was widespread. After his visit to Paris, French palaces soon ceased to have high-pitched roofs and imitated the Italian style. JOHANN BERNARD FISCHER VON ERLACH, partially trained in Bernini's entourage, took a Roman, essentially Berninesque sense of architectural design back to Vienna, where it was influential. Bernini's scenography is reflected in interiors by the ASAM BROTHERS in Bavaria, which was partially derived from experience in Rome under Carlo Fontana, Bernini's successor as architect of St. Peter's. GUARINO GUARINI's Palazzo Carignano in Turin is ultimately based on Bernini's first Louvre façade design. Even the Radcliffe Camera at Oxford by JAMES GIBBS reflects the architect's training under Fontana.

The importance of Bernini's architecture is hard to overestimate. He mastered traditional Italian design to the extent that he could employ Renaissance principles and create new works that are organically related to the architectural history of Rome, as in his palace façades. But he did more, using architecture as an active framework for religious dramas and emotional appeals to the senses that employ sculpture and painting, making architecture part of a greater whole. Finally, he created new forms, as in the unique Piazza di San Pietro, which alone would make Bernini one of the great architectural innovators.

HOWARD HIBBARD

WORKS

1624–1626, Santa Bibiana (renovation); 1624–1633, St. Peter's (baldachin); 1627–1629, Barcaccia Fountain, Piazza di Spagna; 1627–1641, St. Peter's (reliquary loggias); 1627–1647, St. Peter's (Tomb of Urban III); 1629–c.1640, Palazzo Barberini (with others); 1630, Santa Maria in Aracoeli (Catafalque for Carlo Barberini); 1634–1639, Cappella dei Re Magi, Palazzo di Propaganda Fide; Rome. 1634–1635, San Paolo (high altar), Bologna, Italy. 1636–1643, Santa Maria in Via Lata (apse and high altar); 1637–1642, St. Peter's (campanili); 1638, Palazzo del Quirinale (benediction loggia); 1640–1644, San Lorenzo in Damaso (apse decoration); 1640–1647, Raimondi Chapel, San Pietro in Montorio; 1641–1649, Santa Maria Nova (confessio); 1642–1643, Triton Fountain; 1644, Api Fountain; 1644, Palazzo di Propaganda Fide (north façade); 1645–1648, St. Peter's (decoration of nave); 1647–1651, Cornaro Chapel, Santa Maria della Vittoria; 1647–1651, Four Rivers Fountain; 1649–1650, Alaleona Chapel, Santi Domenico e Sisto; 1651–1654, Moro Fountain; Rome. 1652–1654, Chapel of Saint Barbara, Cathedral, Rieti, Italy. 1652–1656, Chigi Chapel (restoration), Santa Maria del Popolo; 1653–1655, Palazzo di Montecitorio (Ludovisi); c.1655–?, Santa Maria del Popolo (restoration of interior and façade); 1656–1658, Porta del Popolo (restoration); 1656–1659, Quirinal Palace (extension); 1656–1667, Piazza di San Pietro; 1657–1666, Cathedra Pietri, St. Peter's; Rome. 1658–1661, San Tommaso Villanova, Castel Gandolfo, Italy. 1658–1663, Arsenal, Civitavecchia, Italy. 1658–1664, Chigi Chapel, Cathedral of Siena, Italy. 1658–1670, Sant'Andrea al Quirinale; 1660–1663?, De Silva Chapel, Sant'Isidoro; 1660–1666, Fonseca Chapel, San Lorenzo in Lucina; Rome. 1662–1665,

Church of the Assumption, Ariccia, Italy. 1663–1666, Scala Regia, Vatican Palace; 1664–1666, Palazzo Chigi (Odescalchi; reconstruction); 1668–1670, Ponte Sant' Angelo (reconstruction and decoration); 1671–1675, Altieri Chapel, San Francesco a Ripa; 1671–1678, St. Peter's (Tomb of Alexander VII); 1673–1674, Chapel of the Holy Sacrament (decoration), St. Peter's; Rome.

BIBLIOGRAPHY

BALDINUCCI, FILIPPO (1682)1966 *Life of Gian Lorenzo Bernini.* Translated by Catherine Enggass. University Park: University of Pennsylvania Press.

BERNINO, DOMENICO (1713)1980 *Vita del Cavalier Gio. Lorenzo Bernino. . . .* Ann Arbor, Mich.: University Microfilms.

BIRINDELLI, MASSIMO 1980 *La machina heroica: Il disegno di Gianlorenzo Bernini per piazza San Pietro.* Rome: Università degli Studi di Roma, Istituto de Fondamenti dell'Architettura.

BORSI, FRANCO 1980 *Bernini architetto.* Milan: Electa.

BRAUER, HEINRICH, and WITTKOWER, RUDOLF (1931)1970 *Die Zeichnungen des Gianlorenzo Bernini.* 2 vols. New York: Reprinted Collectors Editions.

CHANTELOU, PAUL FRÉART DE 1885 *Journal du voyage du Cavalier Bernin en France.* Edited by L. Lalanne. Paris: Gazette des Beaux-Arts.

FAGIOLO DELL'ARCO, MAURIZIO, and CARANDINI, SILVIA 1977–1978 *L'Effimero barocco.* 2 vols. Rome: Bulzoni.

LAVIN, IRVING 1980 *Bernini and the Unity of the Visual Arts.* 2 vols. New York: Morgan Library; London: Oxford University Press.

LAVIN, IRVING ET AL. 1981 *Drawings by Gianlorenzo Bernini from the Museum der Bildenden Künste Leipzig.* Princeton, N.J.: Art Museum.

WITTKOWER, RUDOLF (1958)1982 *Art and Architecture in Italy: 1600 to 1750.* 3d ed., rev. Baltimore: Penguin.

BERNOULLI, HANS

Hans Bernoulli (1876–1959), of an old family of Basel, studied architecture in Munich with FRIEDRICH VON THIERSCH with whom he also worked. In 1901, he settled in Berlin where he became familiar with the German garden city movement. In 1912, he returned to Basel to work for a big building society. After 1918, he built a number of new housing developments. His architecture was a simple classicism, reflecting the *Um 1800* movement.

An early enthusiast of CAMILLO SITTE, Bernoulli played an important role in the development of urbanism, serving as consultant for a number of cities, including Warsaw, after World War II. He also taught at the Institute of Technology in Zurich from 1912 to 1939, when his demand that the land of the cities be communalized led to his dismissal for political reasons.

MARTIN STEINMANN

WORKS

1899, Schindler House, Aeschbach, near Lindau, Germany. 1905, Brandenberg House, Berlin. 1907–1908, Social Center for the Chemical Industries, Griesheim, near Frankfurt am Main. 1910, Hotel Baltic; 1911–1912, Mendel Building; Berlin. 1912–1914, Commercial Building, Frankfurt an der Oder, Germany. 1914–1915, Schifflände Building; 1915–1916, C. W. House; Basel. 1917, A. W. House, Bilsteinfluh, near Langenbruck, Basel-Land. 1920, Social Center for the Sandoz Chemical Industries; 1920–1922, Housing Estate, Langen Löhn; 1922–1923, Housing Estate, Lindengarten; Basel. 1924, Grain Elevator, Kleinhüningen, near Basel. 1924–1929, Hirzbrunnen Estate (with August Künzel), Basel. 1924–1929, Hardturmstrasse Housing Estate, Zurich. 1930, Houses in the WOBA Estate (with Künzel); 1939, Eglisee Housing Estate; 1957, Realgymnasium (with Ernst Mumenthaler and Otto Meier); Basel.

BIBLIOGRAPHY

BERNOULLI, HANS   1929   *Städtebau in der Schweiz.* Zurich: Fretz.

BERNOULLI, HANS   1942   *Die organische Erneuerung unserer Städte.* Basel: Wepf.

BERNOULLI, HANS   1946   *Die Stadt und ihr Boden.* Zurich: Verlag für Architektur.

GUBLER, JACQUES   1975   Pages 78–80, 104–109 in *Nationalisme et internationalisme dans l'architecture moderne de la Suisse.* Lausanne, Switzerland: Editions de L'Age d'homme.

SALZMANN, FRIEDRICH (editor)   1951   *Dr. h.c. Hans Bernoulli.* Bern: Verlagsgenossenschaft Freies Volk.

SCHMID, WERNER   1974   *Hans Bernoulli.* Schaffhausen, Switzerland: Meili.

STEINMANN, MARTIN (editor)   1981   "Hans Bernoulli." *Archithese* 6:entire issue.

BERRECCI, BARTOLOMMEO

Bartolommeo Berrecci (?–1537), a native of Pontassieve, Tuscany, was called to Kraków in 1517 to work for Sigismund I Jagellon. His major work for the king was the Sigismund Chapel in Wawel Cathedral (c.1517–1533), a mortuary chapel built on a truncated Greek-cross plan with a humanistic decorative program.

As the first Renaissance building in Poland, the chapel influenced ninety-four other structures over the next two centuries. Berrecci himself built a smaller version for the Bishop of Kraków, Piotr Tomicki (1524–1530). Certainly, the tomb figure, a *statue accoudée,* and the decorative program demonstrate that he had worked in Rome.

Berrecci also made renovations in Wawel Castle, and his high wages between 1524 and 1530 suggest that he was chief royal architect. Further, his role as a sculptor in the Sigismund Chapel and elsewhere has prompted the attribution of several Renaissance statues in Poland to him.

DOROTHY LIMOUZE

WORKS

c.1517–1533, Sigismund Chapel, Wawel Cathedral, Kraków, Poland. c.1521–1524, Cistercian Priory, Mogila near Kraków, Poland. 1522–1537, Royal Palace (rebuilt); 1524–1530, Funerary Chapel of Piotr Tomicki, Wawel Cathedral; Kraków, Poland. 1525, Tomb of Louis Nicolas Szydłowiecki, Collegiate Church, Opatow, Poland. 1534, Pleasure Palace, Wola near Kraków, Poland.

BIBLIOGRAPHY

BIAŁOSTOCKI, JAN   1967   "The Sea-Thiasos in Renaissance Sepulchral Art." Pages 69–74 in *Studies in Renaissance and Baroque Art Presented to Anthony Blunt on His 60th Birthday.* London: Phaidon.

BIAŁOSTOCKI, JAN   1976   *The Art of the Renaissance in Eastern Europe.* Ithaca, N.Y.: Cornell University Press.

BURNATOWA, IRENA   1964   "Ornament renesansowy w krakowie." *Studia Renesansowe* 4:5–243.

FISCHINGER, ANDREZEJ   1978   "Ze studiów nad rzeźba figuralna kaplicy zygmuntowskiej." *Studia do Dziejów Wawelu* 4:215–244.

KALINOWSKI, LECH   1961   "Treści artystyezne i ideowe kaplicy zygmuntowskiej." *Studia do Dziejów Wawelu* 2:1–129.

KALINOWSKI, LECH   1976   "Motywy antyczne w dekoracji kaplicy zygmuntowskiej." *Folia Historiae Artium* 12:67–94.

KOZAKIEWICZOWA, HELENA   1961   "Z badań nad Bartłomiejam Berreccim." *Biuletyn Historii Sztuki* 23 no. 4:311–327.

REWSKI, ZBIGNIEW   1962   "Głos dyskusyjny do artykułu H. Kozakiewiczowej p. t. z badań nad Bartłomiejem Berreccim." *Biuletyn Historii Sztuki* 24 no. 2:216–220.

WILIŃSKI, STANISŁAW   1970   "Zygmunt stary jako Salomon z listów Erazma z Rotterdamu." *Biuletyn Historii Sztuki* 32 no. 1:38–48.

WILIŃSKI, STANISŁAW   1976   "O renesansie wawelskin." Pages 213–225 in *Renesans:sztuka i ideologia.* Warsaw: Państwowe Wydawnictwo Naukowe.

BERTOLA, ANTONIO

Antonio Bertola (1647–1719), architect and military engineer, was born and died in Muzzana, in Piedmont, Italy. Bertola held many ducal posts, was chief engineer during the siege of Turin in 1706, and from 1708 was chief architect and military engineer, the first to hold the post. He designed many fortresses (Brunetta, Fenestrelle, and so on), and from the mid-1690s executed buildings and altars. He worked on at least three buildings which GUARINO GUARINI left unfinished:

Sante Sindone, where he designed the altar and pavement (1692-1996); San Filippo Neri, where he modified the main altar (1699-1704); and the Palazzo Carignano (1699-). He also designed the Castello at San Martino Alfieri (1696) and Santa Croce in Cuneo (1709-1712).

HENRY A. MILLON

WORKS

1692-1696, Sante Sindone (main altar and pavement; completion of work by Guarino Guarini), Turin, Italy. 1696, Castello, San Martino Alfieri, Italy. 1699-1704, San Filippo Neri (modification of main altar; completion of work by Guarini); 1699 and later, Palazzo Carignano (completion of work by Guarini); Turin, Italy. 1709-1712, Santa Croce, Cuneo, Italy.

BIBLIOGRAPHY

BRAYDA, CARLO; COLI, LAURA; and SESIA, DARIO 1963 *Ingegneri e architetti del sei e settecento in piemonte.* Turin, Italy: Società Ingegneri e Architetti.
CARBONERI, NINO 1950 "Antonio Bertola e la Confraternita di S. Croce in Cuneo." *Bollettino Società per gli studi storici, archeologici ed artistici nella provincia di Cuneo* 27:54-70.
LANGE, AUGUSTA 1962-1963 "I progetti dell'architetto Antonio Bertola per la Chiesa di Superga." *Bollettino Società Piemontese di Archeologia e di Belle Arti* 16-17:104-120.
OLIVERO, E. 1929 "L'altare della SS. Sindone ed il suo autore." Volume 2, page 7 in Arturo Midana, *Il Duomo di Torino,* Turin, Italy: Sacra.

BERTOTTI SCAMOZZI, OTTAVIO

The architect, writer, and theorist Ottavio Bertotti Scamozzi (1719-1790) was born in Vicenza, Italy, the city where he always lived and which is closely associated with his name. Bertotti at an early age came under the protection of the Marchese Mario Capra, a learned architectural dilettante. Capra, executor of the celebrated will of the architect VINCENZO SCAMOZZI, used his influence to have its endowment bestowed upon Bertotti, who was thereby enabled to study architecture. In gratitude, Bertotti subsequently appended Scamozzi to his surname.

Bertotti Scamozzi's earliest training in architecture came under Domenico Cerato, a practitioner of the ANDREA PALLADIO-Scamozzi tradition. Later contacts with TOMMASO TEMANZA proved more fruitful, exposing Bertotti to the developing Venetian neoclassical current. Of greater importance, however, were the architect's contacts with many of Europe's intellectual leaders. Among his acquaintances were FRANCESCO MILIZIA, Francesco Algarotti, Giacomo Quarenghi, J. W. von Goethe, and the learned circle which clustered around Elisabetta Turra Caminer, a leader of the Vicentine intelligentsia. Moreover, Bertotti Scamozzi enjoyed a continental reputation as a *cicerone,* and in this capacity he was in close contact with the British architects WILLIAM CHAMBERS and JAMES ADAM and ROBERT ADAM. The Vicentine's useful book, *Il forestiere istruito . . . ,* published in 1761, was a standard guidebook for visitors to the city.

As a practicing architect, Bertotti Scamozzi enjoyed considerable patronage in Vicenza and its immediate vicinity. His buildings before about 1780 show decided Palladian influences, an unsurprising phenomenon given Bertotti's diligent study of Palladio's structures and the former's publication, from 1776 to 1783, of *Le fabbriche e i disegni di Andrea Palladio,* a work of major importance for Palladio studies. Bertotti Scamozzi's assertion that Palladio used musical ratios in his designs demonstrates his keen understanding of Palladian intentions. Ottavio's Casa Muzzi at Riello (1770) closely follows the Palladian model of the Villino Cerato di Montecchio Precalcino, and the Palazzo Franceschini a San Marco (1770) at Vicenza, with its animated façade and elegant sequence of large windows and graceful moldings, closely follows Palladian formulae.

During the last decade of Bertotti Scamozzi's career, he came under the influence of the Italian *illuminismo* movement, a direction which perhaps can be best described in architecture as neoclassical. The Palazzo Braghetta sul Corso (1780) at Vicenza reveals a new severity and rationalism in its simple window pediments and engaged Ionic pilasters. The austere façade of the Teatro Eretenio (1781-1784) displays similar reductive tendencies.

An important figure for understanding many late Settecento architectural currents, Bertotti Scamozzi is best known for his edition of Palladio, a monumental achievement which has largely overshadowed his own architectural contribution.

CHRISTOPHER JOHNS

WORKS

*1758, Wooden Arch in honor of Marino Priuli, Vincenza, Italy. 1760, Villa Trissino, Sandrigo, Italy. 1766, Casa Milani a Santa Lucia, Vincenza, Italy. 1770, Casino Muzzi, Riello, Italy. 1770, Palazzo Franceschini a San Marco, Vincenza, Italy. 1770, Villa Franceschini, Arcugnano, Italy. 1774, Church of San Faustino (façade); 1776, Casa Muzzi sull'Isola; 1780, Palazzo Braghetta sul corso; Vicenza, Italy. *1780, Palazzo Morozzo della Rocca, Turin, Italy. *1781-1784, Teatro Eretenio (façade), Vicenza, Italy.

BIBLIOGRAPHY

BARBIERI, FRANCO 1967 "O. Bertotti Scamozzi."

Volume 9, pages 632–635 in *Dizionario Biografico degli Italiani*. Rome.

BARBIERI, FRANCO 1970 "L'interpretazione grafica del Palladio da porte del Bertotti Scamozzi e le sue consequenze." *Bollettino del Centro Internazionale di Studi di Architettura 'A. Palladio'* 12:140–154.

BERTOTTI SCAMOZZI, OTTAVIO 1758 *Descrizione dell'arco trionfale e della illuminazione fatta nella pubblica piazza di Vicenza la notte del 12 novembre 1758 per la gloriosissima esaltazione alla dignità cardinalizia di Sua Eminenza Reverendissima Signor Antonio Marino Priuli. . . .* Vicenza, Italy.

BERTOTTI SCAMOZZI, OTTAVIO 1761 *Il forestiere istruito delle cose più rare d'architettura e di alcune pitture della città di Vicenza.* Vicenza, Italy: Mosca.

BERTOTTI SCAMOZZI, OTTAVIO 1776–1783 *Le Fabbriche e i disegni di Andrea Palladio raccolti ed illustrati.* Vicenza, Italy.

BERTOTTI SCAMOZZI, OTTAVIO 1785 *Le Terme dei Romani disegnate da Andrea Palladio e ripubblicate con la giunta di alcune osservazioni giusta l'esemplare del Lord conte di Burlington impresso a Londra l'anno 1752.* Vicenza, Italy: Modena

BERTOTTI SCAMOZZI, OTTAVIO 1790 *L'origine dell'Accademia Olimpica di Vicenza con una breve descrizione del suo teatro.* Vicenza, Italy: Rossi.

FRANCO, FAUSTO 1963 "Ottavio Bertotti Scamozzi." *Bollettino del Centro Internazionale di Studi di Architettura 'A. Palladio'* 5:152–161.

OLIVATO, LOREDANA 1975 *Ottavio Bertotti Scamozzi Studioso di Andrea Palladio.* Vicenza, Italy: Pozza.

PANE, ROBERTO 1959 "La storiografia palladiana dell'età neoclassica da Bertotti Scamozzi a Magrini." *Bolletinno del Centro Internazionale di Studi di Architettura 'A. Palladio'* 1:53–56.

BERTRAND, CLAUDE

Architect of the town of Besancon, Claude Joseph Alexandre Bertrand (1734–1797) laid out the Chamars Promenade (1777–1786) and the Granvelle Gardens (1779), built the Church of Saint Pierre (1784–1786), and designed the Fontaine des Dames and the houses surrounding CLAUDE NICOLAS LEDOUX's theater (1780). He established his reputation with the *hôtel* of the Marquis Terrier de Santans, first president of the parliament of Franche-Comté. For the same magistrate, he also designed the Château of Moncley, which ranks among the most beautiful examples of neoclassical architecture and merits comparison with the contemporary Château of Montmusard built by CHARLES DE WAILLY near Dijon. Like Montmusard, the Château of Moncley has a semicircular courtyard, but its central block and portico recall the facade of the Intendance (today the Préfecture) of Besancon designed by VICTOR LOUIS.

Claude Bertrand is often confused with Philippe Bertrand, engineer of bridges and highways in Franche-Comté.

GÉRARD ROUSSET-CHARNY
Translated from French by Richard Cleary

BIBLIOGRAPHY

LAVEDAN, PIERRE 1960 *Le château de Moncley.* Paris.

BESTELMEYER, GERMAN

The work of German Bestelmeyer (1874–1942) had its roots in the Romanesque Revival and neo-Gothic teachings of FRIEDRICH VON THIERSCH and Friedrich von Schmidt, with whom he studied. A native Bavarian, Bestelmeyer combined these styles with elements of the south German architectural tradition. He practiced during the Second Empire, the Weimar Republic, and the Third Reich.

Bestelmeyer held professorships in Dresden, Berlin-Charlottenburg, and Munich, and became, in 1922, president of the Munich Academy of Art. In the late 1920s, he was a leading critic of modern architecture, and after 1933 he joined in Nazi denunciations of modern art. His influence during the Nazi period was, however, relatively slight.

BARBARA MILLER LANE

WORKS

1906–1910, 1922, New Buildings and Remodeling, University of Munich. *1911, German Pavilion, International Art Exhibition, Rome. 1914–1917, Germanic Museum (now Busch-Reisinger Museum of Central and North European Art; built without Bestelmeyer's supervision), Harvard University, Cambridge, Mass. 1921, Reichsschuldenverwaltung Offices, Berlin. 1933–1939, Air Force District Headquarters, Munich. 1933–1939, Chapel, Waldheim, Germany. 1933–1939, Church, Munich.

BIBLIOGRAPHY

HEGEMANN, WERNER 1929 *German Bestelmeyer.* Berlin: Hübsch.

LANE, BARBARA MILLER 1968 *Architecture and Politics in Germany, 1918–1954.* Cambridge, Mass.: Harvard University Press.

PASQUARELLI, SILVIO 1980 "I padiglioni stranieri." Pages 279–284 in *Roma 1911*. Rome: Galleria Nazionale d'arte Moderna.

RITTICH, WERNER 1938 *Architektur und Bauplastik der Gegenwart.* Berlin: Rembrandt.

STAHL, FRITZ 1918–1919 "German Bestelmeyer." *Wasmuths Monatshefte für Baukunst und Städtebau* 3:1–56.

THIERSCH, HEINZ 1961 *German Bestelmeyer: Sein Leben und Werken für die Baukunst.* Munich: Callwey.

BETTINO, ANTONIO

Antonio Bettino (active 1650s–1670s) was first noted in Turin, Italy, in 1657 working on the Santissima Sindone. In 1664, in Chieri, he designed the Church of San Filippo Neri. In 1675, he designed and began construction of San Filippo Neri in Turin, but in 1679, he was superseded by GUARINO GUARINI. In 1678, he built the adjacent Oratorio of San Filippo Neri which was later altered by FILIPPO JUVARRA. In 1679, he prepared designs for the altar and crypt of the Cathedral of Vercelli and, in Turin, designed his masterpiece, Santi Maurizio and Lazzaro.

HENRY A. MILLON

WORKS

1657, Santissima Sindone (partially executed), Turin, Italy. 1664–1673, San Filippo Neri, Chieri, Italy. 1675–1678, San Filippo Neri (Oratory); 1679–1704, Santi Maurizio e Lazzaro; Turin, Italy.

BIBLIOGRAPHY

BRAYDA, CARLO; COLI, LAURA; and SESIA, DARIO 1963 *Ingegneri e architetti del sei e settecento in Piemonte.* Turin, Italy: Società Ingegnerie Architetti.
CHEVALLEY, G. 1942 "Vicende Costrutive della Chiesa di S. Filippo Neri in Torino." *Boll. Centro di Studi Archeologici ed Artistici del Piemonte* 2:63–99.
CHICCO, GIUSEPPE 1943 *Memorie del Vecchio duomo di Vercelli, sua Demolizione e successiva Ricostruzione.* Vercelli, Italy: Gallardi.
POMMER, RICHARD 1967 *Eighteenth-Century Architecture in Piedmont.* New York University Press.
TAMBURINI, LUCIANO 1968 *Le chiese di Torino.* Turin, Italy: Le bouquiniste.

BETTO FAMILY

The Betto Family were three generations of architects who worked in and around Nancy, France, from the late seventeenth to the mid-eighteenth centuries. Jean (1647–1722), the eldest and best-known, was called from Novarre to Nancy by the duke of Lorraine. His interior design of the Cathedral of Nancy (1699–1736) is among the finest examples of French classicism. Little is known about his son, Jacques, or his grandson, also named Jacques (1714–?).

JUANITA M. ELLIAS

WORKS

JEAN BETTO

1681–1684, Congregation of Saint Michel (various buildings); 1699–1736, Cathedral of Nancy (interior; with others); 1723, Premonstratensian Church; Nancy, France.

JACQUES BETTO

1709, Cathedral of Nancy (with others); 1712, Church of Saint Epvre; Nancy, France.

BIBLIOGRAPHY

BAUCHAL, CHARLES 1887 *Nouveau Dictionnaire Biographique et Critique des Architectes Français.* Paris: Librairie Générale de l'Architecture et des Travaux Publics and Daly.
HAUTECOEUR, LOUIS 1950 *Première moitié du XVIIIe siècle: Le style Louis XV.* Volume 3 in *Histoire de l'architecture classique en France.* Paris: Picard.
MAROT, PIERRE (1935)1970 *Le Vieux Nancy.* Rev. ed. Nancy, France: Humbolt.

BEYAERT, HENRI

Henri Joseph François Beyaert (1823–1894), born in Kortrijk, Belgium, and apprenticed there as a mason, was educated in Brussels under the neo-classic architect Tilman Frans Suys. His first major work, the Banque Nationale (1860–1865) in Brussels was done in a robust classicizing style. The severity of Beyaert's classicism in this and other early works was mitigated by the effects of rich ornament, a taste in which the architect indulged particularly in the 1860s and 1870s when his architecture tended increasingly toward the picturesque with designs in neo-Gothic and neo-Flemish Renaissance styles. Of this latter style Beyaert was, along with J. J. Van Ysendyck, one of the principal originators and most convincing practitioners.

Beyaert was a designer not only in several styles but also of a wide range of building types. He was also interested in urban design and was an outspoken proponent of curvilinear street planning.

Beyaert's architectural designs were published in major Belgian professional journals of the late nineteenth century and were thus made familiar to the younger generation of Belgian architects, some of whom were to create the Belgian Art Nouveau. Both VICTOR HORTA and PAUL HANKAR, among dozens of their contemporaries, actually worked in Beyaert's office and were directly exposed to his design practice.

ALFRED WILLIS

WORKS

1860–1865, Banque Nationale; 1869–1870, Porte de Hal (enlargement; with EUGÈNE EMMANUEL VIOLLET-LE-DUC); Brussels. 1872–1880, Banque Nationale, Antwerp, Belgium. 1873–1876, Godefroy House; 1873–1876, "Maison des Chats"; Brussels. 1879, Railway Station and Dependencies, Tournai, Belgium. 1880, Square du Petit Sablon (landscaping and fence; perhaps with Paul Hankar); 1892, Ministry of Railways Office Building; Brussels.

BIBLIOGRAPHY

BEYAERT, HENRI 1877 "Le tracé des voies publiques." *L'Emulation* 3:7-11, 35.

L'Emulation 1874-1875, 1876, 1877, 1879, 1887, 1902, 1903, 1904 1: plates 20-21; 28, 29, 32, 35, 40, 41; 2: plates 1-6; 44-48; 3: plates 1-2; 5: plates 11-13; 12: plates 38-39; 27: plates 41-45; 28: plate 96; 29: plates 24-31.

Exposition de l'oeuvre de Henri Beyaert organisée par ses anciens élèves, avril 1904. 1904 Brussels: Hayez.

"Henri Beyaert." 1894 *L'Emulation* 19:28-32.

KENNES, J.; VANDERPERREN, J.; and VICTOIRE, J. 1978 *L'architecture éclectique d'Henri Beyaert.* Brussels: Banque Nationale de Belgique.

MARTINY, V. G. 1980 *Bruxelles: L'architecture des origines à 1900.* Brussels: Vokaer.

PUTTEMANS, PIERRE 1976 *Modern Architecture in Belgium.* Translated by Mette Willert. Brussels: Vokaer.

Travaux d'architecture exécutés en Belgique par Henri Beyaert, architecte. 1880-1892 Brussels: Lyon-Claesen.

VAN DE VOORT, J. 1956 "De Bouwkunst en de Kunstnijverheid in België van 1800 tot 1950." Volume 3 pages 351-385 in H. E. Van Gelder and J. Duverger (editors), *Kunstgeschiedenis der Nederlanden van de Middeleeuwen tot onze tijd.* Utrecht: De Haan.

VONDENDAELE, RICHARD ET AL. 1980 *Poelaert et Son Temps.* Brussels: Crédit Communal de Belgique.

BIBIENA FAMILY

See GALLI BIBIENA FAMILY.

BIDLAKE, W. H.

William Henry Bidlake (1861-1938) was a pupil of GEORGE F. BODLEY and THOMAS GARNER and practiced in Birmingham. He built churches in a refined and original late Gothic style. His middle-class houses combine the vernacular idiom and workmanship of Arts and Crafts architecture with a dignity and restraint not so typical of that movement.

ALAN CRAWFORD

WORKS

1892-1893, 1900, Saint Oswald's Church, Birmingham, England. 1897, Woodgate, Hartopp Road, West Midlands, England. 1899, Branch School of Art; 1899-1901, Saint Agatha's Church, Stratford Road; 1901, Garth House, Edgbaston Park Road; Birmingham, England. 1901-1902, Redcroft (now Saint Winnow), Ladywood Road, Four Oaks, West Midlands, England. 1903-1904, Bishop Latimer Memorial Church, Winson Green; 1909-1910, Handsworth Cemetery Chapel, Birmingham, England.

BIBLIOGRAPHY

BIDLAKE, W. H. 1891 "Pitfalls on Commencing Practice." *The Builder* 61:351-353, 365-368.

BIDLAKE, W. H. 1897 "The Architect and the Public." *The Builder* 72:194-198.

BIDLAKE, W. H. 1902 "The Study and Delineation of Old Buildings." *The Builder* 83:600-604.

BIDLAKE, W. H. 1906 "The Home from Outside." Pages 13-96 in W. Shaw Sparrow (editor), *The Modern Home: A Book of British Domestic Architecture for Moderate Incomes.* London: Hodder & Stoughton.

DAVEY, PETER 1980 *Arts and Crafts Architecture: The Search for Earthly Paradise.* London: Architectural Press; New York: Rizzoli.

WEBSTER, SUTTON 1976 "W. H. Bidlake 1862-1938." *Architecture West Midlands* 26:17-25.

BIEGANSKI, PIOTR

Piotr Bieganski (1905-) studied architecture at the Technical University of Warsaw and graduated in 1933. He has been active mostly as a restorer of old buildings and as an architectural historian. From 1947 to 1954, he was chief conservation architect for the city of Warsaw in charge of reconstruction work in Warsaw's Old Town after the Germans had deliberately destroyed most ancient buildings during World War II. Other reconstruction work involved early nineteenth-century neoclassical palaces and government buildings.

Bieganski has taught history of architecture at the Technical University in Warsaw since 1945. He is the author of numerous articles and books on the subject.

In 1952, he won first prize in an international competition for the Opera House in Leipzig, Germany.

Bieganski's consideration of the wider environmental context of historic monuments as well as his efforts at conveying through conservation the value of a country's architectural heritage became key points of his work and consequently of general Polish attitudes toward conservation.

LECH KŁOSIEWICZ

WORK

1952, Opera House, Leipzig.

BIBLIOGRAPHY

Warszawska Szkoła Architektury: 1915-1965. 1967 Warsaw: P.W.N.

BIGELOW, HENRY FORBES

Henry Forbes Bigelow (1867-1929), a Boston architect, was known for his conservative application of the neo-Georgian idiom in and around Boston. Born in Clinton, Massachusetts, educated at the Massachusetts Institute of Technology, he joined the office of Winslow and Wetherell, Boston, in 1888 and became a partner in 1889. After the death of the original two, Bigelow in 1900 took Philip Wadsworth into partnership. Bigelow's most prominent buildings included the Shawmut National Bank, Tremont Building, the Hotel Touraine, additions to the Athenæm, all in Boston; the Library at Radcliffe, Cambridge, Massachusetts; and the country houses of Robert Saltonstall, Milton, Massachusetts (n.d.), and J. J. Storrow, Lincoln, Massachusetts.

LELAND M. ROTH

WORKS

n.d., Boston Athenaeum (additions; with Philip Wadsworth). n.d., Hotel Touraine, Boston. n.d., Radcliffe College Library, Cambridge, Mass. n.d., Robert Saltonstall House (grounds by Arthur A. Shurtleff), Milton, Mass. n.d., Shawmut National Bank, Boston. n.d., J. J. Storrow House, Lincoln, Mass. n.d., Tremont Building, Boston.

BIBLIOGRAPHY

ALDRICH, W. T. 1929 "Obituary of Henry Forbes Bigelow." *Bulletin of the Boston Society of Architects* Sept.
"Estate of Robert Saltonstall." 1912 *American Architect* 102, Aug. 28.
"House of Henry Forbes Bigelow." 1916 *American Architect* 109, June 7:369–375.

BIGIO, NANNI DI BACCIO

Nanni di Baccio Bigio (?–1568), Florentine sculptor and architect, began as a sculptor. By 1540, he may have been in the Sangallo (see SANGALLO FAMILY) workshop at Saint Peter's. Giovannoni (1959) attributes to him the Palazzo Farnese at Ronciglioni (1542), and Coolidge (1945–1947) attributed the pair of loggie at the Campidoglio to Bigio in 1544–1547. In 1550, he prepared the first plans for the Jesuit Church and Monastery in Rome. The plan of the Gesù in the Uffizi, first attributed to MICHELANGELO by Popp (1927), is a variant of the original scheme by Bigio (Ackerman, 1964, vol. 2). In 1551, Bigio was granted a patent for a new brick-making process, and he retained an interest in brick for the remainder of his life. He rebuilt the brick foundries for Saint Peter's.

In 1551, Bigio replaced Michelangelo as architect in the strengthening of the Ponte Santa Maria against floods. He probably continued construction of the Palazzo Ricci (now the Palazzo Sacchetti) which was built in 1555–1557. In 1557, the bridge collapsed during a flood.

In 1559, he provided a new plan for the fortification of Fano and was supervising construction there. Two years later, he was at work on the fortifications at Castel Sant' Angelo in Rome. He claimed to have considerable knowledge of structure and was consulted in 1561 about the transport and erection of a column to be taken from the Baths of Caracalla to Florence. The Porta del Popolo was built by Bigio from 1561 to 1564. In 1567, he was appointed architect to the papal palace for life and began what was probably the busiest phase of his career, supervising construction at the palace, Castel Sant' Angelo, Sistine Chapel, San Martino degli Svizzeri (in the Vatican), and the fortifications at Ostia and Civitavecchia.

For most of his life, he hoped to become architect of Saint Peter's. Frustrated in his desire to succeed Antonio da Sangallo in 1546 through the appointment of Michelangelo, Bigio spent the remainder of his life criticizing Michelangelo's undoing of Sangallo's design, Michelangelo's own design, his supervision, structural knowledge, construction practice, and administration, and his assistants, all the while working on the staff until 1558 when he was dismissed.

In 1563, when Michelangelo's assistant was murdered, the ecclesiastical deputies appointed a replacement and reappointed Bigio. After a two-month term, Michelangelo once again had him dismissed. The day after Michelangelo died, Bigio wrote Duke Cosimo de' Medici requesting his support as a candidate to replace Michelangelo in the post. The job was given several months later to PIRRO LIGORIO.

Virtually nothing survives by Bigio in a state that would allow a characterization of his supposedly undistinguished architecture. If the attribution of the Loggie at the Campidoglio is correct, his architecture began in a conservative, Sangallesque manner. The Porta del Popolo at mid-career

*Bigio.
Porta del Popolo.
Rome.
1561–1564*

is a restrained, dry, Doric triumphal arch. His late work remains undefined.

HENRY A. MILLON

WORKS

(A)1542, Palazzo Farnese, Ronciglione, Italy. (A)1544–1547, Campidoglio (loggie); 1553–1557, Palazzo Ricci (completion); 1561–1564, Porta del Popolo (exterior completed; interior unfinished); Rome.

BIBLIOGRAPHY

ACKERMAN, JAMES S. 1964 Volume 2 in *The Architecture of Michelangelo*. 2d ed., rev. London: Zwemmer.

ACKERMAN, JAMES S. 1972 "The Gesù in the Light of Contemporary Church Design." Pages 15–28 in Rudolf Wittkower and Irma B. Jaffe (editors), *Baroque Art: The Jesuit Contribution*. New York: Fordham University Press.

ANDRES, GLENN M. 1976 *The Villa Medici in Rome.* New York: Garland.

BERTOLOTTI, A. 1886 "Nanni di Baccio Bigio." *Arte e Storia* 5:195.

COOLIDGE, JOHN 1945–1947 "The Arched Loggie on the Campidoglio." *Marsyas* 4:69–79.

GIOVANNONI, GUSTAVO 1959 Volume 1, pages 101, 331 in *Antonio da Sangallo, il Giovane*. Rome.

HESS, J. 1961 "Die Papstliche Villa bei Avaceli." Volume 16, pages 239–254 in *Miscellanea Bibliothecae Hertzianae*. Munich: Schroll.

HEWETT, A. E. 1911 "Ancora sul palazzo Sangallo." *Bollettino d'Arte* 1911:439–440.

JANITSCHECK, HUBERT 1879 *Reportorium für Kunstwissenschaft* 2:417–419.

KELLER, FRITZ-EUGEN 1976 "Zur Planung am Bau der römischen Peterskirche im Jahre 1564–1565." *Jahrbuch der Berliner Museen* 18:24–56.

LEWINE, MILTON J. 1969 "Nanni, Vignola, and S. Martino degli Svizzeri in Rome." *Journal of the Society of Architectural Historians* 28, no. 1:27–40.

MARTIN, J. 1974 "Un grand bâtisseur de la Renaissance: Le cardinal Giovanini Ricci di Montepulciano (?1497–1574)." *Mélange Ecole français de Rome* 86, no. 1:251–275.

POPP, ANNY E. 1927 "Unbeachtete Projekte Michelangelos." *Münchner Jahrbuch der Bildenden Kunst* no. 4:389–477.

RONCHINI, A. 1867 "Nanni di Baccio Bigio." *Atti e memorie della RR. Reputazioni di Storia Patria per le provincie modenesie parmensi* 8:351–360.

SALERNO, LUIGI 1975 Pages 292–295 in *Via Giula*. 2d ed. Rome: Staderini.

WITTKOWER, RUDOLF 1968 "Nanni di Baccio Bigio and Michelangelo." Pages 248–262 in A. Kosegarten and P. Tigler (editors), *Festschrift Ulrich Middledorf.* Berlin.

BILHAMER, JOOST JANSZOON

Joost Janszoon Bilhamer or Beeltsnijder (1521–1590) was an architect, sculptor, engraver, sur-

veyor, and fortification engineer in Amsterdam. As an architect he was known for the spire of the Old Church (1565–1566), Amsterdam, with its Renaissance elements, which became the prototype for many Dutch towers.

Bilhamer worked also as a sculptor for the Amsterdam Orphanage (1581), for which he made the porch with a relief. He was fortification engineer for the expansion of the Amsterdam fortresses.

MARIET J. H. WILLINGE

WORKS

1565?, New Church (charnel house); 1565–1566, Old Church (tower); Amsterdam. 1577–1578, New East Gate, Hoorn, Netherlands. 1581, Orphanage (porch with reliefs); 1585, Fortification (with A. Anthonisz. van Alkmaar), Amsterdam.

BIBLIOGRAPHY

FOCKEMA ANDREAE, S. J.; KUILE, E. H. TER; and HEKKER, R. C. 1957 *De Bouwkunst na de Middeleeuwen.* Volume 2 in *Duizend jaar bouwen in Nederland.* Amsterdam: Lange.

"Joost Jansz Bilhamer." 1940 *Amstelodamum: Maandblad voor de kennis van Amsterdam* 27, no. 6:93–94.

MEISCHKE, R. 1975 *Amsterdam Burgerweeshuis.* The Hague: Staatsuitgeverij.

STARING, A. 1964 *Joost Jansz. Bilhamer als Beeldhouwer.* Assen, Netherlands: Opus Musivum.

VERMEULEN, FRANS A. J. 1931 Volume 2 in *Handboek tot de geschiedenis der Nederlandsche bouwkunst.* The Hague: Nijhoff.

BILL, MAX

Max Bill (1908–), born in Winterthur, Switzerland, is known as a sculptor, painter, graphic designer, industrial designer, theoretician of art and design, and teacher. Yet, he thinks of himself primarily as an architect, and his two most important works, the Hochschule für Gestaltung in Ulm, Germany (1951–1955), and the pavilion *Bilden und Gestalten* at the Swiss National Exhibition in Lausanne (1964), amply justify this claim.

Bill learned the craft of silversmith at the Kunstgewerbeschule in Zurich. After travels in France and Italy, he decided, after listening to a lecture by LE CORBUSIER, to move from the crafts to architecture. He studied at the Bauhaus in Dessau (1927–1928) under WALTER GROPIUS and HANNES MEYER, and other Bauhaus masters such as LÁSZLÓ MOHOLY-NAGY, JOSEF ALBERS, Kandinsky, and Klee had a great influence on him as well.

Since 1929, he has lived and worked mostly in

Zurich, with the exception of his years as head of the Hochschule für Gestaltung in Ulm, Germany (1950–1957).

Max Bill does not advocate one universal system of forms over another. On the contrary, the formal organization of Bill's projects and buildings is conceived from scratch as an answer to the specific requirements of the design (costs, resources, social purpose, cultural significance). If there is a unifying principle, it is that of a strictly economic use of elementary formal means toward clearly defined ends. Bill has frequently proposed modular grid structures, especially for exhibition pavilions; such projects reflect his interest in mathematical principles and their relationship to or application in art.

The buildings of the Hochschule für Gestaltung in Ulm (1951–1955) are a European landmark. Within a narrow budget, Bill succeeded in realizing a cluster of cubical units differentiated according to function (dwellings, lecture rooms, studio-workshops, cafeteria) and coordinated into a complex whole. The austere elegance of the buildings and their delicate insertion into a romantic setting recall KARL FRIEDRICH SCHINKEL.

STANISLAUS VON MOOS

WORKS

1932–1933, Bill Studio House, Zurich. *1936, Swiss Pavilion, Triennale, Milan. 1951–1955, Hochschule für Gestaltung, Ulm, Germany. *1961–1964, Art and Design Section, Swiss National Exhibition (parts still extant), Lausanne, Switzerland. 1964–1974, Studio and Administration Building of Radio Zurich, Zurich. 1967–1968, Bill House, Zumikon, ZH, Switzerland.

BIBLIOGRAPHY

BILL, MAX (editor) 1934–1938 Volume 3 in *Le Corbusier et Pierre Jeanneret: Oeuvre complète.* Zurich: Girsberger.

BILL, MAX 1945 *Wiederaufbau.* Zurich: Verlag für Architektur.

BILL, MAX 1948 "Ausstellungen." *Werk* 35, no. 3:65–71.

BILL, MAX 1952 *Form: Eine Bilanz über die Formentwicklung um die Mitte des XX. Jahrhunderts.* Basel: Werner. With an English text.

BILL, MAX 1953 "The Bauhaus Idea: From Weimar to Ulm." *Architect's Year Book* 5:29–32.

BILL, MAX 1955 *Mies van der Rohe.* Milan: Il Balcone.

FRAMPTON, KENNETH 1974 "On Max Bill: A Review of the Albright-Knox Exhibition Catalog." *Oppositions* 4:154–157.

GOMRINGER, EUGEN 1962 "Max Bill: Variety and Unity of the Shaped Environment." *Architect's Year Book* 10:52–74. Originally published in German.

HÜTTINGER, EDUARD 1977 *Max Bill.* Zurich: ABC.

MALDONADO, TOMAS 1955 *Max Bill.* Buenos Aires: Nueva Vision.

STABER, MARGIT 1962 "La scuola di Ulm." *Casabella* 259:2–27.

STABER, MARGIT 1964 *Max Bill.* Sankt Gallen, Switzerland: Erker; London: Methuen.

BILLING, HERMANN

Trained in his native Karlsruhe, Germany, under Joseph Durm and in Berlin, Hermann Billing (1867–1946) established during the first decade of his practice (1897–1907) an international reputation as a sensitive domestic architect and interior designer. Although he began with robust and inventive compositions of regional medieval and even vernacular forms, Billing soon developed an individual *Jugendstil* interior manner, characterized by massive but elegantly simplified forms and rich color harmonies. The Wagnerian ideal of a *Gesamtkunstwerk,* or fusing all the arts and crafts to a unified effect is reflected especially in the interiors he created for the Turin (1902) and St. Louis (1904) exhibitions: in the latter his contribution, appropriately, was a Music Room. Along with Robert Curjel and KARL MOSER, Billing created a specifically Karlsruhe style in which ponderous Romanesque motifs are geometricized, simplified, and animated in plastically handled façades. After a series of unsuccessful competition entries, Billing's winning design for Kiel's City Hall (1903; built 1906–1911) marked his entry into public architecture. The monumental convex entry façade of his Mannheim Kunsthalle (1906–1907) anticipates the symmetrical compositions, emphatic lines, and chaste surface articulation—often in his favored red sandstone—of his mature work. Billing's late expressionistic engravings had few echoes in his architecture which, as in the Karlsruhe Post Office, reflected an increasingly neoclassical sobriety and simplicity.

BARRY BERGDOLL

WORKS

1892–1895, New Weser Bridge, Bremen, Germany. 1897, Lieber House; 1899, Billing House, 23 Eisenlohr Strasse; Karlsruhe, Germany. c.1900, Bolza House, Rastatt, Germany. c.1900, Bausback, Meckel, and Mees Houses, Karlsruhe, Germany. c.1900, Hotel Klingenberg, Neckarelz, Germany. 1901–1905, Apartment Houses and Six Houses, Baischstrasse, Karlsruhe, Germany. *1902, Reception Hall, International Exhibition, Turin, Italy. *1902, Rhine Bridge, Ruhrort, Germany. *1902, Ruhr Bridge, Mülheim, Germany. c.1903, Administration Building, Maschine Factory, Bruchaal, Germany. *c.1903, Brother Beckh Brewery House, Pforzheim, Germany. *1903–1907, Gasthof zum Grünen Baum, Karlsruhe, Germany. *1904, Study and Music Room, Exhibition, St. Louis, Mo. c.1905, Melanchton Memorial House, Bretten, Baden, Germany. 1906–1907, Kunsthalle, Mannheim, Germany. *1906–1911, Town Hall, Kiel, Germany. *1907, Kunsthalle in der Flora, Kunstausstellung, Cologne, Germany. 1907–1909, Kunsthalle, Baden-Baden, Germany. 1907–1911, New University Buildings (with Friedrich Ratzel), Freiburg im Breisgau, Germany. 1909, Villa Weber, Gernsbach, Germany. 1911, Hofapotheke; 1924–1928, Post Office Administration Building; *1927, Municipal Fire Station, Ritterstrasse; c.1930, Houses, Kolpingplatz; 1932–1934, Houses (with H. Zippelius), Beiertheimer Allee; Karlsruhe, Germany.

BIBLIOGRAPHY

BERINGER, JOSEPH AUGUST 1912 "Das Kollegiengebäude der Universität zu Freiburg i. Br. von Hermann Billing." *Moderne Bauformen* 11:349–380.

BILLING, HERMANN 1904a *Architekturskizzen.* Stuttgart, Germany: Waldner.

BILLING, HERMANN 1904b *Der Musikraum in der Weltausstellung, St. Louis, 1904.* Stuttgart, Germany: Hoffmann.

BILLING, HERMANN 1935 *Verkleinerte Tafelzeichnungen aus meinen Vorträgen über Gestaltungslehre an der Technischen Hochschule Karlsruhe.* Karlsruhe, Germany.

COMMICHAU, FELIX 1902–1903 "Hermann Billing als Innen-Künstler." *Deutsche Kunst und Dekoration* 11–12:105–116.

GRIESELMANN, REINHARD 1969 "Zur Geschichte der modernen Architektur—Hommage à Billing." *Bauen und Wohnen* VII, 3–4.

GÜNTHER, SONJA 1971 *Interieurs um 1900.* Munich: Fink.

HARBERS, G. 1939 "Die neue Reichspostdirektion in Karlsruhe." *Baumeister* 37:105–107, plate 29.

"Hermann Billing." 1898 *Deutsche Kunst und Dekoration* 3:90–91.

LEHMANN, A. 1907 "Architektur auf der Jubiläumsausstellung Mannheim 1907." *Moderne Bauformen* 6.

MARTIN, K. 1930 *Hermann Billing.* Berlin: Hübsch.

"Neue badische Architektur." 1904 *Deutsche Bauzeitung* 38:477–478, 501–502, 525–526, 537–538.

PLEHN, A. L. 1903 "Erste internationale Ausstellung für moderne dekorative Kunst in Turin." *Kunstgewerbeblatt* 14:1–7.

RIECKE 1949 *Hermann Billing: Sein Werk als Beitrag zur Formensprache moderner Architektur.* Schöntal, Germany.

SCHIRMER, W., and GÖRICKE, J. 1975 "Architekten der Fredericiana, Skizzen und Entwürfe seit Friedrich Weinbrenner." *Fredericiana, Zeitschrift der Universität Karlsruhe* 18:87–99.

WIDMER, KARL 1901–1902 "Hermann Billing-Karlsruhe." *Deutsche Kunst und Dekoration* 9–10:423–453.

WIDMER, KARL 1904 "Moderne Baukunst in Karlsruhe—Hermann Billing." *Moderne Bauformen* 3:1–9.

WIDMER, KARL 1910 "Professor Hermann Billing." *Moderne Bauformen* 9:527–548.

WIDMER, KARL 1912 "Das Kieler Rathaus von Hermann Billing." *Moderne Bauformen* 11:57–104.

BILLINGS, HAMMATT

Charles Howland Hammatt Billings (1818–1874) was among the most versatile artists of nineteenth-century America. Best remembered now as a magazine and book illustrator (*Uncle Tom's Cabin,* 1852 and 1853), he was also a painter, sculptor, architect, and designer of furniture, monuments, landscapes, and fireworks and other displays. In his own day, the range of his talent earned him the title of MICHELANGELO, of his time.

Born in Milton, Massachusetts, Billings trained in graphic design with Abel Bowen and in architecture with ASHER BENJAMIN and AMMI B. YOUNG. His architectural work was the mirror of the age, stretching from the Boston Museum (1846–1848), among the earliest palazzo façades in America, through the Gothic Tremont Street Methodist Episcopal Church, Boston (1860–1862), to Wellesley College (1869–1875), including the layout, College Hall, and the gate lodges. College Hall was Billings's crowning achievement. A vast, colorful, eclectic pile riding the crest of a low hill above Lake Waban, it was a major work of the picturesque in America.

Billings's reputation as architectural designer has been obscured because few of his works survive and because he often worked with or for others, including his brother, Joseph E. Billings, George F. Meacham, and GRIDLEY J. F. BRYANT.

JAMES F. O'GORMAN

WORKS

*1846–1847, Boston Museum. *1846–1852, Church of the Saviour (Second Unitarian); 1849–1850, Temple Club; Boston. *1855–1859, Canopy over Plymouth Rock, Mass. 1855–1889, National Monument to the Forefathers, Plymouth, Mass. *1857–1860, Massachusetts Charitable Mechanic Association Building; 1860–1862, Tremont Street Methodist Episcopal Church (New Hope Baptist); Boston. *1869–1875, College Hall; 1869–1875, Gate Lodges; Wellesley College, Mass. 1870–1871, Wesleyan Association Building; Boston. 1873–1874, Thayer Library (now Water Works), Braintree, Mass.

BIBLIOGRAPHY

STODDARD, RICHARD 1972 "Hammatt Billings: Artist and Architect." *Old-Time New England* 62:57–65, 76–79.

BINAGO, LORENZO

Following the deaths of MARTINO BASSI and PELLEGRINO TIBALDI in the 1590s, there was something of a lull in Milanese architecture. Lorenzo Binago (1554–1629) was one of the three architects, the others being Fabio Mangone (see MAN-

GONE FAMILY) and G. A. Mazenta, who formed the next generation although they did not achieve their predecessors' stature.

Born in Milan, Binago became a Barnabite monk in 1572. He was ordained as a priest in 1578. From 1579 to 1593, he lived and worked in Casale Monferrato in the province of Alessandria. There he worked first as an architect on the construction of San Paolo in Casale (1586–1594). From 1593 to 1599, he lived in Zagarolo near Rome where he helped in the construction of the Barnabite Church and College of Santissima Annunziata (1593–1596). In 1599, he was recalled to Milan where, with the exception of a few side trips, he spent the rest of his life.

Like that of fellow Milanese Mangone, Binago's work is cool, crisp, and classical. In the massing of an early work, such as San Paolo in Casale this is already evident. Yet, despite this early Renaissance feeling there is a lightness and fragile elegance to the surface that recalls mannerist architects such as GALEAZZO ALESSI or GIACOMO BAROZZI DA VIGNOLA.

Binago's masterpiece was the Church of Sant'Alessandro in Milan. Work was begun in 1602 when the first stone was laid by CARLO BORROMMEO, the leader of the Milanese Counter-Reformation movement. Borrommeo especially approved of Binago's restrained style. The church is laid out as a Greek cross with an extended choir. Binago combined elements from DONATO BRAMANTE's St. Peter's in Rome (the freestanding piers supporting the cupola) with a delicate clarity and elegance that recalls Alessi's Santa Maria di Carignano, Genoa. Binago was not totally immune to the baroque currents from Rome. The lighting, mysterious, even quasi-theatrical, recalls contemporary work in Rome by FRANCESCO BORROMINI. As it stands today, the Church of Sant'Alessandro reflects only partly Binago's intentions. In 1627, the cupola, which threatened to collapse, was destroyed and a new one was built in 1693 by Giuseppe Quadrio. The upper level of the façade was built by Marcello Zucca (1704–1711).

Binago was also the author of a treatise, now lost, on the nature of religious architecture, *De fabrica et supellectili ecclesiastica,* begun around 1593.

NICHOLAS ADAMS

WORKS

1586–1594, San Paolo, Casale Monferrato, Italy. 1593–1596, Church and College of Santissima Annunziata, Zagarolo, Italy. 1602, Sant'Alessandro, Milan. 1607, Church and College of San Marco, Novara, Italy.

BIBLIOGRAPHY

MEZZANOTTE, G.   1961   "Gi architetti Lorenzo Binago e Giovanni Ambrogio Mazenta." *L'Arte* 60:231–294.

WITTKOWER, RUDOLF   (1958)1972   *Art and Architecture in Italy: 1600–1750.* 3d ed., rev. Harmondsworth, England: Penguin.

BINDESBØLL, GOTTLIEB

The Danish architect Michael Gottlieb Birkner Bindesbøll (1800–1856) was the designer of the Thorwaldsen Museum (1834–1848) in Copenhagen, one of the strongest designs produced in Europe during the 1840s.

Bindesbøll was born in the small town of Ledøje in Jutland, where his father was the Protestant minister. In 1815, he was sent to Copenhagen to study engineering and there he entered the broad cultural environment of Tonas Collin, the patron of Hans Christian Andersen. In the winter of 1822–1823, he traveled to Hamburg, Berlin, Munich, Weimar (where he paid the obligatory visit to Goethe, discovering there the first plates of Sulpiz Boisserée's vision of the completion of Cologne Cathedral), and Paris. In Paris, Bindesbøll spent several weeks with FRANZ CHRISTIAN GAU, a friend and admirer of Boisserée. This experience deeply impressed him, evidently because of Gau's ideas concerning Pompeii and polychromatic decoration which in 1826–1830 were also to impress another student of Gau, GOTTFRIED SEMPER.

Returning to Copenhagen determined to pursue architecture, Bindesbøll spent from 1824 to 1833 working in the office of Jørgen Hansen Koch and studying at the Royal Academy of Art. In 1833, he won the Gold Medal with a traveling stipend and left in the summer of 1834 for Rome, going by way of Berlin, Dresden, and Munich, where he admired the latest works of German Romantic classicism (especially the Residenzkapelle by LEO VON KLENZE). The following summer and fall he devoted to a trip to Naples, Sicily (where he admired the Byzantine churches), Athens, and Istanbul. The years 1836 and 1837 he spent in Rome, making the acquaintance of the respected Danish sculptor Bertel Thorwaldsen. In the summer of 1838, he journeyed back to Copenhagen through Munich again and down the Rhine to Amsterdam.

Upon his return the great enterprise of Bindesbøll's career, the Thorwaldsen Museum, begun to unfold. A museum in Denmark for all the sculptor's works had been proposed—by Collin, among others—in the early 1830s and was formally authorized by King Frederick VI on February 5, 1834. Before he left for Italy later in that year, Bindesbøll had exhibited an ideal project for it and while in Rome he had made a series of studies in cooperation with Thorwaldsen himself and in communication with Collin. Soon after his return to Copenhagen (and that of Thorwaldsen that same year), Frederick VI contributed a carriage and theater-scene storehouse erected by CHRISTIAN FRIEDRICH HANSEN behind his Christiansborg chapel on the canal north of Christiansborg Palace in the center of the city. Designs were solicited from Koch, Gustav Friedrich Hetsch, and Bindesbøll. Bindesbøll's was chosen in May 1839, his project approved by the king on November 13, 1839, and final drawings were completed on August 29, 1840. Construction was begun in that year and completed in 1844, the year Thorwaldsen died and was buried in the courtyard.

In spite of the power and consistency of the impression the building makes, it was simply a reconstruction of an existing structure: the interior was repartitioned and vaulted, two major spaces were added at the front and back, and the exterior was refaced in stucco. The "Etruscan" splayed doors which comprise the sole adornment of its four façades make neither historical nor functional sense (since they principally enframe windows), and the frieze—exploded in size and dropped to ground level—is unprecedented. But these are perfectly scaled to the blocklike mass of the structure, part museum, part tomb. The low, barrel vaulted interior spaces painted alternately red, green, and ochre are more reminiscent of the partially excavated Golden House of Nero or the Stabian Baths at Pompeii than of the open, neoclassical-shaped rooms of von Klenze's Glyptothek in Munich, but they complement the white marble of Thorwaldsen's sculptures perfectly and make the open central court—its walls painted away with huge images of oaks, palms, and bay trees—a magic space around Thorwaldsen's tomb.

Before his death in 1856, Bindesbøll executed a number of smaller works with the same sense of broad, scenographic effect: the city halls at Thisted (1851–1853), Flensburg (1852), Stege (1853–1854), and Naestved (1855–1856); the summer bathing establishment at Klampenborg (1844); the hospital at Oringe (1853–1857); the church at Hobrø (1850–1851); and the Royal Veterinary and Agricultural School in Copenhagen (1856). He almost had the opportunity to show the full extent of his mature powers when in 1852 and 1855–1856 he produced a series of projects for the University Library in Copenhagen, but the commission went to JOHAN DANIEL HERHOLDT. Bindesbøll saw the building as a warehouse for books in 1852, conceiving a long, narrow and infinitely elegant brick box penetrated by banks of windows. From this idea, he moved in 1855–1856 to a monumental image, making the structure T-shaped with banks of stacks flanking tall glass-roofed central spaces all departing from three sides of a central dome, enclosing staircases that rose from the ground to the second floor in dramatic straight runs.

DAVID T. VAN ZANTEN

WORKS

1834–1848, Thorwaldsen Museum, Copenhagen. 1839, Thorwaldsen Studio, Nysø, Denmark. 1844, Bathing Establishment, Klampenborg, Denmark. 1850–1851, Church, Hobrø, Denmark. 1851–1853, City Hall, Thisted, Denmark. 1852, City Hall, Flensburg, Germany. 1853–1854, City Hall, Stege, Denmark. 1853–1857, Hospital, Oringe, Denmark. 1855–1856, City Hall, Naestved, Denmark. 1856, Royal Veterinary and Agricultural School, Copenhagen.

BIBLIOGRAPHY

BRAMSEN, HENRIK 1959 *Gottlieb Bindesbøll: Liv og Arbejder.* Copenhagen: Selskabet til udgivelse af okrifter om danskte mindesmaerker.
BRUUN, CHARLES, and FENGER, L. P. 1892 *Thorvaldsens Musaeums Historie.* Copenhagen: Philipsen.
JØRGENSEN, LISBET 1972 "Thorvaldsen's Museum: A National Monument." *Apollo* New Series 96:198–205.
MILLECH, KNUD 1960 *Bindesbølls Museum.* Copenhagen: Thorvaldsens Museum.
MILLECH, KNUD 1961 *J. D. Herholdt og Universitetsbibliotekt i Fiolstraede.* Copenhagen: Paludan.
WANSCHER, VILHELM 1903 *Arkitekten G. Bindesbøll.* Copenhagen: Køster.
WANSCHER, VILHELM 1932 "Gottlieb Bindesbøll." *Artes* 1:53–185.

BIZZACHERI, CARLO

Carlo Francesco Bizzacheri (1655–1721) was born in Rome and studied under CARLO FONTANA, the leading architect of the Roman late baroque. He was accepted into the Accademia di San Luca in 1697 and also became a member of the Congregazione de' Virtuosi al Pantheon. Bizzacheri was architect of the Tribunale delle Strade of Rome, of a number of convents, and to the Pamphili family. He died in Rome in the first days of February 1721, having remained active in his profession to the end, and leaving at least one student of merit, Tommaso de Marchis.

Bizzacheri's work is more representative of the early stages of Roman rococo architecture than that of such contemporary architects as Giovanni Battista Contini (see CONTINI FAMILY), LUDOVICO RUSCONI SASSI, or ALESSANDRO SPECCHI, whose styles were more strongly tied to that of the second half of the seventeenth century. The influence of Carlo Fontana can be felt only occasionally and marginally in his work; on the other hand, the buildings of FRANCESCO BORROMINI had a great impact on his architecture, particularly as sources for pedimental forms, ornamental motifs, and for the treatment of moldings. Borrominesque in inspiration also are Bizzacheri's avoidance of right-angle corners in interiors and exteriors, the layering of the wall, and the use of interconnecting bands as both articulation and ornament of the wall surface. In adopting these particular elements of Borromini's art, Bizzacheri moved toward what would soon become general practice.

Since Bizzacheri did not execute any church from the ground up, only the design of several chapels can indicate his approach to the decoration of ecclesiastical interiors. His choice of predominantly light-colored marbles instead of the deep, somber range preferred by his master Fontana anticipates the light tonality prevalent in later eighteenth-century interiors. His designs for door or altarpiece frames, with "pagoda"-shaped or broken, curving pediments, and his pervasive use of imaginative and delicate stucco decoration are features that would become ubiquitous later in the century.

His two most significant works, the façade of San Isidoro (1704–1705), Rome, and the fronts of the convent of San Luigi dei Francesi (1709–1712), Rome, already show many of the characteristics of the Roman rococo style. In these works we find the preference for varied floral and vegetal motifs in low relief as ornament for the frames around wall openings, and the emphasis on the linear quality of the mobile ribbons of stucco used as moldings that are typical of architectural design in the following half-century. The imaginative resources of the artist are concentrated on these decorative frames and on the low-keyed play of thin surface layers that enliven the wall and its articulation. Bizzacheri's approach soon became pervasive; his work not only established an early precedent for the new manner but also made important contributions to its repertory of forms.

NINA A. MALLORY

WORKS

1679, Chapel of Sant' Anna, Santa Maria in Montesanto; 1680–1684, Convent of Santa Maria Maddalena; 1681–1688, Chapel of San Antonio di Padova, San Isidoro a Capo le Case; c.1694, Chapel of the Pietà, San Salvatore in Lauro; 1694–1696, Chapel of San Nicolò di Bari, Santa Maria Maddalena; after 1695–c.1707, Chapel, Monte di Pietà; Rome. Before 1699, Villa Aldobrandini (garden wall and gate), Frascati, Italy. 1704–1705, San Isidoro a Capo le Case (façade); 1707, Tomb of Cardinal Cinzio Aldobrandini, San Pietro in Vincoli; 1709–1712, Convent of San Luigi dei Francesi; Rome. After 1715, Palazzo Nuzzi, Orte, Italy. 1717–1719, Fountain of the Tritons, Rome.

BIBLIOGRAPHY

MALLORY, NINA A. 1974 "Carlo Francesco Bizza-
cheri (1655–1721)." *Journal of the Society of Architectural Historians* 33:27–47.
MALLORY, NINA A. 1977 *Roman Rococo Architecture from Clement XI to Benedict XIV (1700–1758).* New York and London: Garland.
PORTOGHESI, PAOLO (1966)1970 *Roma Barocca: The History of an Architectonic Culture.* Translated by Barbara Luigia La Penta. Cambridge, Mass.: M.I.T. Press.

BJERKE, ARVID

Arvid Bjerke (1880–1952) born in Göteborg, Sweden, studied in Stockholm between 1899 and 1905, first at the Royal Institute of Technology and then at the Royal Academy. He traveled abroad during the next fifteen years, studying continental European architecture. With R. O. Swensson, Ernst Torulf, and SIGFRID ERICSON, Bjerke founded the Ares Consortium which directed the Jubilee exhibition of 1923 in Göteborg. Although best known for his participation in designing this exposition, which was the first comprehensive display of modern Swedish design, Bjerke was responsible for many hospitals, schools, and private houses.

JUDITH S. HULL

WORKS

1911, Lindholm School; 1914, Nordhem School; 1919–1923, Exhibition Hall (with Sigfrid Ericson), Jubilee Exhibition; 1919–1923, Museum of Fine Arts (with Ericson); 1924, Carlander Hospital; Göteborg, Sweden.

BIBLIOGRAPHY

BJERKE, ARVID, and ERICSON, SIGFRID 1930 *Göteborgs jubileum, 1923, Utställningens arkitektur.* Stockholm: Generalstabens litografiska anstalt.
NYMAN, THURE, and PERGAMENT, NOEMI 1942 "Arvid Bjerke." Volume 1, page 326 in *Svenska Män och Kvinnor.* Stockholm: Bonniers.

BLACKALL, CLARENCE H.

Clarence Howard Blackall (1857–1942), a native of New York, trained at the University of Illinois and the Ecole des Beaux-Arts. In 1884, he joined PEABODY AND STEARNS and in 1889 began practice with James F. Clapp and Charles A. Whittemore. Known nationally for his theaters, Blackall also designed Boston's first entirely steel-framed office structure, the Carter (later Winthrop) Building (1893–1894).

FREDERIC C. DETWILLER

WORKS

1889, Church of Our Saviour, Roslindale, Mass. 1891–

1892, Bowdoin Square theater; 1893–1894, Carter (later Winthrop) Building; 1894, Castle Square Theater and Hotel; 1895, Tremont Temple; 1899–1900, Colonial Theater; 1912, Copley Plaza Hotel (with HENRY J. HARDENBERGH); 1912, Washington Street Olympia; 1914, Modern Theater; 1914, Wilber Theater; 1915, Hotel Kenmore; 1916–1917, Little Office Building (with Little and Russell); 1922–1923, New Studio Building; Boston. 1926, Oxford Court Apartments, Cambridge, Mass. 1928, Temple Ohabei Shalom, Brookline, Mass. 1928, Yale University Theater, New Haven.

BIBLIOGRAPHY

FOX, PAMELA, and KOCH, MICKAIL 1980 *Central Business District Inventory.* Boston Landmarks Commission.
TUCCI, DOUGLASS SHAND 1978 *Built in Boston, City and Suburb, 1800–1950.* Boston: New York Graphic Society.

BLACKBURN, JAMES

James Blackburn (1803–1854) was an inspector of sewers in London, convicted of forgery and transported to Hobart, Tasmania, in 1833. He was particularly influenced by the pattern books of J. C. Loudon and others, designing churches in conventional Gothic and in Norman with Doric overtones, Greek Revival public buildings, and Tudor and picturesque Italianate houses. In 1849 he emigrated to Melbourne, where he was appointed city surveyor.

MILES LEWIS

WORKS

c.1839, Church of Saint Mark, Pontville; c.1840–1843, Government House, Hobart; 1840–1847, Holy Trinity Church; Hobart; 1840–1849, Bridgewater Bridge; 1846–1850, Rosedale, Campbell Town; c.1848–1849, The Grange, Campbell Town (with James Thompson); Tasmania, Australia.

BIBLIOGRAPHY

BROADBENT, JAMES 1981 "James Blackburn, 1803–1854." In Howard Tanner (editor) *Architects of Australia.* Melbourne: Macmillan.
Catalogue of the Library of James Blackburn. 1888 Melbourne: Privately published.
GROVE, JANE 1981 "James Blackburn." Unpublished B. Arch. thesis, University of Melbourne.
PRESTON, HARLEY n.d. "The Life and Work of James Blackburn." Unpublished M.A. thesis, University of Melbourne.

BLACKBURN, WILLIAM

William Blackburn (1750–1790), a native of London, rose from studies in the Royal Academy

Schools to become architect of the Watermen's Livery Hall (1778–1780). There he ably combined Adamesque interior decoration with aquatic façade symbolism. After winning first prize from THOMAS LEVERTON in the 1782 Penitentiaries Competition, he applied himself almost exclusively to designing jails. They feature advanced radial planning, later used by JOHN HAVILAND, but they lack the drama of the earlier Newgate Prison by GEORGE DANCE THE YOUNGER.

PIERRE DE LA RUFFINIÈRE DU PREY

WORKS

1778–1780, Watermen's Livery Hall, London. 1786–1789, City Jail, Oxford. 1786–1790, County Jail, Ipswich, England. *1787–1790, New Bailey Prison, Salford, England. 1788–1790, County Jail, Monmouth, England. 1788–1790, County Jail (not completed until 1791), Gloucester, England. 1789–1790, County Jail (not completed until 1795), Dorchester, England. *1789–1790, County Jail (not completed until 1795), Exeter, England.

BIBLIOGRAPHY

DAVIES, CELIA 1974 "Skilled Boatmen of the Thames. The Company of Watermen and Lightermen." *Country Life* 156:1488–1489.
FAIRWEATHER, LESLIE et al. 1975 *United Nations Social Defence Research Institute Prison Architecture.* London: Architectural Press.
HOWARD, JOHN 1789 *An Account of the Principal Lazarettos in Europe. . . .* Warrington, England: Eyres.
HUTCHINS, JOHN 1796–1815 Volume 2, pages 24–26 in *The History and Antiquities of the County of Dorset.* 4 vols. 2d ed. London: J. Nichols.
MARKUS, THOMAS 1954 "Pattern of the Law." *Architectural Review* 116:251–256.
PEVSNER, NIKOLAUS 1976 *A History of Building Types.* Princeton University Press.
WEINSTOCK, M. B. 1956 "Dorchester Model Prison 1791–1816." *Proceedings of the Dorset Natural History and Archaeological Society* 78:94–103.

BLANQUI, ANDRÉS

Andrés Blanqui (1677–1740) was born near Rome in 1677. He entered the Jesuits in 1716 and was assigned to Argentina. He had practiced as an architect in Italy, designing a project for a Roman basilica, and was quite well known in his profession when he entered the order.

He arrived in Rio de la Platte in 1717, eventually settling in Buenos Aires. His works were primarily religious commissions, but his technical knowledge and expertise allowed him to extend the scope of his work.

His churches in Buenos Aires integrated conservative scholarly treatises with late baroque novelties. In Córdoba, he designed the portico of the town cathedral (1728–1740) and in Buenos Aires, he commenced the building of Saint Catherine's (1739).

RAMÓN GUTÍERREZ

WORKS

1719–1723, College of the Jesuits, La Calera, Argentina. 1723, College of the Society of Jesuits; 1725, Church of Saint Ignazio; 1726, Church of Pilar; 1727–1729, Church of Mercy; Buenos Aires. 1728–1730, La Caroya Estate (addition); 1728–1738, Convictorio College; 1728–1740, Cathedral (façade and portico); Córdoba, Argentina. 1729, Cathedral (façade); 1729–1740, Cabildo; Buenos Aires. 1730–1737, College of Monserrat; 1730–1738, Estate of the Jesuits of Alta Gracia and Jesús María (partially constructed); Córdoba, Argentina. 1739, Convent of Saint Catherine, Buenos Aires.

BIBLIOGRAPHY

BUSCHLAZZO, MARIO J. 1959 *Argentina*. Volume 2 in *Monumentos históricos y arqueológicos*. Mexico City: Instituto Panamericano de Geografía e Historia.
FURLONG, GUILLERMO 1946 *Arquitectos argentinos durante la dominación hispánica*. Buenos Aires: Editorial Huarpes.
GRACIA, JOAQUÍN 1940 *Los jesuítas en Córdoba*. Buenos Aires: Espasa Calpe argentina.
GRENON, PEDRO 1941 "La Catedral de Córdoba." *Boletín de la Comisión Nacional de museoa y de Monumentos y Lugares históricos* 4:71–133.
LASCANO GONZALEZ, ANTONIO 1941 *Monumentos religiosos de Córdoba Colonial*. Buenos Aires.

BLEROT, ERNEST

Born and educated in Brussels, Ernest Blérot (1870–1957) enjoyed a successful architectural practice as a popularizer of the Art Nouveau style. Although his private houses in Brussels lack the profound complexity of VICTOR HORTA's works, they are nevertheless generally characterized by lively compositional invention.

ALFRED WILLIS

WORKS

1897, House, 30 rue du Monastère; 1898–1900, Houses, 12–19, 22 rue E. Solvay, 15, 17, 18, 19 rue St. Boniface; 1900–1903, Houses, 1–25 rue Vanderschrick; *1901–1908, Blérot House; Brussels.

BIBLIOGRAPHY

BORSI, FRANCO 1977 *Bruxelles 1900*. New York: Rizzoli.
DELEVOY, ROBERT et al. 1971 *Bruxelles 1900—Capitale de l'Art nouveau*. Brussels: Ecole Nationale Supérieure d'Architecture et des Arts Visuels.
PUTTEMANS, PIERRE 1976 *Modern Architecture in Belgium*. Translated by Mette Willert. Brussels: Vokaer.

REHME, WILHELM 1901–1902 *Architektur der Neuen Freien Schule*. Leipzig: Baumgärtner.
REHME, WILHELM 1902 *Ausgeführte Moderne Bautischler-arbeiten*. Leipzig: Baumgärtner.
RUSSELL, FRANK (editor) 1979 *Art Nouveau Architecture*. New York: Rizzoli.

BLEVE, JEAN LOUIS

Architecte-expert juré du roi in Paris (1766–1792), Jean Louis Blève (?–c.1807) built numerous townhouses. In 1799, he was *chef de service* at the Palais Bourbon and architect to the Tribunat at the Palais Royal. In both posts he was soon replaced by Gisors le jeune (see GISORS FAMILY) and Claude Etienne Beaumont, respectively.

MYRA DICKMAN ORTH

WORKS

*1768, Hôtel de Saule au Petit-Bercy; *1771, Grand Hôtel de Persan; *1771, Hôtel de Persan; 1772, Immeuble Doublet de Persan; 1777, Immeuble Pierre Guérard; *1790 Immeuble des Consorts Cavaignac; 1801, Salle du Tribunat (executed by Claude Etienne Beaumont), Palais Royal; Paris.

BIBLIOGRAPHY

BOYER, FERDINAND 1936 "Le Palais-Bourbon sous le Premier Empire." *Bulletin de la Société de l'Histoire de l'Art Français* 1936:91–123.
GALLET, MICHEL 1964 *Les Demeures parisiennes: L'Epoque Louis XVIᵉ*. Paris: Le Temps.
HAUTECOEUR, LOUIS 1953 *Révolution et Empire: 1792–1815*. Volume 5 in *Histoire de l'architecture classique en France*. Paris: Picard.
LABORDE, DE 1771 "Fichier." Unpublished manuscript copy of a document, linking Jean Louis Blève to J. Martus, a flower painter who was a member of the Academy of Saint Luke, Bibliothèque Doucet (Arch. Châtelet Y 4957), Paris.

BLOMFIELD, REGINALD

Scholar and architect, Reginald Theodore Blomfield (1856–1942) was articled to his uncle, Sir Arthur Blomfield, in 1881, but he left within two years. After a sketching tour in France and Spain, he discovered that he had "never really cared for Gothic," and thereafter his preference for classical architecture was confirmed. Beginning practice in 1884, he was occupied for many years with small commissions and turned his interest to architectural history. His *History of Renaissance Architecture in England* (1897) not only was influential in furthering the vernacular neoclassic revival but also brought him numerous commissions. In the early 1900s, his style underwent a change toward a purer classicism on the French model. His outstanding work was the redesigning of the Regent Street Quadrant, Piccadilly Circus (1910–1930), London. He was professor of architecture at the Royal Academy from 1906 to 1910 and president of the Royal Institute of British Architects from 1912 to 1914. He was knighted in 1919.

BETTY ELZEA

WORKS

1896, Wordsworth Building, Lady Margaret Hall, Oxford. 1900, Warehouse for the Army and Navy Stores, Westminster; 1908, United Universities Club, Pall Mall East; 1910–1930, Regent Street Quadrant (remodeling) and Piccadilly Circus (remodeling of the west side); London. 1926, Menin Gate War Memorial, Ypres, France.

BIBLIOGRAPHY

BLOMFIELD, REGINALD T. 1892 *The Formal Garden in England.* London: Macmillan.
BLOMFIELD, REGINALD T. 1897 *History of Renaissance Architecture in England: 1500 to 1800.* 2 vols. London: Bell.
BLOMFIELD, REGINALD T. (1911)1974 *History of French Architecture.* Reprint of 1921 ed. 2 vols. New York: Hacker.
BLOMFIELD, REGINALD T. 1932 *Memoirs of an Architect.* London: Macmillan.
BLOMFIELD, REGINALD T. 1934 *Modernismus.* London: Macmillan.
BLOMFIELD, REGINALD T. 1938 *Sebastien Le Prestre de Vauban: 1633–1707.* London: Methuen.
BLOMFIELD, REGINALD T. 1940 *Richard Norman Shaw.* London: Batsford.
RICHARDSON, A. E. 1943 "Sir Reginald Blomfield, R. A." *Journal of the Royal Institute of British Architects* Series 3 50:65–67.
SERVICE, ALASTAIR 1977 *Edwardian Architecture.* London: Thames & Hudson.

his social and ethical concerns into an ascetic but human architecture: still, the work remains very Finnish. As a graphic artist, he also contributed to the applied arts. He was one of the founders of the journal *Le Carré Bleu.* He received the Finnish State Prize in Architecture in 1977.

PIRKKO-LIISA LOUHENJOKI

WORKS

1951, Apartment House, Asesepänkaru. Turku, Finland. 1954, Ketju Terrace Houses; 1954, Kolmirinne Apartment House; 1955, Artists' Terrace Houses; 1956–1957, Apartment House, Nallenpolku; 1958, Aulis Blomstedt Studio; Tapiola, Espoo, Finland. 1959, Workers' Institute (annex), Helsinki. 1961, Apartment House, Riistapolku; 1964, Terrace Houses, Leppäkertuntie; 1965, Kaskenkaataja and Allakka Apartment Houses; Tapiola, Espoo, Finland. 1974, Puntarpää Apartment House, Soukka, Espoo, Finland.

BIBLIOGRAPHY

Finnish Architecture. 1975 The Hague: Museum of Finnish Architecture and the Netherlands Congress Center. Exhibition catalogue.
PALLASMAA, JUHANI (editor) 1980 *Aulis Blomstedt. Architect. Thought and Form. Studies in Harmony.* Helsinki: Museum of Finnish Architecture. Exhibition catalogue.
RICHARDS, J. M. 1978 *800 Years of Finnish Architecture.* Newton Abbot, England: David & Charles.
SALOKORPI, ASKO 1970 *Modern Architecture in Finland.* London: Weidenfeld & Nicolson.
SUHONEN, PEKKA 1980 "Blomstedt, Aulis." Pages 99–100 in Muriel Emanuel (editor), *Contemporary Architects.* New York: St. Martin's.
TEMPEL, EGON 1968 *New Finnish Architecture.* Translated by James C. Palmes. London: Architectural Press.
WICKBERG, NILS ERIK (1959)1962 *Finnish Architecture.* Helsinki: Otava. Originally published in Finnish.

BLOMSTEDT, AULIS

Aulis Blomstedt (1906–1979), a Finnish architect, received his education in classical architecture but became a functionalist. He did not design many buildings—the first major ones only in the 1950s—but he had a strong influence on Finnish architecture as its foremost theoretician and as an influential teacher at Helsinki University of Technology from 1958 to 1966. Blomstedt has often been seen as a counterpart to ALVAR AALTO in his emphasis on the theoretical background of architecture. From the 1930s on, he studied systems of measurement based on the dimensions of the human body and on musical harmony, called Canon 60, and experimented with these systems in industrial building. In his architecture, Blomstedt combines the classical clarity of his systems with

BLONDEL, FRANÇOIS

Nicolas-François Blondel (1618–1686) came from a family belonging to the upper strata of the bourgeoisie. At an early age, he joined the army, rising to the rank of captain in the *corps des ingénieurs du roi* in which capacity he inspected fortifications in Provence. As a reward for these activities and his distinguished career as a commanding officer in naval battles at the Spanish and Italian coast he was made a *maréchal des camps* and also appointed professor of mathematics at the Collège de France. At the same time, the minister of foreign affairs offered him the post as tutor to his son whose education was thought to be best achieved by extensive traveling. Thus, from 1652 to 1655 Blondel visited with his charge almost every important town in western Europe, proceeding from Germany to Holland, Scandinavia, and Finland and then via Riga, Danzig, Warsaw, Prague, and Vienna to Venice, Florence, and Rome. The wider outlook gained and the contacts made through these travels were undoubtedly the qualifications that led Cardinal Mazarin to send him on diplomatic missions to Brandenburg, Sweden, and also Constantinople. While the negotiations with the Turkish vizier dragged on, Blondel made use of waiting time to visit Greece and Egypt. Returning to France in 1659, he was appointed ambassador to Denmark, a post he held for four years.

Thereafter, it was Jean Baptiste Colbert who availed himself of Blondel's services, this time in the capacity of *ingénieur du roi*. Foreseeing a war with England, he charged Blondel with the inspection of the coastal defenses and the planning of fortified ports. As part of this program, Blondel restored and strengthened the Ancien Pont des Saintes (1665), modernized the Fort de la Prée on the Ile de Ré, and submitted plans for the important town of Rochefort (1666). In fact, the layout of this new town was carried out after his design, as were the buildings of the Arsenal and the Corderie.

Returning to Paris and his academic chair, he was, in 1669, elected to the mathematical section of the Académie des Sciences and, two years later, appointed director of the newly formed Académie d'Architecture, an institute that was controlled by Colbert. Being obviously experienced in the academic education of young people, he was chosen in 1673 as teacher in mathematics to the Dauphin in which capacity he wrote two treatises, of which one, dealing with a novel manner of fortification, was widely discussed.

His major work, however, and the one that made him widely known as an authority on classical doctrine, was the publication of lectures he gave twice weekly at the Academy before an audience of young architects. Since good taste and classical architecture were then considered to be synonymous, it is hardly surprising that the system he expounded knew of no other models than those of Roman antiquity, although today it strikes us as extraordinary that the artistic outlook of someone who had traveled as extensively as no other architect before him remained unaffected by what he had seen and learned on these journeys. In five parts, Blondel surveyed in great detail the proportional rules and interdependence of all the formal elements of classical architecture: the five orders, the intercolumniation and multistoried buildings, but also the arches, doors and windows, vaults and domes, bridges and staircases. Methodically, he

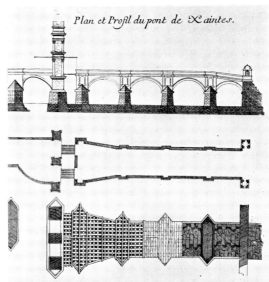

Plan et Profil du pont de Xaintes.

François Blondel.
Drawing of Pont des
Saintes.
France.
1665

François Blondel.
Frontispiece to Cours (*Parts
II and III*).

reviewed the rules laid down by VITRUVIUS and those prescribed by the great masters of the Cinquecento: GIACOMO BAROZZI DA VIGNOLA, ANDREA PALLADIO, and VINCENZO SCAMOZZI. He accepted them equally as authorities and only occasionally advised against an unorthodox arrangement. His principal aim was to make the young architect acquainted with the variations in the measurements of the orders and in this way to help him form his taste and judgment. This made Blondel's *Cours d'Architecture* (1675) unique and distinguished it from the writings of his predecessors; it presented, for the first time, a complete account of the official academic teaching. In the

*François Blondel.
Composé de Scamozzi
(Part I).*

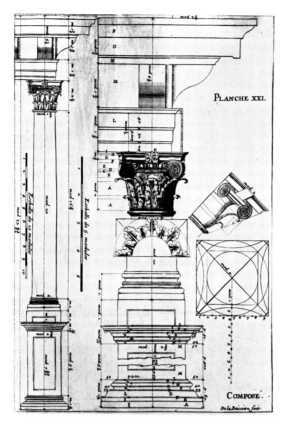

*François Blondel.
Plan of the city of
Dunquerque.*

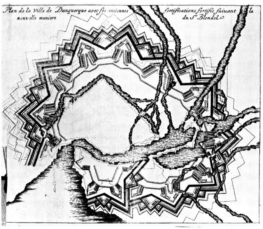

the cosmic order, and that the feeling for harmony and the pleasure derived from it are inborn in man. Perrault, in contrast, believed that it is only through the all powerful force of custom that proportions are thought to be the cause of beauty: seeing them constantly in company with richness of material, precise workmanship, and symmetrical arrangement all of which produce beauty, one unconsciously transfers their quality of being beautiful to something that is not. Blondel thought this an absurd notion which he refused at length. In conclusion and as final proof that proportions alone create beauty, he referred to Santa Giustina in Padua as an example of those simple but well-proportioned buildings that, though lacking any decorative embellishment, are beautiful, and, surprisingly, to the Gothic façade of Milan Cathedral with its almost classical proportions which, in spite of foul decoration, break through the surrounding confusion, calling forth our admiration and pleasure. In another context, the gap between the two opponents widened and reached down to a deeper level. From his premise that proportions are not determined by unalterable laws of nature, Perrault concluded that it is up to man to contain them within definite rules. Blondel no doubt agreed with this laudable aim. Yet, Perrault went further and demanded that, once proportions had been fixed, they must not be changed for any reason whatsoever. Blondel rejected this precept outright. The dispute was about a problem that had been under discussion ever since Vitruvius—should an architect try to counteract the effect of perspective? As far as this touched on a physiological function, namely that of vision, Perrault had the upper hand; but when the discussion moved to purely artistic considerations, Blondel stood his ground. Since the aim of architecture, he argued, is to please, architects would fail in their calling if they used the same proportions in all kind of situations. The admirable variety of ancient monuments is proof that the ancients deliberately made adjustments, not, as Perrault thought, that they blindly fumbled. Only through long experience will the architect be able to judge the permissible limits and thus succeed in giving his work the indefinable and indispensable quality of *grâce*—certainly not by mechanical application of Perrault's proposed proportions, rationally arrived at by working out an average.

Although Blondel had been in the service of the king and of powerful ministers from Richelieu to Colbert, he was never charged with the design of a major building. This was partly due to the fact that for many years his time was taken up by giving expert advice on fortifications where any buildings connected with these belonged of neces-

concluding chapters he widened his view and dealt with basic principles. He discussed proportions in general, showed through careful analysis that the Renaissance architects achieved aesthetic unity by means of a system of mathematical ratios which they applied to the inside as well as to the outside, and deduced from this survey that proportions are the cause of beauty in architecture. It was at this point that he clashed with CLAUDE PERRAULT who in his notes on Vitruvius had expressed quite different views. Since the difference of opinion was of a basic nature, the Blondel–Perrault dispute occupies an important place in the history of architectural theory.

Blondel was convinced that architectural proportions, like musical consonances, emanate from sity to the class of civil engineering. This was the character of the few buildings already mentioned and must also have been that of a design which, if tradition is to be trusted, he made for an armory in Berlin (not pertaining to the present *Zeughaus*, begun only thirty or forty years later). The stables of the Château Chaumont Laguiche (c.1650), an early and quite remarkable work, were built in a more decorative, though by Parisian standards old-fashioned, style. Later, when he settled in Paris for good, he was available for commissions. But by then, in 1667, Colbert's great building program was well under way. A few years later, when the ramparts of Paris were dismantled, it was the municipality that sought his services, in particular to embellish the entries to the city. The program included the erection of a new Porte Saint-Denis (1671). It became Blondel's masterwork, admired at the time for the originality of its decoration and its size: it was the biggest arch ever built until surpassed by the Arc de Triomphe. Blondel also modernized the Porte Saint-Antoine (1671) and the Porte Saint-Bernard (1671), constructed the section of the Seine quai from Nôtre Dame to the Hôtel de Ville, and produced with the assistance of PIERRE BULLET, his pupil, a plan of Paris to serve as basis for future town development. It was published in 1673. After that date, he does not seem to have been actively engaged as an architect.

In any case, it was not through his architectural works but almost exclusively through his work as a teacher and director of the Academy that Blondel was able to exert considerable influence on the development of French classical architecture.

WOLFGANG HERRMANN

WORKS

c.1650, Stables Château Chaumont Laguiche, Saône et Loire, France 1665, Pont des Saintes sur la Charente, France. 1666, Town, Arsenal, and Corderie, Rochefort, France. 1671, Porte Saint Antoine; 1671, Porte Saint Bernard; 1671, Porte Saint Denis; Paris.

BIBLIOGRAPHY

BLOMFIELD, REGINALD (1921)1974 *A History of French Architecture.* Reprint. New York: Hacken.

BLONDEL, FRANÇOIS (1673*a*)1696 *The Comparison of Pindar and Horace . . . English'd by Sir Edward Sherburne.* London: Thomas Bennet.

BLONDEL, FRANÇOIS (1673*b*)1736 *Résolution des quatre principaux problèmes d'architecture.* Amsterdam: Mortier.

BLONDEL, FRANÇOIS (1675)1698 *Cours d'Architecture enseigné dans l'Académie royale d'Architecture.* 2d ed. Paris: The author.

BLONDEL, FRANÇOIS (1682)1699 *Histoire du calendrier romain . . . .* Paris: The author.

BLONDEL, FRANÇOIS (1683*a*)1699 *L'Art de jetter les bombes.* Paris: The author.

BLONDEL, FRANÇOIS (1683*b*)1699 *Cours de mathématique contenant divers traitez composez et enseignez à Monseigneur le Dauphin.* 2d ed. Paris: The author.

BLONDEL, FRANÇOIS (1683*c*)1711 *Nouvelle manière de fortifier les places.* The Hague: de Voys.

BRÖNNER, WOLFGANG 1972 "Blondel-Perrault." Unpublished Ph.D. dissertation, Rheinische Friedrich-Wilhelms-Universität, Bonn.

FICHET, FRANÇOISE (editor) 1979 *La théorie architecturale à l'age classique.* Brussels: Mardaga.

GERMANN, GEORG 1980 *Einführung in die Geschichte der Architekturtheorie.* Darmstadt, Germany: Wissenschaftliche Buchgesellschaft.

HAUTECOEUR, LOUIS 1948 *Le règne de Louis XIV.* Volume 2 in *Histoire de l'architecture classique en France.* Paris: Picard.

HERRMANN, WOLFGANG 1973 *The Theory of Claude Perrault.* London: Zwemmer.

KAMBARTEL, WALTER 1972 *Symmetrie und Schönheit.* Munich: Fink.

MAUCLAIR, PLACIDE, and VIGOREUX, C. 1938 *Nicolas-François de Blondel.* Laon, France: Imprimerie de l'Aisne.

TATARKIEWCZ, WLADYSLAW 1974 Volume 3, pages 416ff. in *History of Aesthetics.* The Hague.

TEYSSÈDRE, BERNARD 1967 *L'art français au siècle de Louis XIV.* Paris: Le Livre de Poche.

Elevation de la Porte Saint Denis, vue du côté de la Ville Exécutée sur les desseins de François Blondel.

Plan.

*François Blondel.
Engraving of Porte Saint Denis.
Paris.
1671*

BLONDEL, GEORGES FRANÇOIS

Georges François Blondel (c.1730–c.1790) was the son of JACQUES FRANÇOIS BLONDEL from whom he received training in architectural drawing before studying in Rome. In London from 1764 until his return to Paris in 1774 he is known to have exhibited drawings and etchings of architectural subjects and to have made unexecuted designs for Stowe House, Buckinghamshire.

MICHAEL MCCARTHY

BIBLIOGRAPHY

HARRIS, JOHN 1964 "Blondel at Stowe." *Connoisseur* 155, no. 625:173–176.

LEJEAUX, JEANNE 1936 "Georges-François Blondel: Engraver and Draughtsman." *Print Collector's Quarterly* 23, no. 4:260–277.

MCCARTHY, MICHAEL 1973 "The Rebuilding of Stowe House, 1770–1777." *Huntington Library Quarterly* 36, no. 3:267–298.

BLONDEL, JACQUES FRANÇOIS

The most influential teacher of architecture in eighteenth-century France, Jacques François Blondel (1705–1774) developed a theory of architecture based on rational analysis which he used to reinforce the primacy of traditional French design in the face of both rococo and neoclassical challenges. His students applied his teachings to a wide range of problems, sometimes arousing his criticism. He taught his theory through a case study method in which he emphasized the particular character and circumstances of the individual building problem. From his early career, he stressed the importance of national culture, history, and experience in influencing the character of architecture.

Born in Rouen, France, into a family of architects and building tradesmen, Jacques François Blondel began the formal study of architecture with his uncle, learning as well to draw and engrave. In his early career, in addition to building, he began to publish his engravings, first as part of the work of others and later in his own books. Publishing and then teaching supplanted his desire to build. Founding his own school of architecture in 1746, he was later named professor at the Academy of Architecture, his principal professional activity for the remainder of his life.

Blondel's personality is unanimously described as friendly, open, generous, and devoted to family and profession. Blondel married Marie Anne Garnier in 1729 Their son, GEORGES FRANÇOIS BLONDEL, was born in 1730. There was also a daughter, Claudine Angelique. Blondel's wife died in 1755. In 1760, Blondel married Marie Madeleine Balletti, a child of the famous comédienne Sylvia Balletti. Their son Jean Baptiste was born in 1764. Georges practiced as an engraver; Jean was an architect whose principal position was as architect for the city of Paris.

Blondel first studied architecture with his uncle, JEAN FRANÇOIS BLONDEL, and later with GILLES MARIE OPPENORD. From the former he acquired great respect for traditional French design and from the latter great facility in the new picturesque, or rococo, manner. He also developed fine techniques as an engraver. Although he traveled throughout France, there is no record of travel to other countries. His knowledge of the history of architecture outside France was extensive and based on the study of published sources. His knowledge of architecture in France, its history and techniques, was wide and based on a deep familiarity with the literature and with the buildings of France.

Blondel's reputation rests largely on his activities other than building. Knowledge of his built work is small for two reasons. First, no major project was done in Paris or any equivalent center. Second, relatively little of his executed work survives. The designs he published show a diagrammatic clarity and competency. His design for the reorganization of Metz, France, in which a series of public and other institutional structures are coherently and precisely related through a series of public squares, is his finest work. While pieces of it fell to nineteenth-century medievalizing, enough remains to give a clear impression of Blondel's sophistication and sensitivity.

Blondel's writings and engravings were published throughout his career, with the engravings concentrated in the earlier decades and the writings increasing toward the end. As in his teaching, Blondel reached three distinct audiences in his publications, although the books themselves often had broad appeal. First, there were publications for an amateur audience, such as *De la Distribution des Maisons de Plaisances* (1737–1738), *Description des Festes . . .* (1740), his articles contributed to the *Encyclopédie* (1750–1776), the 1767 edition of GIACOMO BAROZZI DA VIGNOLA, and *L'Homme du Monde Éclairé par les Arts* (1774). Second, there were publications aimed at educating bureaucrats whose responsibilities included initiating and supervising public building. *L'Architecture Française* (1752–1756), with its extensive analyses of circumstantial as well as formal problems and solutions, is most precisely intended for this relatively small audience. It's sumptuous scale and quality gave it wide appeal as well. Third, there were publications directed at students, including his two pamphlets on the study of architecture and his multivolume *Cours d'Architecture* (1771–1777). The extensive and favorable notice his work received in the popular journals demonstrates that all categories of his writings appealed to a wide audience. A fourth category of his writings, although not published, often had a direct influence. These are his reports, often prepared with his colleagues, accomplished as part of his duties as a member of the Academy of Architecture. From an assessment of new techniques of encaustic to the surveying of the royal castle at Blois, Blondel's work in this area demonstrates the broad range of his expertise.

Because Blondel's most important contribution comes from his teaching, the reasons for his founding an independent school of architecture, in the face of some initial official opposition, are noteworthy. His fundamental innovation was the establishment of an extensive and carefully organized curriculum which sought to comprehend the great range of architectural theory and technique. Since he had to secure the approval of the Academy of Architecture, which conducted its own school, to open his school, one may know his criticisms of existing teaching largely by the special virtues he claims for his own school. It would have been clearly impolitic to attack the school of the Academy of Architecture when petitioning the Academy itself. The biggest weakness in the training of architects, Blondel often said, is the haphazard nature of their training, leaving some without the ability to realize successfully an entire project. Blondel incorporated and expanded the Academy's best known pedagogical device, the competition, while severely reducing the role of the sponsoring architect as a teaching resource. Blondel used competitions for virtually every level of student advancement. He wanted very much for students, even at the lowest levels, to have the sense of accomplishment and mastery entailed in the completion of an entire project, regardless of size.

By bringing all his students together in his school, Blondel also sought to control what and how they learned, and at what rate. He further sought to insure that all students would become competent in all areas of their profession. Although the use of calculus and the analysis of materials were not entirely new aspects of the curriculum, Blondel provided practical training in the application of these techniques. He did much of the teaching himself, but he also made extensive use of other professionals, both in narrow professional topics, such as engineering, and in the fields of painting and sculpture.

Assessing the impact and influence of a great teacher is difficult. The number of Blondel's students who later distinguished themselves is both large and representative of a broad range of theory, form, and practice. Among them are ETIENNE LOUIS BOULLÉE, WILLIAM CHAMBERS, CLAUDE NICOLAS LEDOUX, and CHARLES DE WAILLY.

Blondel's influence rests largely on three as-

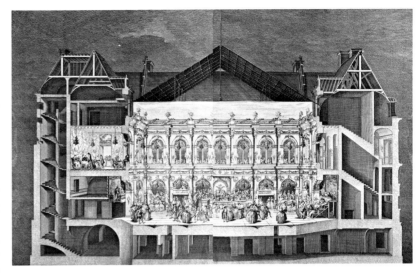

Jacques François Blondel.
Hôtel de Ville.
Engraving from
Description des Festes.

pects: (1) the importance of rational analysis in problem solving; (2) the importance of the particular problem in influencing the solution in addition to the character of the problem in relation to others of its type; and (3) the importance of attention to detail, from inception to completion of a task. Although Blondel's own taste was traditional, he clearly placed that preference in its cultural context, thus urging upon his students not a form of correct architectural expression but a means of rational analysis that was intended to foster progressive and responsible change. He never attacked rococo or neoclassical forms themselves, only the application of those forms in an inappropriate social context.

Although the Academy of Architecture denied Blondel's initial request for permission to conduct his school on the grounds that it would duplicate resources already available at the Academy of Architecture itself, subsequent relations between the two schools appear to have been tolerant. The Ecole des Ponts et Chaussées, from its inception in 1747, sent its students to Blondel for the architectural portion of their training rather than to the school of the Academy. No record or evidence of objection on the part of the Academy to this decision is known. Blondel's talents and innovations must have been appreciated because Blondel was appointed professor at the Academy school in 1762, after which his methods were introduced to its curriculum. Also, following his election to the Academy of Architecture in 1755, Blondel's students were eligible to enter the Rome prize competitions.

In addition to his professional architectural students, Blondel sought to reach three other audiences with his teaching. These audiences for his teaching paralleled those for which he wrote. First, there were professionals and craftsmen in the building trades whom Blondel taught on Sunday,

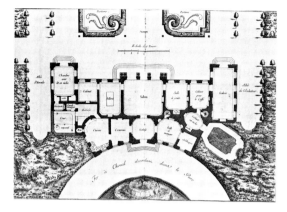

Jacques François Blondel. Ground plan with gardens. Design from De la Distribution des Maisons de Plaisances.

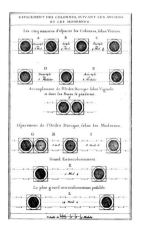

Jacques François Blondel. Variety of Intercolumniation. Plate from Cours d'Architecture.

their day off. He would discuss the latest approved techniques of construction, decorating, finishing, or other, usually practical, topics of professional concern. In addition to these technical matters, Blondel also sought to demonstrate the rationale for his analysis with special emphasis on the importance of *convenance* (suitability, decorum). As with all others he taught, Blondel believed that a wide audience of sophistication and reason would be proof against architectural unreason and transitory fashion. Blondel also conducted public lectures on architectural theory and led tours of buildings, both under construction and completed, for the other two categories of students: amateurs—those who might either intend to build or simply find architecture interesting; and bureaucrats in a position to influence and supervise government building.

When Blondel became professor at the Academy of Architecture in 1762, thus ending his own school, he introduced his comprehensive curriculum. The atelier system, through which students had sponsors and special training, continued, but Blondel did not give up any of his technical courses. In this way, he insured that each student would be trained in all facets of their profession. In expanding the competition system, one of his major reforms, he also encountered his chief obstacle. The *Procès Verbaux d'Académie Royale d'Architecture* is regularly dotted with reports that the marquis de Marigny, the royal director of building and Blondel's bureaucratic supervisor, refused to authorize the medals for a new or expanded competition. Blondel's own statements stressed the importance of the competitions for student advancement; the denials ignored Blondel's rationale and simply complained of the cost of the medals. However, except for this obstacle, there is no other evidence in the records of the Academy to indicate resistance to Blondel's curricular innovations.

From the time Blondel was elected to the second class of the Academy of Architecture in 1755, he was an active and contributing member. He regularly participated in debates. His own writings continued to be read at open sessions, to the praise of his fellows. His interest in technical innovation meant that he was often a member of a committee investigating and reporting on such matters. Although no direct evidence can be adduced, Blondel's activities, which often challenged or pushed the established manner of the Academy, may have contributed to his not being advanced to the first class of the Academy of Architecture. He was often among those nominated to the first class, but never among those actually advanced. Blondel was only the second professor of the Academy not to be elected to the first class. One may infer that because his reforms, his challenges, and his leadership, a certain level of personal resentment emerged which combined to deny Blondel official recognition which his activities, judged on any scale, entitled him.

To understand Blondel's theory, it is important to separate it from his own taste. His taste was for traditional forms sanctioned by long and carefully developed experience. The theory was more flexible, and this flexibility contributed to his success as a teacher even when his students did not accept Blondel's taste. Blondel believed that architecture was a public and visible expression of order. This expressed order was dependent on the particular circumstances and history of each culture. The authority that these ideas achieved derived from their accurate reflection of the culture that made it and not from any sort of absolute rule. Blondel believed that CLAUDE PERRAULT had clearly shown the absence of rules and the importance of custom in making architecture. Architects thus became continually responsible to tradition, the changes occasioned by the passing of time and the development of new techniques and ideas. In placing great emphasis on his concept of *convenance,* he indicated that the social continuum from most public to most private must be understood and respected in architectural terms. Because this was seen as an inherently flexible continuum, Blondel had a means to introduce new ideas into architecture. The gradual acceptance of a new idea could move, slowly, from its original point of introduction to more or less private or public spheres. Most important was that a sense of the relation between the elements on a continuum be clear. Thus, the residence of the monarch provided a standard below which could devolve the residences of all his subjects in a proper hierarchical arrangement. Blondel stressed that the hierarchy that would be appropriate to one time and place would likely not be applicable elsewhere. In order to impress this on his students and the readers of his books, Blondel favored a case study method whereby an individual building was studied in detail and depth, making

Blondel's rationale for his judgments concrete and tangible. Not only were the overall hierarchy and the place of the particular building in it reinforced, but the logic of the situation—the particular reasons for the particular decisions—was also explained.

In addition to his case study method, Blondel emphasized the importance of process. His sense of the fluid character of reason, coupled with an absence of absolute authority, also strongly influenced Blondel's sense of process as a means to describe and record the complex sequence of events, both physical and social. Blondel recognized that reason itself implies an orderly process to approach and solve a problem. He understood also that the ability to reason well depended on experience and study. He further emphasized that this process should not be an abstract element but instead closely related to the particular circumstances of the problem at hand.

Beyond the importance of such general topics as the debate of absolute versus relative rules, the character of change, and the role of progress, he also had strong opinions on the meaning and role of genius as he frequently declared that genius must be tempered by taste. Blondel recognized that taste was relative, based on custom or tradition, and he could also point to examples by which taste had changed in a measured, progressive manner. Blondel recognized as well that such evolutionary change might be progressive or regressive. When discussing the Gothic, whose ornamental forms he found unattractive, he emphasized that these forms satisfied those who made them. In fact, it was the ease with which Blondel believed architects could lapse into bad taste that caused him to stress reason, reflection, and consideration upon those seeking to make change.

Because Blondel believed that taste based on reason was so crucial to the progress of architecture, he maintained a wary view of genius. His view was in part the result of the general shift in the meaning of genius during his lifetime. Although Blondel recognized that the individual of great talent was capable of transforming taste with positive and progressive results, he believed that this would occur only rarely. In the vast majority of cases, he argued, the claim that genius was the source of creativity actually masked an unwillingness to think and reason deeply, creating results that were positively damaging to the orderly practice of architecture and to the culture of which it was so visible a component. In political terms, Blondel believed that the social order was a greater value than individual license. Blondel's development of a rational technique to incorporate change into the process of a vital national taste allowed

him to claim the ability to maintain an ordered public image of architecture that was also expected to respond to the changes occurring in modern society.

Because Blondel's theory sought to develop a rational method applicable to changing circumstances, his influence extended very broadly. A few examples may be offered here in conclusion. To read Denis Diderot's discussion of FRANÇOIS MANSART's Château Maisons, some years after editing Blondel's contributions to the *Encyclopédie,* is to encounter very clearly Blondel's intentions about the social and hierarchical role of architecture, accurately perceived by an amateur. To read his fellow encyclopedist, Jean François Marmontel, who was also a secretary to Marigny in the royal bureaucracy, is to get an indication of his influence among bureaucrats charged with responsibility for building. To read his student William Chambers's demands for reason and his attacks on absolute rules is to understand that Blondel's ideas had currency beyond France. To read the title of another student's major publication, Ledoux's *L'Architecture Considérée sous le Rapport de l'Art des Moeurs et de la Legislation,* in which architecture is understood in terms of the laws and customs of a people, is to find Blondel's ideas having influence beyond changing taste.

Toward the end of his final illness, Blondel asked that he be taken to his classrooms at the Louvre. There, among his books, his models, and his students, he died.

KEVIN HARRINGTON

Jacques François Blondel.
Three ways of treating a
*   ceiling.*
Plate from Cours
*   d'Architecture.*

WORKS

1745, Porte Saint Martin (decoration); Paris. 1748, Archbishop's Palace, Cambrai, France. 1748, Blondel House (remodeling), Rue du Croissant. 1748, Gallery (decoration), Hôtel de Choiseul (formerly the Hôtel de Crozat), Rue de Richelieu; Paris. *1761–1771, Cathedral (principal portal), Metz, France. 1767–?, Cathedral (*aubette* and screen), Strasbourg, France. n.d., Hôtel de Marivat, Place Dauphine, Besançon, France, n.d., Orangery, near Florence.

BIBLIOGRAPHY

ALEMBERT, JEAN LE ROND D'   1963   Page 133 in *Preliminary Discourse to the Encyclopedia of Diderot.* Indianapolis, Ind.: Bobbs-Merrill.

BAROZZIO DE VIGNOLE, JACQUES 1767 *Livre Nouveau ou Règles des Cinq Ordres d'Architecture . . . . , Nouvellement Revu . . . par Monsieur B*** Architecte du Roy. . . .* Paris: Petit.

BLONDEL, JACQUES FRANÇOIS (1737–1738)1967 *De la Distribution des Maisons de Plaisance et de la Décoration des Edifices en General.* 2 vols. Reprint. Farnborough, England: Gregg.

BLONDEL, JACQUES FRANÇOIS 1740 *Description des Festes Données par la Ville de Paris a l'Occasion du Mariage de Madame Louise-Elizabeth de France, & de Dom Philippe, Infant & Grand Amiral d'Espagne les vingt-neuvieme & trentieme Août mil sept cent trent-neuf.* Paris: Le Mercier.

BLONDEL, JACQUES FRANÇOIS 1747 *Discours sur la Manière d'Etudier l'Architecture, et les Arts qui sont Relatifs a celui de Bastir.* Paris: Mariette.

BLONDEL, JACQUES FRANÇOIS 1750–1776 Numerous articles on architecture in volumes 1–7 in Denis Diderot and Jean le Rond d'Alembert (editors), *Encyclopédie.* Paris: Briasson. A selection of titles of Blondel's significant articles includes agrafe, amortissement, arabesque ou moresque, arc, architecte, architecture, architrave, aspect, balustrade, balustre, bâtiment, cabinet, cannellures, caprice, chambre, chapelle, chapiteau, cheminée, claveau, clé, colonnade, colonne, comble, convenance, décoration, denticule, dessein, développement, distribution, dôme, école, entablement, façade, génies, and goût.

BLONDEL, JACQUES FRANÇOIS (1752–1756)1904–1905 *L'Architecture Françoise, ou Recueil de Plans, d'Elevations, Coupes et Profils. . . .* 8 vols. Reprint. Paris: Librairie Centrale des Beaux-Arts.

BLONDEL, JACQUES FRANÇOIS 1754 *Discours sur la Nécessité de l'Etude de l'Architecture. . . .* Paris: Jombert.

BLONDEL, JACQUES FRANÇOIS 1771 *De l'Utilité de Joindre à l'Etude de l'Architecture, celle des Sciences et des Arts qui lui Sont Relatifs.* Paris: Desaint.

BLONDEL, JACQUES FRANÇOIS (1774)1973 *L'Homme du Monde Eclairé par les Arts.* Reprint. Geneva: Minkoff.

BLONDEL, JACQUES FRANÇOIS, and CONTANT D'IVRY, PIERRE 1757 "Extrait de L'Enregistrement Concernant la Rapport." *Mercure de France* June:169–171.

BLONDEL, JACQUES FRANÇOIS, and PATTE, PIERRE 1771–1777 *Cours d'Architecture, ou Traité de la Décoration, Distribution & Construction des Bâtiments; Contenant les Leçons Données en 1750, & les Années Suivantes. . . .* 9 vols. Paris: Desaint. Patte prepared the last two volumes of text and one volume of plates for publication following Blondel's death. Although following Blondel's topical plan, Patte rewrote extensively much, but not all, of Blondel's material.

BRAHAM, ALAN 1980 *The Architecture of the French Enlightenment.* Berkeley: University of California Press.

COURAJOD, LOUIS 1874 "Introduction: L'Enseignement de l'Art Français aux Différentes Epoques de son Histoire." Pages LXVIII–LXXIX in *L'Ecole Royale des Eleves Protégés.* Paris: Du Moulin.

DÉZALLIER D'ARGENVILLE, A. N. (1787)1972 "Jacques François Blondel." Volume 1, pages 467–473 in *Vies des Fameux Architectes depuis la Renaissance des Arts, avec une Description de leurs Ouvrages.* Reprint. Geneva: Minkoff.

ERIKSON, SVEND 1974 *Early Neo-Classicism in France.* London: Faber.

FRANQUE, FRANÇOIS 1774 "Eloge de J-F Blondel." *Journal des Beaux-Arts et des Sciences* Mar.:559–570.

GALLET, MICHEL 1972 *Stately Mansions: Eighteenth Century Paris Architecture.* New York: Praeger.

HARRINGTON, KEVIN 1981 "Architectural Relationships: Changing Ideas on Architecture in the Encyclopedie, 1750–1776." Unpublished Ph.D. dissertation, Cornell University, Ithaca, N.Y.

HAUTECOEUR, LOUIS 1950 *Première moitié du XVIIIe siècle: Le style Louis XV.* Volume 3 in *Histoire de l'architecture classique en France.* Paris: Picard.

HERRMANN, WOLFGANG 1962 "Jacques François Blondel." Appendix 9 in *Laugier and 18th Century French Theory.* London: Zwemmer.

KAUFMANN, EMIL 1949 "The Contribution of J-F Blondel to Mariette's *Architecture Françoise.*" *Art Bulletin* 31:58–59.

KAUFMANN, EMIL (1955)1968 *Architecture in the Age of Reason: Baroque and Post-Baroque in England, Italy, and France.* Reprint. New York: Dover.

LEJEAUX, JEANNE 1927a "Jacques François Blondel: Professeur d'Architecture." *L'Architecture* 40:23–27.

LEJEAUX, JEANNE 1927b *La Place d'Armes de Metz.* Strasbourg, France: Istra.

LEJEAUX, JEANNE 1931 "La Cathédrale de 1750 à 1870 et l'Oeuvre de Blondel à Metz." Chapter 2 in Marcel Aubert (editor), *La Cathédrale de Metz.* Paris: Picard.

LENÔTRE, G. 1910 "J-F Blondel, et l'Architecture Française." *L'Architecte* 5:5–8.

LESUEUR, PIERRE 1910 "Jacques François Blondel: Admirateur de l'Architecture Gothique." *Chronique des Arts* Sept. 24:244.

LESUEUR, PIERRE 1931 "Un Ouvrage Inédit de Jacques François Blondel."

MIDDLETON, ROBIN 1959 "Jacques François Blondel and the *Cours d'Architecture.*" *Journal of the Society of Architectural Historians* 18:140–148.

PROST, AUGUSTE 1860 *Jacques François Blondel et Son Oeuvre.* Metz, France: Rousseau-Pallez.

SAMARAN, CHARLES 1914 Pages 206–211 in *Jacques Casanova: Venetien.* Paris: Calman-Levy.

STURGES, W. KNIGHT 1952 "Jacques François Blondel." *Journal of the Society of Architectural Historians* 11:16–19.

BLONDEL, JEAN FRANÇOIS

Jean François Blondel (1683–1756) belongs to the second rank of architects, consolidating and extending the creative achievements of others. He was born in Rouen, France, the uncle of JACQUES FRANÇOIS BLONDEL. Jean's training and career before 1719 is not clear. At that time he appears in

Paris. From 1721 to 1723, he resided in Geneva, and then returned to Paris. He was elected to the second class of the Academy of Architecture in 1728. Always competent, rarely inspired, his work in Paris has not survived. What remains in Rouen and Geneva demonstrates his considerable skills. The Maison Lullin at Genthod, Switzerland (1723–1725) translates the prevailing taste for careful siting, ordered planning, and discrete ornament from the scale of great models to that of a well-to-do bourgeois. Such flexibility is in accord with the tenets of decorum in French design as codified from the beginning of the Academy of Architecture. Following the completion of his Consulate in Rouen (1732–1739), Blondel is not associated with any completed building, suggesting that such occupations as controller of buildings in the Royal Military School, his activities in the Academy of Architecture, as well as his engraving and publications had come to take all his time. By establishing in his own work a level of excellence in support of traditional ideas as well as incorporating, usually in interior finishes, new and changing tastes, Blondel stressed the measured assimilation of new ideas in a stable environment. Through his later activities he was able to enforce such a point of view in the projects that he reviewed.

KEVIN HARRINGTON

WORKS

*1719–1724, Saint Jean en Grève (high altar and choir), Paris. 1721, Gedeon Mallet House, Geneva. 1723, Cramer House, Cologny, Switzerland. 1723–1725, Aimé Lullin House and Gardens, Genthod, Switzerland. *1724, Grand Charonne House, near Paris. *1730–1733, Communion Chapel, Saint Jean en Grève, Paris. 1730s, Madeleine (work), Besançon, France. 1732, Rouillé House (enlarging and remodeling), Paris. 1732–1739, Consulate (later Bourse), Rouen, France. *c.1737, Saint Saveur (remodeling), Paris.

BIBLIOGRAPHY

BLONDEL, JACQUES FRANÇOIS (1752)1904 Volume 2, book 4, pages 114–116 in L'Architecture Françoise, ou Recueil de Plans, d'Elevations, Coupes et Profils. . . . Reprint. Paris: Librarie Central des Beaux-Arts.

BLONDEL, JACQUES FRANÇOIS 1774 Volume 6, page 468 in Cours d'Architecture, ou Traité de la Décoration, Distribution & Construction des Bâtiments; Contenant les Leçons Données en 1750, & les Années Suivantes. . . . Paris: Desaint.

BLONDEL, JEAN FRANÇOIS 1745 Fêtes publiques données par ville de Paris, à l'occasion du mariage de Monseigneur le Dauphin les 23 et 26 fevrier 1745. Paris.

BLONDEL, JEAN FRANÇOIS 1747? Fête publique donnée par ville de Paris à l'occasion du mariage de Monseigneur le Dauphin le 13 fevrier 1747. Paris.

BLONDEL, JEAN FRANÇOIS 1755 Fragmens d'architecture . . . du Louvre. . . . Paris: Chérau.

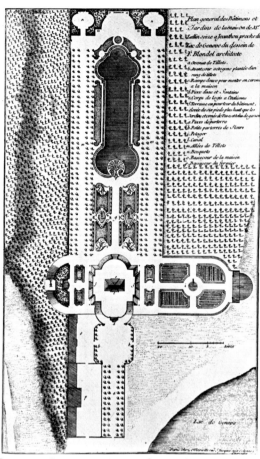

Jean François Blondel.
Aimé Lullin House and
Gardens (site plan).
Genthod, Switzerland.
1723–1725

BLONDEL, LOUIS 1924 "L'influence de l'architecture française à Genève au XVIIIe siècle, les oeuvres de Jean François Blondel." Volume 2, pages 219–225 in Actes du Congrès d'histoire de l'art. Paris: Presses universitaires de France.

BOFFRAND, GERMAIN 1745 Livre d'architecture. Paris: Cavelier.

BRISEUX, CHARLES ETIENNE (1743)1966 Art de bâtir les maisons de campagne. Reprint. Farnborough, England: Gregg.

HAUTECOEUR, LOUIS 1950 Pages 98–103 in Première moitié du XVIIIe siècle: Le style Louis XV. Volume 3 in Histoire de l'architecture classique en France. Paris: Picard.

LEJEAUX, JEANNE 1927 "Jean-François Blondel, architecte, (1663–1756)." L'Architecture 40:395–400.

LEMONNIER, HENRI (editor) 1911–1930 Procès verbaux de l'Academie Royale d'Architecture. 10 vols. Paris: Schemit.

MARIETTE, JEAN (1727)1927–1929 L'Architecture Française. 3 vols. Reprint. Paris: Vanoest. Hautecoeur reports that Blondel's work is shown on pages 410–421. Lejeaux reports that Blondel's work is to be found in volumes 1 and 3. In the set at the Burnham Library of the Art Institute of Chicago, which was part of the Percier and Fontaine Library, work by Blondel is to be found in the second volume. The plates 4, 5, 6 show the house at Charonne; 155, 156, 157, 158, 159, 160, 161 show the Mallet house; 162, 163 show the Cramer house; 164, 165, 166 show the Lullin house; and 167–168, 169, 170, 171, 172 show a project for a country house near Geneva.

SCHLUMBERGER, EVELINE 1955 "Une villa du XVIIIᵉ siècle au bord du lac de Genève." *Connaissance des Arts* 15, Oct.:42–47.

VIGNOLA, GIACOMO BAROZZI DA 1752 *Règles des cinq ordres . . . reduites de grand en petit par Monsieur Blondel, Architecte du Roy, en 1752, ...* Paris: Charpentier.

BLORE, EDWARD

Edward Blore (1787–1879), son of lawyer and topographer Thomas Blore, was raised in Stamford, England. He developed an interest in medieval architecture and became a skilled draftsman and engraver illustrating some twenty-two topographical works. Walter Scott helped him obtain his earliest commissions. He became a friend of THOMAS RICKMAN and although he had no formal training he established a practice in London by the early 1820s. He was elected a fellow of the Society of Antiquaries and of the Royal Society, was a founder of the Royal Archaeological Institute, and was awarded a D.C.L. by Oxford University. Appointed special architect to William IV and Queen Victoria, he worked at Windsor Castle (1839–1850), and after completing Buckingham Palace (1830–1850) was offered a knighthood, which he refused. He had an extensive practice designing country houses and the cheaper sort of church; his preferred style was Gothic, although he also adopted Jacobethan for some houses. His detail is based upon extensive research, evidenced by forty-eight volumes of antiquarian drawings, but there is an attenuation and lack of depth in his designs which betrays their actual date. In 1849, he retired from practice a wealthy man. WILLIAM BURGES, Henry Clutton, and P. C. HARDWICK were his most distinguished pupils.

JILL ALLIBONE

WORKS

1826–1836, Canford Manor, Dorset, England. *1828–1841, Goodrich Court, Herefordshire, England. 1829–1833, Lambeth Palace; 1830–1850, Buckingham Palace; London. 1832–1840, Aloupka, Crimea, Russia. 1833–1837, Bedford School, Bedfordshire, England. 1837–1843, Crewe Hall, Cheshire, England. 1839–1850, Windsor Castle, Berkshire, England. 1841–1843, College of Saint Mark, London. 1843–?, Glasgow Cathedral, Strathclyde, Scotland. 1845–1848, Marlborough College, Wiltshire, England.

BIBLIOGRAPHY

CROOK, J. MORDAUNT, and PORT, MICHAEL HENRY (editors) 1973 Volume 6 in *The History of the King's Works.* London: Her Majesty's Stationery Office.

EASTLAKE, CHARLES LOCK (1872)1970 Pages 138–141 in *A History of the Gothic Revival.* London: Longmans; New York: Humanities.

"The Late Mr. Edward Blore, Architect." 1879 *The Builder* 37:1019.

"The Late Mr. Edward Blore, F.R.S." 1879 *Illustrated London News* 75:279.

MELLER, HUGH DAVID 1975 "Blore's Country Houses." Unpublished M.A. thesis, University of London.

MELLER, HUGH DAVID 1977 "The Architectural History of Goodrich Court, Herefordshire." *Transactions of the Woolhope Naturalists' Field Club* 42, part 2:175.

STEPHEN, LESLIE, and LEE SIDNEY (editors) 1917 Volume 2, pages 699–700 in *The Dictionary of National Biography.* London: Oxford University Press.

BLOUET, G. ABEL

G. Abel Blouet (1795–1853) was academically trained in Paris and Rome; he was a protégé of ANTOINE QUATREMÈRE DE QUINCY. Blouet supervised the completion of the Arc de l'Etoile (1831–1836). After visiting America, he published an influential report on the design of penal institutions (1837). In 1848, he became restoration architect at Fontainebleau.

LISA B. REITZES

WORKS

1831–1836, Arc de Triomphe de l'Etoile (completion), Paris. 1840, Penal Colony, Mettray, France. 1848–1853, Whitehorse Courtyard (restoration), Sully Pavilion, and François I Gallery, Château at Fontainebleau, France.

BIBLIOGRAPHY

HAUTECOEUR, LOUIS 1943–1957 *Histoire de l'Architecture classique en France.* 7 vols. Paris: Picard.

VAN ZANTEN, DAVID 1970 "A French Architect in America in 1836." *Journal of the Society of Architectural Historians* 29:255.

BLUNTSCHLI, A. F.

Alfred Friedrich Bluntschli (1842–?), architect of the eclectic school, was born in Zurich, where he studied architecture under GOTTFRIED SEMPER. He subsequently studied under C. A. QUESTEL at the Ecole des Beaux-Arts in Paris. In 1870, Bluntschli settled in Frankfurt, where he established a successful practice with C. Jonas Mylius, building mainly houses and villas, but also the Hotel Frankfurter Hof in Frankfurt and the Kreditbank in Mannheim, Germany.

Bluntschli and Mylius became well known for their prize-winning designs for major competitions, including the City Halls for Munich, Hamburg, and Vienna, the Reichstag in Berlin, the Swiss Parliament in Bern, and the Railroad Station in Frankfurt (none built). In 1881, Bluntschli was appointed professor at the Polytechnikum in Zurich.

RON WIEDENHOEFT

BOARI, ADAMO

Born in Ferrara, Italy, Adamo Boari (1865–1928) traveled to South America, the United States, and finally to Mexico where he lived the rest of his life. He was a friend of Porfiro Diaz and was the main architect of the dictator's "Europization" of the country. His buildings are in a variety of revived and revival styles.

JOHN H. WILSON

WORKS

1904–1934, Teatro Nacional (now the Palacio de Bellas Artes); 1910, Correos Central; Mexico City.

BIBLIOGRAPHY

"Boari, Adamo." 1968 Biografías 1, volume 3 in Enciclopedia del Arte en America. Buenos Aires: Bibliográfica OMEBA.
TERRY, T. PHILIP 1935 Terry's Guide to Mexico. Boston: Houghton Mifflin.

BOBERG, FERDINAND

One of the most prestigious of Swedish architects until about 1905, when his influence was displaced by the National Romantic movement, Ferdinand Boberg (1860–1946) welded together diverse styles in works of a unique individuality. Although his earliest buildings showed the influence of H. H. RICHARDSON, Boberg's mature works were very different; rich in decoration and materials, with exotic (or, as his critics liked to put it, "oriental") touches, they were also simple in their massing and symmetrically organized, in keeping with the indigenous neoclassical tradition. Boberg was also a well-known painter and furniture designer, and made a significant contribution to many of the crafts. In 1916, he withdrew from architectural practice in order to pursue these other interests.

BARBARA MILLER LANE

WORKS

1882–1883, Rosenborg House Offices; 1891–1893, Värta Gas Works; Stockholm. 1892 Stockholm Electrical Works. 1896, Churches in Alnö, Medelpad, Sweden. 1898–1904, Central Post Office; 1899–1900. Carlsberg House (now LO House Offices); 1902–1904 Rosenbad; 1902–1905 Kronoberg Railroad Station; 1904–1905, Thielska Art Gallery; 1905, Djurgård Railroad Station; 1905–1906, Villa Bergsgarden; 1908–1909, Exposition Buildings; Stockholm. 1912, Exposition Buildings, Venice, Italy. 1912?–1913, Church, Saltsjöbaden, Sweden. 1912–1915, Nordiska Company Offices, Stockholm. 1914, Baltic Exposition Buildings, Mälmo, Sweden.

BIBLIOGRAPHY

AHLBERG, HAKON 1925 Swedish Architecture of the Twentieth Century. London: Benn. Originally published in Swedish.
ANDERSON, HENRIK O., and BEDOIRE, FREDRIC 1973 Stockholms Byggnader. Stockholm: Prisma.
EATON, LEONARD K. 1972 American Architecture Comes of Age: European Reaction to H. H. Richardson and Louis Sullivan. Cambridge, Mass.: M.I.T. Press.
FISKER, KAY 1960 "Internationalism contra Nationalromantik." Arkitekten (Denmark) 62, no. 22:369–387.
JOHANSSON, BENGT O. H. 1970 "Svensk arkitekturpolitik under 1900-talets första decennium." Pages 35–62 in Sju Uppsatser i Svensk Arkitektur Historia. Volume 2 in Rudolf Zeitler (editor), Studier utgivna av Konsthistoriska Institutionen vid Uppsala Universitet. Uppsala, Sweden: Weilands Boktryckeri.
JOHNSSON, ULF G. 1970 "Mot en ny stil—svensk arkitekturdebatt omkring 1900." Pages 7–34 in Sju Uppsatser i Svensk Arkitektur Historia. Volume 2 in Rudolf Zeitler (editor), Studier utgivna av Konsthistoriska Institutionen vid Uppsala Universitet. Uppsala, Sweden: Weilands Boktryckeri.
JOSEPHSON, RAGNAR 1958 "Arkitekten Ferdinand Boberg." Pages 40–104 in Bobergiana. Stockholm: Nordisk Rotogravyr.

BÖBLINGER, HANS, and BÖBLINGER, MATTHÄUS

Hans Böblinger the Elder (1412–1482) headed a southern German family of architects. He acquired his mason's mark in Constance in 1435. Sponsored by MATTHÄUS ENSINGER, he moved to Esslingen to work on the Frauenkirche in 1440. There he married and had five sons who became architects and a daughter who married a builder. Active in civic and professional events, Hans signed the Mason's Declaration in Regensburg in 1459. After the death of Ensinger in 1463, the elder Böblinger was appointed master of construction of the Frauenkirche in Esslingen. He died there in 1482, leaving a pattern book which, in light of recent research, is considered an important testament to cross-disciplinary activities of engravers, sculptors, goldsmiths, and architects.

Hans Böblinger's second oldest and most famous son, Matthäus Böblinger (?–1505), studied in Cologne and was an apprentice at the Frauenkirche in Esslingen. In 1477, Matthäus was hired as consultant at Ulm and in 1480 he was hired for life when he replaced ULRICH VON ENSINGEN as master. Matthäus was dismissed in 1492 for structural shortcomings and returned to Essinglen to work on the Frauenkirche.

JEANINE CLEMENTS STAGE

WORKS
HANS BÖBLINGER
1440–1482, Frauenkirche, Esslingen, Germany. 1460–1464, Church (tower), Mohringen near Stuttgart, Germany.

MATTHÄUS BÖBLINGER
c.1470, Church of Saint Martin (baptismal font), Laugenau, Germany. c.1474, Mount of Olives Monument; 1478–1492, Cathedral (tower of the minister); Ulm, Germany. 1502–1505, Frauenkirche, Esslingen, Germany.

BIBLIOGRAPHY

BUCHER, FRANÇOIS 1980 Volume 1 in *Architector: The Lodge Books of Medieval Architects*. New York: Baris.
KOEPF, HANS 1980 "Die Esslinger Frauenkirche." *Esslinger Studien* 19:3–46.

BODLEY, GEORGE F.

The buildings of George Frederick Bodley (1827–1907) represent the climax of the Gothic Revival in England. He developed a Decorated style of extreme elegance and refinement, continuing English medieval Gothic, as it were, after it had stopped with the Tudor accession and the Reformation. The Bodleys claimed descent from the founder of the Bodleian Library at Oxford and the right to use his coat of arms.

Bodley was first sent as a pupil in 1845 to GEORGE GILBERT SCOTT. He served a five-year apprenticeship with Scott, but subsequently reacted against Scott's brand of Gothic. The publication of JOHN RUSKIN's *The Seven Lamps of Architecture* (1849), followed by *The Stones of Venice* (1851–1853), had considerable influence on him. GEORGE E. STREET was also in Scott's office, as was WILLIAM H. WHITE; they shared the same religious views and were able to discuss their architectural theories and their wish to strike out on new lives. Street, who was three years older than Bodley, wrote a book, *Brick and Marble Architecture of North Italy* (1855), an important book in connection with Bodley's early work.

One of Bodley's first clients was the Reverend Thomas Keble, a well-known Tractarian. He was vicar of Bisley in Gloucestershire, with other churches in his care, one of which was Bussage

which had been built in 1846, paid for largely by a group of High Church Oxford undergraduates. To this church Bodley was invited to add a south aisle in 1854. The breakaway from Scott is hardly noticeable, but the influence of Ruskin is evident. His next church for Keble, at France Lynch (1854–1857), however, was an innovation in his first use of French Gothic tracery. The *Ecclesiologist* approved and said that "the whole design shows great merit." Other French Gothic churches followed. At Scarborough, Bodley employed the pre-Raphaelites to decorate the church and gave WILLIAM MORRIS his first chance to make ecclesiastical stained glass. In the 1860s, his style changed to forms with much interior enrichment. In 1869, THOMAS GARNER became his partner, and they did some domestic buildings. But primarily an ecclesiastical architect all his life, in 1869 also, Bodley designed Saint Augustine's Pendlebury (1870–1874), probably his greatest achievement, never surpassed in Victorian church building.

This was quickly followed by another great church in late Gothic style, Holy Angels, Hoar Cross (1872–1876), which is the ideal product of Bodley's mature fourteenth-century manner. In 1886, Bodley told the students of the Royal Academy that the golden age in England was the fourteenth century, and he showed them how he had progressed from plate tracery to the ogee line. He invented the word refinement in architecture. His pupils included NINIAN COMPER and HENRY VAUGHAN.

Bodley's later churches, such as Clumber (1886–1889) and Eccleston (1899), show a high perfection of skillful detail. He wielded greater influence on church architecture than any other English architect during the last part of the nineteenth century and the beginning of the twentieth. In 1906, Bodley was commissioned to design Washington Cathedral with his former assistant Henry Vaughan of Boston. His drawings are preserved in the Cathedral. He traveled to America in the autumn of 1906, but died on his return a year later.

DAVID VEREY

WORKS
1854, Saint Michael and All Angels (south aisle), Bussage; 1854–1857, Saint John the Baptist, France Lynch; Gloucestershire, England. 1858–1862, Saint Michael and All Angels (south aisle), Brighton, England. 1861–1863, Saint Martin-on-the-Hill, Scarborough, England. 1870–1874, Saint Augustine, Pendlebury, Lancashire, England. 1872–1876, Holy Angels, Hoar Cross, Staffordshire, England. 1886–1889, Saint Mary, Clumber, Nottinghamshire, England. 1899, Saint Mary, Eccleston, Chesire, England. 1902, Holy Trinity (chancel, nave, and south aisle), Prince Consort Road, London.

BIBLIOGRAPHY

G. F. Bodley's unpublished correspondence is in the France Lynch Church, Gloucestershire, England.

ADDLESHAW, G. W. O. 1967 "Architects, Sculptors, Painters, Craftsmen, 1660–1960, Whose Work is to Be Seen in York Minster." *Architectural History* 10:89–119.

ANSON, PETER F. 1960 *Fashions in Church Furnishings: 1840–1940.* London: Faith.

BRANDON-JONES, J. 1965 "Letters of Philip Webb and his Contemporaries." *Architectural History* 8:52–72.

CLARKE, B. F. L. (1938)1969 *Church Builders of the Nineteenth Century.* Reprint. Newton Abbot, England: David & Charles.

EASTLAKE, CHARLES L. (1872)1970 *A History of the Gothic Revival.* Reprint. Leicester (England) University Press.

SEWTER, A. C. 1974–1975 *The Stained Glass of Morris and his Circle.* 2 vols. New Haven and London: Yale University Press.

SIMPSON, F. M. 1908 "George Frederick Bodley." *Journal of the Royal Institute of British Architects* Series 3 15:145–158.

THOMPSON, PAUL 1967 *The Work of William Morris.* New York: Viking.

VEREY, DAVID 1973 "The Victorian Architects' Work in Gloucestershire." *Transactions of the Bristol and Gloucestershire Archaeological Society* 92:5–11.

WARREN, EDWARD 1910 "The Life and Work of George Frederick Bodley." *Journal of the Royal Institute of British Architects* Series 3 17:305–340.

BOETTO, GROVENALE

Grovenale Boetto (1603–1678), engraver and architect, who was born and died in Fossano, Italy, probably worked with ERCOLE NEGRO DI SANFRONT at Savigliano. His early work, however, shows greater affinity to the simple forms of ASCANIO VITOZZI. San Francesco Saverio, Mondovi Piazza (1665–1677), and San Agostino, Cherasco (1668–1687), his most successful works, are longitudinal in plan with a pronounced cross axis covered by a pendentive dome. Extensive fresco decoration is integral to Boetto's conception for these churches.

HENRY A. MILLON

WORKS

1641–1648, Santurario dell'Apparizione, Savigliano, Italy. 1643–1659, Assunta, Bene Vagienna, Italy. 1648–1656, San Biagio, Pamparato, Italy. 1665–1677, San Francesco Saverio, Mondovi Piazza, Italy. 1668–1687, Sant'Agostino (frescoes by ANDREA POZZO), Cherasco, Italy. Begun 1680, San Rocco, Cavallermaggiore, Italy.

BIBLIOGRAPHY

BAUDI DI VESME, ALESSANDRO 1963 "Boetto, Giovenale." Volume 1, pages 143–148 in *Schede Vesme.* Turin, Italy: Stamperia Artistica Nazionale.

BRAYDA, CARLO; COLI, LAURA; and SESIA, DARIO 1963 Page 18 in *Ingegneri e architetti del sei e settecento in Piemonte.* Turin, Italy: Società degli ingegneri e degli architti.

CARBONERI, NINO; GRISERI, ANDREA; and MORRA, CARLO 1966 Pages 9–29 in *Giovenale Boetto.* Fossano, Italy: Risparmio.

Bodley.
Saint Augustine.
Pendlebury, Lancashire, England.
1870–1874

BOFFRAND, GERMAIN

Germain Boffrand (1667–1754) was the greatest French architect in the first half of the eighteenth century: his first independent work dates from 1700 and his last from 1753. He was curiously outside of his time—looking back to the early French classicism of LOUIS LE VAU and being the teacher and forerunner of the neoclassicist generation that followed him—but he also produced that perfect example of the fashionable rococo style of his own days, the upper oval salon of the Hôtel de Soubise in Paris.

Born in Nantes as the son of a minor sculptor and architect, Boffrand went to Paris to learn the same arts with the leading men in those fields, François Girardon and JULES HARDOUIN MANSART. Having had his apprenticeship in the vast royal building organization headed by Mansart, he became, before the turn of the century, curator of its archives and project manager at Place Vendôme.

Apart from the court, the second milieu which was decisive for his life was that of men of law, the Parliament, and later on the Hôpital Général.

In 1700, Boffrand built the Hôtel LeBrun in Paris; in 1702, Mansart sent him to Nancy as his substitute. There, in the last independent state inside present-day France, he soon took over from Mansart, and during the next twenty years, he planned and executed most of the major tasks a princely court could offer—the Palais Ducal at Nancy (1715–1722), the Château of Lunéville (1702–1722), and the Malgrange (1711–1717). He also provided projects and advice to the local nobility (foremost to the princes Craon and Vaudémont); he was involved in the completion of Mansart's Primatiale Church; and he probably had a decisive part in the elaboration of the plans for Saint-Jacques at Lunéville. Named first architect to the duke of Lorraine in 1711, after the death of Mansart in 1708, he was also reemployed in the royal building office and was received directly in the first class of the Academy in 1709.

The first two decades of the century were the happiest in Boffrand's life as an architect: there were not only his monumental works in Lorraine and less important ones for the elector Max-Emmanuel of Bavaria in Brussels and Paris, but he also built and modernized numerous townhouses in Paris. His clients included Anne de Bavière, princesse de Condé; the prince de Rohan; the mistress of the duke of Orléans; and the president De Mesme; but his most interesting Paris hôtels were built on his own account and sold afterward to ministers, marshals, and ambassadors. Thus, he played a major role in the development of the fauborgs Saint-Germain and Saint-Honoré and the Place Vendôme. With the last of these speculative operations—the proposal for a unified building scheme for the grounds of the Hôtel de Soissons—he overstrained his means in 1718 and was ruined in 1719 by the crash of Law's Mississippi Company.

After 1720, Boffrand's career took a different turn. Because of political changes, Lorraine patronage ceased, and he had no part in the next expansive phase of Paris hôtel building. The administrative aspect of his work predominated; he also wrote and developed vast urban schemes.

Although he was consulted by the prince-bishop of Würzburg on his residence, working with JOHANN BALTHASAR NEUMANN during the latter's sojourn in Paris and producing a plan for a cascade for another Schönborn, the archbishop of Mainz, Boffrand's hopes for a second court career did not materialize.

His only major work in private architecture during this phase was the decoration of the two main apartments in the Hôtel de Soubise (1732–1739) with the addition of a corner pavilion housing the famous oval salons. He started again to speculate, but apparently less on construction or sites than on objects such as the Picardie channel or the exploitation of a patent for the processing of lead for the building trade.

His Paris connections gave Boffrand the opportunity to redecorate the Grande Chambre of the Palais de Justice for the coming-of-age of Louis XV and to take over the restoration of Notre Dame, where he made a new rose window in the north transept and a funerary chapel for the archbishop (1725–1727).

In 1724, he had become the architect and a member of the board of the highly influential Hôpital Genéral (the administration of most Paris hospitals headed by the archbishop and members of Parliament); for this body he produced his most admired technical work, the well and reservoir at Bicêtre (1733–1740), and his last architectural achievement, the Foundling Hospital (1746–1751) opposite Notre Dame, including the reorganization of the square in between. In 1732, already at an advanced age, he entered the Departement Ponts des Chaussées (the central administration of French highways) and continued to move slowly up the ranks, becoming in 1742 *premier ingénieur* and in 1743 *inspecteur général;* he built several bridges (another technical accomplishment of his was the invention of steam pumps).

In 1745, Boffrand published a book on the

Boffrand.
Oval Salon, Hôtel de
Soubise.
Paris.
1732–1739

general principles of architecture illustrated by plans and elevations of existing buildings in France and abroad. In the Academy he had taken an active interest in theoretical questions since the beginning.

In 1748, he submitted three projects in the open competition for a Place Royale in Paris and got wide support for his proposals; in 1753, in the closed competition for the final site—the future Place de la Concorde—it was again he who produced the solution for the way to deal with such an unusual open space.

This last attempt is quite revealing insofar as it demonstrates the architect's ability to deal individually with each problem, his inventiveness, and his originality. As a consequence, his oeuvre at first glance shows less coherence than that of ROBERT DE COTTE with its closely knit network of forms. De Cotte, Boffrand's main rival, depository and refiner of the French heritage, and its official representative as successor of Jules Hardouin Mansart, was subdued in his plans and elevations; Boffrand preferred bolder and seemingly simpler choices and worked toward a strong central accent and the great form. He liked volumes and intact wall surfaces on the one hand and the classical orders on the other, but he did not contaminate them in a baroque sense, emphasizing thus the academic and symbolic value of the orders by their separate existence. Having never been to Italy, he was nevertheless the most Italianate architect of his time, and his debt to ANDREA PALLADIO has always been recognized.

Boffrand stressed the horizontal continuity by cornices which not only separate the floors but also link the segmental arches of the windows and the imposts of semicircular openings, thus creating undulating lines. The semicircular arch is one of his guiding forms, applied equally outside and inside. Arches and cornices running in a broad rhythm around a room give a strong feeling of spatial unity. Thinking architectonically, Boffrand arrived equally—and earlier than the mere decorators—at the complete fusion of forms that characterized rococo interiors. Other elements in this fusion are the reinforcement of frame moldings, the presence of garlands, and the unification of the coving. Tending in rectangular rooms to obscure the angles, Boffrand cherished the oval and circular room: from the Bouchefort Hunting Lodge (1704–1706) and the Malgrange to the Pavilion of the duchess of Maine at the Arsenal, Paris (1729). He also introduced salons of that form in preexisting structures such as the Hôtel de Canillac (1708), the Château of Croismare (1710–1712), the Château of Bugnéville, and most splendidly at the Hôtel de Soubise.

It is a distinctive mark of Boffrand that he added significant and monumental units to a less accentuated or neutral context. He was charged to do just this with the main block of the Château of Commercy, where the prince was dissatisfied with the undistinguished ensemble produced by his architects. This was also the case with the grand attic elevation surmounted by cannons and trophies he put on the center part of the rather utilitarian façades of the Paris Arsenal. Counterproof is provided by the great *hôtel* Boffrand built on his own and sold to the Marquis de Torcy; the buyer, splendid minister that he was, still asked for the elimination of the gallery on the first floor and its division into apartments.

Monumentality and dignity are to be found in the use of classical porches, from the early Hunting Lodge at Bouchefort to the late Foundling Hospital; in the giant order at Lunéville and at Malgrange; and in the elevations of the Palace Ducal in Nancy and his late Parisian urban projects.

The Hôtel LeBrun is a nude and isolated block, dignified only by a fine entablature and the pedi-

Boffrand.
Château.
Lunéville, France.
1702–1722

Boffrand.
Pétit Luxembourg.
Paris.
1709–1711

ments—an emblematic beginning. In spite of the frequent use of the giant order, the horizontal dimension remains predominant during Boffrand's central period; only in his late works a certain verticalism can be observed. Despite horizontalism and a search for monumentality, Boffrand's buildings are not heavy: smooth surfaces and fine lines preserve the general stylistic outlook of this period. His most elegantly decorated façades were probably those of the early Hôtel d'Argenton (1704–1705). The chapel of the Lunéville Château with its widely spaced, superimposed fluted columns proves the lightness of which he was capable.

Boffrand was a master of plans. The most famous one is that of the Hôtel d'Amelot (1712–1714), where the court is a perfect oval and the wings are graded down logically from the giant order of the central part; in the interior the curve is perfectly assimilated and leads to interesting room plans. Both elements—the giant order in the *hôtel particulier* and the rounding off of the corners between corps-de-logis and wings—have precedents in the French architecture of the mid-seventeenth century, but never before was such a complete fusion attempted. The Hôtel de Torcy (1713–1715) is the largest one, with two imposing axes; here as elsewhere, Boffrand attributed great value to proper sequences of proportions in his apartments. The Petit Luxembourg (1709–1711) in Paris gives another testimony of his inclination toward the great form: confronted with certain restrictions of the site, Boffrand chose to isolate a highly representative suite and to place the kitchen on the other side of the street, connected by an underground passage.

His most original plans Boffrand devised for a *maison de plaisance,* the Malgrange, a prototype revision of Le Vau's Vaux-le-Vicomte with two small interior courts. Malgrange is on the same lines as JOHANN BERNARD FISCHER VON ERLACH'S garden-palace Althann and FILIPPO JUVARRA'S Stupinigi. A minor *maison de plaisance* at Saint-Ouen can be described as a synthesis of ideas from Mansart's Trianon, Marly, and Château du Val, adjusted for a different age.

For the residences of the duke of Lorraine, Boffrand chose the Louvre and Versailles as models in a nearly iconic acceptance. His "Louvre" is a severely classical four-wing building, of which only the slight concavity of the main façade on the Carrière square seems baroque. (This can be explained more legitimately in the light of its urbanistic position; ideas announcing the ensemble later realized by EMMANUEL HÉRÉ DE CORNY probably were already in the air.) The Château of Lunéville differs from its model, Versailles, in that the central pavilion is a kind of empty gesture, since it does not contain the sovereign's bedroom (the ducal apartment was situated in the garden wing). The concept of an open axis from the court to the gardens goes back to ideal plans by Jean Androuet du Cerceau (see DU CERCEAU FAMILY) and Jean Marot and had been realized in LeBrun's country house at Montmorency.

In his early salons, Boffrand followed the line that goes from Vaux-le-Vicomte to Marly: they are two-storied with herms or ignudi. His paneling is not diffuse but accentuates the center motif and frame, with forceful lines and naturalistic ornament. Whereas the decoration of the Petit Luxembourg provided an incunabula of the Regence style, in the Hôtel de Soubise Boffrand created a dense synthesis of animated paneling, with sculpture and painting as highlights in the oval salons. Boffrand continued in his interiors the Louis XIV tradition of illusionistic painting: the gallery of the Hôtel du Premier Président (1712–1714) ended in a perspective by Boyer, and the entire chapel of the Foundling Hospital was painted by Brunetti and Natoire to be a ruin with nuns and children shown as looking at the Nativity and Adoration of the Magi (Natoire was Boffrand's favorite collaborator as a painter).

Complementary to his role as decorator, Boffrand might be seen as the principal representative in his times of the great French tradition of stonecutting: the projecting salons of the Hôtel de Canillac and of the Arsenal pavilion were supported by squinches and consoles respectively; the kitchen of the Petit Luxembourg and the reservoir at Bicêtre have most impressive vaults.

With regard to theory, Boffrand proved to be

orthodox, defending the *règles* and the *beau réel,* opposed to fashion (against rococo excesses, yet slightly open to Gothic). He insisted on *convenance,* on the role of nation and patron. Boffrand's fame is based on his Paris *hôtels* and on his historical role as the man who brought classical architecture to Lorraine.

JÖRG GARMS

WORKS

1700, Hôtel LeBrun, Paris. 1702–1722, Château, Lunéville, Lorraine, France. *1704–1705, Hôtel d'Argenton, Paris. *1704–1706, Hunting Lodge, Bouchefort, near Brussels. *(A)1708, Château de Bugnéville, Lorraine, France. *1708, Hôtel de Canillac (additions); 1709–1711, Petit Luxembourg; Paris. *1710–1712, Château de Croismare, Lorraine, France. 1711–1714, Hôtel de Duras, Paris. *1711–1717, La Malgrange, near Nancy, France. 1712, Château de Commercy (central pavilion), Lorraine, France. 1712, Château d'Haroué, Lorraine, France. 1712, Hôtel de Craon, Nancy, France. 1712–1714, Hôtel d'Amelot; *1712–1714, Hôtel du Premier Président (modernization), Palais de Justice; 1713–1715, Hôtel de Torcy (now German Embassy); Paris. *1715–1722, Palais Ducal, Nancy, France. 1715–1725, Arsenal (river wing), Paris. *1717, Maison du Prince de Rohan, Saint-Ouen, near Paris. 1725–1727, Notre Dame (restoration); *1729, Pavilion of the duchess of Maine, Arsenal; Paris. (A)1730–1747, Saint-Jacques, Lunéville, France. 1732–1739, Hôtel de Soubise (oval salons), Paris. 1733–1740, Well and Reservoir, Hospital, Bicêtre, near Paris. *1746–1751, Foundling Hospital, Paris.

BIBLIOGRAPHY

BABELON, JEAN-PIERRE 1958 *Musée de l'Histoire de France.* Volume 1 in *Historiques et description des bâtiments des Archives Nationales.* Paris: Imprimerie Nationale.
BABELON, JEAN-PIERRE 1969 "Les façades sur jardin des palais Rohan-Soubise." *Revue de l'art* 4:66–73.
BABELON, JEAN-PIERRE 1970 "Le Palais de l'Arsenal à Paris." *Bulletin Monumental* 128:267–310.
BERCKENHAGEN, ECKHART (editor) 1970 *Die französischen Zeichnungen der Kunstbibliothek Berlin. Kritischer Katalog.* Berlin: Hessling.
BLOMFIELD, REGINALD (1921)1974 *A History of French Architecture from the Death of Mazarin to the Death of Louis XV: 1661–1774.* Reprint. New York: Hacker.
BLONDEL, JACQUES-FRANÇOIS 1752–1756 *Architecture Française.* 4 vols. Paris: Jombert.
BOFFRAND, GERMAIN (1745)1969 *Livre d'Architecture.* Reprint. Farnsborough, England: Gregg.
BOUDON, FRANÇOISE 1973 "Urbanisme et spéculation à Paris au XVIIIᵉ siècle: Le terrain de l'Hôtel de Soissons." *Journal of the Society of Architectural Historians* 32:267–307.
BRICE, GERMAIN 1971 *Description de la ville de Paris.* Reprint. Geneva: Droz; Paris: Minard.
COCHE DE LA FERTÉ, ETIENNE 1969 "Le Faubourg Saint Germain dans l'Orient séditieux." *L'Oeil* 176–177:20–27.
DEZALLIER D'ARGENVILLE, ANTOINE NICOLAS 1787 *Vie des fameux architectes et sculpteurs.* Paris: Debure.
GARMS, JÖRG 1962 "Studien zu Boffrand." Unpublished Ph.D. dissertation, University of Vienna.
GARMS, JÖRG 1964a "Boffrand à l'église de la Merci." *Bulletin de la Société d'Histoire de l'Art Français* 1964:184–187.
GARMS, JÖRG 1964b "L'aménagement du parvis de Notre Dame par Boffrand." *Art de France* 4:153–157.
GARMS, JÖRG 1967a "Les projets de Mansart et de Boffrand pour le Palais Ducal de Nancy." *Bulletin Monumental* 125:231–246.
GARMS, JÖRG 1967b "Projects for the Pont Neuf and the Place Dauphine in the First Half of the 18th Century." *Journal of the Society of Architectural Historians* 26:102–113.
GARMS, JÖRG 1969 "Der Grundriss der Malgrange I von Boffrand." *Wiener Jahrbuch für Kunstgeschichte* 22:184–188.
GRANET, SOLANGE 1961 "Le Livre de Vérité de la Place Louis XV." *Bulletin de la Société d'Histoire de l'Art Français* 1961:107–113.
HAUTECOEUR, LOUIS 1950 *Première moitié du XVIIIᵉ siècle: Le style Louis XV.* Volume 3 in *Histoire de l'Architecture Classique en France.* Paris: Picard.
HERRMANN, WOLFGANG 1962 *Laugier and Eighteenth Century French Theory.* London: Zwemmer.
KALNEIN, WEND, AND LEVEY, MICHAEL 1972 *Art and Architecture of the Eighteenth Century in France.* Harmondsworth, England: Penguin.
KAUFMANN, EMIL 1955 *Architecture in the Age of Reason.* Cambridge, Mass.: Harvard University Press.
KIMBALL, FISKE (1943)1964 *The Creation of the Rococo.* Reprint. New York: Norton.
LA FONT DE SAINT-YENNE (1749)1752 *L'ombre du Grand Colbert.* Rev. ed. The Hague.
MIDDLETON, R. D. 1962 "The Abbé de Cordemoy and the Gothic Ideal." *Journal of the Warburg and Courtauld Institutes* 25:278–320.
MOREY, MATHIEU PROSPER 1866 *Notice sur la vie et les oeuvres de Germain Boffrand.* Nancy, France: Raybois.
PATTE, PIERRE 1754 *Discours sur l'Architecture.* Paris: Quillau.
PATTE, PIERRE 1765 *Monumens érigés à la gloire de Louis XV.* Paris: The author.
RAMBAUD, MIREILLE (editor) 1964–1971 *Documents du Minutier Central concernant l'histoire de l'art (1700–1750).* 2 vols. Paris: S.E.V.P.E.N. Volume 3 forthcoming.

BOGARDUS, JAMES

James Bogardus (1800–1874), a prolific mechanical and structural inventor, was born in Catskill, New York on March 14, 1800. Typical of the "ingenious Yankees" of the early and middle years of the nineteenth century, Bogardus received an irregular education on only the elementary level, which terminated in 1814, when he was apprenticed to a watchmaker in his native town. Although he appears to have been successful in learning the trade, he eventually moved to New York City, where in a few years his career offered the perfect exemplification of the American success story. Before he reached middle age he had been granted patents for a succession of mechanical inventions, chief of which were new types of clocks (1830), improvements in the machinery for spinning cotton thread (1830), an eccentric sugar mill (1831), a clock-striking mechanism (1832), and the eversharp pencil in a metal tube (1835). In the following year he made a trip to England, and in 1839 the British government awarded him a prize of two thousand dollars for an engraving machine which he had first developed, though without securing a patent, in 1831. Other inventions came in 1840–1847, following his return to the United States—a mill for grinding the white lead oxide used in paint, a rice mill, and a dynamometer for stationary engines.

At this juncture Bogardus turned to the structural arts. In 1848 he established a foundry in New York for casting, among other objects, the structural elements and the utilitarian and decorative details of buildings. There was nothing novel about the use of cast-iron members for a primary role in construction: they had been introduced in England as early as 1772; several foundrymen in New York, Boston, Rochester, and other cities, most notably DANIEL BADGER, had anticipated Bogardus in the production of columns, beams, smaller structural shapes, and enclosing elements. What set these two iron manufacturers apart from their competitors was the thoroughgoing exploitation of the technique that led to radical alterations in the traditional structural character of multistory buildings. It must be realized, however, that the novel forms of buildings for which Bogardus manufactured the components were the work of architects as much as that of the inventor.

Bogardus.
Factory Patent Drawing.

In 1849 he was granted a patent for the first complete iron building: sills on stone foundations, columns, and primary girders were to be made of cast iron, and floor beams, tie rods, floor plates, and probably roof trusses were to consist of or to be assembled from wrought iron elements, although the floor plates, perforated to reduce weight, could have been cast. No evidence exists that such an all-iron building was ever constructed, but Bogardus possessed an unbounded enthusiasm for its potentialities, going so far as to suggest that iron buildings could be carried to a height of ten miles.

The chronology of the earliest structural works for which the inventor manufactured the iron components has not been precisely determined. The pioneer essays were both erected in the years 1848–1849: the Bogardus factory was built in stages over both years, whereas the first building erected for an independent owner, the unified group known as the Laing Stores in New York, appears to have completed before the end of the earlier year. In both cases timber girders (and very likely timber flooring on brick arches) took the place of the comparable elements of iron in the patent description. The factory was carefully designed to be a demountable structure and hence answered all the esential criteria for a prefabricated building. By far the most important work with which Bogardus was associated was the printing plant of Harper and Brothers, erected on Franklin Square in New York in 1854 after the plans of the architect JOHN B. CORLIES. The entire façade was an open framework of cast-iron columns, arched lintels, and spandrels enclosing the large floor-to-ceiling windows. The interior flooring and floor arches were supported by wrought-iron floor beams spanning between arched cast-iron girders with wrought-iron ties, the composite forms carried in turn by hollow cast iron columns. The floor beams were part of the first lot of 7-inch wrought iron beams to be rolled in the United States, the successful manufacturer in this prolonged effort being the Trenton Iron Works in New Jersey. Except for the thin party walls at the sides and rear, the Harper plant was a shell of glass supported by an iron frame. Bogardus erected a number of closely similar buildings in other cities, most notably newspaper plants in Philadelphia and Baltimore.

Possibly more prophetic than the iron-framed, iron-fronted buildings were a project for the Crystal Palace of the New York Exposition of 1853 and a series of free-standing iron-framed towers (1851, 1853, 1855). The exposition building would have been the first suspended structure in the United States, while the towers might be regarded as a minor but valuable step in the direction of the skeleton construction appropriate to the skyscraper. The first three were fire lookout towers which consisted of an open, free-standing iron framework of columns arranged in a square plan and of beams acting as ties set at vertical intervals, an internal iron stairway, and an observation deck. More advanced than these simple frames were the towers erected for the manufacture of shot, of which the most impressive was constructed for the McCullough Shot and Lead Company in 1855. Having the over-all form of an upward-tapering octagonal prism, the primary structure consisted of eight stands of columns tied at intervals by beams, the various members joined by bolted connections. The open interior was enclosed by brick walls supported as individual panels by the beams and columns of the frame. The brick screen was thus a primitive form of the multistory curtain wall. Other structures followed the shot tower, but Bogardus's major works were concentrated in the 1850s. He remained active through the succeeding decade and died in New York on April 13, 1874.

CARL W. CONDIT

WORKS

*1848, Laing Stores; *1848–1849, Bogardus Foundry and Manufactory; *1851, Fire Tower; *1853, Fire Tower; *1854, Harper and Brothers Printing Plant; *1855, Fire Tower; *1855, McCullough Shot Tower; New York.

BIBLIOGRAPHY

BANNISTER, TURPIN C. 1956–1957 "Bogardus Revisited." *Journal of the Society of Architectural Historians* 15, Dec.:12–22; 16, Mar.:11–19.
BOGARDUS, JAMES 1856 *Cast Iron Buildings: Their Construction and Advantages.* New York: Harrison.
"Bogardus, James." 1929 Volume 2, pages 407–408 in *Dictionary of American Biography.* New York: Scribner.
CONDIT, CARL W. 1968 *American Building: Materials and Techniques from the First Colonial Settlements to the Present.* University of Chicago Press.

BOGNER, WALTER FRANCIS

Walter Francis Bogner (1899–) was a member of that generation of architects who were trained in the traditional Beaux-Arts methods but who practiced, wrote, and taught during the halcyon years of modernism in America. Born in Providence, Rhode Island, he studied at the State Technical School, Austria (1914–1919), and at the Harvard School of Architecture (1922–1923), where he taught from 1929 to 1966. After the formation of the Graduate School of Design at Harvard in 1937,

Bogner became a colleague and follower of WALTER GROPIUS and associated with Gropius and the Boston Center Architects for the Boston Back Bay Development plan of 1953.

ANTHONY ALOFSIN

WORKS

1939, Walter F. Bogner House, Lincoln, Mass. 1940, Garett Birkhoff House, Cambridge, Mass. 1941, May L. Jacobs House, Lincoln, Mass. 1941, E. J. Kingsbury House, Keen, N.H.

BIBLIOGRAPHY

FORD, JAMES, and FORD, KATHERINE 1940 *The Modern House in America.* New York: Architectural Book Publishing.

BOHIGAS, MARTORELL, and MACKAY

José Oriol Bohigas Guardiola (1925–) was born in Barcelona, Spain, and graduated from the School of Architecture there in 1951. He received a doctorate in architecture in 1963 and has been teaching architecture in Barcelona. He has many publications to his name.

José Martorell Codina (1925–) was born in Barcelona and graduated from the School of Architecture there in 1951, together with Bohigas with whom he founded the "Grupo R" and with whom he established an office in 1952. He received a doctorate in architecture in 1963.

David Mackay (1933–) was born in Eastbourne, Sussex, England. He joined the Bohigas and Martorell office in 1960.

This group of architects has realized a great number of houses, public buildings, schools, and factories. The group does not have a defined style since it has always attempted to be at the forefront of the most advanced trends in the world. In certain works, the influence of the English Brutalists appears; in others, one detects that of LE CORBUSIER, PHILIP C. JOHNSON, and Aldo Rossi. Their posture has always been to play with the style dominant in a country at that moment. In 1952, they initiated the fight against classicism and in 1965 against rationalism. Their buildings are intentionally polemical and in many cases pretend to demonstrate ideas of progressive social and political character even when the majority of their commissions come from the bourgeoisie and the government. Their work has been discussed in many Spanish and foreign journals and has been commented on by critics throughout the world.

JUAN BASSEGODA NONELL
Translated from Spanish by
Judith E. Meighan

WORKS

1952–1962, Bloque Escorial; 1959–1962, House, Cahner; 1962–1965, 28 La Vanguardia, Pelayo Street; Barcelona, Spain. 1969–1973, Bloque La Salut, San Feliu de Llobregat, Spain. 1971–1973, Pals Golf Houses, Gerona, Spain. 1978, Banco de España (additions), Madrid. 1980, Parque de España, Rosario, Argentina. 1981, Parque Sarmiento, Cordoba, Argentina.

BIBLIOGRAPHY

BENEVOLO, LEONARDO (1960)1971 *History of Modern Architecture*. 2 vols. Cambridge, Mass.: M.I.T. Press.
BOHIGAS, ORIOL 1976 "Actualidad de la arquitectura Catalana." *Arquitecturas/bis.* nos. 13–14:2–26.
"Casa Heredero." 1970 *Cuadernos de Arquitectura* no. 75:25–32.
"Comentario al Pueblo Español." 1961 *Arquitectura* 3, no. 35:14–25.
FLORES LOPEZ, CARLOS 1961 *Arquitectura española contemporánea*. Madrid: Aguilar.
HERNÁNDEZ CROS, J. E. 1978 *Guía de Arquitectura de Barcelona*. Barcelona, Spain: Colegio de Arquitectos.

BÖHM, DOMINIKUS

Dominikus Böhm (1880–1955), the German pioneer of modern Roman Catholic church architecture, was born in the Swabian town of Jettingen. From his father, an architect, and his mother, whose family maintained a tradition of rural handicrafts, he imbibed a strong feeling for the inherent properties of materials. After his father's death, his older brother took over the architectural office in which Dominikus worked while attending the Bauschule in Augsburg. He then studied at the Technische Hochschule in Stuttgart under the revered THEODOR FISCHER, who developed further his sense of the proper use of materials and building methods.

In 1907, Böhm began teaching at the Bauschule in Bingen. The following year, some models and drawings which he exhibited at Darmstadt elicited an invitation from Hugo Eberhard, head of the School of Architecture and Applied Arts at Offenbach am Main, to join his faculty. Böhm taught at Offenbach for eighteen years, building a reputation as a masterful teacher.

At Offenbach, Böhm was introduced to the liturgical movement by his student Martin Weber, an oblate or lay associate of the Abbey of Maria Laach. This abbey was a leading center of the movement, whose aim was to stimulate more active and conscious participation in the public worship of the church. The ideals of the liturgical movement, colored by the Germanic sense of the sacred, led Böhm to regard the church building as the visible expression of the mystery of Christian worship, whose design exacted from the architect the very highest standards.

There is nothing remarkable about the relatively few commissions Böhm carried out before his service in the German army in 1918. But his first executed church, the "temporary" Saint Joseph in Offenbach (1919–1920), a transformed barracks, attracted critical attention for the frank expression of its wooden construction and the spatial unity of the interior. It already manifested his lifelong concern with light as a primary element of church design in the accent the altar received from large windows on both sides. Similar qualities appeared in the village church of Saints Peter and Paul (1922–1923), Dettingen, but now with walls of sandstone—Böhm's first work executed in association with Martin Weber. The two also collaborated on the large Saint Benedict's Abbey (1922–1924) in Vaals, Holland, where Böhm set the tabernacle in the apse wall, leaving the altar to stand free as a simple table in front of it.

Certain exaggerated Gothic references in these three works show in Böhm an Expressionist tendency that reached its peak in his Saint John the Baptist (1921–1927), Neu-Ulm, Germany. The massive stone façade has a central tower whose stubbiness is emphasized by the three tall pointed arches sheltering the doors. Inside, creased-paper-like cellular vaults resemble contemporary Expressionist movie sets in their psychological intensity. They also attest to Böhm's inventive handling of materials, since they were executed in reinforced concrete by a novel method that dispensed with formwork. Böhm used conventional formwork for his brick and concrete church of Christ the King (1926) in Bischofsheim. Here, the unity of the congregation with the altar is stressed by a continuous parabolic vault that binds nave and sanctuary into one unbroken space, articulated by cross vaults for the windows. He introduced an arrangement for the choir which he used frequently thereafter, emphasizing its liturgical role by locating it in a side gallery directly overlooking the altar.

In 1927, a design by Böhm and RUDOLF SCHWARZ, who had joined the faculty at Offenbach in 1925, won the competition for the Frauenfriedenskirche in Frankfurt. The pair conceived an unadorned rectangular room, with the congregation ordered in a double column toward the sanctuary. The latter was undifferentiated from the nave except by its dramatic elevation and large windows, the only breaks in the side walls, to illuminate the single table altar. This radical break with historical church styles was never executed, but its basic concept appears in Böhm's modest cubic white vacationers' church (1931) at Norderney.

The competition project signaled a new phase in Böhm's career. In 1926, he had accepted the invitation from Konrad Adenauer, then mayor of Cologne, to head the division of church art at the Cologne Werkschule at the same time that RICHARD RIEMERSCHMID was named the school's director. Böhm held this position until the Nazis removed him in 1934; he later returned to teach there from 1947 to 1953. His early years in Cologne were intensely active. He supervised the Roman Catholic section of the famed Pressa Exhibition of 1928, for which he designed the cylindrical Immaculate Conception Chapel. He executed private homes, including his own house in Cologne (1931–1932), business and industrial buildings, and a number of Roman Catholic hospitals and other institutions with attached churches. All of these manifest the same simplicity and stress on pure geometric shapes which characterized the Frauenfriedenskirche design and, indeed, the emerging International style.

The characteristics of Böhm's style at this time are summed up in the brick Saint Joseph Church (1930–1931), Hindenburg. Its continuous flat ceiling stresses the unity of the interior space, despite the elevation of the sanctuary for visibility. A series of side chapels is created by projecting wall segments, pierced by arches at their bases to form processional passages. This type of passage appeared frequently in his churches, as did the stacked tiers of brick arches that curtain the ambulatory behind the altar and that also provide the dominant façade motif, enclosing a quiet atrium between the flanking blank towers.

Böhm had also entered a circular plan in the Frauenfriedenskirche competition. This plan was further developed in his Saint Engelbert Church (1930–1932) in Cologne-Riehl. The congregation is gathered under a ring of clustered parabolic vaults which are clearly expressed on the exterior. Yet the dialogic nature of the Roman Catholic liturgy is acknowledged by placing the altar not in the center of the circle, but under another parabolic vault which projects from the circumference and is strongly lighted from a side window to give it added focus.

Under the National Socialist regime, with its increasing restrictions on church bulding, Böhm resorted to radical simplifications of traditional German forms, especially of the Ottonian and Romanesque periods. Probably his best from these years is the Village Church (1935–1936) at Ringenberg. For the first time, he grouped the assembly closely in three arms around the altar, which stands under a massive square crossing tower. A second table above and behind the tabernacle on the altar enables the priest to celebrate mass facing the people as well as in the traditional manner with his back to them. A large window behind the altar here as in other Böhm churches suggests that light emanates from the altar itself.

The aerial bombardment of World War II left an enormous number of German churches in ruins. In the rebuilding projects entrusted to him, Böhm sought to preserve what he could of what remained and to integrate it with frankly modern additions re-ordered for better liturgical participation. In Saint Joseph (1948–1950), Duisburg, the still-standing neo-Gothic aisle was retained as a confessional chapel opening alongside the new rectangular eucharistic hall with its screenlike window filling the wall behind the altar. In both Saint Martin (1949–1951), Cochem, and the Roman Catholic church in Geilenkirchen-Hünshofen (1950–1951, built in association with his son GOTTFRIED BÖHM), new, larger worship halls were built at right angles to surviving Gothic choirs, which became specialized chapels attached to one side.

Böhm was also active designing new churches in the postwar period. His Saint Mary's (1951–1953), Ochtrup, is a bright, wide rectangular space which unites the congregation easily with the action at the altar. Its subtly curved shell vaults are carried on delicate struts which offer little visual obstruction. The baptistery is in the base of the powerful tower which stands before the left-hand corner of the wide-gabled façade, with its dominating circular window. Böhm's best postwar church is Mary the Queen in Cologne—Marienburg (1953–1954). It is a nearly square room with a low platform extending forward from a shallow apse to bring the simple table altar into intimate relationship with the assembly. The south wall is entirely of stained glass in a gray–green leaf pattern over which play the shadows cast by the surrounding trees. This window is punctured near the sanctuary by a glassed-in passage leading to the depressed circular baptistery, entirely sheathed in colored glass. Böhm, a master stained-glass worker, designed the windows for many of his churches, but none is more effective than this.

Böhm's influence had spread internationally through publications of his work, through his competition design for San Salvador Cathedral (1953, unexecuted), and through his many students and collaborators. His son, Gottfried Böhm, who had shared his practice since 1952, took over his father's office.

HOWARD V. NIEBLING

WORKS

*1919–1920, Temporary Church of Saint Joseph, Offenbach am Main, Germany. 1921–1927, Saint John the Baptist Church, Neu-Ulm, Germany. 1922–1923,

Saints Peter and Paul Church (with Martin Weber), Dettingen am Main, Germany. 1922–1924, Abbey of Saint Benedict (with Weber), Vaals, Netherlands. 1926, Christ the King Church, Mainz—Bischofsheim, Germany. *1928, Immaculate Conception Chapel, Pressa Exhibition, Cologne, Germany. 1929, Saint Camillus Workers' Welfare Home; 1929, Savings Bank; 1929, Technical School; Hindenburg, Germany. 1929–1930, General Secretariate of the Kolping Works, Cologne, Germany. 1929–1931, Catholic Seminary, Limburg an der Lahn, Germany. 1929–1931, Saint Camillus Asthma Hospital and Church, Mönchengladbach, Germany. 1930–1931, Saint Joseph Church, Hindenburg, Germany. 1930–1931, Zanders Paper Factory, Bergisch—Gladbach, Germany. 1930–1932, Caritas Institute Hospital Church of Saint Elisabeth, Cologne—Hohenlind, Germany. 1930–1932, Saint Engelbert Church, Cologne-Riehl, Germany. 1931, Summer Church, Norderney, Germany. 1931–1932, Diaspora Church, Marienburg, Germany. 1931–1932, Dominikus Böhm House, Cologne-Marienburg, Germany. 1933–1934, Country Home for Youth, Voiswinkel near Bergisch—Gladbach, Germany. 1934–1936, Saint Engelbert Church, Essen, Germany. 1935, Saint Marien Church, Nordhorn-Frenswegen, Germany. 1935–1936, Village Church, Ringenberg, Germany. 1936, Heart of Jesus Church, Bremen-Neustadt, Germany. 1937–1939, Holy Cross Church, Dülmen, Germany. 1938–1940, Saint Wolfgang Church, Regensburg-Kumpfmühl, Germany. 1939–1940, Dominikus Böhm House, Jettingen, Germany. 1948–1950, Saint Joseph Church (reconstruction), Duisburg, Germany. 1948–1950, Saint Wendelin Church, Dirmingen, Germany. 1949–1951, Saint Martin Church (reconstruction), Cochem, Germany. 1950–1951, Roman Catholic Church (with Gottfried Böhm; reconstruction), Geilenkirchen-Hünshofen, Germany. 1951–1953, Saint Mary's Church, Ochtrup, Germany. 1953–1954, Church of Mary the Queen, Colgne-Marienburg, Germany. 1954–1955, Holy Spirit Church, Hagen-Emst, Germany. 1955, Saint Joseph Church (not completed until 1956), Cologne-Rodenkirchen, Germany.

BIBLIOGRAPHY

HABBEL, JOSEF (editor) 1943 *Dominikus Böhm, ein deutscher Baumeister.* Regensburg, Germany: Habbel.

HOFF, AUGUST; MUCK, HERBERT; and THOMA, RAIMUND 1962 *Dominikus Böhm.* Munich: Schnell & Steiner.

LÜTZELER, HEINRICH 1950 "Dominikus Böhm—Siebzig Jahre Alt." *Das Münster* 3:294–299.

MAGUIRE, ROBERT, and MURRAY, KEITH 1965 *Modern Churches of the World.* New York: Dutton.

"St. Joseph's Church, Hindenburg, Germany." 1935 *Architectural Forum* 63:108–116.

SCHWARZ, RUDOLF 1927 "Dominikus Böhm und sein Werk." *Moderne Bauformen* 26:226–240.

SCHWARZ, RUDOLF 1955 "Dominikus Böhm—Kirchbauten aus vier Jahrzehnten." *Baukunst und Werkform* 8:72–83.

STALLING, GESINE 1974 *Studien zu Dominikus Böhm.* Bern: Herbert Lang; Frankfurt: Peter Lang.

BÖHM, GOTTFRIED

Gottfried Böhm (1920–), son of the architect DOMINIKUS BÖHM, attended the Munich Institute of Technology (1942–1946) and the Munich Academy of Sculptural Arts (1947). He worked in his father's office in Cologne for eight years, with the exception of a year's sojourn in New York, before opening his own office in 1955.

From the start, Böhm's architecture has been marked by a synthesis of technological achievement and artistic form and by a sympathy toward surrounding structures. These qualities are exemplified in Böhm's best known building, the Town Hall of Bensberg, in which the office floors and expressionistic tower harmoniously coexist with adjacent medieval buildings.

Böhm uses the modern materials of steel and concrete in a manner that gives rise to organic and biological analogies. The sculptural quality inherent in the shaped concrete of Bensberg's Town Hall is reminiscent of crystalline rock formations, while the twelve metal vaults of the Wigratzbad Pilgrimage Church (1972–1976) are like molecules that coalesce to form a larger structure.

Böhm is considered one of Germany's leading contemporary architects. His multivalent architecture often retains a Germanic character while achieving a modern synthesis of functionalism, form, and urban sensitivity.

IVAN S. FRANKO

WORKS

1949, Saint Columba's Church, Cologne, Germany. 1955, Church in Ching Liau, Taiwan. 1957, Herz Jesu Church, Schildgen, Germany. 1958, Saint Christopher's Church, Oldenburg, Germany. 1958, Queen of Grace Church, Kassel-Wilhelmshöhe, Germany. 1959, Corpus Christi Parish Center, Porz-Urbach, Germany. 1959, Saint Joseph Parishioners' Center, Kierspe, Germany. 1962, Housing for the Elderly, Garath, Düsseldorf, Germany. 1962, Thomas Morus Parishioners' Center, Gelsenkirchen, Germany. 1962–1968, Church of the Pilgrimages, Neviges, Germany. 1962–1969, Town Hall, Bensberg, Germany. 1963, Church of the Annunciation, Impekoven, Germany. 1963–1964, Children's Village, Refrath, Bensberg, Germany. 1963–1970, Resurrection Church, Melaten, Cologne, Germany. 1965, Children's Village, near Lake Bracciano, Italy. 1965, Saint Ludwig Church, Saarlouis, Germany. 1966, Dr. Paul Böhm House, Munich. 1969–1972, Kauzenburg-Ruine (renovation and restaurant), Bad Kreuznach, Germany. 1969–1975, Diocesan Museum, Paderborn, Germany. 1969–1975, Housing Complex, Chorweiler, Cologne, Germany. 1969–1976, State Bureau for Data Processing and Statistics, Düsseldorf, Germany. 1972–1976, Pilgrimage Church, Wigratzbad, Germany. 1973, City Hall and Cultural Center, Bocholt, Germany. 1973, Saint Matthew Parishioners'

Center, Kettwig, Essen, Germany. 1975, Neckermann Store (façade and renovation), Braunschweig am Altstadtmarkt, Germany.

BIBLIOGRAPHY

BODE, PETER M.   1978   "Expressive Kraft und schöpferische Humanität des Architekten Gottfried Böhm." *Architecture and Urbanism* 89, no. 3:37–48.

RAEV, SVETLOZAR   1978   "Architecture of Synthesis: Remarks on the Architecture of Gottfried Böhm." *Architecture and Urbanism* 89, no. 3:5–7.

SACK, MANFRED   1980   "Böhm, Gottfried." Pages 108–110 in Muriel Emanuel (editor), *Contemporary Architects.* New York: St. Martin's.

BOILEAU, LOUIS AUGUSTE

Louis Auguste Boileau (1812–1896), born in Paris, was one of the most curious architects of his time and a controversial pioneer in the use of iron in architecture. Educated as a craftsman, he appears to have been a self-trained architect. His early notoriety was based upon the construction of Saint-Eugène, Paris (1854–1855), a church combining Gothic forms with light-weight iron construction in so literal a fashion as to arouse the ire of such important critics as CÉSAR DENIS DALY and EUGÈNE EMMANUEL VIOLLET-LE-DUC. In particular, the latter was upset that Gothic forms had been rendered in a new material, and a lively exchange developed between the critic and the architect. (Indeed, it was this controversy that led Viollet-le-Duc to reconsider his views on iron construction and ultimately develop the ideas and schemes that appeared in his *Entretiens sur l'Architecture,* 1863–1872.) On the interior, Saint-Eugène was composed of iron columns and vaults, while the exterior was a conventional masonry shell that gave no hint of the novel interior.

Boileau's concept was based upon his so-called *cathédrale synthétique,* a model of which was exhibited in 1850, as well as upon a design for a chapel in Saint-Denis of the same year. Similar schemes were illustrated in his various tracts from *La Nouvelle Forme Architecturale* of 1853 to his *Histoire Critique de l'Invention en Architecture,* published in 1886. Boileau continued to build neo-Gothic churches in iron throughout the 1860s, one of his more notable being the now destroyed Notre-Dame-de-France, Leicester Square, London (1868). His remaining work of considerable fame is the iron-and-glass interior of the Bon Marché Department Store, Paris (1869–1879), which he designed in collaboration with his son, LOUIS CHARLES BOILEAU, and with GUSTAVE EIFFEL. Here, the forms and spaces are academic rather than medieval in inspiration. The centerpiece of the Bon

Marché's interior is a great stair contained within a glazed light well surrounded by galleries on all sides that is, in its distinctive way, comparable to CHARLES GARNIER's *grand escalier* in the Paris Opera. The interiors of this commercial palace (which seems to be more the work of Louis Charles than of his father) were to serve as a model for the design of Parisian department stores such as Printemps, Samaritaine, and the Galeries Lafayette for a half-century.

JOHN JACOBUS

WORKS

1854–1855, Saint-Eugène, Paris. 1863–1865, Church, Le Vésinet, France. 1868, Notre-Dame-de-France, Leicester Square, London. 1869–1879, Magasins du Bon Marché (interiors), Paris.

BIBLIOGRAPHY

FOUCART, B.   1969   "La Cathédrale Synthétiqué de Louis-Auguste Boileau." *Revue de l'Art* 3:49–69.

JACOBUS, JOHN   1956   "The Architecture of Viollet-le-Duc." Unpublished Ph.D. dissertation, Yale University, New Haven.

BOITO, CAMILLO

Camillo Boito (1836–1914) was an architect and theorist of the Italian Gothic revival. Born in Rome, he moved to Venice at an early age and studied at the Accademia with Francesco Lazzari and Pietro Selvatico. In 1856, he was awarded a government fellowship to study medieval architecture in Rome and Florence. Thereafter, he was active as a teacher at the Brera in Milan and as an architect, building in a simplifed form of Italian Gothic, known as *Stile Boito,* which is similar to English and American High Victorian Gothic. Also active as a writer and polemicist, like many medievalists such as EUGÈNE EMMANUEL VIOLLET-LE-DUC, Boito wrote on restoration theory and architectural history. His most distinguished pupil was LUCA BELTRAMI.

NICHOLAS ADAMS

WORKS

1865, Cemetery; 1871, Hospital; Gallarate, Italy. 1872–1874, Palazzo delle Debite; 1879, Municipal Museum; 1892–1896, Church of San Antonio (restoration of the choir); Padua, Italy. 1899, Casa Verdi, Milan.

BIBLIOGRAPHY

BOITO, CAMILLO   1877   *Scultura e pittura d'oggi.* Turin, Italy: Bocca.

BOITO, CAMILLO   1880   *Architettura del Medio Evo in Italia.* Milan: Hoepli.

BOITO, CAMILLO   1882   *I principii del disegno e gli stili dell'ornamento.* Milan: Hoepli.

MEEKS, CARROLL L. 1966 *Italian Architecture, 1750–1914.* New Haven: Yale University Press.

BON, GIOVANNI; BON, BARTOLOMEO; and BON, BARTOLOMEO (BERGAMASCO)

The Venetian stonemason Giovanni Bon (c.1362?–1443), son of Bertuccio, is first recorded in documents of 1382/1385–1388. He seems to have lived successively in the neighboring parishes of San Canciano, Santa Sofia, San Felice, and (after c.1424) San Marcilian, now called San Marziale. He first worked locally, especially for the *Scuole* of which he was a member, the Misericordia (reconstructed in 1411–1412) and San Cristoforo (in the Madonna dell'Orto, itself rebuilt from c.1392). He had a substantial shop, with apprentices and associated masters equally accomplished in architectural and figural carving, and specialized in ensembles (usually applied to existing buildings) that combined both techniques. His attractive but unremarkable late Gothic style would hardly be remembered were it not for the emergence of his son, Bartolomeo as a far more gifted artist, concurrently with their patronage by the wealthy procurator Marin Contarini, whose extravagantly carved and gilded palace of the *Ca'd'Oro* (1424–1431) brought the Bons a prominence that secured their state commission for a monumental entrance to the Ducal Palace. The resulting *Porta della Carta* (1438–1443) is a tall and richly ornamented frontispiece with elaborate figural sculptures; together with the *Ca'd'Oro,* it marks the apogee of the floriated late Gothic in Venice.

Bartolomeo Bon (c.1405–c.1467) (who signed the ducal portal) finished his apprenticeship by 1422, and wrote his will in 1464; but worked continued two years longer on his great classicizing door for the Madonna dell'Orto (1460–1466), and his Morosini tomb (apparently suspended since 1445/46) was completed by a colleague in 1467/68: thus a document that mentions his having died by 28 April 1467 probably indicates the event as recent. During the last year of his father's life, Bartolomeo undertook one more purely Gothic commission, the Church of the Carità (1441/1442–1452) in Venice, and he may have directed work on portals similar to the Carità's at Santo Stefano, San Polo, and the Frari (all possibly 1440s). But in an astonishing development, he invented a wholly new style in the years around mid-century (attracting, for example, the friendship of Donatello in 1453), as attested by three extraordinary masterworks: the reliably attributed *Arco Foscari* at the Ducal Palace (1440–1464/1467), together with his documented portal for Santi Giovanni e Paolo (1458–1463) and his splendid commencement (1456/1457) of Palazzo Corner on the Grand Canal, interrupted as a partially finished basement by its purchase in 1460 as a Venetian *Ca'del Duca* for Francesco Sforza of Milan. These latter works combine huge Antique columns with weighty framing elements to create a Renaissance monumentality with native Venetian forms. They are as precocious as they are compelling: the *Ca'del Duca's* diamond rustication, indeed, initiates the use of an element that was to influence profoundly the classical revolution of succeeding generations. They thus encourage the more problematic attribution to Bartolomeo of the Arsenal Gate (1460–1462?), on whose triumphal arch an accurate recreation of antiquity makes its first decisive appearance in Venetian dominions.

The Venetian family of the Bons should not be confused with a younger Lombard architect who worked there: Bartolomeo Bon called Bergamasco (1463?–1529) was architect to the Venetian Signoria from 1492 and of the Procuratia di San Marco from 1505 until his death. He was a skillful follower of MAURO CODUCCI, best remembered for his beautiful ground floor of the Scuola di San Rocco (1516–1524).

DOUGLAS LEWIS

WORKS

GIOVANNI AND BARTOLOMEO BON

1411–1441?, Scuola Vecchia della Misericordia (portal and windows); 1424–1425, Palazzo Barbaro, San Vidal; 1424–1431, Palazzo Contarini (Ca'd'Oro; with Marco Di Amadio and Matteo Raverti), Grand Canal; 1424–1438, Ducal Palace (Piazzetta façade and wing; with the Porticato Foscari); Early 1430s, Palazzo Corner, Santa Fosca, *1437–1443, Scuola Grande di San Marco (portals); *1437–1447, Twenty Almshouses for Baseggio and Signolo estates, Corte Novo, San Marziale; 1438–1443, Ducal Palace (Porta della Carta); (A)late 1430s–1445, Church of the Madonna dell'Orto (Morosini Chapel and façade; portal, reworked by Bartolomeo in 1460–1466, not completed until 1438 by others); (A)1440s?, Santa Maria Gloriosa dei Frari (Cornaro Chapel portal?); (A)1440s?, Santa Stefano (portals); (A)1440s?, San Polo (portal on flank); Venice, Italy.

BARTOLOMEO BON

(A)1440s–1464/1467, Arco Foscari, Ducal Palace; 1441/1442–1452, Santa Maria della Carità (converted 1807–1811 into storerooms and galleries for the Accademia di Belle Arti); 1445–1467?, San Gregorio (tomb of Bartolomeo Morosini; not completed until 1467–1468 by Guido Bianco); *1451, Hospice of Santa Maria della Scala (windows), San Biagio, 1456/1457–1460, Palazzo Corner (basement), San Samuele, Grand

Canal; 1458–1463, Santi Giovanni e Paolo (also known as San Zanipolo; main portal); (A)1460–1462?, Arsenal (main portal); Venice, Italy.

BARTOLOMEO BON (BERGAMASCO)

1489–1508, San Rocco (nave rebuilt 1725–1743 by Giovanni Antonio Scalfarotto; façade rebuilt 1765–1771 by Bernardino Maccoruzzi); (A)1496–1499, 1502–1506, Torre dell'Orologio (including wings; with others), (A)c.1500?–?, Palazzo Treviso-Cappello in Canonica; 1510–1514, Campanile (belfry and steeple collapsed 1902, rebuilt 1902–1912), Piazza San Marco; 1513–1526, Procuratie Vecchie (with Guglielmo Dei Grigi), Piazza San Marco; 1516–1524, Scuola Grande di San Roco (not completed until 1524–1527 by Sante Lombardo, 1527–1549 by Scarpagnino, and 1549–1560 by Gian Giacomo Dei Grigi); *1510s?, San Geminiano (high altar); 1520, San Rocco (high altar); Venice, Italy.

BIBLIOGRAPHY

ARSLAN, EDOUARDO (1970)1971 *Gothic Architecture in Venice*. Translated by Anne Engel. London: Phaidon; New York: Praeger.

GALLO, RODOLFO 1961–1962 "L'Architettura di transizione dal Gotico al Rinascimento e Bartolomeo Bon." *Atti dell'Istituto Veneto di Scienze, Lettere, ed Arti* 120:187–206.

HOWARD, DEBORAH 1981 *The Architectural History of Venice*. New York: Holmes & Meier; London: Batsford.

LEWIS, DOUGLAS 1972 "Un disegno autografo." *Bollettino dei Musei Civici Veneziani* 17, nos. 3–4:7–36.

MCANDREW, JOHN 1980 *Venetian Architecture of the Early Renaissance*. Cambridge, Mass.: M.I.T. Press.

PAOLETTI, PIETRO 1893 *L'Architettura e la scultura del Rinascimento in Venezia*. Venice, Italy: Ongania-Naya.

PINCUS, DEBRA 1976 *The Arco Foscari: The Building of a Triumphal Gateway in Fifteenth Century Venice*. New York: Garland.

ROMANO, SERENO 1980 *The Restoration of the Porta della Carta*. Edited by Ashley Clarke and Philip Rylands. Venice, Italy: Armena.

SCHULZ, ANNE MARKHAM 1978 "The Sculpture of Giovanni and Bartolomeo Bon and their Workshop." *Transactions of the American Philosophical Society* 68, part 3:1–81.

TEMANZA, TOMMASO (1778)1966 "Vita di Mastro Bartolommeo Buono scultore ed architetto." Pages 98–105 in Liliana Grassi (editor), *Vite dei più celebri architetti e scultori veneziani*. Reprint. Milan: Labor.

BONANNO

A native of Pisa, Bonanno (12th century) is known for the bronze doors of Pisa Cathedral (those for the façade were lost in the fire of 1595; another pair in the south transept is still extant) and of Monreale in Sicily (1186). His burial within the leaning tower of Pisa has led some to attribute to him its design.

CHRISTINE SMITH

WORK

(A)1174, Campanile (leaning tower), Pisa, Italy.

BIBLIOGRAPHY

BOECKLER, ALBERT 1953 *Die Bronzetüren des Bonanus von Pisa und des Barisanus von Trani*. Berlin: Deutscher Verein für Kunstwissenschaft.

CARLI, ENZO 1956 *La Piazza del Duomo di Pisa*. Firenze, Italy: Casini.

BONATZ, PAUL

Born in Lorraine, Paul Bonatz (1877–1956) studied at Munich with Karl Hocheder and FRIEDRICH VON THIERSCH. He then associated himself closely with THEODOR FISCHER, first in the Municipal Planning Office in Munich and next as Fischer's assistant at the Stuttgart Technische Hochschule. In 1908, when Fischer was called to Munich, Bonatz succeeded him as professor at Stuttgart, and remained there for most of his career. Having been briefly associated with the Social Democratic Party in the early years of the Weimar Republic, Bonatz was in danger of losing his position during the last years of the Third Reich. He fled from Germany to Turkey in 1943 and was professor of architecture at Istanbul from 1946 to 1953. In 1953, he returned to Stuttgart.

Bonatz was deeply influenced by Fischer's massive rough-cut masonry buildings and carried Fischer's teachings forward in a modernized form. His transformation of Fischer's legacy can be seen in the successive projects for the Stuttgart Railway Station (1911–1928), in which Bonatz collaborated with F. E. SCHOLER. The first proposal of 1911 incorporated many historical references including a miniature temple at the top of the main tower. The final version of 1913, which arranged the wings asymmetrically around a massive tower, was relatively free from historical references and resembled in many respects the contemporary work of WILHELM KREIS and EDMUND KÖRNER in Germany and H. P. BERLAGE in Holland.

Bonatz continued to employ this monumental yet modern masonry style in designs for bridges (under the Third Reich, his principal commissions were bridges for the Autobahn network). Concurrently, he developed a modest and refined neoclassicism, deriving in part from the vernacular traditions of South German architecture, for less monumental buildings. The University Library at Tübingen, constructed from 1909 to 1912, exem-

Bonatz.
Railroad Station (with
Scholer).
Stuttgart, Germany.
1911–1928

plifies this highly personal aspect of Bonatz's work: faced with plain stucco, crowned by a tiled roof and lit by rows of tall windows, the building makes a rich yet subdued impression, which is enhanced by the marble floors and stucco-work ceilings of the interior. The Tübingen Library has been consistently admired by architects of every artistic and ideological persuasion.

Bonatz's commissions after World War I were few, but he achieved a consistency throughout his career which escaped most of his contemporaries. He did not, like Kreis, adopt the vocabulary of the International style, but he also refrained from becoming an opponent of the modern movement, as GERMAN BESTELMEYER and PAUL SCHMITTHENNER did. From 1908 to 1943, Bonatz distinguished himself as a teacher at Stuttgart, where several generations of students learned from him to revere fine materials and workmanlike design. In his memoirs, Bonatz claimed that it was his popularity with his students which protected him from persecution under the Third Reich.

ALBERT SPEER, on the other hand, asserted in *Inside the Third Reich* that he and FRITZ TODT protected Bonatz and secured commissions for him. Bonatz's monumental buildings were greatly admired by many Nazi officials and architects; the Nazi Ordensburgen, for example, were influenced by the Stuttgart Railway Station. But Bonatz himself was able to retain his integrity in a period when many of his colleagues sacrificed theirs to ambition or ideology.

BARBARA MILLER LANE

WORKS

1904?, Hirschbergstrasse School (with Theodor Fischer), Munich. 1905, School, Rottweil, Germany. 1905–1910, Courthouse, Mainz, Germany. 1905–1910, Hospital (extension), Strasbourg, Germany. 1907, School, Schweinfurt, Germany. 1908–1909, Lagerhaus Henckell, Biebrich bei Wiesbaden, Germany. 1909–1912, University Library, Tübingen, Germany. 1911–1928, Railroad Station (with F. E. Scholer), Stuttgart, Germany. 1914?, Stadthalle (with Scholer), Hannover, Germany. 1922, Stumm Company Office Building, Düsseldorf, Germany. 1926–?, Locks and Bridges, Nekar River, Germany. 1931, Art Museum, Basel, Switzerland. 1935–1941, Autobahn Bridges, Germany. 1943, Theater, Ankara. 1956, Opera House (reconstruction), Düsseldorf, Germany.

BIBLIOGRAPHY

BONATZ, PAUL (1950)1954 *Leben und Bauen.* Stuttgart, Germany: Spemann.
ECKART, H. P. 1957 "Zum Tode von Prof. Paul Bonatz." *Die Bauzeitung: Deutsche Bautzeitung* 62:30–31.
GRAUPNER, G. 1931 *Paul Bonatz und seine Schüler.* Stuttgart, Germany.
HAENSELMANN, J. F. 1914–1915 "Professor Paul Bonatz." *Wasmuths Monatshefte für Baukunst und Städtebau* 1:205–222.
LANE, BARBARA MILLER 1968 *Architecture and Politics in Germany: 1918–1945.* Cambridge, Mass.: Harvard University Press.
"Münchener Schulhausneubauten." 1905 *Zentralblatt der Bauverwaltung* 25:441–444.
Paul Bonatz: Ein Gedenkbuch der Technischen Hochschule Stuttgart. 1957 Stuttgart, Germany: Deutsche Verlagsanstalt.
RITTICH, WERNER 1938 *Architektur und Bauplastik der Gegenwart.* Berlin: Rembrandt.
SPEER, ALBERT (1969)1970 *Inside the Third Reich: Memoirs.* Translated by Richard and Clara Winston. New York: Macmillan.
"Zum Wettbewerb des Stuttgarter Hauptbahnhofe." 1911 *Zentralblatt der Bauverwaltung* 31:333–335.

BONAVENTURA

The presence of Bonaventura (13th century), probably from Lombardy, in Massa Marittima, Italy, is documented in 1231. At that time, a large number of masons from the Lake Como region were working in this city. Projects in which they were involved include the Cathedral (begun 1228 by Maestro Enrico, perhaps from Campione), Baptistery (begun by Giroldo da Como in 1267), the Palazzo Pretorio (begun c.1230), and the city walls.

CHRISTINE SMITH

BIBLIOGRAPHY

PETROCCHI, LUIGI 1900 *Massa Marittima; arte e storia.* Florence: Venturi.

BONET, ANTONIO

Vanguard of the modern architecture movement in Argentina, Antonio Bonet (1913–) moved to Buenos Aires in 1938 after working for JOSEP LLUIS SERT in his native Barcelona from 1932 to 1936 and spending two years with LE CORBUSIER in Paris.

In 1939, he put together the AUSTRAL group, responsible for espousing the ideas of functional orthodoxy but with a regional consciousness that considered Argentina's economical and cultural necessities. From 1945 to 1948, Bonet put to use Austral's theories in the development of Punta Ballena, Uruguay. At the Berlingieri House (1947) and the Hotel-Restaurant La Solana del Mar (1947), he used local stone and stucco vaulting that displayed his lucid handling of plastic forms.

Frustrated by the Argentine government's anachronistic view of architecture, Bonet began to accept commissions in Spain in 1949. In 1963, he opened offices in both Barcelona and Madrid winning soon thereafter the FAD award for his dog track and stadium in Meridiana. Bonet's work in Spain exhibits a unique regionalism, as displayed at the Cruylles House (1968), which is roofed with vaults conscribed in truncated domes. The application of modern techniques with historical precedents has made Bonet an innovator in both Argentina and Spain.

ELIZABETH D. HARRIS

WORKS

1937, Spanish Pavilion, Paris. 1942–1944, Four Houses, Martinez, Buenos Aires. 1947, Berlingieri House; 1947, La Solana del Mar Hotel and Restaurant; Portezuelo, Uruguay. 1957, Oks House, Mar del Plata, Argentina. 1958–1963, Terraza Palace Apartments, Mar del Plata, Argentina. 1962, Canodromo, Barcelona, Spain. 1965, Castanera House; 1966, Golf Club Puigcerda; Gerona, Spain. 1967, Rubio House, Murcia, Spain. 1968, Cruylles House, Gerona, Spain. 1971, Urquinaona Tower, Barcelona, Spain.

BIBLIOGRAPHY

BULLRICH, FRANCISCO 1969 *New Directions in Latin American Architecture.* New York: Braziller.
ORTIZ, FEDERICO, and BALDELLOU, MIGUEL 1978 *La Obra de Antonio Bonet.* Buenos Aires: Ediciones Summa.

BONET GARÍ, LUIS

Luis Bonet Garí (1893–) was born in Argentona, north of Barcelona, Spain. He collaborated with ANTONIO GAUDI I CORNET on the works of the Sagrada Familia in Barcelona, of which he was co-

director. He has realized studies on popular architecture in Catalonia and has collaborated on the restoration of the monasteries of Poblet, Tarragon.

JUAN BASSEGODA NONELL
Translated from Spanish by
Judith E. Meighan

WORKS

1922, Casa Armengol, 103 Clarís; 1951, Banco Vitalicio; 1955, Instituto Nacional de Previsión; n.d., Capilla del Cros., Argentona; n.d., Casa Patxot., Paseo de la Reina Elisenda; n.d., Casa rectoral de Teià; Barcelona, Spain.

BIBLIOGRAPHY

JARDÍ, E. 1980 *El Noucentisme.* Barcelona, Spain.
RÀFOLS, JOSÈ F. 1955 Volume I in *Diccionario biográfico de artistas de Cataluña.* Barcelona, Spain: Millá.

BONNARD, JACQUES CHARLES

A student of Jean Renard and Henri Watelet, Jacques Charles Bonnard won the Academy's *second premier prix* (1788). He studied briefly in Rome (1790) and returned to Paris only to be compelled to flee to England (1792–1795). Bonnard was the architect of the Ministry of Foreign Affairs (1810–1814) in Paris, finished in 1838 by his pupil Jacques Lacornée. In 1816, Bonnard was elected to the new Académie des Beaux-Arts.

MYRA DICKMAN ORTH

WORK

*1810–1814, Ministry of Foreign Affairs (on the site of the present Gare d'Orsay), Paris.

BIBLIOGRAPHY

FONTAINE, PIERRE, and PERCIER, CHARLES 1809 *Choix des plus célèbres maisons de plaisance de Rome.* Paris: Didot.
HAUTECOEUR, LOUIS 1953–1955 Volumes 5 and 6 in *Histoire de l'architecture classique en France.* Paris: Picard.
LEGRAND, J. G., and LANDON, C. P. (1808)1818 Volume 2, page 238 in *Description de Paris.* Paris: Treuttel.
LEMONNIER, HENRY 1926 Volume 9, pages 235, 238–241 in *Procès-verbaux de l'Académie Royale d'Architecture: 1671–1793.* Paris: Schmit.

BONOMI, JOSEPH

Born in Rome and educated at the Collegio Romano, Joseph Bonomi (1739–1809) appears to have been a pupil of the architectural amateur Girolamo Teodoli before his departure for Lon-

Bonomi.
Great Packington.
Warwickshire, England.
1789–1792

don, where he arrived in 1767. Although he is reputed to have been brought there by ROBERT ADAM and JAMES ADAM, the only evidence for this are payments to him in the Adam bank accounts in 1770 and 1771. After work with Adam, he worked for THOMAS LEVERTON, then began an independent career, in which he was especially noted as a country house architect. This was interrupted near its beginning by a trip to Italy in 1783–1784, probably together with an important patron of his, the fourth earl of Aylesbury.

For Aylesbury, he created interiors for Packington Hall, Warwickshire (c.1782–c.1788), including the gallery with its Pompeian decoration (though the painting there is probably by J. F. Rigaud and may date from around 1800), and the very impressive Church of Great Packington (1789–1792). The design of this church, with its Greek-cross-in-square plan, austere exterior without any orders, and powerful stone-vaulted interior with four Greek Doric columns, may owe a great deal to the patron; but the contribution of Bonomi was not insignificant.

Related to this facet of Bonomi's work are the pyramidal mausoleum at Blickling, Norfolk, of 1794; such powerful, unfluted porticoes as that at Longford Hall, Shropshire (1789–1794); and Roseneath Castle, Dumbartonshire (1803–1806), which features a tall cylindrical projecting tower ending atop the house as a belvedere, as well as parades of columns and relatively unusual capitals.

In other works, and especially in his earlier interiors, he employed an elegant neoclassicism, though usually not quite as delicate and refined as that of Adam. Typical of this are the interiors at Packington Hall, which can be seen not only in

the house itself but in his drawings for it, and the designs (c.1782) for the destroyed Great Room at Montagu House, Portman Square, London.

Elected an associate of the Royal Academy in London in 1789, he was also an associate of the Accademia di San Luca in Rome and the Accademia Clementina in Bologna, as well as an honorary architect of St. Peter's, Rome, an honor acquired in 1804. One of his sons, Ignatius, followed him as an architect; another, Joseph, Jr., was a noted Egyptologist and second curator of Sir JOHN SOANE's Museum, London. Bonomi himself died in London, where his career had been centered.

DAMIE STILLMAN

WORKS

c.1782–c.1788, Packington Hall, Warwickshire, England. *c.1782–c.1790?, Montagu House (Great Room), Portman Square, London. *1784–1788, Dale Park, Sussex, England. *1789–1790, Bavarian Chapel, Warwick Street, London. 1789–1792, Great Packington Church, Warwickshire, England. 1789–1794, Longford Hall, Shropshire, England. *1792–1793, Barrells, Warwickshire, England. *1793–1796, Spanish Chapel, Manchester Square, London. *1793–1800, Eastwells Park, Kent, England. 1794, Mausoleum, Blickling, Norfolk, England. *c.1796–1797, Lambton Hall, County Durham, England. 1796–1799, Laverstoke Park, Hampshire, England. *1799, Sandling House, Kent, England. *1803–1806, Roseneath Castle, Dumbartonshire, Scotland.

BIBLIOGRAPHY

"The Life and Works of Joseph Bonomi." 1843 *Architect, Engineer and Surveyor* 1843:70–71.
PAPWORTH, WYATT 1868–1869 "Memoir." *Transactions of the Royal Institute of British Architects* 19:123–134.
STILLMAN, DAMIE n.d. "English Neo-classical Architecture." London: Zwemmer. Forthcoming publication.

BONSIGNORE, FERDINANDO

Ferdinando Bonsignore (1760–1843), born in Turin, Italy, was a major neoclassic architect of the early nineteenth century. He studied for fifteen years in Rome (1783–1798) before returning to practice in Turin. He was professor of architecture at the university there from 1805. He designed the Pantheon-like Temple of the Gran Madre di Dio in Turin (1818–1831), built to commemorate the return of Vittorio Emanuele I after Napoleon's downfall. For the prince of Carignano, he designed the entrance doors and three rooms in the Palazzo Carignano as well as a circular temple/pavilion in the garden at Racconigi.

HENRY A. MILLON

WORKS

1818–1831, Gran Madre di Dio, Turin, Italy. n.d., Palazzo Caragnano (entrance doors and three rooms), Turin, Italy. n.d., Temple/Pavilion, Racconigi, Italy.

BIBLIOGRAPHY

BAUDI DI VESME, ALESSANDRO 1963 Volume 1, pages 156–159 in *Schede Vesme*. Turin, Italy: Società Piemontese di Archeologia e Belle Arti.
BRAYDA, CARLO; COLI, LAURA; and SESIA, DARIO 1963 *Ingegneri e architetti del sei e settecento in piemonte*. Turin, Italy: Società Ingegneri e Architetti.
MEEKS, CARROLL L. V. 1966 *Italian Architecture: 1750–1914*. New Haven: Yale University Press.

BONVICINI, PIETRO

Pietro Bonvicini (1741–1796) was an assistant and follower of FILIPPO NICOLIS DI ROBILANT. Bonvicini's interest in the late works and classical references of di Robilant and BERNARDO ANTONIO VITTONE are manifest in the hexagonal Church of San Michele, his major work in Turin, Italy. He also assisted CARLO AMEDEO RANA in the Church of Santi Michele and Solutore at Strambino, Italy.

HENRY A. MILLON

WORKS

*1783–?, San Processo e San Martiniano (renovation and new façade); 1785–1791, San Michele Church and Convent; Turin, Italy.

BIBLIOGRAPHY

BRAYDA, CARLO; COLI, LAURA; and SESIA, DARIO 1963 Pages 19–20 in *Ingegneri e architetti del sei e settecento in Piemonte*. Turin, Italy: Società degli ingegneri e degli architetti.
LANGE, AUGUSTA 1941 "La Chiesa di S. Michele dei Trinitari Scalzi e i disegni di Pietro Bonvicini." *Bollettino storico—bibliografico subalpino* 43, no. 4:299–307.
ROSSI GRIBAUDI, ELISA 1964 *La chiesa di Strambino*. Ivrea, Italy.
TAMBURINI, LUCIANO 1968 *Le chiese di Torino*. Turin, Italy: Le bouquiniste.

BORELLA, CARLO

Little is known about the early life of Carlo Borella (1661–1707). An architect from Vicenza, Italy, he represents a hybrid architectural tradition that mixed, in the eclectic manner of the late seventeenth century, a baroque style of architectural plan and decorative scheme with a strain of classicism inspired by antique and Renaissance precedents. The former current is best exemplified in the work of FRANCESCO BORROMINI whom Borella admired, and the latter can be witnessed in the work of VINCENZO SCAMOZZI.

Controversy has centered on his Santa Maria d'Araceli in Vicenza (1675–1680), first falsely attributed to GUARINO GUARINI by FRANCESCO MILIZIA and then accredited by the Italian scholar P. Portoghesi (1957) to Borella, based on a design by Guarini. During his short life, Borella was active in and around Vicenza designing secular as well as ecclesiastical buildings.

TINA WALDEIER BIZZARRO

WORKS

1675–1680, Santa Maria d'Araceli (not consecrated until 1743), Vicenza, Italy. 1676–1680, Palazzo Barbieri-Piovene, San Marco, Italy. 1688–1703, Sanctuary of Monte Berico, Italy. 1698, Stable House for the Nanti Family, Valdagno, Italy.

BIBLIOGRAPHY

CEVESE, RENATO 1962 "Il Barocco a Vicenza: Revese-Pizzocaro-Borella." *Bollettino del Centro Internazionale di Studi di Architettura—Andrea Palladio* no. 4:129–145.
FRANCO, FAUSTO 1934 "La scuola architettonica di Vicenza." *I Monumenti italiani* 3.
FRANCO, FAUSTO 1937 "La scuola scamozziani 'di stile severo' a Vicenza." *Palladio* 1:59–70.
Guida d'Italia del Touring Club Italiano: Veneto. (1952)1954 4th ed. Milan: Vallardi.
PORTOGHESI, PAOLO 1957 "Guarini a Vicenza: La Chiesa di S. Maria d'Araceli" *Critica d'Arte* no. 20:108–128; no. 21, part 2:214–229.
WITTKOWER, RUDOLF (1958)1980 *Art and Architecture in Italy: 1600 to 1750*. 4th ed., rev. Harmondsworth, England: Penguin.

BORGO, FRANCESCO DEL

Francesco del Cereo di Borgo San Sepolcro (?–1468) was born in Borgo San Sepolcro (Tuscany), Italy. He is first mentioned in 1450 as a member of the financial staff of the Apostolic Chamber and of the secret treasury of Nicholas V (1447–1455). Climbing quickly through the levels of the financial bureaucracy at the papal court, he became, in 1460, papal vice-treasurer. By 1457, at the latest, he was *scriptor apostolicus,* and in 1465 he was named *scriptor bullarum.* Precious manuscripts of Latin translations of Archimedes, Euclid, Ptolemy, and Muhamid Ibn Musa al-Khuwarzimi were illustrated by Francesco and decorated at his behest in 1457–1458. He must have belonged to the circle of humanists around LEON BATTISTA ALBERTI who had been a member of the papal court from the time of Eugene IV (1431–1447). Alberti may have taught Francesco architecture and engineering.

Alberti may have recommended Francesco to

Pius II (1458–1464) who charged him with the design of the benediction loggia in front of St. Peter's and with the reshaping of St. Peter's square. Francesco planned to substitute the temporary wooden pulpit in front of the old atrium, from which the earlier popes had blessed the crowd, by a two-storied marble loggia of eleven bays. Its elevation recalled the design of the exterior of Roman theaters (Colosseum, Theater of Marcellus). Instead of half-columns, however, antique marble shafts articulated the arcades. It was the first thorough-going imitation of Roman imperial architecture and the first forum building *all'antica* of post-antique times. It was probably inspired by Alberti's comments, in *De re aedificatoria* (1452), on fora, on theaters, and on triumphal arches. As against the Tuscan formal language of BERNARDO ROSSELLINO's contemporary piazza in Pienza, Francesco's loggia marks the beginning of an autonomous Roman Renaissance, the architectural expression of the new imperial aspirations of the Roman *pontifex maximus*. When Pius II died in August of 1464, only four arcades of the ground-floor of the loggia had been executed, the nearby tower above the entry to the papal palace and the crowning story of the old campanile had been redone, and a fountain and the leveling of the square had been begun. Work on the loggia was continued until around 1510 but it was never finished, and the structure was destroyed in 1600. Other works which Francesco probably designed for Pius II are the still existing tabernacle near Ponte Milvio in Rome on the spot where Pius received the skull of Saint Andrew in 1462; a chapel in the outer left nave of Old St. Peter's with a two-storied tabernacle for the skull of Saint Andrew; and the fortress of Tivoli (1461–1462).

In 1465, Pius's successor, Paul II (1464–1471), charged Francesco with the enlargement of the palace he had begun while a cardinal. It was to become his new papal residence, today the Palazzo Venezia. At Francesco's death the irregularly shaped Basilica of San Marco had been transformed into a symmetrical church with pillars supporting vaulted aisles, with semicircular chapels, transepts ending in exedras, an elevation articulated in the nave by half-columns and, in the aisles, by pilasters, and a rich coffered ceiling roofed with gilded lead tiles. The old portico was replaced by a two-story benediction loggia of only three bays but similar to that of Pius II. In front of the loggia, a regular piazza was laid out, one side of which was defined by the new Palazzetto Venezia. This was a hanging garden for the pope surrounded by porticoes which have typological similarities with medieval cloisters. Here, Francesco's innovations can be seen in the tripartite entabla-

tures in both stories and in the exquisite proportions of the sober exterior. The northern front of the Palazzetto and the eastern façade of the Palazzo defined the huge Piazza Venezia which became the focus of the Via Flaminia and the main site of the Roman carnival. The earlier palace was incorporated in the east wing of the papal palace; new halls of enormous size, a vestibule with a coffered barrel vault, and staircases were added in accord with the ceremonial disposition of the Vatican. The huge angular tower of the Palazzo Venezia was added after Francesco's death, and the two large portals and the fragmentary courtyard date from after Paul's death.

Historians have often doubted that Francesco could have been both a financial expert and a great architect. His activities for the two popes are, however, documented by a nearly completely preserved series of accountbooks, and the two chroniclers of Paul II's reign praise Francesco as the *architectus ingeniosissimus* of the Palazzo Venezia. Stylistically, he stands between Alberti's revival of Roman imperial architecture and the more conservative language of MICHELOZZO DI BARTOLOMEO and Rossellino. Francesco's literal imitation of antique prototypes and his relatively abstract detailing may be explained by his formation not as a painter or sculptor but as a humanist and intellectual. Like Alberti and LUCIANO DA LAURANA, Francesco represents the new type of the learned "Vitruvian" (see VITRUVIUS) architect. His many followers dominated Roman architecture for the next decades and were superseded only by DONATO BRAMANTE's arrival in 1499.

CHRISTOPH LUITPOLD FROMMEL

WORKS

1460–1464, St. Peter's (loggia of benediction and upper story of the campanile); 1460–1464, Vatican Palace Entrance Tower; Rome. 1461–1462, Fortress, Tivoli, Italy. 1462, Edicola, near Malvien Bridge, Italy. 1462–1464, Saint Andrew's Chapel, St. Peter's; 1465, Chapel of San Patronilla (renovation), St. Peter's; 1465–1468, San Marco (reconstruction of interior and groundfloor loggia of the new façade); 1466–1468, Palazzetto (with hanging garden). 1466–1468, Palazzo Venezia (enlargement); 1466–?, Knights of Rhodes (reconstruction of palace and loggia); *1467–?, Jacopo Gottifredi House, Piazza Pasquino; Rome.

BIBLIOGRAPHY

CASANOVA, MARIA LETIZIA 1980 *Palazzo Venezia: Paolo II e le fabbriche di S. Marco.* Rome: DeLuca. Exhibition catalogue.
DENGEL, IGNAZ PHILIPP 1913 *Palast und Basilika San Marco in Rom.* Rome: Loescher.
DENGER, IGNAZ PHILIPP; DVOŘÀK, MAX; and EGGER, HERMANN 1909 *Der Palazzo Venezia in Rom.* Vienna: Malota.

FROMMEL, CHRISTOPH LUITPOLD 1981 *Der Palazzo Venezia als Papstresidenz.* Dusseldorf, Germany: Westdeutscher.

FROMMEL, CHRISTOPH LUITPOLD 1982 "Francesco del Borgo—Architekt Pius' II. und Pauls II.: I. Der Petersplatz und weitere römische Bauten Pius' II. Piccolomini." *Römisches Jahrbuch für Kunstgeschichte* 20.

MÜNTZ, EUGÈNE 1879 Volume 2, pages 33ff. in *Les arts à la cour des papes pendant le XVe et le XVIe siècle.* Paris: Thorin.

OLITSKY RUBINSTEIN, RUTH 1967 "Pius II's Piazza S. Pietro and St. Andrew's Head." Pages 22–23 in D. Fraser, Howard Hibbard, and M. J. Lewine (editors), *Essays in the History of Architecture presented to Rudolf Wittkower.* London: Phaidon.

RUYSSCHAERT, JOSÉ 1968 Page 263 in Dominico Maffei (editor), *Enea Silvio Piccolomini Papa Pio II.* Siena, Italy.

SPOTTI TANTILLO, ALDA 1975 "Inventari inediti di interesse librario." *Archivio della Società Romana di Storia Patria* 98:77–94.

TOMEI, PIERO 1942 Pages 72ff. in *L'architettura a Roma nel Quattrocento.* Rome: Palombi.

ZIPPEL, GIUSEPPE 1910 "Paolo II e l'arte." *L'Arte* 13:241–258.

ZIPPEL, GIUSEPPE 1921 "Ricordi romani dei Cavalieri di Rodi." *Archivio Società Romana di Storia Patria* 44:169–205.

BORING, WILLIAM A.

William Alciphron Boring (1858–1937) was born in Carlinville, Illinois. The son of a builder, Boring briefly attended the architecture school of the University of Illinois before moving to California in 1882, where he was a draftsman and a partner with C. B. Ripley. In 1886, Boring attended the School of Architecture at Columbia University, but left the next year to attend to the Ecole des Beaux-Arts in Paris, where he entered León Ginain's atelier. In 1890, Boring returned to New York and worked briefly for McKIM, MEAD, AND WHITE before forming a partnership with Edward L. Tilton. In 1895, the firm won the competition for the United States Immigration Station on Ellis Island, New York, their best known work. He was active in architectural education serving the American Academy in Rome, the Society of Beaux-Arts Architects, and from 1915 as a professor in the School of Architecture at Columbia University. In 1931, he became the school's first dean.

DENNIS McFADDEN

WORKS

1895–1902, United States Immigration Station (with Edward L. Tilton), Ellis Island, N.Y.

BIBLIOGRAPHY

The manuscript of William A. Boring's "Memories of the Life of William Alciphron Boring" is in the Avery Architectural Library, Columbia University, New York.

BORRA, GIOVANNI BATTISTA

Giovanni Battista Borra (1712–1786), who came from Piedmont, Italy, trained with BERNARDO ANTONIO VITTONE and BENEDETTO ALFIERI. He is the author of a treatise on the structure of vaults (1748) and of *Views of Turin* (1799). He traveled with Dawkins and Wood in 1750–1751 as draftsman on a voyage to Baalbek and Palmyra, returning with them to England to prepare drawings for the plates. Borra may have remained in England until late 1755, receiving commissions from Lord Temple for work at Stowe (1752—but also in 1758 and 1760, probably sent from Turin) and from the duke of Norfolk for the decoration of his house in St. James' Square (1755). By April 1756, he returned to Piedmont, where he worked for the prince of Carignano at Racconigi (south façade and pavilions) and in Turin (façade of Teatro Carignano).

HENRY A. MILLON

WORKS

1752–1760, Stowe (Temple of Victory and Concord, Garden Pavilions, south front exterior stair, and state bedroom and dressing room), Buckinghamshire, England. 1755–?, Castello (main salon, south façade pavilions and stair, and (A)north façade stair), Racconigi, Italy. 1756–?, Teatro Carignano (façade); 1761, Church of the Sudario (façade), Turin, Italy.

BIBLIOGRAPHY

BAUDI DI VESME, ALESSANDRO 1963 "Borra, Giovanni Battista." Volume 1, pages 177–178 in *Schede Vesme.* Turin, Italy: Stamperia Artistica Nazionale.

BRAYDA, CARLO; COLI, LAURA; and SESIA, DARIO 1963 Pages 20–21 in *Ingegneri e architetti del sei e settecento in Piemonte.* Turin, Italy: Società degli ingegneri e degli architetti.

CARBONERI, NINO 1949 "Prodromi di neoclassicismo nell'architettura piemontese del Settecento." *Bollettino della Società per gli Studi Storici, Archeologia ed Artistici nella Provincia di Cuneo* no. 26:41–62.

BORROMEO, CARLO

Archbishop of Milan, Carlo Borromeo (1538–1584) was a leading Church reformer following the Council of Trent. His *Instructionum Fabricae et supellectilis ecclesiasticae libri duo* (1577) prescribed rules for the design and decoration of the church. Seeking the dignity and splendor of early Christian traditions, Borromeo justified the presence and form of each ecclesiastical feature according to its effectiveness in promoting the faith. He condemned circular churches as pagan, favored the Latin-cross plan, and commended rich decoration only insofar as it served to inspire devotion. As a patron, Borromeo employed PELLEGRINO TIBALDI as his personal architect. He was canonized in 1611.

RICHARD J. TUTTLE

BIBLIOGRAPHY

BORROMEO, CARLO (1577)1857 *Saint Charles Borromeo's Instructions on Ecclesiastical Building.* Translated and edited by George J. Wigley. London: Dolman. Originally published with the title *Instructionum Fabricae et supellectilis ecclesiasticae libri duo.*

DEROO, ANDRÉ 1963 *Saint Charles Borromée, cardinal réformateur, docteur de la pastorale (1538–1584).* Paris: Editions Saint-Paul.

JEDIN, HUBERT 1971 *Carlo Borromeo.* Rome: Istituto della Enciclopedia Italiana.

BORROMINI, FRANCESCO

Francesco Borromini (1599–1667) was the great innovative genius of Italian seventeenth-century architecture and the major influence in the formation of the baroque style. Born in Bissone on Lake Lugano, now in southern Switzerland, he was originally named Francesco Castello. His first training came from his father, Giovanni Domenico Castello-Brumino, a builder in the service of the Visconti family of Milan. Possibly as early as the age of nine, Francesco was sent to Milan to learn the trade of stonecutter. He seems to have worked on decorative details of the cathedral. Milan was then governed by a Spanish viceroy, and throughout his life Borromini was to remain a partisan of the pro-Spanish party in Roman politics. Even his style of dress was considered Spanish. In Milan, Borromini would have become acquainted with the artistic and architectural doctrines of CARLO BORROMEO, the great post-Tridentine reformer of the archdiocese. He would have studied the work of an older generation of Lombard architects, particularly PELLEGRINO TIBALDI and MARTINO BASSI. The great architectural event of this period in Milan was the rebuilding of the early Christian Church of San Lorenzo (after 1573), a complex structure which would later leave its stamp on Borromini's churches of Sant'Ivo and San Carlo alle Quattro Fontane. Among the younger generation, Borromini may have had contact with FRANCESCO MARIA RICCHINO, whose buildings often show curved façades, oval plans, and other features similar to Borromini's Roman work.

In late 1619, Borromini moved to Rome, taking up lodging with Lombard relatives who were involved in the workshop of St. Peter's and soon securing employment there himself. A number of surviving drawings that show details from St. Peter's testify to the truth of a statement made by Borromini's early biographers that he would often forsake the company of his fellow workers at lunchtime to draw fragments of this great exemplar and to give himself an architectural education in the process. During the early years in Rome he changed his name from Castello to Borromini, probably to distinguish himself from the many northern workmen called Castelli then active in the Roman building trades.

The major formative influence on Borromini during these years of apprenticeship was CARLO MADERNO, a distant relative and then the official architect of St. Peter's and the most important architect in Rome. At first, Borromini exercised his original trade as a decorative stonecutter (*scarpellino*) for Maderno, doing angels' heads and other details in the new portico of St. Peter's, decorative details in the frame of the Porta Santa, and designs for the monumental bronze gate of the Cappella del Coro (now installed in the Cappella del Santo Sacramento in the nave). However, it was as a draftsman that Borromini eventually proved of greatest talent, and over the early 1620s Maderno gradually delegated most of his drafting and eventually even designing to his young assistant. In 1621, Borromini produced a drawing for Maderno's water cascade at the Villa Ludovisi in Frascati and several projects for the façade of Sant'Andrea della Valle; both show small innovations of detail within the generally conservative framework of Maderno's style. However, Borromini was allowed a free hand in the design of the lantern of Sant'Andrea, and there he introduced the unorthodox feature of a single, broad, animated capital to link together each pair of columns (1623). Further works drafted for Maderno include the campanile of the Monte di Pietà (1624) and a plan for the church of Sant'Ignazio with an unusual number of columns articulating the side chapels.

During the early years of the pontificate of Urban VIII (1623–1644), Borromini came into direct contact with his brilliant contemporary, the sculptor GIOVANNI LORENZO BERNINI, by working as draftsman for the construction of the baldachin of St. Peter's (1624–1626 and 1631–1633). The baldachin is as much a work of architecture as of sculpture, and its origins go back to the destruction of the apse of the old Constantinian basilica under Pope Clement VIII in 1591. In Constantine's church, the altar in the apse had been close to the tomb of the saint; given the Greek-cross plan and the immense dimensions of the new church, the new apse was far removed from the tomb, and separate visual forms were devised to decorate each place. The altar in the apse was decorated with a canopy supported on spiral columns of early Christian origin, while the saint's tomb under the crossing was decorated with a tasseled baldachin supported by four staves held by angels. The canopy was architectural, while the baldachin recalled temporary devices used in processions to protect persons of honor. Under Paul V, Maderno produced a project for reuniting the two forms under the crossing; it seems to have introduced the idea of a hybrid form, combining colossal spiral columns, possibly in bronze, with a tasseled baldachin. These ideas were taken much further under Bernini's direction. The four bronze spiral columns were cast and erected in 1623–1626, using in part ancient bronze beams removed from the Pantheon porch; the bronze superstructure of the baldachin was planned in 1628–1629 and carried out, with modifications, in 1631–1633. Although Bernini was in charge, Borromini was responsible for all the working drawings and, in addition, for some of the details on the vine leaves, tassels, and composite columns. His workshop was responsible for the execution of the four marble bases with their eight elaborate Barberini shields. He may also have suggested the change from semicircular ribs to the more dynamic volutes of the present canopy and the lowering of the tasseled bands which makes the whole design much more an architectural structure. Finally, after studying the effect of the baldachin within the cavernous space of the crossing of St. Peter's, shown in a series of beautiful perspective studies, Borromini devised the high impost blocks that make the upper members of the structure align with the entablature of the church when seen from several privileged points of view.

Borromini's last major project under Maderno was the Palazzo Barberini, planned after the purchase of the older Sforza Palace in 1625 and mostly built in 1628–1632. The site was located between the Piazza Grimani (now Piazza Barberini) and the Quattro Fontane, on a steep hillside outside of the built-up area of the city; both terrain and location suggested a combination palace-villa. The planning began with the submission of a number of memoranda by gentlemen and amateurs in the Barberini entourage; for the most part their advice tended toward the academic and Vitruvian (see VITRUVIUS), but one, Michelangelo Buonarroti the Younger, offered an interesting arrangement of stairs and bridges designed to deal with the steep terrain, and another suggested an oval room and a nymphaeum of the sort that found its way into the final palace. Maderno's earliest projects, drawn by Borromini, envisage an unimaginative blocklike palace modeled on the Farnese. The jump to a more interesting design seems to have come in 1628 when the earlier ideas were synthesized into new projects by PIETRO BERRETTINI DA CORTONA, Bernini, and Borromini, all working under Maderno's direction until his death in early 1629. Cortona's contribution seems to have been to take the river loggia of the Palazzo Farnese as a model, a decision which resulted in the open arcade that is such a singular feature of the present palace façade. The doors and windows were drawn by Borromini but at first represented Maderno's ideas until construction reached the uppermost story, when details (like the grotesques in the entablature, the pilaster clusters, and especially the small windows with diagonal volutes that seem to shape the space around them) began to reflect an active collaboration between Borromini and Bernini, one that continued in the door frames in the main *salone*. Bernini alone, however, may have been responsible for the sculptural details of the façade (the coat of arms and the metopes), and the oval plan of the *galleria* facing the garden. Cortona's last contribution to the architecture was the design of the riding court on the north side of the palace, shown in drawings by Borromini of 1631 but later converted to the Barberini theater. In 1631–1632, the two main factions within the family, Taddeo Barberini inhabiting the north wing and Cardinal Francesco Barberini inhabiting the south wing, began to build features in their own respective areas which ruined the unified skyline of the palace, especially when seen from the rear. Borromini attempted to maintain a unified design but, frustrated with the difficulties, left the commission in 1631.

During the period of collaboration with Bernini on the baldachin and the Palazzo Barberini, Borromini moved in the direction of greater freedom and expressiveness in his drawing style and in the design of architectural details. But he also seems to have developed a growing resentment of Bernini, who was making considerably more money out of these projects in spite of a weak grounding in the technical side of architecture, who was taking credit for the entire designs, and who tended to ridicule Maderno, Borromini's mentor. Later, these resentments would boil over into one of the great rivalries of the baroque age, but the final split had still not quite developed in the early 1630s. One of the last recorded incidents of friendly contact between them came in September 1632, when Bernini recommended Borromini for the post of architect of the Sapienza, the university of Rome. However, it was not until 1642 that work began on the university chapel of Sant'

Ivo; in the early 1630s, Borromini was still without tangible commissions.

In 1634, Borromini began work on the commission that would eventually blossom into his early masterpiece, the Church and Monastery of San Carlo alle Quattro Fontane, popularly known as San Carlino because of its diminutive size. The patrons of this church were a group of Spanish monks known as Discalced Trinitarians (*Trinitarii Scalzi*) who had arrived in Rome in 1610 and had purchased a small house at the Quattro Fontane in 1611. The Trinitarians were an older, established order, founded in 1198 for the redemption of Christian captives from the infidel. The Discalced Trinitarians, however, were a reforming offshoot of the main order and on the worst of terms with it; they were austere and unremitting in their insistence on a return to the primitive austerity of the founders. They installed a small church in a makeshift way in their house at the Quattro Fontane and dedicated it to the newly canonized San Carlo Borromeo as well as to the Trinity, the standard dedication of all of the order's churches. The monks lived in conditions of austerity, but gradually forged links with important figures in Roman society. In 1628, Padre Giovanni della Annunzia-

tione, the superior, became confessor to Cardinal Francesco Barberini; and in 1636, Urban VIII recognized the full independence of the *Scalzi* from the older, orthodox Trinitarian order. These were the conditions of patronage when Borromini assumed the commission: severe poverty, but at the same time proximity to the papal court and the order's ambition to establish its own autonomy.

In 1634–1635, Borromini built the dormitory quarters at the back or south side of the complex, including a refectory (now used as the sacristy), fourteen cells, and a capacious library. In 1635–1636, the small cloister was built connecting the dormitory with the Via Pia. Work did not begin on the church until February 1638, and shortly beforehand there was a crisis in which the majority of the monks refused to assent to Borromini's design, which they thought was too elaborate, and demanded instead a church costing about one-fifth as much. Padre Giovanni della Annunziatione called in Cardinal Francesco Barberini, and with his help convinced the monks to go along with the design, presumably in a modified version. The bare fabric of the church took somewhat more than one year to build, while the stuccoes of the interior were carried out in 1640–1641. The church was officially consecrated in 1646. The exterior was decorated over a long span of time: the side façade along the Via Felice was designed in 1641; the convent façade on the Via Pia was carried out in 1662–1664; the lower story of the church façade was built in 1665–1667, as one of Borromini's last works before his death in 1667; his original triangular campanile was replaced by the present four-sided campanile between 1667 and 1670; and finally, the upper story of the church façade was carried out on a modified design by the architect's nephew in 1675–1677.

All visitors to San Carlo are struck by the novelty and intricacy of the plan. The early drawings show Borromini working out the shape of the church in a series of revisions, one drawn on top of another in pencil, until the reworkings become almost too dense to read. The basic plan was a centralized church with a circular cupola and four crossing piers, each curving inward on the model of late antique buildings like the Oratory of the Sante Croce at the Lateran. This original plan was later expanded into a much larger quatrefoil, with four apsed spaces bulging outward from the crossing piers, rather like a design by MICHELANGELO for the Sforza Chapel in Santa Maria Maggiore. In the final revision the quatrefoil was compressed and the circular cupola squeezed into an oval to produce the present plan. Not only did the plan go through these complex changes, but the interior was made still more difficult to comprehend by the way in which architectural membering was used. The walls of the church appear to be in constant motion. The crossing piers are hollowed out at their lowest level, creating a skeletal effect of spaces glimpsed beyond the normal perimeter of the interior. Sixteen columns are set in front of the walls, as though an open pavilion of columns had been squeezed into an exotic shape by walls pressing against it. From one point of view, the columns can be read as members designed to frame the crossing piers, from another, as parts of aediculae framing the altars; the ambiguity between these two readings appears to be deliberate. The small space of the church is enlarged in an optical sense by a perspectival trick: the coffers of the apses and of the main cupola diminish in size as they recede, making the surfaces that they cover seem farther away than they really are. Everywhere there are unconventional details: capitals with inverted volutes, an egg-and-dart motif in which the "eggs" have been changed into angels' faces, altarframes in which palm fronds are mixed with animated rinceau motif. The small Barberini Chapel to the left of the high altar is decorated with very florid motifs taken from late antique architectural ornament, and the effect of this tiny space is that one is standing in a columnar sarcophagus turned inside out.

The intensely animated effect of the upper church is completely reversed in the crypt, which represents the plan of the church with an almost mathematical abstraction. There is no decoration beyond simple moldings, and the impression made on the spectator, particularly by the little octagonal space underneath the Barberini Chapel, is one of pure voids and volumes. The side spaces of the crypt were used by the monks for burial, and in April 1666 they granted Borromini permission to select a space in the crypt to construct a chapel and altar for his own tomb. To judge from markings made on a plan of the crypt, Borromini wanted to use the space directly under the high altar, although nothing was done about the matter by the time of his death.

Whereas the interior of San Carlo is Borromini's early masterpiece, the façade must be viewed as his last great work. The façade appears in plan on many of the early drawings but it gives the impression of having been added to the design later. Furthermore, it is built on a sinusoidal curve, with smooth changes of direction rather than the abrupt shifts between the concave and convex curves of his early façades. The upper story was not built until 1675–1677 and shows several uncharacteristic traits, such as the disproportionate height, the abrupt shifts in curvature, and the Berninesque angels carrying a painting aloft; there is every rea-

Borromini. San Carlo alle Quattro Fontane (central dome). Rome. 1634–1641

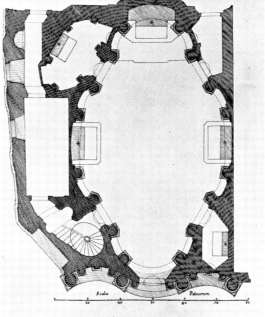

VESTIGIVM TEMPLI S. CAROLO DICATI AD QVATVOR FONTES Eq. Francisco Borromino Architecto.

Borromini. Plan of San Carlo alle Quattro Fontane. Rome. 1634–1641

son to think that this stage was designed by the architect's nephew, Bernardo Borromini.

Soon after the church was completed it began to attract attention, and there were many requests, particularly from visiting foreigners, for printed copies of the plan. Borromini never seems to have complied. Nevertheless, there are some churches or church projects close enough to be considered near-copies: the project of 1652 by Giovanni Battista Mola for a church at the northern end of Piazza Navona; a set of projects by Bernardo Borromini for a church dedicated to Sant'Eustacchio, probably done around 1665 but once thought to be preparatory drawings for San Carlo; and finally a crude provincial copy, Santa Maria del Prato in Gubbio, begun in 1662.

If San Carlo is the great ecclesiastical commission of Borromini's early career, the Oratory and Residence of the Filippini is the great domestic commission. The Filippini, or followers of Saint Philip Neri, were priests who devoted their time to confessions and to a form of devotion known as the oratory, in which men would gather to listen to informal sermons and to devotional music. Eventually, the music displaced the sermons and evolved into the genre known as oratorio. The service did not require a church and could be conducted anywhere, from private rooms to a stable, but nevertheless between 1575 and 1606, Saint Philip and his followers built the large basilica of Santa Maria in Vallicella to shelter the crowds that their apostolate was beginning to attract. The priests themselves lived in a number of older, dilapidated houses alongside the new church. Early in the seventeenth century, there were already projects for a large and dignified new residence, but the real planning did not get underway until 1624, when an elaborate series of projects was produced by the congregation's architect, PAOLO MARUSCELLI. Maruscelli's projects give the impression of being a cross between a palace and a monastery, and in fact he seems to have been given instructions to avoid both excessive austerity and excessive splendor. The middle ground he hit upon drew partly on the model of ANDREA PALLADIO's Convent of the Carità in Venice, partly on the model of Milanese ecclesiastical residences, and partly on the new type of Roman building known as the palace of a *famiglia* or princely household. He also planned an oratory but hid it inside the building without an ecclesiastical façade of its own. Maruscelli's project was approved in 1627, and over the next few years, small parts of it were put into execution, in particular the sacristy attached to the transept of Santa Maria in Vallicella.

When Borromini took over the commission in early 1637 a complete and detailed project was thus already in effect, and although changes could be introduced with special permission, wholesale innovation was out of the question. Borromini began by redesigning the oratory, which was kept in the same position as in Maruscelli's project but was made into a more skeletal structure, with singers' and cardinals' choirs at the two ends for the more elaborate musical performances, and with a delicate ribbed vault over the central space. He gave the oratory an elaborate ecclesiastical façade, which stood on the south wing of the building immediately next to the façade of Santa Maria in Vallicella. Permission was granted for this innovation on the condition that the oratory façade not compete in splendor with its older neighbor, and so it was built in brick with an extraordinarily restrained type of composite order on the lower story. Its main innovations lie in the use of fine brickwork, modeled on Roman imperial terra cotta architecture, and in the gentle curve of the plan. After the first story of the façade had been completed in 1638, there was a change in plan involving the addition of a large library to the upper floors and the expansion of the whole façade from five to seven bays wide. The façade as it appears on the present building reflects both this change and a further expansion of 1665, done after Borromini's departure.

During the construction of the residential and functional wings of the building, Borromini introduced many features into the design that tend to give the building a more palatial or aulic tone than Maruscelli had intended: a type of stairs modeled on the Palazzo Farnese in Rome, giant niches taken from the Palazzo Farnese in Piacenza, a colossal order adapted from either Palladio's Palazzo Iseppo da Porto in Vicenza or Michelangelo's Capitoline Palaces in Rome, and so forth. At the rear of the building, a special façade was built around a monumental clocktower, which was positioned to catch the eye of the traveler crossing the bridge from the Vatican and approaching along the city's busiest thoroughfare. In this adaption of a tower to possible avenues of approach Borromini seems to have anticipated some of the more interesting urban effects of CHRISTOPHER WREN's City churches. But he also seems to have been concerned to outfit the building with all the possible accouterments of an older aristocratic palace, including towers. Eventually the Filippini reached a consensus that the imagery of their residence was becoming more aristocratic than they had originally intended. This factor, combined with difficulties of personality and the temporary absence of Borromini's great protector in the congregation, VIRGILIO SPADA, led to Borromini's loss of the commission in 1650–1652 and replacement by the more docile Camillo Arcucci, who completed the remaining east and west wings.

The church generally considered to be Borromini's masterpiece is Sant'Ivo alla Sapienza, the chapel attached to the Roman university, called the Arciginnasio or Sapienza (meaning literally "Wisdom"). Although Borromini was appointed the official architect of the university in 1632, the construction of the church did not begin until 1642, after both the Oratory and San Carlo had been finished. The site for the church was a small area at the eastern end of a long, narrow courtyard that had gradually been built over the course of the entire sixteenth century, principally by the architects PIRRO LIGORIO and GIACOMO DELLA PORTA. At the eastern end of the courtyard stood a curved screen that was to constitute the chapel façade, and behind this screen, della Porta had planned a simple, circular church surmounted by a low drum and cupola. Borromini thus had to adapt his plans to the curved screen and the restricted site; in response to the challenge, he produced one of the most complex and exotic spaces in the history of Western architecture. His plan may be described as a triangle with three apses, each apse centered on one of the three sides; it has precedents on a very small scale in sketches by BALDASSARE PERUZZI and Maderno.

Borromini originally planned three altars, all in the eastern half of the church, and each one visible on a line of sight from three entrances on the western side; in the final church these would be compressed into a single altar. Early sources close to Borromini connect the plan with the shape of a bee, the six points of the interior space (three apses and three points of the triangle) corresponding roughly to the 6 parts of the insect (head, tail, and four wings); but this is probably a postfactum gloss on the plan designed to attract the sympathy and the finances of the Barberini, under whose patronage the church was begun. Urban VIII died in 1644, at about the time the basic structure was being vaulted; the exotic superstructure and decoration dragged on for more than two decades, and eventually came to reflect the family heraldry of two additional pontificates. The lantern and spiral were built in 1652, and they are appropriately crowned with the Pamphilj dove and orb to reflect the patronage of Pope Innocent X. Finally, the stucco decoration of the interior of the cupola reflects the Chigi heraldry of Pope Alexander VII, who subsidized the completion of the church in 1659–1660 and the construction of the neighboring Biblioteca Alessandrina, the university library, in 1660–1666. The painting over the high altar was begun by Cortona but was finished long after his death by a disciple, Giovanni Ventura Borghese, in

1683. The original marble altarframe, now removed, was designed by Giovanni Battista Contini (see CONTINI FAMILY) in 1684–1685. The twelve niches on the interior of the church were filled with stucco statues of the apostles in 1699 or shortly thereafter; the sculptor was Francesco Galesini, working under Contini's supervision; these statues were shown in a print of 1720 but were later removed. The whole interior was somewhat disastrously restored in the mid-nineteenth century, when most of the surface was painted to resemble fictive marble. Now the interior has been restored to a uniform white.

Sant'Ivo is a relatively small church, but it creates an effect of tremendous splendor and power, particularly on the spectator who enters it for the first time. Giant pilasters rise from floor to cornice, and the dome begins to spring immediately above the cornice, without the usual intermediate drum. The source for this special type of structure is to be found in Lombardy; and the drumless cupola of San Lorenzo in Milan, as re-

Borromini.
Sant'Ivo alla Sapienza.
Rome.
1642–1660

built by Martino Bassi after 1573, certainly influenced Borromini. For the most part, the lower zone of Sant'Ivo is windowless, and light floods into the church from above, through the lantern and six windows set into the rising curve of the dome. Before the nineteenth-century restorations, light also streamed down over the high altar from a hidden source above, after entering from the east and being reflected down with the help of steel mirrors. According to Borromini himself, the use of hidden lighting was modeled on Bernini's Cornaro Chapel. The extraordinary plan seems to set the walls of the church in motion, while the spectator's eye is drawn relentlessly upward. The motion of the walls is continued into the cupola, which at first sight appears like a billowing tent, but which also recalls the so-called pumpkin vaults familiar from Hadrianic architecture, such as the Piazza d'Oro in Hadrian's Villa at Tivoli. This strong Roman feeling of Sant'Ivo, which in the end dominates over the various Lombard and Gothic elements in the design, is most evident on the exterior of the cupola. The drum bulges outward, only to be pushed back in by buttresslike pilasters like those found at the so-called Temple of Minerva Medica; the lantern (called a tempietto in the documents) has concave scallops around the sides like the Temple of Venus in Baalbek and also, most probably, like ancient funerary monuments once standing in the vicinity of Rome but now vanished.

Unraveling the iconography of Sant'Ivo has proved a complex task, and conflicting theories abound. On the earliest plan for the church, Bor-

Borromini.
Sant'Ivo alla Sapienza.
Rome.
1642–1660

romini inscribed some verses from Proverbs 9: "Wisdom has built herself a house—She has erected seven columns—She has laid her table." The last of these verses, which was to have been inscribed on the pedestal of a statue over the high altar, suggests that the moral emphasis of the Old Testament sapiential literature is being given eucharistic overtones, with the table of the verse standing for the altar on which mass is celebrated. The bees drawn at the center of this plan, aside from their role as Barberini dynastic symbols, can be taken as symbols of a more secular or literary kind of wisdom. The geometry of the plan has been taken as a reference to the Star of Solomon, the Temple of Solomon, and the *Domus Sapientiae* or House of Wisdom. The iconography of the exterior is still more complex. From the Biblical text alone one might have expected an extravagant crowning feature: "Wisdom has proclaimed from the city's heights, 'Who is ignorant? Let him step this way.'" On top of the lantern, Borromini designed a spiral that winds upward in counterclockwise fashion for a little more than three full turns. At the top is a flaming laurel wreath, surmounted by an iron framework carrying the Pamphilj globe, dove, *fleur-de-lys,* and cross. The spiral was originally designed with a parapet to protect anyone walking around it. The whole affair suggests an arduous ascent to an enflamed or inspired goal. More specific interpretations have been advanced based on various visual comparisons. They include, in descending order of probability, the *pharos* or ancient lighthouse of Alexandria, the Tower of Babel, the column of fire that guided the Israelites in the desert, and Mount Purgatory as described by Dante. Whatever the original reference, it seems to have been altered shortly after construction by the introduction of stucco gems, pearls, and other ornaments that suggest a crown or papal tiara. The new image is somewhat awkward, since neither crowns nor tiaras wind in spirals. Possibly the change is to be connected with the introduction of many heraldic and dynastic motifs under Alexander VII, which include jewel-encrusted crowns among the stuccoes on the interior of the cupola.

All of the commissions discussed thus far were begun under the pontificate of Urban VIII. However, Borromini's period of greatest official favor and renown came during the subsequent pontificate of Innocent X Pamphilj (1644–1655). Innocent X came into office as part of a wave of reaction against the Barberini and their protégés. Bernini suffered a temporary eclipse in prestige, and soon his campanile on the south side of the façade of St. Peter's was under attack for overloading the foundations. Borromini's criticisms eventually contributed to the decision to dismantle the campanile. Furthermore, the new political climate under Innocent X tended to be pro-Spanish, and Borromini's Milanese origins and Spanish sympathies fitted this outlook perfectly. Although the Pamphilj continued to work with a number of different architects, Borromini soon emerged as their dynastic architect par excellence, and he was able to dominate the two major commissions of the pontificate: the rebuilding of the Lateran basilica and the conversion of the Piazza Navona into a Pamphilj Forum.

In 1646, Innocent X put Virgilio Spada in charge of two of the major basilicas of Rome: San Paolo fuori le mura and San Giovanni in Laterano. Little was done at San Paolo beyond repairs to the roof, but the Lateran became the object of a major restoration amounting almost to a total rebuilding of the nave, carried out between 1646 and 1650. The Lateran was the official cathedral of Rome, but due to its outlying location and to the continued residence of the popes at the Vatican since their return from Avignon it suffered from neglect. The transept was entirely rebuilt for the Holy Year of 1600 by Pope Clement VIII, but the nave, hard hit in the middle ages by several fires and an earthquake, was still in ruinous condition, with the north wall leaning precipitously inward. Borromini would probably have enjoyed the opportunity for a total reconstruction, but the keynote of the design, according to the pope, was to be restoration of what he thought was the Constantinian basilica, preserving as much as possible of the old structure and even retaining the roof and coffered ceiling that was thought to be a work of Michelangelo. In his respect for the old building Innocent X was following broader intellectual currents, founded particularly in the writings of Cardinal Baronius and other Oratorians, who insisted on veneration for the incunabula of the early Christian past.

Borromini began by drafting three alternative schemes for the reconstruction of the nave, each modeled in a loose way on Michelangelo's design for the Capitoline palaces. All of them involved consolidating the ruinous old walls and opening up large new arches to connect the nave with the side aisles. In the final design, pairs of pilasters were used to form enormous piers that stretch from floor to coffered ceiling, with large arches and generous windows opened up between them. The reconstruction was a remarkable feat of engineering. The arches had to be cut in the side walls while the old roof and ceiling still stood above them; and the leaning north wall had to be chained to a new outer wall to prevent its collapse. Probably in the hope that some future pope would give permission to remove the coffered ceiling and crown the nave with a massive vault, Borromini

built the beginnings of buttresses that were intended, when completed, to take the thrust that the vault would exert. A recently discovered section drawing shows a remarkably classical barrel vault with coffers as Borromini's first idea; possibly, if the opportunity had been given him, he would have allowed the shape to evolve into something more like the vault of the Propaganda Fide.

Thus, without the planned vault, the Lateran nave is to be viewed as a fragment of a larger design. On the other hand, it is in the side aisles that Borromini shows his consummate skill in dramatic lighting and in the shaping of space. He was allowed to dismantle the old side aisles completely; twenty-four of the thirty-six columns of *verde antico* marble that had supported the old roofs were reused in the statue niches of the nave. The two inner side aisles were built with alternating barrel and sail vaults and lit by ingenious "light boxes" that convey illumination indirectly into the interior; the two outer aisles were covered by flat architraves. The whole area is full of interesting oblique perspectives, and the cherubs' heads that are used instead of the normal inanimate brackets to support the flat architraves make it seem as though the earthly space had been invaded by an intense angelic presence.

The decoration of the main nave was an important part of the reconstruction, and in general it was intended to augment the Constantinian flavor of the whole design. On the top of the side walls were a series of large oval openings that in the eighteenth century were filled with paintings of the prophets, but that originally were intended as enormous reliquaries, showing the fragments of the Constantinian (really late medieval) walls beneath. They were meant to prove that the old basilica had been truly preserved. In the middle level were a series of twelve stucco reliefs by followers of Alessandro Algardi showing scenes from the Old and New Testaments paired typologically. The program was based on texts of the seventh century which purported to describe the original Constantinian decorative program. Finally, on the lower level of the nave Borromini installed twelve sumptuous niches that protrude out "like a human breast" from the nave walls. Originally these niches were meant to contain statues of the four evangelists, the four Latin, and the four Greek fathers of the church (a mixture that recalls Bernini's Chair of St. Peter). But very early on it was decided to install statues of the twelve apostles instead. In the rear of each niche is a marble door, and the overall effect would have been to suggest the Heavenly City of Jerusalem, entered by the Apostles through twelve doors. As it was, the decoration of the nave had to be carried out in great haste to meet the deadline of 1650, the Holy Year when 700,000 pilgrims would visit the shrines of the city; there was no time even to begin such an extensive sculptural program, and the statues of the apostles were not carried out until the early eighteenth century. Other embellishments that are mentioned in the sources were designs for a series of houses leading to the basilica from Santa Maria Maggiore, a piazza in front of the church, and a two-story façade with benediction loggia rivaling that of St. Peter's. Borromini's façade designs apparently were still extant in the early eighteenth century but were subsequently lost; possibly distant reflections of them may be seen in the façade of Santa Maria in Via Lata by Cortona (1658–1662) and in CARLO RAINALDI's unexecuted façade project for Santa Maria in Campitelli (1658).

Work continued on the Lateran even after Innocent X's death. Alexander VII commissioned Borromini to design frames and ornament to surround many late medieval tomb fragments which had been removed from the old basilica but were to be reinstalled in the new side aisles. These designs show an interesting use of perspective to simulate depth, and a new level of fantasy inspired by the medieval fragments. Similarly exotic frames were designed for a fresco, attributed to Giotto, showing Pope Boniface VIII instituting the Jubilee of 1300, and for an inscription commemorating Alexander VII's predecessor and namesake, Alexander III. Although they make ingenious use of Chigi heraldry, the designs were criticized by the pope himself as being too Gothic.

The project closest to Innocent X's heart was the transformation of the Piazza Navona into a Pamphilj Forum. The Piazza Navona was originally the Stadium of Domitian, built in A.D. 92–96 with a straight south end and a curved north end according to the Greek practice; it was not a circus and did not have an obelisk. Abandoned after the barbarian invasions and partly hidden by a steadily rising ground level, the stadium saw a rebirth of activity in the fifteenth century and the construction of many noble palaces on top of the arches that lined its periphery. The first Pamphilj Palace was built at the southwest corner in 1471–1497. Innocent X's projects began with a rebuilding of this palace in 1645–1648, beginning a steady expansion northward that would eventually result in the rebuilding of most of the western side of the piazza. The official architects of the palace were GIROLAMO RAINALDI and Carlo Rainaldi, but Borromini presented alternative designs which made use of a giant order and showed projects for an open loggia or viewing-box on top of the roof. The palace was finished according to the Rainaldis'

design, but in 1646 Borromini built a long thin gallery on the north side of the palace, using his idea of a viewing-box with a Serlian motif for the gallery façade. The imagery of the gallery façade, drawn from the papal benediction loggia shown in RAPHAEL's *Fire in the Borgo* and from imperial circus loggias shown on late antique consular diptychs, is built around the idea of the palace as a new Vatican. The Serlian motif functions as a symbol of the ideal presence of the pope, and it is recorded that near the end of his life Innocent X actually intended to transfer the papal court to the Piazza Navona. Also involved is a creative archeological mistake, in which the stadium is reinterpreted as a circus and the palace as a new Palatine. The missing obelisk was supplied by Borromini's design for a fountain of 1647, in which the obelisk of the Circus of Maxentius is shown standing over a pedestal with four lions' faces spewing water; soon afterward, however, the design was transferred to Bernini and evolved into the famous Four Rivers Fountain.

By 1652, Innocent X decided on a total rebuilding of the small shrine of Sant'Agnese, which stood immediately to the north of Borromini's gallery. The commission would change hands many times before the church was complete. Foundations were laid according to the designs of the Rainaldi workshop, and the crossing piers and façade begun according to their direction. Borromini took over the commission in 1653 and attempted to redesign the crossing piers by giving them convex faces, like his earliest plan for San Carlo. In the end, the piers were left with straight faces and the interior space articulated by columns. On the exterior, Borromini demolished the beginnings of the Rainaldi façade and built his own façade up to the cornice level. It was designed along a concave, oval curve with broad campanili on either side; by the time of Innocent X's death in 1655 it was completed up to the level of the pediment and cornice. The loss of his great patron was a severe blow to Borromini, however, and the years 1655–1657 mark a psychological low point in his career. He refused to direct the work at Sant'Agnese, browsing in the bookstalls of the area while the crews of workmen went idle for want of instructions. Finally in 1657, he was replaced by a committee of architects, including Carlo Rainaldi, who continued the church on a revised design. What one sees today is Borromini's façade and campanili up to the level of the main cornice; a classicizing pediment designed by Bernini in 1666 to replace Borromini's pediment; and Rainaldi's cupola and upper stories of the campanili.

Around the time of the Palazzo Pamphilj, Borromini was also responsible for three major palace remodelings, specifically the Palazzo Carpegna, the Palazzo Falconieri, and the Palazzo Spada. Between 1638 and 1643, he produced an extensive series of designs for Count Ambrogio Carpegna, who had acquired a smaller palace and larger plots of adjacent property near the Trevi Fountain. Borromini incorporated the older palace into the projects for the new building and ingeniously concealed the irregularities of the site by the use of curved walls, niches, and many examples of fictive symmetry that derive from the ruins of Hadrian's Villa. The most interesting plans show a large oval courtyard at the center of the scheme, surrounded by an arcade on paired columns resembling the recently completed cloister of San Carlo alle Quattro Fontane. In 1641, he even prepared a design that would have called for the oval courtyard to span a public street and continue onto an adjacent property. As it was, Ambrogio Carpegna died in 1643 and the palace was completed on less ambitious designs by his brother Cardinal Ulderico Carpegna. The one feature of note is the large spiral ramp that gives access to the upper floors. The first two turns of the ramp are concealed behind an elaborate display of stucco ornament that contains many iconographical references appropriate to the family: the winged Medusa shield, abundant flowers, and inverted cornucopias drawn from Ripa's emblem of Hospitality. The cornucopia on the left pours forth symbols of the family's succession and nobility, such as crowns and a baby; while the cornucopia on the right pours forth fruits and pomegranates.

The Palazzo Falconieri on the Via Giulia contains still more elaborate references to family iconography and imagery drawn from emblem books. In 1638, Orazio Falconieri bought a sixteenth-century palace behind the Palazzo Farnese that consisted of a symmetrical, seven-bay façade with a central portal. The neighboring property was later acquired, and in 1646, Borromini enlarged the Via Giulia façade, adding a false portal and three additional bays. The façade was covered with new rustication and the whole broad front was crowned with a cornice full of antique emblems of victory; at either end, two large herms with realistic falcon's heads provide strong boundaries to the design as well as references to the Falconieri family. On the river side of the palace, Borromini designed a U-shaped courtyard and a rooftop loggia that echoes, in a very baroque way, Giacomo della Porta's nearby river loggia in the Palazzo Farnese. On the interior, Borromini built a new staircase, with a vestibule on the *piano nobile* recalling the Palazzo Farnese, and many interesting door frames in rich colored marbles. But the main innovation on the interior was a series of vaulted ceilings with

stucco designs drawn from sixteenth-century emblem books, symbolizing Justice and other themes relating to Orazio Falconieri's official career. In the nineteenth century the palace passed into the hands of the Medici del Vascello family, and much of the interior reflects their rebuilding campaign of 1891–1895. Most of Borromini's ceilings survive, but they exhibit a color scheme (gilt, with deeply saturated reds and blues) closer to the world of ROBERT ADAM than to seventeenth-century taste. In 1927, the palace was acquired by the Hungarian government as the seat of their Roman academy; it was extensively restored in 1973–1979.

The Palazzo Spada contains one of Borromini's best known works, the small colonnade with a built-in perspectival distortion that makes the space seem much longer than it really is. Cardinal Bernardino Spada, the older brother of Virgilio Spada, bought the older Renaissance palace of Cardinal Capodiferro, near the Palazzo Farnese, in 1632. He first employed Maruscelli to adapt it to his needs, and over the next decade Maruscelli redesigned the atrium, gardens, and staircase, and in addition built a picture gallery and a meridian gallery or elaborate solar clock and calendar. Cardinal Spada was deeply interested in perspective and knew several of the famous mathematicians attached to the French Minim convent at the Trinità dei Monti. Maruscelli painted some sort of fictive perspective design on a garden wall in 1640–1642, which was the forerunner of the present colonnade. Borromini became Spada's architect in about 1650, and in 1652, he and his assistant Francesco Righi built the present colonnade, using the perspectival expertise and probably the designs of an Augustinian priest, Giovanni Maria da Bitonto. An inscription that formerly stood above the colonnade gives some idea of the irony that Cardinal Spada saw in it: just as the length of the colonnade is not what it seems, so too all worldly *grandezza* is illusory. Borromini's other important contribution to the palace was the design of a painted backdrop for the piazza, which included medieval crenellations such as a rural castle, fictive diamond-shaped rustication of the sort found on villa gates, and an *Abundance* fountain modeled on the image of a woman spouting water from her breasts then visible in the Villa Farnesina across the Tiber.

Borromini's two great late works, Sant'Andrea delle Fratte and the Propaganda Fide, stand in close proximity to one another in a newly developed area of Rome known as *Capo le case* (end of the houses) or *Le fratte* (the hedges), both names reflecting the recent urbanization of the district. Sant'Andrea was an old church which had been given to the order of Minims of San Francesco di

Paola by Pope Sixtus V in 1585. A new church was begun on the site in 1604 on the designs of Gaspare Guerra (see GUERRA FAMILY) of Modena, an architect in the service of Ottavio del Bufalo, a nobleman who offered to finance the completion of the church but who died in 1612 without leaving sufficient funds. The Minims themselves completed the nave vault, but then work stagnated. In 1653, Ottavio's son, the Marchese Paolo del Bufalo, offered to complete the church and retained Borromini as his architect. Paolo directed the patronage of the work from his base in Florence, but the full documentation has never been found, and there are only vague indications of a certain amount of conflict between del Bufalo and the Minims. The campanile of the church was built between 1653 and 1659. It is one of Borromini's most fantastic designs, beginning from a square base, rising through a circular tempietto and then a story made up of eight angelic herms arranged around four concave niches, and terminating in a bizarre device that combines the arms of the Minims with those of the del Bufalo family (a buffalo with a ring through his nose). The drum and cupola were underway by around 1660, but had advanced only one story by 1665, and work was completely stopped by the time of Borromini's death in 1667. The cupola was finished in a makeshift way under Mattia de' Rossi in 1686–1691. The standard Roman construction procedure was to raise scaffolding outside the building as the basic structure rose, and then to apply the coat of decorative stucco as the scaffolding came down. Thus, the crude, rough brickwork of the cupola of Sant'Andrea, in spite of its undeniable power, would have given way to a more elegant stucco finish if Borromini had been able to complete the building; in fact, drawings exist showing the embellishment of some of the rough window frames with details like buffalo heads. Other drawings suggest that the cupola was to have at least one more story, more dramatic in its use of curved forms than the lantern of Sant'Ivo; and a drawing by Juvarra, who may have seen a model of Borromini's design, suggests that Borromini intended to use hidden lighting, channeled down into the top of the cupola interior, to illuminate four windows with the motto of the Minims, "Charitas." Even in its unfinished state, however, the drum appears as one of Borromini's most powerful creations. Echoing the complexities of ancient sepulchral architecture (in particular, the tomb known as the Conocchia on the Via Appia near Capua), and based on a complex geometrical plan, the drum of Sant'Andrea is shaped by the intersection of deep convex and concave curves, close in spirit to the late style of the façade of San

Carlo alle Quattro Fontane.

The Propaganda Fide was the great institutional commission of Borromini's late career, analogous in many ways to the Oratory and residence of the Filippini, but more highly evolved and self-assured in style. The building was to be the home of two related institutions: the Congregation of the Propagation of the Faith (Propaganda Fide), a missionary organization founded in 1622; and the Collegium Urbanum, a missionary college founded by Urban VIII in 1627. The original building was a late sixteenth-century palace near the southern edge of the Piazza di Spagna, the Palazzo Ferratini. A small oval chapel was built on the same block near this palace by Bernini in 1634; and in 1644, the façade of the palace facing the Piazza di Spagna was redesigned and reinforced, in part with Bernini's advice. In 1639–1645, the architect Gaspare de' Vecchi built a long dormitory wing on the eastern side of the block. De' Vecchi died in 1644 while work was in progress, and in 1646, Borromini took his place as the Congregation's architect. His first overall plan for the entire block dates from 1652, but work progressed slowly, with many changes in plan. The west wing was built between 1655 and 1662; Bernini's Chapel of the Three Wise Men (Re Magi) was demolished about 1660 and replaced by Borromini's present chapel and façade, which was completed about 1664 and stuccoed about 1665. The uppermost story of the façade, an addition to the original design, was finished by 1666, and minor decorative work was still going on by the time of Borromini's death.

Borromini's Re Magi Chapel represents a rethinking of many of the themes of the Oratory of the Filippini. It is a highly skeletal structure, with perforated piers and passages winding around it on the upper level. The elevation, although it features capitals and moldings of a typically Borrominesque stamp, is a paraphrase of Palladio's façade of the Palazzo Valmarana in Vicenza, where the main theme was also the triple superposition of the orders. The vault is the most dynamic in Borromini's work, with ribs that create diamond or alpha patterns as they interlock across its surface. The façade is a starkly powerful composition, using giant pilasters of no recognizable order that bend and turn along arcs that seem to radiate from the spectator's eye as he moves down the adjacent street. The windows are powerful sculptural forms that alternate between concave and convex shapes, with the central window acting as a kind of summation of both types. Like the Oratory façade, it uses a degree of camouflage: the left half covers the Re Magi Chapel; the right half covers functional spaces such as staircases and shops; the central door opens onto a loggia along one side of the main courtyard. But unlike the Oratory façade, that of the Propaganda is not easily recognizable as a church façade; it seems more appropriate for a palace, and in fact its closest contemporary relative is Bernini's façade for the Palazzo Chigi a Piazza Santi Apostoli of 1664.

Borromini was something of a melancholy genius, and his personality had its dark and difficult side. Patrons complained about his "impossible" nature; he was jealous of rivals; and there were stormy periods even with friends and protectors like Virgilio Spada. Basically, he was a stonecutter who aspired to artistic independence and then to nobility, changing professions twice and suffering all the tensions that would normally be associated with this sort of rapid rise in seventeenth-century society. There were several periods of acute crisis in his life. In 1649, a man named Marco Antonio Bussoni was murdered by workmen in the Lateran for tampering with the marbles; Borromini was held responsible, but because of his special services to the basilica he incurred only a brief removal from Rome. In 1652, he was received into the Order of Christ with the rank of Knight, but in 1655 his great patron Innocent X died, and the depression and irascible conduct of the next two years cost Borromini the commission of Sant'Agnese. By 1657, he was functioning once more, but a psychological crisis arrived again in late July 1667 and eventually led to his dramatic suicide on August 2, 1667, when he wrote his will by candlelight and then fell on his sword, in the manner of the ancient Stoics.

Aside from his extraordinary innovations in architecture, such as curving walls and façades, complex geometrical plans, the revival of intricate Hadrianic shapes and of complex patterns of ancient brickwork, and unlimited innovations in the realm of architectural detail, Borromini also brought about a revolution in architectural draftsmanship. He was the first to use the graphite pencil as a medium for presentation drawings in place of the traditional ink and wash. As a result, his drawings show several layers of rethinking at the same time, and some of the most complex elevations almost give the effect of seeing through a building, as in an X-ray. He saved his drawings religiously and considered them his "children"; in 1665, he refused to enter the Louvre competition because he did not want his children sent forth begging into the world, as he put it. At several points during his career, he considered publishing his work through the medium of engravings. In 1647, he collaborated on a detailed description of the Oratory and Residence of the Filippini with Virgilio Spada, but then withheld the drawings that he had promised

to provide so that the manuscript remained unpublished. In the 1650s, his outlet for publishing both his ideas and his drawings was the medium of guidebooks, especially those written by his friend Fioravante Martinelli. In about 1660, he conceived the idea of publishing his complete works, both the actual buildings and unexecuted projects. He commissioned a series of engravings from the Frenchman Domenico Barrière, showing plans and elevations of the Oratory and Sant'Ivo. But the project was never completed, and some of the material assembled was burned just before his suicide. Several engravers and publishers had access to the remaining drawings, but the most ambitious publication was undertaken in 1720–1725 by Sebastiano Giannini, who published all the surviving plates of Sant'Ivo, adding many of his own. He later added the text of the manuscript of 1647 on the Oratory of the Filippini, which he also translated into Latin and called the *Opus Architectonicum.* Giannini also prepared a publication of San Carlo alle Quattro Fontane, which exists in only one proof copy, and possibly envisaged one further volume of unknown content. In 1730, the entire corpus of drawings was acquired by Baron Philipp von Stosch and brought to Florence; in 1769, it passed to the Vienna Hofbibliothek as part of Stosch's enormous encyclopedic geographical *Atlas,* and today the bulk of the drawings are preserved in the Albertina, Vienna.

Borromini certainly had an articulate architectural theory, but because of the nature of the publications there is no single, uncomplicated statement of it. From the text of the *Opus Architectonicum* it is clear that he venerated ancient Roman architecture, and his work testifies to an intense study of Hadrian's Villa and numerous other remains. He also declares his allegiance to "Michelangelo, Prince of the Architects," but his work reveals borrowings not only from Michelangelo but also from a broad spectrum of sources, particularly sixteenth-century masters such as DONATO BRAMANTE, Raphael, SEBASTIANO SERLIO, Palladio, and GIACOMO BAROZZI DE VIGNOLA. All of his contemporaries revered Michelangelo, but this great breadth of architectural erudition is unique to Borromini. While respecting Vitruvius and the sixteenth-century textbooks, he stressed the need for creative innovation both in spatial forms and in details; by the end of his life, the cumulative impact of his innovations was beginning to give him the reputation of an architectural heretic. Although he had an assistant, Francesco Righi, he had no students or immediate followers. His nephew, Bernardo Castelli-Borromini, inherited his drawings and attempted to establish himself as his uncle's successor, but failed due to his utter lack of talent. Although many of Borromini's characteristic details gradually entered the Roman vocabulary and although there was an interesting revival of his style in Rome in the early eighteenth century, the person who best understood his principles of design was an outsider, the Theatine monk GUARINO GUARINI, whose churches in Turin show Borromini's heritage at its most profound.

JOSEPH CONNORS

WORKS

1619–1623, St. Peter's (decorative details); 1623, Sant'Andrea della Valle (lantern); 1623–1624, Carlo Maderno Tomb, San Giovanni dei Fiorentini; 1624, Monte di Pietà (campanile); 1624–1633, St. Peter's (decorative details and volutes of baldachin); 1627, St. Peter's (grille of the Cappella del Sacramento); 1628–1632, Palazzo Barberini (decorative details); 1634–1641, San Carlo alle Quattro Fontane; 1637–1652, Filippini Residence and Oratory; 1638–1639, Santa Lucia in Selci (Cappella Landi); Rome. 1638–1642, Santi Apostoli (Filomarini Altar), Naples. 1638–1643, Palazzo Carpegna; 1642–1660, Sant'Ivo alla Sapienza; 1643–1646, Santa Maria dei Sette Dolori; 1646, Pamphilj Gallery; 1646–1650, San Giovanni in Laterno (rebuilding of nave and aisles); 1646–1656, Palazzo Falconieri (remodeling and enlargement); 1647, Palazzo di Spagna (staircase remodeling); 1650, Ceva Memorial, Lateran Baptistery; c.1650, Palazzo Giustiani (portal and remodeling); c.1650?, Villa Giustiani al Laterno (façade remodeling); 1650–1653, Palazzo Spada-Capodiferro (colonnade, piazza, and remodeling); 1652–1667, Propaganda Fide; 1653–1657, Sant'Agnese in Piazza Navona (interior and façade to cornice level); 1653–1667, Sant'Andrea delle Fratte (unfinished cupola and campanile); 1655–?, Lateran Tombs; 1657, Lateran Baptistery (frieze); before 1659, Sant'Anastasia (tribune); 1659, Piazza Sant'Agostino; 1659, San Giovanni in Oleo (remodeling); 1660–1666, Biblioteca Alessandrina alla Sapienza; 1661–1662, Palazzo del Banco di Santo Spirito a Piazza Monte Giordano (later Palazzo Spada); 1663–1666, Collegio Innocenziano a Piazza Navona; 1665–1667, San Carlo alle Quattro Fontane (lower story of façade); Rome. 1667?, Villa Falconieri, Frascati, Italy. *n.d., Villa of Fioravante Martinelli a Monte Mario, Rome.

BIBLIOGRAPHY

ACCADEMIA NAZIONALE DI SAN LUCA 1967 *Studi sul Borromini.* Rome: De Luca.
ANTONAZZI, GIOVANNI 1979 *Il Palazzo di Propaganda.* Rome: De Luca.
BLUNT, ANTHONY 1979 *Borromini.* Harmondsworth, England: Penguin; Cambridge, Mass.: Harvard University Press.
BORROMINI, FRANCESCO, and SPADA, VIRGILIO (1720–1725)1964 *Opus Architectonicum.* Reprint. London: Gregg.
CONNORS, JOSEPH 1980 *Borromini and the Roman Oratory: Style and Society.* Cambridge, Mass.: M.I.T. Press.
DE BERNARDI FERRERO, DARIA 1967 *L'opera di Fran-* cesco Borromini nella letteratura artistica e nelle incisioni dell'otà barocca. Turin, Italy: Albra.
EIMER, GERHARD 1970 *La fabbrica di S. Agnese in Navona.* Stockholm: Almqvist & Wiksell.
GÜTHLEIN, KLAUS 1979 "Quellen aus dem Familienarchiv Spada zum römischen Barock." *Römisches Jahrbuch für Kunstgeschichte* 18:173–246.
HEIMBÜRGER RAVALLI, MINNA 1977 *Architettura scultura e arte minori nel barocco italiano. Ricerche nell'Archivio Spada.* Florence: Olschki.
HEMPEL, EBERHARD 1924 *Francesco Borromini.* Vienna: Schroll.
HIBBARD, HOWARD 1971 *Carlo Maderno and Roman Architecture: 1580–1630.* London: Zwemmer.
INCISA DELLA ROCCHETTA, GIOVANNI 1967 "Un dialogo del p. Virgilio Spada sulla fabbrica dei Filippini." *Archivio della Societa Romana di Storia Patria* 90:165–211.
MARTINELLI, FIORAVANTI (1660–1662)1969 *Roma nel seicento.* Edited by Cesare D'Onofrio. Florence: Vallechi. Originally published with the title *Roma ornata dall'architettura, pittura e scultura.*
NEPPI, LIONELLO 1975 *Palazzo Spada.* Rome: Editalia.
OST, HANS 1967 "Borrominis römische Universitätskirche S. Ivo alla Sapienza." *Zeitschrift für Kunstgeschichte* 30:101–142.
PIAZZO, MARCELLO DEL (editor) 1968 *Raguagli borrominiani.* Rome: Ministero dell'Interno.
PORTOGHESI, PAOLO 1964 *Borromini nella cultura europea.* Rome: Officina.
PORTOGHESI, PAOLO 1967 *Borromini. Architettura come linguaggio.* Rome: Bozzi.
PREIMESBERGER, RUDOLF 1976 "Pontiflex romanus per Aeneam praesignatus: Die Galleria Pamphilj und ihre Fresken." *Römisches Jahrbuch für Kunstgeschichte* 16:221–288.
STEINBERG, LEO 1977 *Borromini's San Carlo alle Quattro Fontane: A Study in Multiple Form and Architectural Symbolism.* New York: Garland.
THELEN, HEINRICH 1967 *Francesco Borromini: Die Handzeichnungen.* Graz, Austria: Akademische Druck- u. Verlagsanstalt.
THELEN, HEINRICH 1967 *Zur Entstehungsgeschichte der Hochalter-Architektur von St. Peter in Rom.* Berlin: Mann.
WITTKOWER, RUDOLF (1967)1975 "Francesco Borromini, his Character and Life." In *Studies in the Italian Baroque.* London: Thames & Hudson.

BOSSAN, PIERRE

Born in Lyons, Pierre Marie Bossan (1814–1888) was the son of a stonemason. He was trained in the atelier of HENRI LABROUSTE, to whom he became greatly devoted. Appointed *architecte diocésain* in Lyons in 1844, he erected several medievalizing buildings, most notably the Church of Saint-Georges (1844) and the Hôtel Blanchon (1845).

He spent the years from 1847 to 1852 in Italy and Sicily pursuing business speculations, but upon returning to Lyons he began designing churches in a striking Byzantinizing *néo-Grec* style, beginning with that at Couzon of 1854 and culminating with those at Ars of 1862, La Louvesque of 1865, and the massive votive church at Fourvière above Lyons (1866–1888).

DAVID T. VAN ZANTEN

WORKS

1844, Church of Saint-Georges; 1845, Hôtel Blanchon; Lyons, France. 1854, Parish Church, Couzon, France. 1856, Church of the Immaculate Conception, Lyons, France. 1859, Parish Church, Nandax, France. 1862, Pilgrimage Church of Saint Philomène, Ars, France. 1865, Pilgrimage Church of Saint François Regis, La Louvesque, France. 1866, Notre-Dame-de-la-Roche, Sauvage, France. 1866–1888, Notre Dame de Fourvière (not completed until 1891 by Louis Jean Sainte-Marie Perrin), Lyons, France.

BIBLIOGRAPHY

SAINTE-MARIE PERRIN, LOUIS JEAN 1889 *Pierre Bossan, architecte.* Lyons, France: Mougin-Rhjand.
SAINTE-MARIE PERRIN, LOUIS JEAN (1896)1912 *La Basilique de Fourvière.* Lyons, France: Vitte.
THIOLLIER, FELIX 1891 *L'Oeuvre de Pierre Bossan, architecte.* Montbrisson, France: Brassart.

BOSSE, ABRAHAM

An appreciated engraver, Abraham Bosse (1602–1676) also published many treatises on perspective and art theory including the theory of architecture. From 1648 to 1660, Bosse taught perspective at the French Royal Academy of Painting and Sculpture. Adapting the new geometrical perspective method of Gerard Desargues to fine arts, Bosse was the first art theorist in France to develop a systematic art doctrine.

WALTER KAMBARTEL

BIBLIOGRAPHY

BLUM, ANDRÉ 1924 *Abraham Bosse et la société française au dix-septième siècle.* Paris: Morancé.
BOSSE, ABRAHAM 1643 *La pratique du trait à preuves de M. Desargues pour la coupe des pierres en l'architecture.* Paris: Des-Hayes.
BOSSE, ABRAHAM 1659 *Représentations géométrales de plusieurs parties de bastiments faites par les reigles de l'architecture antique et de qui les mesures sont réduittes en piedz, poulces et lignes, afin de s'accomoder à la manière de mesurer la plus en uzage parmy le commun des ouvriers.* Paris: The author.
BOSSE, ABRAHAM 1664a *Des ordres de colonnes en l'architecture et plusieurs autres dépendances d'icelle.* Paris: The author.
BOSSE, ABRAHAM 1664b *Traité des manières de dessiner les ordres de l'architecture antique en toutes leurs parties. . . .* Paris: The author.
BOSSE, ABRAHAM 1665 *Traité des pratiques géométrales et perspectives enseignées dans l'Académie Royale de la Peinture et Sculpture.* Paris: The author.
KAUFFMANN, GEORG 1960 *Poussin-Studien.* Berlin: de Gruyter.

BOSWORTH, WILLIAM WELLES

William Welles Bosworth (1869–1966), born in Marietta, Ohio, received his early education at the Marietta Academy. He subsequently entered the Massachusetts Institute of Technology, graduating in 1889. He then worked for SHEPLEY, RUTAN, AND COOLIDGE; FREDERICK LAW OLMSTED; and WILLIAM ROTCH WARE. Following a European tour with Ware, he began his own practice. Bosworth then returned to Europe to study with Alma-Tadema in London and at the Ecole des Beaux-Arts in Paris. Upon his return to America in 1900, he worked briefly for CARRÈRE AND HASTINGS before starting out on his own again. By World War I, he had developed an extremely successful practice, designing the gardens for John D. Rockefeller's estate (1908–1910) at Pocantico Hills, New York, the main buildings for the Massachusetts Institute of Technology (1913) in Cambridge, Massachusetts, the house of John D. Rockefeller, Jr. (1914) in New York, as well as remodeling a Fifth Avenue mansion for Cartier's (1917). He served in France during World War I and returned to the United States briefly before leaving again for Paris to oversee the work of the Comité Franco-Americain pour la Restauration des Monuments. Except for the years of World War II, Bosworth remained in France until his death.

STEVEN MCLEOD BEDFORD

WORKS

1908, New York Magdalen Benevolent Association Asylum. 1908–1910, Gardens for John D. Rockefeller, Pocantico Hills, N.Y. 1909, L'Enfant Memorial, Washington. 1912, Gardens of Samuel Untermeyer, Tarrytown, N.Y. 1913, Main Buildings, Massachusetts Institute of Technology, Cambridge, Mass. 1914, John D. Rockefeller, Jr., House; 1917, American Telegraph and Telephone Headquarters; 1917, Cartier Building (remodeled); New York. 1919, Scarboro-on-Hudson School, Scarborough, N.Y. 1925–1939, Cathedral of Chartres (restoration), France. 1925–1939, Cathedral of Reims (restoration), France. 1925–1939, Palace at Fontainebleau (restoration), France. 1925–1939, Palace of Versailles (restoration), France.

BIBLIOGRAPHY

SWALES, F. S. 1925 "Master Draftsman IX: Welles Bosworth." *Pencil Points* 6:59–64.

BOULLEE, ETIENNE LOUIS

As a builder, teacher, and theorist, Etienne Louis Boullée (1728–1799) was one of the greatest eighteenth-century architects. During Boullée's lifetime, he was highly acclaimed for the design of the elegant Hôtel de Brunoy (1774–1779) along the Champs-Elysées. Today, Boullée's fame rests primarily on the more than one hundred beautiful drawings of ideal public buildings executed on a large format and on the theoretical essay on the "art" of architecture which they illustrate. Writing in an age which sought to understand first principles, Boullée explored through writings and designs the importance of an architecture of pure forms intended to stimulate deep feelings. Like the work of Jean-Jacques Rousseau on man's underlying nature and on the origins of society, Boullée's inquiries into the fundamentals of architectural form and of aesthetic experience have a universal value not limited to their time.

Boullée was born in Paris to Louis-Claude Boullée, architect, and to Marie-Louise Boucher, possibly a relative of the celebrated painter François Boucher. Boullée's life was dominated by a passionate desire, developed in his youth, to be a painter. His father, though, obliged him to become an architect, preparing him to follow the same career as an *architecte expert* who appraises and registers the drawings for new constructions and who certifies the completed work. Although Boullée was forced to leave the studio of the painter Jean-Baptiste Pierre and to continue his architectural education, first with JACQUES FRANÇOIS BLONDEL and then with Pierre Etienne Lebon, JEAN LAURENT LEGEAY, and GERMAIN BOFFRAND, he soon found his calling as a teacher. When Boullée was nineteen, his studio already had an illustrious reputation. In August 1762, Boullée was admitted to the second class of the Académie Royale d'Architecture.

Between that time and his promotion to the first class in December 1780, Boullée pioneered the low lying horizontal house with the appearance of a single story praised by Thomas Jefferson when he lived in Paris. In all of Boullée's major houses—Hôtel Alexandre (1763–1766), Château de Chaville (1764–1766), the grand Hôtel de Monville (1764), Hôtel de Brunoy (1774–1779)—the principal façade presented a horizontal block with an attic supported by Ionic columns over the center. Instead of a single entry, Boullée used a series of French doors which either extended across the entire façade or whose forms were echoed by tall windows to either side. This serial repetition of the same geometric element Boullée would develop even further in his public architecture of the 1780s.

The idea of creating a contrapuntal vertical movement with an attic supported by columns at the middle of an otherwise horizontal composition Boullée first applied in his project (1759–1760) for the new royal mint. Although Boullée lost the commission to Jacques-Denis Antoine, the younger architect utilized this motif in the actual Hôtel de la Monnaie (1768–1775). In one variant of his own design for the mint as well as in his project (1764) for the reconstruction of the Palais-Bourbon, Boullée placed a pyramidal, stepped *amortissement* above the attic to dramatize further the central sculptural grouping. This he repeated in the celebrated Hôtel de Brunoy where the elevated statue of Flora presided over the house and the gardens which, through the use of a trench or ha-ha, appeared to extend into the adjacent Champs-Elysées.

Contemporaries praised the imaginative design of the Hôtel de Brunoy which made the house seem like a three-sided arcade wrapping around the vertical temple of the goddess. In the gardens two sunken allées covered with an arched bower and bordered by aromatic plants extended from the Champs-Elysées to the house where they terminated in an elevated, open *salle de verdure* whose walls were the projecting wings of the house covered with trellises. With the building raised above the garden and the allées partially submerged, the owner was afforded an uninterrupted view of the Champs-Elysées.

In 1782 Boullée resigned from his official charges as *Contrôleur des bâtiments à l'Hôtel Royal des Invalides* and *à l'Ecole Militaire* to devote himself primarily to his work as an academician, theoretician, and educator. His mature style emerged at this time and contributed to the flowering of neoclassical architecture through a purity of contour and a simplicity of form. At this point, Boullée became a painter in the sense that Hubert Robert was an architect. These two kindred spirits invented architectural forms whose regular geometries, large uninterrupted walls, and long rows of columns made their buildings seem both grandiose and serene. A fascination with the very substance of stone, the play of light and shadow, and the overall ambiance of the site with its particular topography, vegetation, and even weather, made Robert's canvasses and Boullée's architectural drawings into a type of landscape painting in which the protagonist was the building itself.

The epigram to Boullée's essay, *Architecture, Essay on the Art,* which was completed by 1793, was Antonio da Correggio's famous profession of faith, "I too am a painter." The deepest meaning of this line, which pervades Boullée's entire text as it did his life, was aptly expressed by the wife of one of Boullée's greatest pupils, ALEXANDRE THÉODORE BRONGNIART, when she wrote to her husband after a visit in 1794 to the sixty-six-year-old master: "You spoke of this several times, but I never imagined that one could produce moral effects in architecture as in painting." The three projects which most impressed Madame Brongniart—the *Métropole* (church), the Cenotaph to Sir Isaac Newton, and the cemetery—were precisely those which Boullée considered to be his most important designs. Like the paintings by RAPHAEL (the School of Athens and the Creation) which Boullée so admired, Boullée's architectural drawings for these projects conveyed truths about the sublimity of the creation, the immensity of nature, and the awesomeness of divine intelligence. These insights were not purely intellectual but rather came simultaneously through enraptured feelings. Madame Brongniart herself felt "electrified" as she listened to Boullée explain his work.

In writing on the "art" or "poetry" as opposed to the "science" of architecture, Boullée followed the example of NICOLAS LE CAMUS DE MÉZIÈRES to explain the effects of architectural form on a viewer according to a theory of geometrical bodies understood through their analogy to the human psyche. The architect's task was to combine simple, stereometric forms so as to prompt an immediate feeling in the observer appropriate to the building's purpose. The idea that every building had to have a suitable "character," dependent upon the massing as opposed to the decorative use of the classical orders, was a basic tenet in the writings of Boullée's former teachers, Boffrand and Blondel. Both Le Camus de Mézières and Boullée, though, transformed this earlier definition of character, intended primarily to enable one to identify a building by its aspect, by extending it into the realm of feelings. In this matter, these two architects were influenced by the ideals of the picturesque landscape garden as it was developing in France in the 1770s–1780s in which each scene was intended to evoke a different emotion. Only Boullée, though, applied the theory to the design of an entire series of ideal projects for public buildings.

In his architecture, Boullée followed the lead of the landscape poets and theorists who drew inspiration from the changing character of the seasons. To the deists and pantheists of the time, nature was the "universal book" of wisdom. Departing, though, from the common cyclical understanding of the seasons, Boullée posited a bipolar opposition between three seasons of life and one of death (winter).

Virtually all of Boullée's projects for public buildings are organized around this duality, with the forms and lighting providing two diametrically opposed but complementary worlds. For the city of the living, Boullée used free-standing columns in unbroken, regular series, balanced by vast, severe walls with little decoration, the whole to be seen under the sun. For the funerary world, Boullée developed an "architecture of shadows" with images of columns obtained from dark shadows cast into recesses cut into a stone surface viewed in the moonlight. His "buried architecture" employed forms which seemed partially buried and which also appeared to be sliding down into the ground, thereby teaching a lesson about human mortality.

In both the world of the living and the world of the dead, Boullée's monumental forms were imbued with a pantheistic fervor. Even in the cemetery, the large central pyramid rose, as Jean Starobinski has observed, in triumph as if it were the embodiment of nature itself. Boullée's ultimate expression of religious feelings came in the Métropole (c.1781–1782) or church project (the "epic poem of architecture") and in the project for a Cenotaph to Sir Isaac Newton (1784). Both buildings were designed to provide the experience of a union with divinity in a manner analogous to Rousseau's communion with the Supreme Being as recounted in the *Reveries of a Solitary Walker* and in the "Third Letter to Malesherbes": "my heart, constrained within the limits of its human frame, wanted to bound into infinity"; "In my transports I cried out several times, 'Oh Great Being,' and could not think or say anything more."

The methods of attaining the sublime which Boullée used in these two buildings correspond closely to the mechanisms of the "artificial infinite" described by Edmund Burke in his *Philosophical Enquiry into the Origin of Our Ideas of the Sublime and Beautiful* (London, 1757; French translation, 1765). In the Métropole, Boullée used the seemingly infinite field of columns, and in the Cenotaph, the continuous surface of the sphere, to have the celebrant identify with the immensity of nature. To this experiential aspect of architecture Boullée often added a symbolic, metaphorical, or allegorical dimension which provided a suitable characterization: the circular opera conceived as a temple to Venus, the palace of justice arranged to teach the triumph of Virtue over Vice, the library as an amphitheater of the Manes of the greatest thinkers of the past, the museum as a temple of Fame, and the Cenotaph to Newton with its star-filled spherical cavity presenting in a microcosm the universe whose single underlying and unifying law, gravity, Newton had discovered.

All of Boullée's urban projects, when considered together, constitute a comprehensive image of a new Paris directly related to the contemporary enthusiasm for *embellissement,* or urban design. In their specifics, Boullée's building programs responded to commonly perceived needs for new public edifices, and in their totality, to the current idea of the city which would banish the cemetery from its traditional home near the parish church to the periphery where it would form a self-contained world. In this sense, Boullée's treatise and drawings rank along with CLAUDE NICOLAS LEDOUX's writings and designs for the ideal town of Chaux as the two most complete visions of a new physical world conceived during the late Enlightenment.

Boullée's influence extended beyond the training of his most talented pupils such as Brongniart and JEAN FRANÇOIS CHALGRIN. His architectural style and his painterly manner are evident throughout the Grand Prix designs of the late eighteenth century. JEAN NICOLAS LOUIS DURAND, perhaps Boullée's most famous student, carried on the pedagogical calling of his master. Unlike Boullée, though, with his richly symbolic mind and his sense of the ineffable, Durand was a utilitarian whose simplified, rational design methodology was to dominate the educational system of the Ecole des Beaux-Arts throughout the nineteenth century.

RICHARD A. ETLIN

WORKS

*1752–1754, Altar for the Chapelle du Calvaire and the Chapelle de la Vierge, Eglise Saint-Roch; 1762, Maison Tourolle (decorations); 1763, Chapelle Saint-Geneviève and another chapel in the transept, Eglise Saint-Roch; 1763–1766, Hôtel Alexandre; *1764, Hôtels Racine de Monville; *1764–1766, Château de Chaville; *1768–1770, Hôtel de Pernon; *1769–1771, Hôtel de Thun; *1774–1779, Hôtel de Brunoy; *1780–1782, Prison de la Grande Force; Paris.

BIBLIOGRAPHY

ETLIN, RICHARD A. 1983 "Cities of the Dead: From Charnel House to Elysium in Eighteenth-Century Paris." Cambridge, Mass.: M.I.T. Press. Forthcoming publication.

KAUFMANN, EMIL 1939 "Etienne Louis Boullée." *Art Bulletin* 21, no. 3:212–227.

KAUFMANN, EMIL 1952 *Three Revolutionary Architects: Boullée, Ledoux, and Lequeu.* Philadelphia: American Philosophical Society.

LANKEIT, KLAUS (1968)1973 *Der Temple der Vernunft: Unveröffentlichte Zeichnungen von Etienne-Louis Boullée.* 2d ed. Basel and Stuttgart, Germany: Birkhäuser.

LE CAMUS DE MÉZIÈRES, NICOLAS 1780 *Le Génie de l'architecture ou l'Analogie de cet art avec nos sensations.* Paris: The author.

PÉROUSE DE MONTCLOS, JEAN-MARIE (editor) 1968 *Etienne-Louis Boullée, Architecture, Essai sur l'art.* Paris: Hermann.

PÉROUSE DE MONTCLOS, JEAN-MARIE 1969 *Etienne-Louis Boullée (1728–1799): De l'Architecture classique à l'architecture révolutionnaire.* Paris: Arts et Métiers Graphiques.

PÉROUSE DE MONTCLOS, JEAN-MARIE 1974 *Etienne-Louis Boullée, 1728–1799; Theoretician of Revolutionary Architecture.* Translated by James Emmons. New York: Braziller.

ROSENAU, HELEN (editor) 1953 *Boullée's Treatise on Architecture.* London: Tiranti.

ROSENAU, HELEN 1976 *Boullée and His Visionary Architecture.* London: Academy; New York: Harmony.

ROSSI, ALDO (editor) 1967 *Etienne-Louis Boullée, Architettura. Saggio sull'arte.* Padua, Italy: Marsilio.

STAROBINSKI, JEAN 1964 *The Invention of Liberty; 1700–1789.* Translated by Bernard C. Swift. Geneva: Skira.

SZAMBIEN, WERNER 1981 "Notes sur le Recueil d'Architecture privée de Boullée (1792–1796)." *Gazette des Beaux-Arts* 97:111–124.

Visionary Architects: Boullée, Ledoux, Lequeu. 1968 Houston, Tex.: University of Saint Thomas. Exhibition catalogue.

VOGT, ADOLF MAX 1969 *Boullées Newton-Denkmal: Sakralbau und Kugelidee.* Basel and Stuttgart, Germany: Birkhäuser.

BOULOGNE, JEAN AMEL DE

Jean Amel de Boulogne (?–1395) was probably born in Antwerp, Belgium. There has been some confusion regarding his distinction from and relation to Peter Appelman(s), documented as master of works of Antwerp Cathedral. Jean seems to have taken part in the construction of Saint George, Antwerp, nearing completion at the time of his death, and he also seems to have worked on the choir of Antwerp Cathedral, begun around 1353, the design of which is sometimes attributed to him.

ELIZABETH SCHWARTZBAUM

WORKS

1353–1395, Cathedral of Our Lady (choir); Before 1395, Saint George; Antwerp, Belgium.

BIBLIOGRAPHY

VAN BRABANT (1972)1977 *De Onze-Lieve-Vrouwkathedraal van Antwerpen.* 2d ed. Antwerp, Belgium: Vlaamse Toeristen-bond.

BOULTON and WATT

Matthew Boulton (1728–1809), James Watt (1736–1819), Charles Bage (1752–1822), and William Strutt (1756–1830) all came from different backgrounds and had different primary interests. But they were brought together by a shared interest in the textile industry and were responsible for the construction of a sequence of mill buildings during the last decade of the eighteenth century that might be regarded as the first ancestors of the modern steel skyscraper. Earlier mills had been built with timber floors supported (between the outer masonry walls) by timber columns. They were frequently destroyed by fire. William Strutt introduced fireproof construction in mills in Derby and Belper in 1792–1793, with brick jack-arch floors spanning between protected timber beams carried by cruciform iron columns. Charles Bage at Shrewsbury Mill (1796–1797) then substituted iron beams of a similar though more slender form for the timber beams, and finally Boulton and Watt at Salford Mill (1799–1801) adopted the more efficient forms of an inverted "T" for the beams and a hollow tube for the columns.

ROWLAND MAINSTONE

WORKS
BOULTON AND WATT
1799–1801, Salford Mill, England.

CHARLES BAGE
1796–1797, Shrewsbury Mill, England.

WILLIAM STRUTT
1792–1793, Belper Mill, England. 1792–1793, Derby Mill, England.

BIBLIOGRAPHY
SKEMPTON, A. W., and JOHNSON, H. R. 1962 "The First Iron Frames." *Architectural Review* 131:175–186.

BOURGEAU, VICTOR

Victor Bourgeau (1809–1888) can be regarded as one of the most successful architects in Canadian history. His career was an extraordinary coincidence of a popular new style (the baroque Revival), unprecedented demand for new buildings (from the foundation of scores of new farming parishes in the province of Quebec), and a social phenomenon (the rising nationalism of French Canada in the mid-nineteenth century). Born in Lavaltrie, Quebec, Bourgeau trained himself as a sculptor, a builder, and finally as an architect. His four great works are in Montreal: the new interior of the Church of Notre-Dame, the Hôtel-Dieu Hospital, the Convent of the Soeurs Grises, and the Church of Saint-Jacques. During a sixty-year career, Bourgeau also built dozens of rural parish churches.

FRANKLIN TOKER

BIBLIOGRAPHY
ALLARD, MICHEL ET AL. 1973 *L'Hôtel-Dieu de Montreal: 1642–1973.* Montreal: Hurtubise HMH.
GOWANS, ALAN 1955 "The Baroque Revival in Quebec." *Journal of the Society of Architectural Historians* 14:8–14.
TOKER, FRANKLIN 1970 *The Church of Notre-Dame in Montreal.* Montreal: McGill-Queen's University Press.

BOURGEOIS, VICTOR

Born in Charleroi, Belgium, Victor Bourgeois (1897–1962) received his architectural education at the Académie Royale des Beaux-Arts of Brussels (1914–1919). Apart from the academic principles of composition with which he came in contact, Bourgeois also studied the works of innovative modern architects such as FRANK LLOYD WRIGHT and HENRI SAUVAGE, and embraced the social theories of TONY GARNIER.

From 1921 to 1922, he was an architect-in-training with the Service Technique de la Société Nationale des Habitations à Bon Marché (the engineering division of the national society for low-cost housing). The position gave him the opportunity to confirm his ideas about workers' housing and to realize with mastery, at the age of twenty-five, three hundred units of "La Cité Moderne" in Berchem-lez-Bruxelles (1922–1925). This was the first example after World War I of a development on a grand scale combining flexible planning with the use of simple architectural forms. An ardent activist, he was a member of the avant-garde artistic and literary movements of Brussels. He befriended the painters René Magritte and Fernand Léger, and with his brother, the poet and man of letters Pierre Bourgeois, he founded the polemical reviews *Au Volant* (1919) and *Le Geste* (1920). With funding from the newly formed cooperative for publishing and artistic propaganda, *L'Equerre,* they later produced *7 Arts,* a weekly of news and criticism that became the official journal of the Neoplasticists in Brussels from 1922 to 1928.

In 1923, together with the urban planner Louis Van der Swaelmen, Bourgeois established the Société Belge des Urbanistes et Architectes Modernistes. He collaborated with the best contemporary Belgian modernists in the design of a garden-city displayed at the Exposition Internationale des Arts Décoratifs of 1925 in Paris. Following this, his activities became increasingly international. In 1927, he was invited to build a house in rhe model city of Weissenhof for the exposition organized by the German Werkbund.

He conducted the debates and was a co-signer of the manifesto of the first Congrès Internationaux

Bourgeois.
La Cité Moderne
   (preliminary drawing).
Berchem-Sainte-Agathe,
   Belgium.
1922–1925

Bourgeois.
La Cité Moderne
   (construction stage).
Berchem-Sainte-Agathe,
   Belgium.
1921

d'Architecture Moderne (CIAM) at La Sarraz in 1928. Under his leadership, the third CIAM was organized in Brussels in 1930 to mark the centennial of Belgian independence, and the meeting's "Journées de l'Habitation Minimum" reunited the representatives of economic and political interests by rationalizing the building industry.

When the Institut Supérieur des Arts Décoratifs was established in 1927, HENRY VAN DE VELDE invited Bourgeois to take charge of the course on "pure form." He also taught a course on practical aesthetics in construction until 1938, when he became the head of the atelier of architecture, a post he held until 1962.

Associated with the Belgian socialist movement (he designed the monument to the sculptor Constantin Meunier), he organized many conferences and polemical exhibitions on architecture and urbanism between 1928 and 1932 based on research and theoretical studies he directed on the development, improvement, and defense of the capital city of Brussels. To this end, he founded the review, *Bruxelles* (1933–1935), in which questions regarding the redevelopment, growth, and embellishment of the city were addressed with the intention of acquainting the public with the problems of urban development. In 1939, he built the Belgian pavilion at the World's Fair in New York, collaborating with Van de Velde and Léon Stijnen.

After World War II, he participated in the reconstruction of Belgium by designing many buildings for the public health services and for industry.

MAURICE CULOT
Translated from French by
Shara Wasserman

WORKS

1922–1925, La Cité Moderne (three hundred dwellings, town planning), Berchem-Sainte-Agathe, Belgium. 1925, Victor Bourgeois House, Brussels. 1927, Belgian House, Weisenhof, Stuttgart, Germany. 1928, Oscar Jespers House, Woluwe-Saint-Lambert, Belgium. 1938–1940, D'Hofstade Square, Brussels. *1939, Belgian Pavilion, World's Fair, New York. 1947, General Stores (for the Society of Baume and Marpent), Haine-Saint-Pierre, Belgium. 1957, Cultural House, Namur, Belgium. 1958, Etenit Tower, International Exposition, Brussels. 1962, Ray of the Sun Hospital, Montignies-Charleroi, Belgium.

BOYCEAU, JACQUES

Jacques Boyceau de la Barauderie (17th cent.), French royal garden designer and treatise writer, probably designed Marie de' Medici's great Luxembourg Gardens in Paris. In his *Traité du jardinage* of 1638, he not only proposed a formal garden of great monumentality, elaborateness, and "organic regularity," but also, by emphasizing the aesthetic over the practical, helped to establish garden design as an art as opposed to a craft.

RICHARD O. SWAIN

WORKS

The dates listed below for each garden are the founding dates.
(A)c.1615, Luxembourg Gardens, Paris. (A)c.1615–1620, Château-Neuf, Saint Germain-en-Laye, France. (A)c.1623, Tuileries, Paris. (A)c.1631, Versailles, France.

BIBLIOGRAPHY

BOYCEAU DE LA BARAUDERIE, JACQUES 1638 *Traité du jardinage: Selon les raisons de la nature et de l'art.* Paris: Vanlochom.
HAZLEHURST, F. HAMILTON 1966 *Jacques Boyceau and the French Formal Garden.* Athens: University of Georgia Press.

BOYLE, RICHARD

See BURLINGTON, EARL OF.

BOYINGTON, WILLIAM W.

William W. Boyington (1818–1898), born in Southwick, Massachusetts, designed the first locomotive cab, for the Boston and Albany Railroad in 1840. By midcentury, he had designed several cotton mills in Massachusetts.

Boyington's major architectural career began in Chicago in 1853. His work before the Chicago Fire of 1871 displays a diverse range of Gothic Revival styles and includes Chicago University (1857–1865) and the Illinois State Penitentiary (1857–c.1862) Joliet (both with O. L. Wheelock), and the celebrated survivor of the fire, the Water Tower and Pumping Station (1867–1869).

The fire brought an influx of architects, most of whom were better trained than the pioneer master-builders of the 1850s and 1860s. Nonetheless, Boyington was a principal rebuilder of the devastated city, designing commercial buildings, hotels, and railroad stations. For the massive Board of Trade Building (1881–1885), Boyington employed a "floating foundation" of timbers in concrete. He had long experimented with foundations, and was instrumental in introducing improved technology and fireproofing practices to Chicago's architecture.

Active professionally in Chicago for forty-five years, Boyington was eclipsed in his last years by the notable achievements of a new generation of Chicago architects.   THOMAS L. SLOAN

WORKS

*1856, Terrace Row, Chicago. 1857–c.1862, Illinois State Penitentiary (with O. L. Wheelock), Joliet. *1857–1865, Chicago University (with Wheelock). *1865, Crosby's Opera House; 1867–1869, Water Tower and Pumping Station; *1871–1872, Grand Pacific Hotel; *1881, Wells Street Depot (Chicago and North Western Station); *1881–1885, Board of Trade Building; *1881–1885, United Passenger Station; *1883, Royal Insurance Company Building; *1892, Columbus Memorial Building; *1893, Illinois State Building, Columbian World's Exposition; Chicago.

BIBLIOGRAPHY

BOYINGTON, WILLIAM W. 1886 "Foundations." *The Inland Architect and Builder* 8, Dec.:69–71.
CONDIT, CARL W. 1964 *The Chicago School of Architecture: A History of Commercial and Public Building in the Chicago Area, 1875–1925.* University of Chicago Press.
ERICSSON, HENRY (1942)1972 *Sixty Years a Builder: The Autobiography of Henry Ericsson.* Reprint. New York: Arno.
NEWCOMB, REXFORD 1950 *Architecture of the Old Northwest Territory: A Study of Early Architecture in Ohio, Indiana, Illinois, Michigan, Wisconsin, and Part of Minnesota.* University of Chicago Press.
RANDALL, FRANK A. (1949)1972 *History of the Development of Building Construction in Chicago.* Reprint. New York: Arno.
TALLMADGE, THOMAS EDDY (1941)1975 *Architecture in Old Chicago.* University of Chicago Press.

BRADLEE, NATHANIEL J.

Nathaniel Jeremiah Bradlee (1829–1888), a Boston native and a founder of the Boston Society of Architects, was trained as a draftsman in the office of George M. Dexter. After 1853, Bradlee independently designed numerous commercial and several public buildings in Boston and vicinity. He was later associated with Walter T. Winslow and with George H. Wetherell, who, with HENRY F. BIGELOW, succeeded him.

FREDERIC C. DETWILLER

WORKS

*1847–1853, Fitchburg Railroad Station (with George M. Dexter); 1858, South End Ros House Blocks; 1860–1862, South Congregational Church (now Saint John the Baptist Greek Orthodox Church); Boston. 1863, Gray's Hall, Harvard University, Cambridge, Mass. *1867, Boston and Maine Railroad Station (remodeling), Haymarket Square; (A)1869, Fort Hill Standpipe; Roxbury, Mass. 1872, House, 37–39 Commonwealth Avenue; *1872, Rialto Building; 1872–1874, Second Unitarian Church; *1873, New England Mutual Life Insurance Company Building; Boston. 1875, State Insane Asylum, Danvers, Mass. 1875, Young Men's Christian Union; 1879, Residence, 119 Commonwealth Avenue; 1880–1881, Marlboro Building (with Walter T. Winslow); Boston.

BIBLIOGRAPHY

BUNTING, BAINBRIDGE 1967 *Houses of Boston's Back Bay.* Cambridge, Mass.: Belknap.
COTE, RICHARD n.d. "Bibliography: Nathaniel Jeremiah Bradlee." Unpublished manuscript, Society for the Preservation of New England Antiquities, Boston.
FOX, PAMELA, and KOCH, MICKAIL 1980 *Central Business District Inventory.* Boston Landmarks Commission.
KAY, JANE HOLTZ 1980 *Lost Boston.* Boston: Houghton Mifflin.
TUCCI, DOUGLASS SHAND 1978 *Built in Boston, City and Suburb, 1800–1950.* Boston: New York Graphic Society.

BRADLEY, LUCAS

Lucas Bradley (1809–1889) was born in Cayuga County, New York. After having learned the building trade from his father, he established himself in St. Louis in 1838 as a builder and architect.

He achieved success with the Second Presbyterian Church (1840) which he designed in the style of CHRISTOPHER WREN. By 1845, he had acquired a lumber yard; its loss by fire and poor health conditions in St. Louis precipitated his move to Racine, Wisconsin, where he remained until his death.

DONALD MARTIN REYNOLDS

WORKS

1840, Second Presbyterian Church, St. Louis, Mo. 1850s, Buildings, Beloit College, Wisc. 1850s, Buildings, Racine College, Wisc. 1850s, Private Residences, Beloit, Wisc. 1852, First Presbyterian Church; 1852–1874, Public School Buildings; Racine, Wisc. 1862, First Congregational Church, Beloit, Wisc. *1868, Taylor Orphanage, Racine, Wisc.

BIBLIOGRAPHY

Primary material on Bradley is available in the Bradley Family Records, Dodge City, Kansas; the archives division of the State Historical Society of Missouri, Columbia; a taped interview with Clarinda Winslow (Bradley's niece), December 17, 1973, no. UC523A, in the division of iconographical records, the State Historical Society of Wisconsin, Madison; and an unpublished biographical sketch of Bradley in the division of archives and manuscripts, the State Historical Society of Wisconsin, Madison.

BRADLEY, JOHN ALBURY (editor) 1928 *Missouri's Contribution to American Architecture.* St. Louis, Mo.: Architecture Club.

BRADLEY, JOHN ALBURY 1934 "Outstanding Architects in St. Louis Between 1804 and 1904." *Missouri Historical Review* 28, no. 2:83–90.

PATTON, HELEN 1974–1975 "Lucas Bradley: Carpenter, Builder, Architect." *Wisconsin Magazine of History* 58, no. 2:107–125.

PERRIN, RICHARD W. E. 1967 *The Architecture of Wisconsin.* Madison: State Historical Society of Wisconsin.

PERRIN, RICHARD W. E. 1976 *Historic Wisconsin Architecture.* Milwaukee: Wisconsin Society of Architects.

BRADY, JOSIAH R.

Josiah R. Brady (c.1760–1832) was described as a practical builder, ingenious draftsman, and contract writer by ALEXANDER JACKSON DAVIS, his apprentice from 1826 to 1827. Beginning his practice in New York City before 1800, Brady is now known for such early Gothic Revival churches as Saint Luke's (1824–1828), Rochester, New York.

GWEN W. STEEGE

WORKS

*1824, Merchants' Exchange; c.1824, Saint Thomas's Protestant Episcopal Church; New York. 1824–1828, Saint Luke's Church, Rochester, N.Y.

BIBLIOGRAPHY

Additional information on Josiah R. Brady is in Alexander Jackson Davis's manuscript of the Davis entry for Dunlap's History of the Arts of Design in the United States in the Davis Collection I, F–2, Avery Architectural Library, Columbia University, New York.

NEWTON, ROGER HALE 1942 *Town and Davis Architects.* New York: Columbia University Press.

PIERSON, WILLIAM H., JR. 1978 *American Buildings and Their Architects: Technology and the Picturesque. The Corporate and the Early Gothic Styles.* Garden City, N.Y.: Doubleday.

BRAEM, RENAAT

Born and educated in Antwerp, Belgium, Renaat Braem (1910–) traveled widely in Europe during the 1930s and worked for a time in the office of LE CORBUSIER. A member of the CIAM (1936–1950), he became one of the leading Belgian urbanists of that period. Braem's architectural designs owe much to the stark aesthetic of the International style, although those of the 1960s and 1970s incorporate curvilinear elements derived from the formal vocabulary of Belgian Art Nouveau. His interest in the Art Nouveau was tied to his efforts to develop an "organic" architecture based on natural forms.

ALFRED WILLIS

WORKS

1950, Apartment Block (with V. Maeremans and R. Maes), Antwerp-Kiel, Belgium. 1959–1970, Exhibition Pavilion, Middelheim Sculpture Museum, Antwerp, Belgium. 1970, House, Pastorijstraat, Buggerhout, Belgium. 1974, Apartment Block, Boom, Belgium.

BIBLIOGRAPHY

BONTRIDDER, ALBERT 1963 *L'architecture contemporaine en Belgique, le dialogue de la lumière du silence.* Antwerp, Belgium: Helios.

BRAEM, RENAAT (editor) 1950–1962 *Bouwen en Wonen.* Includes many articles by Braem.

BRAEM, RENAAT 1963 "De 'Libre Esthétique' te Antwerpen." *Bouwkundig Weekblad* 81:477–483.

BRAEM, RENAAT 1968 *Het Lelijkste Land ter Wereld.* Louvain, Belgium: Davidsfonds.

BRAEM, RENAAT 1969 *De "Art Nouveau" en Wij.* Mededelingen van de Konivklÿke Vlaamse Academie voor Wetenschapen, Letteren, en Schone Kunsten van België, vol. 31, no. 1. Brussels: Paleis der Academiën.

PUTTEMANS, PIERRE 1976 *Modern Architecture in Belgium.* Translated by Mette Willert. Brussels: Vokaer.

SMETS, MARCEL 1977 *L'Avènement de la Cité-jardin en Belgique.* Brussels: Mardaga.

BRAGDON, CLAUDE F.

Claude Fayette Bragdon (1866–1946) believed that architecture should express the vitality of

American democracy. In this and in his insistence on organic rather than arranged architecture and ornament and in his rejection of eclecticism he firmly belongs to the ideological tradition of LOUIS H. SULLIVAN and FRANK LLOYD WRIGHT. Bragdon, who described himself as having four distinct lives—architectural, theatrical, literary, and occult—was born in Oberlin, Ohio. Graduation from Oswego High School in New York marked the end of his formal education. Bragdon became an expert draftsman, working for numerous architects including Charles Ellis, whose brother, HARVEY ELLIS, would later become one of Bragdon's friends and mentors. In 1889, Bragdon accepted employment with BRUCE PRICE in New York City, and in 1890, with the firm of Green and Wicks (see E. B. GREEN) in Buffalo, New York. In 1901, Bragdon established an architectural practice in Rochester, New York. Private residences, railway stations in the United States and Canada, and several civic buildings including the Rochester Chamber of Commerce (1917) constitute Bragdon's architectural oeuvre. His largest commission was for the design of the New York Central Railroad Station in Rochester (1912–1913). Although the exterior was rather conventional, the plan was exemplary. In 1923, Bragdon gave up his practice, moved to New York City (where he remained until his death), and became the set designer for Walter Hampden, a stage actor. Bragdon's career as a lecturer on architectural themes began in 1901 with an address before the Architectural League of America entitled "Mysticism and Architecture." Bragdon wrote a total of sixteen books on architecture, theosophy, the fourth dimension, and ornament in addition to contributing numerous articles to professional journals.

SUSAN STRAUSS

WORKS

1907, Albert Eastwood House; 1912–1913, New York Central Railroad Station; 1917, Rochester Chamber of Commerce; Rochester, N.Y. 1918, Hunter Street Bridge, Peterborough, Ontario.

BIBLIOGRAPHY

BRAGDON, CLAUDE (1910)1922 *The Beautiful Necessity: Seven Essays on Theosophy and Architecture.* 2d ed. New York: Knopf.

BRAGDON, CLAUDE 1913a "The New York Central Railway Station at Rochester." *The Brickbuilder* 22:263–266.

BRAGDON, CLAUDE 1913b *A Primer of Higher Space (the Fourth Dimension).* Rochester, N.Y.: Manas Press.

BRAGDON, CLAUDE 1913c "The Rochester Passenger Station." *American Architect* 104:237–242.

BRAGDON, CLAUDE 1916 *Four-Dimensional Vistas.* New York: Knopf.

BRAGDON, CLAUDE 1918a *Architecture and Democracy.* New York: Knopf.

BRAGDON, CLAUDE 1918b "Architecture and Democracy, Before, During and After the War." *Architectural Record* 44:75–84, 125–131, 253–258.

BRAGDON, CLAUDE 1925 *Old Lamps for New: Ancient Wisdom in a Modern World.* New York: Knopf.

BRAGDON, CLAUDE 1932 *The Frozen Fountain: Being Essays on Architecture and the Art of Design in Space.* New York: Knopf.

BRAGDON, CLAUDE 1938 *More Lives Than One.* New York: Knopf.

BRAGDON, CLAUDE 1940 "The Exceptional Failure." *Architects' Journal* 91:503.

CONNELY, WILLARD 1960 *Louis Sullivan As He Lived: The Shaping of American Architecture.* New York: Horizon.

"The Rochester Chamber of Commerce." 1917 *Architectural Forum* 27:157–164.

BRAMANTE, DONATO

Donato (or Donnino) di Angelo di Antonio, called Bramante (1444?–1514), was born in what is now called Fermignano, near Urbino, in the Marches of Central Italy. His family name is said to have been Lazzari, but there is no positive evidence of this: the nickname Bramante (ardent, intensely desiring), however appropriate, had already been given to his maternal grandfather and was also borne by others in the family. He was to become the embodiment of the High Renaissance style in architecture, parallel to MICHELANGELO and RAPHAEL in sculpture and painting, although he belonged to an older generation (he was perhaps as much as forty years older than Raphael, to whom he may have been related).

The date of his birth is unknown. GIORGIO VASARI, writing some thirty years after Bramante's death, says that he was seventy when he died and that he was buried in St. Peter's. We know that he died on April 11, 1514, so he was presumably born about 1444. Unfortunately, his grave was lost in 1543, when the pavement of St. Peter's was raised, and we can only speculate that Vasari had seen it and read an inscription giving his age as seventy. Vasari is not always reliable in such matters, and there is no other evidence for so early a date as 1444. If correct, it would make Bramante older than LEONARDO DA VINCI (born 1452), with whom he worked in Milan, and contemporary with such early Renaissance artists as Perugino, Botticelli, and Signorelli (all born around 1445). This makes the modernity of his achievements around the turn of the century even more remarkable, and it also highlights the problem of his early years up to 1477, when he is first recorded as a painter.

In contrast to his peers Leonardo, Michelangelo, and Raphael, we know very little about his life and training, and some of what we do know is contradictory. CESARE DI LORENZO CESARIANO, the editor of VITRUVIUS, described himself as Bramante's pupil (1521) and called Bramante *patiente filio de paupertate,* which seems to imply that he was the son of poor peasants (Cesariano also refers to him as illiterate as does at least one other writer of the time), but Bramante's family seems to have been fairly comfortable (to judge from their wills), and Bramante himself was to write some rather mediocre poetry and was certainly well-read in Dante. Toward the end of his life he is known to have spent hours discussing Dante with his great patron, Pope Julius II, who would certainly not have done this with an illiterate peasant.

We also know from Vasari (1568 edition only) that Bramante had a liking for hieroglyphs and similar punning allusions and that he tried to persuade Julius to have an inscription in hieroglyphs on the wall of the Vatican. This, like his idea of moving the Tomb of Saint Peter, was firmly rejected by the pope, who clearly knew his man. Bramante seems to have been extremely impulsive and was given to changing his mind about buildings almost daily, so that the early history of the rebuilding of St. Peter's will probably never be elucidated. He was also far too eager to pull down old buildings and erect new ones, sometimes so hastily constructed that they fell down. He was called *Maestro Rovinante,* and a contemporary satire (*Simia,* 1517) represents him as trying to persuade Saint Peter to allow him to pull down Heaven and rebuild it more commodiously.

There is no evidence that Bramante ever married. Certainly, he was unmarried in 1513 when the Pope gave him the Piombo, a virtual sinecure involving a good salary in return for the supervision of the leaden seals attached to papal bulls. This office had to be held by a celibate, and it was supposed to be a condition that the holder knew no Latin, but it is difficult to believe that Bramante did not know any Latin, which is the usual meaning of "illiterate" in the sixteenth century.

By the time of his death, Bramante had trained many of the new generation of architects—Antonio da Sangallo the Younger (see SANGALLO FAMILY), JACOPO SANSOVINO, BALDASSARE PERUZZI, and Raphael—and was recognized as the reviver of ancient architecture and the creator of the new classical style. SEBASTIANO SERLIO (1537) wrote that "it may be said that he revived the good architecture which had been buried from the days of the Ancients until now," and ANDREA PALLADIO (1570) describes the decline of Rome, and therefore of architecture, until modern times when

"Bramante was the first to bring to light the good and beautiful architecture which had been hidden from the time of the Ancients until then"; he includes Bramante's Tempietto in his Fourth Book, along with the ruins of Antiquity, as an example of the good style. Vasari , in his editions of 1550 and 1568, uses similar expressions in his life of Bramante, which is the fullest near-contemporary biography.

Bramante's fame was thus assured, but he achieved it through his influence on the architects of the first half of the sixteenth century, many of whom actually worked in the office at St. Peter's and through the wide dissemination of Serlio's and Palladio's treatises, rather than through his actual buildings, few of which have survived intact. His great masterpiece, the new design for St. Peter's, has to be reconstructed from drawings and other indications, since almost nothing, except the gigantic scale and the disposition of the dome piers, can be attributed to him.

To return to Bramante's early years, the splendid palace at Urbino was being built in the 1460s and 1470s for Federigo da Montefeltro, duke of Urbino, and LUCIANO DA LAURANA, Piero della Francesca, and LEON BATTISTA ALBERTI were all closely connected with him. It was the most significant building in Italy in the 1460s, and it is natural to suppose that Bramante, who was born only a few miles away, would have worked on it as a young man. He may have done so, but attempts have been made to attribute specific parts of the palace to him, notably the Cappella del Perdono (almost certainly executed by A. Barocci) and the duke's Studiolo, as well as the nearby Church of San Bernardino. There are, however, strong objections against all of these attributions. First, the style of all these buildings is different from—and more maturely classical than—the earliest architectural works by Bramante in Milan, including the engraving of 1481. Second, FRANCESCO DI GIORGIO MARTINI was certainly active in Urbino at that time, and San Bernardino, at least, is much closer to his style than to that of Bramante at any time. Third, the rhymed Chronicle by Raphael's father, Giovanni Santi, written between 1482 and 1494, which records many artists active locally and may be presumed to have recorded a local artist if possible, makes no mention of Bramante (this is also an additional reason for doubting the date of Bramante's birth as 1444). Finally, we have the evidence of a contemporary that Bramante was trained as a painter and did not take up architecture until later. This evidence is contained in Sabba Castiglione's *Ricordi,* published in Venice in 1549. Sabba (1480–1554) was born in Milan and joined the Order of Saint John of Jerusalem in 1505, spending the years 1508–1515 in Rome, that is, Bramante's last years. It is likely that as a Milanese with an interest in the arts Sabba would actually have known Bramante at that time. His *Ricordo* CXI is entitled *Cerca il creare de i figluoli* (On bringing up children), and contains the following passage on Bramante: "Bramante from the slopes of San Marino, a man of great ingenuity, a cosmographer, a poet in the vernacular, and an able painter, as a disciple (*discepolo*) of Mantegna, and a great perspectivist, having been brought up (*creato*) by Piero del Borgo; but in architecture so excellent that it may be said that he was the first in our time to recall to light the ancient architecture, buried for many years, as many of his buildings testify, among them the famous Temple of St. Peter's at Rome, which is justly numbered among the most celebrated and antique buildings of Rome or Greece, even though some people called him Maestro Guastante and others Roinante."

Sabba's references to Mantegna and Piero della Francesca as forming Bramante's style in painting and perspective can be confirmed from the earliest surviving work by him, a fresco of the philosopher Chilon, painted on the facade of the Palazzo del Podestà in Bergamo (now in the Museo Civico), datable to 1477. The fresco is now in a ruinous state, but it still clearly shows the influence of Mantegna in the steep perspective, decorative details, and general figure style. The influence of Piero is less noticeable, but it is manifest in a series of other fresco fragments (now in the Brera, Milan). These are not documented, but they are certainly by Bramante and probably date from the 1480s. It has been suggested that Bramante may have assisted Piero with the architectural background of the *Madonna and Child with Saints and Federigo of Urbino* (Brera, Milan), datable to the mid-1470s, but the only evidence for this is the similarity of the shell-niche in the painting to the one in the engraving, certainly designed by Bramante, of 1481. This very large engraving, which exists now in only two examples (British Museum, London, and Perego Collection, Milan), can be shown to have exercised great influence as far away as Spain and England. A contract, dated October 24, 1481, exists, binding the engraver, Bernardo Prevedari, to make an engraving from a drawing by Bramante which was provided and which he undertook to return. The contract, unfortunately, describes the subject of the drawing merely as buildings and figures (*cum hedifitijs et figuris*), but the print bears Bramante's name and the phrase IN MLO, that is, *in Mediolano, Milan.* The actual subject is certainly connected with the rise of Christianity in the Roman Empire (in which Milan played an important part) and the decay of paganism, symbolized by the ruined temple. The small cross on the baluster column, the kneeling monk, and the cardinal are part of the Christian aspect of the subject. Three firm conclusions can be drawn from the print: (1) Bramante's style in 1481 (or slightly earlier, since we do not know the date of the drawing itself, which is lost) was still highly pictorial, and his feeling for architecture was that of a stage designer rather than a builder; (2) the architectural forms employed do not correspond with anything in Urbino; and (3) the subject and the reliefs represented indicate the love of mystification and hieroglyphs Bramante is known to have possessed, which is equally evident in a fresco fragment of *Heraclitus and Democritus* of about the same date (Brera, Milan).

On the other hand, the elaborate detailing, the capitals, and the profiles of the moldings are close to those in Santa Maria presso San Satiro in Milan, where Bramante is recorded between 1482 and 1486, although it is probable that he began work there somewhat earlier. The plan shows the unique treatment of the choir, which is actually almost flat, but is represented perspectively to give the impression of depth. Such illusionism again reminds one of Piero and Mantegna, and it confirms the painterly approach still characteristic of Bramante; the plan, however, also reveals a new, essential element in the development of Bramante's architecture. The ninth-century chapel of San Satiro was remodeled by Bramante and incorporated into the new church. It has a complex central

Bramante.
*Detail of baptistery
    decoration in Santa
    Maria presso San Satiro.
Milan.
c.1480*

plan, based on a square with four apses projecting from the centers of each side to form a Greek cross, and the whole is contained within a circle. Such central plans, like the sacristy designed by Bramante on the other side of the church, derive ultimately from early Christian churches, the most important example in Milan being the fifth- (or fourth-?) century church of San Lorenzo. This basilica was rebuilt in the late sixteenth century, but the original forms can be reconstructed and were one of the most important influences on Bramante's attempts to revive ancient Roman architectural forms in a Christian context. In Santa Maria presso San Satiro (c.1480), Bramante combined these complex central plans with a long-nave design, which seems to indicate knowledge of both FILIPPO BRUNELLESCHI's and Alberti's Latin-cross church plans. It is not clear how he could have known these buildings in Florence and Mantua (especially Sant' Andrea in Mantua, which was not designed until 1470 and was hardly begun by 1472, when Alberti died), but since we know so little about his early life, he may have been active as a journeyman painter in several parts of Italy. Alberti certainly visited Urbino more than once, and it is possible that Bramante may have met him on one such occasion.

Leonardo da Vinci arrived in Milan about 1482 and soon began to work for the Sforza court. Probably, he met Bramante immediately, and both men worked for the duke until 1499. Leonardo painted his *Last Supper* in the refectory of the monastery of Santa Maria delle Grazie, at the same time that Bramante remodeled the eastern part of the church, the 1490s—although there are no documents recording his activity. He rebuilt the choir, crossing, and transepts to form a tribune at the end of the Gothic nave, apparently originally intended as a mausoleum for the Sforzas. Much of the fussy terra-cotta detailing on the exterior of the apse was executed after Bramante left Milan, but the impressive massing with large rectangular blocks and half-cylinders abutting them is evidence of his increasing sense of monumentality. Inside, the decorative elements are surprisingly light and elegant, but the same grand and simple massing is dominant. The contrast between the low, rather dark, Gothic nave and the soaring lightness of the dome is particularly striking and must be deliberate.

Somewhat earlier than this, Bramante had been consulted on the planning of Pavia Cathedral in 1488, and a very large wooden model (now in the Museo del Castello at Pavia) seems to reflect Bramantesque ideas, particularly in the crossing and east end. The actual cathedral—which is still incomplete—is also strongly Bramantesque in the crossing and crypt. Perhaps the most interesting

Bramante.
Sant' Ambrogio (canonica).
Milan.
1492–?

aspect of Pavia Cathedral is that it is known to have been designed with Hagia Sophia in Constantinople in mind, although the resemblance is not very clear. It may even be that Bramante first became aware of the great Byzantine church through drawings seen at Pavia: certainly Hagia Sophia is one of the elements in the genesis of the new St. Peter's.

In 1490, Bramante wrote a memorandum on the *tiburio* or crossing tower of Milan Cathedral, but the actual building has nothing to do with him. By this time, however, he was clearly regarded as an expert on building matters and was consulted on fortification and other technical problems. One of the most interesting of his activities at this period was the planning of the huge piazza at Vigevano, along with work there on the Palazzo delle Dame, a Sforza residence. Unfortunately, both have been considerably altered, but the layout of the piazza is larger and grander than usual. The arcades which run around the sides are derived from prototypes such as Brunelleschi's Loggia degli Innocenti in Florence, but the illusionistic paintings of triumphal arches and the clever management of the streets entering the piazza mark a new stage in urban planning. The work at Vigevano seems to have been done between about 1492 and 1494. The date 1497 is incised (rather crudely) on the entrance arch of Santa Maria Nascente at Abbiategrasso, between Milan and Vigevano. This arch is traditionally attributed to Bramante, but it is not one of his more successful works. It was fitted into an existing cloister and starts with coupled columns of the same height as the cloister, on top of which were mounted a second pair of coupled columns, and from them springs a large semicircular arch. There is now a gable roof, presumably not original, but the effect is markedly topheavy and the detailing is coarser than the contemporary work at Sant' Ambrogio.

During his last years in Milan, Bramante was occupied with the three cloisters at Sant' Ambrogio which are generally regarded as the prelude to his *ultima maniera,* the style he was to perfect in Rome. On one side of the great church, he began, but never completed, the Porta della Canonica (c.1492) intended as a closed court, probably square, with residences for the canons above the arches; only the range next to the church was actually built. It consists of a large central arched opening, flanked by smaller arched bays which rise to half the height of the whole: they were intended to carry pilasters above the columns, thus creating an effect close to that in the court of the palace at Urbino, the most distinguished example of the form based on Brunelleschi's Innocenti. The basic design of high arch supported by pilasters on high pedestals and flanked by a lower arcade is similar to that at Abbiategrasso, but the effect is much more harmonious, since the relationship of the upper part to both the great arch and the rest of the arcade is better proportioned. A peculiarity of the Porta della Canonica is the use of columns, at the angles and inside the central arch, that have shafts carved to resemble tree trunks with the branches sawn off close to the trunk. This unusual and picturesque feature presumably derives from the Vitruvian idea of the origin of columns from trees used to support the roofs of primitive huts; if so, it is evidence that Bramante was studying Vitruvius (the text of which, in Latin, had recently become available in printed form), and this would have been at about the same time that Leonardo made his famous drawing of "Vitruvian Man" (Accademia, Venice), which illustrates the Vitruvian theory of human proportion. The influence of Leonardo on Bramante, and vice versa, can be demonstrated from the fact that Leonardo, during his stay in Milan, began to work on an architectural treatise and was clearly interested in the planning of imaginary churches based on central plans of the type found in Lombardy, but rendered as complex as possible to explore the maximum spatial potential. These drawings probably arose from his interest in anatomy and were to provide a new form of architectural draftsmanship which was to be exploited in the sixteenth century, but which, at this time, must have provided Bramante with a new means of imagining space. Leonardo's universal curiosity must have been one of the factors in the creation of Bramante's mature style, together with his experience of early Christian architecture in Lombardy, contemporary architecture in Urbino and elsewhere, and the architecture as well as the architectural theory of ancient Rome, which he could have experienced in the north as well as in Rome itself, although his Roman studies after 1500 were decisive in the formation of High Renaissance style.

In fact, Bramante was twice absent from Milan, without leave in 1492 and 1493, and it is possible that he was in Rome then. The importance of this Roman visit, if it (or they) took place, lies in the fact that the Palazzo della Cancelleria in Rome and a revised version of it, the Palazzo Giraud-Torlonia, have been connected with Bramante at least since the sixteenth century. The Cancelleria, however, was largely complete by the mid-1490s and is, in any case, stylistically quite different from the cloister at Santa Maria della Pace, one of Bramante's first works in Rome. The architect of the Cancelleria is unknown, and there is a temptation to assign it to a major figure; on balance, however, it is difficult to accept Bramante.

The two other cloisters at Sant' Ambrogio are very much larger than the Porta della Canonica and lie on the other side of the church, forming part of the monastery (now the Catholic University of Milan). Bramante is known to have worked there in 1497–1498, but he may well have designed the cloisters before then. The Doric cloister was probably begun and partly executed before Bramante left Milan, but the Ionic (which is a repeat of the Doric with the order changed) was not completed until much later and may not even have been begun by Bramante, although he may have made a model.

The Doric cloister resembles the Porta della Canonica in that it consists of a wide, airy arcade carried on slender columns reminiscent of Brunelleschi's Innocenti arcade and quite different from the truly Doric character of the Tempietto. Whereas the Canonica has a single bay on the upper floor corresponding to each ground-floor bay, the Doric cloister has a pair of windows over each bay of the arcade. These windows are spaced between three pilasters with arches, so that the ground floor bays consist of column/arch/column, but the *piano nobile* has pilaster/arch and window/pilaster/arch and window/pilaster in the same width. The windows have straight entablatures, and all the moldings are sharply and sparely profiled, emphasizing the flat planes, so that there is no attempt at sculptural modeling to disguise the discrepancy in scale. As at Urbino, the whole composition depends on the precise adjustment between the various elements. It is particularly noticeable that the upper story has two elements to every one below, providing a central pilaster above the crown of the arch in violation of the rule that solids should not appear above voids. However, the so-called Crypta Balbi in Rome (as represented in Giuliano da Sangallo's Codex Barberini) shows just such a feature in an ancient building, and it was to recur in Bramante's cloister at Santa Maria della Pace in Rome only a few years later. The rigor of the proportions and the austere detailing clearly foreshadow the purer classicism of Bramante's Roman works, and his *ultima maniera* may be said to have begun in Milan at precisely the same time that Leonardo ushered in the High Renaissance with his *Last Supper*.

The French armies entered Milan in September, 1499. Bramante may have seen what was coming and left earlier; he was certainly in Rome by 1500, when he painted a fresco (now lost, but known from a drawing in the Albertina, Vienna) at San Giovanni Laterano for the Jubilee of 1500. According to Vasari (who was better informed about Bramante's Roman years than about his earlier life), he had accumulated some money in Milan and was able to live on it for some time while he made an intensive study of the remains of ancient Rome in the city itself, the Campagna, and as far south as Naples. Vasari's description of him as wandering *solitario e cogitativo* certainly corresponds with the idea of him refining and classicizing his style by close contact with the greatest of the remains of classical antiquity. Buildings such as the Pantheon, the Colosseum, the Basilica of Constantine, and the Baths of Diocletian were on a scale that could hardly be paralleled elsewhere, and the simplicity of the bare ruins, stripped as they were of all their original ornamentation, must have made a profound impression on anyone with a feeling for architecture. By then, he may have been in his late fifties (if he was born in 1444), an age at which few artists are prepared to make great stylistic changes, but there can be no doubt that his last works are far purer and grander in style than anything he achieved in Lombardy. It should be remembered that the great change in Raphael's style, so clearly visible in his Vatican frescoes, took place when he was still in his middle twenties.

About 1500, there appeared a small book called *Antiquarie prospettiche romane,* dedicated to Leonardo da Vinci and dealing with Roman antiquities, by "Prospectivo Milanese depictore." It is difficult to imagine who else but Bramante could have written it, and it may be the fruit of his wanderings. During the fourteen years Bramante lived in Rome, and especially after the election of Julius II in 1503, he was occupied on many buildings at the same time, and, from 1505 at least, on the greatest undertaking of the age, the rebuilding of St. Peter's. It is impossible to establish the exact chronology of such major works as the Tempietto and the House of Raphael, but it is clear that Bramante's Roman works can be divided into those that were not commissioned by Julius II and those that were, these all dating from about 1504 onward. The only work certainly datable before 1504 is the cloister at Santa Maria della Pace, which bears an inscription dated 1504 and records Cardinal Carafa as the donor, while a document of 1500 names Bramante as the designer. Cardinal Carafa was the representative in Rome of the interests of both Naples and Spain, and this connection may have been responsible for Bramante's involvement with the Spanish national church in Rome, San Giacomo degli Spagnuoli in the Piazza Navona, although nothing now indicates his activity there; more important, it may have led to the commission for the Tempietto, perhaps as early as 1502.

The Pace cloister, like its predecessor at Sant' Ambrogio in Milan, presented Bramante with a problem arising from the existing site and buildings, limiting his freedom of action. The court itself is square but placed in such a way that the entrance is at one corner and the main view is therefore on a diagonal, emphasizing the corner. Perhaps for this reason, Bramante abandoned the simple arcade form he had previously employed and adopted the much more "Roman" solution of arches supported by heavy piers, with pilasters on pedestals set against the piers as a decorative rather than a structural motif. The ancient prototypes for this more monumental solution were numerous and included the Colosseum and the Theater of Marcellus, while in more recent times the idea had been revived (perhaps under Alberti's influence) in the cortile of the Palazzo Venezia. The adoption of piers meant that the angles seemed to be strengthened, since the L shape formed by the junction of two arcades at the angles gives an appearance of solidity which is markedly lacking in the single column found, for example, at Sant' Ambrogio. Like the Doric cloister, however, the upper range has two bays to each one below, and the result is that colonnettes now stand over the crowns of arches (a point that Vasari probably had in mind when he criticized the Pace cloister). Once again, the proportions are very carefully adjusted, and the heavy entablature at the top, combined with the horizontal emphasis provided by the beautiful and correctly antique Roman letters of the inscription, creates a grid of verticals and horizontals giving a heavier and more classical feeling to the whole court than the one in Milan. The difference between these closely comparable structures is often used as a touchstone for the *gravitas* which was an essential part of Bramante's *ultima maniera.*

On October 31, 1503, Giuliano della Rovere was elected pope as Julius II and almost immediately, he began a career as one of the greatest of all patrons of the arts. At first, however, Giuliano da Sangallo, who had been his architect while he was a cardinal, continued to be employed by him, although it was clear to the new pope that in Bramante he had a collaborator who would be capable of matching his own grandiose vision of a restored Roman *imperium* with art equal to that of antiquity created by such men as Michelangelo, Bramante, and, later, Raphael. From 1505, or perhaps even 1504, Bramante's time was increasingly taken up with work for Julius, who was notorious for wanting everything done at once (compare Michelangelo's problems with the Julius Tomb). Julius was aware that he had only a limited life expectancy (in fact, nearly ten years) in which to achieve his huge program of reform and reconstruction, and it must be admitted that his impatience and Bramante's own volatility led to the failure of parts of the structure of the Belvedere court, and, more important, the failure to draw up a definitive plan for the new St. Peter's, which could be put into effect only over a longer period of time than either Julius or Bramante could reasonably expect to live.

There are, however, several buildings not connected with Julius and not adequately documented that are of the greatest importance as manifestations of the new classicism. The two most significant are the Tempietto (1502?), an *exemplum* of a centrally planned martyrium, and the Palazzo Caprini, better known as the House of Raphael (1509–?), the *exemplum* of a town palace in the ancient manner and the progenitor of most of the important sixteenth-century Italian palaces. (The *exemplum* of a classical villa—the Belvedere—was actually commissioned by Julius.)

One of the better preserved of Bramante's Roman buildings is the circular martyrium, known as the Tempietto, in the courtyard of the Franciscan convent of San Pietro in Montorio, on the top of the Janiculum Hill (also known as Mons Aureus, Montorio). The principal problems connected with this very small building are those of date, siting, and patronage, all of which have a bearing on the meaning of the chapel as a *memoria*. In the crypt, there is a stone slab inscribed: *Sacellum Apostolor. Princi. Martirio. Sacrum. Ferdinand. Hispan. Rex Et. Helisabe. Regina. Catholici. Post. Erectam. Ab. Eis. Aedem. Poss. An. Sal. Kriane. M.D.II.* From this it seems clear that the Tempietto was erected by Ferdinand and Isabella of Spain in honor of the martyrdom of Peter, Prince of the Apostles, in the year 1502. We know that the ground on which the Franciscan convent and the Church of San Pietro in Montorio stand had been given, some thirty years earlier, to Spanish Franciscans under Amedeo Meñez da Silva (in fact, the Spanish Academy in Rome still occupies part of the buildings), but it is not immediately obvious why Ferdinand and Isabella should wish to build, in 1502, a small separate chapel only a few feet away from the church itself, and awkwardly sited in a small courtyard. The date is probably that of the decision to build on the part of the Catholic sovereigns rather than that of completion. Until recently, 1502 was accepted as the date of building, but there are reasons for rejecting this: first, Francesco Albertini, in his guidebook to Rome, written in 1509 and published in 1510, refers to the church of San Pietro in Montorio and its Spanish connection, but does not mention the Tempietto at all; second, the Tempietto is thought to be stylistically later than the Pace cloister of 1500–1504. The most likely date, however, is probably before the early plans for St. Peter's, so it is possible that, following a vow made in 1502, the sovereigns got a design from Bramante, perhaps between 1502 and 1506, which was executed sufficiently slowly

for Albertini in 1509 not to feel it necessary to mention it. The supervision of this building was entrusted to another Spaniard, Cardinal Carvajal. It has recently been shown by J. Huskinson that an unfounded theory concerning the location of the crucifixion of Saint Peter was current from the mid-fifteenth century on and is reflected in the bronze doors made for Old St. Peter's by Filarete. According to this theory, the spot on which Peter was martyred was *inter duas metas,* which was interpreted as meaning between the Meta Romuli and the Pyramid of Cestius, further interpreted as on the top of the Janiculum. This hypothesis did not last long, but it was probably enough to persuade the Spanish royal couple to assert a claim to the possession of a sacred spot on Spanish soil, which in turn explains the choice of shape of the building, as well as its location. Vitruvius had laid down that temples should be built according to decorum, that is, the Doric Temple is appropriate to male, heroic gods such as Hercules or Mars; the Corinthian for virgin goddesses such as Diana or Vesta. It is noteworthy that the Tempietto is the earliest example of a fully worked-out Doric Temple in the Renaissance, and the following passage from Serlio (Book IV, 1537) is crucial in this respect:

The Ancients dedicated this Doric Order to Jove, Mars, Hercules and other robust gods, but after the Incarnation it is right that we Christians should proceed differently if we have to make a temple to be consecrated to Jesus Christ our Redeemer, or to Saint Paul or to Saint Peter, or to Saint George or to any saint of that kind, who, not being soldiers by profession, yet had a virile and strong expression of their lives for Christ—for all these the Doric is suitable. . . . And this was observed in the works of Bramante in the buildings he made in Rome. And we should give credence to Bramante, seeing that it was he who was the inventor and light of all good architecture which had been buried until his time, the time of Julius II.

The Tempietto is therefore to be regarded as a classical Christian martyrium, in the same tradition as a classical pagan *memoria*. Confirmation of this interpretation can be found in the frieze of the Temple of Vespasian, which is known to have been above ground in the sixteenth century. It is carved with a variety of pagan sacrificial instruments. The frieze of the Tempietto, being Doric, has triglyphs alternating with metopes, and the metopes are carved with various liturgical and symbolical objects: thus, above the entrance, there is a chalice and paten; other metopes have candlesticks, incense-boats and other liturgical objects used in the celebration of the Eucharist or symbolic of sacrifice; there are also crossed keys, which are a specific reference to the Petrine Primacy.

A drawing (A 135) in the Uffizi, Florence, attributed to Bramante, is called a study for the Tempietto, but it is much more likely to date from the second half of the sixteenth century; a recent attribution to F. Barocci, for a painting by him which has the Tempietto in the background, seems probable. This drawing differs from the extant building in several respects, including the fact that the metopes are shown as carved with classical paterae instead of liturgical objects. It should also be noted that the plans and sections illustrated by Serlio and Palladio, as well as several early sixteenth-century drawings (for example, the Codex Coner in the Soane Museum, London), differ among themselves as well as from the executed building. Some of these discrepancies may be ascribed to the alterations made to the building in 1536 and 1605, when the dome was considerably altered, but other factors, such as the number of entrances and the disposition of the internal pilasters cannot be so explained. The disposition of the internal pilasters shown by Serlio, according to Bruschi, may reflect an early project which Bramante abandoned in execution. Also in Serlio's treatise is a site plan that was probably never executed because the court itself is too small to accommodate the extra ring of columns and the deep niches in each corner. This plan does, however, indicate that Bramante was thinking in terms of a complete environment, a complex series of interrelated central plans based on a square, a Greek cross and concentric circles, looking back to San Lorenzo in Milan and forward to the project for the new St. Peter's in Rome. The combination of ancient Roman forms with Christian symbolism was, like St. Peter's itself, intended as an affirmation of the idea of the Christian Roman *imperium* which Bramante shared with Julius II. There is, however, one vital difference between the Tempietto and St. Peter's: the Tempietto was a pure martyrium, intended solely to commemorate what was thought to be the place of the Apostle's martyrdom, and is indeed far too small to be of much practical use. For this reason it had to be centrally planned, since the vast majority of such commemorative buildings were so planned, as Bramante would have known from San Satiro, for example. Of all central forms the circle was held to be the most perfect, and this seems to have been the general view throughout the sixteenth century. St. Peter's, on the other hand, was certainly also a martyrium, since it was the site of the Apostle's Tomb and had been so venerated at least since the fourth century; but it was also a major basilica with the need to provide for very large crowds during the great feasts. The need to express two different functions was perhaps the greatest of the problems Bramante faced when he began to work seriously on the project for rebuilding the ancient basilica, and it was never, as far as we know, satisfactorily solved by him.

If the Tempietto was to be regarded as the

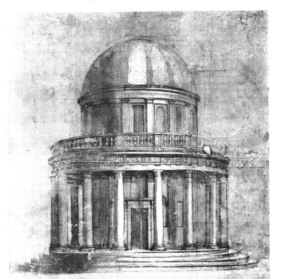

Bramante.
Drawing of the Tempietto.
Rome.
1502?

Bramante.
Tempietto.
Rome.
1502?

Bramante.
Drawing of the Belvedere
Court by Serlio.

model for a martyrium, then the *exemplum* for domestic building was provided by Bramante's design for the Palazzo Caprini, usually called the House of Raphael. This building, which is known only from an engraving by Lafreri of 1549 and one or two drawings, nevertheless exerted a great influence on town palaces for centuries to come. The palace is obviously based on the ancient Roman *insula,* a freestanding block with evenly arranged openings on the ground floor for shops and apartments on the upper floors. This arrangement survived into modern times (for example, in Florence in the fourteenth century) because it provided a well-off family with imposing headquarters, with the ground floor used either as offices for the family business or rented to others to provide an income. The *piano nobile* above served as a residence for the head of the family, and the upper floor(s) were servants' quarters or accommodation for poor relations. From this point of view, Bramante's design was a failure (it is significant that both Bramante and Raphael were bachelors); the *piano nobile* provides a splendid sequence of large state rooms with identical windows, but there is nowhere room for a kitchen and servants' quarters. The drawing, once attributed to Palladio (Royal Institute of British Architects, London) provides a clue which the engraving does not, for it shows some of the metopes in the frieze as openings, presumably garrets. This confirms the view that the design was intended as a manifesto rather than a practical solution to an everyday problem, since there are only two stories (instead of three or more), sharply differentiated. The basement or podium is heavily rusticated but has no order. It is subdivided by a course of ashlar masonry at the level of the springing of the arches, marking the mezzanine rooms over the shops, which are symmetrically disposed about the central axis. The

piano nobile above has ashlar masonry with coupled Doric columns separating each window bay, giving an identical repetition of units. The contrast between the massive bosses of rustication on the lower level and the precision and elegance of the upper story was intended to reflect the commercial and noble purposes of the respective floors. From the London drawing it seems clear that the rustication was heavy, and Vasari specifically informs us that the construction was of brick and stucco "cast in a novel way," similar to that used by Bramante at Santa Maria del Popolo and St. Peter's itself, where the great crossing arches were cast in concrete, like their Roman prototypes. The use of cast stucco or concrete seems to have been revived by Bramante as a result of his studies of Roman remains, and it may help to determine the date of the House of Raphael. There is no firm evidence for this, and dates ranging from 1500 to 1512 have been suggested, but it seems unlikely that it could be earlier than the Tempietto, and the use of cast material may indicate a date around 1509 or later.

The third classical *exemplum*—the villa—is represented by the Belvedere Court of the Vatican, begun in 1505. Adjoining it is the Cortile di San Damaso, the only range built of a series of loggie intended as part of a complete rebuilding of the Vatican Palace. The existing range, which contains the famous decorations by Raphael and his assistants, consists of three superimposed loggie (originally open, but now glazed to protect the frescoes) of a type similar to the Benediction Loggia of Old St. Peter's. Nearby and extending uphill for some 300 yards is the Belvedere Court, connecting the Vatican Palace with the small villa of the Belvedere built by Innocent VIII. As its name implies, this commanded a fine view and was used to contain the ever growing collection of ancient statues discovered in Rome (the most famous was the *Laocöon,* discovered in 1506). Basically, the Belvedere Court consists of two very long ranges, starting at the palace end as a three-story block and enclosing a garden about 200 feet wide; this changes to two stories when the first terrace is reached, and finally to a single story at the top level, where the Belvedere itself stands. There are thus two very long corridors on three levels connected by elaborate ramps and steps, and culminating in a hemicycle at the end, which disguises the fact that the Belvedere villa is at an awkward angle to the main axis. Unfortunately, the court as we now have it is not at all what Bramante intended. The hemicycle, and especially the famous semicircular steps, were rebuilt by Michelangelo and PIRRO LIGORIO in the sixteenth century, and the general effect was ruined by the building, in the eighteenth century, of the Braccio Nuovo, a wing of the new museum which cut the court in half and destroyed the intended vista from the palace to the villa. The building also suffered from the impatience of Julius, who had it carried on by day and night, with the result that parts of it collapsed and had to be rebuilt later. The Temple of Fortuna Primigenia at Palestrina (Praeneste) was almost certainly the model for the rising terraces culminating in a hemicycle at the top, but the general effect was thought of as a villa, perhaps like Hadrian's at Tivoli. Both Tivoli and Palestrina must have been known to Bramante from his excursions in the Campagna, but it is difficult to be sure how much ancient work was then visible.

The most celebrated feature of the Belvedere, however, is the open spiral ramp which winds up from ground level to the Belvedere itself, with a series of columns changing from Doric at the bottom to Corinthian at the top.

Julius II was elected pope at the end of October, 1503. Given our knowledge of his character, it may be assumed that he intended to do something about St. Peter's, even if it was no more than repair work. The problem was an old one: in the pontificate of Nicholas V (1447–1455) a survey had shown walls badly out of true, and there was a real risk that the next earth tremor would bring the 1,100-year old building down in ruins. As a result of this report, BERNARDO ROSSELLINO began foundations for a new, larger choir extending from the transept of the old building considerably to the west of the original choir—St. Peter's is orientated to the west—while retaining the central position of the Apostle's Tomb with the Constantinian Memoria above it. These foundations were begun on the south side only and were discontinued after Nicholas's death, but enough had been done for Bramante to be instructed to avoid waste by including them in his own project.

We know that well before April 1506, a firm decision had been taken to rebuild on a grand scale, so it is reasonable to suppose that the first projects were discussed between Bramante and the pope, each encouraging the other to grander and more expensive schemes, but without taking definite decisions, perhaps as early as 1504. The first definite proposal was probably made in the summer of 1505: unfortunately, the whole history of the rebuilding is bedeviled by the fact that no truly definitive decisions were ever taken, nor are there any records of deliberations. At this time, the architectural profession was only just coming into existence and Bramante had no established office to record and execute such decisions; besides, both Julius and he were conscious of the need for haste, since they were both old men and needed to commit their successors by building so much that it would be cheaper to go on than to withdraw (neither could have foreseen the financial troubles and the Sack of 1527).

The only primary evidence for this first project is a drawing (Uffizi A 1, "The Parchment Plan"), together with the medal by Caradosso dated 1506. The drawing shows a half-plan of a building with a large central dome and two subsidiary Greek-cross chapels, also domed, in the angles of what appears to be half of a large Greek cross. On the back, in what is certainly the handwriting of Antonio da Sangallo the Younger, is the statement that it is by Bramante (*di mano di Bramante*) and that it was not executed. It is thus the only certainly authentic drawing by Bramante, but since it is not freehand it affords no indication of Bramante's style as a draftsman. According to Vasari, Bramante was unable to draw in his later years because of paralysis in the hand, so that he employed others—Sangallo the Younger, Sansovino, and especially Peruzzi—to realize the projects he visualized. This is the principal reason for the confusion over Bramante's intentions: there are large numbers of early sixteenth-century drawings and many, perhaps most, are unofficial. Specifically, the existence of Greek-cross and long-nave designs implies only that no final decision had been taken when Bramante died. Serlio (Book III) reproduces a Greek-cross plan as by Peruzzi (which is more likely to be a revision by Bramante of his own Parchment Plan) and a long-nave version, reminiscent of Santa Maria delle Grazie, which he attributes to Raphael, Bramante's designated successor at St. Peter's.

The Caradosso medal is equally important. On the obverse it has a profile of Julius II with the date 1506; the reverse shows an elevation of the new

Bramante.
An early plan of St. Peter's.
Rome.

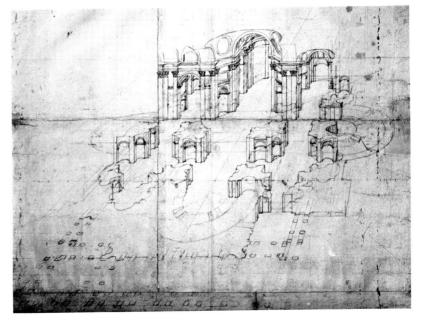

building with the inscription: TEMPLI PETRI INSTAURACIO. VATICANUS M. The word *instaurare* is highly significant. It occurs in the Bible and in other liturgical contexts with the meaning "to make new, to restore," and it provides clear evidence of the intention, not to replace, but to restore the Vatican Basilica to its former, ancient, glory. The building as shown is dominated by a huge dome of the same type as the Pantheon, flanked by two tall campanili (since it is an elevation the intention may have been to have four towers, one in each angle). San Lorenzo in Milan is the prototype for such a building in the early Christian tradition. The new St. Peter's would thus be a martyrium like the Tempietto, but on an enormous scale. Old St. Peter's, however, was a unique combination of a centrally planned martyrium over the Tomb itself, with a very large nave and four aisles converting it into a basilical plan and allowing adequate space for the great crowds of pilgrims and for processions on major feasts. This practical aspect weighed heavily with the clergy and was probably decisive in the final conversion of Michelangelo's central plan into the present shape. Many of the drawings made by Leonardo in Milan show complex central plans joined to naves in exactly the same way as Santa Maria delle Grazie, so it is probable that, up to his death, Bramante never finally decided which he wanted.

Since we know that examples of the medal were buried at the base of the northwest (Veronica) pier when the foundation stone was laid by Julius II on April 18, 1506, the medal itself must have been made before then and the project behind it may therefore date from 1505: certainly, modifications soon became necessary. The most obvious was the need to support a dome of the size and type of the Pantheon on something more than four small piers with minimal abutment. The sheer scale of the undertaking—since Bramante had fixed the position of the piers—was similar to the Pantheon and Florence Cathedral, and the Roman masons would have had no experience with the problems of statics. The second, so-called Peruzzi, plan published by Serlio already shows the piers thickened with heavier abutments, and a drawing (Uffizi A 20) made about the time of Bramante's death shows the old building with the new plan superimposed, the original Veronica pier more or less as it was in 1506, but all the others much larger and heavier. In fact, the process of enlarging the piers and increasing the abutments continued until the dome was finally built (by GIACOMO DELLA PORTA and DOMENICO FONTANA) in 1585–1590.

Progress on the huge undertaking was necessarily slow, in spite of the desire for haste on the part of Julius and Bramante himself, and, after

their deaths in 1513 and 1514, it became even slower, although Raphael was appointed to succeed Bramante. Nevertheless, the storm raised by Luther meant that financial support was dwindling, and Julius's successors, Leo X, Hadrian VI, and Clement VII, lacked the burning desire to see the basilica finished as a symbol of papal imperial Rome. The Sack of Rome in 1527 meant that all work ceased for many years. The drawings made in the 1530s by the Dutch painter Maerten van Heemskerck show the building still in much the same state as Bramante had left it except for the weeds and bushes sprouting out of it, which made contemporaries think of it as just another Roman ruin. There are several drawings, by Heemskerck and others, which provide evidence of this before serious rebuilding started under Sangallo. They also show the *tegurio,* or temporary shelter, which Bramante designed in 1513 to cover Saint Peter's Tomb while it was exposed to the elements: like the Tempietto, it was a Doric temple. It was destroyed when the dome was built above it.

The most important facts provided by these drawings are that the size and scale of all future building were determined by Bramante when he established the position of the piers and the height of the pilasters facing the piers, together with the great arches, coffered in the Roman manner, that join them. In fact, the present building has decreased the height of the original pilasters because the floor level has been raised; otherwise, the form, though not the decoration, of the crossing below the springing of the dome is Bramante's. Perhaps the best idea of his conception of the building as an austerely classical space can be gained from the architecture in Raphael's *School of Athens,* painted in 1509–1511.

Traditionally, Bramante is supposed to have expressed the desire to set the dome of the Pantheon on the vaults of the Temple of Peace (the Basilica of Constantine); and there can be no doubt that the Foundation Medal expressed the desire, shared by Bramante and Julius alike, to revive the imperial Roman age and to create a building expressive of the *pax romana cristiana:* it is not without significance that Hagia Sophia in Constantinople had been the embodiment of such an idea; since it had fallen to the Turks in 1453, it was necessary to reassert its significance by erecting a high martyrium over the Tomb of the Prince of the Apostles: *Templi Petri instauracio.*

Apart from the Caradosso medal we have little evidence for the external appearance of Bramante's design, but there are two important pointers. Serlio (Book III) refers to a model which Bramante had made, but which was imperfect in some respects (*il modello rimase imperfetto in alcune parti*);

by itself, this might mean no more than a lost sketch, but, writing about 1570, Onofrio Panvinio refers specifically to a wooden model (*e ligno fabricato*) by Bramante. A recently discovered sketchbook, attributed to Menicantonio de Chiarellis and now in the Paul Mellon Collection, contains a drawing of the elevation and section which may be based on the lost model. Chiarellis (if he was the draftsman) was active in Bramante's lifetime in the *Fabbrica* of St. Peter's, so he had ample opportunity to see any model. His general accuracy seems to be confirmed by other drawings representing works by Bramante and especially by a plan showing the surroundings of the new basilica treated like a Roman bath complex, which is very close to a drawing from the Bramante circle in the Uffizi (A 104). Other reflections of these projects may be found in works by members of the Bramante circle, as well as what may have been trial runs by Bramante himself. The most important of these are the churches at Montepulciano, Todi, and Loreto; and Santa Maria del Popolo, Santi Celso e Giuliano, San Biagio alla Pagnotta and Sant' Eligio degli Orefici, all in Rome.

The Madonna di San Biagio at Montepulciano was begun by Antonio Sangallo the Elder after Bramante's death, but probably derives from the Caradosso medal; Santa Maria della Consolazione at Todi is a centrally planned building connected in some way with both Bramante and Leonardo, and the medal of 1509 showing the façade of the Basilica at Loreto represents a domed church with two campanili which was certainly designed by Bramante. Santa Maria del Popolo has a choir with cast coffering, finished by 1509, which seems to have been a small-scale experiment in the casting of arches like those for St. Peter's; Santi Celso e Giuliano and San Biagio (which was part of a projected Palace of Justice complex) are both variations on the Greek-cross theme, designed from about 1508–1509 and now lost. Sant' Eligio is a later Greek-cross building, still extant, on which Raphael and Peruzzi also worked: it is not clear whether Bramante himself actually had a hand in the design, but it is certainly connected with the centrally planned variations on St. Peter's.

St. Peter's is the lost masterpiece of the High Renaissance, as Michelangelo himself recognized when he wrote in a letter of January 1547: "One cannot deny that Bramante was as skilled in architecture as anyone since the time of the ancients. He it was who laid down the first plan of St. Peter's, not full of confusion, but clear, simple, luminous and detached in such a way that it in no wise impinged upon the Palace. It was held to be a beautiful design, and manifestly still is, so that anyone who has departed from Bramante's arrangement,

Bramante.
St. Peter's.
In School of Athens by
Raphael.

as Sangallo has done, has departed from the true course" (Ramsden, 1963, no. 274). And Michelangelo disliked Bramante, blaming him, after all those years, for the difficulties he experienced with Julius II, who drove them both so hard.

PETER MURRAY

WORKS

1477, Palazzo del Podesta (fresco now in Museo Civico), Bergamo, Italy. c.1480, Santa Maria presso San Satiro, Milan. 1488 and later, Pavia Cathedral (adviser), Italy. 1492–?, Piazza, Vignevano, Italy. 1492–?, Santa Maria delle Grazie (tribune); 1492–?, Sant' Ambrogio (canonica); Milan. 1497, Santa Maria Nascente (entrance), Abbiategrasso, Italy. 1497–1498 and later, Sant' Ambrogio (cloisters), Milan. 1500–1504, Santa Maria della Pace (cloister); 1502?, Tempietto; 1504?, Belvedere Court; 1505–1506, St. Peter's (first proposals for renovation and reconstruction); 1505–1509, Santa Maria del Popolo (choir); *1508–?, San Biagio; before 1509, Court of San Damaso; *1509–?, House of Raphael; *1509–?, Santi Celso e Giuliano; (A)*1509–?, Sant' Eligio; *1513, Tegurio (shelter for St. Peter's Tomb); Rome.

BIBLIOGRAPHY

ACKERMAN, JAMES S. 1954 *The Cortile del Belvedere.* Vatican City: Biblioteca apostolica.
ALBERTINI, FRANCESCO (1510)1972 "Opusculum de mirabilibus urbis Romae." In Peter Murray (editor), *Five Early Guides to Rome and Florence.* Reprint. Farnsborough, England: Gregg.
BRUSCHI, ARNALDO 1969 *Bramante architetto.* Bari, Italy, and Rome: Laterza.
BRUSCHI, ARNALDO 1977 *Bramante.* London: Thames & Hudson.
CESARIANO, CESARE (1521)1968 *Di Lucio Vitruvio Pollione de Architectura.* Reprint. New York and London: Blom.

Congresso internazionale di studi bramanteschi. 1974 Rome: DeLuca.

FIENGA, DORIS 1974 "Bramante Autore delle *Antiquarie Prospettiche Romane. . . .*" *Studi Bramanteschi* 1974:417–426.

GUARNA, ANDREA DA SALERNO (1517)1970 *Scimmia.* Translated by E. and G. Battisti. Rome: DeLuca. Originally published in Latin as *Simia.*

HUSKINSON, J. M. 1969 "The Crucifixion of St. Peter." *Journal of the Warburg and Courtauld Institutes* 32:135–161.

MURRAY, PETER 1962 "Bramante Milanese: The Prints and Drawings." *Arte Lombarda* 7, no. 1:25–42.

MURRAY, PETER 1963 "Leonardo and Bramante." *Architectural Review* 134:347–351.

MURRAY, PETER 1967 "Menicantonio, du Cerceau, and the Towers of St. Peter's." In *Studies in Renaissance and Baroque Art Presented to Anthony Blunt.* London: Phaidon.

PALLADIO, ANDREA (1570)1965 *The Four Books of Architecture.* Translated by Isaac Ware. Reprint. New York: Dover.

PASTOR, LUDWIG VON (1891)1950 Volume 6 in *The History of the Popes.* London: Kegan Paul.

RAMSDEN, E. H. 1963 Volume 2, letter 274 in *The Letters of Michelangelo.* 2 vols. London: Owen.

SANGIORGI, FERT 1970 *Bramante hasdrubaldino.* Urbino and Fermignano, Italy: Comitato nazionale per le celebrazione bramantesche.

SERLIO, SEBASTIANO (1537–1540)1964 Books 3–4 in *Tutte l'opere d'architettura, pospetiva.* Ridgewood, N.J.: Gregg. Originally published with the title *Regole generale di Architeturra.*

SHEARMAN, JOHN 1974 "Il Tiburio di Bramante." *Studi Bramanteschi* 1974:567–573.

VASARI, GIORGIO (1568)1973 *Le opere di Giorgio Vasari, con nuove annotazioni e commenti.* 9 vols. Edited by G. Milanesi. Reprint. Florence: Sansoni. Originally published in 1550 with the title *Le vite de più eccelenti architetti.* There are many English translations and selections from Vasari's *Lives;* the standard one by G. du C. de Vere was published in ten volumes in London by the Medici Society in 1912–1915.

BRAMANTINO

Bartolommeo Suardi (c.1455–1536), known as Bramantino, was born in Milan. His first master was probably Butinone, but the greatest influence was his contact with LEONARDO DA VINCI and DONATO BRAMANTE. Primarily a painter, Bramantino was somewhat involved in architecture, taking part in the discussions concerning the planning and building of the Cathedral of Milan in 1503. Working in Rome between 1508 and 1513, he apparently completed drawings of the antiquities and is later assumed to have sketched all of the ancient buildings in Milan. Although GIORGIO VASARI and Lomazzo both relate this information, none of the drawings has survived.

Bramantino's work as an architect does not seem to have been prolific. His paintings typically show a high degree of certainty in architectural handling of the backgrounds. A rather frequent display of monumental architectonics in conjunction with a unique style of perspective may attest to an understanding of architecture. His only remaining architectural achievement is the original design of the Trivulzio Burial Chamber in Milan. In 1525, as a reward for political loyalty, Bramantino was appointed court painter and architect by Duke Francesco Sforza.

JEFFREY HUGHES

BIBLIOGRAPHY

SUIDA, WILLIAM E. 1953 *Bramante pittore e il Bramantino.* Milan: Ceschina.

BRANDON, DAVID

David Brandon (1813–1897) was predominantly an architect of country houses which he designed and restored in the Jacobethan style. From 1828 to 1833, he was articled to GEORGE SMITH of Mercer's Hall. In 1832, Brandon was awarded the Silver Medal of the Royal Academy for the best drawings of the Bank of England. From 1838 to 1851, he was in partnership with THOMAS HENRY WYATT, their major work being the *Rundbogenstil* Church of Saints Mary and Nicholas in Wilton, Wiltshire (1840–1846). In 1851, Brandon began his independent and prolific practice, designing country houses, churches, hospitals, and schools.

MARGARET RICHARDSON

WORKS

1840–1846, Church of Saints Mary and Nicholas, Wilton, England. 1845, 18–19 Kensington Palace Gardens and Entrance Lodges, London. 1850–1853, Saint John's Hospital, Stone, Buckinghamshire, England. *1851, Falconhurst Lodge, Cowden, Kent, England. *1854, Colesbourne Park, Gloucestershire, England. 1865, Corn Exchange, Market Square, Aylesbury, England. 1861–1863, Chilham Castle (restoration; partly demolished), Kent, England. *1866–1869, Junior Carlton Club, Pall Mall, London. 1881, Foxbury, Chislehurst, Kent, England.

BIBLIOGRAPHY

GIROUARD, MARK (1971)1979 *The Victorian Country House.* Rev. ed. New Haven: Yale University Press.

"Obituary." 1897 *Journal of the Royal Institute of British Architects* 4:144–145.

BRASINI, ARMANDO

A Roman, largely self-taught, Armando Brasini (1879–1965) was a prolific designer of buildings mostly in a neobaroque style; he was also a city planner, a restorer of historical monuments, and the author of many extravagant, unrealized projects. From his scenic entrance pavilions for the Rome Zoo (1909–1910) to the numerous enterprises of his old age such as the Messina Straits Bridge and a fairyland palace for the Saudi royal family, he spurned transalpine modernism. Although in the fascist period he largely ignored the official style, he was successful because his intoxication with a Piranesian monumentality appealed to those who wished to see Roman traditions implied once again by magniloquent architecture in Italy and Italian possessions overseas. His sources were Mannerism, FRANCESCO BORROMINI, the late baroque and, above all, his singular vision of the grandeur of ancient and papal Rome. He was an indefatigable worker, entering into competitions and controversies with equal zest.

If his work has a common quality it is theatricality; he may have been the last architect to produce monumental neobaroque buildings. He smoothly infused his designs with ancient and baroque themes, producing a powerful sense of drama as at the convent of Buon' Pastore in Rome (1930). He was eclectic in that he frequently made use of others' forms, but his sense of drama was largely his own, and his scenic silhouettes and highly articulated surfaces, though by no means to everyone's taste, do carry the grand Italian tradition of theatrical effect to a kind of logical if sometimes overpowering conclusion. These qualities show up even more strongly in the imaginative renderings of his grandiose schemes, which sometimes verge on the fantastic. He seems to have turned with ease from feasible projects such as completing Saint Ignazio in Rome, the dome of which had never been built, to proposals for leveling large sections of the historic center of Rome in order to construct imperially-scaled plazas flanked by mammoth buildings the Caesars might have envied. These defiant proposals caused much controversy, but the fact that both Brasini's supporters and critics took them seriously for a while fairly sets the man in his time. To romantics, his buildings often have an appealing side; for cooler temperaments, his work at Tripoli (city planning and the fine seaside boulevard, for example), his restorations, and his Museum of the Risorgimento (1924–1939) in Rome will seem more attractive.

WILLIAM L. MACDONALD

WORKS

1909–1910, Zoo (gateway); Sets for Guazzoni's *Quo Vadis;* Rome. 1920s, Castello (restoration), Tripoli. 1920s, House of Italo-Japanese Culture, Tokyo 1920s, Stadium, Rio de Janeiro, Brazil. 1924–1939, Monument to Victor Emmanuel (completion of the Museum of

Brasini.
Convent of Buon' Pastore.
Rome.
1930

the Risorgimento and the Monument to the Unknown Soldier), Rome. 1925, Italian Pavilion, Paris Fair. 1930, Convent of Buon' Pastore, Rome. 1930s, City Hall, Foggia, Italy. 1930s, Prefecture, Taranto, Italy. 1931, Italian Pavilion, Colonial Exhibition, Paris. c.1938, Forestale, EUR (unfinished); 1940, Saint Rita's Church (moved); 1951, Ponte Flaminio; 1955, Church of the Immaculate Heart of Mary; Rome.

BIBLIOGRAPHY

BRASINI, LUCA (editor) 1979 *L'opera architettonica e urbanistica di Armando Brasini.* Rome: Columbo.
CLINTON, DONALD, and WILKIN, CLARA 1979 *Armando Brasini: Roma imperiale.* Edmonton Art Gallery.
ORANO, P. 1916 *Urbe Massima. L'architettura e la decorazione di Armando Brasini.* Rome: Formiggini.
PANI, S. RAFFO 1972 Volume 14, pages 64–66 in *Dizionario biografico degli Italiani.* Edited by Alberto M. Ghesalberti. Rome: Istituto della Enciclopedia italiana.

BRATKE, OSWALDO

Born in São Paulo, Brazil, Oswaldo Bratke (1907–) has concentrated on the human factor in architecture, whether for a new town in the Amazonian jungle or a simple suburban residence. He graduated from the University of Mackenzie when architecture existed as a minor course for civil engineers, and he began his career as a builder in 1932. In 1945, he turned to architecture as a profession after having built over 400 popular dwellings.

Attracted by the problem of public housing in Brazil, Bratke devoted part of his career to the creation of new towns in remote areas of the Amazon and the State of Amapa—from initial layouts to actual construction of urban networks. Above all, he stresses the need for simple design in conjunction with materials that can be easily maintained.

For Bratke, modern architecture implies a new lifestyle demanding smaller single-family houses with open planning and vertical multiple-family dwellings that can be adapted for modern appliances, and houses that are secure against crime. Winner of several architectural awards, the most recent being the Mario Andrade Medal given by the State of São Paulo, Bratke is a thoughtful architect who has dedicated himself to creating a peaceful yet efficient environment for man.

ELIZABETH D. HARRIS

WORKS

1938, Grande Hotel, Campos do Jordão, Brazil. 1943, Apartment Building, Rua General Jordim; 1947, Aricanduva Pavilon; 1950, Livio Gomes House; 1951, Office Building, Rua Major Sertório; 1952, Gilberto Freire's House; 1953, Bratke Workshop; 1953, Morumbi Infant Hospital; São Paulo, Brazil. 1956–1965, Vilas Industriais Amazonas, Amapa State, Brazil. 1960, Jockey Club Headquarters; 1961, Legislative Assembly; São Paulo, Brazil. 1965, Town Hall, Santo Andre, Brazil.

BIBLIOGRAPHY

FERRAZ, GERALDO 1957 "Osvaldo Bratke." *Habitat* 45:21–37.
MINDLIN, HENRIQUE 1956 *Modern Architecture in Brazil.* New York: Reinhold.

BREBION, MAXIMILIEN

Maximilien Brébion (1716–1796) won the *premier prix* at the French Academy in 1740 and was appointed to membership by the marquis de Marigny in 1755. He became inspector of the buildings of the Louvre in 1757. A faithful disciple of JACQUES GERMAIN SOUFFLOT, with whom he had worked since 1770, Brébion carried out his master's plans for the dome of Sainte-Geneviève from 1780. That year, in the context of the adaptation of the Louvre as a museum, Brébion carried out Soufflot's plans for a monumental staircase leading to the Salon Carré. He also pierced an archway from the Cour Carré (1780?) toward the Pont des Arts. Between 1781 and 1785, he planned and constructed the Marché Sainte-Catherine. Brébion was also involved in projects to build the Opéra between the Louvre and the Tuileries. With Jean Renard, he began the restoration of the Observatory (1786). In 1792, he was asked to help transform the Salle des Machines of the Tuileries into an assembly room. In 1791, he was among the Academicians who proposed a National Academy of the Arts. Two years later, he renounced his royal diplomas to join the Commune des Arts in spite of failing eyesight.

MYRA DICKMAN ORTH

WORKS

1780?, Arched passage from Cour Carré of the Louvre toward the Pont des Arts; *1780, Monumental Stair to Salon Carré, Louvre; 1780–1796, Sainte Geneviève (dome; later the Panthéon); *1781–1785, Marché Sainte-Catherine; 1786, Observatory (restoration; with Jean Renard); Paris.

BIBLIOGRAPHY

BRAHAM, ALLAN 1980 *The Architecture of the French Enlightenment.* London: Thames & Hudson.
BRIÈRE, GASTON 1950 "Iconographie du Palais du Louvre: Une vue d'Hubert Robert." *Musées de France* 10:229–231.
GALLET, MICHEL 1964 *Les Demeures parisiennes: L'Epoque Louis XVIe*. Paris: Le Temps.
HAUTECOEUR, LOUIS 1952 *Seconde moitié du XVIIIe siècle: Le style Louis XVI, 1750–1792.* Volume 4 in *Histoire de l'architecture classique en France.* Paris: Picard.
LEPAUZE, HENRY 1903 *Procès-verbaux de la Commune générale des arts de peinture, sculpture, architecture, et gravure (18 juillet 1793...) et de la Société populaire et républicaine des arts (2 nivose II-28 floréal III).* Paris: Imprimerie nationale.
LEMONNIER, HENRY (editor) 1918–1926 Volumes 5–9 in *Procès-verbaux de l'Académie Royale d'Architecture: 1671–1793.* Paris: Schmit.
PEROUSE DE MONTCLOS, JEAN MARIE (1969)1974 *Etienne-Louis Boullée (1728–1799).* Translated by James Emmons. New York: Braziller.
PETZET, MICHAEL 1961 *Soufflots Sainte-Geneviève und der französische Kirchenbau des 18. Jahrhunderts.* Berlin: de Gruyter.

BREGNO, ANDREA

Andrea Bregno (1418–1506) was one of the most distinguished of many Lombard masons and sculptors to move south to Tuscany and Lazio during the fifteenth century. In 1464–1465, during the pontificate of the Venetian Paul II Bregno seems to have come to Rome, where he made his career by successfully blending northern decorative imagery, classical ornament, and Tuscan architectural form into large-scale sculpture. From then until his death there, Bregno was the head of a prominent sculptural workshop.

Bregno's fine ornament, highly finished surfaces and delicate lines were much favored by aristocratic patrons. In tomb sculpture, particularly, Bregno forced aside the Tuscan sculptor Mino da Fiesole, then the most popular in Rome. The quality of Bregno's work at this time is demonstrated by the tomb for Cardinal Louis d'Albret in the church of Santa Maria d'Aracoeli (1465) in Rome. Another notable work is the Piccolomini Altar in the Duomo (1481–1485), Siena, remarkable for the classical ornament and delicate garlands carved on the pilasters. But Bregno's work lost its original strength as his increasing work load forced the intervention of the shop.

From an architectural point of view Bregno's importance is hard to measure. His shop provided sculpted architectural ornament for many Roman buildings during the fifteenth century, such as the Hospital of Santo Spirito in Rome (1474–1482). Bregno's study of Roman ornament provided a perfect foil for the new Renaissance architecture of Rome. As a result, his name has been proposed as the architect of one of the largest palaces of the Roman fifteenth century, the Cancellerial (1475). No evidence exists to support this attribution, although his tomb sculpture is replete with architectural elements.

Bregno was able to mix relatively easily in humanistic circles. The humanist Platina was one of his friends and his collection of Roman antiquities was highly prized. As an indication of his social standing, his tomb in the church of Santa Maria sopra Minerva in Rome includes not only an epitaph in which he is praised as a new POLYKLEITOS but also a portrait—an unusual honor for an artist at that time. Thus Bregno, through his study of the classical past as well as his intellectual standing, is a model for the artists of the high Renaissance, such as RAPHAEL.

NICHOLAS ADAMS

WORKS

1465, Tomb of Cardinal d'Albret, Santa Maria d'Aracoeli; 1474–1482, Hospital of Santo Spirito (portal); 1475, Tomb of Cardinal Coca, Santa Maria sopra Minerva; 1479, Tomb for Cristoforo delle Rovere, Santa Maria del Popolo; Rome. 1481–1485, Piccolomini Altar, Duomo, Siena, Italy. 1490, Santa Maria della Quercia (tabernacle), Viterbo, Italy. 1495–1498, Savelli Tomb, Santa Maria d'Aracoeli, Rome.

BIBLIOGRAPHY

BATTISTI, EUGENIO 1959 "I Comaschi a Roma nel Primo Rinascimento." Pages 3–61 in Edoardo Arslan (editor), Arte e Artisti dei Laghi Lombardi. Volume 1 in Architetti e Scultori del Quattrocento. Como, Italy: Antonio Noseda.
POPE-HENNESSY, JOHN 1958 Italian Renaissance Sculpture. London: Phaidon.

BRETTINGHAM, MATTHEW

Matthew Brettingham (1699–1769) was born in Norwich, England, the son of a bricklayer or mason. He began his career as a surveyor and building contractor but he is best known for the supervision of the building of Holkham Hall, Norfolk (1734 onward), for the earl of Leicester, to the designs of WILLIAM KENT; his personal

claims to the design may be exaggerated. He designed or altered a number of country houses, mainly in East Anglia, and several townhouses in Norwich and for the aristocracy in London. He was in the second rank of Palladian (see ANDREA PALLADIO) architects, not displaying flair in the manner of LORD BURLINGTON or WILLIAM KENT, but designing handsome, well-proportioned houses.

ANNE RICHES

WORKS

1740–1750, Langley Park, Norfolk, England. 1748–1751, Saint James's Square (stonefaced in 1854); 1756–1760, Egremont House (now the Naval and Military House), 94 Piccadilly; London.

BIBLIOGRAPHY

BRACKETT, OLIVER 1927 "Langley Park, Norfolk." Country Life 62:16–22.
HUSSEY, CHRISTOPHER 1954 "Holkham Hall, Norfolk." Country Life 1954:40–47.
SHEPPARD, F. H. W. 1960 The Parish of St. James Westminster. Part One: South of Piccadilly. Volume 29 in Survey of London. London: Athlone.

BRETTINGHAM, MATTHEW

The son of MATTHEW BRETTINGHAM I, Matthew Brettingham II (1725–1803) traveled in Italy and Greece with JAMES STUART and NICHOLAS REVETT, studied architecture in Rome, and served as a dealer in antique sculpture and paintings. His career began as an outgrowth of his father's, supervising the construction of Holkham in the late 1750s. Few of Brettingham's designs were ever executed, but his remodeling of and additions to Charlton House (1772–1776) reveal that he was competent.

RICHARD LORCH

WORKS

1772–1776, Charlton House (rebuilding two façades, remodeling, additions, redecorating interior), Wiltshire, England.

BIBLIOGRAPHY

HUSSEY, CHRISTOPHER 1933 "Charlton Park." Country Life 74:388–394, 420–425, 483.
NICHOLS, JOHN 1919 Volume 3 of Illustrations of the Literary History of the Eighteenth Century. London: Nichols, Son, and Bentley.

BRETTINGHAM, ROBERT

Born Robert William Furze (1755?–1820), Brettingham assumed his maternal relations' illustrious name, but failed to enhance the family reputation. Brettingham's Royal Academy classmate JOHN SOANE tutored him in Italy to no great avail. In succession to WILLIAM BLACKBURN, Brettingham's practice consisted chiefly of provincial jails. He also did some minor alterations.

PIERRE DE LA RUFFINIÈRE DU PREY

WORKS

*1789, Downpatrick Jail, County Down, Ireland. 1790, Temple of Concord, Audley End, England. *1791–1794, County Jail, Northampton, England. *1793–1794, County Jail, Reading, England.

BIBLIOGRAPHY

BOLTON, ARTHUR T. (editor) 1927 *The Portrait of Sir John Soane.* London: Sir John Soane's Museum Publications.

BRETTINGHAM, WALTER 1969 "The Brettingham Family of Norfolk." *Blackmansbury* 6, nos. 3 & 4:51–55.

DU PREY, PIERRE DE LA RUFFINIÈRE 1977 *John Soane's Architectural Education 1753–80.* New York: Garland.

BREUER, MARCEL

Marcel Lajos Breuer (1902–1981), a doctor's son, was a native of Pécs, Hungary, where he attended school. From 1920–1924, he was a student in the furniture design workshop at the Weimar Bauhaus. When the Bauhaus moved to Dessau, he became a "young master" in the same studio, remaining there until 1928. It was during this time at the Bauhaus that he designed his famous steel tube chair which he named, after his friend Kandinsky, the Wassily chair. Though Breuer became impatient with the program of the Bauhaus and later disclaimed its influence, WALTER GROPIUS recalled: "I believe that the preliminary course of the Bauhaus curriculum (Itten and Albers) and the subsequent experiences in the workshop had more to do with Breuer's finding himself as a crea-

tive artist than any other influence including the 'Stijl.' . . . His preoccupation has always been structural and I don't remember him to have been under anyone's spell for long" (Gropius to Peter Blake, January 10, 1949). Between 1928 and 1931, Breuer worked as an architect in Berlin. One house commission in Wiesbaden was for a wealthy manufacturer, Harnischmacher, for whom Gropius had already designed a house, in the course of which he had introduced Breuer. This was followed by a four-year period of travel and study in France, Spain, Morocco, Switzerland, Germany, Hungary, and Greece, terminating in 1935 when Gropius arranged for Breuer to come to England where he worked as a designer for Isokon Laminated Furniture and subsequently as an architect in partnership with FRANCIS R. S. YORKE. In 1937 Breuer followed Gropius to Harvard University to assist him as a research associate in the Master's class. Breuer became an associate professor in 1938 and remained in that position until 1947. His educational philosophy was similar to Gropius's own—that of developing each individual student's own potential and of experimenting with many different solutions. Their students became prominent in architecture and planning education and practice; among them are EDWARD L. BARNES, I. M. PEI, ELIOT NOYES, EDUARDO CATALANO, Charles Burchard, HARRY SEIDLER, Arthur Davis, Frederic Day, EMILIO DUHART, Louis Fry, John Harkness, Ernest J. Kump, Samuel Hurst, and John C. Parkin.

The two architects were in private practice together until 1941 when an incident in a faculty meeting led to the end of their collaborative work, but not of their communication nor of Gropius's support of Breuer. When the UNESCO committee to select architects for the new Paris headquarters building attempted every artifice on behalf of LE CORBUSIER, himself a member of the committee, Gropius, also a member, persuaded it to accept Breuer, BERNARD ZEHRFUSS, and PIER LUIGI NERVI. Gropius wrote about Breuer: "His out-

Breuer.
Breuer House.
New Canaan, Connecticut.
1947

standing quality was his completely unbiased mind and the independence and boldness with which he attacked technical and aesthetic problems" (letter to Peter Blake, January 10, 1949). Lines credited to Breuer are said to describe his approach to design:

> Colors which you can hear with ears;
> Sounds to see with eyes;
> The void you touch with your elbows;
> The taste of space on your tongue;
> The fragrance of dimensions;
> The juice of stone.

In 1973, the Metropolitan Museum of Art in New York held its first one-man architecture show; it was on Breuer's work. His work in that exhibition ranged from chairs to country houses that appear to grow out of the ground, to huge monoliths and reflected Breuer's diversified ability in both precise detailing and massive buildings, which had become increasingly sculptural. Contrast also marked Breuer's work in the use of materials, for example, glass against rough stone.

REGINALD R. ISAACS

WORKS

1931–1932, Harnischmacher House, Weisbaden, Germany. 1938, Haggerty House (with Walter Gropius), Cohasset, Mass. 1942, Defense Housing Development (with Gropius), New Kensington, Pa. 1945, Geller House, Lawrence, N.Y. 1947, Breuer House, New Canaan, Conn. 1949, Clark House, Orange, Conn. 1950, Cooperative Dormitory, Vassar College, Poughkeepsie, N.Y. 1950–1952, Arts Center, Sarah Lawrence College, Bronxville, N.Y. 1953–1957, De Bijenkorf Department Store (with A. Elzas), Rotterdam, Netherlands. 1953–1958, UNESCO Secretariat Building and Conference Hall (with PIER LUIGI NERVI and BERNARD ZEHRFUSS), Paris. 1954–1962, Annunciation Priory, Dickens, Bismarck, N. Dak. 1957–1958, Van Leer Headquarters, Amstelveen, Netherlands. 1963–1966, Whitney Museum of American Art (with H. Smith), New York. 1963–1967, Jacques Koerier House, Lago Maggiore, Switzerland. 1963–1968, United States Department of Housing and Urban Development Headquarters (with H. Beckhard), Washington. 1967–1970, Cleveland Art Museum (with Smith), Ohio. 1973, Ministry of Finance Building, The Hague.

BIBLIOGRAPHY

ARGAN, GIULIO CARLO 1957 *Marcel Breuer: Desegno industriale e architettura.* Milan: Görlich.
BLAKE, PETER 1949 *Marcel Breuer, Architect and Designer.* New York: The Architectural Record and the Museum of Modern Art. Exhibition catalogue.
BREUER, MARCEL 1955 *Sun and Shadow: The Philosophy of an Architect.* Edited by Peter Blake. New York: Dodd.
BREUER, MARCEL 1962–1963 "Les buts de l'architecture." *Architecture, formes et fonctions* 9:6–29.
BREUER, MARCEL 1966 "Genesis of Design." Pages 120–125 in Gyorgy Kepes (editor), *The Man-made Object.* New York: Braziller.
HITCHCOCK, H. R. 1938 *Marcel Breuer and the American Tradition in Architecture.* Cambridge, Mass.: M.I.T. Press.
JONES, CRANSTON (editor) 1962 *Marcel Breuer: Buildings and Projects, 1921–1961.* New York: Praeger.
PAPACHRISTOU, TICIAN 1970 *Marcel Breuer: New Buildings and Projects.* New York: Praeger.

BRIDGEMAN, CHARLES

Charles Bridgeman (?–1738) is a key figure in the evolution of the English landscape garden which—as *le jardin anglais, der englische Garten,* or *il giardino inglese*—was to sweep eighteenth-century Europe. As such, Bridgeman played a crucial role in the transition from the geometric layouts of the late 1600s and early 1700s to the freer designs of WILLIAM KENT and LANCELOT ("Capability") BROWN.

Bridgeman's chief official post was as royal gardener to George II and Queen Caroline from 1728 to 1738, in which he was successor to HENRY WISE, who had held the position under Queen Anne. While he was involved between 1726 and 1738 with the royal gardens and parks at Hampton Court, Kensington, Hyde Park, and Richmond, Bridgeman simultaneously worked for private patrons at such houses as Blenheim, Eastbury, Wimpole, Marble Hill, and Stowe in Buckinghamshire. Stowe was the seat of Richard Temple, first viscount of Cobham, and the most celebrated landscape of the day. Numerous poems and guidebooks attest to its glories, and in 1733–1734 Bridgeman commissioned Jacques Rigaud and Bernard Baron to prepare their sumptuous series of views of Stowe, which were published in 1739. Whereas Bridgeman's royal work was essentially formal in character, Stowe was much more adventurous and incorporated a judicious use of walks, ha-has, regular and irregular planting, waterscape, and numerous temples, many of them embodying historical, political, and mythological themes.

Such ideas must have stemmed, in part at least, from Lord Cobham, but they also reflect Bridgeman's own friendship and collaboration with architects such as JOHN VANBRUGH, JAMES GIBBS, and Kent, writers such as Alexander Pope and Matthew Prior, and painters such as John Wootton and Philip Mercier. Through them and also through his membership in the exclusive Saint Luke's Club of artists to which he was elected in 1726, Bridgeman would be conversant with the progressive thinking of the day. Similarly, on horticultural matters, the gardener and writer STEPHEN SWITZER must have been influential.

When Bridgeman died in 1738 at his home in Kensington, the gardening revolution was all but won, and in 1755 the journal *The World* could only note its positive delight at "the rapid progress of this happy enthusiasm."

PETER WILLIS

WORKS

Begun c.1709, Blenheim Palace, Oxfordshire, England. Begun c.1716, Stowe, Buckinghamshire, England. Begun 1720s, Chiswick, Middlesex, England. Begun 1720s, Claremont, Surrey, England. Begun 1720s, Eastbury, Dorset, England. Begun 1720s, Houghton, Norfolk, England. Begun 1720s, Rousham, Oxfordshire, England. Begun 1720s, Wimpole, Cambridgeshire, England. Begun 1724, Marble Hill; 1726–1738, Hampton Court; Middlesex, England. 1726–1738, Hyde Park; 1726–1738, Kensington Gardens; London. 1726–1738, Richmond Gardens, Surrey, England. 1726–1738, Windsor, Berkshire, England. Begun c.1730, Amesbury, Wiltshire, England.

BIBLIOGRAPHY

WILLIS, PETER 1977 *Charles Bridgeman and the English Landscape Garden.* London: Zwemmer.

BRIGHAM, CHARLES

Charles Brigham (1841–1925) is best known for his huge, late works—public buildings in Boston and Fairhaven, Massachusetts, executed with Charles Coveney and Henry K. Bisbee. The earlier, twenty-year partnership of this prolific architect with the English-educated JOHN HUBBARD STURGIS gave him, however, the breadth of vision, architectural sophistication, and self-confidence which made possible his later achievement.

After drafting for Calvin Ryder of Cambridge in the late 1850s, Brigham joined GRIDLEY J. F. BRYANT and ARTHUR D. GILMAN as their Boston City Hall and Arlington Street Church were being erected. Here, he met Sturgis with whom he formed a partnership following service in the Civil War. From 1866 to 1886, Sturgis and Brigham designed notable Queen Anne Revival buildings which established their role as purveyors of English artistic standards for Boston. Although the brilliant Sturgis was prime designer, Brigham's capability to manage both aristocratic clients and the labor force enabled their structurally and decoratively innovative practice to flourish. After 1886, Brigham quickly gained prominence with his sensitive extension to CHARLES BULFINCH's Massachusetts State House (1887–1895), conceptually a pace-setter in Colonial Revival design and influential on such later state capitols as CASS GILBERT's in St. Paul, Minnesota (1893–1904). The huge ribbed dome of Brigham's Christian Science Mother Church Extension (1904–1909), like Gilbert's St. Paul Capitol, is a free transcription of the European Renaissance architecture which Brigham saw only late in life. Unique in the Back Bay is the Loire valley grandeur of his stone Albert Burrage House (1899).

The buildings designed by Brigham for Fairhaven, Massachusetts (under the patronage of H. H. Rogers of Standard Oil), finally provided his greatest architectural opportunity. In the 1890s were erected a painterly Queen Anne mansion for Rogers, the vibrant Millicent Library, and the Fairhaven Town Hall which incorporated Richardsonian (see H. H. RICHARDSON) allusions. Ultimately, however, an English image reappeared in his half-timbered Tabitha Inn (1896) and Parish House, Elizabethan High School (1904), and Gothic Unitarian Church (1901–1903), a miniature cathedral in stone.

MARGARET HENDERSON FLOYD

WORKS

1867, Edward Codman House, 53 Marlborough Street, Boston. 1867, Wadsworth Monument, Geneseo, N.Y. *1868, Bureau of Charities, New Chardon Street, Boston. 1868, Robert Cushing House, Ocean Avenue, Newport, R.I. 1868–1869, Pinebank (Edward N. Perkins House), Jamaica Plain, Mass. 1869, Frances Hunnewell House, 278 Clarendon Street; 1869, Hollis H. Hunnewell House, 315 Dartmouth Street; 1870, Museum of Fine Arts, Copley Square; Boston. 1886, Charles Brigham House, 84 Garfield Street, Watertown, Mass. 1886, H. A. Whitney House, 261 Beacon Street, Boston. 1886–1888, *Bellwood* (S. S. Howland House), Mount Morris, N.Y. 1886–1888, Railroad Station, Stoughton, Mass. 1886–1888, H. H. Rogers House, New York. 1887–1895, Massachusetts State House (extension), Boston. 1888–1889, Inebriates Hospital, Foxborough, Mass. 1888–1889, Presbyterian Church, Roxbury, Mass. 1888–1889, Railroad Station, Roxbury Crossing, Mass. 1890, H. H. Rogers House; 1891–1893, Millicent Library; Fairhaven, Mass. 1892–1894, New Bedford Institution for Savings, Mass. 1892–1894, Town Hall; 1896, Tabitha Inn; Fairhaven, Mass. 1897–1899, Subway Stations at Adams Square and Scollay Square Central and North; 1899, Albert Burrage House, 314 Commonwealth Avenue; Boston. 1901–1903, Unitarian Church, Parish House and Rectory; 1904, High School; Fairhaven, Mass. 1904, High School, Watertown, Mass. 1904–1909, Christian Science Mother Church (extension), Boston.

BIBLIOGRAPHY

BUNTING, BAINBRIDGE 1967 *Houses of Boston's Back Bay.* Cambridge, Mass.: Harvard University Press.

DAMRELL, CHARLES 1895 *A Half Century of Boston's Building.* Boston: Hager.

FLOYD, MARGARET HENDERSON 1973 "A Terra-Cotta Cornerstone for Copley Square: Museum of Fine Arts, Boston, 1870–1876, by Sturgis and Brigham." *Journal of the Society of Architectural Historians* 32, no. 2:83–103.

FLOYD, MARGARET HENDERSON n.d. "John Hubbard Sturgis of Boston and the English Architectural Image." Unpublished manuscript.

GILLINGHAM, JAMES L., and HUNT, CYRUS D. ET AL. 1903 *Brief History of the Town of Fairhaven.* New Bedford, Mass.: Standard Print.

HITCHINGS, SINCLAIR H., and FARLOW, CATHERINE H. 1964 *A New Guide to the Massachusetts State House.* Boston: John Hancock Mutual Life Insurance Company.

HERNDON, RICHARD 1892 *Boston of Today.* Boston: Post.

HITCHCOCK, H. R., and SEALE, WILLIAM 1976 *Temples of Democracy.* New York: Harcourt.

KING, MOSES (1878)1889 *King's Handbook of Boston.* 9th ed. Boston: The author.

WILLIAMSON, MARGARET 1939 *The Mother Church Extension.* Boston: Christian Science Publishing Society.

BRISEUX, CHARLES ETIENNE

An academically rather than practically oriented architect, Charles Etienne Briseux (1660–1754) was born in Baume-les-Dames in the Franche-Comté region of France, not far from Switzerland. He was active during the transitional stylistic period between the Regency of Louis XV (d.1723) and the birth of the rococo in France, but his contribution to architectural history resides mainly in his theoretical writings: *l'Architecture moderne ou l'Art de bien bâtir* (1728; published by his editor Jombert under his name), *l'Art de bâtir des maisons de campagne* (1743), and *Traité du Beau essentiel dans les arts* (1752). The 1743 work served, along with works by FRANÇOIS BLONDEL, as practical handbooks or architectural catalogues with choices for building schemes as well as decorative ideas for the aristocrats and wealthy bourgeoisie whose taste for frivolous and idyllic country estates shaped the architectural style known as "le style Louis XV."

TINA WALDEIER BIZZARRO

BIBLIOGRAPHY

BRISEUX, CHARLES ETIENNE (1743)1966 *L'art de bâtir des maisons de campagne.* Reprint of 1761 ed. Farnborough, England: Gregg.

KALNEIN, WEND GRAF, and LEVEY, MICHAEL 1972 *Art and Architecture of the Eighteenth Century in France.* Harmondsworth, England: Penguin.

BRITTON, JOHN

John Britton (1771–1857) "did more to promote the due appreciation of Mediaeval Art than any contemporary writer" (Eastlake, 1970, p. 86); his *Architectural Antiquities of Great Britain* (1807–1826) and *The Cathedral Antiquities* (1836) being major source books for the British and American Gothic Revivals. Born in Kingston Saint Michael, Wiltshire, Britton moved in 1787 to London, where he began his career as topographical publisher, preparing the *Beauties of Wiltshire* (1801–1825), then, with E. W. Brayley, the more scholarly *Beauties of England and Wales* (1801–1816). Britton's numerous, popular publications fostered English art and engraving, though he died poor in London. He campaigned for governmental protection of ancient monuments and for the founding of the Royal Institute of British Architects.

R. WINDSOR LISCOMBE

BIBLIOGRAPHY

BRITTON, JOHN 1801–1825 *The Beauties of Wiltshire.* 3 vols. London: Dewick.

BRITTON, JOHN 1807–1826 *The Architectural Antiquities of Great Britain.* London: Longman.

BRITTON, JOHN 1823 *Graphical and Literary Illustrations of Fonthill Abbey.* London: Britton.

BRITTON, JOHN 1825–1828a *The Architectural Antiquities of Normandy.* Measured and drawn by Augustus Pugin. London: Longman.

BRITTON, JOHN 1825–1828b *Illustrations of the Public Buildings of London.* Drawings by Augustus Pugin. London: J. Taylor. A supplement, edited by William Henry Leeds, was issued in 1838.

BRITTON, JOHN 1827 *The Union of Architecture, Sculpture and Painting . . . With Descriptive Accounts of the House and Gallery of John Soane.* London: Britton.

BRITTON, JOHN 1832 *Descriptive Sketches of Tunbridge Wells and the Calverly Estate.* London: Britton.

BRITTON, JOHN 1836 *The Cathedral Antiquities of England.* London: Nattali.

BRITTON, JOHN 1838 *A Dictionary of the Architecture and Archaeology of the Middle Ages.* London: Longman.

BRITTON, JOHN 1850 *The Autobiography of John Britton, F. S. A.* London: Britton.

BRITTON, JOHN, and BRAYLEY, E. W. 1801–1816 *The Beauties of England and Wales.* London: Vernor and Hood.

BRITTON, JOHN, and BRAYLEY, E. W. 1836 *The History of the Ancient Palace and Late Houses of Parliament at Westminster.* London: J. Weale.

BRITTON, JOHN, and SHEPHERD, THOMAS 1829 *Bath and Bristol.* London: Jones.

BRITTON, JOHN, and SHEPHERD, THOMAS 1831 *Modern Athens . . . Edinburgh in the Nineteenth Century.* London: Jones.

CROOK, J. MORDAUNT 1968 "John Britton and the Genesis of the Gothic Revival." Pages 98–119 in John Summerson (editor), *Concerning Architecture.* London: Allen Lane.

EASTLAKE, CHARLES LOCK 1970 Pages 80–90 in J. M. Crook (editor), *A History of the Gothic Revival.* New York: Humanities Press.

FERRIDAY, PETER 1957 "John Britton 1771–1857." *Architectural Review* 122:367–369.

BRODERICK, CUTHBERT

Cuthbert Broderick (1822–1905) is esteemed for a handful of classical buildings, all in Yorkshire, England. Born at Hull in the same county, he was articled to HENRY FRANCIS LOCKWOOD, toured Europe and returning to Hull designed the Royal Institution (1852). The following year he achieved renown with the design of Leeds Town Hall, a model for many others. It combines a full range of chambers in a monument of civic splendor, characterized by a giant Corinthian order, repeated to support a noble tower. Other works in Leeds followed: the Corn Exchange (1860–1863) and the Mechanics' Institute (1860–1865) are especially notable as is his Scarborough hotel (1862–1867), but his career did not develop and after a stay in London he abandoned architecture to live in France and then Jersey where he died.

A. P. QUINEY

WORKS

*1852, Royal Institution, Hull, England. 1853–1858, Town Hall; 1860–1863, Corn Exchange; 1860–1865, Mechanics' Institute (now Civic Theatre); Leeds, England. *1861, Town Hall, Hull, England. 1862–1867, Grand Hotel, Scarborough, England. *c.1862, Warehouse, King Street, Leeds, England.

BIBLIOGRAPHY

LINSTRUM, DEREK 1967 "Architecture of Cuthbert Broderick." *Country Life* 141:1379–1381.
LINSTRUM, DEREK 1978 *West Yorkshire: Architects and Architecture*. London: Lund Humphries.
"Obituary of Cuthbert Broderick." 1905 *The Builder* 88:272.

BROEBES, JEAN BAPTISTE

The architect and engraver Jean Baptiste Broebes (c.1660–1720) was born in Paris. He studied fortification and civil architecture and learned copper engraving under the guidance of Jean Marot. He contributed engravings to illustrate FRANÇOIS BLONDEL's *Cour d'Architecture* (1683). In 1685, Broebes, who was a Huguenot, fled to Bremen where he was employed by the municipal council as architect for the restoration of the city gate on the Weser Bridge and to build the Stock Exchange. In 1692, he suddenly left Bremen and entered the service of Prince-Elector Frederick III of Brandenburg, first, until 1697, as fortifications engineer in Pillau (East Prussia) and thereafter, from 1699 on, as professor of military and civil architecture at the Academy of Arts in Berlin. He renovated and extended the castle in Schlobitten (East Prussia) for Count Alexander Dohna.

Although not active as an architect in Berlin,

he kept a keen and critical watch on contemporary palace and country-seat architecture and recorded his observations, together with his own projects and proposed improvements, in engravings which he planned to publish. In 1720, he went to Barby (Anhalt) to complete the palace that Giovanni Simonetti had begun, but he died that same year. His widow sold the copper plates of the *Vues* to the publisher who had them printed without alteration. The significance of the collection lies in its documenting portions and their value as a source for the building history of the Brandenburg-Prussian baroque palaces. Broebes's own, in part quite insignificant, projects often consist of proposals for buildings already planned or in progress that are stylistically connected to contemporary French architecture. His design, conceived around 1702, for the organization of the Schlossplatz (palace square) in Berlin is famous. It goes beyond the concrete situation to develop theoretical concepts for the center of a baroque court capital.

FRITZ-EUGEN KELLER
Translated from German by
Beverley R. Placzek

WORKS

*1685–1692, City Gate on the Weser Bridge (renovation); *1685–1692, Stock Exchange; Bremen, Germany. 1695–1697, Count Dohna's Castle (remodeling and expansion; heavily damaged in 1945), Schlobitten, East Prussia.

BIBLIOGRAPHY

BROEBES, J. B. 1733 *Vues des Palais et Maisons de Plaisance de Sa Majesté le Roy de Prusse*. Augsburg, Germany: Merz.
COLOMBIER PIERRE DU 1956 Volume 1, pages 110–111 in *L'Architecture française en Allemagne au XVIIe siècle*. Paris: Presses Universitaires de France.
GROMMELT, CARL, and MERTENS, CHRISTINE von 1962 *Das Dohnasche Schloss Schlobitten*. Stuttgart: Kohlhammer.
GURLITT, C. 1884 "Zur Baugeschichte Berlins." *Kunst-Chronik (Bei-Blatt zur Zeitschrift für bildende Kunst)* 19:292–298, 311–314.
LADENDORF, HEINZ 1935 *Der Bildhauer und Baumeister Andreas Schlüter*. Berlin: Deutscher Verein für Kunstwissenschaft.
MÜLLER, HANS 1896 *Die Königliche Akademie der Künste zu Berlin 1696 bis 1896*. Berlin: Bong.

BROGGI, LUIGI

Luigi Broggi (1851–1926) was a figure of prime importance in the architectural development of Milan at the beginning of the twentieth century. A pupil of CAMILLO BOITO and professor of architecture at the Accademia di Brera, Broggi was an eclectic who also worked in the Italian "Liberty" style. The Contratti Department Store (1902–1903) in Milan, an experiment in reinforced concrete, metal, and glass, is generally considered his best work.

ELLEN R. SHAPIRO

WORKS

1889, Società d'Assicurazioni Italia Building (with GIUSEPPÈ SOMMARUGA), Milan. 1898, Grand Hotel delle Terme, Salsomaggiore, Italy. 1899–1901, Stock Exchange (now the Postal Service Offices); 1902, Credito Italiano Bank; 1902–1903, Contratti Department Store; Milan, Italy. 1904–1907, Palazzo Bellini (restoration), Novara, Italy. 1907–1912, Banca d'Italia (with C. Nava); *1908, Verdi Conservatory (central hall; with Nava), Milan. 1909, Cassa di Risparmio Bank, Alessandria, Italy. 1914–1915, Royal Villa, Bordighera, Italy.

BIBLIOGRAPHY

BORSI, FRANCO 1966 *L'Architettura dell'Unita d'Italia.* Florence: Le Monnier.

BOSSAGLIA, ROSSANA 1968 *Il Liberty in Italia.* Milan: Mondadori.

MEEKS, CARROLL L. V. 1966 *Italian Architecture 1750–1914.* New Haven and London: Yale University Press.

MEZZANOTTE, PAOLO, and BASCAPE, GIACOMO (1948)1968 *Milano nell'arte e nella storia.* Milan: Bestetti.

PATETTA, LUCIANO 1975 *L'Architettura dell Eclettismo fonti, teorie, modelli 1750–1900.* Milan: Mazzotta.

REGGIORE, FERDINANDO 1947 *Milano 1800–1943.* Milan: Edizioni del Milione.

REGGIORE, FERDINANDO 1970 *Milano liberty, panorama di architettura.* Milan: Mediocredito Regionale Lombardo.

BRONGNIART, ALEXANDRE THEODORE

Alexandre Théodore Brongniart (1739–1813) was trained by JACQUES FRANÇOIS BLONDEL and ETIENNE LOUIS BOULLÉE. Although he never won a grand prix and never went to Italy, he became a fashionable architect of townhouses in the 1770s and played an important role in the development of new residential districts of Paris: the Chaussée d'Antin and the area south of the Invalides. Brongniart's *hôtels* combine features of the French tradition with the new taste for geometric clarity and Palladian (see ANDREA PALLADIO) characteristics. He often isolated the corps de logis, used colossal orders and relief sculpture (by Clodion) on the façades, and set his houses into imaginatively designed gardens. At his first larger building, the Monastery of Saint Louis d'Antin (1779–1782), he professed a purer neoclassicism by using the base-less Doric order for the cloister.

Brongniart succeeded Boullée as architect and *contrôleur* at the Invalides and the Ecole Militaire. He finished the latter in 1786. The Revolution cost him his post and his private collection of art, and he was forced to spend the years of the Terror in Bordeaux. Back in Paris in 1795, he was named to the Conseil des Bâtiments Civils and became consultant for the Pantheon, but he soon again lost these posts. Lacking architectural commissions, he worked as a porcelain designer for Sèvres.

In 1804, he was recalled to government service and as chief of public works in Paris designed the Père Lachaise Cemetery (1805). He used the terrain judiciously to create a necropolis and provide Parisians with a public park. His last building, the Stock Exchange (Bourse or Temple du Commerce; 1808–1813), testifies to Brongniart's adaptability. Without abandoning the rational design principle of his earlier buildings, he adjusted his neoclassicism to coincide with Napoleon's taste for Roman Corinthian temples.

CHARLOTTE LACAZE

WORKS

*1769–1773, Hôtel de Mme. de Montesson; *1771, Hôtel de Taillepied de Bondi; *1772–1774, Hôtel du Duc d'Orléans; 1774–1777, Hôtel de Monaco; *1775, Hôtel de Bouret de Vézelay; 1779–1782, Monastery of Saint Louis d'Antin (now in part the Lycée Condorcet); 1780–1781, Hôtel de Montesquiou; 1780–1783, Hôtel de Bourbon-Condé; 1781, Maison Brongniart; 1785–1786, Ecole Militaire (stables and observatory; after plans by ANGE JACQUES GABRIEL); 1787, Hôtel Masserano; 1788–1789, Hôtel de Boisgelin; Paris. 1792, Château de Trilbardon, Seine et Marne, France. *1797, Montesson House, Romainville, France. 1805, Père Lachaise Cemetery, Paris. *1808, Petits Appartements (interior decoration), Saint-Cloud, France. 1808–1813, Stock Exchange (not completed until 1825), Paris.

BIBLIOGRAPHY

ANDIA, BÉATRICE DE 1978 *De Bagatelle à Monceau, 1778–1978: Les Folies du XVIIIᵉ Siècle à Paris.* Paris: Musée Carnavalet. Exhibition catalogue.

ANDIA, BÉATRICE DE 1980 *Le Faubourg Saint-Germain: La Rue de Grenelle.* Paris: Société d'Histoire et d'Archéologie du VIIᵉ Arrondissement. Exhibition catalogue.

BIVER, MARIE LOUISE 1963 *Le Paris de Napoléon.* Paris: Plon.

BRAHAM, ALLAN 1980 *The Architecture of the French Enlightenment.* Berkeley and Los Angeles: University of California Press.

BRONGNIART, ALEXANDRE-THÉODORE 1814 *Plans du Palais de la Bourse de Paris et du cimetière Mont-Louis.* Paris: Capelet.

EGBERT, DONALD DREW 1980 *The Beaux-Arts Tradition in French Architecture.* N.J.: Princeton University Press.

ERIKSEN, SVEND 1974 *Early Neo-Classicism in France.* London: Faber.

ETLIN, RICHARD A. 1977 "Landscapes of Eternity: Funerary Architecture and the Cemetery, 1793–1781." *Oppositions* 8:14–31.

FREGNAC, CLAUDE, and ANDREWS, WAYNE 1979 *Great Houses of Paris.* New York: Vendome.

GALLET, MICHEL 1964 *Demeures Parisiennes: L'Époque de Louis XVI.* Paris: Le Temps.

GALLET, MICHEL 1980 *Claude-Nicolas Ledoux.* Paris: Picard.

HÉBERT, MONIQUE 1964 "Les demeures du duc d'Orléans et de Madame de Montesson à la Chaussée d'Antin." *Gazette des Beaux-Arts* 64:161–176.

HAUTECOEUR, LOUIS 1952–1953 Volumes 4 and 5 in *Histoire de l'architecture classique en France.* Paris: Picard.

Jardins en France: 1760–1820. 1978 Paris: Edition de la Caisse Nationale des Monuments Historiques et des Sites. Exhibition catalogue.

KALNEIN, WEND GRAF, and LEVEY, MICHAEL 1972 *Art and Architecture of the Eighteenth Century in France.* Harmondsworth, England: Penguin.

KAUFMANN, EMIL (1955)1968 *Architecture in the Age of Reason.* New York: Dover.

LAUNAY, LOUIS DE 1940 *Une Grande Famille de Savants: Les Brongniart.* Paris: Rapilly.

OTTOMEYER, HANS 1974 "Autobiographies d'Architectes Parisiens: 1759–1811." *Bulletin de la Société de l'Histoire de Paris et de l'Ile de France* 98:141–206.

PARISET, FRANÇOIS-GEORGES 1962 "L'architecte Brongniart, les activités à Bordeaux et à La Réole (1793–1795)." *Bulletin et Mémoires de la Société archeologique de Bordeaux* 62:1–59.

PÉROUSE DE MONTCLOS, JEAN MARIE 1969 *Etienne-Louis Boullée, 1728–1799: De l'architecture classique à l'architecture révolutionnaire.* Paris: Arts et Métiers Graphiques.

RIVIÈRE, CLÉRY 1939 *Un village de Brie au XVIIIe siècle: Mauperthuis.* Paris: Picard.

ROSENBLUM, ROBERT 1967 *Transformations in Late Eighteenth Century Art.* N.J.: Princeton University Press.

SILVESTRE DE SACY, JACQUES 1940 *Alexandre Théodore Brongniart 1739–1813: Sa Vie—Son Oeuvre.* Paris: Plon.

Soufflot et Son Temps. 1980 Paris: Edition de la Caisse Nationale des Monuments Historiques et des Sites. Exhibition catalogue.

WIEBENSON, DORA 1978 *The Picturesque Garden in France.* N.J.: Princeton University Press.

BROOKS, JAMES

James Brooks (1825–1901) was one of the foremost Victorian church architects. Born at Hatford, Berkshire, he moved to London in 1847 and became a pupil of Lewis Stride; in 1849 he entered the Royal Academy Schools.

The churches that made his reputation were built in the East End of London in an austere Gothic Revival style. Many are built of brick. The early ones show the influence of WILLIAM BUTTERFIELD. His mature style is characterized by a very personal and powerful interpretation of early French Gothic.

In 1895, Brooks received the Gold Medal of the Royal Institute of British Architects. Among his pupils was ARTHUR H. MACKMURDO.

ROGER DIXON

WORKS

1863–1865, Saint Michael's, Shoreditch; *1865–1866, Saint Saviour's, Hoxton; 1867–1870, Saint Andrew's, Plaistow; 1868–1869, Saint Chad's, Haggerston; 1868–1869, Saint Columba's, Haggerston; 1876–1898, Church of the Ascension (completed by J. T. MICKLETHWAITE and SOMERS CLARKE), Battersea; 1880–1886, Church of the Transfiguration, Lewisham; 1892–1901, Church of All Hallows (completed by GILES GILBERT SCOTT), Gospel Oak; London.

BIBLIOGRAPHY

ADKINS, J. S. 1910 "James Brooks: A Memoir." *Journal of the Proceedings of the Royal Institute of British Architects* Series 3 17:493–516.

DIXON, ROGER 1976 "The Life and Works of James Brooks 1825–1901." Unpublished Ph.D. Thesis, Courtauld Institute of Art, London University.

DIXON, ROGER, and MUTHESIUS, STEFAN 1978 *Victorian Architecture.* London: Thames; New York: Oxford University Press.

EASTLAKE, CHARLES L. (1872)1978 *A History of the Gothic Revival.* Edited by J. Mordaunt Crook. 2d ed. England: Leicester University Press; New York: Humanities.

BROSSE, SALOMON DE

See DE BROSSE, SALOMON.

BROWN, A. PAGE

Arthur Page Brown (1859–1896), born in Ellisburg, New York, studied architecture at Cornell University for approximately a year. He joined McKIM, MEAD, AND WHITE's office soon after it was formed. Under the patronage of Mrs. Cyrus McCormick, Brown began independent practice in 1884. He moved to San Francisco five years later where he enjoyed a flourishing business until his death. Brown and his chief draftsman A. C. SCHWEINFURTH pioneered in developing a regional mode derived from California's Franciscan missions and other Hispanic sources.

RICHARD W. LONGSTRETH

WORKS

*1885–1886, Trask House, Saratoga Springs, N.Y. *1887–1890, Museum of Historic Art; 1888–1892, Whig and Clio Halls; Princeton University, N.J. *1889–1891, Crocker Building; *1890–1891, Towne House; *1892–1893, Atkinson Building; San Francisco. *1892–1893, California Building, World's Columbian Exposition, Chicago. 1894–1895, Church of the New Jerusalem, San Francisco.

BIBLIOGRAPHY

LONGSTRETH, RICHARD W. 1977 "Architects on the Edge of the World: Ernest Coxhead and Willis Polk in San Francisco During the 1890s." Unpublished Ph.D. dissertation, University of California, Berkeley.
"Obituary of A. Page Brown." 1896 *American Architect and Building News* 51:57–58.
WOODBRIDGE, SALLY (editor) 1976 *Bay Area Houses.* New York: Oxford University Press.

BROWN, CAPABILITY

Lancelot Brown (1716–1783), architect and landscape designer, was to become widely known by his nickname of "Capability," acquired through his habit of referring to the capabilities of the places on which he was consulted. Succeeding to the mantle of WILLIAM KENT, whom HORACE WALPOLE hailed as "the father of Modern Gardening," Brown became the second great figure in the landscape movement which flourished in England for nearly a hundred years and exerted considerable influence on the continent.

Brown was born in 1716 in Kirkharle, a remote Northumbrian village set in a countryside of rolling hills and fertile valleys which may well have contributed subconsciously to the variety and scale which was later to be a feature of his works. His forebears were of farming stock, and his own acquaintance with land and horticultural management was developed when, after attending school at nearby Cambo, he worked on William Loraine's estate at Kirkharle. Loraine, a man of learning, who was also reputed to be "skilled in architecture and physic," was then remodeling his house and laying out its surroundings in accordance with the "natural" concept of gardening then spreading northward. This concept had already transformed the grounds of Castle Howard and Studley Royal in Yorkshire. Brown's participation in Loraine's activities, and in due course his responsibility for laying out a considerable area of previously rough land on the estate, provided the practical experience invaluable for the independent career he later followed. In 1739, when the work at Kirkharle was completed, he moved to the south of England.

It was almost certainly through an introduction to Loraine's father in law, Richard Smith of Preston Bissett, that Brown is next heard of in the Buckinghamshire-Oxfordshire area. Here his first recorded commission came from Charles Browne (who was no relation) at Kiddington where the little river Glyme was dammed to form a lake at the foot of a sloping garden. By the beginning of 1741 Brown had come to the notice of Lord Cobham of Stowe, who needed to replace his recently departed head gardener. Stowe was already famous for its gardens: JOHN VANBRUGH and CHARLES BRIDGEMAN had contributed designs in previous years, while JAMES GIBBS and Kent were currently designing further embellishments. Brown began work at first as head gardener, but soon assumed the duties of clerk of the works and paymaster. In the ensuing years he was thus able to study at first hand Kent's and Gibbs's theories of landscaping as well as their garden buildings, with whose construction he was closely involved. These included the Queen's and Gothic Temples, and the lofty prospect column which some years later was to be adapted as a memorial to Cobham. Gibbs's Gothic Temple was, in fact, to be a source of inspiration for several of Brown's subsequent designs in the Gothic style.

The increasing ill-health of both Gibbs and Kent, and the latter's reluctance to travel, meant that Stowe saw little of either as the decade progressed and Brown consequently shouldered much of the responsibility for the execution of their designs. It is also evident that the formation of the Grecian Valley on the northeast of the estate grew out of deliberations between Cobham and Brown alone. Cobham was, moreover, lending Brown to a few close friends or relations for the improvement of their gardens, notably at Wotton (1742), which belonged to his nephew Richard Grenville, and at Newnham Paddox where in 1745 Brown "serpentined" the great canal and planted the "hanging slopes" round one of the park ponds for Lord Denbigh. Following Kent's death in 1748 he undertook the completion of the house and grounds designed by the former for the duke of Grafton at Wakefield Lodge, some four miles to the northeast of Stowe.

With the death of Cobham in 1749 Brown resolved to set up his own practice, and although he did not leave Stowe for another three years, he was already supplying garden schemes and making internal alterations at Warwick Castle. Walpole wrote of his visit to Warwick: "The view pleased me more than I can express, the river Avon tumbles down a cascade at the foot [of the Castle]. It is well laid out by one Brown who has set up on a few ideas of Kent and Mr. Southcote," (Kent's client). Commissions for the grounds of Petworth in Sussex and Packington in Warwickshire were received by Brown in 1751, and in the late autumn he left Stowe for Hammersmith, on the outskirts of London, where he settled with his family.

Brown's immediate success lay partly in his ability to catch the spirit of Kent's "Albano scenes," and partly in his sound knowledge of horticulture and building. As several of Kent's patrons had learned to their cost, the designs of that amiable character, while so beguiling on paper, were not infrequently found wanting in execution, because he gave instructions "when he was full of claret." Although Brown never acquired the delicacy and freedom of draftsmanship which Kent perfected after his long training as an artist, he taught himself to express his ideas with clarity, the buildings being set out with architectural accuracy and the landscapes in a characteristic style. Clients would be supplied either with designs to be carried out by their own estate workmen, or would enter into contracts whereby Brown would supervise the execution—sending one of his foremen to take charge—and visit the work from time to time, often over a period of several years. Almost all his architectural works were devised as part of a landscaped scene, and there can be no doubt of the correctness of WILLIAM MASON's observation that Brown turned to architecture "from a kind of necessity having found the great difficulty which must frequently have occurred to him in forming a picturesque whole, where the previous building had been ill-placed or of improper dimensions."

This would certainly have been his experience when building a new mansion at Croome in Worcestershire (1750–1752) for Lord Coventry, an early commission which he owed to an acquaintance from Stowe days, Sanderson Miller of Radway, by whom he was also recommended to Lord Dacre of Belhus in Essex for garden work, and probably to Lord Exeter for whom his alterations to Burghley House and its grounds in Northamptonshire extended over many years. At Croome his assignment was to replace Lord Coventry's damp and inadequate Jacobean house. This first involved draining a water-logged site with brick culverts leading to a newly-formed serpentine lake. For the house itself, built in 1752, he designed a Palladian block with corner turrets and, on the south façade, a giant tetrastyle Ionic portico—a theme which he also adopted for several subsequent houses. The landscaping proceeded throughout the 1750s at the end of which he also undertook the rebuilding of the church of Saint Mary Magdalene on rising ground within the park. At Burghley work began in 1754 and involved remodeling the south front and altering several of the principal rooms as well as building new stables, an orangery, a bridge over the new lake, and a lakeside pavilion.

Only one of Brown's account books survives although it is evident that there must have been several others. From this and other material it is known that more than thirty commissions had been completed or were still in hand by 1758, the year in which fourteen of his influential clients petitioned that he should be given a royal preferment. However, probably due to the notorious procrastination of the duke of Newcastle as patronage secretary, nothing came of this until 1764 when Brown was appointed royal gardener at Hampton Court and Richmond. At the former he wisely declined to interfere with the seventeenth century layout in the grounds, but at Richmond Old Park (now part of the Royal Botanic Gardens at Kew), he made several changes, sweeping away Merlin's Cave—the extravaganza Kent designed for Queen Caroline—and setting out the winding walk now known as the Rhododendron Dell.

In the same year as his royal appointment, Brown began work on one of his most celebrated works, the gardens and park of Blenheim Palace (1764–c.1769). His plan survives and was closely followed in execution, many of the clumps of trees still being prominent features in the landscape. The most important feature was the damming of

Capability Brown.
Blenheim Palace.
Oxfordshire, England.
1764–c.1769

Capability Brown.
The Great Lake, Blenheim
*   Palace.*
Oxfordshire, England.
1764–c.1769

the river Glyme, which had hitherto provided an insignificant trickle of water, to form the great lake. Most of the work had been completed by the end of the decade, including the rebuilding of the castellated High Lodge in the park, and a spectacular cascade at the south end of the lake by which THOMAS JEFFERSON, who was not lavish in his praise of English gardens, was particularly delighted in the course of his tour of 1786.

Realizing that none of his three sons had any desire to follow his vocation, Brown looked elsewhere for help with the commissions which continued to arrive, particularly with those involving architecture. The answer was provided by the son of a prosperous London builder whom Brown had known for many years, HENRY HOLLAND. The latter had been trained in his father's firm and already showed promise as a designer. His first work with Brown involved the internal decoration in 1771 of Claremont, the house which Capability had designed for Lord Clive and the foundations of which were laid in 1769. As the walls rose it became apparent that Brown had by this time foresaken the heavy Palladianism of Croome, Newnham Paddox, and Fisherwick (1768) for a more compact villa form, with the principal rooms ranged round an inner, top-lit, staircase hall. This theme was soon to be used for the house at Benham (1774), in the construction and decoration of which Holland also participated. He had in the former year strengthened his ties with Brown by marrying his daughter.

Brown's practice extended to almost every county and it is indisputable that through his own designs, and through the influence which he exerted on landscape designs in general, he brought about the transformation of vast areas of hitherto rough countryside into the lush parkland for

which England was to become renowned. Like his predecessor Kent, he never put his theories into print, but in 1773 he set out in a letter to the Reverend Thomas Dyer the principles by which he was guided in the art of gardening and what he called "place-making." To achieve good results, he maintained, it was necessary to have "a good plan, good execution, and a perfect knowledge of the country and the objects in it, whether natural or artificial, [also] infinite delicacy in the planning etc., so much Beauty depending on the size of the trees and the colour of their leaves to produce the effect of light and shade so very essential." Attention to such details would ensure that the English garden would be "exactly fit for the owner, the Poet and the Painter."

Brown was fully occupied with commissions until his sudden death in London on February 6, 1783. His funeral took place at Fenstanton in Huntingdonshire, where he had a small estate. Here, in the church of Saint Peter and Saint Paul, his monument is inscribed with the eulogistic verse composed by his old friend, the poet William Mason.

DOROTHY STROUD

WORKS

1742, Wotton (landscaping), Buckinghamshire, England. 1745, Newnham Paddox (house and landscaping); 1749, Warwick Castle (alterations and landscaping); Warwickshire, England. 1750–1752, Croome (house and landscaping), Worcestershire, England. 1751, Packington (landscaping), Warwickshire, England. 1751, Petworth (landscaping), Sussex, England. 1754, Burghley (house and landscaping), Northamptonshire, England. 1757, Bowood (landscaping); 1757, Longleat (landscaping); Wiltshire, England. 1758, Harewood (landscaping), Yorkshire, England. 1759, Ashridge (landscaping), Hertfordshire, England. c.1760, Alnwick (landscaping), Northumberland, Eng-

Capability Brown.
Claremont (with Holland).
Surrey, England.
1769–1770

Capability Brown.
Proposed plan for Moccas
  Courts.
Hertfordshire, England.

land. 1760, Chatsworth (landscaping), Derbyshire, England. 1760, Corsham (house and landscaping), Wiltshire, England. 1761, Castle Ashby (landscaping), Northamptonshire, England. 1762, Temple Newsam (landscaping), Yorkshire, England. 1763, Redgrave (house and landscaping), Suffolk, England. 1763, Milton Abbey (landscaping and village), Dorset, England. 1764, Broadlands (house and landscaping), Hampshire, England. 1764, Luton Hoo (landscaping), Bedfordshire, England. 1764, Richmond Park (alterations), Surrey, England. 1764–c.1769, Blenheim Palace (house and landscaping), Oxfordshire, England. 1766, Sandbeck (landscaping), Yorkshire, England. 1766, Thorndon (landscaping), Essex, England. 1767, Ashburnham (landscaping), Sussex, England. 1767, Wimpole (landscaping), Cambridgeshire, England. 1768, Fisherwick (house and landscaping), Staffordshire, England. 1769–1770, Claremont (house and landscaping; with Henry Holland), Surrey, England.1771, Brocklesby (landscaping), Lincolnshire, England. 1773, Wardour Castle (landscaping), Wiltshire, England. 1774, Benham (house and landscaping; with Holland), Berkshire, England. 1775, Sherborne Castle (landscaping), Dorset, England.

BIBLIOGRAPHY

CLARKE, GEORGE 1971 "Lancelot Brown's Work at Stowe." *The Stoic* (Stowe [England] School Magazine).
HUSSEY, CHRISTOPHER 1967 *English Gardens and Landscapes, 1700–1750.* London: Country Life.
STROUD, DOROTHY 1975 *Capability Brown.* Rev. ed. London: Faber.
WALPOLE, HORACE 1785 *Essay on Modern Gardening.* London: Strawberry Hill.

BROWN, DAVID

For eighteen years, Canadian David Brown (?–1970), a retired embalmer, designed a complex of buildings, lookout towers, bridges, and walkways, made entirely of oblong embalming fluid bottles. Laid in mortar, like bricks, the bottles with their tops left on provided for insulation and illumination. Work is continued by his son.

JANET KAPLAN

WORK

1952–1970, David Brown House, Boswell, British Columbia.

BIBLIOGRAPHY

WAMPLER, JAN 1977 Pages 16–23 in *All Their Own: People and the Places They Build.* Cambridge, Mass.: Schenkman.

BROWN, GLENN

Glenn Brown (1854–1932) had a distinguished architectural practice in Washington; he was equally noteworthy for the role he played in improving the quality of public art and architecture in the capital and throughout the country. As secretary-treasurer of the American Institute of Architects (and an admirer of the PIERRE CHARLES L'ENFANT plan), he was instrumental in the formation of the McMillan Commission and its 1902 plan for Washington. Through the Institute, he worked to establish the U.S. Commission of Fine Arts and to open up the design of government buildings to private architects. He initiated the A.I.A.'s purchase of WILLIAM THORNTON's Octagon.

Born in Fauquier County, Virginia, Brown was the grandson of North Carolina's Senator Bedford Brown. He was educated at Washington and Lee University, worked for N. G. Starkweather in Washington, then completed the special course in architecture at the Massachusetts Institute of Technology (1877). First employed by O. W. Norcross as clerk of the works on H. H. RICHARDSON's Cheney Building, he opened his Washington office in 1880; he took his son, Bedford, into partnership around 1909. Brown's practice was a varied one; he was also an author. His writings ranged from technical articles to the two-volume *History of the United States Capitol* (1900–1903).

SUE KOHLER

WORKS

*1884, Alderney Dairies Plant; 1899, 1909, House, 1732 Massachusetts Avenue, N.W.; 1890, National Union Fire Insurance Building; Washington. 1894, Christ Church (interior restoration), Alexandria, Va. *1897, Zebu House, National Zoo; 1898, Holt House (restoration), National Zoo; 1898, House, 2012 Massachusetts Avenue, N.W.; 1907, House, 2301 Massachusetts Avenue, N.W.; Washington. 1907–c.1920, Pohick Church (interior restoration); 1912, Gunston Hall (restoration and modernization); Fairfax County, Va. 1914, Dumbarton (Q Street) Bridge, Washington.

BIBLIOGRAPHY

For additional information on Brown, see the Glenn Brown collection in the American Institute of Architects Archives, Washington.

AMERICAN INSTITUTE OF ARCHITECTS 1913 *Proceedings of the Forty-Seventh Annual Convention* 47:101–102.
BROWN, GLENN 1900–1903 *History of the United States Capitol.* 2 vols. Washington: G.P.O.
BROWN, GLENN (compiler) 1901 *Papers Relating to the Improvement of the City of Washington, District of Columbia.* Washington: G.P.O.
BROWN, GLENN 1925 "The Proposed Marine Barracks at Quantico, Va." *Architectural Record* 57:510–516.
BROWN, GLENN 1931 *1860–1930, Memories: A Winning Crusade to Revive George Washington's Vision of a Capital City.* Washington: Roberts.
"Glenn Brown." 1932 *American Architect* 141:44.

MOORE, CHARLES 1932 "Glenn Brown: A Memoir." *Journal of the Royal Institute of British Architects* 39:858.

UNITED STATES COMMISSION OF FINE ARTS 1973–1975 Volume 1, pages 355–378 and volume 2, pages 79–90 in *Massachusetts Avenue Architecture.* Washington: G.P.O.

Joseph Brown.
First Baptist Meeting
House.
Providence, Rhode Island.
1774–1775

BROWN, JOSEPH

Joseph Brown (1733–1785) was an eighteenth-century gentleman–amateur architect and scientist. A member of the illustrious Brown family of Providence, Rhode Island, he was born in that city on December 3, 1733. He began a successful business career in the family firm of Nicholas Brown and Company but, although not college educated, he soon devoted himself to scholarly pursuits in science, mechanics, mathematics, astronomy, and architecture. He also played an important role in Rhode Island College (now Brown University) established in 1764. He served on the building committee for the new College Edifice (later known as University Hall); as a trustee from 1769; and later as professor of experimental philosophy. He was also elected to the Academy of Arts and Science.

Brown's brief career in architecture began after 1770 when, as the colony's commercial center shifted from Newport, Providence experienced a period of great prosperity. During these years his name was associated with five of the city's most important buildings—the College Edifice (1770–1771), the Market House (1773–1777), and the First Baptist Meeting House (1774–1775), as well as his own house at 50 South Main Street (1774) and his brother's at 52 Power Street (1786–1788).

Brown's inventory included two architectural books: JAMES GIBBS's *Book of Architecture* (1728), and ABRAHAM SWAN's *Designs* (1745), while two other works, William Salmon's *Palladio Londonensis* (1748) and one of BATTY LANGLEY's mid-eighteenth century handbooks, belonged to the Providence Library Company. The influence of such books, out-of-fashion in England since the 1750s, helped contribute to the *retardataire* aspect of his work.

For the College Edifice the committee, composed of Brown, Stephen Hopkins, and President James Manning, agreed on a somewhat simplified version of Old Nassau Hall in Princeton designed by Robert Smith of Philadelphia. Although the design has always been ascribed to Brown, a plan recently discovered among the building papers is signed by Smith.

For the First Baptist Meeting House, the building committee (Brown, Comfort Wheaton, and Jonathan Hammond) interpreted into wood designs from Gibbs for a structure eighty-feet square with a tower and a steeple. The spire itself is an almost exact copy of one of the rejected spires for Saint Martin's-in-the-Fields, while the interior follows the scheme of coved ceiling and balconies intersecting the orders in the Marylebone Chapel in London. Full-scale working drawings were made by James Sumner, master workman from Boston.

For his own brick house, Brown used a baroque ogee form for the gable pediment, while the interior treatment resembles smaller early eighteenth-century English houses like Rainham Hall in Essex. Mantels and window treatments were drawn from plates in Gibbs and Salmon.

Brown died in 1785 before his brother's house on Power Street was begun, but he has always been credited with the design. A large three-story hip-roofed brick structure with a one-story columniated portico set in front of a projecting pedimented pavilion, it was considered one of the most magnificent mansions of its day. In Providence it set the key for later elaborate houses, introducing features like the pedimented pavilion and the portico. The richly decorated interiors reflect some of the influence of the brothers Adam (see ADAM FAMILY) and other more contemporary design concepts, but the building essentially belongs as did Brown's other work to the waning academic manner.

ANTOINETTE F. DOWNING

WORKS

1770–1771, The College Edifice (University Hall); 1773–1777, Market House; 1774, Joseph Brown House;

1774–1775, First Baptist Meeting House; 1786–1788, John Brown House; Providence, R.I.

BIBLIOGRAPHY

CADY, JOHN HUTCHINS 1952 "The Providence Market House and Its Neighborhood." *Rhode Island History* 11:97–116.

CADY, JOHN HUTCHINS 1957 *The Civic and Architectural Development of Providence, 1636–1950.* Providence, R.I.: Book Shop.

DOWNING, ANTOINETTE F. 1937 *Early Homes of Rhode Island.* Richmond, Virg.: Garrett.

GUILD, REUBEN A. 1887 *History of Brown University with Illustrative Documents.* R.I.: Providence Press.

HITCHCOCK, H. R. 1939 *Rhode Island Architecture.* Providence, R.I.: Museum Press.

ISHAM, NORMAN MORRISON 1925 *The Meeting House of the First Baptist Church in Providence: A History of the Fabric.* Providence. R.I.: Akerman-Standard.

"Joseph Brown." 1881 Pages 50–51 in *The Biographical Cyclopedia of Representative Men of Rhode Island.* Providence, R.I.: National Biographical Publishing.

WILSON, J. WALTER 1945 "Joseph Brown: Scientist and Architect." *Rhode Island History* 4:67–79, 121–128.

BROWNE, GEORGE

George Browne, (1811–1885) was born in Belfast, Ireland, evidently the son of an architect of the same name. He emigrated to Quebec City, Lower Canada, in 1830 and practiced architecture there for the next decade. His great opportunity came in 1841 when Kingston, Upper Canada, was made the capital of the newly united provinces of Upper and Lower Canada (the present Ontario and Quebec). Browne went there as government architect, but he also obtained many civic and private commissions. His Kingston work shows the development of a personal style, stemming from JOHN SOANE's classicism but with a greater sense of mass. Its simplicity and the consistent use of the Tuscan order give it a primitive flavor which ultimately recalls CLAUDE NICOLAS LEDOUX. The building that most strongly exemplifies this style is the City Hall and Market Buildings (1842–1844) which cost $80,000 and was perhaps the largest structure of its kind in North America at this time. Browne won the commission in a competition against eleven other architects.

In 1844, the capital moved to Montreal, and Browne went with it. He seems to have remained there for the rest of his life, executing mostly domestic and commercial work, including two grand terraces (Wellington Terrace, 1855–1856; and the Prince of Wales Terrace, 1861). Both were destroyed in the redevelopment of the 1960s. Perhaps his finest Montreal building is Molson's Bank (1864–1866; now Bank of Montreal), a superb essay in the Second Empire style.

George Browne was one of the finest architects working in Canada in the first half of the nineteenth century. His Kingston buildings are perhaps his greatest achievement. There, he produced work whose primitivism and triumphal exuberance both derive from British and European tradition. Yet, the combination was especially apt for a confident, expanding society which had only recently emerged from the pioneering phase.

J. DOUGLAS STEWART

WORKS

1832–1833, 9 Haldimand Street, Quebec City. 1841, Saint Andrew's Presbyterian Church Manse; 1842–1844, City Hall and Market Buildings; 1844, Bank of Montreal (now the Frontenac Apartments); Kingston, Ontario; 1852–1853, Chalmers-Wesley Church, Quebec City. *1855–1856, Wellington Terrace; *1861, Prince of Wales Terrace. 1864–1866, Molson's Bank (now the Bank of Montreal); Montreal.

BIBLIOGRAPHY

ANGUS, MARGARET 1963 "Architects and Builders in Early Kingston." *Historic Kingston* 11:25–26.

ANGUS, MARGARET 1966 *The Old Stones of Kingston.* University of Toronto Press.

BORTHWICK, J. DOUGLAS (1875)1892 *History and Biographical Gazeteer of Montreal.* Montreal: Lovell.

MACRAE, MARION 1963 *The Ancestral Roof.* Toronto: Clarke, Irwin.

RICHARDSON, A. J. H. 1970 "Guide to the . . . Buildings . . . of Quebec, with a Biographical Dictionary of Architects and Builders." *Bulletin of the Association for Preservation Technology* 2, nos. 3–4:41–45, 76–77.

STEWART, J. DOUGLAS 1974 "Controversies, Myths and Realities." Pages 4–10 in *Kingston City Hall.* Kingston: Corporation of the City.

STEWART, J. DOUGLAS 1976 "Architecture for a Boom-Town: The 'Primitive' and the 'Neo-Baroque' in George Browne's Kingston Buildings." Pages 37–61, 346–351 in Gerald Tulchinsky (editor), *To Preserve and Defend: Essays on Kingston in the Nineteenth Century.* Montreal: McGill-Queen's University Press.

STEWART, J. DOUGLAS 1982 "George Browne." In *Dictionary of Canadian Biography.* University of Toronto Press.

STEWART, J. DOUGLAS, and WILSON, IAN E. 1973 *Heritage Kinston.* Kingston, Ontario: Agnes Etherington Art Centre, Queen's University.

BROWNE, JOHN JAMES

During the last half of the nineteenth century, Montreal could boast no more versatile nor prolific an architect than John James Browne (1837–1893). Born in Quebec City, he personally credited his success to his extensive travels throughout Europe. *The American Architect and Builder's Monthly,* in commenting on one of his designs in 1870, delivered a critique which serves as a general statement on his architecture: "It shows much careful thought and fertility of invention. . . . The carving is good and the general design shows a freedom not foreign to this architect's other works."

JULIA GERSOVITZ

WORKS

*c.1865, Jesse Joseph House (Dilcoosha), Sherbrooke Street West; *c.1865, Robert MacKay House, Sherbrooke Street West; 1870, Christ Church Cathedral Rectory; 1870, John Foulds House (Rockmount), Summerhill Avenue; 1870, Gothic Cottages, MacGregor Avenue; 1870, Warehouse, Recollet and Saint Helen Streets; *c.1872–1875, A. F. Gault House (Rokeby), Sherbrooke Street West; *1878, Weslleyan Church, Dorchester Street; 1881, Morrice Hall, McGill University; 1882, Thomas Craig (or Corby's) House, 1202 Sherbrooke Street West; 1888, Nordheimer Building, 359–363 Saint James Street West; 1889, Peter Lyall House, 1445 Bishop Street; Montreal. 1890, Central Chambers, Elgin Street, Ottawa.

BIBLIOGRAPHY

BORTHWICK, J. DOUGLAS 1875 *Montreal: Its History to Which Is Added Biographical Sketches with Photographs.* Montreal: Drysdale.
BORTHWICK, J. DOUGLAS 1892 *History and Biographical Gazetteer of Montreal to 1892.* Montreal: Lovell.
McCONNIFF, JOHN 1894 *Illustrated Montreal: The Metropolis of Canada.* Montreal: The author.
"Montreal Building Notes." 1908 *Engineering and Contract Record* 22, Sept. 16:23.
"Obituary." 1893 *Canadian Architect and Builder* 6, no. 8:87.
"Stray Notes on Street Architecture in Montreal." 1870 *American Architect and Builder's Monthly* 1, Nov.:13–16.

BRUAND, LIBERAL

Libéral Bruand (or Bruant) (c.1635–1697) was born into a Parisian family of architects and government officials. His father was *Maître Général des Bâtiments et des Ponts et Chaussées* and *Maître Général des Oeuvres de Charpenterie du Roi.* Libéral's elder brother, Jacques, was architect to Gaston d'Orléans and an *architecte du roi.* Libéral inherited his father's positions, became *architecte du roi* in 1663, and was a charter member of the Académie Royale d'Architecture. By the time of his death in 1697, he had been ennobled and awarded several honorary appointments to the court of Louis XIV including those of *écuyer, conseiller,* and *secrétaire du roi.* Bruand was not an innovator of architectural

Bruand.
Engraving of the Hôtel des Invalides.
Paris.
1670–1677

form, but he was an architect equally comfortable with the arts of building and design.

Early in his career, Bruand worked as site architect on the Church of Notre Dame des Victoires in Paris executing the plans of PIERRE LE MUET. Following Le Muet's death in 1669, Bruand succeeded him as director of works at the hospital for mendicants known as the Salpetrière, and in 1670 he designed its central-plan chapel. That same year, the marquis de Louvois invited him, along with six or seven other architects, to submit plans for a veterans' hospital. Bruand won the competition, and in 1671 he signed the contract for the construction of the Hôtel des Invalides. Dedicated in 1674, the Invalides provided a monumental setting for a model facility devoted to the care of wounded and indigent soldiers.

Bruand's role in the design of the Church of Saint-Louis des Invalides (Eglise des Soldats) remains uncertain. Between 1673 and 1675, he had lost favor with Louvois amidst charges of having taken payments for work not completed, and after 1675 his involvement with the Invalides was minimal. The church, called for in the contract of 1671 but not built with the rest of the *hôtel,* was constructed by JULES HARDOUIN MANSART after 1676. It is likely that Hardouin Mansart used studies by Bruand as the basis for his own design.

Apart from designing the portal of the monastery of the Feuillants in Paris (1677), Bruand received no major commissions for public buildings after 1675. This scarcely diminished his activity, however, for he remained a regular participant in the business of the Académie, and he continued to build houses for private patrons and to supervise the works of the department of bridges and roads.

The full extent of Bruand's residential practice is not known. He prepared a project for a country house intended for the duke of York in 1662. Four years later, he remodeled the Parisian *hôtel* of the duc de Vendôme. During the 1670s, he designed houses in Versailles for members of the aristocracy, and he undertook some speculative building in Paris. His own house, begun in 1683, follows a conventional plan but has a striking façade recalling the superimposed arcades of the main courtyard of the Invalides.

RICHARD CLEARY

WORKS

*1666, Hôtel Vendôme (remodeling); 1670, Chapel of the Hospital of the Salpetrière; 1670–1677. Hôtel des Invalides; *1677, Monastery of the Feuillants (portal); 1683, Libéral Bruand House, rue de la Perle; Paris.

BIBLIOGRAPHY

HAUTECOEUR, LOUIS 1948 *Le règne de Louis XIV.* Volume 2 in *Histoire de l'architecture classique en France.* Paris: Picard.
JARRY, PAUL 1929 *Les vieux hôtels de Paris: Le quartier Saint-Antoine; Architecture et décorations intérieures.* Paris: Contet.
REUTERSWÄRD, PATRIK 1962 "A French Project for a Castle at Richmond." *Burlington Magazine* 104:533–535.
REUTERSWÄRD, PATRIK 1965 *The Two Churches of the Hôtel des Invalides: A History of Their Design.* Stockholm: National-museum.
STRANDBERG, RUNAR 1966 "Libéral Bruand et les problèmes que soulèvent l'Eglise des Soldats et le Dôme des Invalides." *Konsthistorisk Tidskrift* 35:1–22.

BRUBAKER, CHARLES WILLIAM

Charles William Brubaker (1926–) was born in South Bend, Indiana, and attended Purdue University and the University of Texas at Austin. He has been a partner in the firm of Perkins and Will of Chicago since 1950.

Brubaker is a humanist whose primary interest is the design of educational institutions. He believes that schools are "principal community centers" and that colleges are "principal cultural centers." He advocates the building of colleges in shopping malls so as to unite culture and commerce.

MARY D. EDWARDS

WORKS

1963, Eckerd College, St. Petersburg, Fla. 1966, School of Technology, Southern Illinois University, Carbondale. 1972, Disney Magnet School; 1974, Whitney Young High School; Chicago. 1978, Robert Morgan Technical-Vocational Institute, Miami, Fla. 1978, Oakton Community College, Des Plaines, Ill.

CHARLES W. BRUBAKER IN
COLLABORATION WITH OTHERS.

1963, National College of Agriculture, Chapingo, Mexico. 1964, Cairo–American College. 1965, First National Bank, Chicago. 1966, New Trier High School, Winnetka, Ill. 1967, Sandhill College, Southern Pines, N.C. 1968, First National Bank Plaza, Chicago. 1968, Orchard Ridge College, Farmington, Mich. 1970, Richland College, Dallas, Tex. 1976, Arvada Center, Colo. 1976, Fort Hayes Career Center, Columbus, Ohio. 1978, Augustana College Center, Rock Island, Ill. 1978, Grand Rapids Junior College, Mich. 1978, Lake County Public Library, Merrillville, Ind.

BIBLIOGRAPHY

BRUBAKER, CHARLES W. 1968 "How to Create Territory for Learning in the Secondary School." *Nation's Schools.*
BRUBAKER, CHARLES W. 1973 "Long Island: 2001." *Newsday* June 24.
BRUBAKER, CHARLES W. 1977 *Planning Flexible Spaces.* New York.
BRUBAKER, CHARLES W. ET AL 1967 *Schools for America.* Washington.
BRUBAKER, CHARLES W. ET AL 1968 *The Schoolhouse in the City.* New York.
CONWAY, DONALD J. (editor) 1977 *Human Response to Tall Buildings.* Stroudsburg, Pa.: Dowden, Huychinson & Ross.
REDSTONE, L. G. 1976 *The New Downtowns.* New York: McGraw-Hill.

BRUCE, WILLIAM

William Bruce (c.1630–1710) was the younger son of a small Perthshire, Scotland laird, Robert Bruce of Blairhall. Little is known of his early life, but his knowledge of architecture and horticulture was probably acquired mainly by private study and travel. Like most of his relations, Bruce was a Royalist and his activities during negotiations for the Restoration gained him the favor of Charles II and the Earl of Lauderdale. A knighthood and baronetcy soon followed, together with a series of official appointments, including that of surveyor of the King's Buildings in Scotland. The death of Charles II brought an end to Bruce's government career and his last years were clouded by political alienation, family estrangement, and debt; he died in Edinburgh on New Year's Day 1710.

Although he held the surveyorship for a short period, during which he rebuilt the royal palace of Holyroodhouse (1671–1679), Bruce cannot be regarded primarily as a professional architect, for most of his country houses were designed for patrons, relatives, or friends. Initially, he had to be content to remodel existing buildings (Balcaskie, c.1668–1674; Thirlestane, c.1670–1677), and in these cases he invariably introduced a simple axial plan and formal courtyard layout of a kind then new to Scotland. With his designs for Dunkeld (c.1676–1684) and Moncreiffe (1679), however, he began to experiment with the type of "oblong square" plan recently developed in England, and this led to the erection of a distinctive group of mature classical houses, for some of which (Kinross, 1686–1693; Hopetoun, 1699–1703) he also provided well-integrated garden layouts.

Beside being the founder of classical architecture in Scotland and a pioneer in planting and landscape design, Bruce helped to shape the ideas and careers of a younger generation of native architects, notably Robert Mylne, Alexander Edward, and JAMES SMITH.

JOHN G. DUNBAR

WORKS

c.1668–1674, Balcaskie House (remodeling), Fife, Scotland. c.1670–1677, Thirlestane Castle (remodeling), Berwickshire, Scotland. 1671–1679, Holyroodhouse (rebuilding), Edinburgh. 1672–1674, Brunstane House (remodeling), Midlothian, Scotland. 1673–1674, Lauder Church, Berwickshire, Scotland. 1673–1677, Lethington (now Lennoxlove) East Lothian, Scotland. *1676–1684, Dunkeld House; *1679, Moncreiffe House; Perthshire, Scotland. *1680–1682, The Exchange, Edinburgh. 1686–1693, Kinross House, Kinross-shire, Scotland. c.1695–1699, Craigiehall House; 1699–1703, Hopetoun House; West Lothian, Scotland. 1702–1707, Auchindinny, Midlothian, Scotland. 1703–, Mertoun House, Berwickshire, Scotland. 1703–1705, The Town House, Stirlingshire, Scotland. *c.1709–1710, House of Nairne (not completed until 1712), Perthshire, Scotland.

BIBLIOGRAPHY

DUNBAR, JOHN G.   (1966)1778   *The Architecture of Scotland.* Rev. ed. London: Barsford.
DUNBAR, JOHN G.   1970   *Sir William Bruce, 1630–1710.* Edinburgh: Scottish Arts Council. Catalogue of a Scottish Arts Council exhibition, Edinburgh, 1970.
FENWICK, HUBERT   1970   *Architect Royal: The Life and Works of Sir William Bruce, 1630–1710.* Kineton, England: Roundwood.
MYLNE, ROBERT SCOTT   1893   *The Master Masons to the Crown of Scotland and their Works.* Edinburgh: Scott.

BRUKALSKA, BARBARA, and BRUKALSKI, STANISŁAW

Barbara Sokołowska Brukalska (1899–1980) and Stanisław Brukalski (1894–1967) were a husband-and-wife team of architects active in Warsaw. Barbara Brukalska studied architecture at the Technical University in Warsaw and graduated in 1934. Stanisław Brukalski studied first at the University of Milan and later at the Technical University in Warsaw, where he graduated in 1925.

The Brukalskis were pioneers of the Modern movement in Poland, building many housing developments for the Warsaw Housing Cooperative (WSM). Both were members of the Polish avant-garde group "Praesens" and were active in the Congrès Internationaux d'Architecture Moderne. From 1927 to 1938, they also designed many interiors of passenger ships.

From 1939 to 1944, Stanisław Brukalski was interned in a German P.O.W. camp where he stayed active by conducting architectural courses. After the war, both Barbara and Stanisław became professors in the architecture department of the Technical University in Warsaw.

The work of the Brukalskis is characterized by a sense for human scale and a sensitivity to the natural environment as well as a rational use of building materials. Initially, their style was subordinated to the dicta of the International style, but later their work became more organic and individual. Their work after World War II turned more toward historically inspired forms.

LECH KŁOSIEWICZ

WORKS

BARBARA BRUKALSKA AND STANISŁAW BRUKALSKI

1927–1938, Passenger Ships Batory, Piłsudski, Sobieski, and Chrobry (interiors). 1927–1939, Fourth, Seventh and Ninth WSM Housing Developments; Zoliborz; 1945–1960, Eleventh, Twelfth, and Thirteenth WSM Housing Developments, Zoliborz; 1946–1955, Old Town Reconstruction Design; Warsaw.

BARBARA BRUKALSKA

1962, Senior Citizens' Home; 1964, House of Parliament (interior); Warsaw.

STANISŁAW BRUKALSKI

1928–1931, Brukalski House, Niegolewskiego Street; 1952–1956, Zoliborz Cultural Center and Theater; Warsaw.

BIBLIOGRAPHY

"Architektura Pospolita."   1939   *Pion* 1939: no. 3.
BIEGÁNSKI, PIOTR   1971   *Uźródel Architektury Współczesnej.* Warsaw: P.W.N.
BRUKALSKA, BARBARA, and BRUKALSKI, STANISŁAW   1936   "Nasza Praca Nad Mieszkaniem Robotniczym." *Osidle Mieszkaniowe* Series 1 no. 8:10–11. Also published in *D.O.M.* 1936, nos. 10–11.
"Kuchnia Wspołczesna."   1929   *D.O.M.* 1:8.
BRUKALSKA, BARBARA   1948   *Zasady Społecznego*

Profektowania Osiedli Mieszkaniowych. Warsaw: Ministry of Education.

The Polish Avant-Garde, 1918–1939: Architecture-Town Planning. 1981 Warsaw: Interpress. Exhibition catalogue originally published in Polish.

Warzawska Szkoka Architektury: 1915–1965. 1967 Warsaw: P.W.N.

WISŁOCKA, IZABELLA 1968 *Awangardowa Architektura Polska: 1918–1939.* Warsaw: Arkady.

BRUNEL, ISAMBARD K.

Isambard Kingdom Brunel (1806–1859) was one of the leading engineers of the early Victorian period in England. He was an imaginative and confident designer who turned his hand to everything from tunnels, railways, and bridges to harbors, prefabricated buildings, and even ships. He was born in Portsmouth, the son of an almost equally famous engineer, Sir Marc Isambard Brunel. Young Brunel was sent to France to complete his schooling before entering his father's office in 1822, and, while in Paris, he absorbed something of the spirit of the architecture of the *Grand Siècle.*

Brunel served his final apprenticeship assisting his father in the early stages of the construction of the Thames Tunnel (1824–1842), proving himself such an apt learner that he was soon given the position of engineer in charge. This apprenticeship was suddenly terminated in 1828 when the river broke through the tunneling shield and he was lucky to escape with his life. During convalescence in Clifton, he submitted several designs against stiff competition for a bridge over the Avon Gorge at Clifton. One of these designs—for a suspension bridge crossing the gorge in a single span between masonry towers reminiscent, as originally detailed, of the pylons of Egyptian temples—was declared the winner. It embodied lessons learnt from a close study of THOMAS TELFORD's Menai Bridge and from his father's experience in designs for the French government. He was formally given the commission for the bridge in 1831, but construction was not completed until 1860–1864 after his death, and much of the Egyptian detailing of the pylons was omitted.

In 1833, Brunel was appointed chief engineer of the new Great Western Railway. This was to call not only for the construction of many miles of track—for which he adopted a broader gauge than other engineers to permit higher speeds—but also for numerous tunnels, bridges, and two large terminal stations in Bristol and London. Outstanding was the Maidenhead Bridge over the Thames (1837–1838) with two unusually flat brick arches of elliptical profile. Later came the Saltash Bridge (1857–1859), carrying a single track high above the river Tamar on two wide spans, each a unique combination of arched wrought-iron tube and suspension chains (some of which had originally been fabricated for the Clifton Bridge whose construction was then halted for lack of money). The train shed at Temple Meads station in Bristol (1839–1840) was roofed in a single wide span by timber arches of a slightly pointed profile with added decoration giving a hammer-beam appearance. At Paddington, the London terminal (1852–1854), the train shed was roofed with wrought-iron arches in three parallel bays intersected by two transepts. Here the young MATTHEW DIGBY WYATT with whom he had worked on the preparation for the Great Exhibition of 1851 served as Brunel's architectural collaborator.

Brunel's shipbuilding activities (Great Western [1837], Great Britain [1843], and Great Eastern [1858]) are of less architectural relevance but demonstrate again his originality, his energy, his creative ability, and his ruthless pursuit of what he saw as the fundamental logic of a situation—even when, as here, he made excessive calls on current technology and anticipated markets that did not yet exist.

Though Brunel had numerous loyal assistants, none was of his stature. His lasting contributions were the examples he set by his own works and, just as importantly, by his professional standards. He did as much as anyone to establish the profession of civil engineer as we now know it.

ROWLAND MAINSTONE

WORKS

1831–1859, Clifton Suspension Bridge (not completed until 1864), England. 1837–1838, Maidenhead Bridge, England. 1839–1840, Temple Meads Station, Bristol, England. 1852–1854, Paddington Station, London. 1857–1859, Saltash Bridge, near Plymouth, England.

BIBLIOGRAPHY

NOBLE, CELIA BRUNEL 1938 *The Brunels: Father and Son.* London: Cobden Sanderson.

PUGSLEY, ALFRED (editor) (1976)1980 *The Works of Isambard Kingdom Brunel: An Engineering Appreciation.* New York: Cambridge University Press.

ROLT, L. T. C. (1957)1970 *Isambard Kingdom Brunel.* Reprint. Harmondsworth, England: Penguin.

BRUNELLESCHI, FILIPPO

Filippo Brunelleschi (1377–1446) was born in Florence, the son of Ser Brunellesco Lippi, a notary and middle-level public official in the Florentine state apparatus. He died sixty-nine years later, a celebrated member of a technological and artistic elite that had made and continued to make substantial contributions to the well-being of the Florentine state on both the military and the economic levels and, more particularly, to Florentine prestige internationally.

Brunelleschi's life and career are best understood in this historical context. In the last quarter of the fourteenth century, Florence was engaged in a peninsula-wide struggle for political and economic survival and supremacy with the competing powers of Lombardy, Venice, Naples-Sicily, and the papal state. The struggle to develop viable regional or national states, a necessary response to the failure of the medieval city-states to provide an adequate economic base for the expanding urban populations at the end of the thirteenth and the beginning of the fourteenth centuries, may be at the heart of what is summarily described as "the Renaissance." Technical and artistic talent to meet the competitive challenges in military engineering and architecture, in shipbuilding and weaponry, in industry and financial management, were at a premium in this struggle. The state capable of producing and/or attracting and holding the oustanding creative minds, the men of *ingegno,* that is to say, the engineers, was at a distinct advantage.

The changing historical situation led to the formation of a new upper class of political and economic managers generally, but not exclusively, from the old patrician families, increasingly restricted in number, but proportionally richer, more powerful, and, consequently, increasingly demanding in matters of housing, material well-being, and the outward expression of their personal identity. The convenient means for this expression was in the patronage of humanists and artists who could provide the larger and more elaborate palaces, with their decorations and furnishings, as well as in patronized institutional architecture and burial churches and chapels in the *all'antica* style suitable to a new era of large scale comparable to the architecture of Roman antiquity. Brunelleschi's career and achievement may be seen as an integral part of this new era.

The chronological facts of Filippo's life are fairly well-known and documented. To round out the picture we have the polemical but informative biography by Antonio di Tuccio Manetti written in the fifteenth century. As the son of a reputable public official and of a mother from an old patrician banking family, the Spini, Filippo received a basic *abbaco* school education with the addition of readings in Latin literature. An early penchant for drawing led him to the most elegant of the design professions: he was matriculated as a master goldsmith in the Silk guild in 1404, following a six-year term of service as a journeyman. Specimens of his work survive in several silver figures of proph-

ets on the gilded altar of San Jacopo in Pistoia. Of several works in wooden sculpture, his crucifix in Santa Maria Novella remains an interesting piece of comparison to Donatello's Santa Croce crucifix.

Brunelleschi grew up amid major building projects sponsored or financially supported by the Florentine state: the Loggia dei Signori, Or San Michele, Santa Croce, Santa Maria Novella, and, most crucial, the Cathedral of Santa Maria del Fiore. Santa Trinita, the first major parish church in Florence to be surrounded by a ring of uniform chapels, grew up along with the adolescent Brunelleschi. By family tradition, Filippo was a member of the Florentine political establishment (the so-called *reggimento*), not in a leading position, but at its periphery. From 1400 on, he sat in the city councils. In 1404, he was a member of an advisory commission of citizens and masters consulting on an alleged error committed by the *capomaestro* of Santa Maria del Fiore, Giovanni d'Ambrogio, in constructing one of the buttresses of the first (northern) tribuna arm of the cathedral. Filippo's name continued to appear occasionally in the books of the cathedral *opera* until 1417 when he became directly and permanently involved in the planning and construction of the great cupola of Santa Maria del Fiore.

The Ospedale degli Innocenti

In 1419, the Silk guild committed itself to build an asylum for abandoned infants and called on Brunelleschi, a guild member, to provide a design for the new Ospedale degli Innocenti, to be built on the Piazza de' Servi. Brunelleschi complied with a measured elevation drawing of the portico façade of the building and assumed supervision of the project during the following years. The decision to enlarge the building in 1427 led to alterations in Filippo's design, most notably the addition of an outer bay on the right-hand (southern) side of the portico. His first formal architectural design, the Innocenti elevation, with its portico of

Brunelleschi. Ospedale degli Innocenti. Florence. 1419

round arcades on monolithic Corinthian columns flanked by outer bays with giant Corinthian pilasters, established the hallmarks of Brunelleschi's architectural style: traditional schemes, derived from traditional Florentine building types, expressed in a very personal and restrained language of details *all'antica*. The very gradual completion of the Innocenti project led to the omission of some parts of Filippo's design, such as the paired *pilastrelli* over the giant pilasters of the lower story, and to the introduction of some non-Brunelleschian elements, particularly the "bent" architrave at the end of the southern addition, following a motif found in the Florentine Baptistery.

San Lorenzo

The reconstruction and enlargement of San Lorenzo, the parish church of the richest quarter in Florence, began in 1418. Brunelleschi was involved in the project almost from the outset. First he provided a design for the sacristy, which Giovanni di Bicci de' Medici was committed to patronize. From there it was nearly inevitable that

Brunelleschi.
San Lorenzo (sacristy).
Florence.
1418–1429

Filippo should seek to integrate his novel sacristy design into the larger context of a church conforming to his own clear vision. The nature of that vision will become apparent if we understand Filippo's preferred project in the context of a program that required a plan substantially identical to that of Santa Trinità. What Filippo intended was a transept and nave with vaulted aisles flanked by square vaulted side chapels with one single-bay chapel at either end of the transept. All chapels were to be identical in plan and elevation, each lit by a window. The problematic chapels in the corners between the aisles and the transept were to have been open toward both transept and aisles (as in Santa Trinità) and lit laterally. That this was Brunelleschi's preferred solution may be inferred from Antonio Manetti's (1970) criticism of the church as executed, contained in his *Life of Brunelleschi* (lines 1176ff.) The resultant building would have complied with Filippo's ideal in several respects: (1) the fewest number of different parts; (2) complete identity of identical parts; and (3) homogeneity of lighting achieved by allotting to each part a proportionately scaled window. Insurmountable were the difficulties implied in the Santa Trinità model. Transept and nave with aisles could not be wholly integrated. The three-step elevation of the chapels led to shorter pilasters responding to the nave columns. Some of the problems were of Brunelleschi's own making. He preferred to make the fluted pilasters of the crossing piers identical in width to the pilasters between the chapels. This led to excessively slim crossing piers and subsequent problems with the dome over the crossing which, for structural reasons probably, had to spring directly over the pendentives. Sunk into the surrounding roofs, it could be lit only through the oculus in its apex, contrasting with Brunelleschi's ideal of homogeneous lighting.

Brunelleschi's design at San Lorenzo was frustrated almost from the beginning. For reasons probably related to the conflict of political factions in Florence in the 1420s, just enough patrons were found for the transept chapels. The project with nave chapels was abandoned, the corner chapels were closed toward the nave, and the end chapels of the transept became double-bay chapels. When the nave chapel project was revived in 1434 (during Cosimo de' Medici's brief exile), chapels quite different from the transept chapels were proposed. The nave chapels eventually executed resemble those proposed in 1434: shallow, lower than the transept chapels and unlit. Brunelleschi was probably out of the San Lorenzo project after the completion of the sacristy in 1429 and the death of Giovanni di Bicci. Cosimo's favorite architect,

MICHELOZZO DI BARTOLOMMEO, may have been connected with the nave chapel project of 1434 and he was probably in charge of completing the sacristy and church from the time of Cosimo's return from exile in August 1434 up to his fall from favor in the early 1450s. Antonio Manetti Ciaccheri is the architect of record thereafter, completing the transept with its dome over Cosimo's intended tomb (the first Renaissance copy of the Pantheon dome, perhaps following a suggestion of LEON BATTISTA ALBERTI). The nave and its chapels were completed in the 1460s and 1470s. The location of Cosimo's tomb directly under the dome turned the church, in essence, into the family chapel of the Medici—a revolutionary and decisive turn in church patronage. Antonio di Tuccio Manetti's criticisms of the finished building must be read in the light of this building history.

The Pazzi Chapel

The close personal, political, and business alliance between Andrea de' Pazzi and the Medici family may explain the origins and character of Brunelleschi's project for the chapter house which was to be built as part of the large-scale cloister reconstruction underway at Santa Croce after a dormitory fire in 1423. The Medici had shown the flag in the camp of their political opponents in the Santa Croce quarter by endowing the Novitiate of Santa Croce in about 1425 (built from the mid-1430s on). They may have found it opportune to convince their rich but stingy friend and partisan, Andrea de' Pazzi, to assume the patronage over the chapter house which was to rival not merely the celebrated chapter house of Santa Maria Novella (the so-called Spanish Chapel) but also to emulate the Medici sacristy at San Lorenzo in character and style. The commission went inevitably to Brunelleschi. His design may have been ready as early as 1424. Andrea made his formal commitment to build the chapel in 1429.

Allowing for the functional requirements of the chapter house (rectangular chapter room, altar chapel, outer portico to continue the line of the cloister portico, all in the tradition of the Spanish Chapel), the Pazzi Chapel repeats the major motifs of the San Lorenzo sacristy. Regardless of their varying liturgical functions as sacristy and chapter hall, both buildings served, perhaps primarily, as family mausolea. In the Medici sacristy, this function assumed a revolutionary form: a twelve-partite melon dome on pendentives with tholos lantern (modeled on the Baptistery lantern) directly over the exposed marble sarcophagus of Giovanni di Bicci and his wife Piccarda de' Bueri set under the marble sacramental table in the center of the sacristy. The capitular functions of the

Brunelleschi.
Pazzi Chapel.
Florence.
c.1425–1428 (executed
after 1442)

main room of the Pazzi chapter hall made similar burial arrangements there an impossibility, and the Pazzi crypt was located under the adjacent raised altar room. In all other respects—melon dome on pendentives with roundels, wall articulation with Corinthian pilasters, dome altar chapel, and an elaborate sculptural decorative program—the Pazzi Chapel emulates and equals the Medici sacristy.

Recent theories implying that the portico and its façade are later additions to Brunelleschi's design are based on an erroneous interpretation of the archeological evidence. The portico as executed is substantially that projected by Brunelleschi. It may be, however, that Filippo did not plan the executed central dome on pendentives in the central bay of the portico, but a pendentive vault (such as those of the Innocenti portico or the aisle vaults of San Lorenzo and Santo Spirito) instead. That device would have allowed the arrangement of a shed roof over the vaults of the portico in such a way as to allow full exposure of the façade oculus over the portico and a satisfactory front elevation instead of the unfortunate existing porch roof, raised on stone piers to clear the high central dome on pendentives.

Andrea de' Pazzi's chronic reluctance to commit funds to the chapter house project prevented its execution during his lifetime, and he was buried in his family vault in the transept of Santa Croce. Serious building efforts did not begin until 1442, presumably under pressure from the Medici. Completed around 1465, it is executed substantially according to Brunelleschi's intentions, except for the portico dome and its roof. The interior is clearly and harmonically articulated into narrower and wider bays by carefully designed Corinthian pilasters. The pilasters sustain a system of arches and cornices curving under the central pendentives and the dome and, laterally, under flanking narrow barrel vaults articulated by flat coffers. The narrow bays toward the cloister are penetrated by arched windows. Blind arches in the corresponding bays around the main chapter room suggest homogeneous lighting throughout. The wider bays around the room, corresponding to the altar chapel on the east side, impart a suggestion of centrality and equivalence. Round windows in the spandrel arches under the pendentives were either intended to have access to light or are blind windows due to flanking buildings. The altar room is lit by a large stained-glass window, appended almost like an altar retable under the entablature of its eastern wall. The small round windows at the base of the twelve-partite melon dome and its lantern-covered oculus complete the framework of homogeneous illumination.

The marble steps and pavement of the altar room and the marble altar itself may be the product of a collaboration between LUCA DELLA ROBBIA (the artist of the chapter hall roundel reliefs) and Brunelleschi's stepson and heir, Andrea di Lazzero Cavalcanti, called Buggiano, executed in the late 1450s. Buggiano probably also executed the altar and the Medici sarcophagus in the San Lorenzo sacristy. The stained-glass window of the Pazzi altar room has been attributed to Baldovinetti. The intarsia portal wings are by GIULIANO DA MAIANO. Execution of the chapter hall after about 1450 was probably in the hands of the shop of BERNARDO ROSSELLINO.

The Barbadori Chapel in Santa Felicità

No project among the relatively few works of Brunelleschi is minor in conception or quality of execution. The chapel, dedicated to the Santissima Annunziata, located in the front right-hand corner of Santa Felicità, which Brunelleschi designed and executed for the Barbadori family (perhaps following a commitment by Bartolommeo di Gherardo Barbadori), is unique both in form and in function. Manetti suggests that it was begun about the time of the Innocenti or a little later, which would indicate a date in the early 1420s. The chapel, somewhat like the intended corner chapels at San Lorenzo, is open in two directions. A corner pier and Corinthian pilasters at the sides flank an engaged smaller order of Ionic columns carrying arches and support an upper entablature. The interior is vaulted by a dome (truncated by eighteenth-century alterations) on pendentives with roundels. One-sixth pilaster fragments appear in the interior corners between the engaged Ionic half-columns, rising up to disappear into the pendentives.

The reason for building this chapel may explain its form. It appears that the miraculous completion of the Annunciation fresco by the angel which gave the Servite church of Santissima Annunziata its name and importance, was believed to have reoccurred in various churches (San Marco, Santa Maria Novella, Ognissanti, and Santa Felicità), all of which have Annunciation frescoes on one side or another of their inner façade walls. The original Annunziata fresco was replaced in the late fourteenth-century by the present version (the original may have been rubbed away by the faithful). The earlier version in Santa Maria Novella shows an Annunciation taking place in an open loggia. The Virgin is visible through one opening of the loggia while the Angel Gabriel is seen addressing the Virgin through the other arcade. Brunelleschi's design for the chapel baldachin that was to frame the (lost) version of this scene on the façade of Santa Felicità, appears to be a three-dimensional projection of the miraculous painting. Michelozzo's similar framework for the original martyrium in Santissima Annunziata, built around 1450, is derived from Brunelleschi's conception.

The chapel passed to the Capponi in 1525. The great "Deposition" panel by Pontormo which was subsequently installed over the altar on the southern side of the chapel, may be considered to be a miraculous vision seen by the Virgin Annunciate painted on the façade wall by Pontormo, presumably an echo of the original Annunciation.

Palazzo di Parte Guelfa

Florentine political and administrative institutions, both large and small, followed a common model: the Signoria. The architectural framework of these institutions, likewise, was modeled on the great buildings of deliberation, judgment, and administration of the Florentine republic, the Palazzo del Podestà (Bargello) and the Palazzo della

Signoria. The essential characteristic of these buildings is a great hall for deliberations, flanked by subsidiary administrative chambers, set over a vaulted ground floor story, accessible by narrow, wholly or partially exterior stairs for reasons of security. Such was the pattern of the great council rooms of the Signoria until the late fifteenth century when the creation of the Council of Five-Hundred and its new enormous hall east of the old palace made the construction of a more convenient interior staircase a necessity. The present elaborate staircase was constructed by GIORGIO VASARI in the wholly changed political conditions of the duchy of Cosimo I.

The Parte Guelfa had its roots in the factional struggles that led to the formation of the republic in 1293. Together with the church and the guilds, it remained one of the ideological pillars of the Florentine state. At the height of its power in the middle of the fourteenth century, its captains—mostly from archconservative patrician families—considered themselves the guardians of Guelf loyalty in all branches of the government. At times, it acted like a government within the government, proscribing its opponents as Ghibellines and dictating both internal and external policy. Shaken by the struggle between Florence and the papacy in the so-called War of the Eight Saints in the 1370s, its prestige and power were curtailed under the guild government which emerged from the turmoil of the Ciompi rebellion in 1378–1382. It was revived and modernized by a far-reaching reform in 1413. Its post-1422 building program, in which the characteristically modest residence of the formerly all-powerful Parte was to be doubled in size, was a final bid for consolidation and integration by a declining institution.

The sparse documents indicate that the vaulted lower story of the new building east of the old residence was built in the years after 1422. The war years, 1426–1431, and the subsequent factional quarrels seem to have interrupted the project. After 1442, work on the upper story continued, to be interrupted permanently in 1459 when Cosimo de' Medici decided on the permanent degradation of the old institution. It was at this time also that the Parte lost the patronage over its niche at Or San Michele.

Brunelleschi's contribution, the design of the great hall of the upper story and its adjoining *udienza* and passageway to the old wing, might have been made as early as the mid-1420s. Its main feature was a great hall with a ceiling, probably to be coffered, with four large round-arched windows on its eastern and two on its shorter southern side facing the Via di Terme. The upper reaches of the hall were lit by large round windows over each of the arched windows below. The ceiling was probably to rest on a classical entablature supported by pilasters (fluted, Corinthian?) between the windows. None of these interior elements were completed during Brunelleschi's lifetime. The exterior of the great hall was completed to half the height of the roundels over the arched windows. The existing interior pilasters were executed by Maso di Bartolommeo, an associate of Michelozzo, in the late 1450s.

The exterior façade of great arched windows with profiled surrounds *all'antica* in *pietra forte* was flanked by giant unfluted pilasters, left incomplete without capitals. A Corinthian order with upper entablature may be assumed.

Again, Brunelleschi resolved the problem of this design by following the traditional model (Sala dei Dugento), reducing the number of differentiated parts to the minimum (even number of identical windows, no central accent) with the elements expressed in simple *all'antica* style. The adjoining *udienza* and corridor, insofar as they were executed under Filippo, were handled in similar manner.

Santa Maria degli Angeli

Brunelleschi's concern with homogeneity, assimilation, and equivalence, frustrated to some extent in his earlier projects, was bound to lead him to central symmetry—already implicit though sublimated in his San Lorenzo sacristy and Pazzi Chapel designs. The four major projects initiated during the last fifteen years of his life—the lantern of the cupola of Santa Maria del Fiore, the so-called *tribune morte* on the piers under the cathedral cupola, the Church of Santo Spirito, and the Church of Santa Maria degli Angeli—are all centrally symmetrical in substance or in essence.

The documentation concerning the Angeli project is extremely sparse and the early descriptions (Manetti, Fortunio) are garbled or ambiguous. A donation by members of the Scolari family, left in trust with the Calimala guild, was to be applied to the building of an oratory dedicated to the Virgin and the Twelve Apostles in the Florentine monastery of the Camaldolese order, Santa Maria degli Angeli. Why the commission for this design was given to Brunelleschi is not known. Building according to his project began in 1434, to be interrupted three years later when the funds were appropriated by the state. Nothing further was done until 1503 when the building fragment was roofed. The building functioned briefly as the seat of the ducal Academy of Design in the 1560s. Thereafter it served various secular uses and became a sculptor's studio in the nineteenth century. In 1934, it was isolated from its context and "com-

Brunelleschi.
Santa Maria degli Angeli
  (not completed).
Florence.
1434

pleted" according to a scheme of the architect Rodolfo Sabatini. It serves presently to store institutional files.

Given the limited documentation and the fact that the building never functioned as intended, it is very difficult to define just what that intention was and the reason for Filippo's design, which had no precedent in Florentine architecture. Scholars are still debating whether the building was to have had a portal toward the street or whether it was to be accessible solely from the interior of the monastery. Manetti's comments can and should be understood to the effect that the monks' choir was to be in the octagonal center of the building, under the eight-partite groin-voluted dome shown in the sixteenth-century Laurenziana drawing. The intended function of the surrounding chapels and their patronage (members of the Scolari family; others?) remain moot points. The proposed dedication of the oratory to the Virgin and the Apostles made a central plan based on antique prototypes such as the Pantheon and the Minerva Medica or one of the antique mausolea flanking Saint Peter's an iconographical desideratum. Just how such a building might serve in the context of a monastic community is indicated by the somewhat later project for the rotunda choir of Santissima Annunziata.

Even though, in Manetti's words, the building was "completely *al modo antico* inside and outside," it was characteristic of Brunelleschi's manner that no specific antique building was imitated. The final result is a balanced mix of elements from the two buildings which were Filippo's primary sources: the Florentine Baptistery and the cathedral of Santa Maria del Fiore, neither of them antique, both of them in the mainstream of the Florentine architectural tradition.

Our visual sources for the reconstruction of the elevation are the partial elevation in Giuliano da Sangallo's (see SANGALLO FAMILY) Vatican sketchbook (Vat. Lat. 4424, fol. 15v) and the sectional view in the Laurenziana codex (Ashburn-

ham, 1828, App. fol. 85). Fortunio's description of 1579, based on a drawing unknown to us, gives measurements for the elevation. The central, probably groin-vaulted, octagon was surrounded by eight square chapels, flanking massive triangular piers in the corners. The piers were hollowed out toward the chapels and toward the sixteen-sided exterior by large arched niches and bent around the corners of the octagon. Fluted, probably Corinthian pilasters flanked the octagon corners and the arched openings into the chapels. Narrow passages, angled through the corner piers, connected the chapels. Each chapel was lit by a narrow rectangular window high up (8 braccia = 4.67 meters) over the chapel floor (following the rules of the order) and covered by a barrel vault running radially to the octagon. The arches over the chapel openings sustained an entablature at the base of a drum. Large oculi in the drum, framed by profiled arches, lit the interior at mid-height. The drum arches sustained an upper entablature from which the eight-partite groin vault rose in a pointed dome to an octagonal oculus topped by a lantern. As with his other designs, the Angeli oratory satisfied Filippo's basic stylistic criteria: a minimum number of differentiated parts, identity of similar parts, and homogeneous illumination.

The connection of the *tempio* to the adjoining buildings including the monastery church remains problematic. The rectangular room which appears as a kind of adjunct to the building in Giuliano da Sangallo's plan has generally been identified as the choir (and is so labeled in several later copies after Sangallo's plan). It has recently been proposed that this space is not the choir (which was to be in the central octagon) but a vestibule, possibly intended for the laity. In any event, it provided the only entrance indicated on Giuliano's plan and, following Fortunio's description, would have faced east, toward the old monastery church on Via de' Alfani which had a similar vestibule-narthex for the laity accessible from the street.

Santo Spirito

"When Filippo had made the model and founded a part of [the Church of Santo Spirito] he said at some point that, insofar as the composition of the building was concerned, it seemed to him that he had begun a church in accordance with his intentions" (Manetti, 1970, lines 1536ff.). Filippo's expression of contentment contrasts with his dismay at the alterations in his Innocenti design (ibid., lines 1069ff.) and his disappointment at the impossibility of realizing his first project for San Lorenzo (ibid., lines 1218ff.). Brunelleschi's intentions become clear when we consider again the insuperable problems inherent even in Filippo's ideal solution with chapels for San Lorenzo. Transept and nave were two differentiated parts of a composed whole as they had been in every church of this type derived from the model of Constantinian Saint Peter's. Fluted pilasters, three steps over the aisles, responded to the unfluted nave columns. There was the uncomfortable choice of making the crossing pier pilasters wider than the pilasters between the chapels or constructing piers too slim to sustain the load of a cupola which rose high enough to be lit at its base. The dome, centralizing in its form and implications, was located at one end of the building, giving that end clear predominance in the composition.

Brunelleschi's Santo Spirito design resolved all of these difficulties. The domical center of the building is flanked on four sides by equivalent arms surrounded by vaulted aisles with side chapels, semicircular in plan with apsidal vaults. The only concession to asymmetrical expediency was the addition of six additional bays on the southern (entrance) side to accommodate both the large congregation of what was the major parish church of the quarter and the large number of family chapels, all equal in form and nearly equivalent in prominence of position, which made this church a classic expression of the fourteenth-century Florentine ideal of *reggimento* by a patriciate of leading families of equivalent power and standing. Half-columns between the chapels, one (column plinth) step over the aisles responded as perfect equivalents to the aisle columns. The crossing pier pilasters, being unique elements in the composition, could be given adequate width to allow for piers of sufficient strength to sustain pendentives bearing an interior drum which lifted a melon dome with round windows at its base and a lantern-covered oculus over the roofline of the arms flanking the crossing.

The assimilation of parts characteristically faced its ultimate challenge at the corners between arms flanking the crossing. Filippo's ideal solution at San Lorenzo—chapels opening in the direction of both transept and nave—could not change the fact that one opening faced the aisles while the other flanked the wide expanse of the transept. Filippo resolved this dilemma at Santo Spirito with identical chapels flanking a shared three-quarter engaged column at the corner. The party wall between the corner chapels was reduced to a minimum. It was, as Manetti infers, the kind of church which Brunelleschi had waited a lifetime to build.

Filippo achieved his ideal of homogeneous lighting to an unprecedented degree in his Santo Spirito design. Arched windows in the chapels, similar arched windows in the clearstory, the roundels at the base of the dome, and the lantern-cov-ered oculus give each level of the building its proportionate share of illumination. The under-the-roof spaces over the pendentive vault-covered side aisle bays are lit by exterior round windows.

The Cupola of Santa Maria del Fiore

Brunelleschi's long involvement with the construction of the cupola of Santa Maria del Fiore (1417–1434) is the central fact and event in his busy and productive life. Perhaps one-half of Manetti's biography of Filippo is concerned with it. It is the supreme building and engineering achievement of the fourteenth and fifteenth centuries. Its complexity and sheer size put Filippo's other building efforts into the shadow. It must be said, nonetheless, that even though the cupola project challenged all of Filippo's formidable abilities as an inventor, engineer, organizer, and problem solver, it offered only limited opportunities for the expression of his formal ideals. Its basic form, its curvature, its exterior appearance as well as many aspects of its internal structure were determined decades before Filippo came on the scene. He was constrained by specific guild legislation to accept the existing cathedral model. His task and that of his collaborators was not to improve the design, but to bring it to execution. One should not interpret this situation, however, as implying grudging acceptance or muted disapproval. On the contrary: there is no indication whatever that Filippo was in conflict with any aspect of the predicated form of the cupola. All of the aesthetics of the design and the very process of almost universal

Brunelleschi.
Santa Maria del Fiore
*   (cupola).*
Florence.
1417–1434

Brunelleschi.
Santa Maria del Fiore
   (*cupola*).
Florence.
1417–1434

Brunelleschi.
Santa Maria del Fiore
   (*lantern of the cupola*).
Florence.
1436

consultation by which it came to approval must have been congenial to Brunelleschi's very traditional Florentine view of things.

His chance to add touches of his own design conceptions to the cathedral complex came with the revised design for the so-called *tribune morte* and the final competition concerning the design of the great lantern, the culmination of the great man-made mountain of the dome.

The cupola lantern.   The lantern is the more important and chronologically earlier of these two projects. On the one hand, it has the qualities of an exquisite work of the goldsmith's art in marble, a turret reliquary. On the other, it is the ultimate expression and termination of the internal structural system of the cupola: the rising lantern is the equivalent and extension of the interior cupola shell and the pierced buttresses with their rising decorated volutes abutting inner piers represent the continuation of the eight interior corner piers. This emphatic distinction of the corners is continued upward through the spire. Corner piers with baluster finials alternate with profiled niches at the base of the spire. Pyramidally diminishing angle strips alternate with convex panels. The composition is closed by the gilded knob, ball, and cross.

The tribune morte.   An exterior structure to terminate the great piers under the cupola and to make a transition to the drum had been part of the 1367 cathedral model which was demolished as no longer valid in 1431. Following the general lines of the building, these terminations were polygonal in shape like the adjacent clearstories and vaults of the octagon arms. In 1439, with the cupola completed, Brunelleschi presented a revised design for these terminations (called *tribune morte,* that is, blind or nonfunctional *tribune* by contrast to the *tribune vive,* the functional adjoining octagon arms): semicircular in shape with five shell-vaulted niches divided by paired engaged Corinthian pilasters supporting a classical entablature and terminated by a conical tiled roof. Niches and pilasters were all identical in form, in line with Brunelleschi's avoidance of differentiated systems. Covered by thin hemispheric domes on their interior, the *tribune morte* served to cover the stairways leading up from the ground on the outer side of the piers with passage upward continuing in the adjoining foot of the drum.

Lost architectural works

Manetti reports that Brunelleschi was connected with the building of a house for his kinsman Apollonio Lapi on the Canto de' Ricci. The building on the site contains octagonal columns and masonry from the first half of the fifteenth century. Whatever remained of a chapel that Filippo built for Schiatta Ridolfi in San Jacopo Oltrarno disappeared in a baroque reconstruction in 1709. According to Manetti, it was next to the main chapel, open toward two sides (like the Barbadori Chapel) and covered with a melon dome (*a creste e a vela*). A rod, anchored at the center of curvature, was used to control the form of the vault during execution. The office of the Ufficiali del Monte (the funded debt of the state) in the Palazzo della Signoria was built by Brunelleschi in 1429. Manetti claims it was still to be seen at the end of the fifteenth century. Possible remains of a house near the Ponte Vecchio which, according to Manetti, Filippo built for the Barbadori in the Borgo San Jacopo were blown up by German sappers during World War II.

The perspective panels

Interest in the two perspective panels painted by Brunelleschi and described by Manetti has never waned. The frontal view of the Baptistery as seen from the cathedral was intended as a graphic illustration of the proportional relationships between similar visual triangles at a scale of about 1:60. Whether the perspective was constructed according to the procedure described in Alberti's *Della Pittura* is questionable. Brunelleschi may have painted over the reflection of the building mirrored in the silvered back of the half-braccia square panel described by Manetti. The proper distance effect was achieved by looking through a hole in the back of the panel and viewing the painting reflected in a mirror held half an arm's length away. It was the correct illustration of the proportional principle, not the perspective illusion which probably interested Brunelleschi. A second panel, showing the Palazzo della Signoria at an angle, cut out to be seen against real sky, had similar didactic purposes. The two panels, which were inventoried in the Medici collection at the end of the fifteenth century, have long since disappeared.

Works ascribed to Brunelleschi

The Vasari tradition, sometimes well-founded, often spurious, dies hard. The Palazzo Pazzi, the Palazzo Pitti, and the Badia in Fiesole continue to be listed, with more or less emphatic caveats, as works of Brunelleschi. We will discuss them here briefly in order to reject them all as works of the master.

Palazzo Pazzi. This important palace of Jacopo Pazzi, the son of Andrea Pazzi who commissioned the chapter house of Santa Croce, was probably begun around 1474 when the Pazzi became papal bankers and began their dissent from the Medici party which ended in the conspiracy of 1478 and tragedy. Plan, elevation, and detail, particularly the dolphin-decorated column capitals of the courtyard, indicate that this may be Giuliano da Sangallo's first major architectural commission upon his return from his youthful studies in Rome. Neither the attribution to Brunelleschi or to Giuliano da Maiano is sustainable.

Palazzo Pitti. If uniformity were a criterion of Brunelleschi's style, the Palazzo Pitti would qualify. But even though Brunelleschi restrains his vocabulary to the least number of differentiated parts, he is never monotonous nor does large scale in itself become the essence of his statements. The elements of the Palazzo Pitti amount to no more than this: a massive expanse of façade wall of enormous, almost cyclopic rusticated stone blocks, is penetrated on the ground level by three arched openings and four smaller rectangular mezzanine windows. The two upper floors are each broken by seven identical arched windows framed by rusticated arches and flanked by very slim, almost imperceptible jamb pilasters. There is none of the subtle play of profiled relief against smooth ashlars and of the proportional division of illuminative labor and the clear separation of wall, window, and pilaster-entablature functions which characterizes the simple but eloquent *sala magna* façade of the Palazzo di Parte Guelfa. It was built after 1458 and there is no basis whatever for assuming that an old Brunelleschi design was revived twelve years after Filippo's death.

Badia in Fiesole. That few scholars still attribute this complex to Brunelleschi is not surprising. That the church should ever have been connected with Filippo is a tribute to the persistence of the Vasari tradition in the face of a concept which is in complete contrast with all characteristic aspects of Brunelleschi's style in those buildings unquestionably designed and built by him. Once superficial similarities in arch profiles and Corinthian pilaster capitals are discounted, we have a barrel-vaulted nave lit by a cluster of three rectangular façade windows flanked by pendentive vaulted side chapels one step over the nave, each with an arched window. The transept, up four steps over the nave, is divided into three distinct parts: a central crossing bay covered with a pendentive vault, flanked by barrel-vaulted arms lit by clustered windows in their end walls. The choir, one step over the transept and wider than the nave, is barrel-vaulted and lit by a window cluster in its end wall. It was originally intended to receive additional illumination from side windows, high up under the entablature. No two adjoining spaces would have had the same plan, vaulting, or illumination. Not assimilated but sharply distinct parts make up this complex and variegated whole. It is novel, important, and influential. It is probably based on a concept or design of Leon Battista Alberti. Church and monastery were probably executed by the shop and circle of Bernardo Rossellino in the years between 1456 and 1466. It has nothing to do with Filippo Brunelleschi.

Brunelleschi and Florentine politics

The struggles between archiguelfs and new men (the recently wealthy without old family connections), the conflict between the established members of the Wool guild and the Ciompi, and the suppressed proletariat of wool industry workers were past history before Filippo was five years old. In the period from 1382 to 1434 a conservative government was in power, dedicated to rule by an inner circle of some two hundred old-line families and to the defense of Florentine interests abroad against the encroachments of Lombardy, Naples, Hungary, Venice, Genoa, and Siena. Filippo's father served this government and his son grew up in sympathy with its ideals and objectives. He served regularly in its councils from his twenty-third year and sat as a member of its highest executive organ, the Priors, in the May to June term of 1425. As chief architect of the cathedral cupola, he was called on repeatedly to counsel and supervise on the construction of fortifications (Pisa, Vicopisano) entrusted to the cathedral workshop. Brunelleschi received a patent from the Signoria for a wheel-driven river barge in 1421. He eventually held a contract for hauling marble from Pisa up the Arno for the cathedral *opera,* but the boat broke down near Empoli. His complex engineering project for diverting a river against Lucca during the war in 1430 failed, largely due to faulty dike construction beyond Filippo's control.

The subsequent decline in Brunelleschi's political career (he no longer appeared in the councils) has been attributed to the failure of the Lucca project. But the matter may be more complex than that. Brunelleschi was of the generation of his early architectural patrons, Giovanni de' Medici and Andrea de' Pazzi. These were men in the conservative and frugal tradition of fourteenth-century Florentine bankers, sound and competitive businessmen little given to pomp and luxury. They were Florentine patriots of the traditional stripe, groaning under their taxes, ready to avoid them if they could, but equally ready to pay when they had to preserve the republic. Everything we know about Brunelleschi indicates that he was in profound sympathy with the views and attitudes of this generation: ready to confront all problems with old-fashioned Florentine ingenuity and persistence, fundamentally attuned to the corporate ideals of the Florentine fourteenth century.

The revolutionary aspects of the San Lorenzo sacristy complex (burial of Giovanni di Bicci and Piccarda Bueri in the sarcophagus under the sacristy table) may be due to the particular intentions of Cosimo de' Medici. Filippo was outraged by the decorative additions made to the sacristy by Donatello and Michelozzo. Brunelleschi was apparently no longer associated with the building of San Lorenzo after the death of Giovanni di Bicci in 1429 and he received no further Medici commissions. The rumor of a rejected Brunelleschi project for the Medici Palace (based on a late source) accords with this fact. Aside from the early Medici and Pazzi commissions and the minor works for the Barbadori and Ridolfi, all other Brunelleschi projects were in the public domain: the Innocenti for Brunelleschi's own Silk guild; the offices for the Monte officials in the Palazzo della Signoria; the *sala* for the Parte Guelfa (perhaps allocated to him due to the influence of Andrea Pazzi, a prominent Guelf captain); the Angeli oratory for the Camaldolese order under the leadership of Ambrogio Traversari, a humanist in sympathy with Brunelleschi's ideas; Santo Spirito, financed with city money and, of course, the cupola of Santa Maria del Fiore and its appurtenances.

We have no basis for suggesting that Filippo's political sympathies were anti-Medicean. But his connections on his mother's side were with families (Spini and Aldobrandini) who suffered financial ruin and exile with the rise of the Medici party. His connections, personal and political, were with men of the older generation. His architectural vision appealed more to the men of that generation than to the rising younger group. The sons of Giovanni di Bicci and Andrea Pazzi had a taste for the more colorful variegated architectural style of Michelozzo and the shops which emanated from that circle such as Bernardo Rossellino's, all of them under the influence of the revolutionary architectural thought of Leon Battista Alberti. Brunelleschi's late commissions came either from the cathedral *opera* in which he was dominant or were in the public domain (Angeli and Santo Spirito) where the influence of strong independent personalities such as Fra Ambrogio Traversari and Neri di Gino Capponi, the major figure in the Santo Spirito quarter, may have proven decisive. The Santo Spirito design was for a church containing forty identical and equivalent chapels, following the older traditions of a republican partriciate of equivalent men.

It was less a matter of politics than of generations. Brunelleschi's architectural vision was basically an up-dated version of traditional Florentine schemes and this is what gave it its appeal. This conservative trend remained endemic in Florentine taste and reappeared in the last quarter of the fifteenth century in the architectural designs of Giuliano da Sangallo. Brunelleschi was, in the best sense, a man of the old school. Not Brunelleschi but Leon Battista Alberti was to be the revolutionary architectural theorist of the early Renaissance.

HOWARD SAALMAN

WORKS

The list of works was prepared by Shirley Stark.

1417–1434, Church of Santa Maria del Fiore (cupola); Begun c.1418, Church of San Lorenzo; 1418–1429, Church of San Lorenzo (sacristy); 1419, Ospedale degli Innocenti; Early 1420s, Barbadori Chapel, Church of Santa Felicita; Mid-1420s–early 1440s, Palazzo di Parte Guelfa (upper story; not completed); c.1425–1428, Pazzi Chapel (executed after 1442), Church of Santa Croce; 1429, Uffizzi del Monte, Palazzo Becchio; 1434, Church of Santa Maria degli Angeli (not completed); 1436, Church of Santo Spirito (completed after Brunelleschi's death); 1436, Santa Maria del Fiore (lantern of the cupola); 1439; Santa Maria del Fiore (*tribune morte*); Florence.

BIBLIOGRAPHY

The bibliography was prepared by Shirley Stark.

ARGAN, GIULIO C.   (1955)1978   *Brunelleschi.* Reprint. Milan: Mondadori.

Atti del Convegno Internazionale di Studi Brunelleschiani (Firenze, 16–22 ottobre 1977).   n.d.   Forthcoming publication.

Atti del I Congresso Nazionale di Storia dell' Architettura (Firenze, 20–31 ottobre 1977).   1978   Florence: Sansoni.

BATTISTI, EUGENIO   1976   *Filippo Brunelleschi.* Milan: Electa.

BENEVOLO, LEONARDO; CHIEFFI, STEFANO; and MAZZETTI, GIULIO   1968   "Indagine sul S. Spirito di Brunelleschi." *Quaderni dell' Istituto di Storia dell' Architettura, Università di Roma* 15:85–90.

BOZZONI, CORRADO, and CARBONARA, GIOVANNI 1977–1978   *Filippo Brunelleschi: Saggio di Bibliografia.* 2 vols. Rome: Istituto di Fondamenti dell' Architettura.

BRUCKER, GENE   1977   *The Civic World of Early Renaissance Florence.* N.J.: Princeton University Press.

BRUSCHI, ARNOLDO   1972   "Considerazioni sulla 'Maniera matura' del Brunelleschi: Con un' appendice sulla Rotonda degli Angeli." *Palladio* New Series 22:89–126.

BURNS, HOWARD   1971   "Quattrocento Architecture and the Antique: Some Problems." Pages 269–287 in R. R. Bolgar (editor), *Classical Influences on European Culture, A.D. 500–1500: Proceedings of an International Conference Held at King's College, Cambridge, April 1969.* Cambridge University Press.

BURNS, HOWARD   1979   "San Lorenzo in Florence Before the Building of the New Sacristy: An Early Plan." *Mitteilungen des kunsthistorischen Institutes in Florenz* 23:145–154.

CABLE, CAROLE   1981   *Brunelleschi and His Perspective Panels.* Monticello, Ill.: Vance.

DOUMATO, LAMIA   1980   *Filippo Brunelleschi: 1377–1446.* Monticello, Ill.: Vance.

ELAM, CAROLINE   1979   "The Site and Early Building History of Michelangelo's New Sacristy." *Mitteilungen des kunsthistorischen Institutes in Florenz* 23:155–186.

FABRICZY, CORNELIUS VON   1892   *Filippo Brunelleschi.* Stuttgart, Germany: Cotta.

FABRICZY, CORNELIUS VON   1907   "Brunelleschiana." *Jahrbuch der königlich preussischen Kunstsammlungen* 28:1–84.

FANELLI, GIOVANNI   1977   *Brunelleschi.* Florence: Becocci.

Filippo Brunelleschi: L'uomo e l'artista. Mostra documentaria.   1977   Florence: Archivio di Stato di Firenze. Exhibition catalogue.

FLORENCE, GALLERIA DEGLI UFFIZI, GABINETTO DEI DISEGNI E DELLE STAMPE   1977   *Disegni di fabbriche brunelleschiane.* Florence: Olschki. Exhibition catalogue.

FOLMESICS, HANS   1915   *Brunelleschi: Ein Beitrag zur Entwicklungsgeschichte der Frührenaissance-Architektur.* Vienna: Schroll.

GINORI-CONTI, PIERO   1940   *La Basilica di S. Lorenzo di Firenze, e la famiglia Ginori.* Florence: Olschki.

HERZNER, VOLKER   1974   "Zur Baugeschichte von San Lorenzo in Florenz." *Zeitschrift für Kunstgeschichte* 37, no. 2:89–115.

HEYDENREICH, LUDWIG HEINRICH   1931   "Spätwerke Brunelleschis." *Jahrbuch der preussischen Kunstsammlungen* 52:1–28.

HOFFMANN, VOLKER   1971   "Brunelleschis Architektursystem." *Architectura* 1:54–71.

HORSTER, MARITA   1973   "Brunelleschi und Alberti in ihrer Stellung zur römischen Antike." *Mitteilungen des kunsthistorischen Institutes in Florenz* 17, no. 1:29–64.

HYMAN, ISABELLE   1972   "Brunelleschi, Filippo." Volume 14, pages 534–545 in *Dizionario Biografico degli Italiani.* Rome: Istituto della Enciclopedia Italiana.

HYMAN, ISABELLE   1974   *Brunelleschi in Perspective.* Englewood Cliffs, N.J.: Prentice-Hall.

HYMAN, ISABELLE   1977   *Fifteenth Century Florentine Studies: The Palazzo Medici and a Ledger for the Church of San Lorenzo.* New York: Garland.

KEMP, MARTIN   1978   "Science, Non-science and Nonsense: The Interpretation of Brunelleschi's Perspective." *Art History* 1 no. 2:134–161. Contains a summary of earlier research on Brunelleschi's perspective panels.

KENT, DALE   1978   *The Rise of the Medici: Faction in Florence, 1426–1434.* Oxford University Press.

KLOTZ, HEINRICH   1970   *Die Frühwerke Brunelleschis und die mittelalterliche Tradition.* Berlin: Mann.

LASCHI, GIULIANO; ROSELLI, PIERO; and ROSSI, PAOLO A.   1962   "Indagine sulla Capella dei Pazzi." *Commentari* 13:24–41.

LUPORINI, EUGENIO   1964   *Brunelleschi: Forma e ragione.* Milan: Edizioni di Comunità.

MAINSTONE, ROWLAND   1977   "Brunelleschi's Dome." *Architectural Review* 162:156–166.

MANETTI, ANTONIO   1970   *The Life of Brunelleschi.* Introduction, notes, and critical text by Howard Saalman. Translated from Italian by Catherine Enggass. University Park: Pennsylvania State University Press.

Manetti, Antonio 1976 *"Vita di Filippo Brunelleschi" preceduto da "La Novella del Grasso."* Edited by D. de Robertis and G. Tarturli. Milan: Polifilo.

Mendes Atanasio, M. C., and Dallai, G. 1966 "Nuove indagine sullo Spedale degli Innocenti a Firenze." *Commentari* 17:83–106.

Miarelli-Mariani, Gaetano 1974–1976 "Il Tempio fiorentino degli Scolari: Ipotesi e notizie sopra una irrealizzata immagine brunelleschiana." *Palladio* New Series 23–25:45–74.

Molho, Anthony 1977 "Three Documents Regarding Filippo Brunelleschi." *Burlington Magazine* 119:851–852.

Nyberg, Dorothea F. 1957 "Brunelleschi's Use of Proportion in the Pazzi Chapel." *Marsyas* 7:1–7.

Prager, Frank D., and Scaglia, Gustina 1970 *Brunelleschi: Studies of His Technology and Inventions.* Cambridge, Mass.: M.I.T. Press.

Ragghianti, Carlo L. 1977 *Filippo Brunelleschi: Un uomo, un universo.* Florence: Valleschi.

Saalman, Howard 1958 "Filippo Brunelleschi: Capital Studies." *Art Bulletin* 40:113–137.

Saalman, Howard 1959 "Early Renaissance Architectural Theory and Practice in Antonio Filarete's Trattato di Architettura." *Art Bulletin* 41:89–106.

Saalman, Howard 1978 "San Lorenzo: The 1434 Chapel Project." *Burlington Magazine* 120:361–364.

Saalman, Howard 1980 *Filippo Brunelleschi: The Cupola of Santa Maria del Fiore.* London: Zwemmer.

Saalman, Howard n.d. *Filippo Brunelleschi: The Buildings.* Forthcoming publication.

Sanpaolesi, Piero (1941)1977 *La cupola di S. Maria del Fiore. Il progetto. La costruzione.* Reprint. Florence: Edam.

Sanpaolesi, Piero 1951 "Ipotesi sulla conoscenze matematiche, statiche e meccaniche del Brunelleschi." *Belle Arti* 2:25–54.

Sanpaolesi, Piero 1962 *Brunelleschi.* Milan: Il Club del Libro.

Thoenes, Christof 1972 "Sostegno e adornamento: Zur sozialen Symbolik der Säulenordnung." *Kunst Chronik* 25:343–344.

Waddy, Patricia 1970–1972 "Brunelleschi's Design for S. Maria degli Angeli in Florence." *Marsyas* 15:36–45.

Zervas, Diane Finiello 1979 "Filippo Brunelleschi's Political Career." *Burlington Magazine* 121:630–639.

BRUNNER, ARNOLD WILLIAM

Arnold Brunner (1857–1925), born in New York City, received his early education in New York and England before he entered the Massachusetts Institute of Technology in 1877. Upon graduation in 1879, he entered the office of George B. Post, where he remained for five years. He then spent the years 1883–1885 studying abroad. Upon his return to New York, he formed a partnership with Thomas Tryon. This alliance produced the Studio of Daniel Chester French (1888) and Temple Beth-El (1890) in New York. In 1898, the year after the dissolution of his partnership, Brunner won the competition for Mount Sinai Hospital in New York, the 1901 competition for the Cleveland Federal Building, and the 1910 competition for the Department of State Building in Washington (never built). Upon winning these commissions, he became known as an architect who specialized in large, severe schemes, executed in a style that owed much to Roman classicism. Brunner was also well-known as a city planner, providing plans or studies for Baltimore; Denver, Colorado; and Rochester and Albany, New York.

Steven McLeod Bedford

WORKS

1888, Daniel Chester French Studio (with Thomas Tryon); 1890, Temple Beth-El (with Tryon); 1898, Mount Sinai Hospital; New York. 1901, Federal Building, Cleveland, Ohio. 1906, Public Baths; 1913, Montefiore Hospital; *1915, Lewisohn Stadium; 1917, Barnard Hall, Barnard College; New York.

BIBLIOGRAPHY

Aitken, R. I. (editor) 1926 *Arnold Brunner and His Work.* New York: American Institute of Architects.

BRUYN, WILLEM DE

Architect, engineer, and magistrate and son of a head mason at court, Willem De Bruyn (1649–1719) became city architect of Brussels in 1685, a position he held until his death. His responsibilities included the reconstruction of the city after the bombing by the French in 1695. His architectural style adapted the classical edicts to the Flemish taste and followed the more moderate principles of the baroque of Brabant.

Pierre Lenain
Translated from French by Shara Wasserman

WORKS

*1696–1697, Butcher Market (reconstruction); 1696–1698, Crab House (restoration); 1696–1698, Fortune House (restoration); 1696–1698, Hermitage House (restoration); Brussels.

BIBLIOGRAPHY

Fierens, Paul 1945 *La Grand Place de Bruxelles.* Brussels: Cercle D'Art.

Martiny, Victor Gaston 1980 *Bruxelles: L'Architecture des origines à 1900.* Brussels: Vokaer.
Van Ackere, Jules 1972 *Belgique Baroque et Classique.* Brussels: Vokaer.

BRYANT, GRIDLEY J. F.

Gridley James Fox Bryant (1816–1899), a leading figure in the Boston Granite school, pioneered in the development of the large architectural office, through building type specialization, and the use of labor saving devices such as the standardized plan. He presided over the largest architectural office in Boston in the third quarter of the nineteenth century enjoying a practice that was regional if not national in scope.

The eldest child of Gridley Bryant, the engineer, railroad pioneer, and granite contractor and trained in the office of Alexander Parris and Loammi Baldwin (c.1832–1837), Bryant dated his professional success from the Mechanics Bank Building in South Boston, commissioned while still in Parris's employ. On his own by the fall of 1837, Bryant designed his first commercial blocks in the 1840s, the most important being perhaps the massive granite Long Warf Bonded Warehouse (1846). Railroad termini, however, seem to have been his first area of specialization. In 1847, he designed the Boston and Maine Depot at Salem, Massachusetts, and he is generally credited with the innovative station of the Old Colony Railroad in Boston in the same year. By the early 1850s, Bryant had added school and courthouse design to his office's area of expertise, but he achieved his greatest success of the decade in asylum architecture. His Charles Street Jail (1848–1851) in Boston, designed in conjunction with the penal reformer Louis Dwight, integrated the cumbersome inside cell block of the "Auburn System of Prison Discipline" with the radial plan of the rival "Pennsylvania System." The resulting cruciform configuration received immediate acclaim as a seminal design and became the first executed American project to be published in the British architectural periodical *The Builder.* Bryant adapted the Charles Street plan to a wide range of institutional types starting with the Deer Island Almshouse (1849) and by 1870 comprising a total of thirty asylum projects.

As a commercial architect, Bryant was responsible for 152 buildings in Boston's central business district that was devastated by the fire of 1872; he was commissioned to rebuild 111. Bryant's practical brand of architecture was popular with Boston merchants and led to such major commissions as the massive Beebe Block (1861). A statistical as-

*Bryant.
City Hall.
Boston.
1861–1865*

sessment of his other work, counts nineteen state capitol and city hall projects, ninety-five courthouses, asylums, or schools, sixteen custom houses or post offices, and eight churches. Preferring to superintend construction in later years, Bryant seems to have given his associates a free hand in design. Hence, such important office commissions as the Boston City Hall (1861–1865) have been attributed to his collaborator Arthur D. Gilman. The two major figures associated with Bryant were Gilman and Louis P. Rogers. Charles A. Cummings was among the many who began their careers in the Bryant office.

Robert B. MacKay

WORKS

1838, Abbot Lawrence House; *1846, Long Warf Bonded Warehouse; Boston. *1847, Boston & Maine Depot, Salem, Mass. *1847, Old Colony Railroad Station; 1848–1851, Suffolk County (Charles Street) Jail; 1849, City Almshouse, Deer Island; Boston. *1850, Massachusetts State Prison Extension, Charlestown, Mass. 1850–1851, City Almshouse, Cambridge, Mass. 1851, Norfolk County Jail, Dedham, Mass. 1851, State Reform School, Cape Elizabeth, Maine. 1851–1852, Hampshire County Jail, Northampton, Mass. 1853, Essex County Jail, Lawrence, Mass. 1853, Mount Auburn Cemetery Tower, Cambridge, Mass. *1853–1854, Massachusetts State House Extension; 1855–1857, Mercantile Wharf Building; Boston. 1856–1857, Androscoggin County Courthouse and Jail, Auburn, Maine. 1856–1857, Maine State Seminary, Lewiston. 1857, State Street Block, Boston. 1857–1859, Kennebec County Jail, Augusta, Maine. 1858, Cheshire County Courthouse, Keene, N.H. *1858–1859, Iowa State Penitentiary Extension, Fort Madison, Iowa. *1861, Beebe Block; *1861–64, Boston City Hospital; 1861–1865, City Hall; Boston. 1864, New Hampshire Statehouse Extension, Concord, N.H. *1865, Horticultural Hall, Boston. *1870, Michigan State Prison Extension, Jackson, Mich. *1870, Mutual Life Insurance Company,

Hartford, Conn. *1880, Cony High School, Augusta, Maine. 1884, Parker House Extension, Boston.

BIBLIOGRAPHY

BAILEY, HENRY T. 1901 "An Architect of the Old School." *New England Magazine* 25:326–348.

BRYAN, JOHN M. 1972 "Boston's Granite Architecture." Unpublished Ph.D. dissertation, Boston University.

BUNTING, BAINBRIDGE 1967 *Houses of Boston's Back Bay.* Cambridge, Mass.: Belknap.

CUSHMAN, EDWARD WESLEY (compiler) n.d. "A Complete Catalogue of Plans, Specifications, Architectural Drawings, Photographs, etc. The Property of Gridley J. F. Bryant, Esq. Architect, 28 State Street, Boston. In custody of Henry T. Bailey, North Scituate, Mass., 1890." Unpublished manuscript, University of Oregon, Eugene.

GIEDION, SIGFRIED 1941 *Space, Time and Architecture.* Cambridge, Mass.: Harvard University Press.

HITCHCOCK, H. R., and SEALE, WILLIAM 1976 *Temples of Democracy: The State Capitols of the U.S.A.* New York: Harcourt.

KILHAM, WALTER H. 1946 *Boston After Bulfinch.* Cambridge, Mass.: Harvard University Press.

MACKAY, ROBERT B. 1980 "The Charles Street Jail: Hegemony of a Design." Unpublished Ph.D. dissertation, Boston University.

BRYCE, DAVID

Born into the world of small builders in late Georgian Edinburgh, David Bryce (1803–1876) rose largely through his own talent and industry to become the undisputed head of the architectural profession in Victorian Scotland and the principal of its most influential teaching office. In independent practice for almost fifty years, he was to work on over 120 country house commissions, many for clients of the very first rank. His known commissions exceed 230 buildings.

Bryce was a bachelor, large, self-confident, brusque in manner, and driven by an almost demonic energy in his pursuit of architectural success. Between 1829 and 1850, he was closely associated with WILLIAM BURN, first as a clerk (though he already undertook private work) and from 1841 as Burn's junior partner. From Burn, who was very much a professional architect, he acquired precise business habits and much of the art of design, yet his distinctive contribution to the vocabulary of Victorian forms—the Scottish Baronial style—was in essence Bryce's creation alone. In the Scottish Baronial mansion—designs like Kimmerghame (1851), The Glen (1855), Craigends (1857), or Castlemilk (1863)—Bryce pioneered the development of large, loosely disposed houses, carefully planned to serve exactly the needs of their various inhabitants—family, servants, and guests—yet romantically composed as a mixture of the more flamboyant elements of Scottish sixteenth-century architecture. R. W. Billings's *Baronial Antiquities of Scotland,* published between 1845 and 1852, provided much of the detail of these designs, such as crow-stepped gables, armorial plaques, towers, and turreted bartizans, yet the admixture and bold arrangement of elements by Bryce was quite new and was to have reverberations reaching throughout Britain and even to Australia, Canada, and the United States.

Though celebrated for his country house design, Bryce was careful to preserve a practice that was broadly based with commissions for ecclesias-

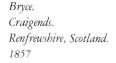

Bryce.
Craigends.
Renfrewshire, Scotland.
1857

tical and commercial work and for public buildings as well. For these, he usually employed an Italianate classical style, at first closely modeled on the palazzo manner of CHARLES BARRY, then modulating into a more vigorous nineteenth-century baroque which reached its apogee in Saint George's West Church (1867–1869) and in the Head Office of the Bank of Scotland (1864–1871), both in Edinburgh. Bryce was also one of the first British architects to revive the French château style, a trend which developed naturally out of his Scottish Baronial work and which left two major monuments in the great country house of Kinnaird Castle, Brechin, Angus (1853–1857) and the famous Scottish public school, Fettes College, Edinburgh (1863–1869). Bryce became a Fellow of the Royal Institute of British Architects in 1845 and was elected a Fellow of the Royal Society of Edinburgh and of the Royal Scottish Academy in 1856. He was architect to the Masonic Order in Scotland and a member of the exclusive New Club, Edinburgh, whose premises he enlarged in 1859. Bryce had a large collection of European architectural pattern books; it was acquired by the Art and Architecture Library of George Washington University, St. Louis, Missouri, in 1932.

ALISTAIR ROWAN

WORKS

1841, Seacliffe, East Lothian, Scotland. *1846, Western Bank; 1846–1849?, British Linen Bank; Saint Andrew Square, Edinburgh. 1846–1850, Balfour Castle, Orkney, Scotland. *1847, Inchdairnie, Fife, Scotland. 1847, 1854, Capenoch, Dumfriesshire, Scotland. 1848–1852, Hamilton Palace Mausoleum, Lanarkshire, Scotland. *1851, Kimmerghame, Berwickshire, Scotland. *1852, Panmure House, Angus, Scotland. 1853–1857, Kinnaird Castle, Angus, Scotland. 1855, 1874, The Glen, Peebleshire, Scotland. 1856, Shambellie, Kirkcudbrightshire, Scotland. 1856, Torosay Castle, Isle of Mull, Scotland. *1857, Craigends, Renfrewshire, Scotland. 1858–1861, Cullen House, Banffshire, Scotland. *1859, New Club, Princes Street; Edinburgh. 1863–1869, Castlemilk, Dumfriesshire, Scotland. 1863–1869, Fettes College; Edinburgh. 1864–1869, Ballikinrain Castle Stirlingshire, Scotland. 1864–1871, Bank of Scotland Head Office, The Mound; 1867–1869, Saint George's West Church; Edinburgh. 1869, Broadstone Castle, Renfrewshire, Scotland. 1869, Meikleour, Perthshire, Scotland. *1870, Cortachy Castle, Angus, Scotland. 1872, Gala House, Selkirkshire, Scotland. 1874–1876, Union Bank, George Street, Edinburgh.

BIBLIOGRAPHY

BILLINGS, ROBERT W.   1845–1852   *The Baronial and Ecclesiastical Antiquities of Scotland.* Edinburgh: Blackwood.

FIDDES, VALERIE, and ROWAN, ALISTAIR (compilers) 1976   Pages 11–131 in *David Bryce 1803–1876: Catalogue of an Exhibition to Mark the Centenary of Scotland's Great Victorian Architect.* University of Edinburgh, Talbot Rice Arts Centre.

"The Late Mr. David Bryce, R.S.A."   1876   *The Builder* 34:507–508. Includes a list of 116 works.

ROWAN, ALISTAIR   1970   "Capenoch, Dumfriesshire." *Country Life* 148:394–397.

ROWAN, ALISTAIR   1977   "Castlemilk, Dumfriesshire." *Country Life* 162:350–353, 422–425.

ROWAN, ALISTAIR   1982   *The Building of Shambellie: The Story of a Victorian Building Contract.* Edinburgh: Royal Scottish Museum.

BRYDON, J. M.

Born in Dunfermline, Scotland, John McKean Brydon (1840–1901) studied in Liverpool, Italy, and with DAVID BRYCE of Edinburgh before joining Campbell Douglas and JOHN JAMES STEVENSON in Glasgow (c.1863–1866). After working (1867–1869) for WILLIAM E. NESFIELD and R. NORMAN SHAW in London, Brydon helped to found the firm of Wallace and Cottier, furniture designers and decorators, before enjoying a successful architectural practice. His first major building, Saint Peter's Hospital, Covent Garden (1883–1884), reflected interest in Queen Anne, but Chelsea Vestry Hall (1885–1887), London, anticipated the revival of English baroque in the 1890s which Brydon advocated in his timely lecture, "The English Renaissance" (1889), and in his designs for Chelsea Polytechnic (1891–1895) in London and important municipal buildings in Bath. Brydon died before his major commission, the Local Government Board Offices, London (1898–1901), had risen above the foundations.

HILARY J. GRAINGER

WORKS

1883–1884, Saint Peter's Hospital, Covent Garden; 1885–1887, Chelsey Vestry Hall; 1887, Congregational Church (with James Cubitt), West Kensington; 1889, The Free Library, Chelsea; 1889–1890, Hospital for Women, Euston Road; London. 1891–1895, Municipal Buildings, Bath, England. 1891–1895, South West London (Chelsea) Polytechnic, London. 1896–1897, Victoria (Municipal) Art Gallery and Library, Bath, England. 1896–1899, London School of Medicine for Women, Handel Street; 1898–1901, Local Government Board Offices (not completed until 1912 by Henry Tanner), Parliament Square; London.

BIBLIOGRAPHY

"Architecture—A Profession or an Art?"   1891   *The Architect* Nov. 27:330–331.

BRYDON, J. M.   1889   "The English Renaissance." *The Builder* 56:147, 168.

GIBSON, JAMES SIVEWRIGHT   1900–1901   "The Late John McKean Brydon." *Journal of the Royal Institute of British Architects* 8:400–405.

GIROUARD, MARK 1977 *Sweetness and Light: The Queen Anne Movement, 1860-1900.* Oxford: Clarendon.

LOFTIE, WILLIAM JOHN 1905 "Brydon at Bath." *Architectural Review* 18:3–9, 50–59, 146–154.

MINTY, E. ARDEN 1906–1907 "London's New Public Buildings." *Architectural Review* 10:210–218.

PHYSICK, JOHN FREDERICK, and DARBY, MICHAEL 1973 *Marble Halls: Drawings and Models for Victorian Secular Buildings.* London: Victoria and Albert Museum.

STAMP, GAVIN, and AMERY, COLIN 1980 *Victorian Buildings of London: 1837–1887, An Illustrated Guide.* London: Architectural Press.

BRYGGMAN, ERIK

Erik Bryggman (1892-1955) was second only to ALVAR AALTO as a pioneer in Finland of the international modern style first seen there at Turku's seventh-centenary exhibition of 1929 on which the two architects collaborated. Bryggman's work was influenced especially by that of the Swedish GUNNAR ASPLUND, but retains echoes of the neoclassicism strongly established in Finland throughout the preceding century by CARL LUDWIG ENGEL. Later, his architecture became more romantic.

Bryggman practised in Turku where most of his important buildings are located. Best known is his concrete-framed white-walled Resurrection Chapel (1939–1941) on the southeastern outskirts of the city, notable for its lyrical interior with views into the forest outside.

J. M. RICHARDS

WORKS

1929, Hospits Betel (hotel), Turku, Finland. 1929–1936, Sports Institute, Vierumäki, Finland. 1933–1936, Library, Åbo Akademi; 1938, Sampo Insurance Offices; 1939–1941, Resurrection Chapel; Turku, Finland.

BIBLIOGRAPHY

RICHARDS J. M. 1978 *800 Years of Finnish Architecture.* Newton Abbot, England: David and Charles.

WICKBERG, NILS ERIK 1962 *Finnish Architecture.* Helsinki: Otava.

BUCHSBAUM, HANNS

Hanns Buchsbaum (c.1390–c.1456), whose name is also spelled Puchsbaum, Puchspaum, Puxbaumb, and Buxbom, was a late Gothic Austrian architect who worked in the Danube region. He is first mentioned in an Ulm lodgebook in 1418. His life and work are not documented again until 1443, when he designed and directed the building of the parish church in Steyr. In 1446, he was appointed master of the works at the Cathedral of Saint Stephen in Vienna. In 1451 and 1452, he and Lorenz Spenyng rebuilt the *Spinnerin am Kreuz,* a monument outside Vienna. In 1456, Spenyng was appointed master of the works at Saint Stephen's and hence it is presumed that Buchsbaum died shortly before that date.

There is controversy over the role Buchsbaum played at the Cathedral of Vienna and which extant plans can be attributed to him. The years between 1430 and 1443 are not documented, but Bruno Grimschitz placed Buchsbaum at Saint Stephen's during this period. Hans von Prachatitz, who was *parlier* under his father Peter between 1420 and 1429, was master from 1430 until his death in 1439. Grimschitz suggests that Buchsbaum worked as *parlier* possibly from 1430 and more certainly after 1440 until he became master of the works in 1446. Thus, it would be possible to attribute to Buchsbaum the Puchlein baldachin dated 1434 and the early plans for the building of the north tower, made before the first corner stone laying in 1444. Buchsbaum has also been credited with the vaulting of Saint Stephen's and the designs for the Barbara Chapel.

More recently, Hans Koepf has challenged Grimschitz's attributions, questioning Buchsbaum's connection with Saint Stephen's between 1430 and 1446. He has also removed from Buchsbaum's oeuvre the Zapolya Chapel in Donnersmark which he dates to 1478. Until Buchsbaum's contribution at Saint Stephen's is outlined more securely, it remains difficult to assess his importance as an architect.

JOANNE E. SOWELL

WORKS

1443–1446, Parish Church, Steyr, Austria. (A)1446–1456, Saint Stephen (vaulting and Barbara Chapel), Vienna. 1451–1452, Spinnerin am Kreuz, near Vienna.

BIBLIOGRAPHY

GRIMSCHITZ, BRUNO 1947 *Hans Buchsbaum.* Vienna: Wolfrum.

KOEPF, HANS 1969 *Die gotischen Planrisse der Wiener Sammlungen.* Vienna: Böhlaus.

Die Kunst der Donauschule. 1965 Linz, Austria: Abbey of Saint Florian. Exhibition catalogue.

PERGER, RICHARD 1970 "Die Baumeister des Wiener Stephansdomes im Spätmittelalter." *Wiener Jahrbuch für Kunstgeschichte* 23:66–107.

BUCKLAND, WILLIAM

Born in Oxford, England, and apprenticed for seven years to a London joiner, William Buckland (1734–1774) produced woodwork of exceptional quality and undertook design and construction in Virginia and Maryland. The scope of his activity is indicated by the varied work force of craftsmen he apprenticed and indentured and by his sizable collection of fifteen architectural books.

Buckland was engaged in 1755 to finish George Mason's Gunston Hall (1755–1759) in northern Virginia, for which he devised fashionable Palladian (see ANDREA PALLADIO) and even Chinese and Gothic motifs. Endorsed by Mason (on the back of the indenture) as "a complete Master of the Carpenter's & Joiner's Business," Buckland by 1761 was at work not far away in Richmond County at Mount Airy (1761–1764). There he received payment from John Tayloe apparently for the elaborate woodwork, of which only a few fragments survived the fire of 1844. Nearby, Buckland's workmen contributed minor updating to Landon Carter's Sabine Hall (1766). Buckland remained until 1772 in Richmond County, where he also undertook small public buildings.

Other construction in Virginia's Northern Neck possibly involved Buckland and his shop: Elmwood (after 1767), Nanzatico (1767–1769), Menokin (1769–1771), and Blandfield (1769?–1772?) all are handsomely finished houses built by relations of Mason, Tayloe, and Landon Carter when Buckland lived in the vicinity. His letter of 1771 to Robert Carter III of Nomini Hall verifies an interest in such commissions for which he had available "some of the Best Workmen in Virginia."

During this same period, in Maryland the Upton Scott (begun 1762?) and John Ridout (begun 1765?) Houses in Annapolis and Governor Horatio Sharpe's Whitehall (begun 1764) were each finished with elaborate woodwork that Buckland's shop certainly was capable of producing. The uncertainty about these and other poorly documented projects is underscored at the Annapolis house of the Brice family (begun 1766), the important parlor carving of which has recently been reattributed from Buckland's hand to a William Frampton on evidence in a newly discovered account book.

In 1771, Buckland was engaged by Edward Lloyd of Annapolis to provide some of the grand interiors for the unfinished house he had purchased from Samuel Chase. This important commission (1771–1773), for which Buckland supervised part of the construction, caused him to relocate in the growing Maryland capital. He produced equally magnificent carving across the street at the Hammond-Harwood House (1773–1774), for which he also provided the design rendered in his portrait.

Buckland's death at age forty prematurely ended an important career that had advanced beyond the bounds of his early training.

WILLIAM M. S. RASMUSSEN

WORKS

1755–1759, Guston Hall (interior woodwork and porches), Fairfax County, Va. 1761–1764, Mount Airy (interior woodwork), Richmond County, Va. 1771–1773, Chase-Lloyd House (interior woodwork); 1773–1774, Hammond-Harwood House; Annapolis, Md.

BIBLIOGRAPHY

BEIRNE, ROSAMOND RANDALL, and SCARFF, JOHN HENRY 1958 *William Buckland, 1734–1774: Architect of Virginia and Maryland.* Baltimore: Maryland Historical Society.
MONROE, ELIZABETH BRAND 1975 "William Buckland in the Northern Neck." Unpublished M.A. thesis, University of Virginia, Charlottesville.
PIERSON, WILLIAM H., JR. 1977 "The Hammond-Harwood House: A Colonial Masterpiece." *Antiques* 3:186–193.
TATUM, GEORGE B. 1977 "Great Houses from the Golden Age of Annapolis." *Antiques* 3:174–185.
WATERMAN, THOMAS TILESTON 1946 *The Mansions of Virginia: 1706–1776.* Chapel Hill: University of North Carolina Press.

BUCKLIN, JAMES C.

James C. Bucklin (1801–1890) is chiefly known for his reserved and monumental Greek Revival buildings which, as noted by TALBOT HAMLIN, (1964) "showed what truly urbane and reticent grandeur the Greek Revival could produce with simple means." Born in Pawtucket, Rhode Island, he was apprenticed to JOHN HOLDEN GREENE and in 1822 went into partnership with William Tallman. The firm was responsible for some of the outstanding buildings not only in Providence but in other parts of the country. RUSSELL WARREN joined the firm in 1827 and THOMAS A. TEFFT did so for a short time in the 1850s, but Bucklin always played a key role. Documents, together with his handsome drawings, indicate that he was largely responsible for an impressive number of the firm's projects, including the Westminster Street front of the Providence Arcade (1828), the Westminster Congregational Street Church (1829, and Manning Hall (1833, modeled after the Temple of Diana Prophylea in Eleusis), all dignified full-porticoed temples; the monumental Washington Row Buildings (1843); and Brown University's President's House (1840), Rhode Island Hall (1840), and the Rhode Island Historical Society Cabinet (1843), the last three stuccoed non-porticoed Greek Revival structures.

Throughout his career, Bucklin's work retained the monumental dignified quality of his Greek Revival buildings. Representative are the Providence Marine Corps Artillery Company (1840), a heavy stuccoed-over-stone Gothic Revival building with twin crenelated fore-turrets for which there is a drawing signed by Bucklin; the massive red-brick Greek Revival-derived Providence High School (1842–1843); the third Howard Building, with its pared-down Italianate detailing (1859); and the magnificent granite Victorian Hoppin-Homestead Building (1875).

ANTOINETTE F. DOWNING

WORKS

1828, Chatham County Courthouse (with William Tallman and Russell Warren); 1828, Clarke Slater House; Savannah, Ga. 1828, Westminster Street (front), Providence Arcade; *1829, Westminster Street Congregational Church; *1831, James Bucklin House; 1833, Manning Hall, Brown University; 1836, Beneficient Congregational Church (alterations); 1838–1844, Shakespeare Hall; 1838–1845, Exchange Bank Building; *1840, President's House, Brown University; *1840, Providence Grammar School; 1840, Providence Marine Corps Artillery; 1840, Rhode Island Hall, Brown University; *1842–1843, Providence High School; 1843, Rhode Island Historical Society (cabinet); *1843, Washington Buildings; *1859, Third Howard Building; *1860, Blackstone Building; 1860, Phenix Building; 1867, Providence Athenaeum (alterations); *1869, Thomas Davis House; *1870, Reynolds Block; c.1870, S. S. Sprague House; *1875, Hoppin-Homestead Building; Providence, R.I.

BIBLIOGRAPHY

BELL, DONNA 1969 "The Green Revival Architecture of James C. Bucklin." Unpublished M.A. thesis, University of Delaware, Newark.

CADY, JOHN HUTCHINS 1957 *Civic and Architectural Development of Providence: 1636–1950.* Providence: Book Shop.

FEDERAL WRITERS PROJECT 1937 *Rhode Island: A Guide to the Smallest State.* Boston: Houghton Mifflin.

The Greek Revival in the United States. 1943 New York: Metropolitan Museum of Art.

HAMLIN, TALBOT F. (1944)1964 *Greek Revival Architecture in America.* Reprint. New York: Dover.

Historic American Buildings Survey Catalog. 1941–1963 Washington: National Park Service.

HITCHCOCK, H. R. (1939)1969 *Rhode Island Architecture.* Cambridge, Mass.: M.I.T. Press.

James C. Bucklin. 1908 Volume 2 in *Representative Men and Old Families of Rhode Island.* Chicago: Beers.

PIERSON, WILLIAM H., JR. (1970)1976 *American Buildings and Their Architects: The Colonial and Neo-Classical Styles.* New York: Anchor.

STONE, EDWIN MARTIN 1860 *Mechanics' Festival.* Providence, R.I.: Knowles.

WRISTON, BARBARA 1941 "Thomas Tefft: Progressive Rhode Islander." *Collections of the Rhode Island Historical Society* 34, no. 2:60–61.

BUFFINGTON, LEROY SUNDERLUND

Leroy Sunderlund Buffington (1847–1931) was born in Cincinnati, Ohio. After graduation from high school, he entered the architectural office of Anderson and Hannaford in Cincinnati. By the end of 1869, he had worked as a draftsman in Cincinnati, in Terre Haute, Indiana, and in Cleveland, Ohio, and had been both student and teacher at the Ohio Mechanics Institute. Buffington moved to Saint Paul, Minnesota, in 1871 to serve as superintendent of the United States Customs House and superintendent of construction on government buildings. Shortly after moving to Saint Paul, he entered into partnership with Abraham M. Radcliffe. The partnership continued until the mid-1880s, but there is no evidence that the partners ever collaborated as designers.

Buffington established his Minneapolis office in 1873 and met with immediate success. The design of his 1874 mansion for Charles F. Pettit was heavily influenced by the LUDOVICO VISCONTI and HECTOR M. LEFUEL additions to the Louvre of 1852–1857 and by RICHARD MORRIS HUNT's house for the Wetmore family in Newport, Rhode Island, of 1872–1873. The Pettit house was not an original or noteworthy design, but it was not carpenter-vernacular architecture; in Minneapolis, it established Buffington as an arbiter of taste. Between 1877 and 1888, he designed mansions for John, George, Charles, and Fred Pillsbury, a publishing plant for the Minneapolis Tribune, schools, hotels, office buildings, and a theater. The designs for both the West Hotel (1881–1884) and the Pillsbury "A" Mill (1880–1882) were noted in the national press. Buffington's greatest success was confined to the 1870s and 1880s, but he continued to practice until near the time of his death in 1931. Very few of the commissions from the major period of practice survive, but Pillsbury "A" Mill, the large productive capacity of which made Minneapolis the primary flour milling center of the world from 1882 until after World War I, survives, and four buildings on the Minneapolis campus of the University of Minnesota still stand.

Buffington's national reputation in the late nineteenth century stemmed largely from his claim to have invented the system of metal skeleton construction that made the modern high building possible. In May 1888, he was granted patents on his system of metal frame construction, and he subsequently devoted much time to unsuccessful litigation in protection of his patent rights. These claims again attracted national attention briefly at the end of the 1920s, when Rufus Rand, an old friend and owner and developer of the Rand (now

Dain) Tower, voluntarily paid fees to Buffington in recognition of his patent rights. However, research carried out in the 1930s and published in *The Art Bulletin* seems to offer conclusive proof that Buffington's system never saw application.

DONALD R. TORBERT

WORKS
*1874, Charles F. Pettit House; *1877–1878, George Pillsbury House; *1877–1878, John Pillsbury House; 1880–1882, Pillsbury "A" Mill; *1881–1884, West Hotel; *1881–1886, Boston Block; *1883–1884, Minneapolis Tribune Publishing Company; 1885–1886, Eddy Hall, University of Minnesota; 1887–1889, Pillsbury Hall (designed by HARVEY ELLIS), University of Minnesota; *1888, Fred Pillsbury House (designed by Ellis); 1889, Nicholson Hall (designed by Ellis), University of Minnesota; 1893–1895, Burton Hall, University of Minnesota; Minneapolis, Minn.

BIBLIOGRAPHY
BRANHAM, MURIEL B.(editor) 1941 "Memories of Leroy S. Buffington." Unpublished M.A. thesis, University of Minnesota, Minneapolis.
BRANHAM, MURIEL B. 1944 "How Buffington Staked His Claim." *Art Bulletin* 26, Mar.:13–24.
MORRISON, HUGH 1944 "Buffington and the Invention of the Skyscraper." *Art Bulletin* 26, Mar.:1–2.
TSELOS, DIMITRI 1944 "The Enigma of Buffington's Skyscraper." *Art Bulletin* 26, Mar.:3–12.

BULFINCH, CHARLES

Charles Bulfinch (1763–1844) was America's first native-born professional architect. During a practice that spanned the crucial forty years between the Constitutional Convention and the election of Andrew Jackson, he developed a national style expressive of the simplicity, frugality, and aspiring dignity of the new United States. Because of his many and varied public and private commissions, as well as his innovative ideas on town planning, structural materials, heating, and sanitation, his work served as the model for architectural construction in the Federalist and Republican periods. Bulfinch was not simply a New England architect, and his national reputation culminated in his appointment as architect of the Capitol. His style was carried by overland pioneer builders to the frontier settlements as far west as the Missouri River and reached the Pacific coast through the memory of Massachusetts seafarers. Working from a pragmatic combination of colonialism, patriotism, and economy, Bulfinch shaped an American architecture that successfully met the building requirements of the first generations engaged in developing the material and spiritual resources of the new nation.

Bulfinch was born into a wealthy and cultivated Boston family whose divided loyalties mirrored those of the colonies at large. His maternal grandfather, Charles Apthorp, known as an ardent gentleman practitioner of architecture, began the library that was an important stimulus in the architectural development of his grandson. He also assisted in obtaining from his acquaintance PETER HARRISON the design for King's Chapel (1749–1758), one of the few structures of architectural significance in pre-Revolutionary Boston. Bulfinch's first known architectural effort, a sketch of a Corinthian column done when he was ten years old, might be a representation of the double row of coupled columns in King's Chapel, where his family worshipped.

More directly traceable is the influence of his uncles, Charles Ward Apthorp and the Reverend East Apthorp. The former was a talented amateur builder and the possessor of an important architectural library; the latter was assumed by contemporaries to be in line for the first American bishopric. Bulfinch was probably impressed by the important house his uncle built in Cambridge in 1765. Still called Apthorp House by its present owner, Harvard University, the building is believed to have been designed by Harrison. Apthorp House was one of the region's first buildings to embody English Palladianism, which, with the usual two-generation time lag, reached the American colonies at mid-eighteenth century. This self-consciously modern and stylistically striving house must have exerted considerable influence upon the young dilettante in search of models. Harrison's Boston and Cambridge work, along with the architectural folios in the libraries of Apthorp relatives, prepared Bulfinch for his impending encounter with Europe.

In contrast to the extreme royalist inclinations of the Apthorps, the Bulfinchs were patriots in the War of Independence. Bulfinch's life can be read in part as an attempt to promote the architectural reputation of his country both at home and abroad. He graduated from Harvard College in 1781, where he received training in mathematics and perspective, and discovered, through the folios of ROBERT WOOD and ROBERT ADAM, the neoclassical sources which informed his early work. It was probably at this time, too, that Bulfinch became acquainted with THOMAS DAWES, master builder, patriot, and future governor of Massachusetts. The degree of practical instruction given Bulfinch by Dawes is not known; what is certain is that they collaborated on Bulfinch's second recorded commission, the Washington Arch (1789) erected to commemorate the visit to Boston of the newly inaugurated president.

When Bulfinch was twenty-two years old, he embarked on a grand tour of Europe. This journey, planned in part by THOMAS JEFFERSON, included England, France, and Italy. The most surprising thing about this experience is that Bulfinch was captivated not by Europe's historic buildings but rather the most contemporary ones, especially those of Robert Adam, WILLIAM CHAMBERS, JAMES WYATT, JOHN SOANE, and ROBERT MYLNE. While staying in Paris as the protégé of Jefferson, Bulfinch was also impressed with modern French planning, particularly its organization for function and convenience.

Bulfinch introduced European neoclassical ideas into New England with the country house constructed in Somerville, Massachusetts, in 1792–1793, for Joseph Barrell. With this house, and the pavilion designed several years later in nearby Dorchester for the Francophile James Swan (1796), Bulfinch first differentiated room shapes and heights, compressed the traditionally wide colonial stairhall into a narrow enclosed space, and gave unusual attention to facilities for entertainment and service. Neoclassical planning had long been assimilated by those British designers who influenced Bulfinch. It is certain that what he saw in Europe, particularly in England, provided the inspiration for an American version of neoclassicism that brought, first to Boston and then to the country, a modest but luminous architecture expressive of republican priorities and aspirations.

Bulfinch returned to Boston in 1787 at a time when interstate rivalry was expressed in architecture in the construction of new state capitols, each intended as a material representation of the assumed pretensions of the former British colonies.

Implicit in this rivalry was the emergent problem of American cultural identity, which in architecture involved the search for a building form most appropriate to a new and independent nation, still acutely conscious of its colonial past. Virginia presumed to lead with construction of a capitol (1784–1789) at the newly created town of Richmond from a model by Jefferson. Based upon a recently restored ancient temple in the south of France, the Virginia capitol rejected the English tradition and proclaimed instead Augustinian Rome as the model for the new nation. Massachusetts, whose commercial interests identified her with England, and where every Virginian challenge was vigorously contested, turned to Bulfinch for a design that drew not upon antiquity but the most recent public buildings in London and Paris. Bulfinch's design rather than Jefferson's was the model for most subsequent state capitol construction.

The Massachusetts State House (1795–1797) is not only Bulfinch's most celebrated and influential work, it may be one of his earliest. Bulfinch submitted a design for the capitol in 1787; an elevation and plan survives, representing the State House substantially as built, but whether this represents the 1787 scheme is conjectural. The strongest possibility is that Bulfinch prepared only one basic design, and its subsequent alterations resulted from the inflation in building costs and the decision, in 1795, to change the location from a site adjoining the Common to one beneath the summit of Beacon Hill—an eminence already dominated by Bulfinch's Memorial Column (1790–1791). The Beacon Hill site could also explain the expansion of the State House dome from

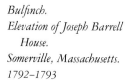

Bulfinch.
Elevation of Joseph Barrell
House.
Somerville, Massachusetts.
1792–1793

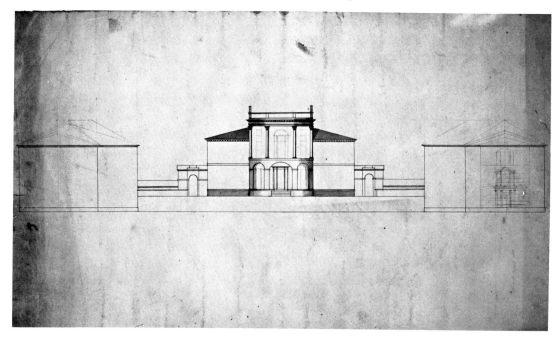

Bulfinch.
Massachusetts State House.
Boston.
1795–1797

one of typically shallow neoclassical proportions to the commanding hemisphere that stood out against the barren mound that then was the highest elevation in Boston.

Although the date of the actual working design of Bulfinch's capitol is unknown, its stylistic origins are determinable. None of Bulfinch's seventy or more subsequent projects reveal so clearly the influence of his European experience. The source of the design is the central portion of the river front of William Chambers's Somerset House (1776–1786) in London, admired for its monumentality and modernity. It is significant that Bulfinch, who is widely held to have been an architectural conservative, was so favorably affected by such a contemporary building. Like most architects in his time, he used classical precedents; but within this universal design formula, he was exceptional in his acceptance of whatever was new in the nature of style, usage, materials, and domestic economy. Because of this, and because he was so responsive to the nation's new social demands, he became a leader of the newly developed profession of architecture in the United States.

Bulfinch chose Somerset House as a model for the first modern building in the United States because it was designed for governmental offices and not, as in colonial precedent, merely a gentleman's house enlarged. And if, as has been suggested, he

was also influenced by the Ministry of Marine in the Place de la Concorde in Paris (completed 1763), it was because the monumental scale and bureaucratic planning of ANGE JACQUES GABRIEL's civic masterpiece represented another of the latest and most splendid means of housing the political life conceived by the ambitious young architect for his native state. Obviously inspired by neoclassicism in England and France, when Bulfinch was asked for a plan for what was destined to be the most important building in New England, he used the occasion to introduce this style to America. With the completion of the Massachusetts State House hardly ten years after that of its European prototype, the prevailing two-generation culture lag between the Old and New Worlds was reduced to a decade. Bulfinch's earliest designs therefore were revolutionary in helping to eliminate the historic–stylistic time lag between England and America.

The extravagant hopes that Bulfinch had for his country's architectural future were dramatically revealed in the Franklin Place project, completed in part between 1793–1795. The most ambitious urban housing scheme yet undertaken in the United States was conceived as an ellipse formed of two identical crescents each containing sixteen connected townhouses and facing one another for almost five hundred feet on either side of an en-

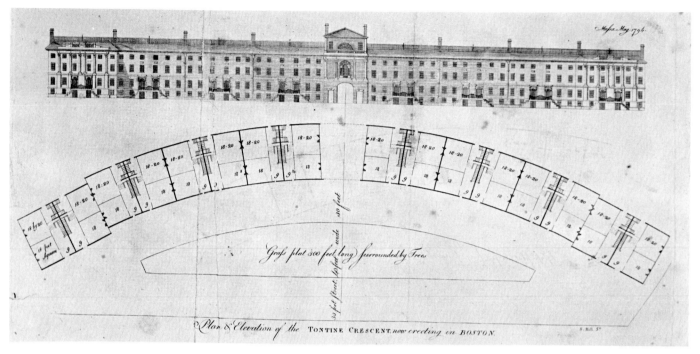

Grass plat 300 feet long, surrounded by Trees

Plan & Elevation of the TONTINE CRESCENT *now erecting in* BOSTON

Bulfinch.
Plan and elevation of the
Tontine Crescent.
Boston.
1793–1794

closed tree-lined oval of grass. Because of adverse economic conditions only one side of the ellipse was constructed: the Tontine Crescent (1793-1794).The complementary space was occupied by four double houses instead of a crescent, and the revised complex was graced at the eastern end by Boston's first theater (1793–1794).

The buildings in Franklin Place were uniform in scale and material, and reflected the stylistic movement in England to which the young Bostonian was particularly attracted. The crescent had two possible sources: the unexecuted plan by Robert Adam for two half circles of connecting houses designed as an extension of Portland Place in London, and the earlier crescents Bulfinch saw in Bath, whose impressions were preserved by a folio of engravings he carried home from Europe. Tontine Crescent was demolished in 1858; the curved section of Franklin Street alone bears testimony to that project which, according to the architect's follower and imitator ASHER BENJAMIN, "gave the first impulse to good taste; and to architecture, in this part of the country" (1833, preface). It also introduced neoclassical urban planning into the United States. Using this as his model, over the next two decades Bulfinch created a modern cityscape of terraced townhouses and business complexes, all executed in a unified design formula that made the Boston of his time the most beautiful city in America.

The Tontine Crescent was Bulfinch's most interesting and audacious scheme; even London did not then contain an oval plan of terraced houses. However, it exhausted the architect's financial resources and in 1795, with less than half of the

houses in the crescent sold, he was forced into bankruptcy. Bulfinch then attempted unsuccessfully to support his family as a professional architect fully committed to his practice, a role which he had come to initially as an amateur. By 1799, the leaders of Boston, sensible to the important civic but unremunerative role Bulfinch played in the development of their town, created the permanent posts of chairman of the Board of Selectmen and superintendent of police for him. Thus began an extraordinary conjunction of architect and administrator that continued for almost twenty years and is without parallel in modern history. As the Board of Selectmen constituted Boston's highest administrative body and almost its only source of authority, Bulfinch had to subordinate his architectural pursuits to his new public duties. While architecture continued to be part of his life—perhaps the most rewarding—his time, energy, and talent were increasingly expended in civic responsibility for health, safety, education, and planning. No part of the public life of his town was outside of Bulfinch's concern; Josiah Quincy, one of the early mayors of Boston wrote: "During the many years he presided over the town government, he improved its finances, executed the laws with firmness, and was distinguished for gentleness and urbanity of manners, integrity and purity of character" (1850, pp. 26–27).

This intimate relationship with the life of his town at every level gave Bulfinch a sense of the human dimensions of public planning and design where previously he had been concerned only with stylistic and technical considerations. This was earliest demonstrated in the Boston Almshouse

(1799–1801), designed in the first year of Bulfinch's appointment and then considered to be second in importance only to the State House among the buildings of Federalist Boston. The design shows the five-part plan and elevation, believed to have derived from Wyatt, subsequently used in most of Bulfinch's important public commissions. Typically, much of the contemporaneous praise for the Almshouse centered upon the attention Bulfinch gave to the convenience, comfort, and sanitary facilities of his administrative wards—the town's poor.

Bulfinch fulfilled his police duties in a similarly thorough and complete manner, transforming Boston's rudimentary police office into the town's most efficient administrative agency. He also designed county courthouses and state and county jails. The most important of these judicial structures was the Suffolk County Courthouse (1810–1812), the first of several splendid granite buildings. Bulfinch always preferred to use stone in civic and commercial commissions, and he prescribed it for the Hartford State House (1793–1796) as early as 1792. He had to wait for more than a decade, however, until the completion of the Middlesex Canal, when Chelmsford granite could be ferried from the interior, before he could employ it in the State Prison at Charlestown (1804–1805). He waited almost another decade before Boston's growth in wealth and power was reflected in significantly increased building budgets to enable him to specify its use for the Suffolk County Courthouse. This was a bold and austere design in which the somewhat thin neoclassical details, formerly employed for architectural effect, were subordinate to the material itself. Bulfinch introduced heavy, ornamental iron balconies as a foil to the stark simplicity of hammered granite surfaces. The Courthouse was a transitional building pointing the way to the great Greek Revival structures by

Bulfinch and his followers ALEXANDER PARRIS and SOLOMON WILLARD.

In other areas of civic life, the same pattern of architect and public servant prevailed. Bulfinch not only supervised the administration of Boston's unrivaled system of public education but designed many school buildings. Most notable was the Third Latin School (1812), a rational granite structure whose plain façade complemented the neighboring Suffolk County Courthouse. This was followed by another academic commission, Harvard's University Hall (1813–1814), for which Chelmsford granite was likewise prescribed. This handsome, understated building with large, many-paned windows, presaged the last structures Bulfinch designed for Boston: New South Church (1814) and Massachusetts General Hospital (1818–1823). The octagonal plan of New South was characteristic of the neoclassical era, recalling as it did the circular and octagonal spaces of ancient Rome; and its bold, textured walls were not only similar to the austere masonry of neoclassical England and France, but also repeated the similar treatment in the Suffolk County Courthouse. Because Boston churches by tradition required a steeple, Bulfinch adapted a simplified version of one of JAMES GIBBS's alternative designs for Saint Martin-in-

Bulfinch.
Drawing of Suffolk County
*   Courthouse.*
Boston.
1810–1812

Bulfinch.
Massachusetts General
*   Hospital.*
Boston.
1818–1823

the-Fields, London (1721–1726). However, the principal feature—a slender Roman Doric portico—is also a device remindful of English neoclassicism of the late eighteenth century. Saint Chad's, Shrewsbury (1796) is typical; and Saint Chad's is a circular church which relates it even further to New South.

The Massachusetts General Hospital was an even more forceful statement of the neoclassical plain style that began to distinguish American architecture in the early nineteenth century. Its design recalled the five-part plan of the Suffolk County Courthouse, as well as its cylindrical dome and sharply defined, unadorned openings. The major design element, however, was the portico which was similar to the one on New South Church except that it was larger and displayed a Greek Ionic order. The building is therefore a major example of the Greek Revival in the later work of Bulfinch. Although completely his design, the actual construction of the hospital was supervised after his departure for Washington by his pupil, Parris.

The plan, which reflected the humanitarian considerations that developed with the architect's experience in administering the affairs of his town, provided for a greater number of private rooms than was usual as well as smaller wards with special attention given to the patients' comfort and the convenience of the nursing staff. The Massachu-

Bulfinch.
India Wharf.
Boston.
1803–1807

setts General Hospital was one of the most universally esteemed buildings of the early republic, praised equally for the exterior beauty of the portico and the interior efficiency of the clinical amphitheater and advanced systems of lighting, ventilation, heating, and sanitation. The Bulfinch pavilion of this greatly expanded facility survives as one of the first and finest monuments to the American phase of Greek Revival architecture.

The greatest transformation worked upon Boston by Bulfinch resulted from the architect's responsibility for planning town growth. He leveled part of Beacon Hill to provide a better site for the State House and adjacent freestanding mansions designed for his friends. He also developed market squares and enormous complexes of wharves, stores, and warehouses; straightened streets, laid out parkways and malls, filled in the old water boundaries, and firmly shaped the outlines of the modern city.

The India Wharf project (1803–1807), for which Bulfinch supplied the plans, laid out the streets, and designed the buildings, was unrivaled in America at the time for scale and environmental consistency. Together with an addition on Broad Street, the complex consisted of more than one half mile of wharves, warehouses, and stores extending southeasterly from the foot of State Street facing the harbor. Because Chelmsford granite was not available in sufficient quantity when the enterprise was planned, brick was used above a stone basement; the trim was marble and sandstone. The design recalled the earlier Tontine Crescent with the central pavilion suppressed to a dominant bay arching a cross street. The over-all impression, especially as seen from the water, was one of massive solidity which conveyed an immediate sense of Boston's maritime importance. This same quality was evident at the Common, along whose eastern confines stretched Park Row (1803–1805) and the Colonnade (1810–1812). The latter contained nineteen houses built to a master architectural plan that specified uniformity in height and style, the whole complex held together by a continuous iron balcony at the second-story level supported by a line of slender stone columns. The eastern end of the Common has an affinity with the State House and the private dwellings Bulfinch designed for Beacon Hill.

Bulfinch's Beacon Hill houses also reflected the neoclassical buildings of England and France. The three houses designed for Harrison Gray Otis (over a period of thirteen years) best demonstrate the maturation of Bulfinch's characteristic residential architecture. The first (1795–1796), at the northern base of the hill, was originally enhanced, according to the architect's elevation, with several distinctive neoclassical forms that were omitted in the actual construction. The result is a foursquare colonial mansion with a hipped roof, the traditional Palladian window, and an old-fashioned plan with central hall and corner rooms. But when Otis commissioned a design several years later for a site on the southern slope of the hill, in Mount Vernon Street, the architect's scheme was more resolutely followed and the completed house (1800–1802) was a bold and ambitious expression of American neoclassicism. The rear entrance freed the front, with its view over the Common and the harbor, for a range of rooms whose importance was conveyed by modulated window heights. The façade was based upon the late eighteenth-century English townhouse pattern of a high, arched basement carrying above it several stories within an architectural order. Bulfinch's use of recessed arches on the ground floor and a balustrade to conceal the low line of the roof were much duplicated in subsequent Beacon Hill residential architecture. The third Otis house (1805–1808), further down the hill, was remarkable for the contrast between the entrance level and the monumental scale of the second or principal floor. A full story higher than Otis's previous house, the importance of the second floor was emphasized by the triple-hung windows Bulfinch here introduced to America. These huge windows, framed by attenuated pilasters and bracketed entablatures (the central one displaying the iconographic eagle and shield of the republic) gave the mansion the lofty, vertical appearance for which it became famous. The asymmetrical plan, conceived for comfort and privacy as well as for entertainment, followed the break with formal colonial precedent earlier utilized by Bulfinch. Long admired and much copied, the third Otis house represents the culmination of Bulfinch's efforts to establish a Federal residential style that complimented, equally with his public architecture, the promise of the newly independent nation.

The Church of Christ, Lancaster, Massachusetts (1816), served as Bulfinch's valediction to his native commonwealth. Almost his last significant structure in Massachusetts, the Lancaster church has been the subject in recent years of enthusiastic comment and inquiry. Its most celebrated component—the coeval arches of the portico—is not part of the original design but apparently an intuitive alteration by the master builder who supervised the work. The thin brick piers are a refinement of the basement arcade of the State House. The equally admired cupola was taken from an unexecuted design for Harvard's University Hall and used with characteristic economy for a different type of structure; the fan-patterned consoles repeat those first used in the Church of the Holy Cross,

Bulfinch.
Drawing of Colonnade.
Boston.
1810–1812

Bulfinch.
Third Harrison Gray Otis
House.
Boston.
1805–1808

Boston (1800–1803). The plan is essentially the same as one devised for the Congregational Church in Pittsfield, Massachusetts (1791–1793), an early Bulfinch design that definitively altered the plan and appearance of the traditional New England meetinghouse. Still in its rural setting

Bulfinch.
Church of Christ.
Lancaster, Massachusetts.
1816

and pristine condition, the Lancaster church is an outstanding example of integrity, simplicity, and economy.

Bulfinch's appointment by President James Monroe as architect of the Capitol in January 1818, led to a twelve-year residency in Washington which he later called the happiest period of his life. During this time, he was honored as the leader of his profession in America and welcomed equally into the ruling and contending political and social circles. With John Quincy Adams, John C. Calhoun, and Daniel Webster, Bulfinch formed the Unitarian Society, and designed its first church (1821–1822). He received the commission for the Federal Penitentiary, Washington (1827–1828), but it was to the task of completing the Capitol that Bulfinch most conspicuously brought the qualities of professional skill and experience and personal modesty and adaptability. By accepting political decisions that ran counter to stylistic preferences, such as increasing the height of the Capitol's dome, he brought to fulfillment a project

that had been stalled by controversy for a quarter of a century. Bulfinch's achievement was chiefly the harmonious completion of a scheme evolved by preceding architects; his direct contributions being limited to the design of the western portico, the old Library of Congress (burned 1851), the Dome, and the Capitol grounds.

The Maine State House (1829–1832; altered repeatedly after 1851) was Bulfinch's final architectural commission. The design was submitted a year before his return to Boston in 1830, where he passed the remaining fourteen years of his life. The similarity between the Maine and Massachusetts state houses was fostered by a legislative directive that the Augusta capitol replicate its famous Boston prototype on a reduced scale. The building material, however, was stone rather than brick, and expressed the full development of Bulfinch's expertise in the use of granite from its early employment in the Suffolk County Courthouse through the decade of work on the national Capitol.

As Bulfinch's last commission, the Maine State House provides a summation of his mastery of forms during an architectural education and practice of more than half a century. The earliest of these forms, the Palladian, is revealed in the proportion of the portico to the general scheme; the next, or neoclassical, is denoted in plan, scale, and detail; the final, or Greek Revival, is evinced in the lower dome and the use of the tholos as cupola. Bulfinch's formula—hemispherical dome and columnar frontispiece, and the use of granite as the most suitable building material—was virtually unchallenged as the mode for public architecture; it directly influenced the construction of subsequent state capitols nationwide. What Bulfinch began in Boston in the late eighteenth century as a regional idiom expressing the federal ideal became, in the nineteenth century, the prevailing architectural symbol of American democracy.

HAROLD KIRKER

WORKS

*1787–1788, Hollis Street Church; *1789, Washington Arch; *1790–1791, Beacon Hill Memorial Column; *1791–1792, Joseph Coolidge, Sr., House; Boston. *1791–1793, Congregational Church, Pittsfield, Mass. *1792–1793, Joseph Barrell House, Somerville, Mass. *1793, Charles Bulfinch House; *1793–1794, Theater; *1793–1794, Tontine Crescent; Boston. 1793–1796, State House, Hartford. 1795–1796, Harrison Gray Otis House; 1795–1797, State House; Boston. *1795–1799, Elias Hasket Derby House, Salem, Mass. *1796, James Swan House, Dorchester, Mass. 1796, Perez Morton House, Roxbury, Mass. *1798, United States Bank; *1799–1801, Almshouse; 1800–1802, Harrison Gray Otis House; *1800–1803, Church of the Holy Cross; 1802–1804, New North (now Saint Stephen's) Church; *1803, Suffolk Insurance Office; 1803–1804, Thomas

Amory House; 1803–1805, Park Row; *1803–1807, India Wharf; *1804–1805, Thomas Perkins House; Boston. *1804–1805, State Prison, Charlestown, Mass. 1804–1805, Swan Houses; 1805–1808, Harrison Gray Otis House; *1809, Boylston Hall and Market; *1810–1812, Colonnade; *1810–1812, Suffolk County Courthouse; *1812, Third Latin School; Boston. 1813–1814, University Hall, Harvard University, Cambridge, Mass. *1814, New South Church; *1814–1815, Blake–Tuckerman Houses; Boston. 1816, Church of Christ, Lancaster, Mass. 1817–1818, Pearson Hall, Andover, Mass. 1818–1823, Massachusetts General Hospital, Boston. 1818–1829, Capitol (completion); *1821–1822, Unitarian Church; *1827–1828, Federal Penitentiary; Washington. 1829–1832, State House (alterations), Augusta, Maine.

BIBLIOGRAPHY

BENJAMIN, ASHER (1833)1972 *Practice of Architecture.* Reprint. New York: Da Capo.

BULFINCH, ELLEN SUSAN (1896)1973 *The Life and Letters of Charles Bulfinch, Architect.* Reprint. New York: Franklin.

HITCHCOCK, H. R., and SEALE, WILLIAM 1976 *Temples of Democracy: The State Capitols of the USA.* New York: Harcourt.

KIRKER, HAROLD 1969 *The Architecture of Charles Bulfinch.* Cambridge, Mass.: Harvard University Press.

KIRKER, HAROLD, and KIRKER, JAMES 1964 *Bulfinch's Boston, 1787–1817.* New York: Oxford University Press.

PICKENS, BUFORD 1970 "Wyatt's Pantheon, the State House in Boston and a New View of Bulfinch." *Journal of the Society of Architectural Historians* 29:124–131.

PIERSON WILLIAM, H., JR. 1970 *American Buildings and Their Architects.* Garden City, N. Y.: Doubleday.

PLACE, CHARLES A. (1925)1968 *Charles Bulfinch: Architect and Citizen.* Reprint. New York: Da Capo.

QUINCY, JOSIAH 1852 *A Municipal History of the Town and City of Boston during Two Centuries.* Boston: Little, Brown.

BULLANT, JEAN

Overshadowed by PHILIBERT DELORME, Jean Bullant (c.1515/1520–1578) is known primarily for conferring a sense of grandeur on French Renaissance architecture. His birthplace is unknown, but it is probably Amiens, where he is descended from a long line of master masons in Picardy. From 1556 until his death in 1578, he resided at Ecouen. In the preface to his *Reigle géneralle d'architecture* (1564), he states that he made drawings of ancient monuments while in Rome (probably c.1540–1545); these include the "five orders of columns . . . which I have measured from the ancients." From c. 1553 he is recorded as architect in the service of the Connétable Anne de Montmorency at his Château of Ecouen, and it is here that he produced his major works. His earliest building here may be the North Wing, completed c. 1555, noted as much for its classical quotations as for its license in their transcription to both the terrace and court façades. On the latter the Tuscan and Doric orders correspond to the ideal of these orders "according to the doctrine of VITRUVIUS," but in reality, Bullant is copying the orders directly from ancient Roman models (Hoffmann, 1973–1974, p. 65). Bullant's Entry Pavilion on the east wing (1555–1560), no longer extant, but known through Du Cerceau's (see DU CERCEAU FAMILY) engraving, was designed to display the equestrian statue of the Connétable and express thereby his military élan—a portrait type which harks back to that of the king in the entry of the Louis XII wing at Blois. In its use of a triumphal arch motif and superimposed orders, the Ecouen pavilion is reminiscent of both Delorme's portal at Anet and the Porte Dorée at Fontainebleau. But Bullant's innovation is fully manifest in the frontispiece of the Court Portico of the south wing (c.1560), where for the first time in France the colossal order is used (its precedent probably in a façade with colossal pilasters for Fontainebleau, designed by Delorme in 1558; see Blunt, 1958, pp. 59–60); its details are based on the Corinthian order of the Pantheon's portico, but the total concept is anticlassical. In the niches of the Ecouen portico were the two white marble slaves of Michelangelo originally designed for Julius II's tomb, and presented to Montmorency by Francis I.

A penchant for monumental scale and sensitivity to site are also evident in Bullant's design of a Roman-type viaduct with its superimposed galleries built to span the valley at Fère-en-Tardenois, and thus to connect the château with its dependencies (1552–1562). The dramatic view created by arches twenty meters high bridging the ravine provides a romantic and picturesque context for the old thirteenth-century fortified castle in this hunting terrain acquired by Montmorency in 1528. The disposition of the façade with windows breaking through the entablature and the interlocking system of pediments over the windows at Fère is repeated in the gallery at Chenonceau. It is further developed with increasingly complex refinements in the Petit Château built for Montmorency at Chantilly (c.1560). Here is a French type of mannerism which finds its parallel in ANDREA PALLADIO's contemporary works in the Veneto.

When not preoccupied with commissions from Montmorency, Bullant profited from this respite in building activity to theorize about various technical matters. The writings he produced

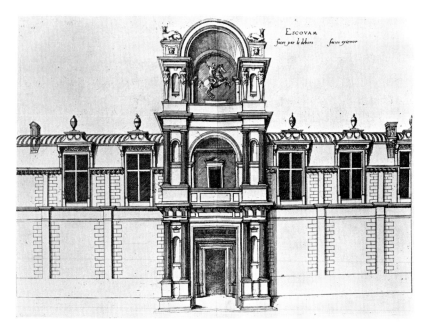

Bullant.
Engraving of Entry
*   Pavilion, Château*
*   Ecouen.*
France.
1555–1560

show him to be a compiler of extant works rather than an original thinker. The *Recueil d'horlogiographie* (1561) is compounded of tracts by S. Münster, O. Finé, and A. Dürer; the *Reigle géneralle d'architecture* is based on Jean Martin's translations of Vitruvius and LEO BATTISTA ALBERTI and on Barbaro's commentary on Vitruvius, although its format is modeled on that of SEBASTIANO SERLIO's books on architecture. In his preface to the *Reigle,* Bullant makes clear that he is writing for practicing architects, to whom he wishes to present a rational means of constructing the orders. To this end his magnificent illustrations present exact details of ancient orders. Bullant's concluding sonnet, "Aux architectes françois," instructs them to seek in the "oldest remains the true forms of ancient buildings."

Bullant first appeared in the royal accounts in 1557–1559 as "Supervisor of the King's Buildings." He does not reappear until after Delorme's death in 1570, at which point he became the architect to Catherine de' Medici. Much of his work under the queen mother is still in doubt—for example, his role in the construction of the Chapel of the Valois in Saint Denis, where Bullant was in charge of the execution of FRANCESCO PRIMATICCIO's original plan from 1572 to 1578. In the Tuileries (1571), Bullant probably completed the pavilion to the south (and perhaps, too, the one to the north) of Delorme's wing; this pavilion bears his stamp in the inventive arrangement of parts and in the superimposed orders of columns. Bullant's design of the Hôtel de la Reine (1572–1578) for the Queen is secure; its only remaining feature near the Halle au Blé (Corn Exchange) is the singular Doric column, twenty-five meters high, which was once supposedly used as an observatory,

a vestige of Catherine's astronomical interests. Bullant also supervised works in progress such as the schemes to enlarge the Château of Saint Maur (1575–1579) and added a gallery to the bridge over the Cher at Chenonceau (1576).

In Bullant's work, we are struck by the extraordinary refinement and beauty of the details (as was Charles Percier in 1794: "But what details! I have never seen among the moderns any better executed; they could be placed alongside the finest works of antiquity." Hoffmann, 1970, p. 87). Of note, however, is the fact that Bullant's ornamentation is not an organic part of the architecture. Nowhere is this more apparent than in his works at Ecouen, where despite the elegance of the parts, there is a lack of harmony within the ensemble. For the most part, Bullant's work is based on that of Delorme. Modern criticism has underscored as well his pedantic use of the orders which alternates with his delight in a certain fantasy and license manifest, for instance, in the surfeit of interlocking elements—perhaps the domain of a *maître maçon* or a stonecutter in the French Gothic tradition. In the late sixteenth century, this spirit is allied with a form of mannerism and a younger generation of architects; hence Blunt's proposal of 1520/1525 as a more likely birthdate (Blunt, 1953, p. 135).

NAOMI MILLER

WORKS

1546, Hôtel de Ligneris (now the Hôtel Carnavalet; with Pierre Lescot), Paris. 1552–1562, Viaduct and Gallery, La Fère-en-Tardenois, France. c.1555, North Wing; *1555–1560, Entry Pavilion; Château of Ecouen, France. 1558–1578, Hôtel Neuf de Montmorency; Paris. 1560, Court Portico, south wing, Château of Ecouen, France. 1560, Petit Château, Chantilly, France. 1562, Drawbridges, Château of Ecouen, France. 1568–1578, Tombs of the Connétable Anne de Montmorency, Church of Saint Martin, Montmorency; Paris. 1568–1573, Château of Gandelu (alterations), France. *1571, Southwest Pavilion, Tuileries; *1572–1578, Chapel of the Valois, Saint Denis; *1572–1578, Hôtel de la Reine (later the Hôtel de Soissons; column remains); Paris. 1573–1579, Château of Saint Maur (enlargement; supervisor), France. 1576, Chenonceau (enlargement of gallery over bridge; supervisor), France.

BIBLIOGRAPHY

BAUCHAL, CHARLES 1887 "Jehan II Bullant." Pages 83–86 in *Nouveau dictionnaire des architectes français.* Paris: André, Daly.
BERTY, ADOLPHE 1860 *Les grands architectes français de la Renaissance.* Paris: Aubry.
BLUNT, ANTHONY (1953)1977 *Art and Architecture in France: 1500–1700.* Harmondsworth, England: Penguin
BLUNT, ANTHONY 1958 *Philibert De l'Orme.* London: Zwemmer.
BLOMFIELD, REGINALD (1911)1974 *History of French*

Architecture: 1494-1661. Reprint of 1921 ed. 2 vols. New York: Hacker.

BULLANT, JEAN 1561 *Recueil d'Horlogiographie, contenant la description, fabrication, et usage des horloges solaires.* Paris: Sertenas.

BULLANT, JEAN 1562 *Petit Traicté de Géométrie et d'Horlogiographie pratique.* Paris: Cavellat.

BULLANT, JEAN (1564)1619 *Reigle générale d'Architecture des cinq manières de colonnes à scavoir, Tuscane, Dorique, Ionique, Corinthe, & Composite, à l'exemple de l'antique suivant les reigles & doctrine de Vitruve.* 2d ed., enl. Paris: De Marnef.

ERLANDE-BRANDENBURG, ALAIN 1981 *Musée National de la Renaissance: Château d'Ecouen.* Paris: Editions de la Reunion des Musées Nationaux.

GEBELIN, FRANÇOIS 1927 *Les Châteaux de la Renaissance.* Paris: Les Beaux-Arts.

HOFFMANN, VOLKER 1970 *Das Schloss von Ecouen.* Berlin: de Gruyter.

HOFFMANN, VOLKER 1973-1974 "Artisti francesi a Roma: Philibert Delorme e Jean Bullant." *Colloqui del Sodalizio* Series 2 4:55-68.

JAMES, FRANÇOIS-CHARLES 1968 "Jean Bullant: Recherches sur l'architecture française du XVIᵉ siècle." Pages 101-109 in *Ecole Nationale des Chartres: Positions des thèses . . .* Paris: Ecole des Chartres.

MONTAIGLON, ANATOLE DE 1857-1858 "Jehan Bullant architecte: Analyse du compte des dépenses faites pour le château des Tuileries en 1571." *Archives de l'Art Français* 9:1-13.

MONTAIGLON, ANATOLE DE 1858-1860 "Jean Bullant, architecte du connétable de Montmorency; actes extraits des registres de la mairie d'Ecouen (1556-1578)." *Archives de l'Art Français* 11:305-339.

PATTISON, MRS. MARK 1879 Volume 1 in *The Renaissance of Art in France.* London: Kegan Paul.

PLANAT, PAUL 1903 Volume 1 in *Encyclopédie de l'Architecture et de la Construction.* Paris: Dujardin.

BULLET, PIERRE

Pierre Bullet (1639-1716) was a favored student of FRANÇOIS BLONDEL, whose strict and sober French classical style he continued. Successful in Paris as a private architect, Bullet likewise worked on urban projects as architect to the king and the city of Paris. He was also active as an engineer and the author of several books, of which his *L'Architecture pratique* (1691) was the most influential. His skill as a draftsman involved him in work with JULES HARDOUIN MANSART. Bullet's much admired austere simplicity was eased by his son, JEAN BAPTISTE BULLET.

MYRA DICKMAN ORTH

WORKS

1669, Hôtel Jabach; 1672, Porte Saint Denis (with François Blondel); 1673-1679, Quai le Pelletier; 1674, Chapel of the Sorbonne (high altar); 1674, Porte Saint Martin; 1675, Saint Germain des Prés (transept chapels); 1681, Chapel of the Visitation Sainte Marie de Chaillot; Paris. 1681-1686, Archbishop's Palace (entry wing only); Bourges, France. *1681-1686, Château d'Issy, Issy-les-Molineux, France. 1682-1688, Chapel for the Novitiate of the Jacobins (now Saint Thomas Aquinas); *1684, Fountain Saint Michel; 1686, Hôtel Pelletier de Saint Fargeau; 1699-1707, Hôtel Crozat (now the Ritz Hotel), Place Vendôme; 1699-1707, Hôtel d'Evreux (now the Credit Foncier), Place Vendôme; 1700-1710, Hôtel de Terrat; 1701, Hôtel de la Force; 1702-1704, Hôtel Amelot de Chaillou; n.d., Hôtel de Chavigny; n.d., Hôtel de Montmorency; n.d., Hôtel de Vauvray; Paris.

BIBLIOGRAPHY

BABELON, JEAN-PIERRE 1978 "Une Oeuvre mal connue de Pierre Bullet à Paris: L'Hôtel Amelot de Chaillou puis de Tallard." *Bulletin Monumental* 136:325-339.

BIER, ERICH 1945 *Från Ludvig XIV's Paris: Pierre Bullet's originalritningar i Nationalmuseum.* Stockholm: Nationalmusei utställningskatalog.

BULLET, PIERRE 1665, 1675 *Maps of Paris.* Paris.

BULLET, PIERRE 1675 *Traité de l'usage de pantomètre.* Paris: Prallard.

BULLET, PIERRE 1688 *Traité de nivellement.* Paris: Langlois.

BULLET, PIERRE (1691)1973 *L'Architecture pratique.* Reprint. Geneva: Minkoff.

BULLET, PIERRE 1695 *Observations sur la nature et sur les effets de la mauvaise odeur des lieux ou aisances.* n.p.

HAUTECOEUR, LOUIS 1948 *Le règne de Louis XIV.* Volume 2 in *Histoire de l'architecture classique en France.* Paris: Picard.

LANGENSKIÖLD, ERIC 1959 *Pierre Bullet: The Royal Architect.* Stockholm: Almqvist & Wiksell.

STRANDBERG, RUNAR 1971 *Pierre Bullet et J.-B. de Chamblain à la lumière (des dessins) de la Collection Tessin-Hårleman du Musée National de Stockholm.* Stockholm: Faibografiska.

BULLET DE CHAMBLAIN, JEAN BAPTISTE

The Parisian architect, Jean Baptiste Bullet de Chamblain (1665-1726), began his career by assisting his father, PIERRE BULLET, in the construction of townhouses on the Place Vendôme in Paris behind the façades already erected by JULES HARDOUIN MANSART. Among these, Chamblain was solely responsible for the hôtel of Poisson de Bourvalais (1703-1707), and for the first great example of the *maison de plaisance,* the Château de Champs (1703-1707). Despite its dependency on the plan of LOUIS LE VAU's Château de Vaux-le-Vicomte (1656-1661), with an oval salon protruding from the garden façade, Champs was truly modern in its intimate scale, commodious arrangement of space, and simplicity of exterior decoration. Chamblain's achievements include ingenious variations on the rococo interior (Hôtel Dodun, Paris [after 1715]). His projects for the façades of Saint Roch (1722) and Saint Sulpice, Paris (after 1722), followed the two-storied rectilinear designs of FRANÇOIS MANSART's Convent of the Minimes, Paris (1657), and Hardouin Mansart's Primatiale in Nancy (1706).

ROBERT NEUMAN

WORKS

*1700, Hôtel Reich de Pennautier (with Pierre Bullet); 1703–1707, Château de Champs; 1703–1707, Hôtel de Poisson de Bourvalais; after 1715, Hôtel Dodun; Paris.

BIBLIOGRAPHY

HAUTECOEUR, LOUIS 1950 *Première moitié du XVIIIe siècle: Le style Louis XV.* Volume 3 in *Histoire de l'architecture classique en France.* Paris: Picard.

KALNEIN, WEND GRAF, and LEVEY, MICHAEL 1972 *Art and Architecture of the Eighteenth Century in France.* Baltimore: Penguin.

STRANDBERG, RUNAR 1962 "Jean-Baptiste Bullet de Chamblain: Architecte du roi." *Bulletin de la Société de l'Histoire de l'Art français* 1962:193–255.

STRANDBERG, RUNAR 1963 "Le Château de Champs." *Gazette des Beaux-Arts* 61:81–100.

STRANDBERG, RUNAR 1965 "Les Dessins d'architecture de Pierre Bullet pour la Place Vendôme et l'Hôtel Reich de Pennautier-d'Evreux." *Gazette des Beaux-Arts* 65:71–90.

BULLRICH, FRANCISCO

Francisco Bullrich (1929–) is an Argentine architect, painter, and critic. In 1962, together with CLORINDO TESTA and Alicia Cazzaniga, he designed the National Library in Buenos Aires, which has become a milestone in the development of contemporary architecture in Argentina.

FEDERICO F. ORTIZ

WORKS

1962, National Library, Buenos Aires. 1970, Argentine Embassy, Brasilia. 1976, Banco del Oeste Headquarters Building, Buenos Aires.

BIBLIOGRAPHY

BULLRICH, FRANCISCO 1963 *Arquitectura Argentina Contemporánea.* Buenos Aires: Ediciones Nueva Visión.

BULLRICH, FRANCISCO 1969a *Arquitectura Latinoamericana.* Buenos Aires: Editorial Sudamericana.

BULLRICH, FRANCISCO 1969b *New Directions in Latin American Architecture.* New York: Braziller.

BUNNING, JAMES BUNSTONE

Born in London, James Bunstone Bunning (1802–1863) was district surveyor of Bethnal Green and of the Foundling Hospital Estate from 1825. In 1839 he succeeded STEPHEN GEARY as architect to the London Cemetery Company. Appointed clerk of the works of the City of London in 1843, he designed a number of distinguished buildings, including the Coal Exchange (1847–1849).

JAMES STEVENS CURL

WORKS

1834, Royal Humane Society's Receiving House; *1835–1837, The City of London School; 1839–1840, Cemetery of Saint James at Highgate (Egyptian Avenue and chapels); *1847–1849, Coal Exchange; *1849–1851, City Prison; 1850–1855, Metropolitan Cattle Market (partly demolished); London.

BIBLIOGRAPHY

BOASE, FREDERIC 1965 Volume 1, column 474 in *Modern English Biography, Containing Many Thousand Concise Memoirs of Persons Who have Died Between the Years 1851–1900.* London: Frank Cass.

BUNNING, JAMES BUNSTONE 1839 *Designs for Tombs and Monuments.* London.

CANSICK, FREDERICK TEAGUE 1869 *A Collection of Curious and Interesting Epitaphs Copied From the Existing Monuments of Distinguished and Noted Characters in the Cemeteries and Churches of Saint Pancras, Middlesex.* London: J. Russell Smith.

CURL, JAMES STEVENS 1977 *Nunhead Cemetery, London. A History of the Planning, Architecture, Landscaping, and Fortunes of a Great Nineteenth-Century Cemetery.* London: Ancient Monuments Society.

CURL, JAMES STEVENS 1980 *A Celebration of Death. An Introduction to Some of the Buildings, Monuments, and Settings of Funerary Architecture in the Western European Tradition.* London: Constable.

BUNSHAFT, GORDON

Gordon Bunshaft (1909–) was born in Buffalo, New York, the son of Russian immigrants. After earning bachelor's and master's degrees in architecture at the Massachusetts Institute of Technology, he traveled through Europe and North Africa on a Rotch Traveling Fellowship from 1935 to 1937. In the fall of 1937, Bunshaft went to work for Louis Skidmore of Skidmore and Owings (Merrill joined the firm in 1939; see SKIDMORE, OWINGS, AND MERRILL) as a designer; he became a partner after he returned from service in World War II in 1946.

Bunshaft's first major building was the twenty-four-story Lever House (1952, New York), which opened a new era in skyscraper design. A glazed and masonry slab rests on a one-story mezzanine, supported by pilotis, that extends to the property boundaries above an open arcade with garden at the ground level. An open well over the garden admits light from above and permits a view of sky and building from below. The third floor is recessed setting off the tower from the mezzanine. The top three floors of the tower, housing machinery and equipment, are visually set off by a horizontal band in the curtain wall retaining a reference to the traditional skyscraper design of base, shaft, and capital.

By using only 25 percent of the available air space for its tower, Bunshaft introduced a new relationship between the skyscraper and its urban setting that had many imitators. An innovation in *architecture parlante,* Lever House is a gigantic advertisement for making "cleanliness commonplace," William Hasketh Lever's stated goal inscribed on a steel plaque on the building. When the building is cleaned, the glazed curtain walls that surround Bunshaft's slab on three sides are washed down (negotiated by movable scaffolding invented for this function) with the same product Lever markets to clean windows and kitchen fixtures in the home (Handy Andy was used first).

Innovative design and rich materials are hallmarks of Bunshaft's buildings, and one of his aims has been to promote an architectural vernacular appropriate to his time. His Manufacturers Hanover Trust Building (1954, New York) applied the glass cage to bank design, and the W. R. Grace Building (1973, New York) and the 9 West 57th Street Building (1974, New York) introduced the sloping façade as a new solution to the setback to satisfy zoning regulations. As a variant on the blank box, Bunshaft's National Commerical Bank (1982; Jeddah, Saudi Arabia) is an immaculate travertine tower from the outside. An equilateral triangle in plan, it surrounds a central environment with seven floors of glass-walled offices protected from direct sun by deep loggias.

Although best known for his skyscrapers, Bunshaft has said, "I like architecture you don't have to lie on your back to see," which is exemplified in the H. J. Heinz Company Plant in Pittsburgh (1952) and the headquarters for the Connecticut General Life Insurance Company (1957, Bloomfield). The Connecticut General Life complex of modern glass cages is adapted to a 250-acre landscaped garden reminiscent of the Picturesque tradition, with sculpture and a lake. It became influential as a suburban office building type. The American Institute of Architects gave it its first honor award in 1958, and numerous other citations for it have included those from the American

*Bunshaft.
Lever House.
New York.
1952*

Association of Nurserymen and Administrative Management Magazine.

The importance of environment applies to his urban projects as well. Although the design for the Chase Manhattan Bank and its plaza (1961, New York) was dictated largely by zoning considerations, aesthetic ones were also significant in relating the plaza to the surrounding area. To emphasize that, Bunshaft favors a vantage point from the southwest corner of 140 Broadway (Marine Midland Bank, 1967, New York) with its glazed black tower rising from an ample plaza, where Isamu Noguchi's red perforated cube dramatically punctuates the space. Looking eastward into the Chase plaza, Jean Dubuffet's great treelike sculpture, installed after 140 Broadway was completed, was placed on the axis of Cedar Street that unites these two sites.

Among Bunshaft's other major buildings are the Olivetti Building (originally Pepsi-Cola Building, 1960, New York), Emhart Corporation (1963; Bloomfield, Connecticut), Beinecke Rare Book and Manuscript Library (1963, Yale University; New Haven, Connecticut), Banque Lambert (1965; Brussels), American Can Company (1970; Greenwich, Connecticut), The Lyndon Baines Johnson Library and Sid W. Richardson Hall (1971, University of Texas; Austin), and The Hirshhorn Museum and Sculpture Garden (1974; Washington).

DONALD MARTIN REYNOLDS

WORKS

1952, H. J. Heinz Company Plant, Pittsburgh. 1952, Lever House, New York. 1957, Connecticut General Life Insurance Company, Bloomfield, Conn. 1960, Olivetti Building (originally Pepsi-Cola Building); 1961, Chase Manhattan Bank and Plaza; New York. 1963, Beinecke Rare Book and Manuscript Library, Yale University, New Haven. 1963, Emhart Corporation, Bloomfield, Conn. 1965, Banque Lambert, Brussels. 1967, Marine Midland Bank, New York. 1970, American Can Company, Greenwich, Conn. 1971, Lyndon Baines Johnson Library and Sid W. Richardson Hall, University of Texas, Austin. 1973, W. R. Grace Building, New York. 1974, Hirshhorn Museum and Sculpture Garden, Washington. 1982, Haj Terminal, King Abdul Aziz International Airport; 1982, National Commercial Bank; Jeddah, Saudi Arabia.

BIBLIOGRAPHY

"Banque Lambert, Brussels." 1966 *Architectural Review* 139, Mar.:193–200.
"Bâtiment de Bureaux, Bloomfield, Connecticut, Etats-Unis." 1965 *L'Architecture d'Aujourd'hui* 35, Mar.:8–10.
DREXLER, ARTHUR 1979 *Transformations in Modern Architecture.* New York: Museum of Modern Art.
FORGEY, BENJAMIN 1974 "An Auspicious Beginning." *Art News* 73, no. 8:40–42.
"Genetrix." 1957 *Architectural Review* 121, May:336–386.
"Heinz Centre, Hayes." 1965 *Architect and Building News* 228:255–261.
HITCHCOCK, H. R. (1958)1967 *Architecture: Nineteenth and Twentieth Centuries.* Baltimore: Penguin.
JACKSON, HUSON 1952 *New York Architecture: 1650–1952.* New York: Reinhold.
JACOBS, DAVID 1972 "The Establishment's Architect-plus." *New York Times Magazine,* July 23, pp. 12–23.
"The Library-Museum at Lincoln Center." 1966 *Progressive Architecture* 47, Apr.:176–183.
"L'Immeuble 'Lever House' à New York." 1953 *Techniques et Architecture* 12, nos. 3–4:6–9.
"Making It on Tobacco Road." 1976 *Progressive Architecture* 57, no. 6:78–83.
McCALLUM, IAN 1959 *Architecture U.S.A.* London: Architectural Press.
"No Corn in Iowa." 1966 *Progressive Architecture* 47, Feb.:144–151.
"Offices and Laboratories." 1965 *Architects' Journal* 142, Aug.:329–342.
STOLOFF, CYRIL 1975 "Art Gallery and Sculpture Garden, Washington, D.C." *Architect and Builder* 25, Mar.:18–20.
"The Team Approach." 1958 *Industrial Design* 5, Sept.:48–57.

BUONAMICI, GIANFRANCESCO

Gianfrancesco Buonamici (1792–1859) was the greatest exponent of the provincial architectural culture that took over in the northern regions of the papal states in the wake of their growing political and economic importance. His activity was centered in Ravenna, Rimini, Urbino, Pesaro, and Fano. These cities, all places favored by archbishops and papal legates, were to be given new ecclesiastic buildings and infrastructures. At first serviced from Rome, they came increasingly to rely on native artists until finally, in the second half of the eighteenth century, under the banner of early neoclassicism, decisive impulses went in the opposite direction, from the northern region to Rome.

In this respect, Buonamici's rise from a provincial to an academically recognized architect at the end of his career is typical. Although at first he was overshadowed by the achievements of the papal architect LUIGI VANVITELLI in the southern part of the Marches, in the end he took the latter's place in the region. His architectural undertakings nevertheless remain rather modest, in keeping with the amount of building possible. In his work, Buonamici ranges from close adherence to the Roman baroque in a variant of the Sant'Ignazio solution, as seen in the reshaping of the Ravenna Cathedral (the former Basilica Ursiniana) to original, small, centrally planned churches (Sant'Eufemia, Ravenna, 1742–1747; Santa Giustina, Ravenna, 1745–1747; San Bernardino, Rimini, 1759). In these, he shows a virtuosity in the command of curvilinear spatial construction and simple but effective profiling of door jambs, window jambs, and vaults which is reminiscent of the contemporary but qualitatively superior churches of BERNARDO ANTONIO VITTONE in the Piedmont. Buonamici's Peschiera (1746–1747) in Rimini was praised even by FRANCESCO ALGAROTTI. Numerous utilitarian buildings (lighthouse, Rimini, 1754; harbor, Pesaro, 1749) and restorations round out the work of Buonamici.

WERNER OECHSLIN
Translated from German by
Beverley R. Placzek

WORKS

1734–1745, Cathedral of Ravenna (remodeling and portico), Italy. 1741–1760, Church of the Hermit, Monte Giove, Fano, Italy. 1742–1747, Sant'Eufemia; 1745–1747, Santa Giustina; Ravenna, Italy. *1749, Harbor Buildings (lighthouse, warehouses, casino), Pesaro, Italy. 1754, Lighthouse; 1759, San Bernardino; Rimini, Italy. n.d., Harbor Works, Senigallia, Italy.

BIBLIOGRAPHY

BUONAMICI, GIANFRESCO 1748 *Metropolitana di Ravenna, Architettura del Cavaliere Gianfresco Buonamici Riminese, Accademico Clementino, co'disegni dell'antica Basilica, del Museo Arcivescovile, e della Rotunda fuori delle mura della città.* Bologna, Italy.
BUONAMICI, GIANFRESCO 1754 *Fabbriche fatte sul porto di Pesaro sotto la Presidenza dell'Eminentissimo e Rev. do Principe Sig. Cardinale Gianfresco Stoppani, Architettura del Cavaliere Gianfresco Buonamici.* Bolo-

gna, Italy: Lelio della Volpe.

OECHSLIN, WERNER 1969 "Contributo alla conoscenza dell'architettura barocca in Romagna: Fra G. Merenda e G. Buonamici." Pages 265–272 in *Atti del Congresso internazionale sul barocco, barocco europeo, barocco italiano, barocco salentino*. Lecce, Italy.

BUONAROTTI, MICHELANGELO

See MICHELANGELO.

BUONTALENTI, BERNARDO

Bernardo Buontalenti (1531–1608) served the Medici grand dukes in every conceivable form of artistic endeavor. His responsibilities covered all aspects of courtly life: civil and military architecture, sculpture, painting, mechanical devices, pyrotechnical displays, and even jewelry derived from Ming dynasty porcelains. His executed buildings were no less diverse. Fantasy and severity were mixed in almost equal measure, particularly in the invention of extravagant and ingenious architectural ornaments. Doors and windows fuse themes from nature and architecture, and sometimes natural elements overwhelm an entire structure. The Michelangelesque (see MICHELANGELO) forms which he developed were the point of departure for Florentine baroque architecture, and their influence extended to Roman projects like FRANCESCO BORROMINI's window studies for the Collegio di Propaganda Fide (1646–1667) in Rome.

Born in Florence, Buontalenti was adopted by the Medici court in 1547 after the death of his parents. He began his long career as a military architect with work on a number of notable Tuscan fortresses, among them Porto Ferraio (1560), Terra del Sole and Porto Ercole (1565), Pistoia (1575), and Livorno (1576, 1587–1589). With the growing political importance of Prince (later Grand Duke) Francesco de' Medici, whom he accompanied on a trip to Spain in 1563, Buontalenti's career was secure. In 1568, he was placed in charge of hydraulic engineering for Tuscany's canals and rivers.

Buontalenti's first major architectural commission was the renovation of a medieval house on the Via Maggio in Florence for Bianca Cappello (1567–1574), Francesco's mistress. The changes were not radical; a row of round windows were added in the attic, and the façade was decorated in graffiti by Bernardo Poccetti, likely from Buontalenti's own designs. The most remarkable elements, however, were the ground floor windows which were the first examples of Buontalenti's taste for unconventional detail (bats, shells) within a traditional design.

Buontalenti's masterpiece, the villa and garden at Pratolino, near Florence, was begun in 1569. The inconvenient, mountainous site tested his technical skills—the nearest water was five miles away—but it was particularly appropriate for Prince Francesco who prized solitude. The villa was placed roughly at the center of the property, thus taking advantage of a sharply sloping site with a magnificent view toward Florence. The two sectors of the garden were separated by a wall, and any visitor wishing to reach one from the other had to pass through the villa and the grottoes located in its base. The garden's true focal points—an informal arrangement of fountains, watercourses, statues, and grottoes—were found to either side of the main axis which ran through the entire complex. With a view toward Pratolino's splendor and magnificence, contemporaries rightly claimed that it rivaled the Villa d'Este in Tivoli.

The villa showed the more practical side of Buontalenti's architecture. Its plain, blocklike forms recalled Giuliano da Sangallo's (see SANGALLO FAMILY) Medici Villa at Poggio a Caiano (1485), and this included a tall base which raised the structure to take advantage of sunlight. Pratolino's T-shaped villa plan offered all rooms an exterior exposure. The configuration of the main apartments—a central hall flanked by separate suites—was derived from both Poggio a Caiano and the residential wing in BARTOLOMEO AMMANNATI's addition to the Pitti Palace. This planning feature was repeated in modified forms at the Artimino and Belvedere villas. Unfortunately, both the villa and garden at Pratolino were remodeled beyond recognition in the nineteenth century.

Villa design continued to be one of Buonta-

*Buontalenti.
Painting of Medici Villa and Gardens by Utens.
Pratolino, Italy.
Begun 1569*

Buontalenti.
Grotto, Boboli Gardens.
Florence.
1583–1593

lenti's main concerns throughout his career. In the sixteenth century the Medici court was away from Florence as often as it was in the city, moving from villa to villa according to the changing seasons. In general, the villas closest to Florence were used for the entertainment of both visiting dignitaries and the granducal family; more distant examples were less elaborate. Unlike ANDREA PALLADIO's villas which can be categorized by plan types, Buontalenti's villa plans follow no formal pattern. Most projects involved the remodeling of existing structures, and in many cases, the evidence of his participation is fragmentary at best. The early villa at Seravezza (c.1561–1565) is an example: the attribution to Buontalenti is based upon simple massing and rhythmic window patterns. At La Magia (1585) and Marignole (1587), modesty and simplicity were probably determined by existing constructions which were transformed into granducal hunting lodges. At Petraia (1575–1590), a castellated structure was transformed into a compact block with a symmetrically located tower and garden; at Castello (1592) alterations were executed on the existing villa, and the garden begun by Niccolo Tribolo and continued by GIORGIO VASARI was completed with a symmetrical series of terraces and parterres.

Apart from his villa renovations, Buontalenti continued to allow *quattrocento* models to suggest the form of later projects. The central loggia within a blocklike form, derived from Poggio a Caiano, was repeated in different ways at both the Belvedere villa in Florence (1594–1595) and at Artimino (1594). The first example, located atop a fortress adjacent to the Boboli gardens, served three important functions: a retreat where the Medici could enjoy splendid views of both city and countryside from its back-to-back loggias, a place of refuge for the granducal family in time of revolt, and the location of the Medici treasury. An earlier building, however, existed on the same site, and the extent of its influence on the Belvedere's form is uncertain.

Artimino, on the other hand, was conceived by Grand Duke Ferdinando I de'Medici as a hunting lodge commodious enough to accommodate the entire court. Of all Buontalenti's villas, it is the clearest derivation from Poggio a Caiano, but here bastions have been added to the villa's exterior corners, a visual conceit without any apparent necessity. Artimino's plan is otherwise elegant and functional, accommodating multiple suites of apartments on several floors with a minimum of vertical circulation.

Buontalenti's official commissions in Florence were even more varied. The plan of the Casino Mediceo (1574), Francesco's personal retreat, resembles the layout of the Pitti Palace, and its plain exterior is similar to Buontalenti's villas. Its architectural ornament, however, entered the realm of fantasy. In the ground floor windows, pediments and frames are supported by the heads of goats and bats respectively. The molding surrounding the main doorway appears to stand free of adjacent rustication; other details seem to have been cast and not carved. In both examples traditional elements of architectural grammar have been given new life by emphasizing the expressive qualities of stone, and in the case of the main portal, the frontispiece has been combined with a balcony to create a new door type.

At the same time, Buontalenti's ingenuity was directed toward a series of temporary architectural decorations which have long since disappeared. For the funeral of Cosimo I de' Medici in 1574, he designed a baldachin modeled on a Spanish *capella ardente* with a pyramidal canopy supported by herms at each of the four corners. Imitating Michelangelo's sculptures in San Lorenzo's New Sacristy, figures tenuously recline on volutes. The baldachin which he designed for the funeral of Francesco (1587) was scarcely different. For the baptism of Filippo de' Medici (1577), the Florentine Baptistry was to have been transformed with a series of monumental pilasters on volutes, but this proved to be too extravagant. For the main altar, a sense of movement was suggested in a series of concave and convex staircases, but available space did not permit this. The final solution employed straight staircases bent at angles.

In 1574 Buontalenti succeeded Vasari as architect of the Uffizi in Florence. The lower levels of this ingenuous project contained offices in the Florentine Magistracies, but the upper level as executed by Buontalenti was conceived as a private exhibition area for the most important pieces of the Medici art collection. His most important contribution was the Tribuna (1586), an octagonal room surmounted by a cupola and derived from VITRUVIUS's description of the Tower of Winds in Athens. Other additions to Vasari's design included a hanging garden with fountains on the roof of the Loggia dei Lanzi (1583), a staircase in the west arm which permitted access to the gallery and artist's workshops on the upper floors, and the first permanent theater in Florence (1586).

Buontalenti's most evocative and influential piece of architectural ornament, the Porta delle Suppliche (1580), was built at the end of one of the Uffizi's ground floor arcades. Its purpose was mainly ceremonial, since here Tuscans deposited their personal petitions to the Grand Duke. Early designs experimented with traditional elements such as curved and triangular pediments, but the executed project employed reversed scrolls to form a broken, V-shaped pediment over the main doorway. This curious solution was inspired by Michelangelo's tombs in the New Sacristy, but it may have had deeper significance as well. A contempo-

rary chronicler refers to broken frontispieces as indications of misfortune and death, and Buontalenti had already employed this motif in the baldachins for the funeral of Cosimo I to whom the doorway originally may have been dedicated. The connection between death and this motif escaped Buontalenti's followers who indiscriminately adapted it to palace portals and windows.

Even more exotic effects were achieved in the Grotta Grande (1583–1593) adjacent to the Pitti Palace, begun by Vasari in 1556. Pumice stone covers the vestige of a pediment and threatens the structural logic of an arch supporting reclining figures. The interior is no less bizarre with hidden sources of illumination, satyrs, and other figures.

Buontalenti's only known urban planning project in Florence was the unexecuted renovation of the square in front of the Pitti Palace. Likely the result of a competition sometime after 1590, it would have created a grandiose setting for the granducal palace. Practical requirements for carriages demanded an easy ascent up a sharp slope, and in all schemes this is achieved with symmetrical, curved ramps reminiscent of the Nymphaeum of the Villa Guilia in Rome.

Buontalenti's residential and ecclesiastical projects are less inspiring. In the Palazzo Non-Finito (1593–1600), only the boldly rusticated ground floor was completed. The new altar stairs for Santa Trinità (1574), now in Santo Stefano, were an architectural tour de force; the illusionistic carving of the steps made the main face too shallow for use while the stairs to the tribune were hidden to either side. After the demolition of the unfinished Gothic façade of Florence Cathedral in 1587, Buontalenti's entry in the competition for its replacement diminished the scale of the project with its tracerylike pattern of architectural ornament. A new façade of Santa Trinità (1592) was a weak derivation of LEON BATTISTA ALBERTI's façade for Santa Maria Novella. The Cappella dei Principi, the funerary chapel of the Medici grand dukes, occupied the last years of his life.

Throughout his career, Buontalenti provided stage designs and costumes for theatrical productions at the Medici court. In 1565, he assisted Vasari in the preparation of various intermezzi performed inside the Palazzo Vecchio, and in 1569, he provided costumes for Baldassare Lancia's production of *La Vedova*. The stage designs created in 1586 for the opening of the Medici theater surmounted technical difficulties by presenting scenes in hell and at sea; the 1589 intermezzi created in honor of Ferdinando's wedding included an artificial mountain designed to collapse at the end of the performance.

Artistic success did not bring financial rewards.

After six decades of service to the Medici, Buontalenti was aged, infirm, and had to beg for funds owed him. A letter to Ferdinando (1606) indicates that he had been overlooked, and Buontalenti, lacking food, refers to his poor household.

LEON SATKOWSKI

WORKS

1560, Fortress, Porto Ferraio, Italy. c.1561–1565, Medici Villa, Seravezza, Italy. 1565, Fortress, Porto Ercole, Italy. 1565, Fortress, Terra del Sole, Italy. 1567–1574, Bianca Cappello House (renovation), Florence. *Begun 1569, Medici Villa and Gardens, Pratolino, Italy. 1571, Bastion for Fortress, Pistoia, Italy. 1571, Fortress, San Piero, Sieve, Italy. *1574, Baldachin (for funeral); 1574, Casino Mediceo; 1574, Santa Trinità (altar stairs and choir; now in Santo Stefano); Florence. 1575, Fortress, Pistoia, Italy. 1575–1590, Medici Villa, Petraia, Florence. 1576, 1587–1589, Fortress, Livorno, Italy. 1578–1583, Villa, Poggio Francoli, Italy. 1580, Porta delle Suppliche, Uffizi; *1583, Loggia dei Lanzi (roof garden); Florence. 1583–1588, Granducal Palace, Pisa, Italy. 1583–1593, Grotto, Boboli Gardens; 1584, Santa Trinità (cloister); Florence. 1585, Medici Villa, La Magia, Italy. 1586, Theater; 1586, Tribuna; Uffizi, Florence. 1587, Baldachin (for funeral), San Lorenzo, Italy. 1587, Medici Villa, Marignole, Italy. 1588, Palazzo Vecchio (additions), Florence. 1592, Medici Villa, Castello, Italy. 1592, Santa Trinità (façade); 1593–1600, Palazzo Non-Finito; 1594, Corsini Palace; Florence. 1594, Medici Villa, Artimino, Italy. 1594–1595, Belvedere Villa; 1596, Santa Maria Maggiore (organ loft); Florence. 1605, Loggia dei Banchi, Pisa, Italy.

BIBLIOGRAPHY

BERTI, LUCIANO 1967 *Il principe dello studiolo: Francesco I dei Medici e la fine del Rinascimento fiorentino.* Florence: Edam.

BOTTO, IDA MARIA 1968 *Mostra di disegni di Bernardo Buontalenti (1531–1608).* Florence: Olschki.

FARA, AEMILIO 1979 *Buontalenti: architettura e teatro.* Florence: La Nuova Italia.

NAGLER, ALOIS 1964 *Theatre Festivals of the Medici: 1539–1637.* New Haven: Yale University Press.

VENTURI, ADOLFO 1939 "Bernardo Buontalenti." Volume II, part 2, pages 455–546, in *Storia dell'arte italiana.* Milan: Hoepli.

BURBA, GARIBALDI

Born in Vicenza, Italy, Garibaldi Burba (?–1925) was an engineer-architect known for his work in Rome, where he took part in the experiment of overcoming the traditional themes of the classicistic national style. He combined elements of northern eclectic and floral language with principles of modernism and internationalism and, as such, broke with the local architectonic culture, which was locked in an academical historicism. Above all in his villas (or rather in the *villino,* a new type of house for the upper middle class in Rome), he opposed the romantic re-evaluation of the medieval style. His best known work, Villino Cagiati (1913–1918) shows freedom of masses and pre-Raphaelite ornamentation. His design for a new square near Piazza Colonna was not built and that for the Convitto Nazionale's Palace was unfinished. The construction of his most monumental experiment, the Corte dei Conti Palace in Piazza Verdi, was halted for several years and completed for different use by an other architect.

ANTONINO TERRANOVA

WORKS

1886, House, via Q. Sella; 1913–1918, Corte dei Conti Palace (now the Poligrafico dello Stato; not completed until 1924 by others), piazza Verdi; 1913–1918, Cagiati villino, 25 via Orsini; Rome. 1918?, Palazzo della Fonte Hotel and Thermal Baths, Fiuggi, Italy.

BIBLIOGRAPHY

ACCASTO, GIANNI; FRATICELLI, VANNA; and NICOLINI, RENATO 1971 *L'architettura di Roma capitale: 1870–1970.* Rome: Golem.

DE GUTTRY, IRENE 1978 *Guida di Roma moderna: Architettura dal 1870 ad oggi.* Rome: De Luca.

PORTOGHESI, PAOLO 1968 *L'eclettismo a Roma.* Rome: De Luca.

SAPORI, FRANCESCO 1953 *Architettura in Roma, 1901–1950.* Rome: Belardetti.

BURGES, WILLIAM

The most brilliant art architect of his generation, William Burges (1827–1881) was born in London, the eldest son of Alfred Burges, a leading marine engineer. He was educated at King's College School, London, where his near contemporaries included Dante Gabriel Rossetti and William Michael Rossetti. Their drawing master was probably John Sell Cotman. Burges stayed on at King's College to study engineering but left after one year, in 1844, to take up articles in the office of EDWARD BLORE. Five years later, he moved to MATTHEW DIGBY WYATT's office as an "improver." In 1851, Burges formed an informal partnership with a fellow enthusiast for Gothic, Henry Clutton. But the influence of A. W. N. PUGIN was greater than any of these: Burges always revered that "wonderful man."

From 1849 onward, Burges traveled regularly and extensively in Europe: northern and southern France; Italy and Sicily; Greece and Turkey; Belgium, Holland, Switzerland, Germany, and Spain. He also studied vicariously the arts of Japan, India,

Scandinavia, and North Africa. During the 1850s and 1860s, he built up an international reputation as a medieval archaeologist—though he lacked EUGÈNE EMMANUEL VIOLLET-LE-DUC's systematic atic mind—and developed a highly personal style, an eclectic compound based on French, Italian, Arabic, Japanese, Pompeian, and Assyrian sources. He was especially intrigued by the Islamic permeation of Gothic and by pagan survivals in Christian art. The thirteenth century, in particular, was Burges's chosen field, and he modeled his style of draftsmanship on the famous sketchbook of VILLARD DE HONNECOURT in the Bibliothèque Nationale, Paris. For visionary drawings, however, notably his "St. Simeon Stylites" (1860), his model was Albrecht Dürer.

Burges's career was astonishingly diverse but unhappily brief. His early competition triumphs (Lille Cathedral [1855]; Crimea Memorial Church [1856]) proved abortive. He won his first major commission for Saint Finbar's Cathedral in Cork in 1863, but he died in 1881. His style did not develop from commission to commission. Once established after twenty years' preparation, his design language had merely to be applied, and he applied and reapplied the same vocabulary with increasing subtlety and gusto. Like Tennyson, he reused and refashioned his favorite dodges again and again. His range was formidable: he designed not only buildings, but stained glass, metalwork, ceramics, mosaic, sculpture, textiles, jewelry and furniture. Several of his most extraordinary designs remained unexecuted: a multidomed art school for Bombay in "a kind of . . . quasi-Orientalising Gothic" (1865–1866); a controversial scheme to decorate the interior of Saint Paul's Cathedral, London, with polychrome marble and Byzantine mosaics (1870–1877); and a competition project for London's new Law Courts (1866–1867) which, in planning and silhouette, combined lucidity and drama to an exceptional degree. Such missed opportunities had their saving grace: Burges was rescued from GEORGE GILBERT SCOTT's prolixity, from GEORGE E. STREET's overproduction.

As an architectural theorist, Burges was neither original nor consistent. But his very confusion is valuable: in numerous lectures and public statements he spoke on behalf of the mid-Victorian generation, a generation bewildered by novelty and confused by change, a generation of architects whistling in the dark. Despite his engineering background, Burges's aesthetic was essentially atectonic. He would have applauded EDWIN LUTYENS's aphorism: "architecture begins where function ends." "The Civil Engineer," Burges admitted, "is the real nineteenth-century architect." But engineering alone, he believed, was not

Burges.
Castell Coch.
Near Cardiff, Wales.
1875–1881

architecture. In his early years he followed A. J. Beresford-Hope's doctrine of "progressive eclecticism." And early French—rather than Italian or English Gothic—seemed to him the most suitable matrix for a Victorian style. He admired especially its "boldness, breadth, strength, sternness and virility." But in the 1860s, the excesses of popular Gothic led him to despair: the New style, he admitted in 1865, "may perhaps take place in the twentieth century, it certainly . . . will not occur in the nineteenth." During the 1870s, however, Burges refused to follow his contemporaries in rejecting Gothic for Queen Anne. In 1875, he described the new fashion as "the very dregs of the Renaissance." "I have been brought up," he announced, "in the thirteenth-century belief, and in that belief I intend to die." Toward the end of his life he retained only one last vestige of evolutionary optimism: the future of architecture must lie in a renaissance of the minor arts, hence Burges's position as proto-high-priest of the Arts and Crafts movement. Generally speaking, however, he shared in the aesthetic flaccidity of the 1870s. He gave up wrestling with eclectic theory and concentrated on private rather than public, decorative rather than structural design. He escaped into a world of architectural fantasy: Cardiff Castle (1868–1881); Castell Coch (1875–1881); Tower House (1875–1881). He abandoned doubts for dreams.

Burges was a pre-Raphaelite architect in all but name. He was friendly with most of the movement's leaders and employed a number of pre-Raphaelites and peripheral pre-Raphaelites in the

Burges.
Yatman Cabinet.
1858

groups: the Institute of British Architects, the Archaeological Institute, the Architectural Museum and Architectural Exhibition Society, the Architectural Association and the Ecclesiological Society. His bohemian lifestyle seems to have kept him out of the Royal Academy until just before his death and he never joined the Society of Antiquaries.

Burges never ran a large office. His style had many imitators (especially popular were his Law Courts and Skilbeck's Warehouse designs), but he founded no school: his pupils were devotees rather than disciples. Two of them, however—JOSIAH CONDER and WILLIAM EMERSON—carried Burgesian eclecticism across the world. Burges's influence can be traced to the United States. His design for Trinity College, Hartford, Connecticut (1873–1882), remained incomplete: less than one-sixth of the quadruple-quadrangled masterplan was constructed, and even that was diluted in execution by its two local architects, FRANCIS H. KIMBALL and G. W. Keller. Still, through Kimball, through Keller, and—most of all—through H. H. RICHARDSON, not a little of Burges's genius lives on in America. His influence on Richardson is a matter for debate. But Richardson's only English work—Lululaund, Bushey, Hartfordshire (1886–1894), for Sir Hubert Herkomer—seems almost a tribute to Burges.

Burges's leading patrons were Roman Catholics (Lord Bute and Lord Ripon) or High Anglican (A. J. Beresford-Hope), but his own approach to religion was aesthetic rather than theological. As ROBERT KERR put it, "[WILLIAM] BUTTERFIELD was High Church, Scott Low Church, and Burges no church." In his art and in his writings, he emphasized the visual rather than the metaphysical side of religion. He loved ceremony almost for its own sake. Hence perhaps the fact that he was an enthusiastic Freemason and may well have been a Rosicrucian.

A lifelong bachelor, enthusiastic, jokey, voluble, and gregarious, Burges was a popular figure in the mid-Victorian art world. Short-sighted, stocky, chubby, and cherubic in appearance, usually known as Billy, he died suddenly, at the height of his powers, in the same year as his contemporary and rival, George E. Street. Besides numerous lectures and essays, he published *Art Applied to Industry* (1865) and *Architectural Drawings* (1870). He was, an omnivorous collector and bequeathed many items—armor, *objets d'art,* and illuminated manuscripts—to the British Museum.

J. MORDAUNT CROOK

WORKS

Items of furniture and metalwork designed by Burges are in

production of mural decoration, stained glass, and painted furniture. D. G. Rossetti, E. Burne-Jones, J. E. Millais, Simeon Solomon, Henry Holiday, N. J. N. Westlake, Albert Moore, Thomas Morten, Charles Rossiter, Frederick Smallfield, J. A. Fitzgerald, W. F. Yeames, E. J. Poynter, H. W. Lonsdale, W. Gualbert Saunders, Fred Weekes, Stacy Marks, Charles Campbell, Axel Herman Haig—all these worked at different times under Burges's direction. And several (notably Burne-Jones) acknowledged a considerable debt to Burges at the start of their careers. With their assistance, Burges produced the earliest and most striking examples of painted Gothic furniture; and with the help of Saunders, Lonsdale, and Weekes, in particular, he produced stained glass that surpassed in originality and brilliance even the finest work of Morris and Company. He also excelled in a field Morris never entered: jewelry and metalwork. Working with several different silversmiths Burges inspired work that excelled in scholarship even that of his master Pugin and anticipated in range and virtuosity the triumphs of the Arts and Crafts phase.

Burges was a key member of several fringe pre-Raphaelite coteries: the Hogarth Club, the Medieval Society, the Arts Club, and the Foreign Architectural Book Society. He also played a leading role in a number of more obviously professional *the following public collections: Victoria and Albert Museum, London; Fitzwilliam Museum, Cambridge; Cecil Higgins Museum, Bedford, England; Manchester City Art Gallery, England; Leeds City Art Gallery, England; Birmingham City Art Gallery, England; British Museum, London.*

1858–1865, Gayhurst (alterations), Buckinghamshire, England. 1859–1877, Waltham Abbey (restoration), Essex, England. 1860–1862, All Saints, Fleet, Hampshire, England. 1863–1881, Saint Finbar's Cathedral (not completed until 1904), Cork, Ireland. 1864–1879, Worcester College (chapel and hall), Oxford. 1865–1866, Skilbeck's Warehouse, London. 1866–1868, Holy Trinity, Templebrady, Cork, Ireland. 1867–1868, Saint Michael, Lowfield Heath, Surrey, England. 1867–1874, Knightshayes, Devonshire, England. 1868, 1871–1873, 1881, Saint Faith, Stoke Newington, London. 1868, 1892–1899, Saint Michael (extensions), Brighton, England. 1868–1881, Cardiff Castle (reconstruction), Wales. 1870–1876, Christ the Consoler, Skelton; 1870–1878, Saint Mary, Studley Royal; Yorkshire, England. 1871–1877, Harrow School (speech room), Middlesex, England. 1873–1882, Trinity College (incomplete), Hartford. 1875–1881, Castel Coch, near Cardiff, Wales. 1875–1881, Tower House, London.

BIBLIOGRAPHY

CROOK, J. MORDAUNT 1970 "Patron Extraordinary: John, 3rd Marquess of Bute." In P. Howell (editor), *Victorian South Wales.* London: Victorian Society.
CROOK, J. MORDAUNT 1975–1976 "Knightshayes, Devon: Burges versus Grace." *National Trust Yearbook* 1:44–55.
CROOK, J. MORDAUNT 1981 *William Burges and the High Victorian Dream.* Forthcoming book.
HANDLEY-READ, C. 1963a "Notes on William Burges's Painted Furniture." *Burlington Magazine* 105:496–509.
HANDLEY-READ, C. 1963b "William Burges." In P. Ferriday (editor), *Victorian Architecture.* London: Jonathan Cape.
HANDLEY-READ, C. 1967 "Cork Cathedral." *Architectural Review* 107:422–430.

BURGH, THOMAS

Thomas Burgh (1670–1730) was born in Ireland and educated at Trinity College, Dublin. He served, probably as an engineer, in the Williamite wars (1689–1691) and in the Low Countries (1692–1695). In 1697, he was on the staff of WILLIAM ROBINSON. He was appointed surveyor-general of Ireland, which post he held until his death. His country seat, Oldtown, County Kildare, is still occupied by his descendants, and there are two portraits of him there. His work at Dublin Castle consisted mainly in executing designs by his predecessor Robinson. The Dublin Custom House (1704–1706) was an original design of somewhat Dutch character. The Library of Trinity College,

his most important building, begun in 1712, was finished only in 1733. He also designed Dr. Steevens' Hospital, Dublin (1718), the Royal Barracks in Dublin (1701–1707), and his own house at Oldtown (c.1715), of which only the wings were built. Attributions include Oakley Park, Celbridge (c.1720), Ballyburley, County Offaly, and Celbridge Collegiate School (1730). His style was straightforward classical without Palladian (see ANDREA PALLADIO) elements.

MAURICE CRAIG

BIBLIOGRAPHY

LOEBER, ROLF 1977 "Biographical Dictionary of Engineers in Ireland: 1600–1730." *Irish Sword* 13, no. 51:106–122.
PAKENHAM-WALSH, W. P. 1907 "Lieutenant-Colonel Thomas Burgh, Chief Engineer of Ireland, 1700–1730." *Royal Engineers' Journal* 6:69–74.

BURKE, EDMUND

Edmund Burke (1850–1919) was born in Toronto and was trained by Henry Langley, his uncle, who was his partner from 1872 to 1892. After 1894, Burke's practice with J. C. B. Horwood produced some exceptional department store designs, particularly Robert Simpson's, Toronto (1895), and the Hudson's Bay Company, Calgary, Alberta (1911–1918), and Vancouver, British Columbia (1911–1916).

STEPHEN A. OTTO

BIBLIOGRAPHY

A collection of Edmund Burke's drawings is in the Horwood Collection, Ontario Archives, Toronto.
"Obituary." 1919 *The* (Toronto) *Globe,* Jan. 3, p. 6.

BÜRKLEIN, FRIEDRICH

As FRIEDRICH VON GÄRTNER's assistant on the Ludwigstrasse in Munich, Georg Christian Friedrich Bürklein (1813–1872) was nurtured in the quest for a modern architecture developed from an analytical synthesis of past styles. His City Hall at Fürth (1840–1843) is based on its typological model, the Palazzo Vecchio in Florence. A more synthetic approach underlies the polychromatic Lombardic Romanesque Munich Central Railroad Station (1847–1849), whose iron train shed led to numerous commissions for the Bavarian Royal Railroad. As King Maximilian II's favored architect, Bürklein was charged, after an international competition in 1851, with devising a new architectural style to be pioneered in the Maximilianstrasse, a monumental eastward expansion of the city. The *Maximilianstil* façades of brick and terra cotta are based predominantly on English and German late Gothic models preferred by Maximilian. The skeletal bay structure with pronounced vertical articulation rejects the integral wall plane of Gärtner's Ludwigstrasse, just as the broad forum at the end of the Maximilianstrasse suggests a new approach to boulevard design which incorporates nature and variety.

BARRY BERGDOLL

WORKS

1840–1843, City Hall, Fürth, Germany. *1843–1848, Main Railroad Station, Hof, Germany. *1847–1849, Main Railroad Station; 1852–1875, Maximilianstrasse; 1853–1856, Frauenklinik, Sonnenstrasse; Munich. 1856–1859, Protestant Church, Passau, Germany. 1856–1860, National Theater (extension on the Maximilianstrasse); 1857–1861, Maximilianeum (completed 1874 by another architect); 1859–1863, Mint; 1871–1874, Head Customs Administration Building, Munich.

BIBLIOGRAPHY

DRÜCKE, EBERHARD 1978 "Die Maximilianstrasse in München: Zum Problem des neuen Baustils." Pages 107–119 in Monika Steinhauser and Michael Brix (editors), *Geschichte allein ist Zeitgemäss.* Giessen, Germany.
"Freidrich Bürklein." 1873 *Deutsche Bauzeitung* 7:18–19.
HAHN, A. 1953 "Der Maximilianstil." Pages 92ff. in Hans Gollwitzer (editor), *Hundert Jahre Maximilianeum: 1852–1952.* Munich: Pflaum.
HEDERER, OSWALD 1959 "Friedrich Bürklein." Volume 3, page 1 in *Neue-Deutsche Biographie.* Berlin: Duncker & Humblot.
HEDERER, OSWALD 1976 *Friedrich von Gärtner 1792–1847; Leben, Werk, Schüler.* Munich: Prestel.
HOJER, GERHARD (1972)1974 "München-Maximilianstrasse und Maximilianstil." Pages 33–65 in Ludwig Grote (editor), *Die Deutsche Stadt im 19. Jahrhundert.* Originally published in *Festschrift für Nikolaus Pevsner.* Munich: Prestel.
KARLINGER, HANS 1933 *München und die deutsche Kunst des 19. Jahrhunderts.* Munich: Bayerische Heimatbücher.

BURLE MARX, ROBERTO

Brazilian landscape architect, painter, jewelry maker, sculptor, and costume and scenery designer Roberto Burle Marx (1909–) discovered the inherent beauty and diversity of Brazilian flora in the Dahlem Botanical Gardens while studying in Germany in 1928. He has since used the lush tropical vegetation of Brazil to reproduce three-dimensional painting in landscape gardening the world over. Born in São Paulo, Brazil, he moved to Rio de Janeiro as a youth and studied painting with Candido Portinari and architecture at the National School of Fine Arts. He designed his first garden in 1933 for a house planned by LÚCIO COSTA and GREGORI WARCHAVCHIK. A year later, his natural ability and vast botanical knowledge led to his appointment as director of parks and gardens in Recife. From 1935 to 1938, he filled the city with parks and plazas, creating the first ecological gardens in Brazil. Burle Marx's philosophy of landscape architecture respects the existing ecological balance and tries to enhance it with plants and flowers that flourish in a particular environment. He often includes small ponds filled with Amazonian lilies whose border foliage provides nourishment and shelter for local birds.

Again in Rio, he elaborated the gardens for the Ministry of Education Building in 1938. Designed by the vanguard of modern Brazilian architecture with LE CORBUSIER as consultant, the building was a showcase of the arts and Burle Marx's gardens added the finishing touch, giving the building an atmosphere of its own and bringing nature to the urban cityscape.

In 1947, he designed Odette Monteiro's garden in Petropolis, Brazil, his favorite and first award-winning garden that he still visits, annually replanting certain sections. Here as in all of his gardens, he composed a three-dimensional painting by applying color, texture, and design with his rich knowledge of horticulture.

Since 1950, Burle Marx has maintained a farm and greenhouse near Rio where he cultivates plants and flowers from every continent. He has designed gardens throughout Latin America, Europe, and the United States. In Venezuela at Parque del Este (1960–1961), he interspersed common plant forms, some considered to be weeds, into the park's 2,500,000 square feet, giving emphasis to plants whose beauty often goes unnoticed.

Burle Marx's jewelry, painting, and other artwork reflect his landscapes which in themselves parallel modern movements in painting. In the 1940s, formal elements of composition dominated his gardens. At Pampulha (1943), a suburban recreation development that surrounded an artificial lake, Burle Marx's plants and flowers highlighted OSCAR NIEMEYER's Church of Saint Francis of Assisi, the yacht club, a casino, and a restaurant. In the late 1950s, Burle Marx designed the Aterro which curves along a million square yards of Rio beachfront and exhibits the free-flowing liberty of movement with the staccatoed color of abstract Expressionism. After the gardens were planted, pedestrians were allowed to make their own path-

Burle Marx.
Odette Monteiro Garden.
Petropolis, Brazil.
1947–1948

ways; once well established, the walkways were covered over with asphalt.

Burle Marx likes to refer to himself as a gardener, but his ability to create a ubiquitous sense of surprise and exaltation with nature's raw materials marks him as a true artist of landscape architecture.

ELIZABETH D. HARRIS

WORKS

1935, Arthur Costa Square Gardens, Recife, Brazil. 1938, Gardens, Ministry of Health and Education (now Palácio da Cultura), Rio de Janeiro, Brazil. 1943, Pampulha Park and Gardens, Belo Horizonte, Brazil. 1947–1948, Odette Monteiro Garden, Petropolis, Brazil. 1952, Airport Gardens, Santos Dumont, Brazil. 1955–1956, Museum of Modern Art Landscaping; 1955–1962, Beach Landscaping; Rio de Janeiro, Brazil. 1958–1960, Defino Garden; 1960–1961, Parque del Este, Caracas. 1963, UNESCO Gardens (six), Paris. 1965, Ministry of Foreign Relations Gardens (Itamarati); 1976, Vice-President's Residence Gardens, Brasília.

BIBLIOGRAPHY

BARDI, P. M. 1964 *The Tropical Gardens of Burle Marx.* New York: Reinhold. Originally published in Portuguese.
MUSÉE GALLIERA *Roberto Burle Marx.* Paris: The museum.

BURLINGTON, EARL OF

Richard Boyle, third earl of Burlington and fourth earl of Cork (1694–1753), "the architect earl," was in every respect a fortunate man. Endowed by nature with a strong though reserved personality, a keen intellect, and a true passion for music, the arts, and especially architecture, he was born at the right time into the right social class, and he knew how to make the most of his innate gifts and the privileges of his rank. Heir to vast estates in Ireland and Yorkshire, owner of valuable properties in and near London, he was considered one of the richest peers of the realm. Successor to a string of titles and high offices, member of the court society, he was, moreover, related by blood or marriage to some of the most influential politicians of his time. A Whig by family tradition and inclination, he had the advantage of living during the long era of the Whig party's dominance, an era of peace, economic growth, and cultural reawakening after the troubled years of the civil wars.

Burlington's father, Charles, second earl of Burlington, died in 1704, and the upbringing of his only son and heir, together with that of his four daughters rested, in accordance with his last will, in the hands of his widow, the dowager Countess Juliana, by all accounts a serious-minded woman. She saw to it that the young earl received that all-round education advocated most persuasively by Lord Shaftesbury—an education which included, apart from the study of the classical authors, a knowledge of French and Italian and a grounding in mathematics, music, the arts, and architecture. Thus turned into "a Man of Breeding and Politeness," the earl was sent on the Grand Tour to Italy there to train his eyes and enrich his mind by contemplating "the right Models of *Perfection*." This meant first and foremost to study in

Rome of "the truest pieces of Architecture, the best remains of Statues, the best Paintings of a Raphael or Carache"—in short to acquire that concord of morality and taste which lends distinction to a true virtuoso and accomplished connoisseur.

So Burlington, like some aspiring noblemen before and many after him set out to the fountainhead of classical learning and polite manners. Traveling in great style as befitted his station in life, he left England in May 1714, arrived in Rome in September, spent the winter there, and returned home in May 1715, the year of his coming of age. This was also the year of two epoch-making publications: the first volume of *Vitruvius Britannicus* by COLEN CAMPBELL and the first installment of an English translation of *I quattro libri dell'architettura* by GIACOMO LEONI. These two volumes were to prove of the utmost importance for what Lord Burlington almost immediately came to consider his vocation in life: to revive the gospel of true architecture as laid down by VITRUVIUS, interpreted by ANDREA PALLADIO, and anglicized by INIGO JONES.

Even before Burlington had set out on his Italian travels he had begun to modernize his town residence, the Jacobean house acquired by his grandfather in 1667 and subsequently known as Burlington House, Piccadilly. Redecoration of the interior was started as early as 1713. Soon after, the remodeling of the exterior was almost certainly entrusted to JAMES GIBBS, a highly regarded architect who had studied several years in Rome. After his return to England, Gibbs tried to adjust his style to the rising classical taste, but he could never quite shake off his Italian baroque training. This, in all likelihood, must have seemed too old-fashioned to Burlington. He promptly dismissed him and in 1717 handed over the modernization of his house to Colen Campbell who, taking the Palazzo Porto Colleoni in Vicenza as his model, turned the old mansion into the first strictly Palladian building in London. It was a resounding success.

There can be little doubt that Burlington's decision to take up architecture seriously dates from the time he employed Campbell. It was under his tutelage that he erected, in 1717, his first building to his own design, the Bagnino, a small garden pavilion on the grounds of Chiswick.

First, however, realizing that his knowledge of Palladio was totally insufficient, based as it was on not entirely satisfactory publications, he decided to spend several months in Vicenza and Venice in order to study the master's actual works on the spot. By a stroke of luck he was able to buy there more than sixty original Palladio drawings, apart from prints and books. These were the nucleus of his constantly growing collection and the chief

guide and inspiration for his own work and that of his followers. No wonder that with Burlington House as a shining example of his successful departure from the traditional English façades of private homes and, now, with his firsthand and unequaled knowledge of Palladian buildings, he became the acclaimed leader of progressive owners of stately homes who eagerly sought not only his advice but also his designs for the remodeling of their residences.

In March 1721, Burlington married Dorothy Savile, oldest daughter and co-heir of William Savile, Marquess Halifax. It proved a happy union. Lady Burlington shared her husband's enthusiasm for Italian arts and music. She was a good hostess to his friends and many visitors and, though given to occasional stormy tempers, never interfered with her husband's architectural activities which began to occupy a great deal of his time.

The decade between 1721 and 1731 was the most active and fruitful period in Burlington's life. In 1721, he built what was originally planned as a hunting lodge in Tottenham Park, Wiltshire, for his brother-in-law, Lord Bruce, for which a number of sketches and drawings still survive. The design of the main front, drawn by HENRY FLITCROFT, is inscribed as "front of Tottenham Park 1721 Burlington ar."—the first time that a peer of the realm proclaimed himself a professional. The building consisted of a simple central block flanked by four towers each adorned by a tripartite window, a type first published by SEBASTIANO SERLIO and frequently used by Palladio, hence variously called a Serliana, a Palladian, or a Venetian window. This motif became almost a hallmark of all Burlingtonians. The building was demolished and replaced in 1826.

The majority of Burlington's buildings suffered a similar fate: they were either remodeled out of recognition or pulled down, victims of their later owners' changed taste or their selling out to speculators. Lost are Lord Bruce's Warwick House, Saint James, London (destroyed 1827) and his Round Coppice, Iver Heath, Buckinghamshire (demolished 1954). The adjoining houses for Lord Mountrath (c.1721) and General Wade (1723), London, are gone. Both were demolished in 1935. General Wade's residence was built after an unpublished original Palladio drawing in Burlington's collection. It was a beautiful building and nothing more authentic could be imagined, but it was not a livable house. Burlington was concerned more with reviving the eternal classical rules than with the convenience of the occupant.

The same was true of his design for the Dormitory of Westminster School, London (1722–1730), which had been for long in a ruinous condition. In

the early years of the century the rebuilding was first entrusted to CHRISTOPHER WREN, then to NICHOLAS HAWKSMOOR. The final decision to call on Lord Burlington for a design was the first official sanction of the rising taste for "that simple and chaste style in architecture which never fails to please." Pleasing to the eye as the building was, it had some serious practical drawbacks. The originally open arcade of the ground floor proved unsuitable for the English climate. It was enclosed in 1846. The small square windows above the plain niches in the main floor did not provide enough light for the long bare room in which the boys lived and slept. In 1895, large windows were broken into every second niche. The building was heavily damaged during World War II but was rebuilt in 1947 in its nineteenth-century form.

Three of the lesser buildings executed during this period are the extensive remodeling of Northwick Park, Worcestershire (c.1728–1730) for Sir John Rushout; the partial rebuilding of Richmond House (c.1730); and Foxhall, the banqueting house for fox hunters at Charlton, Sussex (1730 or 1732), both the properties of Charles, second duke of Richmond. By far the most important buildings of that decade are Chiswick House, dating from its beginning, and the Assembly Rooms at York, designed at its end.

The Chiswick property with its Jacobean mansion was acquired by Burlington's grandfather in 1682. In the early eighteenth century, the neighborhood had become extremely fashionable, partly because of its pleasant scenery along the Thames, partly because at a time when much of the traffic went by waterways the river afforded easy access to the court whether the king resided in London, at Hampton Court, or Windsor. As Burlington's design for the bagnino indicated, plans to turn

Chiswick into a showplace for his architectural creed must have occupied him from the very beginning of his career. Oddly enough, despite the many documents, drawings, and letters preserved, we have few definite dates either for the remodeling of the old house, or for the building of the famous new structure, or for the revolutionary layout of the garden, but it seems safe to date the actual building period between 1725 and 1730, although deliberations of what to do and how to proceed may, of course, have started earlier. His plan was threefold: (1) to modernize the street (south) front of the Jacobean mansion, but leave its main body, as he did at Burlington House, Piccadilly, essentially untouched; (2) to erect next to the old house, which remained the residential quarter, a new structure, small in scale and definite in purpose, and link it with the dwelling house by a carefully proportioned two-storied wing; (3) to redesign the layout of the entire grounds.

Burlington's architectural method never varied. He was not an inventor of imaginative novel forms, but, not unlike Palladio himself, he was an extremely skillful, learned, and, to a certain degree, dogmatic manipulator of what he conceived to be the basic elements of classic Roman architecture. Yet, he was an innovator insofar as he used those elements in ever varying combinations, and he took them from whatever source suited his purpose. Nowhere is this more apparent than in his designs for Chiswick and for the Assembly Rooms at York.

At Chiswick Villa, everything, from the conception of the whole down to the minutest detail is based on precedents. The general idea—a perfect square with a central domed hall, fronted by a free-standing portico—derives from Palladio's Villa Rotonda, yet it was by no means a mere copy of the prototype. Burlington's deviations from his model are, however, not free inventions, but are frequently based on other authorities, mainly VINCENZO SCAMOZZI, the follower and popularizer of Palladio's ideas, and Inigo Jones. It is not possible here to enumerate all the particulars. A few examples, chosen more or less at random, have to suffice.

The octagonal drum and the saucer dome, for instance, hark back to Scamozzi's Villa Pisani with the difference that Scamozzi used one step to separate dome and drum while Burlington, on the authority of ancient Roman temples (Vesta, Pantheon), uses four. From Villa Pisani, too, comes the idea of giving the chimney pots over the lateral fronts the shape of pyramids—an idea often found in Scamozzi's but never in Palladio's buildings.

The segmental mullioned windows in the drum come from Roman thermae. They occur in Scamozzi's central structure in Villa Molin, but were probably better known to Burlington from a Palladio drawing in his collection. Also from Villa Molin are the windows over balusters at each side of the portico of the main façade.

In the portico itself Burlington followed Palladio's interpretation of the classical tradition in the height of the columns, the intercolumniation, and the entablature. But he departed from the classical rule of widening the distance between the two central columns. His intercolumniation is of entirely equal width. His source for this deviation was French, exemplified by CLAUDE PERRAULT and JACQUES FRANÇOIS BLONDEL.

The right choice of the orders was of great importance, indeed, until quite recent times. Palladio liked the simple, Ionic order for his villas; Burlington preferred the more festive Corinthian order for Chiswick. The crowning capitals he cop-

ied from those of the Castor and Pollux temple in Rome, but not the rather extravagant entablature: for this he followed the more traditional system published by Palladio.

The one entirely unorthodox feature is the grandiose staircase, extending across the whole width of the main front. Nothing like it is to be found in Burlington's usual models. It probably reflects contemporary Italian designs such as GUARINO GUARINI's staircase at Racconigi near Turin which he may have seen when he spent some days in the Piedmontese capital on his Grand Tour.

The garden front is a composite of two drawings in Burlington's collection. The starkly plain wall with its carefully proportioned three recessed Venetian windows and two small, arched niches between them became one of the most influential façade designs in eighteenth-century England, down to ROBERT ADAM.

Likewise, in the interior every decorative element, every door case, window frame, freeze, chimneypiece, had a precedent. But whereas the exterior design was exclusively Burlington's own work, assisted only by a clerk of works, a certain Samuel Savil, and by Flitcroft who turned Burlington's clumsy, amateurish sketches into finished drawings, he had found in WILLIAM KENT a sympathetic, richly gifted, and versatile collaborator for the interior design. Kent, a failed history painter who had first been introduced to Lord Burlington in Rome in 1714–1715, proved an ideal choice for endowing the rooms with sparkle and glamor for the intimate parties and informal gatherings of friends for which the house was planned. It was Kent also who was mainly responsible for turning Burlington's early rather timid plans for redesigning his grounds into the first typically

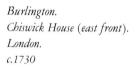

Burlington.
Chiswick House (east front).
London.
c.1730

English landscape garden with winding paths, vistas ending in small temples (designed by Burlington), obelisks, statues, and the almost obligatory grotto.

The ground plan of Chiswick differs entirely from Palladio's plan for the Rotonda. The long passage leading from the portico to the cupola room occurs in Palladio's Palazzo Thiene in Vicenza, and the sequence of round, apsidal, and octagonal rooms facing the garden and known as "the gallery" follows Palladio's reconstruction of Roman thermae where such arrangements were not uncommon.

After Burlington's death in 1753, the estate passed to his daughter Charlotte, his sole heir, and through her marriage to Lord Hartington into the possession of the dukes of Devonshire. Later owners had no use for the old mansion. It was pulled down in 1788. At the same time, the villa was enlarged by JAMES WYATT and quite thrown out of proportion by the addition of wings to the side fronts. In 1892, house and gardens were let to a doctor for use as a private lunatic asylum. In 1929, the Middlesex County Council purchased the estate, turned the gardens into a public park, and let the house slowly fall into disrepair. Bombs caused further damage during World War II. Finally, the Ministry of Works undertook the restoration of the house with great care. Wyatt's wings were damaged beyond redemption and were pulled down.

The austere splendor and novelty of the architecture at Chiswick were surpassed even by Lord Burlington's most revolutionary design—that for the Assembly Rooms at York. The need for a proper place to entertain the visitors to the Assizes and Races at York as well as for the year-round use of the local and county nobility had existed for a long time, but only in 1726 a site was bought for the erection of a suitably festive building. After the death of the first architect chosen for the task, the directors of the Assemblies wrote to Lord Burlington on May 4, 1730, beseeching him to supply a design for their building. They promised to "entirely leave it to your Lordship in what manner you think proper." What they desired was "a large Dancing Room, not less than 90 ft. long, another large Room for Cards and play, another for Coffee and Refreshments and a Kitchen or place to make Tea in, with a Retiring place for the Ladies. And somewhere about the entrance, perhaps underground, a place with a chimney for footmen. . . ."

Burlington seems to have accepted the commission with alacrity. He saw here a unique opportunity to solve an old antiquarian puzzle. He could build what Vitruvius had described as a spacious hall built in "the manner of the Egyptians" and what Palladio in his *Quattro Libri* had tried to reconstruct in a cross-section and part of a ground plan. But the plan showed only the width of the aisles and intercolumniation, not the length of the hall, and in his descriptive text Palladio says no more than that "the Egyptian Hall . . . resembles basilicas very much." Now in his reconstruction of a Roman basilica six columns wide with narrow aisles, he stipulated a length of eighteen columns,

Burlington.
White Hall, Chiswick
  House.
London.
c.1730

Burlington.
Assembly Rooms.
York, England.
c.1731–1732

and as it happened, height, width, and length of the two reconstructions combined fitted perfectly into the rather awkward site available for the York Rooms and was literally taken over by Burlington. He made use, too, of other Palladian features, such as the small rectangular, octagonal, and apsidal rooms flanking the hall, or the façade with its open-arched, segmental portico between two wings and mullioned windows set into lunettes.

In a letter of November 18, 1730, the directors gratefully acknowledged the receipt of his Lordship's drawings and again assured him "that no alteration shall be made in your design, but the same shall be strictly executed." Yet, Burlington was still wary. He sent one of his own clerks to reside on the spot, and he himself frequently came to supervise the execution of his wishes. Progress was rapid. On March 1, 1731, the foundation stone was laid. In August 1732, the building was finished except for minor details.

The general reaction to this most rigidly classical building in England and, indeed in Europe, was either glowing praise or outright disapproval, even ridicule. As so often, Burlington had been more concerned with theory than with practicalities.

Burlington.
Assembly Rooms.
York, England.
c.1731–1732

Consequently, many distorting changes were made by and by in the interior, and the façade, whose protruding porch obstructed the growing traffic, was pulled down in 1828 and replaced by a nondescript new façade with a stereotypical flat portico.

The York Assembly Rooms were Lord Burlington's last great enterprise. In 1733, he suddenly resigned all his court employments without ever revealing his reason to anyone except his wife, and she kept as strictly silent about his motivation as he did. From then on, he occasionally still obliged friends and acquaintances with designs or suggestions for alterations for or additions to their houses. He gave advice to Kent for his designs for the Horse Guards, the Royal Mews, the Treasury, and his project for the rebuilding of the Houses of Parliament (c.1733), and he collaborated with ROGER MORRIS at Kirby Hall (begun c.1747), but the drive and the urgency were gone.

He seems practically to have retired from life in London to spend more time at Chiswick which became the focal point of his social and what remained of his professional life. He transferred most of his collection of paintings and drawings from Burlington House, Piccadilly, to the villa in the ground floor of which he had installed his treasured library of a few thousand books.

Burlington was not a bibliomaniac. In size and scope, his library cannot compare with those of such passionate contemporary collectors as Sir Hans Sloane, Lord Harley, or Thomas Coke, earl of Leicester, to mention only a few. From his early acquisitions on, Burlington obviously planned to build up a smaller but well-defined specialized collection. A carefully compiled catalogue, dated January 1742, shows that most of his books were works on architecture, antiquities, sculpture, history, and allied subjects, although classical and contemporary authors were not missing. It clearly was first and foremost a working library and one not only for his own use but intended as an indispensable means for demonstrating, buttressing, and spreading his vision of architecture. It was also meant to be a freely accessible teaching tool. The introduction to the catalogue states explicitly that the index and the shelving of the books have been arranged in such a way that "any Person not acquainted with ye Library" would have no difficulty in finding what he was looking for. And indeed, the library provided invaluable source and study material for practitioners and theorists alike. Among many others, publications such as Kent's immensely influential *The Designs of Inigo Jones* (2 vols., 1727), Robert Castell's learned *Villas of the Ancients* (1728), ISAAC WARE's painstakingly correct edition of *The Four Books of Architecture by*

Andrea Palladio (1738), with the English translation of the text revised and corrected by Burlington himself, could never have gone into print without Burlington's unstintingly given access to his collection. In 1730, he himself had published a magnificent facsimile edition of Palladio's reconstruction of Roman thermae from the drawings he owned. A second volume, planned but never realized, was to contain his Palladio drawings of arches, theaters, temples, and other ancient buildings.

Lord Burlington lived to see the learned, carefully selected, and costly publications written or sponsored by him and his devoted adherents being turned into a veritable flood of cheap, often plagiarized and vulgarized productions. There was a new market for this kind of book because there was a growing public that wanted and needed it—the newly rich middle class, minor architects, builders, masons, carpenters, joiners. He also saw the emergence of an entirely unprecedented type of small-sized books, inaugurated in 1724 by WILLIAM HALFPENNY's *Practical Architecture,* the preface of which states that it is "brought out in such a size as may without burthen be carried in the pocket and be always ready for use."

The pocketbook was born. It found scores of imitators and was indeed a handy guide for anyone to build a modest but stately and fashionable home in town or country, including even farmhouses, in the prevailing classical idiom. The titles of two works by BATTY LANGLEY, one of the most successful and notorious popularizers, will have to suffice to indicate the tenor of a host of similar productions: *The Builder's Jewel: or the Youth's Instructor, and Workman's Remembrancer. Explaining short and easy rules, made familiar to the meanest capacity* (1741), and *The Workman's Golden Rule for drawing and working the Five Orders in Architecture* (1750). Whatever the literary merit of the pocketbooks, it was surely owing to them that the British standard of aesthetically pleasing anonymous architecture was so high and so widely diffused for two or three generations.

In his letters, Burlington never once referred to the unexpected effect of his own propagandist efforts. Socially one of the least prejudiced men, was he pleased to see this democratization of his high ideals? Or did his own reaction find expression in Pope's lines in his *Epistle to Lord Burlington:*

Yet shall (my Lord) your just, your noble rules
Fill half the land with imitating Fools;
Who random drawings from your sheets shall take
And of one beauty many blunders make.

After his retirement from the court and the curtailment of his architectural practice, Burlington spent more time than ever at Londesborough. He had always liked to go there for a few weeks during the hunting season. Now he often extended his stay into late November. In contrast to Burlington House and the old house at Chiswick, he never faced Londesborough Hall (begun in the latter part of the sixteenth century) with a Palladian front but restricted himself to modernizing parts of the interior. Now, too, with more leisure than he had ever had before, he turned with passionate devotion and much expense in time and money and with the help of Thomas Knowlton, a renowned gardener and botanist, to develop the extensive grounds into a park and gardens of imposing magnificence. He entertained a great deal. His many guests included most of the local gentry whose visits he reported to Lady Burlington in his frequent letters with indulgent, never bitter, sarcasm. He was a contented man.

For about half a century, Lord Burlington's influence on architecture remained alive and reached far beyond the confines of his native land into Europe as well as America. His name lived on as that of a powerful patron, but in the nineteenth century his role as an active architect was first doubted, then refuted altogether. Not before our own time and not without much digging into half-forgotten archives was this unusual peer restored to his rightful place in the history of architecture.

MARGOT WITTKOWER

WORKS

*c.1721, Mountrath House, London. 1721, Tottenham Park, Wiltshire, England. 1722–1730, Dormitory (later rebuilt), Westminster School; *1723, Wade House; London. c.1728–1730, Northwick Park (remodeling), Worcestershire, England. c.1730, Chiswick House; *c.1730, Richmond House (partial rebuilding); London. 1730?, 1732?, Foxhall House, Charlton, Sussex, England. c.1731–1732, Assembly Rooms, York, England. Begun c.1747, Kirby Hall (with Roger Morris), Northamptonshire, England.

BIBLIOGRAPHY

Ackerman's History of the Colleges of Winchester, Eton, and Westminster. 1816 London.
Apollo of the Arts: Lord Burlington and his Circle. 1973 Nottingham, England: University Art Gallery. Exhibition catalogue.
CHARLTON, JOHN 1958 *A History and Description of Chiswick House and Gardens.* London.
DRAKE, FRANCIS 1736 *Eboracum, or, the History and Antiquities of the City of York.* York, England.
GOODALL, IAN H. 1970 "Lord Burlington's 'Piazza'." In *Annual Report of the York Georgian Society.* York, England.
LYSONS, DANIEL 1800–1811 *The Environs of London.* 5 vols. London.

NEAVE, DAVID 1977 *Londesborough: History of an East Yorkshire Estate Village.* Londesborough, England.

PEVSNER, NICHOLAS 1951 *The Buildings of England.* London.

SAXL, F., and WITTKOWER, RUDOLF 1969 *British Art and the Mediterranean.* London: Oxford University Press.

SHAFTESBURY, EARL OF 1710 *Advice to an Author.*

WHEATLEY, HENRY B. 1891 *London Past and Present.* London.

WILLIS, PETER 1977 *Charles Bridgeman and the English Landscape Garden.* London.

WITTKOWER, RUDOLF 1974 *Palladio and English Palladianism.* London:

WITTKOWER, RUDOLF n.d. *The History of the York Assembly Rooms.* York, England.

Wren Society 1934 11.

BURN, WILLIAM

The foremost master of early Victorian country house planning, William Burn (1789–1870) studied in London under ROBERT SMIRKE. He returned to his native Edinburgh in 1812 to build his master's neoclassical Kinmount House. His earliest commissions were Grecian public buildings, but in 1818 he commenced a country house practice averaging four a year. His first large commission, Saltoun Hall (1818–1826), East Lothian, was enlarged into a neo-Tudor pile with a towered central saloon modelled on Kinmount. WILLIAM WILKINS's Dalmeny in Midlothian inspired Burn's East Anglian Tudor at Blairquhan (1820–1824), Ayrshire, and Carstairs House (1822–1824), Lanarkshire. At Grecian Camperdown House (1821, 1824–1826), Angus, Burn developed a continuous enfilade of private and principal apartments along the garden frontages, almost concurrently with Wilkins at Dunmore. He perfected this arrangement at Jacobean Dupplin Castle (1828–1832), Perthshire, into more asymmetrically disposed plan types, the larger usually with symmetrical garden fronts at the main blocks, in which high central saloons were now superseded by hall corridors. Comfort, privacy, and segregation of service became the paramount considerations, a height of two stories and attics was seldom exceeded, and family and servants wings became both more clearly defined and more sophisticated in plan.

Stylistically Burn progressed to Cotswold cottage houses at Snaigow (1824–1827), Perthshire, parallel with EDWARD BLORE at Corehouse; to English Jacobean at Fettercairn House (1826–1827) in Kincardineshire, and, infused with Scottish features, at Milton Lockhart (1829–1836), Lanarkshire; and to Scottish baronial, particularly when incorporating old houses, at Stenhouse

(1835), Stirlingshire. The commission to complete ANTHONY SALVIN's Harlaxton, Lincolnshire, in 1838 greatly expanded his Jacobean repertoire, leading to his finest sequence of houses, Falkland House (1839–1844) in Fife, Whitehill Hall (1839–1844) in Midlothian, Stoke Rochford House (1841–1843), and Revesby Abbey (1844) in Lincolnshire, and Dartrey (1844–1846), Monaghan. Harlaxton (from 1838) included an unprecedented illusionist baroque stairwell; Stoke and Revesby had Louis XV and German baroque décor.

From 1844 Burn concentrated exclusively on country house work from London, but only Montagu House (1853–1859), London, matched earlier achievements. DAVID BRYCE remained his Edinburgh partner until 1850, largely inheriting the Scottish practice. His later pupils included R. NORMAN SHAW and WILLIAM E. NESFIELD.

DAVID M. WALKER

WORKS

1814–1816, North Leith Parish Church; 1816–1818, Saint John's Episcopal Church; Edinburgh. 1817–1818, Custom House, Greenock, Scotland. 1818–1826, Saltoun Hall, East Lothian, Scotland. 1820–1824, Blairquhan, Ayrshire, Scotland. 1821, 1824–1826, Camperdown House, Angus, Scotland. 1822–1824, Carstairs House, Lanarkshire, Scotland. *1824–1827, Snaigow House, Perthshire, Scotland. 1825–1828, John Watson's Hospital (now the National Gallery of Modern Art), Edinburgh. 1826–1827, Fettercairn House, Kincardineshire, Scotland. *1826–1827, Garscube House, Dunbartonshire, Scotland. *1828–1832, Dupplin Castle, Perthshire, Scotland. 1829–1830, Tyninghame House, East Lothian, Scotland. *1829–1836, Milton Lockhart, Lanarkshire, Scotland. 1832–1834, Madras College, Saint Andrews, Fife, Scotland. *1834, New Club, Edinburgh. 1834–1835, The County Hall, The Castle, Inverness, Scotland. 1834–1839, The Crichton Royal Lunatic Asylum, Dumfries, Scotland. *1835, Stenhouse, Stirlingshire, Scotland. From 1838, Harlaxton Manor (completed with additions), Lincolnshire, England. 1839–1843, Muckross Abbey, Kerry, Ireland. 1839–1844, Falkland House, Fife, Scotland. 1839–1844, Whitehill Hall, Edinburgh. 1841–1843, Stoke Rochford House; 1844, Revesby Abbey; Lincolnshire, England. *1844–1846, Dartrey, Monaghan, Ireland. 1848–1852, Idsworth, Hampshire, England. *1849–1852, Poltalloch, Inverness-shire, Scotland. *1851–1852, Dunira, Perthshire, Scotland. 1851–1855, Sandon Hall, Staffordshire, England. *1852–1854, Buchanan House, Stirlingshire, Scotland. *1853–1859, Montagu House, London. *1856, Fonthill Abbey, Wiltshire, England. 1856–1861, Lynford Hall, Norfolk, England. *1865–1868, Whittlebury Lodge, Northamptonshire, England.

BIBLIOGRAPHY

FAWCETT, JANE (editor) (1976)1977 *Seven Victorian Architects.* University Park: Pennsylvania State University Press.

FIDDLES, VALERIE, and ROWAN, ALISTAIR (compilers)
1976 *David Bryce, 1803–1876.* University of Edinburgh.

GIROUARD, MARK (1971)1979 *The Victorian Country House.* Rev. ed. New Haven: Yale University Press.

HITCHCOCK, H. R. (1954)1972 *Early Victorian Architecture in Britain.* 2 vols. Reprint. New York: Da Capo.

HUSSEY, CHRISTOPHER 1958 *English Country Houses: Late Georgian, 1800–1840.* London: Country Life.

KERR, ROBERT 1864 *The Gentleman's House.* London: John Murray.

LINDSAY, IAN GORDON (1948)1973 *Georgian Edinburgh.* 2d ed., rev. Edinburgh and London: Scottish Academic Press.

MACAULEY, JAMES 1975 *The Gothic Revival: 1745–1845.* Glasgow and London: Blackie.

Burnet.
McGeoch's Store.
Glasgow, Scotland.
1905–1910

BURNET, J. J.

The Scottish architect John James Burnet (1857–1938) was one of the most celebrated designers of the Edwardian era, with a widespread reputation and practice. He was born in Glasgow, the son of a prosperous architect there. At the age of seventeen he went to the Ecole des Beaux-Arts in Paris and trained for three years in the studio of JEAN-LOUIS PASCAL, whose influence can be seen clearly in Burnet's early work. He joined his father's practice on his return from Paris in 1878, and immediately gained recognition with his design for Glasgow's Fine Art Institute, built during that year.

In 1886, JOHN ARCHIBALD CAMPBELL, who had studied with Burnet in Paris, became a partner in the firm, which for the next twelve years was known as Burnet, Son, and Campbell. The two younger partners collaborated on a number of important Glasgow buildings during this period, notably the Athenaeum Theatre of 1891–1892.

In 1896, Burnet went to the United States where he met Charles F. McKim (see McKIM, MEAD, AND WHITE), who became a close friend, and LOUIS H. SULLIVAN. He was greatly inspired by the new structural techniques he saw being developed for large buildings, particularly in Chicago, and began experimenting with them when he returned to Scotland. Indeed, the influence of this visit can be seen in Burnet's work in Glasgow over the next ten years, which reached full maturity with the design of McGeoch's Store (1905–1910). As in much of his work there was classical detailing on the elevations of McGeoch's. However, this was both controlled and refined, the overriding sensation being one of massive power in the clear vertical articulation of the façades. McGeoch's was an architectural masterpiece of its period and a totally convincing attempt by Burnet to express the structure and function of a building on its exterior.

Burnet was awarded the prestigious commission for the King Edward VII Galleries at the British Museum (1904–1914) and he transferred his main office from Glasgow to London. Shortly afterward, THOMAS TAIT joined the London firm, which then became Burnet and Tait (later Burnet, Tait, and Lorne), and together they designed the innovative Kodak Building in London's Kingsway (1910–1911). With its bold and functional expression of a steel frame, the Kodak became the model solution for a large number of office buildings built in Britain during the 1920s.

Burnet's final pioneering work was the Wallace Scott Tailoring Institute (1913–1916) in his native Glasgow. Now sadly mutilated by extensions, the original building marked the culmination of Burnet's development toward a rational style and was a fine example within the tradition of Glasgow industrial architecture.

Burnet was knighted on the completion of his British Museum work in 1914 and was awarded the Royal Institute of British Architects' Gold Medal in 1923. Although Tait became the principal designer after World War I, Burnet remained actively involved in the practice until his retirement in 1935. However, the simplicity of expression which had marked Burnet's earlier work is missing in the series of lavish and fairly ostentatious neoclassical office buildings which his firm produced in London between the wars.

A popular and respected member of his profession who had spent more than fifty years in practice, Burnet died in 1938. It can be said that CHARLES RENNIE MACKINTOSH was the soaring genius of the next generation of Scottish designers, but Burnet was certainly the premier figure of his own age; for indeed "Sir John was all things to all people, a cultured charmer, an excellent Classicist, a skillful Goth, and a substantial modernist" (Rankin, 1953, p. 6).

JOHN MCASLAN

WORKS

1878, Fine Art Institute; 1886–1890, Barony Church (with John Archibald Campbell); Glasgow, Scotland. 1890, Garmoyle (with Campbell), Dumbarton, Scotland. 1890–1891, Charing Cross Mansions (with Campbell); 1891–1892, Athenaeum Theatre (with Campbell); 1894, Glasgow Stock Exchange; 1895–1896, Saving Bank of Glasgow; Glasgow, Scotland. 1896–1900, Gardner Memorial Church, Brechin, Angus, Scotland. 1899, Atlantic Chambers; 1901, Elder Library; Glasgow, Scotland. 1903–1907, Civil Service and Professional Supply Building, Edinburgh. 1904–1914, King Edward VII Galleries, British Museum, London. *1905–1910, McGeoch's Store, Glasgow, Scotland. 1906–1910, Forsyth's Department Store, Edinburgh. 1909–1911, General Buildings, London. *1910–1911, Alhambra Theatre, Glasgow, Scotland. 1910–1911, Kodak Building (with Thomas Tait), London. *1913–1916, Wallace Scott Tailoring Institute (with Norman Dick); 1922, Cenotaph; 1923, University of Glasgow (by Burnet, Son, and Dick); Glasgow, Scotland.

BIBLIOGRAPHY

BURNET, JOHN JAMES 1923 "The Royal Gold Medal Address." *Journal of the Royal Institute of British Architects* 30:513–514.
GOMME, ANDOR, and WALKER, DAVID 1968 *Architecture of Glasgow.* London: Lund Humphries.
GOODHART-RENDEL, H. S. 1923 "The Works of Sir John Burnet, Royal Gold Medalist." *Architects' Journal* (London) 57:1066–1110.
PATERSON, ALEXANDER 1938 "Obituary: Sir John Burnet, R. A." *Journal of the Royal Institute of British Architects* 45:893–894.
RANKIN, ROBERT 1953 "Sir John J. Burnet and his Works." *Royal Incorporation of Architects in Scotland Quarterly Journal* 94:6,27–39.
SERVICE, ALASTAIR (editor) 1975 *Edwardian Architecture and its Origins.* London: Architectural Press.
SERVICE, ALASTAIR 1977 *Edwardian Architecture.* London: Thames & Hudson.

BURNHAM, DANIEL H.

Daniel Hudson Burnham (1846–1912) captured the essence of his own life and work in his famous aphorism: "Make no little plans, they have no magic to stir men's blood. . . . Make big plans . . . remembering that a noble, logical diagram once recorded will never die but long after we are gone will be a living thing asserting itself with ever growing insistency" (Hines, 1974, p. 401). Burnham's importance in the history of architecture lies chiefly in his ability to stimulate and direct the design efforts of others. Working with his several partners and associates in his own successive architectural offices, with collaborators on various city planning schemes, and as an international cultural entrepreneur, Burnham choreographed large efforts indeed.

Born in Henderson, New York, to parents of old-stock, Anglo-American lineage, the family moved to Chicago in 1854. Burnham's scholarship was less impressive than his social, managerial, and artistic skills, and he was rejected by both Harvard and Yale universities. To prepare him for the abortive college examinations, however, his parents had sent him to Massachusetts for private tutoring with Tilly Brown Hayward, who introduced him to architectural history and theory. This interest, coupled with his drawing skills, was sufficient to get him work with the Chicago office of Loring and Jenney. There, in 1867 and 1868, with the great engineer WILLIAM LEBARON JENNEY, Burnham had his first experience and training as an architect. Still feeling restless and unfulfilled, Burnham left for two unrewarding years as a silver speculator in Nevada. He returned to Chicago in 1870, where he worked in a succession of small architectural offices and looked for a better position.

In 1872, he secured that better job in the office of Carter, Drake, and Wight, which was busily engaged in rebuilding the burned-out city. Peter B. Wight was a sympathetic and influential mentor, but in 1873, Burnham and JOHN WELLBORN ROOT, a fellow Wight draftsman, formed their own partnership. The two men sensed the differing but reciprocal qualities of temperament and talent which, integrated, would form the ideal partnership. Brilliant, quick-witted, and amiable among friends, Root was shy and reserved in public. His myriad talents and interests, moreover, served frequently as distractions and excuses for procrastination. Burnham, on the other hand, toughened by his earlier failures, had grown increasingly aggressive, determined, and persuasive, and ultimately became the firm's chief administrator, planner, and liaison with clients. He was also, Root acknowledged, chiefly responsible for the planning and layout of most of the firm's buildings, and served as a perceptive critic of the architectural designs, which the two considered Root's special domain.

In 1874, the firm obtained its first major residential commission from the stockyards magnate John B. Sherman, a fortuitous event in Burnham's personal and professional fortunes since it resulted in his marriage to the client's daughter, Margaret. She and the five children they produced provided for Burnham lifelong happiness and stimulation. The acknowledged success of the Sherman design and the vast social connections of the Sherman family led, moreover, in the 1870s and 1880s, to important commissions, particularly residences, for such Chicago luminaries as music critic Reginald DeKoven (1888–1890), and such prominent businessmen as Edward Ayer (1885–1886). Related in scale and ambience to the residential commissions were small public and commercial structures, and numerous small train stations throughout the Middle West.

Attracted in their residential designs to the Queen Anne idiom and in their small public buildings to the Romanesque Revival, Burnham and Root took their cues from R. NORMAN SHAW and H. H. RICHARDSON. Like Richardson with the Romanesque and Shaw with the Queen Anne, Burnham and Root borrowed selectively from other eras and traditions but seldom allowed other styles to dominate their own developing synthesis.

Though they never made sufficient break with the past to signal a real revolution in house design, Burnham and Root's smaller work, in its inexorable trend toward greater simplicity, marked both the end of an older order and, in several late houses, a transition to the work of FRANK LLOYD WRIGHT and his contemporaries. Yet, as Burnham had confided to LOUIS H. SULLIVAN, he was "not going to stay satisfied with houses; my idea is to work up a big business, to handle big things, deal with big businessmen, and to build up a big organization" (Sullivan, 1956, pp. 285–286). And indeed it was the big things that counted most in Burnham's ultimate achievement, the tall build-

ings for the big businessmen which would come to be called skyscrapers.

Although Burnham and Root emulated Jenney's demonstration of the metal-cage, weight-bearing concept of the mid-1880s, and although they built numerous steel-framed buildings in the late 1880s and 1890s, their most famous skyscrapers, ironically, were three wall-bearing structures, all built in Chicago for the developers Peter and Shepherd Brooks. The ten-story Montauk Building (1881–1882) was virtually without traditional historic references, adumbrating in its stern obeisance to "functionalism" much of the ethic and aesthetic of the subsequent Modern movement. The Montauk was demolished to make way for the First National Bank Building (1903) of D. H. Burnham and Company. The Rookery Building (1885–1887) was a more consciously elaborate structure with Root's lush ornament highlighting the Romanesque styling. Its logical internal plan, attributed to Burnham, with four connecting wings surrounding a light court, would long serve as a model for skyscraper layout. The dark, stark Monadnock Building (1889–1891) eschewed ornament even more explicitly than the Montauk. Despite the anachronism, demanded by the client, of its elegantly flared wall-bearing structure, the Monadnock would become another favorite monument of Modernism. The Mills Building (1890–1891) in San Francisco reflected an important synthesis of elements: a steel-frame, four-winged plan around the central light court and the orderly Chicago school proportions as accented by Root's exuberant ornament.

Following Root's premature death in 1891, the

*Burnham.
Rookery Building.
Chicago.
1885–1887*

*Burnham
Monadnock Building.
Chicago.
1889–1890*

Burnham.
Reliance Building.
Chicago.
1891–1894

Burnham.
Union Station.
Washington.
1903–1907

office, reconstituted as D. H. Burnham and Company, widened its stylistic parameters to include buildings of the reemerging Beaux Arts neoclassical persuasion. Until his death in 1895, CHARLES B. ATWOOD replaced Root as the firm's major designer. After that, several architects carried design responsibilities, chief among whom was Pierce Anderson.

The Reliance Building in Chicago (1891–1894), commissioned in 1890, owes greater debts to Burnham's collaboration with Atwood than to Root's preliminary studies. Carrying the possibilities of the steel skeleton several steps beyond that of any existing structure, Burnham and Atwood produced a breathtaking glass tower of fourteen stories. The slim shaft contained no light court. Obviously resting on the Chicago frame, the building's façade was a tightly stretched skin of glass and terra cotta that confined and articulated the crisp, shallow bays. Over two-thirds of the street front wall surface was glass—a radically prophetic ratio that heralded the glass architecture of the twentieth century.

Eschewing the crystalline image of the Reliance Building for a sturdier monumentality, the beautifully proportioned and richly ornamented Fuller or Flatiron Building in New York (1903) towered above Broadway as a great triangular rock. The Railway Exchange Building (1903) and the Butler Brothers Warehouse (1913), both in Chicago, carried forward the ordered functionalism of the Chicago school tradition.

On the other side of the Burnham repertoire were templelike, Beaux Arts libraries, museums, and railroad stations. Union Station in Washington (1903–1907), epitomized this ceremonial mode, which came to be known as "Burnham Baroque." A fitting "vestibule" to the nation's capital, the station was one of the largest projects Burnham's office ever handled and constituted its most successful essay in the neoclassical mode. Omitting the usual high-arched train sheds at the rear, the building contained two primary elements: the central train, or midway, concourse,

leading onto the open train platforms, and the elaborate main waiting room or passenger concourse at the front. Rising high above the arched entrance porch, the vast barrel vault of the main waiting room ceiling was explicitly expressed as the building's dominant exterior feature.

Much of the Union Station's success and significance lay in its deference to the Washington plan. As such it was an integral component of the City Beautiful movement—the dominant trend and motivating force in American urban design from the 1890s to the 1920s. The City Beautiful was an ambitious and at times naïve and contradictory effort to achieve for American cities something approaching a "cultural parity" with the great urban centers of an older and grander European civilization. Not surprisingly, the American movement used those cities as models for its own remodeling efforts. Burnham was the movement's acknowledged father and leader.

However important the work of FREDERICK LAW OLMSTED and his contemporaries in earlier park and landscape architecture, the single most important catalyst in the launching of the City Beautiful was the 1893 Chicago World's Columbian Exposition. The White City became a microcosm of the City Beautiful movement on pragmatic, aesthetic, and ideological levels. For in addition to the splendor of the spectacle, with its formal Court of Honor and its allegiance to varieties of neoclassical architecture, the builders of this temporary city groped with many of the real problems of cities—from the efficiency of streets, sidewalks, waterfronts, and bridges to the problems of transportation, sustenance, and sewage. Whereas the relatively informal lagoon area to the north reflected the picturesque aesthetic that had characterized Olmsted's work, the court to the south formed the seminal image of the City Beautiful mentality. It was also prophetic that Burnham, the operator supreme, should choreograph the whole enterprise.

Meeting in Chicago for several crucial planning sessions in early 1891, the board of architects,

chaired by RICHARD M. HUNT, had agreed on the need for a formal court, determined the size and exact location of buildings, court, canal, and lagoons, and agreed upon a maximum cornice line for the buildings of the court. These general criteria led, with seeming inevitability, to a consensus in favor of Renaissance, Baroque, and other neoclassical stylistic motifs. Several of the architects, including Hunt and Charles McKim (see MCKIM, MEAD, AND WHITE), had trained at the Ecole des Beaux-Arts and had garnered their penchant for classicism there. All were acquainted with the formal, ordered, and axially oriented imperatives generally associated with Beaux-Arts aesthetics—a point of view that would dominate most City Beautiful architecture. And in 1893 the results seemed remarkable. In the same year that historian Frederick Jackson Turner proclaimed the "end" of the American frontier at one of the fair's numerous professional congresses, American architects and urban planners received from the White City a suggestive vision of things to come—new frontiers indeed of twentieth-century urbanism.

Over the next two decades, Burnham and his colleagues took the aesthetic and pragmatic lessons of the White City to the real cities of Washington, Cleveland, San Francisco, and Manila in the newly Americanized Philippines. Such critics as Sullivan decried the results and lamented the blow dealt the Modern movement by the neoclassical "contagion." Yet, then and later, Burnham and the City Beautiful had their champions and defenders.

Burnham and EDWARD H. BENNETT's *Plan of Chicago* (1909) achieved, of all plans of the period, the most significant integration of aesthetic and pragmatic strands. The substantive proposals encompassed the development of the whole Chicago area within a sixty-mile radius of the city's center, including a system of radial and concentric boulevards connecting the center with its outlying suburbs and linking the suburbs one with another. The plan also proposed numerous changes in the width, function, and general appearance of individual streets throughout the city. One of the most prescient recommendations was the call for what came to be the modern world's first double-level boulevard, one level for commercial traffic, the other for regular traffic. The Chicago River was to be straightened and enhanced for more efficient water transportation and river-borne commerce. The stations and tracks of the numerous connecting rail lines would also be relocated and consolidated into one or more union stations. A useful and beautiful park system would run twenty miles along Lake Michigan and throughout the city in an integral park network. The plan's elegant formal culmination in downtown Grant Park would be eastwardly inflected toward the new inner harbor development with breakwater causeways stretching far into the lake. Beaux Arts aesthetics would pervade the landscaping and public buildings. Although the proposed civic center was never completed, a remarkable percentage of Burnham and Bennett's proposals were later realized. The Chicago plan was Burnham's "largest" achievement.

Burnham grew very interested in cultural philanthropy and was a staunch supporter and board member of the Chicago Symphony Orchestra and the Art Institute of Chicago. He was one of the founders and lifelong benefactors of the American Academy in Rome. Of all the honors conferred upon him, the one he valued most was his appointment by President William H. Taft in 1910 as the first chairman of the national Commission of Fine Arts.

Burnham's "big" architecture and "no little" plans were components indeed of an even larger life.

THOMAS S. HINES

WORKS
BURNHAM AND ROOT
*1874, Sherman House; *1881–1882, Montauk Building; *1881–1883, Calumet Clubhouse; Chicago. 1883–1885, Montezuma Hotel, Las Vegas, Nev. *1885–1886, Ayer House; 1885–1887, The Rookery Building; *1886–1887, Art Institute; Chicago. *1887, Train Station, Kewanee, Ill. 1887-1888, Lakeview Presbyterian Church; *1888–1889, Valentine House; 1888–1890, DeKoven House; *1888–1890, Rand–McNally Building; Chicago. 1888–1890, Society for Savings Bank, Cleveland, Ohio. 1889–1890, Monadnock Building; *1890–1891, Herald Building; Chicago. 1890–1891, Mills Building, San Francisco. *1890–1892, Equitable Building, Atlanta, Ga. *1890–1892, Masonic Temple; *1890–1892, Woman's Building; Chicago.

D. H. BURNHAM AND COMPANY
1891–1894, Reliance Building, Chicago. 1901, Frick Building; 1902, Union Station; Pittsburgh. 1902, Marshall Field Retail Store; *1903, First National Bank; Chicago. 1903, Fuller (Flatiron) Building; New York. 1903, Railway Exchange Building; Chicago. 1903–1907, Union Station, Washington. 1904, Union Station, El Paso, Tex. 1905, Orchestra Hall, Chicago. 1905, Schmidlapp Memorial Library, Cincinnati, Ohio. 1909, Wanamaker's Store, Philadelphia. 1910, Claridge Hotel, New York. 1910, People's Gas Building; 1913, Butler Brothers Warehouse (built after Burnham's death); Chicago.

BIBLIOGRAPHY
BURNHAM, DANIEL H., and BENNETT, EDWARD (1909)1970 *Plan of Chicago*. Reprint. New York: Da Capo.
HINES, THOMAS S. (1974)1979 *Burnham of Chicago,*

Architect and Planner. 2nd ed. University of Chicago Press.

HOFFMANN, DONALD 1973 *The Architecture of John Wellborn Root.* Baltimore: Johns Hopkins University Press.

MONROE, HARRIET 1966 *John Wellborn Root: A Study of His Life and Work.* Park Forest, Ill.: Prairie School Press.

MOORE, CHARLES (1921)1968 *Daniel H. Burnham: Architect, Planner of Cities.* Reprint. New York: Da Capo.

SULLIVAN, LOUIS HENRY 1956 *The Autobiography of An Idea.* New York: Dover.

BURNS, FRED

Building a little at a time with driftwood and rusted nails found on the beach, Fred Burns (1890–) constructed his home (1941–?) in Belfast, Maine. It is a haphazard series of rooms, covered with irregularly sized wooden slats brilliantly painted with the variegated colors he could find in cans of left-over paint.

JANET KAPLAN

BIBLIOGRAPHY

WAMPLER, JAN 1977 Pages 166–175 in *All Their Own: People and the Places They Build.* Cambridge, Mass.: Schenkman.

BURROUGH, JAMES

James Burrough (1691–1764) was a serious if conservative follower of JAMES GIBBS's Palladianism, tempered by local baroque tastes. His reputation at Cambridge, where he lived and worked, was considerable: "The public Buildings of this University alone will convey a sufficient Idea to Posterity of his Knowlege in the polite Arts, & approved Abilities in Architecture" (*Cambridge Chronicle,* 1764).

TERRY F. FRIEDMAN

WORKS

*1732–1734, Queen's College (hall); 1736–1742, New Building, Peterhouse College; 1738, Great Saint Mary's Church (pulpit); 1742–1745, Trinity Hall (hall and quadrangle); 1749–1752, Sidney Sussex College (hall); *1751–1754, Great Saint Mary's Church (gallery); Cambridge. 1754, Assembly Rooms (interior), Norwich, Norfolk, England. 1754–1756, Peterhouse College (quadrangle); 1763, Clare College (chapel); Cambridge.

BIBLIOGRAPHY

William Coles's unpublished notes, including the Cambridge Chronicle *of August 11, 1764, are in the British Library, London.*

HUDSON, T. P. 1972 "James Gibbs's Designs for University Buildings at Cambridge." *Burlington Magazine* 114:842–848.

BURTON, DECIMUS

Although the long working career of Decimus Burton (1800–1881) ran from 1818 to 1864, his reputation today rests on a few buildings erected in London during the 1820s and on his great, bubble-like iron-and-glass conservatory for the Royal Botanic Gardens (1844–1848) at Kew. Unquestionably, his Regent's Park terraces and villas, his arch and screen at Hyde Park Corner and his Athenaeum Club building represent his finest work, all in the classical revival style although interpreted through the rigorist design discipline of J. N. L. Durand.

Born in London, he was the tenth child of JAMES BURTON, the builder–architect, in whose office he worked as an assistant while attending the Royal Academy schools. Through his father he was personally acquainted with such established professionals as HUMPHRY REPTON, George Maddox (with whom he studied drawing), and JOHN NASH, whose protégé he became. Under Nash's supervision he produced imaginative designs for Cornwall (1821–1823) and Clarence (1822–1823) terraces, Regent's Park, before establishing himself in independent practice in 1823. As a founding member of the Athenaeum Club, whose building he designed (1827–1830), he became personally known to many of the most influential men in government. His club membership provided him with a source of commissions for the rest of his professional life.

He applied the Regent's Park experience in the design of a large-scale, self-contained community to his planning on the Calverley Estate (1827–c.1840) at Tunbridge Wells, Kent. Burton placed buildings of a rather severe, stripped-down classical style on the regular sections of the plan, while classical, Gothic, and Italianate villas were situated within a landscaped park, following the dictates of picturesque practice as popularized by Nash and Repton. Also in Kent and nearby Sussex, he designed a number of country houses, those of the 1820s in an attractive Regency classical mode, whereas those of the 1830s were usually Tudor or rustic Gothic. His seven churches were essentially of an earlier classical form but dressed up in simple Gothic detail. One senses that Burton adopted these nonclassical styles after 1830 more to satisfy contemporary fashion than out of any genuine conviction as to their appropriateness.

He frequently provided designs for the specu-

lative development of estates made newly accessible through the rapid spread of the railway network, but few materialized. As an inland resort, his Beulah Spa (1828–1831), Upper Norwood (south London), in the rustic mode, was very popular in the 1830s. He handled the new port of Fleetwood, Lancashire (1835–1843), in essentially the same manner as that of the commercial section of his earlier Calverley Estate.

One of the most interesting aspects of his later career was as a designer of large conservatories. These came about through collaboration, however, as in the Great Conservatory at Chatsworth (1836–1840), where he worked with the landscape architect JOSEPH PAXTON. In designing one of the most beautiful early conservatories extant, the Palm Stove at Kew (1844–1848), he was assisted by the Dublin engineer RICHARD TURNER, with whom he worked again on the Winter Garden, Regent's Park (1845–1846). At Kew, he later added the more conventional Temperate House (1859–1862).

He was a Fellow of the Royal Society, of the Society of Antiquaries, and a vice-president of the Royal Institute of British Architects. He traveled in Spain, Italy, Greece, and even to Canada and the United States. He retired in 1869 and died in London, a lifelong bachelor.

PETER J. BOHAN

WORKS

1821–1823, Cornwall Terrace, Regent's Park; 1822–1823, Clarence Terrace, Regent's Park; 1822–1824, Grove House, Regent's Park; *1823–1827, The Colosseum, Regent's Park; 1825, Hyde Park (entrance archways); 1825, Hertford Villa, Regent's Park; London. 1827–1829, Holy Trinity, Kent, England. 1827–1830, Athenaeum Club, London. 1827–c.1840, Calverley Estate, Kent, England. *1828–1831, Beulah Spa, London. 1835–1843, Port of Fleetwood, Lancashire, England. *1836–1840, Great Conservatory, Chatsworth, Derbyshire, England. 1844–1848, Palm Stove (with Richard Turner), Royal Botanic Gardens, Kew, England. *1845–1846, Winter Garden Conservatory, Regent's Park (with Turner), London. 1859–1862, Temperate House Conservatory, Royal Botanic Gardens, Kew, England.

BIBLIOGRAPHY

BOHAN, PETER n.d. *The Architecture of James and Decimus Burton, 1784–1860.* Forthcoming book.
BOLTON, A. T. 1913 "Grove House." *Country Life* Mar. 22:11–16.
BRITTON, JOHN 1832 *Descriptive Sketches of Tunbridge Wells and the Calverley Estate.* London: The author.
Designs of Ornamental Gates, Lodges, Palisading, and Iron Work of the Royal Parks. 1841 London: Weale.
ELMES, JAMES 1827 *Metropolitan Improvements; or London in the Nineteenth Century.* London: Jones.
HIX, JOHN 1974 *The Glass House.* Cambridge, Mass.: M.I.T. Press.
HONOUR, HUGH 1953 "The Regent's Park Colosseum." *Country Life* 113:22–24.
HUSSEY, CHRISTOPHER 1940 "Grimston Park, Yorkshire." *Country Life* 87:276–280.
McRAE, J. F. 1927 "Burton's Tunbridge Wells." *Architect's Journal* 65:214–216, 249–250.
MONKHOUSE, C. 1975 "Fleetwood, Lancashire." *Country Life* 158:126–128, 290–293.
NARES, GORDON 1951 "The Athenaeum." *Country Life* 109:1018–1022.
RAMSEY, STANLEY C. 1913 "The Athenaeum Club, London." *Architectural Review* 34:54–58.
"St. Dunstan's Lodge, Regent's Park." 1936 *The Architect and Building News* 145:supplement.
SUMMERSON, JOHN (1935)1949 *John Nash: Architect*

to King George the Fourth. 2d ed. London: Allen and Unwin.

SUMMERSON, JOHN (1945)1978 *Georgian London.* 3d ed. Cambridge, Mass.: M.I.T. Press.

TAYLOR, G. C. 1939 "Holme House, Regent's Park." *Country Life* 86:444–448.

TAYLOR, G. C. 1940 "A House in Regent's Park." *Country Life* 87:416–418.

BURTON, JAMES

Born in London where his Scottish father was a builder, James Burton (1761–1837) rose to prominence and wealth between 1792 and 1816 as the principal speculative builder in the development of the great Bloomsbury estates. From 1817 to 1825 he supported JOHN NASH in the Regent's Street and Park scheme. This is reflected in his picturesque town planning for Saint Leonard's-on-Sea, Sussex, which he founded in 1828 and developed until his death.

PETER J. BOHAN

WORKS

*1784, Leverian Museum; 1792–1802, Foundling Estate (housing); 1798–1803, Bedford Estate (housing); *1802, The Russell Institution; 1807–1816, Skinners' Estate (housing); 1808–1814, Lucas Estate (housing); *1817, 1820–1824, Regent's Street buildings; 1818, The Holme, Regent's Park (with DECIMUS BURTON); 1818–1823, Eyre Estate (housing); 1822, York Terrace (eastern half); 1825, Chester Terrace; London. 1828–1832, Town of Saint Leonard's-on-Sea (Hotel, James Burton House, *Baths, Assembly Rooms, South Lodge, Clock Tower, *Saint Leonard's Church, Gloucester Lodge, Quarry House, North Lodge), Sussex, England.

BIBLIOGRAPHY

BAINES, J. MANWARING 1956 *Burton's St. Leonards.* Hastings (England) Museum and Art Gallery.

BOHAN, PETER n.d. *The Architecture of James and Decimus Burton, 1784–1860.* Forthcoming book.

OLSEN, DONALD J. 1964 *Town Planning in London: The Eighteenth and Nineteenth Centuries.* New Haven: Yale University Press.

SUMMERSON, JOHN (1935)1949 *John Nash: Architect to King George IV.* 2d ed. London: Allen and Unwin.

SUMMERSON, JOHN (1945)1978 *Georgian London.* 3d ed. Cambridge, Mass.: M.I.T. Press.

BUSBY, CHARLES AUGUSTUS

Charles Augustus Busby (1788–1834) was born in London and attended the Royal Academy School of Drawing. Bankruptcy interrupted his promising architectural career in 1814 and he visited America. After a disagreement with the architect FRANCIS GOODWIN, for whom he worked briefly on his return, he moved to Brighton in 1822 and entered into partnership with the local architect and builder Amon Wilds. During the 1820s, they transformed the appearance of Brighton and Hove in Sussex through two major architectural projects, Kemp Town and Brunswick Town. Busby was largely responsible for the design and Wilds for the execution.

J. M. RUTHERFORD

WORKS

1807, Nightingale Cottage, Nightingale Lane, Clapham Common, Surrey, England. 1810–1811, Commercial Rooms, Corn Street, Bristol, England. *1813–1814, Episcopal Jews' Chapel, Bethnal Green, London. c.1823, Gothic House (with Amon Wilds), Western Road; 1823–c.1830, Brunswick Town (with Wilds); 1823–c.1830, Kemp Town (with Wilds); 1824–1825, Saint George's Chapel (with Wilds); 1824–c.1830, Portland Place (with Wilds); Brighton, England.

BIBLIOGRAPHY

BUSBY, CHARLES AUGUSTUS (1808)1835 *A Series of Designs for Villas and Country Houses Adapted with Economy to the Comforts and to the Elegancies of Modern Life, with Plans and Explanations to Each.* 2d ed. London: Taylor.

BUSBY, CHARLES AUGUSTUS 1810 *A Collection of Designs for Modern Embellishments, Suitable to Parlours, Dining and Drawing Rooms, Folding Doors, Chimney Pieces, Varandas etc.* London: Lumley.

DALE, ANTONY 1947 *Fashionable Brighton: 1820–1860.* London: Country Life.

PORT, MICHAEL 1958 "Francis Goodwin (1784–1835): An Architect of the 1820s. A Study of His Relationship with the Church Building Commissioners and His Quarrel with C. A. Busy." *Architectural History* 1:60–72.

BUSCHETO

Named in a sepulchral inscription on the façade of Pisa Cathedral as an engineer/architect whose skill rivaled that of Daedalus, Buscheto (11th–12th centuries) is generally credited with the design (c.1064) and most of the execution (up to c.1115) of this fabric. Since the only documentary references to Buscheto occur in the first decade of the twelfth century, some reservations must be entertained about the likelihood of his presence, sixty years earlier, as designing architect. These references, moreover, may suggest an activity as administrator rather than as architect. Perhaps, having overseen the decisive constructional period of the project in the late eleventh century, he was credited on his tomb with having built it.

CHRISTINE SMITH

WORK

c.1064–1115, Cathedral of Pisa, Italy.

BIBLIOGRAPHY

SANPALOESI, PIERO 1975 *Il Duomo di Pisa.* Pisa, Italy: Nistri-Lischi.

SCALIA, GIUSEPPE 1972 "'Romanitas' pisana tra XI e XII secolo." *Studi medievali* Series 3 2:791–843.

BUTLER, WILLIAM F.

William Frederick Butler (1867–1918) was born in St. John's, Newfoundland and received his architectural education at the Technical School in Toronto. After working in Toronto he went to Chicago in 1893 as a works superintendent during the World's Fair. Returning to St. John's in late 1894 he started a partnership with James MacDonald of Sydney, Nova Scotia. Despite the fact that he had arrived at the end of the 1892 Fire building boom, Butler was nonetheless able to build a substantial practice involving both commercial and residential building.

He was responsible for most of the great Queen Anne style mansions built throughout St. John's after 1900 which are striking by virtue of their size and the quality of their workmanship—if not by their design. His commercial buildings are more sedate. An early Newfoundland member of the Canadian Architect's Association, Butler was drowned in the wreck of the S.S. *Florizel* in 1918.

SHANE O'DEA

WORKS

1894, Delgado Building; 1902, Kedra; 1905, Winterholme; 1912, King George V Institute; 1912, James Ryan House; St. John's, Newfoundland.

BUTTERFIELD, WILLIAM

William Butterfield (1814–1900) was the eldest son of a fairly well-to-do London chemist. His personal life seeems to have been particularly uneventful. Although, of course, he mixed with clients, churchmen, and other architects, and was a member of the Athenæum Club from 1858, he was hardly a public figure like some of his professional brethren, such as CHARLES BARRY, GEORGE GILBERT SCOTT, or even George E. STREET. Unlike almost all his contemporaries he did not strive hard for business. He never took part in public competitions, nor did he normally exhibit the new kind of spectacular perspectives of his works and projects. He did not produce books or articles in support of his views, and he had very few pupils. He was singularly independent of criticism of his work, in fact, he became increasingly adverse to it. But his individualism was not that of what one could call the "picturesque extremists," or "Rogue architects," like E. B. LAMB or SAMUEL S. TEULON; it was rather premonitory of that of his friend and lifelong admirer PHILIP S. WEBB. Zealous professionalism and scrupulous attention to planning and building were his main concerns.

His early training as builder and then as architect is of little significance. About his travels to the continent we know very little. He set up practice in 1840 and his first job was Highbury Chapel in Bristol (1842). The major and decisive event is the beginning, in the same year, of his close involvement with the Cambridge Camden (from 1845, Ecclesiological) Society, which brought the strongly "catholic" ritualistic element into Church of England design. Virtually all Butterfield's work—and his output, like that of many other church architects, was considerable—came under this patronage. Amongst the outstanding supporters of the High Church Movement were A. J. Beresford-Hope, who paid for most of All Saints, Margaret Street, London (1849–1859) and the seventh Viscount Downe, who financed most of the Yorkshire commission (1853–1854).

High Church Ritualism demands a meticulous attention to planning detail, clearly marking out internally and externally the features of the nave, chancel, the altar, the font, the tower or bell turret, as well as the more practical implements such as fireplaces. In many of his churches, even in Saint Ninian's Cathedral, Perth, begun 1847, Butterfield proudly shows a long external flue for the fireplace. A clear accentuation of differing practical functions is also prevalent in his church-related buildings, like chapels, vicarages, schools, convents. Butterfield normally insisted in designing all the internal fittings, as well, especially in churches, using a great variety of materials and techniques. Beginning with his first major works, Saint Saviour Church and Vicarage, Gloucestershire (1844–1845), and Saint Augustine's College, Canterbury (1844–1873) Butterfield makes use of a rather severe and solid looking "Middle Pointed" Gothic. All this was clearly influenced by what A. W. N. PUGIN was doing in those years. Butterfield, in fact, was the most faithful follower of Pugin, in that he, unlike Scott and Street, never looked outside Gothic.

Butterfield did, though, become the champion of a new and extremely influential movement in Victorian architecture, "constructional polychromy," that is polychromatic effects inside and outside a building achieved by varying materials of facing and construction, fulfilling the rationalist–moralist demand of truthfulness. The writings of JOHN RUSKIN and Street, and the works of many church architects are also important in the early development of this mode, but Butterfield's contribution to it is the most varied and probably the most outstanding, often characterized as "ugly" by modern critics like John Summerson (1949). An account of his work is to a large extent a description of the intricacies of decorations and materials. The first full-scale building is All Saints. The outside is far from spectacular, but very remarkable from the point of view of fitting a variety of functions into a very cramped space. The variation of materials on the outside is still comparatively modest, black brick diaper work on red brick—the latter a very unorthodox choice in London at that date. Inside, there is the full blaze of checkerboard patterns—mainly inlaid and tile work—virtually each part of the elevation and construction is a different material. In addition there are strongly colored stained glass and murals, and in the chancel the emphasis is on darkly glowing gilded work. In the 1850s Butterfield goes on with both more restrained polychromy, as in his small Yorkshire churches at Balne, Hensall, and Cowick (all 1853–1854), where he just varies the color of brick a little on the outside and whitewashes—the normal procedure—the inside; and with more strident polychromy in the small, but precious chapel of Bailliol College, Oxford (1854–1857), the building that gave rise to the well-known characterization "streaky bacon-style." Throughout the 1860s and 1870s—after which his output slowed down considerably—Butterfield adhered to his vivid polychrome patterning, at a time when most of his fellow church architects had already turned away from it toward a heavier and simpler style. Keble College, Oxford (1866–1886), is his most lavish work. Red brick—again, not the usual choice of material in Oxford—with black brick and limestone banding and diaper work. The major aim is to show the chapel soaring over the quad, and the decor is subservient to this purpose, for example, the way in which the interminable horizontal bands keep the dormitories to the ground in contrast with the blazing-out of decor on the upper parts of the chapel. All Saints, Babbacombe Torbay, Devon (1865–1874) also shows exuberantly complicated decoration inside and out. In many of his works Butterfield does show a sensitivity to the *genius loci*. Babbacombe church is placed amongst lush, almost southern trees; Saint Augustine's Penarth, Cardiff (1864–1866) straddles a cliff, defying the elements with its rough local Pennant stone and with a severe and heavy interior. Gradually, mid-Victorian interest in colored patterning is moving into Arts and Craftslike sensitivity for textural effects.

STEFAN MUTHESIUS

WORKS

1842, Highbury Chapel, Bristol, England. 1844–1845, Saint Saviour Church and Vicarage, Coalpitheath, Gloucestershire, England. 1844–1873, Saint Augustine's College, Canterbury, England. Begun 1847, Saint Ninian's Cathedral, Perthshire, Scotland. 1847–1878, Anglican Cathedral, Adelaide, Australia. 1849–1859, All Saints, Margaret Street, London. 1850–1863, Saint Dunstan's Abbey, Plymouth, England. 1853–1854, Church, School, and Vicarage, Balne, Pollington, England. 1853–1854, Church, School, and Vicarage, Cowick; 1853–1854, Church, School, and Vicarage, Hensall; Yorkshire, England. 1853–1856, Milton Ernest Hall, Bedfordshire, England. 1854–1857, Chapel, Bailliol College, Oxford. 1862–1866, Saint Cross, Clayton, Manchester, England. 1863–1868, Royal Hampshire County Hospital, Winchester, England. 1864–1866, Saint Augustine, Penarth, Cardiff, Wales. 1865–1874, All Saints, Babbacombe Torbay, Devon, England. 1866–1886, Keble College, Oxford. 1870–1877, Saint Augustine, Queen's Gate, London. 1877–1886, Saint Paul's Anglican Cathedral, Melbourne.

BIBLIOGRAPHY

BUTTERFIELD, WILLIAM 1850–1852 *Instrumenta Ecclesiastica*. 2 vols. London: Ecclesiological Society.

SUMMERSON, JOHN 1949 "William Butterfield, or the Glory of Ugliness." In *Heavenly Mansions, and Other Essays on Architecture*. London: Cresset Press.

THOMPSON, PAUL RICHARD 1971 *William Butterfield*. London: Routledge.

BUTTON, S. D.

Stephen Decatur Button (1813-1897) is best known for his work in Philadelphia and Camden, New Jersey between 1850 and 1880. Born in Preston, Connecticut, Button was early apprenticed to his uncle, and later at age twenty-one, became an assistant in the New York firm of George Purvis. For a decade afterward, he designed houses in Hoboken, New Jersey. In 1845, he moved to Florida and then Georgia and the following year, he won the competition for the Alabama State Capitol (1847) in Montgomery. In 1848, he moved to Philadelphia and formed a partnership with his brother in law, Joseph C. Hoxie. Although the firm was dissolved around 1852, Button maintained a flourishing career in Philadelphia and Camden through the late 1870s; he was also active with the Philadelphia Chapter of the American Institute of Architects.

ANTOINETTE J. LEE

WORKS

*1847, State Capitol, Montgomery, Ala. 1850–1851, John Brock, Sons, and Co. Building; 1855, Charles Leland Building; *1856, Dale, Ross and Withers Building; *1856–1858, Pennsylvania Railroad Building; 1859?, Spring Garden Lutheran Church; Philadelphia. 1874–1875, City Hall, Camden, N.J.

BIBLIOGRAPHY

TEITELMAN, EDWARD, and LONGSTRETH, RICHARD W. 1974 *Architecture in Philadelphia: A Guide.* Cambridge, Mass.: M.I.T. Press.
WEBSTER, RICHARD JAMES 1963 "Stephen D. Button: Italian Stylist." Unpublished M.A. Thesis, University of Delaware, Newark.
WEBSTER, RICHARD JAMES (editor) 1976 *Philadelphia Preserved: Catalog of the Historic American Buildings Survey.* Philadelphia: Temple University Press.
WEISMAN, WINSTON 1961 "Philadelphia Functionalism and Sullivan." *Journal of the Society of Architectural Historians* 20, no. 1:3–19.

BY, JOHN

John By (1779–1836), builder of the Rideau Canal in what was then designated the province of Upper Canada, now Ontario, was born in London. In 1799, he was commissioned in the Royal Engineers. In 1826, he was appointed superintendent of the Rideau Canal project, with the rank of lieutenant-colonel.

The objective was a navigable waterway through a 126-mile forested and malarial wilderness between Kingston, on Lake Ontario and the juncture of the Rideau with the Ottawa River, at the site of the nation's future capital. Completed in 1832, despite the ravages of fever and a high death toll, the Rideau Canal comprises 16.5 miles of artificial channel by-passing nonnavigable stretches in the natural waterway. The forty-seven limestone and sandstone locks, measuring 134 by 33 feet, raised the navigable channel 162 feet from Kingston to the height of land, thence dropping it 273 feet to the level of the Ottawa River. Twenty-four masonry dams controlled the water level. The two most formidable works were the 49-foot high Hog's Back Dam, whose initial design was modified following a washout, and the 62-foot high and 350-foot long Jones Falls Dam, embodying a novel keywork design and at the time the loftiest structure of its kind on the continent. Colonel By was the chief architect of these works, assisted by officers of the Royal Engineers and a small civilian staff. The work was let by contract.

By was recalled to England in 1832 under the pall of a parliamentary inquiry, the cost of the project having exceeded his estimates, unavoidably because of the time and place. Although cleared of all charges, By never received any recognition from the Crown, and he died a disappointed man.

EDWARD F. BUSH

BIBLIOGRAPHY

CAMP, R. A. 1971 "Canada's Tribute to Lieut. Colonel John By, Royal Engineers." *Royal Engineers Journal* 85:236–242.
FROME, EDWARD CHARLES 1844 "Account of the Causes Which Led to the Construction of the Rideau Canal. . . ." *Papers on Subjects Connected with the Duties of the Corps of Royal Engineers* 1:69–98.
HARRINGTON, LYN 1947 "Historic Rideau Canal." *Canadian Geographical Journal* 35:278–291.
HIND, EDITH J. 1965 "Troubles of a Canal-Builder: Lieut.-Col. John By and the Burgess Accusations." *Ontario History* 58:141–147.
LEGGET, ROBERT FERGUSON 1955 *Rideau Waterway.* University of Toronto Press.
MACTAGGART, JOHN 1829 *Three Years in Canada: An Account of the Actual State of the Country. . . .* 2 vols. London: Colburn.
MORGAN, H. R. 1925 "The Story of Colonel By, Founder of the City of Ottawa." *Saturday Night,* Aug. 29.
RAUDZENS, GEORGE 1970 "The British Ordnance Department in Canada: 1815–55." Unpublished Ph.D. dissertation, Yale University, New Haven.

BYRNE, BARRY

Francis Barry Byrne (1883–1968) received his architectural training under the apprentice system in the Oak Park Studio of FRANK LLOYD WRIGHT in Chicago from 1902 to 1909. After four years in Seattle, in 1913, he left for California where JOHN LLOYD WRIGHT and LLOYD WRIGHT, sons of Frank Lloyd Wright, introduced him to the sculptor Alfonso Ianelli, who later became his collaborator. In late 1913, Byrne took over the practice of his former fellow-pupil at the Oak Park Studio, WALTER BURLEY GRIFFIN, who was going to Australia. His own construction firm, formed in 1922, dissolved after the stock market crash in 1929. Byrne then opened a small office in Wilmette, Illinois, in 1930, where he worked until opening an office in New York in 1932. He returned to Chicago in 1945.

Although Byrne remained faithful to the organic principles of Wright's philosophy of architecture, and to Wright's method of designing a building in plan to meet the spatial needs for the use of each building, he developed an original style early in his career. Byrne's predilection for clean surfaces and motifs formed from the natural geometric patterns inherent in brickwork are reflected in the Kenna apartments (1916) in Chicago. Unlike Wright, Byrne used the wall as an undisguised functional element, articulated and decorated by well-proportioned door and window groupings.

Byrne's chief contribution to American architecture was his revolutionary change in the design of modern churches. He found the traditional long rectangular form unsuitable to the modern feeling that a church is a place for communal celebration. For the Church of Saint Thomas the Apostle (1922) in Chicago, he designed a light, airy, single-span interior and began the process of integrating the nave and sanctuary spaces which he pulled together even more closely in the churches that followed, Saint Patrick's (1924) in Racine, Wisconsin, and the Church of Christ the King (1926) in Tulsa, Oklahoma, and which achieved complete integration in the concrete Church of Christ the King (1928) in Cork, Ireland. This principle of a unified space for the priest and the people was given further expression in his later churches. Byrne was forty years ahead of his time, as it was not until the early 1960s that the reforms of the New Liturgy in the Roman Catholic Church made such integration a requisite element in church design.

In the 1920s, Byrne began an adjunct career as a serious writer on architectural subjects. His critical acumen was unfettered by preconceptions or prejudices, and he published articles on architecture in general, church architecture in particular, art criticism, and architectural history. His later essays were perceptive in analysis and at times prophetic of the course of modern architecture.

SALLY CHAPPELL

WORKS

1909, C. H. Clark House, near Seattle, Wash. 1914, J. B. Francke House, Fort Wayne, Ind. 1915, Chemistry Building, University of New Mexico, Albuquerque. 1916, Kenna Apartment Building; 1921, Immaculata High School; 1922, Church of Saint Thomas the Apostle; Chicago. 1924, Saint Patrick's, Racine, Wis. 1925, Clark College, Dubuque, Iowa. 1926, Church of Christ the King, Tulsa, Okla. 1928, Church of Christ the King, Cork, Ireland. 1936, Michael Williams House, Westport, Conn. 1939, Church of Saints Peter and Paul, Pierre, S.D. 1949, Church of Saint Francis Xavier, Kansas City, Mo. 1951, Saint Benedict's Abbey, Atchison, Kan. 1951, Saint Columba, Saint Paul, Minn. 1958, Holy Redeemer College, Windsor, Ontario. 1962, Saint Procopius College Library, Lisle, Ill.

BIBLIOGRAPHY

The Barry Byrne Papers are in the Chicago Historical Society.

BROOKS, H. ALLEN, JR. 1960 "The Early Work of the Prairie Architects." *Journal of the Society of Architectural Historians* 19:2–10.

BROOKS, H. ALLEN, JR. 1966 "'Chicago School': Metamorphosis of a Term." *Journal of the Society of Architectural Historians* 25:115–118.

CHAPPELL, SALLY 1966 "Barry Byrne, Architect: His Formative Years." *Prairie School Review* 3, no. 4:5–23.

CHAPPELL, SALLY 1968 *Architecture and Writings.* Unpublished Ph.D. dissertation, Northwestern University, Evanston, Ill.

CHAPPELL, SALLY 1969 "Barry Byrne: His Church Architecture." *Inland Architect* 11, no. 5:7–9.

CONDIT, CARL W. 1964 *The Chicago School of Architecture: A History of Commercial Building in the Chicago Area, 1875–1925.* University of Chicago Press.

LAVANOUX, MAURICE 1935 "St. Patricks Church, Racine, Wisconsin." *Liturgical Arts* 4, no. 2:91–100.

McCOY, ROBERT C. 1968 "Rock Crest/Rock Glen: Prairie Planning in Iowa." *Prairie School Review* 5, no. 3:5–39.

PEISCH, MARK L. 1964 *The Chicago School of Architecture: Early Followers of Sullivan and Wright.* New York: Random House.

RYAN, JOHN F. 1930 "Modernism Goes to Church." *American Architect* 138:50–53, 86.

SCANLON, JOHN HOLLY 1951 "Art and the Parish." *Liturgical Arts* 19:62, 71.

SWEENEY, JAMES JOHNSON 1932 "Barry Byrne and New Forms in Church Construction." *Creative Art* 11:61–65.

CABOT, EDWARD CLARK

Edward Clarke Cabot (1818–1901), president of the Boston Society of Architects from 1867 to 1901, was the first Bostonian to enter the profession from art rather than engineering. His first work and masterpiece, the Italianate Boston Athenæum (1847), suggests the simplicity of George M. Dexter, from whom he learned construction, and style and scale of ARTHUR D. GILMAN, his associate in the 1850s.

With James Elliot Cabot, he produced in stone the restrained, academic Second Boston Theater (1852), researched in Milan at La Scala. After 1875 with Francis W. Chandler, his distinguished, cutbrick Queen Anne Revival designs increasingly reflected Richardsonian (see H. H. RICHARDSON) overtones, lessening applied ornament using quarry-faced ashlar. Forming lastly Cabot, Everett, and Mead in 1888, he retired from his fifty-year practice in 1896.

MARGARET HENDERSON FLOYD

WORKS

1847, Boston Athenæum. *1848, Second Church First Parish, Brookline, Mass. *1849, Massachusetts Eye and Ear Infirmary (with J. Preston); *1852, Second Boston Theater (with Preston, J. C. Cabot, and Noury); 1860, Gibson House; Boston. *1860, Harvard University (President's House and Rogers Gymnasium), Cambridge, Mass. 1860, Russel House, Boston. 1873, Walter C. Cabot House, Brookline, Mass. 1878, Lee House, Beverly Farms, Mass. 1879, Lowell House, Boston. 1880, Insurance Company of North America, Philadelphia. 1880, Lee House; Boston. *1880, Torrey House, Dorchester, Mass. 1882, Hubbard Estate, Weston, Mass. 1883, Simes House; 1886, Allen Gymnasium; Boston. 1889, Johns Hopkins University Hospital, Baltimore.

BIBLIOGRAPHY

American Architect and Building News 1901 71:9.
The Boston Almanac. 1851 Boston: Collidge.
BOSTON ATHENÆUM 1976 *Change and Continuity.* Boston Athenæum.
BRIGGS, LLOYD VERNON 1927 *History and Genealogy of the Cabot Family 1475–1927.* 2 vols. Boston: Goodspeed.
CABOT, JAMES ELLIOT 1904 *Autobiographical Sketch.* Boston: Ellis.
ELIA, RICHARD 1978 "Edward Clarke Cabot: Watercolorist." *Antiques* 11:1068–1075.
LEWIS, ARNOLD, and MORGAN, KEITH (editors) (1886)1975 *American Victorian Architecture.* Reprint. New York: Dover. Originally published in French.
WHITEHALL, WALTER MUIR 1967 "Boston Society of Architects 1867–1967: A Centennial Sketch." Pages 15–72 in *Boston Society of Architects: The First 100 Years, 1867–1967.* Boston Society of Architects.

WITHEY, HENRY F., and ELSIE RATHBURN (1956) 1970 *Biographical Dictionary of American Architects* (*Deceased*). Los Angeles: Hennessey & Ingalls.

CABRERO, FRANCISCO

Francisco Cabrero (1912–) is a member of the first generation of post-Civil War Spanish architects. His work is largely monumental in style, recalling the traditional architectural vocabulary of Spain. Cabrero won a competition for the Casa Sindical in Madrid in 1949 and executed a number of housing projects throughout the 1940s and 1950s. In the depressed economic environment of postwar Spain, he was innovative in his use of traditional building materials such as brick and clay in the absence of unavailable iron armatures. His Virgen del Pilar housing project of 1948–1949 in Madrid represents innovations in concrete and approaches the functionalist tendencies of mid-century.

ELIZABETH A. T. SMITH

WORKS

1942–1944, Virgen del Casteñar Housing Project, Béjar, Spain. 1943, Monument to Reform (with R. Aburto); 1945, Housing Project, Madrid. 1946–1947, Workers' Housing Unit, San Rafael, Segovia, Spain. 1948, Buildings for First National Country Fair (with J. Ruiz); 1948–1949, Virgen del Pilar Housing Project; 1949, Casa Sindical (with R. Aburto); 1952–1953, Cabrero Residence, Ciudad Puerta de Hieno; 1954–1955, Grupo San Nicolás Housing Project; 1958–1959, National Hotel School (with J. Ruiz); 1959, Pavilion of the Ministry of Housing (with J. Ruiz), Fourth National Country Fair; Madrid.

BIBLIOGRAPHY

BOZAL, VALERIANO 1972 *Historia del arte en España*. 2 vols. Madrid: ISTMO.
CABRERO, FRANCISCO 1948 "Residencia de trabajadores en San Rafael (Segovia)." *Revista Nacional de Arquitectura* 8:317–320.
CABRERO, FRANCISCO 1953 "Bloque de Viviendas Protegidas en Madrid." *Revista Nacional de Arquitectura* 13:12–13.
FLORES LOPEZ, CARLOS 1961 *Arquitectura española contemporánea*. Bilbao, Spain: Aguilar.

CACCINI, GIOVANNI BATTISTA

Best known as a sculptor and follower of Giambologna, Giovanni Battista Caccini (1556–1612) was probably a student of Giovanni Antonio Dosio. He prepared projects for the façade of San Stefano, Pisa, Italy, and for the choir of Pisa Cathedral. In Florence, he designed the choir balustrade, high altar, and ciborium for Santo Spirito. At the Church of Santissima Annunziata, he built the Pucci Chapel and completed Antonio da Sangallo's (see SANGALLO FAMILY) portico. The tribune of San Domenico, Fiesole, Italy, may be his work. He also played a small part in the construction of the Palazzo Non Finito, Florence.

GARY M. RADKE

WORKS

1590s, Santo Spirito (choir decorations and ciborium); 1601–1604, Santissima Annunziata, Florence. 1603–1606, San Domenico (tribune), Fiesole, Italy. 1604–1615, Pucci Chapel, Santissima Annunziata, Florence.

CADY, J. C.

Born in Providence, educated at Trinity College, and trained by an unknown German architect, Josiah Cleveland Cady (1837–1919) was a leading exponent of the Romanesque Revival. In 1868, Cady established a New York City office (later J. C. Cady and Co; then as Cady, Berg, and See). Cady's early work was High Victorian, but, under the influence of the German Romanesque Revival and the work of H. H. RICHARDSON, he developed a powerful, generally monochromatic style popular for institutional buildings. Most notable are Cady's austere churches, particularly the New York Avenue Methodist Episcopal Church (1889–1892) in Brooklyn, New York, which exhibits Cady's masterful use of brick, and the Hampton Memorial Church (1886) in Virginia. Both employ the massive square towers Cady favored. He is best known as architect of the old Metropolitan Opera House in New York (1881–1884) and of the south wing of the American Museum of Natural History (1891–1908).

ANDREW SCOTT DOLKART

WORKS

*1870–1872/1873, Brooklyn Academy of Design (Brooklyn Art Association), N.Y. 1873, Oyster Bay Presbyterian Church, N.Y. *1881–1884, Metropolitan Opera House; *1884–1885, Broome Street Tabernacle; New York. 1884–1885, Saint Paul's Evangelical Lutheran Church, Brooklyn, N.Y. 1886, Hampton Memorial Church, Va. *1887, Church of the Covenant, Washington. 1888, Chittenden Hall, New Haven. 1888, Morgan Hall, Williamstown, Mass. *1888–1892, Presbyterian Hospital, New York. 1889–1892, New York Avenue Methodist Episcopal Church, Brooklyn, N.Y. 1891–1908, American Museum of Natural History (south wing); 1893–1894, Hudson Street Hospital; New York. 1894, Sheffield Laboratory, New Haven. 1894, Fayerweather Gym, Middletown, Conn. 1894–1895, Grace Methodist Episcopal Church, New York. 1894–1897, Yale Law School, New Haven.

BIBLIOGRAPHY

SCHUYLER, MONTGOMERY 1897 "The Works of Cady, Berg & See." *Architectural Record* 6:517–556.

CAGNOLA, LUIGI

Luigi Cagnola (1762–1833), a leading exponent of the neoclassical style in Italy, was born in Milan. After the invasion of Italy by Napoleon, he was in Venice and studied the work of JACOPO SANSOVINO and ANDREA PALLADIO. Both his own villa at Inverigo (1813–1833) and a project for the ex-empress Josephine at Malmaison (1812) show Cagnola working in a conscious but rather severe Palladian manner. His sober interpretation of antiquity is witnessed in the Pantheon-inspired Rotonda at Ghisalba (early 1800s) and the Propylaea-inspired Porta Ticinese (1801–1814) in Milan. For the Arco del Sempione (1806–1838) in Milan, Cagnola desired a slightly more ornate combination of sculpture and architecture. Approximately one thousand drawings and watercolors by him and his assistants are preserved in the Musei Civici, Milan.

GARY M. RADKE

WORKS

1801–1814, Porta Ticinese; 1806–1838, Arco della Pace (del Sempione); Milan. Early 1800s, Ghisalba (Rotonda), Italy. 1813–1833, Villa Cagnola d'Adda, Inverigo, Italy. After 1821, Duomo Nuovo (cupola), Brescia, Italy.

BIBLIOGRAPHY

ALBERICI, CLELIA 1963 "Disegni e stampe dell'Archivio Cagnola ora in deposito presso la Raccolta delle stampe Achille Bertarelli nei Musei Civici di Milano." *Arte Lombarda* 8:143–150.
HUBERT, GÉRARD 1976–1977 "Cagnola: Architecte de l'impératrice Joséphine? (à propos d'un projet pour Malmaison)." *Gazette des Beaux Arts* Series 6 88, Oct.:137–144; 89, Feb.:79.
MEEKS, CARROLL L. V. 1966 *Italian Architecture: 1750–1914.* New Haven: Yale University Press.
MEZZANOTTE, PAOLO 1930 *Le architetture di Luigi Cagnola.* Milan.

CAILLTEAU, PIERRE

See LASSURANCE, PIERRE.

CAIUS, JOHN

John Caius (1510–1573) was an important patron and amateur designer at a time when the professional architect hardly existed in England. A humanist physician (he studied with Vesalius in Padua), he refounded Gonville Hall in Cambridge as Gonville and Caius College in 1557, became Master in 1559, and began a new court in 1565. The remarkable feature of his expansion of the college was a series of three gates symbolizing the student's progress through the university. Though eclectic and residually Gothic, the gates were highly advanced for the time in England in the sophistication of their classical details. The college *Annals* (begun by Caius) state that the Gate of Honour was fashioned "according to the very form and figure which Doctor Gaius himself during his lifetime had prescribed to the architect." This was presumably the obscure Fleming Theodore Haveus (de Have), who executed Caius's monument in the college chapel.

IAN CHILVERS

WORKS

1565, Gate of Humility (moved from college entrance to the master's garden); 1567, Gate of Virtue; 1573–1575, Gate of Honour; Gonville and Caius College, Cambridge.

BIBLIOGRAPHY

CAIUS, JOHN 1904 *The Annals of Gonville and Caius College.* Edited by John Venn. Cambridge Antiquarian Society.
CAIUS, JOHN 1912 *The Works of John Caius, with a Memoir of His Life by John Venn.* Edited by E. S. Roberts. Cambridge University Press.
OSVALD, ARTHUR 1934 "Gonville and Caius College, Cambridge." *Country Life* 75:248–254.
PEVSNER, NIKOLAUS (1954)1970 *The Buildings of England: Cambridgeshire.* 2d ed. Harmondsworth, England: Penguin.
ROYAL COMMISSION ON HISTORICAL MONUMENTS, ENGLAND 1959 Part 1, pages 72–81 in *An Inventory of the Historical Monuments in the City of Cambridge.* London: H.M. Stationary Office.
SUMMERSON, JOHN (1953)1977 *Architecture in Britain 1530 to 1830.* 6th ed., rev. Harmondsworth, England: Penguin.
VENN, JOHN 1901 Volume 3, pages 30–62 in *Biographical History of Gonville and Caius College.* Cambridge University Press.
WILLIS, ROBERT, and CLARK, J. W. 1886 Volume 1, pages 157–185 in *The Architectural History of the University of Cambridge.* Cambridge University Press.

CALAMECH, ANDREA

Andrea Calamech (1514–1578) was born into a family of artists and spent his early days in Carrara, Italy, whose indigenous white marble provided raw material for many Renaissance sculptors. Andrea, too, began as a sculptor. At first, Calamech (Italianized as Calamecca) worked in Tuscany as head sculptor at the Cathedral of Orvieto. Later, he was in Florence sculpting statues for MICHELANGELO's obsequies under BARTOLOMEO AMMANNATI. In Messina, Sicily, he earned his fame as architect. Sometime around 1565, he was chosen by the Senate of Messina to direct the architectural and sculptural programs of the Cathedral of Santa Maria (12th–16th cents.).

TINA WALDEIER BIZZARRO

WORKS

c.1565–1578, Santa Maria; *1565?–1578?, Ospedale Civico; *1565?–1578?, Palazzo Reale; *1565?–1578?, Palazzo Senatorio; Messina, Italy.

BIBLIOGRAPHY

CALANDRA, E. 1948 *Breve Storia dell-architettura in Sicilia*. Bari, Italy.
CONDIVI, ASCANIO 1746 *Vita di Michelangolo Buonarroti, pittore scultore, architetto e gentiluomo fiorentino, pub. mentre viveva dal suo scolare Ascanio Condivi*. Florence: Albizzini.
Guida d'Italia del Touring Club Italiano, Sicilia. 1953. Milan: Allegretti.
HEYDENREICH, LUDWIG, H., and LOTZ, WOLFGANG 1964 *Architecture in Italy: 1400 to 1600*. Harmondsworth, England: Penguin.
SAMONA, G. 1950 "L'Architettura in Sicilia dal secolo XIII a tutto il Rinascimento." In *Atti VII° Congresso Nazionale della Storia Architettura*. Palermo, Italy: The congress.
VASARI, GIORGIO (1568)1973 *Le opere di Giorgio Vasari, con nuove annotazioni e commenti*. 9 vols. Edited by G. Milanesi. Reprint. Florence: Sansoni. Originally published in 1550 with the title *Le vite de più eccelenti architetti*. There are many English translations and selections from Vasari's *Lives;* the standard one by G. du C. de Vere was published in ten volumes in London by the Medici Society in 1912–1915.

CALDERARI, OTTONE

The architecture of Ottone Calderari (1730–1803) dots the cityscape of Vicenza and other parts of the Veneto in Italy. A native of Vicenza, the home town of ANDREA PALLADIO, Calderari began his studies of architecture under the Jesuit Domenico Cerato, who founded, in 1748, a school devoted to the study of Palladian principles of architecture. Calderari achieved great fame during his lifetime and was dubbed by his contemporaries "prince of modern architects." He was applauded and commemorated by poets, other artists, and historians. He designed many illustrious secular and ecclesiastical buildings as well as altars. His architectural drawings and writings were published after his death.

TINA WALDEIER BIZZARRO

WORKS

1774, Villa, Vivaro, Italy. 1776, Palazzo Cordellina (now Scuola Media), Vicenza, Italy. 1780, Church of Sant'Orso, Italy. n.d., Palazzo del Seminario, Verona, Italy. n.d., Villa, Breganze, Italy. n.d., Villa, Marostica, Italy.

BIBLIOGRAPHY:

ANTI-SOLA, S. 1804 *Un dolente tributo di versi*. Vicenza, Italy.
DIEDO, A. 1811 "Elogio di Ottone Calderari." In *Atti d. Accad. di belle arti*. Venice: The academy.
Guida d'Italia del Touring Club Italiano, Veneto. 1954 Milan: Vallardi.
RUMOR, S. 1905 Volume 1 in *Gli scritt. vic. del sec. 18 e 19*. Venice, Italy.

CALDERINI, GUGLIELMO

Born in Perugia, Italy, Guglielmo Calderini (1837–1916) attended the local Academy before studying engineering in Turin with CARLO PROMIS. He served as civil engineer of Perugia (1862–1870) and director of monuments for Rome, Aquila and Chieti (1870–1876) and taught in Perugia, Pisa, and Rome. Calderini entered all the major public competitions in Italy. His most significant work, the monumental Palazzo di Giustizia in Rome (1888–1910), was designed in a richly ornamented neobaroque style.

JOY M. KESTENBAUM

WORKS

*1879–1881, Palazzo delle Belle Arti, Turin, Italy. 1880–1886, Duomo (façade), Savonna, Italy. 1887–1888, Palazzo Bianchi; 1888–1889, San Costanzo (reconstruction); Perugia, Italy. 1888–1890, Public Baths, Fontecchio, Italy. 1888–1910, Palazzo di Giustizia; 1893–1910, Quadriportico of San Paolo fuori le mura; Rome. 1907–1909, Palazzo Cesaroni, Perugia, Italy.

BIBLIOGRAPHY

CALDERINI, GUGLIELMO 1890 *Il Palazzo della Giustizia in Roma*. Rome: Ripamonte.
MARCONI, PAOLO 1974 *Calderini*. Rome: Editalia.
MEEKS, CARROLL L. V. 1966 *Italian Architecture: 1750–1914*. New Haven: Yale University Press.
MILANI, GIOVANNI BATTISTA 1917 *Le Opere Architettoniche di Guglielmo Calderini*. Milan: Bestetti & Tumminelli.

CALZA-BINI, ALBERTO

Born in Rome, Alberto Calza-Bini (1881–1957) graduated from the Accademia di Belle Arti of Rome in 1900. Active in the fields of restoration and housing, he held numerous important positions in various professional, educational, and political organizations.

DENNIS DOORDAN

WORKS

1926–1932, Theater of Marcellus (restoration); 1928, Istituto Case Popolari Headquarters; Rome. 1933, Istituto Nazionale Assicurazioni Housing, Bari, Italy. 1933, Palazzo Gravina (restoration), Naples.

BIBLIOGRAPHY

"Alberto Calza-Bini." 1974 Volume 17, pages 50–52 in *Dizionario Biografico degli Italiani.* Rome: Istituto della Enciclopedia Italiana.
CENNAMO, MICHELE 1973 *La Prima Esposizione Italiana di Architettura Razionale.* Naples: Fausto Fiorentino.

CAMBIO, ARNOLFO DI

See ARNOLFO DI CAMBIO.

CAMERON, CHARLES

Charles Cameron (c.1740–1812), the son of a London mason and associate of ISAAC WARE, was responsible for an English interpretation of neoclassicism that was one of the varieties of that style which flourished in Russia in the late eighteenth century.

Cameron's architectural ideas are best seen in *Baths of the Romans* (1772), the fruit of his study in Rome from about 1766 to 1769. A piece of scholarly self-advertisement, the work sought to continue and correct ANDREA PALLADIO's work on Roman antiquity, following LORD BURLINGTON's *Fabbriche Antiche* (1730), and anticipated but was inferior to OTTAVIO BERTOTTI SCAMOZZI's monumental *Fabbriche ci disegni di Andrea Palladio,* begun in 1776. The book prompted an invitation from Catherine II for Cameron to come and work in Russia. He was essentially her architect, and Cameron's career virtually ended with her death in 1796. His work as court architect was concentrated on the two palaces of Tsarskoe Selo and Pavlovsk with only a handful of outside commissions, such as Batourin (c.1790s).

Many of Cameron's designs for both Tsarskoe Selo and Pavlovsk have survived. His substantial collection of prints and drawings was broken up in 1812, and it was from these and from subsequent sales that drawings in Russian collections and the Soane Museum, London, are derived. The designs themselves, in pen and ink and watercolor, are attractive and sophisticated but below the standard of JACQUES-LOUIS CLÉRISSEAU or ROBERT ADAM, and as a draftsman Cameron was certainly inferior

to his successor GIACOMO QUARENGHI.

At Tsarskoe Selo, Cameron added to BARTOLOMMEO RASTRELLI's Summer Palace (1750–1755) a series of private apartments (1780–1784), the Agate Pavilion (1782–1785) and the Cameron Gallery (1783–1785). In these additions, the change of style from Rastrelli's baroque was abrupt physically as well as visually. The Agate Pavilion was a cautious essay in the Louis XVI style, and the Cameron Gallery was closely derived from West Wycombe Park (c.1764). The unifying element was Cameron's feeling for the Picturesque, which made a brilliant composition from terrace, staircases (notably the Pente Douce), and the lakeside setting. This quality was again apparent at Pavlovsk, where a Palladian villa of the Trissio a Meledo type was set in a landscaped park with an ideal town in the true neoclassic spirit at its gates.

At both palaces, Cameron produced a series of apartments of unmatched splendor and importance. Starting with a simple and conventional room he used glass, bronze, agate, and malachite to create an exotic art worthy of Fabergé. His style is seen at its richest in the Lyons Drawing Room (1784), with its painted decoration by Ivan Scotti, and at its most chaste in the Cold Bath of the Agate Pavilion, both at Tsarskoe Selo.

A. A. TAIT

WORKS

1780–1784, First-Fifth Apartments (later restored), Summer Palace, Tsarskoe Selo, Russia. 1781–1796, Pavlovsky Palace (later restored by Cameron), Pavlovsk, Russia. 1782–1785, Agate Pavilion; 1782–1787, Cathedral of Saint Sophia; 1783–1785, Cameron Gallery, Summer Palace, Tsarskoe Selo, Russia. 1785–1796, Garden Pavilions and Town, Pavlovsky Palace, Pavlovsk, Russia. c.1787, Bakhtchi-Serai; 1790s, Batourin (restored in 1911); Crimea, Russia.

BIBLIOGRAPHY

BERTOTTI SCAMOZZI, OTTAVIO (1776–1783)1968 *Fabbriche di disegni di Andrea Palladio.* 4 vols. Reprint of 1796 ed. London: Tiranti.
BURLINGTON, LORD 1730 *Fabbriche Antiche disegnate da Andrea Palladio Vincentino.* London.
CAMERON, CHARLES 1772 *The Baths of the Romans.* London: Scott.
LOUDOMSKI, GEORGES (1740–1812)1943 *Charles Cameron.* London: Nicholson & Watson.
RICE, T. TALBOT, and TAIT, A. A. 1967–1968 *Charles Cameron.* London Arts Council. Exhibition Catalogue.

CAMPANINI, ALFREDO

Born in Gattatico di Praticello (Reggio Emilia), Italy, Alfredo Campanini (1873–1926) died in

Milan where he had worked since 1896 when he graduated from the Accademia di Brera. For a short period, he was one of the leading interpreters of the Milanese Stile Liberty, beginning with a house on Via Petrella (1902) and followed by the Villino Verga (1904) and his own house on Via Bellini (1906). After 1909, he designed a neorococo building on Via Senato and the Istituto San Vincenzo in Milan and executed many restoration works including the Castle of Borgo Grazzano Visconti.

MANFREDI G. NICOLETTI

WORKS

1902, House, Via Petrella; 1904, Villino Verga; 1904-1906, Casa Campanini; 1909, Istituto San Vincenzo; 1910-?, Castle of Borgo Grazza Visconti (restoration); Milan.

BIBLIOGRAPHY

BOSSAGLIA, ROSSANA 1968 *Il Liberty in Italia.* Milan: Mondador.
MEEKS, C. L. V. 1966 *Italian Architecture: 1750-1914.* New Haven: Yale University Press.
NICOLETTI, MANFREDI 1978 *L'Architettura Libery in Italia.* Bari, Italy: Laterza.
REGGIORI, FERDINANDO 1947 *Milano: 1800-1943.* Milan: Edizioni del Milione.

CAMPBELL, COLEN

Colen Campbell (1676-1729) was born in Boghole, Nairnshire, Scotland. How he acquired his knowledge of architecture is not known for certain: he at least claimed to have studied architecture both in England and abroad for several years. It is possible that he was infected with an interest in Palladianism by JAMES SMITH, the most prominent Scottish architect of the time, from whom he subsequently inherited a set of pseudo-Palladian drawings; conceivably he was encouraged in the direction of his studies by GEORGE CLARKE and WILLIAM BENSON, both members of the Commission for Fifty New Churches and both already interested in the academic revival of INIGO JONES. Just as important in the formation of Campbell's taste would seem to be the instinctive interest in simple geometrical forms, the repetition of elements and boxlike outlines, evident even in his earliest, non-Palladian drawings. Possibly it was a result of his upbringing, a touch of prudent Scottish Calvinism; else his training as a lawyer made him judicious and methodical. ANDREA PALLADIO, anyway, was a natural source to turn to: Godfrey Richards's 1663 translation had appeared in successive impressions and even JOHN VANBRUGH was

trying to obtain a copy of the French edition in 1703.

Campbell's first work was Shawfield Mansion (1711), Glasgow, built for a fellow member of the Campbell clan. It was, in architectural type, extremely conservative, a reversion to the Restoration style of Belton house though with a faintly detectable mannerism in the window surrounds. In the following year, he presented to the Commission for Fifty New Churches a set of designs which look like academic exercises, curiously jejune, with a method of composition that is characteristically additive. In 1713, he made his first drawings for Wanstead. Why Sir Richard Child should have entrusted this major commission to an unknown Scot is hard to fathom. The earliest designs are the most elementary outlines. Presumably, Campbell was a convincing salesman and possibly his method appealed to his client's sense of economy. It should be remembered that, in his *Discourse on Trade,* Child's father had written that "Luxury and Prodigality are as well prejudicial to Kingdoms as to private Families"; and it is significant that Campbell later wrote that he was "confined as to the Dress of the windows," suggesting that it was his employer who stipulated the lack of decoration. Maybe Child regarded plainness as an appropriate accompaniment to his collection of antique statuary or else was reluctant to indulge in nouveau riche display. In form, Wanstead (c.1714-1720) was a simplified version of Castle Howard, with the proportions distended to accord with a taste for more static design: it was a triumphant success, much visited, admired for the ingenuity of its planning and the richness of its interiors, and it was the model for a succession of other houses, including Wentworth Woodhouse, Nostell Priory, Prior Park.

In 1716, Campbell capitalized on this success by publishing plates of Wanstead among the masterpieces of British architecture in the first volume of his *Vitruvius Britannicus.* It appears to have been much more a piece of entrepreneurial self-advertisement than a statement of architectural faith. Though it praises "the great Palladio" as "the ne plus ultra of his art" and condemns FRANCESCO BORROMINI for having "endeavoured to debauch Mankind with his odd and chimerical Beauties," it does not, as had Shaftesbury, dismiss the School of CHRISTOPHER WREN: indeed, Campbell is happy to illustrate the works of Vanbrugh, NICHOLAS HAWKSMOOR, and THOMAS ARCHER alongside his own oversimplified pastiches. The first plates show Saint Paul's juxtaposed to Saint Peter's, a clear indication of its chauvinist, rather than purist, intention, and Inigo Jones is praised for his "Addition of Beauty and

Majesty," an implicit condemnation of too great simplicity. Much more important than its text was the fact that *Vitruvius Britannicus* established reproduction by outline engraving, which inevitably encouraged axial, geometrical, and unornamented composition. Moreover, it fostered a competitive interest in architecture among the aristocracy and provided a repertory of designs.

The years immediately following the Treaty of Utrecht and the Hanoverian Accession were extremely prosperous. The building industry enjoyed an unprecedented boom and Campbell was employed in a spate of country house commissions. In 1716, he was asked by Sir Charles Hotham, a successful soldier also known as a classical scholar, to design a town house in Beverley. It was a cubic block, topped with balustrade and urns and flanked by side wings. In 1718, Campbell designed Ebberston Lodge for William Thompson, Member of Parliament for Scarborough and a brother-in-law of Hotham. Here again, he mitigates the severity of the outline by incorporating a certain amount of decorative ornament: entrance capitals with frostwork banding, keystones carved with female heads, a rusticated basement and a cupola since removed. In 1720, work began on Newby Park, a villa commissioned by Sir William Robinson, a prominent York merchant who wanted a rural retreat. Like the later Stourhead, it was modeled on the Villa Emo at Fanzolo, though, once again, with impure details.

Through this circle of Yorkshire gentry, Campbell must have met LORD BURLINGTON, a neighbor and friend of the Hothams, already engaged in reconstructing his London House; and Burlington, looking for an outlet for his colossal wealth and presumably liking Campbell's work, adopted him as his protégé. Campbell was responsible for the gateway to Burlington House (1718–1719), soon to be satirized by Hogarth for its Italianate pretention; he designed 31–34, Old Burlington Street (1718–1723), and himself leased Number 32, after Pope had rejected his scheme for a *palazzotto* on the grounds of expense. He "presented a draught" for the Burlington School for Girls (1719–1721), although he seems not to have supervised the construction. Lord Hervey described number 31 as "the smuggest, sprucest, cheerfulest thing I ever saw," a commendation which suggests an anthropomorphic view of Palladianism.

In 1722, Campbell was at the peak of his career and was invited to design Houghton House for Sir Robert Walpole and Mereworth for the Honorable John Fane. In these he reveals his divergence from the more dogmatic ideas of Lord Burlington. At Houghton, the windows are strongly rusticated in the manner of the Palazzo Thiene and in the course of construction, domes were added, closely comparable to the one at Mereworth (1722–1725), giving an air of theatricality to the design; the interiors were of a superlative lavishness. Mereworth should be compared with Chiswick House, Burlington's contemporary interpretation of the Villa Rotunda: it is much less severe, less meticulously ordered; the intercolumniation is wider and the pediment cartouche and garlands and the swelling shapes of the dome create an effect of fantasy very

Campbell. Mereworth Castle. Kent, England. c.1722–1725

different from Chiswick. It seems that thereafter Campbell was dropped by Lord Burlington, replaced by WILLIAM KENT.

In the last few years of his life, Campbell designed comparatively little, making alterations to Compton Place (1726–1727), Eastbourne, and advising John Aislabie on additions and alterations at Waverley and Studley Royal. He had perhaps been overtaken by fashion and was unsuited to the more doctrinaire Palladianism of LORD PEMBROKE and Lord Burlington: though he prepared an edition of Palladio more scholarly than GIACOMO LEONI's, he appended to it a set of plates and an ornamental frontispiece that suggest that he was becoming less, rather than more, restrained in his decorative effects: the chimneypieces, cornices, and doorcases are festooned with foliage, surrounded by cherubs, supported by herms. It should be noted that even in his most sparse drawings, he frequently added figures of a Hogarthian lightheartedness. It seems that his adoption of Palladio was less rigid, less fervent than current taste dictated; and by the time of his death in 1729 his career was already effectively at an end.

As an architect, Campbell appears less of a pioneer than used to be supposed. By the time of Wanstead, Shaftesbury had already called for a national style, and amateurs and academics alike were turning to Inigo Jones. Campbell's success must be attributed to the fact that he grasped the requirements of his clients: architecture was, to some extent, conceived as a language of social status and Campbell supplied a formula that was neat, easily reproducible, an instant badge of respectability without the supposed coarseness of Vanbrugh. Certainly, he had a natural inclination for rectilinear shapes and seems to have been incapable of manipulating a building plastically; but he was not averse to using decoration as a garnish. The Earl of Oxford described him as an ignorant rascal. He died a rich man.

CHARLES SAUMAREZ SMITH

WORKS

1711–1712, Shawfield Mansion, Glasgow, Scotland. *c.1714–1720, Wanstead House, Essex, England. 1716–1717, House for Sir Charles Hotham, Beverley, Yorkshire, England. 1717–1724, The Rolls House, Chancery Lane, London. 1718, Ebberston Lodge, Scarborough, Yorkshire, England. 1718–1719, Gateway to Burlington House, Piccadilly; 1718–1723, 31–33, Old Burlington Street; 1719–1721, Burlington School for Girls, Boyle Street, London. 1720–1728, Newby Park, Yorkshire, England. c.1720–1724, Stourhead, Wiltshire, England. 1722–1729, Houghton Hall, Norfolk, England. c.1722–1725, Mereworth Castle, Kent, England. 1724, Pembroke House, Whitehall, London. c.1725, Waverley Abbey, Surrey, England. 1726–1727, Compton Place, Eastbourne, Sussex, England. 1728, House for Stamp Brooksbank, Hackney, Middlesex, England.

BIBLIOGRAPHY

BOYNTON, L. 1970 "Newby Park, Yorkshire: The First Palladian Villa in England." Pages 97–105 in H. M. Colvin and John Harris (editors), *The Country Seat: Studies in the History of the British Country House Presented to Sir John Summerson.* London: Allen Lane.

BREMAN, P., and ADDIS, D. 1972 *Guide to Vitruvius Britannicus.* With a foreword by John Harris. New York: Blom.

CAMPBELL, COLEN (1716–1725)1967 *Vitruvius Britannicus or The British Architect.* 3 vols. Reprint. New York: Blom.

CAMPBELL, COLEN 1728–1729 *Andrea Palladio's Five Orders of Architecture.* London: S. Harding.

COLVIN, H. M. 1974 "A Scottish Origin for English Palladianism?" *Architectural History* 17:5–13.

CONNOR, T. P. 1977 "The Making of Vitruvius Britannicus." *Architectural History* 20:14–30.

CONNOR, T. P. 1979 "Colen Campbell as Architect to the Prince of Wales." *Architectural History* 22:64–71.

GOODFELLOW, G. L. M. 1964 "Colin Campbell's Shawfield Mansion in Glasgow." *Journal of the Society of Architectural Historians* 23, no. 3:123–128.

GOODFELLOW, G. L. M. 1966 "Colin Campbell." *Architectural Review* 140, Aug.:145–146.

GOODFELLOW, G. L. M. 1969 "Colin Campbell's Last Years." *Burlington Magazine* 111, Apr.:185–191.

McMAHON, K. A. 1965–1968 "The Beverley House of the Hotham Family." *Transactions of the Georgian Society for East Yorkshire* 4, no. 3:37–49.

STUTCHBURY, H. E. (1967)1972 *The Architecture of Colen Campbell.* Manchester (England) University Press.

CAMPBELL, JOHN ARCHIBALD

The early life of John Archibald Campbell (1859–1909) is obscure, but he was apprenticed to the Glasgow firm of Burnet and Son from 1877 to 1880. He then trained in Paris at the Ecole des Beaux-Arts, returning to Glasgow in 1883. From 1886 to 1897, he was in partnership with JOHN J. BURNET, with whom he designed the city's famous Athenaeum Theatre in 1891.

Campbell was in independent practice from 1897 until 1907, when he took A. D. Hislop into partnership. Campbell designed a number of striking office buildings in Glasgow as well as several country houses on the outskirts of that expanding city before his early death in 1909.

Campbell's major work is the Northern Insurance Building (1908–1909). Although the street façade is unexceptional, the functional rear elevation of that building was pioneering in its bold and expressive articulation of the steel frame structure.

JOHN McASLAN

WORKS

1886–1890, Barony Church (with J. J. Burnet); 1888, Shawlands Old Parish Church; Glasgow, Scotland. 1890, Garmoyle (with Burnet), Dumbarton, Scotland. 1890–1891, Charing Cross Mansions (with Burnet); 1891–1892, Athenaeum Theatre (with Burnet); Begun 1898, Britannia Building; 1899, 71–75 Robertson Street; Begun 1900, 3, 7–23 Kirklee Road; 1902, 157–167 Hope Street; 1904, United Kingdom Providence Building; 1905, 50 Argyle Street; 1908–1909, Northern Insurance Building; Glasgow, Scotland.

BIBLIOGRAPHY

GOMME, ANDOR, and WALKER, DAVID 1968 *Architecture of Glasgow.* London: Lund Humphries.
SERVICE, ALASTAIR (editor) 1975 *Edwardian Architecture.* London: Architectural Press.

CAMPEN, JACOB VAN

See VAN CAMPEN, JACOB.

CAMPORESE FAMILY

Pietro Camporese (1726–1781) and his two sons, Giulio Camporese (1754–1840) and Giuseppe Camporese (1763–1822), were all members of the Accademia di San Luca. Pietro started the Subiaco Cathedral, finished by his sons, and worked at the Vatican Musea where Giuseppe built the sculpture galleries (1786). Giuseppe's cathedrals of Genzano and Carbognano show compromise between the academic tradition and the new neoclassic modes. His offices included the directorship of the Highways and Bridges Commission and of excavation of the Roman and Trajan forums.

Pietro Camporese the Younger (1792–1873), son of Giulio, also was a member of the Accademia di San Luca. He became director of the first commission after the unification of Italy to study the enlargement of Rome and was a member of the jury for the façade competition of Florence Cathedral. His work is characterized by strong urbanistic research, especially in the façade of San Giacomo degli Incurabili Hospital, Rome (1843) balanced by antiquarianism in the façade of the Palazzo Wedekind, Rome (1838) built with columns from Vei, and in the Renaissance handling of the palazzetto in Piazza Nicosia, Rome.

MARTHA POLLAK

WORKS

1745, Santa Maria in Aquiro (façade); 1786, Vatican Musea (sculpture galleries); 1825–1829, San Paolo fuori le Mura (reconstruction); 1834, San Vito e Modesto (restoration); 1837, Argentina Theater; 1838, Palazzo Wedekind (façade); 1843, San Giacomo degli Incurabili Hospital (façade); 1869, San Thomas of Canterbury; Rome, n.d., Carbognano Cathedral, Italy. n.d., Collegio Germanico, via della Scrofa, Rome. n.d., Genzano Cathedral, Italy. n.d., Instituto di belle arti, via Ripetta; n.d., Orfanelli Hospital, Piazza Capranica; n.d., Palazzetto, Piazza Nicosia; n.d., Palazzo dei Senatori (council hall); n.d., Santa Maria in Monserrato (rebuilding of convent and church); n.d., Spanish Embassy to the Vatican (decoration of second floor); Rome. n.d., Subiaco Cathedral, Italy.

BIBLIOGRAPHY

LAVAGNINO, EMILIO 1961 Volume I in *L'arte moderna dei neoclassici ai contemporanei.* Turin, Italy: Unione Tipografico-Editrice Torinese.
MEEKS, C. L. V. 1966 *Italian Architecture, 1750–1914.* New Haven: Yale University Press.

CANDELA, FELIX

Master shell builder Felix Candela (1910–) has specialized in the construction of light concrete roofs, creatively exploiting the tensile strength of reinforced concrete. For his advancements in the field of architecture and engineering he has won many awards.

Born in Madrid, Candela studied architecture at the Escuela Superior de Arquitecture and was continually fascinated by structural theories. He focused his studies on analytic geometry, trigonometry, as well as on German innovations in laminated structures. He graduated in 1935 and after working as an engineer for a year he joined the Republican forces in the Spanish Civil War. In 1939, he was taken prisoner and sent to Mexico. He soon adopted Mexico as his own country and began experimenting with shell construction and foam concrete, assuming that structural resistance came from form and not mass.

At first, engineers turned down his designs convinced that earthquakes and defective subsoil made them impractical, but eventually a friend let him design a bowling alley, and Candela's career was launched. In 1951, he came to the aid of the university in Mexico City when it needed a pavilion for the study of cosmic rays with a roof of 1.5 centimeters in thickness. Thought to be impossible, Candela's hyperbolic paraboloid that vaulted the small laboratory shook when people jumped on it but refused to buckle. The success of his shells brought many lecture invitations and commissions. In 1951, he formulated his new philosophy of structure, analyzing reinforced concrete in terms of its inherent potential as a shell form and rejecting its application in traditional post-and-lintel support system.

Candela.
Cosmic Rays Pavilion.
University City, Mexico
*   City.*
1951

Candela's greatest satisfaction has been in the ability of concrete shells to be aesthetically pleasing and to cover habitable spaces economically. Ideal for covering large areas such as markets or factories, Candela's shells have been used successfully for low-cost single-family dwellings, churches, restaurants, and even television posts. The Xochimilco Restaurant (1958), Candela's favorite work, is composed of octagonal groin vaults formed by four intersecting hyperbolas while Lomas de Cuernavaca Chapel (1958–1959) used a thin shell in a saddle shape to cover an outdoor amphitheater. As one of Candela's most unusual designs, it brings to life the Mexican tradition of open chapels. In the Church of the Miraculous Virgin (1954), Candela reflects ANTONIO GAUDÍ's use of hyperbolic paraboloids. Architecture for Candela becomes an art only when it is scientific.

Candela has completed over 900 shell structures in Mexico varying from umbrella shapes to inverted mushrooms and other bizarre forms exhibiting his genius and the creative potential of reinforced concrete.

ELIZABETH D. HARRIS

WORKS
1948, Bowling Alley; 1951 Cosmic Rays Pavilion, University City; Mexico City. 1952, Novedades Houses, Jardín de Pedregal, Mexico. 1954, Church of the Miraculous Virgin; 1955, Exchange Hall; 1956–1957, Coyoacan Market; Mexico City. 1957, La Jacaranda Cabaret, Juárez, Mexico. 1957, Texas Instruments Factory, Dallas, Tex. 1957–1958, Beach Club, Playa Azul, Venezuela. 1958, Xochimilco Restaurant, Mexico City. 1958–1959, Chapel Lomas de Cuernavaca, Mexico. 1959–1960, Synagogue, Guatemala City. 1960–1963, Baccardi Brewing Company, Cuatitlán, Mexico. 1966, Santa Monica Church; 1968, Olympic Stadium; Mexico City.

BIBLIOGRAPHY
FABER, COLIN   1963   *Candela: The Shell Builder.* New York: Reinhold.
SMITH, CLIVE BAMFORD   1967   *Builders in the Sun: Four Mexican Architects.* New York: Architectural Book Publishing Company.

CANDILIS JOSIC WOODS

The partnership of Candilis Josic Woods in Paris between 1955 and 1969 produced some of the most important theoretical and built projects of the postwar European reaction to the orthodox modernist urbanism of LE CORBUSIER and of the Congrès Internationaux d'Architecture Moderne.

The association began in the late 1940s in the office of Le Corbusier, with the meeting of Georges Candilis (1913–), a Russian-born Greek trained in architecture at the Technical Institute in Athens, and Shadrach Woods (1923–1973), an American trained in engineering in New York and in philosophy at Trinity College, Dublin. In 1951, they organized an architectural and engineering office in Tangier for the ATBAT (Atelier des Bâtisseurs) organization. In the following several years, the office completed a number of significant projects, principally housing in North Africa. By 1955, Candilis and Woods had returned to Paris and were joined by Alexis Josic (1921–), a Yugoslav trained in architecture at Belgrade University. Their practice was dominated by commissions for large-scale public works including housing, universities, and new communities. A number of unbuilt competition entries, such as the Bochum University competition (1962) and the Frankfurt competition (1963), were widely publicized.

Through realization of a large number of built projects, a theoretical position gradually evolved, principally around Woods. The CIAM urbanism of point-towers in parklike settings was challenged by a move toward more continuous organization. It attempted to respond more closely to human activity as form generator. At the time of the competition entry for Berlin University (1963), these principles began to exert a wide influence in Europe, especially through the forum of the Team 10 group. In 1969, the partnership was dissolved. Candilis and Josic remained in Paris in separate practice. Woods returned to the United States where his ideas had gained recognition especially in academic circles and among an emerging group of young architects whose interests were frequently associated with the public realm. Before his untimely death in 1973, Woods practiced in New York. His most significant project was a study for Cooper Square housing on the Lower

East Side (1972). He also taught at Harvard, Yale, and Washington Universities, and wrote on urbanism.

RICHARD A. PLUNZ

WORKS

1956, Housing, Blanc Mesnil, France. 1956, Housing, Gagny, France. 1956, Housing and Market, Bois Colombes, France. 1956–1961, New Community, Bagnols sur Cèze, France. 1957, Housing, Bobigny, France. 1957, Housing, Chatenay Malabry, France. 1958, Gymnasium, Cachan, France. 1958, Housing, Lyon, France. 1958, Housing, Nimes, Tour l'Evêque, France. 1958, Housing, Paris. 1959, Housing, Marseille, France. 1960, Hotel, Cesaeria, Israel. 1960, Housing, Pau, France. 1961, Housing, Avignon, France. 1961, Housing, Monosque, France. 1961, Housing, Nîmes, France. 1961, New Community, Toulouse le Mirail, France. 1962, Artisans Workshops, Sevres, France. 1962, Primary School, Balata, Martinique. 1962, Primary School, Geneva. 1962, Radiology Center for the Fondation Rothschild, Paris. 1962, Urban Renewal, Fort Lamy, Chad. 1963–1973, Free University of Berlin.

BIBLIOGRAPHY

CANDILIS, GEORGES 1973 *Recherches sur l'Architecture des Loisirs.* Paris: Editions Eyrolles.
CANDILIS, GEORGES 1975 *Toulouse le Mirail.* Stuttgart, Germany: Krämer.
CANDILIS, GEORGES 1977 *Bâtir la Vie: Une Architecte Témoin de son Temps.* Paris: Stock.
WOODS, SHADRACH (editor) 1968 *Candilis, Josic, Woods: Building for People.* New York: Praeger.
WOODS, SHADRACH 1970 *What U Can Do.* Houston, Tex.: Rice University.
WOODS, SHADRACH 1975 *The Man in the Street.* Baltimore: Penguin.
WOODS, SHADRACH, and PFEUFER, JOACHIM 1968 *Stadtplanung Geht Uns Alle An.* Stuttgart, Germany: Krämer.

CANEVARI, RAFFAELE

Trained in engineering and bridge construction, Raffaele Canevari (1825–1900) was one of the most active and innovative of Roman architects of the period 1870–1890. He was responsible for the first great monumental building of the new, unified Italy: the Ministry of Finance in Rome (1872–1875), a large, impressive, highly decorated building, showing considerable Beaux-Arts influence. In his Museum of Agriculture (1873; now the Ufficio Geologico), Canevari experimented with glass-and-iron construction in ways which opened up the interior and allowed interpenetration between interior and exterior. In this aspect of his work, he was a forerunner of GIULIO DE ANGELIS and Giulio Podesti.

BARBARA MILLER LANE

WORKS

1872–1875, Ministero delle Finanze; 1873, Museo dell' Agricoltura (now the Ufficio Geologico); 1881–1883, Palazzetto, via Gregoriana; Rome.

BIBLIOGRAPHY

ACCASTO, GIANNI; FRATICELLI, VANNA; and NICOLINI, RENATO 1971 *L'architettura di Roma capitale: 1890–1970.* Rome: Golem.
BORSI, FRANCO 1966 *L'architettura dell' unita d'Italia.* Florence: Le Monnier.
GUTTRY, IRENE DE 1978 *Guida di Roma moderna: Architettura dal 1870 ad oggi.* Rome: De Luca.
MEEKS, CARROLL L. V. 1966 *Italian Architecture: 1750–1914.* New Haven: Yale University Press.
PAOLIS, SAVERIO DE, and RAVAGLIOLI, ARMANDO 1971 *La Terza Roma.* Rome: Palombi.
PORTOGHESI, PAOLO 1968 *L'eclettisomo a Roma: 1870–1922.* Rome: De Luca.

CANINA, LUIGI

Luigi Canina (1795–1856), after GIUSEPPE VALADIER, was the most important among the architects who helped bring about the triumph of archeological classicism in Rome in the first half of the nineteenth century. Not only was he an international champion of classicist architecture as established in a precise canon of rules of Greek, Roman, and also Egyptian derivation, he was equally active as an archeologist, a researcher of buildings, and an architectural historian. His vigorous defense of dogmatic classicism in no way impeded him either in adapting ancient Christian styles to the modern purposes of church building or in conceding that new technical possibilities and modern building materials had their uses. Insofar as Canina based his architectural system on firm rules and sure historical-archeological knowledge, he also claimed that it was generally applicable and that it could be generalized, amplified, and integrated.

Canina was born in Casale Monferrato and received his training with FERDINANDO BONSIGNORE in Turin. In 1818, he went to Rome on a scholarship. Here he came in contact with archeology, and in 1822, on the strength of his archeological architectural work ("L'Anfitheatro Flavio descritto, misurato e restaurato"), he was received into the Accademia di San Luca. Restoration work brought him into contact with Valadier, whose double orientation, to both architecture and archeology, he took over with even greater intensity. From 1822 onward, he was concerned with projects for the Parco Borghese in Rome, and in 1825 he succeeded ANTONIO ASPRUCCI and Marco Asprucci as the Borghese family architect. In this capacity, Canina produced his most important architectural legacy, primarily monuments for the Parco Borghese, ranging from obelisks and Roman triumphal arches to bridges in the shape of Egyptian propylaea. The high point among these are the great propylaea forming the entrance gate to the park from the Piazza Flaminia. This literal reproduction of the Ionic order of the Temple of Poseidon on Cape Sunion, coupled as it is with a simultaneous typological flexibility, constitutes, so to speak, Canina's manifesto on rule and freedom in classicist building. The building, erected in 1827/1828, is part of an international tradition of gateway building—from the Brandenburger Tor by CARL GOTTHARD LANGHANS (1789–1794) to Charles PERCIER AND Pierre Leonard FONTAINE's Arc de Triomphe du Caroussel (1806–1807), to LUIGI CAGNOLA's Porta Ticinese in Milan (1814), LEO VON KLENZE's Tor on the Königsplatz in Munich (1817), and DECIMUS BURTON's Propylaea at Hyde Park Corner in London (1828) whose stylistic closeness to Canina's work shows the related archeological orientation of English and Italian classicism. Canina had personal ties to England and intended to defend the values of classical architecture through a European union. He traveled there three times, both for that purpose and in the hope of carrying out his projects for the duke of Northumberland.

Still, the fact that JOSEPH PAXTON had used iron in his Crystal Palace did not mislead Canina into rejecting the possibilities of modern technology; as a result of his openness to technology, he had himself earlier invented an elevator (*sedia meccanica*). Rather, he attempted to give modern iron architecture an artistic (classical) dimension, which he legitimized through archeologically documented domestic and utilitarian architecture (see his *Particolare genere di architettura proprio degli usi domestici,* Rome, 1852).

As a result of a journey to Turin as an attendant of Queen Maria Cristina of Spain he obtained the commission to the Turin Cathedral and the square on which it fronts, a project which he took as a starting point for fundamental reflections on church architecture and on the basilical system. The position he assumed was once more in partial approval of the solutions of LOUIS HYPPOLITE LEBAS, JACQUES IGNACE HITTORF, and WILLIAM INWOOD, but it sharply rejected A. W. N. PUGIN's neo-Gothic style. And here, too, Canina advocated the expansion of modern architecture on solid classic and archeological foundations. His reconstruction of the Fortuna temple in Palestrina quite possibly had an effect on GIUSEPPE SACCONI's monument to Vittorio Emanuele II and thus serves to illustrate the continued impact of his ideas for which he had hoped.

Apart from the above-mentioned works for the Borgheses, which were largely confined to restorations inside the Palazzo Borghese, and with the exception of the modernized Casino Vagnuzzi, (1839–1840) Canina's work remained without visible architectural result. He gained all the more prominence in his various academic, archeological, and even political functions. In 1839, he succeeded A. Nibby in the important office of *Commissario alle antichità* and in this capacity led the archeological excavations in the Forum, on the Esquiline, the Via Appia, and in Veij. Finally, Canina consolidated his leading position as an archeologist through large editorial enterprises. In 1827, his *Architettura Greca* appeared as the first volume of the monumentally conceived *Architettura dei principali popoli antichi considerata nei monumenti,* which was modeled on the historiographic achievements of Winckelmann, SEROUX D'AGINCOURT, Cicognara, and Hirt. Together with the parts on *Architettura romana* (1830ff.) and *Architettura egiziana* (1839ff.), the work forms a corpus of ancient architecture which—in emulation of D'Agincourt—was to be illustrated by the monuments themselves. The arrangement consists of a chronological description of the most important monuments (*Storia dell'arte*), a typological history together with comments on insights derived from the sources (*Teorica dell'arte*), and a monographic presentation of selected works (Descrizione dei monumenti). In 1848–1851, *Gli Edifizj di Roma antica cogniti per alcune reliquie descritti e dimostrati nell'intera loro architettura* appeared as the second of his chief monumental works.

Almost all Canina's archeological campaigns were accompanied by sumptuous publications: Cere (1838), Campagna romana (1839), Tusculo (1841), Veij (1847), Etruria marittima (1851), Via Appia (1853). This extremely rich publication activity—to which the standard reference work, the *Indicazione topografica di Roma antica* (Rome, 1831; fourth edition, Rome, 1850) must be added—was guaranteed by his own printing operation. This commitment was sustained by the conviction that classical architecture was grounded in precise archeological knowledge. In fact—despite the relatively small size of his built oeuvre—the archeological classicism of the first half of the nineteenth century reached a high point under Canina.

WERNER OECHSLIN
Translated from German by Beverley R. Placzek

WORKS

1825–1827, Bridges, Obelisks, and Triumphal Arches, Parco Borghese; 1827–1828, Gateway, Via Flaminia;

Parco Borghese; 1830–1833, Temple of Aeschylus, Parco Borghese; c.1839, Casino Vagnuzzi; Rome.

BIBLIOGRAPHY

BENDINELLI, G.   1953   "Luigi Canina." *Rivista di storia, arte e archeologia per la provincie di Alessandria e Asti* 62:1–431.

CANINA, LUIGI   1828   *Le nuove fabbriche della Villa Borghese denominata.* Rome: Pinciana.

CANINA, LUIGI   (1843)1846   *Richerche sull'architettura più propria dei tempi cristiani, ed applicazione della medesima ad una idea di sostituzione della Chiesa cattedrale di S. Giovanni in Torino.* Rome.

CANINA, LUIGI   1852   *Particolare genere di architettura domestica decorato con ornamenti di svelte forme ed imimpiegato con poca varieta dai più rinomati popoli antichi ora solo ordinato con metodo e proposto alla applicazione delle fabbriche moderne in parte costrutte col legno e ferro fuso.* Rome: Bertinelli.

DONALDSON, T. L.   1856   *A Brief Memoir of the Late Commendatore Canina, Architect.* London.

HOFFMAN, P.   1965   *La casina Vagnuzzi sulla Flaminia.* Rome: Instituto di Studi Romani.

MEEKS, CARROLL L. V.   1966   *Italian Architecture, 1750–1914.* New Haven: Yale University Press.

OECHSLIN, WERNER   1977   "Dekor und Architektur, Canina's Kritik an Paxton's Crystal Palace." *Kunstchronik* 30:120–122.

RAGGI, O.   1857   *Della vita e delle opere di L. Canina, architetto e archeologo di Casal Monferrato.* Casal Monferrato, Italy: Nani.

CANO, ALONSO

Alonso Cano (1601–1667) presents the paradox of an artist acclaimed as a great architect, although almost no work of architecture or architectural theory can be attributed to him. Also an outstanding painter and sculptor, Cano is recognized as one of the great figures of the baroque in Spain.

Born in Granada in 1601, Cano received his earliest training from his father Miguel, a moderately successful maker of altarpieces. In 1614 the family moved to Seville where Miguel Cano established a workshop and apprenticed his son to Francisco Pacheco, a leading painter in Seville, an art theorist, and a member of an intellectual elite who met as an informal academy to discuss the arts. The experience was decisive in shaping Cano's style and career, as he was exposed to an exalted view of art and of the artist which contrasted with his own provincial and artisan background. Cano also became friends with Diego Velázquez, then finishing his apprenticeship with Pacheco, and when he became a master in the painters' guild in 1626, he was also training as a sculptor, probably with Juan Martínez Montañes.

In the 1620s Cano assisted his father in designing altarpieces and by 1629 he and his father were accepting commissions jointly. His father also signed contracts which he turned over to his son. Many of Cano's works of this time are lost or destroyed, but those that survive show that Cano had already developed the harmonious and elegant manner—what has been called a classicizing baroque style—which he later practiced in Madrid.

Cano left Seville in 1638 for a position as *ayudante de camara,* in effect painter in residence, to the Count-Duke Olivares in Madrid. Until 1652, Cano remained in the capital, where he joined the confraternity of painters and moved in the circle of court artists around Velázquez.

In spite of his being very well placed, Cano's career in the capital may not have lived up to his expectations. He was a famous artist of the court but no major commission seems to have come his way. Cano was always in debt and he was further distressed in 1644 when his young second wife was murdered. He went briefly to Valencia, seemingly with the intention of taking holy orders there, but returned to Madrid where Philip IV arranged for his appointment as a prebendary at the Cathedral of Granada. Thus began years of bitter controversy between Cano and the canons of the cathedral. From 1652 until 1657 Cano was in Granada engaged on paintings for the cathedral, but the canons refused to confirm his appointment and he traveled to Madrid to plead his case successfully before the king. In 1660 Cano returned to Granada where he remained working on projects for the cathedral until his death. He painted the series of scenes from the life of the Virgin in the apse and designed the Cathedral façade.

There is no evidence that Cano ever took formal training as an architect or that he practiced architecture in the usual sense. But he was not a complete amateur. As early as 1635, Cano was described as "a painter, sculptor and architect" in the contract for the altarpiece for Santa Paula in Seville. In 1643 Cano also applied for the position of master of the works at the Cathedral of Toledo. He was not appointed but his application suggests his competence as an architect. Palomino de Castro y Velasco's assertion that Cano was a master of the works in the royal bureaucracy is thought to be false, but Cano was unquestionably considered an architect by the king. In 1651, Philip IV described Cano as "a great architect, an excellent painter and sculptor."

It is not clear to what extent this reflected Cano's practice as an architect. *Retableros* and *ensambladores*—the designers and producers of altarpieces—were not usually styled architects since they practiced a trade, but architects did design altarpieces. Since an altarpiece required an architectural framework, it is likely that Cano learned the rudiments of Renaissance architectural vocabulary from his father. He certainly pursued his studies independently, since in 1645 he deposited a large collection of architectural books, prints, and moldings (perhaps models of decorative elements) in the Cistercian monastery in Valencia. No trace of an architectural commission from his years in Seville has been found. His only recorded architectural work in Madrid is the temporary festival arch at the Puerta de Guadalajara, designed for the entry of Mariana of Austria in 1649. However this arch created a sensation among the artists of the capital who apparently appreciated its novel, unclassical proportions and decorative motifs.

No visual record of the arch survives and thus the evaluation of Cano's position as an architect rests upon his designs for altarpieces, his drawings (which are largely figure studies or for altarpieces and decorative works), and his design for the façade of the Cathedral of Granada (1667).

Cano's altarpiece for the church of Santa Maria in Lebrija (1629–1632) is the masterpiece of his early years. Cano's sculpture and design are considered the prototypes for the development of the baroque altarpiece in Spain. Instead of the complex, Italianate architectural motifs, usually found in Sevillian altarpieces, Cano used a colossal order of four spirally fluted Composite columns to create a tryptych form. A decorated attic is substituted for the second story. Architecture now dominates the painting and sculpture and gives the altarpiece a new authoritative scale and unity. Cano's design may owe something to the altarpieces of Martínez Montañes and even more to the Jesuit architect Alonso Matías whose altarpiece in the Jesuit house in Seville (1604–1606) was certainly familiar to Cano.

Cano's decorative vocabulary was always full-bodied but restrained. His favorite garlands of fruit and leaves and his elegant curved moldings can be studied in his drawings, many of them from his years in Madrid. The extent of Cano's influence on architecture and decoration in the capital is still unclear. The style he formed in Seville was not inconsistent with contemporary trends in Madrid. The emphasis is upon an open articulated structure and a colossal order appear in Hermano Bautista's nave of San Isidro in Madrid. Tovar Martin has noted the impact of Cano's decoration upon a number of architects in Madrid; on the other hand, Cano's altarpieces in Getafe outside Madrid (1645) seems influenced by the classicizing decorative vocabulary of Giovanni Battista Crecenzi.

Cano's design for the façade of the Cathedral of Granada has been criticized as an amateurish overscaled altarpiece by Fernando Chueca Goita but it is praised by most historians. George Kubler considers it "one of the most original and personal works in all Spanish architecture" (Kubler & Soria, 1959, p. 25). Cano himself died shortly after the church canons accepted his design, but his scheme was followed in its essentials. The façade was not completed until the eighteenth century. The division of the façade into three bays was dictated by DIEGO DE SILOE's existing foundations and pedestals, but Cano rejected the system of superimposed orders which had characterized earlier projects and designed a two-storied triumphal arch, effectively eliminating the orders altogether. "Cano's is the entire system of pilasters, layered planes, and of swags and bosses hanging like wasps nests from the upper horizontal members. One is reminded of muscle and tissue interweaving over an animal's skeleton." (*Ibid.,* 1959, p. 25) Cano's façade is a splendid match to the open verticality of Siloe's interior. Its steep proportions and novel decoration transcend classical canons yet the effect is strikingly classical in its structural coherence.

Cano's most important followers were Sebastián Herrera de Barnuevo and Juan Luis Ortega who executed Cano's designs for the Angel Custodio in Granada (1653–1661) and who designed the churches of Las Angustias (1664–1671) and the Magdalena (1677–1694) in Granada, both of which were once attributed to Cano.

CATHERINE WILKINSON

WORKS

1629–1632, Church of Santa Maria (altarpiece), Lebrija, Spain. 1635, Santa Paula (altarpiece), Seville, Spain. 1645, Gatafe Altarpieces, Spain. 1649, Arch at the Puerta de Guadalajara, Madrid. 1667, Cathedral of Granada (façade; not completed until eighteenth century), Spain.

BIBLIOGRAPHY

BERNALES BALLESTERUS, JORGÉ 1976 *Alonso Cano en Sevilla.* Seville, Spain: Disputación Provincial.
Centenario de Alonson Cano. 1969 Granada, Spain: Patronato de la Alhambra y Generalife. See in particular articles by José Camon Aznar, Fernando Chueca Goitia, Maria Elena Gomez-Moreno, Alfonso R. Gutiérrez de Ceballos, and José Manuel Pita Andrade.
KUBLER, GEORGE 1957 *Arquitectura de los siglos XVII y XVIII.* Madrid: Editorial Plus-Ultra.
KUBLER, GEORGE and SORIA, MARTIN 1959 *Art and Architecture in Spain and Portugal and their American Dominions, 1500 to 1800.* Baltimore: Penguin.
PALOMINO DE CASTRO Y VELASCO, ACISCLO ANTONIO 1947 *El Museo Pictorico, y escala óptica.* Reprint. Madrid: Aguilar.
ROSENTHAL, EARL 1961 *The Cathedral of Granada.* N.J.: Princeton University Press.
TOVAR MARTÍN, VIRGINIA 1975 *Arquitectos madri-*

leños de la segunda mitad del siglo XVII. Madrid: Instituto de estudios madrileños.

WETHEY, HAROLD EDWIN 1955 *Alonso Cano: Painter, Sculptor, Architect.* N.J.: Princeton University Press.

CANO LASSO, JULIO

Julio Cano Lasso (1920–) was born in Madrid and received the title of architect from the Technical Superior School of Architecture in Madrid in 1949. His work consists mostly of large-scale projects for the Central Administration. Removed from the cultural polemic, he values architecture as art and subscribes to rationalist tenets. He has a predilection for austerity and maximum economy in the means of his expression derived from the Castilian mysticism of the sixteenth century. One recognizes in his work the influence of the Amsterdam school and he demonstrates his admiration for WILLEM MARINUS DUDOK in his use of brick.

JOSEP MARTORELL
Translated from Spanish by
Judith E. Meighan

WORKS

1958–1959, Julio Cano Lasso House (including studio); 1971–1974, Apartments, Basilica Street; Madrid. 1973–1974, Trade University, Almeria, Spain. 1974–1975, Trade University, Albacete, Spain. 1974–1975, Trade University, Orense, Spain.

BIBLIOGRAPHY

CANO LASSO, JULIO 1977a *Dibujos y notas.* Madrid: Taller de Ediciones JB.
CANO LASSO, JULIO 1977b *Fuentelareina: Tres propuestas de arquitectura naturalista.* Madrid: Taller de Ediciones JB.
CANO LASSO, JULIO 1980 *Julio Cano Lasso, arquitecto.* Madrid: Xarait.
Construcciones en ladrillo. 1970 Barcelona, Spain: Gilli.
DOMENÈCH, LLUIS 1968 *Arquitectura española contemporánea.* Barcelona, Spain: Blume.
FLORES LOPEZ, CARLOS 1961 *Arquitectura española contemporáanea.* Madrid: Aguilar.

CANONICA, LUIGI

Born at Tesserete, near Lugano, Switzerland, Luigi Canonica (1762–1844) proceeded early on to Milan where he first studied under GIUSEPPE PIERMARINI and then entered the Royal Academy of Architecture. Already a laureate architect and professor of architecture at the Collegio Imperiale dei Nobili in his twenties, he earned the title of Government Architect and Inspector of Buildings under Napoleon I. He was knighted in 1810.

Most noteworthy, in addition to his various imperially sponsored projects such as villas, garden landscapes, altar designs, and urban plans, is the colossal Amphitheater or Civic Arena in Milan (1805–1807), capable of accommodating a crowd of 30,000. Canonica went on to design many other theaters throughout Italy.

TINA WALDEIER BIZZARRO

WORKS

1805–1807, Civic Arena; 1831–1844?, Brentano Palace (now Banca Commerciale); Milan.

BIBLIOGRAPHY

Guida d'Italia del Touring Club Italiano: Milano e Laghi. 1956 Milan: Vallardi.
MERZARIO, GIUSEPPE 1893 Volume 2 in *I Maestri Comacini: Storia Artistica di Mille Duecento Anni (600–1800).* Milan: Agnelli.
MONTI, D. SANTO 1922 *l'Italia Monumentale: Como.* Florence: Alinari.

CANTACUZINO, GHEORGHE MATEI

Gheorghe Matei Cantacuzino (1899–1960) graduated from the Ecole des Beaux-Arts in Paris in 1927. He was a professor at the Institute of Architecture in Bucharest from 1942 to 1948. His large public buildings are rendered in a mixture of historical styles, whereas his domestic architecture uses a modern idiom. Cantacuzino was active in the restoration and remodeling of old structures. He was an active journalist and wrote many books and articles.

CONSTANTIN MARIN MARINESCU

WORKS

1920, Mogosoaia Palace (restoration), near Bucharest. 1928, Chrissoveloni Bank (with others; now the State Bank); 1933, Office Building, University Square; 1933, Mǎrul de Aur Restaurant; 1935, Urban Development Plan; *1936, Apartment Building Carlton; Bucharest. *1939, Rumanian Pavilion (with others), International Exhibition, New York. 1939, International Hotel, Mamaia, Rumania. 1940, Hotel Belona, Eforie, Rumania.

BIBLIOGRAPHY

IONESCU, GRIGORE 1965 Volume 2 in *Istoria Arhitecturii in Romania.* Bucharest: Editura Academiei Republicii Romañe.
IONESCU, GRIGORE 1969 *Arhitectura in Romania: Perioda anilor 1944–1969.* Bucharest: Editura Academiei Republicii Socialiste Romañía.
IONESCU, GRIGORE 1972 "Saptezeci si cinci de ani de la infiintarea invatamintului de arhitectura din Romania." *Arhitectura* 20:35–42.
MAMBRIANI, ALBERTO 1969 *L'Architettura Moderna*

nei Paesi Balcanici. Bologna, Italy: Capelli.

PATRULIUS, RADU 1973–1974 "Contributii Romanesti in Arhitectura Anilor '30." *Arhitectura* 21, no. 6:44–52; 22, no. 1:53–59.

SASARMAN, GHEORGHE 1972 "Inceputurile gindirii teoretice in arhitectura românească (1860–1916)." *Arhitectura* 20, no. 6:44–46.

CAPORALI, GIOVAN BATTISTA

A Perugian-born painter and architect, Giovan Battista Caporali (c.1476–1560) received his architectural formation on a 1508–1509 visit to Rome, during which he met DONATO BRAMANTE, BALDASSARE PERUZZI, and Giuliano da Sangallo (see SANGALLO FAMILY). He is best known for a 1536 translation of VITRUVIUS, based on CESARE CESARIANO's version of 1521. Caporali painted in the successive styles of Perugino, RAPHAEL, MICHELANGELO, and GIULIO ROMANO.

HOWARD SHUBERT

BIBLIOGRAPHY

SCARPELLINI, P. 1975 "Caporali, Giovan Battista." In *Dizionario Biografico degli Italiani.* Rome: Enciclopedia Italiana.

WITTKOWER, RUDOLF 1971 *Architectural Principles in the Age of Humanism.* New York: Norton.

CAPPONI, GIUSEPPE

Born in Cagliari, Sardinia, Giuseppe Capponi (1893–1936) was one of the early proponents of the Modern movement in Rome, participating in the first exhibit of Rationalist architecture in 1928. His Apartment House on the Tiber in Rome (1926) is perhaps his finest work, displaying a tendency toward the baroque combined with the Expressionism of ERIC MENDELSOHN and HANS SCHAROUN.

THOMAS L. SCHUMACHER

WORKS

1926, Apartment House, Lungotevere Arnaldo di Brescia; 1932–1935, Department of Botanical Research; 1932–1935, Department of Pharmaceutical Research; University of Rome.

BIBLIOGRAPHY

ARGAN, GIULIO CARLO 1940 "Giuseppe Capponi." *Le Arte* 2, no. 3:195–196.

DANESI, SILVIA, and PATETTA, LUCIANO 1976 *Il Razionalismo e L'Architettura in Italia Durante il Fascismo.* Venice, Italy: La Biennale di Venezia.

PICA, AGNOLDOMENICO 1936 *Nuova Architettura Italiana.* Milan: Hoepli.

CAPRAROLA, COLA DA

Cola da Caprarola (?–1518) worked under Antonio da Sangallo the Elder (see SANGALLO FAMILY) on the fortress at Città Castellana (1494). Attributed to him is one of the first centrally planned churches of the High Renaissance, Santa Maria della Consolazione, Todi (1508–1512, completed 1606).

HOWARD SHUBERT

BIBLIOGRAPHY

HEYDENREICH, LUDWIG H., and LOTZ, WOLFGANG 1974 *Architecture in Italy, 1400–1600.* Translated by Mary Hottinger. Harmondsworth, England: Penguin.

ZÄNKER, JÜRGEN 1971 "Die Wallfahrtskirche Santa Maria della Consolazione in Todi." Unpublished Ph.D. dissertation, Rheinischen Friedrich-Wilhelms-Universität, Bonn.

CAPRIANI DA VOLTERRA, FRANCESCO

See VOLTERRA, FRANCESCO CAPRIANI DA.

CAPRIANO DA VOLTERRA, FRANCESCO

Francesco Capriano da Volterra (c.1535–1595) was born in Volterra, Italy. Originally a woodcarver and cabinetmaker, he went to Rome around 1558–1559 and became the private architect of the Gaetanis. Around 1565, he built the Villa Belvedere in Frascati for the physician Pier Antonio Contugio of Volterra. In the same year, he entered the service of Duke Cesare Gonzaga, in whose ducal town, Guastalla, he straightened streets, completed the Palazzo Ducale, and remodeled the municipal palace and the church of San Pietro. In 1570, he returned to Rome where during the next two and a half decades he developed a lively building practice. Besides the Gaetani, his most important clients were the Lancellotti and the Rustici as well as the cardinals Ippolito d'Este, Niccolo Salviati and Ptolomeo Galli. Occasionally, he took over the construction of buildings designed by others as, for instance, the Ospedale di San Giacomo or the foundations for the nave of Sant' Andrea della Valle. He was active in garden and fountain design and erected the villa of Cardinal Ptolomeo Galli in Frascati, a building with a complex arrangement of spaces and a characteristically steep central façade. His Roman palace buildings for the Lancellotti, the Salviati, and the Cardelli remained committed to the organizational scheme and the façade developed by Antonio da Sangallo (see SANGALLO FAMILY) for the Palazzo Farnese.

In the course of the brisk ecclesiastical building activity of the Counter Reformation, Capriano received important commissions for church buildings. The main façades of the Roman churches of San Lorenzo in Panisperna, Santa Chiara, Santa Maria in Monserrato, Santa Maria della Scala, and San Giacomo in Augusta, erected or begun by him, clearly show the development of his post-Vignola (see GIACOMO BAROZZI DA VIGNOLA) style. Using the two-story façade scheme of Antonio da Sangallo as his basis and in reaction to the buildings of Vignola (upper story of the façade of Santa Maria dell'Orto), he developed—contemporary with GIACOMO DELLA PORTA—a façade shaped by a clear organization of pilasters and a strongly emphasized stepped projection in the middle. Furthermore, by neglecting any connection with the wings, this organization accentuates a vertical unity at the center of the façade that reaches over both stories. With this concentration on verticality in the shaping of the façade, Capriani prepared the way for early baroque formulations such as those found in the work of CARLO MADERNO.

Inspired by the example of Vignola, he preferred to use an oval ground plan in church architecture, both for the domed choir section of single-hall churches (San Silvestro in Capita (1591–1595); restoration of Santa Pudenziana (1587–1588), where, furthermore, in the vaulting of the nave there is a latent reference to late baroque solutions) and for the whole centralized and domed church space of San Giacomo in Augusta (1582–1592) where, for the first time, the oval ground plan was applied on a grand scale and was combined with a rhythmically arranged pier-arcaded wall with superimposed orders, a system developed from triumphal arch motifs. San Giacomo is thus the starting point for the rich tradition of high and late baroque oval churches that spread throughout the whole of Europe. Capriani used spare, planar architectural ornamentation giving the same impression of dryness as does the brittleness of the drawings that have been preserved.

In 1557, Capriani became a member of the Virtuosi al Pantheon, and in 1594 he was made a member of the Accademia di San Luca. However, he turned down an invitation of the latter to talk about architectural theory, a sign of the practitioner's dislike of theoretical discussions. After his death, Carlo Maderno took over the greater part of his unfinished buildings.

FRITZ-EUGEN KELLER
Translated from German by
Beverley R. Placzek

WORKS

*c.1565, Villa Belvedere, Frascati, Italy. 1565–1570, Municipal Palace (alteration); 1565–1570, Palazzo Ducale (alteration); 1569–1570, San Pietro (alteration); Guastalla, Italy. 1574, San Lorenzo in Panisperna (façade); 1576–1577, Santa Maria dell'Orto (upper story of façade); Rome. *1578–1579, Cardinal Galli's Villa, Frascati, Italy. *1582, Santa Chiara, Rome. 1582–1584, Cathedral (coffered ceiling of central nave), Volterra, Italy. 1582–1592, Ospedale di San Giacomo in Augusta (execution of older plans); 1582–1593, Santa Maria in Monserrato (lower story of façade); 1585–1593, Santa Maria in Via (convent and church); 1587–1588, Santa Pudenziana (restoration); 1590–1591, Santa Maria in Aquiro; 1591–1593, Sant'Andrea della Valle (foundations of nave); 1591–1595, Lancellotti Palace (completed by Carlo Maderno); 1591–1595, San Silvestro in Capite (completed by Maderno); Rome.

BIBLIOGRAPHY

BAGLIONE, GIOVANNI (1642)1933 *Le vite.* Reprint. Rome: Calzone.
GIOVANNONI, GUSTAVO (1931)1935 *Saggi sulla architettura del Rinascimento.* 2d ed. Milan: Fratelli.
HEYDENREICH, L. H., and LOTZ, WOLFGANG 1974 *Architecture in Italy: 1400–1600.* Translated by Mary Hottinger. Harmondsworth, England: Penguin.
HIBBARD, HOWARD 1971 *Carlo Maderno and Roman Architecture: 1580–1630.* University Park: Pennsylvania State University Press.
KELLER, F. E. 1980 *Zum Villenleben und Villenbau am römischen Hof der Farnese.* Berlin: The author.
LOTZ, WOLFGANG 1955 "Die ovalen Kirchenräume des Cinquecento." *Römisches Jahrbuch für Kunstgeschichte* 7:58–61, 74–76.
ZOCCA, MARIO 1936 "L'architetto di San Giacomo in Augusta." *Bollettino d'Arte* 29:519–529.

CAPRINO, MEO DA

Meo da Caprino (1430–1501) was a Florentine stonecarver and architect, one of the many masters who worked in Rome first as stonecarvers (*scalpellini*) then architects in the last quarter of the fifteenth century. His presence is documented in Ferrara in 1453–1461 working as a *scalpellino*. In Rome from 1462, his name appears in the registers at San Marco (1467), the Benediction Loggia (1467–1470), and other work at the Vatican. He also worked on the Palazzo Venezia from 1462 and served on the jury for the façade of Florence Cathedral (1491).

There are few secure attributions of designs among the significant buildings in Rome in the last quarter of the fifteenth century. Although individuals are often cited in the documents, it is difficult to distinguish supervisors from collaborators or the directing architect (who often may not be cited in documents).

There is no reason, therefore, to accept or reject Federico Hermanin's (1948, p. 19) and Adolfo Venturi's (vol. 7, pp. i, 439) view that Meo collaborated at the Palazzo Venezia with Giuliano di Francesco da Firenze, who may have been Giuliano da Sangallo (see SANGALLO FAMILY) nor should G. Milanesi's view be accepted that works attributed to BACCIO PONTELLI by GIORGIO VASARI be assigned to Meo (Vasari ([1568] 1973, vol. 2, pp. 659–665).

One building, not in Rome, can be securely given to Meo, the Cathedral of Turin (1491–1498), commissioned by Cardinal Domenico della Rovere, brother of Pope Sixtus V, and bishop of Turin from 1482 to 1501. The building is Roman, not Piedmontese, of basilican plan, fusing aspects of Santa Maria del Popolo and San Agostino in Rome, with which it can be compared favorably. The nave is covered by a barrel vault with penetrations. The side aisles are groin-vaulted. The piers contain half-round columns that rise, with attic extensions, well above the middle of the clearstory window, appearing to support the vault independently of the clearstory wall. An octagonal drum and cloister vaulted dome at the crossing are supported on squinches as at Santa Maria del Popolo in Rome. The masonry and sparse carving (entrance doors) are of notable quality.

HENRY A. MILLON

WORKS

(A)1462, Palazzo Venezia, Rome. (A)1467, San Marco, Venice, Italy. (A)1467–1470, Benediction Loggia, Rome. 1491, Florence Cathedral (façade; with others). 1491–1498, Turin Cathedral, Italy.

BIBLIOGRAPHY

HERMANIN, FEDERICO 1948 *Il Palazzo di Venezia.* Rome: Libreria della Stato.
HEYDENREICH, LUDWIG H., and LOTZ, WOLFGANG (1947)1974 *Architecture in Italy: 1400–1600.* Translated by Mary Hottinger. Harmondsworth, England: Penguin.
MAGNUSON, TERGIL 1958 *Studies in Roman Quattrocento Architecture.* Stockholm: Almqvist & Wiksell.
MARCHINI, GIUSEPPE 1942 *Giuliano da Sangallo.* Florence: Sansoni.
MIDANA, ARTURO 1929 *Il Duomo di Torino.* Turin, Italy: Sacra.
SOLERO, SILVIO 1956 *Il Duomo di Torino.* Pinerolo, Italy: Alzani.
TOMEI, PIERO 1942 *L'Architettura a Roma nel Quattrocento.* Rome: Palumbi.
URBAN, GUNTER 1961–1962 "Der Dom von Turin und seine Stellung zur römischen Architektur des Quattrocento." *Römisches Jahrbuch für Kunstgeschichte* 9–10:245–287.
URBAN, GUNTER 1961–1962 "Die Kirchenbaukunst des Quattrocento in Rom." *Römisches Jahrbuch für Kunstgeschichte* 9–10:73–244.
VASARI, GIORGIO (1568)1973 *Le opere di Giòrgio Vasari, con nuove annotazioni e commenti.* 9 vols. Edited by G. Milanesi. Reprint. Florence: Sansoni. Originally published in 1550 with the title *Le vite de piv eccelenti architetti.* There are many English translations and selections from Vasari's *Lives;* the standard one by G. du C. de Vere was published in ten volumes in London by the Medici Society in 1912–1915.
VENTURI, ADOLFO (1901)1967 *Storia dell'arte Italiana.* Milan: Hoepli.

CARAMUEL DE LOBKOWITZ, JUAN

Juan Caramuel de Lobkowitz (1606–1682) is one of the astonishing figures of universal learning who generated the classically inspired Catholicism of the seventeenth century. On the borderline of what Roman Catholic theology deemed tolerable but short of the definitive defection of scientifically oriented Cartesian modernism, Caramuel aimed at producing a universal systematization of the sciences with speculative results scarcely second to those of Athanasius Kircher.

Born in Spain, Caramuel was descended from a family whose members were related to Bohemian and Flemish nobility. His grandfather came to Spain as a minister to Charles V; Caramuel's father, an astronomer, provided his son with the best possible education which Caramuel continued in Spanish theological institutions. A career as a theologian, together with the appropriate professional responsibilities and offices—leading finally in 1673 to the bishopric of Vigevano—guaranteed Caramuel unlimited travel in Roman Catholic Europe. After 1634, he was active chiefly in the Spanish Netherlands and the Palatinate, along the newly drawn religious battlefront of the Thirty Years War. He used the opportunity, both in Louvain and in Mainz, for theological disputation, which later, on account of his "probabilistic" position, brought him into repeated difficulties with the orthodox Roman Catholic position. He was called from Mainz to Vienna and Prague where he was also active, under orders from Emperor Ferdinand III, as an adviser in the fortification of the Hungarian front. He went to Rome in 1655 as the mediator for the Bohemian nobles and there for a time enjoyed the favor of Pope Alexander III. However, in 1657 he was removed to Naples as bishop of Campagna and Satriano. Caramuel remained in contact with the Habsburg crown, for instance, by participating in the coronation of Emperor Leopold I in Frankfurt in 1658. In the Neapolitan Accademia degli Investiganti he gained new access to open forms of scientific activity (including experiments in the natural sciences!). Not until 1671 did he return to Rome from his "exile," after which, in 1673, he took up residence in Lombardy as bishop of Vigevano. He became blind and died there on September 8, 1682.

Essentially, Caramuel's career was shaped by his often controversial theological positions. In addition, he concerned himself with all imaginable branches of knowledge: grammar, prosody, secret writing, mathematics, law, history, and the arts, producing altogether more than 260 scientific works. He held that all the sciences should be brought together into a system of the "catena aurea" (golden chain); thus architecture, too, was to be conceived of not as an independent science in the Vitruvian sense but rather as part of a system encompassing all branches of knowledge, a part whose fundamentals, methods, and characteristics of classification would depend upon a higher "forma mentis," most particularly the mathematical.

This larger framework is essential to the understanding of Caramuel's architecture and architectural theory. Moreover, it indicates a position that was characteristic of the architect–scholar of the seventeenth century as seen in Nikolaus Goldmann and even CHRISTOPHER WREN. Mathematics and the confrontation with Cartesian thought play a decisive, often even a dominant role.

It is not surprising then that Caramuel's major achievement in architecture is in the area of theory, as set forth in his work, *Architectura civil, recta y obliqua, considerada y dibuxada en el Templo de Ierusalem* (Vigevano, 1678–1681; Latin edition: *Templum Salomonis, Rectam et obliquam architecturam exhibens*). According to the author, this work was the fruit of many years of wrestling with the issues. Caramuel himself traced the development of his "discovery" of *architectura obliqua* back to the years 1624 and 1630. Two lines of interconnected thought—the mathematical-scientific and the historical-theological—characterize this work. The historical-theological view is often used to legitimatize systematic arguments. Nevertheless, Caramuel also recognized Spain's cultural interests, praising the Escorial as the eighth wonder of the world. In doing so, he made use of Hochelaga's plan and of examples from the architecture of the native inhabitants of America. In this section, which preceded that on Logarithmics ("Tratado III") introduced by a quotation from Kepler, he emphasized the accomplishments of the "moderns," most particularly the conquest of the New World as the "non plus ultra" breakthrough.

Of primary importance to any historical discussion is the Temple of Jerusalem—the "primer principio de toda buena architectura"—as the founding principle of architecture. This biblically inspired point of view is comparable to that of Goldmann who, in a similar way, maintained the importance of supplementing the Vitruvian (see VITRUVIUS) doctrine with a theological-historical viewpoint. Both men were part of a tradition that runs from Villalpando and Prado to Isaac Newton's discussion of the Solomonic temple.

Accordingly, Caramuel begins his work, in a "Tratado Proemial," with a discussion of the age of the world and the history of creation—and not without exposing Aristotle's errors. He connects the origins of civil and military architecture—in chronological order—with the Temple of Jerusalem. There follows an extremely detailed description of the temple itself, including its individual parts, based mostly on Villalpando. Only in the "Tratado I" is the subject itself introduced, together with an indication of what the architect must known ("Facultades Literarias"). Caramuel refers to Vitruvius's recommendations but then expands encyclopedically on them, mentioning, in addition to orthography and poetry, Trithemius's art of secret writing and even the squaring of the circle. "Tratados II–IV" deal equally amply with the mathematical foundations of arithmetic, logarithmics (extolled here as the discovery of his own century!), and geometry.

In "Tratado V," the discussion of architecture

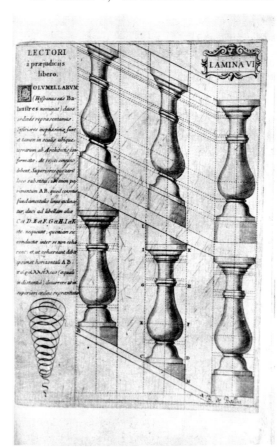

Caramuel de Lobkowitz. Plate from Architectura civil, recta y obliqua. *1678–1681*

proper begins, which Caramuel, in an original classification, divides into "Architectura recta" and "Architectura obliqua." Under the former, Caramuel discusses architectural fundamentals, purpose, aesthetic qualities, imitation of the ancients, and development. It is noteworthy that he expands the discourse far beyond the Vitruvian framework to explore the building techniques of various peoples, including the practices of nomadic tribes. Caramuel even takes up the architectonic phenomena of the American colonies. It is surprising to find here a consideration of primitive living habits as adduced from the way huts are built, along with a discussion of Hochelaga's layout, which is significant in the context of plans for the ideal city. Under "architectura recta en particular," Caramuel deals with the architectural orders in the widest sense and attempts—in typical encyclopedic manner—to expand on the Vitruvian groundwork. He offers seventeen different solutions for the construction of Ionic volutes including those of MICHELANGELO on The Capitol and the inventions of Goldmann and Carlo Cesare Osio. He expands the rule of the classical orders to include the "Orden Tyrio," derived from the Temple of Jerusalem; the "Orden Attico," formed from elements of the remaining orders into a "system" and to be discerned in the "claustro ionico" in Sant' Ambrogio in Milan; the "Orden Gothico"; the "Orden Mosayco"; the "Orden Atlantico"; and the "Orden Paranymphico."

The heart of the treatise, is the "architectura obliqua," a problem that, as the author himself declares, had concerned him since 1630. The "architectura obliqua" is the most characteristic result of Caramuel's mathematical "forma mentis," and includes all the irregularities brought about by nonrectangular, curvilinear, and perspective deformations, listed systematically. What makes sense in connection with the spindles of sloping bannisters, Caramuel insists on, without exception, for all comparable situations where slopes, basic oval shapes, and other such forms deviate from the rectangular and hence, as a logical consequence, require oblique capitals, pillars set above oval sectional figures, and so forth. This rigorism, with its theoretical bias, led, not unexpectedly, to polemics and was discarded as impractical even by GUARINO GUARINI, who was otherwise open to mathematical thinking and who, more than any other, grappled with Caramuel. On the other hand, it is also by reason specifically of the "architectura obliqua" that Caramuel's work belongs in the series of scientifically oriented architectural treatises. Indeed, as Fernandino Galli-Bibiena (see BIBIENA FAMILY) avows, his own "Architettura civile" (Parma, 1711) is also built up

on the premises of perspective.

In "Tratado VII," Caramuel comes back to Vitruvius's requirement that architects be educated in other sciences, discussing in particular the related arts of painting, sculpture, physiognomy, perspective, music, astronomy, and military architecture. His obsession with mathematical-scientific problems is also illustrated in this section when he discusses the doubling of the square, already identified by Vitruvius as a classic problem.

Apart from the text that explains the plates, "Tratado VII" appears to be the final section. Here, under the title "Architectura Practica," Caramuel summarizes his historical considerations. They contain an enumeration of the wonders of the world, set forth at encyclopedic length, as well as of other great architectural accomplishments of the ancient world. Basing himself on Jacobus Laurus and Casalius, Caramuel describes the buildings of ancient Rome and adds a lengthy discussion of St. Peter's in Rome. The superiority of the first Christian building over the ancient wonders of the world is emphasized; again based on Casalius, the "errores" in the construction of St. Peter's are also presented. Caramuel also criticizes GIOVANNI LORENZO BERNINI's colonnades, which he wishes had been shaped according to the principles of his own "architectura obliqua." The attack on Bernini, whom, in the same chapter, he celebrates as "the Phidias of our century," remains a theoretical exercise.

With the exception of Guarini's "Architettura civile" (1737), which discusses in detail the mathematical conditions set by Caramuel, the latter's theoretical work, for all its scholarship and wealth of historical material had hardly any major significance for later periods. The material is pieced together too haphazardly, and Caramuel too readily disregarded the architectonic realities of his day. His only architectural work, the façade of the Vigevano Cathedral (1673–?), seems amateurish in spite of its virtuosity and skill. It corrects the irregular relationship of the cathedral to the square in the Renaissance layout and makes it symmetrical by means of a skillful illusion created by the addition of an axis to the façade where a side-street flanks the cathedral. The formal result cannot be integrated into the stylistic evolution of the highly developed Italian art of façade building. On the other hand, the eclecticism of the form recalls—yet again—related configurations of N. Goldmann ("second example of a church") and Christopher Wren (Saint Peter Cornhill).

WERNER OECHSLIN
Translated from German by
Paul A. Bernabeo and
Beverley R. Placzek

BIBLIOGRAPHY

Bernardo Ferrero, D. de 1965 "Il conte I. Caramuel de Lobkowitz, vescovo di Vigevano, architetto e teorico dell'architettura." *Palladio* 15:91ff.

Bernardo Ferrero, D. de 1966 *I 'disegni d'architettura civile et ecclesiastica' di Guarino Guarini e l'arte del Maestro.* Turin, Italy: Albra.

Caramuel de Lobkowitz, Juan 1967-1681 *Architectura civil, recta y obliqua.* Vigevano, Italy: Corrado.

Guarini, Guarino (1737)1968 *Architettura Civile.* With an introduction by Nino Carboneri and critical notes by Bianca Tavassi la Greca. Milan: Il Polifilo.

Guidoni-Marino, A. 1973 "Il colonnato di Piazza S. Pietro: Della architettura obliqua del Caramuel al 'classicismo' bernniano." *Palladio* 23:81ff.

Lotz, W. 1974 "La piazza ducale di Vigevano." Pages 205-221. in *Studi Bramanteschi.* Rome: De Luca.

Oechslin, Werner 1970 "Osservazioni su Guarino Guarini e Juan Caramuel de Lobkowitz." In *Guarino Guarini e l'internazionalità del Barocco.* Turin, Italy: Accademia delle Scienze.

Pastine, D. 1975 *Juan Caramuel: Probabilismo ed Enciclopedia.* Florence: La nuova Italia.

Tadisi, J. A. 1760 *Memora della vita di Mons. G. Caramuel.* Venice, Italy.

CARIMINI, LUCA

Trained as a stonemason and active in sculpture and painting as well as architecture, Luca Carimini (1830-1890) combined the massive rustication of Quattrocento palazzos with complex surface patterns in brick and travertine, producing a refined and urbane style which was much admired and imitated in Rome from 1890 to 1914.

BARBARA MILLER LANE

WORKS

1871, Priest's House, Santa Maria di Loreto; 1873, House, via Panisperna; 1877, Church of Sant'Ivo dei Bretoni; 1878, Church of San Giacomo degli Spagnoli; 1880-1896, Palazzo Brancaccio; 1884-1888, Church and College of Sant' Antonio; 1888, Church and College of San Giuseppe di Cluny; 1888-1889, Palazzo Blumensthil, Rome.

BIBLIOGRAPHY

Accasto, Gianni; Fraticelli, Vanna; and Nicolini, Renato 1971 *L'architettura di Roma capitale 1870-1970.* Rome: Golem.

Callari, Luigi (1907)1944 *I palazzi di Roma.* Rome: Apollon.

De Guttry, Irene 1978 *Guida di Roma moderna dal 1870 ad oggi.* Rome: De Luca.

Piacentini, Marcello, and Guidi, Francesco 1952 *Le vicende edilizie di Roma dal 1870 ad oggi.* Rome: Palombi.

Portoghesi, Paolo c.1968 *L'eclettismo a Roma, 1870-1922.* Rome: De Luca.

CARLONE FAMILY

The Carlone were a family of Italian Lombard artists, masons, stuccoists, and painters whose influence spanned from the first half of the sixteenth to the first half of the eighteenth century. The family is divided into two branches: one from Rovio, near Mandrisio, and the other from Scaria, near Como; the latter settled in Austria in the late seventeeth century. The different members of the family worked in Italy, Austria, Germany, Switzerland, Spain, and France.

Antonio di Battista Carlone, architect and sculptor, designed the portal of the Pallavicini Palace in Genoa (1503). He worked on the Corpus Domini Chapel in Chieri (1509) and designed a tomb in Turin's Cathedral.

Giacomo Carlone from Scaria, who was an architect and sculptor in Carrara (1538-1550), participated in the construction of the Cathedral in Genoa.

Pietro Carlone worked in Graz and Kreuz, Austria, around 1556.

Taddeo Carlone (1543-1613), an architect and painter who was born in Rovio and died in Genoa, designed the Church of San Pietro in Banchi (1570-1576) and the Fountain of Soziglia in Genoa (1578). The mannerist style of his façade of the Sanctuary in Savona contrasted with his more sober designs for parts of several palaces in Genoa.

Sebastiano Carlone, architect and sculptor, worked mainly in Graz, Austria (Chapel of the Castle, 1599); in Seckau, Austria (Abbatical Church, 1589-1612); and in Judenburg, Austria.

Giovanni Battista Carlone (?-1645) undertook restoration work on the Palace of Ferdinand II in Vienna and participated in the construction of Saint Michael's Church there (1626).

A. Silvestro Carlone (c.1610-1671), who was born in Scaria, worked on the completion of Scozzesi Church (1646) and on the construction of Saint Michael's Church in Vienna. He designed the façade of the Jesuit Church am Hof in Vienna (1662) which shows a baroque sense of movement.

Pietro Francesco Carlone, who built churches in Styria, Austria, later moved to upper Austria where he designed Garsten Church (1667), completed by his son Carlo Antonio.

Domenico Carlone (1615-1679) worked in Vienna on the completion of Saint Maria-Brun Church (1645) and on the extension of Grafenegg Castle (1647).

Carlo Martino Carlone (1616-1679) worked

on the Imperial Castle in Vienna and erected a column for the Blessed Virgin there.

Giovanni Battista Carlone (c.1650–?), born in Scaria, was the son of Pietro Francesco Carlone. He worked as an architect and sculptor in Germany, designing the chapel of Garsten Convent (1696) and the Cathedral of Passau (1689). As a stuccoist, he decorated Saint Michael's Church in Passau. The ornamentation he designed for Saint Maria del Soccorso in Amberg illustrated what is referred to as the Carlone baroque style in a harmonious and colorful deep-relief stucco.

Carlo Antonio Carlone (?–1708), son of Pietro Francesco Carlone, was born in Milan and completed his father's project for Garsten Church. He worked on the Cistercian Church of Schlierbach; the Capital Hall of Admond, Graz (c. 1681); and designed the Jesuit Church of Passau, using massive proportions softened by the elaborately stuccoed façade. His masterpiece was the Austin Priory Church in Saint Florian Monastery, Austria, on which he worked from 1686 and where he died.

Silvestro II Carlone (?–c.1708), who was born in Como and died in Prague, practiced in Germany, designing the Convent of Premonstrat and the Prelatur in Mülhausen (1695).

Giovacchino Carlone designed the Convent of Pollau near Graz between 1701 and 1709.

Diego Carlone (1647–1750), stuccoist, son of Giovanni Battista Carlone, practiced in Germany and developed a unique stucco style which he applied to the chapel of Ludwigsburg Castle and the chapel of Saint Florian Monastery in Austria. His ornamentation for Wiengarten Church (1715–1722), Germany; Einsiedeln Church, Switzerland; and Santa Maria di Carignano in Genoa placed him as an original stuccoist.

MARC DILET

CARLU, JACQUES

Born in Bonnières-sur-Seine, France, Jacques Carlu (1890–) established his reputation as both a good designer and a fine draftsman by the age of twenty. After some early training at the Ecole des Beaux-Arts in Paris Carlu traveled to Bucharest where, with a Rumanian architect, he won the design competition for the Palais du Sénat. In 1913, he was employed by the Canadian planner THOMAS HAYTON MAWSON and contributed to various designs in Calgary and Ottawa. By the age of twenty-nine, Carlu had won both the Prix Roux at the Ecole des Beaux-Arts and the most important French architectural award, the Premier Grand Prix. Also at this time, he was named director of architecture at the Fontainebleau School of Fine

Arts. In 1924, he went to the United States where he became professor at the Massachusetts Institute of Technology; he has continued to teach ever since in various capacities both in the United States and in France.

Carlu is perhaps best known for the Palais de Chaillot in Paris which he designed along with two other French architects, LOUIS HYPPOLITE BOILEAU and LÉON AZÉMA. Unashamedly monumental, the Palais de Chaillot—which was the centerpiece of the 1937 Exposition Universelle in Paris—reflects to a large extent the severe neoclassicism popular in the 1930s. Proportionally, however, the building is not overwhelming and, because its shape is contoured to the terrain, neither does it aggressively dominate the surrounding landscape.

Following World War II, Carlu designed a number of institutional buildings across France such as universities, secondary schools, hospitals, and churches. His philosophy on building reflects a fundamental debt to "the forms of civilization" combined with "an intelligent understanding of the program to be interpreted and the skilled use of material in an adaptable manner" (Campbell, 1926, p. 283).

PETER L. DONHAUSER

WORKS

1931, T. Eaton and Company Department Stores, Toronto and Montreal. 1937, Palais de Chaillot (with Louis Hyppolite Boileau and Léon Azéma); 1951, United Nations General Assembly; Paris. 1953, Cité de Carreire (with M. Babin and M. Joly); 1953, Cité de Claveau (with Babin and Joly); Bordeaux, France. 1954, Maison de la Radio (with Joly), Rennes, France. 1956, Apartment Buildings, Cité de la Benauge (with Babin and Joly), Bordeaux, France. 1957, NATO Building, Paris. 1961, Lycée Mixte, Libourne, France. 1964, Lycée Mixte, Montreuil, France. 1965, Ecole Nationale Supérieure des Arts et Métiers, Bordeaux-Talence, France. 1965, Faculté des Lettres et Sciences Humaines, Paris. 1969, Maison de la Culture (with Joly), Rennes, France.

BIBLIOGRAPHY

CAMPBELL, EDMUND S. 1926 "French Comrades in America: Jacques Carlu." *Pencil Points* 7:266–289.
CARLU, JACQUES 1931 "The T. Eaton & Co. Department Stores in Toronto and Montreal." *Architectural Record* 69:447–456.
CARLU, JACQUES 1932 "Falaise—The Heart of Normandy." In *The Tuileries Brochures.* New York: Marchbanks.
CARLU, JACQUES 1965 "New Buildings of the University of Paris Faculté des Lettres et Sciences Humaines de Paris-Centre Censier." *L'Architecture Française* nos. 275–276:83–85.
CARLU, JACQUES, and AZÉMA, LÉON 1938 "New State Theater, Paris." *Architect's Journal* 88:370–372.

LADOUÉ, PIERRE 1937 "Le Nouveau Trocadéro; Carlu, Boileau et Azéma, Architectes." *L'Architecture* 50:69–78.

CARMONTELLE, LOUIS CARROGIS

Amateur, dilettante, playwright, and garden designer, Carmontelle (1717–1806) began his career as tutor to the children of the marquis d'Armentières, and later became reader to the duc d'Orléans, for whom he wrote dramatic renderings of proverbs. He designed several gardens, including the Parc de Monceau (1773–1778) for the duc de Chartres. Carmontelle advocated an artificial and theatrical style of design for French gardens, in which countless diversions would be planned for the spectators. In his book on Monceau (1779) he emphasized the relation of garden design to that of the opera: a scene from Servandoni's *Pyramis et Thisbe* was included at the Parc de Monceau.

DORA WIEBENSON

WORK

1773–1778, Parc de Monceau, Paris.

BIBLIOGRAPHY

CARMONTELLE (LOUIS CARROGIS) 1779 *Jardin de Monceau, près de Paris.* Paris: Delafosse.
FRÉNILLY, A. F. F. DE 1908 Page 5 in *Souvenirs du Baron de Frénilly, pair de France (1768–1828).* Paris: Plan-Nourrit.
Louis Carmontelle, lecteur du Duc d'Orléans. 1933 Paris. An exhibition catalogue.
OULMONT, CHARLES 1908 "Un gentilhomme artiste: Carmontelle. D'Après deux documents inédits." *Gazette des Beaux-Arts* Series 3 40:254–260.
WIEBENSON, DORA 1978 Pages 76–77, 91–98 in *The Picturesque Garden in France.* N.J.: Princeton University Press.

CARNEVALE, PIETRO

Born in Piedmont, Pietro Carnevale (1839–1895), whose name is sometimes spelled Carnevali, studied with A. Cipolla in Rome. He practiced in Rome as both architect and sculptor, specializing in residences. His was an eclectic, often delicate and elegant style, in which he combined both neo-Gothic and Renaissance motifs. The Casa Ruboli on the via IV Novembre (1886) is an example of Carnevale's best work.

BARBARBA MILLER LANE

WORKS

1879, Palazzo Pasucci; 1885, Palazzo, Piazza dell'Esquilino; 1886, Casa Ruboli, via IV Novembre; 1886, Palazzo, Piazza Dante; n.d., Palazzo, via Firenze; n.d., Palazzo, via Nazionale; n.d. Palazzo, via Arenula; n.d., Galleria Pasucci; Rome.

BIBLIOGRAPHY

ACCASTO, GIANNI; FRATICELLI, VANNA; and NICOLINI, RENATO 1971 *L'architettura di Roma capitale: 1890–1970.* Rome: Golem.
CARNEVALE, PIETRO 1885 "La vecchia e nuova Roma." *L'Italia* Nov.:82.
GUTTRY, IRENE DE 1978 *Guida di Roma moderna: Architettura dal 1870 ad oggi.* Rome: De Luca.
PORTOGHESI, PAOLO 1959 "La vicenda romana." *La Casa* 6; no. 55:42–95.

CARNILIVARI, MATTEO

Matteo Carnilivari (fifteenth century), a native of the Sicilian city of Noto, was one of a number of little-known architects and *capomaestri* who worked in Palermo. It was in the 1490s that he directed the construction of the Palazzo Abatellis in Palermo, his most important work, which shows him much under the sway of Spanish late Gothic ornamental styles, on the one hand, with an Italian sense of balance and unified palace design, on the other.

STEPHEN TOBRINER

WORKS

1487, Misilmeri Castle (restoration and amplification), near Palermo, Italy. 1488, Santa Maria della Vittoria (reconstruction); 1489–1495, Palazzo Abatellis; 1491–1494, Palazzo Aiutamicristo (portions), Palermo, Italy. 1494, Castle of Augusta (repairs), Italy.

BIBLIOGRAPHY

MELI, FILIPPO 1958 *Matteo Carnilivari e l'architettura del Quattro a Cinquecento in Palermo.* Rome: Palombi.
ROTOLO, FILIPPO 1964 "Nuovi documenti su Matteo Carnilivari." *Archivio storico per la Sicilia* Series 3 15:83–88.

CARPENTER, J. E. R.

James Edwin Ruthven Carpenter (1867–1932) was an influential designer of luxury apartment houses in New York and was often credited with the innovation of the foyer-centered, rather than the "long hall" apartment plan. Carpenter was involved financially with many apartment developments and he was responsible for the 1921 lawsuit which opened Fifth Avenue to apartment house construction.

CHRISTOPHER S. GRAY

WORKS

1913–1914, 640 Park Avenue; 1915–1916, 907 Fifth Avenue; 1916–1917, 550 Park Avenue; 1922, 920 Fifth Avenue; 1924–1926, 175 Riverside Drive; 1929, 623 Park Avenue; New York.

CARPENTER, R. C.

Richard Cromwell Carpenter (1812–1855) was educated at Charterhouse, and articled to John Blyth. The son of a deputy lieutenant of Middlesex, he became a friend of A. W. N. PUGIN and through his introduction was associated from its foundation with the Cambridge Camden Society (later the Ecclesiological Society). He entered practice in London, later becoming a member of the consulting committee of architects of the Incorporated Church Building Society and consulting architect to Chichester Cathedral. Toward the end of his life, he was assisted by his first pupil, William Slater.

Carpenter was one of the best and most successful church architects of his generation. From an early age he demonstrated architectural precocity. His friendship with Pugin was of great significance in the development of the Gothic Revival in the Church of England. Under his influence, Carpenter developed experience in the design of painted glass, polychromatic decoration, church furniture, and metalwork. It was he who pre-eminently brought Pugin's innovations into the mainstream of Anglicanism. His work is distinguished by exquisite colors, harmony, scholarship, and control.

His most influential churches are Saint Paul's, Brighton (1846–1849) and Saint Mary Magdalene, Munster Square, London (1849–1852), both models of ecclesiological planning for which Pugin designed painted glass. They are designed in the Camden Society's approved fourteenth-century Decorated style. *The Ecclesiologist* regarded Saint Mary Magdalene's as "the most artistically correct new church yet consecrated in London."

Carpenter's most extensive work was his design for Lancing College, Sussex (begun 1854, completed by Slater, his son, R. H. Carpenter, and S. E. Dykes Bower), a boys' public school founded on Tractarian principles by Nathaniel Woodard. In 1844, he designed three churches for Tasmania and colonial cathedrals for Jamaica and Colombo. Inverness Cathedral (the designs for which were exhibited at the Paris Exhibition, 1855) was begun at the end of his life and completed after his death by Slater and Alexander Ross.

ANTHONY SYMONDSON

WORKS

1838–1842, Lonsdale Square, Islington, London. 1840–1841, Saint Stephen's Church and School; 1844–1846, Saint Andrew's, Bordesley; Birmingham, England. 1846–1849, Saint Paul's (tower and spire by R. H. Carpenter), Brighton; 1848, Saint Peter's, Chichester; Sussex, England. 1849–1852, Saint Mary Magdalene's, Munster Square, London. 1851–1853, Saint John's College (chapel by R. H. Carpenter), Hurstpierpoint, Sussex, England. 1851–1855, Beresford Parsonage and Tomb, Kilndown, Kent, England. 1852, Saint John's, Bovey Tracey, Devon, England. 1854–1856, Saint Stephen's School and Parsonage, Burntisland, Fife, Scotland. 1854 and later, College of Saint Mary and Saint Nicholas (completed by William Slater, Carpenter, and S. E. Dykes Bower), Lancing, Sussex, England. 1855, Inverness Cathedral (completed by Slater and Alexander Ross), Scotland.

BIBLIOGRAPHY

CLARKE, BASIL F. L. 1938 *Church Builders of the Nineteenth Century.* London: Society for Promoting Christian Knowledge.
DIXON, ROGER, and MUTHESIUS, STEFAN 1978 *Victorian Architecture.* London: Thames & Hudson; New York: Oxford University Press.
The Ecclesiologist 1855 16:119, 137–142.

CARR, JOHN

John Carr (1723–1807) of York, perhaps the most successful provincial architect of the eighteenth century in England, was born in the village of Horbury in the county of Yorkshire. He left school at about the age of fourteen to assist his mason father, Robert, who, operating on occasion as contractor, designer, itinerant director of works and surveyor of bridges, provided his son with a background of practical training.

About 1750, the ambitious Carr moved to the city of York, center of communications and metropolis of the north. Here his success as an architect attracted attention and he was elected to civic office, becoming an alderman, magistrate, and twice Lord Mayor.

Three episodes can be said to have influenced his development as an architect: first, his supervision of the building of Kirby Hall (c.1750), designed by the progenitor of eighteenth-century Palladianism, Richard Boyle, LORD BURLINGTON, with his assimilation of the conventions of Palladianism there forming the background to his work; second, his receiving the plum commission for the stand on York's popular racecourse, which brought him to the notice of the nobility and gentry; and third, his association with ROBERT ADAM over the design of Harewood House (1759–1771) which led him to reject the rich rococo of earlier years, that he had used particularly for his interiors, and to adopt with accuracy the graceful decoration of the Adamesque.

His range of commissions was extensive—mansions, stables, churches, racestands, law courts, and hospitals—but as surveyor of bridges to the West Riding authority and later to the North Riding authority he also made an exceptional contribution to the design of bridges throughout Yorkshire. Hard-working, practical, and sensible but no trend-setter, he himself best expressed his achievement in a letter to the Board of Leeds Infirmary claiming simply "to arrange the necessary conveniencys with some degree of art."

R. B. WRAGG

WORKS

1748, Huthwaite Hall; 1750–1754, Arncliffe Hall, Ingleby Arncliffe; Yorkshire, England. *1754–1757, Racestand, York, England. 1756, Church, Ravenfield; 1757–1764, Everingham Hall; Yorkshire, England. 1757–1764, Lytham Hall, Lancashire, England. 1759–1771, Harewood House (staterooms designed by Robert Adam); 1760–1763, Church, Kirkleatham; Yorkshire England. 1760–1767, Tabley Hall, Cheshire, England. 1762–1768, Constable Burton Hall, Yorkshire, England. 1763–1765, Castlegate House, York, England. 1766, Royds House, Halifax, Yorkshire, England. *1767–1771, Thoresby House, Nottinghamshire, England. 1769–1771, Infirmary, Leeds, Yorkshire, England. 1770–1799, Hospital of San Antonio, Oporto, Portugal. 1771, Chesters, Hexham, Northumberland, England. 1772, Aston Hall, Yorkshire, England. 1772–1777, County Assize Courts, York, England. 1773, Rutherford Bridge; 1773, Greta Bridge; Yorkshire, England. 1774, Leventhorpe Hall, near Leeds, Yorkshire, England. 1774–1776, Town Hall, Newark, Nottinghamshire, England. 1774–1777, County Lunatic Asylum, York, England. 1776, Norton Place, Bishop Norton, Lincolnshire, England. 1776, Basildon Park, Berkshire, England. 1776–1777, County Hospital, Lincoln, England. *1777, Racestand, Nottingham, England. *1777–1781, Racestand, Doncaster; 1777–1780, Middleton Lodge, Middleton Tyas; 1778, Denton Park; *1779–1781, Thornes House, Wakefield; *1780, Wiganthorpe Hall, Malton; Yorkshire, England. 1780–1783, Female Prison, York, England. 1780–1790, Crescent, Buxton, Derbyshire, England. 1781–1787, Grimston Garth, Aldbrough, Yorkshire, England. 1782–1784, Church, Ossington, Nottinghamshire, England. 1783–1785, Clifton House, Rotherham; *1786–1789, Eastwood House, Rotherham; 1786–1790, Farnley Hall, Otley; 1791–1793, Church, Horbury; 1797–1804, Bridge, Ferrybridge; Yorkshire, England. 1799–1807, Coolattin Park, Shillelagh, Ireland. 1800–1803, Morton Bridge, Yorkshire, England.

BIBLIOGRAPHY

ATKINSON, J. B. 1853 "John Carr." Volume 2, page 36 in *The Dictionary of Architecture*. London: Architectural Publication Society.

DAVIES, ROBERT 1877 "A Memoir of John Carr, Esq., Formerly of York, Architect." *Yorkshire Archaeological and Topographical Journal* 4:202–213.
KITSON, SYDNEY D. 1910–1911 "Carr of York." *Journal of the Royal Institute of British Architects* Series 3 17:241–266.
WRAGG, R. B. 1957 "John Carr: Early Years and the Meeting with Robert Adam." *Journal of West Riding Society of Architects*. 17, part 3:8–12.
WRAGG, R. B. 1957 "John Carr: Late Life and Achievements." *Journal of West Riding Society of Architects* 17, part 4:11–16.
YORK GEORGIAN SOCIETY 1973 *The Works in Architecture of John Carr*. York, England: The Society.

CARRERE and HASTINGS

John Merven Carrère (1858–1911) and Thomas Hastings (1860–1929) met as students at the Ecole des Beaux-Arts in Paris in the early 1880s before returning to New York to work as draftsmen for MCKIM, MEAD, AND WHITE. Henry Flagler, a Florida developer, encouraged them to form an office in 1885 to design and supervise two hotels and two churches at Saint Augustine, Florida. Hastings was the chief designer throughout the firm's history, while Carrère directed the office and dealt with the clients and official agencies.

From the start, Carrère and Hastings represented many aspects of the Beaux-Arts movement in America, and epitomized the best parts of the French system—its adherence to functional planning and the appropriate use of materials—and avoided the obvious excesses of ornament and modish composition. The Ponce de León Hotel at Saint Augustine (1888) was the first lesson in French planning by members of their generation. The building's functional success led to commissions for the Laurel-in-the-Pines Hotel (1889–1890), at Lakewood, New Jersey, and Hotel Jefferson (1893–1894) in Richmond, Virginia.

The New York Public Library (competition

Carrère and Hastings.
Ponce de León Hotel.
Saint Augustine, Florida.
1888

1897, construction 1902–1911) marked the first major acceptance of their ideas, and also the first success of the Beaux-Arts movement in America. The façades were Parisian, the front based on a prototype associated with museums and libraries, and the rear the result of the bookstacks and the main reading room. By 1904, Carrère and Hastings had altered their style to a more general French classicism, which they considered a modern descendant of Renaissance and eighteenth-century architecture.

The firm enjoyed a huge and prosperous practice until 1915, and their intellectual rather than stylistic method of design enabled them to handle a diversity of building types: the New (later Century) Theater (1907–1909), the Manhattan Bridge and Approaches (1904–1911), the Staten Island Ferry Terminals (1901), the Richmond Borough Hall (1903–1906), and County Courthouse (1913–1919), the U.S. Rubber Building (1911–1912), Arden House for E. H. Harriman (1905–1910), and the Henry Clay Frick House (1913–1914), in New York. The firm also had many country house commissions in which they emphasized the whole estate, its landscape, gardens, and outbuildings, as well as the house itself.

After 1918, Hastings, the doyen of the profession in America, designed many large office buildings, some speculative such as the Fisk Building (1920–1922) and the Liggett Building (1919–1920) as well as more prestigious efforts such as the Standard Oil Building (completed 1926), the Macmillan Building (1924), the Cunard Building (1919–1921), and Devonshire House (1925–1926) in London. In these, he demonstrated his interpretation of the 1916 New York Zoning Law with its set-back provisions as well as his conception of the tall building. Guided by Beaux-Arts principles, Hastings conceived of the skeleton frame and the exterior sheathing as separate entities because of differing functions, one for support and the other for enclosure. As early as 1894, he had used the term "curtain wall" as we now know it and in the Blair Building (1902) had expressed the façade as a thin marble veneer devoid of structural meaning.

In many areas of their work, Carrère and Hastings demonstrated the relevance of the best features of the Beaux-Arts system for later architectural phases.

CHANNING BLAKE

WORKS

1888, Ponce de León Hotel, Saint Augustine, Fla. 1889–1890, Laurel-in-the-Pines Hotel, Lakewood, N.J. 1893–1894, Hotel Jefferson, Richmond, Virginia. 1901, Staten Island Ferry Terminals; 1902, Blair Building, New York. 1902–1911, New York Public Library. 1903–1906, Richmond Borough Hall; 1904–1911, Manhattan Bridge and Approaches; 1905–1910, Arden House; 1907–1909, New (later Century) Theater; 1911–1912, U.S. Rubber Building; 1913–1914, Henry Clay Frick House; 1913–1919, Richmond County Courthouse; 1919–1920, Liggett Building; 1919–1921, Cunard Building (with Benjamin W. Morris); 1920–1922, Fisk Building; 1924, Macmillan Building; New York. 1925–1926, Devonshire House, Piccadilly, London. Completed 1926, Standard Oil Building, New York.

BIBLIOGRAPHY

"The Works of Carrère and Hastings." 1910 *Architectural Record* 27, Jan.:1–120.

CARSTENSEN, GEORG

Algerian-born Georg Johan Bernard Carstensen (1812–1857) graduated from the University of Copenhagen, studied law, served in the king's bodyguard, and worked as a journalist before he founded and designed the famous Tivoli Gardens (1842–1843) in the bed of Copenhagen's ancient moat. After serving with Danish forces in the Virgin Islands, Carstensen spent three years in America. He and Charles Gildemeister won the competition for the New York Crystal Palace (1852–1853). Of glass and iron, painted olive with gilding, it was shaped like a Greek cross and had an imposing dome. The interior, with ornate iron galleries and staircases, was painted in polychromy. Fire destroyed the building in 1858.

MARGOT GAYLE

WORKS

1842–1843. Tivoli Gardens; *1845–1847, The Casino; Copenhagen. *1852–1853, New York Crystal Palace (with Karl Gildemeister).

BIBLIOGRAPHY

"Carstensen, G. J. B." 1934 *Dansk Biografisk Leksikon.* Copenhagen: J. H. Schultz.
CARSTENSEN, GEORG JOHAN BERNHARD, and GILDEMEISTER, CHARLES 1854 *New York Crystal Palace: Illustrated Description of the Building.* New York: Riker.
SILLIMAN, BENJAMIN, JR., and GOODRICH, C. R. (editors) (1853)1854 *The World of Science, Art and Industry.* New York: Putnam. First published as *The Illustrated Record of the Industry of All Nations: New York Exhibition.*

CARTAUD, JEAN

Jean Silvain Cartaud (1675–1758) was born in Paris in 1675. He was named a member of the Royal Academy in 1742 and served as architect to both the duke of Berry (1711–1714) and the duke of Orleans (1752–1758).

Cartaud studied in Rome in 1695. This Italian influence is suggested in his plans for the Hôtel Crozat in Paris (1704) and the elevations of the Château de Montmorency in Paris (1708). Most of his designs, however, reflect the elegant simplicity of the Mansart school. This can be seen particularly in two of his better known works, the Hôtel de Janvry, Paris (1732–1733), and the Château de Bourneville in La Ferté-Milon. Recalling the style of ROBERT DE COTTE, Cartaud preferred the use of rusticated pilasters to monumental orders and harmoniously integrated this motif into his reserved and dignified designs.

Described as intelligent and educated by his contemporaries, Jean Cartaud was popular with patrons and executed numerous domestic and ecclesiastical designs during his long career.

KATHLEEN RUSSO

WORKS

1703, Barnabites Church (portal; later altered); 1704, Hôtel Pierre Crozat; 1705, Houses, rue de la Planche; 1708, Château de Montmorency; 1715–1745, Palais Royal (service buildings); 1723, Maison Guillot; 1732–1733, Hôtel de Janvry; 1738, Notre Dame des Victoires (portal); 1740, Maison des Orfèvres; Paris. 1741, Château d'Argenson, Neuilly, France. 1744, Château de Bourneville, La Ferté-Milon, France.

BIBLIOGRAPHY

BLOMFIELD, REGINALD (1911)1974 Volume 2 in *A History of French Architecture.* Reprint of 1921 ed. 2 vols. New York: Hacker.
BLONDEL, JACQUES FRANÇOIS (1752–1756)1904–1905 *L'Architecture française.* 4 vols. Reprint. Paris: Lévy.
BRICE, GERMAIN (1698)1971 Volume 1 in *Nouvelle Description de la ville de Paris.* 9th ed. Geneva: Droz; Paris: Minard.
CHAMPIER, VICTOR, and SANDOZ, ROGER 1900 *Le Palais-Royal.* 2 vols. Paris: Société de propagation des livres d'art.
DÉZALLIER D'ARGENVILLE, ANTOINE JOSEPH (1749)1813 *Voyage pittoresque de Paris.* Paris: De Bure père.
GALLET, MICHEL 1972 *Paris Domestic Architecture of the Eighteenth Century.* London: Barrie & Jenkins.
HAUTECOEUR, LOUIS 1950 *Première moitié du XVIIIe siècle: Le Style Louis XV.* Volume 3 in *Histoire de l'architecture classique en France.* Paris: Picard.
KALNEIN, WEND GRAF, and LEVEY, MICHAEL 1972 *Art and Architecture of the Eighteenth Century in France.* Baltimore: Penguin.
MARIETTE, JEAN (1727)1927–1929 *L'architecture française.* Edited by Louis Hautecoeur. 3 vols. Reprint. Paris and Brussels: Van Oest.

CARTER, JOHN

John Carter (1748–1817) is not remembered as an architect, although Lea Castle, Worcestershire (c.1816), is an extraordinary example of neo-Romanesque architecture, but rather as one of the principals in the conversion of English "Gothick" to Gothic, substituting archeology for romanticism. Some of the drawings made for the *Builder's Magazine* (1774–1786) are of considerable antiquarian interest, but Carter's great achievement are his drawings of Bath Abbey, Saint Stephen's Chapel, Westminster, and of Saint Albans and Gloucester Cathedrals, made for the Society of Antiquaries and published between 1795 and

1813, as well as his *Ancient Architecture of England* (1795–1814).

JOHN HARRIS

WORKS

c.1775, Midford Castle, Somerset, England. c.1810, Exeter Cathedral (west window), Devonshire, England. c.1816, Lea Castle, Worcestershire, England.

BIBLIOGRAPHY

CARTER, JOHN 1774–1786 *Builder's Magazine.* London.

CARTER, JOHN 1795–1814 *Ancient Architecture of England.* London.

CASTELLAMONTE, AMEDEO DI

Amedeo di Castellamonte (1610–1683) was a Piedmontese count, ducal architect, and military engineer and the son of CARLO DI CASTELLAMONTE. From 1659, Amedeo was general superintendent of works and fortifications and councillor of state. In 1678, he was appointed first engineer to the duke. He assisted his father until his death in 1641. By 1646, he designed San Salvario, a church with an unusual longitudinal octagon plan and corner towers enclosing an octagonal cloister vault dome. Ten years later, his plan for the chapel of the Sindone was accepted and work was carried forward nearly to the level of the main entablature before GUARINO GUARINI replaced him. In 1658, he redesigned the principal façade of the Palazzo Reale in Turin, and a year later, he planned the second enlargement of the city toward the Po river.

Castellamonte's main achievement is the hunting palace of Venaria Reale (from 1660) about which he published a book (1672) cast as a dialogue between himself and the visiting GIOVANNI LORENZO BERNINI. Of the extensive gardens (known from the publication) and palace little remains due to ravagement by French troops in 1693. Venaria began to be rebuilt by MICHELANGELO GAROVE but was enlarged and renewed by FILIPPO JUVARRA. Castellamonte's integration of castle, gardens, and support town is insufficiently appreciated. His large-scale developments (Venaria; the second enlargement of Turin; Piazza Carlo Emanuele; via Po) are handled with facility though with neither grace nor monumental dignity.

His sober side can be seen in the Palazzo Trucchi di Levaldiggi in Turin (1673–1675) and the Palazzo Reale, while his puckish, late mannerist tendencies appear in the nearby Palazzo Beggiono di San Albano (Palazzo Lascaris) (from 1665). Altars by Castellamonte number among the finest of the period.

HENRY A. MILLON

WORKS

1646, San Salvario; 1656, Santi Sindone (not completed until later by Guarini); 1658, Royal Palace (façade); Turin, Italy. 1660 and later, Palace and Gardens, Venaria Reale, Italy. 1665, Palazzo Beggiono di San Albano (Palazzo Lascaris); 1673–1674, Palazzo Trucchi di Levaldigi; 1678, Piazza Carlo Emanuele; Turin, Italy.

BIBLIOGRAPHY

BAUDI DI VESME, ALESSANDRO 1963 Volume 1, pages 285–291 in *Schede Vesme.* Turin, Italy: Società piemontese di archologia e belle arte.

BRINO, G., DE BERNARDI, ATTILIO ET AL. 1966 *L'opera di Carlo e Amedeo di Castellamonte nel XVIII secolo.* 2d ed. Turin, Italy: Quaderni di Studio.

BRAYDA, CARLO; COLI, LAURA; and SESIA, DARIO 1966 *Ingegneri e architetti del sei e settecento in piemonte.* Turin, Italy: Società Ingegneri e Architetti.

CARBONERI, NINO 1963 Volume 1, pages 30–31 in *Architectura: Mostra del Barocco Piemontese.* Turin, Italy: Catalogo a cura di Vittorio Viale.

TAMBURINI, LUCIANO 1968 *Le Chiese di Torino.* Turin, Italy: Le bouquiniste.

CASTELLAMONTE, CARLO

The career of Carlo Castellamonte (1560–1641) is paradigmatic of the formative stage of the modern Savoy dukedom. Belonging to the Cognengo branch of the Castellamonte counts, he fulfilled the functions of ducal engineer (1615), member of the Fabriche e Fortificationi council (1621), superintendent of fortresses, councillor of state, and lieutenant of artillery (1637). He was a close collaborator of ASCANIO VITOZZI, whose work he largely implemented, and he may have briefly visited Rome (1605). He made a fundamental contribution to the urbanism of Turin, to the military landscape of Piedmont, and to the development of

Amedeo di Castellamonte. Palazzo Beggiono di San Albano (Palazzo Lascaris). Turin, Italy. 1665

the local palace type. His liaison role between the duke and the city councillors in building matters was much appreciated by both sides, but his numerous ducal commissions and honors awoke the animosity of his colleagues.

Castellamonte worked on numerous buildings. The major extant ones are San Carlo, Santa Cristina, and the Valentino Villa, all in Turin. San Carlo (1619) and Santa Cristina (1635–1638) are the twin churches on Piazza San Carlo, both with single-aisled rectangular plan and façades that were finished much later, Santa Cristina in 1715 by FILIPPO JUVARRA and San Carlo in 1834 by Caronesi. In the Valentino Villa (1630–?), the hands of Carlo and of his son, AMEDEO DI CASTELLAMONTE are hard to distinguish, but the central part of the main pavilion can be safely attributed to Carlo. The architectural vocabulary he inherited from Vitozzi was somewhat dry and static, which the Palladian (see ANDREA PALLADIO) ideas he employed helped to enliven. Although the Vitozzian lack of dynamism resulted in undistinguished single façades, it served very well in large-scale urban design. Castellamonte designed the Piazza San Carlo (1639) and the Piazza San Giovanni (1622) in Turin. The latter survives greatly altered although the dimensions of the post-World War II building are faithful to the original porticoed structure. Piazza San Carlo (1619) is a masterpiece of urban design. It echoes the organization of the Piazza del Popolo in Rome in the use of the twin churches, but in its original conception the square was intended for residential use. Piazza San Carlo was part of a major enlargement of Turin, whose purpose was to improve the defenses of Turin and to glorify the house of Savoy. Castellamonte's achievement in urban design is his seamless blending of what might seem self-exclusive objectives. His city planning was influenced by order, economy, and discipline, the hallmarks of military architecture. His work of fortification exceeded his architectural concerns in the amount of time he dedicated to it and in its importance for the dukedom. He was responsible for the rebuilding of Verrua, Momigliano, and Savigliano, three major but now destroyed fortresses. In addition, his manuscript, *Parere sopra la fabrica dell'imboccatura da farsi al naviglio che scorre da Ivrea a Vercelli . . .* of 1616, proves Castellamonte's ability as a hydraulic engineer.

MARTHA POLLAK

WORKS

1598, Sanctuary (with Ascanio Vitozzi), Vicoforte di Mondovì, Italy. 1602, Eremo dei Camaldolesi, Turin, Italy. 1604, San Sudario, Rome. 1619, San Carlo (with M. Valperga); 1620, Citta Nova (expansion south); *1622, Piazza San Giovanni; 1630–?, Valentino Villa; 1635–1638, Santa Cristina; c.1636, Palazzo Isnardi di Caraglio (Accademia Filarmonica); 1639, Piazza San Carlo; Turin, Italy.

BIBLIOGRAPHY

BAUDI DI VESME, A.   1932   "L'arte negli stati sabaudi." *Atti SPABA* 14:742.
BERTAGNA, U.   1974–1976   "Vicende costruttive delle chiese del Corpus Domini e dello Spirito Santo in Torino." *Palladio* 23–25:75–113.
CARBONERI, NINO   1966   *Ascanio Vitozzi: Un architetto tra manierismo e Barocco.* Rome: Officina.
LOTZ, WOLFGANG   1955   "Die ovalen Kirchenräume des Cinquecento." *Römisches Jahrbuch für Kunstgeschichte* 7:9–99.
PROMIS, CARLOS   1871   "Gli ingegneri militari." *Miscellanea di Storia Italiana* 12:584–591.
SCOTTI, AURORA   1969   *Ascanio Vitozzi: Ingegnere ducale a Torino.* Florence: La nuova Italia.

CASTELLI, DOMENICO

Lombard by birth, Domenico Castelli (c.1582–1657) moved to Rome around 1611 where he remained until his death. His reputation is based chiefly on the supervisory and collaborative roles he played as architect of the Camera Apostolica during the pontificates of Urban VIII and Innocent X. In various executive capacities Castelli's name is associated with nearly four dozen civic and ecclesiastical commissions in and around the papal city. These include projects ranging from the upkeep of public fountains to the restoration of the Lateran Baptistery. Among the architects he assisted in such undertakings were CARLO MADERNO, FRANCESCO BORROMINI, PIETRO BERRETTINA DA CORTONA, GIOVANNI LORENZO BERNINI, and especially LUIGI ARRIGUCCI.

Castelli's relatively few independent commissions tend to be rather conservative in outlook. His masterpiece in Rome is undoubtedly the façade of San Girolamo della Carità (1647–1657), a tasteful work which in all but a few respects relies entirely upon the Roman conventions of the late sixteenth century.

JOHN VARRIANO

WORKS

1638, Sante Cosma e Damiano (high altar); 1639, Duomo of Monterotondo; c.1640, San Isodoro; c.1640, Santa Anna (portico and chapel); 1647–1657, San Girolamo della Carità (façade; not completed until 1660); 1653–1657, Biblioteca Angelica, San Agostino (rebuilt in the eighteenth century); Rome. 1654–1657, Sanctuary of Cibona, near Tolfa, Italy.

BIBLIOGRAPHY

BAGGIO, CARLO, AND ZAMPA, PAOLA   1979   *Quaderni dell' istituto dell'architettura* 25:21–44.

BAGLIONE, GIOVANNI (1642)1935 Pages 180–183 in *Vite de pittori, scultori et architetti.* Reprint. Rome: Calzone.

D'ANNUNZIO, M. R. 1978 "Domenico Castelli." Volume 21, pages 708–711 in *Dizionario biografico degli Italiani.* Rome: Istituto della Enciclopedia Italiana.

PIAZZO, MARCELLO DEL 1968 *Ragguagli Borrominiani.* Rome: Ministero dell'interno.

POLLAK, OSCAR 1928 Volume 1 in *Die Kunsttätigkeit under Urban VIII.* Vienna: Filser.

VARRIANO, JOHN 1974 "Domenico Castelli's Facade for S. Girolamo della Carita in Rome." Pages 139–145 in Robert Enggass and Mary Stokstael (editors), *Hortus imaginum: Essays in Western Art.* Lawrence: University of Kansas.

CASTELLI, FILIPPO

Filippo Castelli (1738–1818) was born in San Damiano d'Asti, Italy, and died in Turin. He studied in Turin and Rome, where he followed archeological interests. After his return to Turin in 1763, he worked on the Hospital of San Giovanni. Among his works of greater importance are Santa Michele at Cavaglià (1779–1787), San Martino at Azeglio (1784–1790), the new stables for the Carignano Palace in Turin (1790; now the façade of the Biblioteca Civica), and San Francesco in Moncaliere (1787). His work shows that special Piedmontese blend of classicism and late baroque structuralism also found in his contemporaries LUIGI MICHELE BARBERIS and GIOVANNI BATTISTA FEROGGIO.

HENRY A. MILLON

WORKS

c.1763 and later, Hospital of San Giovanni, Turin, Italy. 1779–1787, Santa Michele, Cavaglia, Italy. 1784–1790, San Martino, Azeglio, Italy. 1787, San Francesco, Moncalieri, Italy. 1790, Palazzo Carignano (stables; now the façade of the Biblioteca Civica), Turin, Italy.

BIBLIOGRAPHY

BRAYDA, CARLO; COLI, LAURA; and SESIA, DARIO 1963 *Ingegneri e architetti del sei e settecento in piemonte.* Turin, Italy: Società Ingegneri e Architetti.

CARBONERI, NINO 1963 Volume 1, pages 86–87 in *Architettura, Mostra del Barocco Piemontese.* Turin, Italy: Catalogo a cura di Vittorio Viale.

GAMERINO, FRANCESCO 1947 "Architettura barocca nel monferrato." *Bollettino Società Piemontese di Archeologia e di Belle Arte* 1:116–127.

CASTIGLIONE, ENRICO

Enrico Castiglione (1914–) was born in Busto Arsizio near Milan where he did most of his work.

Graduating in 1934 from the Engineering School of Milan, he became registered as an architect in 1936. His early designs in the 1950s showed an interest in concrete structures which later became his original trademark.

His entry for the design competition of the Naples Train Station (1954) was the starting point of an ongoing research in expressionist architecture using such elements as thin reinforced concrete slabs, vaults, and arches. The use of structures to create an organic feeling related closely to such architects as LUIGI NERVI and FELIX CANDELA. His talented capacity to handle materials, light, and space was clearly present in his Sempione School design in Busto Arsizio (1958) and his Necropolis project (1965). The plasticity of the overall appearance of the Prospriano Church in Varese (1965) exhibits a strong sculptural interest which has been referred to as neobaroque. The poured-in-place massive curved piers of the Polytechnic Institute in Turin (1966) created a quality of Brutalism often seen in Italian architecture at this period as a development of the Modern movement.

MARC DILET

WORKS

1953, Housing Complex; 1954, Catholic Cultural Hall; 1955, Housing Sempione, Busto Arsizio, Italy. 1957, Lamberti Offices, Albizzate, Italy. 1958, Sempione Elementary School, Busto Arsizio, Italy. 1959, Artea Industrial Complex, Parabiago, Italy. 1965, Prospriano Church, Varese, Italy. 1966, Gallarete Housing, Varisino, near Milan. 1966, Polytechnic Institute, Turin, Italy.

CASTIGLIONI, ACHILLE, and CASTIGLIONI, PIER GIACOMO

The brothers Achille Castiglioni (1918–) and Pier Giacomo Castiglioni (1914–) are Italian architects renowned for their designs of world's fair pavilions throughout Europe during the 1950s and 1960s. These pavilions were intended to represent the most contemporary Italian architectural concepts as well as the latest graphic and industrial designs. The small number of building elements used to compose these small pavilions gave them a sense of spatial transparency. The Castiglioni designs were based on geometrical forms developed from the Bauhaus vocabulary. The RAI pavilion at the 1965 Milan Fair had an abstract sculptural expression and became a structure reused for consecutive fairs. The architectural mastery can be found in this opposition between the permanent and the temporary features. A similar design attitude of austerity and clarity underlay the Castiglionis' interior architecture of the Watchmaker's Shop in Milan (1970).

MARC DILET

WORKS

*1965, Montecatini Pavilion; *1965, RAI (Italian Radio and Television) Pavilion; Milan Fair; 1970, Watchmaker's Shop; Milan.

CASTLE, RICHARD

Richard Castle (c.1695–1751), Ireland's most prolific Palladian architect, was born in Kassel, Hesse, Germany. Arriving in Dublin in 1728 from London, where he had probably established contact with LORD BURLINGTON's circle, he became the assistant and protégé of EDWARD LOVETT PEARCE, the leading Irish Palladian. Pearce died prematurely in 1733 and, as his worthy though more stolid successor, Castle was the designer of an impressive series of country houses, often lavishly fitted-out. In Dublin, he designed public buildings and several important aristocratic *palazzi,* notably Leinster House (1745–1751). His Palladian style is distinctively robust and masculine and influenced particularly—apart from Pearce—by JAMES GIBBS.

NICHOLAS SHEAFF

WORKS

1731, Hazlewood, County Sligo, Ireland. 1731, Westport, County Mayo, Ireland. 1731–1740, Powerscourt, County Wicklow, Ireland. 1733, Ballyhaise, County Cavan, Ireland. 1734, Printing House, Trinity College; 1736–1737, 80 Saint Stephen's Green; Dublin. 1737, Knockbreda Church, Belfast, Ireland. 1738, 85 Saint Stephen's Green, Dublin. 1739–1745, Carton, County Kildare, Ireland. *1740, Fishamble Street Music Hall; 1740, Tyrone House; Dublin, c.1742, Belvedere, County Westmeath, Ireland. 1742–1755, Russborough, County Wicklow, Ireland. 1745–1751, Leinster House, Dublin. c.1750, Bellinter, County Meath, Ireland. 1750–1757, Rotunda Lying-in Hospital, Dublin.

BIBLIOGRAPHY

CASTLE, RICHARD c.1729 "An Essay on Artificial Navigation." Unpublished Manuscript, National Library of Ireland, Dublin.
GLIN, KNIGHT OF 1964 "Richard Castle, Architect, His Biography and Works: A Synopsis." *Irish Georgian Society Quarterly Bulletin* 7:31–38.
"History of the Fine Arts in Ireland—Richard Castle." 1793 *Anthologia Hibernica* 2:242–243.
SADLEIR, T. U. 1911 "Richard Castle: Architect." *Journal of the Royal Society of Antiquaries of Ireland* Series 6 1:241–245.
SHEAFF, NICHOLAS 1979 *Iveagh House: An Historical Description.* Dublin: Department of Foreign Affairs.

CATALANO, EDUARDO

Eduardo Catalano (1917–), an American architect who employs dramatic structural forms in his imposing buildings, is an outspoken advocate of systematic design methods. He criticizes the conventional practice of treating each building as a unique case, and suggests instead that architects design generic structural and functional elements, capable of adaptation to varying circumstances. Catalano further believes that schools of architecture, working together with industry, must take the initiative in developing such rational methods of building and urban design.

Born in Buenos Aires, he graduated with architectural degrees from the University of Pennsylvania in 1944 and, the following year, from Harvard University. He began an independent practice in Buenos Aires before emigrating to the United States in 1951. Studies in warped surface structures led to the design of the Raleigh House in Raleigh, North Carolina (1954), whose open spaces are formed under a single hyperbolic paraboloid roof spanning 82 feet. This early building embodies features found in many of his larger structures, such as the Student Center at the Massachusetts Institute of Technology (M.I.T.) in Cambridge (1963) and the Governmental Center in Greensboro, North Carolina (1970). The plan is simple and regular if not symmetrical; the form is large-scaled; and the roof extends horizontally, affording shelter, yet lifting outward. Catalano taught at the University of North Carolina in Raleigh from 1951 to 1956, and from 1956 to 1977 at M.I.T.

MICHAEL HOLLANDER

Catalano.
Governmental Center
(*courthouse*).
Greensboro, North
Carolina.
1970

WORKS

1954, Raleigh House, Raleigh, N.C. 1963, Student Center; 1965, Married Student Housing; Massachusetts Institute of Technology, Cambridge. 1968, Juilliard School of Music, Lincoln Center for the Performing Arts (with PIETRO BELLUSCHI and Helge Westermann), New York. 1970, Governmental Center, Greensboro, N.C. 1973, Hall of Justice, Springfield, Mass. 1974, United States Embassy, Buenos Aires. 1976, Cambridge High School, Mass. 1976, La Guardia High School, New York.

BIBLIOGRAPHY

CATALANO, EDUARDO 1960 "Structures of Warped Surfaces: Combinations of Units of Hyperbolic Paraboloids." *North Carolina State University School of Design Student Publication* 10, no. 1: entire issue.
CATALANO, EDUARDO 1969 "A Case for Systems." *Progressive Architecture* 50, no. 5:162–166.
CATALANO, EDUARDO 1978 *Buildings and Projects.* Edited by C. Gubitasi and A. Izzo. Rome: Officina Edizioni.
HEYER, PAUL 1966a *Architects on Architecture.* New York: Walker.
HEYER, PAUL 1966b "M.I.T. Student Center: Eduardo Catalano Starts with Systems and Creates Architecture." *Architectural Record* 139, Mar.:125–132.

CATANEO, PIETRO

Pietro Cataneo (1510?–1574?) was a Sienese architect whose reputation rests on his architectural treatise, *I Quattro Primi Libri di Architettura* (1554). Cataneo appears to have been a student or assistant to the Sienese artist–architect BALDASSARE PERUZZI and may well have helped Peruzzi on designs for the Bruna River Dam (1530). He was also active as a fortification engineer throughout the Sienese republic (late 1540s–early 1550s). His civil architecture has yet to be securely identified.

Cataneo's treatise considers both military and civil architecture together. The treatise, which has yet to be systematically studied, is important for many reasons, among them the fact that the city plan and its walls are viewed as a unified defense organism rather than just the walls. This section was most significant for the future of military planning. Cataneo reissued *I Quattro Primi Libri* with the addition of four new books in 1573 as *De Architectura di Pietro Cataneo Senese*.

NICHOLAS ADAMS

BIBLIOGRAPHY

CATANEO, PIETRO (1554)1964 *I Quattro Primi Libri di Architettura.* Reprint. Ridgewood, N.J.: Gregg.
DE LA CROIX, HORST 1960 "Military Architecture and the Radial City Plan in Sixteenth Century Italy." *Art Bulletin* 42:263–290.
MARCONI, PAOLO 1973 *La Città come forma simbolica.* Rome: Bulzoni.

CATTANEO, CESARE

An exponent of the Modern movement in both abstract and symbolically Christian terms, Cesare Cattaneo (1912–1943) was one of the three major architects (along with GIUSEPPE TERRAGNI and PIETRO LINGERI) of the Como school of the 1930s in Italy. His major works are few but important, the Casa d'Affito in Cernobbio (1938–1939), his masterpiece, being one of the most sophisticated buildings of the interwar period.

THOMAS L. SCHUMACHER

WORKS

*1935, Rowing Room, Sports Show, Palazzo dell'Arte, Milan. 1935–1936, Giuseppe Garbagnati Nursery School, Asnago, Italy. 1936, Camerlata Fountain (with Mario Radice), Como Italy. 1938–1939, Casa d'Affito (apartment house), Cernobbio, Italy.

BIBLIOGRAPHY

CATTANEO, CESARE 1941 *Giovanni e Giuseppe; Dialoghi d'Architettura.* Milan: Libreria Artistica Salto.
"Cesare Cattaneo (1912–1943)." 1961 *L'Architettura* 6, no. 9:636–639; no. 10: 708–711; no. 11:780–783; no. 12:852–855.
DANESI, SILVIA 1977 "Cesare Cattaneo." *Lotus International* 16:88–121.
PICA, AGNOLDOMENICO 1941 *Architettura Moderna in Italia.* Milan: Hoepli.
SARTORIS, ALBERTO (1948)1954–1957 *Encyclopedie de l'architecture nouvelle.* 2d ed., rev. New York: Hoepli.

CAUCHIE, PAUL

Paul Cauchie (1875–1952), born in Ath, Belgium, and educated at the Brussels Academy of Fine Arts, was not a professional architect but a mural painter. His frescoes and sgraffiti came to be commissioned as façade and interior embellishments for many Art Nouveau buildings in Brussels. His own house in Brussels (1905) had a rather severe rectilinear façade enlivened with large-scale figurative sgraffito panels in his distinctive Art Nouveau style. Cauchie's later career was devoted to furniture design, interior decoration, and to the design of some small cottages in the Netherlands.

ALFRED WILLIS

WORK

1905, Cauchie House, Brussels.

BIBLIOGRAPHY

BORSI, FRANCO 1977 *Bruxelles 1900.* New York: Rizzoli.

DELEVOY, ROBERT ET AL. 1971 *Bruxelles 1900 Capitale de l'Art nouveau.* Brussels: Ecole Nationale Supérieure d'Architecture et des Arts Visuels.

PUTTEMANS, PIERRE 1976 *Modern Architecture in Belgium.* Translated by Mette Willert. Brussels: Vokaer.

RUSSELL, FRANK (editor) 1979 *Art Nouveau Architecture.* New York: Rizzoli.

CAUDILL, ROWLETT, and SCOTT

Founded in 1947 by William Wayne Caudill (1914–), professor, theorist, principal architect, the Houston-based firm of Caudill, Rowlett, and Scott (CRS) has grown steadily since its inception from two members to over one thousand employees and affiliates. Best known for its innovative educational, commercial, and health care architecture, the firm has built both in the United States and abroad.

CRS has been a leader in management and technological advances, pioneering the team concept in architecture. Their interdisciplinary teams, comprised of architects, technologists, designers, and site specialists, strive to develop a total design concept which often involves clients in direct participation with the building process. In its commitment to a humanistic and energy conservation approach to building design, concerns for natural light and ventilation and careful consideration of environmental and regional factors are articulated within the formal modernist tradition of form following function. Thus, the step-back construction method in which upper floors serve as overhangs to shade lower floors serves as a solar control device. Thermal buffer zones, pressure walls, earth berms, open plans, and multi-use spaces are all designed to reduce energy. A variety of fenestration techniques not only enhance the aesthetic qualities of a structure but also carefully orient the building to both its site and its intended usage. CRS's design objectives extend to a postoccupancy discussion and questionnaire to determine the relative success or failure of the completed project.

Several members of the firm, most notably Caudill, publish books on design and theory. In the 1974 edition of *A Bucket of Oil,* by Caudill, Frank D. Lawyer, and Thomas A. Bullock, the aspirations of the firm are summed up best: "Our challenge for the future is to conserve energy, yes. But we must at the same time preserve the dignity of man."

JAN AVGIKOS

WORKS

1969, CRS Office Building, Houston, Texas. 1970, Four College Science Center, Claremont, Calif. 1973, Desert Samaritan Hospital, Phoenix, Ariz. 1974, Hyatt Regency Hotel, Houston, Texas. 1974, Salanter-Akiba Riverdale Academy, Bronx, N.Y. 1975, Thomas E. Leavey Student Activity Center, University of California at Santa Clara. 1977, Rochester General Hospital, N.Y. 1977, Tulane University Hospital and Teaching Center, New Orleans, La. 1978, Bahrain Monetary Building, Manama, Saudi Arabia. 1979, International Business Machines Office Building, Houston, Tex.

BIBLIOGRAPHY

BULLOCK, THOMAS A.; CAUDILL, WILLIAM W.; and LAWYER, FRANK D. 1974 *A Bucket of Oil.* Boston: Cahners.

CAUDILL, WILLIAM W. 1971 *Architecture by Team.* New York: Van Nostrand.

MURPHY, JAMES 1977 "The Corporate Architect." *Progressive Architecture* 58, May:63–65.

MURPHY, JAMES 1979 "Silver Bell: Switching Facility." *Progressive Architecture* 60, July:66–69.

MURPHY, JAMES 1981 "Corral in the Sun: Federal Correctional Institution, Bastrop, Texas." *Progressive Architecture* 62, Apr.:126–131.

CEINERAY, JEAN BAPTISTE

Born in Paris, where at the Académie Royale d'Architecture he was probably the student of FRANÇOIS FRANQUE, Jean Baptiste Ceineray (1722–1811) established himself in Nantes after 1760 as an *architecte-voyer* (architect–surveyor of roads). His master plan for the city received final approval in 1766 and was immediately put into effect under his direction. Ill, Ceineray left his position in 1780 to his student MATHURIN CRUCY, who continued and considerably expanded his mentor's work in a more original style. The rather austere architecture of Ceineray exemplifies in the provinces the aesthetic of ANGE JACQUES GABRIEL and JACQUES FRANÇOIS BLONDEL, two masters of the *style Louis XV* as tempered by a regard for rigorous classicism. His most ambitious building remains the Chambre des Comptes (1762–1782), the present Préfecture of Nantes.

DANIEL RABREAU
Translated from French by Shara Wasserman

WORKS

1762–1780, City to the West (extension); 1762–1780, Quay, Public Square, and Promenade at the site of the ancient embankment; 1762–1782, Hôtel de la Chambre des Comptes; 1764–1767, Brancas Quay; 1772–1776, Flesselles Quay; 1772, Place du Bouffay; 1774, Place d'Armes et des Cours Saint-Pierre et Saint-André; Nantes.

BIBLIOGRAPHY
LELIÈVRE, PIERRE 1942 *L'urbanisme et l'architecture à Nantes au XVIIIe siècle.* Nantes, France: Durance.

CELER

See SEVERUS and CELER.

CELLERIER, JACQUES

Jacques Cellérier (1742–1814) was born in Dijon, France, and studied architecture under JACQUES FRANÇOIS BLONDEL and JULIEN DAVID LEROY. He made his reputation designing fashionable houses in a neoclassical style for a clientele including aristocrats, actresses, and theater directors. His activities in speculative building precluded his election to the Académie Royale d'Architecture, but he served the *ancien régime,* the revolutionary governments, and the Empire as an architect and administrator. In 1810, he designed the elephant fountain planned for the Place de la Bastille. A friend of CLAUDE NICOLAS LEDOUX, Cellérier wrote the first biography of that architect in 1806.

RICHARD CLEARY

WORKS

*1777, Duc de Laval's Weekend House; *1779, Hôtel Nicolai; *1786, Hôtel de l'Infantado (stables); *1787–1788, Hôtel de Soubise (Hôtel Soyecourt); *1808, Théâtre des Variétés; Paris. 1810, Theater, Dijon, France.

BIBLIOGRAPHY
BRAHAM, ALLAN 1980 *The Architecture of the French Enlightenment.* London: Thames & Hudson.
GALLET, MICHEL 1972 *Stately Mansions: Eighteenth Century Paris Domestic Architecture.* New York: Praeger.
HAUTECOEUR, LOUIS 1952–1953 Volumes 4 and 5 in *Histoire de l'architecture classique en France.* Paris: Picard.
J. [ACQUES] C. [ÉLLÉRIER] 1806 *Notice rapide sur la vie et les ouvrages de Claude-Nicolas Ledoux.* Paris: Imprimerie des Annales de l'architecture et des arts.
KRAFFT, J. CH., and RANSONNETTE, N. c.1801 *Plans, coupes, élévations des plus belles maisons et des hôtels construits à Paris et dans les environs.* Paris: Clousier.

CELSING, PETER

Peter Celsing (1920–1974), the most prominent and artistically gifted Swedish architect after World War II, after studies at the Royal Institute of Technology and at the Academy of Arts in Stockholm, was employed at a contracting and trading company in Beirut (1946–1948). During the next four years, he was the architect of the Stockholm Subway System. He used concrete in a beautiful manner, combined with glass and steel.

During the following decade, however, his main task was to design churches, which well fitted his artistic nature. Dark red brick became the characteristic material of his churches during the 1950s, for which his inspiration came from the architecture of Swedish National Romanticism (see RAGNAR ÖSTBERG). Typical of the ecclesiastical architecture of Celsing is a highly sophisticated expression and a devotional spirit, sometimes with a postmodern approach, such as in the Crematorium of Ludvika where the brick front is treated as a thin screen. Also characteristic is an advanced collaboration with artists, painters, and sculptors and the very high quality in the treatment of materials. His tendency toward the mannerist and the sublime is especially evident in his last church, Nacksta (1963–1969) in Sundsvall, and in the building for the Bank of Sweden (1965–1976), Stockholm, where the heavy Renaissance palace is transformed to a modern office with an expressively rusticated front of granite. The theater building in the complex of the House of Culture (1965–1976) in Stockholm is an outstanding example of a modern city architecture with a lustrous front of stainless steel.

From 1960 to 1969, Celsing was a professor at the Royal Institute of Technology in Stockholm.

FREDRIC BEDOIRE

WORKS

1948–1952, Stations for Stockholm Subway System. 1953–1962, Saint Thomas Church, Vällingsby, Sweden. 1953–1962, University Library (rebuilding), Uppsala, Sweden. 1954–1958, Crematorium at Ludvika, Dalarna, Sweden. 1955–1961, Stockholm Opera House (restoration). 1956–1959, Almtuna Church, Uppsala, Sweden. 1957–1959, Härlanda Church, Göteborg, Sweden. 1963–1969, Nacksta Church, Sundsvall, Sweden. 1964–1970, Swedish Film Institute; 1965–1974, Bank of Sweden (not completed until 1976); 1965–1974, House of Culture; Stockholm. 1970–1974, Humanistic Center (not completed until 1975), Uppsala University, Sweden.

BIBLIOGRAPHY
LARSSON, L. O. ET AL. (editors) 1980 *Peter Celsing: En bok om en arkitekt och hans verk.* Stockholm: Förlag.

CENDRIER, FRANÇOIS-ALEXIS

François-Alexis Cendrier (1803–1893) studied at the Ecole des Beaux-Arts in Paris under ANTOINE

L. T. VAUDOYER and LOUIS HIPPOLYTE LEBAS and
won a Second Grand Prix in 1827. He worked as
an architect for the Orléans Railway Company
(1837–1840) and was chief architect of the Paris-
Lyons Railway Company (1840–1859), designing
both principal and secondary stations.

ANN LORENZ VAN ZANTEN

WORKS

1837, Félix de Beaujour Tomb, Père Lachaise Cemetery;
*1847–1852, Gare de Lyons; *1852, Palais de l'Industrie
(with Alexis Barrault; altered and completed by J. M. V.
Viel); Paris. 1855–1857, Central Railway Station,
Lyons-Perrache, France.

CEPPI, CARLO

Carlo Ceppi (1829–1921) was born and died in
Turin, Italy. A pupil of CARLO PROMIS, he was one
of the most important architects of the last quarter
of the nineteenth century in Turin. When Ceppi
won one of three first prizes in the competition for
a new façade of Santa Maria del Fiore in Florence
(1863), his career was launched. His design for the
Railroad Station (1866–1868) at Porta Nuova in
Turin with ALESSANDRO MAZZUCCHETTI showed
his openness to innovation, later confirmed by the
early use of reinforced concrete in the Bellia Building on via Pietro Mica (1894–1898), Turin. He
worked ably in neobaroque as well, designing the
peripheral connecting chapels of the Consolata
(1899), the Palazzo Ceriani-Peyron (1878–1879),
the façade of San Tomaso (1890), and a commemorative tablet crowning the façade of the Palazzo
Carignano (c.1880), all in Turin.

HENRY A. MILLON

WORKS

1866–1868, Railroad Station (with Alessandro
Mazzuccheti), Porta Nuova; 1876, San Gioacchino;
1878–1879, Palazzo Ceriana-Peyron; c.1880, Palazzo
Carignano (commemorative tablet crowning façade);
1894–1898, Casa delle Imprese Bellia; 1896, San Tomaso
(façade); 1896, Consolata (enlargement); Turin, Italy.

BIBLIOGRAPHY

BRUNO, E. 1928 "Ricordando il Maestro." L'Archi-
tettura Italiana 23, no. 10: 109–112.
HITCHCOCK, H. R. (1958)1977 Architecture: Nine-
teenth and Twentieth Centuries. 4th ed., rev. Baltimore:
Penguin.
MEEKS, CARROL L. V. 1966 Italian Architecture:
1750–1914. New Haven: Yale.
SPURGAZZI, GIOVANNI 1922 Della vita e degli studi del
Conte Carlo Ceppi architetto Torinese. Turin, Italy:
Celanza.

CERDÁ, ILDEFONSO

Ildefonso Cerdá (1815–1876), author of the plan
of reform and enlargement of Barcelona, Spain,
was the first to attempt to make urban planning a
science. He laid out his principles in a monumental work, The General Theory of Urbanization
(1867).

Born in Centellas, Barcelona, he studied in
Madrid to become a civil engineer (1835–1841).
From 1841 to 1849, he worked as an engineer for
the state, mostly on public roads. In 1849, an unexpected inheritance enabled him to put his career as
civil servant behind him and to dedicate himself
completely to urbanization, a word he invented.
Cerdá, in developing his theory of urbanization,
took into consideration many disciplines, including history, law, economics, statistics, architecture,
and engineering. Since Cerdá above all wanted his
theory to have practical application, he was careful
to distinguish between what was theoretically perfect and practically possible. He applied both to
the case of Barcelona, trying to reduce to a minimum the arbitrariness inherent in each plan
(1859). This solicitude guided him in a project of
reform and enlargement that was as much egalitarian as flexible. As proposed by Cerdá, the plan for
Barcelona would look like a homogeneous checkerboard, disposed on an axis, which, without reinforcing its centrality, would incorporate the old
Barcelona into a new modern city. Buildings were
grouped in blocks that, in general, occupied two
of the four sides of a square. Placing and designing
the blocks in various ways, Cerdá created unities
that were visually different but endowed with the
same features. On the other hand, he deliberately
shied away from zoning and designed the squares
in such a way that each could accommodate living,
industry, gardens, or commerce. Congruently, the
building ordnances were flexible.

This plan, its elaboration, and its management
occupied some twenty years of Cerdá's life. It
marked decisively the development of Barcelona
and served as a model for other Spanish city enlargements (Madrid, Bilbao, San Sebastían, Saba-
dell, Pamplona) and inspired in part the Law of
Enlargements of Population Centers (1864).

After the General Theory of Urbanization, Cerdá
sketched a "general theory of ruralization" whose
object was the "reforms and enlargement" of rural
space. Shortly before his death, it was proposed to
integrate both in a theory of the "colonization" of
territory of an entire country. Of these two last
theories no more than fragments and allusions are
known.

The integration of the urban and the rural pursued by Cerdá influenced another well-known

Spanish urbanist, ARTURO SORIA Y MATA, the designer in 1882 of the Linear City.

ARTURO SORIA Y PUIG
Translated from Spanish by
Judith E. Meighan

BIBLIOGRAPHY

CERDÁ, ILDEFONSO 1968 *Teoría general de la urbanización. Madrid: 1867.* Reprint. Madrid: Instituto de Estudios Fiscales.
DIERNA, SALVATORE 1974–1975 "Il Pla Cerdá e il processo di formazione della città moderna a Barcelona." *Rassegna dell'Istituto di Architettura e Urbanistica* 1974–1975:29–32.
ESTAPE, FABIAN 1971 *Vida y obra de Ildefonso Cerdá.* Madrid: Instituto de Estudios Fiscales.
MILLER, BERNARD 1977 "Ildefonso Cerdá. An introduction." *Architectural Association Quarterly* 1:12–22.
RODRIGUEZ-LORES, JUAN 1980 "Ildefonso Cerdá: Die Wissenschaft des Städtebaues und der Bebauungsplan von Barcelona (1859)." *Städtebau um die Jahrhundertwende. Materialien zur Entstehung der Disziplin Städtebau.* Cologne, Germany.
SORIA Y PUIG, ARTURO 1979*a* "Arbitrariedad, igualdad y flexibilidad en la planificación. Algunas consideraciones sobre el plan de Cerdá para Barcelona." *Revista de la Universidad Complutense* 115:279–292.
SORIA Y PUIG, ARTURO 1979*b* *Hacia una teoría general de la urbanización. Introducción a la obra teórica de Ildefonso Cerdá.* Madrid: Colegio de Ingenieros de Caminos.

ČERNÝ, FRANTIŠEK M.

František M. Černý (1903–1978) was born and worked in Prague, Czechoslovakia. His style, issuing from the principles of functionalism, displays a wide architectural invention and is characterized by the application of both natural and synthetic materials. His most important architectural work is the new façade with two towers of the Emauzy Monastery in Prague (1965–1968).

VLADIMÍR ŠLAPETA

WORKS

1928, Apartment House, Vinohrady District; 1937, Low-income Housing (with K. Ossendorf), Holešovice District; 1938, Dr.-Ing. Moezler, Dejvice District; Prague. 1946–1950, Hospital, Kolín, Czechoslovakia. 1965–1968, Emauzy Monastery (front façade with two towers), Prague.

BIBLIOGRAPHY

ŠLAPETA, VLADIMÍR 1973 "F. M. Černý = 70 let." *Československý architekt* 19, no. 26:4.
ŠLAPETA, VLADIMÍR 1978 "Frantíšek M. Černý." *Arkkitehtiopiskelija* 1978, no. 1:34–37.

CERUTI, GIOVANNI

Giovanni Ceruti (1842–1907) was born in Valpiana, in the region of Valsesia, Italy. He studied at the Universities of Pavia and Torino, and received his degree in engineering from the Polytechnic Institute of Milan in 1867. Later, he got an advanced degree in architecture at the Academy of Fine Arts in Brera. Ceruti belongs to that generation of Milanese architects who developed from and followed the teachings of CAMILLO BOITO, a dominant figure in Milanese culture of the second half of the nineteenth century. Of all the trends then available in the eclectic architecture of the period, Ceruti selected the neo-Romanesque, reinterpreting elements and decorative motifs of the Lombard-bramantesque (see DONATO BRAMANTE) style. His first great professional opportunity occurred at the Italian Exposition in Milan in 1881, for which he designed the urban plan and several of the buildings. Between 1888 and 1893, Ceruti designed the Museum of Natural History of Milan in which he merged Romanesque and Gothic elements with rich taste. Elements of Italian medieval and Renaissance architecture are incorporated also in the façade of the Basilica dell'Assunta in the Sanctuary of the Sacro Monte of Varallo, and in the local cemetery, both built between 1891 and 1897. He was a member of the commission in charge of the restoration of the Duomo of Milan and of the commission for the conservation of monuments of the Lombard province.

LUCIANO PATETTA
Translated from Italian by
Richard Koffler

Černý.
Emauzy Monastery (front
façade with two towers).
Prague.
1965–1968.

BIBLIOGRAPHY

MEEKS, CARROLL L. V.   1966   *Italian Architecture: 1750–1914.* New Haven: Yale University Press.

PATETTA, LUCIANO   1976   *Il Razionalismo e l'architettura in Italia durante il fascismo.* Venice: Biennale di Venezia.

CESARIANO, CESARE DI LORENZO

Cesare di Lorenzo Cesariano (1483–1543) was born and died in Milan. A painter, architect, illustrator, and commentator of VITRUVIUS, he is important chiefly for his edition of Vitruvius's *De architectura* (1521), the first vernacular translation of and commentary on Vitruvius's treatise. Cesariano's own annotated copy has been untraceable since 1948. His biography is known principally from his annotations and from his commentary. Until he was sixteen, Cesariano studied with DONATO BRAMANTE in Milan; whether he studied painting, architecture, or both is not known. Thereafter, Cesariano worked as a painter (frescoes, sacristy, San Giovanni Evangelista, Parma [1508]; altarpiece, Santa Eufemia, Piacenza [c.1506]) and as an architect (forecourt, Santa Maria presso San Celso, Milan [1513]), and studied enough Latin and other academic subjects to give him sufficient confidence to attempt a Vitruvius translation and commentary.

Cesariano's commentary reveals little knowledge of Roman monuments; he never visited Rome, despite GIORGIO VASARI's passing remark that he did so. Cesariano did not understand Vitruvius thoroughly, so that much of the commentary is merely a lengthy restatement of the intelligible portions of Vitruvius's text. Collaborators finished the commentary after carta 154v in an incomplete and ignorant way and printed Cesariano's remaining illustrations without the necessary explanations.

Despite its flaws, Cesariano's edition offers insights into aspects of the Italian Renaissance. Because he did not understand the architecture of Vitruvius's time, Cesariano had to invent suitable buildings with which to illustrate Vitruvius's work. He did so by modifying Romanesque and early Italian Renaissance architecture and thereby showed how he and others created the many varieties of Renaissance architecture out of locally available sources. His text tells us who and what impressed a contemporary observer in Renaissance Milan. His commentary and illustrations show us some developments made in technology since Vitruvius's times. The book as a luxurious product was probably designed for sale not only to architects but also to rich laymen; thus it suggests that architecture had become a subject that the wealthy were inclined to study.

The illustrations of greatest interest include Cesariano's autobiographical allegory and the plan, section, and elevation of Milan Cathedral, which show only what the words mean (they do not present the cathedral as a Roman building and do not give the true measurements of the cathedral).

Cesariano's volume, although employing a scheme of illustration based on that of FRA GIOCONDO's Latin Vitruvius editions of 1511 and 1513, went so far beyond its predecessors in the elaboration of the pictures, in translating and commenting on the text, that the 1521 Vitruvius edition itself became the model for several subsequent editions and treatises, for example, those by Francesco Lutio Durantino (1524, 1535) and Walter Ryff (alias Rivius, 1543).

In his later years, Cesariano was a consultant to the Milan Cathedral officials concerning north transept portal projects and was the designer of the once famous (but obsolete and later destroyed) fortifications, the *Tenaglia* at the Castello Sforzesco in Milan.

CAROL HERSELLE KRINSKY

BIBLIOGRAPHY

CESARIANO, CESARE DI LORENZO (editor)   (1521)1969   *Vitruvius, De architectura.* (*Nachdruck der kommentierten ersten italienischen Ausgabe von Cesare Cesariano [Como, 1521], with an Introduction and Index by Carol Herselle Krinsky*) (*Bilddokumente, Quellenschriften und ausgewählte Texte zur europäischen Kunstgeschichte*). Edited by Friedrich Piel. Munich: Wilhelm Fink.

GATTI, SERGIO   1971   "L'attività milanese del Cesariano dal 1512–13 al 1519." *Arte Lombarda* 16:219–230.

KRINSKY, CAROL HERSELLE   1971   "Cesariano and the Renaissance without Rome." *Arte Lombarda* 16:211–218.

PAGAVE, VENANZIO DE   1878   *Vita di Cesare Cesariano.* Milan: Casati.

QUINTAVALLE, A. G.   1959   "Un dipinto di Cesare Cesariano a Piacenza." *Paragone* 10, no. 109:51–53.

VERZONE, PAOLO   1971   "Cesare Cesariano." *Arte Lombarda* 16:203–210.

CESSART, LOUIS ALEXANDRE DE

Born in Paris, Louis Alexandre de Cessart (1719–1806) embarked on a military career in 1742, but in 1747 he enrolled in the Ecole des Ponts et des Chaussées and worked thereafter for that institution, rising to inspector general in 1783. He perfected techniques for caisson foundations and experimented daringly, if unsuccessfully, with timber cone structures for Cherbourg's breakwater. He is renowned as the designer of the first cast-iron bridge to be built in France.

R. D. MIDDLETON

WORKS

1756–1770, Pont Cessart (begun by Bentivoglio, known in France as Jean de Voglie), Saumur, France. 1776–1779, Harbor, Dieppe, France. *1776–1780, Harbor and quays, Rouen, France. 1776–1782, Harbor, Le Havre, France. 1778–1780, Sluice Gate, Le Tréport, Seine Inférieure, Paris. *1783–1789, Breakwater, Cherbourg, France. *1801–1802, Pont des Arts (erection supervised by Jacques Dillon), Paris.

BIBLIOGRAPHY

ARNEUVILLE, DUBOIS DE (editor) 1806–1808 *Description des travaux hydrauliques de Louis Alexandre de Cessart, ouvrage imprimé sur les manuscrits de l'auteur.* 2 vols. Paris: Baudouin.
CACHIN, JOSEPH MARIE FRANÇOIS 1820 *Mémoire sur la digue de Cherbourg comparée au breakwater ou jetée de Plymouth.* Paris: Firmin-Didot.
CESSART, LOUIS ALEXANDRE DE 1844 "Projet d'un rouleau de fonte pour comprimer les chaussées d'empierrement." *Annales des Ponts et Chausées* First Semester 1844:134–136.

CETTO, MAX

Max Cetto (1903–) was born in Germany of Mexican parentage and was educated at the Technical Universities of Darmstadt, Munich, and Berlin, at the latter under HANS POELZIG. A founding member of the Congrès Internationaux d'Architecture Moderne (CIAM) in 1928, Cetto practiced in Germany until emigrating to the United States in 1938. He worked with RICHARD JOSEF NEUTRA in San Francisco for a year before emigrating to Mexico. Cetto settled in Mexico City. He taught at the school of architecture of the Universidad Nacional Autonoma in Mexico City and since 1945 has been in private practice. Cetto has also written a great deal and is best known for his book, *Modern Architecture in Mexico* (1960).

ELIZABETH GREENE

WORKS

1947, Quintana Weekend House, Lago de Tequesquitenge, Morelos, Mexico. 1949, Max Cetto House, 130 Calle del Agua, El Pedregal; 1951, Bedrecio House, 140 Calle Fuentes, El Pedregal; 1955, Office Building of the Aseguadora Reforma; Mexico City. 1967–1968, Morelos Tanning Company, Cuautla, Morelos, Mexico. 1968–1971, Office Building, 629 Obrero Mundial, Mexico City. 1970–1979, German Club of Mexico, Tepepan, Mexico. 1975, Cold Rolled Company Office Building, Ixtapalapa, Mexico.

BIBLIOGRAPHY

CETTO, MAX (1960)1961 *Modern Architecture in Mexico.* New York: Praeger.
CETTO, MAX 1978 "Architecture Mexicaine." *Techniques et Architecture* 320:119–146.
HITCHCOCK, H. R. 1955 *Latin American Architecture since 1945.* New York: Museum of Modern Art.
MYERS, IRVING EVAN 1952 *Mexico's Modern Architecture.* New York: Architectural Book.
RODRIGUEZ, IDA 1980 "Cetto, Max." Pages 144–146 in Muriel Emanuel (editor), *Contemporary Architects.* New York: St. Martin's.

CHADIRJI, RIFAT

Rifat Chadirji (1926–), an Iraq architect, has complemented his Western education with an understanding of traditional Arab architecture and its methods of construction which he acquired through some of the government posts he has held and through personal interest. In his architectural production, this interest has manifested itself in a gradual movement away from the International style to an attempt to combine modern technology with traditional Arab forms. The outcome has been a highly individual style which has had a great impact on Arab architects.

MEHRANGIZ NIKOU SEXTON

WORKS

1968, Iraqi Federation of Industries Building; 1968, Rafidain Bank, Mansur Branch; 1970, Rafidain Bank, Salhiyah Branch; 1975, Reinsurance Company Building; Baghdad. 1976, Cabinet of Ministers Building; 1977, National Theater, Abu Dhabi; United Arab Emirates.

BIBLIOGRAPHY

BAZAROV, KONSTANTIN 1978 "Modern Arab Architecture." *Arts and Artists* 13, no. 2:4–7.
BAZAROV, KONSTANTIN 1980 "Chadirji, Rifat." Pages 146–147 in Muriel Emanuel (editor), *Contemporary Architects.* New York: St. Martin's.
MASON, WILLIAM 1978 "Arab Architecture at Home: Exhibition of Iraqi Architect Rifat Chadirji's Work." *Building Design* no. 392:22–23.
TOWN, PETER, and RABENECK, ANDREW 1978 "Individuality at a Cultural Crossroads: Rifat Chadirji." *Middle East Architectural Design* 1, no. 1:12–13.

CHALGRIN, JEAN FRANÇOIS THERESE

Jean François Thérèse Chalgrin (1739–1811), although from a poor family, became one of the most prominent neoclassical architects in France. He studied architecture with GIOVANNI NIC-

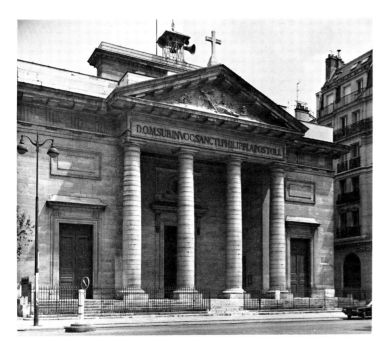

Chalgrin.
Saint Philippe du Roule.
Paris.
1764–1784

Chalgrin.
Arc de Triomphe.
Paris.
1806–1836

COLÒ SERVANDONI, ETIENNE LOUIS BOULLÉE, and PIERRE LOUIS MOREAU-DESPROUX, and won the Prix de Rome in 1758. Returning to France in 1763, he joined the Bâtiments de la Ville de Paris. He was elected to the Académie d'Architecture in 1770 and was promoted to the first class in 1791. Chalgrin attracted several powerful patrons, becoming architect to the comte de Provence in 1775 and *intendant des bâtiments* of the comte d'Artois in 1779. This association with the higher levels of the nobility led to Chalgrin's imprisonment during the French Revolution, but he survived with his reputation intact. He went on to serve the Directoire and the Empire as a member of the Conseil des Bâtiments (appointed 1795), and he succeeded CHARLES DE WAILLY in the Institut de France in 1798.

Chalgrin's first major building was the Hôtel Saint-Florentin in Paris (1767–1770). He followed plans prepared by ANGE-JACQUES GABRIEL for the exterior elevations, but the courtyard screen, the portal, and the interior decoration are from his own designs and illustrate his commitment to the neoclassical revival, previously evidenced in his Rome drawings.

The comte de Saint-Florentin secured for Chalgrin the commission for his most important work, the Church of Saint Philippe du Roule in Paris. Designed in 1764 but not completed until 1784, this was the first new basilican church built in Paris. Together with the contemporary basilica-plan churches designed by NICOLAS MARIE POTAIN and LOUIS FRANÇOIS TROÙARD, it initiated a style of ecclesiastical architecture that remained influential on the Continent through the nineteenth century.

From 1776 to 1788, Chalgrin worked on the Church of Saint Sulpice in Paris. He built the north tower and fluted the porch columns, giving the façade a more classical appearance than that envisioned by its original architect, Servandoni. In the interior, Chalgrin designed the baptistry and the organ case.

Chalgrin's private commissions included inventive designs for gardens *à l'anglais, hôtels,* and furniture. The rotunda of his elegant Pavillon de Musique built in Versailles for the wife of the comte de Provence (1784), for example, has *trompe l'oeil* painting creating the illusion that the room is in the midst of a garden. He also built a pavilion and laid out a garden in Versailles for the comte's mistress, Madame de Balbi.

During the Directoire, he remodeled the Palais du Luxembourg for use as the seat of the government (c.1795–c.1797). Among his additions are the debating chamber and the ceremonial staircase. His last important work was the Arc de Triomphe in Paris commissioned by Napoleon in 1806. Although not completed until 1836, the arch follows Chalgrin's design except for the decoration and the attic. It issues from a long lineage of triumphal arches reaching back through the *ancien régime* to antiquity, but Chalgrin realized it on a colossal scale. Dominating the grand axis of the Champs-Elysées, the arch remains the most powerful monument of French imperial ambitions.

RICHARD CLEARY

WORKS

1767–1770, Hôtel Saint-Florentin; 1764–1784, Saint Philippe du Roule; 1768, Chapelle du Saint-Esprit; Begun 1768, Hôtel de Langéac; *1770, Assembly Hall for the Comte de Mercy Argenteau; 1776–1777, Saint Sulpice (north tower, entry, and organ case); 1780–1784, Collège de France; 1780–1788, Saint Sulpice (baptistry); Paris. *1781–1784, Gardens of the Comtesse de Provence; 1784, Music Pavilion of the Comtesse de Provence; Begun 1786, Gardens and *Pavilion of Madame de Balbi; Versailles, France. c.1795–c.1797, Palais du Luxembourg (remodeling); 1806–1836, Arc de Triomphe; Paris.

BIBLIOGRAPHY

BRAHAM, ALLAN 1980 *Architecture of the French Enlightenment.* London: Thames & Hudson.
CHALGRIN, JEAN FRANÇOIS THÉRÈSE n.d. *Plan, coupes et élévations de l'église de St Philippe du Roule.* n.p.
GAEHTGENS, THOMAS W. 1974 *Napoleons Arc de Triomphe.* Göttingen, Germany: Vandenhoeck & Ruprecht.
GAEHTGENS, THOMAS W. 1976 "Four Newly Discovered Designs for the Arc de Triomphe by J-F Chalgrin." *Print Review* 5:58–68.
GALLET, MICHEL 1972 *Paris Domestic Architecture of the Eighteenth Century.* Translated by James C. Palmes. London: Barrie & Jenkins.
HAUTECOEUR, LOUIS 1943–1957 *Histoire de l'architecture classique en France.* 7 vols. Paris: Picard.
RICE, HOWARD C. 1947 *L'Hôtel de Langéac: Jefferson's Paris Residence.* Monticello, Va.: Thomas Jefferson Memorial Foundation.
SCOTT, BARBARA 1972 "Madame's Pavillon de Musique." *Apollo* 95:390–399.

CHAMBERLIN, POWELL, and BON

The partnership of Chamberlin, Powell, and Bon was established in 1952 by Peter Chamberlin (1919–1978), Geoffrey Powell (1920–), and Christoph Bon (1921–). The architects won the Golden Lane housing competition in London, and this success led to the commission to rebuild the Barbican housing development which had been flattened during World War II. The Barbican redevelopment, inspired by postwar idealism and the promise of prosperity, was the largest work ever built in the City of London by a single architectural firm and, as such, presented an unusual opportunity to design a cultural and residential enclave. Consequently, the Barbican has been Chamberlin, Powell, and Bon's major oeuvre over a period of twenty-seven years, although they designed numerous other buildings, notably New Hall, Cambridge, and several buildings for the University of Leeds. The Barbican Development Plan, initiated in 1955 and built in stages until completion in 1982, encompasses residential accommodation for 6,500 people in flats and maisonettes, offices, a school of music and drama, and a

mammoth arts center of concert hall, theater, cinema, library, art gallery, conference facilities, and restaurants. The architectural strategy reflects a 1950s approach to monumentality in both scale and materials, further reinforced by the unfortunate burying of numerous buildings beneath an above-street podium into a structure of giganticism. Nonetheless, the firm has been lauded with numerous awards.

RICHARD LORCH

WORKS

1955, Bousefield Primary School, South Kensington, London. 1955, Cooper Taber Factory, Witham, Essex, England. 1955–1982, The Barbican, City of London; 1957, Golden Lane Estate, Finsbury; 1957, Rossdale House; 1960, Trinity Saints Primary School; 1960, Two Saints Primary School; London. 1962–1966, New Hall, Cambridge. 1963, Henry Price Buildings, University of Leeds, England. 1963, Shipley Salt Grammar School, Yorkshire, England. 1965, Vanbrugh Park Housing, Greenwich, London. 1966, Physical Education Centre, University of Birmingham, England. 1966, Physical Education Centre; 1967, Mathematics Building and Senior Common Room; 1967, Charles Morris Hall of Residence; 1968, Television Centre; 1969, Biology Building; 1969, Biophysics Building; 1969, Physics Building; 1969, Students' Union (extension); 1969, Saint George's Fields Gardens; 1970, Lecture Theatre Block; 1971, Computer Laboratory (extension); 1971, Medical Building; University of Leeds, England. 1971, Welfare Insurance Company Building; 1971–1974, Flats and Maisonettes; Folkestone, Kent, England. 1972, Arts Block; 1974, Physics Centre; 1974, School of Physiotherapy; 1975, Undergraduate Library, Block 19; University of Leeds, England.

BIBLIOGRAPHY

"Arts and Towers." 1980 *Country Life* 167:75.
"Barbican Development, City of London." 1974 *Architecture and Urbanism* 4, no. 38:13–24.
GOLDSTEIN, BARBARA 1977 "English Encampments." *Progressive Architecture* 58, no. 7:58–67.
KNOBEL, LANCE 1981 "Barbican Arts Centre." 1981 *Architectural Review* 170, Oct.:238–254.
"Lecture Theatre Block: University of Leeds." 1979 *Architecture and Urbanism* 9, no. 108:73–78.
"Sounds in the City: Guildhall School of Music and Drama." 1977 *Architects' Journal* 166, no. 44:834–837.
STEVENS, ANTHONY; CORBETT, B.; and STEELE, A. 1977 "Barbican Arts Centre: The Design and Construction of the Substructure." *Structural Engineer* 55:473–485.
STEVENS, ANTHONY; CORBETT, B.; and STEELE, A. 1979 "Barbican Arts Centre: The Design and Construction of the Substructure." *Structural Engineer* 57:24–27.
STEVENS, TED 1980 "Great White Hope: Barbican Arts Centre." *Building* 238, no. 7128:24–26.
"University of Leeds." 1979 *Architect and Builder* 29, no. 2:2–7.

WATERS, BRIAN 1978 "The Final Stage: The Barbican Arts Centre." *Building* 234, no. 7041:84–90.

WEBB, MICHAEL 1969 *Architecture in Britain Today.* Feltham, England: Country Life.

WRIGHT, LANCE 1974 "University of Leeds." *Architectural Review* 155, Jan.:2–30.

CHAMBERS, WILLIAM

William Chambers (1723–1796) was the son of a Scottish merchant established in Göteborg, Sweden, where he was born. Although he was educated in England, probably in Ripon, Yorkshire, he returned to Sweden in 1739 to enter the service of the Swedish East India Company. He made three voyages, the first to Bengal and two to Canton, one from 1743 to 1745, the other from 1748 to 1749. It was during these travels that he discovered his interest in architecture and made studies of Chinese buildings and customs. In 1749, he decided to make architecture his "sole study and profession," and to this end went to Paris to attend JACQUES-FRANÇOIS BLONDEL's Ecole des Arts. In this context, Chambers should be regarded as a Continental student, not an English one: the Swedes would study in Paris, whereas the English would go straight to Rome. Blondel's école set the cast for Chambers's affiliations, nearly always Gallic, and for most of his life he treasured the friendships made in Paris with CHARLES DE WAILLY and his likes, all of whom were to be leaders of French neoclassicism in the 1760s and 1770s. In 1750, Chambers set off for Rome where he spent four years of intense study, again orientated with the French Academy rather than with English circles. In March 1753, he married Catherine More, whose origins are somewhat obscure, but who may have been a "milliner girl" who followed Chambers from London to Paris to Rome.

Chambers's decision to settle in London may have been conditioned by an earlier friendship with Frederick, Prince of Wales, who died in 1751, and there is circumstantial evidence that Chambers might have designed the House of Confucius (1749) in Kew Gardens, Surrey, en route in 1749 from Sweden to Paris via London. By 1756, Chambers had achieved the remarkable coup of becoming architect to Augusta, Dowager Princess of Wales, and by 1757 he had become tutor in architecture to George, Prince of Wales, the future George III. The influence of John, third earl of Bute, is possible but not certain. Chambers was responsible for laying out Kew Gardens with an astonishing variety of temples and objects, including many exotic ones: the Mosque, the Gothic-laced Alhambra, and Kew's most famous object,

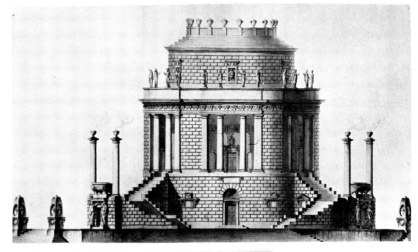

Chambers.
Design for Mausoleum for
 Frederick, Prince of
 Wales.
1751

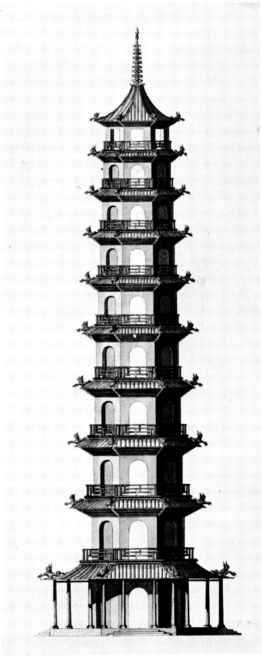

Chambers.
Chinese Pagoda, Kew
 Gardens.
Surrey, England.
1763

the Chinese Pagoda. Kew was completed by about 1763, and was commemorated in a folio paid for by George III titled *Plans, Elevations, Sections and Perspective Views of . . . Kew* (1763). Already in 1757, Chambers had published his *Designs of Chinese Buildings,* a book most influential on chinoiserie on the continent, although not so important in England where chinoiserie had reached its apogée of influence in the 1740s. The garden section in this book was of special importance and even saw a Russian edition. Chambers was interested in garden design to an unusual extent, and the horticultural parts of Kew were of pioneering importance in the layout of flower gardens, hothouses, and ancillary buildings, prefiguring the framing ground and composite garden of JOHN CLAUDIUS LOUDON's day in the early nineteenth century. In 1759, Chambers produced his most important book, the *Treatise on Civil Architecture,* in which was collected a "Series of Sound Precepts and good Designs," and thought rightly by HORACE WALPOLE to be the "best book and the most exempt from prejudice that ever was written in that science." A second edition appeared in 1768 and a third in 1791 when its title was changed to *A Treatise on the Decorative Part of Civil Architecture,* the "constructive" part never having been written. The treatise was undoubtedly the most influential book in its day, and its influence was exceeded only by English editions of ANDREA PALLADIO's *Four Books of Architecture.* In the *Treatise,* Chambers shows himself an eclectic, not at all doctrinaire. All this activity and the great reputation Chambers was gathering led to his appointment in 1761 to the Office of Works as one of the two Joint Architects to the King. The other was ROBERT ADAM, for whom Chambers had little time, and there was not a small spice of antagonism between these two great architects. From this time on, Chambers, not Adam, dominated work for the king and royal family, remodeling Buckingham House, London, from 1762 to 1773, building the Observatory in Richmond Gardens in 1768, and altering the White House at Kew in 1772.

In 1756, Chambers lost the commission for rebuilding Harewood House, Yorkshire, with a design that was thoroughly Franco-Roman. From that point on he decided to compromise with the neo-Palladian tradition, so strong in England that it could not be ignored, and his country houses are expositions upon models laid down by COLEN CAMPBELL as well as recent ones by second-generation architects such as ISAAC WARE. The villa theme was Chambers's ideal, beginning with Castle Hill, Dorset (c.1760) and Lord Bessborough's Roehampton, Surrey (1760). Very quickly, Chambers arrived at his ultimate villa with Lord Abercorn's Duddingston House, Midlothian (1763), marvelously elegant, with a portico laid on the ground like a temple portico. There were, however, many departures from these basically neo-Palladian exercises, notably certain houses built for friends who were willing to allow Chambers to design what he wished. He was able to do this with Lord Charlemont at the casino at Marino House, Dublin (1758–1776), one of the most exquisite small buildings in the whole of Europe. It is Franco-Italianate in inspiration with a columnar exercise that belongs to experiments carried out by a small group of young French students at the French Academy in Rome. Other departures from the Palladian norm were Trent Place, Middlesex (c.1777), a neoclassical lodge; the vast Gothic house at Milton Abbey, Dorset (1771–1776), as well as plans for the model village there, built by LANCELOT BROWN from 1774; and Teddington Grove, Middlesex (c.1765), which may have been an uncompromising villa in the style of Palladio's in the Veneto.

At the same time Chambers was building many townhouses, his best being Gower House, Whitehall (1765–1774), and Melbourne House, Piccadilly (1771 to 1774). He also built townhouses outside London, notably Dundas House, Edinburgh (1771) and Charlemont House, Dublin (1763), the latter containing a gallery in the garden terminating in a museum building for Lord Charlemont's collections. Chambers was also active on public buildings. He built the Town Hall, Woodstock, Oxfordshire (1766) and the Observatory at Richmond (1768), the latter incorporating advanced techniques. He designed the theater and chapel at Trinity College, Dublin (1775, 1777–1786). The Trinity buildings are Gallic-flavored, a reminder that in 1774 Chambers visited Paris to study the latest and most modern public buildings there. The reason was almost certainly that he was hoping to wrest the job of building public offices at Somerset House in London from a minor architect, William Robinson, who then conveniently died in 1775, leaving the field clear for Chambers.

Somerset House (begun 1776) represents Chambers's triumph, for here, in his maturity,

Chambers.
Llanaeron (unexecuted
design).
Cardiganshire, Wales.
1761

there was now no need to compromise with patrons who wanted to impose their tastes upon him. Somerset House can stand comparison with any other public building of the neoclassic era and was handled by Chambers in a most exquisite manner. On the Strand front he paid homage to INIGO JONES (in fact, JOHN WEBB) by adopting the theme of Webb's Somerset House Gallery of 1662, demolished by Chambers with great sadness, for not only did he recognize its quality, but it had housed the rooms of the Royal Academy from 1768. Elsewhere, however, all the details of Somerset House are Parisian, and nothing could be more so than the handling of the courtyard elevations, creating here no less than a large urban square, with ornamental details taken from JACQUES DENIS ANTOINE, de Wailly, CLAUDE NICOLAS LEDOUX, and other friends in Paris.

Chambers also tackled the site problem with ingenuity, for not only was it cut on one side by a public way to the water gate on the Thames, but it was not possible to acquire all the Strand frontage, and there was a considerable drop in levels from the Strand to the river. Due to this drop Chambers was able to create great Piranesian vaults (see GIOVANNI BATTISTA PIRANESI) under the courtyard and was able to give depth to his river elevation, divided into three sections by transparent colonnades and set above a huge embankment with Roman style watergates. The major criticism that must be made of Somerset House is that the proportions of the central dome suited the elevation to the courtyard, but looked like a small cupola when seen from across the river. The interiors of the Strand Block, housing the Royal Academy and antiquarian societies, were in the most advanced Louis Seize style, paying no lip service to English decoration. Before 1776, Chambers had been slowly developing this taste, first at Buckingham House in the 1760s, then at Peper Harrow, Surrey (c.1765), and triumphantly so in the reception rooms of Gower House, Whitehall, in the 1770s.

Somerset House also displays another of Chambers's unsung skills, that as a designer of complex staircases. There had been Gower House, based upon BALDASSARE LONGHENA's stair in the monastery of San Giorgio Maggiore, Venice, but made spatially more complex; then there was the Melbourne House, Piccadilly, one, in which the stairs hang on the wall with a crossing flier; and then the apogee at Somerset House, with the two Strand Block stairs, the one on the Royal Academy side having a theatric, Borrominesque (see FRANCESCO BORROMINI) basement, and the Navy Stair, twisting and winding up its oval well.

Chambers's real achievement at Somerset House was, however, the bringing together under one roof of a multitude of public offices, although the inspiration may have been Edmund Burke's, for as Chambers wrote him, "tis a child of your own." Others would see his achievement in more material terms, for there can be little doubt that Chambers deliberately intended Somerset House to be a display of the best in English craftsmanship and design. Throughout his career, he paid particular attention to the quality of stone carving, and this he learned from the French.

Chambers's progression up the ladder of the Office of Works was predictable. He succeeded as Comptroller of the Works in 1769 and through the reorganization of the works conducted by Burke, he became the first holder of the combined post of Comptroller and Surveyor General. He was an able and humane administrator, fair to the high and the low in life, and can be regarded as one of the most distinguished of all government architects from that day to the present.

In the role of administrator, it is not surprising that Chambers played a formative part in the founding of the Royal Academy of Arts in 1768, and became its first treasurer, responsible only to the king. As its first president, Sir Joshua Reynolds declared, "Sir William was Viceroy over him," a reminder that Chambers had been made Knight of the Polar Star by King Gustav of Sweden and had been permitted by George III to assume the rank and title of an English knight.

At Kew, Chambers had laid out a garden composed of episodes in which ornamental buildings enlivened the scene, a combination of nature simple and nature improved by art. He despised the growing fashion under Capability Brown for smooth lawns reaching up to the house and for an unornamented prospect. In fact, Kew was the last great garden laid out by the breed of architect gardener, from JOHN VANBRUGH on. As a riposte to Brown's popularity, Chambers composed his *Dissertation on Oriental Gardening* (1772), in which he attacked Brown under the literary camouflage of Oriental dress. It rather misfired, for the public imagined that Chambers was, in fact, advocating Chinese gardens, and in 1773, there appeared the anonymous (by William Mason) *An Heroic Epistle to Sir William Chambers,* really intended as an attack upon the Tory court of George III. Chambers's *Dissertation,* however, had great influence in later generations, especially on the blending of colors in gardening as espoused by Gertrude Jekyll, and on the more modern concept of planning the environment.

Chambers's great activity brought him great wealth and affluence. He lived in ducal style in the Duke of Argyll's Palladian villa at Whitton, Middlesex, where he amassed a fine collection of works of art and furnished the house elegantly, a reminder that he was also the designer of furniture and objects. He was frequently portrayed, notably by Reynolds in his Royal Academy Diploma piece, and by the Swedish painter Carl Frederik Von Breda.

JOHN HARRIS

WORKS

(A)1749, House of Confucius, Kew Gardens, Surrey, England. Completed 1757, Kew Gardens (garden works), Surrey, England. 1757, Wilton House (triumphal arch and casino), Wiltshire, England. 1758–1776, Marino House (casino), Dublin. c.1760, Castle Hill, Dorset, England. 1760, Parksted, Roehampton, Surrey, England. 1762–1773, Buckingham House (remodeling), London. 1763, Charlemont House, Dublin. 1763, Chinese Pagoda, Kew Gardens, Surrey, England. 1763, Duddingston House, Midlothian, Scotland. c.1765, Peper Harrow, Surrey, England. c.1765, Teddington Grove, Middlesex, England. 1765–1774, Gower House, Whitehall, London. 1766, Woodstock Town Hall, Oxfordshire, England. 1767, Woburn Abbey (remodeling), Bedfordshire, England. 1768, Observatory, Richmond Gardens, Surrey, England. 1771, Dundas House, Edinburgh. 1771–1774, Melbourne House, Piccadilly, London. 1771–1776, Milton Abbey, Dorset, England. 1772, White House (alterations), Kew Gardens, Surrey, England. 1775, 1777–1786, Trinity College (theater and chapel), Dublin. 1776, Queen's Lodge, Windsor Castle, Berkshire, England. Begun 1776, Somerset House, London. 1777, Trent Place, Middlesex, England. 1778, Hedsor Lodge, Buckinghamshire, England.

BIBLIOGRAPHY

CHAMBERS, WILLIAM (1757)1968 *Designs of Chinese Buildings.* Reprint. New York: Blom.
CHAMBERS, WILLIAM (1759)1968 *A Treatise on the Decorative Part of Civil Architecture.* Reprint of 3d ed. New York: Blom. Originally published with the title *Treatise on Civil Architecture.*
CHAMBERS, WILLIAM (1763)1966 *Plans, Elevations, Sections and Perspective Views of the Gardens and Buildings at Kew in Surrey.* Reprint. Farnborough, England: Gregg.
CHAMBERS, WILLIAM (1772)1972 *Dissertation on Oriental Gardening.* Reprint. Farnborough, England: Gregg.
HARRIS, JOHN 1970 *Sir William Chambers.* London: Zwemmer.
MASON, WILLIAM (1773)1972 *An Heroic Epistle to Sir William Chambers.* Reprint of 14th ed. Farnborough, England: Gregg.

CHAMBIGES FAMILY

The Chambiges were a dynasty of master masons active in the Ile-de-France and Champagne from 1490 to 1643. Martin Chambiges (?–1532) and his son Pierre (?–1544), masters of late Gothic architecture, are central figures in discussions of Italian influences on sixteenth-century French architecture. The principal biographer of the family, Marius Vachon, who regarded the French Renaissance as developing from native traditions, cast the Chambiges as designing architects on all projects. This interpretation has been contested by historians who emphasize Italian sources of the French Renaissance. Surviving documents do not disclose in many cases if the Chambiges built according to their own designs.

Martin Chambiges, probably active in Paris during the 1480's, is first named in 1490 as the designer of the transept of Sens Cathedral (1490–1513). In 1500 Martin was commissioned to design the transept of Beauvais Cathedral, and from 1502–1503 he designed the west front of Troyes Cathedral, begun in 1507. In 1509, Martin installed in the Troyes workshop his nephew Leger or Legier Chambiges, his son Pierre I Chambiges, his son-in-law Jean de Damas or de Soissons, and Jean's brother Pierre. Jean de Damas directed the workshop from 1516–1531, succeeded by his son-in-law Jean II Bailly (?–1559). Other works are attributed to Martin Chambiges on stylistic grounds. The traditional attributions of the southwest tower of Saint-Jacques-la-Boucherie and the choir of Saint-Gervais, Paris to Martin have been rejected (Nelson, 1973).

Pierre Chambiges was apprenticed as a master mason in his father's workshops at Troyes (1509) and Beauvais (1511) where he was appointed comaster in 1518. From 1521 to 1527, he supervised construction of the transept of Senlis Cathedral. At Anne de Montmorency's Château of Chantilly, Pierre built and possibly designed two wings in the triangular court with an exterior stair rising to a loggia and an arcaded gallery (1528–1531). He is cited in documents as *maçon et voyer* of the bishop of Paris in 1533 and as *maistre des oeuvres de la maçonnerie et pavement de la Ville de Paris* in 1536 in which capacity he directed construction of the Hôtel de Ville (1533–1544) designed by Domenica da Cortona. Pierre was paid in 1538–1539 for designs of an unexecuted Collège des Trois Langues and in 1540 for unspecified work at Fontainebleau and Saint-Germain-en-Laye. Vachon attributed the design of the *cour du cheval blanc* and the peristyle of the *cour ovale* at Fontainebleau as well as the entire Château of Saint-Germain-en-Laye to Pierre on stylistic grounds. Pierre was architect and builder of François I's hunting lodge *La Muette* (1541–1544) and may have designed the Château of Saint-Ange at Challuau (c.1540) as well.

Guillaume Guillain (?–1586) continued the work of his father-in-law at *La Muette* (1544–

1548), Saint-Germain-en-Laye (1544–1546) and the Hôtel de Ville in Paris (1549–1551). He held the office of master of masonry works for the city of Paris which he passed to his son Pierre Guillain (1530–c.1614) in 1573. Augustin I Guillain (?–1636) replaced his father as master mason for Paris in 1611 and was succeeded by his son Augustin II Guillain (?–1643?), the last Chambiges tenant of the office.

HILARY BALLON

WORKS

MARTIN CHAMBIGES

1490–1513, Sens Cathedral (transept), France. 1500–1532, Beauvais Cathedral (transept; not completed until 1549), France. Begun 1507, Troyes Cathedral (west front), France.

PIERRE CHAMBIGES

1521–1527, Senlis Cathedral (transept; supervision), France. *1528–1531, Château of Chantilly (two wings), France. *1533–1544, Hôtel de Ville (supervision), Paris. (A)1539–1544, Château of Saint-Germain-en-Laye (not completed until 1546), France. (A)c.1540, Château of Fontainebleau (cour du cheval blanc and peristyle of the cour ovale), France. *(A)c.1540, Château of Saint-Ange, Challuau, France. *1541–1544, La Muette (not completed until 1548), Saint-Germain-en-Laye, France.

GUILLAUME GUILLAIN

1544–1546, Château of Saint-Germain-en-Laye (supervision of completion); *1544–1548, La Muette (supervision of completion); Saint-Germain-en-Laye, France. *1549–1551, Pavillon de l'arcade Saint-Jean, Hôtel de Ville, Paris.

BIBLIOGRAPHY

BLOMFIELD, REGINALD (1911)1974 Volume 1 in *A History of French Architecture from the Reign of Charles VIII till the Death of Mazarin, 1494–1661.* Reprint of 1921 ed. New York: Hacker.

GUIFFREY, JULES 1915 *Artistes parisiens des XVIe et XVIIe siècles.* Paris: Imprimerie nationale.

HAUTECOEUR, LOUIS (1943)1963 *La formation de l'idéal classique.* Volume 1 in *Histoire de l'architecture classique en France.* Rev. ed. Paris: Picard.

HELIOT, PIERRE 1944 "Pierre Chambiges et les égouts de Paris." *Bibliothèque de l'Ecole des Chartres* 105:191.

MURRAY, STEPHEN 1975 "The Completion of the Nave of Troyes Cathedral." *Journal of the Society of Architectural Historians* 34:121–139.

MURRAY, STEPHEN 1977 "The Choir of Saint-Etienne at Beauvais." *Journal of the Society of Architectural Historians* 36:111–121.

NELSON, ROBERT J. 1973 "Martin Chambiges and the Development of French Flamboyant Architecture." Unpublished Ph.D. dissertation, The Johns Hopkins University, Baltimore.

NELSON, ROBERT J. 1974 "A Lost Portal by Martin Chambiges?" *Journal of the Society of Architectural Historians* 33:155–517.

SANFAÇON, ROLAND 1971 *L'Architecture flamboyante en France.* Quebec: Presses de l'Université Laval.

VACHON, MARIUS 1907 *Une famille parisienne de maistres-maçons aux XV, XVI, XVII siècles. Les Chambiges.* Paris: Librairie La Construction Moderne.

Pierre Chambiges.
Château of Chantilly (two wings).
France.
1528–1531

CHAMBLESS, EDGAR

Roadtown, published in 1910, was envisioned by its author and inventor, Edgar Chambless (?–1936), as an entirely new concept of a "decentralized city in the country."

Theoretically, it embodied the principle of redistribution of populations through linear communities, with transportation, social features, and industry combined within the structure and extended along lines in a single organism. The transportation roadway would be at a sunken level, leaving the two open vertical sides facing lawns and gardens. Within this road would be the monorails, auto lanes, and transmission cables for distributing supplies, food, parcels, freight, and so on, to individual dwellings, institutional buildings, shops, industries built overhead on separate foundations. The flat roof would be the street or promenade with shade and weather protection provisions.

In 1918, Chambless launched the Laws of Centripetal and Centrifugal Social Force formulae in a paper entitled "Laws for Reversing the Trend of Population" which he read by invitation before the American Association for the Advancement of Science in November 1924 in Washington. Dr. W. J. Spillman, director of farm management of the Department of Agriculture, said: "He has really discovered the reason for the terrific congestion of our large cities, he shows me quite clearly how to obviate it."

In 1934, federal agencies requested Chambless to present his plans for the building of a 10-mile Roadtown structure between Baltimore and Washington before the Senate Committee; they were also interested in his rural repatriation movement to relieve the cities of their vast burden of unemployment, stressing rural resources development with part-time farming and industrial employment in Roadtown's environment.

The rejection of Chambless's many efforts led to his untimely death on Memorial Day, 1936.

HARRY SINGER

BIBLIOGRAPHY

CHAMBLESS, EDGAR   1910   Roadtown. New York: Roadtown.
CHAMBLESS, EDGAR   (1931)1944   Roundtown to Roadtown. Edited by Harry Singer. 2d ed. New York.
COLLINS, GEORGE R.   1968   "Linear Planning: Its Forms and Functions." Forum 20, no. 5.
HASTINGS, MILO   1914   "The Continuous House." Sunset Jan.:110–116.
REINER, THOMAS A.   1963   The Place of the Ideal Community in Urban Planning. Philadelphia: University of Pennsylvania Press.

CHAMBON, ALBAN

A Frenchman educated at the Ecole des Beaux-Arts, Paris, Alban Chambon (1847–1928) moved to Belgium in 1868, where his designs included theaters and other leisure facilities. His eclectic style was sumptuous, richly detailed, and exotic—vaguely Islamic—in effect. He also worked in England and the Netherlands.

ALFRED WILLIS

WORKS

*1885–1888, Théâtre de la Bourse; 1894, Hotel Métropole (interiors); Brussels. 1894–1900, Villas, Westende, Belgium. *1890–1906, Casino, Ostende, Belgium. *1903–1908, Casino, Spa, Belgium.

BIBLIOGRAPHY

"Alban Chambon: Le Casino de Spa—Projets 1903–1908." Bulletin des Archives de l'Architecture Moderne en Belgique June:20–23.
Belgian Art 1880–1914.   1980   New York: Brooklyn Museum. Catalogue of an exhibition at the museum.
CULOT, MAURICE   1975   "Alban Chambon (1847–1928)." Bulletin des Archives de l'Architecture Moderne en Belgique Dec.:6–7.
RANIERI, LIANE   1973   Léopold II, urbaniste. Brussels: Hayez.
RUSSELL, FRANK (editor)   1979   Art Nouveau Architecture. New York: Rizzoli.

CHAMPNEYS, BASIL

Architect and littérateur, Basil Champneys (1842–1935) was a late practitioner of the Gothic style. Born in London, the son of a clergyman, he studied under JOHN PRICHARD, the diocesan surveyor of Llandaff Cathedral. He began practice in 1867 and largely specialized in educational buildings, including several in Oxford, Cambridge, and London. His Indian Institute (1884), Oxford, first brought him attention, but his most important and elaborate work was the Rylands Memorial Library (1890–1899), Manchester, England, based on his earlier library at Mansfield College, and carried out in stone in the late Gothic style.

BETTY ELZEA

WORKS

1884, Indian Institute; 1888, Mansfield College; Oxford. 1890–1899, Rylands Memorial Library, Manchester, England.

BIBLIOGRAPHY

BLOMFIELD, REGINALD   1934–1935   "Basil Champneys." Journal of the Royal Institute of British Architects Series 3 42:737–738.
CHAMPNEYS, BASIL   1875   A Quiet Corner of England. London: Seeley.
CHAMPNEYS, BASIL   1901   Memoirs and Correspondence of Coventry Patmore. London: Bell.
GOODHARD-RENDEL, H. S.   1953   English Architecture Since the Regency: An Interpretation. London: Constable.
SERVICE, ALASTAIR   1977   Edwardian Architecture: A Handbook to Building Design in Britain, 1890–1914. New York: Oxford University Press.

CHANTRELL, ROBERT DENNIS

Robert Dennis Chantrell (1793–1872) was representative of the early nineteenth-century architects who found profitable employment in the developing industrial North of England. Born in Newington, Southwark, he was articled to JOHN SOANE for seven years (1807–1814). Five years after completing his articles, he set up practice in Leeds. His first designs were for small neoclassical public buildings: the Philosophical Hall (1819–1820), Public Baths (1819–1820), and the more ambitious South Market (1823–1824) which was built around a central, double-colonnaded circular Market Cross. The 1818 First Church-building Act brought Chantrell an opportunity to develop another building type and style, and he became a serious student of Gothic architecture. His work was confined to the West Riding of Yorkshire, where he designed, restored, or remodeled between twenty and thirty churches. Although most of his new designs followed the conventional rectangular plan form of the Commissioners' Churches, Chantrell varied the details and silhouettes with some ingenuity and sited the buildings skillfully.

Slender cast-iron arcades and galleries were frequently inserted within the dark, hard millstone-grit exteriors. Chantrell's masterpiece is the historically important Saint Peter's Church, Leeds (1837–1841), in which the chancel, long abandoned in worship, was brought back into use. The plan, in which chancel and nave balance one another to the east and west of a central north tower facing an organ in the south transept, influenced the design of churches in the United States and Australia (most notably in Saint Andrew's Cathedral, Sydney). The *Ecclesiologist* (1847, vii, 46) described Saint Peter's as "the first really great undertaking of the present age," and the *Church Intelligencer* (September 11, 1841) singled out "the magnificent Church at Leeds" as a model to be followed. Chantrell left Leeds in 1846.

DEREK LINSTRUM

WORKS

*1819–1820, Philosophical Hall, Park Row; *1819–1820, Public Baths, Wellington Road; *1823–1824, South Market; *1823–1826, Christ Church, Meadow Lane; Leeds, England. 1828–1829, All Saints, Netherthong; 1828–1829, Emmanuel Church, Lockwood; 1828–1829, Saint Stephen, Kirkstall; 1829–1830, Saint Peter, Morley; West Riding, Yorkshire, England. 1829–1832, Saint Matthew, Holbeck; *1837–1838, Saint Michael, Headingley; 1837–1841, Saint Peter; 1839, Holy Trinity (new steeple); Leeds, England. 1839, Saint Wilfrid, Pool-in-Wharfedale; 1839–1840, Saint David, Holmbridge; 1840, Saint Lucius, Farnley Tyas; 1840–1841, Holy Trinity, Batley Carr; West Yorkshire, England. 1841–1842, Saint Paul, Shadwell, Leeds, England. 1842–1843, Saint Mary, Honley; 1843–1846, Saint Paul, Denholme Gate; 1844–1846, All Saints, Roberttown; *1845–1847, Saint Paul (steeple extant), King Cross, Halifax; West Riding, Yorkshire, England. *1845–1847, Saint Philip, Wellington Street, Leeds, England. 1846–1852, Saint Mary, Middleton; 1846–1848, Saint Andrew, Keighley; 1847–1848, Saint Paul, Armitage Bridge; West Yorkshire, England.

BIBLIOGRAPHY

LINSTRUM, DEREK 1978 *West Yorkshire Architects and Architecture.* London: Lund Humphries.

CHAREAU, PIERRE

Pierre Chareau (1883–1950) was born in Bordeaux, France, into a family of shipowners from Le Havre. He studied painting, music, and architecture from 1900 to 1908 and became an apprentice in furniture design in the firm of Waring and Gillow (1908–1914) in Paris. He spent the war years as a soldier and came back to Paris in 1918 to establish his own practice.

His first commission was for the remodeling of the apartment of Dr. and Mrs. Dalsace, which included the design for a set of original furniture that he exhibited the following year at the Salon d'Automne. Unusual for the time, his furniture designs included such materials as plywood, ebony, palm, and metal tubes. In his "Suite for an Ambassador," the set that he designed for the Exposition des Arts Décoratifs in 1925, the furniture pieces were large and took on a rather architectural nature with curved and angular forms, abstract and bare but strong and robust looking. At the Salon, he met Bernard Bijvoet who became his associate (1925–1935). With Bijvoet, Chareau built the Beauvallon Clubhouse near Saint-Tropez; the house was composed of four white volumetric spaces with a direct link displaying a functional spatial continuity.

In 1928, the Dalsaces asked Chareau to design a house in Paris that would be placed within the first three floors of an eighteenth-century building. The glass block façade (hence the name Maison de Verre) enclosed both an office and an apartment. Completed in 1932, the house plan and details were complex. Chareau had considered the nature of all elements constituting the house and given them his interpretation. Movable partitions, translucent screens, and a steel structure created an aesthetic flow between the different rooms and floors.

In 1934, Chareau designed the interior of the telephone company in Paris, including all the furnishings which were made of rosewood, palm wood, walnut, and mahogany. As one of the founders of the Union des Artistes Modernes (UAM), he participated actively in the national development of the arts in a more comfortable way than was possible for him in the universalist Congrès Internationaux d'Architecture Moderne. In 1937, he took part in the exhibit of the UAM showing his furniture.

His nonacademic, uncompromising attitude and his lack of interest in groups isolated him. Receiving fewer commissions with the onset of World War II, Chareau moved to New York in 1940 where he organized shows for the services of the French Cultural Center. He designed two houses near New York, one of which was for the painter Robert Motherwell, but these commissions were too small to challenge what was to remain his masterpiece, the Maison de Verre.

MARC DILET

WORKS

1918–1919, Dalsace Apartment (interiors), rue Saint-Germain; *1925, Embassy Office (interiors), Salon des Arts Décoratifs; Paris. 1927, Golf Club (with Bernard Bijovet), Beauvallon, France. 1928, Hôtel (interiors), Tours, France. 1928–1931, Dalsace House (Maison de Verre), rue Saint-Guillaume; 1931–1932, Compagnie du Téléphone; Paris. 1937, Djemel Anik Country House, near Paris. 1937, Ministry of Foreign Affairs (office interiors); *1937, Pavillon de l'Union des Artistes Modernes, International Exposition; 1939, Soldier Colonial Foyer, Grand Palais; Paris. n.d., Chareau House, East Hampton, N.Y. *n.d., Exhibition layouts for the French Cultural Center; n.d., Monteux-Laughin House (alterations), New York. n.d., Robert Motherwell House, near New York.

BIBLIOGRAPHY

CHAREAU, PIERRE 1929 *Meubles.* Paris: Moreau.
CHAREAU, PIERRE 1935 "La Creation artistique et l'imitation commerciale." *L'Architecture d'Aujourd'hui* no. 9:68–69.

CHARES OF LINDOS

A pupil of the renowned sculptor Lysippus, Chares of Lindos (?–270 B.C.) designed the largest statue of the ancient world—one of its seven wonders—the Colossus of Rhodes. About 120 feet high, of bronze cast around a masonry core, the Colossus (a representation of Apollo) was built between 292 and 280 B.C. Standing on a seawall in the harbor of Rhodes, it was intended apparently for use as a lighthouse, but neither this nor most other details are certain as it was toppled by an earthquake in 224 B.C. It was known through most of antiquity only as a stupendous ruin.

B. M. BOYLE

WORK

*292–280 B.C., Colossus of Rhodes, Greece.

BIBLIOGRAPHY

English translations of the ancient texts can be found in the volumes of the Loeb Classical Library series, published by Harvard University Press and Heinemann.
PLINY, *Historia naturalis,* Book 34.41.
STRABO, *Geographikon,* Book 14.652.

CHÂTEAUNEUF, ALEXIS DE

The son of a French noble émigré, Alexis de Châteauneuf (1799–1853) was born in Hamburg and trained under Carl Ludwig Wimmel (see WIMMEL AND FORSMANN), ACHILLE LECLERE in Paris, and FRIEDRICH WEINBRENNER in Karlsruhe. Pioneering the revived brick tradition in Hamburg, he combined North German medieval motifs and structural techniques with North Italian Romanesque and early Renaissance forms.

Despite the influence of his plans for redesigning Hamburg after the 1842 fire, Châteauneuf received few public commissions, and thus sought clients in England and later Norway. English influence permeates his domestic design, although the interiors of his finest house, the Abendroth House in Hamburg (1832–1836), pay homage to PERCIER AND FONTAINE and KARL FRIEDRICH SCHINKEL. Its Renaissance-style façade was widely imitated in Hamburg.

BARRY BERGDOLL

WORKS

*1826, Three Houses, 31–33 ABC-Strasse; *1830–1831, Post Office; Hamburg, Germany. 1830–1831, Sieveking House and outbuildings, Hamm, Germany. *1832–1836, Abendroth House, Neuer Jungfernstieg, Hamburg, Germany. c.1837, Bucholz House, Lübeck, Germany. 1839–1840, Amalienstift Saint Georg (alms house); *1840–1842, Railroad Station, Hamburg-Bergedorf Railroad Line; Hamburg, Germany. 1841–1842, Railroad Station, Bergedorf, Germany. 1844, Alster Arcades, Hamburg, Germany. 1844, Hornheimer Anstalten (sanatorium), near Kiel, Germany. 1844–1848, Petrikirche and Parsonage (restoration); 1845, Hudtwalker House, 14 Hermannstrasse; 1846, Children's Hospital of Saint George; 1846, Main Post Office, Poststrasse; *1846–1849, Railroad Station, Hamburg-Berlin Company; Hamburg, Germany. 1848–1849, Holy Redeemer Church (remodeling); 1850–1859, Church of the Apostles (executed largely by von Hanno), Christiania; Oslo.

BIBLIOGRAPHY

"The Career of Alexis de Châteauneuf," 1919 *Architectural Review* 45:53–56.
CHÂTEAUNEUF, ALEXIS DE 1839 *Architectura Domestica.* London: Ackerman.
CHÂTEAUNEUF, ALEXIS DE 1860 *Architectural Publica.* Berlin: Ernst & Korn.
LANGE, GUNTER 1965 *Alexis de Châteauneuf: Ein Hamburger Baumeister (1799–1853).* Hamburg: Verlag Weltarchiv.
MADSEN, STEPHAN T. 1965 *The Works of Alexis de Châteauneuf in London and Oslo.* Oslo: Foreiningen Til Norske Fortidsminnesmerkers Bevaring.
MADSEN, STEPHAN T. 1966 "Châteauneuf in London." *Architectural Review* 140:366–368.
SCHUMACHER, FRITZ 1923 "Die neuen Regungen des Hamburger Backsteinbaus in der Mitte des 19. Jahrhunderts." *Zentralblatt der Bauverwaltung* 43:61–65, 73–78, 85–86, 113–138.
SPECKTER, HANS 1952 *Der Wiederaufbau Hamburgs nach dem Grossen Brande von 1842.* Hamburg, Germany: Boysen & Maasch.

CHAUSSE, JOSEPH ALCIDE

Joseph Alcide Chausse (1868–1944), a Montreal architect born and educated in Quebec province, was apprenticed to Alphonse Raza of Montreal. He began his own practice in 1888. He was city architect of Montreal from 1900 to 1918, and founded the Royal Architectural Institute of Canada in 1907. His work includes Place Viger Terminal Warehouse, Montreal (1919), and the Kent Picture Theatre, Montreal (1924).

ROBERT HILL

BIBLIOGRAPHY

ADAMSON, ANTHONY 1939 "Vive Monsieur Chaussé." *Journal of the Royal Architectural Institute of Canada* 16:89–90.

NOBBS, PERCY 1944 "Obituary." *Journal of the Royal Architectural Institute of Canada* 21:287–288.

CHAWNER, THOMAS

Thomas Chawner (1774–1851) studied with JOHN SOANE between 1788 and 1794. He designed few buildings, being employed as a surveyor in the Land Revenue Department and thereafter in the Offices of Woods and Forests and of Works; he was elected president of the Surveyors' Club in 1811. His "more *urban* and builder like" scheme for Marylebone (afterward Regent's) Park, London (1811), with THOMAS LEVERTON, was rejected for JOHN NASH's "enchanting *rural* plan" (Elmes, 1827, p. 11).

R. WINDSOR LISCOMBE

WORKS

1807–1809, Chertsey Church (rebuilding), Surrey, England. 1819, Brixton Prison; *1836–1837, Cox's Hotel (with Henry Rhodes), 53–55 Jermyn Street; London.

BIBLIOGRAPHY

ELMES, JAMES (1827)1968 *Metropolitan Improvements.* Reprint. New York: Blom.

PORT, MICHAEL H., and CROOK, J. MORDAUNT 1973 Volume 6, page 367 in *A History of the King's Works.* London: H.M. Stationery Office.

SUMMERSON, JOHN 1980 Pages 63–64, 65, 68, 71, 76, 80, 81 in *The Life and Work of John Nash.* London: Allen.

SUMMERSON, JOHN 1977 "The Beginnings of Regent Park." *Architectural History* 20:56–62.

SUMMERSON, JOHN (1945)1978 Pages 178–179 in *Georgian London.* Cambridge, Mass.: M.I.T. Press.

"Survey of London" 1956 Volume 26, pages 103–104 in F. H. W. Sheppard, *Parish of St. Mary Lambeth: Part II. Southern Area.* London: Athlone.

"Survey of London." 1960 Volume 29, page 275 in F. H. W. Sheppard, *Parish of St. James, Westminster: Part I. South of Piccadilly.* London: Athlone.

CHEDANNE, GEORGES

Born in Maromme, France, Georges-Paul Chedanne (1861–1940) studied with JULIEN GUADET at the Ecole des Beaux-Arts in Paris. At the Ecole, Chedanne won many distinctions and prizes, including, in 1887, the Grand Prix for his restoration drawings of the Pantheon in Rome. Chedanne then pursued his studies of the Pantheon in Rome itself. He was the first to provide convincing evidence dating the Pantheon to the reign of Hadrian, an achievement which led immediately to the discovery of the remains of Agrippa's Pantheon.

Chedanne returned to Paris to practice independently. His work was influenced by Art Nouveau to a certain extent, and displays parallels to the work of CHARLES PLUMET and FRANTZ JOURDAIN, but his style remained highly individual. Some of his buildings were characterized by bare and undulating surfaces; others, by a very extensive and severe use of glass and iron; still others employed massive masonry forms to achieve a heavy and monumental appearance. In addition to the inspiration of ancient Rome, Chedanne drew upon the traditional motifs and materials of Parisian architecture. His French Embassy in Vienna (1904–1909) recapitulated the Parisian yellow limestone, iron balconies, and metal-covered roofs in different materials and new forms to produce a building which was both radically new in appearance and distinctively French.

BARBARA MILLER LANE

WORKS

1899, Élysée Palace Hôtel (now the Crédit Commercial de France); 1903–1904, Hôtel Mércèdes; 1903–1904, Le Parisien libéré, 124 Rue de Réaumur; Paris. 1904–1909, French Embassy, Vienna. n.d., French Legation, Peking. n.d., Foreign Affairs Ministry Archives; n.d., Galeries Lafayettes; n.d., Hôtel Dehaynin; Paris. n.d., Hôtel Riviera, Monte Carlo. n.d., Hôtel Royal, Ostend, Belgium. n.d., Hôtel Terminus, Lyon, France.

BIBLIOGRAPHY

EMERY, MARC 1971 *Un Siècle d'Architecture Moderne en France: 1850–1950.* Paris: Horizons de France.

FAVIER, JEAN 1938 "Salon 1938; la Rome des Flaviens par Georges Chedanne, architecte." *Construction Moderne* 53, no. 31:504–509.

FRATELLI, ENZO 1958 "1904: Una costruzione in ferro a Parigi." *Casabella continuità* 222:55.

GUILLAUME, EUGENE 1892 "Le panthéon d'Agrippa, a propos de découvertes récentes." *Revue des deux Mondes* Series 3 112:562–581.

LOERKE, WILLIAM C., JR. n.d. "The Discovery of Agrippa's Pantheon." Forthcoming publication.

MARX, ROGER 1904 "A propos d'une construction récente de M. Chedanne." *Art et Décoration* 16:156–164.

MOISY, PIERRE 1974 "L'ambassade de France à Vienne, manifeste d'un art nouveau officiel." *Revue de l'Art* 23:42–53.

NORBERG-SCHULZ, CHRISTIAN 1972 "Le Parisien Arkitekt Georges Chedanne." *Byggekunst* 54, no. 6:190–191.

SPIERS, R. PHENÉ 1895 "Monsieur Chedanne's Drawings of the Pantheon, Rome." *Journal of the Royal Institute of British Architects* Series 3 2:175–182.

CHERMAYEFF, SERGE IVAN

Serge Ivan Chermayeff (1900–) began his architectural career as one of the most important of the pioneers of the modern movement in England in the 1930s. He later became a distinguished educator in the United States, pursuing writing and research in addition to design activity.

Born Sergius Ivan Issakovitch near Grozny in the Caucasus, he was sent to England for education at age ten and graduated from Harrow in 1917. Plans to continue his studies at Trinity College, Cambridge, were disrupted by the Russian Revolution which left him without family support. He remained in England and began his architectural career as an interior designer in 1924 after pursuing a variety of other interests. In 1928, Chermayeff organized the first exhibition of modern furnishings in England at Waring and Gillow, where he had become director of the modern furnishing department. During the next several years, he completed many important interior design commissions, primarily under the aegis of Waring and Gillow. Included were the interiors of the Cambridge Theatre, London (1930), and the widely publicized interiors for the British Broadcasting Corporation, London (1932).

In 1930, Chermayeff formed his own architectural office in London, although he continued to design industrial objects and furnishings. Between 1933 and 1936, he executed some commissions in partnership with the German émigré ERIC MENDELSOHN. They won the competition for an entertainment hall (1935) at Bexhill, Sussex; they also built two houses in partnership. Chermayeff's largest commissions of the period were an office building for W. and A. Gilbey, Ltd. (1937), London, and the Dyestuffs Research Laboratory for the Imperial Chemical Industries (1938), Manchester. But perhaps his best known work was his own house (1938) at Halland, Sussex.

With the threat of Nazi Germany, Chermayeff and his family emigrated to the United States in 1940. They settled in San Francisco, where he executed two house commissions. In 1942, he was appointed chairman of the Department of Art at Brooklyn College. He created the Department of Design, which was the first reform of an existing fine arts curriculum in the nation. In 1946, he became president of the Chicago Institute of Design after the death of LÁSZLÓ MOHOLY-NAGY. At Chicago, he expanded the curricular concerns most notably in the areas of architecture and environmental design. In the 1940s, Chermayeff attempted to organize a practice in the United States. He executed numerous small commissions and maintained an office in New York with KONRAD WACHSMANN in 1947. He organized several exhibitions, most notably "Design for Use" at the Museum of Modern Art in 1944, and he exhibited his own paintings in several important abstract expressionist shows.

In 1951, Chermayeff taught briefly at the Massachusetts Institute of Technology and then at Harvard University, where he revised the first-year curriculum and began a long period of research activity concerned primarily with housing. In 1959, with Christopher Alexander, he began work on *Community and Privacy* (1963). Chermayeff left Harvard for Yale in 1963, where he directed the Master's Class in Environmental Design, ultimately completing a second book, *Shape of Community,* in 1971, with Alexander Tzonis, a former Yale student.

Throughout his two decades at Harvard and Yale, Chermayeff maintained a small practice, completing a number of houses and other small structures; together with painting this activity complemented his more theoretical work. Most significant was the Payson House, Portland, Maine

Chermayeff.
Chermayeff House.
Halland, Sussex, England.
1938

(1952), and a series of houses on Cape Cod which dealt with reinterpretation of traditional materials and forms of the region. He embellished his well-established reputation as an architectural critic and has continued to write and lecture profusely. His concerns have remained steadfast in their wedding of architectural issues with more general societal concerns. He has always seen architecture as a public art, with attendant public responsibilities.

RICHARD A. PLUNZ

WORKS

1930, Cambridge Theatre (interior); 1930, Chermayeff House (interior); 1932, BBC Studios (interiors); London. 1933, Shann House, Rugby, England. 1935, Entertainment Hall (with Erich Mendelsohn), Bexhill, England. 1935, Nimmo House (with Mendelsohn), Chalfont, Cuckinghamshire, England. 1936, Cohen House (with Mendelsohn); 1937, W. and A. Gilbey Office Building; 1937, Heywood-Lonsdale Flat (interior); London. 1938, Chermayeff House, Halland, Sussex, England. 1938, Imperial Chemical Industries Laboratory Building, Manchester, England. 1942, Horn House, Marin County, Calif. 1942, Mayhew House, Oakland, Calif. 1945–1972, Chermayeff Family Compound, Truro, Mass. 1951, Cape Codder Offices and Plant, Orleans, Mass. 1952, Payson House, Portland, Me. 1953, Sigerson House; 1953, Wilkinson House; 1956, O'Connor House; Truro, Mass. 1963, Chermayeff House, New Haven.

BIBLIOGRAPHY

The Serge Chermayeff Archive is in the Avery Architectural Library, Columbia University, New York.

CHERMAYEFF, SERGE, and ALEXANDER, CHRISTOPHER 1963 *Community and Privacy: Toward a New Architecture of Humanism.* Garden City, N.Y.: Doubleday.
CHERMAYEFF, SERGE, and TZONIS, ALEXANDER 1971 *Shape of Community. Realization of Human Potential.* Baltimore: Penguin Books.
PLUNZ, RICHARD 1972 "Projects and Theories of Serge Chermayeff: Chronology and Bibliography." Unpublished manuscript in the Frances Loeb Library, Harvard University, Cambridge, Mass.

CHERPITEL, MATHURIN

Mathurin Cherpitel (1736–1809), who was born in Paris, began his architectural training in the office of ANGE JACQUES GABRIEL and later attended the school of JACQUES FRANÇOIS BLONDEL. A co-winner of the Prix de Rome with JEAN FRANÇOIS CHALGRIN, Cherpitel studied in Italy from 1759 to 1765 and enjoyed recognition for his drawings of Rome and ancient monuments. His earliest commissions were for residences for clients in provincial cities, notably Bordeaux, and outside France, but the comte du Châtelet's patronage during the 1770s assured his success as a designer of neoclassical townhouses in Paris. Cherpitel was elected to the Académie Royale d'Architecture in 1776.

RICHARD CLEARY

WORKS

1770–1776, Hôtel du Châtelet (now the Ministère du Travail); *1775–1777, Hôtel de Neckar; 1776–1778, Hôtel de Damas (now the Korean Embassy); 1776–c.1782, Hôtel de Rochechouart (now much altered as the Ministère de l'Education); *c.1779–c.1790, Church of the Gros Caillou; Paris.

BIBLIOGRAPHY

BRAHAM, ALLAN 1980 *The Architecture of the French Enlightenment.* London: Thames & Hudson.
GALLET, MICHEL 1972 *Paris Domestic Architecture of the Eighteenth Century.* Translated by James C. Palmes. London: Barrie & Jenkins.
HAUTECOEUR, LOUIS 1952 *Seconde moitié du XVIIIe siècle: Le style Louis XVI.* Volume 4 in *Histoire de l'architecture classique en France.* Paris: Picard.
MAGNY, FRANÇOIS 1976–1977 "Mathurin Cherpitel (1736–1809)." *Bulletin de la Société de l'Histoire de Paris et de l'Ile-de-France* 103–104:95–113.

CHERSIPHRON OF KNOSSOS

Chersiphron of Knossos (?–540 B.C.) was architect of the colossal Ionic temple of Artemis at Ephesos, the fourth on the site. Together with THEODOROS, Chersiphron laid the foundations around 565 B.C. and began the colonnade, which was finished only after 500 B.C. The entablature was completed by his son, Metagenes. Father and son wrote a book on the building, now lost; they were famous for devising means of moving great stones. The temple itself was burned in 356 B.C.; only the base and fragments of the original superstructure survive.

B. M. BOYLE

WORK

*Begun c.565 B.C., Fourth Temple of Artemis (with Theodoros of Samos and Metagenes), Ephesos, Greece.

BIBLIOGRAPHY

English translations of the ancient texts can be found in the volumes of the Loeb Classical Library series, published by Harvard University Press and Heinemann.

ASHMOLE, BERNARD 1972 *Architect and Sculptor in Ancient Greece.* New York: New York University Press.
COULTON, J. J. 1977 *Ancient Greek Architects at Work.* Ithaca, N.Y.: Cornell University Press.
DINSMOOR, WILLIAM B. (1902)1975 *The Architecture of Ancient Greece.* Reprint of 1950 ed. New York: Norton. Originally published with the title *The Ar-

chitecture of Ancient Greece and Rome.
LAWRENCE, ARNOLD W. (1957)1975 *Greek Architec-
ture.* Harmondsworth, England: Penguin.
PLINY, *Historia naturalis,* Books 7.125 and 36.95.
STRABO, *Geographikon,* Book 14.640.
VITRUVIUS, *De architectura,* Books 3.2.7 and 7. Praef. 12.

CHEVAL, FERDINAND

After failed careers in baking and farming, and a
sojourn in Algeria, Ferdinand Cheval (1836–1924)
became a rural postman in 1874 in Hauterives in
the Drôme area of France. From 1879 to 1905, he
built his *Palais Ideal,* a fantasy castle of cement and
stone whose form was first suggested to him in a
dream around 1864. The building recalls Romantic illustrations and Cambodian temples, is encrusted with figural, animal, and plant decoration,
and embodies a complex symbolic program in its
two main façades and interior passages. It incorporates and draws inspiration from odd rocks found
by Cheval along his route. The postman built the
palace singlehandedly and inscribed it with poems
to the immortal glory of his will-to-labor as a solitary peasant. It first attracted attention around
1900, was venerated by the Surrealists, and was
classified a historical monument in 1969 by André
Malraux (minister of culture), who felt it was the
supreme example of *naif* architecture. Cheval's
only other work is the tomb he built for himself,
from 1913 to 1915, in the Hauterives cemetery.

KIRK VARNEDOE

CHEVOTET, JEAN-MICHEL

Winner of the Prix de Rome in 1722 and admitted
to the Royal Academy of Architecture in 1732,
Jean-Michel Chevotet (1698–1772) worked for
private patrons in and around Paris. His most important surviving buildings, the Château de
Champlatreux and the Pavilion de Hanovre, both
from the 1750s (the latter removed to the Parc de
Sceaux in 1933), show him still favoring the varied
forms and rich contours of the early Louis XV period.

CHRISTOPHER TADGELL

CHIATTONE, MARIO

Mario Chiattone (1891–1957), painter and futurist
architect, was active in the circle of ANTONIO
SANT'ELIA in Milan. In 1914, he took part in the
exhibition of the *Nuove Tendenze.* His projects
from this period, all unrealized, are derived from
the Viennese Secession and are closely related stylistically to the work of Sant'Elia, although much
less complex. The cathedral is a preferred theme of
his many studies of single monumental buildings.

After World War I, the architect lost contact
with the Milan architectural scene and returned to
his native Switzerland, where he realized numerous works in a predominantly neoclassical style,
abandoning his former call for a radical renewal in
architecture.

ELLEN R. SHAPIRO

WORKS

1934, Country House, Condra, Switzerland. 1945, In-
door Market, Mendrisio, Switzerland. *1947, Pavilion,
Exhibition; 1949, Columbarium; Giubiasco, Switzerland.

BIBLIOGRAPHY

ARATA, GIULIO 1919 "Giovane architettura e giovani
architetti: Mario Chiattone." *Emporium* 49, no.
294:298–307.
VERONESI, GIULIA 1962 "Disegni di Mario Chiattone, 1914–1917." *Comunità* 16, no. 98:47–67.
VERONESI, GIULIA (editor) 1965 *L'opera di Mario
Chiattone, architetto.* Pisa, Italy: Lischi & Figli.
VERONESI, GIULIA 1969 "I disegni di Mario Chiattone." Pages 12–20 in *Profili disegni, architetti strutture, esposizioni.* Florence: Vallecchi.

CHIAVERI, GAETANO

Born in Rome, Gaetano Chiaveri (1689–1770)
pursued his career in foreign lands. Nothing is
known about his life or work before 1717 when he
entered the service of Peter the Great. In the recently founded city of Saint Petersburg he was primarily active as an assistant to DOMENICO TRES-
SINI. His unexecuted independent projects—a
church of the Holy Trinity at Korostyn (1721–
1722), commissioned by Catherine I, and a proposal to rebuild the façades of the Academy of Sciences (1724)—reveal Chiaveri's mastery of the
Roman high baroque style and his predilection for
the work of FRANCESCO BORROMINI.

After a ten-year stay in Warsaw following the
death of Catherine I in 1727, Chiaveri went to
Dresden, Germany. In September 1738, August
III, elector of Saxony and king of Poland, charged
him with the construction of the Hofkirche
(1737–1753). As a result of the marriage of the
elector's daughter into the Hapsburg family earlier
in the same year, the position of the Roman Catholic court in the predominantly Protestant city had
been greatly strengthened, affording Chiaveri considerable freedom in preparing his designs. Chiaveri successfully conflated a basilican plan with the

elevation of the chapel at Versailles and the Germanic tower façade, producing a late baroque structure. He boldly aligned the tower façade to the head of the bridge over the Elbe, thereby making the Hofkirche the new focal point of the city. The placement of the façade with respect to the river was perhaps suggested by Tressini's project of 1715 for the Alexander Nevsky Lavra in Saint Petersburg. Although tower façades had also recently been revived in Potsdam and Berlin, Chiaveri's design was principally inspired by GIOVANNI LORENZO BERNINI's ill-fated campanili of St. Peter's.

Chiaveri's grandiose schemes for a new residence in Dresden were never realized, but his plan of 1740 for the enlargement of the Saxon palace in Warsaw formed the basis of Johann Christoph Knöffel's executed project. In 1742, Chiaveri published his proposal for the reinforcement of the dome of St. Peter's in which motifs derived from Bernini and CARLO FONTANA were combined to create a sculptural structure more akin in spirit to Borromini. His designs for portals and windows, published in 1742–1743, also reveal Chiaveri's continued interest in Borromini's contributions.

In recognition of his achievement Chiaveri was made a member of the prestigious Roman Academy of Saint Luke on October 4, 1746. However, he never received any commissions in Rome, where he resided between late 1748 and 1766. The plastic, exuberant baroque style of Chiaveri was no longer in vogue. After his move to Foligno until his death in 1770 Chiaveri's only known activity consisted of revising his proposal for St. Peter's.

Chiaveri's sole executed work was not without influence. The Marienstern at Nebelschitz, begun in 1740, reflects his plan, and the church at Mikulynzi in the Ukraine (1746–1795) is a much simplified version of the Hofkirche. His accomplishment was also appreciated in Protestant circles as is evidenced by the Kreuzkirche in Dresden, begun in 1762.

CATHIE C. KELLY

WORKS

1737–1753, Hofkirche; *1742, Catafalque for Queen Maria Josepha; 1742–1743, Ornamenti Diversi; Dresden, Germany.

BIBLIOGRAPHY

CHIAVERI, GAETANO 1742 *Sentimento sopra la pretesa reparazione di danni della cupola di San Pietro in Vaticano.* Rome.
CHIAVERI, GAETANO 1743–1744 *Ornamenti Diversi di Porte e Finestre.* 2 vols. Dresden, Germany: Lorenzo Zucci.
CHIAVERI, GAETANO 1767 *Breve Discorse . . . circa i danni riconosciuti nella portentosa Cupola di S. Pietro di Roma.* Pesaro, Italy: Amatina.
FASOLO, FURIO 1962 "Review of Eberhard Hempel, Gaetano Chiaveri: Der Architekt der katholischen Hofkirche zu Dresden." *Palladio: rivista di storia dell'architettura* 12:93–98.
HEMPEL, EBERHARD 1955 *Gaetano Chiaveri: Der Architekt der katholischen Hofkirche zu Dresden.* Dresden, Germany: Wolfgang Jess Verlag.
HEMPEL, EBERHARD 1957 "Gaetano Chiaveri, supplementi alle opere dell'architetto romano." *Palladio: rivista di storia dell'architettura* 7:172–178.
HEMPEL, EBERHARD 1965 *Baroque Art and Architecture in Central Europe.* Baltimore: Penguin.
NORBERG-SCHULZ, CHRISTIAN 1974 *Late Baroque and Rococo Architecture.* New York: Abrams.
PORTOGHESI, PAOLO (1966)1970 *Roma Barocca: The History of an Architectonic Culture.* Translated from the Italian by Barbara Luigia La Penta. Cambridge, Mass.: M.I.T. Press.

CHISHOLM, ROBERT F.

Robert Fellowes Chisholm (1840–1915) was the leading Victorian architect to practice in Madras, where he designed several public buildings. Although his earliest buildings are in the Renaissance and Gothic styles, in the 1870s he became an advocate of Indo-Saracenic for buildings in India and, as head of the Madras School of Art, employed Indian craftsmen on his buildings. Chisholm first practiced in Calcutta and, around 1865, became consulting architect to the government of Madras. In the 1880s, he moved to Baroda, where he completed the new palace begun by Major Mant (1848/49–1881). Chisholm left India in 1900. He resumed practice in Britain in 1902 and retired in 1912.

GAVIN STAMP

WORKS

1870s, Chepauk Palace (later the Board of Revenue Offices), Madras, India. c.1872–1880, Napier Museum, Trivandrum, India. c.1872–1880, Post Office; 1874–1879, University Senate House; Madras, India. c.1881–1883, New College, Baroda, India. 1883–1888, Victoria Public Hall, Madras, India. c.1892–1894, Museum, Baroda, India. 1904–1909, First Church of Christ Scientist, Chelsea, London.

BIBLIOGRAPHY

CHISHOLM, ROBERT F. 1882–1883 "New College for the Gaekwar of Baroda." *Transactions of the Royal Institute of British Architects* Series 1 22:141–146.
CHISHOLM, ROBERT F. 1896 "Baroda Palace." *Journal of the Royal Institute of British Architects* Series 3 3:421–433.
"Obituary: Mr. R. F. Chisholm." 1915 *The Builder* 108:528.
STAMP, GAVIN 1981 "British Architecture in India: 1857–1947." *Journal of the Royal Society of Arts* 129:357–377.

CHMIELEWSKI, JAN OLAF

Jan Olaf Chmielewski (1895–1974) studied architecture at the Technical University of Warsaw and graduated in 1930. From 1930 to 1939, Chmielewski was chief planner for Warsaw's Regional Planning Office. During this time, he wrote extensively on urban, regional, and country planning and developed a pioneering study on the idea of functional belts.

After World War II, from 1945 to 1949, he was vice-chairman of the Country Planning Authority in Warsaw. From 1947 until his death, he taught in the department of architecture at the Technical University of Warsaw.

In collaboration with others, he designed several housing estates in Warsaw. Together with H. Górska, he designed two mountain resort hotels: one in the Koscieliska Valley (1948) and one in the Five Ponds Valley (1948) of the Tatra Mountains. The hotels are done in a semivernacular style and are remarkably integrated into the surrounding scenery.

LECH KŁOSIEWICZ

WORKS

1948, Hotel (with H. Górska), Koscieliska Valley, Poland. 1948, Hotel (with Górska), Five Ponds Valley, Tatra Mountains, Poland.

BIBLIOGRAPHY

WISŁOCKA, IZABELLA 1968 *Awangardowa Architektura Polska: 1918–1939.* Warsaw: Arkady.

CHOCHOL, JOSEF

Josef Chochol (1880–1956) was one of the leading representatives of Czech cubism. After a short initial period when he was influenced by the Wagnerian (see OTTO WAGNER) modern trend, Chochol drew his inspiration from cubism and designed and built a number of cubistically conceived houses in Prague below Vyšehrad Hill (1911–1913) that are the purest documents of cubism in Czech architecture. Already before World War I, he reduced the façades in his drawings to elementary forms and thus anticipated the Czech postwar purism. In the 1920s, he was strongly influenced by Soviet Constructivism; this inspiration manifested itself particularly in his nonrealized design for the Liberated Theater in Prague (1927).

VLADIMÍR ŠLAPETA

WORKS

1910, Old Town Hall (Session Hall interior); 1911–1912, House, Vyšehrad District; 1912–1913, Triple House, Vyšehrad District; 1913, Apartment House, Vyšehrad District; 1926–1928, Trojský Bridge; 1937–1939, Low-income Housing (with R. F. Podzemný), Vysočany District; 1939, Apartment House, Holešovice District; Prague.

BIBLIOGRAPHY

ŠVÁCHA, ROTISLAV 1980 "Josef Chochol: 1880–1980." *Umění* 28, no. 6:545–552.

CHOISY, AUGUSTE

François-Auguste Choisy (1841–1904) was an engineer, explorer, and teacher who above all was an architectural historian and archeologist. Choisy's mathematical bent led him first to the Ecole Polytechnique and then to the Ecole des Ponts et Chaussées in Paris where he completed his training as a civil engineer. He then joined the government Département des Ponts et Chaussées where for many years he was engineer in chief. Though he remained on the staff there all his life (retiring with the title of *inspecteur général*), he soon began teaching.

His lectures on architectural history provided the material for his major work—*Histoire de l'Architecture* (1899). Illustrated with more than seventeen hundred engravings made from Choisy's drawings, this history provided a brilliant and cohesive analysis of building construction through the ages.

Choisy concluded that form and style were not the result of taste, chance, or inspiration but the way talented builders used tools, manpower, and materials to create structures epitomizing a society at a given time—the people, place, history, economics, politics, customs, needs, and ideals.

The theory underlying Choisy's work derives from the writings of EUGÈNE EMMANUEL VIOLLET-LE-DUC, and Choisy's writings were important to the leaders of the modern movement in France—AUGUSTE PERRET and LE CORBUSIER.

PERCIVAL GOODMAN

BIBLIOGRAPHY

CHOISY, AUGUSTE 1866 *Note sur la courbure dissymmétrique des degrés qui limitent au couchant la plateforme du Parthénon.* Paris: Donnaud.
CHOISY, AUGUSTE 1873a *L'Art de bâtir chez les Romains.* Paris: Boucher.
CHOISY, AUGUSTE 1873b *Essai sur l'organization des classes ouvrières chez les Romains.* Paris: Cusset.
CHOISY, AUGUSTE 1876 *L'Asie Mineure et les Turcs en 1875: Souvenirs de voyage.* Paris: Didot.
CHOISY, AUGUSTE 1881 *Le Sahara: Souvenirs d'une mission à Goléah.* Paris: Plon.

CHOISY, AUGUSTE 1883a *L'Art de bâtir chez les Byzantines.* Paris: Librairie de la Société anonyme de publications périodiques.

CHOISY, AUGUSTE 1883b *Etudes sur l'architecture grecque.* Paris: Librairie de la Société anonyme de publications périodiques.

CHOISY, AUGUSTE 1890–1895 *Chemin de fer transsaharien: Documents relatifs à la mission dirigée au sud de l'Algérie.* Paris: Imprimerie nationale.

CHOISY, AUGUSTE 1899 *Histoire de l'Architecture.* Paris: Gauthier-Villars.

CHOISY, AUGUSTE 1904 *L'Art de bâtir chez les Egyptiens.* Paris: Rouveyre.

CHOISY, AUGUSTE 1910 *Vitruve.* Paris: Lahure.

CHRISTOPHERSEN, ALEJANDRO

Alejandro Christophersen (1866–1946), Norwegian by nationality, was born in Cádiz, Spain, when his father was consul there. He studied at the Royal Academy of Fine Arts in Antwerp, Belgium, and at the School of Fine Arts in Paris. From 1888, he carried out the greater part of his profuse professional work in Buenos Aires and held, among other offices, the presidency of the Central Society of Architects. As a founding professor of the School of Architecture (1900) of the University of Buenos Aires, he was admired by his students, with whom he shared, in 1915, the founding of the *Review of Architecture,* which attained a wide dissemination and to which he contributed assiduously.

Considered the major representative of academic eclecticism in Argentinian architecture, he handled with great success monumental scale, ostentatious and sensational resolution of interior spaces, and a great diversity of styles: Louis Treize in his design for the National Congress competition (1895); neo-Gothic in the Chapel of the Holy Union (1899–1900); Art Nouveau in the *petit-hôtel* Coelho (1900?); ancient Muscovite in the Russian Orthodox Church of the Most Holy Trinity (1900–1901, based on a previous project received from St. Petersburg); Scandinavian National Romanticism in the Norwegian Church (1918–1920).

A favorite of the high society of Buenos Aires, he let the mansions of classical French style predominate in his domestic architecture. The best example is the Anchorena Palace (1906), a triple residence (for the mother, the widow, and her two married sons), all jointly surrounded by an oval-shaped *cour d'honneur,* with a railing front, thus creating a reciprocal transparency with the green contour of Plaza San Martín.

His works of greater monumentality are the Commercial Stock Exchange (1916), in the style of Louis Seize, and the Santa Rosa Church (1926–1934), in Byzantine neo-Romanesque with centralized interior space, both in Buenos Aires.

ALBERTO S.J. DE PAULA
*Translated from Spanish by
Florette Rechnitz Koffler*

WORKS

1899–1900 Chapel, College of the Holy Union of the Sacred Hearts 772 Esmeralda; 1900?, Coelho (*petit hôtel*), 1780 Alvear Avenue; 1900–1901, Russian Orthodox Church of the Most Holy Trinity; 1903, Ledesma Palace (now Italian Circle), 1266 Libertad; 1905, Belgian–American Mortgage Society, Alem y Mitre Avenue; c.1908, Anchorena Palace (now San Martin Palace), 761 Arenales; Buenos Aires. c.1915, Buen Retiro, Carrasco Square, Montevideo. 1916, Commercial Stock Exchange, Buenos Aires. c.1917, Félix Ortiz de Taranco (El Portazgo), Melilla, Montevideo. *1918–1920, Norwegian Church and Mission to Sailors; 1921, Banco de la Nación Branch, San Jose de Flores; Buenos Aires. *1922, Argentinian Pavilion, International Exposition, Río de Janeiro. 1926–1934, Sanctuary of Santa Rosa de Lima, Buenos Aires.

BIBLIOGRAPHY

BUSCHIAZZO, MARIO J. 1967 *Architecture in Argentina.* Buenos Aires: Valero.

ORTIZ, FEDERICO F. ET AL. 1968 *The Architecture of Liberalism in Argentina.* Buenos Aries: Sudamericana.

CHURCH, THOMAS D.

Thomas Dolliver Church (1902–1978) was born in Boston and attended the University of California at Berkeley and the Harvard Graduate School of Landscape Architecture. He was professor of landscape architecture at Ohio State University (1927–1929) and at the University of California, Berkeley (1929–1930). From 1933 to 1978, he was a principal of Thomas D. Church and Associates, San Francisco (1933–1978). He served as consultant landscape architect at Stanford University (1957–1977) and at the University of California at Berkeley and at Santa Cruz (1959–1977).

Church's private gardens are characterized by intimacy achieved by use of fences and hedges, flower beds raised above the primary level, sun decks often pierced by trees, and trellises with exaggerated orthogonals.

MARY D. EDWARDS

WORKS

Thomas D. Church designed nearly two thousand private gardens in the United States from 1930 to 1977.
1935, War Memorial Opera House Garden Court; 1940,

Exposition Garden, Golden Gate International Exposition; 1941–1950, Park Merced; San Francisco. 1945, General Motors Research Center Gardens, Detroit, Mich. 1946, Des Moines Art Center Gardens, Iowa. 1946, El Panama Hotel, Panama City. 1958, Stanford Medical Center Gardens, Palo Alto, Calif. 1958, Stuart Pharmaceutical Company Gardens, Pasadena, Calif. 1964, Caterpillar Tractor Company, Peoria, Ill.

BIBLIOGRAPHY

CHURCH, THOMAS D. 1955 *Gardens Are for People.* New York: Reinhold.
CHURCH, THOMAS D. 1969 *Your Private World: A Study of Intimate Gardens.* San Francisco: Chronicle Books.
LAURIE, MICHAEL 1973 "Thomas Church and the Evolution of the California Garden." *Landscape Design* no. 101:8–12.
MESSENGER, PAM-ANELA 1977 "Thomas D. Church: His Role in American Landscape Architecture." *Landscape Architecture* 67, no. 2:128–139, 170–171.

CHURRIGUERA FAMILY

In 1661, José Rates y Dalmau (?–1684), a Catalan sculptor of wooden retables or altarpieces, in collaboration with the Portuguese carver Manual Pereira, completed a decorated galley for the new lake of the Buen Retiro palace for Philip IV of Spain. Probably soon after, Rates was joined in Madrid by his son or stepson, José Simon Churriguera (?–1679), also Catalan. His wife furthermore bore him five sons, three of whom were to be famous: José Benito (1665–1725), Joaquin (1674–1724), and Alberto (1676–c.1740). About the sons' formative years little is known but something may be inferred. Both Rates and Simon on occasion executed other men's designs. In 1673–1674, they carved a retable for the Hospital of Montserrat in Madrid from the designs of Francisco de Herrera the Younger, a painter/architect with Italian experience who had been appointed court painter in 1672. The retable, destroyed in 1903 but surviving in photographs, had four Salomonic columns garlanded with vine leaves, the outer two projected on consoles. They framed a deep, stagelike recess with the seated Virgin of Montserrat. The effect was very like Pineda's altarpiece at the Caridad Hospital in Seville of 1670. Herrera had quite certainly seen this, but he was already familiar with the Salomonic column as he had used the form in the frescoed dome of the church of Atocha in Madrid in 1665. Another family acquaintance was José Ximenez Donoso, another painter/architect who was a witness in 1679 to José Simon's will. These two and their associates with courtly connections and skills both in painting and architecture probably provided the three youths with a firm background in their craft; through books, drawings, and engravings a knowledge of work elsewhere in Spain as well as in Italy was probably obtained.

José Benito de Curriguera, as his superb drawings show, must have been an apt pupil. On the death of Rates, he became the head of the family, already rather well off financially. In July 1686, José Benito contracted jointly with Juan de Ferraras, architect and resident of Madrid, for a retable in the Ayala Chapel of the Cathedral of Segovia, also intended as the *sagrario* or parish church, to be finished in eight months. Paired Salomonic columns on projecting consoles frame a complex polychromed mass of active putti crowned by an image of Faith all under an elaborate canopy of simulated cloth, colored in red and purple. Columns and canopy recall GIOVANNI LORENZO BERNINI and the theatrical presentation of the altarpiece at Montserrat. In 1689, José Benito won a competition for a catafalque to be erected for the funeral of Queen Maria Louisa of Orleans, first wife of Charles II. The monument was four-sided like Pineda's for the canonization of Ferdinand in Seville of 1571, but unlike the model, eight *estípites* or ornamented pilasters on projecting consoles loomed outward from the base as do the columns in the Ayala Chapel.

In 1690, José Benito was appointed *ayuda trazador de las obras reales,* essentially the position of an architectural draftsman who worked quite possibly from the designs of others. Until 1696, he received no remuneration but after this date he was salaried until his death. Apparently he was seldom active and may have had disagreements with Teodoro Ardemans, named chief draftsman of the royal works in 1702. This is, however, our first evidence of his activity as an architect.

In January 1692, José Benito contracted to build the enormous retable of San Esteban at Salamanca. For the two years of the contract, the patron agreed to make a monthly payment to his wife, Isabel de Palomares, in Madrid and to provide him with food and lodging in the monastery at Salamanca. The general form is quite reminiscent of the high altar of the Clerecia in Salamanca of 1673–1676 by Juan Hernandez in the vertical disposition of its parts, Salomonic columns on consoles, and recessions, but it is far more dramatic and has greater unity. In 1693–1694, José Benito added the retable of the Virgin of the Rosary in the north transept.

José Benito seems never to have given up residence in Madrid, and his later works were all in its close vicinity. In San Salvador in Leganés, 20 kilometers southeast of the city, he bid in 1702 for a retable designed by Manuel de Arredondo of Madrid and revised by José Jimenez. The work, finished in 1704, seems, nevertheless, close to his altarpiece for San Esteban. In 1717–1720, he executed two more retables for Legañes which conform to his usual formula.

Despite his continuing salary as an assistant draftsman, there is no evidence that José Benito maintained any influence as an architect in the court itself. His works in architecture were for a private patron, the banker Juan de Goyeneche, for whom he planned and built the town of Nuevo Baztan in 1709–1713. With its three plazas, palace, and church void of a rigid symmetry, the plan continues the tradition of the cities of Lerma and Alcalá de Henares. The two-towered church returns to the style of JUAN DE HERRERA modified by Palladian (see ANDREA PALLADIO) revivals distinctly retardataire for the period. He probably also designed Goyeneche's townhouse in Madrid, now the Academy of San Fernando, and drastically remodeled by Diego de Villanueva in 1773. Villanueva's drawing shows the original state with a rusticated ground floor rising from artificial rock work like Bernini's in Rome and giant pilasters articulating the two upper stories.

A signed drawing of superb quality in the Academy of San Fernando dated 1717 was for the now lost retable of the Church of San Basilio in Madrid. The retable was completed in 1720 by Nicholas, José's son. Here, the columns were of a fluted Composite order, wreathed but not Salomonic, the center two on consoles framing a *custodia* or shrine for the monstrance. Above this was a complex allegorical sculpture with Saint Basil, rather like that for the Ayala Chapel at Salamanca. In 1720, on the recommendation of Teodoro Ardemans, José Benito was given the contract for a retable of rather similar design for the Church of Calatrava in Madrid, which was completed in 1723–1724. Here, a drawing and a photograph of the completed work survive. The columns are of the same fluted Composite order as those of San Basilio but instead of being garlanded in spirals they are draped in skeins of what appears to be twisted cloth or even leather and have lost all semblance of the Salomonic. Furthermore, each pair supports a section of straight entablature from which an arch rises in a much more architectonic manner than at San Basilio. Whether the work at Nuevo Baztan had moved him toward a more classicizing style or whether some other influence was at work, José Benito would appear to have given up in his later years the rich chiaroscuro which had made him famous.

Joaquin de Churriguera already described himself as a resident of Salamanca when he contracted

José Benito de Churriguera.
Retable.
San Esteban.
Salamanca, Spain.
1692–1694

for the retable of Santa Clara with Pedro de Gamboa in 1702 and for the retable of Santo Tomas in San Esteban in 1705. Both are close to José Benito's style but even more burdened with lavish ornament which eats away the architectural frame. When in March 1714 Joaquin was made master of the works of Salamanca Cathedral, he had probably already submitted his design for the crossing lantern. Here, he carried his brother's architectural revivalism at Nuevo Baztan to a logical conclusion by returning to the baluster columns and surface enrichment of the sixteenth-century Plateresque. The lantern, incomplete in 1724, survives in a drawing of 1745 but was dismantled and rebuilt except for the inner octagon after 1755. Shortly before 1715, Joaquin began the Hospederia of the Colegio de Anaya in Salamanca, whose patio repeats that of the Colegio de Nobles Irlandeses of 1529–1534. Only Joaquin's more accentuated chia-

José Benito de Churriguera.
Nuevo Baztan.
Spain.
1709–1713

Alberto de Churriguera.
Plaza Mayor.
Salamanca, Spain.
1729–1733

roscuro and more robust Tuscan order below and Corinthian above mark this work as eighteenth rather than sixteenth century. In 1717, Joaquin began the Collegio de Calatrava, whose two-towered façade with a strong emphasis on the center portal recalls the works of RODRIGO GIL DE HONTAÑON, DIEGO DE SILOE, and ALONSO DE COVARRUBIAS. Incomplete in 1725, the work was continued by Pedro de Gamboa and Alberto Churriguera.

Alberto de Churriguera's early years were overshadowed by the fame of his brothers, and his early works are few. He assisted José Benito in a retable for the Church of San Sebastian in Madrid in 1710–1715. In Salamanca in 1719–1720, he built an orphanage whose richly scrolled portal, though more restrained, suggests the work of PEDRO DE RIBERA, having nothing of the conservative Palladianism of José Benito or the Plateresque revival of Joaquin. In 1725, he was appointed master of the works of Salamanca Cathedral to replace Joaquin. It is possible that the enclosure of the choir and the choir stalls themselves had already been designed by Joaquin in 1724 as the choir enclosure shows, evidence of his attraction to the Plateresque. The project was probably finished by 1733 when the church was finally consecrated. Another possible late work of Joaquin is the altar of the Assumption of the Virgin in the Cathedral of Plasencia. Joaquin was there in April 1724. When he died later in the same year, the chapter wrote to José Benito in Madrid but he died in 1725; the chapter then contracted with Alberto in April of the same year. He completed the work in December 1726. The four columns are not Salomonic but heavily encrusted like those of the Salamanca choir enclosure.

In 1728, Alberto began his first independent work, the Plaza Mayor of Salamanca. Work began with the west range in 1729, continuing counterclockwise to the east range with its royal pavilion completed in 1733. The arcades with tondi recall Joaquin but the next two stories, articulated with giant pilasters and the upper floor with its own pilasters, are more typical of Alberto. He also provided the design in 1729–1733 for the upper portion of the west front of Herrera's unfinished Cathedral for Valladolid, providing, as George Kubler (1957) has pointed out, an allegro to Herrera's andante.

The present parish church of the Cathedral of Salamanca, San Sebastian, was begun by Alberto in 1731, assisted by José de Lara Churriguera. The single nave and octagonal lantern recall the chapel of San Isidro at San Andres in Madrid. The retable of San Sebastian now in San Martin has *estípites,* rare in the work of the Churriguera. The portal, with its graceful moldings and rich foliage, epitomizes all that is best in his style without the oppressive elaboration of the choir enclosure in the new cathedral. In 1738, Alberto told the Salamanca chapter that since there was little work for him in Salamanca he wished to move to Madrid, retaining his title of master of the works and a token salary. At the same time, there had been a dispute over Pedro de Ribera's plans for the tower of Salamanca which were by this time reactionary and opposed to Alberto's own style. At any rate, he refused to return to Salamanca though he did not resign his title. In 1738, two new projects were begun, a parish church for Orgaz in the province of Toledo, and the Church of Saint Thomas at Rueda in the province of Valladolid. Neither were finished in his lifetime but both are stamped with his peculiar grace, a truly Spanish rococo, most unlike that which the Bourbon court had imposed from without. Alberto's death probably occurred about 1740 or 1741 as in November of 1741 Manuel de Lara Churriguera, his nephew, was received as master of the works at Salamanca.

JOHN DOUGLAS HOAG

WORKS

JOSÉ BENITO DE CHURRIGUERA

1686–1687, Ayala Chapel (retable), Cathedral of Segovia, Segovia, Spain. 1689, Catafalque, Funeral of Maria Louise of Orleans, Madrid. 1692–1694, San Esteban (retables), Salamanca, Spain. 1701–1704, San Salvador (retables), Leganés, Spain. 1709–1713, Nuevo Baztan, Spain. (A)1709–1713, Juan de Goyeneche House; *1710–1715, San Sebastian (retable); *1717–1720, San Basilio (retable); Madrid. 1717–1720, San Salvador (retables), Leganés, Spain. *1720–1724, Church of Calatrava (retable), Madrid.

JOAQUIN DE CHURRIGUERA

1702, Santa Clara (retable); 1714, Santo Tomas in San

Esteban (retable); *1714, Crossing Lantern, Salamanca Cathedral; 1715, Hospederia, Colegio de Anaya; 1717 Colegio de Calatrave; Salamanca, Spain.

ALBERTO DE CHURRIGUERA

1719–1720, Orphanage; 1724–1733, Cathedral of Salamanca (choir), Spain. 1725–1726, Cathedral of Plasencia (retable of the Assumption), Spain. 1729–1733, Plaza Mayor (west, south, and east ranges), Salamanca, Spain. 1729–1733, Cathedral of Valladolid (west façade), Valladolid, Spain. 1731–1738?, Parish Church, Orgaz, Spain. 1738–1740, Saint Thomas, Rueda, Spain.

BIBLIOGRAPHY

BONET CORREA, ANTONIO 1962 "Los retablos de las Calatravas de Madrid." *Archivo Español de Arte* 35, no. 137:21–49.
CHUECA GOITIA, FERNANDO 1951 *La catedral nueva de Salamanca.* Spain: University of Salamanca.
GARCIA Y BELLIDO, A. 1929 "Estudios del barroco español, avances para un monografía de los Churrigueras." *Archivo Español de Arte y Arqueologia* 5, no. 13:21–86.
GARCIA Y BELLIDO, A. 1930 "Estudios del barroco español, avances para un monografía de los Churrigueras, nuevos aportaciones." *Archivo Español de Arte y Arqueologia* 6, no. 17:135–187.
GUTÍERREZ DE CEBALLOS, ALFONSO RODRÍQUEZ 1971 *Los Churriguera.* Madrid: Instituto Diego Velázquez, Consejo Superior de Investigaciones Cientificas.
GUTÍERREZ DE CEBALLOS, ALFONSO RODRÍGUEZ 1972a *El Colegio de la Orden Militar de Calatrava de la Universidad de Salamanca.* Salamanca, Spain: Centro de Estudios Salmantinos.
GUTÍERREZ DE CEBALLOS, ALFONSO RODRÍGUEZ 1972b "Los retablos de la parroquia de San Salvador de Leganés." *Archivo Español de Arte* 45, no. 177:23–32.
IGARTUA MENDIA, MARIA TERESA 1972 *Desarrollo del Barroco en Salamanca.* Madrid: Edita Revista Estudios.
KUBLER, GEORGE 1957 *Arquitectura de los Siglos XVII y XVIII.* Madrid: Plus Ultra.
VERRIE, E. P. 1949 "Los barceloneses Xuriguera." Volume 8 in *Divulgacion Historica.* Barcelona, Spain.

CHUTE, JOHN

John Chute (1701–1776) was entrusted by his intimate friend HORACE WALPOLE with the designing of the exterior, and some of the interior, of Strawberry Hill and of the Chapel-in-the-Woods at Strawberry Hill (1753–1768), both major monuments of the Gothic Revival. He also designed Chalfont House, Buckinghamshire (c.1755), and Donnington Grove, Berkshire (c.1770). All his Gothic designs, including those made for his own house, The Vyne, Hampshire (1754), show dependence on the publications of BATTY LANGLEY. His classical designs for Hagley Hall (1752), for the staircase at The Vyne (1770), and for the monument to Challenor Chute at The Vyne (from 1754), were largely dependent on SEBASTIANO SERLIO.

MICHAEL MCCARTHY

WORKS

1753–1758, Strawberry Hill, Middlesex, England. Begun 1754, The Vyne (alterations), Hampshire, England. 1755, Chalfont House (since overbuilt), Buckinghamshire, England. c.1770, Donnington Grove, Berkshire, England. 1770, The Vyne (staircase), Hampshire, England.

BIBLIOGRAPHY

BEARD, G. W., and FOLKES, J. H. 1952 "John Chute and Hagley Hall." *Architectural Review* 3:199–200.
HARRIS, JOHN 1971 *A Catalogue of British Drawings for Architecture, Decoration, Sculpture and Landscape Gardening, 1550–1900, in American Collections.* Saddle River, N.J.: Gregg.
HUSSEY, CHRISTOPHER 1958 "Donnington Grove, Berkshire." *Country Life* 124:588–591, 654–657, 714–717.
MCCARTHY, MICHAEL 1975–1976 "John Chute's Drawings for the Vyne." *National Trust Year-Book* 1975–1976:70–80.
MCCARTHY, MICHAEL 1976 "The Building of Hagley Hall." *The Burlington Magazine* 118:214–225.

CIAMPI, MARIO

Born in San Francisco, Mario Ciampi (1907–) studied in San Francisco, at Harvard University, and at the Ecole des Beaux-Arts in Paris. In addition to design and planning, Ciampi has served as a judge for projects in the San Francisco area and has lectured at the University of California and Stanford University. Ciampi's firm has developed master plans for universities, school districts, and private developments, and has served as urban consultant for the general redevelopment of San Francisco.

PATRICIA C. PHILLIPS

WORKS

1970, University Art Museum, University of California, Berkeley. 1971, Embarcadero Plaza-Ferry Park (with Lawrence Halprin and Associates and John S. Bolles and Associates), San Francisco.

BIBLIOGRAPHY

Some of the information in this article was provided by Mario Ciampi and Associates.
SKY, ALISON, and STONE, MICHELLE 1976 *Unbuilt America.* New York: McGraw-Hill.

CIONE, ANDREA DI

See ORCAGNA.

CIVITALI, MATTEO DI GIOVANNI, and FAMILY

The Civitalis worked mainly in Lucca, Italy, primarily as sculptor–architect–engineers. Matteo di Giovanni Civitali (1436–1501) probably studied portrait sculpture in Florence. He developed a style of high realism and architectonic severity for tomb monuments (for example, Pietro Noceto's, completed 1472, Cathedral of Lucca). With FRANCESCO DI GIORGIO MARTINI, Matteo supplied plans for the new fortifications of Lucca (1491–1492). His son Niccolao di Matteo Civitali (1482–1560?) worked on the designs of several palaces in and around Lucca. Niccolao's son, Vincenzo di Niccolao Civitali (1523–1597), a goldsmith, is best known as military engineer of Lucca (1559–1562, 1584–1589).

HOWARD SHUBERT

CLARKE, G. SOMERS

George Somers Clarke (1825–1882) was a pupil of Sir CHARLES BARRY, in whose office he developed a sound sense of composition and a dexterity, very like his master's, in the handling of Gothic and Renaissance ornament. In London, his most important surviving work is the former General Credit Building, Lothbury (1868), a five-story office block detailed in Venetian Gothic. The Auction Mart, which adjoined it in Tokenhouse Yard (1867), was in a Cinquecento style. His country houses include Wyfold Court, Oxfordshire (1873–1874), a brilliant fusion of Elizabethan and François I styles, while the Turkish Baths in Jermyn Street, London (1862), blended Gothic timber construction with Arab ornament.

JOHN SUMMERSON

CLARKE, GEORGE

George Clarke (1661–1736), fellow of All Souls and Tory Member of Parliament for the University of Oxford, was a well-known virtuoso who advised on many architectural projects. His drawings for these, along with his architectural library and his collection of drawings by INIGO JONES and JOHN WEBB, are in the library of Worcester College, Oxford.

JOHN BOLD

WORKS

1704–1706, Warden's House, All Souls College, Oxford. c.1710, Cokethorpe House (alterations), Oxfordshire, England. 1710–1721, Queen's College (with NICHOLAS HAWKSMOOR); 1713–1716, Chapel (refitting), All Souls College; 1717–1736, Christ Church Library (not completed until 1738); 1720–1736, Worcester College (with William Townsend; not completed until 1759); Oxford. 1723, Rectory, Kingston Bagpuize, Berkshire, England. 1733–1734, New Buildings, (with Townsend), Magdalen College, Oxford.

BIBLIOGRAPHY

SHERWOOD, JENNIFER, and PEVSNER, NIKOLAUS 1974 *Oxfordshire.* Harmondsworth, England: Penguin.

CLARKE and BELL

William Clarke (?–1878) and George Bell the Elder (1814–1887) met around 1830 in the combined offices in Edinburgh of DAVID BRYCE, to whom Clarke had been articled, and WILLIAM BURN, who employed Bell after the death of Archibald Elliott, his first employer. They appear to have entered a number of architectural competitions together, being premiated in the competition for the Free Church College, Edinburgh, in the 1840s. In 1842, they won the competition for the City and County Buildings, Glasgow, Scotland, moving to Glasgow shortly afterward to set up practice there. The office produced buildings varying enormously in style and quality.

BRUCE WALKER

WORKS

1842–1844, City and County Buildings (southern and central sections), 40–50 Wilson Street; 1853, Shops and Offices, 102–104 Saint Vincent Street; 1855, Merchants' Hall; 1856, Granby Terrace, 2–28 Hillhead Street; 1871, City and County Buildings (northern section; altered in 1892); 1873, Fish Market, 64–76 Clyde Street; 1873?, Hillhead Burgh Hall; Glasgow, Scotland. 1885, Sheriff Courthouse; 1890, County Buildings, Saint James Street; Paisley, Scotland.

BIBLIOGRAPHY

GOMME, ANDOR, and WALKER, DAVID 1968 *Architecture of Glasgow.* London: Lund Humphries.

CLASON, ISAK GUSTAF

Isak Gustaf Clason (1856–1930) studied at the Royal Institute of Technology and the Academy of

Arts, both in Stockholm, partly as a pupil of FREDRIK WILHELM SCHOLANDER. After his studies, he spent several years on journeys in France, Italy, and Spain. Very soon he became predominant in his profession, and as a president of the Swedish Architects Association he remained so to the beginning of the twentieth century. From 1890 to 1904, he was the professor of architecture at the Royal Institute of Technology. Early inspired by the British Arts and Crafts movement, he proclaimed the use of "true materials" (stone and brick instead of plaster) at the same time that the stone industry was developed in Sweden. He also dissociated himself from the classical symmetrical building plans, and some of his works were closely connected to British and American villa architecture. Eclectic all his life, Clason at first used historic styles in a very free way, for example, French and Spanish Renaissance, but from around 1895 he very consciously chose Swedish national styles, mainly from the seventeenth century. His architecture was no longer modernistic and picturesque but associative and historicizing, and in that sense he was a forerunner of the Swedish national movement (see RAGNAR ÖSTBERG).

FREDRIC BEDOIRE

WORKS

1885–1889, Östermalms Market Hall (with Kasper Salin); 1886–1888, Bünsowska House, 29–33, Strandvägen; 1889–1907, Nordish Museum; 1893–1898, Hallwyl Palace; 1915–1927, Carpenters' Hall, Stockholm. 1916–1920, Adelsnäs Manor House, Östergötland, Sweden. 1920–1922, Mårbacka Manor House, Värmland, Sweden.

BIBLIOGRAPHY

Edestrand, Hans, and Lundberg, Erik 1968 *Isak Gustaf Clason*. Stockholm: Norstedt.

CLAYTON, A. B.

Arthur Bowyer Clayton (1795–1855) studied painting with William Etty before turning to architecture. A Greek and Gothic Revivalist, he assisted D. R. ROPER, notably on Saint Mark's Church, Kennington, London (1822–1824) and, from 1827, GEORGE SMITH, with whom he designed the Corn Exchange, London (1827–1828). From 1833 on, he was in independent practice.

R. WINDSOR LISCOMBE

WORKS

1834, Christ Church, Herne Bay; 1836, Brook House, near Reculver; Kent, England. 1845, Norley Hall (alterations and additions), Cheshire, England.

CLAYTON, NICHOLAS J.

Vigor and boldness characterize Nicholas J. Clayton's (1849–1916) work although he was personally quiet and modest. Born in Cork, Ireland, Clayton emigrated to the United States in 1851. After serving in the navy he was trained in architecture in Memphis, Tennessee, by W. H. Baldwin. Late in 1872, Clayton moved to Texas and established practice in Galveston. A devout Roman Catholic, he received a number of commissions from the Texas church. Clayton fused elements from such diverse styles as Romanesque, Queen Anne, the Second Empire, and high Victorian into a colorful and personal elaboration. He designed churches, convents, civic and commercial structures, and extravagant residences, many subsequently damaged or destroyed by Texas storms or by fire. He is best known for the exuberant Gresham House (1888) and stout polychromatic University of Texas Medical School Building (1889–1890) in Galveston.

ROXANNE WILLIAMSON

WORKS

1874–1884, Saint Mary's, The Cathedral of Austin, Tex. 1881–1882, Kauffman and Runge Building (Stewart Title Building); 1881–1882, Trueheart–Adriance Building; Galveston, Tex. *1882–1883, Ursuline Convent, Dallas, Tex. *1883, The Beach Hotel, Galveston, Tex. 1883–1884, Galveston News Building, Tex. 1884, Church of the Annunciation (remodeling), Dallas, Tex. 1888, Gresham House (Bishop's Palace), Galveston, Tex. *1888–1889, Saint Edward's University, Austin. 1889–1890, University of Texas Medical School Building (Ashbel Smith Hall); *1891–1894, Ursuline Convent; Galveston, Tex.

BIBLIOGRAPHY

A selection of Nicholas J. Clayton's drawings are in the Architectural Drawings Collection of The University of Texas at Austin.

ALEXANDER, DRURY BLAKELY   1966   *Texas Homes of the Nineteenth Century.* Austin: University of Texas Press.

BARNSTONE, HOWARD   1966   *The Galveston That Was.* New York: Macmillan.

ROBINSON, WILLARD E.   1974   *Texas Public Buildings of the Nineteenth Century.* Austin: University of Texas Press.

CLEAVELAND, HENRY W.

Henry William Cleaveland (1827–1919) was a propagandist for suburban living. Son of Bowdoin College's Nehemiah Cleaveland, he apprenticed with RICHARD UPJOHN and adopted ANDREW

JACKSON DOWNING's philosophy. He toured the world, visited California in 1850, then practiced in New York, where he wrote *Village and Farm Cottages* (Cleaveland, Backus, & Backus, 1856) arguing the moral and practical advantages of owning a small house outside the unhealthy city. Readers could buy patented plans. In San Francisco after 1859, he designed residences, especially Italian villas with ample grounds. Edward Swain's partner from 1882 to 1885, Cleaveland retired to Poughkeepsie, New York.

ANNE BLOOMFIELD

WORKS

*1861, Jonathan Hunt House, San Francisco, *1862–1863, Hotel, Napa Springs, Calif. 1865, John Bidwell Mansion; *1870, Bidwell Memorial Presbyterian Church; Chico, Calif. *1872, Niantic Hotel, San Francisco. *1874–1876, Charles L. Low's Country Villa and Horse Farm, Alameda, Calif. *1877, I. L. Requa House, Piedmont, Calif. *1882, Row Houses for J. P. Hale (with Edward Swain); *1884, Hobart Building (with Swain); San Francisco.

BIBLIOGRAPHY

Architectural plans, letters, and other papers of Henry W. Cleaveland are in the collections of the California Historical Society, San Francisco, and in the Special Collections, of the University Library, California State University, Chico, California.

CLEAVELAND, HENRY W.; BACKUS, WILLIAM; and BACKUS, SAMUEL D. (1856)1976 *Village and Farm Cottages.* Reprint. Watkins Glen, N.Y.: American Life Foundation.

KIRKER, HAROLD (1960)1973 *California's Architectural Frontier.* Reprint. Santa Barbara, Calif.: Peregrine Smith.

MCINTOSH, CLARENCE FREDERIC 1968 *Bidwell Memorial Presbyterian Church: Its First Century, 1868–1968.* Chico, Calif. Privately printed.

MCINTOSH, CLARENCE 1978 "Bidwell's Architect, Henry William Cleaveland." *Bidwell Mansion State Historic Park News Notes* Spring:3.

SNYDER, JOHN 1976 "A Partial Index to *The California Architect & Building News.*" Unpublished M.A. thesis, University of California, Davis.

CLERE, F. DE J.

Frederick de Jersey Clere (1856–1952) was born in Lancashire, England. He worked with the ecclesiastical architect Edmund Scott of Brighton and with R. J. Withers of London and then emigrated to New Zealand. He became Wellington diocesan architect and practiced into his ninetieth year. He was most notable for his churches and country houses.

JOHN STACPOOLE

WORKS

1881, Saint John's Church, Fielding, New Zealand. 1884, Overton House, Marton, New Zealand. 1885, Saint George's Church, Patea, New Zealand. 1891, Harbour Board Offices, Wellington. 1894, Wanganui Collegiate School, New Zealand. 1898, Highden House, Awahuri, New Zealand. 1907, Tututotara House, Marton, New Zealand. 1919, Boys' High School, Palmerston North, New Zealand. 1919, Saint Mary of the Angels Church; 1921, Saint Andrew's Presbyterian Church; 1925, A.M.P. Society Building; Wellington. 1926, Woodford House Chapel, Havelock North, New Zealand. 1930, Saint Patrick's College, Silverstream, New Zealand. 1931, Saint Andrew's Presbyterian Church, New Plymouth, New Zealand. 1932, Saint Gerard's Monastery, Wellington.

BIBLIOGRAPHY

STACPOOLE, JOHN, and BEAVEN, PETER 1972 *New Zealand Art: Architecture, 1820–1970.* Wellington: Reed.

CLERISSEAU, CHARLES-LOUIS

Charles-Louis Clérisseau (1721–1820), architect, archeologist, and artist, is an important figure in the genesis and diffusion of the neoclassical style in architecture and decoration, particularly in his relationship to such key figures as GIOVANNI BATTISTA PIRANESI and Johann Joachim Winckelmann and to pupils such as ROBERT ADAM and JAMES ADAM, WILLIAM CHAMBERS, and FRIEDRICH WILHELM VON ERDMANNSDORFF. Furthermore, his exact role in the invention and spread of the decorative style variously known as the Pompeian, Louis XVI, Adam, Arabesque, or Cameronian style from Italy to France, England, Germany, and Russia is still not completely clear. More than his actual architectural works, it is his thousands of drawings of ancient decorative details and real and imaginary ruin compositions and ancient-style buildings which helped create the neoclassical style.

Clérisseau was first trained as an architect in Paris under GERMAIN BOFFRAND and, after winning the Grand Prix in 1746, spent the years 1749–1754 at the French Academy in Rome. Leaving after the first of many unpleasant scenes which occurred throughout his life, Clérisseau briefly became the teacher of William Chambers and in 1755 began a long and complex association with Robert Adam, first as teacher cicerone and later as employee in the study of ancient architectural and decorative forms and their adaptation to a new architectural style. Together, they visited Diocletian's Palace in Spalato (Split, Yugoslavia); Adam's book on the palace, with unacknowledged plates

by Clérisseau, appeared in 1764. Few of Clérisseau's projects of his Italian years, 1749–1767, were executed. The ancient ruin garden for Abbé Fracetti at Sala (1767) exists only in a description. Others, such as the decoration for the café on the Villa Albani in Rome (1764), which may be one of the first uses of groteschi in the new style, have not survived. The one exception is the painted monastic cell for Père LeSueur resembling an ancient room at Santa Trinità dei Monti, Rome (c.1766), a tour de force even today without its original furniture.

His projected château for Louis Borély of Marseilles (1767) was not executed as planned but reveals the sensitive use of ancient motifs. On his return to France, he began a study of Roman France, producing a volume on the monuments of Nîmes in 1778. Returning to Paris in 1767, he was admitted to the Academy of Painting and Sculpture in 1769 as a painter of architecture. During the early 1770s, the Adam brothers finally allowed him to come to England to help on their projects (they had paid him to stay away before this) but his design for the Landowne Library of 1774 was rejected. He returned to France and designed for Catherine the Great of Russia an enormous Roman villa which she rejected in 1773 (drawings survive in the Hermitage). The great contretemps which this caused was resolved by Catherine by purchasing over a thousand drawings which influenced later Russian architecture. A triumphal arch for the same patron in 1782 was also rejected but a model and complete drawings survive. Also in the 1770s, Clérisseau decorated two salons for Laurent Grimod de la Reynière in Paris, variously dated but not the first use of grotteschi decoration in the Louis XVI style as has been suggested. Clérisseau's one complete building, the Palais du Gouverneur (now Palais de Justice), Metz, France (1776–1789), is an enormous but somewhat dull structure relieved by classical trophies flanking the entrance. Clérisseau's exact role in the design of THOMAS JEFFERSON's Virginia Capitol, Richmond, Virginia (1785–1790), is not clear aside from his greater architectural and ancient expertise and knowledge of its prototype, the Maison Carrée. His salon for the Palace at Weimar of 1792 was not executed.

Clérisseau's later years were not artistically active ones but were filled with honor. In 1804, he published a second edition of his Nîmes book, with text by his son-in-law, J. G. Legrand. In 1810, he was made a member of the Academy of Rouen and in 1815 a member of the Legion of Honor. He died in 1820 nearly 100 years old. Clérisseau's greatest role was that of a teacher and as an artist-archeologist who helped diffuse neoclassicism throughout Europe and the United States.

THOMAS J. McCORMICK

Clérisseau.
Monastery (painted ruin room), Santa Trinità dei Monti.
Rome.
c.1766

Clérisseau.
Hôtel Grimod de la Reynière (salon decoration).
Paris.
1775–1777

WORKS

*1764, Villa Albani (café decoration); c.1766, Monastery (painted ruin room), Santa Trinità dei Monti; Rome. *1775–1777, Hôtel Grimod de la Reynière (salon decoration), Rue Grange-Batelière, Paris. 1776–1789, Palais du Gouverneur, Metz, France. 1780–1782, Hôtel Grimod de la Reynière (salon decoration), Rue Boissy d'Anglas, Paris. 1785–1790, Virginia State Capitol (with Thomas Jefferson), Richmond.

BIBLIOGRAPHY

ACADEMY DE FRANCE À ROME 1976 *Piranese et les Français: 1740–1790.* Edited by A. Chastel and G. Brunel. Rome: Edizioni dell'Elefante.
BRAHAM, ALLAN 1980 *The Architecture of the French Enlightenment.* Berkeley: University of California Press.
CLÉRISSEAU, CHARLES-LOUIS 1778 *Monumens des Nismes.* Part 1 in *Antiquités de la France.* Paris: Phillipe-Denys-Pierres.
CROFT-MURRAY, EDWARD 1963 "The Hôtel Grimod de la Reynière: The Salon Decorations." *Apollo* 78:377–383.
FLEMING, JOHN 1958 "The Journey to Spalato." *Architectural Review* 123:102–107.
FLEMING, JOHN 1962 *Robert Adam and His Circle in Edinburgh and Rome.* London: Murray.

GALLET, MICHEL 1972 *Stately Mansions: Eighteenth Century Paris Architecture.* New York: Praeger.

McCORMICK, THOMAS J. 1964 "Virginia's Gallic Godfather." *Arts in Virginia* 4:2–13.

McCORMICK, THOMAS J. 1967 "Charles-Louis Clérisseau." *Papers of the American Association of Architectural Biographers* 4:9–16.

McCORMICK, THOMAS J. 1978 "Piranesi and Clérisseau's Vision of Classical Antiquity." *Actes du colloque Piranèse et les Français* 1978:305–314.

McCORMICK, THOMAS J., AND FLEMING, JOHN 1962 "A Ruin Room by Clérisseau." *Connoisseur* 159:239–243.

MIDDLETON, ROBIN, and WATKIN, DAVID 1980 *Neoclassical and 19th Century Architecture.* New York: Abrams.

CLINTON, CHARLES W.

Charles William Clinton (1838–1910) was born in New York City. He trained as an architect in the office of RICHARD UPJOHN and practiced in New York until his death. Early in his career, Clinton was associated with Anthony B. McDonald, Jr. and with EDWARD T. POTTER. In 1894, he and William Hamilton Russell formed the firm of Clinton and Russell.

DENNIS McFADDEN

WORKS

1877–1879, Seventh Regiment Armory; 1906–1908, Apthorp Apartments (with William Hamilton Russell); 1907, Hudson Terminal Building (with Russell); New York.

BIBLIOGRAPHY

"Charles W. Clinton, Dead." 1910 *New York Times* Dec. 2, p. 9.

STURGIS, RUSSELL 1897 "A Review of the Work of Clinton and Russell." *Architectural Record* 7, no. 2:1–61.

CLINTON and RUSSELL

The New York firm of Clinton and Russell was composed of Charles W. Clinton (1838–1910) and William Hamilton Russell (1854–1907). Clinton apprenticed with RICHARD UPJOHN and was first associated with EDWARD T. POTTER before entering into partnership with Russell in 1894. Russell was a great-nephew of JAMES RENWICK, in whose office he was a partner before 1894. Although the firm designed a few churches and residences, Clinton and Russell's prolific practice was mainly in the commercial field where their designs followed LOUIS H. SULLIVAN's prescription for tall buildings. After Russell's death, Clinton practiced under the firm name until his own death.

GWEN W. STEEGE

WORKS

1896, Hudson Terminal Building; 1899, Cheeseborough Building; c.1902, Astor Hotel; 1903, Wall Street Exchange; *1905, Seventy-first Regiment Armory; n.d., Bank of America; n.d., Broad Exchange Building; n.d., New York Athletic Club; New York.

BIBLIOGRAPHY

HUTCHINS, WILLIAM 1902 New York Hotels. II. The Modern Hotel." *Architectural Record* 12:621–635.

KOCH, ROBERT 1955 "The Medieval Castle Revival: New York Armories." *Journal of the Society of Architectural Historians* 14:23–29.

SCHUYLER, MONTGOMERY 1906 "Two New Armories." *Architectural Record* 19:259–264.

STURGIS, RUSSELL 1904 "The Warehouse and the Factory in Architecture." *Architectural Record* 15:122–133.

CLOQUET, LOUIS

Trained as an engineer, Louis Cloquet (1849–1920) was a leading figure in the later phases of the Gothic Revival in Belgium. Following the theories of EUGÈNE EMMANUEL VIOLLET-LE-DUC, he promoted Gothic architecture as a rational structural system eminently suited for modern constructions. As an architectural educator at the University of Ghent and the Academy of Fine Arts in Antwerp, Cloquet influenced many young Belgian architects, including HUIB HOSTE, who were to achieve significance as Modernists after World War I.

ALFRED WILLIS

WORKS

1899–1905, Pharmacodynamic, Physiological, Polyclinical, and Rommelaere Institutes, University of Ghent; 1902–1912, Post Office; 1912, House, 1 Recollettenlei; 1913, Sint-Pieters Railway Station; Ghent, Belgium.

BIBLIOGRAPHY

CAMPUS, RICHARD 1957 "Cloquet (Louis)." Volume 29, columns 458–461 in *Biographie Nationale publiée par l'Académie Royale des Sciences, des Lettres, et des Beaux-Arts de Belgique.* Brussels: Bruylant.

CLOQUET, LOUIS 1898–1901 *Traité d'architecture.* 5 vols. Paris: Baudry.

MOUTON, H. 1978 "Ingenieur-architect Louis Cloquet (1849–1920): Zijn werk in opdracht van de Rijksuniversiteit te Gent." Unpublished Ph.D. dissertation, University of Ghent, Belgium.

SMETS, MARCEL 1972 *Huib Hoste: Propagateur d'une*

architecture renouvelée. Brussels: Confédération Nationale de la Construction.

VAN TYGHEM, FRIEDA   1980   "De universitaire instituten van L. Cloquet te Gent." *Vlaanderen* 21, Jan.–Feb.:37–39.

CLUSKEY, CHARLES B.

A native of Ireland, Charles Blaney Cluskey (1806?–1871) emigrated to New York in 1827. From 1829, he worked as architect and builder in Savannah, Georgia, being appointed city surveyor in 1845. He designed a number of houses and the noble Medical College of Georgia at Augusta (1834–1835) in the Greek style. In 1848, he went to Washington, both to ascertain the fate of his 1845 design for the Savannah Custom House and to compile an official report on the eight Public Buildings. Unsuccessful in the 1850 Capitol extension competition, Cluskey later claimed that his projected rotunda with cast-iron columns had influenced THOMAS U. WALTER's dome. Beside laying out streets on the west line of the east wing of the Patent Office, he won few subsequent commissions. He is supposed to have completed some houses in New Orleans before 1856, when he went to Galveston, Texas, hoping to secure the Custom House commission. After acting as contractor with Edwin W. Moore, he returned in 1858 to Washington, where he died.

R. WINDSOR LISCOMBE

WORKS

1834–1835, Medical College of Georgia, Augusta. *1836–1840, Main Building, Oglethorpe University, Atlanta, Ga. 1837–1838, Governor's Mansion, Milledgeville, Ga. 1839?, Daniel R. Tucker House (Lockerly), Irwinton Road, near Milledgeville, Ga. (A)1840?, Henry McAlpin House (The Hermitage), near Savannah, Ga. *1840–1843, Exchange (additions east side); (A)1841, Francis Sorrel House; 1843–1844, Aaron Champion House (third floor added 1896); 1843–1844, Moses Eastman House; Savannah, Ga.

BIBLIOGRAPHY

CLUSKEY, CHARLES B.   1849   "Public Buildings &c." *House Report 90.* 30th Cong., 2d sess., Feb. 13. Washington: Government Printing Office.
CORLEY, FLORENCE F.   1976   "The Old Medical College and the Old Governor's Mansion." *Journal of the Richmond County Historical Society* 8, no. 2:5–22.
LEHMAN, DONALD J.   1973   Pages 18–43 in *Lucky Landmark: A Study of a Design and Its Survival.* Washington: United States Public Buildings Service.
NICHOLS, FREDERICK D.   1976   Pages 57–59, 318–329 in *The Architecture of Georgia.* Savannah, Ga.: Beehive Press.

CLUYSENAAR, J. P.

Jean Pierre Cluysenaar (1811–1880) was educated at the Academy of Fine Arts, Brussels, and received practical training under Tilman Frans Suys. An accomplished practitioner of neoclassic and neo-Renaissance modes, he was also an imaginative designer in various medievalizing styles. His Galeries Saint-Hubert (1837–1847) in Brussels, with a glazed barrel vault, was, according to J. F. Geist (1969), "the first monumental example of a commercial passage."

ALFRED WILLIS

WORKS

1837–1847, Galeries Saint-Hubert; *1848, Madeleine Market Hall; Brussels. 1852, Theater and Casino, Homburg, Germany. 1872–1877, Royal Conservatory of Music; Brussels.

BIBLIOGRAPHY

GEIST, JOHANN FRIEDRICH   1969   *Passagen, ein Bautyp des 19. Jahrhunderts.* Munich: Prestel.
PUTTEMANS, PIERRE   1976   *Modern Architecture in Belgium.* Translated by Mette Willert. Brussels: Vokaer.
"Der Spielsaal in Homburg."   1855   *Zeitschrift für praktische Baukunst.* 15:337–338, plates 36–38.
STEVENS, J., and DUMONT, A.   1957   "Cluysenaar (Jean Pierre)." Volume 29 of *Biographie nationale . . . de Belgique.* Brussels: Palais des Académies.
VAN DE VOORT, J.   1956   "De Bouwkunst en de Kunstnijverheid in België van 1800 tot 1950." Volume 3 pages 351–385 in H. E. Van Gelder and J. Duverger (editors), *Kunstgeschiedenis der Nederlanden van de Middeleeuwen tot onze tijd.* Utrecht: De Haan.
VONDENDAELE, RICHARD ET AL.   1980   *Poelaert et Son Temps.* Brussels: Crédit Communal de Belgique.

COATES, WELLS

Wells Wintemute Coates (1895-1958) was a pioneer in England of the international modern style promoted in the 1930s by the Modern Architectural Research Group of which he was one of the founders. Born in Japan and educated at McGill University, he came to London in 1924. His buildings are notable for skillful planning for economy of space, as in his poured concrete apartments at Lawn Road (1932–1934), London, and in his own studio–residence in Yeoman's Row (1947), London. His apartment block in Palace Gate (1937–1939), London, has an ingenious split-level duplex section. Coates was an engineer as well as an architect and designed advanced radio-sets and experimental sailing craft. Latterly he was engaged on urban planning projects in Canada.

J. M. RICHARDS

WORKS

1932, British Broadcasting Corporation (studio interiors); 1932–1934, Lawn Road Flats; London. 1936, Apartment Building, Brighton, England. 1937–1939, No. 10, Palace Gate, London. 1938, House (with Patrick Gwynne), Esher, England. 1947, Yeoman's Row (studio–residence); 1951, Cinema, Festival of Britain South Bank Exhibition; London.

BIBLIOGRAPHY

CANTACUZINO, SHERBAN 1978 *Wells Coates*. London: Gordon Fraser.

COBERGHER, WENZEL

A humanist figure, enamored of economics, chemistry, numismatics, and hydraulics, Wenzel Cobergher (16th–17th centuries) was the most brilliant proponent of the Italian style in Belgium. Initially, he studied painting in the studio of M. De Vos the Elder. From 1583 to 1604, he worked in Naples and Rome, where he developed his painting according to the mannerist style and where he was first introduced to architecture. He was called back to Flanders in 1605 to assume the position of architect to the archdukes. In this capacity, he realized his grandest projects, among which were the Mounts-of-Piety in Brussels (1617). His influence was so marked that he became the foremost promoter of the hybrid mannerist style, called the Italo-Flemish, which characterized seventeenth-century Flemish art.

PIERRE LENAIN
Translated from French by
Shara Wasserman

WORKS

1609–1621, Church of Montaigu, Scherpenheuvel, Belgium. 1615–1618, Church of the Augustins, Antwerp, Belgium. 1617, Monts-de-Piété, Brussels. 1618, Monts-de-Piété, Tournai, Belgium. 1620, Monts-de-Piété, Antwerp, Belgium. 1620, Monts-de-Piété, Mons, Belgium. 1620, Monts-de-Piété, Namur, Belgium.

BIBLIOGRAPHY

BORTIER, PIERRE 1875 *Cobergher: Peintre, architecte, ingénieur.* Brussels: Vanderauwera.
PARENT, PAUL 1926 *L'Architecture des Pays-Bas meridionaux aux XVIᵉ, XVIIᵉ, et XVIIIᵉ Siècles.* Paris and Brussels: Van Oest.
VAN ACKERE, JULES 1972 *Belgique Baroque et Classique.* Brussels: Vokaer.

COCCEIUS AUCTUS, LUCIUS

Lucius Cocceius Auctus (?–10 B.C.) was responsible for the so-called Grotto of Cocceius (c.35 B.C.), running from Cumae to Lake Avernus, below Mount Grillo, Italy. A huge tunnel five-eighths of a mile long, it was wide enough to allow passage of two carts at once. It was lit by slanting shafts from above and was paralleled by a subterranean aqueduct. Also attributed to Cocceius is the so-called crypta neapolitana (c.35 B.C.) near Posilipo, Italy, smaller than the grotto but still impressive. These tunnels were typical examples of that skill in architectural engineering which contributed so much to the successes of the Roman Republic and Empire.

B. M. BOYLE

WORKS

(A)c.35 B.C., Crypta Neapolitana, Posilipo, Italy. c.35 B.C., Grotto of Cocceius, Cumae, Italy.

BIBLIOGRAPHY

English translations of the ancient texts can be found in the volumes of the Loeb Classical Library series, published by Harvard University Press and Heinemann.
MAIURI, AMEDEO 1947 *The Phlegraean Fields.* Translated by V. Priestley. Rome: Libreria dello Stato.
PLINY, *Historia naturalis,* Book 34.41.
STRABO, *Geographikon,* Book 14.652.

COCHRANE and PIQUENARD

A civil engineer graduate of the Ecole Centrale in Paris and immigrant to the United States, Alfred H. Piquenard (c.1826–1876) worked several years for the St. Louis architect George I. Burnett and began working for John C. Cochrane (1835–1887) in Chicago in 1867. Cochrane, after an apprenticeship to a builder in his native New Hampshire and a move to the West, had been in practice as an architect in Chicago since 1864. He and Piquenard formed a partnership in 1868 and were the architects for the Illinois Capitol (1869–1887) in Springfield and for the Iowa Capitol (1871–1887) in Des Moines.

WESLEY I. SHANK

WORKS

1869–1887, Illinois Capitol (not completed until 1888), Springfield. 1871–1887, Iowa Capitol, Des Moines.

BIBLIOGRAPHY

GOELDNER, PAUL K. 1970 "Temples of Justice: Nineteenth Century Courthouses in the Midwest and Texas." Unpublished Ph.D. dissertation, Columbia University, New York.
HITCHCOCK, H. R., and SEALE, WILLIAM 1976 *Temples of Democracy: The State Capitols of the U.S.A.* New York: Harcourt.
"The New State Capitol of Illinois." 1868 *American Builder and Journal of Art* 1:opposite p. 20.

"Obituary of John C. Cochrane." 1888 *American Architect and Building News* 23:13.

"Obituary of Alfred H. Piquenard." 1876 *American Architect and Building News* 1:399.

"Public Buildings in Illinois—the New State House." 1877 *American Architect and Building News* 2:61–62.

COCKERELL, C. R.

Charles Robert Cockerell (1788–1863) was one of the most refined and distinguished classical architects of his day in Europe. His Ashmolean Museum (1841–1845), Oxford, branch Bank of England (1844–1847), Liverpool, and unfinished University Library (1837–1840), Cambridge, demonstrate a uniquely imaginative handling of the classical language based on his unrivalled knowledge of antique, Renaissance, Mannerist, and English seventeenth- and eighteenth-century architecture. He is especially memorable for his bold deployment of the orders, for the beauty of his detail and the commanding scale of his buildings. Even a small work like his lodge at Wynnstay (1827–1828), Denbighshire, has this characteristic largeness of scale and air of absolute authority. He wrote to a friend of his Cambridge Library: "Observe the large stones & the attempt at a *large* manner, it being as difficult to be large & noble in archre. as it is to be large & noble in morals" (Watkin, p. 196). Although not thought of as a creator of interior spaces, his elliptical Concert Hall (1851–1854) at Saint George's Hall, Liverpool, is not only a noble and original space but also exquisitely ornamented.

Born in London Cockerell was trained firstly by his father SAMUEL PEPYS COCKERELL, the successful surveyor and architect, and secondly by ROBERT SMIRKE, leader of the Greek Revival in England. He was sent by his father in 1810 on the customary grand tour but extended it to a seven-year period of study in which he helped make sensational archeological discoveries, including the use of entasis on the Parthenon, the frieze of the temple at Bassae, and the pedimental sculpture of the temple at Aegina. This gave him a sense of the sculptural basis of Greek architecture with its springiness of line which separates his work from the Greek Revival as it had been practiced from JAMES STUART and NICHOLAS REVETT to WILLIAM WILKINS and Smirke. His handsome personal appearance at this time is recorded in a fine drawing made in Rome in 1817 by Jean Ingres.

Returning to England in 1817 with a large artistic vision and a nervous romantic sensibility, Cockerell found difficulty in applying his love and knowledge of Greek design to his architectural practice in a climate dominated by the to him insipid style of his old master Smirke. He has left a set of fascinating diaries for the years 1821–1832 which record the introspective process of self-criticism which helped him to establish his personal style by the late 1830s. His early buildings like the Literary and Philosophical Institution (1821–1823) at Bristol, Lough Crew (1821–1829), County Meath, and the National Monument (1824–1829), Edinburgh, are in a dry Smirkelike manner, but already his Hanover Chapel (1823–1825), Regent Street, London, and Holy Trinity Chapel (1829–1830), Hotwells, Bristol, contain centrally-planned domed spaces in which the Greek Revival is enriched by memories of CHRISTOPHER WREN and NICHOLAS HAWKSMOOR. His ambition, as he noted in his diary in 1822, was to unite the "richness of rococo & the breadth & merit of Greek." We can begin to find this richness in a building which marks a turning point in his career, the Westminster, Life and British Fire Of-

Cockerell.
Ashmolean Museum and Taylorian Institution.
Oxford.
1841–1845

Cockerell.
Concert Hall.
Saint George's Hall.
Liverpool, England.
1851–1854

fice in the Strand (1831–1832). Here the theme of the Greek Doric temple has been embedded in a richer sculptural setting which draws on favorite buildings of Cockerell dating from ANDREA PALLADIO's Mannerist phase such as the Villa Barbaro at Maser and the Loggia del Capitaniato at Vicenza. Cockerell brilliantly developed this theme in major works such as his unexecuted project for the Royal Exchange (1839) and his Liverpool Bank of England.

In such buildings Cockerell established the type of classical bank architecture which survived until World War II. His career as an architect of insurance and banking premises is puzzling given his distaste, expressed in letters as a young man to his father, for the commercial and business side of the architectural profession. Nevertheless, he always saw himself primarily as an artist and was also conscious of being a gentleman. His gentlemanly fastidiousness, distinction of manner and appearance, intellectual refinement and obvious scholarly and artistic attainments, made him become as the years went by the uncrowned head of the architectural profession, although he lost most of the architectural competitions he entered, for example, the National Gallery, Houses of Parliament, Reform Club, Royal Exchange, and Carlton Club. In 1819 he succeeded his father as Surveyor to Saint Paul's Cathedral and in 1833 succeeded Sir JOHN SOANE as architect to the Bank of England. He became a Royal Academician in 1839 and professor of architecture at the same institution in the following year. The lectures which he delivered in that capacity from 1841–1856 were widely admired, though his passionate belief in the classical tradition set him apart from the mainstream of architectural taste which was flowing strongly toward Gothic. Antiquity was for him the bedrock and he illustrated his lectures with his own impressive reconstructions of Greek and Roman buildings. However, what he especially emphasized was the continuity of the classical tradition so that he constantly opened the eyes of his pupils to the various beautiful ways in which the orders had been handled by Renaissance, Baroque, and eighteenth-century architects. Though he attempted to influence young architects in these lectures his own method of design was too personal and introspective for him to want to take pupils into his office. This, coupled with the impact of the Gothic Revival, meant that his influence in his lifetime was slight. Since his death he has been a source of inspiration to architects as different as the elder and younger Burnet, ARTHUR BERESFORD PITE, ALBERT RICHARDSON and H. S. GOODHART-RENDEL.

In 1828 he married Anna, daughter of the civil engineer JOHN RENNIE, by whom he had ten children including Frederick Pepys Cockerell who succeeded him in his architectural practice. In 1848 he was the first recipient of the Royal Gold Medal of the Royal Institute of British Architects and in 1860 became the institute's first professional president. He received numerous awards from foreign academies and on his death in London in 1863 was buried in the crypt of Saint Paul's Cathedral.

DAVID WATKIN

WORKS
1819–1836, Oakly Park (remodeling), Shropshire, England. 1821–1823, Literary and Philosophical Institution, Bristol, England. *1821–1829, Lough Crew, County Meath, Ireland. *1823–1825, Hanover Chapel, London. *1824, Derry Ormond, Cardiganshire, Wales. 1824–1829, National Monument, Edinburgh. 1827–1828, Lodge, Wynnstay, Denbighshire, Wales. *1827–1833, Langton House, Dorset, England. 1829–1830, Holy Trinity Chapel, Hotwells, Bristol, England. *1831–1832, Westminster, Life and British Fire Office; *1837–1839, London and Westminster Bank; London. 1837–1840, University Library (unfinished), Cambridge. 1840–1841, Chapel, Killerton, Devon, England. *1841–1842, Sun Fire Office, London. 1841–1845, Ashmolean Museum and Taylorian Institution, Oxford. 1844–1845, Branch Bank of England, Manchester. 1844–1846, Branch Bank of England, Bristol. 1844–1847, Branch Bank of England; 1851–1854, Saint George's Hall (completion of interiors); 1856–1857, Liverpool and London Insurance Company Offices (with F. P. Cockerell); Liverpool, England.

BIBLIOGRAPHY
COCKERELL, CHARLES R. 1830 *Antiquities of Athens and Other Places of Greece, Sicily, etc.* London: Priestley.
COCKERELL, CHARLES R. 1851 *Iconography of the West Front of Wells Cathedral, with an Appendix on the Sculptures of Other Mediaeval Churches in England.* Oxford and London: Parker.
COCKERELL, CHARLES R. 1860 *The Temples of Jupiter Panhellenius at Aegina, and of Apollo Epicurius at Bassae near Phigalein at Arcadia.* London: Weale.
HARRIS, JOHN 1971 "C. R. Cockerell's 'Ichnographical Domestica.'" *Architectural History* 14:5–29.
WATKIN, DAVID 1974 *The Life and Work of C. R. Cockerell.* London: Zwemmer.

COCKERELL, SAMUEL PEPYS

Many architects are known for single great buildings. Samuel Pepys Cockerell (1754–1827) is not. Instead, he designed numerous types competently in a variety of styles. He was a thorough professional, having been trained from the age of fifteen in the office of ROBERT TAYLOR in London. Upon Taylor's death in 1788 Cockerell took over the office. However, as early as 1774 he was working independently as surveyor for the parish of Saint George's, and in 1775 he became clerk of the works at the Tower of London. Several lucrative surveyorships came to him when Taylor died.

Although variations on classicism characterize most of Cockerell's efforts, there are notable exceptions. The church at Tickencote (1792), Rutland, was rebuilt in Norman Romanesque to match the chancel arch retained from a twelfth-century edifice. Daylesford House (1788–1793), Gloucestershire, has an Oriental dome and several interior rooms with Eastern decoration, while most of the exterior is unadorned classicism. The Church of Saint Martin Outwich (1796–1798), London, was strongly under the influence of the French architect CLAUDE NICOLAS LEDOUX who enjoyed the effect of walls with heavily incised lines between stone courses. The nave plan was ovoid. Middleton Hall (1793–1795), Cockerell's handsomest country mansion, near Carmarthen, Wales, was beautifully proportioned in the Ionic order and situated in an extensive park with mineral springs. Still standing is a triangular, Gothic belvedere and banqueting hall.

Sezincote House (c.1805) in the Cotswolds introduced to England the design for a complete mansion in the Indian style. Cockerell's brother Charles had made a fortune in India and spent a large portion on the richly carved exterior of Sezincote. The golden-hued local stone brilliantly enhances the Oriental effect. But the plan is that of a typical Georgian house. The vast garden is also Orientalized.

Number 32, St. James's Square (1819–1821), London, marks the less romantic side of Cockerell's work. Whereas Sezincote has much humor about it, this is a standard townhouse deriving from designs by his master Robert Taylor and from ROBERT ADAM.

Cockerell was descended through his mother from Samuel Pepys, the diarist. His son, CHARLES ROBERT COCKERELL, one of thirteen children, became the most successful classical architect in England. BENJAMIN HENRY LATROBE, the great American architect of the early nineteenth century, learned the profession in Cockerell's office.

PAUL F. NORTON

WORKS

1786–1788, Admiralty House, London. 1788–1793, Daylesford House, Gloucestershire, England. 1792, Tickencote Parish Church, Rutlandshire, England. *1792–1795, Gore Court, Tunstall, England. 1792–1797, Church of Saint Mary's, Banbury, England. *1793–1795, Middleton Hall, Carmarthenshire, Wales. *1796–1798, Church of Saint Martin Outwich; 1802–1803, Church of Saint Anne's Soho (tower); *1804–1805, Westminster Guildhall; London. c.1805, Sezin-

cote House, Gloucestershire, England. 1819–1821, 32, Saint James's Square, London.

BIBLIOGRAPHY

BETJEMAN, JOHN 1931 "Sezincote, Moreton-in-Marsh, Gloucestershire: It's Situation, History and Architecture Described." *Architectural Review* 69:161–166.
HUSSEY, CHRISTOPHER 1958 *English Country Houses: Late Georgian, 1800–1840.* London: Country Life.
NORTON, PAUL F. 1963 "Daylesford: S. P. Cockerell's Residence for Warren Hastings." *Journal of the Society of Architectural Historians* 22:127–133.
WATKIN, DAVID 1974 *The Life and Work of C. R. Cockerell.* London: Zwemmer.

CODERCH Y DE SENTMENAT, JOSÉ ANTONIO

José Antonio Coderch y de Sentmenat (1913–) began his career shortly after the end of the Spanish civil war of 1936–1939 in the climate of disorientation in which Spanish architecture found itself at that time. From his first works—realized in collaboration with Barcelona architect Manuel Valls Vergés—Coderch showed a deep desire to overcome that situation. In trying to develop his own ideas, he created works of great interest such as his Ugalde House in Caldetas (1951). The exemplary nature of Coderch's work in this stage was based not only on the clarity, perfection, and elegance of his architectural solutions but also on the ethical significance of his personal posture on the edge of historicist revivalism and ephemeral styles accepted with the weight of dogma. In his article, *There are no geniuses that we need now,* published in the Italian magazine *Domus* (1961), he defends his concept of architecture as resulting from serious work, complete dedication and an avoidance of the conformist routines and false generalizations. That manifesto summarized his vision of the professional as a member detached from society to which, unavoidably, he must render a service. Coderch has continued to be faithful to these postulates, enriching his language and branching out to the fields of urbanism and design in which works such as the Torre Valentina—which never passed beyond the project stage—or his Coderch Lamp gained worldwide recognition. Since 1961, he has been active in Team 10.

CARLOS FLORES LOPEZ
Translated from Spanish by
Judith E. Meighan

WORKS

1947, Casa Garriga-Nogués, Sitges; 1951, Building, Barceloneta; Barcelona, Spain. 1951, Pabellón de Espana, 9th Triennale, Milan. 1951, Casa Ugalde, Caldetas; 1956, Casa Catasus, Sitges; Barcelona, Spain. 1957, Casa Vallbé, Camprodon, Gerona, Spain. 1958, Building, Calle Bach, Barcelona, Spain. 1962, Casa Rozes, Rosas, Gerona, Spain. 1965, Trade Building; 1968, Cocheras Housing; 1972, Instituto Francés; Barcelona, Spain.

BIBLIOGRAPHY

ANTÓN CAPITEL, JAVIER ORTEGA   1978   *J. A. Coderch: 1945–1976.* Madrid: Xarait.

BOFILL, RICARDO, and GOYTISOLO, J. A.   1975   "Dernier Grand Maître solitaire de l'architecture espagnole." *L'Architecture d'Aujourd'Hui* 177:67–73.

FLORES LOPEZ CARLOS   1961   *Arquitectura española contemporánea.* Madrid: Aguilar.

SORIA BADÍA, ENRIC   1979   *Conversaciones con Coderch.* Barcelona, Spain: Blume.

CODMAN, OGDEN JR.

Born into a wealthy Boston family, Ogden Codman, Jr., (1868–1951) spent his formative years in France, where he was influenced by eighteenth-century neoclassical architecture. He spent a year at the Massachusetts Institute of Technology while apprenticed to his uncle, JOHN HUBBARD STURGIS. In 1891, he launched his career as a society architect and interior decorator in Boston, Newport, and New York, numbering family friends and relations among his clients. Between 1895 and 1920, he designed twenty-one houses, remodeled ten more, and decorated seventy-five others.

He was a close friend of novelist Edith Wharton and decorator Elsie de Wolfe, and of Herbert W. C. Brown and ARTHUR LITTLE, with whom his work can be compared. An early preservationist, Codman left measured drawings of colonial buildings in New England, New York, Philadelphia, and Washington. He saw interior decoration as an integral part of architecture, and with Wharton coauthored a classic book on the subject (1897).

ROBERT L. HOWIE, JR.

WORKS

1893, Edith Wharton House; 1894–1895, Cornelius Vanderbilt House; 1895–1896, Mrs. Charles C. Pomeroy House; *1900, E. Rollins Morse House; Newport, R.I. 1901, Lloyd Bryce House, Roslyn, N.Y. 1901, Alfred Coats House, Providence, R.I. 1902–1903, Frank K. Sturgis House, Newport, R.I. *1904, Oliver Ames House, Prides Crossing, Mass. 1908, John D. Rockefeller, Jr., House, Tarrytown, N.Y. 1908–1910, Martha Codman (Karolik) House, Washington. 1908–1911, J. Woodward Haven House, New York. 1910, Martha Codman (Karolik) House, Newport, R.I. 1910–1912, Bayard Thayer House, Boston. 1912, Ogden Codman, Jr., House; 1913–1915, Archer M. Huntington House; 1915, Lucy Drexel House; 1916, Mrs. Robert Livingston House; New York. 1916–1917, Walter E. Maynard House, Brookville, N.Y. 1926–1927, Ogden Codman, Jr., House, Brie-Comte-Robert, France. 1929–1931, Ogden Codman, Jr., House, Villefranche-sur-Mer, France.

BIBLIOGRAPHY

Personal papers and early architectural drawings and records of Ogden Codman, Jr., are in the Codman Family Manuscripts Collection, Society for the Preservation of New England Antiquities, Boston. Business records and later architectural drawings and records are in the Department of Prints and Photographs, Metropolitan Museum of Art, New York. Other archival materials are in the Avery Architectural Library, Columbia University, New York, and the Boston Athenæum.

CHAPIN, R. CURTIS   1975   "Excavating an Italian Garden in America." *Horticulture* November:35–44.

CODMAN, FLORENCE   1970   *That Clever Young Boston Architect.* Augusta, Maine: The author.

CODMAN, OGDEN, JR.   1939   *La Leopolda: A Description.* Paris: The author.

DRAKE, STUART, A.   1973   "Ogden Codman, Jr.: 1863–1951." Unpublished M.A. thesis, Harvard University, Cambridge, Mass.

METCALF, PAULINE C.   1980   "Interiors of Ogden Codman, Jr." *Magazine Antiques* 118:486–497.

METCALF, PAULINE C.   1981   "Ogden Codman, Jr., Architect-Decorator: Elegance Without Excess." *Old-Time New England* 71. Forthcoming article.

WHARTON, EDITH, and CODMAN, OGDEN, Jr.   (1897)1978   *The Decoration of Houses.* Reprint. New York: Norton.

CODUCCI, MAURO

Mauro Coducci (c.1440–1504), the great pioneer of Venetian Renaissance architecture (often called Mauro Codussi), was born at Lenna (or Lentina) in the Valle Brembana north of Bergamo and died in Venice. In contemporary documents Coducci is called almost exclusively Magister Moro (or Moretto); apparently only in the last document of his life (1501), is he referred to as Mauro (or Maurus). His surname—if it be truly such—is never given in either of the modern forms, but only as a toponymic, usually in a version of the formula *lapicida de Cudussis, civis Bergomi* (mason from Codussi, in the Bergomasco). Since the documents record dictations in Venetian dialect, the double s is probably only a verbal idiosyncrasy, thus making Coducci the best Italian equivalent.

Coducci is one of the most important masters of the early Renaissance of the fifteenth century in northern Italy, but nothing is known of his youth or training. He retained consistent ties with his native Lombardy, as he returned almost every winter to his home near Bergamo, where his family included a brother and two sons who occasionally worked with him. He thus would certainly have been able to study the modern masterpiece of the Cappella Colleoni by GIOVANNI ANTONIO AMADEO, built at Bergamo Cathedral (1470–1473); but his own first work in Venice both precedes it in date and excels it in quality. The Camaldolese Monastery Church of San Michele in Isola (under his supervision 1469–1479), as Venice's first and most impressive monument of mainland Renaissance style is one of the epoch-making designs of Quattrocento architecture. The splendid façade, capped by a curving main pediment flanked by two lower half-curves over the aisles, derives its bold and influential profile from the unfinished *Tempio Malatestiano,* San Francesco, Rimini, by LEON BATTISTA ALBERTI, probably via a foundation medal of 1450 by Matteo de' Pasti. But San Michele's over-all incrustation with smooth, sharply outlined Istrian stone blocks first introduces on a church façade the treatments of Alberti's Palazzo Rucellai (with suggestions also of his pilasters on San Maria Novella) in Florence, and—especially for its uniformly rusticated pilasters— Palazzo Piccolomini at Pienza of 1458–1462 by BERNARDO ROSSELLINO. References to these up to date and sophisticated Tuscan parallels, however, have obscured the relationships demonstrated by Coducci with a regionally more potent proving ground of Albertian design, the great ducal palace at Urbino. This most important and most beautiful of all quattrocento monuments in eastern Italy was achieving its final form in a second campaign, directed by LUCIANO DA LAURANA, under the aesthetic guidance of Piero della Francesco (1465–1472). It is possible that both the young Coducci and Laurana may have been influenced by masters such as Luciano's Dalmatian compatriot, GIORGIO ORSINI DA SEBENICO. Since one of Laurana's principal collaborators and successors at Urbino was Ambrogio Barocci (da Milano), who is reliably named by an early source as executant of Coducci's façade portal of San Michele, it is fully possible that San Michele's revolutionary façade treatment may have influenced the subsequent palace façade at Urbino, for which Barocci has been suggested as supervisor. Certainly reciprocal influences were at work as well, for hallmarks of the "style of Urbino" appear in this first work of Coducci's, to persevere through his last: above all, a breadth of proportion and sureness of scale, with spare, simple surfaces articulated by refined but highly sculptural detail, in a combination at once powerfully architectonic and profoundly expressive of spatial purity, clarity, and poise. These qualities are most incisively evident in San Michele's chaste façade, in the luminous space encapsulated by the taut planes of its high nave and domed chancel, and in the robust energy of its delicate stonecarving, especially on the two transverse marble screens that support a raised choir across the second bay from the entrance.

In the three-year interval before Coducci's next documented work it seems likely that he undertook a remodeling of the Gothic fabric of Palazzo Zorzi at San Severo (c.1479–1482). The palace is interesting for its effort to regularize a haphazard pre-existing plan by imposing a structure of classical order on its exteriors; but these very restrictions limit its wider significance.

A far more ambitious work is Coducci's completion of the great ducal and Benedictine abbey church of San Zaccaria (1483–1491), immediately behind San Marco: its large new building had been begun in 1458 by Antonio Gambello, shortly after whose death in 1481 Coducci reworked the tall, narrow Gothic interior to culminate in a fascinating but somewhat incongruous series of Renaissance saucer domes and also totally redesigned the immense façade, which became his major work in the city center. Above Gambello's simple basement Coducci elaborated four further stories of gleaming stone columns, pilasters, arches, and windows, crowned with the same three curving pediments as at San Michele. The towering front of San Zaccaria is supported by four buttresslike tiers of superimposed double-columnar aediculae that mark the façade with visual correspondences of the outer walls and the sides of the main nave. The powerful projections of these structurally expressive verticals are tellingly balanced by four increasingly elaborate and dominant entablature bands that break forward over the aedicular buttresses in heavy projecting blocks, to emphasize the vertical and horizontal intersections of this organizing grid. The whole is so clearly and brilliantly elaborated in three-dimensional mass and sculptural detail as to provide a persuasive new model for the dramatic development in depth of Venice's formerly quite flat façade walls, and here once again Coducci's pioneering genius helped to inspire generations of successors in both local and distant centers.

Coducci's works of the early 1490s—his completion of the Scuola Grande di San Marco (1490–1495), his rebuilding of the parish church of Santa Maria Formosa (1490–1504), and his presumed construction of Palazzo Lando, called "Corner-Spinelli," on the Grand Canal (before 1493)—are interesting and appealing monuments, but they are less important than the three great masterpieces which the architect in each case developed from these middle-period prototypes, and which in turn

Coducci.
Scuola Grande di San
   Giovanni Evangelista
   (great staircase).
Venice, Italy.
1498–1504

Coducci.
Palazzo Loredan (also
   called Palazzo Non
   Nobis or Vendramin-
   Calergi).
Venice, Italy.
1502–1504 (not completed
   until 1509)

define the internationally significant late style that affords Coducci his distinctive position in the history of Renaissance architecture.

Despite the beauty of the Scuola di San Marco's celebrated façade, begun in 1487 by Pietro, Antonio, and Tullio Lombardo with Giovanni Buora and completed in its eastern and upper portions by Coducci after being hired in their place in 1490, his most influential work there was a great double-branch interior staircase, ascending between inner and outer walls from two landings at opposite extremities of the ground floor meeting hall, in twin flights on a single axis, to culminate pyramidally in a central landing giving onto the center of the upstairs hall. The rival Scuola Grande di San Giovanni Evangelista determined in 1495 to emulate this innovative and impressive model even more grandly, and—after acquiring the necessary land—commissioned Coducci (1498–1504) to outdo his own prototype in creating one of the finest gems of Renaissance architecture. Whereas the execution of the Scuola's scheme at San Marco had been complicated by severe spatial and proportional restrictions, its triumphant development at San Giovanni was uniquely favored by a lavish budget and by a fortuitous widening of the site toward the central landing, so that Coducci's symmetrically broadening flights, ascending from spectacularly decorated entrance landings with saucer domes, give the illusion of miraculously undiminishing breadth as one mounts the beautiful steps toward one of the most sublime yet simple spaces in European architecture. This is the breathtaking upper landing, where a square plan opens under a large, smooth dome through one great arch into the main salone, and through a corresponding one into a large arched window (a Coduccian "signature motif," prefigured in Palazzo Lando and reappearing at Palazzo Loredan), whose twin lights are crowned by semicircular traceries, supporting a smaller full circle inscribed between them and the surrounding arch.

Just before accomplishing this masterpiece of secular design, Coducci had developed one of the most harmonious achievements of early Renaissance ecclesiastical planning in his parish church of San Giovanni Crisostomo, again with a façade of three curved pediments (1497–1504). Its equally inspired simplicity culminates a long quattrocento development by returning to early Medieval and eastern Imperial examples for a central domed cube of space, opening through four arches into the equal barrel-vaulted arms of a regular Greek cross, with four smaller domed compartments in the corners (plus small apsidal and chapel projections). This scheme had to some extent been prefigured in San Maria Formosa, where, however, the apsidal chapels were deeper by a full minor bay, the transepts were extended by one more and the nave by two more large bays, and where there were further additions of deep nave and transeptal chapels. All these latter elements are eliminated at San Giovanni Crisostomo to achieve a centralized clarity of hierarchically ordered curvilinear vaults (unfortunately replaced by a flat ceiling in the chancel) and pure white surfaces sparely articulated with delicate stone moldings, which served to inspire some of the best productions of north Italian church architecture far into the future: a particularly close derivation in Venice is the fine parish church of San Felice of 1531–1535.

Coducci's unquestioned masterwork—which establishes his rank as a genius not only of the harmonious gracility of the early Renaissance but also of the more massive gravity and the more profound authority of high Renaissance architecture, and indeed in the field of monumental palace design makes him an equal talent beside DONATO BRAMANTE and RAPHAEL—is the magnificent Palazzo Loredan (1502–1504) called "Vendramin-Calergi" on the Grand Canal, firmly attributed to Coducci and probably completed by his sons. Early called the Palazzo *Non Nobis,* the building has been accurately understood since its completion, at any rate by Venetians, as adumbrating a wholly new image of scale and grandeur for urban palace design. A clear recognition of its international importance has been curiously slow to emerge—as for that matter has been the general reputation of Coducci—but a comparison of its balanced yet subtly centralized composition with a coeval paradigm such as Raphael's Palazzo Branconio dall'Aquila, or its brilliant precociousness vis-à-vis such a touchstone as Sangallo's (see SANGALLO FAMILY) and MICHELANGELO's Palazzo Farnese, will reveal its decisive influence on many of the determining masterworks of this elevated genre, from JACOPO TATTI SANSOVINO's Palazzo Corner della Ca' Grande through MICHELE SANMICHELI's Palazzo Grimani, to BALDASSARE LONGHENA's Palazzo Pesaro; and, beyond these great descendants in Venice itself, to a widening progeny throughout Italy and the world.

DOUGLAS LEWIS

WORKS

1469–1479, Church of San Michele in Isola; (A)c.1479–1482, Palazzo Zorzi at San Severo (remodeling); 1482–1490, San Pietro di Castello (bell tower); 1483–1491, Church of San Zaccaria (façade and completion of the interior); 1490–1495, Scuola Grande di San Marco (great staircase and completion of façade), Santi Giovanni e Paolo; 1490–1504, Church of Santa Maria Formosa (rebuilding); before 1493, Palazzo Lando (Corner-Spinelli) on the Grand Canal; 1497–1504, Church of San Giovanni Crisostomo (San Zuan Grisostomo) at Rialto; 1498–1504, Scuola Grande di San Giovanni Evangelista (great staircase); 1502–1504, Palazzo Loredan (not completed until 1509; also called Palazzo *Non Nobis* or Vendramin–Calergi) on the Grand Canal; Venice.

BIBLIOGRAPHY

LIEBERMAN, RALPH 1979 "Review of *Mauro Codussi* by Lionello Puppi and Loredana Olivato Puppi." *Journal of the Society of Architectural Historians* 38:387–390.

PAOLETTI, PIETRO 1893–1897 *L'architettura e la scultura del rinascimento in Venezia.* Venice: Ongania-Naya.

PUPPI, LIONELLO, and PUPPI, LOREDANA OLIVATO 1977 *Mauro Codussi.* Milan: Electa.

SOHM, PHILIP L. 1978 "The Staircases of the Venetian Scuole Grandi and Mauro Coducci." *Architectura* 8:125–149.

COIA, JACK

Jack Coia (1898–1981) was a Scottish architect much influenced by his native Italy but perhaps more so by the Glasgow architects of the turn of the century and by CHARLES RENNIE MACKINTOSH whose successor he largely became.

Born in Wolverhampton, Staffordshire, England, he was the eldest of nine children. His father, a sculptor, went to Glasgow shortly after Jack's birth and opened one of the first Italian cafés in that city. Jack worked in the shop but did not enjoy it. He tried engineering, first at Shettleston Bridge Works. In 1915, he became an apprentice to J. Gaff Gillespie, an eminent Glasgow architect of the day. He followed in the steps of the local Glasgow Salmond family of architects and studied with them the so-called Art Nouveau approach to architecture in Scotland. After a brief sojourn in London with Herbert A. Welch, he returned to Glasgow in 1927 and became a partner in the firm of Gillespie, Kidd, and Coia (Kidd had died earlier in the year).

Trained at the Glasgow School of Architecture, then largely under the influence of the Ecole des Beaux-Arts, he combined this training with his Italian background in such buildings as the Ca'doro in Union Street (1927) and with his Art Nouveau influence in a delightful small shop in Saint Vincent Street (1928).

His first real commission was for the Roman Catholic Church, with which he was associated all his life, namely Saint Anne's Church in the east end of Glasgow (1933). It was here that he first worked with artists in stone ceramics and in marble which he continued all his life.

Many other churches followed in Glasgow and surroundings until World War II when his Italian background forced him to stay at home.

The war over, he undertook a great many commissions for the church, some of utilitarian conception. The new town of East Kilbride claimed his help in housing at Freeland Lane (1952). He also undertook housing at Cumbernauld New Town (1960). He took part in the vast school building program of this time and produced a splendid school using a cantilevered concrete frame at King's Park (1956).

In 1956, his advanced ideas in church architecture appeared at Saint Paul's, Glenrothes, Fife (1956-1957). In this, he was ahead of the Second Vatican Council and the ideas of Pope John XXIII. Coia himself pursued this new approach of central grouping of the worshippers around the altar in his churches in Bo'ness, West Lothian (1962); Castlemilk, Glasgow (1961); East Kilbride, Lanark (1963-1964); Easterhouse, Glasgow (1965); Drumchapel, Glasgow (1965-1967); and Faifley, Clydebank, Dunbarton (1963).

Coia's contribution to the Scottish scene is very great. His work for the Roman Catholic Church alone (over thirty churches) would earn him a place in history but to this must be added his schools, the Hospital at Bellshill, Lanark, (1962), and the College at Cardross, Scotland (1966). The inspiration he gave to his young partners McMillan and Metzstein must also be noted.

ROBERT W. K. C. ROGERSON

WORKS

1927, Ca'doro, Union Street; *1928, Leon Shop, Saint Vincent Street; 1933, Saint Anne's, Dennistown; *1938, Chapel and Pavilion, Empire Exhibition; Glasgow, Scotland. 1952, Domino Flats, East Kilbride, Lanark, Scotland. 1956, Coia House (adaptation), Glasgow, Scotland. 1956-1957, Saint Paul's, Glenrothes, Fife, Scotland. 1960, Housing Cumbernauld, Dunbarton, Scotland. 1961, Saint Martin's, Castlemilk, Glasgow, Scotland. 1962, Hospital, Bellshill, Lanark, Scotland. 1962, Saint Mary's, Bo'ness, West Lothian, Scotland. 1963, Saint Joseph's, Faifley, Clydebank, Dunbarton, Scotland. 1963-1964, Saint Bride's, East Kilbride, Lanark, Scotland. 1965, Saint Benedict, Easterhouse; 1965-1967, Saint Benedict, Drumchapel; Glasgow, Scotland. 1966, College, Cardross, Scotland.

BIBLIOGRAPHY

"Architectural Design Project Award: Our Lady's Girls' High School, Cumbernauld." 1964 *Architectural Design* 35, June:279-280.
"Bookish Nook, Wadham College, Oxford." 1977 *Architects Journal* 167, Oct.:620-621.
BROADBENT, GEOFFREY 1967 "Corbusier Influence on the Scottish Hills." *Sunday Times,* Mar. 20.
"Cumbernauld Housing." 1959 *Architectural Prospect* Winter:15.
"Home for Old People, Dumbarton." 1964 *Architectural Review* 135:29.
"Jack Coia: Royal Gold Medalist." 1969 *Journal of the Royal Institute of British Architects* 76, July:281-282.
MCWILLIAM, COLIN 1969 "Jack Coia: Architect of Vision." *The Scotsman,* Jan. 4.
"Seminary, Cardross, near Glasgow." 1961 *Architectural Review* 129:19.
SHARP, DENNIS 1969 "A Craftsman's Architecture." *Country Life* 145, June:1590-1592.
THOMSON, NORMAN 1967 "Building a New Scotland." *Scottish Field* Sept.:46-49.
WEBB, MICHAEL 1967 "Scottish Homage to Le Corbusier." *Country Life* 42, July:212-214.
WILLIS, PETER 1977 *New Architecture in Scotland.* London: Lund Humphries.
WORSDALL, FRANCIS 1967 "The Achievement of Jack Coia." *Scotland's Magazine* Aug.:42-44.

COIT, ELISABETH

Elisabeth Coit (c.1892-) was born in Winchester, Massachusetts, and educated at Radcliffe College, the Massachusetts Institute of Technology, and the Sorbonne in Paris. Early in her career, she specialized in designing low-cost housing, first as an architect employed by GROSVENOR ATTERBURY and later in her own practice based in New York City. In 1942, she designed war housing for the United States Public Housing Authority, and in 1947, she joined the New York Housing Authority as principal project planner, a position she retained until 1962.

EUGENIE L. BIRCH

BIBLIOGRAPHY

TORRE, SUSANA (editor) 1977 *Women in American Architecture: A Historic and Contemporary Perspective.* New York: Whitney Library of Design.

COLE, HENRY

Henry Cole (1808-1882) was one of the able, energetic individuals with wide interests and many accomplishments who flourished in England in the nineteenth century. Born in Bath, England, in 1808, he was educated at Christ's Hospital and entered public service in 1823. Thereafter, he was never without a project or a cause: organizing public records, advocating the use of postage stamps or of uniform gauge railway tracks. In 1841, he began to publish inexpensive books for children illustrated by leading artists. In 1846, he published the first Christmas card. Beginning in 1843, as "Felix Summerly," Cole published illustrated handbooks to Hampton Court, Westminster Abbey, Canterbury Cathedral, and Temple Church, in which the architecture was closely observed and described. A series of railway charts (1846) contained annotated illustrations, often of architectural features on the route.

Cole's involvement with industrial design became evident in 1846, the year he joined the Society of Arts when he won a silver medal for a functional earthenware tea service at the Society's competition. His tea service, when produced, became very popular. This led to the brief life of Summerly's Art Manufactures (1847–1849) and the *Journal of Design* (1849–1852) which emphasized clarity of design and its fitness for use along the lines of A. W. N. PUGIN's pronouncements.

Cole served on the Executive Committee that planned and carried through the Great Exhibition of 1851 and he worked closely with Prince Albert, whose interest in industrial design he shared. As secretary of the government Department of Science and Art, Cole oversaw the establishment of the South Kensington (now the Victoria and Albert) Museum. He established architectural and decorative ateliers there, and he helped to revive the government schools of design. He and FRANCIS FOWKE planned the buildings for the Second International Exhibition of Industrial Arts (1862), but the exhibition was not financially successful, and a large brick building (1861–1862), intended for future exhibitions, was demolished in 1864. He concentrated, however, on building a hall for music in South Kensington, a project favored by Prince Albert, and eventually Albert Hall was erected (1867–1871).

Cole resigned his secretaryship in 1873 but kept busy. He founded the National Training School for Music (1876), the National Training School for Cookery (1874), studied the disposal and utilization of sewage in Birmingham and Manchester (1876–1879), and was laying plans for Guilds of Health when he died in London in 1882.

Henry Cole was knighted in 1875. He was widely acquainted with the leading figures of his day and he was known as an effective man of original ideas and action in the public interest. Prince Albert is said to have remarked: "When we want steam, we must get Cole" (Bradford, 1962, p. 15).

JOSEPH R. DUNLAP

BIBLIOGRAPHY
BINNEY, MARCUS   1971   "The Origins of the Albert Hall." *Country Life* 149:680–683.
BRADFORD, BETTY   1962   "The Brick Palace of 1862." *Architectural Review* 132:15–21.
BURY, SHIRLEY   1967   "Felix Summerly's Art Manufactures." *Apollo* 85:28–33.
COLE, HENRY   1884   *Fifty Years of Public Work.* 2 vols.
London: Bell.
"The Late Sir Henry Cole."   1882   *The Builder* 42:505–507, 562.
PEVSNER, NIKOLAUS   1968   Volume 2, pages 39–40, 72, 94, 95 in *Studies in Art, Architecture and Design.* London: Thames & Hudson.

COLEMAN, G. D.

George Drumgoole Coleman (1795–1844) was born in Ireland of a merchant family. Nothing is known of his architectural training but he was certainly fully conversant with the standards of Palladian and Georgian architecture before he left for Calcutta in 1815. After five years in Calcutta and two in Java, he arrived in 1822 at Singapore, founded only three years before by Sir Thomas Stamford Raffles, where Coleman was largely to spend the rest of his life. Coleman was fully involved, initially with Raffles, in the planning and construction of the city during the most crucial years of its early development.

PAULINE ROHATGI

WORKS
*1822–1823, Residency; *1822–1837, St. Andrew's Church; *1826, D. S. Napier House; 1826–1827, J. A. Maxwell House; 1827, Monument to Sir Thomas Stamford Raffles; 1828–1829, G. D. Coleman's Residence; 1833, Pauper Hospital; 1834–1835, Armenian Church of Saint Gregory; c.1836, Sir John Grant House; 1836–1841, Raffles Institution; c.1840–1841, H. C. Caldwell House; c.1843, North Boat Quay Warehouse; Singapore.

BIBLIOGRAPHY
HANCOCK, T. H. H.   1955   "Coleman of Singapore." *Architectural Review* 117:169–178.

COLLCUTT, T. E.

Thomas Edward Collcutt (1840–1924) was one of the many talented architects to emerge from the office of GEORGE E. STREET, where he overlapped with R. NORMAN SHAW as an assistant. In his work as designer and architect for Collinson and Lock, who pioneered the production of "art furniture" in the 1870s, he developed the Eastlake-Talbert tradition, which received international acclaim. In 1877, Collcutt won the Wakefield Town Hall competition with a design echoing Shaw's New Zealand Chambers. This commission represented a victory for the new Queen Anne style, of which Collcutt rapidly became a leading exponent. The Ludgate Hill City Bank is a characteristic amalgam of large gables, round arches, an asymmetrical angle turret and fenestration, tall chimneys, terra-cotta ornament, and contrasting stripes of brick and stone. As in his furniture, small-scale detail is confined within bold simple forms. His most prestigious building was the Imperial Institute, an imposing free Renaissance composition with eclectic detailing drawn from Spain and the châteaux of the Loire. Like other Queen Anne architects, he developed an "Old English" style for his country houses, incorporating local materials and vernacular traditions. Lloyd's Registry (c.1900) represented a successful move into Arts and Crafts baroque, but many of the designs produced thereafter in partnership with Stanley Hamp lacked his earlier vitality.

JULIET KINCHIN

WORKS

*1870, Marble Showrooms, Pimlico, London. 1872–1874, Blackburn Free Library and Museum, Lancashire, England. *1873–1874, Premises for Collinson and Lock, Fleet Street and Bridge Street; *1877, 36 Bloomsbury Square; London. 1877–1880, Wakefield Town Hall, Yorkshire, England. *1878, Collinson and Lock's House, Paris International Exhibition. *1887–1893, Imperial Institute (only the tower remains); 1888–1890, Royal English Opera House, Cambridge Circus; London. *1890s, Reina Christina Hotel, Algeçiras, Spain. *1890, Grand Hotel, Saint Heliers, Jersey, England. 1890–1900, Bechstein Concert Hall and Showrooms, Wigmore Street; 1891, Ludgate Hill City Bank; London. 1892, Rivernook, Wraybury, Buckinghamshire, England. 1893, Hotel Burlington, Bournemouth, Hampshire, England. *1893, P & O Company Offices, Leadenhall Street; *1894, Holborn Restaurant; London. 1895, Coldharbour, Liphook, Hampshire, England. 1895–1897, The Croft, Totteridge, Hertfordshire, England. *1896–1908, P & O Steamship (interiors). 1899–1906, Walpole House, Waynefield House, Westbury House, and Woton House, Eton College, Buckinghamshire, England. 1900, P & O Company Pavilion, Paris International Exhibition. 1900–1902, Lloyd's Registry, Fenchurch Street; 1903–1904, Savoy Court, The Strand; 1907, Winterstoke Library and Murray Scriptorium, Mill Hill School; London.

BIBLIOGRAPHY

GIROUARD, MARK 1977 *Sweetness and Light—The 'Queen Anne' Movement 1860–1900.* Oxford: Clarendon.

KINCHIN, JULIET 1979 "Collinson & Lock—Manufacturers of Artistic Furniture." *Connoisseur* 201, May:46–53.

COLLECINI, FRANCESCO

Francesco Collecini (18th–19th centuries) was an architect of mild talent, whose chief work was the utopian village of San Leucio near Naples, Italy. At the command of King Ferdinand IV, Collecini turned the dour hamlet into an idyllic setting for a remarkable royal experiment. Here, escaping from the pressures and intrigues of the court, the king could take pleasure in a prospering cottage industry he himself had ordained and could go hunting in the rugged hills, his favorite sport.

San Leucio lay at the edge of the park of the enormous new palace at Caserta, where Collecini as an apprentice architect had been trained in the language of grandiose perspectives formed with icy precision. At San Leucio, he cleverly retained a trace of this, muted to suit a village; at the same time, he adapted and added to the very modest dwellings and barns of the peasants, creating a quiet counterpoint. This fitted perfectly the ideas of the king, who in 1773 had established by fiat a minuscule community of silk workers, spinners, and weavers, whose handsome products were absorbed by the court. The artisans, whom the king addressed as "you, artists," were the erstwhile local peasant farmers; they still alternated tillage with manufacture. Watched over by a superintendent and the parish priest, they elected community leaders in secret balloting and were encouraged to improve their earnings through skill and industry. Their egalitarian clothing and housing were regulated by the royal code which also provided medical care and pensions. Collecini showed admirable restraint in remodeling the row housing strung in an arc facing the main hall where church, school, and council were accommodated along with the royal apartments, often in use. After more than twenty years, the century ended in the clash of Bourbons and Bonapartes, and the king had to flee to Sicily.

When he returned, San Leucio served him mainly for hunting. Meanwhile, in 1805, Collecini built a separate village church in the simplest Gothic forms in contrast to the watered-down classicism of the earlier work. The plan of San Leucio included enlargements that would have effected overall bilateral symmetry, but as these were never built the town kept a picturesque air on its sloping site. It remains a testimony to the charm of an unambitious and incomplete architecture. Many theorists have compared San Leucio architecturally and economically to other utopian communities established in the Western world between 1750 and 1850. The parallels do not hold; there is too pervasive an element of paternalism in the code that governed San Leucio. It was not a co-operative but the dream of an autocrat, and that dream was deftly embodied by Francesco Collecini.

EDGAR KAUFMANN, JR.

BIBLIOGRAPHY

ACTON, HAROLD (1956)1957   *The Bourbons in Naples.*
Rev. ed. London: Methuen.

FUSCO, RENATO DE 1980   *L'architettura dell'ottocento*
(*Storia dell'arte in Italia*). Turin, Italy: Utet.

COLLENS, CHARLES

See ALLEN and COLLENS.

COLLING, JAMES KELLAWAY

Supposed ill health and unusual skill as a drafts-man determined the career of James Kellaway Col-ling (1816–1905), whose fine, though remotely located buildings were less influential than his books. Born in the same decade as A. W. N. PUGIN and JOHN RUSKIN, he emerged in the 1850s as the Gothic Revival secularized. As the moral fervor of the previous decade ebbed, Colling favored a new scientific approach to the visual forms of England's medieval heritage from which he sought inspiration. Relying heavily on geome-try, botanical categorization, and systematic ab-straction from nature, he adapted Gothic foliage to secular use, publishing his theories in five books of drawings, the most important of which was *Art Foliage* (1865).

Son of the clerk of the works at Covent Garden and Hungerford Market, Colling trained initially as an engineer. Opting for architecture, he joined Matthew Habershon in 1832 and then John Brown of Norwich from 1836 to 1840. His draft-ing skill was already considerable when in 1841–1842, while with GEORGE GILBERT SCOTT and W. B. Moffatt, he continued study and sketching of medieval architecture. Serving also as a delinea-tor for other architects, he published in the *Illus-trated London News* between 1849 and 1855. His first book, *Gothic Ornaments* (1848–1850), con-sisted of magnificent chromolithographic plates from his measured drawings.

Colling was a founder first of the Association of Architectural Draughtsmen (1842), and with Robert Kerr of the subsequent Architectural Asso-ciation (1847), for which he delivered the first lec-ture. With George Gilbert Scott, he established the Architectural Museum (1851), an outgrowth of Cottingham's Museum from which he had drawn and published many objects. He was also important as a drawing teacher in the early 1850s, WILLIAM E. NESFIELD (who with R. NORMAN SHAW had joined the Architectural Association) and JOHN HUBBARD STURGIS of Boston (later his

Colling.
Albany Block.
Liverpool, England.
1856

assistant and associate) being his best known stu-dents. He was, by 1856, a member of the Royal Institute of British Architects and a fellow by 1860. His collaboration on the Museum of Fine Arts, Boston (1870–1876), and publication there of his books brought honorary membership in the American Institute of Architects in the 1870s with a contemporaneous transatlantic following. His most significant commissions were The Albany Block (1856), and Saint Paul's Hooten (1858), both for Richard Naylor, a Liverpool industrialist. These are powerful, individualized extensions of Ruskinian theory, combining classical and Gothic motifs while exploiting violent, intense contrast of ornament and ground.

The crisp and simplified style of Colling's drawings had both a theoretical and a visual im-pact on nineteenth-century architecture. From his detailed study of medieval models in the 1840s evolved a system for design of natural foliage from two-dimensional stencilling to three-dimensional carving. His continual focus on placement of orna-ment in context accordingly varied its style be-tween naturalistic and conventionalized form. Colling's *Art Foliage* by 1865 thus replaced his Gothic measured drawings in *The Grammar of Ornament* (1856) as the textbook for architectural sculpture of the 1870s.

MARGARET HENDERSON FLOYD

WORKS

1839–1840, Saint Margaret's, Lee, Kent, England. 1848, Hooten Hall (remodeling); 1853, Hooten Hall Con-servatory; Cheshire, England. 1853, Saint Pancras Alms-houses, Kentish Town, London. 1856, Albany Block, Liverpool, England. 1856–1857, Ashewicke Hall, Marshfield, Gloucestershire, England. 1858, Saint Paul's, Hooten, Cheshire, England. 1859, Nantclwyd Hall (remodeling), Denbighshire, Wales. 1859, Hooten

Hall Picture Gallery, Cheshire, England. 1859, West Walton Church (south porch and tower), Norfolk, England. 1860, New School, Haslinston, near Crewe, Cheshire, England. 1860, Rangemoor Hall (additions), Staffordshire, England. 1861, Cuxwold Hall, Lincolnshire, England. 1861, New Schools, Marshfield, Gloucestershire, England. 1870, Saint Withaburger (restoration), Holkham, Norfolk, England. 1871, Kelmarsh Hall Dining Room, Northamptonshire, England. 1872, Saint Andrew (remodeling), Arthingworth, Northamptonshire, England. 1874, Saint Andrew Scole, Norfolk, England. 1874, Saint Dionysis, Kelmarsh, Northamptonshire, England. 1874–1878, Melbury Church (remodeling), Dorset, England. 1875, Popham Church, Hamptonshire; 1881–1883, Saint Peter's (pulpit and lecturn), Vere Street; London. 1882, Saint Nicolas, Oakley, Norfolk, England. 1891–1894, National Portrait Gallery (remodeling; with Ewan Christian), London. 1898, Cark Hall, Lancashire (?), England. n.d., Chapel of the Mercer's Company, London. n.d., Eye Church (remodeling); n.d., Farnham Hall; n.d., Grammar School, Eye; Suffolk, England. n.d., Saint Andrew's (remodeling), Hingham, Norfolk, England. n.d., New House, Caterham, Kent, England. n.d., New Schools, Coppenhall, Cheshire, England.

BIBLIOGRAPHY

James Kellaway Colling's notebooks are in the Drawings Collection, Royal Institute of British Architects, London. Twelve letters from Collins to John Hubbard Sturgis between 1867 and 1871 are in the Sturgis Papers, Boston Athenaeum.

COLLING, JAMES KELLAWAY 1846–1850 *Gothic Ornaments.* 2 vols. London: Jobbins.

COLLING, JAMES KELLAWAY 1856 *Details of Gothic Architecture from Existing Examples.* 2 vols. London.

COLLING, JAMES KELLAWAY 1859 "On the Application of Natural Foliage to Architecture." *Civil Engineer and Architect's Journal* 22:8–39. Paper delivered at the Liverpool Architectural Society.

COLLING, JAMES KELLAWAY 1865 *Art Foliage.* London: Batsford.

COLLING, JAMES KELLAWAY 1874 *Examples of English Medieval Foliage and Coloured Decoration.* London: Batsford.

COLLING, JAMES KELLAWAY 1879 "Architectural Foliage." *Transactions of the Royal Institute of British Architects* 24, Mar.:137–152.

COLLING, JAMES KELLAWAY 1881 Introduction and text in John Leighton, *Suggestions in Design.* London: Blackie.

FLOYD, MARGARET HENDERSON 1973 "A Terra Cotte Cornerstone for Copley Square: Museum of Fine Arts, Boston 1870–1876 by Sturgis and Brigham." *Journal of the Society of Architectural Historians* 32:83–103.

FLOYD, MARGARET HENDERSON n.d. "John Hubbard Sturgis of Boston and the English Architectural Image." Unpublished manuscript.

FRANKLIN, JILL 1981 *The Gentleman's Country House and Its Plan: 1835–1914.* London: Routledge.

HUGHES, QUENTIN 1964 *Seaport: Architecture and Townscape in Liverpool.* London: Lund Humphries.

JONES, OWEN 1856 Pages 100–103 in *The Grammar of Ornament.* London: Quaritch.

SAINT, ANDREW 1976 Pages 3 and 440 in *Richard Norman Shaw.* London: Yale University Press.

SMITH, J. OSBORNE 1902 "Testimonial to Mr. J. K. Colling: Presentation to the Library of His Sketches and Drawings." *Journal of the Royal Institute of British Architects* Feb.:187–189.

SUMMERSON, JOHN 1947 *The Architectural Association: 1847–1947.* London.

TURAK, THEODORE 1974 "French and English Sources of Sullivan's Ornament and Doctrine." *Prairie School Review* 11, no. 4:5–28.

COLONIA FAMILY

The Colonia Family was a dynasty of late Gothic architects founded by Hans (Juan) de Colonia (1410?–1481) who arrived in Burgos, Spain, around 1440, probably from the lower Rhineland where he may have been recruited by Alonso de Cartegena, bishop of Burgos, who had attended the Council of Basel. From 1442 to 1458, he built the open-work western spires of the cathedral after a German model, perhaps Esslingen. He built the Carthusian Monastery of Miraflores (1452–1488) and, assisted by his son, Simon (1440?–1511), the crossing lantern of Burgos Cathedral (1465–1478), which collapsed in 1539. Simon built, probably from his father's designs, the Church at Miraflores (1478–1488). From his own designs, he built the Constable's Chapel at Burgos Cathedral (1482–1494?). The open tracery at the apex of the ribbed dome, which may reflect that of the lost crossing tower, may be of Islamic inspiration. The enormous escutcheons and the rich pendant tracery of the wall arches, which may have been executed by Gilde Siloe, greatly contributed to the Isabelline style also characteristic of the Toledan works of JUAN GUAS. Around 1495, he contracted with Alonso de Burgos, bishop of Palencia, for the west portal, two interior doors, a retable (lost), and a tomb (lost) at the Dominican Church of San Pablo in Valladolid, all finished by 1505. The complex organization of the multiple ogee arches of the lower portion of this façade, more complex than that of the Constable's Chapel, carried the Burgos school's contribution to the Isabelline style into its final stage and provided the inspiration for JUAN GIL DE HONTAÑON's design of the west front of the new Cathedral of Salamanca begun in 1512. In 1497–1502, Simon built the crossing lantern of the Cathedral of Sevilla, which collapsed in 1511, and shortly before 1499 he may have provided Bishop Alonso de Burgos with designs for the sumptuous and complex choir enclosure for Palencia Cathedral. Work continued on this project until 1519, probably under the direction of Simon's son, Francisco, who was master of works there from 1513 until dismissed for incompetence in 1518. The west portal of Santa Maria in Aranda de Duero may have been designed as early as 1506 when Alonso Enriquez, whose arms it bears, became bishop of Burgo de Osma. If so, it is attributable to Simon and may also have been completed by his son. Francisco (1480?–1542) was primarily an engineer and a builder of other men's designs. However, he broke from the late medieval family tradition with the Puerta de la Pellejeria of Burgos Cathedral (1516–1530), which reflects the earliest introduction of Renaissance forms into Spain from fifteenth-century Milan.

JOHN DOUGLAS HOAG

WORKS

1442–1458, Burgos Cathedral (western spires); 1452–1488, Monastery of Miraflores; 1465–1478?, Burgos Cathedral (lantern; now lost); 1482–1494?, Constable's Chapel, Burgos Cathedral; Burgos, Spain. 1495?–1505, San Pablo (façade), Valladolid, Spain. 1497–1502, Cathedral of Seville (lantern; now lost), Spain. c.1499–1519, Cathedral of Palencia (choir enclosure), Spain. Begun 1506?, Santa Maria (façade), Aranda de Duero, Spain. 1516–1530, Burgos Cathedral (Puerta de la Pellejeria), Spain.

BIBLIOGRAPHY

CHUECA GOITIA, FERNANDO 1953 *Arquitectura del Siglo XVI.* Madrid: Plus-Ultra.
CHUECA GOITIA, FERNANDO 1965 *Historia de la Arquitectura Española, Edad Antigua y Edad Media.* Madrid: Dossat.
LAMPEREZ Y ROMEA, V. 1904 *Juan de Colonia.* Valladolid, Spain.
LOPEX MATA, TEOFILO (1950)1966 *Le Catedral de Burgos.* 2d ed. Burgos, Spain: Hijos de Santiago Rodriguez.
TORRES BALBAS, LEOPOLDO 1952 *Arte y Arquitectura Gotica.* Madrid: Plus-Ultra.

COLONNA, EDWARD

Edward Colonna (1862–1948), who changed his name from Klönne, was born in Mülheim-am-Rhein, Germany. After reputedly studying architecture in Brussels, he emigrated to the United States in 1882. He worked with LOUIS C. TIFFANY and Associated Artists in New York City before moving to Dayton, Ohio. There, he decorated railroad car interiors and published small design books of an original character. Beginning in 1888, he worked in Montreal for William Van Horne and the Canadian Pacific Railroad. From 1898 to 1903, he was one of the principal designers for S. Bing's Parisian store, *L'Art Nouveau,* and gained an international reputation for his elegant furniture and *objets d'art* in the Art Nouveau style. After 1903, he pursued various careers as painter, interior decorator, and antique dealer, then retired to the Riviera.

MARTIN P. EIDELBERG

BIBLIOGRAPHY

COLONNA, EDWARD 1887 *Essay on Broom-Corn.* Dayton, Ohio.
COLONNA, EDWARD 1888 *Materiae Signa.* n.p.
EIDELBERG, MARTIN 1971 "Edward Colonna's 'Essay on Broom-Corn.'" *The Connoisseur* 176:123–130.
EIDELBERG, MARTIN 1981 "The Life and Work of E. Colonna." *Decorative Arts Society Newsletter* 7, no. 1:1–7; no. 2:1–10; no. 3:1–8.

COLONNA, FRANCESCO

Francesco Colonna (1433–1527) was an Italian Dominican friar and the author of the *Hypnerotomachia Poliphilii* (1499), a strange allegorical romance rich in architectural imagery. The complex story line serves as a framework for a series of highly imaginative fantasies about the ancient world; in particular, Colonna recreates the classical monuments with elaborate descriptions and illustrates them with woodcuts. Colonna's approach to the ancient world is quite unlike that of LEON BATTISTA ALBERTI or FILIPPO BRUNELLESCHI in the early Renaissance. Whereas the latter were spare and archeologically precise, Colonna was flighty and imaginative. Motifs from The *Hypnerotomachia Poliphilii* were used in architectural sculpture by FRANCESCO DI GIORGIO MARTINI and Giuliano da Sangallo (see SANGALLO FAMILY) and by painters such as Filippino Lippi. The *Hypnerotomachia Poliphilii* was published in Venice by Aldo Manuzio and is recognized as a masterpiece of the typographical art. An English edition appeared in 1592.

NICHOLAS ADAMS

BIBLIOGRAPHY

BLUNT, ANTHONY (1940)1962 *Artistic Theory in Italy 1400–1600.* New York: Oxford.
COLONNA, FRANCESCO (1499)1976 *Hypnerotomachia: The Strife of Love in a Dream.* Reprint. New York: Garland.

COLTER, MARY

Mary E. J. Colter (1869–1958) moved with her family from Pittsburgh to Saint Paul, Minnesota, as a child and immediately became interested in Indian artifacts. When her father, a city sewer inspector, died, she was seventeen; she went to San Francisco to study for a teaching career in art. There, Colter apprenticed in an architectural office, then taught mechanical drawing in Saint Paul until hired by the Fred Harvey Company and the Santa Fe Railway as architect and decorator, practicing in the southwest until her retirement in 1947. She designed simple indigenous buildings rooted in Indian and Spanish traditions, and stimulated national interest in native American arts and crafts.

SARA HOLMES BOUTELLE

WORKS

1905, Hopi House; 1914, Hermit's Rest; 1914, Lookout; 1922, Phantom Ranch; Grand Canyon. *1930, La Posada Hotel, Winslow, Ariz. 1932, Watchtower; 1935, Bright Angel Lodge; 1936, Men's Dormitory; Grand Canyon. 1937, Westport Room, Union Station, Kansas City. 1937, Women's Dormitory, Grand Canyon.

BIBLIOGRAPHY

COLTER, MARY E. J (1909)1977 Manual for Drivers and Guides Descriptive of the Indian Watchtower at Desert View and Its Relations Architecturally to the Prehistoric Ruins of the Southwest Grand Canyon. Chicago: Harvey.
GEBHARD, DAVID 1963–1964 "Architecture and the Fred Harvey Houses." New Mexican Architect 1962, July–Aug.:11–17; 1964, Jan.–Feb.:18–25.
GRATTON, VIRGINIA L. 1980 Mary Colter: Builder upon the Red Earth. Flagstaff, Ariz.: Northland Press.
National Park Service Rustic Architecture: 1916–1942. 1977 San Francisco: National Park Service.
"La Posada and Harveycars, Winslow." 1932 Hotel Monthly Mar.:24–29.

COLVIN, BRENDA

Brenda Colvin (1897–1981) was a founder member of the Institute of Landscape Architects in Britain and is best known for her pioneering work and advocacy for modern landscape design. As a vanguard of the first generation of English landscape architects, Colvin was educated in horticulture and began a practice of private garden design before landscape architecture was established as a discipline. Her practice later expanded into large-scale public projects involving, for example, the siting and landscaping of power stations for the Central Electricity Generating Board. Colvin prepared a major scheme of land reclamation at Gale Common, Eggborough, Yorkshire, to transform swampy land into an undulating agricultural landscape by recycling industrial wastes from nearby

power stations and coal mines. This project is exemplary of her philosophy that landscape architecture is involved in "long-term issues rather than short-term policy." One of her books, Land and Landscape, is particularly significant in explaining the roles of landscape design for a modern industrial society. First published in 1947, the book has become a standard reference because it addresses landscape design within the issues of ecological balance and long-term planning, technical ability, industrial and town planning, aesthetics, and recreation. Through her varied life of practice, writing, and active advocacy, Colvin established landscape architecture as a rigorous and essential discipline.

RICHARD LORCH

WORKS

1935, West Stowell House, near Marlborough, Wiltshire, England. 1937, Château Zywiec, Poland. 1948, Sutton Courtenay Manor Gardens; 1953, Compton Beauchamp Estate; Oxfordshire, England. 1956, Salisbury Crematorium, Wiltshire, England. 1958, Shotton Steelworks, Cheshire, England. 1959, Drakelow Power Station, Burton-on-Trent, Staffordshire, England. 1961, Eggborough Power Station, Yorkshire, England. 1962, Rugeley Power Station, Staffordshire, England.

BIBLIOGRAPHY

COLVIN, BRENDA (1948)1970 Land and Landscape: Evolution, Design and Control. 2d ed. London: Murray.
COLVIN, BRENDA 1961 "Planting as a Medium of Design." Journal of the Institute of Landscape Architects 77, Aug.
COLVIN, BRENDA 1968a "Landscape Maintenance of Large Industrial Sites." Journal of the Institute of Landscape Architects 84, Aug.
COLVIN, BRENDA 1968b "Gale Common, Eggborough, Yorkshire." Journal of the Institute of Landscape Architects 84, Aug.
COLVIN, BRENDA 1979 "Beginnings." Landscape Design 125, Feb.:8–9.
COLVIN, BRENDA, and GIBBERD, F. 1974a "Power Station, Didcot, Berkshire." Architectural Review 156, Aug.:72–73.
COLVIN, BRENDA, and GIBBERD, F. 1974b "Potash Mine, Boulby, Yorkshire." Architectural Review 156, Aug.:92–100.
COLVIN, BRENDA, and TYRWHITT, JACQUELINE (1947)1961 Trees for Town and Country. 3d ed., rev. London: Lund Humphries.

COMBES, LOUIS

A principal figure of the neoclassicism in Bordeaux, France, Louis Combes (1762–1816) was a district engineer of civil buildings, publicist, theoretician, and pedagogue. He imposed the new style on the public buildings of Bordeaux—the Myer Mansion with a terrace on a peristyle (1795–1797); the Château of Margaux (1810–1812)—and in the restoration of the Cathedral of Saint-André. Other works are the Temple of Liberty (1791) and the European Federapolis (1814), both in Bordeaux.

FRANÇOIS-GEORGES PARISET
*Translated from French by
Shara Wasserman*

BIBLIOGRAPHY

PARISET, FRANÇOIS-GEORGES 1964b "Les théories artistiques d'un architecte du néo-classicisme Louis Combes de Bordeaux." *Annales du Midi* 76:543–554.

PARISET, FRANÇOIS-GEORGES 1964a "L'architecture néo-classique de Bordeaux: L'architecte Combes. *Congrès international d'Histoire de l'art* 3:129ff.

PARISET, FRANÇOIS-GEORGES 1966 "Architekt z Bordeaux Louis Combes." *Biuletyn Historii Sztucki* 28:134–136.

PARISET, FRANÇOIS-GEORGES 1968 Volume 5 in *Histoire de Bordeaux.* Bordeaux, France.

PARISET, FRANÇOIS-GEORGES 1973 "Louis Combes." *Revue Historique de Bordeaux* 22:5–43.

PARISET, FRANÇOIS-GEORGES 1974 *Exposition des dessins de L. Combes.* Bordeaux, France: Bibliothèque Municipale. Exhibition catalogue.

PARISET, FRANÇOIS-GEORGES 1979 "Château de Rastignac." *Actes Congrès Sté Frse d'Archéologie.* Périgord, France: Sarladais.

COMEY, ARTHUR COLEMAN

Arthur Coleman Comey (1886–1954), a pioneer in the American development of professional city and regional planning, commenced in the politically optimistic era of Progressivism, the early decades of the twentieth century. Broadened in focus from the design of mass housing to zoning and to issues of large-scale regional planning, his ideas were overshadowed by parallel developments in planning with more direct European influences.

A graduate of the Harvard School of Architecture in 1907 at the age of twenty-one, Comey was trained as a landscape architect. He opened an independent practice as a consultant in city planning in Cambridge, Massachusetts, in 1911, and two years later, he won second prize in the Chicago City Club competition for the development of a quarter-section within the Chicago city limits. In the same year, as an appointee to the Massachusetts Homestead Commission, Comey designed the first state-sponsored, preplanned housing community in the United States, Billerica Garden Suburb, twenty-one miles from Boston. His plans relied on English Garden City models combined with single-family homes and the concept of "co-partner-

ship," a system of conveying ownership to working class home dwellers. The project, however, was never fully realized. Later in his career, Comey prepared dozens of town plans and zoning ordinances from Boston, Massachusetts, to Tupelo, Mississippi.

Comey was a founding member of the first professional school of city and regional planning at Harvard's Graduate School of Design in 1937. His contribution to American mass housing efforts, zoning, and regional planning has never been properly assessed. His early optimism must have grown dim both professionally and personally, his life ending in suicide.

ANTHONY ALOFSIN

COMPER, JOHN NINIAN

John Ninian Comper (1864–1960) was born in Aberdeen, Scotland, and was educated at Trinity College, Glenalmond. In 1882, he drew for a term at the Ruskin School, Oxford, later working in London as an assistant to the glass-painter and church craftsman C. E. Kempe, at the same time drawing at the South Kensington School of Art. In 1883, he was articled to GEORGE F. BODLEY.

Throughout his life, Comper recognized his debt to Bodley and his partner, THOMAS GARNER. He claimed that it was to Bodley and Garner's unfinished Saint Michael's, Camden Town (1876–1881), that he owed his conversion to architecture. Contemporaries in the office included C. R. ASHBEE.

In 1888, Comper entered into partnership with William Bucknall, establishing a practice that lasted until 1905. The partnership was unequal, for Bucknall lacked Comper's distinctive gifts; but he was a good draftsman, and his structural skills enabled Comper's designs to be executed. From 1905, Comper was assisted by his nephew, Arthur Bucknall, later by his son, Sebastian Comper, and finally by his great-nephew, John Bucknall.

Since childhood, religion had played a decisive part in Comper's life. He was a fervent Anglo-Catholic, and the religious impulse behind his work was always evident. In creating beauty he sought the glory of God; yet he was not merely an aesthete. He was more concerned with the functional purpose of a church than with its aesthetic appearance. "Comper," wrote his obituarist in *The Times,* "designed from the altar outwards; and to the altar every proportion and detail, every reflection of light, every embellishment were subservient."

His work falls into two periods. From 1888 to

1904, Comper worked in a developed, late medieval style, fusing English Perpendicular with Flemish Gothic. His first major work was the Chapel of the Community of Saint Margaret, Aberdeen (1891), a sensitive exercise in Scottish Gothic. In 1893, he began a sequence of scholarly restorations of medieval churches, beginning with Saint Wilfrid's, Cantley, Yorkshire, in which he successfully recreated interiors, glowing with exquisitely modulated color and silver light, modeled upon medieval illuminations and fifteenth-century Flemish panel paintings. His most successful restoration was executed for the seventh duke of Newcastle at Egmanton, in Nottinghamshire, in 1897. Saint Cyprian's, Clarence Gate, Saint Marylebone (1903) marks the culmination of his first period. Here, he created a fully developed expression of a late medieval parish church. "Its design," he wrote, "neither seeks, nor avoids, originality: still less is its aim to reproduce any period of the past, but only to fulfil these and other needs which are ours today, and to do so in the most beautiful manner of all." No architect since A. W. N. PUGIN possessed such an unswerving loyalty to medieval ideals and principles.

But Comper came to differ from Pugin. In 1904, after an extended visit to Italy and the Mediterranean, he began to develop a personal interpretation of architectural comprehensiveness. Through travel and study of buildings on the Continent, he gradually came to believe that the highest expression of beauty can be achieved only through inclusion, not exclusion. His work came to synthesize many decorative and architectural traditions: classic and Gothic, Byzantine, Moorish, and Arabic; but pre-eminently, it was the Sicilian amalgam of Romanesque, Greek, and Saracenic

that led to the evolution of his second period which he described as "unity by inclusion." It is in Saint Mary's, Wellingborough, Northamptonshire (1904–1932) that he fully worked out his synthesis. The exterior is deceptively Perpendicular, but inside it has an unbroken fan vault, octagonal pillars with the entasis and flutes from the Parthenon, an Italianate ciborium decorated in burnished gold and color, and screens combining Greek, Italian, Spanish, and English detail; from the vault is suspended an overscaled Byzantine majestas, executed in shallow relief; the disposition of the aisles is French. "Only to its contemporaries," he declared, "does the church owe nothing."

Comper designed his churches as unities and expected to design every detail, every vestment, every painted window, even the fringes on the purificators and the altar linen. In such unswerving consistency lay much of his success. He had many strong dislikes. Although he adopted modern methods of construction, using steel and concrete skillfully in Saint Andrew and Saint George, Rosyth (1919–1924) and Saint Philip's, Cosham, Portsmouth (1937), he was altogether opposed to modernism in church art. He loathed the modern theory of self-expression and the deliberate aim to express the spirit of the age. Comper was the last fully convinced historicist, untroubled by doubt. He had an extensive practice and produced a body of work which is almost impossible to record. No architect has provided such a strong and all-pervasive back-cloth to early twentieth-century Anglicanism, nor so neatly rounded off the achievements of the Gothic Revival, nor provided such a convincing solution to the battle of the styles. Yet, his many imitators (including his pupils) were unable to achieve the effortless conviction and ethereal beauty of his work. He was knighted in 1950 and died ten years later, still in practice, at the advanced age of ninety-six, his style dying with him. His ashes are buried in the north aisle of Westminster Abbey, below a series of painted windows designed by him.

ANTHONY SYMONDSON

Comper.
Saint Mary.
Rochedale, Lancashire,
England.
1909–1911

WORKS

1888–1890, Saint Margaret's (extensions); 1891, Chapel (for the Community of Saint Margaret); Aberdeen; Scotland. 1893–1903, Saint Wilfrid's (restoration), Cantley, Yorkshire, England. 1896, Workhouse Chapel, Oundle, Northampshire, England. 1897, Saint Mary's (restoration), Egmanton, Nottinghampshire, England. 1898, Saint Peter Mancroft (restoration), Norwich, Norfolk, England. 1898–1905, Saint Braemar, Aberdeenshire, Scotland. 1903, Saint Cyprian (Clarence Gate), Saint Marylebone, London. 1904, Saint John's Home Chapel, Cowley, Oxford. 1904–1905, Saint Crispin, Yerendawna, India. 1904–1932, Saint Mary

Wellingborough, Northamptonshire, England. 1907, All Saint's Church (restoration), Margaret Street, London. 1908, Saint Margaret's (Founder's Aisle), Aberdeen, Scotland. 1909–1901, Westminster Abbey (windows of abbots and kings; not completed until 1961), London. 1909–1911, Saint Mary, Rochedale, Lancashire, England. 1909–1911, Wimbourne Saint Giles (restoration), Dorset, England. 1911, Oriel College (hall restoration), Oxford University. 1912, Saint Gilbert and Saint Hugh, Gosberton Clough, Lincolnshire, England. 1913–1934, Wymondham Abbey (altar screen), Norfolk, England. 1914, Saint John the Baptist (restoration), Lound, Suffolk, England. 1917, Stanton Chantry, Saint Alban, Holborn, London. 1919–1924, Saint Andrew and Saint George, Rosyth, Fife, Scotland. 1928, Welsh National Memorial, Cardiff. 1930, Church, Rothiemurcas, Inverness, Scotland. 1930, House of Prayer Chapel, Burnham Beeches, Buckinghamshire, England. 1931, Westminster Abbey (Warrior's Chapel), London. 1936–1943, Cathedral Church of Saint Andrew (chancel), Aberdeen, Scotland. 1937, Saint Philip's, Cosham, Portsmouth, England. 1952, Westminster Hall (Parliamentary War Memorial window), London. 1959, Shrine of Our Lady of Walsingham (altar and reredos; with William Bucknall), Norfolk, England.

BIBLIOGRAPHY

ANSON, PETER F. (1937)1960 "The Work of John Ninian Comper: A Pioneer Architect of the Modern Liturgical Revival." In *Fashions in Church Furnishings*. London: Faith Press.

BETJEMAN, JOHN 1939 "A Note on J. N. Comper: Heir to Butterfield and Bodley." *Architectural Review* 85:79–82.

COMPER, J. N. 1893 *Practical Considerations of the Gothic of English Altar and Certain Dependent Ornaments*. Aberdeen, Scotland: Albany Press.

COMPER, J. N. 1897 *The Reasonableness of the Ornaments Rubric Illustrated by a Comparison of the German and English Altars*. London: Harrison.

COMPER, J. N. 1933 *Further Thoughts on the English Altar, or Practical Considerations on the Planning of a Modern Church*. Cambridge: Heffer.

COMPER, J. N. 1940 *The Atmosphere of a Church*. London: Shelon Press.

COMPER, J. N. 1950 *Of the Christian Altar and the Buildings Which Contain It*. London: Society for Promoting Christian Knowledge.

FENWICK, HUBERT 1964 "Sir Ninian Comper (1864–1960): Last of the Ecclesiologists." *Anglican World* 1964:20–24.

CONDER, JOSIAH

Josiah Conder (1852–1920), the "Father of Western architecture in Japan," was articled to Thomas Roger Smith. In 1876 while in the office of WILLIAM BURGESS, he won the Soane Medallion. In 1877, Conder went to Japan to work for the Ministry of Public Works and to teach at Engineering

College. His early Japanese buildings were Gothic, followed by Queen Anne and Edwardian styles. He was a bridge, bringing Western know-how and style to Japan while sharing his knowledge of Japanese architecture, theater, painting, gardens, and flower arrangement in Western publications. Conder contributed a paper, entitled "The Condition of Architecture in Japan," before the World Congress of Architects at the Columbian Exposition in Chicago in 1893. He was the first honorary president of the Society of Japanese Architects.

HANNA LERSKI

Conder.
Mitsubishi I.
Marunuochi, Tokyo.
1893–1897

WORKS

*1877–1880, Tokyo Imperial Museum; *1879–1883, College of Law and Literature; *1880–1881, Bank of Japan (Hokkaido Rooms); *1880–1882, Official Guest House, Rokumeikan; *1880–1883, Palace of Prince Arusigawa; *1893–1897, Mitsubishi I, Marunuochi; *1893–1905, Mitsubishi II; 1894–1896, Hisawa Iwasaki Residence; *1895–1896, Tokyo Club; *1896, Italian Embassy; *1897, German Embassy; Tokyo. *1898, Yokohama Royal Hotel, Japan. *1901, Yokohama United Club, Japan. 1910–1912, Mitsui Club; 1913, Furukawa Residence; 1915, Prince Shimazu Residence; Tokyo.

BIBLIOGRAPHY

CONDER, JOSIAH 1877–1878 "Notes on Japanese Architecture." *Sessional Papers of the Royal Institute of British Architects* 1877–1878:179–192.

CONDER, JOSIAH 1879 "Theatres in Japan." *The Builder* 37:368–376.

CONDER, JOSIAH 1883 "Japanese Pagodas, and Their Construction." *Building News* Apr. 20:529.

CONDER, JOSIAH 1886 "The Mausoleum at Nikko." *Transactions of the Royal Institute of British Architects* 2:103.

CONDER, JOSIAH 1887 "Domestic Architecture in Japan." *Transactions of the Royal Institute of British Architects* 3:103–127.

CONDER, JOSIAH 1891 *The Flowers of Japan and the Art of Floral Arrangement*. Tokyo and London.

CONDER, JOSIAH 1893a "An Architect's Notes on the Great Earthquake of October 1891." *Seismological Journal of Japan* 1893:1–92.

CONDER, JOSIAH 1893b "The Condition of Architecture in Japan." *Proceedings of the Twenty-Seventh Annual Convention of the American Institute of Architects held at Chicago* 1893:365–381.

CONDER, JOSIAH 1893c *Landscape Gardening in Japan.* Tokyo: Kelly & Walsh.

CONDER, JOSIAH 1893d *Supplement to Landscape Gardening in Japan.* Tokyo: Kelly & Walsh.

CONDER, JOSIAH 1897 "Japanese Flower Arrangement." *The Studio* 9:14–28, 178–245.

CONDER, JOSIAH 1931 *Collection of the Posthumous Works of Josiah Conder.* Tokyo.

GRAVES, ALGERNON (1905)1972 Volume 2, page 121 in *The Royal Academy of Arts: A Complete Dictionary of Contributors and Their Work from Its Foundation in 1769 to 1904.* Reprint. New York: Franklin.

LERSKI, HANNA 1979 "Josiah Conder's Bank of Japan, Tokyo." *Journal of the Society of Architectural Historians* 38:271–274.

MURAMATSU, T. 1976 "Venture into Western Architecture." Pages 113–125 in Chishoburoh F. Yamada (editor), *Dialogue in Art.* Tokyo: Kodansha.

RICHARDS, J. M. 1964 "Missionary of Japan: An Exhumation of Josiah Conder." *Architectural Review* 136:196–198.

SHIGEKATSU, ONOGI 1979 "Yoshiki no Ishizue." In T. Muramatsu (editor), *West Meets East: The Japanese Introduction to Western Architecture in the 19th and 20th Centuries.* Tokyo: Sanzei-do.

SUZUKI, HIROYUKI 1976 "Josiah Conder: His Concept of Architecture and Japan." Pages 459–507 in *Nihon Kenchiku.* Tokyo: Chuo Koron bijutsu Shuppan.

SUZUKI, HIROYUKI 1976 "Josiah Conder in England." *Kenshicushi Kenkyu* 40, Sept.:1–15.

CONGDON, HENRY M.

Henry Martyn Congdon (1834–1922), architect of many Episcopal churches, practiced in Brooklyn and New York. Following his graduation from Columbia College in 1854, he apprenticed with John W. Priest in Newburgh, New York, and then was associated with Emlen T. Littell from 1859 to 1860. Afterward, except for a collaboration with J. C. CADY from around 1870 to 1872 and a partnership with his son Herbert Wheaton Congdon which lasted from 1901 until 1922, Congdon worked alone.

Bold surface detail, large, dominant towers, and a picturesque grouping of elements characterize Congdon's churches. Trinity Church (1873, 1874–1892) in Portland, Connecticut, in the Victorian Gothic mode, and the strikingly colorful Saint James' Episcopal Church (1888) in Cambridge, Massachusetts, a Richardsonian (see H. H.

RICHARDSON) building, are outstanding examples of his distinctive manner.

SARAH BRADFORD LANDAU

WORKS

c.1870–1872, Calvary Church, Utica, N.Y. 1872–1873, Chapel of the Good Shepherd, Faribault, Minn. 1873, 1874–1892, Trinity Church, Portland, Conn. 1874–1875, Saint Luke's Church, Germantown, Philadelphia. *1878, 1880–1881, Saint Mary's Free Hospital, New York. 1879–1880, Saint Luke's Church, Lebanon, Pa. *c.1879–1882, Christ Church, Portsmouth, N.H. 1881–1883, Christ Church, Danville, Pa. 1888, Saint James's Episcopal Church, Cambridge, Mass. *1889–1891, House of Mercy; 1889–1891, Saint Andrew's Church; New York. Begun 1890, Saint Mary's Chapel and Convent, Peekskill, N.Y. 1893–1896, Calvary Church and Parish House, Summit, N.J. 1894–1896, Christ Church and Parish House, Ansonia, Conn. 1897–1898, Trinity Church, Torrington, Conn. 1902–1904, Twenty Two-family Houses (with Herbert Wheaton Congdon), Union Street, Brooklyn, New York. 1909, Saint Paul's Church (with Herbert Wheaton Congdon), Norwalk, Ohio. 1911–1913, Saint Paul's Episcopal Church (with Herbert Wheaton Congdon), Philipsburg, Pa.

BIBLIOGRAPHY

Avery Index to Architectural Periodicals. 1973 Boston: Hall.

CONGDON, HERBERT WHEATON 1922 "Obituary: Henry Martyn Congdon." *Journal of the American Institute of Architects* 10:134.

COOLIDGE, JOHN PHILLIPS 1935 "The Gothic Revival Churches of the United States." Unpublished M.A. thesis, Harvard University, Cambridge, Mass.

SHINN, GEORGE WOLFE 1889 *King's Handbook of Notable Episcopal Churches in the United States.* Boston: King.

STANTON, PHOEBE B. 1968 *The Gothic Revival and American Church Architecture.* Baltimore: Johns Hopkins.

CONNELL, WARD, and LUCAS

One of the best known of the Modernist practices in England in the 1930s, Connell, Ward, and Lucas was formed in 1933 and disbanded in 1939.

Amyas Douglas Connell (1900–1980) was born in New Zealand. He began his career as an articled pupil with a local firm but after meeting Basil Robert Ward (1902–1978), he decided to emigrate to England. He continued his architectural training at the Bartlett School, University College, London, winning the Rome Prize of the Royal Institute of British Architects in 1926. After returning from Rome, he began his practice with a house for the former director of the British School in Rome at Amersham, Buckinghamshire. This house, variously described as the last of the great British houses or the first of the new style, was called *High and Over* and caused consternation in the conservative architectural circles of the time.

Ward joined Connell in practice in 1932, and Colin Lucas (1906–) in 1933. Work was based on a simple understanding of the white cubic architecture of the Mediterranean with emphasis on thin reinforced concrete external walls.

In the mid-1940s, Connell commenced work in East Africa, first in Tanganyika and later Kenya. His best works are the Aga Khan Jubilee Hospital and Parliamentary Buildings, both in Nairobi.

Ward, the philosopher of the group, was born in New Zealand and educated at Napier College. He placed second in the Rome Prize of 1926, after Connell. After spending time in Rome, he worked in Rangoon, Burma, for three years and eventually returned to England.

After Connell, Ward, and Lucas was disbanded and after service in World War II, Ward became a partner in Murray Ward and Partners, and later was elected first Lethaby Professor of Architecture, Royal College of Art, London. In the mid-1960s, he retired to the Lake District but took up teaching appointments at Manchester Polytechnic School of Architecture and at Lancaster University, which now holds the Basil Ward Memorial Trust Fund in memory of his services to the University.

Lucas was the Englishman in the group. Born in London and educated at Cheltenham and Cambridge, he initially formed his own building company with his father to construct reinforced concrete houses. After the war, he moved into public authority architecture and acted as team leader of the development group within the LCC's Architect's Department.

DENNIS SHARP

BIBLIOGRAPHY

HITCHCOCK, H. R. 1956 "England and the Outside World." *Architectural Association Journal* 72, no. 806:96–97.
HOUSDEN, BRIAN 1956 "Biography." *Architectural Association Journal* 72, no. 806:95.
STEPHENS, THOMAS 1956 "Connell Ward and Lucas: 1927–1939." *Architectural Association Journal* 72, no. 806:112–113.
WARD, BASIL 1967 "Connell, Ward and Lucas." Pages 73–86 in Dennis Sharp (editor), *Planning and Architecture*. London: Barrie & Rockliff.

CONTANT D'IVRY, PIERRE

Born at Ivry-sur-Seine, France, Pierre Contant d'Ivry (1698–1777) studied drawing with Antoine Watteau and architecture with NICOLAS DULIN.

Virtually nothing is known of his early career. His first building dates from 1725, but three years later he was made a member of the Académie d'Architecture, entering the *première classe* in 1742. He established his reputation only after 1741, when he began to work for Maréchal de Belle-Isle at Bizy. Soon after, he was taken up by the duc d'Orléans, whose *premier architecte* he became in 1752. The interiors he designed, in a solemn Louis XIV style, at the Palais Royal, caused a considerable stir in Paris; even JACQUES FRANÇOIS BLONDEL was impressed to the extent of illustrating them in the *Encyclopédie*. Contant d'Ivry did much more of this sort, also a number of formal garden designs: at Saint-Cloud (from 1743), Arnouville (1745), Isle-Adam (after 1746), Brimborion (c.1750), Saint-Ouen (c.1750), and Parma, where he was invited in 1752 to become architect to the duke. However, his reputation rests on his attempt to recreate Gothic structural and spatial effects in classical terms, in particular in his church interiors. Here, he was something of a structural innovator, experimenting with terra-cotta vaulting and other lightweight structures. His most notable pupil was FRANÇOIS-JOSEPH BÉLANGER.

R. D. MIDDLETON

WORKS

*1725, Hôtel de Gouvernet, 16 rue du Coq Héron; *1733, Hôtel Blondel de Gagny, corner rue D'Anjou and rue Saint Honoré; 1738–1741, Apartment Block for the Marquis de Gouffier, corner rue Pagevin and rue Vieux-Augustins (rue Etienne Marcel and rue Herold); Paris. 1741–1749, Château de Bizy (extensions, garden layout, and stables), near Vernon, Eure, France. *1743–1751, Château de la Gaité (Butte de la Brosse), Saint Cloud, Hauts de Seine; 1744–1747, Hôtel Crozat de Tugny (rebuildings and stables; now part of the Ritz Hotel), 17 Place Vendôme; 1744–1747, Hôtel Crozat de Theirs (rebuilding and decoration; now head office of the Crédit Foncier), 19 Place Vendôme; Paris. 1745–1757, Château d'Arnouville (garden layout and orangery), Arnouville-les-Gonesse, Seine-Saint Denis, France. 1747–1774, Abbaye de Penthémont, 104–106 rue de Grenelle and 37 rue de Bellechasse; 1748, Château de Saint-Cloud (garden pavilion), Hauts de Seine; *c.1750, Brimborion-Bellevue (garden pavilion and layout), Hauts de Seine; *c.1750, Château de Saint Ouen (aviary), Seine-Saint Denis; *c.1750–1768, Château de Saint-Cloud (belvedere and garden layout), Hauts de Seine; c.1751, Hôtel de Rohan/Soubise (interior decoration with GERMAIN BOFFRAND), 60 rue des Francs Bourgeois; Paris. 1751–1755, Saint Wasnon (the initial plan was by Frère Louis of Valenciennes, who directed the building of Contant's project), Conde-sur-Escaut, Nord, France. 1752–1777, Palais Royal (enlargement and redecoration), Paris. 1753–1779, Hôtel du Gouvernment (redecoration and extension), rue de l'Abbiette, Lille, Nord, France. 1754, Hôtel Blouin (interior decoration), 31 rue de Faubourg Saint-Honoré; *1755, Pavilion d'Arnouville, Garges-en-France (Garge-les-Gonesse); Seine-Saint Denis; *1763–1777, Sainte Madeleine; Paris. 1775–1777, Saint Vaast (not completed until 1833), Arras, Pas de Calais, France.

BIBLIOGRAPHY

CONTANT D'IVRY, PIERRE 1769 *Les Oeuvres d'architecture.* Paris: Dumont, Huquier, Joullain.
GALLET, MICHEL 1965 "Un modèle pour la Madeleine d'après le projet de Contant d'Ivry." *Bulletin du Musée Carnavalet* 18, no. 1:14–19.
KRETZSCHMAR, FRANK JOACHIM 1981 *Pierre Contant d'Ivry: Ein Beitrag zur französischen Architektur des 18. Jahrhunderts.* University of Cologne (Germany).

CONTINI FAMILY

During the late sixteenth and the seventeenth centuries, the Roman family of the Contini gave rise to several generations of architects. The professional continuity from father and son to grandson and beyond allowed the family to participate in the full cycle of the development of the baroque style. The family's architectural patriarch, Pietro (?–1603) was active in Rome during the late sixteenth century when baroque canons of style were first developing. His son or grandson (the relationship is unclear), Francesco Gaetano (dates unknown), lived and practiced during the middle years of the seventeenth century when the baroque style was in its heyday and the contribution of architects such as GIOVANNI LORENZO BERNINI and FRANCESCO BORROMINI dominated the field. Francesco Gaetano's son, Giovanni Battista (1641–1723), lived at the end of the age, upholding the legacy of Bernini and participating in the diffusion of the baroque style outside of Italy.

Of Pietro Contini little is known aside from the fact that he worked on the building of the Church of Santa Maria in Vallicella. The exact dates of Pietro's participation in the project are unknown; however, perimeters can be set between 1575, the year in which the project was begun, and 1603, the year of the architect's death.

The life of Francesco Gaetano is better documented. Although the exact dates of his service are unclear, it is known that Francesco worked as an architect in the Barberini household around 1650. At this time, he built the Church of Santa Rosalia, Palestrina (inaugurated 1660) and the triangular casino in the garden of the nearby Barberini summer residence. His most frequently mentioned project is the Church of Santa Maria Regina Coeli (1654), which he built for Anna Colonna, the wife of Taddeo Barberini.

The best known member of the Contini family is Francesco's son, Giovanni Battista (Giambattista). Educated in Latin, geometry, and Italian literature, Giambattista was also a devoted student of Bernini. After his mentor's death in 1680, Giambattista remained, along with Mattia dei Rossi, the most faithful practitioner of Bernini's style.

In Rome, Giambattista's specialty was the building of chapels and altars. Between 1674 and 1686, the young Contini completed numerous works of this nature in various churches throughout Rome, among them, the Chapel of Beata Rita at the Church of San Agostino, the Mascaccioni Chapel at Santa Maria del Suffragio, and the high altar in Borromini's Church of Sant' Ivo alla Sapienza. Save for the interior remodeling of the Church of the Stimmate di San Francesco at the much later date of 1708, major architectural commissions in Rome eluded Giambattista. For these, he had to travel elsewhere.

Between 1681 and 1687, Giambattista worked for the monks of the Benedictine monastery at Montecassino, Italy, building the Loggia del Paradiso, a two-story portico, arcaded and open on ground level, enclosed above, and joined to the abbot's residence. This was the young Contini's first major commission for an entire building. In the classical ordering of the façade, with the Doric order below and strip pilasters above, and the rhythm established in the treatment of the balustrades and windows, the architect shows his debt to Bernini.

Contemporary with his work at Montecassino are Giambattista's designs for the campanile of the Cathedral at Sargossa, Spain (1683–1687). This project represents one of the few direct architectural links between Italy and Spain during the seventeenth century. As such it is important for the dissemination of the seventeenth-century Roman style.

Upon his return to Italy, Giambattista executed two major cathedral projects, at Vetrella and Vignanello (both 1720s) as well as the Church of San Domenico (1699–1703), Ravenna.

In conjunction with his work as an architect, Giambattista practiced hydraulic engineering. In this capacity, he worked on diverting the Tiber River at Todi, Italy, and the Po River at Bologna.

For his labors as an architect and an engineer Giambatista was made a cavalier. In addition, he was elected twice to the presidency of the Accademia di San Luca, once in 1683 and again in 1719.

SARAH E. BASSETT

WORKS

PIETRO CONTINI
1575–1603, Santa Maria in Vallicella, Rome.

FRANCESCO GAETANO CONTINI

1650?, Barberini Summer Residence (triangular casino); 1650?, Santa Rosalia; Palestrina, Italy. *1654, Santa Maria Regina Coeli, Rome.

GIOVANNI BATTISTA CONTINI

1671, Chapel of Santa Caterina di Siena, Santa Sabina; 1674–1686, Chapel of Beata Rita, San Agostino; 1675, Chapel De Angelis (restoration and decoration), Santa Maria in Aracoeli; Rome. 1681–1687, Loggia del Paradiso, Monastery of Montecassino, Italy. 1683–1686, Cathedral of Sargossa (campanile), Spain. 1684–1685, Sant' Ivo alla Sapienza (high altar), Rome. 1699–1703, San Domenico, Ravenna, Italy. 1708, Stimmate di San Francesco (interior remodeling), Rome. 1720s, Cathedral, Betralla, Italy. 1720s, Cathedral, Vignanello, Italy.

BIBLIOGRAPHY

HAGER, HELLMUT 1970 "Giovanni Battista Contini e la Loggia del Paradiso dell'Abbazzia di Montecassino." *Commentari* 21:92–117.
KUBLER, GEORGE, and SORIA, MARTIN 1959 *Art and Architecture in Spain and Portugal and Their American Dominions: 1500 to 1800.* Baltimore: Penguin.
PORTOGHESI, PAOLO (1966)1970 *Roman Baroque.* Translated by Barbara Luigia La Penta. Cambridge, Mass.: M.I.T. Press.
WITTKOWER, RUDOLF (1958)1973 *Art and Architecture in Italy.* 3d ed. Baltimore: Penguin.

COOK, ABNER H.

Master builder and contractor, Abner Hugh Cook (1814–1884) is celebrated for some of the finest Greek Revival houses in Texas. Cook was born in North Carolina and worked briefly in Macon, Georgia, and Nashville, Tennessee. He was in Austin, Texas, from the time of its founding in 1839 until his death.

ROXANNE WILLIAMSON

WORKS

1850s, Governor's Mansion; 1850s, Neill-Cochran House; 1850s, Woodlawn; Austin, Tex.

BIBLIOGRAPHY

ALEXANDER, DRURY BLAKELEY 1976 "Cook, Abner Hugh." Volume 3, page 195 in *Handbook of Texas.* Austin: Texas State Historical Association.
WILLIAMSON, ROXANNE 1967 "Victorian Architecture in Austin." Unpublished M.A. thesis, University of Texas, Austin.

COOK, WALTER

Walter Cook (1846–1916) was born in Buffalo, New York. He briefly attended Yale University but transferred to Harvard where he received an A.B. degree in 1869 and an A.M. in 1872. Following his graduation, he left for study in Europe, where he attended the Ecole des Beaux-Arts in Paris and the Royal Polytechnic School in Munich. In 1877, Cook returned to the United States, where he became the prominent partner in three successive New York architectural firms. BABB, COOK, AND WILLARD; Willard, Babb, Cook, and Welch; and Cook and Welch.

Practicing in a variety of styles, Cook executed many commissions, including the De Vinne Press building (1885), the residence of Andrew Carnegie (1899) and the Henry Hudson Memorial Column (1912), all in New York City. He was also responsible for the New York Life Insurance building (1887) in Kansas City, Missouri.

STEVEN MCLEOD BEDFORD

WORKS

1885, De Vinne Press Building, New York. 1887, New York Life Insurance Building, Kansas City, Mo. 1898, F. B. Pratt Residence; 1899, Andrew Carnegie Residence; New York. 1901, Stadium, Station, and Administration Building, Pan-American Exposition, Buffalo, N.Y. 1905, Mott Haven Branch, New York Public Library; 1912, Henry Hudson Memorial Column; 1913, Choir School, Cathedral of Saint John the Divine; New York.

BIBLIOGRAPHY

"Carnegie Residence, Fifth Avenue, New York City." 1899 *Architectural Record* 9:77–81.
"Walter Cook." 1916 *New York Times* Mar. 26.

COOLEY, THOMAS

Thomas Cooley, (c.1740–1784), apprenticed to a London carpenter, worked in the office of ROBERT MYLNE. On winning the competition for the Dublin Royal Exchange (1769–1779), he settled in Dublin, where he remained until his death. Appointed chief government architect in 1775, his dominance among resident Irish architects throughout the 1770s was challenged only by THOMAS IVORY. He was eclipsed after 1781 by JAMES GANDON.

His oeuvre is of uneven quality. At its best, as in the Dublin Exchange, it displays an imaginative eclecticism based on the works of WILLIAM CHAMBERS and, in particular, Robert Mylne, which was important in the formation of neoclassical taste in Irish architecture.

EDWARD MCPARLAND

WORKS

1769–1779, Royal Exchange; *1770–1773, Hibernian Marine School; Dublin. c.1771, Public Library; 1774,

Royal School; Armagh, Ireland. *c.1775–1781, Newgate Prison; 1776–1784, Public Offices; Dublin. 1779, Caledon House, County Tyrone, Ireland.

BIBLIOGRAPHY

"Anecdotes of the Fine Arts in Ireland . . . Mr. Thomas Cooley." 1793 *Anthologia Hibernica* 2:35–36.
CRAIG, MAURICE (1952)1969 *Dublin 1660–1860: A Social and Architectural History.* Dublin: Allen Figgis.
CURRAN, CONSTANTINE 1949 "Cooley, Gandon and the Four Courts." *Journal of the Royal Society of Antiquaries of Ireland* 79:20–25.
MCPARLAND, EDWARD 1972 "James Gandon and the Royal Exchange Competition, 1768–69." *Journal of the Royal Society of Antiquaries of Ireland* 102:58–72.
MCPARLAND, EDWARD 1980 "The Early History of James Gandon's Four Courts." *Burlington Magazine* 122:727–735.

COOPER, EDWIN

Thomas Edwin Cooper (1873–1942) was one of the principal exponents of Edwardian classic and neo-Georgian architecture. He was born in Scarborough, England, and articled there to the firm of Hall and Tugwell. His first important work came to him by competition. He combined a skill in planning on difficult sites with an ability to hit the stylistic note of the time, with grandiose towers and Corinthian columns. The virtues of his work should be sought in planning and organization rather than in the composition of façades, which have unjustly become a byword for the shortcomings of the style he practiced. He was knighted in 1923 and received the Royal Gold Medal for Architecture in 1931.

ALAN POWERS

WORKS

1906–1914, Guildhall, Hull, England. 1912–1922, Port of London Authority, Tower Hill. 1914–1939, Marylebone Town Hall and Library, London. 1921–1924, Star and Garter Home, Richmond, England. 1922–1926, 1933–1934, College of Nursing, Henrietta Place; 1923–1924, Banque Belge, Bishopsgate; *1925–1928, Lloyds, Leadenhall; 1929, National Westminster Bank, Poultry; London.

COPE and STEWARDSON

Walter Cope (1860–1902) and John Stewardson (1858–1896), both born in Philadelphia, are best known for collegiate buildings and campus design, primarily in creative interpretations of the Jacobean and Gothic styles that became fused in popular references as Collegiate Gothic. At Bryn Mawr College (1886–1904), the University of Pennsylvania (1895–1901), and Princeton University (1895–1903), they made formative additions to existing campuses, adapting the Oxford and Cambridge cloister concepts to the more open American circumstances. All included tower entrances to the scholastic precincts.

In 1899, the firm won an invitational competition for a new campus for Washington University, St. Louis, Missouri, after preliminary planning by John Charles Olmstead and FREDERICK LAW OLMSTED, Jr. Cope's thirteen buildings in pink Missouri granite, some completed after his death, established a gateway tower approach to a large quadrangle, with elements beyond as keystones of expansion receptive to subsequent designs. The university leased the first seven buildings to the Louisiana Purchase Exposition of 1904 for administrative offices before beginning its own occupancy in 1905.

John Stewardson studied at Harvard (1877), and at the Atelier Pascal and the Ecole des Beaux-Arts, Paris (1879–1882). In 1883–1884, he was an apprentice with FRANK FURNESS, and with Cope worked as draftsman for Theophilus Parsons Chandler. After his accidental death in 1896, his brother, Emlyn Lamar Stewardson, became a partner.

Cope was graduated from the Germantown Friends School, and began fourteen months of European travel in 1884. The partnership was formed in 1885. Cope was chairman (1896–1898) of the committee on restoration of Independence Hall. After his death at age forty-two, the firm was continued by Emlyn Stewardson, George Bispham Page, and James P. Jamieson.

GEORGE MCCUE

WORKS

Includes works begun by Cope and Stewardson and completed by Emlyn Stewardson, George Bispham, and James P. Jamieson.

1886, Radnor Hall, Bryn Mawr College, Pa. 1887, Roberts Hall and Lloyd Hall, Haverford College, Pa. 1890–1891, Denbigh Hall, Bryn Mawr College, Pa. 1893–1902, Museum (not completed until 1926 with Wilson Eyre, Jr., and Frank Miles Day), University of Pennsylvania, Philadelphia. 1894, Pembroke Hall and Gateway Tower, Bryn Mawr College, Pa. 1895–1897, Blair Hall and Gateway Tower, Princeton University, N.J. 1895–1901, Memorial Tower; 1895–1935, Little Quad and Big Quad (dormitory group); University of Pennsylvania, Philadelphia. 1897–1904, Rockefeller Hall and Gateway Tower, Bryn Mawr College, Pa. 1898, Stafford Little Hall, Princeton University, N.J. 1898–1910, Law School, University of Pennsylvania, Philadelphia. 1900, Busch Hall and University Hall (renamed Brookings); 1902, Ridgley Building and Tower Hall (renamed Lee, then Umrath); Washington University, St. Louis, Mo.

BIBLIOGRAPHY

AMERICAN INSTITUTE OF ARCHITECTS, PHILADELPHIA
    CHAPTER 1961 *Philadelphia Architecture.* New
    York: Reinhold.
CRAM, RALPH ADAMS 1904 "The Work of Cope &
    Stewardson." *Architectural Record* 16:407–438.
JAMIESON, JAMES P. 1941 *Intimate History of the Cam-
    pus and Buildings of Washington University.* St. Louis,
    Mo.: Privately printed.
PICKENS, BUFORD, and DARNALL, MARGARETTA J.
    1978 *Washington University in St. Louis: Its Design and
    Architecture.* St. Louis,, Mo.: Washington University.
STEWARDSON, WILLIAM EMLYN 1960 "Cope & Stew-
    ardson." Unpublished Master's thesis, Princeton
    University, N.J.
STURGIS, R. CLIPSTON 1903 "Walter Cope, Archi-
    tect." *The Outlook* 73:772–778.
TATUM, GEORGE B. 1961 *Penn's Great Town.* Philadel-
    phia: University of Pennsylvania.

CORBETT, HARVEY WILEY

The son of San Francisco physicians, Harvey Wiley
Corbett (1873–1954) broke with family tradition
when he chose to become an architect. After receiving an engineering degree from the University
of California, Berkeley, in 1895, he entered the
Ecole des Beaux-Arts in Paris in 1896, and the atelier of JEAN LOUIS PASCAL, an eclectic who stressed
the mastery of historical styles. Corbett received
his *diplôme* in 1900, then traveled extensively in
France, Italy, and England.

In New York in 1901, Corbett found employment as a draftsman in the office of CASS GILBERT.
Two years later, he began private practice with a
young New York architect, F. Livingston Pell.
Among the buildings they constructed were two
important commissions won by competition: the
Maryland Institute (1905–1908) in Baltimore, a
variation on a Florentine palazzo, and the classical
Municipal Group (1908–1913) in Springfield,
Massachusetts. The fluency in different stylistic idioms that characterized Corbett's work, particularly
before the mid-1920s, was in part attributable to
his French training, but it also typified the pluralis-
tic nature of American architecture during these
years. His long involvement with architectural
education began at this time. An advocate of the
Beaux-Arts system, he directed one of the ateliers
of the Columbia School of Architecture from
1907–1909 and continued as a critic and special
lecturer from 1909–1935 (with an interruption
from 1912–1920).

In 1912, Corbett joined Frank J. Helmle, an
architect with an established practice in Brooklyn.
Following Helmle's retirement in 1928, he headed
a partnership with WALLACE K. HARRISON and

William MacMurray; that firm became Corbett
and MacMurray in 1935, and Harvey Wiley Corbett Associates in 1941.

The Bush Terminal (1916–1917), a thirty-story
tower on New York's Forty-second Street, marked
Corbett's debut as an influential skyscraper designer and theorist. In the early 1920s, collaborating with the delineator HUGH FERRISS, he was one
of the first to explore the potential for new formal
expression suggested by the setback restrictions of
the New York zoning law of 1916. Corbett saw
the skyscraper as the symbol of modern America.
An ardent defender of the tall building in the polemic over its viability for cities, he envisaged increasing building heights and densities while reducing congestion. His plans included "super-
block" skyscrapers, tiered streets, and multilevel
transportation systems. Some hints of these fu-
turistic proposals appeared in two projects of the
1930s: Rockefeller Center (1928–1937) in New
York (Corbett's was one of three associated firms
of the design team) and the planning of the Chicago Fair of 1933, for which he chaired the committee of architects. In general, though, even the
most modernistic of his commissioned buildings,
such as the Roerich Museum and Master Apartments (1928–1929), New York, belie the inventiveness of his visions of the city of the future.

Corbett was active in many professional and
civic organizations and commented frequently in
the architectural and popular press. His most original contributions came in the 1920s through the
mid-1930s when he was one of the leading figures
trying to define a modern, American style; his later
work increasingly was influenced by the International style.

CAROL WILLIS

WORKS

1905–1908, Maryland Institute (with F. Livingston
Pell), Baltimore. 1908–1913, Municipal Group (with
Pell), Springfield, Mass. 1916–1917, Bush Terminal,
New York. 1920–1924, Bush House, London. 1927,
One Fifth Avenue; 1928–1929, Roerich Museum and
Master Apartments; 1928–1937, Rockefeller Center
(with L. A. REINHARD and HENRY HOFMEISTER,
WALLACE K. HARRISON and William H. McMurray,
and JACQUES ANDRÉ FOUILHOUX); 1930–1933, Metro-
politan Life Insurance Company Building; 1937–1939,
Criminal Courts; New York.

BIBLIOGRAPHY

*Between Traditions and Modernism: American Architec-
    tural Drawings from the National Academy of Design*
    1980 New York: The academy.
CORBETT, HARVEY WILEY 1923 "Zoning and the
    Envelope of the Building." *Pencil Points* 4:15–18.
CORBETT, HARVEY WILEY 1926 "New Stones for
    Old." *Saturday Evening Post* 198, Mar. 27:6–7; May

8:26–27; May 15:16–17.

CORBETT, HARVEY WILEY 1941 "The Skyscraper and the Automobile Have Made the Modern City." In *Studies in the Arts and Architecture.* Philadelphia: University of Pennsylvania Press.

KRINSKY, CAROL 1978 *Rockefeller Center.* New York: Oxford.

MIDDLETON, ROBIN DAVID 1962–1963 "The Abbé de Cordemoy and the Graeco-Gothic Ideal: A Prelude to Romantic Classicism." *Journal of the Warburg and Courtauld Institutes* 25:278–320; 26:90–123.

URBAIN, CHARLES, and LEVESQUE, EUGÈNE 1909–1925 Volume 3, pages 539 and 541 in *Correspondance de Bossuet.* Paris: Hachette.

CORDEMOY, JEAN LOUIS DE

Jean Louis de Cordemoy's biography is virtually unknown, but he was almost certainly the fifth son of Gerauld de Cordemoy (1626–1684), the Cartesian philosopher who was author of the *Discours physique de la parole* (1668) and the *Histoire de France* (1685, 1689), which was finished by his eldest son. The dates for Jean Louis de Cordemoy's birth and death in Roman d'Amat's *Dictionnaire de biographie française* are incorrect, being those of his father's widowed sister Nicole, who died at Jean Louis de Cordemoy's house at La Ferté-sous-Jouarre, where he was "prieur-curé" to Saint Nicolas. He was also a canon at Saint Jean des Vignes in Soissons. His importance springs from his authorship of *Nouveau Traité de Toute l'Architecture* (1706), in which CLAUDE PERRAULT's ideas on architecture were encapsulated as a theory of economy and honest expression of structure, criteria derived from an appreciation of both Greek and Gothic architecture. This curious combination was to act as the model for church architecture—Gothic in its structural principle, classical and rectangular in appearance. The column was to resume its original role as a structural support. This was the subject of an exchange of letters between Cordemoy and A. F. FRÉZIER in the *Mémoires de Trevoux* (see Cordemoy, 1714). Not until MARC ANTOINE LAUGIER took up Cordemoy's ideas did they become the accepted basis for church design in France, most notably for JACQUES GERMAIN SOUFFLOT's Sainte Geneviève. They also became the basis for most rationalist theories of architecture.

R. D. MIDDLETON

BIBLIOGRAPHY

CLAIR, PIERRE, and GIRBAL, FRANÇOIS 1968 *Gerauld de Cordemoy (1626–1684): Oeuvres Philosophiques avec une étude bio-bibliographique.* Paris: Presses Universitaires de France.

CORDEMOY, J. L. (1706)1966 *Nouveau traité de toute l'architecture ou l'art de bastir utile aux entrepreneurs et aux ouvriers.* Reprint of 1714 ed. Farnborough, England: Gregg.

LEDIEU, FRANÇOIS 1857 Volume 3, page 433 in *Mémoires et journal sur la vie et les ouvrages de Bossuet.* Paris: Didier.

CORLIES, JOHN

See BOGARDUS, JAMES.

CORMIER, ERNEST

Ernest Cormier (1885–1980) was an extraordinary figure of his time, as an architect and engineer personally involved in every aspect of the art and science of architecture. Removed from the center of architectural discussion and with never more than two or three assistants, he worked at the leading edge of technology, making powerful buildings based on traditional architectural syntax and vocabulary.

Cormier was initially trained as an engineer in Montreal. He worked for the Dominion Bridge Company until 1908, when he was one of the rare Canadians to enter the Ecole des Beaux-Arts in Paris. He joined the studio of JEAN LOUIS PASCAL and studied painting and sculpture. After two years in Rome as the Jarvis Rome Scholar of the Royal Institute of British Architects, he received his diploma in architecture from the Ecole in 1917. In 1918, he returned to Montreal. Within two years he was invited by L. A. Amos and C. S. Saxe to design for them one of the major buildings in Canada, the Criminal Court of Montreal (1923–1926). In 1924, he was awarded the major commission to design on his own the new campus and buildings for the Université de Montréal.

In the Criminal Court Building, Cormier is a full-blown architect; here and in all future work, he shows how profoundly he had absorbed the precepts of JULIEN GUADET in Pascal's studio: simplicity as a rule of composition; the influence of circulation, lighting, aeration; the reciprocal relation of the building exterior and interior; and above all the belief that these basic principles are unchanging in all great architecture beyond and despite stylistic considerations. Cormier's major buildings, the Criminal Court, the Université de Montréal (1928–1955), his own house (1930–1931), and the Supreme Court of Canada (1938–1950), are in essence the same, whether the vocabulary is Beaux-Arts Roman for the Criminal Court or a development from Art Deco for the other three.

All buildings are superbly sited and masterfully detailed in rich, traditional materials, right down to the furniture and fixtures. Most characteristic is the organization and procession of space, from a vast expanding reception space suffused in light (the house) to sepulchral (the Criminal Court). One is then directed through the compressed space of a sinuous stairwell to be delivered into a well-defined volume, the *sanctum sanctorum,* dark and womblike in the house; bathed in clear light in the Criminal Court room.

Ernest Cormier was an architect of concrete. His engineering design was advanced: the Dubrulé Building (1922) is a brick-sheathed, multistory, concrete structural frame; the thin-shell airport hangars (1928) predate the accepted North American landmark Dairy Building, Chicago (1933). In 1948, he began the early curtain-wall-wrapped National Printing Bureau (1950–1958), which was an experiment in environmental control through a form of double glazing. Cormier taught at the Ecole Polytechnique of Montreal (1925–1954), established the Ecole des Arts, but never otherwise wrote on or publicly discussed architecture.

Cormier was recognized internationally when he was chosen as one of seven representatives appointed as design consultants to the United Nations building, New York. However, the paucity of commissions, the restricted budgets for most of his buildings, the pettiness of partisan political patronage, and lack of understanding all are poignant comments on the thinness of resources for an architect of great capacity in a still colonial country. Yet, it was Canada, particularly French Quebec, which both nurtured Cormier's prodigious talent and made it necessary for him to touch personally every aspect of architecture and engineering. The balance between restrictions and opportunity in his work remains to be studied.

PHYLLIS LAMBERT

WORKS

1922, Debrulé Building (with J. O. Marchand); 1922, Ecole des Beaux Arts de Montréal; 1922, Ecole Saint-Arsène; 1923, Eglise Sainte Marguerite-Marie; 1923–1926, Criminal Court of Montreal (with L. A. Amos and C. J. Saxe); *1924–1926, Chambre de Commerce (with J. E. C. Daoust); Montreal. 1925–1926, Saint John the Baptist Church, Pawtucket, R.I. 1925–1928, Eglise Saint Ambroise (unfinished), Montreal. 1926–1927, Notre Dame of the Sacred Heart, Central Falls, R.I. 1928, Pointe-aux-Trembles Airport; 1928–1955, Université de Montréal; 1930–1931, Cormier House; 1934–1935, Eglise Saint Louis de France (modified); Montreal. 1938–1950, Supreme Court of Canada, Ottawa. 1943–1944, Hospice-Orphélinat; 1945–1948, Hôtel Dieu; Sorel, Quebec. 1948, Saint Michael's College; 1949, Basilian Seminary (modified); Toronto. 1950–1958, National Printing Bureau, Ottawa. 1952, General Assembly Building (entrance door), United Nations, New York. 1957–1960, Grand Séminaire de Québec (interior remade to house the National Archives of Quebec), Quebec City, Quebec.

Cormier.
Supreme Court of Canada.
Ottawa.
1938–1950

CORNARO, ALVISE

The Venetian Alvise Cornaro (c.1484–1566), having completed his studies in law, settled in Padua, Italy, where he achieved wealth through the systematic "melioration and bonification" of his inherited estates. He used this wealth to the benefit of his family, the expansion of his house, and the furtherance of literature, theater, and the fine arts. Sometime around 1522, he went to Rome where he studied ancient architecture and art under the guidance of GIOVANNI MARIA FALCONETTO. At the same time, he read the architectural treatises of VITRUVIUS and LEON BATTISTA ALBERTI, training himself in this way as an architectural dilettante. He had Falconetto to build a loggia in the garden of his house to serve as the *scenae frons* for theatrical performances. Around 1530–1533, he had the so-called Odeo built to his own design. For its ground plan he consciously copied the traditional plan of the Villa of Varro near Cassino, and he chose ancient Roman motifs for the architectural ornamentation and the interior decoration of this, his *suburbanum.* As administrator of the bishopric of Padua, he designed the Villa dei Vescovi in Luvigliano (erected c.1535–1542) for Cardinal

Francesco Pisano. Here, too, he used a central hall and the motifs of Roman High Renaissance architecture.

Cornaro pursued agriculture, hydraulics, and architecture as practical sciences and also dealt with them in treatises. The architectural treatise, aimed at a bourgeois public (of which two versions are preserved), treats only of domestic architecture and the techniques connected with it; questions of architectural theory are deliberately omitted. Basing himself on corresponding passages in Alberti, he lays great stress on the application of his rules as being both practical and inexpensive. In this empirical, anti-Vitruvian attitude, Cornaro's is unique among the architectural treatises of the Renaissance. What makes this architectural dilettante significant is that he introduced the "Villa Suburbana," with its central reception room, to the Veneto. He did this by borrowing Roman and ancient motifs and combining them to create a new form which became the starting point for the villas of SEBASTIANO SERLIO and ANDREA PALLADIO.

FRITZ-EUGEN KELLER
Translated from German by
Beverley R. Placzek

WORKS

Begun 1514, Casa Cornaro (extension); c.1530–1533, Odeo Cornaro; c.1535–1542, Villa dei Vescovi, Luvigliano; Padua, Italy.

BIBLIOGRAPHY

BRESCIANI ALVAREZ, GIULIA 1980 "Le fabbriche di Alvise Cornaro." Pages 36–59 in L. Puppi (editor), *Alvise Cornaro e il suo tempo.* Padua, Italy. Exhibition catalogue.
CORNARO, ALVISE 1977 "Architekturtraktat." Volume 3, pages 3134–3161 in Paolo Barocchi (editor), *Scritti d'arte del Cinquecento.* Milan and Naples: Ricciard.
CORNARO, ALVISE 1980 *Scritti sull'architettura.* Edited by P. Carpeggiani. Padua, Italy: Centro Grafico.
FIOCCO, GIUSEPPE (editor) 1965 *Alvise Cornaro: Il suo tempo e le sue opere.* Vicenza, Italy: Pozza.
KELLER, FRITZ EUGEN 1971 "Alvise Cornaro zitiert die Villa des Marcus Terentius Varro in Cassino." *L'Arte* New Series 14:29–53.
LOVARINI, EMILIO 1899 "Le ville edificate da Alvise Cornaro." *L'Arte* 2:191–212.
MENEGAZZO, EMILIO 1980 "Alvise Cornaro: Un veneziano del Cinquecento nella terraferma veneta." Volume 2, pages 513–538 in *Storia della cultura veneta.* Vicenza, Italy: Pozza.
SCHWEIKHART, GÜNTER 1968 "Falconetto und Cornaro." *Bollettino del Museo Civico di Padova* 57:30–62.
SCHWEIKHART, GÜNTER 1980 "La cultura archeologica di Alvise Cornaro." Pages 64–71 in L. Puppi (editor), *Alvise Cornaro e il suo tempo.* Padua, Italy.

CORRALES, JOSÉ ANTONIO, and VAZQUEZ MOLEZUN, RAMON

José Antonio Corrales (1921–) and Ramon Vazquez Molezun (1922–) both graduated in 1948 from the Superior Technical School of Architecture in Madrid.

Belonging to the second generation of the Spanish postwar period, they constitute an example of architects dedicated almost exclusively to the practice of the profession. Together, they have developed an identifiable style, but it is difficult to determine their individual contributions. Their architecture must be understood in the cultural ambiance of Madrid and is considered by members of their generation to express with great efficacy the distinct influences that have conditioned the Spanish panorama in the last three decades while always maintaining a high grade of internal coherence.

Their most outstanding works (Spanish pavilion in Brussels, 1958; Bank union building, 1970; International Telephone and Telegraph Building, 1970; Pastor Bank, 1972) always resolve the most complicated plans in an ingenious manner. The imagery has a formal precision sufficient to exceed the evidence of the artificial. A great part of their work comes from competitions which they have won. Their projects frequently contain certain characteristic dazzling effects which at times seem a bit gratuitous.

Their project versatility is also manifested in the facility with which they have changed styles to adapt to current tastes while retaining a personal character.

MIGUEL ANGEL BALDELLOU
Translated from Spanish by
Judith E. Meighan

WORKS

JOSE ANTONIO CORRALES

1964, Dwellings, Elviña, La Coruña, Spain. 1967, Housing, Balbina Valverde Street, Madrid. 1971, Parish Center, Las Flores, Elviña, La Coruña, Spain.

RAMON VAZQUEZ MOLEZUN

1970, International Telephone and Telegraph Building, Avenue of America, Madrid.

CORRALES AND MOLEZUN

1952, Teaching Institute, Herrera de Pisuerga, Palencia, Spain. 1957, Spanish Pavilion, Exposition Universelle, Brussels. 1958, Children's Home, Saint Gobain in Miraflores de la Sierra, Spain. 1966, Hotel Galua, Manga del Mar Menor, Spain. 1966, Casa de Huarte; 1970, Industrial Bank Union, Paseo de la Castellana; 1972, Pastor Bank, Paseo de Recoletos; Madrid.

BIBLIOGRAPHY

BENEVOLO, LEONARDO (1963)1971 *History of Modern Architecture.* 2 vols. Cambridge, Mass.: M.I.T. Press.

FLORES LOPEZ, CARLOS 1961 *Arquitectura española contemporánea.* Madrid: Aguilar.

Encyclopedia of Modern Architecture. (1963)1970 London: Thames & Hudson.

CORTINI, PUBLIO

Publio Cortini (1802–1888) studied at the Accademia di San Luca with the CAMPORESE FAMILY, and with A. Sarti, whose Albergo Inghilterra he finished. He worked with GIUSEPPE VALADIER and acted as strategic military councillor in the 1870 attack of Rome. After losing papal employments because of his political activities in 1848–1849, his major patrons were the Torlonia and the Del Bufalo, for whom he restored various family properties. His 1880 project for the Vittorio Emanuele monument in the Piazza Termini was appreciated by contemporary critics. He built the interior porch of the Vereno cemetery and designed the baths to be built in front of the Ripetta port.

MARTHA POLLAK

WORKS

n.d., Albergo Inghilterra; n.d., Del Bufalo Courtyard (restoration), via della Valle; n.d., Torlonia Buildings (restoration), vie Borgognona and Belsiana; n.d., Verano Cemetery (interior porch); Rome.

CORTONA, PIETRO BERRETTINI DA

Pietro Berrettini (1596–1669), usually called Cortona after his native town in Tuscany, stands alongside GIOVANNI LORENZO BERNINI and FRANCESCO BORROMINI as one of the trio of great architects who developed the high baroque style in mid-seventeenth-century Rome. Unlike either of his contemporaries, he was primarily a painter, and any treatment of his architectural career would be incomplete without a study of the fictive architecture in his frescoes and the elaborate stucco framework that usually surrounds them.

His first smatterings of architecture came from his father, Giovanni Berrettini, a decorative carver (*scarpellino*) versed in architecture, and his uncle Francesco, an architect in the town of Cortona. When the young Pietro's talents became evident, he was sent to Florence to study painting with Andrea Commodi, and it was Commodi who first brought him to Rome in 1611. That trip was the decisive influence in Cortona's education. He fell under the sway of the antique, copying statues and reliefs, as well as the paintings of Polidoro da Caravaggio and RAPHAEL; from the start, he studied MICHELANGELO's architecture. When Commodi had to leave Rome, Cortona insisted on staying, and in 1614 he entered the studio of another Florentine mannerist, Baccio Ciarpi. These apprenticeships mattered little to a genius who was essentially self-trained. Cortona soon set up a studio on his own, and his great breakthrough came when a fellow Tuscan, the nobleman Marcello Sacchetti, walked in to examine the paintings and showed his enthusiasm for a copy after Raphael's *Galatea.* Cortona entered the Sacchetti circle and benefited from their rapid rise after the election of Pope Urban VIII Barberini in 1623. Through Francesco Barberini, Cortona was introduced to the poet Giambattista Marino, who was in Rome briefly before his voyage to Naples and death in 1625 and who had set up his own collection of paintings in a gallery in the Palazzo Crescenzi near the Pantheon. Cortona was invited to paint a scene from Tasso for Marino's gallery, and the painting (now lost) showed an Enchanted Palace in the background that was modeled on the apses of St. Peter's, which Cortona continually studied. It was his first recorded architectural composition, and it is appropriately based on Michelangelo.

Cortona's earliest executed work in the field of architecture and large-scale decoration was carried out for the Sacchetti in two seaside villas near Ostia, southwest of Rome. The Villa Sacchetti (now Chigi) at Castel Fusano was a conservative, blocklike building given four corner bastions for defensive purposes; in 1626–1627 Cortona frescoed the chapel and the gallery. The designs for the gallery vault, though inevitably influenced by the Sistine Ceiling and the Carracci Gallery in the Palazzo Farnese, show an imaginative personal style in which *quadri riportati* (fictive picture frames) are set into an exuberant ornamental framework, with perspectival illusions at the corners reminiscent of Bolognese ceiling painting. The Villa Sacchetti del Pigneto was a masterpiece of Cortona's early maturity. Though some sources maintain that it was built for Marcello Sacchetti (died 1629), it appears to be a work of the mid-1630s, contemporary with Cortona's Barberini ceiling. It was already somewhat ruinous in 1675; only the grotto was left standing by modern times, and that was destroyed in World War II. To judge from the image preserved in old prints, plans and painted views, the villa was set into a hillside and used a system of ramps and terraces to allow visitors easy ascent to the level of the central casino. Water flowed under the villa to feed a number of pools and gentle cascades. The grotto had a semicircular colonnade standing in a pool; it was guarded by two Tritons, whose broad, muscular torsos later influenced Bernini's Triton Fountain. The casino itself completely broke with the standard Roman format of villas in the form of porticoes with corner towers. Instead, it hearkened back to themes found in DONATO BRAMANTE's Vatican Belvedere, liberally mixed with motifs from ancient Roman architecture. Cortona's great central niche recalled the way PIRRO LIGORIO had transformed Bramante's Belvedere exedra; his ramps recalled Bramante's own model, the temple of Fortune at Praeneste (Palestrina); and the large semicircular rooms at either side of the casino are based on the solaria of ancient baths. There was an elaborate sculptural program, including reliefs in an antique style, busts and statues in niches, and reclining river gods; the vault fresco in the *salone* showed a David cycle amidst a framework of illusionistic architecture. A showpiece in the best sense of the word, the casino set the tone of lively, eclectic invention that would characterize all of Cortona's architecture.

Cortona soon became one of the Barberini's foremost protégés, although he always seems to have stood under the shadow of the slightly younger Bernini. When Bernini directed the restoration of the medieval Church of Santa Bibiana in 1624–1626, Cortona was allowed to share the commission of the nave frescoes with an older Florentine mannerist named Agostino Ciampelli. A quick comparison of frescoes across the nave allows one to see the birth of the high baroque style. Not only are Cortona's frescoes more full-blooded and colorful, with powerful sculptural forms and dramatic diagonal movements, but they also show a knowledge of architecture in the backgrounds and a study of the antique in the representations of altars and statuary. Cortona had come under the influence of the antiquarian and collector Cassiano dal Pozzo, who was then employing artists to sketch the ruins and who wanted to collect these records into a comprehensive "paper museum" of antiquity. In 1627, possibly at Cassiano's suggestion, Cortona designed a tomb project for Cardinal Francesco Barberini, shown in an autograph drawing now in Lille, France. A reclining effigy of the cardinal is shown on top of a sarcophagus, surrounded by columns, caryatid pilasters, and figurative sculpture. Two allegorical statues, Poetry and Justice, stand over two portrait busts on either side of the main sarcophagus. These busts appear to represent two intellectuals in the cardinal's entourage, John Barclay (an English poet) and Bernardo Guglielmi. Both of these personalities reappear, though without the cardinal's tomb, in a double monument erected in the side aisle of San Lorenzo

fuori le mura under Francesco Barberini's patronage in 1627, where Cortona was responsible for the architectural backdrop and the sculptor Francois Duquesnoy for the busts. Even in this early stage, Cortona's architectural style shows the robust strength, the unorthodox manipulation of the orders, and the *amor pleni* that would characterize all his mature work.

The connection with the Barberini led to an invitation to submit a project for the new family palace being designed, nominally under the direction of CARLO MADERNO, in 1625–1628. A source many years later said that Cortona's project pleased Pope Urban VIII enormously, but that it was too expensive to be put into execution. No plans are known that show this early project, and although Rudolph Wittkower thought he found one in 1958, this drawing, showing a giant palace substructure made up of many octagonal compartments, seems more in the style of an architect like GIROLAMO RAINALDI. However, several elevation sketches in the Uffizi show Cortona playing with variants on the river loggia of the Palazzo Farnese, which eventually became one of the most important elements in the Barberini design. Maderno's early designs had shown a palace in the form of a large block, based on the city side of the Farnese. It was apparently Cortona's idea to turn the attention to the Farnese river front, thus opening up the building to the rustic landscape surrounding it and giving it a villalike appearance. Beyond this important initial idea, Cortona had no role in the actual execution of facade, but he did design the riding court (*cavallerizza*) attached in 1631 to the north wing of the palace, near the point where horses and carriages would enter from the piazza. In its early years, the riding court was simply a walled-off area one story high; by around 1638, the wall was incorporated into a new structure designed to house the Barberini Theater; in 1932, the whole affair was demolished and rebuilt, with Cortona's original portal and windows reused once again. Even in their new location these salvaged pieces show Cortona's originality as a designer of architectural detail. Dark tufa stone is cut into characteristically Tuscan patterns of rustication, while light-colored travertine is used for sharp-edged moldings. The combination of curved and straight forms in the pediment of the main portal would later influence Borromini's Oratory facade. Finally, the entablature that runs around the building breaks forward over the window frames, giving them each a monumental hood. Cortona also designed a gate to the Barberini gardens on the Via Pia as well as the nearby fountain, which forms one of the group of Four Fountains (Quattro Fontane) at the intersection of the Via Pia and the Via

Sistina; both show his imaginative variations on the traditional rustic mode used in villa gate design.

Cortona's great contribution to the Palazzo Barberini was in the realm of fictive rather than real architecture, namely, the frescoed vault of the main *salone*. Cortona executed the fresco between 1633 and 1639, but interrupted work for a trip to Florence, Lombardy, and Venice in 1637; after the trip, he supposedly remarked that he would like to redo the whole vault in the true Venetian manner, and it is possible that the original design underwent extensive revision over the last two years of work. Earlier in his career, in the two Sacchetti villas, Cortona had already experimented with ceiling paintings that used fictive architectural frameworks based on Annibale Carracci's Farnese Gallery, complete with stone herms, an interplay between real and stone figures, entwined stone dolphins, and fictive bronze medallions. Both of these vaults are opened up at the corners, so that the sky seems to be visible beyond the fictive architecture. Furthermore, in Castel Fusano the center of the vault was reserved for celestial allegories, while mythological and historical scenes are shown in the *quadri riportati* at the sides. All of these developments are taken much further in the Barberini ceiling. The center of the vault is reserved for a grand celestial allegory, while the "action" scenes are relegated to the sides. But there are no more *quadri riportati;* beyond the architectural framework, the heavens and landscapes are everywhere visible; figures and clouds seem to rise and fall through an open stone cage. The stone is painted to look pitted, like travertine of great age exposed to centuries of weather. In certain parts, especially around the scene of the Fall of the Giants, the stone itself seems to shatter under the impact of the giants' weight and of Minerva's attack. The architecture itself has roots in the innovations of later Florentine Mannerism, particularly the work of Bernardo Buontalenti, Giovanni Bologna, and Giovanni Antonio Dosio, but it goes far beyond them in complexity, abundance of motifs, and dynamic energy, combining a highly elaborate entablature with octagonal coffers around the bronze medallions, laurel swags, paired dolphins, consoles with human faces and grotesque masks, bucrania, vases, shields, and endless variations on the volute. There is a subtle interaction, and occasionally a sexual attraction, between the stone figures of the architecture and the flesh-and-blood figures immediately adjacent to them; stone *ignudi* brush up against terrified harpies, falling giants, sunburned satyrs, and lightly clad female allegories.

The central allegory of the ceiling revolves

around an enormous Barberini coat of arms, which is being assembled by Faith, Hope, and Charity out of its constituent elements (bees and laurel), while Rome and Religion add the tiara and the papal keys. The central figure of the ceiling, Divine Providence, instructs Immortality to add the stellar crown to the arms. Divine Providence is seated above the clouds among eleven allegorical figures, including Chastity, Eternity, Justice, and Modesty, while below her are the Three Fates and Time devouring his children. In one corner, a small putto reaches out to crown the arms with an inconspicuous laurel crown. The scene may be encapsulated by calling it the triple coronation of the Barberini arms, with the laurel crown of poetry, the tiara of the papacy, and the crown of immortality. This last coronation may reflect the birth of two male heirs to Taddeo Barberini in 1630 and 1631, which insured the family against the extinction symbolized by Time and the Fates. Along the sides of the vault are series of action scenes which were linked at any early date, at least in popular interpretations of the ceiling, with the roles and deeds of various

Cortona.
Palazzo Barberini (salon
  ceiling frescoes).
Rome.
1628–1639

members of the Barberini family; whatever the truth of this thesis, there is a suggestive correlation between the scenes and the architectural divisions of the palace. Over the fireplace, on the side of the *salone* closest to Taddeo Barberini's apartment, are fiery scenes having to do with secular government. Vulcan and the Cyclopes forge the arms of war; Peace (?) looks at her own reflection in a mirror held up by Prudence, while dispatching Readiness with a key to close the Temple of Janus; the Fury of War is bound up while Fame hovers overhead. In these scenes, Cortona comes closest to the vocabulary of political allegory established by Rubens in his cycle of paintings for Marie de' Medici. On the opposite side of the *salone,* closest to Cardinal Francesco Barberini's apartment and to the famous Barberini Library, are scenes of poetic allegory. On one side, drunken Silenus is surrounded by bacchantes and satyrs, on the other Venus lies on her couch amidst nymphs bathing in a fountain. Here, Cortona approaches the spirit of revelry found in Carracci's Farnese Gallery, but he shows it as a world superseded. Venus is confronted by a white-veiled figure of Purity with her lilies, while Eros is vanquished by Anteros. Above the tumult rises a cloud with the young Virgin, Wisdom, holding a burning lamp and an open book, and the matronly figure of Religion with a flaming altar. On the short end of the *salone* near the main facade of the palace, facing the city of Rome, Hercules defeats the Harpies, while Justice instructs Abundance to distribute food to a crowd of old men, nursing mothers, and children. On the opposite wall, Minerva topples the giants and crushes them beneath a falling mountain; on her breastplate she wears the Palladium with an image of the Gorgon's head entwined with snakes, corresponding to a similar image sculpted by Bernini on the portal just below.

In addition to the *salone* ceiling, Cortona did several small frescoes in Taddeo Barberini's wing of the palace, including the chapel vault, decorated with instruments of the passion, and a small gallery which contains an interesting scene of Vulcan Recognizing Caeculus, the mythical founder of the Roman city of Praeneste. In the background, Cortona painted a version of his scheme for reconstructing the Temple of Praeneste, which is also known from a drawing in the Victoria and Albert Museum and from prints published by J. Suarez in 1655. The idea of reconstructing Praeneste, at least on paper, goes back to ANDREA PALLADIO and Ligorio, but the Barberini resurrected the idea, possibly with the intention of actually carrying it out, after they had acquired the fief of Palestrina from the Colonna family in 1629. Cortona probably drew up his project in 1636, when he was staying in Palestrina to direct reconstruction work on the Church of San Pietro; and even though the project was shelved, Cortona's hand can still be recognized in some small architectural details in the rebuilt exedra that stands over the ancient temple site.

In the 1630s, Cortona also did a number of small but significant ecclesiastical designs, none of which survives unaltered. In 1633–1635, he designed the Chapel of the Immaculate Conception in San Lorenzo in Damaso, Cardinal Francesco Barberini's church attached to the Cancelleria Palace. Great care was lavished on marble wall revetments; in the vault, stucco putti carried a complicated stucco picture frame aloft, while the rest of the vault was divided into compartments by stucco ribs. The removal of the vault frescoes in 1820 makes it difficult to imagine the play that must have existed between architectonic form and free aerial space. In February 1633, Cortona designed an apparatus for the Forty Hours Devotion for the same church, which was re-erected and dismantled annually at least until 1648, and which is recorded in a drawing in Windsor. Cortona conceived of the devotion as a theatrical event and erected a large stage setting made of columns, pilasters, and statue niches all converging on a central triumphal arch, beyond which the spectator could glimpse angels, bathed in a flood of light, carrying a tabernacle containing the consecrated host. Both clouds and light break out of their confines and flow into the spectator's space, as they do in the Barberini ceiling. In 1634, Cortona prepared a design for the high altar chapel of San Giovanni dei Fiorentini; it was begun on a different design by Francesco Borromini in 1656 and then completed after Borromini's death in 1667 by Cortona's disciple, Ciro Ferri. Cortona's design envisaged a unique fusion of architecture, sculpture, and directed light. At the center stood a relief of the Baptism of Christ in the Jordan, which was lit from the two sides by light entering the church from the rear and flowing around columns set in its path. God the Father made his apparition in a frame set above the altar, while in the pediment appeared an image of the Holy Spirit, resplendent in light, as though made out of stained glass.

Cortona's great commission of the Barberini period was the Church of Santi Luca e Martina on the Roman Forum, next to the Arch of Septimius Severus and the ancient senate house. It was to occupy the artist for his entire life and eventually to house his tomb; it is the only building entirely by Cortona, inside and out. Its double name reflects its origin as two distinct churches. The painters' guild of Rome, the Accademia di San Luca, was founded in 1577 and centered in the small church of San Luca near Santa Maria Maggiore. When San Luca was demolished in 1588 in the course of Sixtus V's street planning, the academy acquired the old Church of Santa Martina, which had been built in the seventh century in the secretariat of the neighboring senate house. Soon, they decided to rebuild Santa Martina entirely, and by 1592 a wooden model for the new church had been submitted by GIOVANNI BATTISTA MONTANO, and several plans by OTTAVIANO MASCHERINO. No immediate steps were taken. In 1623–1624, there was some acquisition of new property, but no offers of immediate finance. In 1634, Cortona was elected *principe* or head of the academy, and he undertook to renovate the crypt of Santa Martina at his own expense. This was a calculated risk which soon paid off with the discovery of the relics of the saint and her companion martyrs, which caused an immediate sensation and led to generous contributions toward the rebuilding, including a gift of 6,000 *scudi* from Cardinal Francesco Barberini for the high altar alone. Construction began in 1635 and continued through Cortona's north Italian trip in 1637; work halted during Francesco Barberini's brief exile in Paris in 1646–1648; the two transverse arms were begun in 1653 and their terminal apses in 1656; Cortona was buried in the crypt in 1669, but there are indications that the façade as it stood then and now was not quite complete.

The problem that bedevils the history of the design of Santi Luca e Martina is the dating of the early drawings. There are a series of circular plans, copied by Domenico Martinelli and others after Cortona originals, that show a church based on Michelangelo's projects for San Giovanni dei Fiorentini, but they are also influenced by Montano's studies of ancient *tempietti* and funereal architecture. Judging from their classicism and other stylistic characteristics, it is conceivable that they could represent projects of the early 1620s. Cortona's only autograph drawing is a section in Munich that shows a much more highly evolved version of the design, one that it would seem natural to date to 1634. However, it shows a papal tomb with a faintly sketched coat of arms that cannot be read as Barberini bees. Either it is the Pamphilj shield (as argued in new research by Anthony Blunt), which would imply that the drawing is really an early project for Sant'Agnese in Piazza Navona; or it is the Ludovisi shield (as argued by Karl Noehles), which would imply the extraordinarily early date of 1621–1623. Whatever the solution to this quandary, both the Munich drawing and the final Church of Santi Luca e Martina present close variants of the same ideas and thus can be subjected to stylistic analysis together. Both show

a modified Greek-cross plan, with a circular central cupola and with transversal arms that are slightly shorter than the arms on the main longitudinal axis. The main innovation in both designs is the use of giant columns in great abundance to articulate the piers and walls. Flat surfaces tend to disappear altogether behind this mobile, plastic screen of columns. The influence of north Italian architecture is very strong, as is that of Michelangelo. Both Palladio's Redentore (1577ff.) in Venice and FRANCESCO MARIA RICCHINO's San Giuseppe in Milan (1607ff.) provide models for the use of giant columns in the church and the way the crossing piers of the drawing are pierced with doors and balconies. But Michelangelo's vestibule in the Laurentian Library in Florence, mixed in with influence from Michelangelo's Palazzo dei Conservatori on the Capitoline hill, is behind Cortona's use of paired columns set in tightly behind the plane of the wall. The rib system of the half-domes over the apses, which creates the effect of an umbrella billowing upward, is based on Michelangelo's famous motif in the apses of St. Peter's, studied and used by all baroque architects. But if the emphasis in Michelangelo's design is on taut surfaces and skeletal structure, in Cortona's it is on rich, vibrant ornament, piled up in a spirit of abundance and *horror vacui,* and the same spirit is evident in the use of ornament elsewhere in the church. The Munich drawing shows a plain cupola suitable for frescoes, but the final cupola was given a system of ribs and coffers that creates the sensation of con-

Cortona.
Santi Luca e Martina.
Rome.
1634–1669

stant movement and negates all sense of rest. Furthermore, there is an abundant use of figurative ornament, from numerous Barberini bees to the lilies and palms of Santa Martina; the four pendentives are richly decorated with evangelist symbols, set over the coat of arms of the academy (brush, chisel, modeling knife set in a triangle) which are crowned with laurel.

While the upper church of Santi Luca e Martina is executed in white travertine and stucco, rich effects of color are displayed in the crypt. The complex system of staircases, dark corridors, and small Hadrianic chambers is meant to evoke the feeling of mystery experienced by seventeenth-century explorers of the crypts and catacombs of early Christian Rome. The altar chapel is lined in precious marbles and alabaster, and the altar itself, in which the body of Santa Martina is displayed, is made of gilt bronze and lapis lazuli, surpassing all contemporary altars in opulence of effect. The chapel is covered with a vault that is almost totally flat but is articulated by coffers to create the illusion of depth; it rests on four flat arches as taut as carriage springs and below them on four columns set against crossing piers.

Since Santi Luca e Martina was set into a cluster of older houses at the rear, the best view was from the Roman Forum in front. If the façade was begun as early as the crypt in 1635, it is the first of the great curved facades of the baroque, antedating Borromini's Oratory of 1637 and the early plans for San Carlo alle Quattro Fontane, which probably date to 1638. It consists of a central portion following a gentle convex curve, held between straight outer bays. The four central columns seem to be pushed into the surface of the facade like stone into clay. Rich ornament alludes to the patron and to the saint, and everywhere there is an energetic multiplication of horizontal moldings and of sharp vertical edges. At present, the facade is two stories high, with a flat top surmounted by torches and a coat of arms. However, a number of graphic sources suggest that it is unfinished; some show a crowning pediment, others an expansion of

the side bays into large fields set at an angle to the main facade. The cupola shows a similar inventive richness, in particular in the way relieving arches are embellished with moldings and volutes.

Between 1637 and 1647, Cortona spent most of his time outside Rome in the service of the grand duke of Florence, Ferdinando II de' Medici. His principal work in Florence was the transformation of the grand-ducal residence, the Pitti Palace, through a typically baroque combination of painting, interior decoration in stucco, architecture, and scenography. The Florentine connection began in 1637, when Cortona interrupted his work on the Barberini ceiling to accompany Cardinal Sacchetti on a trip to northern Italy; possibly he resented Bernini's growing absolutism over the Roman artistic scene and was on the lookout for other opportunities. His tryout commission consisted of two frescoes in a small room in the Pitti known as the Sala della Stufa. The scenes, consisting of the Age of Gold and the Age of Silver, refer to the Vergilian myth of the return of the Golden Age and are to be interpreted in the light of Ferdinando II's marriage to Vittoria della Rovere of Urbino in April 1637 and to Medici expectations of an heir. Cortona's stay was brief, but he returned to Florence in 1640 to finish the two remaining scenes (the Age of Bronze and the Age of Iron) and to undertake one of the major decorative programs of his career, the ceilings of the four (later five) Planetary Rooms, which formed the main ceremonial reception suite of the Pitti Palace. The author of the program for these ceilings was Francesco Rondinelli. The scheme involved treating each room in an enfilade as one of the successive planetary deities of the Ptolemaic universe (in spite of the Medici patronage of Galileo): Venus, Apollo or the sun, Mars, Jove or Jupiter, and later Saturn. As the visitor advanced through the rooms and through the cycle of planets, he also penetrated deeper into the grand-ducal apartment, finally encountering the throne room in the Sala di Giove. The glory of the rooms lies in the combination of rich stucco ornament and illusionistic ceiling fresco. The stucco framework embodies and even exaggerates the architectural stresses and forces of the actual vault, while the central fresco zone opens the vault up to scenes set in luminous, airy skies. The stucco work was actually carried out by a Roman team under the direction of Giovanni Maria Sorrisi, a craftsman who had worked for Borromini at the Oratory of the Filippini; it is full of Borrominian trademarks and of motifs taken from the repertoire of Florentine Mannerism, with Cortona's usual sense of abundance and lavish redundancy of form. The first room, the Sala di Venere, began the allegorical life-story of an ideal-

Cortona.
Palazzo Pitti (Sala di
Venere).
Florence.
1637–1647

ized Medici prince who journeys through life, shunning pleasure and courting virtue, arriving at various degrees of victory, glory, and apotheosis. The young prince is shown snatched by Minerva and Hercules from the couch and banquet of Venus, somewhat unwillingly, to begin his journey; in eight lunettes around the sides of the vault, Cortona depicted mythological scenes of princes who rejected sensual pleasure in favor of virtuous continence. In the next room in the sequence, the Sala di Apollo (actually painted last and left unfinished in 1647), the prince, accompanied by Fame, is shown by Apollo the celestial globe supported by Hercules, while inscriptions and lunette scenes stress themes of learning, wisdom, virtue, and the golden mean. In the third room, the Sala di Marte (1644–1646), the young hero triumphs in battle, while Hercules erects a trophy and captives assemble before a triumphal arch. In the fourth room, the Sala di Giove or Throne Room (1642–1643/1644), Fortune and Hercules present the prince to Jupiter to receive his crown, while allegorical figures representing virtuous governance gather around. In general, the theme of the rooms has to do with the education of the ideal ruler, analogous to the tradition of Mirrors for Princes (*De regimine principum*). The ceilings do not illustrate the career of any particular Medici prince, but they were intended as a message to young Medici princes for generations to come, beginning with Ferdinando II's son, Cosimo III, born in August 1642 as the Sala di Venere was underway. There may be a more specific reference in the Sala di Marte to the recent War of Castro, in which the Barberini were defeated by the Medici in alliance with the Farnese, and papal pretensions to temporal hegemony tarnished.

In addition to the Planetary Rooms, Cortona also offered advice on the modernization of the Pitti Palace, which is reflected in a few undated drawings that have come to light. He envisaged outfitting the street façade (which had been enormously expanded under GIULIO PARIGI in 1618–1635) with a number of features in a heavy rustic style similar to the rustic architecture of the courtyard by BARTOLOMMEO AMMANNATI. These included a three-bay rustic portal with a pediment for the Medici arms and a balcony for the public appearances of the grand duke, and also numerous variants of window frames with inverted volutes in the Buontalenti tradition. He also envisaged the transformation of the entire slope of the Boboli Gardens behind the palace into a unified ensemble, with a courtyard fountain, semicircular exedra, and a kind of belvedere or viewing box crowning the whole composition on the top of the hill. The whole arrangement was meant to be viewed, sceno-

graphically, from the center of the courtyard or from the *piano nobile,* rather like the way in which Bramante meant his Belvedere Courtyard at the Vatican Palace to be viewed. In fact, the whole transformation of the palace has strong Roman imperial overtones, with many references to the combination of palace and garden found on the Palatine Hill in Rome, and surely Cortona was instructed to celebrate Medici pretensions to royal power and simultaneously to challenge papal claims to temporal authority. However, none of these grand schemes was carried out. Cortona's one other contribution to the palace was the decoration and architecture of a small mezzanine suite for the grand duke's brother, Cardinal Giancarlo de' Medici, in about 1644–1647. It consisted of a room with ceiling frescoes of allegorical and biblical scenes by Cortona and Salvatore Rosa, a small nymphaeum with bold and complex architectural detail, and finally a very rustic fountain meant to be seen at the end of a long vista. Both the frescoes and the fountain expressed the theme of the attainment of repose and quiet, familiar also from Cortona's other work for Giancarlo, a fresco representing an allegory of Quiet in the cardinal's casino in the Orti Oricellari.

In the realm of ecclesiastical architecture, Cortona's great project in the Florentine period was the design of the Oratorian Church of San Firenze, which was begun on a grand scale in 1645 but was eventually carried out by other architects in reduced and modified form. The Florentine Congregation of the Oratory of San Filippo Neri was founded in 1632 and transferred to the old church of San Firenze in 1640. The founder, Father Francesco Cerretani, had close connections with the Barberini and the Sacchetti in Rome, as well as with the Florentine aristocracy, including the grand duke himself. He managed to attract the financial support of the nobleman Giuliano Serragli for a new church, and Serragli in turn nominated Cortona as the architect in January 1645. Cortona seems to have been warned off the project in a letter from his friend Cassiano dal Pozzo, but nevertheless went ahead and planned a grandiose basilica in the form of a Latin cross with giant cupola, six chapels flanking the side aisles of the nave, and two chapels flanking the apse. The most expensive element of the design were the thirty-two columns of the nave and crossing. The old church of San Firenze faced east, away from the center of the city, but Cortona reversed the orientation and envisaged a façade facing west, catching the view of travelers approaching from the Palazzo Vecchio and the Piazza della Signoria. The apse was begun in the old Piazza San Firenze in May 1645, but by the end of that year funds had been exhausted and there was a growing feeling among the Oratorians, except for Cerretani, that the project was too grand. In January 1646, Cortona wrote a disillusioned letter to dal Pozzo, saying that he had always had bad luck in matters of architecture, not because he lacked grand visions but because he did not have a knack for intrigue; henceforth, he claimed, architecture would serve only for his diversion. Work stopped in 1646, and when he left Florence in 1647 he left behind drawings and a wooden model that survived into the eighteenth century. Serragli's generous bequest of 1648 refueled Cerretani's ambitions, but by then most Oratorians wanted a smaller church with a conventional pilaster order to replace Cortona's expensive columns. Changes were introduced into Cortona's project in 1658–1660 by Pier Francesco Silvani, and in spite of Cortona's protests from Rome, work was begun on the new project in 1668. Silvani planned to start with a modest oratory, which became the present day Church of San Firenze; he also planned a larger church immediately next door, but like Cortona's project, Silvani's basilica remained on paper.

In spite of his frustrations with the San Firenze project, Cortona remained close to the Oratorian community in Rome, and when he returned to the city in 1647 he began work on the interior decoration of the Oratorian Church of Santa Maria in Vallicella (the Chiesa Nuova), which was to continue for nearly two decades and to embody many ideas already expressed in drawings for San Firenze. In 1647–1651, he frescoed the cupola of the Vallicella with the Trinity in Glory Together with the Instruments of the Passion. To improve visibility of the figures he rebuilt the base of the cupola, opening up four oval windows and creating a rudimentary drum where none had existed before. He raised the lantern to increase the intake of light, and in a beautiful illusionistic manner he made it seem as if frescoed putti were actually bearing the lantern, like a luminous object, in the middle of space. In 1649–1651, he asked for and received permission to extend his elaborate stucco decorations down from the cupola level into the area of the pendentives and the upper zones of the transept. In 1650–1653, he redesigned the small cupola over the Chapel of San Filippo Neri, giving it a pattern of fictive stucco coffers and a lantern that seems to be held in the grip of dynamic stucco ribs. In 1655–1660, he completed the fresco in the apse of the church, the Assumption of the Virgin which takes place amidst a multitude of saints including Filippo Neri, Gregory the Great (to whom the Vallicella was originally dedicated), and Santa Cecilia (the original patron of the musical oratory). In 1662–1664, Ercole Ferrata and Cosimo Fancelli, working under Cortona's direction, completed the elaborate stucco decoration of the nave, and in 1664–1665 Cortona himself, now nearly seventy, did the fresco. The subject was an incident from the early history of the building, when the Virgin miraculously supported some beams which threatened to collapse while the old basilica of the Vallicella (shown with marble columns) was being dismantled. In the background, the new church is seen rising, its piers vaulted only by the sky, a state to which it would one day return thanks to the beautiful illusionism of Cortona's frescoes in the apse and cupola. The whole scene is framed with a gilt stucco cornice that is held aloft by angels, who superimpose the picture over a coffering pattern that seems to run on behind it. In an even more developed way than the Pitti ceilings, the decorations in the Vallicella show a subtle interaction between frame and picture, space and solid, painting and architecture.

Cortona's last great dynastic fresco cycle was the Story of Aeneas, painted in 1651–1654 on the vault of the gallery of the Palazzo Pamphilj in Piazza Navona. The gallery itself had been built by Borromini in 1646 as a long, narrow appendage to the palace; when Innocent X decided to rebuild the Church of Sant'Agnese in 1650, the gallery assumed a pivotal role as the main representational room of the palace and the link between the public rooms and the pope's private suite near the church. In planning its decoration, Cortona referred to his own earlier work in the *sala grande* of the Palazzo Barberini, and he also incorporated in fresco the type of fictive architectural framework built in stucco in the Pitti Palace. In addition, he seems to have contributed to the design of the twelve doorframes that line the gallery and house busts of the twelve Caesars, announcing the imperial-dynastic theme of the decoration as a whole. The frescoes show scenes of the early arrival of Aeneas on Italian soil: *Quos Ego,* the Landing at the Tiber's Mouth, Aeneas and Evander, the Death of Turnus, the Golden Bough, and the Forging of Aeneas's arms. The original Vergilian text was interpreted in the light of Landino's commentaries on it, and the whole story can be read as an allegory on many levels of the three stages of life, of the distant origins of the Pamphilj family, and of the foundation of the papacy. The key seems to be the idea that the Roman pontiff, in particular the Pamphilj pope Innocent X, is prefigured in Aeneas. Interpreted in this way, Cortona's frescoes reflect the same theme as Borromini's architecture, which used the Serlian motif to convey an image of the imperial papacy; both artists must have been aware of the pope's intentions to move to the palace and to transfer the curia there.

With the accession of Alexander VII Chigi to the papacy in 1655, Cortona returned to the world of built architecture and produced two of the most brilliant façades of the baroque era, Santa Maria della Pace and Santa Maria in Via Lata. Santa Maria della Pace was a late fifteenth-century church built by Sixtus IV to commemorate the end of a war between the Medici and the papacy. It was a simple box with an octagonal cupola at one end and a plain façade at the other. It stood in one of the most crowded areas of the city, just west of the Piazza Navona; and one of Alexander VII's intentions was to open up a small piazza in front of the church to facilitate the maneuvering of carriages. In the final design, this piazza is conceived as a small urban stage, and the buildings which bordered on it were given uniform façades; the effect is similar to the small enclosed spaces created by temporary façades in Florentine triumphal processions. The façade itself, built in 1656–1659, is the most complex of all Cortona's architectural designs. The central motif is a semicircular tempietto, supported by paired Tuscan columns. The tempietto expresses the baroque reinterpretation of the original dedication of the church as a temple of peace; it has its sources in paintings by Rubens and Cortona himself, as well as in the way Renaissance archeologists reconstructed ancient structures such as the Baths of Diocletian. The tempietto curves out into the piazza while side wings curve back in, and on an intermediate plane, volutes reach out on either side to link the façade to its wings and to the houses around the piazza. All these themes are restated in compact form in the upper story of the façade, where concave and convex forms intersect amidst a rich and lively ornament of columns and pilasters. Real and fictive windows are used to maintain the appearance of symmetry, while the irregular street system is accommodated through doors that resemble openings in a *scaenae frons* or stage set. Cortona also restored the interior of the church, including the stuccoes of the nave vault and cupola; he rebuilt the Chigi Chapel (first on the right), preserving Raphael's fresco of the Four Sibyls and planning a pendant to it across the nave.

In 1658–1662, Cortona built the monumental façade of Santa Maria in Via Lata on the Corso, Rome's principal thoroughfare. The church had originally been an early Christian *diaconia* that was rebuilt by Pope Innocent VIII in 1491–1508. Bernini designed the high altar chapel in 1636–1643, and the Neapolitan sculptor-architect COSIMO FANZAGO modernized the interior in about 1650. The learned antiquarian Fioravante Martinelli, Borromini's friend and author of several guidebooks to the city, wrote a treatise on the old

Cortona.
Santa Maria della Pace.
Rome.
1656–1659

church in 1655, sparking an interest that led to the restoration compaign under Cortona of 1658. Martinelli explained that the building was not originally a church but a house, or more precisely, the hotel in which St. Peter had first stayed while visiting Rome in A.D. 44; thus, it was the site of the first mass in Rome, the original home of the papacy, and the predecessor of the Lateran as the first papal palace or *reggia*. Cortona's first action in 1658 was to excavate and restore the crypt, which still contains a number of frescoes and cult objects in a medievalizing style by Cortona's shop. The space was organized scenographically, with a vista through a grille to an inner chamber. The church itself was encased in a high wall, and entered at the front through a columnar portico modeled on Renaissance exemplars (especially BALDASSARE PERUZZI's Palazzo Massimi alle Colonne). Inside, the portico was covered with a barrel vault, and two large flat apses were installed on either side, each with a door leading down to the crypt. Ingenious moldings create the impression that the apses could slide in or out, as though on rails. While the portico was under construction, Cortona must have noticed the intense building activity in the palaces immediately around the church, particularly the wing of the Palazzo Doria Pamphilj which stands at the rear; he must have been concerned to insure that his own façade was not dwarfed by the new buildings. Accordingly in 1662, Alexander VII approved the design of a second story for the façade, which incorporates a grand Serlian motif, or more accurately, an arcuated lintel of the sort found in Roman imperial residences. Borromini had used the same motif in

Cortona.
Santa Maria in Via Lata.
Rome.
1658–1662

the gallery of the Palazzo Pamphilj in 1646, drawing on the imagery of the imperial viewing box overlooking the circus of the Piazza Navona. Surely, Cortona and Alexander VII had the same imagery in mind for Santa Maria in Via Lata, except that the circus is now to be understood as the Corso. Indeed, at the time Cortona's façade was nearing completion, the pope placed an inscription further up the street proclaiming it the "hippodrome of the festive city." Santa Maria della Pace and Santa Maria in Via Lata at first sight seem to represent totally opposed styles: the first the exuberant, three-dimensional, restless character one associates with the high baroque; the second, the calm, flat severity typical of late baroque classicism. But on closer examination the process of design is the same. In each the iconographical theme of the project (the temple of peace or the imperial-papal *reggia* overlooking a circus) is expressed through a concrete image that is tied closely to its architectural context and is enriched with Cortona's inimitable exuberance of detail.

In 1664, Cortona was one of four Italian architects who sent projects to Paris for the completion of the Louvre. Bernini was the favored candidate from the start and sent his project first; a month later, in July 1664, Carlo Rainaldi and an otherwise obscure architect named Candiani sent their projects. Cortona, troubled with gout and busy with the Vallicella frescoes, sent his last, through Alexander VII and the grand duke of Tuscany, in September 1664. The pope is said to have esteemed Cortona's projects over all the others, probably because of their tact with regard to French criteria of decorum, but Bernini criticized them as too

expensive, and Bernini's French host Chantelou said they gave the impression more of a palace than a temple. Three of Cortona's elevations are preserved in the *Recueil du Louvre* in Paris, showing his designs for the main east façade (later built by CLAUDE PERRAULT), the court façade behind it, and the west façade facing the Tuileries. All adopt the French idea of a large central pavilion with a crown-shaped vault topped by a pyramidal or onion-shaped finial. Although the sweeping curves of Bernini's early projects were rejected, the west façade does show a very mild version of the combination of concave and convex forms of Santa Maria della Pace. Many of the window frames resemble those of Cortona's project for the Pitti façade; there is a touch of Pitti-style rustication; Borrominian door and window frames sometimes appear; and there are frequent allusions to Michelangelo's Capitoline palaces. Cortona succeeded in grafting robust baroque detail onto the severe straight surfaces and pavilionated plans demanded by the French commission, but even before they arrived in Paris, his drawings had been rejected and plans were afoot for summoning Bernini to supervise the project in person.

Repercussions from the Louvre designs may be seen in Cortona's last project for Alexander VII, namely, the plan to move the show-fountain (*mostra*) of the Trevi aqueduct to the Piazza Colonna and to give it a monumental architectural backdrop. Three façade elevations and a plan in the Chigi Library in the Vatican, datable to early 1667, show the familar motifs of Pitti-style rustication, giant order over a rustic base, central triumphal arch, and, in the most interesting project, a concave façade with a monumental fountain basin at its foot. Although unexecuted, the combination of monumental palace façade with a naturalistic fountain and a giant basin proved a key influence in the final design for the Trevi Fountain, carried out by NICOLA SALVI in 1732–1762.

Cortona's activity under Alexander VII also included a number of small chapel designs. In 1656, he redecorated the Chapel of the Sacrament in San Marco, which includes a curiously coffered vault, similar to the Chapel of San Filippo in Santa Maria in Vallicella, but it is otherwise an undistinguished work. In 1662, he prepared a model for the redecoration of the tribune (called the Chapel of the Apostles) in San Giovanni in Laterano, which included an interesting columnar centerpiece that uses the same illusionistic techniques as Borromini's tombs in the nave and aisles. In addition, it provided a baldachin over the papal throne, a musicians' balcony, and a reliquary for the heads of the apostles Peter and Paul. Like Borromini's own projects for an apostles' reliquary, it remained unexecuted. The Gavotti Chapel in San Nicola di Tolentino was begun on Cortona's designs in 1668. The finest of his small chapels, it exudes a sense of tremendous compression, particularly in the way the Capitoline motif (pair of columns supporting a flat architrave) is squeezed into the limited space of the side walls and in the way the cupola repeats in miniature the theme of the Vallicella frescoes, with painted putti bearing the lantern aloft.

Cortona's last great work of architecture was the cupola of San Carlo al Corso (originally Santi Ambrogio e Carlo), the church of the Lombard community in Rome. The church was begun in 1612 and continued up to the crossing by the architects Onorio Longhi and Martino Longhi the Younger (see LONGHI FAMILY). The large tribune was undertaken in 1662–1663, and among the architects called in for consultations on the strength of the crossing piers in 1665 was Cortona, "who now holds first place in the theory of this profession." His cupola, begun in 1668, is less painterly and more purely architectural than the earlier cupola of Santi Luca e Martina; it uses the Capitoline motif and clusters of pilasters to create a highly skeletal drum, while the zone above is pierced by eight extra oculi that, along with the lantern, allow a flood of light onto the frescoes by Giacinto Brandi (1671ff.) that decorate the interior.

Cortona published no books specifically related to architectural theory. At some point during his Florentine stay, he lent his name to a treatise "on the uses and abuses of painting and sculpture" by a Jesuit named Giandomenico Ottonelli, and although there are indeed a few commonplaces of artistic theory scattered throughout the work, they are drowned amidst Ottonelli's obsession with sex in art, and the result is a generally appalling book. Much more indicative of Cortona's theoretical views is a speech delivered to the Accademia di San Luca in 1634, in which he espoused belief in the academic doctrine of the Idea, with concomitant neohumanistic theories of the creation of man in the image of God. Since he was an autodidact himself, he believed in the necessity of forming one's style on a number of acknowledged masters. Typically Florentine elements are noticeable in his early architectural style, such as the use of neat rustication and a decorative vocabulary borrowed from Mannerists like Buontalenti and Ammannati. But the dominant influence over his architectural development was the great example of Michelangelo. The Capitoline Palaces, the Laurentian Library, and the apses of St. Peter's inspired Cortona throughout his career. In his early vault frescoes, his point of departure was the robust and vigorous style of Annibale Carracci, to which he brought a

strong Venetian sense of color. He favored the epic over the dramatic mode, that is, a style in which the main themes were constantly interwoven with charming episodes rather than one of stern simplicity. If the Barberini ceiling shows the epic style in painting, then a façade like Santa Maria della Pace shows it in architecture: the main themes (tempietto and side wings) are relatively simple, but they are raised to a pitch of great complexity by the constant, ingenious interweaving of subsidiary motifs. There is a feeling of exuberance, strength, and abundance in all his work. There is also a strong interest in scenography; and the use of abundant, directed light, focused vistas, and stagelike backdrops appears both in his permanent architecture and in his ephemeral decorations.

Perhaps Cortona can best be described as the court artist par excellence of the Roman baroque, the closest Italian equivalent to Rubens, whose influence can often be detected both in artistic style and in style of life. Like Rubens he built his own house, and also like Rubens he strove to deepen his knowledge of antiquity from the early friendship with Cassiano dal Pozzo to his very last days, when he is recorded climbing Trajan's Column to sketch the reliefs and visiting recent excavations to copy ancient frescoes. His great church, Santi Luca e Martina, can be described both as a personal monument and as a statement of his convictions about the nobility of the arts of *disegno*.

Among Cortona's students, Ciro Ferri continued his style in Florence and Francesco Romanelli exported it to Paris. However, there was no Cortona school in the same sense as the school which formed around the aging Bernini and which was later guided by CARLO FONTANA. And unlike Borromini, Cortona experienced no marked revival of his style in the eighteenth century.

JOSEPH CONNORS

WORKS

1626–1627, Villa Sacchetti (gallery and chapel frescoes; later the Villa Chigi), Castel Fusano; 1627, San Lorenzo fuori le mura (left side aisle and the monument to Barclay and Guglielmi); 1628–1639, Palazzo Barberini (riding court, chapel, and gallery, and salon ceiling frescoes); 1633, San Lorenzo in Damaso (Forty Hours' Decoration); 1633–1635, Chapel of the Immaculate Conception, San Lorenzo in Damaso; 1634–1669, Santi Luca e Martina; Rome. *Mid-1630s, Villa Sacchetti del Pigneto, near Rome. 1637–1647, Palazzo Pitti (restoration, garden belvedere, grotto with nymphaeum, decoration of planetary rooms, Sala della Stufa, Sala di Venere, Sala di Giove, Sala di Marte, and the Sala di Apollo; completed in 1661 by Ciro Ferri); *1645, San Firenze (executed and modified by others); Florence. 1647–1665, Santa Maria in Vallicella (drum, lantern, cupola frescoes, pendentive and transept chapel stuccoes, San Filippo Neri Chapel cupola and lantern, apse frescoes, and nave stuccoes and fresco); 1651–1654, Pamphilj Gallery (fresco); 1656, Chapel of the Sacrament, San Marco; 1656–1657, Quirinal Palace (Gallery of Alexander VII); 1656–1659, Santa Maria della Pace (piazza, façade, and interior redecoration); 1658–1662, Santa Maria in Via Lata (façade and crypt); 1662, Francesco da Cortona House, Via della Pedacchia; 1668, San Carlo al Corso (cupola); 1668, Gavotti Chapel, San Nicola di Tolentino; Rome.

BIBLIOGRAPHY

ARCHIVIO DI STATO DI ROMA 1969 *Pietro da Cortona. Mostra documentaria. Itinerario.* Rome: Ministero dell'Interno.

BLUNT, ANTHONY 1958 "The Palazzo Barberini: the Contributions of Maderno, Bernini and Pietro da Cortona." *Journal of the Warburg and Courtauld Institutes* 21:256–287.

BRIGANTI, GIULIANO 1962 *Pietro da Cortona o della pittura barocca.* Florence: Sansoni.

CAMPBELL, MALCOLM 1977 *Pietro da Cortona at the Pitti Palace.* N.J.: Princeton University Press.

CASALE, VITTORIO 1969 "Pietro da Cortona e la Cappella del Sacramento in San Marco a Roma." *Commentari* 20:93–108.

CHIARINI, MARCO, and NOEHLES, KARL 1967 "Pietro da Cortona a Palazzo Pitti: Un episodio ritrovato." *Bollettino d'Arte* 52:233–239.

CISTELLINI, ANTONIO 1970 "Pietro da Cortona e la Chiesa di San Filippo Neri in Firenze." *Studi Secenteschi* 11:27–57.

COFFEY, CAROLINE 1978 "Pietro da Cortona's Project for the Church of San Firenze in Florence." *Mitteilungen des Kunsthistorischen Institutes in Florenz* 22:85–118.

FABBRINI, NARCISO 1896 *Vita del Cav. Pietro Berrettini da Cortona pittore ed architetto.* Cortona, Italy.

JACOB, SABINE 1971 "Pierre de Cortone et la décoration de la galerie d'Alexandre VII au Quirinal." *Revue de l'Art* 11:42–54.

LUGARI, GIOVANNI BATTISTA 1885 *La via della Peddacchia e la casa di Pietro da Cortona.* Rome: Befani.

NOEHLES, KARL 1961 "Die Louvre-Projekte von Pietro da Cortona und Carlo Rainaldi." *Zeitschrift für Kunstgeschichte* 24:40–74.

NOEHLES, KARL 1969 "Architekturprojekte Cortonas." *Münchner Jahrbuch der bildenden Kunst* 20:171–206.

NOEHLES, KARL 1970 "Der Hauptaltar von Santo Stefano in Pisa: Cortona, Ferri, Silvani, Foggini." *Giessener Beiträge zur Kunstgeschichte* 1:87–123.

NOEHLES, KARL 1970 *La chiesa dei SS. Luca e Martina nell'opera di Pietro da Cortona.* Rome: Bozzi. With contributions by Incisa della Rocchetta, Giovanni, and Carlo Pietrangeli.

OST, HANS 1971 "Studien zu Pietro da Cortonas Umbau von S. Maria della Pace." *Römisches Jahrbuch für Kunstgeschichte* 13:231–285.

OTTONELLI, GIANDOMENICO, and CORTONA, PIETRO BERRETTINI DA (1652)1973 *Trattato della pittura e scultura: Uso et abuso loro.* With an introduction and notes by Vittorio Casale. Reprint. Treviso, Italy: Canova.

POSSE, HANS 1919 "Das Deckenfresko des Pietro da Cortona im Palazzo Barberini und die Deckenmalerie in Rom." *Jahrbuch der Preuszischen Kunstsammlungen* 40:93–118, 126–173.

RASY, ELISABETTA 1972 "Pietro da Cortona: I progetti per la Chiesa Nuova di Firenze." *Architettura barocca a Roma.* Edited by Fagiolo dell Arco. Maurizio, and Rome, Italy: Bulzoni.

THELEN, HEINRICH 1967 *Francesco Borromini: Die Handzeichnungen.* Graz, Austria: Akademische Drucku. Verlangsanstalt.

VITZTHUM, WALTER 1961 "A Comment on the Iconography of Pietro da Cortona's Barberini Ceiling." *Burlington Magazine* 103:427–434.

WIRBIRAL, NORBERT 1960 "Contributi alle ricerche sul Cortonismo in Roma: I pittori della Galleria di Alessandro VII nel Palazzo del Quirinale." *Bollettino d'Arte* 45:123–165.

WITTKOWER, RUDOLF (1935)1975 "Pietro da Cortona's Project for Reconstructing the Temple of Palestrina." In *Studies in the Italian Baroque.* London: Thames & Hudson.

WITTKOWER, RUDOLF (1967)1973 *Art and Architecture in Italy: 1600–1750.* Harmondsworth, England, and Baltimore: Penguin.

COSENZA, LUIGI

Luigi Cosenza (20th century) emerged in the post–World War II era as the leading proponent of Modern architecture in Naples and the Campania, Italy. Already in active practice in the 1930s (he collaborated with the Milanese Rationalists EDUARDO PERSICO and GIUSEPPE PAGANO), Cosenza showed a renewed interest and commitment in his postwar work to public housing and social and political concerns, even though his most famous work is the Olivetti Plant (1957–1969) in Pozzuoli, Italy.

THOMAS L. SCHUMACHER

WORKS

1930, Fish Market, Naples, Italy. 1934, Villa Oro; 1937, Villa Savarese; Gulf of Naples, Italy. 1946, Residential Quarter, Viale Augusto, Naples, Italy. 1957–1969, Olivetti Factory Buildings, Pozzuoli, Italy. 1961–1969, Politecnico, Naples, Italy.

BIBLIOGRAPHY

L'Architettura 1969 15, no. 1: entire issue.

"Casa Cernia ad Anacapri." 1971 *L'Architettura* 17, no. 7:450–455.

COSENZA, L. 1971 "Il rapporto nord sud." *Casabella* 42, nos. 440–441:40–41.

GALARDI, ALBERTO 1967 *New Italian Architecture.* New York: Praeger.

GREGOTTI, VITTORIO 1968 *New Directions in Italian Architecture.* New York: Braziller.

"Luigi Cosenza 'apriamo i cantieri ai critici." 1977 *L'Architettura* 23, no. 7:356.

COSSUTIUS

The architect who gave the huge Corinthian temple of Olympian Zeus in Athens its definitive form, beginning in 174 B.C., Cossutius is spoken of approvingly by VITRUVIUS in the preface to Book VII of *De architectura*. Columns from his work, brought to Rome in 86 B.C., may have speeded the Hellenization of Roman formal architecture.

WILLIAM L. MACDONALD

COSTA, LÚCIO

Born of a French mother and Brazilian father in Toulouse, France, Lúcio Costa (1902–) studied painting and architecture at the National School of Fine Arts in Rio de Janeiro. After graduating in 1924, he participated in the neo-Colonial Revival popular in Brazil during the 1930s, and to this day he remains one of Brazil's foremost authorities on colonial architecture. His vision and undaunted persistence to evolve the art of architecture in Brazil distinguishes him as the true father of Brazil's modern architectural movement.

When only twenty-eight, Lúcio Costa was appointed director of the National School of Fine Arts to update the antiquated teaching methods. He replaced the Beaux-Arts curriculum with the functionalist approach of the Bauhaus and LE CORBUSIER. Unfortunately, Costa's reforms were too extreme for the government overseers, and a year later he was forced to leave. His students reacted with a six-month strike and victory for the new curriculum. These same students later became the vanguard of Brazil's modern architectural movement. Costa opened a private office with GREGORI WARCHAVCHIC, and students followed in order to discuss the latest architectural theories of WALTER GROPIUS, LUDWIG MIES VAN DER ROHE, and in particular Le Corbusier.

In 1936, Gustavo Capanema, the minister of education, asked Costa to submit a design for the ministry building, having rejected the academic design chosen by a government jury. Once the design was completed, Costa asked Capanema if Le Corbusier could be contracted as a consultant for the ministry design and for the federal university plan. In 1936, Le Corbusier spent three weeks in Rio de Janeiro working with Costa and a group of young architects elaborating plans for both projects. Costa headed the architectural team of the ministry building until 1939 when again, because of political tension, he moved on to other projects.

Costa's architectural output increased during the 1940s and 1950s as his didactic role decreased. From 1948 to 1954, he worked on the award-winning Eduardo Guinle Apartments, and in 1955 he designed the Brazilian Pavilion at the City University of Paris in conjunction with Le Corbusier.

In 1956, Costa's pilot plan for Brazil's new capital, Brasília, was chosen by an international jury for its clarity and directness, integrating monumentality into daily life. Costa described the airplanelike configuration of the plan as the basic gesture which designates possession of a piece of property. In 1968, Costa was asked once again to aid in urbanizing Brazil, this time the Barra da Tijuca, a beach resort and suburban development of Rio de Janeiro. He drew up an extensive plan, preserving the tropical ecology with parks and nature reserves and integrating apartments and houses into the lush terrain. Regrettably, his plan lost out to speculators and has subsequently been abandoned.

Wearied by the polemics of Brazilian architecture, Costa now devotes his time to the Brazilian Society for Historical Preservation in the hope that young Brazilian architects will not forget their own heritage. A shy, retiring individual, Costa has been a tireless force behind the development of modern architecture in Brazil.

ELIZABETH D. HARRIS

WORKS

1931, Gamboa Housing Project; 1936–1939, Ministry of Education and Health (now the Palácio da Cultura; with Carlos Leão, OSCAR NIEMEYER, EDUARDO AFFONSO REIDY, Ernani Vasconcellos, JORGE MOREIRA, and Le Corbusier as consultant); 1942, Hungria Machade House; Rio de Janeiro. 1944–1945, Parque-Hotel Sao Clemente, Nova Friburgo, Brazil. 1948–1954, Parque Eduardo Guinle Apartments, Rio de Janeiro. 1955–1959, Brazil House, Cité universitaire de Paris. 1957, Urban Plan for Brasília; 1959, Bus Station; 1959, Radio and Television Tower; Brasília. 1973, Monument to Estácio de Sá, Rio de Janeiro.

BIBLIOGRAPHY

BULLRICH, FRANCISCO 1969 *New Directions in Latin American Architecture.* New York: Braziller.
COSTA, LÚCIO 1962 *Sôbre Arquitetura.* Pôrto Alegre: Centro dos Estudantes Universitarios de Arquitetura.
MINDLIN, HENRIQUE 1956 *Modern Architecture in Brazil.* New York: Reinhold.

COSTAGUTA, ANDREA

Andrea Costaguta (17th century), Carmelite priest and architect from Chiavari, Italy, resided in Piedmont from 1641 to 1652. Favored architect of Maria Cristina, duchess of Savoy, he designed Santa Teresa, the church of his order (1642–1674), and the Vigna di Madama Reale (1648–1653), both retardataire.

HENRY A. MILLON

WORKS

1642–1674, Santa Teresa; 1648–1653, Vigna di Madame Reale (now the Villa Abegg); Turin, Italy.

BIBLIOGRAPHY

BAUDI DI VESME, ALESSANDRO 1963–1968 Volume 1 in *Schede Vesme*. Turin, Italy: Società piemontese di archeologia e belle arte.
BRAYDA, CARLO; COLI, LAURA; and SESIA, DARIO 1963 *Ingegneri e architetti del sei e settecento in Piemonte*. Turin, Italy: Società Ingegnere e Architetti.
CARBONERI, NINO 1963 Volume 1 pages 26–27 in *Architettura, Mostra del Barocco Piemontese*. Turin, Italy: Catalogo a cura di Vittorio Viale.
MARINI, RICCARDO ADALGISIO 1927 "La Vigna di Madame Reale sul Colle di San Vito presso Torino." *Bolletino della Società Piemontese di Archeologie e Belle Arti* 10:57–127.
TAMBURINI, LUCIÁNO 1968 *Le Chiese di Torino*. Turin, Italy: Le bouquiniste.

COSTIGAN, FRANCIS

Francis Costigan (1810–1865) established his reputation as Indiana's leading Greek Revival architect with the Lanier (1844) and Shrewsbury (1846–1848) houses in Madison. In Indianapolis, his most notable buildings were the Institute for the Blind (c.1851) and Bates House (1852–1853), both Greek Revival, and the Odd Fellows Building (1853), a Gothic Revival building.

GWEN W. STEEGE

WORKS

1844, Lanier House; 1846–1848, Shrewsbury House; c.1850, Madison Hotel; Madison, Ind. *c.1851, Institute for the Blind; 1852–1853, Bates House; 1853, Odd

Fellows Building; 1856–1857, Oriental House; c.1860, Lewis W. Hasselman House; Indianapolis, Ind.

BIBLIOGRAPHY

NEWCOMB, REXFORD 1950 *Architecture of the Old Northwest Territory*. University of Chicago Press.
"Restorations in Indiana: The Lanier House." 1950 *Antiques Magazine* 58:385–386.
SCHERRER, ANTON 1958 "Francis Costigan, Architect, 1810–1865." Edited by Charles E. Peterson. *Journal of the Society of Architectural Historians* 17:30–32.

COTTE, ROBERT DE

See DE COTTE, ROBERT.

COURTONNE, JEAN

Jean Courtonne (1671–1739), the most distinguished member of a Parisian family of architects, was received into the Académie Royale d'Architecture in 1728, where he lectured from 1730 on. His interest in architecture was based on strong theoretical concerns, and his reputation was secured through his *Traité de la perspective pratique, avec les remarques sur l'architecture* (1725), which embodied the new goals in Parisian architecture first practiced during the wave of nonroyal construction commencing around 1700. Courtonne stressed the principle of transparency according to which the exterior of a building should be the logical outcome of the shaping of the interior space.

His two major works, both *hôtels particuliers* (private urban residences), were erected in fashionable Faubourg Saint-Germain in Paris. The Hôtel de Matignon (1720–1724), constructed for Christian-Louis de Montmorency-Luxembourg, prince of Tingry, reflects a knowledge of contemporary developments in *hôtel* design: the visual impression of the garden façade as a free-standing block had been favored by ROBERT DE COTTE, while the projection of oval and angular pavilions from the court and garden façades was a motif used by GERMAIN BOFFRAND. The classical tradition of French architecture is asserted by the pure volumetric forms and refined proportions of the exterior elevations, marked by an emphatically low horizontal cornice crowned by a balustrade, and a barely visible roof. The classical orders are denied a place on the exterior, giving way to the discreet use of small-scale decoration intended to contrast with the rich rococo paneling and stuccos inside (the work of other designers).

Although a less dramatic house in terms of representational display, the smaller Hôtel de Noir-

Courtonne.
Hôtel de Matignon.
Paris.
1720–1724

moutier (1720–1724) follows contemporary planning more closely, maintaining a single path down a central axis through the structure and a more commodious arrangement of the apartments. The court façade is based on de Cotte's Hôtel d'Estrées (1711–1713), located on the same street in Paris.

ROBERT NEUMAN

WORKS

1712, Hôtel de Sillery (additional floor); 1714, Hôtel de Vendôme (extension); 1720–1724, Hôtel de Matignon; 1720–1724, Hôtel de Noirmoutier; Paris.

BIBLIOGRAPHY

COURTONNE, JEAN 1725 *Traité de la perspective pratique, avec les remarques sur l'architecture, suivies de quelques édifices considérables mis en perspective, & de l'invention de l'auteur.* Paris: Jombert.

HAUTECOEUR, LOUIS 1950 *Première moitié du XVIIIᵉ siècle: Le style Louis XV.* Volume 3 in *Histoire de l'architecture classique en France.* Paris: Picard.

KALNEIN, WEND GRAF, and LEVEY, MICHAEL 1972 *Art and Architecture of the Eighteenth Century in France.* Baltimore: Penguin.

LABANDE, LÉON HONORÉ 1935 "L'Hôtel de Matignon à Paris." *Gazette des Beaux-Arts* 13:257–270; 347–363.

COUSE, KENTON

Kenton Couse (1721–1790) was apprenticed to HENRY FLITCROFT and followed a career in the Office of Works which left him little time for private practice. He obtained his first post, as Labourer in Trust at Whitehall, in 1746, and rose through various clerkships to become secretary to the Board in 1775 and Examining Clerk in 1782.

PETER LEACH

WORKS

1757–1758, Saint Margaret's Church (partial reconstruction), Westminster, London. 1764, Normanton Church, Rutland, England. 1765, Botleys, Surrey, England. *1770–1780, Colney House, Hertfordshire, England. 1774–1776, Holy Trinity Church, Clapham; 1778, The Workhouse, Barnes; London.

COUTURE, GUILLAUME MARTIN

Born in Rouen, France, the son of an architect, Guillaume Martin Couture (1732–1799) studied at the school of the Académie Royale d'Architecture in Paris, the pupil of ANTOINE MATHIEU LE CARPENTIER, and traveled thereafter in Italy. He succeeded Le Carpentier at the Académie in 1773 but was an architect of no great distinction or achievement, his most important commission being the completion of PIERRE CONTANT D'IVRY's Madeleine, which he enlarged and revised after 1777. Work was stopped by the Revolution.

R. D. MIDDLETON

WORKS

*c.1766, A. M. Le Carpentier's Pavillon de la Boissière (interior) *c.1770, Hôtel de Saxe, 51 Faubourg Saint-Honoré; c.1773, Pavillon de Coislin, Bellevue, Paris. *1773–1777, Rood screen, Rouen Cathedral (designed by A. M. Le Carpentier), Rouen, France. 1776, Hôtel de Coislin (façades by A. J. Gabriel), 4 Place de la Concorde, Paris. *1786–1789, Caserne, Caen, France.

BIBLIOGRAPHY

SOREAU, J. B. E. B. 1800 "Notice sur Guillaume Martin Couture, architecte." Part 3, pages 505–511 in *Magasin Encyclopédique.* Paris: Millin.

COVARRUBIAS, ALONSO DE

Alonso de Covarrubias (1488–1570) began his career as a decorative sculptor in the style called, in the Spain of his time, *a lo romano.* His early works show an understanding of the playful variations upon antique themes of the school of Siena, and they have even been compared to the designs of FRANCESCO DI GIORGIO MARTINI.

In his youth, Covarrubias enjoyed a high reputation, indicated by his attendance at the important meeting of masters in 1512 to decide upon the placement of the new Cathedral of Salamanca. His early work at Siguenza and Guadalajara made him familiar with the late fifteenth-century Lombard importations of Lorenzo Vazques. This phase of his style culminated in the Chapel of the New Kings which he completed in 1534 in the Cathedral of Toledo, of which he was named master of the works in the same year. A new phase began with his appointment, jointly with Luis de Vega, as architect of the Royal palaces (Alcazares) of Toledo, Madrid, and Seville in October 1537.

Although personal mannerisms and traditional Spanish elements of medieval origin remain, the playfulness disappears in a broader acceptance of the principles of Renaissance design. In 1541, Covarrubias submitted plans to Cardinal Tavera, archbishop of Toledo, for the Hospital de Afuera, founded outside Toledo by that prelate. The façade is unfinished, lacking cornice and portal, but the clear articulation and carefully disposed rustication of windows and corners contrasts sharply with his earlier work. The portal of the Archbishop's Palace in Toledo (1541–1545), with its sober but not academic Ionic order and bold rustication, gives us an idea of how his entrance to the hospital might have appeared. Between the two interior courtyards he planned a double stair, an elaboration of the single open stairs he had designed earlier at the Hospital de la Santa Cruz in Toledo (c.1524–c.1534) and at the Archbishop's Palace at Alcala de Henares (c.1530–c.1540). This was never built, but a similar stair, almost certainly designed by Covarrubias, was completed for the Madrid palace by 1548. This was destroyed in 1734, but its form is recorded in a seventeenth-century plan by JUAN GOMEZ DE MORA.

The north façade of the Toledo Alcazar was executed in 1546–1552, but as it is less severe than the Afuera façade, it might have been designed as early as 1537. Here, the horizontal and vertical articulation is clear and strong, but the bracketed fenestration and suggestion of the traditional *azotea* at the third level give it a very Spanish feeling.

A falling out with Prince Philip's representative over the design of the stair at the Toledo palace in 1553 led to Covarrubias's partial retirement from the works there, but he retained his appointment and pay. His last major work was an outer bastion added to the Visagra Gate in 1559–1560. With the royal blazon of Charles V hung like a tapestry between smooth, semicylindrical towers, the Spanish tradition is strong, but the rusticated arch beneath recalls SEBASTIANO SERLIO. In 1566, Covarrubias was retired as master of the Cathedral works, and the following year, as royal architect. However, he enjoyed the full salary of both positions until his death three years later.

JOHN DOUGLAS HOAG

WORKS

1514–1517, Retablo of Santa Librada and Tomb of Don Fadrique of Portugal, Siguenza Cathedral, Spain. c.1524–c.1534, Hospital de la Santa Cruz (façade and stair), Toledo, Spain. *c.1530–c.1540, Archbishop's Palace (façade and stair), Alcala de Henares, Spain. 1532–1535, Sacristy Cathedral of Siguenza (completed in 1552), Spain. Completed 1534, Chapel of the New Kings, Cathedral of Toledo; 1534, San Clemente el Real (portal); 1541, Hospital de Afuera (unfinished); 1541–1545, Archbishop's Palace (portal); 1546–1552, Alcazar (north façade); Toledo, Spain. *1548, Alcazar (completion of double stair), Madrid. 1559–1560, Visagra Gate (outer bastion), Toledo, Spain.

BIBLIOGRAPHY

CHUECA GOITIA, FERNANDO 1953 *Arquitectura del Siglo XVI.* Madrid: Plus Ultra.
GARCIA REY, V. 1927–1928 "El famoso arquitecto Alonso de Covarrubias." *Arquitectura* 9:167–175, 207–212, 311–319, 375–380; 10:3–7, 95–99, 202–203, 268–269, 331.

WILKINSON, CATHERINE 1975 "The Escorial and the Invention of the Imperial Staircase." *Art Bulletin* 57:65–90.

COWPER, T. A.

Thomas Alexander Cowper (1781–1825) joined the Bombay Engineers as a cadet in 1796. By 1822, he had reached the rank of lieutenant-colonel and became civil engineer of the Bombay presidency. His only known architectural work is the Town Hall, Bombay (c.1820–1833), which was designed to include the Asiatic Society. After his death at Sonapur in 1825, the building was completed by other Bombay engineers, including Charles Waddington.

PAULINE ROHATGI

WORK

c.1820–1833, Town Hall and Asiatic Society (completed posthumously by others), Bombay.

COXHEAD, ERNEST

A native of Eastbourne, England, Ernest Albert Coxhead (1863–1933) received his training from a local engineer and, subsequently, at the Royal Academy and the Architectural Association in London. In 1886, he and his brother established an independent practice in Los Angeles. Four years later, they moved to San Francisco where they maintained their office until retirement. During his initial six years in California, Coxhead specialized in the design of churches; however, his later work was almost entirely residential. Coxhead's most important designs date from the 1890s. Influenced by contemporary English work in both the Arts and Crafts and academic modes, his designs are highly inventive in their interpretation of historical services and their use of space.

RICHARD W. LONGSTRETH

WORKS

1889, Church of the Angels, Los Angeles. 1890–1891, Chapel of Saint John the Evangelist, Monterey, Calif. *1890–1891, Church of Saint John the Evangelist, San Francisco. 1892, Churchill House, Napa, Calif. 1893, Coxhead House; 1895, Osborn House; San Francisco. *1895–1898, Earl House, Los Angeles.

BIBLIOGRAPHY

ANDERSON, TIMOTHY J. ET AL. (editors) 1974 *California Design 1910.* Pasadena: California Design Publications.
GEBHARD, DAVID, and VON BRETON, HARIETTE 1968 *Architecture in California, 1868–1968.* The Art Galleries, University of California, Santa Barbara.

LONGSTRETH, RICHARD W. 1977 "Architects on the Edge of the World: Ernest Coxhead and Willis Polk in San Francisco during the 1890's." Unpublished Ph.D. dissertation, University of California, Berkeley.

WOODBRIDGE, SALLY (editor) 1976 *Bay Area Houses.* New York: Oxford University Press.

COZZARELLI, GIACOMO

Giacomo Cozzarelli (1453–1515) was a painter, sculptor, and architect of the Sienese Renaissance. As an architect, he is associated with designs for the Palazzo del Magnifico in Siena (1508–?) and the church of the Osservanza, near Siena (1474–1490). Both use a refined and restrained technique that recalls other sculptor-architects such as LUCIANO DA LAURANA. Cozzarelli was also noted as a fortification architect.

NICHOLAS ADAMS

WORKS

1474–1490, Church of the Osservanza, near Siena, Italy. 1496, Fortifications, Montepulciano, Italy. 1508–?, Palazzo del Magnifico; 1508–?, Church of the Santo Spirito (cupola); Siena, Italy.

BIBLIOGRAPHY

DEL BRAVO, CARLO 1970 *Scultura Senese del Quattrocento.* Florence: Edam.

HOOK, JUDITH 1979 *Siena: A City and its History.* London: Hamish Hamilton.

CRAIG, JAMES

Born in Edinburgh, Scotland, James Craig (1744–1795) in 1766 achieved celebrity for a plan of new streets and squares for the New Town of Edinburgh competition. His parallelogrammatical plan for the New Town with a scheme for further remodeling the Old Town of Edinburgh was published in a quatro pamphlet in 1786. Craig's architectural genius is evident in Physicians Hall (1774), a pure Grecian-style building in the New Town. He died in debt in Edinburgh.

FARHAD NIROUMAND-RAD

WORKS

1766, Plan of Edinburgh; 1773, Plan of Saint James Square; 1774, Physicians Hall; Edinburgh.

BIBLIOGRAPHY

CRAIG, JAMES 1786 *The Plan for Improving the City of Edinburgh.* Edinburgh: The author.

MEADE, M. K. 1971 "Plans of the New Town of Edinburgh." *Architectural History* 14:40–52.

YOUNGSON, A. J. 1966 *The Making of Classical Edinburgh: 1750–1840.* Edinburgh University Press.

CRAM, RALPH ADAMS

Ralph Adams Cram (1863–1942), the foremost Gothic revival architect of the United States, has been called the American Ruskin. Editorial comment when he died documents the extent to which he exercised a wide national influence. Cram possessed, noted the *Boston Herald,* a "rare combination of qualities which enabled him to maintain for decades an almost unique eminence among Americans of distinction." The *Washington Star* went so far as to complain that "his genius was beyond the reach of ordinary powers of analysis."

Much of his influence derived from the fact that he was a good writer and a respected scholar as well as an ardent polemicist in several allied fields. A founder or editor of four well-known journals (*Knight Errant, Christian Art, Speculum,* and *Commonweal*), sometime art critic of the Boston *Transcript,* author of twenty-four books and well over a hundred articles (with his right hand, as it were: with his left hand he wrote, sometimes under a pseudonym, plays, poems, and short stories, some still reprinted in anthologies today), Cram was in the first place a distinguished medievalist. He was probably the foremost ecclesiologist of the Anglican Communion. It was Cram who first recognized the importance of Henry Adams's *Mont-Saint Michel and Chartres* (1913); prefaced by Cram, it reached the public entirely through his efforts. A founder of the Medieval Academy of America, Cram, along with the Harvard medievalist Kingsley Porter, inspired Kenneth Conant's work at Cluny. Professor of the philosophy of architecture and head of the school of architecture at the Massachusetts Institute of Technology, Cram also wrote widely on contemporary American architecture; in this area he was a contributor to the twelfth edition of the *Encyclopaedia Britannica* (1922). He was also an accomplished scholar of Japanese art; the London *Times* judged his pioneering work in this field, *Impressions of Japanese Architecture and the Allied Arts* (1905), to have "brought new light to bear on the subject." Cram earned as well a wide following as a social theorist; Albert Joy Nock contended that it was only Cram's reputation as an architect that "over-shadowed [his] claims as a philosopher." Cram was, almost uniquely, both thinker and doer: a medievalist who was the pre-eminent Gothic designer of his day; a professor of architecture who was one of the country's leading architects; a Japanese scholar who designed as well in that idiom. As social theorist, he closed the circle, for his work in this field was rooted in his study of the Middle Ages. Yet all these vocations, finally, were the innumerable refractions of a philosophic unity of purpose that centered on architecture and religion—two sides, for Cram, of the same human experience. In fact, Cram nurtured at his writing desk needs that were met at the drafting boards of the firm of Cram and Wentworth, founded by Cram in Boston in 1888.

The extent and diversity of his office activity was remarkable. Though much of the firm's work was concentrated in the eastern United States, its practice extended from Japan and Hawaii to California across North America from Texas and Panama to New England and Nova Scotia and to France, and the designs included nearly seventy-five churches for virtually every religious denomination, not only in every variety of Gothic, but in the Byzantine, Lombard, and classic (including Georgian) idioms as well; the notion, quite without foundation, that Cram thought Gothic the only acceptable style for churches only reflects his particular mastery of that style. Nor did Cram design only churches. Houses, art museums, and office buildings (including an Art Deco skyscraper of 1930 in Boston, the Federal Building) also came from his drafting board; so too did an important early apartment house in Brookline, Massachusetts, Richmond Court (1898–1900). Cram himself lived in this building, probably the first "Tudor-style" open courtyard apartment house in the northeastern United States. Cram's collegiate work was scarcely less important than his church work; he designed several entire campuses and was supervising architect of Princeton and consulting architect of Bryn Mawr, Mount Holyoke, and Wellesley colleges. Cram was also a fellow of the American Academy of Arts and Sciences.

Scion of a distinguished but not well-off New England family who could not afford to send him to college, Cram was sent as a young man from his native Hampton Falls, New Hampshire, to apprentice in the architectural firm of Rotch and Tilden in Boston, where he was quickly caught up in the literary and artistic ferment of the Boston Bohemia of the 1880s along with such figures as Bliss Carman, Louise Imogen Guirey, Fred Holland Day, Bruce Rogers, and Bernard Berenson. Cram was strongly influenced by the work of JOHN RUSKIN and WILLIAM MORRIS, and his Gothic sympathies merged during this decade with his developing high Church Anglicanism. At the same time, though unsympathetic to H. H. RICHARDSON's stylistic propensities, Cram nonetheless became a keen disciple of Richardson, whose originality Cram greatly admired. Stylistically, Cram quickly found a more direct mentor in HENRY VAUGHAN. Sometime chief draftsman of GEORGE F. BODLEY, Vaughan had practiced in Boston since 1882 and probably played a key role in introducing

Cram to the work of the late English Gothicists, which Cram first saw during his trips to England in the 1880s. In the work of Bodley, JOHN D. SEDDING, John L. Pierson, and GEORGE E. STREET particularly Cram saw in the Gothic mode he preferred the same vitality he had admired in Richardson.

This potential for development of Gothic fascinated Cram. It was, he concluded, not dead, only moribund; its decline due not to exhaustion but to the fact that its development had been cut off with many of its possibilities unexplored by the Renaissance and the Reformation; possibilities he saw the English Gothicists beginning to explore. What was needed, Cram thought, was a creative scholarship. Very much in the tradition of A. W. N. PUGIN (Gothic was not a style but a principle) and earnestly advocating structural integrity, Cram diverged from Pugin not only in seeing this potential in styles other than Gothic (in Japanese temple architecture, for instance), but also in his belief that whereas for Gothic one must return to the Middle Ages for inspiration, modern Gothic might well not only develop forward but in the end surpass the medieval achievement.

In this controversial quest he enjoyed a signal success. The design of his office's first church, All Saints, Ashmont (1892–1941), in the Boston suburb of Dorchester, evidenced a remarkable power of original design, and the striking simplicity and grandeur of All Saints thereafter decisively shaped the development of the twentieth-century American parish church. Of his city churches, Saint Thomas, Fifth Avenue (1906–1914), New York City, is his masterpiece. Cram responded keenly to the challenge of the downtown church, necessarily overwhelmed by skyscrapers and thus posing, for the Gothic idiom, a problem essentially modern and without precedent, and it is a measure of his genius that the bold massing and strong profile of Saint Thomas, the tower of which is very low, has held its own with great authority (unlike, for example, Saint Patrick's Cathedral) as newer skyscrapers around it have climbed higher and higher.

Saint Thomas is also an excellent example of the division of labor in his office, now quite fully documented: the over-all plan, massing, and scale were always by Cram, the detail by his partners, of whom the most notable were BERTRAM GROSVENOR GOODHUE (from 1892 to 1914) and Frank Cleveland (from 1914 to 1942). Goodhue, particularly, was a decorative genius, and his great reredos at Saint Thomas, inspired by the high altar screen at Winchester Cathedral, is a splendid instance of the way Goodhue could take a historic model as a point of departure and make it his own, transfiguring it as at Saint Thomas into a wholly new and most distinguished work of art. In this connection it must also be noted that Cram, who insisted on his office designing even the candlesticks of his churches if it was at all possible, depended as well on the skill of a remarkable rank of artist-collaborators, particularly the sculptors Johannes Kirchmayer and John Angel, the glassman Charles Connick, and the ironworkers Samuel Yellin and Frank Koralewski. A founder of the Boston Society of Arts and Crafts, the first to be established in the United States, Cram not only inspired but in at least one case also privately financed the work of his artist-collaborators. In the wake of his enormous success, Cram attracted to himself a group of disciples (they have been called the Boston Gothicists), who included CHARLES D. MAGINNIS, the founder of the architectural firm of Maginnis and Walsh, the leading American architects in the Roman Catholic tradition in the 1900–1940 period, and the firm of ALLEN AND COLLENS, as well as a whole rank of ecclesiastical craftsmen, including the Boston glassmen Wilbur Brunham and Joseph Reynolds.

Of all Cram's work, his designs for the cathedral of Saint John the Divine in New York (1911–1942) are unquestionably his most important. Saint John's takes its place among the great cathedrals of the world as the climax of the American Gothic Revival, comparable with the Anglican Cathedral at Liverpool in Britain. Indeed, Cram's nave at Saint John's so amazed ALFRED D. F. HAMLIN that he wrote: "The cathedrals of Europe may fairly be challenged to surpass or even to equal it. . . . The French Gothic as here used is handled with such originality and boldness of invention as to form in reality a new and distinctly American chapter in its development." Kingsley Porter pronounced Cram's nave "a tenth symphony."

Yet Cram's parish churches, such as Calvary Church, Pittsburgh (1907–1941), The Church of the Sacred Heart, Jersey City, New Jersey (1922–1925), and Saint Stephen's, Cohasset, Massachusetts (1899–1916), as well as such comparable works as the Conventual Church of Saint Mary and Saint John, Cambridge, Massachusetts (1935–1938) and his smaller village churches, such as All Saints, Peterborough, New Hampshire (1913–1925) and Cram's own private chapel, Saint Elizabeth's, Sudbury, Massachusetts (1914), show perhaps better than anything his strengths as a designer. His sense of mass, proportion, and composition in these small churches was almost faultless. These churches were widely copied by

Cram's many imitators, but their clichés no less than Cram's landmarks document the extent to which Cram's career transformed the visual image of American Christianity.

DOUGLASS SHAND TUCCI

WORKS
CRAM AND WENTWORTH
1889–1892, Ide House; 1890–1894, Gale House; Williamstown, Mass.

CRAM, WENTWORTH, AND GOODHUE
1892–1913, All Saints' Church, Ashmont; 1894, Church of the Advent Lady Chapel (sanctuary interior); Boston. 1894–1926, All Saints' Church, Brookline, Mass. 1896–1899, Phillips Church, Exeter, N.H. 1897, Church of Our Savior, Middleborough, Mass.

CRAM, GOODHUE, AND FERGUSON
1898–1900, Richmond Court Apartments, Brookline, Mass. 1899, Deborah Cook Sayles Public Library, Pawtucket, R.I. 1899–1916, Saint Stephen's Church, Cohasset, Mass. 1900–1921, Emmanuel Church, Newport, R.I. 1902–1904, Saint Mary's Church, Walkerville, Ontario.

CRAM, GOODHUE, AND FERGUSON
(BOSTON AND NEW YORK OFFICES)
1903–1914, United States Military Academy, West Point, N.Y. 1906–1914, Saint Thomas Church, New York.

CRAM, GOODHUE, AND FERGUSON
(BOSTON OFFICE)
1904, Harborcourt, Newport, R.I. 1904–1931, Sweet Briar College, Va. 1905–1909, First Unitarian Church, West Newton, Mass. 1905–1928, Calvary Church, Pittsburgh. 1907–1941, Euclid Avenue Church (now Church of The Covenant), Cleveland, Ohio. 1907–1941, Saint Paul's Cathedral, Detroit, Michigan. 1909–1941, Rice Institute (now University) Campus, Houston,

Cram.
Saint Thomas (with Goodhue and Ferguson).
New York.
1906–1914

Cram.
Cathedral of Saint John the Divine (nave; with Ferguson).
New York.
1915–1941

Tex. 1909, Holy Cross Monastery, West Park, N.Y. 1910, Japanese Garden Court, Museum of Fine Arts, Boston. 1910–1930, Saint John the Evangelist (interior), Boston. 1911–1929, Princeton University Chapel and Graduate College, N.J. 1911–1937, Fourth Presbyterian Church, Chicago. 1912–1941, House of Good Hope Church, Saint Paul, Minn. 1913–1917, Swedenborgion Cathedral, Bryn Athyn, Penn. 1913–1925, All Saints' Church, Peterborough, N.H. 1913–1935, Second Unitarian (now Ruggles Street) Church, Boston. 1914, Saint Elizabeth's Chapel (Cram Estate) Sudbury, Mass. 1914–1920, Williams College Chapel and Chapin Hall, Williamstown, Mass. 1914–1932, Phillips Exeter Academy (library, dormitories, gymnasium, inn, and administration building), Exeter, N.H. 1914–1936, Saint Anne's Convent, Arlington, Mass.

CRAM, GOODHUE, AND FERGUSON
(NEW YORK OFFICE)

1903, El Fureidis, Santa Barbara, Calif. 1905, La Santissima Trinity Church, Havana. 1906, All Saints' Cathedral, Halifax, Nova Scotia. 1908, Saint John's Church, West Hartford, Conn. 1909, Rice Institute (now University) Auditorium, Houston, Tex. 1909, Sage Memorial Church, Far Rockaway, N.Y. 1909, Saint Mark's Church, Mount Kisco, N.Y. 1909–1912, First Baptist Church, Pittsburgh. 1910–1914, Chapel of the Intercession, New York. c.1915, Taft School, Watertown, Conn. c.1915, Washington Hotel, Panama Canal Zone.

CRAM AND FERGUSON

1915–1934, Wheaton College (chapel and other buildings), Norton, Mass. 1915–1941, Cathedral of Saint John the Divine (nave, west front, baptistery, chancel remodeling, and miscellaneous buildings), New York. 1916–1931, Mercersbury Academy Chapel, Penn. 1917–1920, Englewood Chapel, Nahant, Mass. 1919–1933, Saint James Church, Lake Delaware, N.Y. 1920–1928, Central Union Church, Honolulu, Hawaii. 1920–1928, Saint George's School Chapel, Newport, R.I. 1921–1924, First Presbyterian Church, Utica, N.Y. 1921–1929, Sacred Heart Church, Jersey City, N.J. 1922–1925, First Presbyterian Church, Tacoma, Wash. 1923, Saint Vincent de Paul Church Chancel (interior), Los Angeles. 1924–1926, Choate School Chapel, Wallingford, Conn. 1924–1929, Saint Mary's Church, Redford, Detroit, Mich. 1926–1931, Holy Rosary Church, Pittsburgh. 1926–1934, United States War Memorial Chapels, Belleau Wood Cemetery, Aisne-Marne, and Oise-Aisne Cemetery, Fere-en-Tardenons, France. 1927, Church of the Ascension, Montgomery, Ala. 1927, Provident Mutual Building, Philadelphia. 1927–1929, Saint Paul's Church, Winston-Salem, N.C. 1928–1932, Desloge Chapel, Saint Louis University School of Medicine, Mo. 1929–1941, Madison Avenue (now Christ) Church, New York. 1930, Federal Building, Boston. 1930–1939, Rollins College, Winter Park, Fla. 1931–1932, Doheny Library, University of Southern California, Los Angeles. 1931–1941, East Liberty Church, Pittsburgh. 1935–1938, Conventional Church of Saints Mary and John, Cambridge, Mass.

BIBLIOGRAPHY

Correspondence with Cram and articles about him, including the obituaries quoted in the text, are in the Architectural Archive of the Boston Public Library.

CRAM, RALPH ADAMS (1901)1924 *Church Building.* 3d ed. Boston: Marshall Jones.

CRAM, RALPH ADAMS (1905)1966 *Impressions of Japanese Architecture and the Allied Arts.* Reprint. New York: Dover.

CRAM, RALPH ADAMS (1913)1936 Preface in Henry Adams, *Mont-Saint Michel and Chartres.* Boston: Houghton Mifflin.

CRAM, RALPH ADAMS (1914)1967 *The Ministry of Art.* Reprint. Freeport, N.Y.: Books for Libraries Press.

CRAM, RALPH ADAMS (1917)1925 *The Substance of Gothic.* 2d ed. Boston: Marshall Jones.

CRAM, RALPH ADAMS 1922 "Architecture—United States." Volume 30, pages 187–189 in *Encyclopaedia Britannica.* 12th ed. Chicago: Encyclopaedia Britannica.

CRAM, RALPH ADAMS 1930 *The Catholic Church and Art.* New York: Macmillan.

CRAM, RALPH ADAMS (1936)1969 *My Life in Architecture.* Reprint. Boston: Little, Brown.

DANIEL, ANN MINER 1980 *The Early Architecture of Ralph Adams Cram: 1889–1902.* Ann Arbor, Mich.: University Microfilms.

HAMLIN, A. D. F. 1924 *A Study of the Designs for the Cathedral of St. John the Divine.* New York: Dean and Chapter of the Cathedral.

MUCCIGROSSO, ROBERT 1980 *American Gothic: The Mind and Art of Ralph Adams Cram.* Washington: University Press of America.

NORTH, ARTHUR TAPPAN 1931 *Ralph Adams Cram.* New York: McGraw-Hill.

SCHUYLER, MONTGOMERY 1911 "The Works of Cram, Goodhue and Ferguson." *Architectural Record* 29:entire issue.

TUCCI, DOUGLASS SHAND 1975a *Ralph Adams Cram: American Medievalist.* Boston: Public Library. Contains an extensive bibliography of more than one hundred known articles by Cram and an undated list of his known buildings, including additions and remodelings.

TUCCI, DOUGLASS SHAND 1975b "Ralph Adams Cram and Mrs. Gardner." *Fenway Court* 1975:27–34.

TUCCI, DOUGLASS SHAND 1978 "Ralph Adams Cram and Boston Gothic." Pages 155–181 in *Built in Boston, City and Suburbs, 1800–1950.* Boston: Little, Brown.

TUCCI, DOUGLASS SHAND 1979 "First Impressions on the Rediscovery of Two New England Galleries by Ralph Adams Cram." *Currier Gallery of Art Bulletin* 1979:2–16.

CRANE, WALTER

Walter Crane (1845–1915), British designer, painter, author, and educator, started life as a wood engraver, but his talent as an illustrator was soon recognized. From their appearance in the late 1860s, his innovative children's picture books in color were highly appreciated; they influenced many aspects of design and decoration at the time. He in turn had been influenced by pre-Raphaelite and Japanese art. The popularity of his illustrations led to commissions to design wallpapers, textiles, carpets, ceramics, stained glass, mosaics, plaster-work, and mural decoration. In the 1880s, much of his energy was spent in furthering art education, socialist political work, and in promoting exhibition facilities for designer–craftsmen. His books on design theory influenced a generation of designers. He had an international following and was rewarded with many honors.

BETTY ELZEA

WORKS

1879, Coombe Bank (gesso decorations for saloon), Sevenoaks, Kent, England. 1883, Vinland (painted frieze for dining room, and library windows), Newport, R.I. 1897, Paddockhurst (plaster frieze for dining room), Worth, Sussex, England.

BIBLIOGRAPHY

"The Art of Walter Crane." 1898 In *The Easter Art Annual.* London: Art Journal.

CRANE, WALTER 1892 *The Claims of Decorative Art.* London: Lawrence & Bullen.

CRANE, WALTER (1898)1925 *The Bases of Design.* 2d ed. London: George Bell.

CRANE, WALTER (1900)1925 *Line and Form.* 2d ed. London: George Bell.

CRANE, WALTER (1907)1968 *An Artist's Reminiscences.* Reprint. Detroit: Singing Tree Press.

KONODY, PAUL G. 1902 *The Art of Walter Crane.* London: George Bell.

CREANGA, HORIA

Horia Creanga (1893–1943) was the spiritual leader of modern architecture in Rumania in the 1930s. He studied at the School of Architecture in Bucharest and graduated from the Ecole des Beaux-Arts in Paris in 1924. Together with his architect wife, Haralamb Georgescu, he proceeded to design a series of landmarks of modern Rumanian architecture that are distinguished by their refined volumetric qualities, their rigorous structural logic, and a judicious use of materials. He was also a sensitive interpreter of the traditional Rumanian architecture. Horizontality is the main characteristic of his work.

Creanga also wrote many articles for different periodicals.

CONSTANTIN MARIN MARINESCU

WORKS

1931, Patria Apartment Building; 1937, Apartment Building, 35 Boulevard North Balcescu; 1938, Metallurgic Factory; Bucharest. 1938, Yacht Club, Eforie, Rumania. 1939, Apartment Building, 101 Calea Victorieu, Bucharest. 1939, Hotel Carpati, Brasov, Rumania. 1939, Restaurant Pescarus, Bucharest.

BIBLIOGRAPHY

CANTACUZEÑE, GEORGE 1934 "Tendances dans l'architecture roumaine." *Architecture d'Aujourd'hui* 5, no. 5:57–62.

IONESCU, GRIGORE 1965 Volume 2 in *Istoria Arhitecturii in Romania.* Bucharest: Editura Academiei Republicii Romañe.

IONESCU, GRIGORE 1969 *Arhitectura in Romania; Perioda anilor 1944–1969.* Bucharest: Editura Academiei Republicii Socialiste Romañia.

IONESCU, GRIGORE 1972 "Saptezeci si cinci de ani de la infiintarea invatamintului de arhitectura din Romania." *Arhitectura* 20:35–42.

MAMBRIANI, ALBERTO 1969 *L'Architettura Moderna nei Paesi Balcanici.* Bologna, Italy: Capelli.

MOITRY-BIZARY, REÑEE 1934 "Architecture en Roumanie: Bucarest." *Architecture d'Aujourd'hui* 5, no. 5:55–56.

NEDELESCU, NICOLAE 1963 "20 de ani de la moartea lui Horia Creanga." *Arhitectura* 11, no. 6:52.

PATRULIUS, RADU 1973–1974 "Contributii Romanesti in Arhitectura Anilor '30." *Arhitectura* 21, no. 6:44–52; 22, no. 1:53–59.

SASARMAN, GHEORGHE 1972 "Inceputurile gindirii teoretice in arhitectura românească (1860–1916)." *Arhitectura* 20, no. 6:44–46.

SOCOLESCU, TOMA T. 1941 "Principii si Indreptari: Catre o arhitectura românească moderna." *Arhitectura* 2:17–18.

CRESWELL, H. B.

An English architect and humorist, Harry Bulkeley Creswell (1869–1960) was articled in the busy late Victorian office of ASTON WEBB. During the Edwardian years, he practiced from Rugby and built one famous work, the Queensferry Turbine Factory (1901) in Wales, sometimes hailed as a precursor of modernism. After 1918, Creswell, now in London, took increasingly to architectural journalism and in 1929 he published (at first in serial form) *The Honeywood File,* a didactic novel concerning the trials of domestic architecture. There were several successors, some almost as memorable. Creswell was a conservative but shrewd critic of architecture. Probably thwarted in his architectural career by lack of opportunity, he redeemed himself by means of literary grace and wit.

ANDREW SAINT

WORKS

1901, Queensferry Turbine Factory, Flintshire, Wales. 1913, Saint Philip's Church, Rugby, England. 1923, Ceylon Government Railway Offices, Colombo.

BIBLIOGRAPHY

CRESWELL, H. B. 1929 *The Honeywood File: An Adventure in Building.* London: Architectural Press.
CRESWELL, H. B. 1930 *The Honeywood Settlement: A Continuation of the "Honeywood File."* London: Architectural Press.
CRESWELL, H. B. 1931 *Jago v. Swillerton & Toomer.* London: Architectural Press.
CRESWELL, H. B. 1935 *Diary from a Dustbin.* London: Faber.
CRESWELL, H. B. 1942 *Grig.* London: Faber.
CRESWELL, H. B. 1943 *Grig in Retirement.* London: Faber.
"Obituary of H. B. Creswell." 1960 *The Builder* 199:108.

CRET, PAUL PHILIPPE

Paul Philippe Cret (1876–1945) was born in Lyon, France, moved to Philadelphia in 1903, and became a United States citizen in 1927.

From 1897 to 1903 he studied at the Ecole des Beaux-Arts in Paris, winning the Prix Rougevin, and a second place in the Concours Chenavard. To the disappointment of his *patron* JEAN LOUIS PASCAL, Cret did not compete for the Grand Prix de Rome, instead accepting a position at the University of Pennsylvania in 1903.

Cret remained there as professor in design, until ill health forced his resignation in 1937. During his tenure, the architectural program enjoyed a nationwide reputation for excellence. Cret's most famous pupil is LOUIS I. KAHN. Cret also served as critic at the Philadelphia T-Square Club and the Pennsylvania Academy of Fine Arts.

As an architect, Cret established a very successful practice, which he characterized in his curriculum vitae as "the planning of important city improvements, the planning of government buildings and important memorial buildings." His success in architectural competitions (he entered twenty-five, winning six and placing in ten), the invitations to serve on competition juries, and the awards he received (culminating in 1938 in the Gold Medal of the American Institute of Architects) testify to his high professional standing.

Cret's writings enhanced his reputation as a designer engaged in the critical issues of the day. Like his architecture, his writings are distinguished by a Beaux-Arts rationalism and French urbanity.

Cret's architectural career can be divided into three phases:

1903–1914. Cret earned a national reputation primarily through his record in architectural competitions. For example, his entry in the competition for the International Bureau of American Republics (1907–1910) was chosen over seventy-eight other designs by a distinguished jury headed by Charles Follen McKim (see MCKIM, MEAD, AND WHITE). The building, with its formal yet inviting promenade, remains one of his most popular works.

He won the Indianapolis Public Library (1914–1917) commission with a Doric colonnaded façade, a concession to American taste, and an interior that is a Beaux-Arts synthesis of up to date functional planning and appropriate civic impressiveness.

1919–1930. Returning to the United States after serving in the French army, Cret entered his most productive years. He received commissions for war memorials and bridges, such as the much publicized Delaware River Bridge (1920–1926).

In 1928 he joined the planning commission for Chicago's Century of Progress Exposition of 1933. However it was the public buildings, most notably the Detroit Institute of Arts (1919–1927) with its innovative galleries designed in styles appropriate to the art on display that established Cret as one of America's foremost architects.

Cret developed a modern classical style for civic architecture that rationalized the classical language in terms of the steel frame. He used two modes of rational classicism. The Greek mode, seen at the Hartford County Building (1926–1930), featured smooth piers and simplified profiles which recall both French Neo-Grec and American Greek Revival antecedents.

In contrast, his planar classicism, used at the Folger Shakespeare Library (1928–1932), reduced piers to fluted strips and eliminated capitals altogether. Cret was so closely associated with modern classicism that one critic suggested that the style "will wane with the passing of Cret, so amazingly does he personify its virile quality" (Allen, 1931, p. 484).

1931–1945. During the Depression and World War II, Cret's practice was increasingly limited to consulting work on government commissions. His last important civic building was the Greek modernist Federal Reserve Board Building (1935–1937), a commission that he won in competition.

ELIZABETH GREENWELL GROSSMAN

WORKS

1907–1910, International Bureau of the American Republics (now the Organization of American States; with Albert Kelsey), Washington. 1914–1917, Indianapolis Public Library (with Zantzinger, Borie, and Medary). 1919–1927, Detroit Institute of Arts (with Zantzinger, Borie, and Medary), Mich. 1920–1926, Delaware River Bridge (with Ralph Modjeski), Philadelphia. 1923–1925, Barnes Foundation Gallery, Merion, Pa. 1925, University Avenue Bridge (with Stephen Noyes), Philadelphia. 1926–1930, Hartford County Building (with Smith and Bassette), Conn. 1926–1930, Rodin Museum (with JACQUES GRÉBER), Philadelphia. 1926–1933, Aisne-Marne Memorial, near Chateau-Thierry, France. 1926–1933, Flanders Field Chapel, Wareghem, Belgium. 1926–1933, Memorial, near Bellicourt, France. 1927–1929, Providence War Memorial, R.I. 1928–1932, Folger Shakespeare Library, Washington. 1930–1937, Naval Memorial, Gibraltar, Spain. 1932–1934, Federal Reserve Bank, Philadelphia. 1935–1937, Federal Reserve Board Building, Washington.

BIBLIOGRAPHY

Among the papers in the Paul Cret Collection at the University of Pennsylvania is Cret's undated curriculum vitae.

ADAMS, RAYNE 1931 "Paul Philippe Cret." *Architecture* 63:263–268.

ALLEN, GEORGE N. 1931 "The Little Master of the Arts: Paul Philippe Cret of Philadelphia, of Pennsylvania, and of the World at Large." *Architectural Forum* 54:483–484.

CRET, PAUL PHILIPPE 1908 "The Ecole des Beaux-Arts: 'What Its Architectural Teaching Means.'" *Architectural Record* 23:367–371.

CRET, PAUL PHILIPPE 1923 "Modern Architecture." Pages 183–243 in *The Significance of the Fine Arts.* Boston: Marshall Jones.

CRET, PAUL PHILIPPE 1928 "The Architect as Collaborator with the Engineer." *Architectural Forum* 49:97–104.

CRET, PAUL PHILIPPE 1933 "Ten Years of Modernism." *Architectural Forum* 59:91–94.

CRET, PAUL PHILIPPE 1941 "The Ecole des Beaux-Arts." *Journal of the Society of Architectural Historians* 1, no. 2:3–15.

GROSSMAN, ELIZABETH G. 1980 "Paul Philippe Cret: Rationalism and Imagery in American Architecture." Unpublished Ph.D. dissertation, Brown University, Providence, R.I.

HARBESON, JOHN 1966 "Paul Cret and Architectural Competitions." *Journal of the Society of Architectural Historians* 25:305–306.

HOAK, EDWARD WARREN, and CHURCH, WILLIS HUMPHREY 1930 *Masterpieces of Architecture in the United States: Memorials, Museums, Libraries, Churches, Public Buildings, Hotels and Office Buildings.* New York: Scribner. With an introduction by Paul P. Cret.

SWALES, FRANCIS S. 1928 "Draftsmanship and Architecture, as Exemplified by the Work of Paul P. Cret." *Pencil Points* 9:688–704.

VAN ZANTEN, DAVID 1978 "Le Systeme des Beaux-Arts." *Architectural Design* 48; no. 5:11–12, 66–79.

WHITE, THEOPHILUS BALLOU 1973 *Paul Philippe Cret: Architect and Teacher.* Philadelphia: Art Alliance.

IL CRONACA

Il Cronaca (1457–1508), whose real name was Simone del Pollaiuolo, was born in Florence and trained, possibly, by Giuliano da Sangallo (see SANGALLO FAMILY). After a time in Rome (1475–1487), he returned to Florence where he was highly respected as a building contractor as well as a designer. Cronaca's most distinguished work was the Church of San Salvatore (or San Francesco) al Monte, Florence (1487–1504). Its simple plan (it is aisleless and timber-vaulted) and the discrete, classically inspired ornament (derived from the Florence Baptistery) give the building a rustic, early Christian feeling. Cronaca's work strongly recalls that of Giuliano da Sangallo whom he assisted on a number of occasions (Palazzo Strozzi, Florence).

NICHOLAS ADAMS

WORKS

1487–1504, Church of San Salvatore (or San Francesco) al Monte; 1488, Church of Santo Spirito (sacristy; with Giuliano da Sangallo); 1490–1504, Palazzo Strozzi (courtyard and third story); 1495, Sala del Cinquecento, Palazzo Vecchio; 1503, Palazzo Guadagni; Florence.

BIBLIOGRAPHY

GOLDTHWAITE, RICHARD A. 1973 "The Building of the Strozzi Palace: The Construction Industry in Renaissance Florence." *Studies in Medieval and Renaissance History* 10:97–104.

HEYDENREICH, LUDWIG H. 1961 "Über den Palazzo Guadagni in Florenz." Pages 43–51 in Eberhard Ruhmer (editor), *Eberhard Hanfstaengl zum 75. Geburtstag.* Munich: Bruckmann.

HEYDENREICH, LUDWIG H., and LOTZ, WOLFGANG 1974 *Architecture in Italy, 1400–1600.* Translated by Mary Hottinger. Harmondsworth, England, and Baltimore: Penguin.

CROSS and CROSS

Cross and Cross, working primarily in New York City, produced corporate and upper class residential buildings combining great character and refinement; they were one of New York's most distinctive native firms.

The work of the two brothers, John Walter Cross (1878–1951) and Eliot Cross (1884–1949), in the 1910s and 1920s was usually in an urbane, neo-Georgian style, of which the Links Club (1916–1917) and the cooperative apartment house at 1 Sutton Place South (1925–1926, designed in association with Rosario Candela) are the best examples. By 1930, their designs became more mannered, and their distinctly Adam-style (see ROBERT ADAM) bank building at 35 East 72nd Street (1930–1931) was one of their first departures from the more conventional work of the previous decades. Their explicitly Art Deco General Electric Building (originally built in 1930–1931 for RCA), with a crown in the form of personified radio waves, ranks as one of the great New York skyscrapers. Later works were executed in a diffuse, *moderne* styling, of which their Egyptoid Tiffany & Company Building (1939–1940) is a well-known example. John Cross was more often the designer in the firm, and Eliot had extensive real estate interests, including the founding of the Webb & Knapp development firm in 1922.

CHRISTOPHER GRAY

WORKS

1912–1913, Commercial Building, 444 Park Avenue South; 1916–1917, Links Club; 1922–1924, Morris Residence, 116 East 80th Street; 1925–1926, Apartments, 1 Sutton Place South (with Rosario Candela); 1926–1927, Barclay Hotel; 1928, Apartments, 25 East End Avenue; 1929–1930, George Whitney Residence, 120 East 80th Street; 1930–1931, General Electric Building; 1930–1931, 35 East 72nd Street; 1939–1940, Aetna Life Insurance Company Building; 1939–1940, Tiffany & Company; New York.

CROWE, SYLVIA

Born in Banbury, England, Sylvia Crowe (1901–) spent her formative years in the Sussex Weald at her father's fruit farm. At Swanley Horticultural College, Kent, she gained a thorough, practical basis, but her formal training in design began while working in Edward White's London office. In 1939, she designed private suburban gardens for Cutbush Nurseries, Barnet. After the war, she began her own practice from BRENDA COLVIN's Baker Street office in London, designing several private gardens. A turning point came when she was consulted over coastal reclamation after wartime defense. Recognition of her combined horticultural knowledge and planning skills resulted in important commissions. Her research and landscape survey reports on the new towns was seminal in the formulation of modern ideas about urban landscaping development.

In the 1950s, she obtained consultancies with the Central Electricity Generating Board, Essex County Council, and Southern and South West Water Authorities. Success in this resulted from her pragmatic but sensitive approach (apparent in her writings) that accepts industrial power but refuses to let it ruin the landscape. Crowe's appointment as consultant to the Forestry Commission (1964–1976) fulfilled her personal ambition and required her wide vision, aesthetic sense, and expert knowledge. Her pioneering writings and her continuous support of professional bodies such as the Landscape Institute, the International Federation of Landscape Architects, the American Society of Landscape Architects, and the Australian Institute of Landscape Architects reflect her dedication to the landscape as a whole.

HILARY J. GRAINGER

WORKS

1939, Cutbush Nurseries (private gardens), Barnet, England. *1946, Public Gardens, Mablethorpe, Lincolnshire, England. 1948–1968, Coastal Reclamation, Sutton-on-Sea, Lincolnshire, England. 1948–1968, Mablethorpe (restoration of gardens), Lincolnshire, England. 1950–1956, Saint Mary's Churchyard, Banbury, Oxfordshire, England. 1950–1956, Gardens, Oxford University. 1957–1966, Washington New Town (landscape master plan), Durham, England. 1957–1966, Warrington New Town (landscape master plan), Lancashire, England. 1966–1976, Commonwealth Gardens (master plan), Canberra, Australia.

BIBLIOGRAPHY

CROWE, SYLVIA 1956 *Tomorrow's Landscape*. London: Architectural Press.
CROWE, SYLVIA 1958 *The Landscape of Power*. London: Architectural Press.
CROWE, SYLVIA 1960 *The Landscape of Roads*. London: Architectural Press.
CROWE, SYLVIA 1966 *Forestry in the Landscape*. London: H. M. Stationery Office.
CROWE, SYLVIA 1978 *The Landscape of Forests and Woods*. London: H. M. Stationery Office.
CROWE, SYLVIA 1977 *The Gardens of Mughal India: A History and a Guide*. London: Thames & Hudson.
CROWE, SYLVIA, and MILLER, ZVI (editors) 1964 *Shaping Tomorrow's Landscape*. 2 vols. Amsterdam: Djambatan.
FESTING, SALLY 1979 "In Person: Lady in the Landscape." *New Scientist* Jan.: 100–103.

CRUCY, MATHURIN

Born in Nantes, where he served his apprenticeship with JEAN-BAPTISTE CEINERAY, Mathurin Crucy (1749–1826) then moved to Paris. As a student of ETIENNE LOUIS BOULLÉE, he received the first prize of the Académie Royale d'Architecture in 1774 for his project for public baths of mineral water. A fellow student of the painter David at the

Académie de France in Rome (1775–1778), Crucy completed his architectural education with the study of the great monuments of antiquity and the Renaissance. Contact with the buildings of AN- DREA PALLADIO was to have a profound effect on his own work. Upon his return to France, Crucy was made architect-surveyor of Nantes, a city which at the time was undergoing considerable expansion. Continuing the urbanistic work of Ceineray, Crucy turned the architecture of Nantes toward a hellenizing neoclassicism that was both sober and vigorous, attesting to the influence of international Palladianism. Crucy's oeuvre, de- rived in part from utopian theories, is the most complete example in France of neoclassicist urban- ism carried out on a grand scale. In 1809, Crucy became architect of the *département* of Loire- Inférieure.

DANIEL RABREAU
Translated from French by
Shara Wasserman

WORKS

1784–1787, Grand Théâtre and Place Graslin; 1786, Corn Exchange; 1786–1790, Place d'Armes; 1787, Place Royale; 1790–1814, Stock Exchange; 1800, Public Baths; 1821, Textile Exchange; Nantes, France.

BIBLIOGRAPHY

LELIEVRE, PIERRE 1942 *Nantes au XVIIIe siècle: Urbanisme et architecture.* Nantes.
RABREAU, DANIEL 1977 "L'oeuvre de Mathurin Crucy à Nantes: Un modèle d'esthétique urbain neoclassique." *Storia della citta* 4.
RABREAU, DANIEL 1980 "Le théâtre de Nantes ou l'urbanisme mis en scène." *Monuments Histor- iques* 108.

CRUNDEN, JOHN

John Crunden (c.1745–1835) first appears as the author of *Designs for Ceilings* (1765). He is better known as a pattern book compiler than as an archi- tect. However, the Boodles Club (1775) in Lon- don was a fine design in ROBERT ADAM's style and was prominent in the metropolis. He popular- ized a weak Palladian (see ANDREA PALLADIO) manner typified in his widely disseminated *Conven- ient and Ornamental Architecture* (1767). His trade was really as a district surveyor.

JOHN HARRIS

WORKS

1767, Brooklands, Surrey, England. 1775, Boodles Club, London. 1775, Bushbridge, Surrey, England. c.1775, Portswood House, Hampshire, England.

BIBLIOGRAPHY

CRUNDEN, JOHN 1765 *Engravings of Designs for Ceil- ings.* Holbern, England: Webley.
CRUNDEN, JOHN 1767 *Convenient and Ornamental Architecture.* London: The author.

CUBITT, THOMAS

The enterprising British builder Thomas Cubitt (1788–1855) is primarily known for having initi- ated the first modern architectural firm. During the course of his active career, he proved that well- designed buildings of sound construction could be efficiently erected without subcontracting. Because of the extent of his speculative building, his inter- est in civic affairs, and his occasional royal commis- sions, Cubitt established a reputable position in Georgian and Victorian London.

Born in Norfolk, Thomas Cubitt began his career as a journeyman carpenter. In 1809, he set up as a master carpenter in London. In 1815, hav- ing contracted to build the London Institution in Moorsfields, Cubitt set up a comprehensive build- ing establishment in order to complete the project more rapidly and efficiently. He installed a com- plex of workshops at Gray's Inn Road and hired carpenters, smiths, glaziers, bricklayers, and so on. His brother, Lewis Cubitt (1799–1883), who was trained as an architect, was enlisted to do most of the designing. In 1832, Lewis joined his other brother, William Cubitt (1791–1863), in a sepa- rate contracting business.

Because Thomas Cubitt had to support a large labor force that worked on a permanent wage basis, he became involved in speculative building. Throughout the 1820s and until his death in 1855, Cubitt developed areas at Highbury Park, Stoke Newington, Islington, and more extensively at Bloomsbury, where his workshops were located. Cubitt took best advantage of the new prestige given to the areas of Belgravia and later Pimlico by virtue of their proximity to Buckingham Palace. These were his greatest building enterprises. In 1828, Cubitt was elected by the proprietors of Kemp Town at Brighton to serve on a manage- ment committee, a position he held until his death. Kemp Town, after JOHN NASH's Regent Park Terraces, is considered the grandest and most homogeneous of the Regency developments.

Occasionally, when called upon, Cubitt took on noble and royal commissions. Largely because his reputation was untainted by controversy, Cubitt was enlisted by Prince Albert in 1845 to design and build Osborne House on the Isle of Wight. From 1846 to 1850, his firm built the east front of Buckingham Palace according to the designs of EDWARD BLORE. From 1852 to 1856, he built the south side of the palace which was designed by JAMES PENNETHORNE. In general, Cubitt's designs for private homes were conventionally Palladian (see ANDREA PALLADIO) or Italianate and of sound construction.

As a public-minded social figure, Cubitt was concerned with issues of planning relating to the rapid expansion of London. Because of his experience he was often called upon to present his views in Parliamentary hearings on such matters as air pollution control, sewage disposal, and the disposition of public parks. The establishment of Battersea Park, much opposed by Disraeli, is credited to Thomas Cubitt's initiative. He also was a financial guarantor of the Great Exhibition of 1851. Indeed, because his speculative building projects were so lucrative, he was able to amass a great fortune. Upon his death in 1855, Cubitt left over £1,000,000.

SOPHIE GOBRAN

WORKS

1815, London Institution, Moorsfields; 1820–1824, Speculative Housing, Highbury Park; 1820–1824, Speculative Housing, Islington (Barnsbury Park); 1820–1824, Speculative Housing, Stoke Newington (Albion Road); 1824–1855, Speculative Housing, Bloomsbury (not completed until 1860); 1824–1855, Five Fields, Belgravia (not completed until 1860); 1824–1855, Five Fields, Pimlico (not completed until 1860); London. 1828–1855, Kemp Town, Brighton, England. 1845–1848, Osborne House, Isle of Wight, England. 1848–1850, Buckingham Palace (east front; designed by Edward Blore); 1852–1855, Buckingham Palace (south side; designed by James Pennethorne; not completed until 1856); London.

BIBLIOGRAPHY

HITCHCOCK, H. R. (1954)1976 *Early Victorian Architecture.* 2 vols. New York: Da Capo.
HOBHOUSE, HERMIONE 1971 *Thomas Cubitt: Master Builder.* London: Macmillan.
SUMMERSON, JOHN (1946)1978 *Georgian London.* 3d ed., rev. London: Barnie & Jenkins.

CUÉLLAR, SERRANO, and GOMEZ

Camilo Cuéllar Tamayo (1909–) graduated in 1934 from the London Architectural Association School. Gabriel Serrano Camargo (1908–) and José Gomez Pinzón (1909–) graduated from the National University of Colombia, Serrano in 1933 in architecture and engineering and Gomez in engineering in 1934 after winning the prestigious Ponce de Leon prize in 1933. Pioneers of Colombian modernism, they engineered, designed, and built Cine Colombia (1945), the country's first structure of reinforced concrete. At the first exhibition of Latin American architecture in New York City, their university preparatory school (1951–1952) was acclaimed, and they have since produced numerous award-winning structures.

ELIZABETH D. HARRIS

WORKS

1942, Adma Factory; 1945, Cine Colombia; 1948, Club Los Lagartos; 1951, Banco de Bogotá; 1951–1952, University Preparatory School; 1952–1953, Colon Building; 1957, El Dorado Airport; 1959, Ministry of Education; 1961, Tequendama Residences; 1962, National University (Department of Medicine); 1964, Flota Mercante Grancolombiana Headquarters; 1968, Latin American Episcopal Council Building; Bogotá. 1969, Intercontinental Hotel, Cali, Colombia. 1970, Distrito Especial Building; 1971, Neurological Institute of Colombia; 1974, Vecol Laboratories; Bogotá.

BIBLIOGRAPHY

ARANGO, JORGE, and MARTINEZ, CARLOS 1951 *Arquitectura en Colombia.* Bogotá: Ediciones Proa.
BERTY, ANNE 1981 *Architectures Colombiennes.* Paris: Moniteur.

CUMBERLAND, FREDERIC WILLIAM

Frederic William Cumberland (1821–1881), a Toronto architect and civil engineer, was born in England and apprenticed to William Tress, a London architect. He arrived in Canada in 1847. His Toronto work includes Saint James Anglican Cathedral (1850–1853) and the Normal School (1852), in partnership with Thomas Ridout. With WILLIAM G. STORM, he executed University College (1856–1858) and Osgoode Hall (1857–1860).

ROBERT HILL

BIBLIOGRAPHY

ROSE, GEORGE M. (editor) (1886–1888)1893 "Cumberland, Frederic William." Volume 1, pages 705–707 in *Cyclopedia of Canadian Biography.* Toronto: Rose.
ROBINSON, C. BLACKETT 1885 "Biographical Notices, City of Toronto: Colonel F. W. Cumberland." Volume 2, pages 36–37 in *History of Toronto and County of York.* Toronto: The author.

CUMMINGS, G. P.

Gordon Parker Cummings (c.1819–1889) designed San Francisco's earliest major office building and, in Philadelphia, the first iron-fronted building in the United States outside New York. A literate, cultured gentleman, his grand tour included sketching in Greece, Syria, and Egypt. Beginning in 1847, he taught at the architectural school sponsored and housed since 1833 by the venerable Carpenters' Company of his native Philadelphia. In his teaching, he emphasized the finest classical and modern examples and precise terminology. Through two extended stays in California he retained the title of professor. THOMAS U. WALTER published three of his designs. His buildings were in a wide variety of exotic styles, from Greek Revival through Egyptian and Imperial Roman Revivals to Italianate and Gothic Revivals. He built in stone (Montgomery Block, San Francisco, 1853–1854), masonry with first-floor iron fronts (Swaim's Building, Philadelphia, 1847–1848) and all iron (Penn Mutual, Philadelphia, 1850–1851). Third of the California Capitol's four architects, he supervised most of its construction.

ANNE BLOOMFIELD

WORKS

*1845, Pair of Houses for Francis Hopkinson; *1847–1848, Hutchinson's Building; *1847–1848, Swaim's Building; 1847–1849, Logan Square Presbyterian Church; *1848, Raikes' Union School Building; *1848–1849, Sansom Street Hall; *1850–1851, Penn Mutual Life Insurance Building; *1851, Grand Lodge of Colored Masons' Hall; Philadelphia. *1853–1854, Montgomery Block; *1853–1854, Union Hotel; San Francisco. 1865–1870, 1872–1874, State Capitol (ornamentation), Sacramento, California. 1870–1872, Saint Patrick's Church, San Francisco. *1876, California Hall, Centennial Exposition, Philadelphia.

BIBLIOGRAPHY

Alta California 1853, 1865, 1869, 1874, 1876 May 19:2; Aug. 2:1; Dec. 18:1; June 25:1; March 7:1.
BUCHANAN, AGNES FOSTER 1906 "Some Early Business Buildings of San Francisco." *Architectural Record* 20, July:15–32.
LANGLEY 1872 Pages 17, 96 in *San Francisco Directory*. San Francisco.
LE COUNT, and STRONG 1854 Pages 190–192 in *San Francisco Directory*. San Francisco: Le Count & Strong.
MASSEY, JAMES C. 1955 "Carpenters' School: 1833–1842." *Journal of the Society of Architectural Historians* 14, May:29–30.
MCKENNEY 1870 Pages 17, 96 in *Sacramento Directory*. Sacramento, Calif.
PETERSON, CHARLES E. 1950 "The Penn Mutual Building, Philadelphia: 1850–51." *Journal of the Society of Architectural Historians* 9, Dec.:24–25.
Philadelphia Public Ledger 1845, 1847, 1848, 1849, 1851 June 17:2; Mar. 24:2; Dec. 7:2; May 22:2; Feb. 6:2; Oct. 5:2; June 16:2. (Courtesy Constance M. Greiff)
TATUM, GEORGE B. 1961 Pages 97, 188 in *Penn's Great Town*. Philadelphia: University of Pennsylvania Press.
WALTER, THOMAS USTICK (editor) 1846 Plates 21, 50, 105 in *200 Designs for Cottages and Villas*. Philadelphia: Cary & Hart (Courtesy The Athenaeum, Philadelphia).

CUMMINGS and SEARS

Charles Amos Cummings (1833–1905) and Willard Thomas Sears (1837–1920) formed one of the leading architectural firms in post-Civil War Boston. The early work of both men before their partnership began in 1867 and the solo practice of Sears from 1890 to 1920 were also distinguished.

Born in Boston, Cummings graduated from the Rensselaer Polytechnic Institute in 1853. Sears was born in New Bedford, Massachusetts, and served an architectural apprenticeship there. Each spent a year in GRIDLEY J. F. BRYANT's office and was a charter member of the Boston Society of Architects. The firm designed numerous commercial buildings in downtown Boston, many in a polychromatic High Victorian Gothic style, several houses in Boston's Back Bay, and the New Old South Church in Copley Square (1874–1876). In 1890, Cummings left professional practice to write on architecture. Sears's later work included Fenway Court (1899) in Boston, now the Gardner Museum, designed for Mrs. John L. Gardner, with her collaboration.

CYNTHIA ZAITZEVSKY

WORKS

CHARLES A. CUMMINGS

*1864–1866, Brechin Hall; *1864–1876, Chapel, Andover Theological Seminary (later part of Phillips Academy); Andover, Mass. *1866–1867, Mason Hamlin Building, Boston.

WILLARD T. SEARS

*1864, Maculler, Williams and Parker Building, Boston.

CUMMINGS AND SEARS

*1868–1869, Sears Building; *1869, Hotel Kempton; 1871, Charles A. Cummings House; 1874–1876, Bedford Building; 1874–1876, New Old South Church; 1881, Charles Sprague House; 1884, Cyclorama Building; Boston.

WILLARD T. SEARS

1894, Eldredge Building, Boston. 1897, Story Chapel, Mount Auburn Cemetery, Cambridge, Mass. 1898, Cambridge Hotel; 1899, Fenway Court (Mrs. John L. Gardner House; now the Gardner Museum); Boston. 1907–1910, Pilgrim Monument, Provincetown, Mass.

BIBLIOGRAPHY

BUNTING, BAINBRIDGE 1967 *Houses of Boston's Back Bay.* Cambridge, Mass.: Belknap.
CUMMINGS, CHARLES A. 1881 "Architecture in Boston." Volume 4, pages 465–488 in Justin Winsor (editor), *The Memorial History of Boston.* Boston: Ticknor.
CUMMINGS, CHARLES A. 1901 *A History of Architecture in Italy from the Time of Constantine to the Dawn of the Renaissance.* 2 vols Boston: Houghton Mifflin.

CUNDY FAMILY

The most talented members of the family, Thomas Cundy I (1765–1825) and his son, Thomas II (1790–1867), were successively surveyors to Lord Grosvenor's London estate between 1821 and 1867, Thomas II during the residential development of Belgravia and Pimplico by the speculative builder and architect THOMAS CUBITT. Thomas I, born in Cornwall, England, was apprenticed to a Plymouth builder before moving to London where he became clerk of works to SAMUEL PEPYS COCKERELL. He first exhibited at the Royal Academy in 1795 and established himself as an architect-builder in Pimlico. From about 1807, he enjoyed success as a country house architect, designing in the Picturesque Gothic and neoclassical styles. He trained Thomas II, with whom he visited Rome in 1816, and practiced until his death. His third son, Joseph (1795–1875), was an architect and speculative builder in Belgravia. Thomas II, a more accomplished designer who also employed both the classical and the Gothic styles, assumed his father's practice in 1825. He was joined in the late 1840s by his son, Thomas III (1820–1895). They designed a series of churches in London, chiefly in the Gothic Revival style and latterly influenced by the Ecclesiological Society, most notably at Saint Barnabus, Pimlico (1847–1850). In 1864, he relinquished the practice to Thomas III and retired to Kent, where he died.

R. WINDSOR LISCOMBE

WORKS

THOMAS CUNDY I
*1806–1810, Middleton Park (major alterations), Oxfordshire, England.

THOMAS CUNDY I AND THOMAS CUNDY II
1807, Bessingby Hall, Yorkshire, England. 1809–1810, Hawarden Castle (remodeling), Flintshire, Wales. 1813–1814, Wassand Hall, Yorkshire, England. *1815, Hewell Grange (major alterations), Worcestershire, England. 1819?, Garbally Park, Ballinasloe, County Gallway, Ireland. 1823?–1826, Tottenham Park (remodeling), Wiltshire, England. *1825–1827, 1842–1843, Grosvenor House (picture gallery and Doric entrance screen), Upper Grosvenor Street, London.

THOMAS CUNDY II AND THOMAS CUNDY III
1840–1843, Saint Paul's Church, Knightsbridge; 1844, Saint Michael's Church, Chester Square; 1846–1847, Saint Mark's Church, Saint John's Wood; 1847–1850, Saint Barnabus's Church, Pimlico; 1864, Saint Savior's Church, Pimlico; London.

BIBLIOGRAPHY

CORNFORTH, JOHN 1967 "Hawarden Castle, Flintshire." *Country Life* 141:1516–1519, 1608–1611, 1676–1680.
CORNFORTH, JOHN 1973 "Old Grosvenor House." *Country Life* 154:1538–1541.
HOBHOUSE, HERMIONE 1969 "The Building of Belgravia." *Country Life* 145:1154–1157, 1312–1314.
HOBHOUSE, HERMIONE 1971 Pages 53, 86, 89, 121–122, 200–201 in *Thomas Cubitt: Master Builder.* London: Macmillan.
SAINT, ANDREW 1977 "The Grosvenor Estate: 2. The Cundy Era." *Country Life* 162:1474–1477.
"Survey of London." 1977 Volume 39, pages 36, 44–46, 53–54, 133–135, 139–140 in F. H. W. Sheppard, *The Grosvenor Estate in Mayfair: Part I. General History.* London: Athlone.

CUTTER, KIRTLAND K.

Kirtland Kelsey Cutter (1860–1939), born in Cleveland, Ohio, studied at the Art Students League of New York and in Europe. Following his arrival in Spokane, Washington, about 1888, he specialized in residential work for wealthy clients and worked in association with John C. Poetz, with whom he collaborated on the award-winning Idaho State Building for the World's Columbian Exposition in Chicago in 1893. In 1895, he formed a long-lasting partnership with Karl G. Malmgren, former draftsman in the Cutter and Poetz office. Cutter and Malmgren produced an extensive body of work in Washington, Idaho, and Montana. In 1923, Cutter moved to southern California, where he continued his practice.

ELISABETH WALTON POTTER

WORKS

1888, James N. Glover House, Spokane, Wash. *1893, Idaho State Building, World's Columbian Exposition, Chicago. 1896, F. Lewis Clark House; 1898, Amasa B. Campbell House; 1898, Patrick F. Clark House; 1898, Daniel C. Corbin House; 1900, John A. Finch House; Spokane, Wash. 1903–1904, Rainier Club, Seattle, Wash. 1905, Kirtland Hall, Sheffield Scientific School, Yale University, New Haven. 1909–1910, Seattle Golf and Country Club, Wash. 1910, L. M. Davenport

House; 1910, Spokane Club; Wash. 1911, Thornewood (Chester Thorne House), American Lake, near Tacoma, Wash. 1913–1914, Davenport Hotel, Spokane, Wash. 1913–1914, Lewis Glacier Hotel, Glacier National Park, Mont. 1923, Chronicle Building (with G. A. Pearson), Spokane, Wash.

BIBLIOGRAPHY

DURHAM, NELSON WAYNE 1912 Volume 2 in *History of the City of Spokane and Spokane County, Washington.* Chicago: Clarke.

VAUGHAN, THOMAS, and FERRIDAY, VIRGINIA GUEST (editors) 1974 *Space, Style and Structure.* 2 vols. Portland: Oregon Historical Society.

WOODBRIDGE, SALLY BRYNE, and MONTGOMERY, ROGER 1980 *A Guide to Architecture in Washington State.* Seattle: University of Washington Press.

CUVILLIES, FRANÇOIS THE ELDER

François Cuvilliés (1695–1768) was the leading exponent in Bavaria of French Régence and rococo decorative styles. Rather than following them faithfully he skillfully adapted them to the more florid expectations of the Munich area, departing considerably from the prevailing severity of French models.

Born in Soignies (Hainaut) near Brussels, Cuvilliés was taken on as court dwarf in 1708 by Max Emanuel, the elector of Bavaria, then in exile at Bouchefort. Here the elector had employed GERMAIN BOFFRAND to build an octagonal hunting lodge. In 1713, Boffrand completed the decoration of a house designed by JOSEF EFFNER, at Saint-Cloud, near Paris, for the elector's move there. As a page in the household, Cuvilliés was thus exposed to the new modes and techniques of Paris itself, and to his patron's unlimited enthusiasm for them.

In 1715, after the Treaty of Rastatt, the elector and his court returned to Munich, and Cuvilliés became a draftsman under Effner, now the chief court architect. In 1707, Max Emanuel sent Effner to Paris for training under Boffrand; in 1720, Cuvilliés was likewise dispatched for four years' training under JACQUES-FRANÇOIS BLONDEL. His return via Rome appears to have had no influence on his subsequent work.

During the later 1720s Cuvilliés gradually became Effner's equal and in the 1730s clearly eclipsed him. But the Munich architect Johann Baptist Gunetzrhainer offered strong competition, and in 1745 succeeded Effner as chief court architect. Not until 1763 did the title pass to Cuvilliés, who had but five years left to enjoy it.

In 1726, Carl Albert succeeded Emanuel as elector and enthusiastically favored Cuvilliés. The first court commission of importance for Cuvilliés, the Palais Piosasque de Non (destroyed in World War II), came in 1726. Two years later Carl Albert sent his protégé to work on his brother's summer palace at Brühl, newly rebuilt by JOHANN CONRAD SCHLAUN. Here Cuvilliés decorated the Yellow Apartment (1728–1730) and designed Falkenlust (1729–1737) in the great park. As falconry was much in favor, he seized the opportunity to introduce, in his stucco work and tiling for Falkenlust, motives derived from nature. This emphasis, already pronounced in Bavarian decoration and notably distinct from French abstraction in such embellishment, was to reach a much higher pitch in Cuvilliés's interior of the Amalienburg Pavilion (1734–1739) in the park of Schloss Nymphenburg then outside Munich. While the exterior of Falkenlust hardly differs from French models of the time, that of the Amalienburg has a new German freedom, especially in the figured stucco ornamentation by Johann Baptist Zimmermann.

In 1729, a fire at the Munich *Residenz* destroyed much of Effner's ceremonial apartments, and both he and Cuvilliés immediately set to work to replace them. The long *Ahnengalerie* was Effner's work, but Cuvilliés designed the ceiling. Its relative freedom and verve again indicate the younger assistant's inventiveness. The Reiche Zimmer (1730–1737) are primarily Cuvilliés's work, as are the Green Gallery (destroyed in World War II, but expertly reconstructed) and a staircase (destroyed in 1764). An additional set of rooms was dismantled in 1745, soon after Cuvilliés completed them. His ornament in the *Residenz* apartments gradually shifts from the delicacies of régence style toward the rocaille exuberance of the rococo, with its asymmetrical C- and S-shapes. Yet the ever growing introduction of naturalistic detail may also derive from Cuvilliés's stuccoist, Zimmermann, and from his woodcarvers, Joachim Dietrich, Adam Pichler, and Wenzel Miroffsky.

Also at this time Cuvilliés worked on the Palais Holnstein (1733–1737) and the Amalienburg (1734–1739). With their complex architectural elements, cartouches, stucco decoration, and elaborate ironwork, these exteriors notably depart from French models of the day. French influence, however, surely accounts for the greater dignity and sophistication that distinguishes them from Cuvilliés's earlier Palais Piosasque de Non, and even more from comparable works by Effner.

The celebrated round salon is the center of Amalienburg—sparkling with mirrors alternating with doors and windows, tinted in subtlest blues, pale grays, and white, overlaid below with silvered woodwork by Dietrich and above with silvered

Cuvilliés the Elder.
Amalienburg Pavilion.
Nymphenburg Park, Munich.
1734–1739

Cuvilliés the Elder.
Residenztheater.
Munich.
1750–1753

stucco by Zimmermann, and complemented by console tables and candelabra to match. Two yellow and silver rooms, a bedroom and a dining room, flank it, and beyond the latter is a kitchen veneered with Dutch tiles that run to blues and whites (the Wittelsbach colors) but also incorporate the yellows of the secondary rooms. No such fairyland exists in France; indeed, the oval salons of Boffrand's Hôtel de Soubise in Paris, offer more contrasts than similarities—too emphatically urged in much of the literature.

Beginning in 1738, Cuvilliés published a series of books of ornamental designs, many of them engraved by his son of the same name and by his pupil, K. A. von Lespilliez. A second series dates from the 1740s and a third, overseen by the son,

from 1756. The influence of these designs throughout central Europe can hardly be exaggerated. In addition to architectural features, they affected furniture-making and porcelain, especially at the Nymphenburg factory.

A surprising dichotomy marks Cuvilliés's later work, indicating his departure from the variant of French rococo that he had established so triumphantly. On the one hand, his rebuilding, in 1756–1757, of Effner's central room of the Schloss Nymphenburg is formally classical, even though Zimmermann's accompanying stucco and fresco ornamentation is almost florid in its use of rococo elements. On the other, Cuvilliés's *Residenztheater* (1750–1753) (destroyed in World War II; but later reconstructed on a new site) may be described as nearly baroque in flavor—this despite the fact that all elements except the massive columns at the proscenium arch are strictly rococo. Color too—translucent raspberry reds over silvered wood surfaces, plus gold, ivory, and white—is rococo; yet in this luxuriant ensemble a new heaviness appears. We have evidence here of a minor countermovement within the general evolution from baroque to rococo in eighteenth-century German style, for a somewhat similar phenomenon appears in the development of DOMINIKUS ZIMMERMANN's architecture.

It would be convenient to explain Cuvilliés's new classicizing trend as a result of his second stay in Paris in 1754–1755, but nevertheless his restrained design for another *maison de plaisance*, Schloss Wilhelmstal (1750–1752), near Kassel (Hessen), predates that trip.

Cuvilliés's activity in church design was of minor significance. In the 1730s he provided a plan for the abbey church of Schäftlarn, south of Munich, but work was soon interrupted and not taken up again until 1751, with JOHANN MICHAEL FISCHER very much in charge. In 1738, Cuvilliés inspected and approved Fischer's project for the collegiate church of Berg-am-Laim, outside Munich. Cuvilliés's last work, 1765–1768, was a refashioning of ENRICO ZUCCALLI's façade of the Munich Theatinerkirche, carried out by his son.

S. LANE FAISON, JR.

WORKS

*1726–1732, Palais Piosasque de Non, Munich. 1728–1730, Schloss Brühl (Yellow Apartment); 1729–1737, Schloss Brühl (Falkenlust); Germany. 1730–1737, Residenz (Reiche Zimmer, Green Gallery, *staircase); 1733–1737, Palais Holnstein; 1734–1739, Amalienburg Pavilion, Nymphenburg Park; Munich. 1747–?, Schloss Haimhausen, near Munich. 1750–1752, Schloss Wilhelmstal, near Kassel, Germany. 1750–1753, Residenztheater; 1756–1757, Schloss Nymphenburg (reconstruction of main salon); Munich.

BIBLIOGRAPHY

BRAUNFELS, WOLFGANG 1938 *François de Cuvilliés, ein Beitrag zur Geschichte der künstlerischen Beziehungen zwischen Deutschland und Frankreich im 18. Jahrhundert.* Wurzburg, Germany: Mayr.

BRÜHL. SCHLOSS AUGUSTUSBURG 1961 *Kurfürst Clemens August, Landesherr und Mäzen des 18. Jahrhunderts. Ausstellung im Schloss Augustusburg zu Brühl, 1961.* Cologne, Germany: Schauberg.

HAGER, LUISA 1955 *Nymphenburg: Schloss, Park und Burgen.* Munich: Hirmer Verlag.

HANSMANN, WILFRIED 1970 "Die Stuckdecken des Gelben Appartements im Schloss Augustusburg zu Brühl." *Beiträge zur rheinischen Kunstgeschichte und Denkmalpflege* 16:241–268.

HANSMANN, WILFRIED 1973 *Schloss Falkenlust.* Cologne, Germany: Schauberg.

LAING, ALASTAIR 1978 Pages 281–287 in Anthony Blunt (editor), *Baroque and Rococo: Architecture & Decoration.* New York: Harper.

LIEB, NORBERT (1953)1958 *Barockkirchen zwischen Donau und Alpen.* 2d ed. Munich: Hirmer Verlag.

THON, CHRISTINA 1977 *Johann Baptist Zimmermann als Stukkator.* Munich: Schnell und Steiner.

WOLF, FRIEDRICH 1967 *François de Cuvilliés: Der Architekt und Dekorschöpfer.* Munich: Historischer Verein von Oberbayern.

CUYPERS, EDUARD

Eduard Gerard Hendrik Hubert Cuypers (1859–1927) was a pupil and assistant of his famous uncle P. J. H. CUYPERS. From 1878 he was an independent architect and interior decorator in Amsterdam with a large practice throughout the country. He owed this to the late industrial development of the Netherlands. Cuypers was a traditional architect, around 1900 temporarily influenced by Belgian Art Nouveau and British Modernism. He was editor of *Het Huis, Oud en Nieuw* (The House, Old and New) from 1903 to 1927. Much of the design in this monthly influenced the Amsterdam school. JOHAN M. VAN DER MEY, MICHEL DE KLERK, and PIETER L. KRAMER were either his pupils or his assistants between 1897 and 1911.

PIETER SINGELENBERG

WORKS

*1894–1896, Railway Station, 's-Hertogenbosch, Netherlands. 1899, Cuypers House, Amsterdam. 1902–1903, Hoog-Laren Sanatorium (enlarged in 1923), near Amsterdam. 1910, De Hooge Vuursche Country House, Baarn, Netherlands. 1926, Canisius Hospital, Nijmegen, Netherlands.

BIBLIOGRAPHY

FANELLI, GIOVANNI 1978 Pages 251–253 in *Moderne Architectuur in Nederland 1900–1940.* The Hague: Staatsuitgeverij.

LELIMAN, J. H. W., and SLUYTERMAN, K. 1922 *Het Moderne Landhuis in Nederland.* The Hague: Nijhoff.

LELIMAN, J. H. W., and VAN DER STEUR, A. J. 1924 *Het stadswoonhuis in Nederland gedurende de laatste 25 jaren.* The Hague: Nijhoff.

Nederlandse Architectuur, 1910–1930: Amsterdamse School. (1975)1979 2d ed. Amsterdam: Stedelijk Museum.

CUYPERS, P. J. H.

Petrus Josephus Hubertus Cuypers (1827–1921) was born in Roermond, a town in the Roman Catholic province of Limburg in the Netherlands. He received his professional training at the Academy of Antwerp, Belgium, and left this institution in 1849 with the Prix d'Excellence. He went for a short period to Paris to follow, as a convinced medievalist in the nineteenth-century sense, the methods of EUGÈNE EMMANUEL VIOLLET-LE-DUC. The well-known pronouncement of the latter that every form not indicated by the structure has to be rejected became his often quoted device. This positivism did not stand in the way of a late romantic idealism and the wish to break with classicist rules.

In 1850, Cuypers started in his native town as an independent architect and designer. Two years later, he founded the studio Cuypers and Stoltenberg to produce sculpture, furniture, and applied arts, mainly for churches. His ideas about architecture, arts, crafts, and the honest use of materials (especially brick) can be compared with those of his contemporary WILLIAM MORRIS. Therefore, Cuypers was the predecessor of the Dutch Modern movement, inaugurated in the 1890s by H. P. BERLAGE and K. P. C. DE BAZEL. His practice was highly promoted by the reinstatement of the episcopal hierarchy in the Netherlands in 1853. The Roman Catholics, for a long period forced to use clandestine churches in Calvinistic country, needed many new buildings, also not least because the Protestants kept the medieval churches. Cuypers built and decorated in a free Gothic way, rather sober in the grammar, but with the spiritual exuberance of a Counter-Reformation.

Cuypers was also involved in secular architecture. In houses and large public buildings, Cuypers generally used formal elements of the French and Dutch Renaissance.

He restored many medieval buildings according to the principles of Viollet-le-Duc, meaning that he often created a correct archeological situation that never existed at any one moment in the past. One of the merits of this work was that it aroused much interest for the past. In this field, he

was strongly encouraged and supported by Victor de Stuers who was in charge of arts and sciences in the Ministry of the Interior from 1875 till 1901. De Stuers was on the whole a promoter of the restoration of monuments of history and art. Cuypers and De Stuers may be compared to the French duo Viollet-le-Duc and Prosper Mérimée.

Cuypers made his fame in particular with the Rijksmuseum (1876–1885) and the Central Station (1885–1889), both in Amsterdam, with the restoration of the Minster in Roermond, and with the rather free re-creation of Château De Haar at Haarzuilens near Utrecht. In 1865, he moved to Amsterdam where he founded the Rijksmuseum-school, later Quellinus-school, and where he taught applied arts and art history. Many young architects started practice in his office in Amsterdam, K. P. C. de Bazel, J. L. M. LAUWERIKS, and H. T. WIJDEVELD among them.

PIETER SINGELENBERG

WORKS

1850–1852, P. J. H. Cuypers House, Maastrichterweg, Roermond, Netherlands. 1855–1862, Saint Lambertus (alterations made in 1915), Veghel, Netherlands. 1858–1908, Saint Servaas (restoration), Maastricht, Netherlands. 1859, Saint Catharina, Eindhoven, Netherlands. *1864–1873, Saint Willibrordus-buiten-de-Veste (later extended), Amsterdam. 1865, Saint Barbara (later extended), Breda, Netherlands. 1870–1873, Heilig Hart, Vondelstraat, Amsterdam. 1870–1884, Minster (restoration), Roermond, Netherlands. 1872–1875, Cathedral Mayence (restoration), Germany. 1873–1900, Nieuwe Kerk (restoration), Delft, Netherlands. 1875, Saint Jacobus Major, Parkstraat, The Hague. 1876–1885, Rijksmuseum and Director's House, Amsterdam. 1876, Houses, 36–42 and 75 Vondelstraat; 1878–1880, Houses, 3–7 Vondelstraat; Amsterdam. 1881–1885, Saint Bonifacius, Leeuwarden, Netherlands. 1883–1886, Fountain Count William II of Holland, Binnenhof, The Hague. 1884–1885, Oud-Leyerhoven II House, Tesselschadestraat–Vondelstraat, Amsterdam. 1885–1889, Central Station (with A. L. VAN GENDT), Amsterdam. 1886, Saint Josef (with Joseph Cuypers), Groningen, Netherlands. 1886–1917, Onze Lieve Vrouwekerk (restoration; with Joseph Cuypers), Maastricht, Netherlands. 1890–1892, Saint Vitus (K. P. C. de Bazel, surveyor), Hilversum, Netherlands. 1891–1896, Château de Haar (restoration; with Joseph Cuypers), Haarzuilens, Netherlands. 1897, Saint Petrus, Oisterwijk, Netherlands.

BIBLIOGRAPHY

CUYPERS, P. J. H., and LUYTEN, FRANS 1910 *Le Château de Haar à Haarzuylens.* Utrecht, Netherlands: Oosthoek.

FANELLI, GIOVANNI 1978 *Moderne architectuur in Nederland: 1900–1940.* Translated from Italian by Wim de Wit.'s Gravenhage, Netherlands: Staatsuitgeverij.

Het Werk van Dr. P. J. H. Cuypers: 1827–1917. 1917 Amsterdam: Van Holkema & Warendorf.

ROSENBERG, H. P. R. 1972 *De 19de-eeuwse kerkelijke bouwkunst in Nederland.* The Hague: Staatsuitgeverij.

STUERS, VICTOR DE (1873)1975 *Holland op zijn smalst.* Reprint. Bussum, Netherlands: De Haan.

D'AGINCOURT, JEAN-BAPTISTE SEROUX

Jean-Baptiste Séroux d'Agincourt (1730–1814) is one of the first art historians. As the author of the vast *Histoire de l'art par les monuments, depuis sa décadence au IVe siècle, jusqu'à son renouvellement au XVIe* (Paris, 1811–1823), often considered the continuation of Winckelmann's famous *Geschichte der Kunst des Alterthums* (Dresden, 1764), he was undoubtedly one of the founders of the new art history of the Middle Ages. Formed by the classical aesthetic opinions of his time, he was impressed by the views of Winckelmann and Mengs. Nevertheless, his strong historical interest led him to work for thirty years on the "decadent" art of the Middle Ages, just as Gibbon or Montesquieu chose to portray the decline in the period of history between antiquity and the Renaissance.

Born in Beauvais, France, d'Agincourt first followed a military career, becoming involved in the cultural and scientific world only after his return to Paris. He was introduced to the study of botany by Bernard de Jussieu and encouraged by Buffon. He met people like Marmontel, La Harpe, the Abbé Morellet, Rousseau, with whom he dabbled in botany, and Voltaire whom he visited in Ferney. He was introduced to the arts by the comte de Caylus, to whom he addressed a late *hommage* in his *Recueil de fragmens de sculpture antique en terre cuite* (Paris, 1814; this work was intended as an appendix to Caylus's *Recueil d'antiquités*). The contacts which he made in that period with the leading artists of France—Boucher, Vien, Robert, Fragonard, Bouchardon, Cochin—were decisive for his later art historical activity. Leading collectors—among them Mariette—inspired him to start collecting, an experience that was crucial for him. In 1776, at first using his interest in geology as an excuse, he began traveling in France. This resulted in a comparative survey and recording of medieval monuments in drawings. In 1777, he traveled to England, Belgium, and Holland, and upon his return to Paris decided to devote his life to examining artistic monuments. On October 24, 1778, he left Paris for good and set off for Italy, arriving via the Piedmont and Genoa in Modena where he made contact with Tiraboschi. He spent his first prolonged period of research in Bologna. A copy of Malvasia's 1776 guide to Bologna, interleaved with notes and commentaries, shows the method he used to record and examine monuments systematically. It shows also the emphasis of his interest on the Middle Ages and the Renaissance, as well as his relatively simple system of classifying the monuments according to type of art and century. In Venice, he made the acquaintance of the

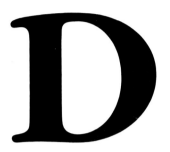

librarian of San Marco, the Abate Morelli, and assisted Cicognara in his bibliographic labors. D'Agincourt reached Rome toward the end of 1779, where he settled down in the Palazzo Zuccari. A few excursions in 1781–1782—to Herculaneum, Pompeii, Paestum, the library in Montecassino, and the Latium—were all that took him out of Rome. In the cultural world of the Rome of the period, d'Agincourt assumed a firm place. He was among the habitual guests at the receptions of Cardinal de Bernis and Nicola d'Azara, and he was esteemed by both Goethe and Stendhal as well as by the circle of artists around Angelika Kauffmann, to whom he was connected by ties of friendship. In this milieu, d'Agincourt was a knowledgeable partner in conversation as well as a catalyst. It is to him that Giovanni Gherardo de-Rossi (*Notizie storiche . . .* , Venice, 1827, pp. 57–58) ascribes the stimulus for the journal *Memorie delle Belle Arti* (1785–1788). The journal, which substantially revived the impulse toward classicist art, was financed by Canova's patron, Don Giovanni Abbondio Rezzonico, and Luigi Lanzi became an additional adviser. D'Agincourt's contacts with the world of scholarship—Della Valle who procured Sienese information for him; Galletti, the specialist in epigraphy; Benedetto Fiandrini who assisted him with the art history of Ravenna—were equally strong and helpful to him in his encyclopedic undertakings. He also entertained relations with the French colony in Rome and with the Académie de France à Rome, where he found the artists he needed to make the drawings of the monuments to be recorded.

This world of broad knowledge and excellent contacts offered d'Agincourt the best external prerequisites for his plan to create a corpus of all art between antiquity and the Renaissance. Himself a mediocre draftsman, he was experienced in the techniques of printing and was able to make use of a great number of artists to make the drawings and do the surveying and on-site checking. Thus, an imposing collection of material was gathered, which included measured plans of even such distant monuments as the Hagia Sophia in Constantinople. The work profited from the services of the best architects, both Italian and French. As a consequence of printing difficulties and the continuation of the research work thus enforced, a younger generation of artists, closer to medieval art, also became active for d'Agincourt.

In his judgments, however, d'Agincourt remained a classicist whose interest in the medieval art of the "decadence" was confined primarily to the importance of individual monuments within the general development. This evaluation provided d'Agincourt with the criteria upon which to base the selection of monuments from his extensive collection (Bibl. Apost. Vat., Cod. vat. lat. 9839–9849, 13477–13480) to be used for publication and engraved by Tommaso Piroli and Giovanni Giacomo Macchiavelli. In this there is both a limitation and a conscious intent to carry the *histoire des monuments* over into a history of art based on aesthetics and to deepen the *histoire matérielle* by referring to historic laws (*ordre*), currents (*enchaînement*), interdependencies (*dépendence réciproque*), and specific characteristics (*caractère spécial*). This is most clearly shown in the break-down of the art under consideration into periods, distinguishing between *Décadence* (fourth to ninth centuries), *Règne du système gothique* (ninth/eleventh to mid-fifteenth centuries), *Renaissance* (mid-fifteenth century) and *Renouvellement* (end of fifteenth/beginning of sixteenth century). Although he appears to envy Winckelmann for the superior subject matter of Greek art history (*Trop heureux Winckelmann!*, I, p. iv), positive value judgments are not alien to him, for instance, in relation to Gothic architecture. Here, he relies on LEON BATTISTA ALBERTI, Muratori, and FRANÇOIS BLONDEL, among others, and recalls his visit to HORACE WALPOLE at Strawberry Hill (1777). In fact, he draws a clear line between Gothic architecture and the preceding "decadence," introducing the former as a system and a new and extraordinary way of building. Finally, in view of later enthusiasm for the Middle Ages, the remark with which d'Agincourt concludes these commentaries on architecture is of some significance, namely, that religion has served architecture as the source of its *plus sublimes pensées* (most sublime thoughts) and its greatest and most enduring works.

Besides the break-down into art-historical periods and the differentiating value judgments this break-down achieved, perhaps d'Agincourt's main and most lasting merit lies in the fact that the monuments themselves were put into the center of consideration. In addition, the quality of the reproductions guaranteed for the first time the actual art-historical evaluation of these dispersed (and inaccessible) works of art. The art-historical examination of the *influence des causes générales* starts with a formal analysis. D'Agincourt makes use both of the comparative method and of conjecture. He establishes typological sequences, as shown in the tables of comparison on the shapes and proportions of columns or the origins and evolution of the divers shapes (Byzantine, Gothic, Persian, Indian) of the pointed arch. This comparative method, using charts, was of great importance for the historical understanding and the architectural theory of the nineteenth century.

The success of d'Agincourt's *Histoire de l'art par les monuments* was correspondingly great, in spite of the delay in its publication. In its main parts, the work was ready for printing in 1790; this was, however, begun only in 1811 and completed only in 1823, after d'Agincourt's death (1814). However, fame preceded its publication. Joseph Forsyth, in his *Remarks on antiquities, arts, and letters during an excursion in Italy in the years 1802 and 1803* (I, p. 287), names d'Agincourt, together with Fea and Zoega, as the leading Roman authority, and Cicognara, in the *Storia della scultura dal suo risorgimento in Italia fino al secolo di Canova* (Venice, 1813–1818), refers to him and to Winckelmann as the predecessors of his own endeavors. Shortly after its first publication, d'Agincourt's work was translated into Italian and brought out in a new edition by Ticozzi (Prato, 1826–1929). There were further Italian editions (Milan and Mantua, 1841) as well as translations into German (Quast, Berlin, 1840) and English (London, 1847).

WERNER OECHSLIN
Translated from German by
Beverley R. Placzek

BIBLIOGRAPHY

D'AGINCOURT, J. B. L. G. SÉROUX (1810)1823 *Histoire de l'Art par les Monumens, depuis sa décadence au IVᵉ siècle jusqu'à son renouvellement au XVIᵉ*. Paris: Treutel & Worte.

D'AGINCOURT, J. B. L. G. SÉROUX 1814 *Recueil de fragmens de sculpture antique en terre cuite*. Paris: Treuttel.

DUMENSIL, J. 1858 Volume 3, pages 1–58 in *Histoire des plus célèbres amateurs français*. Paris: Renouard.

HASKELL, F. 1976 Page 38 in *Rediscoveries in Art*. Ithaca, N.Y.: Cornell University Press.

LOYRETTE, HENRI 1980 "Séroux d'Agincourt et les origines de l'histoire de l'art médiéval." *Revue de l'Art* 48:40–56.

PREVITALI, G. 1964 *La fortuna dei primitivi*. Turin, Italy: Einaudi.

SCHLOSSER, J. (1935)1964 *La letteratura artistica*. Florence: Nuova Italia.

DAKIN, JAMES

One of the most imaginative American architects of the early nineteenth century, James Harrison Dakin (1806–1852) participated in the visionary ferment of the Romantic era. He was born in Dutchess County in upstate New York, where he had learned the carpentry trade.

In 1829, the newly formed architectural firm of TOWN and DAVIS took in James Dakin. Under the tutelage of Alexander Jackson Davis, he developed a drafting and artistic rendering technique uncannily similar to that of Davis. By 1832, Dakin became a full partner. Dakin's work with the firm is not easily discerned, but a few of his buildings are identifiable.

Dakin can be credited, along with Ithiel Town, with the design for New York University (1833–1837). Although Davis did most of the interior detailing of the chapel after Dakin left New York in 1835, the university is one of the earliest and most influential "Collegiate Gothic" designs in the long history of that style in American educational buildings.

Rockaway Marine Pavilion (1833–1834) on Long Island, a gigantic resort hotel in the Greek Revival style, is also Dakin's. While ISAIAH ROGERS is justifiably called "the father of the American hotel," Dakin can also be numbered among the important early hotel builders, with at least five hotels to his credit.

Dakin left Town and Davis in 1833 to establish his own practice in New York. Among his best independent works is the First Presbyterian Church (1834), Troy, New York (now part of Russell Sage College), a Greek Revival building loosely based on the Thesion. For the sides of the church, Dakin employed a favorite Town and Davis device, the "pilastrade," which is a series of square piers faced with pilasters. Rhythmically, the effect is that of a column, but conveying a feeling of great strength.

One of Dakin's most distinguished creations of this period was the Bank of Louisville (1834–

Dakin.
Bank of Louisville.
Kentucky.
1834–1836

Dakin.
Louisiana State Capitol.
Baton Rouge.
1847–1852

1836). The building, attributed erroneously in the past to Gideon Shryock of Kentucky, has a façade which is one of the liveliest and most ingenious examples of the Greek Revival. Battered, Egyptianesque walls, an elliptical coffered ceiling, and an acroterion dominating the parapet all combine to form one of the great monuments of the Greek Revival. The same acroterion motif appeared a year later in plate 25 of MINARD LAFEVER's *Beauties of Modern Architecture,* indicating some influence by Dakin, who drew many plates for two of Lafever's books.

In 1834, Dakin's younger brother, Charles Bingley Dakin, and JAMES GALLIER, SR., both of whom had been hired by James for Town, Davis and Dakin, left New York and set up a practice in New Orleans. The new firm was immediately successful and Charles induced James Dakin to join them, which he did in November, 1835. They soon split up, however, Gallier going his way and the brothers forming the firm of Dakin and Dakin, Architects.

Charles Dakin took over the Mobile, Alabama work left over from his partnership with Gallier, acting mainly as a building supervisor. The Barton Academy (1836) and the exterior of the Government Street Presbyterian Church (1836–1837) were completed from the Gallier and Dakin plans; the interior of the church was by the Dakins. Dakin and Dakin also produced the huge United

States Hotel (1836–1837) which burned in the great fire of 1839, shortly after Charles Dakin's death in Louisiana.

In New Orleans, meanwhile, James Dakin was building the State Arsenal (1839) and Saint Patrick's Church (1838–1840). When a dispute arose over the construction of the church, a board of arbitrators, headed by Gallier, ejected Dakin from the contract, Gallier taking over and finishing the job for himself. Forced into bankruptcy in 1841 from the effects of the Panic of 1837, Dakin rebounded to design the Gayoso House Hotel (1842) in Memphis, Tennessee, the Canal Bank (1843–1844), and the Medical College of Louisiana (1843) in New Orleans, all in the Greek Revival style. In 1845, HENRY HOWARD, later the architect of the plantations Belle Grove, Madewood, and Woodlawn, worked as an apprentice draftsman in Dakin's office.

When the Mexican War broke out, Dakin commanded the "Louisiana Volunteers" and led them to Mexico where they remained for the summer of 1846 without seeing action. On his return, Dakin designed the University of Louisiana (1847–1855), an E-shaped Greek Revival complex which absorbed the Medical College, and later became Tulane University. He also entered a competition for the Louisiana State Capitol (1847–1852) at Baton Rouge, winning with a daring design in the Gothic style. Louisiana thus came to have one of only two Gothic state capitols in the United States to that time.

Dakin supervised its construction from 1847 to 1850, leaving, with only the interior detailing incomplete, when he obtained the position of supervising architect of the U.S. Custom House (1848–1881) at New Orleans. But politics and Creole antagonism toward the American sector of New Orleans led to his ouster in 1851. While there, Dakin had boldly proposed changing A. T. Wood's original plan calling for groined masonry arches to a cast iron frame with the masonry exterior walls merely tied to the frame. Although Isaiah Rogers and others supported him, the original plan was followed. Dakin moved back to Baton Rouge in 1852, where he completed the interior of the Capitol, and died there on May 13, 1852.

James Dakin was one of about a dozen top rank American architects of his generation. His ability to manipulate elements taken from Greek, Gothic and Egyptian sources and his skill in transforming them into new creations, especially for the Bank of Louisville and the Louisiana State Capitol, justify Talbot Hamlin's description of him as "original," "forceful," and "brilliant." Dakin was rarely archeological, but the individual stylistic elements were always "correct" and not a distortion or parody of the original sources.

The regard with which Dakin was held by his peers is indicated by the invitation that he received in 1836 from THOMAS U. WALTER to join him and a few others in forming the American Institution of Architects (forerunner of the American Institute of Architects). While the organization was short-lived, its members included the outstanding men in whose hands American architecture flourished during the Age of Jackson.

ARTHUR SCULLY, JR.

WORKS
*1833–1834, Rockaway Marine Pavilion, N.Y. *1833–1837, New York University. 1834, First Presbyterian Church, Troy, N.Y. 1834–1836, Bank of Louisville, Ky. 1836, Barton Academy (with James Gallier, Sr. and Charles Dakin); 1836–1837, Government Street Presbyterian Church (with Gallier and Charles Dakin); *1836–1837, United States Hotel, Mobile, Ala. 1838–1840, Saint Patrick's Church; 1839, State Arsenal, New Orleans, La. *1842, Gayoso House Hotel, Memphis, Tenn. *1843, Medical College of Louisiana; 1843–1844, Canal Bank; *1847–1855, University of Louisiana; New Orleans, La. 1847–1852, Louisiana State Capitol, Baton Rouge, La. 1848–1881, U.S. Custom House (with several architects), New Orleans, La.

BIBLIOGRAPHY
ANDREWS, WAYNE 1971 "American Gothic." *American Heritage* October: 26–33, 97.
ANDREWS, WAYNE 1975 *American Gothic: Its Origins, Its Trials, Its Triumphs.* New York: Random House.
CARROTT, RICHARD G. 1978 *Egyptian Revival: Its Sources, Monuments, & Meaning, 1808–1858.* Berkeley: University of California Press.
DAVIES, JANE B. 1965 "A. J. Davis' Projects for a Patent Office Building, 1832–1834." *Journal of the Society of Architectural Historians* 24:229–251.
GALLIER, JAMES (1864)1973 *Autobiography of James Gallier, Architect.* Reprint. New York: Da Capo.
GEBHARD, DAVID and NEVINS, DEBORAH (editors) 1977 *200 Years of American Architectural Drawing.* New York: Watson–Guptill.
HAMLIN, TALBOT F. (1944)1964 *Greek Revival Architecture in America.* Reprint. New York: Dover.
LAFEVER, MINARD (1833)1969 *The Modern Builder's Guide: A Reprint of the First Edition—1833.* Reprint. Magnolia, Mass.: Peter Smith.
LAFEVER, MINARD (1835)1968 *The Beauties of Modern Architecture.* 2nd edition. Reprint. New York: Da Capo.
LAUGHLIN, CLARENCE JOHN 1967 "Louisiana Fantasy." *Architectural Review.* 141:330, 383–386.
PATRICK, JAMES A. 1980 *Architecture in Tennessee: Seventeen Sixty-Eight to Eighteen Ninety-Seven.* Knoxville: University of Tennessee Press.
PATTON, GLENN 1969 "Chapel in the Sky: Origins and Edifices of the University of the City of New York." *Architectural Review* 145:177–180.
SCULLY, ARTHUR, JR. 1973 *James Dakin, Architect: His Career in New York and the South.* Baton Rouge: Louisiana State University Press.

DALL' ABACCO, ANTONIO

See ABACCO, ANTONIO DALL'.

DALTON, JOHN

John Dalton (1927–) was born in Leeds, England, and went to Australia in 1950. In 1958, he established practice in semitropical Brisbane. It was Dalton who, through his buildings, writing, and teaching of the 1960s, contributed most to re-establishing a sensitive and responsible architecture attuned to the particular conditions of Queensland.

Dalton describes his architecture as "regional humanism," and his many domestic works exemplify his intent. They are unpretentious buildings designed for the pleasure of their inhabitants. Their white, often bagged masonry walls and dark stained timbers complement the Australian landscape. Dalton obviously delights in the play of light and shadow made possible by the clear skies and strong sun of the region. Shaded courtyards, sheltering verandahs, and careful planning for breeze and sun make for inviting places that are comfortable through the long hot months of the Queensland summer.

His larger buildings, such as University House for Griffith University (1975), Brisbane, demonstrate his successful adaption of the themes of the houses into institutional work. The Halls of Residence for the Kelvin Grove College of Technical and Further Education (1977), Brisbane, most clearly capture the Dalton spirit. Here, in a meandering hillside village of small units, is design for easy living within varied and pleasing architectural forms.

JENNIFER TAYLOR

WORKS
1956, Spinks House, Quentin Street, Indooroopilly; 1957, Young House, Frost Street, Mount Gravatt; 1960, Battersby Flats, Quinton Street, Kangaroo Point, 1961, Mayo House, Droshanne Street, Aspley; 1962, Collier House, Equinox Street, Kenmore; 1963, Arts Theater, Petrie Terrace; 1964, Deignan House, Hoya Street, Holland Park; 1965, Davidson House, Ardell Street, Kenmore; 1966, Buckley House, Fontayne Street, Aspley; 1967, Kaeshagen House, Musgrave Street, Kenmore; 1968, Barclay House, Indus Street, White's Hill; 1969, Bowers House, Castile Street, Indooroopilly; 1970, Cameron House, Bycroft Street and

Heron Road, Pullenvale; 1971, Read House, Lavereigh Street, Indooroopilly; 1972, Myers House, Wonalee Street, Kenmore; 1973, Musgrave House, Roseberry Street, Chelmer; Brisbane, Queensland, Australia. 1974, Arts, Crafts and Music Center, Darling Downs Institute of Technology, Toowoomba, Queensland, Australia. 1975, University House, Griffith University, Nathan; 1976, MacFarlane House, Repton Street, Pullenvale; 1977, Residence Hall, College of Technical Education, Kelvin Grove; Brisbane, Queensland, Australia.

BIBLIOGRAPHY

BOYD, ROBIN 1971 "Architecture in Australia." *Journal of the Royal Institute of British Architects* 78:11–20.

COX, PHILIP 1973 "Housing over the Past 10 Years." *Architecture in Australia* 62, Oct.:53–55.

DALTON, JOHN 1963 "Houses in the Hot Humid Zones." *Architecture in Australia* 52; Mar.:73–80.

FREELAND, JOHN M. 1968 *Architecture in Australia: A History.* Melbourne: Cheshire.

MCKAY, IAN, and BOYD, ROBIN 1971 *Living and Parly Living: Housing in Australia.* Melbourne: Nelson.

SAINI, BALWANT SINGH 1970 *Architecture in Tropical Australia.* Melbourne University Press.

"Seven Just Square." 1968 *Architectural Review* 144:142–143.

Sowden, Harry (editor) 1968 *Towards an Australian Architecture.* Sydney: Ure Smith.

TANNER, HOWARD 1976 *Australian Housing in the Seventies.* Sydney: Ure Smith.

Daly.
Frontispiece from Revue
générale de
l'architecture et des
travaux publics.
1840–1888/1890

DALY, CESAR

César Denis Daly (1811–1894), France's leading architectural journalist and editor, directed the *Revue générale de l'architecture et des travaux publics* (1840–1888/1890) and the weekly, *La semaine des constructeurs* (1876–1897). Born in Verdun, France, the illegitimate son of an impoverished French noblewoman and an Anglo-Irish merchant seaman, Daly was raised in poverty in England. He studied architecture with FÉLIX DUBAN in the early 1830s, but did not attend the Ecole des Beaux-Arts in Paris. His active participation in the Fourierist movement, like his campaign for the Republican Assembly in 1848, was never divulged in the *Revue générale* and neither political commitment survived the Second Empire. Daly was awarded the Royal Institute of British Architects Gold Medal in 1892.

Spokesman for HENRI LABROUSTE and LOUIS DUC, Daly also admired Duban and LÉON VAUDOYER, and published the works of CHARLES BARRY and CHARLES GARNIER. His multivolumed pattern book of domestic architecture, *L'architecture privée au XIXme siècle* (1877), was extremely influential abroad. Critical of the academic and neogothic schools, between 1847 and 1869, Daly developed a theory of "organic architecture" which opposed structural rationalism. Architecture was a language of sentiment, and each age and culture was expressed by a characteristic line. The line of the future he argued was the ellipse, expressive of the complexity of modern society. Designs by Joseph Nicolle and Simon Claude Constant-Dufeux illustrated Daly's theoretical intention in the magazine.

Daly's journal was described as "a monthly magazine, not exactly of architectural news (for such a thing does not exist in France), but of architectural drawings." The *Revue générale,* France's first illustrated architectural magazine, published all types of contemporary and historical architecture, giving not only plans and elevations, but also engravings of large scale details, which were immediately used in the design process. The extremely precise and luxurious steel-engraved plates functioned independently of the text as a means of professional education and communication and the *Revue générale* can be considered the ancestor of the modern, lavishly illustrated architectural magazine.

Daly's reputation as an architectural and social reformer is not entirely justified. His outspoken criticism of the Ecole des Beaux-Arts ceased after its reorganization in 1863. He came to favor higher education for an architectural elite in scientific aesthetics. Partisan of the collaboration of the architect and the engineer, Daly published technical articles only in the *Revue générale*'s early years. His belief in the phalanstery as a model for housing is belied by his housing theory, which espoused the single family suburban villa as the ideal home. His aesthetic theory, however, is derived from Charles Fourier, who also admired the ellipse.

From 1844 to 1877, Daly was the state-appointed architect of the Cathedral of Albi in Tarn, France. His design for the roof, including the addition of turrets, provoked controversy. He restored his eighteenth-century country house in Wissous, France (1860–1882?), introducing an elliptical arch on the street façade and using elliptical lines on the gatehouses, thus making his only original work of architecture and his restoration work conform to his aesthetic theory.

HÉLÈNÈ LIPSTADT

WORKS

1844–1877, Cathedral of Albi (restoration), Tarn, France. 1860–1882?, César Daly House (restoration and refacing of gatehouses), Wissous, France.

BIBLIOGRAPHY

DALY, CÉSAR (editor) 1840–1888/1890 *Revue générale de l'architecture et des travaux publics.* 45 volumes.

DALY, CÉSAR 1848 *Profession de foi du citoyen César Daly.* Paris: Martinet.

DALY, CÉSAR 1864 *L'Architecture privée au XIXme siècle sous Napoléon III: Nouvelles maisons de Paris et des environs.* 3 vols. Paris: Morel.

DALY, CÉSAR 1869 *Motifs historiques d'architecture et de sculpture d'ornement, pour la composition et la décoration extérieure des édifices publics et privés.* 2 vols. Paris: Morel.

DALY, CÉSAR 1871 *L'Architecture funéraire contemporaine.* Paris: Ducher.

DALY, CÉSAR 1872 *L'Architecture privée au XIXme siècle: Deuxième série.* Paris: Ducher.

DALY, CÉSAR (editor) 1876–1897 *La semaine des constructeurs.* 22 volumes.

DALY, CÉSAR 1877 *L'architecture privée au XIXme siècle: Troisième série, Décorations intérieures peintes.* 2 vols. Paris: Ducher.

DALY, CÉSAR 1880 *Motifs historiques d'architecture et de sculpture d'ornement: Deuxième série.* 2 vols. Paris: Librairie générale de l'architecture et des travaux publics.

DALY, CÉSAR n.d. Part 1 in *Motifs divers de Serrurerie.* Paris: André, Daly.

DALY, CÉSAR n.d. Part 2 in *Motifs divers de Serrurerie.* Paris: Ducher.

DALY, CÉSAR, and DAVIOUD, M. GABRIEL 1874 *L'Architecture contemporaine: Les Théâtres de la place du Châtelet.* Paris: Ducher.

LIPSTADT, HÉLÈNE 1975 "Réflexions sur l'habitation bourgeoise à Paris au XIXme siècle: Les écrits de César Daly." Unpublished Mémoir de Maîtrise spécialisée, University of Paris I.

LIPSTADT, HÉLÈNE 1977a "César Daly et l'habitation." *Architecture Mouvement Continuité* 42:37–39.

LIPSTADT, HÉLÈNE 1977b "Housing the Bourgeoisie: César Daly and the Ideal Home." *Oppositions* 8:34–47.

LIPSTADT, HÉLÈNE 1978 "César Daly: A Revolutionary Architect?" *Architectural Design* 48:18–29.

LIPSTADT, HÉLÈNE 1979 "Pour une histoire sociale de la presse architecturale *La Revue générale de l'architecture* et César Daly (1840–1888)." Unpublished Thèse de troisième cycle, Ecole des Hautes Etudes en Sciences Sociales, Paris.

LIPSTADT, HÉLÈNE, and MENDELSOHN, HARVEY 1980 *Architecte et ingénieur dans la presse: Polémique, débat, conflit.* Paris: CORDA-IERAU.

"M. César Daly and the War." 1871 *The Architect* 5:63.

VAN ZANTEN, ANN LORENZ 1977 "Form and Society: César Daly and the *Revue générale de l'architecture.*" *Oppositions* 8:137–145.

VAN ZANTEN, ANN LORENZ 1980 "César Daly and the *Revue générale de l'architecture.*" Unpublished Ph.D. dissertation, Harvard University, Cambridge, Mass.

DAMESME, LOUIS EMMANUEL AIME

A follower of CLAUDE NICOLAS LEDOUX, for whom he served as chief of operations for the construction of the Barrières d'Octroi (toll houses) of Paris (1784–1780), Louis Emmanuel Aimé Damesme (1767–1822) is little known today. Prominent as a designer of houses and apartment buildings in Paris during the Empire, he also built the famous Royal Theater of the Monnaie (1817) in Brussels. Adorned with a portico composed of eight Ionic columns crowned by a grand pediment recalling an antique temple, this building exemplifies Damesme's rather rigid neoclassic style.

DANIEL RABREAU
*Translated from French by
Shara Wasserman*

WORKS

1788, Leduc House; 1795, Property, rue Richard; *1796, Theater of the Olympic Society; Paris. 1817, Royal Theater of the Monnaie, Brussels.

BIBLIOGRAPHY

GALLET, MICHEL 1972 *Paris Domestic Architecture of the 18th Century.* London: Barries & Jenkins.

KRAFFT, J. C., and RANSONNETTE, N. c.1801 *Nouvelle architecture française ou collection des édifices publics et maisons particulières bâties à Paris.* n.p.

DAMIAN, ASCANIO

Ascanio Damian (1914–) graduated from the Institute of Architecture in Bucharest in 1942. He was himself a professor there until 1968. Through his works, Damian tried to promote new social concepts in architecture. Especially his large buildings are expressive and original in structure and outlook. He is the author of a study on LE CORBUSIER.

CONSTANTIN MARIN MARINESCU

WORKS

1947, Baneasa Airport (with others), near Bucharest. 1947, Garment Factory; 1950, Exhibition Pavilion, Herestrau Park; Bucharest. 1952, Rumanian Embassy, Warsaw. *1960, Central Pavilion, Exhibition of National Economy, Bucharest. 1960, Iron Gates Hydropower Plant, Turnu Severin, Rumania.

BIBLIOGRAPHY

DAMIAN, ASCANIO 1969 *Le Corbusier.* Bucharest: Editura Meridiane.

IONESCU, GRIGORE 1965 Volume 2 in *Istoria Arhitecturii in Romania.* Bucharest: Editura Academiei Republicii Romañe.

IONESCU, GRIGORE 1969 *Arhitectura in Romania: Perioda anilor 1944–1969.* Bucharest: Editura Academiei Republicii Socialiste Romănia.

IONESCU, GRIGORE 1972 "Saptezeci si cinci de ani de la infiintarea invatamintului de arhitectura din Romania." *Arhitectura* 20:35–42.

MAMBRIANI, ALBERTO 1969 *L'Architettura Moderna nei Paesi Balcanici.* Bologna, Italy: Capelli.

PATRULIUS, RADU 1973–1974 "Contributii Romanesti in Arhitectura Anilor '30." *Arhitectura* 21, no. 6:44–52; 22, no. 1:53–59.

SASARMAN, GHEORGHE 1972 "Inceputurile gindirii teoretice in arhitectura româneasca (1860–1916)." *Arhitectura* 20, no. 6:44–46.

DAMIANOV, ANGEL

Angel Ivanov Damianov (1909–), the ardent promoter of functionalism and Bauhaus design philosophy, was born in Vidin, Bulgaria, and studied architecture (1927–1931) in Dresden, Germany. He established his private practice (1933–1944) in Sofia. An innovative designer, Damianov introduced in his works of the 1930s open and functional planning, moving partitions and glass walls, and terraces and roof gardens, all expressively molded in personalized forms. In his Library-Museum (1939–1943) in Turnovo, Bulgaria, Damianov captured the spirit, scale, and detail of the ancient capital, creating a model for the following decades of traditions successfully integrated into contemporary architecture.

Despite political limitations, Damianov instilled modern ideals in his students at Sofia Polytechnic Institute through teaching, research, and writing from 1946 until his retirement in 1976.

MILKA T. BLIZNAKOV

WORKS

1934, M. A. Residence, Gornobanski Road, near Sofia. 1935, Doctor S. House, Stara Zagora, Bulgaria. 1936–1939, Ruschev House (now the Egyptian Embassy), 29 Shipka Street; 1939–1940, Housing Cooperative, 17 San Stefano Street; Sofia. 1939–1943, Library-Museum (with A. Khashnov), Turnovo, Bulgaria. 1940–1942, Housing Cooperative, 33 Oborishche Street, Sofia. 1945–1946, Cultural Center, Slatina, near Sofia. 1945–1947, Public Bath Madara; 1948–1950, Ministry of Industry Housing Complex, Graf Ignatiev Street and Evlogi Georgiev Street; 1949–1954, Doctor M. Residence; Triavna, Bulgaria. 1959–1965, Housing and Cinema Complex; 1960–1964, Sports Palace Diana (with Dimitur Tsolov [see VASIL'OV AND TSOLOV] and others); Iambol, Bulgaria. 1965–1975, Recreation Center (with others), Sliven, Bulgaria. 1970–1978, Recreation Complex (with others), Sopot, Bulgaria. 1975–1981, Communist Party Headquarters (with others), Kazanlŭk, Bulgaria.

BIBLIOGRAPHY

BŬLGARSKA AKADEMIIÂ NA NAUKITE 1965 *Kratka istoriia na Bŭlgarskata arkhitektura.* Sofia: The academy.

DAMIANOV, ANGEL 1954 "Arkhitekturno-khudozhestveni vuprosi pri proektiraneto na zhilishchnite sgradi." *Arkhitektura* nos. 5–6:15–22.

DAMIANOV, ANGEL 1957 "Kakva triabva da bude suvremennata sotsialisticheska arkhitektura." *Arkhitektura* no. 1.

DAMIANOV, ANGEL (1959)1978 *Zhilishtni sgradi.* Sofia: Tekhnika.

DAMIANOV, ANGEL 1964 "Za Suvremenniiâ arkhitekturen obraz na zhilishchnite sgradi." *Arkhitektura* no. 8:4–7.

DAMIANOV, ANGEL 1970a "Osnovni nasoki na arkhitekturnoto obrazovanie u nas." *Arkhitektura* no. 8:6–9.

DAMIANOV, ANGEL 1970b "Perspektivi na sportnite sgradi i sŭoruzheniia v Bulgariiâ." *Izvestiia na instituta po gradoustroŭstvo i arkhitektura* 23:195–208.

DAMIANOV, ANGEL 1975 "Khoteli v kurortnite kompleksi po Chernomorieto." In *Arkhitekturata na Norodna Republika Bŭlgariia.* Sofia: Bŭlgarska Akademiia na Naukite.

GREKOV, P. ET AL. 1970 *Arkhitektura Sotsialisticheskoĭ Bolgarii.* Moscow: Stroiizdat.

STOICHEV, GEORGI 1969 "Profesor arkhitekt Angel Damianov na 60 godini." *Arkhitektura* no. 10:22–25.

TANGŬROV, YORDAN S. ET AL. 1972 *The Architecture of Modern Bulgaria.* Sofia: Technika.

TONEV, LUIBEN 1962 *Arkhitekturata v Bulgariiâ: 1944–1960.* Sofia: Bŭlgarska Akademiia na Naukite.

DAMMARTIN FAMILY

Guy de Dammartin (?–1398) participated in the remodeling of the Louvre (1362–1372), directed by Raymond du Temple for King Charles V. Between 1367 and 1372, Guy was retained by Jean, duke of Berry, whose extensive building program Guy supervised until his death. At the Palace of Bourges (1375–1385), Guy designed a single corps-de-logis with rooms enfilade, a significant plan in terms of the development of the urban *hôtel*. He designed two Saintes-Chapelles, one at Riom (c.1380–1389) and one at Bourges (1392–1398) which was largely built by his brother Drouet. Elsewhere, Guy modified pre-existing buildings for the duke. As in the Louvre project, Guy transformed the fortified châteaux of Mehun-sur-Yèvre (1367–1392), Riom (1375–1389), and Poitiers (1382–1390) into residential palaces, removing crenellations and introducing exterior sculptural decoration, fenestration, and dormers.

Drouet de Dammartin (?–1413) also worked for Raymond du Temple at the Louvre (1367–c.1377) before serving the duke of Berry at the Hôtel de Nesle, Paris (by 1377). In 1383, Drouet was appointed *maistre général des oeuvres* of the duke of Burgundy, for whom he built the Chartreuse of Champmol (1384–1391) and directed construction of the Sainte-Chapelle, Dijon (1387). In 1398, Drouet was recalled to Bourges to complete the Sainte-Chapelle. Remaining in the service of the duke of Berry, Drouet probably rebuilt the Château of Concressault and supervised other workshops. Drouet's son, Jean de Dammartin (?–1454), was *maistre des oeuvres* at the Cathedrals of Mans (1421–?) and Tours (1432–?).

HILARY BALLON

WORKS

GUY DE DAMMARTIN

*1362–1372, Louvre (sculptural decoration), Paris. 1367–1392, Château (remodeled), Mehun-sur-Yèvre, France. *1375–1385, Palace, Bourges, France. *1375–1389, Château; c.1380–1389, Sainte-Chapelle; Riom, France. *1382–1390, Château; 1382–1390, Palace; *1385–1395, Gros Horloge (remodeled); Poitiers, France. *1392–1398, Sainte-Chapelle, Bourges, France.

DROUET DE DAMMARTIN

1384–1391, Chartreuse de Champmol, France. *1398–1405, Sainte-Chapelle (completed), Bourges, France. 1402–?, Château, Lusignan, France. *n.d., Château, Concressault, France.

BIBLIOGRAPHY

CHAMPEAUX, ALFRED DE, and GAUCHERY, PAUL 1894 *Les Travaux d'arts exécutés pour Jean de France, duc de Berry.* Paris: Champion.
GAUCHER, PAUL 1898 "L'Influence de Jean de France, duc de Berry, sur le développement de l'Architecture et des Arts à la fin du XIVe siècle et au commencement du XVe siècle." *Congrès archéologique* 1898:255–279.
GAUCHERY, PAUL 1913 "Riom." *Congrès archéologique* 80:144–173.
GAUCHERY, PAUL 1919–1920 "Le Palais du duc Jean et la Sainte-Chapelle de Bourges." *Mémoires de la société des antiquaires du Centre* 39:37–77.
GAUCHERY, ROBERT 1931 "Le Château de Mehun-sur-Yèvre." *Congrès archéologique* 94:338–345.
LEHOUX, FRANÇOISE 1966–1968 *Jean de France, duc de Berry. Sa vie. Son action politique.* 4 vols. Paris: Picard.
ROSENFELD, MYRA NAN 1971 *The Hôtel de Cluny and the Sources of the French Renaissance Palace 1350–1500.* Unpublished Ph.D. dissertation, Harvard University, Cambridge, Mass.

DANCE, GEORGE THE ELDER

Although overshadowed by his gifted son of the same name (see GEORGE DANCE THE YOUNGER), George Dance the Elder (1695–1768) was himself an architect of merit. He was born in the City of London to which his father Giles Dance, a mason of Winchester, had moved ten years before. No doubt attracted to the metropolis by the quantity of building which was to continue for several decades after the Great Fire of 1666, Giles took his son George into partnership in about 1717. Jointly engaged on various City works and in particular on the South Sea Company's premises, they made the acquaintance of John Gould, a surveyor and developer whose daughter George married in 1719. In 1727, George Dance emerged as co-architect with Gould in the designing of Saint Botolph's Church, Bishopsgate, which followed closely the pattern set by CHRISTOPHER WREN's new City churches. Soon after this, George was again associated with his father-in-law in the speculative development, around 1730, of Gould Square near the Minories.

Having established himself as a designer and capable builder, Dance aspired to obtaining the post of clerk of the works to the City of London, an office which had to be purchased but which brought considerable revenue from "fees, profits and commodities" on the work carried out. The previous holder having been dismissed for negligence, Dance was recommended as his successor in 1733, but he had to wait two years for his appointment to be ratified as nineteenth holder of this ancient office. In this capacity, he became responsible for supervising "all the works and edifyings that are or shall be doing," both within the City and in the Corporation's estates in Lewisham, Deptford, and elsewhere.

Following the formation of a committee to consider the building of a new residence for the Lord Mayor, four outside competitors were invited to submit designs and estimates in 1735. None proving satisfactory, Dance was eventually instructed to submit drawings which were adopted in 1737. In these he forsook Wren's influence and took his inspiration from the main façade of COLEN CAMPBELL'S recently completed Wanstead House in Essex, a monumental porticoed essay in Palladian (see ANDREA PALLADIO) revivalism. Apart from some internal details, the building was more or less complete by 1750. Dance was also responsible for several other notable City works including the Fleet Market, the Corn Market, and the Surgeons' Hall, none of which have survived. Of his three London churches, Saint Leonard Shoreditch (1736) and Saint Botolph Aldgate (1741) still stand though much altered, as does his one church outside London, Saint Mary's, Faversham, Kent, rebuilt in 1754.

Dance died on February 17, 1768, a few days after resigning his clerkship in favor of his youngest son George. A number of his drawings for the building of the Mansion house and other works are preserved in Sir John Soane's Museum, London.

DOROTHY STROUD

WORKS

1734, Fleet Market; 1736, Saint Leonard's Church, Shoreditch; 1737, Mansion House; 1741, Saint Botolph's Church, Aldgate; 1743, Saint Matthew's Church, Bethnal Green; 1747, Corn Market, Mark Lane; 1748, Surgeons' Hall, Old Bailey; 1750, Saint Luke's Hospital, Old Street; London. 1754, Saint Mary's Church, Faversham, Kent, England. 1756, London Bridge (rebuilding with Robert Taylor), London.

BIBLIOGRAPHY

PERKS, SYDNEY 1922 *The History of the Mansion House.* Cambridge University Press.
STROUD, DOROTHY 1971 *George Dance, Architect.* London: Faber.

DANCE, GEORGE THE YOUNGER

Although to the discerning, George Dance the Younger (1741–1825) has always been regarded as an outstanding designer and planner, his retiring disposition and preoccupation with work within the City of London caused his remarkable talents to be overshadowed by more flamboyant contemporaries in the profession, such as JAMES WYATT and JOHN NASH. The fifth and youngest son of the elder GEORGE DANCE, architect and Clerk of the City's Works, he was born in Chiswell Street on the fringe of a city dominated by CHRISTOPHER WREN's cathedral and innumerable churches. To this area Dance's father had made his own contri-

butions, notably the Mansion House, Surgeons' Hall, and the rebuilding of London Bridge. Architecture was therefore a familiar background to the boy's life, and he was drawn to it from his early years. Apart from a period of study in Italy and a few short visits to friends, Dance spent his entire life in London. The city was always to be the hub around which his professional life revolved, and for it he produced his finest buildings and schemes. Although some of the latter failed to materialize, and some were subsequently much changed, Dance's innovations had a profound influence, and several of the features which he introduced were to be adopted by other architects as the metropolis expanded.

Having absorbed the rudiments of architecture from his father, Dance was sent to study in Rome where in 1758 he joined his elder brother Nathaniel who was later to become an artist of distinction. There, Dance was duly admitted to the Academy of Saint Luke and became acquainted with current principles of neoclassicism which were to have a profound influence on his designs. In 1763, he entered the Academy of Parma's competition in which his design for a public gallery was awarded a gold medal. Returning to England in December 1764, he at once became his father's assistant, and five months later he entered into competition with several established architects for the rebuilding of All Hallows Church (1765–1767), London Wall, from which he emerged the winner. Although externally a plain brick box, with lunette windows placed high so as to avoid damage by passing traffic in a narrow thoroughfare, the church was given a barrel vault carried over an Ionic order set against the north and south walls. In this order the architrave and cornice of the entablature are omitted, leaving only an enriched frieze, a departure from classical cannon which at first surprised and shocked those critics who were still unfamiliar with the writings of MARC-ANTOINE LAUGIER and other neoclassical theorists.

Nine days before his death in 1768 the elder Dance had submitted his resignation to the City Lands Committee with a request that his son should succeed him as Clerk of the City's Works. This having been agreed, the younger Dance at the age of twenty-six became twentieth holder of an office that went back to the fifteenth century. Although the office offered considerable opportunities for design and planning, these were tempered by many exacting routine duties and constant attendance on committees whose bidding had to be observed.

One of the first development projects concerned a site near the Minories (1767–1768). Although small in extent, Dance's plan for it was to prove of importance as introducing two new forms to London planning, the crescent and the circus, here allied to an older form, the square, which had been used for developments in Westminster and Bloomsbury from 1660 but first appeared in the City in 1730 when Dance's father helped to lay out Gould Square. The idea of the crescent and circus stemmed from John Wood's adaptation of a Roman amphitheater and colosseum in his development of Bath, which Dance visited in 1766 and obviously admired. Given the opportunity of planning the Minories site two years later, he employed these themes but scaled them down to minuscule proportions and translated the building material from stone to stock brick. The project went ahead with building plots being let to various speculators, and *Crescent* and *Circus* (as they were called, without a definitive *The*), together with the adjoining America Square, became prototypes for several of Dance's later and larger schemes in which he sought to break the rigidity of London street layout. Although the actual houses have disappeared in the more important of these groups, notably in Finsbury, at the east end of the Strand, and the crescents to the north and south of Alfred Place, the outlines which they determined have survived in rebuilding.

A scheme which materialized in 1768 after years of discussion and postponement was the rebuilding of Newgate Gaol (1768–1785) for which Dance received instructions two days after his father's death and for which he submitted his first plans on April 15. In these, the massive external walls—windowless for security—enclosed three courts around which were ranged blocks for male and female debtors and male felons, these lit by windows in their inner walls. In the center of the external west wall the Keeper's house was flanked by the prison entrances. Although the imaginative handling of Newgate has often led to comparison with GIOVANNI BATTISTA PIRANESI's *Carceri* designs and although Dance was ac-

Dance The Younger.
All Hallows Church.
London Wall, London.
1765–1767

quainted with him in Rome, there is little in common other than the festoons of chains placed over the entrances in the Newgate building. In fact, the graded courses of rusticated masonry and the massive frames to the niches in the end blocks were derived from ANDREA PALLADIO's Palazzo Thiene at Vicenza. If the total effect left no doubt as to a message of retribution, the internal arrangement of Newgate provided vastly improved conditions for the inmates while the building as a whole was one of the few examples of English architecture considered worthy of inclusion in J. N. L. DURAND's *Recueil et parallèle des edifices* of 1799. Small but distinct echoes of Newgate in the way of rusticated entrances festooned with chains were later to be found in rebuilt prisons as far away as Hereford, King's Lynn, and Dublin. Two other London prisons or "compters" for the detention of debtors were rebuilt by Dance. The Borough Compter in Southwark, designed in 1785, was of

Dance The Younger.
Newgate Prison.
London.
1768–1785

no architectural significance, but the Giltspur Street Compter of 1787–1789, standing only a short distance from Newgate, made a comparable show of strength with three stories of heavily rusticated masonry and battlements to the central and end blocks.

Since the maintenance of the city's Guildhall made constant demands on Dance's time, it was not until 1777 that an innovation of importance came with the building of a new Council Chamber. Here an internal site dictated windows at a high level, a problem which he solved by forming a central space with a top-lit dome resting on four piers. To the north and south of this space were bays, the former being lit by lofty lunettes in its side walls. This spatial arrangement was later to be taken up and developed in the repertoire of Dance's one-time pupil JOHN SOANE. The rebuilding of the main façade of Guildhall in 1788–1789 provided Dance with another opportunity for innovation, the quasi-Oriental character of his design almost certainly owing its inspiration to illustrations in *Select Views of India* published by his friend William Hodges two years earlier. As with All Hallows Church, its novelty invited some criticism, and James Wyatt considered that Dance had "quitted grammatical art for fancies." It was, however, a subtle expression of the building's medieval history, allied to the current importance of Oriental trade maintained through the East India Company. Other Guildhall works of importance were the Chamberlain's Court of 1787 and the separate block of Justice Rooms of 1795.

In 1795, Dance made a major alteration to the Mansion House designed by his father, roofing over the inner courtyard to form a new saloon and lowering the roof of the Egyptian Gallery by inserting a coffered barrel vault. A good deal of his time in the 1790s was taken up with projects connected with the Port of London, the first being a scheme of 1793 to rebuild those docks on the north bank of the Thames known as the Legal Quays for which he proposed an impressive range of warehouses with waterways between them. Neither this nor his imaginative scheme for replacing London Bridge with twin bridges, linked to crescent-shaped layouts on either side of the river, were to materialize, but the rejection of the Legal Quays proposal and the urgent need for more shipping accommodation led to the development of a down-stream site on the Isle of Dogs where Dance's plans, drawn up in consultation with the engineer William Jessop, resulted in the West India Docks, opened in 1802.

During his first twenty years in office, Dance's rigorous schedule allowed little opportunity for other work, and the only early commissions which he undertook were both of a personal nature, the first being two reception rooms added to Pitzhanger Manor in 1768 for his future father in law, Thomas Gurnell. The second was the addition of a ballroom to Cranbury in Hampshire around 1779 for Mr. and Mrs. Dummer, close friends of his brother Nathaniel. His marriage to Mary Gurnell took place in March 1772 and produced three sons, to whom he was devoted. It was probably for their sake that after his wife's death in 1791 he allowed himself more relaxation, indulging his talents as a musician and an artist. He also began to play a more active role in the business of the Royal Academy of which he had been a founder member. Although he delivered no lectures there during his term as professor of architecture from 1798 to 1806, he served as honorary auditor and trustee for several years.

After 1786, when he began remodeling Lansdowne House in London, he began to accept a few private commissions for alterations or additions, but it was only from 1802 that he undertook a handful of important works beginning with Cole Orton, designed in a simplified form of Gothic, followed by the severely classical rebuilding of Stratton Park in 1803. For the nearby village of East Stratton he designed in 1806 an attractive group of semidetached thatched cottages and largely rebuilt the small Gothic Church of All Saints. Four years later, he rebuilt for the same client, Sir Francis Baring, the Church of Saint Mary (1806–1808), Micheldever, which in its octagonal form reflected the London Church of Saint Bartholomew-the-Less, where in 1789 he had added an octagonal nave to a medieval tower.

Dance retired from his City office in 1815 but in that year he continued to visit a large number of country prisons to gather information for a *Report on Inspection . . . of Several Gaols in this Kingdom* (1816). He was succeeded in office by William Mountague who had acted as his assistant since 1814, following the death of Dance's invaluable previous assistant, JAMES PEACOCK. Dance was buried in the crypt of Saint Paul's Cathedral, a few feet from the grave of Sir Christopher Wren. In 1836, his eldest son, Sir Charles Webb Dance, having inherited his father's large collection of architectural drawings, sold them to Sir John Soane in whose London house they have since remained.

Dance's influence on the work of John Soane, who was his pupil for two years, is undoubted. Elsewhere, however, it was mostly confined to his ingenuity in planning and to the effect of his redrafting, in collaboration with Sir ROBERT TAYLOR, of the Building Act of 1774, which tightened the controls over London house-building as to materials and elevations. On the international scene there is little evidence of any impression made by his designs, apart from faint traces in the work of BENJAMIN HENRY LATROBE, with whom he was probably acquainted before the latter left London for America in 1795, and in CHARLES BULFINCH's Tontine Crescent and India Wharf, Boston. A link between Dance and the latter was in fact provided by Peter Banner, a London artisan who had worked on Dance's Finsbury development and later collaborated with Bulfinch.

DOROTHY STROUD

WORKS

1765–1767, All Hallows Church, London Wall; 1767–1768, Crescent, Circus and America Square, Minories; London. 1768, Pitzhanger Manor (additions), Ealing, England. *1768–1785, Newgate Prison; 1768–1816, Finsbury Estate Development; *1769–1774, Sessions House, Old Bailey; *1777–1779, Guildhall (Council Chamber); London. c.1779–1781, Cranbury (additions), Hampshire, England. 1782–1785, Saint Lukes Hospital; 1785, Borough Compter; *1786–1794, Lansdowne House; *1787–1789, Giltspur Street Compter; *1787–1789, Guildhall (chamberlain's court); *1788–1789, Boydell's Shakespeare Gallery; 1788–1789, Guildhall (façade); *1788–1789, Honey Lane Market; 1789–1790, Saint Bartholemew-the-Less (nave); *1790–1807, Skinner Street, Holborn; *1793–1795, Martin's Bank, Lombard Street; *1793–1804; Pickett Place, The Strand; 1795–1796, Mansion House (alterations); *1795–1797, Guildhall (Justice Rooms); 1796–1802, West India Docks and Limestone Canal; *1796–1810, Alfred Place (with north and south crescents); *1798, Billingsgate Market; London. 1802–1808, Cole Orton Hall, Leicestershire, England. *1803–1806, Stratton Park (remodeling: only portico survives), Hampshire, England. 1804–1805, Theatre Royal, Bath, England. 1805–1813, Royal College of Surgeons (columns, now fluted, survive); London. 1806, All Saints Church (rebuilding), East Stratton; 1806–1807, East Stratton Cottages; 1806–1808, Saint Mary's Church, Micheldever; Hampshire, England. 1807–1809, House, 143 Piccadilly, London. c.1812, Laxton Hall (additions), Northamptonshire, England. *1812–1817, Ashburnham Place, Sussex, England. 1814–1815, Kidbrooke (alterations), Sussex, England.

BIBLIOGRAPHY

ANGELL, SAMUEL 1847 "Sketch of the Professional Life of George Dance, Architect." *The Builder* 5:333–335.
FARINGTON, JOSEPH (1923–1928)1978 *The Diary of Joseph Farington.* Edited by Kenneth Garlick and Angus Macintyre. New ed. New Haven: Yale University Press.
HUGO-BRUNT, MICHAEL 1955 "George Dance, the Younger, as Town Planner (1768–1814)." *Journal of the Society of Architectural Historians* 14:13–22.
KALMAN, H. D. 1972 "George Dance the Younger." Unpublished Ph.D. dissertation, Princeton University, N.J.
STROUD, DOROTHY 1971 *George Dance, Architect: 1741–1825.* London: Faber.
SUMMERSON, JOHN 1949 "John Wood and the English Town-planning Tradition." Pages 87–110 in *Heavenly Mansions and Other Essays on Architecture.* London: Cresset.
TEYSSOT, GEORGES 1974 *Cittàe utopia nell'illumimismo inglese: George Dance il Giovane.* Rome: Officina.

DANERI, LUIGI CARLO

Luigi Carlo Daneri (1900–) was one of the few early adherents to the Modern movement in Italy who did not practice in Milan or Rome. Born in Borgofornari, near Genoa, he built some of the most elegant buildings in Italy in the 1930s, his Casa del Fascio, in Sturlo, being the most famous. He also served as professor at the engineering school of the University of Genoa.

THOMAS L. SCHUMACHER

WORKS

1934–1940, Villa Venturini; 1934–1940, Villa Vitale; Genoa, Italy. 1938, Casa del Fascio, Sturlo, Italy. 1952, Condominium Apartments, Quinto, Italy. 1953, INA Casa Residential Unit, Villa Bernabo Brea, Genoa, Italy.

BIBLIOGRAPHY

DANESI, SILVIA, and PATETTA, LUCIANO 1976 *Il Razionalismo e L'Architettura in Italia Durante il Fascismo.* Venice, Italy: La Biennale di Venezia.
GREGOTTI, VITTORIO 1968 *New Directions in Italian Architecture.* New York: Braziller.

D'ANGICOURT, PIERRE

A French knight from Oise or Beauvais, Pierre D'Angicourt (13th century) is often described as the court architect of Charles I of Anjou, as his title *prothomagister operum curie* might suggest. His activity is documented at the castles of Lucera (1270–1284), Canosa (1271), Castelnuovo at Naples (1279), Barletta (c.1280), Villanova and Mola (1281), and at the port of Otranto. In addition, he is assumed to have built the Church of the Grotto at Monte Sant'Angelo in Puglia, the choir of Barletta Cathedral (later replaced), and many churches in Naples, the most important one being San Lorenzo (1266–1324).

Although D'Angicourt has been credited with the diffusion of French Gothic architectural forms in Southern Italy, his documented activity—almost exclusively concerned with military engineering, restoration, and supervision—suggests a more modest assessment of his importance. He is best understood as overseer of royal projects and architectural adviser to the king.

CHRISTINE SMITH

BIBLIOGRAPHY

BERTAUX, EMILE 1905 "Les artistes français au service des rois angevins de Naples." *Gazette des Beaux Arts* Series 3 34:89–114.
FILANGIERI DI CANDIDA GONZAGA, RICCARDO 1934 *Castel nuovo: Reggia Angioina ed Aragonese di Napoli.* Naples: Politecnica E.P.S.A.
RINALDIS, ALDO DE 1927 *Naples Angevin.* Paris: Nilsson.

DANIELL, THOMAS

Thomas Daniell (1749–1840) studied painting at the Royal Academy Schools. As a result of his travels throughout India from 1785 to 1794, he and his nephew published *Oriental Scenery* (1795–1808). Together with their collection of drawings of Indian scenery and monuments, the book was one of the major influences on the Indian phase of architecture and decoration that flourished in England for approximately thirty years.

PAULINE ROHATGI

WORKS

1800, Temple to Warren Hastings, Melchet Park, Hampshire, England. c.1810–1811, Farm Buildings, Temple of Surya, and Bridge, Sezincote, Gloucestershire, England.

BIBLIOGRAPHY

ARCHER, MILDRED 1960 "The Daniells in India and Their Influence on British Architecture." *Journal of the Royal Institute of British Architects* 67:439–444.
ARCHER, MILDRED 1962 *The Daniells in India.* Washington: Smithsonian Institution.
ARCHER, MILDRED 1980 *Early Views of India: The Picturesque Journeys of Thomas and William Daniell, 1786–1794.* London: Thames & Hudson.
COTTON, EVAN 1930 "The Hindu Temple at Melchet Park." *Bengal Past and Present* 40:71–78.
DANIELL, THOMAS, and DANIELL, WILLIAM (1795–1808)1815 *Oriental Scenery.* London: The authors.
HARDIE, MARTIN, and CLAYTON, MURIEL 1932 "Thomas and William Daniell: Their Life and Work." *Walker's Quarterly* 35–36:1–100.
SHELLIM, MAURICE 1979 *Oil Paintings of India and the East by Thomas and William Daniell.* London: Inchcape.
SUTTON, THOMAS 1954 *The Daniells: Artists and Travellers.* London: Bodley Head.

DANNATT, TREVOR

James Trevor Dannatt (1920–) was apprenticed in the office of E. MAXWELL FRY and JANE DREW.

The initial exposure to the architectural polemics of modernism led Dannatt's interests more into the realm of design and building than that of rhetoric and theory. He developed a small but varied practice in postwar England which is noted for its quietly competent ordering of space, handling of materials, and detailing. Dannatt has eschewed monumentality and symbolic images in his work and has favored celebrating the modest and prosaic. The significance of Dannatt's design work is its being a second-generation refinement of the English Modern movement. Dannatt's involvement in the postwar reassessment of modern architecture included his role as the last secretary of the MARS Group (1948–1954) which oversaw the group's dissolution. Although skeptical of theoretical arguments, Dannatt had accepted a new style of building but has emphasized the importance of placing it within the continuum of the traditional role of architecture: crafting space and form. Through his publications and lectures, Dannatt has constantly provided the programmatic and architectural considerations that led to the development of a particular design, thereby elucidating the modern design process and opening it to further discussion. In 1972, Dannatt's practice expanded to a partnership which realized his largest work, a conference center and hotel in Riyadh, the result of an international competition. This project was innovative in architecturally mediating both desert climate and Islamic culture with a sensitive Western approach.

RICHARD LORCH

WORKS

1954, Chapel, Maze Hill; 1957, Congregational Church, Blackheath; 1958, Dobbs House; London. 1958, Laslett House, Cambridge. 1962, Vaughn College and Museum, Leicester, England. 1964, Fellows' Social Building, Trinity Hall, Cambridge. 1964, Needler Hall, University of Hull, England. 1965, Library and Council Chamber, University of Leicester, England. 1965, Science Building and Gymnasium, Rosa Bassett School; 1966, Housing, Poplar High Street; London. 1966, Pitcorthie House, Fife, Scotland. 1969, Old People's Home, Cedars Road, London. 1971, Assembly Hall, Bootham School, York, England. 1971, Children's Reception Home, Davey Street; 1971, Old People's Home, Sumner Road; 1972, Friends' Meeting House, Blackheath; 1972, Meeting Halls, Southwark; 1974, Building Society Offices, Greenwich; London. 1974, Conference Center; 1974, Intercontinental Hotel; 1974, Mosque; 1974, Villas; Riyadh. 1975, Housing and Welfare Home, Union Road, Lambeth; 1976, Meeting Hall, Warwick Estate; London. 1977–1981, Whittington College, Felbridge, Surrey, England. 1981, Colet Court, Saint Paul's Preparatory School; 1981, Playground, Lisson Grove; 1981, Saint John's Vicarage Site; London. 1981, Thames Polytechnic (conversions), Dartford, England. 1981, Wheelchair Housing, Islington, London.

BIBLIOGRAPHY

"Building Society, Board Room Suite." 1976 *Journal of the Royal Institute of British Architects* 83, no. 11:458.

CANTACUZINO, SHERBAN 1975 "Dannatt at Riyadh: Conference Centre and Hotel, Riyadh, Saudi Arabia." *Architectural Review* 157, Apr.:194–219.

DANNATT, TREVOR (editor) 1945–1961 *Architect's Yearbook.*

DANNATT, TREVOR 1959 *Modern Architecture in Britain.* London: Batsford.

DANNATT, TREVOR 1969 "The Architect's Approach to Architecture." *Journal of the Royal Institute of British Architects* 76, no. 3:98–105.

DANNATT, TREVOR 1978 "Hourglass or Quartz Crystal?" *Architectural Review* 164, Dec.:370–376.

HAPPOLD, E.; LIDDELL, W. I.; and WOODWARD, P. A. 1975 "Riyadh Conference Centre and Hotel." *Structural Engineer* 53, no. 12:515–536.

HELLMAN, LOUIS 1973 "From the Cradle to the Grave: North Peckham Children's Reception Centre." *Architect's Journal* 158, Oct.:847–858.

"Meeting Hall, Blackheath, London." 1973 *Architectural Review* 153, Apr.:265–269.

"New for Old." 1975 *Architect's Journal* 161, Jan.:222–225.

"A Palace in the Desert: Hotel and Conference Centre, Riyadh, Saudi Arabia." 1975 *Techniques et Architecture* no. 305, Sept.:95–97.

"School Assembly Hall, York." 1967 *Architectural Review* 141, Mar.:198–202.

"Vaughn College, Leicester." 1963 *Architectural Design* 33, May:226–231.

DANTI FAMILY

During the sixteenth century, the Dantis emerged as the leading family of artist–theoreticians of Perugia, Italy. Nicknamed for his study of the poet Dante, the goldsmith and mathematician Piervincenzo de' Rainaldi (?–1512) gave the family its popular surname. Giovanni Battista Danti (1478–1517), also a mathematician and military engineer, earned the appellation "Daedalus" for his successful aeronautical experiments (Perugia, 1503). Piervincenzo's son, Giulio (1500–1575), was a sculptor who collaborated with GALEAZZO ALESSI on architectural works at Perugia (Rocca Paolina [1547]) and Assisi (Santa Maria degli Angeli [1567]; bronze tabernacle of the lower church of San Francesco [1569]). Giulio's son Vincenzo (1530–1576) achieved fame as a sculptor at Perugia and Florence and in 1567 published a treatise on proportion. He left no major architectural works; however, he prepared a highly regarded project, now lost, for the Escorial of Madrid. Vincenzo's brother was the Dominican friar

Ignazio (1536–1586), an important mathematician and cosmographer active in Florence, Bologna, and Rome. Ignazio published the perspective treatise of GIACOMO BAROZZI DA VIGNOLA with an extensive illustrated commentary and a biography of the architect. His own building activity was modest; he participated in planning the monastery and church of Santa Croce at Bosco Marengo (1563–1572), in restoring the Claudian harbor at Fiumicino (1583), and in erecting the Vatican obelisk (1586).

RICHARD J. TUTTLE

BIBLIOGRAPHY

DANTI, VINCENZO (1567)1960 Volume 1, pages 207–269 in Paola Barocchi (editor), *Trattati d'arte del Cinquecento.* Bari, Italy: Laterza. Originally published in *Il primo libro del trattato delle perfette proporzioni di tutte le cose che imitare e ritrarre si possano con l'arte del disegno.*

Galeazzo Alessi e l'architettura del cinquecento. 1974 Genoa, Italy: Sagep.

PASCOLI, LIONE (1732)1965 *Vite de' pittori, scultori ed architetti perugini.* Reprint. Amsterdam: B. M. Israel.

SUMMERS, DAVID 1980 *The Sculpture of Vincenzo Danti.* New York: Garland.

VIGNOLA, JACOPO BAROZZI DA (1583)1974 *Le due regole della prospettiva pratica . . . Con i comentarij del R. P. M. Egnatio Danti dell'ordine de Predicatori, Matematico dello Studio di Bologna.* Reprint. Vignola, Italy: Cassa di Risparmio.

DAPHNIS OF MILETOS

Together with PAIONIOS, DAPHNIS OF MILETOS (?–300 B.C.) was architect of the colossal Ionic temple of Apollo at Didyma, begun 313 B.C., and notable as much for the extreme richness of its ornament as for its great size. A veritable forest of 120 columns surrounded the unroofed naos, which contained a shrine in the form of a small free-standing Ionic temple. The program was continued until about A.D. 41, leaving the structure still unfinished. It fell around 1493, probably as the result of an earthquake.

B. M. BOYLE

WORK

*Begun 313 B.C., Temple of Apollo (with Paionios of Ephesos), Didyma, Greece.

BIBLIOGRAPHY

English translations of the ancient texts can be found in the volumes of the Loeb Classical Library series, published by the Harvard University Press and Heinemann.

DINSMOOR, WILLIAM B. (1902)1975 *The Architecture of Ancient Greece.* Reprint of 1950 ed. New York:

Norton. Originally published with the title *The Architecture of Ancient Greece and Rome.*

LAWRENCE, ARNOLD W. (1957)1975 *Greek Architecture.* Harmondsworth, England: Penguin.
PLINY, *Historia naturalis,* Book 36.95.
STRABO, *Geographikon,* Book 14.634.
VITRUVIUS, *De architectura,* Book 7.Praef.16.

DARBISHIRE, H. A.

Henry Astley Darbishire (19th century) is one of the most obscure, original mid-Victorian architects. Details of his life and education are unknown. Yet between 1857 and 1868, he designed some of the earliest and best working class tenements for the Peabody Trust. For his principal patroness, the philanthropist Angela, Baroness Burdett Coutts, he built Holly Village, Hampstead, a model village composed of villas set in formal gardens, built for the clerks of Coutts Bank; and a Gothic market hall, of polychromatic brick, iron, and glass, at Columbia Market, Shoreditch.

ANTHONY SYMONDSON

WORKS

1857–1860, Columbia Square Flats, Bethnal Green; 1861, Victoria Park Fountain, Hackney; 1862–1864, Peabody Flats, Commercial Street, Spitalfields; 1865, Holly Village, Swains Lane, Hampstead; 1865, Peabody Flats, Greenman Street, Islington; 1866–1868, Columbia Market, Shoreditch; 1881, Peabody Flats, Wild Street, The Strand; London.

BIBLIOGRAPHY

DIXON, ROGER, and MUTHESIUS, STEFAN 1978 *Victorian Architecture.* London: Thames & Hudson; New York: Oxford University Press.

DARBY, ABRAHAM III

Abraham Darby III (1750–1789), born in Shropshire, England, was the third generation of a dynasty of Quaker ironmasters who spurred the Industrial Revolution. At age eighteen, he began managing the Coalbrookdale Ironworks established in 1708 by his grandfather Abraham I who pioneered melting iron ore with coke instead of charcoal. The works cast parts for early steam engines and cast the first iron rails. Abraham III, not yet thirty, audaciously cast the five 70-foot ribs for the first iron bridge, the earliest engineering or architectural work in the world to use iron structurally. This industrial monument, which was completed in 1779, still spans the Severn River.

MARGOT GAYLE

WORK

1777–1779, The Iron Bridge, Coalbrookdale, Shropshire, England.

BIBLIOGRAPHY

BRACEGIRDLE, BRIAN, and MILES, PATRICIA H. 1974 *The Darbys and the Ironbridge Gorge.* London: David & Charles.
COSSONS, NEIL 1975 *The BP Book of Industrial Archeology.* London: David & Charles.
GLOAG, JOHN, and BRIDGWATER, DEREK 1948 *A History of Cast Iron in Architecture.* London: Allen & Unwin.
IRONBRIDGE GORGE MUSEUM TRUST 1975 *The Coalbrookdale Ironworks: A Short History.* Telford, England: The trust. A pamphlet based on an original text by Arthur Raistrick.

DARLING, FRANK

Frank Darling (1850–1923) was born east of Toronto, the son of an Anglican cleric of advanced Tractarian and architectural tastes. He trained in Toronto with Henry Langley and in London from 1870 to 1873 with GEORGE E. STREET and Arthur Blomfield, before setting up his office in Toronto, in partnership first with Henry Macdougall, then with S. G. Curry, and finally in 1895 with JOHN A. PEARSON. Darling's early Anglican church designs, his buildings for Trinity College (1877–1905), and his winning but unbuilt competition design for the Ontario Parliament Buildings (1880) all reflect the Gothic style of Street and JOHN L. PEARSON. He also designed houses, university, and commercial buildings across Canada in the rich vocabulary of Edwardian classicism. But Darling is most important for his central contribution to the development of a high-quality Canadian bank architecture in a monumental classical style, including head offices, high-rise office towers, and a series of prefabricated wooden branch banks designed for the western provinces. These buildings are distinguished by a lively awareness of the usefulness of architecture in the creation of a recognizable corporate imagery; they were built at a time when Canada's national banks had a very strong sense of their community responsibility.

WILLIAM DENDY

WORKS

1873–1874, Saint Matthias Anglican Church; 1874, Saint Thomas Anglican Church; 1877–1905, Old Trinity College (additions); 1879, Home for Incurables; 1881–1882, Saint Luke's Anglican Church; 1885–1886, Bank of Montreal, 30 Yonge Street; 1888, Toronto Club; 1889, Hospital for Sick Children; Toronto. 1898, Bank of Commerce (main office), Winnipeg, Manitoba. 1900–1901, Joseph Flavelle House; 1901–1923,

University of Toronto (additions); 1902, Bank of Nova Scotia Head Office, Toronto. 1903–1908, Bank of Commerce Main Office, Montreal. 1906–1908, Bank of Commerce Main Office, Vancouver, British Columbia. 1907, Bank of Nova Scotia, Kingston, Jamaica. 1908–1929, Toronto General Hospital (new building), Toronto. 1910–1911, Bank of Commerce Main Branch, Winnipeg, Manitoba. 1912–1914, Dominion Bank Head Office; 1915–1916, North Toronto CPR Station; Toronto. 1916–1929, Sun Life Assurance Building, Montreal. 1919–1924, Shirreff Hall, Dalhousie University, Halifax, Nova Scotia.

BIBLIOGRAPHY

DENDY, WILLIAM 1979 "Frank Darling: 1850–1923." Unpublished M.A. thesis, Columbia University, New York.

D'ARONCO, RAIMONDO

Raimondo D'Aronco (1857–1932) was born in Gemona, Italy, the son of a building contractor. Raimondo's relationship with his family was a source of pain and frustration throughout his life. In 1871, without consulting him, his father arranged an apprenticeship for Raimondo as a mason in Graz, Austria. After three years in this humble occupation, Raimondo returned to Italy and attended classes at the Accademia delle Belli Arte of Venice. After receiving his diploma, he obtained a position in 1880 as a professor of design at the Accademia delle Belli Arte of Genoa. During the next twelve years, he held a variety of teaching positions. While teaching in Messina, Italy, he befriended ERNESTO BASILE. D'Aronco established his professional reputation during these years with a series of widely published competition entries, including a premiated (though unbuilt) design for the Monument to Victor Emmanuel in Rome in 1884.

In 1892, Sultan Abdul Hamid of Turkey called D'Aronco to Istanbul to oversee the design and construction of the First National Ottoman Exhibition. A severe earthquake in Istanbul forced cancellation of the exhibition. As official architect to the sultan, D'Aronco was active in the rebuilding of the damaged city between 1894 and 1898.

In 1901, D'Aronco won the competition for the design of the facilities for the International Exhibition of Decorative Arts scheduled for 1902 in Turin. D'Aronco's designs for the Turin exhibition clearly reflect the influence of contemporary central European work, in particular JOSEPH MARIA OLBRICH's temporary exhibition pavilions in Darmstadt, Germany. However, the Turin pavilions are not without elements of D'Aronco's own approach to design. The central rotonda incorporated elements of Hagia Sophia in Istanbul, with its shallow dome rising above a band of windows. Other pavilions by D'Aronco combine the linearity of Franco-Belgian Art Nouveau with the volumetric clarity of Viennese design. After winning the competition, D'Aronco returned to Turkey. He attempted to direct the execution of his plans for Turin through correspondence from Istanbul. The entire episode was an unfortunate one for D'Aronco. He was bitter about unsanctioned changes in his plans during construction and increasingly sensitive to critical reviews of his work.

In Turkey, he executed a series of important buildings, including the fountain, tomb, and library complex at Yildiz, one of his finest works. D'Aronco returned to Italy in 1908. That same year, he was commissioned to design the Palazzo Comunale of Udine. Due largely to D'Aronco's habit of constantly revising his designs, work on this large project dragged on until his death. The Palazzo Comunale lacks the innovative formal qualities of either the Turin pavilions of 1902 or the work in Turkey.

In 1910, D'Aronco was elected a member of the Italian Parliament. Between 1911 and 1917, he was associated with the Politecnico of Naples. During these years, he also held the position of vice-superintendent of the excavations in Pompeii. Following a long illness he retired to San Remo, where he died.

DENNIS DOORDAN

WORKS

1896, Tophane Fountain, Istanbul, Turkey. *1902, Exhibition Pavilions, International Exhibition of Decorative Arts, Turin, Italy. 1903, Fountain, Tomb, and Library Complex, Yildiz, Turkey. 1905, Italian Embassy Summer Residence, Therapia, Turkey. 1907, Santoro House, Istanbul, Turkey. 1908–1932, Palazzo Comunale, Udine, Italy.

BIBLIOGRAPHY

NICOLETTI, MANFREDI 1955 *Raimondo D'Aronco.* Milan: II Balcone.
NICOLETTI, MANFREDI 1978 *L'Architettura Liberty in Italia.* Bari, Italy: Laterza.
NICOLETTI, MANFREDI. 1982 *D'Aronco e l'architettura liberty.* Bari, Italy: Laterza.
PEVSNER, NICOLAUS, and RICHARDS, J. M. (editors) 1973 *The Anti-Rationalists.* London: Architectural Press.

DAVIDSON, J. R.

Julius Ralph Davidson (1889–1977) was born in Berlin. Turning from art to architecture while employed as a delineator in Berlin, he continued his apprenticeship in London (1910–1913) as a detailer and designer of interiors of yachts and Cunard liners. His style was distinguished by fine craftsmanship, a liberal use of color (an influence of the *fauves* in Paris), and intricate floor planning whose source, he said, was the Swedish village house. In his office in Berlin (1919–1923), he developed novel methods of lighting, which he introduced in Los Angeles where he emigrated in December 1923. Among his large houses in the International style was the Stothart House, Santa Monica, California (1937). In the 1940s, wood, stone, and sloping roofs began to appear, and form became more subservient to plan (Dr. Jokl House, Los Angeles, 1958).

ESTHER MCCOY

DAVILER, CHARLES

Born in Paris of a family from Nancy, Charles Augustin Daviler (1653–1700) was one of the first students at the newly formed Royal Academy of Architecture. In 1674, he was nominated as a royal pensionary for the Academy at Rome. Daviler reached Rome in 1676 together with his fellow student and friend ANTOINE DESGODETZ. He spent four years in Rome. In 1680, Daviler seems to have returned to Paris, where he presented the Academy of Architecture with a plan of the church and colonnade of St. Peter's in Rome. Daviler made researches into the life and work of GIACOMO BAROZZI DA VIGNOLA, the preface of which he read to the Academy in 1683.

In 1684, Daviler entered the office of JULES HARDOUIN MANSART as one of his draftsmen, where he continued until 1689. In 1685, he published a French translation of the sixth book of VINCENZO SCAMOZZI's architectural theory. In 1691 follows his *Cours d'Architecture qui comprend les Ordres de Vignola*. This book included a life of Vignola, a description of buildings by him and by MICHELANGELO, and a dictionary of architectural terms. Daviler also gave practical advice for the design and construction of buildings. His book contained plans and elevations of a typical house and designs of all architectural details such as doorways, entrances, and windows, including even the design of gardens. In his dictionary of terms, Daviler noted the modern distinction between *simmetrie respective* (symmetry) and *simmetrie uniforme* (proportion). In the eighteenth century, Daviler's book was the standard work for architects, and many editions and translations were published.

In 1691 Daviler accepted an invitation from the town of Montpellier, France, to undertake the supervision of a triumphal arch to Louis XIV, to be built there from the designs of FRANÇOIS D'ORBAY, the Porte du Peyrou. Daviler settled at Montpellier, where in 1693 he was appointed *architecte de la province* of Languedoc. As provincial architect, Daviler was employed at Béziers, Carcassonne, Nîmes, Montpellier, and Toulouse. This architectural practice, especially the commissions for buildings of the Roman Catholic church, must be seen in the light of the historical background of the revocation of the Edict of Nantes (1685) and the therein documented increased absolutism of the French monarchy. Beside buildings for the church, such as the archbishop's palaces in Toulouse and Béziers and the churches in Montpellier, Daviler designed private buildings for the urban aristocracy. The Hôtel Deydé in Montpellier gives a characteristic stylistic detail of Daviler's architecture, the so-called *courbe Davilerte*, a sort of flattened arch. Beautifully sculptured portals also marked his buildings. Daviler's designs corresponded to the strong classicism demanded in his *Cours*.

WALTER KAMBARTEL

WORKS

1691, Porte du Peyrou (design by François D'Orbay); 1693, Chapelle des Pénitants blancs; 1693, Hôtel Deyde, Montpellier, France. 1693–1713, Archbishop's Palace, Béziers, France 1693–1713, Archbishop's Palace, Toulouse, France. 1698, Church of Saint Denis, Montpellier, France.

BIBLIOGRAPHY

BLOMFIELD, REGINALD T. (1911)1974 *History of French Architecture.* 2 vols. New York: Hacker.
D'AVILER, CHARLES 1685 *Les cinq ordres d'architecture de Vincent Scamozzi . . . VIe livre de son Idée générale d'architecture.* Paris: Coignard.
D'AVILER, CHARLES (1691)1750 *Cours d'architecture qui comprend les Ordres de Vignole.* Edited by P. J. Mariette. Paris.
DE LA ROQUE, L. 1877 *Montpellierains peintres, sculpteurs, architectes.* n.p.
FLICHE, AUGUATIN 1935 *Montpellier.* Paris: Laurens.
HAUTECOEUR, LOUIS 1943–1952 *Histoire de l'architecture classique en France.* 7 vols. Paris: Picard.

DA VINCI, LEONARDO

See LEONARDO DA VINCI.

DAVIOUD, GABRIEL

Jean-Antoine-Gabriel Davioud (1823–1881) studied at the Ecole des Beaux-Arts in Paris under LÉON VAUDOYER and won a Second Grand Prix de

Rome in 1849. He enjoyed considerable success as a government architect, designing a number of opulent fountains and rustic park pavilions for the city of Paris under the Second Empire, as well as such important buildings as the two theaters on the place du Châtelet (1864) and the Palais du Trocadéro for the 1878 International Exposition. The Châtelet theaters, his best designs, are straightforward, satisfying works of highly rationalized historicism, but much of the rest of his oeuvre lapsed into a florid eclecticism.

ANN LORENZ VAN ZANTEN

WORKS

1855–1867, Buildings in Buttes Chaumont Park; 1858–1860, Fontaine Saint-Michel; 1864, Théâtre Sarah Bernhardt and Cirque Impérial (now Theatre du Châtelet); 1867, Magasins Réunis Department Store; 1868–1874, Fontaine de l'Observatoire (with J. B. Carpeaux); 1876–1878, *Mairie* of the Nineteenth Arrondissement (with J. D. Bourdais); *1878, Palais du Trocadéro (with Bourdais); Paris.

BIBLIOGRAPHY

DALY, CÉSAR, and DAVIOUD GABRIEL 1865 *Architecture contemporaine: Les Théâtres de la place du Châtelet.* Paris: Ducher.

DESTORS 1881 "Notice sur la vie et les ouvrages de G. Davioud." *Bulletin Mensuel de la Société Centrale des Architectes* Series 5 4:233–244.

DAVIS, ALEXANDER JACKSON

The great romantic of American nineteenth-century architecture, Alexander Jackson Davis (1803–1892) was among the most original and influential architects of his period. Proudly American in a period of intense nationalism, he searched for new forms and effects, creating free interpretations of many styles, both neoclassical and picturesque. Although his designs for public buildings and residences in Greek and Tuscan Revival styles were distinctive, boldly rational, and often prophetically experimental beyond historicism, he is probably best known for his country houses in Gothic Revival, Italianate, and bracketed styles. He was a leader in introducing and developing these styles in America, designing prototypal and individualistic cottages and villas that had a marked effect on the evolution of the American house.

Highly imaginative, Davis was always primarily a designer. Light fascinated him; he used large expanses of window, introducing a multistoried, vertically unified type he called Davisean, and experimented with overhead lighting. He attained mastery of asymmetrical massing and control of proportion and scale, together with restrained, meticulous detailing. A strong pictorial sense gave him a feeling for bold and dramatic effects and a concern for the harmony of buildings with their settings.

Davis was born in New York, but most of his early years were spent in Newark, New Jersey, and on the edge of the central New York frontier, in Utica and Auburn, towns booming with building activity. From his father, an impecunious bookseller, editor, and publisher of theological books and periodicals, he gained an ardent love of books. When about fifteen, he was sent to Alexandria, Virginia, to learn the printing trade in a half-brother's newspaper office. Adept but bored, he read romantic literature voraciously and acted in amateur theatricals.

In 1823, Davis returned to New York, where he lived almost all the rest of his life. Deciding to be an artist and supporting himself at first by typesetting, he studied in the meager facilities of the American Academy of Fine Arts (where John Trumbull apparently helped him), the New-York Drawing Association, and the Antique School of the new National Academy of Design (of which he became an associate in 1831, though later in the 1830s he returned to the rival American Academy as an officer). Advised by Rembrandt Peale to concentrate on architecture, he quickly developed skill in drawing buildings, and over the next several years he delineated many in New York and New England; numerous views were printed by prominent publishers and form valuable records.

This background and skill as an architectural illustrator had a determinant effect on Davis's architectural career. Design, not structure or theory, was his chief interest and strength. The temperament and eye of an artist gave his work much of its imaginative, special quality. A superb watercolorist and one of the finest American architectural draftsmen of his day, he did most of his own drafting, able to express his ideas brilliantly and directly in his drawings.

In 1826, he began architectural drafting, working for JOSIAH R. BRADY briefly and for builders and proprietors; within the next two years, he also did some drawing, of uncertain nature and extent, for MARTIN E. THOMPSON and ITHIEL TOWN. Eagerly, he studied architectural books in Town's "Architectural Room" and, during two Boston sojourns in 1827–1828, at the Boston Athenaeum. He set up an office and started to create designs, calling himself an "architectural composer" (a term he later dropped) and exhibiting designs, as well as views, at the National Academy.

Davis's architectural career opened in January

1829 with his first executed design for James A. Hillhouse's Highwood (later Sachem's Wood) on the outskirts of New Haven, Connecticut (1829–1831). A mature design of monumental quality, it brought Davis immediate recognition, as well as entrée into New Haven's intellectual circle.

The next month, Ithiel Town took Davis into partnership. The firm of TOWN AND DAVIS existed for six years, until May 1835, and seven years later it was revived for another year, March 1842 to July 1843. For eighteen months (May 1832 until November 1833), JAMES H. DAKIN was added, while Davis spent two periods of several months in temporary branch offices in Washington and Baltimore.

Partnership with Town gave young Davis extraordinary opportunities. It brought him immediately to the forefront of American architecture under the aegis, guidance, and influence of a prominent architect and bridge engineer almost twenty years his senior. Town was an innovative leader in the new Greek Revival movement, a pioneer in the American Gothic Revival, and an expert in construction, well known as the inventor of the lattice truss for covered bridges. Moreover, he had by far the best architectural library in America.

During six formative years with Town, Davis learned much about architectural form and structure, gained experience, and rapidly developed into a brilliantly original designer. Studying avidly in Town's library, he explored many styles and experimented widely in adventurous designs. He was responsible for much of the drafting and detail and, especially during Town's long absences, played an increasing role in the firm's designs; some of their dramatic quality is probably attributable to Davis. He taught drawing and architecture to several students, the most important of whom were Dakin and John Stirewalt. He began an illustrated book on Greek architecture and jointly with Town, one on American architecture, although neither was completed.

The firm designed many distinguished and influential buildings of widely different types. Most of their designs were strong expressions of the Greek Revival style, with deep porticoes of giant columns and ranges of massive antae. Severely rational and powerful, structural as well as aesthetic, the anta-type square piers appear in most of the firm's designs and in Davis's work throughout his career: as free-standing square pillars; as deeply projecting, austere pilasters; or as structural piers in skeleton construction. They formed bold pseudoperistyles on two monumental buildings modeled after the Parthenon: Indiana's State Capitol in Indianapolis (1831–1835) and New York's Custom House (1833–1842; modified by others in execution). They give character to the end elevations of North Carolina's cruciform Capitol in Raleigh (1833–1840; begun by WILLIAM NICHOLS, finished by David Paton).

A strikingly original, rational feature of Davis's neoclassical designs, from at least 1831 throughout his career, was the vertically unified window type he later called Davisean: multistoried, recessed, and paneled at floor levels, it anticipated the strip window. One of the first executed uses was in the Lyceum of Natural History, New York (1835–1836). In a remarkable design for a Patent Office (1834), he used long ranges of antatype piers with his Davisean windows as virtual window walls, an early example of vertical skeleton construction.

Town and Davis's handsome Ionic French Church du Saint Esprit in New York (1831–1834) was unusual, with a high dome and an interior modeled after Saint Stephen Walbrook, London. Most of their other churches were versions of the distyle-in-antis pattern, apparently introduced by Town in New Haven, which became a standard church façade; especially influential was the West Presbyterian Church on Carmine Street, New York (1831–1832). Many years later, Davis designed the County Courthouse (1848–1849) in Powhatan, Virginia, on this pattern.

Of their New York City houses nothing certain survives. Town and Davis were among the first in New York to introduce Greek columns and pilasters for townhouse doorways, and their house for Samuel Ward with its art gallery (1831–1833) was outstanding. Davis made a number of interesting, exploratory designs for rows and terraces, which may have influenced the work of others. For New Haven they created several distinctive houses, including an Ionic temple with wings for Aaron N. Skinner (1831–1833?). Davis used giant square pillars with impressive effect on a new front sec-

Davis.
Indiana State Capitol
(with Ithiel Town).
Indianapolis.
1831–1835

tion for Robert C. Johnson's Vesper Cliff (1834) in Owego, New York.

Davis was working in other styles also. The bold severity and the great, wide cantilevered eaves of the Tuscan order (as transmitted by INIGO JONES) appealed to his dramatic eye, his rational sense, and his need for economical monumentality. Borrowing its broad eaves and simplicity, he teamed it with Davisean windows in designs of stark austerity, as in his design for the Lunatic Asylum on Blackwell's Island, New York (1834–1835, 1837–1839, 1847–1848); only partially built, it was executed by others in altered style, and a single octagon survives.

With Gothic and Egyptian he had long experimented. Of his first Gothic villa little is known, but drawings exist for Robert Gilmor's Glen Ellen (1832–1834?), Towson, Maryland, for which he did extensive detailing, though it was mostly planned by Town and Gilmor. Davis was in Washington when the New York University Building was planned in 1833, but he later designed and supervised its elaborate Chapel (1835–1837). An Egyptian façade in his Halls of Justice competition entry (awarded a second premium, 1835) he said influenced JOHN HAVILAND's final design.

After Town and Davis discontinued their association on May 1, 1835, they remained friendly. Davis drew occasionally for Town; they jointly entered the Illinois Capitol competition (1837); the Ohio Capitol premium designs were revised and a new design (1839) proposed apparently in both names, though the work was chiefly by Davis. He purchased books from Town and gradually acquired a sizable library.

Soon needing help with problems of structure, Davis in August 1835 "joined interests" with RUSSELL WARREN of Providence, Rhode Island. The association lasted less than a year, but a hotel, several houses, and two fine churches were realized, the Greek Revival Dutch Reformed Church (1835–1837) in Newburgh, New York, and the Gothic First Unitarian Church (1835–1838) in New Bedford, Massachusetts.

Henceforth, Davis practiced alone, except for his few collaborations with Town and the year of revived partnership (1842–1843). Expert draftsman that he was, Davis did nearly all of his own drafting, only at very busy periods employing a draftsman. Most of the time, he ran a one-man office, without even a clerk. A few students came sporadically, seem not to have stayed long, and, except for J. C. CADY (a few months in 1861–1862), did not attain distinction. Davis remained primarily an architectural designer, supervising construction of only a few of his larger houses. He was a leader in the founding of the short-lived American Institution of Architects in 1836–1837.

The second half of the 1830s was a turning point in Davis's career: he was frustrated in most of his large public building projects, but he laid the foundations for the designing of romantic country and suburban houses, henceforth the dominant, though not exclusive, aspect of his career. Some of his large schemes—like his circular and hexagonal designs for a Brooklyn City Hall and his impressive Gothic project for the University of Michigan—were too adventurous. The Panic of 1837 and hard times thwarted others. Only his Gothic chapel for the New York University Building and a few small churches and chapels were realized, though his extravagant design for the Ohio Capitol (1839) probably influenced its final form.

Meanwhile he was evolving many of the basic patterns and salient features that characterized his later domestic architecture, both neoclassical and picturesque. Several houses were built in New Haven, mostly versions of the Grecian mode with individualistic features, like the two giant Corinthian columns fronting Mary Prichard's House (1836–1837?) and the graceful semicircular portico for Henry Whitney's Belmont (1836–1839). But they also included ornamental verandas, touches of Egyptian and Oriental exoticism, unexecuted designs for Gothic and "Palmyrean" villas, and, for Abby Salisbury, a Tuscan house (1835–1836) with a low-pitched roof, wide cantilevered eaves, and Davisean windows. Over the years, Town and Davis contributed much to the architectural distinction of New Haven and influenced local builders and architects, including HENRY AUSTIN.

The Hudson River Valley, inspiration of American writers and its first school of landscape painters, was the setting in which Davis evolved his early interpretations of the picturesque for villas and cottages in America. Davis, his clients, and ANDREW J. DOWNING were influenced by the English aesthetic theory of the picturesque, a point of view that admired the wilder, irregular aspects of nature. Its followers sought to emulate these

*Davis.
Belmont.
near Belleville, New Jersey.
1850–1852*

pictorial effects in landscaping the grounds of country houses and insisted that the houses be designed in harmony with their settings, with irregularity, variety, contrast, and rough texture, visual qualities found especially in the Gothic, Italianate, Swiss, and Oriental styles.

In mid-1836 at Blithewood, the estate of Robert Donaldson in Barrytown, New York, Davis created designs of far-reaching influence on the American house. Two years earlier, he had created for Donaldson, a New York merchant and landscape-gardening enthusiast, a Gothic villa design intended for a different site, which Donaldson sold before building. Now Davis and his client transformed a Federal-style house into a bracketed *cottage orné* by adding novel features: an expansive ornamental veranda and decorative brackets on boldly projecting eaves. As a gatehouse, Davis designed the prototype of the American Gothic cottage. Symmetrical but irregular, it had front and rear projections, high gables and chimney pots, vergeboards, drip molds, a bay window, and mullioned, diamond-paned windows. He sheathed it in vertical board-and-batten siding, here used deliberately for aesthetic effects of rusticity and

roughness. Both houses are now gone, as are most of the other picturesque structures Davis devised for Donaldson's estates over more than two decades.

Encouraged by Donaldson and Hillhouse, in the spring of 1836 Davis began work on his *Rural Residences,* the first American book about country houses. Illustrated with handsome, hand-colored lithographs, it is the key to the beginnings of picturesque architecture in America, remarkable in its new concepts and innovative designs.

Its brief preface drew a sharp distinction between urban and rural architecture, rejecting the Greek temple form for country residences. Davis deplored "the bald and uninteresting aspect of our houses . . . [with] defects . . . not only in the style of the house but in the want of connexion with its site" and praised the "picturesque Cottages and Villas of England" for their pictorial effects and variety of plan and outline.

His designs presented imaginatively free interpretations of various styles, Gothic, bracketed, Oriental, Tuscan, and "American": the asymmetrical villa design for Donaldson and his rustic gatehouse; a *cottage orné* and a villa with touches of Oriental exoticism and ample verandas; a board-and-batten, bracketed farmhouse; a loghouse (in the form of a Tuscan temple); a Gothic village church; and a board-and-batten, windowless schoolhouse with clearstory lighting.

Because of hard times only two of six proposed parts were issued, in 1838 (despite the 1837 title-page date), and relatively few copies were sold. Yet the publication of *Rural Residences* had a strong effect on Davis's career.

In the next few years, Davis designed a number of villas and cottages along the Hudson in which he developed patterns and details basic to his fu-

ture work. Although English books afforded ideas and illustrated specimens of medieval details, Davis used his sources freely and created imaginative American interpretations that were very much his own, adapted to American limitations of size, materials, craftsmanship, and expenditure. English designs, he once wrote, were "not suited to the taste and wants of the American people . . . the English plans are on a scale far more extended and expensive than we can accomplish with our limited means or . . . too inconsiderable and humble for the proper pride of republicans." An impression of romantic styles had to be conveyed for Americans through a few forms and details, judiciously chosen and carefully scaled.

Davis's first major villa, one of the most important of his career, was for William and Philip R. Paulding near Tarrytown, New York (1838–1842), the nucleus of the present Lyndhurst. Asymmetrical in massing and plan, imaginatively varied in feature and detail, it established his basic Gothic-villa vocabulary. Its dramatically high, arcaded central block and its sweeping veranda became favorite themes; the interior spaces were ingeniously arranged and ceilings were vaulted with plaster and open-timber patterns; Davis also made fifty designs for furniture. Another significant early villa was Kenwood (1842–1845, 1848–1849) for Joel Rathbone, south of Albany, New York, more compact in mass, but fashioned with great variety and a radiating plan of fluid spaces.

In several cottages of 1838–1842, Davis developed the ideas inherent in Donaldson's gatehouse into his basic American interpretations of the "English cottage style." He enlarged it for charming and ornamental moderate-sized dwellings—in the concept of the *cottage orné*—intended for substantial citizens as summer retreats or permanent homes in country or village. Usually increasing the central projection, he raised its gable to dramatic height, forming complicated roof shapes, and added a veranda and various embellishments, sometimes an oriel, arcaded entrance, or dormers. Especially influential were Henry Sheldon's Millbrook (1838–1840), near Tarrytown, New York, and the design for Doctor Federal Vanderburgh at Rhinecliff (1841). Lively and irregular in outline and silhouette, the cottages were usually symmetrical, though a larger one for Samuel E. Lyon (1842–1844) in White Plains, New York, was gently asymmetrical.

Davis developed the new bracketed mode (suggested by Anglo-Swiss models) in a variety of structures, including the surviving Blithewood second gate lodge (1841), and he made experimental designs for bracketed, board-and-batten cottages that Downing soon put to use.

Through more than a decade (1839–1850), Davis collaborated with Downing on his influential books and on the *Horticulturist,* drawing most of the architectural illustrations and delineating them with a charm that greatly increased the effectiveness of Downing's persuasive texts. For the *Treatise on . . . Landscape Gardening* (1841, expanded 1844 and 1849) Davis drew views of country houses, many of which were his own recent villas and cottages. Downing's two subsequent books were house pattern books (1842 and 1850); for these and the *Horticulturist* (1846–1850) Davis contributed several designs of his own and revised Downing's rough amateur sketches, correcting proportions, supplying details (as well as landscape backgrounds), and sometimes making major changes.

Downing was strongly influenced by Davis's picturesque cottages and villas. He used Davis's basic patterns and derived several designs directly from specific Davis drawings (though others, particularly in Italianate style, he adapted from models in English books); he adopted and espoused the bracketed style and board-and-batten siding; and he was dependent on Davis for most details.

Downing's influential writings, enhanced by Davis's skillful drawings, popularized in America the ideas and styles of the picturesque. The impact on Davis's career was tremendous. His reputation was greatly extended, and many commissions came to him through Downing's recommendations and contacts; the two even worked together on a few projects, although most did not materialize. Downing created the cultural environment in which Davis's work could flourish.

For more than two decades at mid-century, Davis was the leading American architect of romantic country houses, designing many of America's finest examples in the picturesque styles. Over a hundred of his villas and cottages are known to have been built, chiefly in the Gothic and Italianate modes. Summer homes or year-round dwellings in the country, village, or suburb, they were scattered along the Hudson and from Maine to North Carolina and westward to Michigan, Ohio, and Kentucky. The distant work was usually carried on by correspondence: the amount depended on the client's requests and varied from a single reply with a sketched elevation for a cottage in Virginia to a lengthy series of letters conveying design changes, basic drawings with specification, working drawings, and advice for a major villa in Kentucky. For some houses Davis drew numerous interior details, even occasionally designing furniture, and for several large villas near New York he supervised construction at least partially.

Davis.
William J. Rotch House.
New Bedford,
*   Massachusetts.*
1845–1847?

Most of the smaller houses were versions of the picturesque "English cottage style," which Davis developed with imaginative virtuosity from his earlier patterns. No two were ever exactly alike. These spirited cottages had dramatically high gables, fancifully carved vergeboards, ample bay windows, and delicately ornamented verandas. Two fine surviving examples are the board-and-batten cottage (1844) for Henry Delamater, Rhinebeck, New York, with a beautifully elaborated veranda, and the larger, elegantly ornamented cottage villa (1845–1847?) for William J. Rotch, New Bedford, Massachusetts. Usually symmetrical, these moderate-sized dwellings achieved irregularity through upward and outward projections, divergence of roof levels, and diversity of elements. A few of the larger cottage villas had a subtle asymmetry, such as Cottage Lawn (1849) for Niles Higinbotham at Oneida, New York, and Oakwood (1849–1851) for George W. Penney, Newark, Ohio; the latter was based on an unexecuted design planned jointly by Davis and Downing.

Although detailing on most of Davis's cottages was Gothic, he sometimes used Italianate, Romanesque, bracketed, Swiss, or classical motifs. A board-and-batten "Tuscan cottage" of 1848 for Lewis B. Brown in Rahway, New Jersey, twice published by Downing, proved so popular that Davis called it his "American style."

The larger romantic villas show Davis's special gifts for design—his strong pictorial sense, his eye for scenic effects, and his skill in the picturesque grouping of asymmetrical masses. In designs full of movement, masses advanced and receded, rising and descending from a dramatic central climax, and sometimes stretched out almost like a stage set. Ample verandas added grace, a connecting link with the surrounding landscape, and a distinctly American quality.

In a series of evocative Gothic villas Davis matured ideas broached in his early designs for Donaldson and Paulding, adding expressive features and evolving new patterns. Towers and turrets, crockets and finials, dripstones and discreet crenellations, oriels, bays, and traceried windows suggested to Americans the romance of medieval times and afforded the architect opportunities for picturesque compositions. Basically, Davis carried out his own personal lines of development, although he continued to find inspiration and details in English books, chiefly Regency ones known to him early in his career, for he was relatively untouched by designs in the more recent books of the Victorian period.

The "Suburban Gothic Villa" (1844–1845) on New York's Murray Hill for W. Coventry H. Waddell initiated one of Davis's important individualistic façade patterns, where large and small octagonal towers flanked a central gabled projection. Its finest expression was Henry K. Harral's Walnut Wood in Bridgeport, Connecticut (1846–1848) and it survives in Francis Key Hunt's Loudoun in Lexington, Kentucky (1850–1852). Another group of villas, characterized by a single large, off-center octagonal tower, is represented by William P. Chapman's Whitby (1852–1854) in Rye, New York; and Edwin B. Strange's Ingleside (1854–1857), Dobbs Ferry, New York. For wild and rocky hill sites, Davis designed a few castellated villas of rough-cut stone, usually dominated by a massive round tower; the most romantic was John J. Herrick's Ericstan, overlooking the Hudson at Tarrytown (1855–1859); the sole survivor is Castlewood (1857–1860) for Joseph Howard in Llewellyn Park, West Orange, New Jersey.

Culminating more than a quarter-century's experience, in 1865–1867 Davis enlarged Paulding's Knoll for George Merritt, creating the present-day Lyndhurst, a masterpiece of intricately balanced composition and elegant detailing. With skill and assurance he integrated the new, more elaborate and expansive features into the old innovative design and created a new focal point in a great high tower, which he evolved from his tower for Philip St. George Cocke's Belmead (1845–1848) on the James River in Virginia.

One of the first American architects to undertake a picturesque Italian villa, Davis contributed significantly to the development of that style in this country. His earliest venture (1836) was

Davis.
Walnut Wood.
Bridgeport, Connecticut.
1846–1848

Davis.
Grace Hill.
Brooklyn, New York.
1854–1857

halted because of expense, but he drew an elaboration of it for Downing's *Treatise,* where also appeared his remodeling of Governor John M. Morehead's Blandwood (1844), Greensboro, North Carolina, prototype for the widespread pattern of rectangular block with central front tower. When the versatile Italianate style became increasingly popular in the late 1840s and the 1850s, some thirty villas by Davis were built. The finest of his "Americanized Italian" villas were strong compositions of bold geometric masses, relieved by sweeping verandas, and detailed with restraint; plans were varied, often radiating from, or around, a central core (usually skylighted), and some were ingeniously arranged on split levels. A favorite pattern featured the juxtaposition of two towers of divergent height, breadth, and shape, as in Llewellyn S. Haskell's Belmont (1850–1852), opposite Belleville, New Jersey; Edwin C. Litchefield's Grace Hill (1854–1857) in Brooklyn, New York, where detailing was enriched to accord with the pseudo-Corinthian corn-and-wheat order of the veranda's colonnade; and Winyah (1851–1852), New Rochelle, New York, of Richard Lathers (for whom and for whose friends Davis designed numerous houses in various styles). On Richard O. Morris's Hawkwood (1851–1854), Green Springs, Virginia, the encircling veranda became an arcade, a pattern Davis later varied at Llewellyn Park.

Perhaps the ultimate in American picturesque, Llewellyn Park in West Orange, New Jersey, is a hillside residential park, where landscape and rural architecture united in total romanticism. Probably Davis shared with Llewellyn S. Haskell in originating the concept and overall plan of this influential suburb, and he made many designs for houses and park structures there. Not all the early houses were by Davis, but surviving ones of his design include the rustic gate lodge, a Gothic cottage, a castellated villa, and one of his infrequent mansard-roofed houses.

A few of Davis's country and suburban houses were neoclassical in taste. Notable is Montgomery Place (1843–1867) in Barrytown, New York, where Davis transformed the severity of a Federal-

Davis.
Ericstan.
Tarrytown, New York.
1855–1859

style block into graceful elegance, adding a semicircular Corinthian portico, an arcaded pavilion, terraces, and finely detailed ornamentation (1843 and 1863).

To embellish this estate and several others, Davis created over the years numerous imaginative smaller structures in a variety of styles—farmhouses, gate lodges, and carriage houses, chapels and schoolhouses, gates, rustic seats and bridges, conservatories, springhouses and fountains, garden houses, temples, arbors, pedestals, and prospect and observatory towers: for example, a Chinese seat, an Italianate chicken house, an Egyptian toolhouse.

During the years of his mature career, Davis's New York City houses were not numerous, but they were outstanding, influential, and distinctive. One of the most elegant townhouses of its decade was his neoclassical "palace" for John Cox Stevens (1845–1848), which he superintended and provided with much of its exquisite detailing, interior as well as exterior. In other townhouses he introduced features carried over from his country-house designing: bracketed eaves, bay windows, and ornamental porches. His twin houses for James W. Phillips and Charles C. Taber (1847–1848), among the city's first in Renaissance Revival style, initiated an Italian palazzo pattern with low stoop that others adapted for larger rows. Of Davis's many designs for rows and terraces, the only ones built

Davis.
John Cox Stevens House.
New York.
1845–1848

Davis.
North Carolina Hospital
(elevation and plan).
Raleigh.
1850–1855

were the London Terrace (1845–1846), New York City, 800 feet of antae and Davisean windows, apparently based on drawings by Davis, and the House of Mansions (1858–1859), a castellated block of eleven independent dwellings unified as one edifice. All that now remains of this work are the elaborate cast-iron porches across two houses on Gramercy Park (1843).

Throughout his career, Davis continued to design public buildings of various types. Symmet-

rical, with clean, crisp lines, fine proportions, and restrained detailing, almost all were characterized by his multistoried windows, which gave to his designs a strongly personal quality, transcending the historicism of stylistic allusions in other features. Usually, the styles were rationally neoclassical, although in a few instances he used Gothic, notably for his ingeniously unified façade (with traditional windows) for Hartford's Wadsworth Atheneum (1842–1844), built on a plan by Henry Austin, and for Yale's Alumni Hall (1851–1853).

Several small churches were built, and in the South three large collegiate schemes were partially carried out. Most nearly realized was his Gothic campus for the Virginia Military Institute in Lexington (1848; 1850–1861), where two villalike houses and the great Barracks, rebuilt after Civil War destruction and completed in 1923 by BERTRAM G. GOODHUE, are still standing. At the University of North Carolina, Chapel Hill, Davis created forceful new fronts in bracketed style for two earlier buildings (1844–1848) and a temple with corn-and-wheat capitals (1850–1852). Of the vast quadrangle he envisioned for Davidson College, also in North Carolina, only Chambers Building (1856–1859) was constructed; a colossal Tuscan portico dramatically accented the long ranges of three-story windows. Somewhat similar in overall effect was his North Carolina Hospital for the Insane in Raleigh (1850–1855) which had

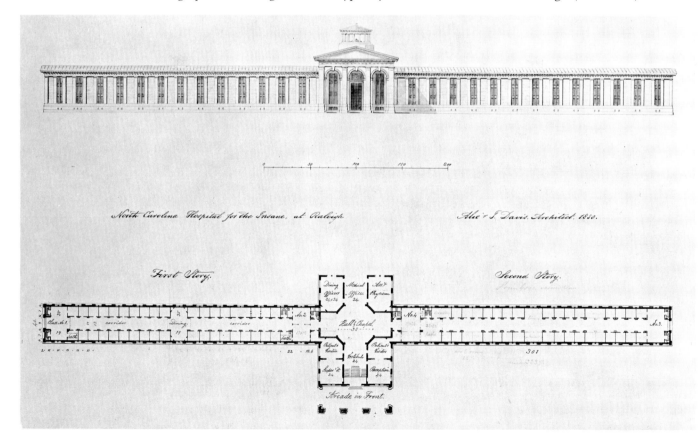

three giant arches as the central focus.

Nominally Tuscan was the Town Hall and Courthouse for Bridgeport, Connecticut (1853–1854), where Davis placed his windows between massive antae used as structural piers, a concept that harked back to his Patent Office project of 1834 and that he also employed in the Rome, New York, Academy of 1848. He explored the rational potentialities of this skeleton, window-wall construction in numerous studies and unexecuted projects, notably designs for an Astor Library (1843), a Merchants' Exchange (1862), and a round Post Office for New York (1867).

The Civil War interrupted Davis's practice, and it never recovered. He was unsympathetic to the High Victorian Gothic and Second Empire styles and to most of the younger architects. He dropped out of the American Institute of Architects, of which he had been an original trustee in 1857. Lyndhurst and Montgomery Place were climaxes, but his work dwindled. Continuing to envision large projects, devising variants of his villa and cottage designs, copying and revising earlier drawings, he kept until 1878 the office where he had chiefly lived as well as worked, totally engrossed in his architecture. In 1890, he moved with his family to a cottage built by his son overlooking Llewellyn Park, where his summer lodge had burned six years before. There, he died on January 14, 1892.

JANE B. DAVIES

WORKS

*1829–1831, Highwood (later Sachem's Wood), New Haven. *1831–1832, West Presbyterian Church (with Ithiel Town), New York. 1831–1833?, Aaron N. Skinner House, New Haven. *1831–1833, Samuel Ward House (with Town); *1831–1834, French Church du Saint Esprit (with Town); New York. *1831–1835, Indiana State Capitol (with Town), Indianapolis. *1832–1834?, Glen Ellen (with Town), Towson, Md. 1833–1840, North Carolina State Capitol (with Town and others), Raleigh. 1833–1842, United States Custom house (with Town and others), New York. 1834, Vesper Cliff (remodeling), Owego, N.Y. 1834–1835, 1837–1839, 1847–1848, Lunatic Asylum (partially built, executed by others), Blackwell's Island; *1834–1848, Pauper Lunatic Asylum (one octagon extant; partially built, executed by others); *1835–1836, Lyceum of Natural History (with Town); New York. *1835–1836, Abby Salisbury House, New Haven. 1835–1837, Dutch Reformed Church (with Russell Warren), Newburgh, N.Y. *1835–1837, New York University Chapel. 1835–1838, First Unitarian Church (with Warren), New Bedford, Mass. *1836, Wyllys Warner House; 1836–1837, Mary Prichard House; *1836–1839, Belmont; New Haven. 1836–1851, Blithewood (remodeling and structures; second gatehouse extant), Barrytown, N.Y. *1838–1840, Millbrook; 1838–1867, Lyndhurst; Tarry-

town, N.Y. *1841, Federal Vanderburgh Cottage, Rhinecliff, N.Y. *1842–1844, Samuel E. Lyon House, White Plains, N.Y. 1842–1844, Wadsworth Atheneum (façade; with Town), Hartford, Conn. *1842–1849, Kenwood, Albany, N.Y. *1843–1844, Henry H. Elliot and Robert C. Townsend Houses, New York. 1843–1844, Church of the Holy Cross (with N. B. Warren), Troy, N.Y. 1843–1867, Montgomery Place (additions and structures; some destroyed), Barrytown, N.Y. 1844, Henry Delamater Cottage, Rhinebeck, N.Y. 1844, Blandwood (remodeling), Greensboro, N.C. *1844–1845, W. Coventry H. Waddell House, New York. 1844–1852, University of North Carolina (additions and Smith Hall), Chapel Hill. *1845–1846, London Terrace, New York. 1845–1847?, William J. Rotch House, New Bedford, Mass. 1845–1848, Belmead, Powhatan County, Va. *1845–1848, John Cox Stevens House; *1846–1847, Charles A. Davis House; New York. *1846–1847?, Henry A. Kent House, Brooklyn, N.Y. *1846–1848, Walnut Wood, Bridgeport, Conn. *1847–1848, James W. Phillips and Charles C. Taber Houses; New York. *1848, Lewis B. Brown House, Rahway, N.J. *1848, Academy, Rome, N.Y. 1848–1849, County Courthouse, Powhatan, Va. 1848–1849, Malbone, Newport, R.I. 1848–1861, Virginia Military Institute (some buildings destroyed), Lexington, Va. 1849, Cottage Lawn, Oneida, N.Y. 1849–1851, Oakwood, Newark, Ohio. *1850–1852, Belmont, near Belleville, N.J. *1850–1852, Elm Street Arsenal, New York. 1850–1852, Loudoun, Lexington, Ky. 1850–1855, North Carolina Hospital for the Insane (partially destroyed), Raleigh. 1851–1852, Locust Grove (remodeling; with Morse), Poughkeepsie, N.Y. 1851–1852, Winyah, New Rochelle, N.Y. *1851–1853, Yale College Alumni Hall, New Haven. 1851–1854, Hawkwood, Green Springs, Va. 1852–1854, Whitby, Rye, N.Y. 1853–1854, Town Hall and Courthouse (now altered), Bridgeport, Conn. 1853–1863, Edgewater (addition and structures; some destroyed), Barrytown, N.Y. 1854–1855, John Munn House, Utica, N.Y. *1854–1856, Vinewood, Detroit, Mich. 1854–1857, Grace Hill, Brooklyn, N.Y. 1854–1857, Ingleside, Dobbs Ferry, N.Y. *1855–1859, Ericstan, Tarrytown, N.Y. *1856–1859, Chambers Building, Davidson College, N.C. 1858–1860, Castlewood; 1857–1866, Llewellyn Park (gatehouses and other structures; many destroyed); West Orange, N.J. *1858–1859, House of Mansions, New York. 1859–1860, Edward W. Nichols Cottage, West Orange, N.J. 1859–1874, Sans Souci, New Rochelle, N.Y.

BIBLIOGRAPHY

The chief manuscript sources for Alexander J. Davis are in the Davis collections of the Avery Architectural Library, Columbia University, New York; the Metropolitan Museum of Art, New York; the New-York Historical Society; the New York Public Library; and the Henry Francis du Pont Winterthur Museum, Delaware.

ALLCOTT, JOHN V. 1973 "Architect A. J. Davis in North Carolina: His Launching at the University." *North Carolina Architect* 20, nos. 11–12:10–15.

ANDREWS, WAYNE (1947)1978 *Architecture, Ambi-*

tion and Americans: A Social History of American Architecture. Rev. ed. New York: Free Press.

DAVIES, JANE B. 1965 "Alexander J. Davis: Architect of Lyndhurst." *Historic Preservation* 17, no. 2:54–59.

DAVIES, JANE B. 1965 "A. J. Davis' Projects for a Patent Office Building, 1832–1834." *Journal of the Society of Architectural Historians* 24:229–251.

DAVIES, JANE B. 1975 "Blandwood and the Italian Villa Style in America." *Nineteenth Century* 1:11–14.

DAVIES, JANE B. 1975 "Llewellyn Park in West Orange, New Jersey." *Antiques* 107:142–158.

DAVIES, JANE B. 1977 "Gothic Revival Furniture Designs of Alexander J. Davis." *Antiques* 111:1014–1027.

DAVIS, ALEXANDER J. (1838)1980 *Rural Residences.* With an introduction by Jane B. Davies. Reprint. New York: Da Capo.

DONNELL, EDNA 1934–1936 "A. J. Davis and the Gothic Revival." *Metropolitan Museum Studies* 5:183–233.

DOWNING, ANDREW J. (1841)1849 *A Treatise on the Theory and Practice of Landscape Gardening.* New York: Putnam.

DOWNING, ANDREW J. (1842)1873 *Cottage Residences.* New ed. New York: Wiley.

DOWNING, ANDREW J. (1850)1968 *The Architecture of Country Houses.* With an introduction by George B. Tatum. Reprint. New York: Da Capo.

DUNLAP, WILLIAM (1834)1965 *History of the Rise and Progress of the Arts of Design in the United States.* 3 vols. Reprint. New York: Blom.

NEWTON, ROGER HALE 1942 *Town & Davis, Architects: Pioneers in American Revivalist Architecture, 1812–1870.* New York: Columbia University Press.

PIERSON, WILLIAM H., JR. 1970 "The Colonial and Neoclassical Styles." Volume 1 in *American Buildings and Their Architects.* Garden City, N.Y.: Doubleday.

PIERSON, WILLIAM H., JR. 1978 *Technology and the Picturesque: The Corporate and the Early Gothic Styles.* Volume 2A in *American Buildings and Their Architects.* Garden City, N.Y.: Doubleday.

TATUM, GEORGE B. 1950 "Andrew Jackson Downing: Arbiter of American Taste, 1815–1852." Unpublished Ph.D. dissertation, Princeton University, N.J.

DAVIS, ARTHUR JOSEPH

Arthur Joseph Davis (1878–1951), an English architect, was trained at the Ecole des Beaux-Arts in Paris. In 1900, he joined the international practice of the Parisian CHARLES F. MEWÈS. Their work was Beaux-Arts in principle, *Dix-huitième* in taste. The dandified elegance of the Ritz Hotel (1903–1906), the crisp embellishment of Inveresk House (1906–1907), and the rather obvious luxury of the Royal Automobile Club (1908–1911) struck a note of Parisian *chic* new to Edwardian London. The Cunard Building (1914–1916), a grave palazzo on Liverpool's Pier Head, heralded the Italian Renaissance inspiration of Davis's postwar banks and offices in the City of London, notably the Westminster Bank in Threadneedle Street (1922).

ALAN CRAWFORD

WORKS
*1901, New Restaurant and Palm Court, Carlton Hotel; 1903–1906, Ritz Hotel, Piccadilly; 1906–1907, Inveresk House, The Strand; 1908–1911, Royal Automobile Club, Pall Mall; London. 1914–1916, Cunard Building, Pier Head, Liverpool, England. 1922, Westminster Bank, 51 Threadneedle Street; 1925, Morgan Grenfell's Bank, 23 Great Winchester Street; 1928–1929, Hudson's Bay Company Building, 52 Bishopsgate; 1930, Cunard House, 88 Leadenhall Street; London.

BIBLIOGRAPHY
DAVID, ARTHUR J. 1914 "The Architecture of the Liner." *Architectural Review* 35:87–110.

FLEETWOOD-HESKETH, PETER 1971 "The Royal Automobile Club." *Country Life* 150:966–969.

MASSINGBERD, HUGH MONTGOMERY, and WATKIN, DAVID 1980 *The London Ritz: A Social and Architectural History.* London: Aurum.

REILLY, CHARLES 1931 *Representative British Architects of the Present Day.* London: Batsford.

SERVICE, ALASTAIR 1975 "Arthur Davis of Mewès and Davis." Pages 432–442 in Alastair Service (editor), *Edwardian Architecture and Its Origins.* London: Architectural Press.

DAVIS, BRODY, and ASSOCIATES

Founded in New York City in 1952, Davis, Brody, and Associates is a firm of urban architects with a strong commitment to the environmental and social context of their architecture. The firm is best known for housing and university buildings and for their innovative use of brick. The senior partners in the firm are Lewis Davis (1925–) and Samuel M. Brody (1926–).

Davis and Brody's sensitivity to community context can best be seen in their housing projects: Riverbend Houses (1966–1968), East Midtown Plaza (1973–1974), Waterside Houses (1972–1974), and Ruppert Houses (1973–1975), all in New York. Their ability to work within governmental budgets and constraints has resulted in uncommonly handsome subsidized housing. The firm pays particular attention to the site and designs pleasing urban spaces, always respectful of the surrounding neighborhood. A mix of low-rise and high-rise buildings combined with multilevel plazas and outdoor passageways provide a sense of privacy and security while breaking down large masses to establish a sense of scale.

At Riverbend Houses, Davis and Brody introduced large-scale bricks, first developed as an economic alternative to the standard-sized brick. Using a variety of sizes and colors, the firm has transformed brick wall construction into a fully integrated design element.

Using their urban approach, the firm also has designed a number of highly successful suburban and rural academic buildings. The Joseph Ellicott Complex, State University of New York at Buffalo (1970–1975), Buffalo, New York, is a city in the country, using towers with multilevel plazas, pedestrian streets, and overscaled outdoor staircases to make an urban sense of place in an otherwise open landscape. Other academic buildings included the Robert Crown Recreational Center, Hampshire College (1972–1975), Amherst, Massachusetts, and the Massachusetts Institute of Technology Athletic Facility (1975–1981), Cambridge, Massachusetts.

Although both architects are design partners, Davis is responsible for all housing and urban design and Brody is responsible for educational and institutional facilities. Alan Schwartzman is the firm's business partner.

Davis, Brody, and Associates have won over forty-five awards including the Louis H. Sullivan Award for Architecture (1977) and the AIA Thomas Award for Pioneering in Housing (1981).

JANE CAROLAN

WORKS

1966–1968, Riverbend Houses; 1967–1970, Westyards Building; New York. 1967–1976, Long Island University, Brooklyn Center, N.Y. 1968–1970, United States Pavilion, 1970 World's Fair, Osaka, Japan. 1970–1975, Joseph Ellicott Complex, State University of New York, Buffalo. 1971–1973, 100 Williams Street; 1972–1974, Waterside Houses; New York. 1972–1975, Robert Crown Recreational Center, Hampshire College, Amherst, Mass. 1973–1974, East Midtown Plaza; 1973–1975, Ruppert Houses; New York. 1975–1981, Massachusetts Institute of Technology Athletic Facility, Cambridge, Mass. 1976–1981, Biochemical Science Library, Princeton University, N.J. 1977–1981, W. C. Decker Engineering Building, Corning Glass Works, N.Y.

BIBLIOGRAPHY

BRENNER, DOUGLAS 1970 "A Meeting of Minds at Corning." *Architectural Record* 147, May:79–85.
DEAN, ANDREA O. 1975 "Profile: Davis, Brody of New York: The 1975 Firm Award Recipient." *Journal of the American Institute of Architects* 63, no. 5:44–48.
DEAN, ANDREA O. 1976 "Waterside, N.Y.C. Architects: Davis, Brody & Associates." *Journal of the American Institute of Architects* 64, Apr.:46–47.
DEAN, ANDREA O. 1981 "University Arena Finely Crafted of Brick." *Journal of the American Institute of Architects* 69, May:198–200.
DIXON, JOHN MORRIS 1975 "College Town." *Progressive Architecture* 56, Dec.:52–61.
HOYT, CHARLES K. 1976a "Waterside." *Architectural Record* 159, Mar.:119–124.
HOYT, CHARLES K. 1976b "L.I.U. Library: A Final Campus Link." *Architectural Record* 160, July:93–98.
HOYT, CHARLES K. 1981 "New Landmark for M.I.T.: Davis, Brody & Associates' Hockey Rink and Field House." *Architectural Record* 169, Feb.:78–83.
"A New Focus on the Princeton Campus." 1980 *Architectural Record* 167, Mar.:81–88.
STEPHENS, SUZANNE 1975 "Judicious Juxtapositions." *Progressive Architecture* 56, Oct.:86–91.
"To Save a Landmark: A Bold Proposal with Even Bolder Implications." 1980 *Architectural Record* 167, Jan.:121–124.
"A Warehouse Too Handsome to Remain One." 1970 *Architectural Record* 147, May:113–118.
"Where the Twain Have Met." 1970 *Progressive Architecture* 51, Aug.:61–67.

DAVUD AGHA

Davud Agha (?–1598/1599), one of the foremost architects of Ottoman Turkey, was active during the last four decades of the sixteenth century, when wealthy and eager patrons still had access to good building materials. He also had the good fortune to have the great architect SINAN as his mentor and supervisor. Davud Agha succeeded Sinan as the chief architect of the royal court (*bash-* or *ser-mimar*), and proved himself a distinguished successor.

Davud Agha's life is known only through short entries by Ottoman court recorders (or chroniclers) and copies of official correspondence regarding his office. To discuss his professional activities as architect, buildings that are attributed to him or bear his name in their dedicatory inscriptions must be examined. Several meticulously kept "expense books," drawn up during construction of his buildings, have come to light recently, describing the financial side of his activities.

Davud Agha's date and place of birth are not known. A member of the Janissary corps, he was, like his teacher Sinan, conscripted to the Ottoman army at a young age and trained at the court schools, rising to chief architect through the ranks, not by birthright. Davud Agha maintained his links with the military–governmental offices throughout his professional life, which was consistent with the nature of the Ottoman hierarchy. His death is shrouded in mystery. According to the most often repeated version, Davud Agha died of the plague in Istanbul in 1007 H./1598. Another version gives his death date as 1008 H./1599, and the cause as execution for antireligious sentiments.

Davud Agha was active during the reigns of three sultans: Selim II (1566–1574), Murad III (1574–1595) and Mehmed III (1595–1603). The sultan, as the supreme head of the empire, was the ultimate employer of the architect. Davud Agha's name first appears in the Ottoman records as a member of the architect–engineering corps, working under Sinan's supervision. The first mention in 1575 lists him as the "supervisor of waterworks" (*su yollari naziri*) and gives his rank as *chavush*, equivalent to the military rank of sergeant. A later document (1577) records complaints against Davud Chavush for diverting public water to private houses in exchange for gifts. His official post and rank meant that he was moving rapidly to the top since the directorship of water maintenance was an influential post.

In many of the documents Davud is referred to as architect (*mi'mar*), but in some he is also called engineer (*muhendis*). Apparently the duties of the corps of official architects included supervision of the waterways. Davud's responsibilities included the laying and maintaining of water channels and pipes, the building of fountains, and the supplying of water to public buildings. He also repaired certain bridges and street pavements in and around Istanbul.

In 1583 Sinan appointed Davud Chavush to supervise a group of 4070 masons, carpenters, and artisans during the Ottoman campaign against Iran. When Davud returned a year later he resumed his post as the supervisor of waterworks, with additional responsibility for building of a number of rooms and a *hammam* (bath) in the main part of the Topkapi palace in Istanbul.

When Sinan died in 1588, Sultan Murad III appointed Davud as chief architect, with the rank of *agha* (master). Murad had reportedly been very pleased with Davud's work at the Topkapi Palace.

After his promotion Davud Agha assumed the business management of his structures. His clients included members of the Ottoman house, as well as influential and wealthy officials of the administration. He hired workers, determined wages (only large-scale constructions had appointed comptrollers), handled complaints against his staff, and ordered materials. As a result of an edict that "the Iznik factories should manufacture tile revetments for the royal and official structures; only upon their completion production of tiles for private enterprises can resume," he reprimanded a tile and brick factory outside of Istanbul whose products were not to the official specifications. He inspected the possibilities of excavating a canal to connect the River Sakarya (Sangarius) with the Bay of Izmit (Nicomedia) on the Marmara Sea, before the controversial project was abandoned due to financial difficulties and the sultan's change of heart. He also supervised the allocation of land to poor people.

In order to evaluate Davud Agha's accomplishments, his relationship to Sinan must be examined, as well as his relationship to his patrons.

Sinan's greatness rests not on the revolutionary or personal expressions he brought to Ottoman architecture, but on his utilization of classical forms and elements of Ottoman architecture in a manner never to be surpassed. He enforced the public aspect of architecture: the viewers of Sinan's buildings are not challenged by the new, but share in the enjoyment of the classical clarity and monumentality of the structures. Davud Agha, quite definitely Sinan's pupil, continued to build according to existing Ottoman conventions. For example, a mosque is never confused with a mausoleum. The symmetry and scale of parts in a structure remain restful. Unconventional materials and decorative elements, or transfers from other art forms, do not appear in Davud Agha's works as they would in later periods of Ottoman architecture.

Yet, there are differences in the buildings of Sinan and Davud Agha. Sadly, Davud Agha's buildings fall short of his master's great works, as he did not have the same creative energy to search for variations on given forms. This may be the result of the changing political and economic conditions in the Ottoman world of his time, as well as a consequence of the patronage that extended to him.

Sinan's royal patrons, Suleyman the Magnificent and his son Selim II, were greatly interested in and supported monumental architecture. Members of the Ottoman royal house (*vezirs*) and a number of prominent individuals commissioned works from Sinan during most of the sixteenth century. Although Sinan is credited with more than three hundred large-scale structures, undoubtedly other architects, including Davud Agha, carried out most of the actual supervision of the constructions. When Davud Agha succeeded Sinan, the economic and political conditions in the Ottoman Empire were no longer as promising. The empire had begun to lose territory. Campaigns and vast architectural undertakings had drained the treasury. Moreover, the sultans of Davud's era were not as interested in architecture as were Sinan's patrons.

While still under Sinan's supervision, Davud Agha had worked on several areas of the Topkapi Palace. As chief architect, his most celebrated works were also within the precinct of the palace grounds. Unfortunately, his earlier works in the palace proper cannot be identified due to alterations; his later edifices are no longer fully extant. Davud Agha's kiosks and apartments within the Topkapi Palace contributed greatly to his personal style.

Although G. Goodwin (1971, p. 304) speaks of Davud Agha's ". . . tendency towards complication and clutter . . . ," this "style" was an outcome of the patronage extended to him. The Topkapi Palace complex is a vast maze of connected or freestanding apartments and kiosks of one or more rooms, built over a period of four hundred years. Many architects made additions to the complex at different periods with no concern for stylistic or spatial continuity. The concern was for the situation of public, semi-public or private areas, and their functions. The rooms, even reception halls or audience rooms, are surprisingly small and unassuming compared to Western palaces. Aside from functionally specific rooms, the architecture and furnishings were not differentiated until the eighteenth century. A sitting room could comfortably be converted to a sleeping area at night or dining room at meal times. In that respect the architecture of the Topkapi Palace was not very different from other domestic structures. The internal decoration and detail of these rooms were more significant than the structure itself. Therefore, it is not surprising that Davud Agha, a preferred builder of the Ottoman sultans for their residences, concentrated on detail or architectural ornamentation. Moreover, lack of interest or funds deterred him from building edifices of monumental scale.

"Pleasure domes" or small kiosks/pavilions are scattered within the private gardens of the Topkapi Palace. These small structures were mostly used as sitting rooms and for viewing the scenery of the Bosphorus, the Golden Horn, or of the gardens. Two of his praised kiosks, built for Murad III, were known as the Incili Köshk (the kiosk with pearls) and the Yali Köshkü (the waterside kiosk). Sinan Pasha—a man of legendary wealth and cunning appointed as grand *vezir* five times—paid the expenses of both structures, which he presented to his sultan.

The work on the Incili Köshk commenced in 998 H./1590. At the periphery of the Topkapi Palace grounds, abutting the sea walls of Istanbul which dated to the Byzantine period, the kiosk was raised over the ruins of the church of Saint Savior Philantropos. The site must have been selected for two reasons: its commanding view of the Bosphorus and Asian shores, and the presence of a spring. Davud Agha utilized both features in his architectural designs. He situated the kiosk partially on

Davud Agha.
Incili Köshk.
Istanbul, Turkey.
1590–1591

existing walls and partially on enormous exposed stone vaulting on the three foundation piers. In front of the center pier he built an impressive water fountain. The epigraphic panel which gives the date and the names of the sultan, Sinan Pasha, the sponsor, and the architect is above the delicately worked marble fountain façade.

The exposed vaulting system which bears the weight of the kiosk is incorporated into the overall architectural scheme. Sinan had used such a system in one of his Topkapi kiosks, and Davud Agha's successors continued it. The exposed vaulting was supposed to raise the kiosk well above ground level, especially when the terrain is uneven, and to incorporate the foundation section into the kiosk by placing a pool or fountain on this level. The foundation vaulting is the only part of the kiosk still extant.

The kiosk, which consisted of three main and several auxiliary rooms, was demolished in the nineteenth century when the upkeep of the royal palace became too burdensome. According to Sedad H. Eldem (1974–1976), Davud Agha's architectural ingenuity was to compose a symmetrical structure with large windows facing the front view. It consisted of a light and expansive looking main floor over massive yet seemingly elastic foundations. The central room of the kiosk was domed from within and had a pitched roof outside. This was the *divan* (reception) room. There was a large golden ball encrusted with pearls hanging from the dome, hence the name of the kiosk. The proportions of the rooms (3.25 m x 2.90 x 3 m), as reconstructed by Eldem, are indeed intimate. While not an imposing structure, it contained much carefully detailed ornamentation as seen by some tile revetments for the interior saved from demolition. In addition to precious jewels and colorful tiles, the rooms were furnished with expensive textiles. When Murad III arrived at the opening of the Incili Köshk (999H./1591), he honored his chief architect Davud Agha with robes and flattery (Refik, 1924, pp. 59–80).

The *Yali Köshkü* (the kiosk on the shore) on

Davud Agha.
Yali Köshkü.
Istanbul, Turkey.
1592–1593

Davud Agha.
Public Fountain Building
and Mausoleum of Sinan
Pasha.
Istanbul, Turkey.
1593

the Golden Horn, in Istanbul, was at the edge of the palace grounds. Built in 1000–1001 H./1592–1593 to replace an older kiosk known as the Bayezid Köshkü (dating from the last years of the fifteenth century), it has totally disappeared. The kiosk served as a resting place as well as a reception hall. A reconstruction of the kiosk, proposed by Eldem (1974, pp. 173–207), shows a small kiosk, based on a cruciform plan, the center of which was domed with arms covered by vaults. The kiosk had a view of the harbor on three sides; on the south it was linked to the palace proper by a road. The kiosk was surrounded by a deep arcade, which was sheltered by a wide sloping roof. Curtains enveloping the arcade gave the kiosk the appearance of a

large tent. Tile revetments were used on the interior walls. The exterior walls, which could be glimpsed through marble columns of the arcading, were covered with marble panels.

Reception or audience halls with cruciform plans had been a traditional part of Islamic palatial architecture, since the early eighth century. The Ottomans used the plan in an earlier and larger kiosk in Istanbul (1472). Davud Agha applied it to the Yali Köshkü, and it was repeated at the Baghdad Köshkü (1638). The Yali Köshkü and the Baghdad Köshkü share the surrounding arcading which does not appear in earlier buildings.

It was for Sinan Pasha that Davud Agha created his architecturally most complete and satisfying work in 1002 H./1593 in Istanbul. This ensemble, consisting of a *sebil* (public fountain), a *turbe* (mausoleum), and a *dar'ul-hadis* (school), is modest in size, particularly compared to royal building complexes in Istanbul. It lacks a mosque and the large classroom of the school was used as the prayer hall. On the other hand, Sinan Pasha's ensemble is situated at a choice site, on the Ottoman processional road (*Divan yolu*). The *sebil*, a small polygonal building set on a square base that is the showpiece of the ensemble, is practically on the street. The large windows of the *sebil* are covered with elegant bronze grills which display variations of arabesque patterns. Thirsty passers-by would dip their bowls into the marble basins along the inner edge of the windows and presumably give their thanks to Sinan Pasha. The *sebil* from outside has a squat dome, and wide eaves which give the structure a sculpturelike quality.

The *sebil* projects out to the street since its function is directed to the citizens. The mausoleum and the school which accommodate a small number of people are pulled back and separated from the street by a high enclosure wall. The mausoleum looms right behind the *sebil*. It is also a polygonal structure, but larger than the fountain building. The mausoleum—the conventional type of the classical Ottoman architecture—is distinguished by the heavy ornamental cornice where the dome meets the shaft. The horizontal line of the cornice merges with the capitals of the engaged columns that separate the faces of the polygonal shaft. This successful use of architectural elements toward decorative ends increases the sculptural effect of the mausoleum and repeats that of the fountain building.

Davud Agha was a master architect who could lend a distinguishing feature to a small and conventional building through carefully thought out and worked decoration. His sense for enriching surfaces must have developed while he worked on various projects at the Topkapi Palace. His attention to detail sets him apart from other followers of Sinan.

ÜLKÜ U. BATES

WORKS

1585, Mosque and Mausoleum of Kizlar Aghasi Mehmed, Charshamba, Turkey. 1585, Topkapi Palace (throne room? and bathhouse), Istanbul, Turkey. 1588/1589, Selimiye Complex (covered bazaar), Edirne, Turkey. *1590–1591, Kiosk of Pearls, Istanbul, Turkey. 1592–1593, Muradiye Complex (school, hostel, commercial building, and soup kitchen), Manisa, Turkey. *1592–1593, Kiosk on the Shore; (A)1593, Mosque of Nishanji Mehmed Pasha; 1593, Public Fountain Building, Mausoleum, and School of Sinan Pasha; 1595–1599, Mausoleum of Sultan Murad III; 1598, New Queen Mother's Mosque (not completed until 1664); (A)1598, Public Fountain Building, Mausoleum and School of Gazanfer Agha; Istanbul, Turkey.

BIBLIOGRAPHY

ASLANAPA, OKTAY 1971 *Turkish Art and Architecture.* New York and Washington: Praeger.
ELDEM, SEDAD H. 1974–1976 *Koskler ve Kasirlar.* (A Survey of Turkish Kiosks and Pavilions) 2 vols. English summary. Istanbul, Turkey: Devlet Guzel Sanatlar Akademisi.
ERDOĞAN, MUZAFFER 1955 "Mimar Davud Aga'nin Hayati ve Eserleri." (Architect Davud Agha's Life and Works) *Istanbul Universitesi Türkiyat Enstitüsü Türkiyat Mecmuasi* 12:179–204.
GOODWIN, GODFRY 1971 *A History of Ottoman Architecture.* Baltimore: Johns Hopkins University Press.
MAYER, LEO A. 1956 *Islamic Architects and Their Works.* Geneva: Kundig.
REFIK, AHMET 1924 *Alimler ve Sanatkârlar (900–1200).* (Scholars and Artists, 900–1200) Istanbul, Turkey: Kitaphane-i Hilmî.
REFIK, AHMET 1931 *Hicri Onbirinci Asirda Istanbul Hayati.* (Life in Istanbul in the Eleventh Century of the Hijra) Istanbul, Turkey: Devlet Matbaasi.
REFIK, AHMET 1935 *Onaltinci Asirda Istanbul Hayati, 1553–1591.* (Life in Istanbul in the Sixteenth Century) Istanbul, Turkey: Devlet Matbaasi.
REFIK, AHMET 1936 *Turk Mimarlari.* (Turkish Architects) Istanbul, Turkey: Devlet Matbaasi.

DAWES, THOMAS

Colonel Thomas Dawes (1731–1809) of Boston was architect, builder, and legislator. A principal figure in New England Palladianism (1750–1800) Dawes bridged the gap between loyalist designers like PETER HARRISON and the patriot builders of the American Revolution. A member of the American Academy of Arts and Sciences, Dawes influenced Federal architect CHARLES BULFINCH with whom he worked on a number of projects including the Massachusetts State House (1787–1798).

FREDERIC C. DETWILLER

WORKS

1762–1763, Hollis Hall; 1764–1766, Harvard Hall (with Francis Bernard); Cambridge, Mass. *1768, Boston Regiment Artillery Company Gun House; *1772–1773, Brattle Square Church; Boston; *1777, Springfield Armory, Mass. *1800, South Row, Boston.

DAY, FRANK MILES

Frank Miles Day (1861–1918), a native Philadelphian, achieved his greatest professional success in the area of college architecture. Much of his earlier residential and small-scale commercial work displayed an original blend of early Renaissance and English Shavian eclecticism, reflecting the influence of three years of foreign study. But with the commission of Weightman Hall (1902) for the University of Pennsylvania, Day began to concentrate on collegiate design. His firsthand knowledge of English Gothic building, and his experience with local fieldstone construction, prepared him well for his greatest work, Princeton University's Freshman Dormitories and Dining Halls (1909–1917). This acclaimed design brought his firm of Day and Klauder (see CHARLES Z. KLAUDER) commissions at Cornell University and Wellesley College, among others.

PATRICIA HEINTZELMAN KEEBLER

WORKS

1881–1892, Philadelphia Art Club; 1892, Harry K. Cummings House; 1894–1896, Horticultural Hall; 1895–1899, Free Museum of Science and Art; 1896–1899, American Baptist Publishing Society; 1902, Weightman Hall, University of Pennsylvania; Philadelphia. 1909–1917, Freshman Dormitories and Dining Halls, Princeton University, N.J. 1913–1918, Freshman Dormitories (not completed until 1923), Cornell University, Ithaca, N.Y. 1915–1918, Wellesley College (plan), Mass. 1915, University of Delaware (plan), Newark. 1917, University of Colorado (plan), Boulder.

BIBLIOGRAPHY

CRAM, RALPH ADAMS 1904 "The Work of Messrs. Frank Miles Day & Brother." *Architectural Record* 15:397–421.
CRAM, RALPH ADAMS 1918 "Holder and the Halls: An Appreciation." *Architecture* 37, Feb.:29–32.
KEEBLER, PATRICIA 1980 "The Life and Work of Frank Miles Day." Unpublished Ph.D. dissertation, University of Delaware, Newark.
KIDNEY, WALTER C. 1974 *The Architecture of Choice: Eclecticism in America, 1880–1930.* New York: Braziller.

DEANE, THOMAS

Sir Thomas Deane (1792–1871), the son of a builder in Cork, founded one of the most successful nineteenth-century Irish architectural firms. He began practicing at the age of fourteen in 1806, and in 1811 won his first major commission for the Cork Commercial buildings (1811–1813) in a competition against the London architect WILLIAM WILKINS. In the 1820s and 1830s, Deane became the principal architect and builder in Cork, where he executed a number of banks and other civic structures in a conventional but competent neoclassical style. His one Gothic work of this period, Dromore Castle (1831–1836) in Kenmare, was a rambling castellated neo-Tudor pile. The firm's later Gothic work of the 1840s and 1850s was executed with his son THOMAS N. DEANE AND BENJAMIN WOODWARD with whom Deane formed a partnership in 1851. After this Deane ceased to play an active role in the firm. Involved in local politics he was elected high sheriff (Mayor) of Cork in 1815 and 1830, at which time he was knighted for his public services.

EVE M. BLAU

WORKS

1806–1822, Naval Dockyard and Supply Depot, Haulbowline Island, Ireland. 1811–1813, Cork Commercial buildings; *1824, Old Savings Bank; Cork, Ireland. 1831–1836, Dromore Castle, Kenmare, Ireland. 1832–1835, County Court House portico; 1836–1840, Bank of Ireland; 1840–1842, New Savings Bank; Cork, Ireland.

BIBLIOGRAPHY

BENCE-JONES, MARK 1967 "Old Towns Revisited: Cork II—Two Pairs of Architect Brothers." *Country Life* 142:306–309.
BLAU, EVE M. 1979 "The Earliest Work of Deane and Woodward." *Architectura* 9:170–192.
BLAU, EVE M. 1981 *Ruskinian Gothic: The Architecture of Deane and Woodward, 1845–1861.* Princeton, N.J.: Princeton University Press.
COLEMAN, JAMES 1915 "Sir Thomas Deane, P.R.H.A." *Journal of the Cork Historical and Archaeological Society* 21:180–186.
MCNAMARA, T. F. 1960 "The Architecture of Cork, 1700–1900." *Yearbook of the Royal Institute of the Architects of Ireland* 1960:15–39.
"Sir Thomas Deane, Architect." 1871 *Builder* 29:804.

DEANE and WOODWARD

The Irish firm of Deane and Woodward occupies an important position in the Gothic revival in Victorian England. The first significant exponents of JOHN RUSKIN's precepts, the firm was responsible for shaping a Ruskinian Gothic style in the 1850s that was distinct both in form and theoretical basis from the concurrently evolving High Victorian Gothic.

The firm was an outgrowth of the practice of THOMAS DEANE. Benjamin Woodward (1816–1861) the designer of the firm's Ruskinian masterpieces of the 1850s, entered Deane's office in 1845. Born in Tullamore, Woodward trained as a civil engineer, but a passionate interest in medieval architecture led him to change professions. Woodward's earnest commitment to his art as well as his study of Irish medieval architecture and the work of the Gothic Revivalists—A. M. N. PUGIN in particular—are reflected in the firm's two major Gothic structures of the 1840s: Queen's College, Cork (1846–1849) and the Killarney Lunatic Asylum (1847–1850).

In 1850, Thomas Newenham Deane (1828–1899), born in Cork and educated at Trinity College, Dublin, joined his father's practice. A year later both he and Woodward were made partners.

Trinity College Museum (1852–1857), Dublin, the first major building of the new partnership, secured the reputation of this firm. The embodiment of Ruskin's richly embellished, monumental, symmetrical, classicizing formal ideal, the museum was acknowledged by Ruskin as the first significant expression of his architectural principles, and established the fundamental character of Ruskinian Gothic.

An important aspect of Deane and Woodward's architecture was the independent role assigned the decorative carvers, a practice first adopted by the firm at Trinity. The elaborate naturalistic and richly associational carving, a striking feature of all their buildings, was the work of the Irish stonecarvers, James and John O'Shea. These craftsmen, following Ruskin's dicta, designed the details of the ornament and to a certain extent determined their subjects.

The Oxford Museum (1855–1861), Deane and Woodward's most famous building and the first secular Gothic building of public character in Victorian England since the Houses of Parliament (1836–1866), created a new image of monumental secular Gothic architecture that persisted for more than two decades. Here Ruskin was an active participant in the design and planning of the building's decorative scheme.

Deane and Woodward did a number of other buildings in Oxford, most notably the Oxford Union (1857), with its famous ill-fated murals by the pre-Raphaelites.

The firm also made significant contributions in civic, commercial, and domestic architecture. The Crown Life Assurance Company Office (1855–

Deane and Woodward.
Oxford Museum.
London.
1855–1861

1857) and Government Offices Competition design (1857) extended Ruskin's influence to London, and established a Ruskinian urban mode characterized by regular classicizing plans, broad simplified forms, Italian Gothic detail, and an emphasis on structural polychromy and elaborate sculptural ornament. The firm's houses of the late 1850s and the Kildare Street Club in Dublin (1858–1861) likewise constitute a Ruskinian domestic mode in the richness of the decoration, the emphasis on craft and materials, the tendency toward simple contained masses, and the interest in window design.

The partnership ended in 1861 with Woodward's death, but Deane continued to practice until his death, mainly in Dublin and Oxford. In 1878 he formed a partnership with his son Thomas Manly Deane who took over the practice.

EVE M. BLAU

WORKS

1846–1849, Queen's College, Cork, Ireland. 1847–1850, Killarney Lunatic Asylum, Ireland. 1852–1857, Trinity College Museum, Dublin. *1855–1857, Crown Life Assurance Company Office, London. 1855–1857, Dundrum Police Court and Barracks, Dublin. 1855–1861, Oxford Museum. *1856–1858, Llys Dulas, Anglesey, Wales. *1856–1858, Saint Anne's Parochial Schools, Dublin. 1857, Government Offices Competition Design, London. 1857, Oxford Union. 1857–1859, Dundrum Schools, Dublin. 1857–1859, Middleton Hall, Oxford. 1858–?, Brownsbarn, Thomastown, Ireland. 1858–?, Clontra; 1858–?, Glandore; County Dublin. 1858–1859, Saint Austin's Abbey, County Carlow, Ireland. 1858–1861, Kildare Street Club, Dublin. 1858–1863, Kilkenny Castle (extensive alterations), Ireland. *1859–1861, 15 Upper Philmore Gardens, London. 1860–1862, Trinity College Library, Dublin.

BIBLIOGRAPHY

ACLAND, HENRY, and RUSKIN, JOHN 1859 *The Oxford Museum*. London: Smith, Elder.
BLAU, EVE 1981 *Ruskinian Gothic: The Architecture of Deane and Woodward, 1845–1861*. Princeton, N.J.: Princeton University Press.
COOK, E. T., and WEDDERBURN, ALEXANDER (editors) 1903–1912 *The Works of John Ruskin*. 39 vols. London: George Allen.
CURRAN, C. P. 1940 "Benjamin Woodward, Ruskin, and the O'Sheas." *Studies* 29:255–268.
EASTLAKE, CHARLES (1872)1970 *A History of the Gothic Revival*. Reprint. New York: Humanities Press.
FERRIDAY, PETER 1962 "The Oxford Museum." *Architectural Review* 132:409–416.
HERSEY, GEORGE L. 1972 *High Victorian Gothic: A Study in Associationism*. Baltimore: Johns Hopkins University Press.
HITCHCOCK, H. R. (1954)1972 "Ruskin or Butterfield: Victorian Gothic at the Mid-century." Chapter 17 in *Early Victorian Architecture in Britain*. Reprint. New York: Da Capo.
MUTHESIUS, STEFAN 1972 *The High Victorian Movement in Architecture 1850–1870*. London: Routledge.
RICHARDSON, DOUGLAS 1978 *Gothic Revival Architecture in Ireland*. New York: Garland.

DE ANGELIS, GIULIO

Giulio De Angelis (1850–1906) was born in Rome and studied architecture in Perugia. After his return to Rome, he became director of the Regional Office for the Preservation of Historic Monuments. In this position, he was deeply involved in the restoration of historic Roman buildings, a task of great importance to Italian nationalism in the newly unified state.

In his own practice, De Angelis specialized in *palazzine*—two- or three-story single family dwellings in the newly developing areas on the periphery of the old city—and in department stores and shopping galleries in the old center. In both types of buildings, De Angelis employed the heavy blocky forms of the Renaissance palazzo, but he opened them up to the street through extensive use of iron and glass. His famous I Grandi Magazzini Boccioni (1886, now La Rinascente), the first department store in Rome, displayed its goods in glassed arches three stories high. In the Palazzo Chauvet (1887) and at Via delle Muratte (1895), De Angelis employed exterior iron columns with glass behind them, combining this wall treatment in the Via delle Muratte with exterior fresco decorations in floral patterns that prefigured Art Nouveau work. Some of the *palazzine* achieved an analogous effect of openness through multistory iron balconies. The interiors of De Angelis's larger buildings were also exceptionally open. The Magazzini Boccioni adapted an interior space similar to that of the Bon Marché in Paris—an interior well, surrounded by shopping balconies—to a much more monumental scale, in keeping with its Renaissance and baroque context. In his conception of the department store and the shopping gallery, De Angelis was also influenced by the Galleria Vittorio Emanuele II, built in Milan from 1863–1867 by GIUSEPPE MENGONI. De Angelis's work was closely related to that of three contemporary Roman architects, RAFFAELE CANEVARI, GIULIO PODESTI, and Raffaele Ojetti.

BARBARA MILLER LANE

WORKS

1876, Palazzini Bonghi; 1876, Palazzini, via Magenta; 1876, Palazzini, via dei Mille; 1883, Palazzo and Galleria Sciarra, via Minghetti; *1885, Villini, via Nicola Fabrizi; 1886, I Grandi Magazzini Boccioni (now La Rinascente); 1887, Palazzo Chauvet, via Due Macelli; 1895, Palazzo, via Minghetti, via delle Muratte, and via delle Vergini; 1899, Palazzina Borghese, via Ripetta and via Tomacelli; Rome. n.d., Teatro nuovo Morlacchi, Perugia, Italy.

BIBLIOGRAPHY

ACCASTO, GIANNI; FRATICELLI, VANNA; and NICOLINI, RENATO c.1973 *L'architettura di Roma capitale: 1890–1970.* Rome: Golem.
GUTTRY, IRENE DE 1978 *Giuda di Roma moderna dal 1870 ad oggi.* Rome: De Luca.
MEEKS, CARROLL L. V. 1966 *Italian Architecture: 1750–1914.* New Haven: Yale University Press.
PAOLIS, SAVERIO DE, and RAVAGLIOLI, ARMANDO 1971 *La Terza Roma.* Rome: Palombi.
PORTOGHESI, PAOLO 1968 *L'eclettismo a Roma: 1870–1922.* Rome: De Luca.

DE BAUDOT, ANATOLE

See BAUDOT, ANATOLE DE.

DE BAZEL, K. F. C. DE

See BAZEL, K. F. C. DE.

DE BODT, JEAN

Jean de Bodt (1670–1745) was born in Paris, the son of the Mecklenburg nobleman Andreas von Bodt. On the strength of a talent for mathematics, drawing, and architecture which de Bodt evinced at an early age, FRANÇOIS BLONDEL is reputed to have given him private instruction. After the revocation of the Edict of Nantes (1685), de Bodt, a Huguenot, fled to Holland. There, he entered the service of William of Orange (1687–1688) who appointed him captain of artillery and, upon his accession to the English throne (1689), took him to England. As captain of artillery and a member of the Corps of Engineers, de Bodt took part in William's campaigns. In 1698/1699, he moved to Berlin, having entered the service of the Elector of Brandenburg, soon to be King Frederick I of Prussia. The king gave him a guard company and put him in charge of all royal building and, in 1706, promoted him to chief of artillery. In 1715, Frederick's successor, Frederick William I, appointed him major general and commandant of the city of Wesel, on the Rhine, where he now moved to oversee the construction of the fortifications. In 1728, disappointed in the service of Prussia, he transferred to the court of Saxony in Dresden, where he became chief of the Saxonian Corps of Engineers, lieutenant general and superintendent of military and civil construction, and, in 1734, commandant of Dresden-Neustadt. In 1741, he became deputy-governor of Dresden.

In keeping with his mathematical and theoretical talents, the officer-architect was successful both as a military and civil engineer and as a builder. The collection of his plans preserved in Dresden attests to his wide-ranging activities in both areas. Plans for Whitehall and for a home for disabled veterans (Greenwich?) survive from his English service. In Brandenburg, Prussia, he was involved in many of the numerous buildings and projects of the young kingdom. Among these are his major works in military architecture: the Zeughaus (arsenal) in Berlin, which had been begun by JOHANN ARNOLD NERING and was continued by ANDREAS SCHLÜTER; the fort in Wesel with the Berliner Tor (Berlin Gate) as the outstanding artistic edifice of the city. Designs for a home for disabled veterans; expert reports and projects for the fortifications of Putzig near Danzig (1704), Berlin (1708), and Magdeburg (1711); and tours of inspection to the Prussian forts round out this area of his activities. The Fortuna Portal of the *Stadtschloss* (town residence) in Potsdam was de Bodt's most important civilian building for the court. In addition, he erected a number of private dwellings and commercial buildings in Berlin on the west side of the

Stechbahn, and the Schwerin House (1700–1702) and the Rademacher House (1701–1704). In the years between 1700 and 1714, four East Prussian country seats were built after his designs. Around 1709, he drew up designs for the eastern wing of Wentworth Castle in Stainborough Park, Yorkshire, for Thomas Wentworth, third Lord Raby, the English minister at the Prussian court. In 1713, the tower of the parochial church in Berlin was built after his design. De Bodt's most ambitious Berlin project was his design for a cathedral next to the palace (1712–1713) based on a Greek-cross plan with a double tower façade intended as a sermon hall. This complex was combined with an adjoining memorial hall for the Brandenburg-Prussian rulers, surmounted by a high drum and steeply curved dome of towerlike proportions. In Saxony, De Bodt's tasks consisted of fortifications and military buildings. As general superintendent of Saxony's civilian architecture, he was in charge of Matthäus Daniel Pöppelmann, Zacharias Longuelune, and Johann Christoph Knöffel. He participated with the first two in building the Japanese Palace, for the eastern front of which he designed the central façade and the entrance hall (1730). His magnificent designs for the expansion of the Zwinger and for a new royal residence in Dresden remained on paper.

With his roots in the school of Sebastian le Prestre de Vauban and Blondel, de Bodt remained close to the tradition of the French academy in his use of columnar orders, his composition and proportioning of façades, and his stylistic detailing. He selected the motifs for his designs from among the chief examples of contemporary European architecture, applying them skillfully to the task at hand: the plans for the Home for Disabled Veterans combine Libéral Bruant's Parisian Maison des Invalides with Christopher Wren's Hospital plans; an Italian-English tower motif appears on the Potsdam Fortuna Portal but with French proportions; the Berlin cathedral project combines motifs from Wren's Saint Paul's, the Dome des Invalides by Jules Hardouin Mansart, and Gianlorenzo Bernini's towers for St. Peter's in Rome; the plans of the palace for the Roman Catholic court in Dresden appear as an academic synthesis of French palace architecture (Louvre, Versailles) and Italian palazzo architecture (the Louvre project by Bernini, the Palazzo Madama by Filippo Juvarra in Turin). The importance of de Bodt consists in his having spread the classical baroque of the French academy to Prussia and Saxony.

Fritz-Eugen Keller
Translated from German by
Beverley R. Placzek

WORKS

1699–1710, Zeughaus, Berlin. *1700–1701, Fortuna Portal, City Palace, Potsdam, Germany. 1700–1702, Schwerin House; 1701–1704, Rademacher House; Berlin. *1709–1714, Friedrichstein Castle; 1710–1716, Dönhoffstaedt Castle; East Prussia. 1713, Parochial Church (tower), Berlin. 1713–1728, Fortifications and Military Buildings; 1718–1722, Berlin Gate; Wesel, Rhineland, Germany. c.1730, Japanese Palace (central façade and entrance hall), Dresden, Germany. 1734–1736, Citadel (inner gate and spring-house), Königstein, Saxony, Germany.

BIBLIOGRAPHY

Du Colombier, Pierre 1956 Volume 1, pages 101–108, 113–116, 118–121 in *L'Architecture française en Allemagne au XVIIIe siècle*. Paris: Presses Universitaires de France.
Harris, John 1961 "Bodt and Stainborough." *Architectural Review* 130, no. 773:34–35.
Hempel, Eberhard 1965 *Baroque Art and Architecture in Central Europe*. Harmondsworth, England: Penguin.
Löffler, Fritz (1955)1966 *Das alte Dresden*. 5th ed. Frankfort: Weidlich.
Lorck, Carl von (1933)1972 Pages 50–56, 102–110 in *Landschlösser und Guthäuser in Ost- und Westpreussen*. 4th ed. Frankfurt: Weidlich. Originally published with the title *Herrenhäuser Ostpreussens*.
Schiedlausky, Günther 1942 *Martin Grünberg*. Burg bei Magdeburg, Germany: Hopfer.
Sponsel, Jean Louis 1924 *Der Zwinger, die Hoffeste und die Schlossbaupläne zu Dresden*. Dresden, Germany: Stengel.
Steche, Rudolf 1891 *Pläne für das Zenghaus und ein königliches Marstallgebäude in Berlin. Aus dem Nachlass des Generals de Bodt*. Berlin.

DE BROSSE, SALOMON

Salomon de Brosse (c.1571–1626) was undoubtedly a very important architect in early seventeenth-century France, yet it is difficult to appreciate his significance because most of his buildings are lost and none of the surviving ones remains unaltered. Documents, drawings (no working ones and none certainly attributable to him), descriptions, and engravings (often inaccurate) are some help, but they cannot give a balanced view, and much remains conjectural.

He was born around 1571, presumably at Verneuil-sur-Oise where his father Jehan worked for Anne d'Este and Jacques de Savoie from 1575 onward on the château (begun 1558). His mother was a daughter of Jacques I Androuet du Cerceau, (see Du Cerceau Family), celebrated architectural engraver, and both families, like many of their circle, were Protestants. Salomon was no doubt first trained at Verneuil, then after his father's death (c.1585) worked for his uncle, Jacques II Androuet du Cerceau. He married (c.1592) Florence Métivier, through whom he became connected with Charles Du Ry (see DU RY FAMILY), later his principal assistant.

We have no record of de Brosse at work until 1597, when, aged twenty-seven, he was with his uncle at the château of Montceaux, near Meaux. This late start may be attributable to the religious war of the Ligue in the 1580s; there were few opportunities for architects until after the accession of Henry IV in 1589. Thenceforward his career was short, twenty-eight years, during the last four of which he was semiretired.

In 1600 de Brosse was back at Verneuil to complete the château, now owned by Henri IV's mistress, Henriette d'Entragues. Verneuil was demolished in 1734, but one entrance gate, evidently de Brosse's work, survived until World War II. Its style showed the influence of his grandfather's designs and of engravings in GIACOMO BAROZZI DA VIGNOLA's *Architettura,* a combination persisting almost throughout his career.

Verneuil, built on a courtyard plan (main block, wings, closing screen, entrance pavilion, and pavilions at the four angles) in both plan and elevation was to have a considerable influence on de Brosse.

Next, de Brosse returned to Montceaux (begun 1547, continued 1597–1599), which since 1601 had belonged to Marie de Medicis, Henri IV's queen. He was officially in charge of its completion (1608–c.1615). Montceaux was destroyed during the French Revolution, but among surviving fragments is the ruin of de Brosse's entrance pavilion, with a fine oval chapel on its upper floor. His forecourt chapel survives, its façade miraculously intact. Though generally deriving from an engraved design by SEBASTIANO SERLIO, this façade so specifically resembles the Vignolesque church at Capranica, Italy, that mere coincidence is improbable. De Brosse never went to Italy, but we must assume his knowledge of drawings brought back by traveling contemporaries.

At various times de Brosse worked on town architecture, in 1609 providing elevations, some of which, though much modified, survive, for the "ideal" town of Henrichemont, near Bourges, founded by the duc de Sully (1605). Between 1608 and 1618, he enlarged several Paris hôtels (large townhouses), including the hôtels de Soissons (1611–1612), de Bouillon (1612–?), and Begnine-Bernard (1615). All have now disappeared, but at the hôtels de Soissons and Bernard he built Vignolesque *portes cochères* (entrance portals) that became celebrated and were recorded in drawings or engravings.

In about 1611–1612 de Brosse provided designs for the château of Blérancourt in Picardy (1611/1612–c.1619), the work being carried out Charles Du Ry. Here he had a knowledgeable and demanding patron, Charlotte de Vieuxpont, wife of the owner, Bernard Potier, wealthy descendant of a family of merchant furriers. Wealthy herself, Charlotte was a bluestocking; she had probably traveled in Italy, certainly admired Vignola, and apparently collected contemporary French and sixteenth-century Italian architectural drawings, all matters of significance for de Brosse. The contracts for Blérancourt were unusually exigent regarding "correct" classical detail.

The château was designed on a large, compact block plan, basically H-shaped, but with the side elevations recessed in the center so that angle pavilions were formed. The block plan, ultimately Italian in origin, and then known in France chiefly through Serlio's and du Cerceau's engravings, had been used for châteaux in the late sixteenth and early seventeenth centuries, but never on the scale or with the sophistication of Blérancourt. Moreover, to stress classical aspirations, Blérancourt was expensively built entirely of stone, including its gates and detached pavilions.

Surviving detail drawings of the château show the elevations to have been much influenced by the classicist PIERRE LESCOT's façade on the Square Court of the Louvre in Paris (begun 1546) and scarcely at all, except in the outer gate, by the exuberant mannerism of the du Cerceau tradition. In plan and elevation, Blérancourt was crucial to the subsequent development of the block château type, notably in the work of FRANÇOIS MANSART.

After the main château was destroyed in World War I, a part of the ground floor of the southeast pavilion was rebuilt to house the Musée Franco-Américain. Two moat pavilions and three entrance gates survive, all having marked Vignolesque features.

At Coulommiers-en-Brie (1613), his next important château, for the Duchesse de Longueville, de Brosse reverted to the Verneuil-type plan. The entire exterior of the building was rusticated; this and the design of the circular entrance pavilion can be seen as a trial run for the Luxembourg Palace in Paris, a supposition strengthened by the intimacy of the duchess and Marie de Medicis. De Brosse's original designs for Coulommiers were engraved by Jean Marot (1655). The Coulommiers entrance pavilion clearly derived from the Valois Mausoleum at Saint-Denis, designed by JEAN BULLANT (based on a project by FRANCESCO PRIMATICCIO in the 1560s), where another of de Brosse's uncles, Baptiste du Cerceau, had been in charge (1582–1585). The courtyard façades were as elaborate as

De Brosse.
Luxembourg Palace.
Paris.
c.1614–?

the exterior was severe, and, like Blérancourt, showed the influence of Lescot's Louvre.

Charles Du Ry, left in charge of the work at Coulommiers, modified the design somewhat, and by 1631 the entrance pavilion and screen were abandoned and replaced by two small pavilions and a balustrade designed by François Mansart. In the interior of the main block, the great staircase, rising through two floors round a large vaulted vestibule, was of an unusual design; some if not all of its supporting piers were replaced by twin female caryatids of considerable size. The huge château, never really completed, was pulled down in 1738. Almost nothing survives save the ruins of curved arcades in the courtyard which linked the main block to the wings, a motif which probably inspired the similar arrangement by Mansart in his courtyard façade at Blois (1635–1638).

After a public competition, de Brosse was commissioned to build the Paris palace of the Queen-Regent, Marie de Medicis (begun c.1614). In the Luxembourg, the queen desired a reminder of her Florentine girlhood home, the Medicis' Pitti Palace. However, the rustication of the whole building and de Brosse's incorporation into it of some elements taken directly from BARTOLOMMEO AMMANNATI'S work at the Pitti (1560–1577) were the only concessions to this requirement.

The main block at the Luxembourg has the same plan as Blérancourt, but here it forms part of a Verneuil–Coulommiers-type courtyard arrangement, unsatisfactorily so because the double pavilions of this block and the single ones terminating the wings cause a curious asymmetry in the side elevations. Originally, the palace was more compact. In the nineteenth century, two more pavilions were added to the main block and the garden front was extended southward, de Brosse's exterior

being reproduced but his interior completely altered. Unfortunately, since it is that rarity, a building by de Brosse actually still standing, the palace was more than once altered at various times in varying degrees; the exterior proportions have been much spoiled and almost nothing survives of de Brosse's interior.

The part of the Luxembourg which gives us the best idea of de Brosse's achievement are the entrance and wing pavilions. (The screen, originally solid, was pierced with arcades in the early nineteenth century.) In the entrance pavilion, the three superimposed circular spaces are articulated with the same skill and imagination as in the Montceaux entrance chapel and the design for the Coulommiers entrance pavilion.

Before the Luxembourg was completed, de Brosse was dismissed from the work, which, in 1624, was taken over by Marin de La Vallée. De Brosse, unwisely, had been both architect and contractor, an error which led him into severe financial difficulties. In April 1621, Rubens's agent wrote that he feared proceedings against de Brosse for bad technical advice, bad financial management, and unwarranted delay in the building program. Certainly by this time de Brosse was sick and inadequately supervising the execution of his projects.

In Paris he also built a new Hall for the Palais de Justice (begun 1618), which survives, though with some later alterations. He also provided a classical west front for the church of Saint-Gervais (begun 1616). This proved to be a successful and influential solution, not before achieved in France, to the problem of how to combine a high, Gothic nave with a classical façade. The result, fortunately, can still be seen. It combines two prototypes: the Roman type of church façade deriving from Vignola's design for the Gesù in Rome (c.1568) and the three-tier type of frontispiece introduced by PHILIBERT DELORME at the château of Anet (before 1550).

After 1618, de Brosse's health appears to have deteriorated further, though he was still making designs for various commissions, one being to provide his coreligionists with a new place of worship—a *temple* at Charenton, near Paris (1623). Based on VITRUVIUS's description of a basilica, the *temple* later influenced both Reformed Church and synagogue architecture in Europe.

De Brosse's outstanding late work was the completion of the Palais du Parlement in Rennes, Brittany (now the Palais de Justice), begun in 1609 by Germain Gaultier. De Brosse visited Rennes in August 1618, remaining for two weeks. He never returned and left Gaultier to execute his designs, which must have been familiar to the young François Mansart, Gaultier's brother-in-law, who worked for a time in Rennes.

The removal, in the eighteenth century, of the exterior steps and terrace, seen in earlier engravings, has unbalanced the horizontal composition of de Brosse's façade, but it remains extremely impressive. Perhaps his most advanced, classical, and sophisticated work, it is influenced in form by the *aile de la belle cheminée* (c.1568; usually attributed to Primaticcio) at Fontainebleau and in detail by Vignola, but in character it is unmistakably French.

The often exuberant influence of the du Cerceau circle in which de Brosse was born and raised was modified in his work by that of de L'Orme, Lescot, and, most important, by Vignola's "learned" mannerisms. De Brosse was no innovator in planning, though he was skillful with small, centralized spaces; his interest appears to have been in the composition and articulation of his elevations. The style which he evolved is chiefly important for the influence it had on the development of François Mansart, the outstanding architect of the next generation.

ROSALYS COOPE

WORKS

*1600–1608, Château of Verneuil (completion), Oise, France *1608–c.1615, Château of Montceaux (completion), Seine-et-Marne, France. *1611–1612, Hôtel de Soissons (enlargement), Paris. *c.1611/1612–c.1619, Château of Blérancourt, Aisne, France. *1612–?, Hôtel de Bouillon (enlargement), Paris. *1613, Château of Coulommiers, Seine-et-Marne, France. c.1614–?, Luxembourg Palace (later altered); *1615, Hôtel Bégnine-Bernard (enlargement); 1616, Saint-Gervais (west front); 1618–?, Salle des Pas Perdus, Palais de Justice; Paris. 1618, Palais du Parlement (principal front and rooms; now Palais de Justice), Rennes, France. *1623, Temple, Charenton, France.

BIBLIOGRAPHY

ANDROUET DU CERCEAU, JACQUES (1559)1965 *Les trois livres d'architecture.* Reprint. Ridgewood, N.J.: Gregg.

Arts de l'Ouest: études et documents. 1979 Rennes, France: Université de Haute Bretagne. Includes articles by A. Mussat, F. Loyer, F. Hamon.

BLOMFIELD, REGINALD 1911 *A History of French Architecture, from the Reign of Charles VII till the Death of Mazarin.* London: Bell.

BLUNT, ANTHONY (1953)1970 *Art and Architecture in France 1500–1700.* 2d ed. Baltimore: Penguin.

COOPE, ROSALYS 1972 *Salomon de Brosse and the Development of the Classical Style in French Architecture from 1565 to 1630.* London: Zwemmer; University Park: Pennsylvania State University Press.

MAROT, JEAN (1655)1969 *Recueil des plans, profils et élévations de plusiers palais, châteaux, églises, sépultures, grotes et hostels bâtis dans Paris.* Facsimile ed. Farnborough, England: Gregg.

PANNIER, JACQUES 1911 *Un architecte français au commencement du XVIIe siècle, Salomon de Brosse.* Paris: Eggimann.

VIGNOLA, GIACOMO BAROZZI 1562 *Regola delle cinque ordini d'architettura.* Rome.

DE CARLO, GIANCARLO

Giancarlo De Carlo (1919–), architect, planner, and writer, born in Genoa, and professor of architecture at the University of Venice, is one of the major post-World War II architects in Italy. Through participation in Team 10 during the final sessions of the Congrès Internationaux d'Architecture Moderne (CIAM); De Carlo developed a range of international professional contacts which, when coupled with the respect engendered by his tenaciously stated and argued views, resulted in many teaching and lecture appointments abroad. De Carlo developed a practice that was equally divided between planning and architecture, a distinction he would not recognize. In addition, he published expositions of work underway, including the analyses that led to recommendations for implementation, and he edits an architectural journal, *Spazio e Società,* dedicated to the view that any physical intervention must be studied in its largest context and in conjunction with the intended inhabitants or users. In 1975, De Carlo formed an International Laboratory of Architecture and Urban Design in Urbino which each fall gathers a group of students and faculty from one architecture school in each of seven countries (Belgium, Italy, Norway, Spain, Switzerland, United States, and Yugoslavia) to examine common problems in the field.

Notable among his many master plans and buildings are workers' housing in the Comasina

Quarter (1953–1955) and the Feltre Quarter (1957–1958) of Milan; a summer camp for children in Riccione (1963); and university buildings in Urbino. De Carlo sees regional planning as inseparable from architecture. He also argues that although there can be no successful architectural or planning decisions that omit social, political, and economic considerations, the field should not and cannot rely solely on technologically sound solutions, but must renew itself by posing formal hypotheses that intersect with social and political theory. De Carlo's work shows an early adherence to Italian rationalism that gives way to experimentation with forms of Corbusian (see LE CORBUSIER) origin, but with a heightened concern for the relationship between use and form.

HENRY A. MILLON

WORKS

1953–1955, Housing Units, Comasina Quarter; 1957–1958, Housing Units, Feltre Quarter; Milan. 1962–1965, 1973–1979, Residential Colleges, Urbino University, Italy. 1963, Summer Camp, Riccione, Italy. 1966–1968, Law School, Urbino University; 1967–1969, Pineta Housing; 1968–1976, School of Education, Urbino University; Urbino, Italy. 1971–1974, Bologna Master Plan, Italy. 1971–1974, Milan Master Plan. 1971–1974, Padua Master Plan, Italy. 1971–1974, Palermo Master Plan, Italy. 1971–1974, Pavia Master Plan, Italy. 1971–1974, Rimini Master Plan, Italy. 1971–1974, Siena Master Plan, Italy. 1971–1974, Villaggio Matteotti, Terni, Italy. 1972–1979, Municipal Art School (incomplete), Urbino, Italy. 1976, Nuovo Villaggio Matteotti, Terni, Italy.

BIBLIOGRAPHY

CARLO, GIANCARLO DE 1947 *William Morris*. Milan: Il Balcone.
CARLO, GIANCARLO DE 1965 *Questioni di Architettura e urbanistica*. Urbino, Italy:
CARLO, GIANCARLO DE (1966)1970 *Urbino: The History of a City and Plans for its Development*. Cambridge, Mass.: M.I.T. Originally published in Italian.
CARLO, GIANCARLO DE 1968 *Pianificazione e disegno delle università*. Rome: Universitarie italiane.
COLOMBO, CESARE 1964 *Giancarlo De Carlo*. Milan: Bassoli.
NICOLINI, PIERLUIGI 1978 "Conversazione su Urbino." *Lotus International* no. 18:4–41.

DE CAUS, ISAAC

Isaac de Caus (?–c.1656) was a garden designer, hydraulic engineer, and architect who worked with INIGO JONES in the 1620s and 1630s. Of French birth, he was the son or nephew of Salomon de Caus, likewise a designer of gardens and waterworks, and stayed in England after Salomon left the employment of the English royal family in 1612, becoming naturalized in 1634. His career is somewhat obscure and he is remembered primarily in connection with the celebrated south front of Wilton House. De Caus was executive architect, but he had the "advice and approbation of Mr Jones" (Aubrey, 1847). The south range was damaged by fire in 1647/1648 and was rebuilt by JOHN WEBB, again with Jones's advice; it is very difficult to determine the creative shares of the three men in the present structure. De Caus published *Nouvelle invention de lever l'eau. . .* in 1644 (English translation in *New and Rare Inventions of Water-Works. . . ,* 1659) and a set of engravings entitled *Wilton Garden* in about 1645.

IAN CHILVERS

WORKS

*1623–1624, Grotto, Banqueting House, Whitehall, London. (A)c.1630, Grotto, Woburn Abbey, Bedfordshire, England. 1630s, Grotto (surviving façade incorporated in the Park School House), Wilton House, Wiltshire, England. *1630–1633, Grotto, Somerset House, London. 1636, Wilton House (south front), Wiltshire, England.

BIBLIOGRAPHY

AUBREY, JOHN (1847)1969 *The Natural History of Wiltshire*. Edited by John Britton. Reprint. New York: Kelley.
COLVIN, HOWARD 1955 "The South Front of Wilton House." *Archaeological Journal* 111:181–190.
HARRIS, JOHN; ORGEL, STEPHEN; and STRONG, ROY 1973 *The King's Arcadia: Inigo Jones and the Stuart Court*. London: Arts Council of Great Britain.
HARRIS, JOHN, and TAIT, A. A. 1979 *Catalogue of the Drawings by Inigo Jones, John Webb and Isaac de Caus at Worcester College, Oxford*. Oxford: Clarendon Press.
LEES-MILNE, JAMES 1953 *The Age of Inigo Jones*. London: Batsford.
PEVSNER, NIKOLAUS (1963)1975 *The Buildings of England: Wiltshire*. Revised by Bridget Cherry. 2d ed. Harmondsworth, England: Penguin.
TAIT, A. A. 1964 "Isaac de Caus and the South Front of Wilton House." *Burlington Magazine* 106:74.

DECKER, PAUL THE ELDER

Born in Nuremberg, Germany, Paul Decker the Elder (1677–1713) at his death in Bayreuth was building superintendent to the margrave. He received his training at the Painters' Academy in his native city from 1695 to 1699 under Georg Christoph Elmmart and thereafter was instructed "in architectonicis" by ANDREAS SCHLÜTER during the building of the Berlin Castle. Paul Decker the Elder excelled above all as an imaginative empirical architectural theoretician. Particularly with his idealized projects in the work *Fürstlicher Baumeister* (Masterbuilder to Princes; 1711, 1713, 1716), he influenced the aristocratic architectural patrons of central Europe and their architects in the building of their palace residences. In the history of German architectural theory his building and decorative ideas, disseminated in engravings without textual commentary, constitute a turning point toward a purely artistic representational style.

HANS REUTHER
Translated from German by
Beverley R. Placzek

BIBLIOGRAPHY

The drawings of Paul Decker the Elder can be found in the Germanisches National Museum, Nuremberg, Germany, and in the Kunstbibliothek Berlin West of the State Museums (Stiftung Preussischer Kulturbesitz).

DECKER, PAUL c.1707–1710 *Folge von Altarentwürfen.* Nuremberg, Germany.

DECKER, PAUL 1711–1716 *Fürstlicher Baumeister.* 3 vols. Augsburg, Germany: Wolff.

DECKER, PAUL 1720? *Ausführliche Anleitung zur Civilbau-Kunst.* Nuremberg, Germany: Weigel.

HABICHT, VICTOR CURT 1918 "Die deutschen Architekturtheoretiker des 17. und 18. Jahrhunderts." *Zeitschrift für Architektur und Ingenieurwesen* 64, no. 5:157ff., 201ff.

DE COTTE, ROBERT

One of the most influential French architects of the eighteenth century, Robert de Cotte (1656–1735) entered the architectural field as an entrepreneur and contractor for masonry. By 1676 he was working in the office of JULES HARDOUIN MANSART, who in 1681 became premier architecte to Louis XIV. In the following year de Cotte married Mansart's sister-in-law, and rapidly became Mansart's most valued assistant in the Service des Bâtiments du Roi. His architectural education was capped by a six-month sojourn in Italy. When Mansart was named surintendant des bâtiments in 1699, he enlarged the Bureau de Dessins, creating three offices in Versailles, Paris, and Marly. De Cotte became architecte ordinaire (second in command) and director of both the Département de Paris, the most strategic spot in the organization, and the Académie Royale d'Architecture. He was ennobled in 1702. After Mansart's death in 1708, de Cotte assumed the position for which he had been groomed, remaining premier architecte for twenty-five years. However, the financial strain resulting from the Sun King's costly wars limited royal undertakings. Therefore, de Cotte and his staff turned to new centers of culture replacing Versailles—Paris, the provincial capitals, and foreign courts.

The evidence of the new sources of patronage consists of several thousand architectural drawings housed primarily in the Bibliothèque Nationale and the Bibliothèque de l'Institut de France, Paris. De Cotte's draftsmen produced the presentation drawings, but as head of the office, he claimed responsibility for the designs. The presence of his scribbled notes and rough sketches indicates his involvement with the work. In a period stressing synthesis and resolution, de Cotte's goal was to perfect a repertory of French architectural motifs that had developed during the Renaissance and the baroque. He shared with his contemporaries a keen sense of *bienséance,* the appropriateness of a specific language of forms to individual building types. The layout and general character of his buildings were intended to convey an idea of function through the symbolic attributes of sharply differentiated forms.

De Cotte's stylistic debt to Mansart is most evident in the realm of urban planning. In 1692, when de Cotte supervised the completion of the Place des Victoires, Paris, he followed the lines strictly designated by Mansart. Eighteenth-century writers credit Mansart with the design of the Place Vendôme, Paris, but de Cotte's claim of responsibility for the definitive octagonal plan of 1699 suggests that he no longer considered himself the anonymous executor of Mansart's ideas. It was certainly Mansart who determined the basic shape of the Place du Dôme des Invalides, Paris, as early as 1676, but when the square was close to realization in 1698, de Cotte, as overseer of the work, was in a position to fix its final form (his project was not executed). In the case of the Place Bellecour in Lyons, the city magistrates rejected Mansart's purely visionary project (1700) and de Cotte struggled for a more viable solution (1711–1714).

For the elevations of the *places* de Cotte generally followed the example of the Place des Victoires, for reasons of aesthetics and royal symbolism. There was more than a hint of megalomaniacal grandeur reflecting the garden front of Versailles in the prodigious size of the royal squares, especially the project for Bordeaux (1728). In defining the vast space of the Place Royale to be created west of the Jardin des Tuileries in Paris (c.1717), de Cotte proposed numerous devices—moats, obelisks, sculpture—which were later incorporated in the Place Louis XV. When embellishments for public promenades were needed, as in the region extending from the Tuileries to the Cours-la-Reine and the Champs-Elysées, de Cotte conceived triumphal arches, gates, aviaries, and garden buildings of a type unknown to

Mansart: airy, delicate, full of wit and charm, they were highly appropriate for *endroits délicieux.*

The projects for town houses date primarily from the 1720s, during the rapid expansion of the western boundary of Paris. De Cotte respected the rules unique to the urban mansion since the French Renaissance, and in general he followed the layouts employed by Hardouin Mansart and PIERRE LASSURANCE. In the instance of the Hôtel du Lude (1710), de Cotte's organizational principles gave precedence to pomp and display, whereas for the Hôtel d'Estrées (1711–1713) his plan emphasized convenience, offering considerable flexibility in the use of the various public rooms and *appartements,* depending on the time of day, the season, or the presence of important guests.

De Cotte came closest to his ideal statement of a private house in the designs for the Hôtel de Torcy (c.1713), one of a series of five unexecuted proposals forming a homogeneous group. The plans are marked by a consistent interest in giving the main living quarters (*corps-de-logis*) the appearance of a free-standing block. For the elevations, he followed a formula drawn from Mansart and château architecture, consisting of a simple rectilinear volume distinguished by reticent end pavilions and a beautifully articulated frontispiece. The originality of his compositions lay in the flatness and delicacy of the forms and in the unification of the elements by means of the large simple shape of the roof, from which the French dormer was eliminated (for example, the Hôtel du Maine, garden elevation [1716–1719]). This suavity and elegance were in marked contrast to the more stark and robust style of de Cotte's chief rival in Paris, GERMAIN BOFFRAND.

De Cotte's contribution to the development of the rococo interior was slight. He left the design of the wall paneling to independent contractors or to artists in the Bâtiments, notably PIERRE LE PAUTRE and FRANÇOIS ANTOINE VASSÉ. In supervising the remodeling of François Mansart's Hôtel de la Vrillière (1713–1719), de Cotte entrusted the design and execution of the details to Vassé, whose Galerie Dorée is one of the masterpieces of the Régence.

The *hôtel* form provided the basis for three city mansions of the clergy, the Palais Épiscopaux of Châlons-sur-Marne (1719–1720; never completed), Verdun (1724–1735), and Strasbourg (planned 1727–1728, erected 1731–1735), although they were differentiated from the *hôtels* through the incorporation of palatial devices. In the Palais des Rohan, Strasbourg, de Cotte stressed hierarchical order by contrasting the modest apartment of the Prince-Bishop, located on the court side, with the magnificent *Grand Appartement* re-

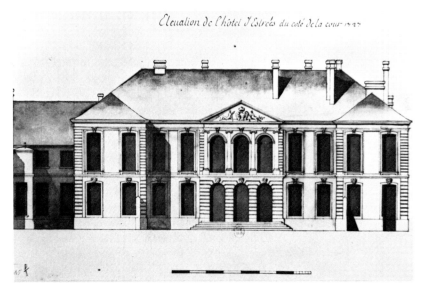

served for the king, which occupied the prestigious river side. The splendid river front, with its giant order and *dôme à l'imperiale,* is one of de Cotte's chief triumphs—decorous and elegant.

De Cotte's reputation outside of Paris was the result of his château designs for European nobility. Although few of these were actually built, their significance lies in having communicated to an international audience an exemplary type of palatial architecture. The ultimate source for the plans was the Palace of Versailles, with its governing principle of the longitudinal axis along which were organized radiating avenues, courts, stables, and gardens. For the dwelling proper, de Cotte employed one of three basic types of configurations, all firmly rooted in French tradition: the isolated block, used for the Duke of Savoy's Château de Rivoli (c.1700); the U-shaped plan, the basis for Chanteloup, the country house of Princess Orsini (1711); and the central plan, a revival of the Italianate form which had flourished during the

De Cotte.
Hôtel d'Estrées (courtyard façade).
Paris.
1711–1713

De Cotte.
Palais de Rohan (river front).
Strasbourg, France.
1731–1735

French Renaissance. The latter provided the starting point for the plans for the Château of Poppelsdorf, Bonn (1715–1723), the Château of Tilburg in the Netherlands (c.1715), and the Palais Bourbon, Paris (1720–1722). The X-shaped scheme for the hunting lodge of Compiègne (1729–1732), the sole major commission from Louis XV, reflected the international character of de Cotte's designs. The layouts of all these buildings featured impressive state chambers, but unlike their seventeenth-century models they were marked by a more functional arrangement of the private rooms and a greater number of small stairs and connecting corridors. For the elevations of the larger palaces, de Cotte drew from three examples—the garden front of Versailles, Hardouin Mansart's Grand Dessein, and the south front of the Louvre.

De Cotte's conception of the perfect princely residence found expression in the two alternatives offered Philip V of Spain, grandson of Louis XIV, for a palatial retreat outside Madrid (1715). Both the U-shaped Buenretiro I and the gigantic cross-in-square of Buenretiro II complied with the royal couple's request for a double pair of apartments to be inhabited alternately in summer and winter and serviced by a single suite of dressing rooms. These and other ideal schemes echoed the Grand Siècle and anticipated the visionary architecture of the later eighteenth century.

De Cotte also designed complexes which were essentially barracks housing large communities. The length of a wall was punctuated only by the monotonous repetition of windows, dormers, and blind arches, as in the grid of wings added by Mansart and de Cotte to the Hôtel des Invalides (c.1690–1750) and the pair of garrisons built in Paris for the Mousquetaires Noires (1699) and the Mousquetaires Gris (1716–1720). De Cotte successfully exploited these austere formal elements,

however, in the monastic quarters at Saint-Denis (1700–1765). Combining suitable iconographic references from different building types—mass-dwelling, convent, and palace—the master produced a barracks whose monumental size and grand sweeping spaces strongly impressed contemporaries.

Although few new religious foundations and churches were built in France during the early eighteenth century, de Cotte undertook the supervision of two of the great decorative projects of the late years of Louis XIV's reign, the Chapel of Versailles (1708–1710) and the choir of Notre Dame, Paris (1708–1714), for which the designs were chiefly by Pierre Le Pautre. For the cathedral of Orléans, de Cotte proposed a façade (1708–1709) in the late Gothic style. His masterpiece in the religious field is the portal of Saint Roch, Paris (c.1731–1735). Although its ultimate source is the Roman aedicular façade, the portal is one of the highpoints in a sequence of French facades beginning with SALOMON DE BROSSE's Saint Gervais, Paris (1616), and including Hardouin Mansart's Dôme des Invalides (1680–1691), as is apparent in the recessing of the central bay, the sparse robustness of the columnar accents, and the rhythm of highlights and shadows created by the blocky sections of entablature.

Robert de Cotte's work was the perfect embodiment of *la belle architecture* as defined by the French in the eighteenth century; an architecture whose noble and simple beauty was the result of a harmonious relationship of the parts and whose purpose was clearly defined through the adroit use of an expressive vocabulary of forms. His buildings fulfilled the needs of a clientele desiring comfortable, smart quarters at home and an impressive setting for the ceremonies of public life.

ROBERT NEUMAN

De Cotte.
Plan of the Abbey of Saint-
*   Denis.*
France.
1700–1735

WORKS

c.1690–1750, Hôtel des Invalides (wings; with Jules Hardouin Mansart); c.1691, Hôtel des Invalides (Infirmary); *1699, Hôtel des Mousquetaires Noirs (with Mansart); 1699, Place Vendôme (definitive plan); Paris. 1700–1735, Abbey of Saint-Denis (not completed until 1765), France. *1703, Hôtel de Pontchartrain (interior remodeling), France. *1706, Hôtel de Beauvais (remodeling), Paris. 1707–1710, Chapel (decoration), Versailles, France. 1708–1709, Sainte Croix (west portal; constructed after 1742), Orléans, France. c.1708–1722, Cathedral of Montauban (additions to portal), France. *1710, Hôtel du Lude, Paris. *1711, Château de Chanteloup, France. 1711–1713, Hôtel d'Estrées, Paris. 1713–1715, Château of Bonn (additions). 1713–1719, Hôtel de la Vrillière (remodeling), Paris. 1714–1717, Hôtel de Caumont, Aix-en-Provence, France. c.1715, Château of Tilburg, Netherlands. *1715, Pompe de la Samaritaine, Paris. 1715–1723, Château of Poppelsdorf (altered), Bonn. *1716–1719, Hôtel du Maine; *1716–1720, Hôtel des Mousquetaires Gris; 1717, Hôtel de Bourvalais (remodeling); *1719, Château d'Eau; Paris. 1719–1720, Palais Episcopaux (unfinished), Châlons-sur-Marne, France. 1720–1722, Palais Bourbon, Paris. 1721–1722, Château de Saverne (decoration), France. *1721–1722, Robert de Cotte House; 1721–1735, Cabinet des Medailles (not completed until 1741), Bibliothèque du Roi (with Jules Robert de Cotte); Paris. 1724–1735, Palais Episcopal (not completed until 1739), Verdun, France. *1727–1735, Palais Thurn and Taxis (not completed until 1736), Frankfurt. 1729–1732, Hunting Lodge of Compiègne, France. c.1731–1732, Chapel of the Charité (portal; partially destroyed); c.1731–1735, Saint Roch (portal; not completed until 1738); Paris. 1731–1735, Palais des Rohan (not completed until 1742), Strasbourg, France. *1734, Hôtel d'Armagnac, Paris.

BIBLIOGRAPHY

BLONDEL, JACQUES FRANCOIS   (1752–1756)1904–1905   L'architecture française. 4 vols. Reprint. Paris: Levy.

BRUNEL, GEORGES   1972   "Würzburg: Les Contacts entre Balthasar Neumann et Robert de Cotte." Actes du XXIIe Congrès International d'Histoire de l'Art (Budapest, 1969). Budapest: The congress.

CHRIST, YVAN   1966   "Ce Saint-Denis méconnu: Un chef d'oeuvre du classicisme français." Jardin des Arts 134:12–23.

Exposition de dessins et de souvenirs de Robert de Cotte, premier architecte du roi (1656–1735).   1937   Paris: Hôtel des Invalides.

GARDES, GILBERT   1974–1975   "La Décoration de la Place Royale de Louis le Grand (Place Bellecour) à Lyon, 1686–1783." Bulletin des Musées et Monuments Lyonnais 5:185–388.

GUIFFREY, JULES   1881–1901   Comptes des bâtiments du roi sous le règne de Louis XIV, 1664–1715. 5 vols. Paris: Imprimerie Nationale.

Hardouin-Mansart et son école.   1946   Paris: Bibliothèque Nationale. Exposition organized by the general Directorship of Architecture on the occasion of the third centennial of his birth.

HAUTECOEUR, LOUIS   1950   Première moitié du XVIIIe siècle: Le style Louis XV. Volume 3 in Histoire de l'architecture classique en France. Paris: Picard.

HAUTTMAN, MAX   1911   "Die Entwürfe Robert-de-Cottes für Schloss Schleissheim." Münchener Jahrbuch 6:256–276.

IBERVILLE-MOREAU, JOSÉ-LUC D'   1972   "Robert de Cotte: His Career as an Architect and the Organization of the Services des Bâtiments." Unpublished Ph.D. dissertation, University of London.

JESTAZ, BERTRAND   1966   Le Voyage d'Italie de Robert de Cotte. Paris: De Boccard.

KALNEIN, WEND GRAF   1956   Das Kürfürstliche Schloss Clemensruhe in Poppelsdorf. Düsseldorf, Germany: Schwann.

KALNEIN, WEND GRAF, and LEVEY, MICHAEL   1972   Art and Architecture of the Eighteenth Century in France. Baltimore: Penguin.

LÜBBECKE, FRIED   1955   Das Palais Thurn und Taxis in Frankfurt am Main. Frankfurt: Kramer.

LUDMANN, JEAN-DANIEL   1979   Le Palais Rohan de Strasbourg. Strasbourg, France: Derniers Nouvelles.

MARCEL, PIERRE   1906   Inventaire des papiers manuscrits du cabinet de Robert de Cotte. Paris: Champion.

NEUMAN, ROBERT   1980   "French Domestic Architecture in the Early 18th Century: The Town Houses of Robert de Cotte." Journal of the Society of Architectural Historians 39:128–144.

NEUMAN, ROBERT   1978   "Robert de Cotte: Architect of the Late Baroque." Unpublished Ph.D. dissertation, University of Michigan, Ann Arbor.

RAUCH-ELKAN, ANNELISE   1958   "Acht Pläne und ein Baumémoire Robert de Cotte's für Schloss Tilburg in Brabant." Brabantia Feb. 2:43–52.

REINHARDT, URSULA   1972   Die bischöflichen Residenzen von Châlons-sur-Marne, Verdun und Strasbourg. Ein Beitrag zum Werk des Ersten Königlichen Architekten Robert de Cotte (1656–1735). Basel.

DECRIANUS

Decrianus (?–130) was an architect and engineer of the time of Trajan and Hadrian. He was responsible, in 121, for moving the colossal statue of Nero from its position in the atrium of the Domus Aurea to a location nearer the Flavian amphitheater to make room for the base of the temple of Venus and Roma. It is said that this feat was accomplished with the aid of twenty-four elephants, the statue being held upright in a massive scaffolding. Today, only the foundation marks the spot where Decrianus placed the statue.

B. M. BOYLE

WORK

121, Colossal statue of Nero (base), Rome.

BIBLIOGRAPHY

English translations of the ancient texts can be found in the volumes of the Loeb Classical Library series, published by Harvard University Press and Heinemann.

NASH, ERNEST   (1961)1968   Volume 1, pages 268–269 in Pictorial Dictionary of Ancient Rome. 2d ed. London: Zwemmer.

SCRIPTORES HISTORIAE AUGUSTAE, Hadrian, Book 19.12–13.

DE CUBAS Y GONZALEZ-MONTES, FRANCISCO

Francisco de Cubas y Gonzalez-Montes, marqués de Cubas y de Fontalba (1826–1899), born in Madrid, is a representative of the stylistic evolution that characterized the Spanish architecture of his time. His evolutionary path led from an Italianizing classicism through historicist medievalism toward rationalism.

A disciple of Narciso Pascual y Colomer, he received the title of architect in 1855. His first works were in a neo-Renaissance style, as reflected in the palace of the Marqués de Alcañicer (1865). This classical tendency was continued in the houses that he constructed for his aristocratic clientele and in the Anthropological Museum in Madrid (1873–1875). Beginning with the Isern House in Madrid (1865), de Cubas developed a different style that pointed toward medievalism, especially in his religious buildings such as the Cathedral of the Almudena (1881–?), an enormous project of which only the crypt was constructed.

This medievalism was purified beginning in 1880, when de Cubas began constructing some very simple buildings of brick in which the gothicism exists almost uniquely as a reference, as in the Convent of the Siervas de María (1883–1885).

HELENA IGLESIAS
Translated from Spanish by
Judith E. Meighan

WORKS

1865, Isern House; 1865, Palace of Marquéz de Alcañicer; 1873–1875, Anthropological Museum; 1878–1881, Houses (for the Marqués de la Torrecilla); 1880, Convent of the Salesas Reales; *1880, Jesuit College of Chamartín; *1880–1886, Asylum of the Sacred Heart; 1881–?, Cathedral of the Almudena (crypt); 1883, Convent of the Siervas de María; Madrid. 1886, Catholic University of Deusto, Bilbao, Spain. 1889–1899, Parish church of Santa Cruz (not completed until 1902 by others), Madrid.

BIBLIOGRAPHY

AMEZQUETA, ADOLFO G. 1969 "Arquitectura Neo-Mudéjar en Madrid." *Arquitectura* 125.

LORENTE, MANUEL 1948 "Don Francisco de Cubas (1826–1899)." *Revista de Arquitectura* 8, no. 81:364.

NAVASCUES, PEDRO 1972 "La obra arquitectónica del Marqués de Cubas." *Villa de Madrid* 34:19–31.

NAVASCUES, PEDRO 1973 *Arquitectura y Arquitectos Madrileños del siglo XIX.* Madrid: Instituto de Estudios Madrilenos.

REPULLES Y VARGAS, E. 1889 "Necrología: El Marqúes de Cubas." *Resumen de Arquitectura* 26, no. 2:13–15.

DE FINETTI, GIUSEPPE

Giuseppe De Finetti (1892–1952) was born in Milan. He studied in Berlin and in Vienna with ADOLF LOOS before World War I. He graduated from the Regio Istituto di Belle Arti in Bologna, Italy, in 1920. His work reflects the intellectual rigor of the Loosian school. His Casa della Meridiana in Milan (1925) is an outstanding example of Novecento architecture. In 1931, he resigned from the Fascist Syndicate of Architects for political reasons. He wrote numerous articles on architecture and urban planning and published Italian translations of essays by Loos and CAMILLO SITTE.

DENNIS DOORDAN

WORKS

1925, Casa della Meridiana; 1930, Apartment Building, via San Calimero; Milan. 1938, Hunting Lodge, Ronchi, Italy.

BIBLIOGRAPHY

CISLAGHI, GIUSEPPE DE; DE BENEDETTI, MARA; and MARABELLI, PIERGIORGIO (editors) 1969 *Giuseppe De Finetti: Milano, costruzione di una citta.* Milan: ETAS Kompass.

DE FINETTI, GIUSEPPE 1934 *Stadi.* Milan: Ulrico Hoepli.

DE' SETA, CESARE 1972 *La cultura architettonica in Italia tra le due guerre.* Bari, Italy: Laterza.

DEGLANE, HENRY

Henri Deglane (1855–1921) was a fashionable teacher at the Ecole des Beaux-Arts in Paris whose American pupils included JOHN MEAD HOWELLS and RAYMOND M. HOOD. His production was small, the best-known work being the Grand Palais for the 1900 Exposition Universelle in Paris. His research of decorative materials, particularly mosaic and wrought iron, was tasteful and timely. His West Africa Palace for the 1906 Colonial Exhibition in Marseilles, France, was an interesting use of massive pisé with machicolations. Sound construction was strong in his atelier and in his own apartment buildings in Paris of 1907 and 1910.

ELIZABETH MCLANE

WORKS

1897, Monument Guy de Maupassant (with Raoul Verlet), Parc Monceau; *1898–1900, Grand Palais, (with A. Louvet and D. Thomas), Exposition Universelle; Paris. *1906, West Africa Palace, Colonial Exhibition, Marseilles, France. 1907, Apartment House, Rue de Grenelle and Rue Saint-Simon; 1910, Apartment Building, Avenue Elysée Réclus; Paris.

BIBLIOGRAPHY

BOILEAU, L. C. 1897 "Causerie: Art et Pratique." *L'Architecture* 10, no. 21:177–180.

DELAIRE, EDMOND 1907 *Les Architectes-Élèves de l'École des Beaux Arts.* 2d ed. With a preface by J. L. Pascal. Paris: Construction Moderne.

MAGNE, LUCIEN 1900 "Les Arts a L'Exposition

Universelle de 1900." *Gazette des Beaux-arts* 1:383–396.
"Monument de Maupassant a Paris." 1898 *Construction Moderne,* 13, no. 14:162.
UHRY, EDUARD   1910   "Le Fer Forge." *L'Architecte* 5:8–11.

DE GROOT, J. H.

J. H. de Groot (1865–1932) had a reputation of being a visionary designer although his actual work never suggested such an image. In fact, he never designed a building, only parts of buildings, and these are known only through his books on composition. From 1890 to 1910, de Groot, K. P. C. DE BAZEL, and J. L. M. LAUWERIKS formed a triumvirate that explored and disseminated proportional systems. These systems were widely considered ways of finding beauty which would link them with ancient civilizations. Never satisfied with Art Nouveau's denial of the past, de Groot was frequently respectful of his ancient predecessors. De Groot published at least seven books on systematic design, but as far as we know he never envisioned a building design. His chief prominence for today is through MICHEL DE KLERK's use of his book *Vormharmonie* (1912). De Klerk employed curvilinear forms as a response to the Art Nouveau and to the curved surfaces in *Vormharmonie.*

SUZANNE FRANK

BIBLIOGRAPHY
DE GROOT, J. H.   (1900)1909   *Iets over evenwicht in de architectuur.* Amsterdam: Van Mantgen & de Does.
DE GROOT, J. H.   1911   *Kleurharmonie.* Amsterdam: Ahrend.
DE GROOT, J. H.   1912   *Vormharmonie.* Amsterdam: Ahrend.
DE GROOT, J. H.   (1922)1926   *Vormcompositie en centraliteit.* Amsterdam: The author.
DE GROOT, J. H.   1926   *Vormcompositie-contrapunt.* Bussum, Netherlands: Dinger.
DE GROOT, J. H., and DE GROOT, JACOBA M.   1896   *Driehoeken bij ontwerpen van ornament: Voor zelfstudie en voor scholen.* Amsterdam: Stenler.
DE MEIJER, JAN   1932   "Jan Hessel de Groot." *Bouwkundig Weekblad Architectura* 53, no. 13:101–102.

DEINOKRATES

Deinokrates (?–320 B.C.), thought to be a Macedonian architect, is known principally from a colorful anecdote recounted by VITRUVIUS. He presented himself, it is said, to Alexander the Great, attired as Hercules, announced an improbable project for the reshaping of Mount Athos, and so

impressed Alexander that he was accepted as a follower. His name has been associated, on no known evidence, with the design of the last temple of Artemis at Ephesos, and with the plan for the city of Alexandria.

B. M. BOYLE

BIBLIOGRAPHY
English translations of the ancient texts can be found in the volumes of the Loeb Classical Library series, published by Harvard University Press and Heinemann.
PLINY, *Historia naturalis,* Book 34.42.
VITRUVIUS, *De architectura,* Book 2.Praef.1.

DE KEY, LIEVEN

Lieven de Key (1560?–1627), born in Ghent, Belgium, emigrated to London because of the Spanish domination of the Southern Netherlands. In 1590, he returned to Holland and settled in Haarlem as a stonemason. He became town mason in 1593 and lived in Haarlem till his death.

De Key, together with the town architect of Amsterdam, HENDRICK DE KEYSER, was the most prominent architect of the Dutch Renaissance. His style was influenced by the decorative style of HANS VREDEMAN DE VRIES, a painter and engraver who lived and worked in the Netherlands and Germany and who was known all over Northern Europe through his books of ornament. Typical of de Key's style was the application of scrolls, festoons, and cartouches and the free use of the classical orders.

The first documented work by Lieven de Key is the rebuilding of the gable of the Vont Chapel of Saint Bavo Church in Haarlem (1593). He must already have achieved some fame, because he was ordered to the town of Leyden in 1594 to submit a design for a new representative façade for the medieval town hall there. He designed a sandstone façade with three gables and a monumental double staircase. The work was executed by Lüder von Bentheim, architect of the town hall façade in Bremen, Germany. In this work, de Key did not yet display all his mastership, although the staircase shows the characteristic features of his later works. The gables with their scrolls, herm pilasters, and obelisks seem to have been derived from the pattern books of Vredeman de Vries.

It is not sure if de Key designed the Weighhouse (1595–1598) in Haarlem, generally attributed to him. The building misses the playful ornaments and is more classical than his other works. Typical of de Key, though, are the joint windows, the heavy consoles, and the frontons.

De Key's most famous work and the best example of the Dutch Renaissance is the Meat Hall in Haarlem (1601–1605). Together with the town carpenter Claes Pietersz, he made two designs for the hall, of which the more classical plan was rejected. The hall has a traditional layout, with rectangular groundplan and a high roof between steep gables. In the interior, the vaults rest on a row of columns, placed in the middle of the building and before the entrances. For the exterior de Key used bricks and stone, which gave a lively effect. The many decorative elements give the building a picturesque and playful character. Here, de Key showed his skill and originality in the free use of the Vredeman de Vries's motifs in scrolls, cartouches, and pinnacles, especially in the gables on the long side and the bold entrances on the short side.

In 1613, de Key designed the elegant tower of Saint Anna's Church in Haarlem. The church itself has been replaced by a church designed by JACOB VAN CAMPEN in 1645. Together with Claes Pietersz, de Key submitted three designs for the extension of the old town hall of Haarlem, of which one was executed in 1620 in the picturesque and lively style characteristic of his other work. With his death, the decorative style of the Dutch Renaissance came to an end.

MARIET J. H. WILLINGE

WORKS

1593, Saint Bavo Church (Vont Chapel), Haarlem, Netherlands. 1594, Town Hall (new façade), Leyden, Netherlands. (A)1595–1598, Weighhouse, Haarlem, Netherlands. 1597, Gemeenlandshuis, Leyden, Netherlands. 1597, Town Hall (staircase); 1601–1605, Meat Hall; 1613, Saint Anna Church (tower); 1616–1620, Town Hall (extension); 1625, Frans Loenenhofje (porch); Haarlem, Netherlands.

BIBLIOGRAPHY

FOCKEMA ANDREAE, S. J.; KUILE, E. H. TER; and HEKKER, R. C. 1957 *De bouwkunst na de Middeleeuwen.* Volume 2 in *Duizend jaar bouwen in Nederland.* Amsterdam: Lange.

JANSSEN, C. F. 1961 "Lieven de Key: Bouwmeester van Haarlem." *Bouw* 16:754–757.

KUILE, E. H. TER 1938 "De werkzaamheden van Lieven de Key te Haarlem." *Oud Holland* 55:245–252.

KUILE, E. H. TER 1939 "Overheidsbouw te Leiden: 1588–1632." *Oudheidkundig Jaarboek* 7:83–87.

VERMEULEN, FRANS A. J. 1931 Volume 2 in *Handboek tot de geschiedenis der Nederlandsche bouwkunst.* The Hague: Nijhoff.

DE KEYSER, HENDRICK

Hendrick de Keyser (1565–1621) was the most distinguished Dutch sculptor and, with LIEVEN DE KEY, the outstanding Dutch architect of the early seventeenth century. He worked mainly in Amsterdam, where in 1594 he was appointed municipal sculptor and architect; his two most important works, the Zuiderkerk and the Westerkerk, are, with their splendid towers, still major landmarks in the city. The Zuiderkerk was Holland's first large Protestant church, focusing attention on the pulpit rather than the altar, and the majestic Westerkerk is, in its ordered spaciousness and dignified sobriety, the fullest expression of de Keyser's mature style, in which he left behind the picturesque Dutch Mannerist tradition and looked forward to the classicism of JACOB VAN CAMPEN. He was much more open to foreign influences than Lieven de Key, and in turn was influential beyond the Netherlands on Protestant church design, his work being described and illustrated in a book which virtually was a contemporary monograph on him: *Architectura Moderna* by the painter and architect Salomon de Bray.

De Keyser was the head of a family of artists. His son Thomas (1596/1597–1667) was the leading portrait painter in Amsterdam before being overtaken in popularity by Rembrandt, and he was also municipal architect from 1662 until his death. Two other sons, Pieter (1595–1676) and Willem (1603–after 1678), are also recorded as architects, but they were active primarily as sculptors. Willem spent part of his career in England, probably initially working with NICHOLAS STONE, the son-in-law and former pupil of Hendrick.

IAN CHILVERS

WORKS

1606–1614, Zuiderkerk; *1608–1611, Exchange; Amsterdam. 1609, Weigh-house, Hoorn, Netherlands. 1618, Town Hall, Delft, Netherlands. (A)c.1620, Bartolotti's House, 170–172 Herengracht; 1620, Mint Tower (rebuilding); 1620–1623, Noorderkerk; 1620–1638, Westerkerk; Amsterdam.

BIBLIOGRAPHY

BRAY, SALOMON DE (1631)1971 *Architectura Moderna ofte Bouwinga van osten tyt.* Facsimile ed. Soest, Netherlands: Davaco.

NEURDENBURG, ELISABETH (1929)1934 *Hendrick de Keyser: Beeldhouwer en Bouwmeester van Amsterdam.* Amsterdam: Scheltema & Holkema.

OZINGA, M. D. 1929 *De Protestantsche Kerkenbouw in Nederland van Hervorming tot Franschen Tijd.* Amsterdam: Paris.

ROSENBERG, JACOB; SLIVE, SEYMOUR; and TER KUILE, E. H. (1966)1977 *Dutch Art and Architecture: 1600–1800.* 3d ed. Harmondsworth, England: Penguin.

HITCHCOCK, H. R. 1978 *Netherlandish Scrolled Gables of the Sixteenth and Early Seventeenth Centuries.* New York University Press.

DE KLERK, MICHEL

Michel de Klerk (1884–1923) was the guiding genius of the Amsterdam school, the expressionist group that dominated architectural production in the Dutch capital from 1915 to 1930 and made its primary contribution in the area of government-supported housing. His buildings for *Eigen Haard* in the Spaarndammerbuurt have been designated historic monuments and were recently restored by the municipality of Amsterdam.

It is fitting de Klerk should have made his mark as a designer of workers' housing, for he himself was of proletarian origins, born in Amsterdam's Jewish Quarter to a diamond worker. Had de Klerk been born a generation earlier, it is doubtful that he would have been able to develop his gifts sufficiently to enter the architectural profession which required education at an academy. But thanks largely to men like P. J. H. CUYPERS, the architectural profession had become more democratic and free trade schools had been established as an alternative to the prestigious academies. At the same time, the architect's sphere of activity had broadened to include the previously unfashionable field of large-scale housing. Both of these transformations would radically affect de Klerk's future.

At the age of fourteen, de Klerk was set upon his career by EDUARD CUYPERS, nephew of the famous Gothic Revivalist. Thunderstruck by the teenager's drafting skills, the younger Cuypers hired him to work in his busy atelier where decorative arts as well as buildings were lovingly, even lavishingly, designed. During his first years there, de Klerk also attended evening classes at the Industrieschool, one of the institutions set up to train workers in the arts and crafts; he always acknowledged the importance of those lessons. But probably even more crucial was the atmosphere in Cuypers's office, where he worked steadily from 1898 to 1910 except for a brief stint in London in 1906. Cuypers believed that architecture was a fine art and that decoration was a fundamental part of its essence, and he encouraged his employees to use his excellent library with its ample assortment of European architectural periodicals. De Klerk was particularly attracted to the English Queen Anne style and to the various manifestations of the Art Nouveau, especially in Austria and Germany. From these sources, from a study of contemporary buildings, from an interest in folk architecture shared with many of his Dutch contemporaries, and from his own richly inventive imagination, de Klerk would forge a personal, striking style, which nevertheless was capable of being assimilated by the admiring colleagues he met first at Cuypers's

studio and then at the powerful club, Architectura et Amicitia, where he was a leading figure from 1916 until his death.

While working for Cuypers, de Klerk entered the numerous competitions that just then in the Netherlands were becoming a significant means of testing young talent. His very first entry, of 1906, for a railroad station, was prophetic in the rather bizarre character of the fenestration but unresolved in the eclectic blend of motifs derived from H. P. BERLAGE and R. NORMAN SHAW. By 1910, in a project for a mortuary chapel given singularity through parabolic windows and exuberant cut-brick trim, de Klerk approached maturity. The jury presciently noted that he sought to symbolize the nature and purpose of the building through the massing and decoration, and awarded him second prize, complimenting him on his lushly picturesque renderings. WILLEM KROMHOUT, whose own appreciation of architectural fantasy made him the closest Dutch predecessor of de Klerk, was one of the jurors.

News of the award came while de Klerk was in Scandinavia, falling under the spell of the rustic vernacular architecture exhibited in the open-air museums outside Stockholm and Copenhagen. On that visit of 1910–1911 he also sketched the uniquely beguiling spires of Copenhagen, one of which—that of ANTON S. ROSEN's Palads Hotel—would be echoed in the tower of his second block for *Eigen Haard*. De Klerk invariably responded to lively silhouettes and dramatic plastic shapes and sought to create these in his own work.

After his return to Amsterdam, de Klerk worked briefly for the Department of Public Works, but he also received an independent commission from the builder Klaas Hille. The result was Hillehuis (1911–1912), a luxury apartment building on the Johannes Vermeerplein, constructed in the material he would make his own, native brick laid in novel patterns. The smooth tile capping of the composition created an unusually forceful sense of three-dimensionality, while the decorative gambrel shapes executed in wood and stone and standing out against the brick surfaces became signature motifs. They appeared again in the Scheepvaarthuis (1912–1916) on the Prins Hendrikkade in Amsterdam. Here J. M. VAN DER MEY, asked to throw a mantel of style and beauty over a concrete skeleton designed by the firm of A. L. VAN GENDT AND SONS, invited the participation of de Klerk and PIETER L. KRAMER, both former colleagues from Cuypers's office, and together they created an office building that was immediately recognized as the harbinger of a new architectural movement. The straining dynamism and the bold scale mitigated by precious and unique details would become hallmarks of the work of the Amsterdam school. De Klerk's contribution can be seen in the side entrance and in the dormers and projecting bay windows at the roof line, whose shapes were prefigured in the mortuary chapel design of 1910.

However, the Scheepvaarthuis is something of an anomaly in de Klerk's *oeuvre,* for its skeletal organization remains visible beneath the virtuoso cladding of brick and stone. De Klerk characteristically shunned such structural revelation, preferring a continuous exterior wall plane that seemed suspended over the interior spaces. More personal, and programmatically of greater moment, is his first block of workers' housing in the Spaarndammerbuurt (1913–1915). The long façade punctuated by a series of parabolic gables owed much to JOSEPH M. OLBRICH's design for the Hotel Konigswart (1902), but de Klerk nationalized the composition by using brick in the taut manner prescribed by Berlage while rejecting the latter's rationalism and austerity. His own contribution lay in the extraordinary way he wove a veritable tapestry from the variety of specially shaped and colored bricks. The oddly shaped, multipaned windows framed in white-painted sash, inspired to some extent by the Queen Anne style, were a feature that would be picked up by other members of the Amsterdam school; they did not interrupt the surface of the wall but seemed an integral part of the smoothly flowing membrane.

De Klerk prepared other designs for Hille but the inflation caused by World War I halted privately financed construction. However, the government, through the Dutch Housing Act of 1901, granted funds to the housing societies so that building could continue, and the social-democratic *Eigen Haard* executed de Klerk's second (1915–1916) and third (1917–1920) housing schemes around the Spaarndammerplantsoen Park. Entries and stairhalls break forward dramatically from the main wall plane, and diverse architectural incidents, some quite whimsical, abound. Bricks are laid vertically and obliquely as well as horizontally, and polychromatic patterns both enliven and unify the surfaces. Red, yellow, purple, and black bricks and black and red tiles are among the diverse materials in de Klerk's arsenal.

The 1917–1920 complex for *Eigen Haard* is a perimeter block triangular in shape and contains 103 dwellings, a post office, and a separate meeting hall. A billowing envelope of towers, turrets, and rounded oriel windows creates the image of a medieval village in miniature. De Klerk sympathized with the workers' expressed hatred of monotonous, barrackslike dwellings and was pre-eminent among the Dutch for devising formal strategies to animate the potentially dreary façades of the standard tenement. The alterations in exterior form are sanctioned by changes in interior space and function. De Klerk did not deny the new scale of the twentieth-century city but he humanized it by modulating the rhythms of façade and silhouette.

De Klerk's next commission (1920–1922), from the predominately Jewish housing society *De Dageraad,* was probably his masterpiece. The blocks facing the two squares, Henriette Ronner- and Therese Schwartzeplein, and those lining the P. L. Takstraat, were designed by de Klerk. These buildings are more disciplined than those in the Spaarndammerbuurt and strike a remarkable balance between the needs of the individual and those of the collective group. An amazing variety of spaces was provided within a fairly fixed program without undue structural strain, and the craftsmanship is superb. These buildings stand as the pinnacle of architectural achievement accomplished by the workers' housing societies with the support of the national and local authorities.

The façades of the housing designed for private entrepreneurs on the Vrijheidslaan (1921–1922) offer a significant contrast. Although de Klerk's design was adjudged architectonically superb by his contemporaries, it did not solve the needs of the tenants, in part because he was obliged merely to place an elevation over standardized builder's plans. The intricate and charming details found in the dwellings of the housing societies were sacrificed to economic considerations. In the more sweeping conception evidenced here, de Klerk comes close to such expressionist contemporaries in Germany as ERIC MENDELSOHN and BRUNO TAUT, who employed large, curving forms and ignored cunning details.

De Klerk did attack programs other than housing, but opportunities for execution were fewer in these areas. Three private houses were built, most notably the Veerhoff-Kothe House in Hilversum (1914), which demonstrated that he could shape the interior with the same panache as the exterior. There is an ingenious compactness to the plan of the house in Hilversum which makes it comparable to the Shingle style cottages of BRUCE PRICE, and there is evidence that Dutch architects were well aware of late nineteenth-century American architecture. American also, at least in its material, is the building for the rowing club. De Hoop (1922), in Amsterdam, destroyed by the Nazis. Here, de Klerk masterfully adapted to wooden construction the rounded, fluid forms he had previously created in brick.

At a time when architecture was increasingly being veiwed as a constructive science with purely pragmatic goals, de Klerk kept alive the poetic ideal of architecture as the supreme art. His buildings communicate the imprint of a romantic and passionate sensibility imbued with a religious devotion to his calling. His ceaseless struggle to realize inspired new visions doubtless contributed to de Klerk's death at the age of thirty-nine, when he was at the height of his powers and his renown.

HELEN SEARING

WORKS

1911–1912, Hillehuis Apartment Block; 1912–1916, Scheepvaarthuis Office Building (with others); 1913–1915, First *Eigen Haard* Housing Estate, Spaarndammerbuurt; Amsterdam. 1914, Veerhoff-Kothe House, Hilversum, Netherlands. 1915–1916, Second *Eigen Haard* Housing Estate, Spaarndammerplantsoen Park; 1917–1920, Third *Eigen Haard* Housing Estate, Spaarndammerplantsoen Park; 1920–1922, Dageraad Housing Estate, Henriette Ronner- and Therese Schwartzeplein and P. L. Takstraat; Amsterdam. 1920–1922, Flower Auction Building, Aalsmeer-Oosteinde, Netherlands. 1921–1922, Housing on the Vrijheidslaan; *1922, De Hoop Clubhouse; Amsterdam. 1923, Barendsen House, Aalsmeer-Oosteinde, Netherlands.

BIBLIOGRAPHY

BANHAM, REYNER (1960)1967 *Theory and Design in the First Machine Age.* 2d ed. New York: Praeger.

FANELLI, GIOVANNI 1968 *Architettura moderna in Olanda: 1900–1940.* Florence: Marchi & Bertolli.

FRANK, SUZANNE S. 1971 "Michel de Klerk's Designs for Amsterdam's Spaarndammerbuurt." *Nederlands Kunsthistorisch Jaarboek* 22:175–213.

PEHNT, WOLFGANG 1973 *Expressionist Architecture.* New York: Praeger.

SEARING, HELEN 1971 "Eigen Haard: Workers' Housing and the Amsterdam School." *Architectura* 2:148–175.

SEARING, HELEN 1978 "With Red Flags Flying: Politics and Architecture in Amsterdam." Pages 230–270 in Henry A. Millon and Linda Nochlin (editors), *Art and Architecture in the Service of Politics.* Cambridge, Mass.: M.I.T. Press.

SEARING, HELEN 1980 "Amsterdam South: Social Democracy's Elusive Housing Ideal." Pages 58–78 in *VIA IV, Culture and the Social Vision.* Cambridge, Mass.: M.I.T. Press.

SHARP, DENNIS 1967 *Modern Architecture and Expressionism.* New York: Braziller.

DE KONINCK, LOUIS HERMAN

Born in Brussels, Louis Herman De Koninck (1896–) is the foremost representative of rational architecture in Belgium. Art Nouveau marked his student work, but from the age of twenty-one he directed his research toward industrial standardization and, later, prefabrication. In 1928, he intro-

duced concrete shell construction to Belgium and from it developed an approach to architecture characterized by formal rigor based on structural necessity, economy, and masterful handling of space often compared to that of VICTOR HORTA. These principles constituted the basis of the important pedagogical mission which he fulfilled at the Ecole de La Cambre in Brussels from 1942 to 1973.

MAURICE CULOT
Translated from French by
Shara Wasserman

WORKS

1924, Louis Herman De Koninck House, Avenue Fond'Roy, Uccle; 1926, Lenglet House, Avenue Fond'Roy, Uccle; 1928, House, Avenue Brassine, Auderghem; 1929, Alban House, Boulevard de Waterloo; Brussels. 1930, Houses (three), Plateau du Tribouillet, Liège, Belgium. 1931, Dotremont House, Avenue de l'Echevinage; 1934, House, Avenue Prince d'Orange; 1936, Housing Complex, Coghen Square; Uccle, Brussels.

DELAFOSSE, JEAN CHARLES

Architect, engraver of designs for ornament, and, at the beginning of his career, sculptor, Jean Charles Delafosse (1734–1791) should be considered above all as one of the originators of the Louis XVI style. In 1767, he presented in his *Iconologie* a repertory of ornament, expanded in subsequent editions, that brought together the Greek key, foliated scrolls, twisted fluting, garlands of laurels and roses, rams' heads, bucrania, and lions' snouts. His *Traité des cinq ordres* mixed Roman examples with his own inventions. Delafosse became a member of the Académie de Bordeaux in 1781. Two Paris residences were built to his designs between 1776 and 1783: the Hôtel Delbarre (later Titon) and the Hôtel Delbarre (later Goix) in the Faubourg Poissonière. His interest in planning on a large scale led to his preparing a project for two necropolises intended for the outskirts of Paris. These schemes sprang from the same imaginative climate that inspired the fantastic funerary architecture of CLAUDE NICOLAS LEDOUX and ETIENNE LOUIS BOULLÉE.

GÉRARD ROUSSET-CHARNY
Translated from French by
Richard Cleary

BIBLIOGRAPHY

GALLET, MICHEL 1963 "Jean-Charles Delafosse, architecte." *Gazette des Beaux-Arts* Series 6 61:157–164.

DE LA FOSSE, LOUIS REMY

Louis Rémy de la Fosse (de Lafosse, Delafosse) (1666–1726) called himself Nicolaus le Rouge. Nothing is known about his early career and training in France; he became known only after 1706 when he moved to central Europe. There, he earned numerous commissions from several German princes for whom he provided studied adaptations of notable French palaces and public buildings.

JUANITA M. ELLIAS

WORKS

1709, Palace, Wilhelmshoehe, Germany. 1716, Palace, Darmstadt, Germany. 1720, Palace, Mannheim, Germany.

BIBLIOGRAPHY

HAUTECOEUR, LOUIS 1950 *Première moitié du XVIIIe siècle: Le style Louis XV.* Volume 3 in *Histoire de l'architecture classique en France.* Paris: Picard.

DELAMAIR, PIERRE ALEXIS

Pierre Alexis Delamair (1676–1745) is best known as the designer of the adjoining Parisian *hôtels* of François de Rohan, prince of Soubise (1705–1709), and Armand Gaston de Rohan, prince-bishop of Strasbourg (1705–1708). The grandiose entry courts were much admired, but the living spaces so lacked the commodiousness achieved by such contemporaries as PIERRE LASSURANCE that Delamair was replaced by GERMAIN BOFFRAND and ROBERT DE COTTE. Finding little other employment, he turned to theoretical writings.

ROBERT NEUMAN

WORKS

1705–1708, Hôtel de Rohan-Strasbourg; 1705–1709, Hôtel de Rohan-Soubise (now Archives Nationales); before 1738, Hôtel de Chanac-Pompadour; Paris.

BIBLIOGRAPHY

BABELON, JEAN-PIERRE 1969a "Les Façades sur jardin des Palais Rohan-Soubise." *Revue de l'Art* 4:66–73.
BABELON, JEAN-PIERRE 1969b *Histoire et description des bâtiments des Archives Nationales.* Volume 1 in *Musée de l'histoire de France.* Paris: Imprimerie Nationale.
HAUTECOEUR, LOUIS 1950 *Première moitié de XVIIIe siècle: Le style Louis XV.* Volume 3 in *Histoire de l'architecture classique en France.* Paris: Picard.
KALNEIN, WEND GRAF, and LEVEY, MICHAEL 1972 *Art and Architecture of the Eighteenth Century in France.* Baltimore: Penguin.
LANGLOIS, CHARLES-VICTOR 1922 *Les Hôtels de Clisson, de Guise et de Rohan-Soubise au Marais.* Paris: Schemit.

DELAMONCE, FERDINAND

Ferdinand Pierre Joseph Ignace Delamonce (1678–1753) was born in Munich and followed his father as an architect, painter, and draftsman. After a stay in Italy, he settled in Lyons, France, in 1731 and joined the local Académie des Beaux-Arts in 1736. Delamonce's *oeuvre* includes projects for a bridge and a quay in Lyons.

RICHARD CLEARY

WORK

1740, Hôtel Tolosan, Lyons, France.

BIBLIOGRAPHY

L'Art baroque à Lyon (1622–1738): Catalogue de l'exposition. 1972 France: Institut d'Histoire de l'Art de l'Université Lyon II.
AUDIN, MARIUS, and VIAL, EUGÈNE 1918 "Ferdinand Delamonce." Volume 1, pages 255–256 in *Dictionnaire des artistes et ouvriers d'art du Lyonnais.* Paris: Bibliothèque d'Art et d'Archéologie.
HAUTECOEUR, LOUIS 1950 *Première moitié du XVIIIe siècle: Le style Louis XV.* Volume 3 in *Histoire de l'architecture classique en France.* Paris: Picard.
PEREZ, MARIE FÉLICE 1979 "Un ultime exemple de l'art baroque à Lyon: Saint Bruno des Chartreux." *Monuments historiques* 101:36–39.
VALLERY-RADOT, JEAN 1963 L'Eglise de l'Oratoire." *Congrès archéologique de France* 121:119–124.

DELANO and ALDRICH

Chester Holmes Aldrich (1871–1940) and William Adams Delano (1874–1960) in 1902 began their collaboration in the office of CARRÈRE AND HASTINGS while that firm was engaged in the construction of the New York Public Library. Aldrich, a Columbia University graduate, had gone to Paris in 1895 to attend the Ecole des Beaux-Arts. Delano, a Yale graduate, attended the school of architecture at Columbia as a special student before leaving in 1900 for Paris to attend the Ecole des Beaux-Arts.

In 1903, a year after Delano returned from Paris, the two set off on their own. Although the firm's first major building was the neoclassically inspired Walters Art Gallery (1910) in Baltimore, Maryland, the firm achieved its greatest success by producing stately homes for the extremely wealthy. Their clients included the Astors, the Burdens, the Havemeyers, the Otto Kahn family, the Pratts, John D. Rockefeller, and the Whitney family. A monograph on their work, *Portrait of Ten Country Houses* (1924), clearly demonstrates that their house plans did not ramble about in a picturesque fashion but rather possessed a general sense of regularity and managed to combine dignity with what Royal Cortissoz has described as "a gracious endearing friendliness." The façades of these houses were derived from architectural sources as diverse as the chateaux of the Loire valley in France and neo-Palladian (see ANDREA PALLADIO) London. In addition to the numerous residences, the firm designed several private clubs and public structures in New York, including the Colony Club (1916), the Union League Club (1936), La Guardia Air Terminal (1940), and the Marine Air Terminal. Their academic commissions included buildings for Yale University and Smith College.

Aldrich was an active member of the American Academy in Rome and was its resident director from 1935 until his death. Before his departure for Rome he had taught at the Columbia University School of Architecture as an assistant to Thomas Hastings.

Following Aldrich's death, Delano continued to practice architecture, winning the competition for the enlargement of the United States Military Academy at West Point (1944).

Delano was a professor at Columbia from 1903 to 1910. In 1924 he was made a member of the National Commission of Fine Arts, and he served as a member of the design board of the 1939 World's Fair in New York.

STEVEN MCLEOD BEDFORD

WORKS

1906–1908, John D. Rockefeller House, Pocantico Hills, N.Y. 1907, Havemeyer House, Syosset, N.Y. 1908, Herter House, Santa Barbara, Calif. 1909, 925 Park Avenue, New York. 1910, Borland House, Mount Kisco, N.Y. 1910, Walters Art Gallery, Baltimore. 1915, Otto Kahn House, Cold Spring Harbor, N.Y. 1916, Burden House; 1916, Colony Club; 1920, Mrs. Willard Straight House; New York. 1922, Astor House, Syosset, N.Y. 1922, Christ Church Parish House, Hartford, Conn. 1926, Vincent Astor House, New York. 1926, Smith College Music School, Northampton, Mass. 1928, Harkness Hall, Yale University, New Haven. 1936, Union League Club; 1939, Walland Hanover Building; New York. 1941, New York City Air Terminal.

BIBLIOGRAPHY

"Colony Club, New York." 1916 *Architecture* 33:1, 59–72.
DELANO, WILLIAM ADAM, and ALDRICH, CHESTER HOLMES 1924 *Portraits of Ten Country Houses.* Garden City, N.Y.: Doubleday.
FISHER, H. T. 1929 "New Elements in House Design." *Architectural Record* 66, Nov.:396–484.
"Obituary" (Aldrich). 1941 *Pencil Points* 22:76.
"Obituary" (Delano). 1960 *Journal of the American Institute of Architects* 33, Mar.:63.

"Residence Harold E. Pratt." 1922 *Architecture* 46:1, 104–108.
"Residence Mrs. Willard Straight." 1920 *Architecture* 41:133–138.

Delano and Aldrich.
Burden House.
Syosset, New York.
1916

DE LA TOUR D'AUVERGNE, BERNARD

Bernard de la Tour d'Auvergne (1923–1976) practiced in his native Paris from 1955 after working with PHILIP JOHNSON and Eugène Beaudouin. His architecture developed the relationships of distinct building elements, characterized by contrasting forms and materials. A rigorous austerity is nevertheless evident in his buildings and his numerous competition projects.

THOMAS G. BEDDALL

WORKS

1952, House, Cuernavaca, Mexico. 1960, Club Martini (with M. Tournon Branly, M. Pechere, and M. Calka), Paris. 1964, National School of Taxes (with Eugène Beaudouin), Clermont-Ferrand, France. 1966, Institut Européen d'Administration des Affaires (with R. Cidrac); 1969, Centre Européen d'Education Permanente; Fontainebleau, France. 1973, National School of Treasury Services (with C. Costantini), Marne-la-Vallée, France.

BIBLIOGRAPHY

"ARC 2000." 1971 *L'Architecture d'aujourd'hui* 43, no. 156:xxiii–xxvi.
"Club aux Champs-Elysées, Paris." 1964 *L'Architecture d'aujourd'hui* 34, no. 112:102–103.
"Concours de Berlin-Capitale." 1958 *L'Architecture d'aujourd'hui* 29, no. 80:47.
"L'Institut Européen d'Administration des Affaires de Fontainebleau." 1967 *L'Architecture de Lumière* no. 16:28–35.

"Parisians Vote on Les Halles Project." 1975 *Progressive Architecture* 56, no. 7:22.

VERNES, MICHEL 1971 "Un ermitage pour cadres supérieurs." *L'Oeil* 203, Nov.:16–21.

DE LA VALLEE, JEAN

Born in France as the son of the architect Simon de la Vallée who in 1639 was appointed royal architect at the court of the Swedish Queen Christina, Jean de la Vallée (1620–1696) very early was trained as an architect, originally by his father but later abroad, in France and Italy. In Sweden again around 1650, he introduced the styles of the Roman Renaissance and mannerist palaces, but his early works also show the influence of Dutch Palladianism (see ANDREA PALLADIO) as well as the modern French palace architecture. Jean de la Vallée, like his father royal architect at the Swedish court, became a mature baroque architect with a strong feeling for sculptural and dynamic features. His clients belonged mainly to the group of very rich field marshalls of the Thirty-Year War, and he satisfied their demands for magnificence. His main work is the House of Nobility in Stockholm, begun in 1641 by his father and later continued by the Dutch architect JOST VINGBOONS. From 1656 to 1674, Jean de la Vallée completed the big building project, to which he applied the impressive curve-shaped roof of his invention as a continuation of the Italian lantern roof. He also designed churches and tried to create an independent architecture for the Swedish Lutheran Church.

FREDRIC BEDOIRE

WORKS

Begun 1653, Oxenstierna Palace, Old Town; begun 1656, Hedvig Eleonora Church; begun 1656, Katarina Church; 1662–1673, Bonde Palace, Old Town; Stockholm. Begun 1666, Mariedal Manor House, Västergötland, Sweden. c.1670, Runsa Manor House, Uppland, Sweden. 1670s, Karlberg Palace, near Stockholm.

BIBLIOGRAPHY

NORDBERG, TORD OLSSON 1970 *De la Vallée—en arkitektfamilj i Frankrike, Holland och Sverige*. Stockholm: Almqvist & Wiksell. Every chapter is summarized in French.

DELAVRANCEA-GIBORY, HENRIETTE

Henriette Delavrancea-Gibory (1894–) graduated from the School of Architecture in Bucharest in 1926. Her main activity was the designing of hospitals and other medical institutions. She also designed many country houses in the mountain regions and on the Black Sea shore. Although she kept up with the modern architecture that was taking root in Rumania, her work is characterized by a personal interpretation of traditional Rumanian architecture.

CONSTANTIN MARIN MARINESCU

WORKS

1934–1935, Villa Albatros; 1934–1935, Villa Rio de Janeiro; 1956–1960, Fudeni Hospital; Balcic, Bulgaria.

BIBLIOGRAPHY

IONESCU, GRIGORE 1965 Volume 2 in *Istoria Arhitecturii in Romania*. Bucharest: Editura Academiei Republicii Romañe.

IONESCU, GRIGORE 1969 *Arhitectura in Romania; Perioda anilor 1944–1969*. Bucharest: Editura Academiei Republicii Socialiste Româña.

IONESCU, GRIGORE 1972 "Saptezeci si cinci de ani de la infiintarea invatamintului de arhitectura din Romania." *Arhitectura* 20:35–42.

MAMBRIANI, ALBERTO 1969 *L'Architettura Moderna nei Paesi Balcanici*. Bologna, Italy: Capelli.

PATRULIUS, RADU 1973–1974 "Contributii Romanesti in Arhitectura Anilor '30." *Arhitectura* 20, no. 6:44–52; 21, no. 1:53–59.

SASARMAN, GHEORGHE 1972 "Inceputurile gindirii teoretice in arhitectura românešca (1860–1916)." *Arhitectura* 20, no. 6:44–46.

DEL DEBBIO, ENRICO

Born in Carrara, Italy, Enrico Del Debbio (1891–1973) distinguished himself in the local Fine Arts Academy and won several prizes for designs, among them the Pensionato Del Monte (1912) and the Pensionato artistico nazionale (1914). He was able to take part in the aristic life of Rome, at Ripetta's Fine Arts Academy and among avant-garde groups of architects and artists. From 1918 on, his professional work was representative of the *Scuola Romana,* with a peculiar inclination toward a neoclassical synthetic taste and a neo-Piranesian (see GIOVANNI BATTISTA PIRANESI) archaism, which allowed him to minimize academical monumentalism even in public works for the Fascist regime.

This peculiarity can be found also—together with a technical correctness in design and in building—in his most important work, the general plan and several buildings in the sports complex of the Foro Mussolini (1930), in which he searched for a simplified language and some approach to Italian Rationalism.

Del Debbio taught architecture from 1920 to 1964 at the School of Architecture in Rome. He was also active in many associations and academies, institutes, and Public Committees, among which the Accademia di San Luca in Rome.

ANTONINO TERRANOVA

WORKS

1923, Torlonia Casale (restoration); 1925, Fiat Palace, Via Calabria; 1930, Foro Mussolini (guest rooms); 1930–1932, Olympic Stadium; 1952–1953, Canova Cafe, Piazza del Popolo; 1957–1960, International Student's House, Foro Italico; Rome. 1961–1965, IFAP Buildings, Terni, Italy. 1968, Thermal Baths, Montesano, Italy.

BIBLIOGRAPHY

ACCASTO, GIANNI; FRATICELLI, VANNA; and NICOLINI, RENATO 1971 *L'architettura di Roma capitale: 1870–1970*. Rome: Golem.

Istituto Nazionale di Urbanistica 1954 *Urbanisti italiani*. Rome: The institute.

VALERIANI, ENRICO 1976 *Del Debbio*. Rome: Editalia.

DEL DUCA, GIACOMO

Giacomo Del Duca (c.1520–1604), who is also known as Jacopo Siciliano or Ciciliano, was born in Cefalu, Italy. Sculptor, bronze caster, and architect, he worked in the Roman workshop of Rafaello di Montelupo. Later, he became an assistant of MICHELANGELO and was the latter's most outstanding and peculiar student, and the only one to remain in Rome after the master's death. Del Duca was one of the finalists in the competition of 1585 for the transportation of the Vatican obelisk. By 1592, he was retained as architect by the city of Messina.

The completion of the construction of the Porta Pia in Rome (1562–1565) is attributed to Del Duca; the zoomorphic arms held by the angels and the large mask mounted on the gate are by him, modeled largely on a design by Michelangelo. His first work of architecture seems to have been the gate of San Giovanni, Rome (1573–1574), whose military design resembles the gates proposed by SEBASTIANO SERLIO and Francesco di Hollanda. The *bugnato* of the arched entryway is intertwined with that of the flanking pilasters supporting a deeply modeled balustrade. At Santa Maria in Loreto, Rome (1573–1577), Del Duca completed the drum, dome, and lantern. The latter, richly detailed and animated with eccentric decoration—small, masklike heads were his specialty—was supported by a double-shell dome. The central window of the drum, framed in layers of Michelangelesque elements, contained also more recent Florentine influences. In respect to the model (St. Peter's), there was a complete transformation of the relationship between the single elements. By contrast, the bell tower is stripped of all decoration and relies on form alone to display a new, tense, and muscular architecture. In the relatively simple façade of Santa Maria in Trivio, Rome (1573–1575), organized by two pairs of Ionic pilasters, the door frame seems squashed between layers of exaggerated detail. The frames of the upper-level windows are squeezed between the capitals of the giant order, reinforcing the quietly tormented quality of the façade.

In his work on the piazza in front of the Palazzo Farnese in Caprarola (1584–1586), Del Duca displayed acute urban design abilities. The change in level is negotiated by a pair of curved ramps and the insertion of a basement at the entry level. The façade of this storage area and the ramps have a strong military aspect, thus adhering to the character of the palace. The masks in the side niches flanking the entry portico give a premonition of things to come in the upper garden of the palace, also laid out by Del Duca. The directional element is the cascading water chain, which is on an axis with the upper garden's pavilion. The ascending water chain leads the visitor to the curved ramps, which, similar to the entrance ramps, negotiate the change of level to the porch of the pavilion. Two further staircases rise from the sides of this level, laid out in various low mazes centered on fountains, to the square behind the pavilion where a flower garden rises further up the hill. The garden sequence repeats in microcosm the sequence of entry and passage through the main palace. The detailing throughout is masterful. The water chain is made of curled dolphins, and the walls flanking the ramps are covered like grottoes with tiny fieldstones. The "glass" fountain at the top of the water chain is flanked by enormous reclining statues on *bugnato* pedestals. The oval ramps are framed by an even-height wall where the *bugnato* pilasters frame niches with huge *maschere* and become shorter as the ramps ascend, as though they continued beneath the ramp; the residual pilaster at the last bay is no more than a midget pilaster. Throughout, the grotesque abounds, in the elaborations of the water chain (Del Duca may have worked on the garden of the Villa Lante in Bagnaia which also had elaborate waterworks), the gigantesque detailing of the ramp, and the size of the masks, for whose design Francesco di Hollanda's *maschere antiche* may have been a model.

Del Duca's greatest merit may be his examination of Michelangelo's proposals with a provincial spirit free of restricting habits and rules, in search of the emotional, the anticanonical essence.

MARTHA POLLAK

WORKS

1562–1565, Porta Pia (mascherone and stemma); 1564–1568, Farnese Tabernacle; 1568, Swiss Guards' Chapel (works in stone), Vatican City; 1570, Savelli Tomb, San Giovanni in Laterano; 1573–1574, San Giovanni (gate); 1573–1575, Santa Maria in Trivio (complex); 1573–1577, Santa Maria di Loreto (drum, dome, and lantern); 1575–1577, Trajan's Column (enclosure); 1575–1583, Public Works; 1576, Orti Farnesiani (wall enclosure); 1582, Palazzo Cornaro; Rome. 1582, Parish Church (presbytery and choir), Compagno, Italy. 1582, Santa Maria Imperatrice (restoration), Rome. 1582–1585, Castle (gates and secret garden), Bracciano, Italy. 1584–1586, Palazzo Farnese (garden, basement, and front piazza); 1584–1586, Palazzo Restituti (garden, basement, and front piazza); Caprarola, Italy. *c.1585, Santi Quirico e Giulitta (restructuring); c.1586, Garden of Cardinal Pio, Palazzo Rivaldi; *c.1586, Villa Mattei; 1586–1587, Mattei Chapel, Aracoeli; *1586–1587, Villa Mattei, Monte Mario; Rome. 1592–1604, San Giovanni di Malta (tribune); *1599, Palazzo Senatorio (sea façade); Messina, Italy.

BIBLIOGRAPHY

BENEDETTI, SANDRO 1967 "L'opera del Giacomo del Duca in S. Maria di Loreto in Roma." *Quaderini, Instituto di Storia dell'Architettura* Series 1479–1484 14:1–40.

BENEDETTI, SANDRO 1970 "Nuovi documenti e qualche ipotesi su Giacomo del Duca." *Palladio* New Series 20:3–37.

BENEDETTI, SANDRO 1973 *Giacomo del Duca e l'architettura del Cinquecento.* Rome: Officina.

HESS, JACOB 1966 "Villa Lante di Bagnaia e Giacomo del Duca." *Palatino* 10:21–32.

SCHIAVO, ARMANDO 1973 "Il michelangiolesco tabernacolo di Jacopo del Duca." *Studi Romani* 21, no. 2:215–220.

SCHWAGER, KLAUS 1967 "Unbekannte Zeichnungen Jacopo del Ducas: Ein Beitrag zur Michelangelo-Nachfolge." Volume 2, pages 56–63 in *Stil und Überlieferung in der Kunst des Abendlandes: Akten des 21. internationalen Kongress für Kunstgeschichte in Bonn.* Bonn: The congress.

DELLA PORTA, GIACOMO

See PORTA, GIACOMO DELLA.

DELLA ROBBIA, LUCA

See ROBBIA, LUCA DELLA.

DEL MORAL, ENRIQUE

Enrique del Moral (1906–) was born in Irapuato, Mexico. The formal and programmatic characteristics of his works make him one of the most dis-

tinguished contemporary architects. He has distinguished himself through a wide range of works: hospitals, office buildings, schools, workers' housing, private houses, public markets, university complexes, and bullfight arenas. Especially notable are his private houses in the cities of Irapuato, Mexico, and Acapulco.

The use of local materials in conjunction with concrete and steel and a consummate comprehension of the problems of Mexico after the revolution of 1910 grant him a distinguished place in international architecture.

Together with the architect MARIO PANI, he designed the University City complex of the National Free University of Mexico (1947–1954).

He was director of the architectural school of the University of Mexico, an international lecturer, and the writer of various notable essays on the style of architecture.

SALVADOR PINOCELLY
Translated from Spanish by
Judith E. Meighan

WORKS

1936, Workers Houses (ten), Acapulco, Mexico. 1939, Andre Guieu House, Cuernevaca, Mexico. 1940–1941, Gama Apartments, Zacatecas y Cordova, Mexico. 1943–1946, Hospital, San Luis Potosi, Mexico. 1947–1954, University City (master plan, with Mario Pani), Mexico City. 1951–1952, Miguel Arias House (with Pani); 1952, Club de Pesca (with Pani); Acapulco, Mexico. 1962–1963, Treasury, Mexico City. 1967–1968, Subway Stations, Tlalpan, Mexico. 1975–1977, Quintana Apartments, Acapulco, Mexico.

DELORME, PHILIBERT

Philibert Delorme (c.1510–1570), whose name is also spelled de l'Orme, de Lorme, and De L'Orme, is acknowledged to be the only architect of the sixteenth century in France on a par with contemporary Italians, yet few buildings bear witness to his impressive achievement. Instead, we are confronted with architectural fragments, a restoration of his principal work, the Château of Anet, and, above all, his treatise on architecture. His most original expressions in building occurred during the reign of Henri II; this period terminated with the king's death in 1559 and Delorme's fall from royal favor.

Life. Born in Lyons, France, Philibert was the son of Jean Delorme, master mason. In his native city, he supervised workers on construction sites. From the age of fifteen, according to his own account, he was in daily charge of more than 300 men; simultaneously, he studied theology. Both his practical and his theoretical training were reinforced throughout his life. Surely, he must have absorbed much of the intellectual atmosphere of Lyons as a leading financial, cultural, and printing center, with its traditions reaching back to Rome and with its proximity to the classical monuments of the Provence. According to references in his treatise, he spent the years 1533–1536 in Rome, where he pursued his studies and inventions in architecture: "in the time of my great youth, I measured buildings and antiquities" ([1567]1648, folio 131r, folio 90v; all folio references are from this work); while thus engaged, he tells of being "discovered" by Cardinal St. Croix, later Pope Marcellus II, learned in sciences and architecture, knowledgeable of antiquities and active in excavations of Hadrian's Villa, favored by Paul III, and an organizer of the Vatican Library. Delorme further relates that he "entered the service of Pope Paul III and received 'une belle charge à St. Martin *dello Bosco,* à la Callabre'" (1860, p. 58). He attended meetings of the Vitruvian Academy, where he was acquainted with SEBASTIANO SERLIO, GIACOMO BAROZZI DA VIGNOLA, GUILLAUME PHILANDER, commentator on VITRUVIUS; and his patron, Georges d'Armagnac, bishop of Rodez. This circle also included Guillaume Du Bellay and his brother Cardinal Jean Du Bellay, humanist and archeologist and ambassador of Francis I. Rabelais, secretary and doctor of the Cardinal, was in Rome in 1534–1535, studying classical monuments and planning a topography of the ancient city. In fact, Blunt (1953, pp. 8–14) hypothesizes that Delorme may well have influenced the detailed description of the Abbey of Thélème in *Gargantua,* published in 1534 (*ibid.,* pp. 8–14). Rabelais's revolutionary abbey reflects the latest Renaissance modes in its references to antiquity and in its emphasis on regularity and ingenious geometry; its innovations extend to the apartment units, similar to those recently designed at Madrid and Chambord. A sketchbook in Munich, largely of modern Roman buildings (1534–1536), has been ascribed by Blunt to Delorme on the basis of the technical ingenuity displayed in the drawings (*ibid.,* pp. 15–17).

Following the advice of the Du Bellays, Delorme returned to France in 1536. At that time, he completed his first known work, the Hôtel de Bullioud in Lyons, for the Minister of Finance and the Treasurer General of Brittany. Only two *trompes* (squinches supporting turrets) remain of this gallery addition to the Hôtel on the rue de la Juiverie (folios 90r,v). Details of the orders are classical but the whole is not. Around 1540, Delorme was called to Paris by Cardinal Du Bellay to work on his newly acquired Château of Saint-Maur-les-Fossés. In 1545, he was appointed inspector of the fortifications in Brittany and was occu-

pied with other aspects of military eningeering. He became architect to the Dauphin, and in 1547 he began work on the Château of Anet.

It was only with the accession to the throne of Henri II in 1547 that Delorme became architect to the king and in effect *surintendant des bâtiments,* thereby assuming charge of all royal buildings with the exception of the Louvre. Among his early commissions was the tomb of Francis I, executed in 1547–1548. One of his few surviving works, in the traditional form of French royal tombs, it is dominated by a noble triumphal arch, as Roman as it is radical; witness the unorthodox intersection of Ionic volutes.

The twelve-year period which Delorme spent in the employ of Henri II was indeed the most productive of his life. But the wheel of fortune turned for Delorme with the death of Henri II in 1559. Immediately, he was deposed as inspector of royal buildings and replaced by Catherine's compatriot and his archrival, FRANCESCO PRIMATICCIO, who, with little experience in architecture, became the royal architect. It was then that Delorme probably wrote the *Instruction de Monsieur d'Yvry, dict de lorme, Abbé de Saint-Sierge, et cestz M^e architecteur du Roy* (Bibliothèque Nationale, Paris; first published by A. Berty, *Les Grands Architectes français de la Renaissance,* Paris, 1860, pp. 49–59), an *apologia pro sua vita* to counter the accusations against him and to exalt his merits. In this brief memorandum, he stresses his many works in the service of his country. Frequently referring to his duties and accomplishments as a military architect, to which he apparently consecrated much of his early years, Delorme cites his inspection of fortresses, galleys, and ships in Brittany twice a year; he enumerates engagements at Brest, Concarneau, Nantes, and places in Picardy and Normandy. In these duties, he was often aided by his brother Jean, who acted as his collaborator and inspector. In his capacity as military engineer, Jean succeeded Philibert in 1549 as superintendent of fortifications in Brittany, and he worked in Italy around 1553; from around 1556–1558, he assisted Philibert in Fontainebleau and Chenonceau. As *escuyer, sieur de Saint-Germain, commissaire député par le roy sur le fait de ses édifices et bastiments,* he shared Philibert's disgrace.

Written as a defense, the memorandum reads like a litany of Delorme's accomplishments in which he calls attention to his inventions in timber framing and roofing and his concern for built-in safety mechanisms. He cites specific works of which he is especially proud—the grand flight of steps "in the low court [at Fontainebleau] which is one of the most beautiful works that could be seen," the temple at Villers-Cotterets, the "chapel at Saint Léger, and La Muette at Saint Germain.

The tone of this remarkable document borders on paranoia, hardly concealing the unabashed anger, outrage, disenchantment, and self-pity as the architect rattles off his ecclesiastical titles and benefices given to him as compensation—namely, the abbeys of Géveton in Brittany, Nantes, Saint Barthélemy of Noyon, Saint Eloi of Noyon, Saint Serge of Angers, with its excellent stone quarries (folio 27r), and Ivry. Further, Delorme notes the lack of hard cash in the form of wages or pensions, even for the models he made as the king's architect. He attributes his disgrace to the divine will who punished him for having rendered more to the service of man than to God. In the time of enforced leisure, he set down his ideas about architecture that would appear in his published works.

Catherine's actions were often capricious and unpredictable. Once again in a position of power when Charles IX succeeded Francis II in 1560, she soon after engaged Delorme on royal projects. Thus he spent his last years on the enlargement of Saint Maur, and, above all, on the palace of the Tuileries, which occupied him until his death in 1570. He was buried in the Cathedral of Notre Dame, where he had recently made repairs and where he had served as canon since 1550.

Works. It was for his sponsor, Cardinal Du Bellay, that Delorme undertook his first major work, the Château de Saint-Maur-les-Fossés. Six miles east of Paris, near Vincennes, it was formerly a Benedictine abbey. Between 1541 and 1544, Delorme built the main corps-de-logis, which, with its terraced roof, has been likened to an Italian villa, more specifically, the Palazzo del Te in Mantua. Whereas classical details, most notably the Corinthian orders, are correct, irregularities persist in the mullion windows (fol. 323r), and traditional elements survive on the interior as well. Saint-Maur was praised by Rabelais as a *Paradis de Salubrité,* and by Jean Goujon as Delorme's most successful work. Acclaimed as the herald of the new classical style in France, Delorme himself proudly declaims that it is he who has "brought into France the manner of good building, removed the barbarous fashions and great gaping joints in the masonry, . . . shown to all how one should observe the measures of architecture . . . and trained the best workmen there are today. . . . let one remember how one built when I began Sainct-Mort" (1860, p. 54); "this is the first built in France to show how one should observe the proportions and measures of architecture" (folio 322r). Elsewhere, Delorme refers to Saint-Maur to illustrate many points in his treatise, such as the practical difficulties of the site, including orientation according to winds and disposition, the soil, the building of foundations at comparatively little

cost by sinking shafts forty feet down to terra firma, and building masonry piers with arches that carried the walls above (folios 46r,v). Here, Delorme applied methods of engineering used in medieval structures.

While in charge of the works at Fontainebleau from 1548 to 1559, Delorme was responsible for the extraordinary horseshoe staircase of the Cour du Cheval Blanc (1558); remarkable for the complexity of its vaulting, it was replaced under Louis XIII. Still extant, however, is the flat wooden ceiling of the ballroom, known as the Galerie Henri II; its Italianate coffered paneling was carved by Scibec de Carpi by order of Delorme in 1550 in place of the elliptical vaulted ceiling originally planned.

In 1548, Delorme enlarged the medieval royal Château of Saint-Léger-en-Yvelines in the forest of Montofort-l'Amaury and built anew the gallery, the small chapel, and the two pavilions (1860, p. 56; folio 322r). As Anet was built for Diane de Poitiers, so in the same years, Saint-Léger was designed for Catherine. Incomplete in 1559, the plan consists of a large court surrounded by four wings, including a brick-and-stone corps-de-logis. The château, to be replaced by a royal stud-farm, was demolished in 1667. Recent excavations and soundings (1977–1979) at the juncture of the wing of the east entry and the southern grand gallery have revealed foundations of Delorme's gallery, and the spacing of the piers agrees with Jacques Androuet Du Cerceau's (see DU CERCEAU FAMILY) plan and elevation as recorded in drawings in the Vatican Library (Chastel, 1980). Part of the vestibule of the central staircase on the west wing has also been found. The remarkable chapel, a centrally domed building on a trefoil plan, recalls those at Anet and Villers-Cotterets.

No undertaking engaged the talents of Delorme more than Anet (1547–1555), the château in Dreux, which the king's mistress, Diane de Poitiers, planned as a memorial to her deceased husband, Louis de Brèze, once Grand Senechal of Normandy. Henri II provided funds for Diane, the duchess of Valentinois, to create a pleasure palace to replace the old fortress. The Latin inscription above the entry proclaims that "By Phoebus has this magnificent dwelling been consecrated to the fair Diana, and Diana offers him in return all that she has been given." The myth of Diana is all pervasive and contributes to the amazingly consistent iconographical program prevalent throughout, from the architecture of the whole to the smallest detail. The presence of Henri and Diane is ubiquitous—their initials intertwined with the royal crown and symbolic crescent, allegorical portraits in the guise of Apollo and Diana.

Funerary symbolism is rampant from the pyramids crowning the chapel's tower to the pervasive use of black and white, to the sarcophagi which function as monumental chimneys—and as fountains. All alludes to the goddess of the chase and the bereavement of Diane de Poitiers. Surely the collaboration of Delorme with Diane is likely.

Anet is Delorme's only work which gives us a glimpse of his genius, though even here most of the buildings were torn down in the Revolution and alterations to the west wing occurred in the seventeenth century. As described by Du Cerceau, "The building is planned in a plain accommodated with all that is needed to make a place perfect, such as a park, woods, canals." Even though the general layout of three wings symmetrically disposed about the court is not new, Delorme's treatment of the three court façades is. For example, there is no loggia on the left wing, which included accommodations for guests and was surrounded by flanking courts and gardens. The right wing contains the chapel, while the center harbors the apartments of Henri and Diane on the first floor. A terrace overlooks a sunken garden reached by a crescent staircase; below the terrace is the cryptoporticus "to go from loggia to the garden" (folio 125r): I remedied not only [the old walls] but also all the old body of the hotel which was very badly founded" (folios 90v–91r).

Still intact are the frontispiece of the central corps de logis (now in the Ecole des Beaux-Arts court, Paris), the entry gate, and the chapel. A paradigm of the French Renaissance, the frontispiece retains the character of the fortified entry to a medieval castle. Strictly an ornamental façade, it does not relate to anything in the main block behind. It does, however, link Anet with Ecouen and the Louvre—the superposition of correct though enriched classical orders, the whole rising to an appropriate crescendo in the statue of Louis de Brèze. But Delorme's inventiveness is most visible in the entrance façade, forming a screen to the three courts behind. Based on a triumphal arch scheme, the mass of the entry gatehouse is comprised of a series of receding volumes on the interior and bastionlike structures on the exterior. In its union of divers units, the whole forms a sculptural entity, enhanced too by the sarcophagi on the terraces of the wings; in the shape of sixteenth-century Italian cassoni, they function as chimneys, but allusions to Diana's bath are not improbable. Most astonishing is the clock at the summit; mechanical contrivances set the stag and two hunting dogs in motion at the striking of the hours, while an astrolabe with its Zodiac records the phases of the moon and wandering stars or planets (folio 247v). The severity of the Doric order adorning the portal is re-

Delorme.
Château of Anet (trompe).
France.
1547–1555.

Delorme.
Chapel, Château of Anet.
France.
1549–1552

deemed by the pierced parapet of interlacing patterns, the colored marbles of triglyphs and metopes, and the bronze nymph by Cellini in the tympanum (now in the Louvre). On either side of the brick-and-stone walls in the center are groups of trees which are incorporated as part of the design and thus contribute to the symbolic, albeit funerary, associations of the ensemble.

Of all the structures at Anet, none is more ingenious than the chapel. A circular space in the tradition of DONATO BRAMANTE's Tempietto, it features a dome supported on a cylindrical structure; ancient examples of coffering are recalled, such as the half-dome of the Temple of Venus and Rome. The dome and lantern are mirrored in the floor design and the lines of the coffering are repeated in the black and white marble pavement, thereby clarifying the whole. There is no prototype in France for this intriguing circular temple form. Although it is Italian in concept, its transformation of ancient and Renaissance ideas is highly original. A circle set within a square forms a shell all around and emphasizes the continuous quality of the wall which is supported by a cylindrical lower structure instead of piers, whose arcs cut into the curves of the dome. Resonances abound of Roman funerary monuments transmitted by fifteenth-century sketchbooks. Roots for this design have been detected in Antonio da Sangallo the Younger's (see SANGELLO FAMILY) funerary chapel in Montecassino for Piero de' Medici the Magnificent and in the ground plan and vaulting of the tepidarium of Diocletian's Bath (Hoffmann, 1973, pp. 133–136), while Blunt cites MICHELE SANMICHELI's Pellegrini Chapel in Verona as the immediate model (1953, p. 40). Delorme undoubtedly knew the central plans in FRANCESCO DI GIORGIO MARTINI's manuscripts, LEONARDO DA VINCI's Vitruvian man, and Serlio's Book V, as well as the built centralized churches of the Renaissance. The plan of the chapel is reflected in ANDREA PALLADIO's Maser Chapel (1577–1580) perhaps known to him via Delorme's treatise. But above all, the play of spatial concepts, the dynamic sense of movement as stressed by cross-axes throughout, and the impression of rotation raised by diagonal segments of the cupola recall MICHELANGELO's plan for San Giovanni de' Fiorentini. The chapel's exterior is comprised of a collection of related parts—segmented pediments at the side, the dome and lantern, the stone pyramid, the spire and the obelisk—elements used in Henri II's entry into Paris in 1549. In fact, both the cupola and the lantern have been interpreted as celestial spheres, allegorizing the imperial ideology of Henri II (Hoffmann, 1973, pp. 35–36).

Even though the entire complex is reminiscent of the Italian mode, Anet is still within the national tradition. Built for a woman, it preserves its feudal character; the seignorial domain and its dependencies are enclosed by a moat with four bastionlike pavilions at the angles. It incorporates a garden and a main court with two side courts at the rear. Delorme surrounded the gardens with galleries of rustic style and included a pool, baths, orangeries and aviaries in the park bordered by canals to drain the swampy terrain (folio 46r). Here were two pavilions with terraced roof where musi-

cians played their cornets and trumpets and other instruments "to give pleasure to the King and princes" (folio 300r). At the end of Diane's park was the Hôtel Dieu, which she ordered to provide lodging for the poor (folio 301r).

Extolled by visitors in its day, Anet was praised by poets and enumerated in such tributes as that given by Joachim Du Bellay in *Les Regrets,* 1558 (ed. Chamard, 179):

De vostre Dianet (de vostre nom j'appelle
Vostre maison d'Anet) la belle architecture,
Les marbres animéz, la vivante peinture,
Qui la font estimer des maisons la plus belle

In 1547, Henri II had given Chenonceaux to Diane de Poitiers. Accounts from 1556–1559 show that Delorme was engaged in building the stone bridge surmounted by a gallery across the river Cher. Delorme's original gallery, including parapets and balustrades, is different from the extant view and from Du Cerceau's engravings; it was completed by JEAN BULLANT in 1576–1578.

Just east of the old château of St. Germain-en-Laye on a site with a fine prospect, unencumbered for once by previous building, Delorme erected a pleasure palace and retreat for Henri II, the Château-Neuf. Begun in 1557, this single-storied palace surrounding a court was conceived as a theater rather than as a château, designed for scenic displays and courtly spectacles—"la maison du théâtre et baignerie" (folio 304r). Based on the contract of 1557 published by Roy, Blunt (1953, pp. 65–67) believes that Delorme's design is markedly different from that shown in Du Cerceau's engravings. The quatrefoil free-standing block preceded by a forecourt and a corps-de-logis with two pavilions containing apartments on each side are within the French mode, thereby forming a link between Madrid and the works of SALOMON DE BROSSE. Works interrupted at Henri II's death and later by the Religious Wars were not resumed until the reign of Henri IV in 1594.

Active in Paris, Delorme executed projects on the site of the Hôtel des Tournelles; a grand domain with a large park, it was the preferred town residence of Henri II. An illustration of a monumental portal serving as entry to the Triumphal Hall in 1559 is the only testimony to Delorme's many designs for festival entries (folio 274r). With the king mortally wounded in the joust held there, the ensemble took on a horror for the royal family and was torn down in 1564. Also in Paris, Delorme worked on public and religious buildings, on bridges and townhouses, and on the upper stories of the Château of Madrid ("on the side where there is no enameled terra cotta" of which he disapproved—[folio 268v]); outside Paris, he worked on the staircase of the Henri II wing of Chambord. At this time (1555–1558), Delorme also built his own house on the rue de Cerisaie, a "building of good grace and without excessive expense" (folios 253r–255r). Illustrations of the street front, the rear of the court and garden façade reveal a cross between Flemish and Italian styles; only the portal is adorned with orders. It is a small townhouse and chapel, simple yet elegant and comfortable.

A few years after the accession to the throne of Charles IX, Delorme was once again engaged in works for the queen mother. In 1563, the unfinished Château of Saint-Maur was sold to Catherine, who instructed Delorme to carry out extensive alterations. The first scheme of enlargement included changes in the gatehouse and two pavilions at each end of the corps-de-logis; linked by a terrace on an arcaded cryptoporticus, the existing buildings remained the same. The second scheme after Delorme's death, as known through Du Cerceau's *Les Plus Excellents Bastiments,* was far more radical—"on three orders of arches . . . is a pediment in the antique manner, and [in its grandness] dazzling." Chenonceau, too, passed on to Catherine; the scheme for its enlargement from around 1576 as known from illustrations by Du Cerceau, may have been planned by Delorme, though Blunt feels that it may well be a fantasy of Du Cerceau (1953, 64).

Delorme's prime commission in his last decade was the building of Catherine's new palace on the site acquired in 1564, formerly occupied by a tile and pottery works, namely, the Tuileries. Because only a small portion was completed at Delorme's death, and this part altered in the seventeenth century and entirely demolished during the Commune in 1871, and because documents are limited, opinions about Delorme's work differ. According to Du Cerceau, the whole was an enormous complex, the palace and gardens designed to be viewed across the moat in relationship to the king's palace, the Louvre; thus, in its attention to the topography of the site, it is analogous to GIORGIO VASARI's joining of the two Medici palaces in Florence. Du Cerceau's detailed drawings also reflect the influence, or rather interference, of Catherine. Her intervention is further corroborated by Delorme, who refers to the work under construction throughout his treatise. While expressing his gratitude to the queen mother for her confidence in him, he notes that it was her taste that was displayed in the rich and elaborate ornament and sculptured pediments, and that she was responsible for the "many incrustations of different kinds of marble, of gilded bronze and mineral stones . . . the stones of this country to enrich the masonry"

Delorme.
Hôtel des Tournelles
   (*monumental portal*).
Paris.
1559

Delorme.
Tuileries (*fragment of
   arcade*).
Paris.
1564–1570

(folio 20r). Her boundless penchant for ostentation led her to change the columns in the course of construction, ordering a "much richer style" commensurate with a most magnificent palace (folio 221r).

Delorme apparently executed the central part of the west garden wing; the south pavilion was completed by Bullant after Delorme's death, and works continued until the time of Louis XIV. The extraordinary staircase in the central pavilion was widely acclaimed. It consisted of two parts: the main flight from the court entry to the first floor, and a section that led from the entrance to a vestibule on the garden side. Known only in descriptions and in surviving drawings (Nationalmuseum, Stockholm; Archives des Monuments Civils, Paris), it appears to have been an astonishing amalgam of medieval ingenuity, mannerist ambiguity, and Catherine's passion for hyperbole. Echoing Lippomano, the Venetian ambassador in 1577, Sauval notes that "one ascends to the great hall . . . by a staircase the most vast, the most comfortable, and the most admirable which exists in the world (1724, vol. 2, p. 54). Sauval describes the cage enclosing an oval staircase, its *trompes* that seemed to produce an almost continuous curving surface, the vaults and convexities, serving as support and foundation to the steps, and the winding spiral stairs not only low and easy, but distinguished by level stretches for even greater facility and propriety. JACQUES FRANÇOIS BLONDEL in his *Cours d'Architecture* (1773, vol. 4, pp. 296–297) cites Delorme's round spiral staircase with ramp suspended in air as "constructed with so much industry and so much art, that it could serve for study to those who wish to learn about the science of the art of stonecutting." Blunt notes the disparity in descriptions between Sauval and Blondel—oval versus round—and further suggests the influence of the staircase of Michelangelo's Laurenziana vestibule completed in 1560, probably known to Delorme via Catherine (1953, pp. 100–107).

The Tuileries had its idiosyncracies, even when compared to sixteenth-century Italian mannerist villas. For example, one notes the absence of a grand entry and, more, the unusual placement of the oval pavilions within the lateral courts; these latter appear to be related to projects of Vignola and Serlio (folios 70v, 71r on oval *traicts;* compare central oval room (c.1542–1545) in Serlio, Book VII, executed when Serlio was at Fontainebleau). Blunt proposes a smaller palace and hypothesizes that Du Cerceau took liberties in his rendering (1953, pp. 92–97). This seems unreasonable; after all, the Tuileries was a royal palace and *Les Plus Excellents Bastiments* is dedicated to the queen. Furthermore, Du Cerceau himself explicitly notes the great size of the building; surely this is in keeping with Catherine's grand schemes at this time and in tune with its role as *the* queen's palace, a palace for entertainment and spectacles, with galleries and gardens to provide vistas and divers pleasures.

Writings.   Nouvelles inventions pour bien bastir et à petits frais (1561) is a short tract largely containing useful advice for building. It considers such matters as correct and incorrect practices in roofing, the construction of beams, their role in sus-

taining the wall instead of vice versa, and the use of iron in masonry. The woodcuts act as diagrams of structural details, illustrating, for example, Delorme's built-up timber roofs; these required no ties or heavy beams but were comprised of trusses composed of small beams pinned together. Throughout, Delorme draws on examples from his own works and from his unexecuted inventions such as the amazing wooden vaulted basilica or *lieu royal* (folio 303r,v); this covered hall with a gallery above and four pavilions was tied by passages with access to the grand hall—a strange hybrid between medieval halls of justice and nineteenth-century railroad sheds. Hardly less incredible is Delorme's project for the roofing of a dormitory as part of the rebuilding of the Montmartre convent, following its destruction by fire in 1559 (folio 304v): a circular structure is surrounded by the three stories of nuns' cells on the periphery; at the center of the cloister, there is a two-story peristyle crowned by an enormous cupola. Delorme here adapts his invention of lightweight construction in wood embodying economy, elegance, and energy to the exigencies of comfort and light. At the summit of the mountain of Montmartre, the spherical form could be viewed by Parisians as a "terrestrial or celestial globe . . . where one marked the hours of the day by the shadow of the sun." Like his contemporaries, Delorme grasped the importance of the *idea* of the sphere, part of the model making of science as well as architecture and part of Henri II's imperial symbolism (Hoffmann, 1978, pp. 37–38).

Le premier Tome d'Architecture (1567) is the most monumental treatise of the time. An essay in architecture, it is closer in spirit to the works of Vitruvius and Palladio (and even ANTONIO AVERLINO FILARETE, in the fantasy of some inventions), than to LEON BATTISTA ALBERTI, and closer to the latter than to contemporary tracts of Serlio and Vignola. Unlike earlier Renaissance treatises, it is addressed to practicing architects rather than to humanists, and it is concerned with practical solutions to the problems of building. Dedicated to King Charles IX, Delorme begins his magnum opus with a paean to the king's father, Henri II, "who provided the useful and necessary conditions for the perfection of architecture to order me to make him a Book so that everyone could understand the ways and means of [building]." He further informs us that publication was prevented by the king's death, but is now possible "since having recovered the liberty of my spirit." Written in the first person, the treatise is an extraordinary amalgam of theory and practice. Based on Delorme's own experiences, it is also very consciously a treatise to enhance the profession of the architect.

More, it is a national treatise to proclaim the birth of a new French architecture, written for the "benefit of my country," "the décor of the kingdom," "the profit of the people," "the public good." It is logical that Delorme is the author of this treatise, for it is he who is the founder of the new French architecture. Knowledge and virtue are constantly evoked, and, more, the grace of God. Tribute is rendered to classical learning and eulogies are given to Plato and to Cicero, but highest praise is reserved for the wisdom of Solomon. It is at the conclusion of the Dedicatory Epistle that Delorme announces the second Tome; never written, this book would explore the Divine Proportions as transmitted by the Old Testament.

Delorme is less dogmatic about the orders than Vitruvius or Serlio or their use in the monuments of antiquity; none of these authorities is infallible. Rather, he turns to another builder: "For God is the only, the great, and wonderful Architect, who has ordered and created by his single word the entire machine of the world, celestial as elementary and terrestrial with an order so great, a measure so grand and proportions so admirable that the human spirit could understand them without his aid and inspiration." These holy and divine measurements were given by God to the Holy Fathers of the Old Testament; to the patriarch Noah to build the ark, to Moses for the tabernacle of the altar, and to Solomon for the Temple of Jerusalem. He wonders why the ancients and moderns did not use these divine measures and proportions ordained from heaven, which co-exist with those derived by measure from the human body. These proportions, based on prime numbers, are applied to the treatment of orders (folios 137vff.) in Books VII and VIII and to specific buildings (folio 235r,v). Both Blunt and Wittkower note the probable influence of Francesco Giorgi, whose memorandum of 1535 for the rebuilding of San Francesco della Vigna contains passages based on proportions of the Old Testament, though admittedly Giorgi was more interested in harmonic proportions derived from music (Blunt, 1953, pp. 132–133; Wittkower, 1949, p. 136ff.).

Following his erudite and literary dedication, Delorme's notice to the reader transfers us directly to the realm of practice. He launches into the difficulty of finding trees large enough to make beams, by explaining his experiment of a new system of *charpente* (timberwork) at La Muette (folio 4v). Necessitated by a lack of beams to support roofs, he devised a system of framing by assemblage, lighter and less costly. To the hunting lodge in the woods of Saint Germain, Delorme added a semicircular timber barrel vault covered with slates; above the terrace roof he made a leaded belvedere

Delorme.
Architect Emerging from Cave.
From Le premier Tome de l'Architecture.

(folio 290v). Twenty years later, Du Cerceau noted that beautiful though it was, the weight of the roofing threatened the safety of the building, which one day would become a total ruin—a prediction fulfilled in the seventeenth century, before it was demolished under Louis XIV.

It is at once apparent that Delorme's intended reader is the architect, the builder, the craftsman to whom he stresses economy and utility. His responsibility to the new profession is never in doubt. Like his other works, the treatise tells much of the man, his proselytization of the new architecture, his contemporaries, and his relationships with them; it confirms his friendship with Rabelais, his difficulties with Ronsard, his jealousy of Palissy. But Delorme's *Architecture* is also a document of its age. Observations throughout note the way the French lived, their economic circumstances, their social models, as well as practices of construction and technology. Like many current books of natural science, architecture too was a natural object of study, and the illustrations were a means of conveying the ideas in the text. From the beginning, the author lays out his plan and tells us precisely where we are going. The treatise is divided into nine books of unequal length, each introduced by a prologue, giving a résumé of the preceding volume and setting forth the contents of the volume at hand. The organization is not always logical or coherent; the style is prolix and repetitive. Comprised of around 600 pages and about 205 woodcuts (with variations in different editions), it is the largest tract to date. Delorme treats the art of building chronologically, starting with the choice of site (taking into account factors of climate, wind direction, terrain), proceeding to the plan and the laying of foundations to the construction of walls, and ending with the placement of the roof, taking care always to include the functional

Delorme.
The Good Architect.
From Le premier Tome de
   l'Architecture.

Delorme.
The Bad Architect.
From Le premier Tome de
   l'Architecture.

and the ornamental. Emphasis on the design process and the means of directing its execution are ever mindful of the role of the *chantier.* Upon this practical armature, Delorme expounds on the importance of geometry and arithmetic and the orders. The author is concerned with general principles and professional knowledge; abstraction— issues of beauty or harmony for their own sake—is not his forte.

Book I presents the dramatis personae: the patron, the architect, and the executants or master masons. Different steps in building the house are then plotted. Delorme discusses the need for expedient relationships between architect and patron. He cautions both to exercise prudence in preliminary negotiations, especially regarding economics. Once the architect is chosen, however, the patron must leave him free from all constraint. He advises the architect to construct a model so that the patron might readily visualize the scheme—in fact, "several [models] concerning all the principal parts of the building" (folios 21b, 22b); according to Delorme, models leave less to ambiguity (folio 23v). Like his Italian predecessors, Delorme focuses on the education of the architect—the patron "must choose a wise, learned and expert architect" (folio 10r); he thereby lifts the profession from the realm of crafts to that of the liberal arts. Pragmatic as he is, Delorme is more reasonable than Vitruvius in regard to the qualifications of a good architect, underplaying the mastery of such disciplines as medicine and law.

Book II is addressed to the mason and is largely concerned with materials and foundations. Geometrical figures are introduced as useful and necessary for laying the groundwork and for cutting stones for vaults. Here and in Book III, Delorme treats of foundations, including staircases and cellars. The importance of geometry and arithmetic is reiterated in Book IV where certain inventions are introduced, such as the vault and *trompe* at Anet. An empirical knowledge of vaulting and carpentry constitutes the principal thrust of the book. The other main concern are the orders to which the larger part of the treatise is consecrated, specifically Books V–VIII. Much attention is given to the composite order and the "French order" in Book VII, while Book VIII examines the application of the orders in triumphal arches, portals, lucarnes, and windows. The last book is devoted to chimneys.

In Book III, Delorme embarks on a discussion of stereotomy, the art of *traict,* of setting and cutting stones for given positions in masonry in specific situations, including such operations as preparation (projections and cuts in spherical and pyramidal forms analogous to descriptive geome-

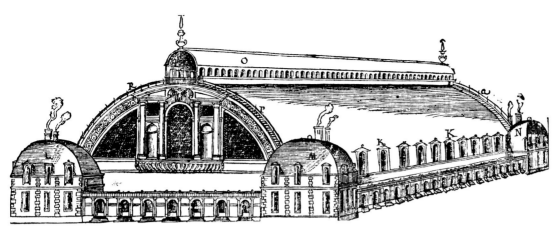

Delorme.
Design for a Basilica.
From Le premier Tome de
l'Architecture.

try) and application, or the execution in the *chantier*. Delorme's analyses are grounded in the secrets of the medieval masons, but he placed stereotomy within the domain of the architect. To demonstrate this art, he cites certain particular works—the twelfth-century barrel-vaulted newel staircase of the Vis Saint Gilles in Languedoc and Bramante's spiral staircase in the Belvedere which he criticizes for not following sloping curves and for using brick instead of stone (folio 123v–124v). In investigating complicated questions of construction and vaulting in Book IV, Delorme's penchant for difficult problems and solutions is apparent; for him, situations created by limitations are particularly challenging. Stereotomy is thus at the core of Delorme's treatise, largely concerned with stone-cutting and timber framing—the surface of arcs, the penetration of volumes. It thereby creates a link with the Middle Ages and ties the architecture of the Renaissance to the great cathedrals, particularly in the accent on the technical construction in vaulting. Equally important is Delorme's emphasis on regularity to mark the transition from the medieval ogival vault to that of the Renaissance.

It is in Book IV, in the context of Anet, that Delorme demonstrates the way in which stone should be cut in the tradition of the medieval masons by illustrating one of his best known inventions, the *trompe* (folios 89v–99r). It was made to bear a cabinet added "to the room where his Majesty King Henri usually lodged" to which he could privately withdraw. In explaining the cutting of the *trompe,* necessitated by a limitation of space and location, Delorme notes the manner in which he arrived at its particular site "without destroying the lodgings or other rooms. . . . to make a vault suspended in the air." He thus ingeniously devised a form of stone corbeling imitating a vault to carry the masonry and loads above; he is mindful, too, of the arching of the lower vault to provide the oval aperture to give light to the staircase. Throughout Delorme's explication of this invention, we are exposed to his creative thought proc-

ess as well as his attention to all practical details. Here, his solution was governed by the need to make available to the king's apartments the requisite comfort without interfering with the geometry of the ensemble. Inserting other examples—a house in Paris on the rue de la Savaterie—he tells us that he writes not for glory, but to teach the ignorant (folios 90r,v). This pedagogical intent informs much of the treatise.

Books V through VIII are devoted to the orders, their measurements, ornaments, and applications. Delorme's references to antique usage are frequent. Although praising Vitruvius—"the opinion of Vitruvius, which pleases me greatly" (folio 142r); "Vitruvius, the incomparable author of architecture" (folio 16v)—he is also ready to point out the confusion, obscurity, and difficulty in the text of the Roman author. Toward Serlio, he is more generous: "It is he who was the first to give to the French, by his books and designs, the knowledge of ancient buildings and many kinds of beautiful inventions . . . I knew him and of great good soul for having given and published of good heart what he had measured, seen and drawn from antiquity" (folio 202v). He is quick, too, to intersperse his treatment of the orders with their application to his own work, testifying once more to his prominent role in French architecture. Discussing the proportions of Saint-Maur, he repeats: "What I have brought to France more than thirty years ago, without taking any glory" (folio 142v).

Expounding on the Ionic order, Delorme introduces the palace of the queen mother, the Tuileries, then under construction: "I wished to accommodate the present order to her said palace because it is seldom used. . . . The other reason . . . is because it is feminine and has been invented according to the proportions and ornaments of females and goddesses" (folios 155v-156r). In the digression in Book V, Delorme repeats Vitruvius who notes the delicacy and greater beauty of the Ionic when compared to the Doric, and the fact that it is more ornate and enriched by singularities

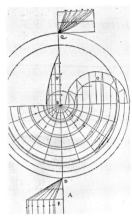

Delorme.
Diagram of the Vault of a
Spiral Staircase.
From Le premier Tome de
l'Architecture.

and hence fitting for a palace of pleasure to give contentment to princes and grand seigneurs. For Delorme, the Ionic had the "charm of novelty," as evident too in his use of this order on the tomb for Francis I (Forssman, 1961, p. 76). In this case, however, Delorme wished to employ this unusual order as an exemplar; above all, it was most appropriate for the queen mother; hence, it was an expressive means, analogous to Serlio's contemporary use of the rustic order.

Delorme had no scruples in making a travesty of the Ionic order by enriching it with bands as if its shafts were of a single cast. He explains his newly devised column: "an invention I have not seen in ancient or modern works, nor in our books of architecture" (folio 156v). It was initially used in the portico of a chapel in the park of Henri II's Château of Villers-Cotterets (1550). "The joints of the foundation are marked by a sculpted band"; "I propose by example our French column, which was made in pieces by certain necessity" (folios 218v, 219v). And like all ancient orders, the French order is inspired by nature itself and adapted to the type and space of stones which one finds in France. Erroneously believing that Greek columns were cut of single shafts of marble, Delorme proposed an expedient solution. Since long shafts of stone were technically unfeasible, four or five drums or decorated bands with splendid ornaments and moldings were superimposed to conceal the joints. His rationale is based on the fact that since the great nations of antiquity had invented new orders, France, a great modern nation, should do the same (folio 218v). From here Delorme proceeds to demonstrate the French version of the five classical orders.

The architect's inventiveness explains in part the emphasis in Book VII on the composite order and his introduction of a column in the form of a tree trunk, justified in terms of ancient writers but probably gleaned from Bramante's column in the Portico della Canonica at Sant' Ambrogio, Milan. In deriving a column from a tree (and in turn comparing a portico to a small forest), Delorme asks why "is it not permitted by imitation of nature to aid us from the first manner of columns drawn from trees" (folios 217r,v).

Throughout the treatise, Delorme considers the gap between texts and reality. Following Vitruvius on ancient architecture, Renaissance architects were creating false solutions. Delorme acts in accord with most Renaissance writers on the orders (aside from Vignola) who admitted the advisability of varying the rules. In Book VI, Delorme presents a digression which includes a warning that cautions against overreliance on the precepts and rules of proportions, measurements, and ornaments of columns (folio 195r; Herrmann, 1973, 102). Delorme's liberty in confrontation with the canon is so extreme that it extended to the necessity to invent different orders. He invites us to seek the "many beautiful inventions hidden in his spirit" (folio 217v) free of prejudice and full of imagination. His text underlies the acceptance of diversity rather than the norm. And it is this inventive spirit in his approach to architectural problems that creates an affinity between Delorme and the masters of the Italian High Renaissance, even Michelangelo.

Delorme constantly asserts the importance of using a variety of measurements, a variety visible in antiquity where he notes that they were "always different: and at all times the buildings were very beautiful to see" (folio 211r). Some were better than others, as "those which approach the most divine proportions and true measures, as we will deduce them some day, God willing." That rules should be applied with freedom and imagination is tied to Delorme's focus on the experience of the professional architect.

Book IX dealing with chimneys seems to end with a whimper. Concerned with function as well as ornament, it is yet another demonstration of the fundamental importance of the practical aspects in Delorme's work. The tome concludes with an allegory as if to remind the reader that one is still emerging from a medieval frame. Here is a moralizing presentation of the good and bad architects—the former superendowed with three eyes, four ears, and four hands, standing in a fruitful garden replete with classical architecture harboring antique fragments; the latter deprived of these physical attributes depicted amidst a barren medieval landscape—which serves to elevate the profession of the architect. The reader has thus come full circle from the dedication, where the good, wise, virtuous, and learned person was opposed to the vicious, bad, and depraved one (folio 3v). The tone of preaching with which the book began is present at its conclusion as well.

Role of the architect. All the theoretical constructions of the treatise directly issue from Delorme's professional practice as a man accustomed to the *chantier.* His wish to impose the domination of the architect on the master mason is the leitmotif of his entire narrative. Thus, Delorme is the first to define the function of the modern architect, in turn artist and man of the *chantier.* Despite Delorme's pragmatic scientific attitude, he never abandons the precepts gleaned in his youth, evident, too, in his references to his inspiration for "divine proportions."

The book stresses the profession of the architect—he who, rather than the master mason, is master of all facets of building and is able to coordinate them. Only the judgment of the skilled architect could decide on the correct proportions. In the preface to Book VI on the Corinthian order, Delorme asserts "that those who wish to make a profession of architecture are sorely mistaken when they have wished to apply the orders of columns, following those they had measured at Rome or elsewhere" without consideration of scale or circumstances (folio 173r). Discussing the Doric capital and the measurement of its parts, Delorme notes that they "must be made according to the good judgment of the architect" and thus correspond with the height and grandeur of the work (folio 145r). The system of the orders thus is a relative system, as is their application, "that is made according to the good and gentle spirit of the architect, who knows how to give the reasons and measures to all his inventions, being well accommodated to the work, which is found always beautiful, admirable and excellent" (folio 152v). What applies to the orders is valid for the construction of the work as a whole. Its beauty and perfection do not come from the application of absolute rules but rather are the function of a specific program.

The treatise is the sum of thirty-five years of experience. To Delorme, professional architecture is synonymous with responsible architecture. Architecture is equated with the social order, for on the quality of architecture depends the material and spiritual well-being of man. Delorme leaves little doubt in the reader's mind that the profile of the profession coincides with his own profile. His idea of the profession is both exalted and down to earth. He is against the practice of amateurs, but he also realizes that the architect is not a universal genius but a professional with adequate skills and knowledge. Geometry is the sine qua non, but besides geometry, the architect must possess the knowledge of materials and know the methods of appropriate construction. Measure and ornament must bow to the "beautiful rules of nature, which concern commodity, usage, and the benefit of the inhabitants, and not to the decoration, beauty, and enrichment of the dwelling, made only for the pleasure of the eyes, without bringing any advantage to the health and life of man" (folio 14r).

Criticism of Delorme. Delorme was not a hero in his time. Enemies of this strong, quarrelsome, uncompromising, arrogant personality included the most eminent artists and poets of the day. Palissy criticized "the god of masons" (1777, II, p. 11) for the failure of his pumps to raise water at Meudon; Primaticcio was the acknowledged competitor and Ronsard vented his anger in such sonnets as the *Epitre à Charles IX:* "J'ay veu trops de

maçons/ Bastir les Tuileries,/ Et en trop de façons/ Faire les momeries." Delorme fared little better in the seventeenth century. In contrast to the reductionism of Vignola and unlike Serlio, who advocated the need to adapt to different circumstances, Delorme invited the architect to explore a new language. This of course ran counter to the academic mentality of the seventeenth century when Fréart de Chambray in 1650 wrote that he looked "upon those excellent things of Rome as it were with Gothic eyes." But by the nineteenth century, rationalist architects would probably agree with EUGÈNE EMMANUEL VIOLLET-LE-DUC, who stated that "more than any of his contemporaries, Delorme was the artist whose taste was surest, whose sentiment the truest, whose principles the most severe . . . [In his work one realizes] an attentive and careful study of proportions, of harmonic relationships" (1858, vol. 1, p. 362). In 1911, Reginald Blomfield, like Lady Dilke before him, focused on his skill in construction rather than on the aesthetics of his architecture (1911, pp. 85–86); "though he had mastered the details of classical architecture, he had not entirely grasped its spirit" (Blomfield, 1905, 189-190). Blunt and Hautecoeur have surely been the most astute critics; Blunt, prone to prove the inaccuracy of Du Cerceau—whether in the Tuileries or in the Château-Neuf at Saint Germain—often questions unexecuted works and details.

Conclusion: the architect. Delorme occupies a singular role in French sixteenth-century architecture, when architecture itself emerged as a discipline in its own right, a new profession. In Delorme, the heritage of the medieval masons fuses with that of the Renaissance humanists. Of all contemporary builders, this merger of theory and practice is closest to that of Palladio; both are classicists hovering on the brink of a new era, though the built legacy and the propagation of an accessible style are absent in Delorme. Instead, we are confronted with an immense fantasy dwelling within the realm of reason, and with an intellectual ambiance permeated not only by the revival of antiquity but by contact with the new experimental scientific world. Well aware of his great Italian predecessors and colleagues, Delorme is more spiritually akin to his friend Rabelais, to the essayist Montaigne, and to the encyclopedic tracts of the sixteenth century, to the new discoveries in the natural sciences, and above all, to the works he alludes to of professors of mathematics at the University of Paris.

However, it is the innovative amalgamation of classicism and medievalism that distinguishes the thought and work of Delorme. Knowledge of antiquity fuses with the absolute logic of vaulting systems of the great cathedrals. It is this legacy derived from the *chantier* that led to his emphasis on building technology and his use of architectural devices in novel ways—the squinch as *trompe,* the new type of truss construction, the attention to stereotomy providing calculable methods for stonecutters. No part of the building process is outside his orbit; he is the designer of ceilings and panelings and the décor of the ensemble.

Most significant, his treatise conveys the emergence of the architect as a modern practitioner. Practical matters are ever present: the role of patron/client, the importance of site and climate and indigenous building materials, and the stress on proportion rather than on decoration, without ignoring the latter. Ultimately, Delorme brought all his talent and knowledge and invention to the service of a new national architecture. "We have an infinity of beautiful *traicts* in France" (folio, 124v); "one will find in France all kinds of marbles, stones and materials to make there the most beautiful and most excellent buildings that one could imagine" (folio 27v). But this new French architecture is open to the liberty as well as to the ratio engendered by Renaissance humanism. Freedom is always tempered by "de bons mesures."

Delorme himself probably best encapsulated the idea of the architect as a learned man and an experienced professional in the allegory portraying the architect given in the prologue of Book III (folios 50r–51v):

Therefore I represent an Architect, dressed as a wise and learned man (as he must be) and as emerging from a cavern or obscure place, that is to say of contemplation, solitude and place of study, so that he can arrive at the true knowledge and perfection of his Art, he tucks up his robe in one hand to show that the Architect must be diligent in all his affairs; and with the other hand he wields and guides a compass with a serpent wound about to signify that he must measure and regulate all his affairs and all his works . . . with a prudence and mature deliberation.

Advancing toward a palm tree, representing glory and honor, the architect encounters ever present caltrops as impediments. But Mercury, author of Eloquence, crowns the emblem. His trophies, the caduceus and the horn, proclaim the fame that the architect will acquire—to which this treatise is a living testament.

NAOMI MILLER

WORKS

1536, Gallery, two *trompes,* Hôtel de Bullioud, Lyons. *1541–1544, Château of St. Maur-les-Fossés, near Paris. c.1545, Altar screen (with Jean Goujon), St. Etienne-du-Mont, Paris (attributed). 1547–1558, Tomb of Francis I (with François Carmoy, François Marchand, Pierre Bontemps), St. Denis. *1547–1556, Arsenal of the King, Paris. 1547–1555, Anêt: *1547–1552, Corps-de-logis opposite entry wing; 1547–1552, Frontispiece (Ecole des Beaux-Arts, Paris); 1547–1549, Crypto-porticus; 1549–1552, Chapel; *1549–1551, Right wing; 1549–1555, Entry; Dreux, France. 1548–1556, Completion of chapel, gallery, Château of Vincennes, Paris. 1548–1559, Ceiling, Gallery of Henri II or Ballroom (with Scibec de Carpi); Henri II's apartments, Pavillon de l'Etang or des Poêles; *Chapelle Haute du roi or St. Saturnin; *Cabinet of the Queen; *Chapelle de la Trinité; *Façades on the Cour de la Fontaine and Cour du Cheval Blanc; *Monumental horseshoe staircase, Cour du Cheval Blanc; *Pavilion of Arms; etc., Fontainebleau. *1548–1559, Grand gallery, chapel, pavilions, Château of St. Léger-en-Yvelines. *1548–1559, Completion of upper stories, fireplaces, Château of Madrid, Paris. *1548–1549, Fountain, triumphal arch, décor for banqueting hall, Hôtel des Tournelles, Paris. *1549, Collaboration, décor for Entry of Henri II to Paris and Coronation of Catherine de'Medici. *1549–1559, Upper story, chapel, Château of La Muette, St. Germain-en-Laye. 1550, Monument for the heart of Francis I (with Pierre Bontemps), St. Denis. *1550–1556, Chapel in the Park, Villers-Cotterets. *1554–1557, Royal stables, Hôtel des Tournelles, Paris. *1554–1558, House of Delorme, rue de la Cerisaie, Paris. *1555–1559, Abbess's quarters, design for new convent, Royal Abbey of Montmartre, Paris. 1556–1559, Bridge and gallery, Château of Chenonceau. *1557–1559, Château-Neuf, St. Germain-en-Laye. *1559, Project for a monumental entry, Hôtel des Tournelles, Paris. *1563, Enlargement, Château of St. Maur. 1564–1569, Repair of vaults, Notre Dame, Paris. *1564–1570, Central pavilion, galleries, monumental staircase, Tuileries, Paris.

BIBLIOGRAPHY

ANDROUET DU CERCEAU THE ELDER, JACQUES (1576–1579)1868–1870 *Les Plus Excellents Bastiments de France.* Reprint. Paris: Levy.

BARDON, FRANÇOISE 1963 *Diane de Poitiers et le mythe de Diane.* Paris: Tresses Universitaires de France.

BERTY, ADOLPHE 1860 *Les Grands Architectes français de la Renaissance.* Paris: Aubry.

BLOMFIELD, REGINALD 1905 *Studies in Architecture.* London: Macmillan.

BLOMFIELD, REGINALD 1911 *A History of French Architecture.* London: Bell.

BLONDEL, JACQUES FRANÇOIS (1773)1913 Volume 4, pages 296–297 in *Cours d'architecture.* 4 vols. Reprint. Paris: Guérinet.

BLUNT, ANTHONY (1953)1981 *Art and Architecture in France; 1500–1700.* Harmondsworth, England: Penguin.

BRIGGS, MARTIN S. 1927 *The Architect in History.* Oxford: Clarendon.

BRION-GUERRY, LILIANE (1955)1960 *Philibert de l'Orme.* Translated by Peter Simmons. New York: Universe.

BRION-GUERRY, LILIANE 1962 *Jean Pélerin Viator: Sa Place dans l'histoire de la perspective.* Paris: Belles Lettres.

CHARVET, E. L. G. 1899 "Philibert Delorme." Pages 275–293 in *Lyon artistique: Architectes*. Lyons, France: Bernoux & Cumin.

CHASTEL, ANDRÉ 1956 "Escalier du château d'Anet." *Bulletin de la Société des Antiquaires de France* 1956:73–74.

CHASTEL, ANDRÉ (editor) 1966 "La Chapelle Saint-Eloi des Orfèvres." *Bibliothèque d'Humanisme et Renaissance* 28:427–438.

CHASTEL, ANDRÉ 1980 "Les Fouilles du château royal de Saint-Léger en Yvelines." *Comptes rendus de l'Académie des Inscriptions et Belles Lettres* Oct.:417–431.

CHÂTELET-LANGE, LILIANE 1973 "Philibert de l'Orme à Montceaux-en-Brie: Le Pavillon de la grotte." *Architectura* no. 2:153–170.

CHEVALIER, M. L'ABBÉ C. 1864 *Lettres et devis de Philibert de l'Orme*. In *Archives Royales de Chenonceau*. Paris: Techener.

CLOUZOT, HENRI 1910 "Un Client de Philibert de L'Orme." *Bulletin du Bibliophile* 1910:352–355.

CLOUZOT, HENRI 1910 *Philibert de l'Orme*. Paris: Plon-Nourrit.

CLOUZOT, HENRI 1917 "Philibert de l'Orme: Grand Architecte du Roi mégiste." Volume 5, pages 75–81 in *Revue du Seizième Siècle*. Paris: Champion.

DELORME, PHILIBERT 1860 "Instruction de Monsieur d'Yvry, dict de lorme, Abbé de Saint Sierge, et cestz Mᵉ architecteur du Roy." Pages 49–59 in *Les Grands Architects français de la Renaissance*. Paris: Berty. Previously unpublished manuscript written c.1560.

DELORME, PHILIBERT (1561)1576 *Nouvelles inventions pour bien bastir et à petits frais*. Paris: Marnef & Cavellat.

DELORME, PHILIBERT (1567)1981 *Le premier Tome de l'Architecture*. With an introduction by Geert Bekaert. Brussels and Liège, Belgium: Mardaga. Facsimile of 1648 edition. All citations in the text are to the 1568 and 1648 editions.

FENTON, EDWARD 1954 "Messer Philibert Delorme." *Metropolitan Museum of Art Bulletin* 13:148–160.

FORSSMAN, ERIK 1956 *Säule und Ornament: Studien zum Problem des Manierismus in den nordischen Säulenbüchern und Vorlageblättern des 16. und 17. Jahrhunderts*. Stockholm: Almqvist & Wiksell.

FORSSMAN, ERIK 1961 *Dorisch, Ionisch, Korinthisch: Studien über den Gebrauch der Säulenordnungen in der Architektur des 16.–18. Jahrhunderts*. Stockholm: Almqvist & Wiksell.

FRÉART DE CHAMBRAY, ROLAND (1650)1733 *A Parallel of the Antient Architecture with the Modern*. Translated by John Evelyn. London: Walthoe.

GÉBELIN, FRANÇOIS 1927 *Les Châteaux de la Renaissance*. Paris: Beaux Arts.

GLOTON, JEAN-JACQUES 1959 "L'Architecture française de la Renaissance: Etat de la question." *L'Information d'Histoire de l'Art* 4, no. 5:133–143.

GRASHOFF, EHLER W. 1940 "Die Schlosskapelle von Anet und die deutsche Barockarchitektur." *Zeitschrift des Deutschen Vereins für Kunstwissenschaft* 7, nos. 2–3:123–130.

GUERRY, LILIANE 1956 "Un Architecte 'moderne': Philibert Delorme." *Le Jardin des Arts* 25:11–18.

GUILLAUME, J. 1982 "Le Traité de De l'Orme." In *Les Traités d'architecture de la Renaissance*. Tours, France: Centre d'Etudes Supérieures de la Renaissance.

HAUTECOEUR, LOUIS 1943 Volume 1 in *Histoire de l'architecture classique en France*. Paris: Picard.

HAUTECOEUR, LOUIS 1961 "Philibert Delorme." Volume 4, pages 302–306 in *Encyclopedia of World Art*. New York, Toronto, and London: McGraw-Hill.

HÉLIOT, PIERRE 1951 "Documents inédits sur le château d'Anet." *Mémoires de la Société nationale des antiquaires de France* Series 9 2:257–269.

HERBET, J. 1894 "Les Travaux de Philibert Delorme à Fontainebleau." *Annales de la Société Historique et Archéologique du Gâtinais* 12:153–163.

HERRMANN, WOLFGANG 1973 *The Theory of Claude Perrault*. London: Zwemmer.

HOFFMAN, VOLKER 1973 "Philibert Delorme und das Schloss Anet." *Architectura* 2:131–152.

HOFFMAN, VOLKER 1973–1974 "Artisti francesi a Roma: Philibert Delorme e Jean Bullant." *Colloqui del Sodalizio* Series 2 no. 4:55–68.

HOFFMAN, VOLKER 1978 "Donec Totum Impleat Orbem: Symbolisme impérial au temps de Henri II." *Bulletin de la Société de l'Histoire de l'Art Français* 1978:29–42.

IVINS, WILLIAM M., JR. 1929 "Philibert de l'Orme's *Premier Tome de l'Architecture*." *Metropolitan Museum of Art Bulletin* 24, no. 5:148–151.

LENORMANT, CHARLES 1840 *Rabelais et l'architecture de la Renaissance*. Paris: Crozet.

MAYER, MARCEL 1953 *Le Château d'Anet*. Paris: Firmin-Didot.

MONTAIGLON, ANATOLE DE 1862 "Philibert et Jean Delorme, architectes (1554–1570): Pièces communiquées par M. Benjamin Fillon et annotées par M. A. de Montaiglon." *Archives de l'Art Français* Series 2 2:314–336.

PALISSY, BERNARD (1777)1888 *Les Oeuvres*. 2 vols. Paris: Niort, Clouzot.

PATTISON, MRS. MARK 1879 Volume 1 in *The Renaissance of Art in France*. London: Kegan Paul.

PÉROUSE DE MONTCLOS, J. M. 1982 "La Stéréotomie dans les traités." In *Les Traités d'architecture de la Renaissance*. Tours, France: Centre d'Etudes Supérieures de la Renaissance.

PFNOR, RODOLPHE 1867 *Monographie du château d'Anet, construit par Philibert de l'Orme*. Paris: The author.

"Philibert De l'Orme." (1890)1903 Volume 4, part 1, pages 130–133 in Paul Planat (editor), *Encyclopédie de l'Architecture et de la Construction*. Paris: Aulanier.

PORCHER, JEAN 1939 "Les Premières Constructions de Philibert Delorme au Château d'Anet." *Bulletin de la Société de l'Histoire de l'Art Français* 1939:6–17.

PRÉVOST, JEAN 1948 *Philibert Delorme*. Paris: Gallimard.

ROY, MAURICE 1913 "La Disgrâce de Philibert De l'Orme à la mort de Henri II." *Annuaire-Bulletin de la Société de l'Histoire de France* 1913:107–122.

ROY, MAURICE 1929 Volume 1, pages 157–392 in *Ar-*

tistes et monuments de la Renaissance en France. 2 vols. Paris: Champion.

SAUVAL, HENRI 1724 Volume 2, pages 54ff. in *Histoire et recherches des antiquités de la ville de Paris.* Paris: Moette.

TOESCA, ILARIA 1956 "Drawings by Jacques Androuet Du Cerceau the Elder in the Vatican Library." *Burlington Magazine* 98:153–157.

VACHON, MARIUS 1887 *Philibert De L'Orme.* Paris: Rouam.

VANAISE, PAUL 1967 "La Construction de la chapelle du parc du chateau de Villers-Cotterêts (1552–1553)." *Bulletin de la Société de l'Histoire de l'Art Français* 1967:27–38.

VIOLLET-LE-DUC, EUGÈNE EMMANUEL (1858)1959 Volume 1, chapter 8 in *Discourses on Architecture.* 2 vols. London: Allen & Unwin. Originally published in French with the title *Entretiens sur l'architecture.*

WARD, WILLIAM H. 1909 *French Châteaux and Gardens in the XVIth Century.* London: Batsford.

WARD, WILLIAM H. (1911)1926 Volume 1 in *The Architecture of the Renaissance in France.* 2 vols. London: Batsford.

WITTKOWER, RUDOLF (1949)1971 *Architectural Principles in the Age of Humanism.* With a new introduction by the author. New York: Random House.

DEMMLER, GEORG ADOLPH

A pupil of KARL FRIEDRICH SCHINKEL, Georg Adolph Demmler (1804–1886) served as court architect to the dukes of Mecklenburg at Schwerin from 1823 until 1848. Schinkel's influence is apparent in the series of monumental representational buildings Demmler built around the Alte Garten in Schwerin. Demmler transformed the Renaissance Schloss (1844–1851) from a collection of structures of various periods to a fanciful and highly picturesque centerpiece of Schwerin and a pioneering landmark of the revival of northern Renaissance forms. His rich exteriors combine forms from the original Schloss, GOTTFRIED SEMPER's 1842 competition design, and French Renaissance châteaux. Due to liberal political involvement, Demmler was replaced in 1851 by FRIEDRICH AUGUST STÜLER who was responsible for the interiors. In his Rathaus façade (1835) and Arsenal (1840–1844), Demmler followed Schinkel's impetus in seeking a synthesis of classical and medieval forms.

BARRY BERGDOLL

WORKS

1823–1834, College Building, Schwerin, Germany. 1828–1829, Theater, Güstrow, Germany. 1831–1836, Theater; 1835, Palace for Grand Duke Paul Friedrich (completed as a museum by L. Willebrand in 1876); 1835, Old Town Hall (façade); 1838–1843, Marstall; 1839–1840, Municipal Hospital; Schwerin, Germany.

1840, Appelationsgericht (now the Zoological Institute), Rostock, Germany. 1840, Feldtor, Wittenburgertor, Gustowertor, Lübeckertor, Wismarschentor, and Berlinertor (all city gates), Commander's House; 1840–1844, Arsenal; (A)1842, Administration Building; 1844–1851, Schloss (exteriors; completed by F. A. Stüler in 1851–1857); Schwerin, Germany. 1850, Glückauf House, Doberan (Kreis Rostock), Germany.

BIBLIOGRAPHY

"G. A. Demmler." 1886 *Deutsche Bauzeitung* 20:51–53, 58–63, 66.

OHLE, WALTER 1960 *Schwerin-Ludwigslust.* Leipzig: Seemann.

MECKLENBURGISCHES LANDESHAUPTARCHIV 1960 Volume 1 in *Schwerin im Spiegel seiner Stadtpläne.* Schwerin, Germany: Die Kleine Reihe des Mecklenburgischen Landeshauptarchivs.

STÜLER, F. A.; PROSCHE, E.; and WILLEBRAND, L. 1869 *Das Schloss zu Schwerin.* Berlin: Ernst and Korn.

DE RENZI, MARIO

The first works of Mario de Renzi (1897–1967), an Italian architect, were fruits of a collaboration with ALBERTO CALZA-BINI, president of the Union of Fascist Architects and director of the IACP (Autonomous Institutes of Popular Houses). In these, there is evidence of the slow acceptance of the Modern movement in Rome. In particular, the Pontifical School (1932) presents a well-calibrated but hardly innovative simplification of the classical styles. Interesting and markedly rationalist is the reorganization of the interior of the German Cultural Institute at Villa Sciarra, Rome (1932). The best works are those done with ADALBERTO LIBERA, secretary of the MIAR (Italian Movement for Rational Architecture); the temporary façade of the Exhibition of the Fascist Revolution (1932) and the Postal Palace for the Aventine district (1933) are among the most significant documents of the history of Italian rational architecture.

SILVIA DANESI SQUARZINA
*Translated from Italian by
Shara Wasserman*

WORKS

1932, Apartment and Movie House, Via XXI Aprile; 1932, German Cultural Center (interior reorganization), Villa Sciarra; *1932, Palace of Expositions (temporary façade), Via Nazionale; 1932, Pontifical School, Fosse di Castello; 1933, Postal Palace, Aventine district; *1933, Italian Pavilion, Chicago Exposition. *1939–1942, Palace of the Armed Forces (with LUIGI FIGINI and GINO POLLINI), E '42 Exposition; 1949–1952, (with SAVERIO MURATORI), Vanco San Paolo and Tuscolano; Rome.

DERISET, ANTOINE

Born in Lyons, Antoine Deriset (1697–1768) studied in Paris and won the first prize of the Academy of Architecture with his project for a Doric palace. In 1723, he moved to Italy as a pensionary at the French Academy in Rome. He was named professor of geometry and perspective at the Academia di San Luca in 1727. As a professor, he developed a strong scholarly interest in theoretical issues and influenced students and contemporaries such as CARLO LODOLI, FRANCESCO MILIZIA, and GIACOMO QUARENGHI.

In 1728, Deriset designed San Claudio dei Borgognoni which evokes GIANLORENZO BERNINI's baroque images and is reminiscent of French and Italian styles in its façades. In 1736, Cardinal Corsini commissioned him to design the Church of Nome di Maria in the Forum of Trajan in Rome. In his design, Deriset used the central components of baroque architecture in order to establish a floating continuity between a focused plan and its exterior envelope. The church is in the form of a small rotunda, and its walls are decorated by the Corinthian order by which Deriset established an original juxtaposition of classical and baroque themes. He introduced eclectic ornamentation in his restoration of the Church of San Luigi dei Francesi. The diverging influences did not result in an homogeneous composition, and the work shows Deriset's limitations as a designer.

Deriset's great contribution to baroque architecture in Rome was in transmitting his wide knowledge as a professor. His interest in the relationship between music and architecture precluded neoclassicist formal preoccupations.

MARC DILET

WORKS

1729, San Claudio dei Borgognoni; 1736–1738, Nome di Maria, Forum of Trajan; 1756, San Luigi dei Francesi; Rome.

DE ROSSI, GIOVANNI ANTONIO

Giovanni Antonio de Rossi (1616–1695) was the son of the stonecutter Lazzaro who had come to Rome from the area of Brambate near Bergamo, Italy, where MARCANTONIO DE ROSSI also originated. The degree of family relationship, if any, still has to be established. Giovanni Antonio received his training from the conservative architect Francesco Peparelli in Rome; he may have collaborated with his master on the construction of Santa Maria della Cima in Genzano (1636–1650), which

he took over as the work proceeded, as is assumed by Gianfranco Spagnesi who established most of the dates of de Rossi's buildings in his basic monograph of 1964, devoted to the architect. Giovanni Antonio's recognition was understandably largely overshadowed by the leading architects of the Roman High baroque. The Church of Santa Maria della Cima, a hall with lateral chapels and an almost square room for the high altar which is detached from the congregational space by strongly projecting lateral piers in a scenographic fashion, is located in the highest part of the city as the terminus of an important urban axis. Giovanni Antonio de Rossi's first work entirely in his own right is Santa Maria in Publicolis (1641–1643), distinguished mainly because of the scenographic qualities of the façade, divided in two stories with the central projection topped by a segmental pediment, and located within the view opened by the funnel-shaped street connection with the Piazza Costaguti, from where the prospect is mainly seen. The rebuilding of San Rocco (1646–1654) on the Tiber embankment near the former Porto di Ripetta, is amazing because of the overtly close affinity with St. Peter's, from which Giovanni Antonio de Rossi adopted the motif of the heavy segmental pediments resting on full columns for the aisles and left open at their bases to increase the strong perspective effect created for the spectator who enters the basilica through either of the two side entrances. His concern for the perception of the spectator is manifest also in his major palaces. The front of the original part of the Palazzo Altieri (1650) on the Piazza del Gesù, which then consisted only of one block, is skillfully broken as it follows the irregular curve of the building and thus to a degree anticipates GIANLORENZO BERNINI's Palazzo Ludovisi (begun 1653). In a similar way, it also "pre-empts" the Palazzo Chigi in Piazza Santi Apostoli (begun 1664) with which it shares the divisioning scheme of a gently projecting center flanked by rather short receding portions. The pilasters by which the center is articulated are so softly divided by the string cornices underneath the windows, that they almost presage Bernini's use of the colossal order under analogous circumstances. The Palazzo Altieri was followed by the Palazzo D'Aste (1658–c.1665), for which Giovanni Antonio corrected the problem of the not fully symmetrical organization on the Corso façade—which is connected with the building site—by employing an equal number of windows on either side of the doorway. However, the palace is mainly famous for its façade toward the Piazza Venezia, where the architect rounded off the corners under Borrominian (see FRANCESCO BORROMINI) inspiration and used the still unusual pa-

Giovanni Antonio De Rossi.
Palazzo Altieri (staircase).
Rome.
1670–1676

Giovanni Antonio De Rossi.
Palazzo Carpegna.
Italy.
1674–1695

goda-shaped window pediments in the uppermost story. The part above the *cornicione* is crowned by a belvedere with a balustrade as the terminating feature. It stands out among Giovanni Antonio de Rossi's works because of the refinement of its proportional system and the neatness of the execution of every detail.

In the service of Roman hospitals, Giovanni Antonio built the Ospedale delle Donne at San Giovanni in Laterano (1655–1656), incorporating an earlier structure, in the traditional style of Italian hospitals, as a barrel-vaulted hall but consisting of one wing only. The altar at one of the small sides is segregated from the main space in Palladian (see ANDREA PALLADIO) style by twin columns with a wider interval in the center (possibly added as late as 1672). Perhaps the most original feature is the double-storied façade which with its triangular pediment intimates a church rather than a hospital front.

The sacristy of the Cathedral in Tivoli, which followed next in the chronology of Giovanni Antonio de Rossi's works (1657), consists of an almost quadrangular hall made interesting because of the vestibule which approximates the effect of a small transverse oval room but in plan is a rectangle enlarged on either side by semicircles.

Giovanni Antonio de Rossi's great hour came when Clement X was elected pope in 1670; his adopted nephew, Cardinal Paluzzo Paluzzi degli Albertoni Altieri, chose him to enlarge the palace in Piazza del Gesù over CARLO FONTANA, who had presented a project evidently less apt for the purpose. The extensions took place in two directions: the original one-winged structure built around 1650 received an arcaded courtyard, for which de Rossi used Bernini's motif of the colossal order from the front of the Palazzo Chigi in great profusion. More conspicuous, even, along the Via del Plebiscito, is the addition parallel to the left flank of the Gesù where during the six years of Clement X's reign (but without his participation) an entirely new structure grew up, realized hastily with workers on night shifts. The addition embraces a deep rectangular courtyard which was conjoined with the previous one by an arcade of four arches. The most spectacular feature of the building is a four-flight staircase, lighted by enormous windows which at that time in Rome had only one equal, Bernini's stairhall of the Palazzo Barberini, which served as the model. Simultaneously, the graceful Villa Altieri (1674, near the Colosseum) was built, which allowed traffic to pass through the central opening of the inferior story, while the *piano nobile* was reached by a horseshoe-curved stairway. This work directly anticipates Giovanni Antonio de Rossi's major building outside Rome, the Palazzo Carpegna at Carpegna in the Marche, first recognized as a work of his by Herbert Siebenhüner in an unpublished article, for which the planning began in the same year. Mainly executed from 1679 until Giovanni Antonio's death, it features an external double-ramped stairway to the principal story which recalls that of the Villa D'Este in Tivoli, or that of the Palazzo Colonna in Marino not to mention the most obvious source, the Palazzo dei Senatori on the Roman Capitol.

After 1674, the circular building of the Cappella Lancellotti at San Giovanni in Laterano was constructed *ex novo*. Although the four pilasters that carry the sail vault are not in a freestanding position but are firmly attached to the wall, a certain similarity with MICHELANGELO's Cappella Sforza in Santa Maria Maggiore has rightly been recognized. Of rare refinement is the integration of the superstructure of the altar into the articulative scheme of the chapel: in Borrominian fashion (lateral altars of San Carlino), the full columns flanking the oval altarpiece, which in form recalls Bernini's altar in Castel Gandolfo, reach the height of the continuous entablature which projects above them and therefore they appear in the frontal view directly associated with the neighboring columns of the chapel which are analogous in shape. The basic scheme in a less sophisticated manner was put to use in Santa Maria in Campomarzio (1682–1685). Close in date (after 1680) is the chapel in the Palazzo del Monte della Pietà, which de Rossi either rebuilt entirely or, less likely, only decorated with colored marble (finished only in 1725 by CARLO FRANCESCO BIZZACCHERI).

Giovanni Antonio de Rossi first planned the church of San Pantaleo (1681–1689), after the precedent of Sant'Agnese in Piazza Navona, as an octagon church with altars set in the niches of the diagonals and spatial extensions along the major axes. The building as it stands now, however, is totally different and reveals the attempt to experiment with the concept of a skeletal structure, evidently under the inspiration of Borromini's Cappella dei Re Magi in the Palazzo della Propaganda Fide. Only the stilted arch above the altar reveals the earlier model of Sant'Agnese.

Between 1682 and 1685, Giovanni Antonio de Rossi replaced the small church of Santa Maria in Campomarzio by a much larger building on a Greek-cross plan which is oriented with its apse toward the opening of the Via degli Uffici del Vicario, where it appears to the spectator as a backdrop, in the fashion of PIETRO BERRETTINI DA CORTONA's portico of Santa Maria della Pace. On the entrance side of the building, Cortona's influence can be felt even more strongly, as de Rossi shaped the interior courtyard (or corridor of the monastery) like a small square, in clear analogy to the Piazza di Santa Maria della Pace.

When in 1695 Giovanni Antonio entered the commission for the Church of the Maddalena, begun by Carlo Fontana in 1668 but interrupted in 1673, he found the room of the high altar and the crossing already determined. In a very competent manner, Giovanni Antonio conjoined the already existing portions of the church with a nave in the form of a longitudinal octagon with side altars positioned in the four diagonal chapels. So as not to divert attention from the high altar, located rather distantly as one enters the church, the architect suppressed the transverse axis (where only niches with statues appear) and used again the motif of the stilted arch as a means to focus attention on the main sanctuary. At the same time, this area is treated as "reserved space" in a manner which brings to mind Carlo Rainaldi's Santa Maria in Campitelli. The Church of the Maddalena was not finished until after de Rossi's death.

During his long career, Giovanni Antonio de Rossi, who like most professionals of his time held various offices and was employed by many noble families and dignitaries, tried to follow a conservative line. This approach, which characterized his work from the beginning, nonetheless did not prevent him from losing touch with the accomplishments of the great masters of his time, Bernini,

Giovanni Antonio De Rossi.
Santa Maria in
* Campomarzio*
* (courtyard).*
Rome.
1682–1685

Borromini, da Cortona, and also Carlo Rainaldi. But his borrowings are careful and selective, and at no time did he associate himself exclusively with the trend of one of the leading architects. Although he did not lack a certain originality, which perhaps appears best in works such as the original building of the Altieri Palace, the Palazzo D'Aste, and the Cappella Lancellotti, de Rossi was most successful when he was bold in his approach to a work by one of the leading masters, as was the case, for instance, with his staircase in the new portion of the Palazzo Altieri and even more so in his forecourt of Santa Maria in Campomarzio, where the quality of his own accomplishment reached at least a level of affinity with the chosen prototype.

HELLMUT HAGER

WORKS

1636–1650, Santa Maria della Cima (with Francesco Peparelli), Genzano, near Rome. 1641–1643, Santa Maria in Publicolis; 1644–1645, Santa Maria Porta Paradisi (interior); 1646–1654, San Rocco (enlargement); 1650, Palazzo Altieri; c.1650, San Francesco di Paola (alteration); 1655–1656, L'Ospedale delle Donne, San Giovanni in Laterano; Rome. 1657, Cathedral (sacristy), Tivoli, Italy. c.1658, Palazzo Gambirasi (alteration); 1658–c.1665, Palazzo d'Aste; c.1660–1662, Palazzo Muti Bussi, Via Aracoeli (courtyard and staircase); *1670, Palazzo Bacelli; 1670–1672, Palazzo Santacroce (enlargement); 1670–1676, Palazzo Altieri (enlargement); 1674, Cappella Lancellotti, San Giovanni in Laterano; 1674, Villa Altieri; Rome. 1674–1695, Palazzo Carpegna, Italy. 1677, Palazzo Nari (doorway, entrance vestibule, and staircase); 1678, Palazzo Celsi (doorway and stairhall); 1678, Palazzo Gomez; 1680, Chapel of Palazzo del Monte della Pietà (not completed until 1725 by Carlo Bizzaccheri); 1681–1689, San Pantaleo; 1682–1685, Santa Maria in Campomarzio (rebuilding); 1695, Santa Maria Maddalena (additions; not completed until 1699 by Giulio Carlo Quadri and Francesco Antonio Bufalini); n.d., Palazzo Astalli; n.d., Palazzo Baldinotti Carpegna; Rome.

BIBLIOGRAPHY

BELLI BARSALI, ISA 1970 *Ville di Roma: Lazio I.* Milan: S.I.S.A.R.

COUDENHOVE-ERTHAL, EDUARD 1930 *Carlo Fontana und die Architektur des römischen Spätbarocks.* Vienna: Schroll.

EIMER, GERHARD 1970–1971 *La Fabbrica di S. Agnese in Navona.* 2 vols. Stockholm: Almqvist & Wiksell.

FAGIOLO DELL' ARCO, MAURIZIO, and CARANDINI, SILVIA 1977–1978 *L'Effimero Barocco: Strutture della festa nella Roma del Seicento.* 2 vols. Rome: Bulzoni.

HAGER, HELLMUT 1967 "Contributi dall'opera di Giovanni Antonio de Rossi per S. Maria in Compo marzio a Roma." *Commentari* 28:329–339.

HAGER, HELLMUT 1967–1968 "Zur Planungs- und Baugeschichte der Zwillingskirchen auf der Piazza del Popolo: S. Maria di Monte santo und S. Maria dei Miracoli in Rom." *Römisches Jahrbuch für Kunstgeschichte* 11:189–306.

HIBBARD, HOWARD 1971 *Carlo Maderno and Roman Architecture: 1580–1630.* University Park: Pennsylvania State University Press.

MALLORY, NINA A. 1977 *Roman Rococo Architecture from Clement XI to Benedict XIV (1700–1758).* New York: Garland.

MORTARI, LUISA 1969 *S. Maria Maddalena.* Rome: Marietti.

PASCOLI, LIONE 1730 Volume 1, pages 316–321 in *Vite de' pittori, scultori, ed architetti: Moderni.* Rome: De'Rossi.

PORTOGHESI, PAOLO (1966)1970 *Roma Barocca.* Cambridge, Mass.: M.I.T. Press.

PREIMESBERGER, RUDOLF 1966–1967 "Entwürfe Pierre Legros für Filippo Juvarras Capella Antamoro." *Römische Historische Mitteilungen* 10:200–215.

SCHIAVO, ARMANDO 1964 *Palazzo Altieri.* Rome: Staderini.

SPAGNESI, GIANFRANCO 1962 "Due opere del primo decennio di ativ̇ità (1640–1650) dell' architetto Giovanni Antonio de Rossi." *Quaderni dell' Istituto di Storia dell' Architettura* 5, nos. 52–53:8–23.

SPAGNESI, GIANFRANCO 1964 *Giovanni Antonio de Rossi: Architetto Romano.* Rome: Officina Edizioni.

TAFURI, MANFREDO 1967 "Un inedito di Giovanni Antonio de Rossi: Il Palazzo Carpegna a Carpegna." *Palatino* 11, no. 2:133–140.

WITTKOWER, RUDOLF (1958)1980 *Art and Architecture in Italy: 1600–1750.* Harmondsworth, England: Penguin.

DE ROSSI, MARCANTONIO

Marcantonio de Rossi (1607–1661), architect and military engineer, was born in or near Bergamo, Italy, and died in Rome. Until rather recently, he was very much an "unknown quantity" whose work had even on occasion been confused with that of FRANCESCO BORROMINI. Minna Heimbürger Ravalli, in her pioneering monograph of 1971, has researched Marcantonio's oeuvre systematically and on a documentary basis. He is the father of two architects: MATTIA DE ROSSI and Domenico de Rossi who died early as the result of an accident which occurred when the statues on the corridor of St. Peter's square were placed in position during the pontificate of Clement XI. Marcantonio held the office of *misuratore della Camera Apostolica* (1658–1661) and was a member of the Accademia di San Luca in Rome. His major work is the urbanistic systemization of San Martino al Cimino near Viterbo (1648–1654) which had become *principato* in 1645 and was placed by Pope Innocent X under the jurisdiction of his sister-in-law, Donna Olimpia Pamphilj. The commission was extended to Marcantonio by her and her son, Don Camillo Pamphilj, and included the urbanization and fortification of the medieval village which is situated on the sloping ridge of a mountain and oriented toward the front of a former Cistercian Abbey dating from the first quarter of the thirteenth century. This church, henceforth referred to as the Cathedral, is situated at the far end on the mountain top and faces the city gate (Porta Viterbese) below. The result of Marcantonio's endeavors is conspicuous as an example of a "planned city" by virtue of the rows of houses built in a uniform pattern, which are flanking the *salita* and are surrounding the church in a hemicycle. In a most remarkable fashion, Marcantonio respected the integrity of the three-aisled basilica and embellished its façade—distinguished by a huge window filled with ornate tracery—with twin bell towers erected *ex novo* in a medievalizing style (begun 1651). The effect of his work is further enhanced by a pre-existing terrace, which he modified, and an open stairway in front of the main portal (1651). Although Marcantonio had been responsible for the system of fortification, the Porta Viterbese, the main entrance into the city, was built to a design by Borromini, but the less ornate Porta della Montagna on the opposite side can safely be considered a work by Marcantonio.

The commission for San Martino al Cimino was preceded by the construction of the fortification walls on the Janiculum under Urban VIII (1643), and connected with it was the building of the Porta di San Pancrazio and also the Porta Portese in Trastevere. Simultaneous with his work for San Martino is de Rossi's participation in VIRGILIO SPADA's project of 1651 to clear the Borgo area in front of Saint Peter's, which would have afforded the present long-distance view of the basilica already at that time, as it was realized anal-

ogously by Marcantonio at San Martino al Cimino. The delightful *Acqua Acetosa* in the north of Rome is also his work, formerly even attributed to GIANLORENZO BERNINI. The steps which lead down to the source guide the visitor to an area which is articulated scenographically and very much in the Berninian spirit by a semicircular screening wall. It has fountains in three round-headed arches which contain the Chigi coat of arms, a motif that reoccurs in the shaped pediment surmounting the composition and cannot fail to reveal Bernini's adornment of the Porta del Popolo as the source of inspiration. The nymphaeum was executed after the architect's death by Andrea Sacchi and Domenico Legendre. This surprising example reveals Marcantonio de Rossi's sensitivity to Berninian concepts, which enabled him to perform not only as a military engineer but also as an architect with a noticeable awareness of the currents of the time, including its Borrominian component, though Marcantonio seems to have been more attracted to Bernini. His limitations, however, become apparent in an accomplishment such as the Porta Portese. With its tripartite division effected by columns and devoid of any motif of vertical culmination, it emulates with a considerable amount of rigidity the scheme of a Roman triumphal arch.

HELLMUT HAGER

WORKS

*1643, Porta di San Pancrazio, Janiculum; 1643, Porta Portese in Trastevere; Rome. 1648–1654, San Martino al Cimino (replanning), near Viterbo, Italy. 1661, Nymphaeum of the Acqua Acetosa (not completed until after Rossi's death), Rome.

BIBLIOGRAPHY

BENTIVOGLIO, ENZO, and VALTIERI, S. 1973 *S. Martino al Cimino.* Viterbo, Italy: Azienda.
EIMER, GERHARD 1970–1971 *La Fabbrica di S. Agnese in Navona.* 2 vols. Stockholm: Almqvist & Wiksell.
HEIMBÜRGER, MINNA RAVALLI 1971 *L'architetto militare Marcantonio de Rossi e alcune sue opere in Roma e nel Lazio.* Rome: Istituto di Studi Romani.
HEIMBÜRGER, MINNA RAVALLI 1977 *Architettura, Scultura e Arti Minori nel Barocco Italiano: Ricerche nell' Archivio Spada.* Florence: Olschki.
ONOFRIO, CESARE D' 1978 *Castel S. Angelo e Borgo tra Roma e Papato.* Rome: Romana società.
PASCOLI, LIONE (1730)1965 Volume 1, page 322 in *Vite dei pittori, scultori ed architetti moderni.* Reprint. Amsterdam: Israel.
PIETRANGELI, CARLO 1974 *L'Accademia Nazionale di San Luca.* Rome: De Luca.

Marcantonio De Rossi. San Martino al Cimino (replanning). Near Viterbo, Italy. 1648–1654

Marcantonio De Rossi. Porta Portese in Trastevere, Rome. 1643

DE ROSSI, MATTIA

Born in Rome, Mattia de Rossi (1637–1695) was the son of MARCANTONIO DE ROSSI from whom he received his first architectural training. His brother was Domenico de Rossi, also an architect, whose death in 1703 was due to an accident. In his *Vita* of Mattia (1730), Lione Pascoli tells us the story of Marcantonio's introduction of his son to his friend GIOVANNI LORENZO BERNINI, who received Mattia in his studio, where the young architect developed into Bernini's favorite assistant who worked for him for the next twenty-five years and whose relationship to Bernini was like that of a son for the rest of his life. We can date Mattia's first connection with Bernini about 1655, and as he

Mattia De Rossi.
Palazzo Rospigliosi.
Lamporecchio, near Pistoia,
*   Italy.*
1668

Mattia De Rossi.
Collegiata Santa Maria
*   dell'Assunta.*
Valmontone, Italy.
1686–1695 (not
*   completed until 1698).*

Mattia De Rossi.
Santa Galla and Hospice
*   (Church and ospizio).*
Rome.
1684–1686

is mainly known as Bernini's assistant, his own career, abruptly terminated by his death at age fifty-seven, has received very limited attention. Mattia de Rossi assisted his master with his churches, Sant'Andrea al Quirinale in Rome, San Tommaso at Castel Gandolfo, the Assunta at Ariccia, and in the modification of Santa Maria di Galloro (near Ariccia). Under Clement IX (1667–1669), he was entrusted with the supervision of the construction of the southern portion of the colonnades of St. Peter's square. Earlier, in 1665, he had accompanied his master to Paris in the matter of the projects for the east wing of the Louvre. Paul Fréart de Chantelou, who kept a diary of Bernini's sojourn, provides us with valuable information about their work and personal relationships. It was Mattia de Rossi who produced the working and presentational drawings from Bernini's rough sketches, although Bernini added the finishing touches himself. Mattia de Rossi also built architectural models for Bernini's projects (for the Louvre and for the likewise unexecuted project for the rear front of Santa Maria Maggiore in Rome, and was supposed to supervise the execution of Bernini's project for the Louvre in Paris before it was discarded. Before

the 1670s, when Mattia de Rossi helped Bernini in the usual fashion with the execution of the monument for Pope Alexander VII and the Tabernacle of the Holy Sacrament in St. Peter's, the aging master already began to rely more heavily on Mattia's assistance, especially in commissions outside of Rome. For Pope Clement IX, he constructed his casino at Lamporecchio (near Pistoia) which, in close analogy to the situation at Ariccia, faces a chapel, the construction of which was imminent in 1668. How far Mattia was dependent on projects by Bernini, however, still has to be determined, although he seems to have had a rather free hand: the longitudinal oval church plan is not what one would necessarily expect from Bernini, who preferred the transverse elliptical form or other centralized schemes, while it is a recurrent feature in Mattia's own work. It occurs in the Hospice Church of Santa Galla in Rome (1684–1686) and at the Collegiate Church adjacent to the Palazzo Pamphilj in Valmontone (1686–1695). The externally rather disadorned palace at Lamporecchio, however, with the arrangement of circular halls contained in the quadrangular center portion of the building superimposed in three stories, may reflect ideas that originated with Bernini. The motif reoccurs in Mattia's oeuvre in his project for a casino with a circular hall in the Accademia di San Luca (1675) which seems to have been submitted when he was formally received as a member, as which he is listed in 1676. CARLO FONTANA followed in 1689 with a project for a casino in the Veneto area which is similar in scheme and also rooted in the tradition of ANDREA PALLADIO's Rotonda. However, an example which demonstrates how far Mattia was able to depart from an original project by Bernini, especially under economic pressure, seems to be the Church of San Bonaventura at Monterano, (1675), which he erected for the Padri delle Scuole Pie. It was commissioned by Cardinal Paluzzo Paluzzi degli Albertoni

Altieri, adopted nephew of Pope Clement X, who owned the nearby palace. The imposing structure as envisaged by Bernini, which in his design culminated in a dome resting on a high drum, was converted in the execution by Mattia to a building with a dome covered by a roof. The major church by de Rossi is the Collegiata at Valmontone, not so much because of the organization of the interior, which is almost a copy of Santa Maria di Montesanto on the Piazza del Popolo in Rome by Carlo Rainaldi and Bernini (1662–1675), but by virtue of its façade, distinguished by a concave trabeated portico, articulated by columns, which is spanned between two bell towers whose rather high open belfries respond scenographically to the surrounding landscape from the top of a mountain. The remodeling of the medieval Basilica of San Francesco a Ripa (1682–1689) was a work of architectural routine dictated by the requirements of a pre-existing situation, again except for the façade, which, in the style of Bernini's modifications to that of Santa Maria del Popolo, is effectively conceived as a building at the end of a street. The same type of façade occurs in Santa Maria delle Vergini, a Greek-cross church with beveled corners, which Mattia de Rossi enlarged or even rebuilt (c.1675) along with the adjoining monastery, and in the front of Sante Croce e Bonaventura dei Lucchesi (c.1692–1696), the design of which may be attributed to him. He also participated in the projectural history of San Giovanni in Laterano, along with GIOVANNI ANTONIO DE ROSSI and others, but no design for this purpose has survived that can be attributed to him. A project for a church to be erected near Sant'Ignazio in Rome for the Padre Garavita was not executed. Ill-fated also was his Church of Santa Francesca Romana a Capo le Case in Rome, which was changed integrally in modern times. Mattia de Rossi also restored the church of Sant'Angelo Custode, which no longer exists.

Mattia de Rossi built numerous altars, all of those in Sant'Andrea al Quirinale (c.1670) were designed by him, variations of the standard type with the superstructure terminating in a triangular or segmental pediment. Others are the High Altar of Santa Maria di Montesanto (1676–1679), where he was also responsible for the flanking niches designed for the busts of the four popes under whom the church had been built; the altar of the Cappella Torre in Santa Maria Maddalena (1690–1696); and the altars of Santa Maria delle Vergini (1675). His model for the High Altar of Sant'Agnese in Piazza Navona, however, was not executed. In Mattia's Cappella Zucchi in Santa Maria in Campitelli (1685–1690), he was tied to the articulative scheme of Carlo Rainaldi's church. In his monument to Clement X in St. Peter's, Mattia de Rossi,

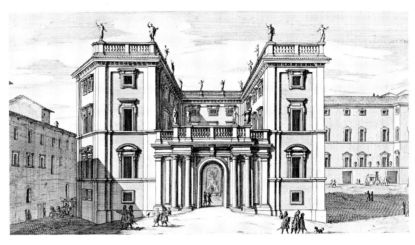

Mattia De Rossi. Palazzo Muti Bussi, Rome. 1675

with Ercole Ferrata's statue of the Blessing Pope (1676–1686) flanked by allegorical statues, follows a long established tradition developed by Bernini, and the same observation can be made with regard to the *Castrum Doloris* for Alexander VIII erected for the ceremony of February 1, 1691, in St. Peter's, which shows the catafalque surrounded by four columns with candles.

In the field of secular architecture, the original building of the Ospizio di San Michele (1686–1689), founded by Innocent XI, a three-winged structure, one side of which is oriented toward the Tiber and the other toward the Cortile dei Ragazzi with a two-storied arcaded loggia, has to be considered his major accomplishment. The building was enlarged by Carlo Fontana who also completed Mattia de Rossi's nearby structure of the Dogana di Ripa Grande (1694). Within the Roman tradition of palace building, rather original in concept is Mattia's Palazzo Muti Bussi (1675) in Piazza della Pilotta, likewise a three-winged structure, the courtyard of which is closed on the front side only by a colonnaded portico one story high. De Rossi completed the building for the Jesuit novices at Sant'Andrea al Quirinale and was also involved in the transformation of Bernini's Palazzo Ludovisi into the Curia Innocenziana (1690–1694) under Innocent XII, where, as Pascoli (1730) says, he may have completed the staircase and the upper story; the main work of the adjustment and enlargement was carried out by Carlo Fontana.

Fontana also succeeded him as architect for Cardinal Benedetto Pamphilj, whom de Rossi served from 1678 to 1681, and for the Principe Marescotti in Vignanello near Viterbo. His project for a palace for Cardinal Rinaldo d'Este remained unexecuted, and his proposals of around 1670 to "embellish" the Rometta Fountain of the Villa d'Este with a waterfall in emulation of Bernini's monumental cascade also remained on paper. The same happened to his interesting though problematic proposal to erect a fountain in the shape of an obelisk on the terrace in front of the Villa d'Este, which would have obstructed the view from the belvedere loggia. Attributable to Mattia de Rossi is a project for the Fontana di Trevi in the Kunstbibliothek in Berlin. It carries the date of 1700 but might have been designed earlier in anticipation of the Holy Year and therefore could be one of Mattia's final and perhaps most felicitous projects: above the cascade, which is reminiscent of Mattia's proposal for the Rometta Fountain of the Villa D'Este at Tivoli, the project envisages a high rising colonnade with projecting columns at the sides and an open interval in the center as a backdrop for a statue of Neptune. Like most of his works, it shows Mattia de Rossi firmly tied to the tradition of Bernini, whose style he continued in congenial and at times rather original fashion after the master's death. His own premature death prevented his becoming a major exponent of this trend, which was to experience its splendid revival in the eighteenth century.

In his lifetime, Mattia de Rossi was highly respected, especially at the Accademia di San Luca, of which he was president in 1681 and 1690–1693. He was also highly esteemed by Bernini's biographer Lione Pascoli and at the Fabbrica di San Pietro in Rome, where he held important offices under Bernini and became his successor as *architetto sovrastante* after Bernini's death in 1680. Chantelou reports that Bernini had the highest esteem for Mattia de Rossi's capabilities and his fine character. He himself considered Mattia de Rossi, among the "four or five" architectural students which Bernini then had, by far the most talented. In 1673, the Swedish architect Nicodemus Tessin the Younger (see TESSIN FAMILY), who visited Rome at that time, considered Mattia de Rossi one of the best architects in Rome and mentioned him in third place after Bernini (after Carlo Fontana, but before Carlo Rainaldi). Undoubtedly, his oeuvre deserves further research.

HELLMUT HAGER

WORKS

1668, Palazzo Rospigliosi (including freestanding chapel), Lamporecchio, near Pistoia, Italy. 1670, Sant'Andrea al Quirinale (altars, sacristy, and building for the novices), Rome. 1675, Santa Bonaventura and Monastery dei Padri delle Scuole Pie, Monterano, near Oriolo, Italy. 1675, Santa Maria delle Vergini (remodeling and altars; now Santa Rita); 1675, Palazzo Muti Bussi, Piazza della Pilotta; 1676, Monument to Clement X, St. Peter's; 1676–1679, High Altar, Santa Maria di Montesanto; 1680, Santa Maria delle Vittoria (organ loft); 1682–1689, San Francesco a Ripa (remodeling); 1684–1686, Santa Galla and Hospice; 1685–1690, Cappella Zucchi, Santa Maria in Campitelli; 1686–1689, Ospizio di San Michele; Rome. 1686–1695, Collegiata

Santa Maria dell'Assunta (not completed until 1698), Valmontone, Italy. 1690–1695, Cappella Torre (altar), Santa Maria Maddalena (not completed until 1696 by CARLO FRANCESCO BIZZACCHERI); 1691, Catafalque for Alexander VIII, St. Peter's; (A)1692–1695, Sante Croce e Bonaventura dei Lucchesi (façade not completed until 1696); 1694, Dogana di Ripa Grande (completed by Carlo Fontana); n.d., Santa Francesca a Capo le Case; Rome.

BIBLIOGRAPHY

ARMELLINI, MARIANO 1942 Volume 1, page 370 in *Le Chiese di Roma dal Sec. IV al XIX*. Rome: Ruffolo.

BALDINUCCI, FILIPPO (1682)1966 *Vita del Cavaliere Giovanni Lorenzo Bernini, Scultore, Architetto e Pittore.* Translated by Catherine Enggass. University Park: Pennsylvania State University Press.

BERNINI, DOMENICO 1713 *Vita del Cavalier Gio. Lorenzo Bernini.* Rome: Bernabò. Excerpts translated on page 40 in George Bauer (editor), *Bernini in Perspective.* Englewood Cliffs, N.J.: Prentice-Hall, 1976.

BORSI, FRANCO 1980 *Bernini Architetto.* Milan: Electa.

BOSCARINO, SALVATORE 1973 *Juvarra Architetto.* Rome: Officina.

BRAHAM, ALLAN, and HAGER, HELLMUT 1977 *Carlo Fontana: The Drawings at Windsor Castle.* London: Zwemmer.

BRAHAM, ALLAN, and SMITH, PETER 1973 *François Mansart.* London: Zwemmer.

BRAUER, HEINRICH, and WITTKOWER, RUDOLF (1931)1970 *Die Zeichnungen des Gianlorenzo Bernini.* New York: Collectors Editions.

BRUHNS, LEO 1940 "Das Motif der ewigen Anbetung in der römischen Grabplastik des 16., 17. und 18. Jahrhunderts." *Römisches Jahrbuch für Kunstgeschichte* 4:253–432.

CASANOVA, MARIA L. 1960 *S. Maria di Montesanto e S. Maria dei Miracoli.* Rome: Marietti.

CHANTELOU, PAUL FRÉART DE 1972 *Journal du voyage du Cavalier Bernini.* With a preface by G. Charensol. New York: Franklin.

COFFIN, DAVID R. 1960 *The Villa D'Este at Tivoli.* N.J.: Princeton University Press.

COUDENHOVE-ERTHAL, EDUARD 1930 *Carlo Fontana und die Architektur des römischen Spätbarocks.* Vienna: Schroll.

DEE, ELAINE EVANS (compiler) 1968 *Views of Florence and Tuscany by Giuseppe Zocchi, 1711–1767: Seventy-seven Drawings from the Collection of the Pierpont Morgan Library.* Meriden, Conn.: Meriden Gravure.

EIMER, GERHARD 1970–1971 *La Fabbrica di S. Agnese in Navona.* 2 vols. Stockholm: Almqvist & Wiksell.

ENGGASS, ROBERT 1964 *The Painting of Baciccio, Giovanni Battista Gaulli, 1639–1709.* University Park: Pennsylvania State University Press.

ENGGASS, ROBERT 1976 *Early Eighteenth-Century Sculpture in Rome.* 2 vols. University Park: Pennsylvania State University Press.

FAGIOLO DELL'ARCO, MAURIZIO, and CARANDINI, SILVIA 1977–1978 *L'Effimero Barocco: Strutture della festa nella Roma del Seicento.* 2 vols. Rome: Bulzoni.

FAGIOLO DELL'ARCO, MAURIZIO, and FAGIOLO DELL'ARCO, MARCELLO 1967 *Bernini: Una introduzione al gran teatro del Barocco.* Rome: Bulzoni.

FASOLO, FURIO 1960 *L'opera di Hieronimo e Carlo Rainaldi.* Rome: Edizioni Ricerche.

GAYNOR, JUAN SANTOS, and TOESCA, ILARIA 1963 *S. Silvestro in Capite.* Rome: Marietti.

GIACHI, G., and MATTHIAE, G. 1969 *S. Andrea al Quirinale.* Rome: Marietti.

GOLZIO, VINCENZO 1939 *Documenti Artistici sul Seicento nell' Archivio Chigi.* Rome: Palombi.

GOLZIO, VINCENZO 1941 "Le Chiese di S. Maria di Montesanto e di S. Maria dei Miracoli a Piazza del Popolo a Roma." *Archivi d'Italia* 8:122–148.

HAGER, HELLMUT 1967–1968 "Zur Planungs- und Baugeschichte der Zwillingskirchen auf der Piazza del Popolo: S. Maria di Montesanto und S. Maria dei Miracoli in Rom." *Römisches Jahrbuch für Kunstgeschichte* 2:251–254.

HAGER, HELLMUT 1973 "La crisi statica della cupola di S. Maria in Vallicella in Roma e i rimedi proposti da Carlo Fontana, Carlo Rainaldi e Mattia de Rossi." *Commentari* 24:300–318.

HAGER, HELLMUT 1975a "On a Project Ascribed to Carlo Fontana for the Façade of San Giovanni in Laterano." *Burlington Magazine* 117:105–109.

HAGER, HELLMUT 1975b "Punctualisazzioni su disegni scenici teatrali e l'architettura scenografica del periodo barocco a Roma." *Bolletino del Centro Internazionale di Studi di Architettura Andrea Palladio* 17:119–129.

HAGER, HELLMUT 1978 "Bernini, Mattia de Rossi and the Church of S. Bonaventura at Monterano." *Architectural History* 21:68–78.

HIBBARD, HOWARD 1965 *Bernini.* Harmondsworth, England: Penguin.

HIBBARD, HOWARD 1971 *Carlo Maderno and Roman Architecture: 1580–1630.* University Park: Pennsylvania State University Press.

JACOB, SABINE 1976 "Zu zwei römischen Architekturzeichnungen der Berliner Kunstbibliothek." *Römisches Jahrbuch für Kunstgeschichte* 16:289–304.

LAMB, CARL 1966 *Die Villa D'Este in Tivoli.* Munich: Prestel.

LORENZ, HELLMUT 1979 "Das 'Lustgartengebäude' Fischers von Erlach—Variationen eines architektonischen Themas." *Wiener Jahrbuch für Kunstgeschichte* 32:59–88.

MENICHELLA, ANNA 1981 *S. Francesco a Ripa.* Rome: Rari Nantes.

MONTALTO, LINA 1955 *Un mecenate in Roma Barocca: Il Cardinale Benedetto Pamphilj (1653–1730).* Florence: Sansoni.

ONOFRIO, CESARE D' 1971 *Castel Sant'Angelo.* Rome: Cassa du Risparmio di Roma.

ONOFRIO, CESARE D' 1978 *Castel S. Angelo e Borgo tra Roma e Papato.* Rome: Romana Società.

PASCOLI, LIONE (1730)1965 Volume 1, pages 322–330 in *Vite de' pittori, scultori ed architetti moderni.* Reprint. Amsterdam: Israel.

PESCI, BENEDETTO 1959 *S. Francesco a Ripa.* Rome: Marietti.

PIETRANGELI, CARLO 1974 *L'Accademia Nazionale di San Luca.* Rome: De Luca.

PINELLI, ANTONIO 1976 "Bernini a Monterano." *Il Seicento: Ricerche di Storia dell'Arte* 1-2:171–179.

SPAGNESI, GIANFRANCO 1964 *Giovanni Antonio de Rossi: Architetto Romano.* Rome: Officina.

WITTKOWER, RUDOLF (1958)1973 *Art and Architecture in Italy, 1600–1750.* 3d ed., rev. Harmondsworth, England: Penguin.

DE SANCTIS, FRANCESCO

Although the name of Francesco De Sanctis (c.1693–1731) is associated with one of the great landmarks of Rome, the stairs of the Piazza di Spagna, very little is known about this architect. He appears for the first time in a professional capacity in 1717, as architect of the convent of San Lorenzo in Lucina, Rome. In the 1720s he also became architect of the convent of San Egidio in Trastevere, of the French Minims, and of the Ospizio della Trinità dei Pellegrini (1723–1724). For the latter, he designed his only other important work of architecture, the façade of their adjoining church (1722–1723).

The façade of the Trinità dei Pellegrini follows a traditional Roman type in its general scheme but reinterprets it with inventiveness. The taut concave curve of the front is amplified by the unusual reversal of emphasis between the center and lateral bays, so that the latter project forward and are more richly articulated and ornamented than the former. Verticality is stressed by various means: through the tall proportions of the whole front, the superimposition of identical orders in both stories, and the continuity of the vertical elements through the entire height of the façade. Although De Sanctis used typically light rococo ornament in the niche frames, the baroque boldness and plasticity of the treatment of the wall and its articulation give this front a monumental character; stylistically, it straddles the gap between the contemporary extremes of purely rococo taste and late baroque architecture.

De Sanctis's masterpiece is the stairs of the Trinità dei Monti (1723–1726), Rome, built for the French Minims, who owned the hillside in front of their church. His project presents a novel and imaginative solution to the design of a grand staircase which was an important urban space as well. The shapes that make up the complex plan of the *scalinata* are, with the exception of the top and bottom runs, fragmentary and mutually dependent. The resulting irregular sequence of curves and breaks, unthinkable outside the rococo idiom, successfully achieves the difficult transition between the unaligned axes of the Trinità façade above and

De Sanctis.
Trinità dei Monti (stairs).
Rome.
1723–1726

the Barcaccia fountain and Via Condotti below. De Sanctis's design also resolved most ingeniously the problem of the arduous climb up the hillside; physically, because he broke the long ascent into short runs of steps and provided comfortable landings at frequent intervals; psychologically, because he made the user visually more aware of the rests than of the climbs. The terraces, in fact, dominate the composition, as the spacious landings and their parapets are played up against the first run of steps. This system of terraces builds up a magnificent base for the façade of the Trinità and provides what has been, from the day of its construction on, a very inviting gathering place for the people of Rome.

Two years after the completion of the stairs, due to a combination of heavy rains and deficient construction, the retaining wall of the Viale del Pincio, built in conjunction with the stairs, collapsed, and the stairs were severely damaged. Although the responsibility for the disaster seems to have rested mainly on the contractors, the blow to De Sanctis's reputation must have been enormous. After 1726, De Sanctis's professional activity was reduced to very modest undertakings as architect of the two churches to which he had long been attached.

NINA A. MALLORY

WORKS

1722–1723, Church of the Ospizio della Trinità dei Pellegrini (façade); 1723–1724, Raimondi Monument, Church of the Ospizio della Trinità dei Pellegrini; 1723–1726, Stairs of the Trinità dei Monti; Rome.

BIBLIOGRAPHY

HEMPEL, EBERHARD 1924 "Die Spanische Treppe." Pages 273–290 in *Festschrift Heinrich Wölfflin.* Munich: Hugo Schmidt Verlag.

LOTZ, WOLFGANG 1969 "Die Spanische Treppe, Architektur als Mittel der Diplomatie." *Römisches Jahrbuch für Kunstgeschichte* 12:39–94.

MALLORY, NINA A. 1977 *Roman Rococo Architecture from Clement XI to Benedict XIV (1700–1758).* New York and London: Garland.

PECCHIAI, PIO 1941 *La scalinata di Piazza di Spagna e Villa Medici, l'obelisco della Trinità, la Cappella Borghese alla Trinità dei Monti.* Rome: Fratelli Palombi.

PORTOGHESI, PAOLO (1966)1970 *Roma Barocca: The History of an Architectonic Culture.* Translated by Barbara Luigia La Penta. Cambridge, Mass.: M.I.T. Press.

DESGODETZ, ANTOINE

Antoine Desgodetz (1653–1728) was born in Paris. Early in life (1669) he entered the service of the Département des Bâtiments. Sent to Rome to further his studies, he measured—apparently on his own initiative—all important ancient monuments. In 1677, he returned with designs which several years later, on order of Colbert, were published in a splendid folio to become a standard work that established his reputation. He served as *contrôleur* in Chambord and Paris, acted as architect for the Collège de Beauvais in Paris, worked on the Château de Vaudreuil (Eure) and submitted a plan for connecting the Louvre and the Tuileries. Nothing is known, however, of any building designed by him. In 1698, he was elected member of the Académie d'Architecture where, from 1719 until his death in 1728, he held the chair of architecture. His lecture course, containing a survey of building types, has survived in several handwritten copies as has an earlier treatise on the orders. Through his teaching at the academy he influenced the next generation of architects.

WOLFGANG HERRMANN

BIBLIOGRAPHY

DESGODETZ, ANTOINE (1682)1771–1795 *The Ancient Buildings of Rome.* London: George Marshall. Originally published with the title *Les Edifices antiques de Rome dessinés et mesurés très exactement.*

DESGODETZ, ANTOINE (1748)1845 *Les Loix des bâtiments suivant la coutume de Paris . . . enseignées par M. Desgodets . . . Avec les notes de M. Goupy.* Edited by P. Lepage. Rev. & enl. ed. Paris: Marescq & Dujardin.

DUPORTAL, J. 1914–1919 "Le 'Cours d'architecture' de Desgodets." *Revue de l'art ancien et moderne* 36:153–157.

HAUTECOEUR, LOUIS 1948–1950 Volumes 2 and 3 in *Histoire de l'architecture classique en France.* Paris: Picard.

HERRMANN, WOLFGANG 1958 "Antoine Desgodets and the Académie Royale d'Architecture." *Art Bulletin* 40:25–53.

LAPRADE, ALBERT 1960 *François d'Orbay.* Paris: Vincent, Fréal.

MIDDLETON, R. D. 1962 "The Abbé de Cordemoy and the Graeco-Gothic Ideal." *Journal of the Warburg and Courtauld Institutes* 25:278–320.

WIEBENSON, DORA 1969 *Sources of Greek Survival Architecture.* London: Zwemmer.

WEND, GRAF KALNEIN, and LEVEY, MICHAEL 1972 *Art and Architecture of the Eighteenth Century in France.* Harmondsworth, England: Penguin.

DESMAISONS, PIERRE

Born into a family of excellent Parisian builders, Pierre Desmaisons (1733–1791) began his career by building a house of daring design at the corner of Rue de La Vrillière and Rue de La Croix-des-Petits-Champs in Paris. He later constructed several buildings for the Grands Augustins and the chapter of Saint-Honoré. Between the Rue de Bourbon and the River Seine, he erected a series of buildings for the Théatins. On the Rue de Lille, an angel resting on a cloud decorates an elegant portal in the style of Louis XVI. The buildings constructed for the chapter of Saint-Honoré have some similarities with the apartments in the form of a prow which he realized at the corner of Rue Dauphine and Rue Mazarine, Paris. In 1770, he remodeled the buildings of the archbishop of Paris. In particular, he designed a remarkable open staircase which delighted his contemporaries. Desmaisons also modified the archiepiscopal residence at Conflans.

After 1770, when he was admitted to the Académie Royale and was ennobled by Louis XV, more sumptuous works were demanded of him. The Cour de Mai in the Palais de Justice in Paris constitutes his most important work, noteworthy for the remarkable composition of the façade and the daring use of interior space.

In 1785, the king named Desmaisons as architect of courts and prisons for Paris. Between 1786 and 1791, he constructed in this capacity the important buildings of the Nouvelle-Force. In old age at the time of the Revolution, he added two important groups of apartment buildings to the long and sinuous façades in the district of the Palais de Justice.

GÉRARD ROUSSET-CHARNY
Translated from French by
Richard Cleary

BIBLIOGRAPHY

GALLET, MICHEL 1959 "L'oeuvre de Pierre Desmaisons: Architecte du roi de 1733 à 1791." *Bulletin de la Société de l'Histoire de l'Art Français* Oct.:91–100.

DESTAILLEUR, HIPPOLYTE-ALEXANDRE-GABRIEL

Born in Paris, the son of François Hippolyte Destailleur, a fashionable architect, Hippolyte-Alexandre-Gabriel Walter Destailleur (1822–1893) studied at the Ecole des Beaux-Arts (1842–1846), the pupil of ACHILLE LECLÈRE. He worked under ETIENNE HIPPOLYTE GODDE, before succeeding his father as architect to the Ministère de la Justice in 1853, and rebuilding and building anew a succession of town and country houses in a florid Renaissance style. His clients were usually rich and titled. Destailleur was a collector of documents and drawings of architecture and of the decorative arts, largely in France, from the sixteenth to eighteenth centuries, most of which passed into national museums in Berlin (1879) and Paris (1890, 1894). His practice was continued by his son, Walter Andre Destailleur.

R. D. MIDDLETON

WORKS

1855, Hôtel de Luttenroth, rue Dumont d'Urville; 1856–?, Hôtel d'Haussonville, 41 rue Saint Dominique; Paris. 1859–1866, Notre Dame de Sacré Coeur, Conflans-Sainte-Honorine, Seine et Oise, France. 1860–?, Maison mère des Dames du Sacré Coeur, Boulevard des Invalides; 1860, Hôtel Saint-Priest, Avenue Montaigne; 1861, Louis Hersent Tomb, Pere Lachaise Cemetery; Paris. 1861–1872, Château de Saint-Aubin, France. 1864, Collard Tomb, Montparnesse Cemetery; 1866–1867, Hôtel Cramail, 118 Boulevard Haussmann; Paris. 1867–?, Château du Mesnil, Yvelines, France. 1867–1869, Hôtel de Mouchy, Boulevard de Courcelles; 1869–1870, 1889–1890, Hôtel de Noailles, 60 Boulevard Latour-Maubourg; Paris. 1868–1890, Château de Mouchy; 1870–1875, Château de Mello; Oise, France. 1873–1876, 1881–1884, Château de Courance (restoration, extension, and outbuildings), Seine et Oise, France. 1874–1876, Hôtel Urbain, 82 rue de l'Université, Paris. *1874–1876, Palais des Fürsten Hans Heinrich XI von Pless, 78 Wilhelmstrasse, Berlin. 1876–1878, 1880–1885, Château du Duc de Massa, Franconville, Oise, France. 1876–1882, Palais d'Albert de Rothschild, 22/26 Prinz Eugen Strasse, Vienna. 1876–1883, 1888–1890, Waddesdon Manor (for Ferdinand de Rothschild), near Aylesbury, Buckinghamshire, England. 1877, Apartment Building, 21 Avenue de l'Opéra; 1877–1878, Hôtel Cramail, rue de Courcelles; Paris. 1877–1880, Château de Vaux-le-Vicomte (restoration and outbuildings), near Melun, Seine et Marne, France. 1878–1880, Hôtel Boivin, 64 rue de Lisbonne; 1878, Hôtel Viollier, rue Rembrandt; Paris. 1880–1882, Palais de Medina-Celi (entrance court and stairhall), Madrid. 1883–1887, Hôtel Cahen d'Anvers, 2 rue Bassano, Paris. 1886, Noailles Mausoleum, Maintenon, Eure et Loire, France. 1887, Apartment Block, 34 rue Bonaparte, Paris. 1887–1889, Priory and Mausoleum for Napoleon III and Family, Farnborough, Hampshire, England.

1887–1895, Château de Vouzeron, Cher, France. 1888–1889, Hôtel Conégliano, 62 rue de Ponthieu; 1889, House, 103 Avenue Malakoff; 1890, Hôtel de Noailles (extension), 131–133 rue de Grenelle; Paris.

BIBLIOGRAPHY

BERCKENHAGEN, EKHART 1970 *Staatliche Museen Preussischer Kulturbesitz: Die Französischen Zeichnungen der Kunstbibliothek Berlin.* Berlin: Hessling.

BERCKENHAGEN, EKHART 1976 "Hippolyte Destailleur." Pages 115–154, in *Fünf Architekten aus Fünf Jahrhunderten.* Berlin: Mann.

DESTAILLEUR, HIPPOLYTE-ALEXANDRE-GABRIEL WALTER 1858–1871 *Recueil d'estampes relatives à l'ornamentation des appartements aux XVIe, XVIIe et XVIIIe siècles.* 2 vols. Paris: Rapilly.

DUPLESSIS, GEORGES 1895 "Notice sur M. Hippolyte Destailleur architecte." Pages i–xvii in *Catalogue de livres et stampes relatifs aux Beaux-Arts provenant de la bibliothèque de feu M. Hippolyte Destailler.* Paris: Damascène Morgand.

DEVEY, GEORGE

George Devey (1820–1886) was born and educated in London. He studied painting under J. S. Cotman and J. D. Harding, then trained as an architect under Thomas Little. His first important commission was at Penshurst, Kent, where from 1850 on he built cottages of a convincingly fifteenth-century appearance. He developed a large, exclusively domestic practice, designing cottages, lodges, village schools, and farms, a few London houses and interiors, and many enormous country mansions. He also restored and enlarged a host of older ones. He pioneered a rambling, informal look and his mansions were generally in a free sixteenth- or seventeenth-century style, but also often included a suggestion of pre-existing medieval work. He died in Hastings, Sussex. CHARLES F. A. VOYSEY worked in his office.

JILL FRANKLIN

WORKS

In the list below, the word "additions" means that Devey's work on an older house was so substantial as to produce an effectively new creation.

1850–1860, Cottages and Village Buildings, Penshurst; 1856–1882, Betteshanger Cottage Hospital; 1856–1882, Betteshanger House; Kent, England. *c.1863, 1870–1874, Coombe Cottage; *c.1863, 1870–1875, Coombe Warren; Surrey, England. 1864, Wickwar Vicarage, Gloucestershire, England. 1867–1868, Akeley Wood, Buckinghamshire, England. *1867–1875, Calverley Grange, Kent. 1867–1875, Wilcote Manor (additions), Oxfordshire, England. 1868–1883, Brantingham Thorpe, Yorkshire, England. 1869–1871, Lillies, Buckinghamshire, England. 1870–1874, 1881–1882, Sway-lands (additions), Kent, England. 1870–1884, Ascott (additions), Buckinghamshire, England. 1871–1872, Send Holme, Surrey, England. 1871–1872, Walmer Castle (restoration of Lord Warden's Quarters), Kent, England. 1871–1873, Wendover Manor, Buckinghamshire, England. *1871–1874, Hall Place, Kent, England. 1871–1875, Bishop Burton, Yorkshire, England. 1871–1875, Denne Hill, Kent, England. 1871–1877, Goldings, Hertfordshire, England. 1871–1877, Stydd House; 1874–1878, Saint Alban's Court; Kent, England. *1875–1886, Ashfold, Sussex, England. 1876–1879, Blakesware, Hertfordshire, England. 1876–1879, Eythrope Pavilion, Buckinghamshire, England. 1877, Betteshanger Parsonage, Kent, England. *1877–1879, Killarney House, Kerry, Ireland. *1877–1879, Membland (additions), Devon, England. *1877–1881, Adderley Hall, Shropshire, England. *1877–1883, Longwood, Hampshire, England. *1880–1884, Durdans (additions), Surrey, England. 1883–1886, Minley Manor (additions), Hampshire, England. 1884–1886, Melbury House (additions), Dorset, England. *1885–1886, Monkshatch, Surrey, England. 1886–1888, Dunraven Castle (additions), Glamorganshire, Wales.

BIBLIOGRAPHY

GIROUARD, MARK (1971)1979 *The Victorian Country House.* Rev. ed. New Haven: Yale University Press.

GODFREY, W. H. 1906 "George Devey FRIBA: A Biographical Essay." *Journal of the Royal Institute of British Architects* Series 3 13:501–525.

GODFREY, W. H. 1907 "The Work of George Devey." *Architectural Review* 21:23–30, 83–88, 293–306.

"Obituary." 1886 *The Builder* 52:728.

DE WAILLY, CHARLES

Charles de Wailly (1730–1798), a contemporary of CLAUDE NICOLAS LEDOUX and VICTOR LOUIS, was born and died in Paris. He was one of the most celebrated architects of his time, not only in France, where he made his official career, but all across the Europe of the Enlightenment, which recognized him as one of the great innovative artists of the epoch. Voltaire and Catherine II were clients of his, and Denis Diderot and Jean d'Alembert published engravings of two of his buildings in the *Encyclopédie.* During the Revolution and Jacques Louis David's domination of artistic affairs, de Wailly's incontestable versatility earned him a position of first rank among the artists of the new regime. An intimate friend of the sculptor Pierre Pajou, a member of the Académie Royale d'Architecture (1767), and—rare achievement for an architect—a member of the Académie de Peinture et de Sculpture (1771), de Wailly, a protégé of the Marquis d'Argenson, pursued the double career of builder and *peintre-architecte.*

His training under GIOVANNI NICCOLO SERVANDONI and JEAN LAURENT LE GEAY predisposed him to become one of the French followers of GIOVANNI BATTISTA PIRANESI, infatuated with the picturesque, the theatrical, and the play of contrasts. His many drawings in wash and in watercolor of imaginary projects or *vedute* worthy of HUBERT ROBERT or Pierre Antoine de Machy (with whom de Wailly exhibited in the Salons du Louvre) are the most striking evidence of his oeuvre, today scattered among the world's principal drawing collections in New York, Leningrad, Paris, Brussels, Vienna, and Berlin. Also a student of the theoretician JACQUES FRANÇOIS BLONDEL, de Wailly won the Grand Prix d'Architecture in 1752. His stay in Italy at the French Academy in Rome (1754–1756) followed by three other trips to that country, some visits to England, to the Netherlands, and to Germany confirm his European connections.

In the early stages of his career, de Wailly was known as an ornament designer and decorator. He published engravings of his designs for vases and furniture, and he worked on ANGE JACQUES GABRIEL's Opéra at Versailles (1767–1700) as well as on some stage settings for Servandoni. Without ever interrupting the creative force that allowed him to produce numerous interior decorations for religious and civil buildings, de Wailly expanded his career to include urban planning and public and private civil architecture (Parisian *hôtels* and châteaux). His aesthetic, springing from both the rationalism of the neoclassicists and a particularly acute sense of the theatrical and the poetic, places him in a position next to ETIENNE LOUIS BOULLÉE and Ledoux among the masters of metaphorical architecture. His passion for antiquity blended with an admiration, rare at the time, for the exuberant display of GIANLORENZO BERNINI. Unfortunately, most of his buildings today are demolished or badly damaged. The Théâtre de l'Odéon in Paris (1769–1782), which he built with his friend Marie-Joseph Peyre (see PEYRE FAMILY) and which still evinces a genius for urban scenography, has been disfigured by fires and unsympathetic restorations.

Included among his students were Antoine-Marie Peyre (see PEYRE FAMILY), LOUIS-FRANÇOIS PETIT-RADEL, and BERNARD POYET, who achieved fame during the Empire.

DANIEL RABREAU
Translated from French by
Shara Wasserman

WORKS

*1762–1770, Hôtel d'Argenson (interior), Paris. *1764–1769, Château de Montmusard, near Dijon, France. *1769, Chapel of the Resting Place, Versailles, France. *1769–1778, Château des Ornes (renovation), Poitou, France. 1769–1782, Théâtre de l'Odéon (with Marie-Joseph Peyre), Paris. *1772–1773, Grand Salon, Palais Spinola, Gênes, France. *1774–1778, Hôtel de Voltaire, rue Richelieu; *1776–1778, Hôtels de Pajou et de Ch. de Wailly, rue de la Pépinière; 1778, Chapel of the Virgin (redecoration), Saint-Sulpice; 1780, Saint-Leu-Saint Gilles (crypt); *1784, La Comédie italienne (new interior arrangement); Paris.

BIBLIOGRAPHY

BRAHAM, ALLAN 1980 *The Architecture of the French Enlightenment.* Berkeley: University of California Press.
MOSSER, MONIQUE, and RABREAU, DANIEL 1979 *Charles De Wailly: Peintre-architecte dans l'Europe des Lumières.* Paris.

De Wailly.
Théâtre de l'Odéon (with Marie-Joseph Peyre).
Paris.
1769–1782

DEWEZ, LAURENT BENOÎT

The foremost promoter of the classical revival in the Belgian provinces, Laurent Benoît Dewez (1731–1812) studied first in Naples and then in Rome with LUIGI VANVITELLI. He continued his education with frequent trips through Europe and to the Near East and through his friendship with ROBERT ADAM. Named architect of the Belgian court in 1767, he undertook, by the example of his own abundant and innovative work, a reform of architecture inspired by the principles of the Louis XVI style.

MAURICE CULOT
Translated from French by
Richard Cleary

WORKS

1762–1763, Church of the Chapter of Andenne, Belgium. 1763–1768, Château de Seneffe, Belgium. 1768–1776, Church and Abbey (reconstruction), Orval, Belgium. 1770–1776, Bonne-Espérance (abbey and cloisters), Belgium. 1776, Herlaimont (reconstruction of the priory), Belgium.

DEXTER, GEORGE MINOT

George Minot Dexter (1802–1872), prominent engineer-architect of mid-nineteenth-century Boston, was much influenced during his European travels in the 1820s by the neoclassical and romantic philosophies of ETIENNE LOUIS BOULLÉE, CLAUDE NICOLAS LEDOUX, and KARL FRIEDRICH SCHINKEL. During the 1830s, together with GRIDLEY J. F. BRYANT, ISAIAH ROGERS, and SOLOMON WILLARD, he trained in Boston as a civil engineer under Loammi Baldwin and ALEXANDER PARRIS. A founder of the American Society of Civil Engineers in 1848, Dexter became its president in 1850.

Although his active practice spanned only sixteen years (1836–1852), drawings for his more than one hundred commissions of all types reveal him as a restrained, vigorous, and skillful draftsman whose stylistic vision reflected his engineering training. His numerous commercial designs, many for the new railroad industry, were impressive. He designed many civic buildings, being an unsuccessful competitor for the Boston City Hall (1838) and the Boston Athenaeum (1845), ultimately serving as engineer for EDWARD CLARKE CABOT on the executed library (1847–1849). Dexter's many residential designs, several executed in collaboration with RICHARD UPJOHN, reflect alternately a Gothic and classical style. His stone Gothic house in Longwood, Brookline, Massachusetts, for Amos Lawrence initiated one of America's first garden suburbs in 1850.

JONATHAN PEARLMAN

WORKS

*1836–1840, Pemberton Square Houses; *1844, Haymarket Station of Boston and Maine Railroad; Boston. 1844, Red Cross Cottage (David Sears House), Newport, Rhode Island. 1844, Stable for Henry Wadsworth Longfellow, Cambridge, Massachusetts. 1844–1846, Massachusetts General Hospital (additions; building by CHARLES BULFINCH), Boston. 1845, Franklin Gordon Dexter House, Manchester-by-the-Sea, Massachusetts. 1845, William H. Prescott House (remodeling), 55 Beacon Street, Boston. *1847, Fitchburg Railroad Station, Causeway Street; 1848–1850, Mill Dam Houses, 92, 93, 94, 95–99 Beacon Street (nos. 92 and 95–99 no longer extant); Boston. 1851, Amos Lawrence House, Longwood, Brookline, Massachusetts.

BIBLIOGRAPHY

The drawings of George M. Dexter, numbering more than twelve hundred, are in the Boston Athenæum.

BUNTING, BAINBRIDGE 1967 *Houses of Boston's Back Bay.* Cambridge, Mass.: Harvard University Press.
"Founding Fathers." 1936 *Journal of the Boston Society of Civil Engineers* 1936:23.
KILHAM, WALTER 1946 *Boston After Bulfinch.* Cambridge, Mass.: Harvard University Press.
KNOWLES, JANE S. 1976 "Changing Images of the Boston Athenæum." In *Change and Continuity.* Boston Athenæum.
LAWRENCE, WILLIAM 1888 *The Life of Amos A. Lawrence.* Boston: Houghton Mifflin.
PEARLMAN, JONATHAN N. 1982 "The Red Cross Cottage and Designs for a Villa in Newport." In William F. Jordy and Christopher Monkhouse (editors), *Buildings on Paper.* Providence, R.I.: Brown University.
WARDWELL, ANNE 1975 "Longwood and Cottage Farm in Brookline." In Pauline Chase Harrell and Margaret Supplee Smith (editors), *Victorian Boston Today.* Boston: Victorian Society.

DIAPER, FREDERIC

One of the most prominent architects in New York in the mid-nineteenth century, Frederic Diaper (1810–1906) was renowned for his Greek Revival commercial architecture and elegantly refined Renaissance Revival mansions. In later works, he skillfully interpreted the Second Empire style as well. Born in Devonshire, England, Diaper studied with ROBERT SMIRKE. He established his own practice and was elected to the Institute of British Architects before emigrating to America at about age twenty-five.

Diaper's partners included HENRY DUDLEY (1864–1869) in New York and ALEXANDER SAELTZER (1869–1871) in San Francisco. Diaper was a founding member of the American Institute of Architects and one of its original trustees. Active in architecture nearly all of his ninety-six years, Diaper died in New Jersey in 1906. Alfred Janson Bloor was one of his students.

JOAN C. WEAKLEY

WORKS

*1838–1840, New York Society Library. c.1840–1842, Beverwyck (Van Rensselaer House), Rensselaer, N.Y. *c.1844, New York Hotel; *c.1845, Aspinwall House; *1845, Bank of America; *1845–1846, Delmonico's Hotel; *c.1846, Minturn House; *c.1846, Seamen's Bank for Savings. *c.1847, Belmont House; *c.1847–1848, City Bank; *c.1848, Union Bank; *c.1848–1850, Howard Hotel; *c.1849, Phenix Bank; *c.1849, Talbot House; *1852, Gihon-Belmont House; *c.1854, D. Parish House; *c.1861, H. Parish House; New York. 1864–1865, Park-McCullough House (with Henry Dudley), North Bennington, Vt. *1870, Mills House (with Alexander Saeltzer), Millbrae, Calif.

BIBLIOGRAPHY

"Annual Address by A. J. Bloor, Fellow." 1877 *American Institute of Architects: Proceedings of the Tenth Annual Convention, 1876.* Boston: Rand, Avery.

BLOOR, ALFRED JANSON 1906 "Frederic Diaper." *American Architect and Building News* 90:94–95.

"Frederick Diaper." 1907–1908 *American Art Annual* 6:108.

DICK, DAVID BRASH

David Brash Dick (1846–1925) was a Toronto architect who trained first with W. L. Moffatt and then with the firm of Peddie and Kinnear in his native Scotland before going to Canada in 1873. Notable among his clients were The Consumers' Gas Company and the University of Toronto. Work for the latter included the Library (1891–1892) and, after a fire in 1890, restoration of University College.

STEPHEN A. OTTO

BIBLIOGRAPHY

A collection of David Brash Dick's drawings is in the Horwood Collection, Ontario Archives, Toronto.

MACTAVISH, NEWTON 1925 *The Fine Arts in Canada.* Toronto: Macmillan.

"Obituary." 1925 *The* (London) *Times,* Sept. 10, p. 140.

DICKINSON, WILLIAM

William Dickinson (1671?–1725), a pupil of CHRISTOPHER WREN, was, as his unexecuted designs show, an architect of competence, but most of his career was spent in working as a surveyor or clerk of works at Saint Paul's Cathedral (from 1696), Greenwich Palace (1696–1701), and Westminster Abbey (1700–1725). He also worked with Wren on the city churches and was briefly a surveyor to the Commissioners for Building Fifty New Churches (1711–1713), before returning to the Royal Works.

JOHN BOLD

BIBLIOGRAPHY

DOWNES, KERRY 1966 *English Baroque Architecture.* London: Zwemmer.

The Wren Society 1924–1943 20 vols.

DIENTZENHOFER, KILIAN IGNAZ

Kilian Ignaz Dientzenhofer (1686–1751) is a major exponent of the last generation of central European baroque architects. He was a contemporary of Dominikus Zimmermann (see ZIMMERMANN BROTHERS), JOHANN BALTHASAR NEUMANN, JOHANN MICHAEL FISCHER, and JOHANN CONRAD SCHLAUN). All these architects in one way or another continued the approach of FRANCESCO BORROMINI and GUARINO GUARINI to space and form. Whereas the others concentrated their attention on particular aspects of this tradition, Kilian Ignaz Dientzenhofer developed its systematic potential. Thus, he created a consistent method of organizing space as an open network of interdependent units. In doing this, he brought the ideas of his father Christoph and his uncle Johann (see DIENTZENHOFER BROTHERS) to their logical conclusion. In addition, he also enriched the vocabulary of Bohemian baroque architecture by means of sensitive detailing and plastic articulation, mostly derivative of LUCAS VON HILDEBRANDT.

Kilian Ignaz Dientzenhofer was born in Prague, and during his childhood and youth he could follow the construction of some of the most important buildings of this city, such as the Saint Nicholas Church in the Lesser Town and the Saint Margaret Church at Břevnov, both designed by his father. In contrast to the older members of the Dientzenhofer family, Kilian Ignaz received a thorough education, and we know that he was well prepared in Latin, philosophy, and theology. In 1707, he was sent to Vienna to study and work, probably under the guidance of Hildebrandt. He remained there for ten years and returned for another visit in 1725, possibly in connection with a trip to Italy. Kilian Ignaz married twice and had nineteen children. From his father he inherited a considerable fortune, and already in 1725 he could afford to build for himself a beautiful mansion in Smichov on the outskirts of Prague, today known as Villa Portheim, from the name of a later owner. In addition to his merits as an architect, Kilian Ignaz was known for having saved Prague from partial destruction when in 1744 he removed the match from a huge mine left by the retiring Swedes. For this heroic deed Empress Maria Theresa offered him a title of nobility, which he did not accept. After his death in 1751, his widow asked the queen for a pension, referring to her husband's faithful services to the country. The request was refused.

The professional career of Kilian Ignaz Dientzenhofer started in 1717 with the construction of a small summer residence for Count Michna, the garden palace Villa Amerika in the New Town of Prague. The layout consists of three pavilions which form an open *cour d'honneur.* The central one is an exceptionally fine essay in Hildebrandtian articulation, combined with a characteristic Bohemian plasticity. In 1719, he got his first commissions for the Church, designing Saint John

Kilian Ignaz Dientzenhofer.
Villa Amerika.
Prague.
1717–1720

Kilian Ignaz Dientzenhofer.
Saint Edwige Church and
*   Monastery.*
Wahlstatt, Czechoslovakia.
1723–1731

Nepomuk on the Hradčany in Prague and the Pilgrimage Church of the Nativity of the Virgin at Nicov in eastern Bohemia. Both churches were built between 1720 and 1728. Being based on similar plans, they make the basic intentions of their architect manifest. Around a dominant central dome, secondary spaces are added as baldachins resting on a skeleton of piers. We recognize a wish for unifying the reduced Greek-cross plan of Hildebrandt's church in Gabel with the wall-pillar system of Christoph Dientzenhofer. More fundamental, however, is the attempt at composing a complex organism by means of centralized open spatial units. Shaped as baldachins, the units seem freely placed within a continuous, extended space. Saint John Nepomuk is in general simpler than Nicov, but in some details it is more advanced. In the narthex, the central baldachin has been given internally convex sides, whereby it seems to contract under the pressure of the adjacent spaces. A pulsating effect is created, which would become a major concern of Kilian Ignaz in his following works.

A series of churches followed in which the problems of pulsating juxtaposition of spaces was systematically studied. Saint Edwige at Wahlstatt in Silesia (1723–1731) may be mentioned as a major example, but several smaller buildings in Bohemia also ought to be remembered. Among them are a group of village churches in the Broumov area, Saint Bartholomew in Prague (1725–1731), and, above all, Saint Adalbert in Počaply near Litoměřice (1724–1726). In Počaply, he based the whole plan on the scheme he had employed in the narthex of Saint John Nepomuk on the Hradčany. The main space is an octagon with longer, internally convex sides on the main axes. A longitudinal direction is created through the addition of transverse ovals on two opposite sides. But the two other sides are also curved in the same way; other ovals could have been added, and the organism must be characterized as a reduced or elongated central church. In Počaply, we also find a more conscious treatment of the exterior plastic articulation, which from now on is mainly used to express the spatial structure of the organism. The transverse axis is thus characterized as open through an interruption of the architrave and frieze, and a gable marks the portal thereby created. The neutral, provisory character of the wall that closes the opening is expressed by a large chasuble-shaped window which naturally has an analogous function when seen from the inside.

Kilian Ignaz Dientzenhofer's search into the *ars combinatoria* of interdependent spaces culminated with three masterpieces: Saint John on the Rock in Prague (1730–1739), Saint Clement in Odolená Voda north of Prague (1732–1735), and Saint Mary Magdalen in Karlsbad (1732–1736). Saint John on the Rock is probably the best known of Kilian Ignaz's works, and it is often considered the Bohemian baroque church par excellence. In no other building is the plastic dynamism and dramatic quality so dear to the country expressed with more ability and conviction. The position of the church on a rock accentuates the effect, and the staircase in front enhances the vertical movement of the façade. The solution is, however, based on a most rigorous composition. The plan repeats the general layout of Počaply, but the greater importance of the later building is emphasized by the addition of a twin-tower front and a circular sanctuary. The central octagon is here slightly elongated, but a series of similar arches over the entablature contribute to the creation of a rotundalike space. Both the centralization and the longitudinal movement are thus strengthened. The entablature is interrupted where the system is open, but it continues from the main space into the secondary ovals for a better integration of the units. Because of the arches which penetrate into the vaults and the windows placed within them, it seems as if the baldachins are immersed in a much higher luminous space. The plastic articulation of the exterior corresponds to the interior organization. Saint John on the Rock in fact constitutes an unsurpassable example of complementary correspondence between inside and outside. Even the diagonally placed campanili are integrated in the spatial disposition.

In Odolená Voda, the characteristics of Saint John on the Rock are further developed. Again, the central space has internally convex sides on the main axes, whereas the diagonals are concave, strengthening the rotundalike centralization as well as the vertical continuity. The double delimitation of the main space is also carried a step further through the addition of shallow secondary spaces on all axes. The aim obviously was to create the impression of one large baldachin within a continuous envelope.

The architect's series of elongated central churches culminated with Saint Mary Magdalen in Karlsbad. Here, the main space is transformed into an oval with an outspoken rotundalike effect. Simultaneously, however, the longitudinal axis is emphasized by the introduction of internally convex zones of transition toward the secondary ovals (narthex and presbytery). The open character of the system is thereby maintained, and the organizing principle is, as usual, pulsating juxtaposition. To prevent the optical dissolution of the diaphanous system, an undulating gallery is carried all around the space. The exterior is related to Saint John on the Rock but, as a logical consequence of the plan, the campanili are frontally disposed. In all, the church may be ranked as the most important architectural achievement of Kilian Ignaz Dientzenhofer.

The churches described above may be characterized as elongated central buildings. In some cases, Kilian Ignaz also tackled the problem of the centralized longitudinal organism. Most important is the Jesuit Church of Saint Francis Xavier in Opařany, built between 1732 and 1735. The nave repeats the scheme of Christoph Dientzenhofer's Saint Clare in Cheb, but a narthex and a presbytery have been added by means of pulsating juxtaposition. The solution also shows a stronger definition of the structural system through the introduction of columns which carry the arches, while the vaults rest on independent pilasters. The skeleton, thus, is plastic, whereas the baldachins appear as surfaces.

This double system is closed off by the usual neutral walls perforated by large chasuble-shaped windows. Together with Saint Mary Magdalen, the church in Opařany represents a stage of consummate mastery.

In 1734–1735, Kilian Ignaz Dientzenhofer made two projects for the great church of the convent of the Ursulines in Kutná Hora. One of the projects repeats the disposition of Opařany in monumentalized form with secondary spaces added along the perimeter. The final version, however, shows the growing interest of the architect in the development of a dominant central rotunda: the main space has become circular and is crowned by a drum and dome. The pulsating juxtaposition has disappeared, but the double delimitation of the space is fully developed. The development of Kilian Ignaz led from the open system of interdependent cells toward the vision of a unitary, seemingly infinitely extended space, in which a large baldachin is immersed. The church in Kutná Hora would have been the crowning achievement of the architect; unfortunately, it was never built, and only a fragment of the large convent was completed.

Kilian Ignaz Dientzenhofer, however, built

Kilian Ignaz Dientzenhofer.
Saint Nicholas in the Old
*   Town.*
Prague.
1732–1737

Kilian Ignaz Dientzenhofer.
Saint Nicholas in the Lesser
*   Town (dome and bell*
*   tower).*
Prague.
1737–1751

Kilian Ignaz Dientzenhofer.
Saint Nicholas in the Lesser
*   Town (dome).*
Prague.
1737–1751

another centralized structure which manifests similar intentions. In Saint Nicholas in the Old Town in Prague (1732–1737), we find a dominant octagonal dome that forms a counterpoint to a strongly emphasized longitudinal axis. The two spatial features are unified by means of a very pronounced double delimitation. The exterior represents a tour de force of plastic articulation. The basic theme is a gradual liberation of the forms in the vertical direction, a solution which is characteristic of Prague in general and the works of Kilian Ignaz in particular. The tripartite façade is united by a continuous basement, while the main story is split apart and the bell towers rise freely toward the sky. The characteristic baroque increase in plasticity toward the middle of the façade contrasts with the linear

treatment of the dome, which appears light and distant. As a result, Saint Nicholas in the Old Town is the most intensely expressive of Kilian Ignaz's buildings.

Another well-known work is the great dome and campanile which he added to his father's nave of Saint Nicholas in the Lesser Town (1737–1751). The strong and picturesque pair of vertical forms does not only represent a great architectural creation, but it is also one of the major landmarks of the city of Prague. In the cityscape it simultaneously acts as a goal to the movement from the Old Town Square across the Charles Bridge toward the Hradčany and as a center to the Lesser Town. At the same time, its plastic articulation expresses the *genius loci* of Prague in a particularly convincing way.

Kilian Ignaz Dientzenhofer was active until the end of his life. His *ultima maniera* shows a characteristic wish for simplification. Examples are the small centralized church of Saint Florian in Kladno (1746–1748) and the longitudinal church in Paštiky near Blatna in southern Bohemia (1747–1751). In these two works, the basic themes of the architect reappear, but the character is less dramatic. Particularly enchanting is the church in Paštiky, where he returned to a simple succession of skeletal baldachins within a continuous outer envelope. Although he was seriously ill, he visited the building site in 1750 to take care of the detailing.

In general, Kilian Ignaz's works show an original synthesis of Bohemian and Austrian traits. Whereas his father concentrated on a few locally rooted types, mainly the *Hallenkirche* with wall-pillars, Kilian Ignaz studied all possible combinations of central and longitudinal plans, exploiting Guarini's ideas as well as the liberating potentiality of the wall-pillar system in a most ingenious way. From Hildebrandt he learned to give his compositions a subtle formal articulation. Kilian Ignaz Dientzenhofer's art was a true expression of its epoch, and it became immensely popular. In Bohemia, his name is still remembered with respect and reverence.

CHRISTIAN NORBERG-SCHULZ

WORKS

1717–1720, Villa Amerika; 1720–1728, Saint John Nepomuk on the Hradčany; Prague. 1720–1728, Nativity of the Virgin Church, Nicov, Czechoslovakia. (A)1720–1730, Churches (with others), near Broumov, Czechoslovakia. 1723–1725, Church and Convent of the Elizabethines, Prague. 1723–1731, Saint Edwige Church and Monastery, Wahlstatt, Czechoslovakia. 1724–1726, Saint Adalbert, Počaply, Czechoslovakia. 1724–1731, Saint Thomas in the Lesser Town (reconstruction); 1725–1728, Villa Portheim; 1725–1731, Saint Bartholomew; Prague. 1726–1738, Benedictine Monastery, Broumov, Czechoslovakia. 1730–1737, Karlin War Invalids Hospice (unfinished); 1730–1739, Saint John Nepomuk on the Rock; Prague. 1732–1733, Star Chapel, Křinice, Czechoslovakia. 1732–1734, Imperial Hospital with Chapel on the Hradčany, Prague. 1732–1735, Saint Clement, Odelená Voda, Czechoslovakia. 1732–1735, Saint Francis Xavier, Opařany, Czechoslovakia. 1732–1736, Saint Mary Magdalen, Karlsbad, Czechoslovakia. 1732–1737, Saint Nicholas in the Old Town, Prague. 1733, Church (with others), Dobrá Voda, Czechoslovakia. 1733, Church (with others), Nepomuk, Czechoslovakia. 1734–1743, Ursuline Convent (unfinished), Kutná Hora, Czechoslovakia. 1736, Saint Charles Borromaeus (with others); 1737, Saint Catherine (with others); 1737–1751, Saint Nicholas in the Lesser Town (dome and bell tower); 1739–1740, Břevov Monastery (gateway and additions); Prague. 1739–1742, Saints Peter and Paul, Březno, Czechoslovakia. 1743–1751, Chapel of the Holy Cross in Stodulky; 1743–1751, Silva-Tarouca Palace; Prague. 1745, Calvary Chapel, Radnice, Czechoslovakia. 1746, Church (with others), Dolni Ročov, Czechoslovakia. 1746–1748, Saint Florian, Kladno, Czechoslovakia. 1747, Loreto Sanctuary Cloisters, Prague. 1747–1751, Saint Martin, Chválenice, Czechoslovakia. 1748, Church (with others), Přeštice, Czechoslovakia. 1748–1751, Saint John the Baptist, Paštiky, Czechoslovakia.

BIBLIOGRAPHY

BACHMANN, ERICH 1964 "Die Architektur und Plastik." Karl Maria Swoboda (editor), *Barock in Böhmen.* Munich: Prestel.

BÜCHNER, JOACHIM 1964 *Die spätgotische Wandpfeilerkirchen Bayerns und Österreichs.* Nuremberg, Germany: Carl.

FRANZ, HEINRICH GEBHARD 1942 *Die Kirchenbauten des Christoph Dientzenhofer.* Brno, Czechoslovakia, Munich, and Vienna: Rohrer.

FRANZ, HEINRICH GEBHARD 1943a *Die deutsche Barockbaukunst Mährens.* Munich: Bruckmann.

FRANZ, HEINRICH GEBHARD 1943b *Studien zur Barockarchitektur in Böhmen und Mähren.* Brno, Czechoslovakia, Munich, and Vienna: Rohrer.

FRANZ, HEINRICH GEBHARD 1947 "Die Klosterkirche Banz und die Kirchen Balthasar Neumanns in ihrem Verhältnis zur böhmischen Barockbaukunst." *Zeitschrift für Kunstwissenschaft* 1:54–72.

FRANZ, HEINRICH GEBHARD 1950 "Gotik und Barock im Werk des Johann Santini Aichel." *Wiener Jahrbuch für Kunstgeschichte* 14, no. 28:65–130.

FRANZ, HEINRICH GEBHARD 1962 *Bauten und Baumeister der Barockzeit in Böhmen.* Leipzig: Seeman.

GRIMSCHITZ, BRUNO (1932)1959 *Johann Lucas von Hildebrandt.* Munich and Vienna.

GRUNDMANN, GÜNTHER 1944 *Das ehemalige Benediktinerkloster Wahlstatt.* Berlin.

GUARINI, GUARINO (1737)1968 *Architettura Civile.* Milan: Il Polifolio.

HAGER, WERNER 1942 *Die Bauten des deutschen Barocks: 1690–1770.* Jena, Germany: Diederichs.

HEGEMANN, HANS W. 1943 *Die deutsche Barockbaukunst Böhmens.* Munich: Bruckmann.

HEMPEL, EBERHARD (1965)1977 *Baroque Art and Architecture in Central Europe.* Harmondsworth, England: Penguin.

HOFFMANN, JOSEF 1898 *Der Barock in Nordwestböhmen.* Carlsbad, Czechoslovakia: Jakob.

KÖMSTEDT, RUDOLF 1963 *Von Bauten und Baumeistern des fränkischen Barocks.* Berlin: Hessling.

KORECKÝ, MIROSLAV 1953 "Poznámy k pražkému Dienzenhoferovu prostoru a klenbám." *Umění* l, no. 4:261–285.

KORECKÝ, MIROSLAV 1958 "Zur Architektur und zum Deckenfresko des Kirchenschiffs von St. Niklas auf der Prager Kleinseite." *Wandmalereien des Spätbarocks.*

KREISEL, HEINRICH 1953 *Das Schloss zu Pommersfelden.* Munich: Nimmer.

KUBIČEK, ALOIS 1946 *Pražské paláce.* Prague: Nakl. V Poláčka.

MADL, KAREL B. 1890 *Die Ville Amerika.* Prague.

MENZEL, BEDA 1934 "Christoph und Kilian Ignaz Dientzenhofer im Dienste der Äbte von Brewnow-Braunau." *Jahrbuch des deutschen Riesengebirgsvereins.*

MENZEL, BEDA 1943 "Der Klosterbau in Braunau." *Zeitschrift für Geschichte der Sudetenländer.*

MÜLLEROVÁ, AUGUSTA, and NOVÁK, J. B. 1948 *Karlínská Invalidovna.* Prague: Výtarný edbor Umélecke besedy.

NEUMANN, JAROMÍR 1969 *Český barok.* Prague: Odeon.

NORBERG-SCHULZ, CHRISTIAN 1968 *Kilian Ignaz Dientzenhofer e il barocco boemo.* Rome: Officina Edizioni.

NORBERG-SCHULZ, CHRISTIAN 1970 "Lo spazio nell'architettura post-guariniana." Volume 2, part 5, pages 411–437 in V. Viale (editor), *Guarino Guarini e l'internazionalita del barocco.* Turin, Italy: Academia delle Scienze.

NORBERG-SCHULZ, CHRISTIAN 1972 *Baroque Architecture.* New York: Abrams.

NORBERG-SCHULZ, CHRISTIAN 1974 *Late Baroque and Rococo Architecture.* New York: Abrams.

PELCL, FRANTIŠEK MARTIN 1773–1782 *Abbildungen böhmischer und mährischer Gelehrten.* 4 vols. Prague: Gerle.

POCHE, EMANUEL 1944 *Pražské portály.* Prague: Pólaček.

POCHE, EMANUEL; BLAŽIČEK, O. J.; and ČEŘOVSKÝ, J. 1944 *Klášter v Břevnově.* Prague.

POCHE, EMANUEL, and PREISS, PAVEL 1973 *Pražské paláce.* Prague: Odeon.

PORTOGHESI, PAOLO 1964 *Borromini nella cultura europea.* Rome: Officini Edizioni.

RADA, OLDŘICH 1955 "Prostor v barokní pohybové architektuře." *Umění* 3:213–240.

ŠAMAL, JINDŘICH 1933–1934 "Pastiky." In *Za starou Prahu.* Prague.

ŠAMAL, JINDŘICH 1941 "Klášter a nemoonice Alžbětinik na Slupi." In *Pokladynárodního umění.* Prague.

SCHMERBER, HUGO 1900 *Beiträge zur Geschichte der Dientzenhofer.* Prague.

SCHMIDT, ADALBERT, and BLASCHKA, ANTON   1930
"Ein Beitrag zur Lebensgeschichte Kilian Ignaz Dientzenhofers und seiner Familie." *Mitteilungen des Vereins für Geschichte der deutschen in Böhmen* 68:47–54.

SCHNELL, HUGO   1961   *Die Stiftskirche Waldsassen.* Munich: Schnell & Steiner.

SCHÜRER, OSKAR   (1930)1940   *Prag.* Munich and Brno, Czechoslovakia: Callwey.

SEDLMAYER, HANS   (1956)1976   *Johann Bernhard Fischer von Erlach.* Vienna: Herold.

STEFAN, OLDŘICH   1926–1927   "Příspěvky k čejinam české barokní architektury." *Památky Archeologické* 35:79–116, 468–545.

STEFAN, OLDŘICH   1959   "Plastický princip v české architektuře barokní počátku 18. věku." *Umění* 7, no. 1:1–17.

SWOBODA, KARL MARIA   1941   *Prag.* Berlin: Deutscher Kunstverlag.

SWOBODA, KARL MARIA (editor)   1964   *Barock in Böhmen.* Munich: Prestel Verlag.

Topographie der historischen und Kunstdenkmale im Königreiche Böhmen: 1897–1934   51 vols. Prague.

WIRTH, ZDENĚK   1941   *Stará Praha.* Prague: Ott.

WIRTH, ZDENĚK   1954   *Prague in Bilden aus fünf Jahrhunderten.* Prague: Artia.

WIRTH, ZDENĚK   1957   *Umělecké památky Čech.* Prague: Nakl.Československé akademievěd.

ZIMMER, HANS   1976   *Die Dientzenhofer.* Germany: Rosenheimer Verlaghaus Forg.

DIENTZENHOFER BROTHERS

The Dientzenhofer family of builders and architects played a decisive role in the development of late baroque architecture in central Europe. The five brothers—Georg (1643–1689), Wolfgang (1648–1706), Christoph (1655–1722), Leonhard (1660–1707), and Johann (1663–1726)—were active in Franconia and Bohemia during the decades just before and after 1700. Although historical information is scanty, we may infer that they kept in contact, and their works in fact make common aims and means manifest. Of particular interest is the general interest in the organization of dynamic groups and sequences of spaces. The more talented of the brothers, Georg, Christoph, and Johann, thus introduced a method of composing with interdependent spatial elements, which was later further developed by Christoph's son KILIAN IGNAZ DIENTZENHOFER. In doing this, they fulfilled what had been promised by FRANCESCO BORROMINI and GUARINO GUARINI, and made possible the great achievement of JOHANN BALTHASAR NEUMANN. The common approach of the Dientzenhofers was, however, also reflected in the use of certain typical forms, such as the so-called Dientzenhofer motif: a large segmented (and usually broken) pediment resting on columns or pilasters.

The Dientzenhofer brothers were born in Upper Bavaria near Rosenheim, as sons of a farmer. They were trained as masons, and in 1676 moved to Prague where work was plentiful. They also brought along a sister, Anna, who in 1678 married ABRAHAM LEUTHNER. Leuthner was a well-studied man and the author of a treatise on architecture. He enjoyed an important position in Prague and was also in charge of the fortification works of the whole country of Bohemia. Undoubtedly, the career of the Dientzenhofers got a flying start because of the connection with Leuthner. Although the brothers had no formal education, they were soon carrying out important works. In 1682, we find Georg, Christoph, and Leonhard in Waldsassen on the border between Franconia and Bohemia, where Georg had been put in charge of Leuthner's project for a large Cistercian monastery. Georg must have done a good job, as two years later he was asked to design an important pilgrimage church in the same area. The Church of the Holy Trinity (1684–1689) on the Glasberg near Waldsassen is generally known as the Kappel. It remains a significant contribution to the history of baroque architecture because of its original plan and articulate form. Georg did not, however, see it finished, as he died in 1689 at the outset of a promising career. The building was completed by his brother Christoph, while Leonhard carried out Georg's last design: the Church of Saint Martin on the Green Market in Bamberg (1689–1693).

The Kappel consists of three apses joined together by a triangular vault and surrounded by an ambulatory. The unusual plan is obviously due to a conscious wish for symbolizing the Holy Trinity. Beyond this meaning, however, it represents a first attempt at composing with interdependent spatial

Georg Dientzenhofer. Kappel (pilgrimage church). Waldsassen, Germany. 1684–1689

cells within an enveloping membranelike wall and thus initiates the systematic search of the Dientzenhofers. In general, the church appears as a centralized structure without a façade. The picturesque silhouette with three campanili crowned by onion-shaped spires unites baroque, Gothic, and Slavic elements, whereas the simple outer walls are related to local folk architecture. The Kappel thus synthesizes an architectural inheritance of a much wider range than the classical tradition.

Being planned in 1684, the Kappel certainly was an original achievement. The Dientzenhofers' further development, however, was strongly influenced by Guarini's ideas, which became generally known after his projects were published in 1686. During the years just after 1700, a group of admirable churches were built in Bohemia, all reflecting the influence of Guarini. We here refer to the Church in Obořiště (1699–1712), the Chapel of the Castle of Smiřice (1700–1713), Saint Nicholas in the Lesser Town in Prague (1703–1711), Saint Clare in Eger, Cheb (1707), and the Church of Saint Margaret at Břevnov near Prague (1709–1715). All these buildings present spatial and formal analogies, and they also represent a certain architectural development. Their author is generally recognized as Christoph Dientzenhofer. According to contemporary sources, Christoph traveled to Marseilles in 1690 in connection with a particular commission, and on the way he probably visited Turin to get direct knowledge of Guarini's buildings. The church in Obořiště has a bi-axial plan which is directly derived from Guarini's church of the Immaculate Conception in Turin (1673), a building which is not included in the publication of the master's works, and in Smiřice, Guarini's plan for San Lorenzo in Turin (1668) reappears. About the same time, however, Guarini's ideas were also introduced in Bohemia by LUCAS VON HILDEBRANDT, who in 1699 started the construction of the Church of Saint Lawrence in Gabel near Prague. Traveling to Gabel, Hildebrandt must have passed through Prague, and it is highly probable that he got to know Christoph Dientzenhofer, who in 1707 sent his son Kilian Ignaz to study with him in Vienna. The plan for Gabel is also derived from San Lorenzo in Turin and represents an important step toward the realization of a group of interdependent spatial cells.

To make a composition with spatial cells effective, it is essential that the primary structure be reduced to a skeleton; that is, the walls should not constitute the spaces, but rather play the role of a secondary "skin" which may be added or taken away at will. Such a system comes close to the structure of Gothic architecture. In Guarini's works the skeletal character is quite pronounced, although he usually maintained a continuous horizontal entablature. In the early baroque architecture of central Europe, however, attempts were made to transform the wall into a true skeleton by using the local wall-pillar construction. Wall-pillars are Gothic buttresses placed inside instead of on the exterior of the building. They are usually filled in by a thin nonsupporting wall, possibly of glass. The adaptation of this type of structure in baroque buildings was realized by Hans Alberthal between 1610 and 1620, and was later developed by the Vorarlberg builders, who created the type of baroque wall-pillar church known as the *Vorarlberger Münsterschema*. The Vorarlbergers, however, did not know the spatial ideas of Guarini, and they applied their structural system to rather conventional longitudinal halls. Because of his knowledge of Guarini's works, Christoph Dientzenhofer could make a more creative use of the wall-pillar construction, and his achievement may in general be understood as an ingenious combination of this type of structure with the method of composing with interdependent spatial cells. Hildebrandt, on the contrary, did not take this decisive step, and later lost interest in this kind of spatial problem.

The Chapel at Smiřice (1700–1711) is the first full-grown expression of Christoph's intentions. It consists of an elongated octagon with internally convex sides. On the longitudinal axis, secondary oval spaces are added, whereas the transverse axis is closed by neutral walls filled in between the slightly projecting wall-pillars. The diagonals are extended by lens-shaped recesses. Thus, the space has been treated as an open system, where cells may be added at will. At Smiřice, this possibility was used to create a highly original synthesis of centralized and longitudinal space. The exterior presents itself as an integrated organism enveloped in a continuous, undulating surface. The potential openness of the main axes, however, is indicated by large segmented pediments. A convincing complementary relationship between interior and exterior is thus realized.

In Saint Nicholas in the Lesser Town in Prague (1703–1711), we confront a much more complex organism, although the longitudinal plan may be understood as a more systematized version of Obořiště. In Saint Nicholas, deep wall-pillars are introduced, between which we find chapels and galleries. The chapels are treated as centralized baldachins with neutral panels filled in toward the outside. Toward the nave, however, the wall-pillars are faced by obliquely placed pilasters from which double-curved arches spring to cross the vault (the arches were taken away later to give room for a large painting). The system has an ambiguous character. It may be understood as a series of inter-

Christoph Dientzenhofer.
Saint Nicholas in the Lesser
Town.
Prague.
1703–1711

penetrating ovals defined by the pilasters and the arches, as well as a normal bay system. The ovals, however, open where the bays meet, and the bays open where the ovals touch each other. Two contradicting spatial definitions are thus realized, creating an effect which has been called "spatial syncopation" or "syncopated interpenetration." The principle represents an original and important invention by Christoph Dientzenhofer, and it was later taken up by Balthasar Neumann. Because of the new principle, Saint Nicholas has a spatial organization that is simultaneously articulate and integrated. Its impact is extraordinary, and it must be counted among the greatest achievements of baroque architecture. As a further development of Smiřice, the façade of Saint Nicholas introduces a note of organic dynamism, which seems to have

Christoph Dientzenhofer.
Saint Nicholas in the Lesser
Town (façade).
Prague.
1703–1711

fitted the Bohemian spirit particularly well.

Saint Clare in Cheb (1707–1711) and Saint Margaret at Břevnov (1709–1715) show a desire for simplification without giving up the spatial richness of the earlier works. At Břevnov, the syncopated interpenetration explored in Saint Nicholas is employed, so that the vault contracts where the space below expands, and vice versa. The nave is, however, reduced to two transverse ovals with smaller ovals added at both ends. The bi-axial organism introduced at Obořiště has thus become fully integrated. The lateral chapels of Saint Nicholas have been omitted in accordance with the simpler nature of the building, illustrating the basically open character of the system. The interior walls at Břevnov thus appear as a succession of tall wall-pillars filled in by secondary neutral surfaces, whereby an effect of strength and clarity is achieved. The exterior is similarly powerful, being kept together by a single giant order of Ionic pilasters. In contrast to Smiřice, however, the outer envelope is split at the entrances to make the spatial system of the interior visible. A convincing relation between outside and inside is thus established by means of a meaningful articulation of the built form.

A close acquaintance with the buildings mentioned above convinces one that they are products of the same creative mind. Their character is essentially different from that of the works of JOHANN SANTINI AICHEL, whom some scholars have proposed as their possible author. Whereas the wall is the constituent element in Santini Aichel's buildings, Christoph Dientzenhofer gives the wall only a secondary role within a primary system of interdependent baldachins. The buildings also form a natural part of the production of the entire Dientzenhofer family. In the works of the youngest brother, Johann, we encounter, in fact, the same basic intentions.

Johann was the only one of the brothers who received a formal education in architecture. An early training at Christoph's in Prague is probable, but before 1700 he moved to Bamberg to assist his brother Leonhard with the rebuilding of the Church of Saint Martin on the Michelberg (1696), and with the New Residenz in the same city (1697–1703). We also know that he visited Italy in 1699 to study Roman baroque architecture. After his return, he was commissioned to reconstruct the Cathedral in Fulda (1704–1712), in central Germany, a fact which gives testimony to the professional position of the Dientzenhofers. After a somewhat hesitant start in Fulda, Johann emerged as a mature artist with the splendid Benedictine Abbey Church of Banz in Franconia (1710–1713, consecrated 1719). The plan is based on

Christoph's Obořiště scheme: two transverse ovals are connected by a narrower intermediate section. The latter is defined by a wide wall-pillar, a solution which had also been used by Christoph in Cheb. Similar sections are added at the extremes of the nave, creating a rhythmical succession of narrow and wide intervals. This rhythm, however, forms a counterpoint to the spaces defined by the double-curved transverse arches, which expand over the narrow intervals and contract over the wide ones, as in Saint Nicholas and Břevnov. We could also say that the spatial units simultaneously contract and expand. The Abbey Church of Banz thus exploits all the spatial possibilities developed by Christoph Dientzenhofer and may be considered the most mature work of the entire group of buildings. The façade is distinguished by a characteristic Dientzenhofer motif.

After Banz, Johann Dientzenhofer was mainly occupied with the planning and construction of the great palace at Pommersfelden (1711–1718) for the elector of Mainz and bishop of Bamberg, Lothar Franz von Schönborn. The basic disposition shows a U-shape with a *cour d'honneur* and corner pavilions. A most impressive novel feature is the dominant central unit which incorporates a great symmetrical staircase, a *sala terrena* (based on interdependent spatial units!), and the Imperial Hall above. The idea of making an unusually large and monumental staircase is supposed to have originated with Lothar Franz himself, but the truly splendid solution must be due to a trained architect. Documentation shows that the interior is mainly the work of the decorative genius of Hildebrandt, whereas the other principal rooms and the exterior clearly show the style of Johann Dientzenhofer. The monumental staircase introduced an element which was to play a prime role in the palaces of Neumann, first of all in the Residenz in Würzburg, where Johann acted as a consultant at the outset of the planning.

When Johann died in 1726, the generation of the Dientzenhofer brothers came to an end. At that moment, however, the son of Christoph, Kilian Ignaz, was already an established and successful architect, and during the following years he continued the Dientzenhofer search into the problems of spatial composition and formal articulation. In general, we may say that the works of the Dientzenhofers represent a most significant interpretation of the aims of the counterreformatory Roman Catholic Church. In their baldachin spaces, Heaven comes down to earth, at the same time that the lateral openness of their spatial systems expresses a symbolic interaction with the surrounding everyday world.

CHRISTIAN NORBERG-SCHULZ

Johann Dientzenhofer.
Benedictine Monastery
Church.
Banz, Germany.
1710–1713

WORKS

GEORG DIENTZENHOFER

1682–1689, Cistercian Monastery (execution of Abraham Leuthner's design), Waldsassen, Germany. 1684–1689, Jesuit College, Amberg, Germany. 1684–1689, Kappel (pilgrimage church), Waldsassen, Germany.

WOLFGANG DIENTZENHOFER

1690–1695, Benedictine Church and Monastery, Michelfeld, Germany. 1692–1698, Abbey Church, Speinshart, Germany. 1693–1699, Salesian Church and Convent, Amberg, Germany. 1695–?, Abbey Church, Ensdorf, Germany. 1705–1707, Frauenbrunndl (pilgrimage church), Straubing, Germany.

CHRISTOPH DIENTZENHOFER

1689–?, Benedictine Monastery, Tapla, Czechoslovakia. 1699–1712, Saint Joseph's Church, Obořiště, Czechoslovakia. 1700–1713, Castle Chapel, Smiřice, Czechoslovakia. 1703–1711, Saint Nicholas in the Lesser Town, Prague. 1707–1711, Saint Clair's Church, Cheb, Czechoslovakia. 1709–?, Ascension of the Holy Virgin Church, Nova Paka, Czechoslovakia. 1709–1715, Saint Margaret's Church, Břevnov; 1716–1722, Saint Loreto's Sanctuary; Prague.

LEONHARD DIENTZENHOFER

1686–1704, Monastery, Ebrach, Germany. 1689–1693, Saint Martin (design by Georg Dietzenhofer); 1696–?, Saint Michael on the Michelsberg (completed by Johann Dietzenhofer); 1697–1703, New Residenz; Bamberg, Germany. 1695–?, Monastery (completed by Johann Dietzenhofer), Banz, Germany. 1698–?, Monastery (completed by B. Schiesser), Schöntal, Germany. 1704?, Castle Weiher (Church of the Holy Savior), Hollfeld, Germany.

JOHANN DIENTZENHOFER

1704–1712, Cathedral; 1704–?, Stadtschloss (City Palace); 1710–?, Bieberstein Castle; Fulda, Germany. 1710–1713, Benedictine Monastery Church, Banz, Germany. 1711–1718, Weissenstein Castle, Pommersfelden, Germany. 1713, Böttingerhaus, Bamberg, Germany. 1714–1719, Schrottenberg Castle, Reichmannsdorf, Germany. 1715, Village Church, Litzldorf, Germany. 1716–1722, Concordia Castle, Bamberg, Germany. 1723, Castle, Kleinheubach, Germany.

BIBLIOGRAPHY

BACHMANN, ERICH 1964 "Die Architektur und Plastik." Karl Maria Swoboda (editor), *Barock in Böhmen*. Munich: Prestel.

BÜCHNER, JOACHIM 1964 *Die spätgotische Wandpfeilerkirchen Bayerns und Österreichs*. Nuremberg, Germany: Carl.

FRANZ, HEINRICH GEBHARD 1942 *Die Kirchenbauten des Christoph Dientzenhofer*. Brno, Czechoslovakia, Munich, and Vienna: Rohrer.

FRANZ, HEINRICH GEBHARD 1943a *Die deutsche Barockbaukunst Mährens*. Munich: Bruckmann.

FRANZ, HEINRICH GEBHARD 1943b *Studien zur Barockarchitektur in Böhmen und Mähren*. Brno, Czechoslovakia, Munich, and Vienna: Rohrer.

FRANZ, HEINRICH GEBHARD 1947 "Die Klosterkirche Banz und die Kirchen Balthasar Neumanns in ihrem Verhältnis zur böhmischen Barockbaukunst." *Zeitschrift für Kunstwissenschaft* 1:54–72.

FRANZ, HEINRICH GEBHARD 1950 "Gotik und Barock im Werk des Johann Santini Aichel." *Wiener Jahrbuch für Kunstgeschichte* 14, no. 28:65–130.

FRANZ, HEINRICH GEBHARD 1962 *Bauten und Baumeister der Barockzeit in Böhmen*. Leipzig: Seeman.

GRIMSCHITZ, BRUNO (1932)1959 *Johann Lucas von Hildebrandt*. Munich and Vienna.

GRUNDMANN, GÜNTHER 1944 *Das ehemalige Benediktinerkloster Wahlstatt*. Berlin.

GUARINI, GUARINO (1737)1968 *Architettura Civile*. Milan: Il Polifolio.

HAGER, WERNER 1942 *Die Bauten des deutschen Barocks: 1690–1770*. Jena, Germany: Diederichs.

HEGEMANN, HANS W. 1943 *Die deutsche Barockbaukunst Böhmens*. Munich: Bruckmann.

HEMPEL, EBERHARD (1965)1977 *Baroque Art and Architecture in Central Europe*. Harmondsworth, England: Penguin.

HOFFMANN, JOSEF 1898 *Der Barock in Nordwestböhmen*. Carlsbad, Czechoslovakia: Jakob.

KÖMSTEDT, RUDOLF 1963 *Von Bauten und Baumeistern des fränkischen Barocks*. Berlin: Hessling.

KORECKÝ, MIROSLAV 1953 "Poznámy k pražkému Dienzenhoferovu prostoru a klenbám." *Umēni* l, no. 4:261–285.

KORECKÝ, MIROSLAV 1958 "Zur Architektur und zum Deckenfresko des Kirchenschiffs von St. Niklas auf der Prager Kleinseite." *Wandmalereien des Spätbarocks*.

KREISEL, HEINRICH 1953 *Das Schloss zu Pommersfelden*. Munich: Nimmer.

KUBIČEK, ALOIS 1946 *Pražské paláce*. Prague: Nakl. V Poláčka.

MADL, KAREL B. 1890 *Die Ville Amerika*. Prague.

MENZEL, BEDA 1934 "Christoph und Kilian Ignaz Dientzenhofer im Dienste der Äbte von Brewnow-Braunau." *Jahrbuch des deutschen Riesengebirgsvereins*.

MENZEL, BEDA 1943 "Der Klosterbau in Braunau." *Zeitschrift für Geschichte der Sudetenländer*.

MÜLLEROVÁ, AUGUSTA, and NOVÁK, J. B. 1948 *Karlínská Invalidovna*. Prague: Výtarný edbor Umélecke besedy.

NEUMANN, JAROMÍR 1969 *Český barok*. Prague: Odeon.

NORBERG-SCHULZ, CHRISTIAN 1968 *Kilian Ignaz Dientzenhofer e il barocco boemo*. Rome: Officina Edizioni.

NORBERG-SCHULZ, CHRISTIAN 1970 "Lo spazio nell'architettura post-guariniana." Volume 2, part 5, pages 411–437 in V. Viale (editor), *Guarino Guarini e l'internazionalita del barocco*. Turin, Italy: Academia delle Scienze.

NORBERG-SCHULZ, CHRISTIAN 1972 *Baroque Architecture*. New York: Abrams.

NORBERG-SCHULZ, CHRISTIAN 1974 *Late Baroque and Rococo Architecture*. New York: Abrams.

PELCL, FRANTTŠEK, MARTIN 1773–1782 *Abbildungen böhmischer und mährischer Gelehrten*. 4 vols. Prague: Gerle.

POCHE, EMANUEL 1944 *Pražské portály*. Prague: Pólaček.

POCHE, EMANUEL; BLAŽIČEK, O. J.; and ČEŘOVSKÝ, J. 1944 *Klāšter v Břevnově*. Prague.

POCHE, EMANUEL, and PREISS, PAVEL 1973 *Pražské paláce*. Prague: Odeon.

PORTOGHESI, PAOLO 1964 *Borromini nella cultura europea*. Rome: Officini Edizioni.

RADA, OLDŘICH 1955 "Prostor v barokní pohybové architektuře." *Umēni* 3:213–240.

ŠAMAL, JINDŘICH 1933–1934 "Pastiky." In *Za starou Prahu*. Prague.

ŠAMAL, JINDŘICH 1941 "Klāšter a nemoonice Alžbětinek na Slupi." In *Pokladynárodního umēni*. Prague.

SCHMERBER, HUGO 1900 *Beiträge zur Geschichte der Dietzenhofer*. Prague.

SCHMIDT, ADALBERT, and BLASCHKA, ANTON 1930 "Ein Beitrag zur Lebensgeschichte Kilian Ignaz Dientzenhofers und seiner Familie." *Mitteilungen des Vereins für Geschichte der deutschen in Böhmen* 68:47–54.

SCHNELL, HUGO 1961 *Die Stiftskirche Waldsassen*. Munich: Schnell & Steiner.

SCHÜRER, OSKAR (1930)1940 *Prag*. Munich and Brno, Czechoslovakia: Callwey.

SEDLMAYER, HANS (1956)1976 *Johann Bernhard Fischer von Erlach*. Vienna: Herold.

STEFAN, OLDŘICH 1926–1927 "Příspēvky k čejinam české barokní architektury." *Památky Archeologické* 35:79–116. 468–545.

STEFAN, OLDŘICH 1959 "Plastický princip v české architektuře barokní počátku 18. věku." *Umēni* 7, no. 1:1–17.

SWOBODA, KARL MARIA 1941 *Prag*. Berlin:

Deutscher Kunsterverlag.

SWOBODA, KARL MARIA (editor) 1964 *Barock in Böhmen.* Munich: Prestel Verlag.

Topographie der historischen und Kunst-denkmale im Königreiche Böhmen. 1897–1934 51 vols. Prague.

WIRTH, ZDENĚK 1941 *Stará Praha.* Prague: Ott.

WIRTH, ZDENĚK 1954 *Prague in Bilden aus fünf Jahrhunderten.* Prague: Artia.

WIRTH, ZDENĚK 1957 *Umělecké památky Čech.* Prague: Nakl. Československé akademievéd.

ZIMMER, HANS 1976 *Die Dientzenhofer.* Germany: Rosenheimer Verlaghaus Forg.

DIESTE, ELADIO

Trained as a civil engineer at the University of Montevideo in 1943, Eladio Dieste (1917–) combined the tensile strength of steel with ceramic in 1948 to create reinforced ceramic shells. A minimum of materials and labor make this construction technique ideal for developing countries, but as a UNESCO lecturer, he has explained its application in any milieu.

Aimed at unifying technical rationality and aesthetics, Dieste's reinforced ceramics gracefully hover above the Salto Bus Station (1972) and undulate in the framing walls of Atlántida Church (1958). Educator and innovator Dieste views architecture as a modification of space in order to make people happy.

ELIZABETH D. HARRIS

WORKS

1958, Church, Atlántida, Uruguay. 1958–1960, Talleres Electronicos Industrial Plant, Montevideo. 1967–1969, St. Peter's Church, Durazno, Uruguay. 1969–1971, Market, Porto Alegre, Brazil. 1972, Bus Station; 1978, Industrial Plant for Refrescos del Norte, Salto, Uruguay. 1979, Agroindustrial Complex, Montevideo.

BIBLIOGRAPHY

BAYÓN, DAMIÁN, and GASPARINI, PAOLO 1977 *Panorámica de la Arquitectura Latino-Americana.* Barcelona, Spain: Blume.

BULLRICH, FRANCISCO 1969 *New Directions in Latin American Architecture.* New York: Braziller.

DIET, ARTHUR STANISLAS

Born in Amboise, France, Arthur Stanislas Diet (1827–1890) entered the Ecole des Beaux-Arts in 1846, and trained in the ateliers of FÉLIX LOUIS JACQUES DUBAN, ABEL BLOUET, and Emile Gilbert, whose daughter he married. Winner of the Grand Prix of Rome in 1853, he stayed only briefly in Italy before returning to take over his father-in-law's practice. He became *architecte en chef de la Ville de Paris* and *inspecteur général* at the Conseil des Bâtiments Civils.

R. D. MIDDLETON

WORKS

1859–1864, Musée de Picardie, Amiens, Somme, France. 1864–?, Aisle d'Aliénés, Charenton; 1864–?, Ecole nationale vétérinaire, 7 rue Jean-Jaurès, Alfort; Seine, France. 1865–1877, Hôtel Dieu, Place du Parvis Notre Dame (executed design by E. Gilbert); *1869–?, Prefecture de Police, Quai des Orfèvres and Boulevard du Palais; Paris. 1869–, Villa Diet, Sevres, Seine et Oise, Paris. 1888–1889, Reservoirs de Montmartre (architectural embellishments), rue Azaïs, Paris.

BIBLIOGRAPHY

DAUMET, P. J. HONORÉ 1890 "Arthur Diet, architecte. Notice sur sa vie et ses oeuvres." *L'Architecture* 1890:394–395.

FOUCART-BORVILLE, JACQUES 1979 "Quelques constructions publiques à Amiens." *Monuments Historiques* 102:46–49.

NORMAND, ALFRED N. 1892 *Institut de France. Académie des Beaux-Arts: Notice sur la vie et les travaux de M. Diet.* Paris: Firmin-Didot.

DIETTERLIN, WENDEL

Wendel Dietterlin (c.1550–1599) was a German Renaissance architect, known for one of the most extraordinary books of fantasies in the history of architecture. Originally named Wendling Grapp, he was born in Pullendorf on Lake Constance; he spent most of his rather short life in Strasbourg where he acquired citizenship in 1571. He specialized as *Architekturmaler,* a fresco painter and decorator who painted façades, ceilings, and wall decorations. None of his works has survived. All the Strasbourg town houses which he decorated have been destroyed. His largest painting was the ceiling for the *Lusthaus* (pleasure palace) of the Duke of Württemberg in Stuttgart. Dietterlin's last years were occupied by the production of the great book on which his fame rests, *Architectura: Von Austheilung/Symmetria und Proportion der Fünff Seulen.* The first part of this work appeared in Stuttgart in 1593, the second in Strasbourg in 1594. An enlarged second edition (the book was obviously what we would now call a success) appeared in Nuremberg in 1598. The plates of *Architectura* are organized around the five orders—in Dietterlin's sequence, Tuscan, Doric, Ionic, Corinthian, and Composite—but the semblance to the classical orders is minimal: nightmarish flights of weird and extravagant forms abound; wild animals and proliferating plants overwhelm

Dietterlin.
Plate from Architectura.

such basic architectural elements as windows, chimneys, door frames, portals, fountains, tombs, and monuments. Dietterlin's book, derived from Dutch and Flemish rather than Italian decorative inventions, contains elements of the late Gothic as well as an anticipation of the powerful northern baroque. But above all, it is a document of the most fantastic aspects of the German Renaissance.

ADOLF K. PLACZEK

BIBLIOGRAPHY

OHNESORGE, KARL 1893 *Wendel Dietterlin: Maler von Strassburg.* Leipzig: Seemann.
The Phantastic Engravings of Wendel Dietterlin. (1593–1594)1968 Reprint of the 1598 ed. With an introduction by Adolf K. Placzek. New York: Dover. Originally published with the title *Architectura: Von Austheilung/Symmetria und Proportion der Fünff Seulen.*
PIRR, MARGOT 1940 *Die Architectur des Wendel Dietterlin.* Gräfenhainichen, Germany: Schulze.

DIMCHEV, EMIL

Emil Dimitrov Dimchev (1926–) was born in Varna, Bulgaria, and graduated from Sofia's Polytechnic Institute in 1950, having studied under Stancho Belkovski, Ivan Danchov (see BELKOVSKI AND DANCHOV), and Dimitur Tsolov (see VASIL'OV AND TSOLOV).

He worked on numerous civic, residential, and commercial buildings, as well as in interior and industrial design. One of his most important ac-complishments, the Hotel Iantra (1956–1959) in Turnovo, Bulgaria, displays the influence of the organic architecture of FRANK LLOYD WRIGHT.

In his works, Dimchev tries to create a contemporary architecture based on the principles of the Bulgarian national revival spirit of the eighteenth and nineteenth centuries.

MARIA POPOVA

WORKS

1956–1959, Hotel Iantra (with Ts. Kolandzhiev and C. Pavlov), Turnovo, Bulgaria. 1971–1972, Department of State (interior); 1972–1973, Council of Ministries (interior); Sofia. 1972–1980, City Civic and Commercial Center; 1974–1981, Historic Preservation and Residential Development; Turnovo, Bulgaria. 1977–1978, Commercial Center (interior), Frankfurt. 1977–1978, Museum and Exhibit, Auschwitz, Poland. *1979, Bulgarian Exhibition Center, Aden. 1980–1981, Bulgarian Exhibition Center, Algiers.

BIBLIOGRAPHY

ANASTOSOV, KHRISTO 1957 "Proekt za predstavitelen Khotel v Turnovo." *Arkhitektura* 4:128–131.
BŬLGARSKA AKADEMIĨA NA NAUKITE 1963–1969 *Kratka Bŭlgarska Entsiklopediĩa* Sofia: The academy.
DIMCHEV, EMIL 1957 "Obzavezhdanetna Korortni Hoteli." *Arkhitektura* 4:119–124.
DIMCHEV, EMIL 1962 "Kompleksut v s. Girginite v Gabrovo." *Arkhitektura* 7:20–23.
DIMCHEV, EMIL 1962 "Obzavezhdaneto na Magazini i Zavedeniĩa u Nas." *Arkhitektura* 8:14–16.
"Mekhana 'Hadzhi Mincho' vuv Veliko Turnovo." 1972 *Arkhitektura* 6–8:66.
STOĨANOV, BORISLAV 1977 *Suvremenna Arkhitektura.* Sofia: Tekhnika.

DINKELOO, JOHN

See ROCHE and DINKELOO.

D'IXNARD, MICHEL

Born in Nîmes, France, Michel d'Ixnard (1726–1798) is best known for introducing French neoclassicism in western Germany, thereby displacing the Italian influence.

Trained as a skilled craftsman-builder, he came to Paris in 1750 through the efforts of Charles de Rohan. He was placed in charge of construction sites for G. N. SERVANDONI and PIERRE CONTANT D'IVRY and met JEAN FRANCOIS BLONDEL. Brought to Strasbourg in 1758 by Cardinal de Rohan (Charles's brother), he designed the Hôtel du Miroir.

From 1764, d'Ixnard practiced in Germany, building and restoring castles, private residences, and convents. After a fire in 1768, he redesigned Saint Blaise Abbey in the Black Forest; its eclectic church, completed in 1780, is considered to be d'Ixnard's masterpiece. The reconstruction of the Gothic church in Buchau (1774–1776) was successfully done in a calm and sober classicism as was Hechingen Church (1776). His original project in 1777 for the vast palace of the Trier's prince elector in Koblenz was reduced to a more severe design and was completed by A. J. Peyre the Younger (see PEYRE FAMILY) in 1779. Back in Strasbourg in 1779, he applied his own order of architecture to the Royal College Library in Colmar.

D'Ixnard's designs were characterized by contradictory influences. His work was new in the German context where neoclassicism reappeared strongly only in the nineteenth century. His most important works were published in a *Recueil d'architecture* (1791).

MARC DILET

WORKS

1758, Hôtel du Miroir, Strasbourg, France. 1764, Hechingen Castle, Germany. 1765, Königseggwald Hunting Castle, Aulendorf, Germany. 1768–1780, Saint Blaise Abbey, Black Forest, Germany. 1769, Convent, Buchau, Germany. 1769–1772, Sickingen Hotel, Freiburg in Breisgau, Germany. 1773–1782, Castle, Ellingen, Germany. 1774–1776, Gothic Church, Buchau, Germany. 1775, Castle, Gammertingen, Germany. 1776–1780, Church, Hechingen, Germany. 1779–1787, Royal College Library, Colmar, Germany.

BIBLIOGRAPHY

D'IXNARD, MICHEL 1791 *Recueil d'architecture*. Strasbourg, France: Treutel.

DOBSON, JOHN

John Dobson (1787–1865) was probably the ablest—and certainly the most prolific—early Victorian architect practicing in the North of England. During the course of his career, he worked on more than fifty churches and nearly one hundred houses, besides playing a key role in the great rebuilding of Newcastle upon Tyne. Dobson was a talented watercolorist, an able engineer, and a meticulous surveyor. He was taught to build by DAVID STEPHENSON of Newcastle; he studied perspective under an Italian refugee artist called Boniface Musso; he learned his skill at watercolors in the studio of John Varley; and his stylistic vocabulary and professional competence stemmed at least in part from his friendship with ROBERT SMIRKE. Few of Dobson's many churches rise above the prosaic level, but several of his neoclassical country houses, notably Longhirst (1824–1828), Nunny-kirk (1825), and Meldon (1832), exhibit a genuine talent for abstraction. And in Newcastle's great Central Railway Station (1847–1850), he triumphantly combined archeology and engineering—Greek Revival detailing plus a formidable glass-and-iron roof—in a way few architects of his generation could match. Even so, Dobson is likely to be remembered best—along with the speculative builder Richard Grainger and a local official, John Clayton—as one of the triumvirate of talents responsible for turning Victorian Newcastle into a rival of Georgian Edinburgh and Regency London. Dobson's drawing of Seaton Delaval, Northumberland (1815), was the first fully colored architectural perspective to be shown at the Royal Academy.

J. MORDAUNT CROOK

WORKS

1822–1831, Morpeth Gaol and Sessions House; 1824–1828, Longhirst House, near Morpeth; 1825, Nunnykirk; Northumberland, England. 1825–1831, Eldon Square (with Richard Grainger), Newcastle, England. 1828, Seaham Harbour, Durham, England. *1831–1832, Royal Arcade, Newcastle, England. 1832, Meldon Park, Northumberland, England. 1835–1836, New Markets; c.1835–1839, Grey Street (with Grainger); Newcastle, England. 1837–1841, Beaufront Castle, Northumberland, England. 1847–1850, Central Railway Station, Newcastle, England. 1853–?, Wallington Hall (central hall); 1855–1857, Ottoburn Church; Northumberland, England.

BIBLIOGRAPHY

DOBSON, MARGARET JANE 1885 *A Memoir of John Dobson*. London: Hamilton-Adams.
GIROUARD, MARK 1966 "Dobson's Northumberland Houses." *Country Life* 139:352–356, 406–411.
WILKES, LYALL 1980 *John Dobson: Architect and Landscape Gardener*. Stocksfield, England: Oriel.
WILKES, LYALL, and DODDS, GORDON 1964 *Tyneside Classical: The Newcastle of Grainger, Dobson and Clayton*. London: J. Murray.

DÖCKER, RICHARD

Richard Döcker (1894–1968), born in Weilheim an der Tieck in Württemberg, Germany, was a proponent of the International style during the 1920s. He studied architecture at the Technische Hochschule in Stuttgart under PAUL BONATZ, whose assistant he became in 1921. He later worked as senior assistant to ERIC MENDELSOHN, developed concepts of terraced construction, designed two houses for the Werkbund exhibition in Stuttgart-Weissenhof in 1927, and served as LUDWIG MIES VAN DER ROHE's construction supervisor for the entire exhibition. Döcker also designed schools and hospitals and was appointed professor at the Stuttgart Technische Hochschule in the late 1920s and again in 1947, where he taught until his death. He was director of reconstruction in Saarbrücken (1941–1943) and of Stuttgart (1946–1950). Döcker planned the rebuilding of the Technische Hochschule in Stuttgart (1948–1951), built the University Library in Saarbrücken, Germany (1951–1953), and prepared the master plan for the university city of Hyderabad, Pakistan (1954–1957).

RON WIEDENHOEFT

BIBLIOGRAPHY

JOEDICKE, JÜRGEN 1980 "Döcker, Richard." Page 208 in Muriel Emanuel (editor), *Contemporary Architects*. New York: St. Martin's.

DODS, ROBIN

Robin Smith Dods (1868–1920) was born in Dunedin, New Zealand, spent his childhood in Britain, and moved to Queensland, Australia, in 1881, where he attended the Brisbane Boys' Grammar School before returning to Britain to study at the Edinburgh Architectural Association. He was articled to the firm of Hay and Henderson in Edinburgh for three years, after which he was employed in the office of ASTON WEBB in London.

Dods returned to Brisbane, Australia, in 1894 and soon formed a partnership with Francis R. Hall. The first commission of Hall and Dods was the Nurses' Home for the Brisbane Hospital (1894), the design of which won first prize for Dods before the partnership was created. Several other hospital commissions followed, and Dods, being the designer in the partnership, soon became recognized in the field of hospital design. At the same time, he also had many ecclesiastical commissions. Dods mostly used face brickwork with stone dressings to create some of his best works as diocesan architect for the Anglican Church in Brisbane.

Dods had a great love of craftsmanship, and this is best seen in his ecclesiastical and domestic work. This personal interest was infused into the artisans carrying out his designs. In this way, Dods did much to raise the standards of building craftsmanship in Queensland.

Dods's awareness of the importance of climatic influences on design led him to redefine the vernacular style of Queensland domestic architecture. Designing to suit the subtropical climate was a primary consideration and his greatest contribution to his profession.

In 1913, Dods moved to Sydney, forming the partnership of Spain, Cosh, and Dods with Alfred Spain and Thomas F. Cosh. Very few works of this partnership show any influence by Dods. After being in ill health for some years, Dods died in Sydney without gaining the recognition that he had enjoyed in Queensland.

PETER NAVARETTI

WORKS

1894, Nurses' Home, Brisbane; 1900, Dods House, New Farm; 1902, Littledyke House, Clayfield; 1905 Saint John's Institute School; 1907, Sun Insurance Building, Brisbane; 1908–1909, Mater Misericordiae Hospital, South Brisbane; 1910, Saint John's Diocesan Office; 1911, Metropolitan Infectious Diseases Hospital; Brisbane; 1912, Bishopbourne Chapel, Milton; 1912–1914, Saint Brigid's Church, Red Hill; 1915, Tamrookum Church, Beaudesert; Queensland, Australia. *1919, South British Insurance Company, Sydney.

BIBLIOGRAPHY

DODS, R. S. 1907 "Notes on Furniture." *Building* Oct.:52–53.
FREELAND, JOHN MAXWELL (1968)1974 *Architecture in Australia: A History.* Harmondsworth, England: Penguin.
JOHNSON, DONALD LESLIE 1980 *Australian Architecture 1901–1951: Sources of Modernism.* Sydney: University Press.
HOGAN, JANET 1978 *Building Queensland's Heritage.* Richmond, Victoria: Richmond Hill Press.
LUND, NEVILLE H. 1958 *Robin S. Dods, the Life and Work of a Distinguished Queensland Architect* 47:77–86.
ROYAL AUSTRALIAN INSTITUTE OF ARCHITECTS 1959 *Buildings of Queensland.* Brisbane, Australia: Jacaranda Press.
"Robin S. Dods." 1920 *Royal Victorian Institute of Architects Journal* July:93.

DOESBURG, THEO VAN

See VAN DOESBURG, THEO.

DOICESCU, OCTAV

Octav Doicescu (1902–1980) graduated from the School of Architecture in Bucharest in 1930. He taught at the Institute of Architecture in Bucharest from 1944 to 1973. Doicescu designed several important industrial buildings that are expressed in simple volumes but are original in structure and outlook. He rejected the eclectic and classicizing currents as well as the "banal forms" of modern Rumanian architecture. He did, however, try to find a creative relationship between past and present architecture. His later works represent a synthesis of contemporary functionalism rendered in classical principles of composition and of traditional Romanian architecture.

Doicescu contributed many articles to cultural and professional journals.

CONSTANTIN MARIN MARINESCU

WORKS

1934, Nautical Club, Snagov, near Bucharest. 1934, IAR Airplane Manufacturing Plant, Brasov, Rumania. 1934?, Tire Factory Victoria, Floresti, Prahova, Rumania. 1936?, Tractor Factory, Brasov, Rumania. 1950, Metallurgic Factory, Colibasi, Rumania. 1953, Opera and Ballet Theater; 1947, Office Building, Calea Victoriei; 1960, Housing Estate Baneasa (with others); 1970, Polytechnic Institute (with others); Bucharest.

BIBLIOGRAPHY

CANTACUZÈNE, GEORGE 1934 "Tendances dans l'architecture roumaine." *Architecture d'Aujourd'hui* 5, no. 5:57–62.
IONESCU, GRIGORE 1965 Volume 2 in *Istoria Arhitecturii in Romania.* Bucharest: Editura Academiei Republicii Romañe.
IONESCU, GRIGORE 1969 *Arhitectura in Romania: perioda anilor 1944–1969.* Bucharest: Editura Academiei Republicii Socialiste Româñia.
IONESCU, GRIGORE 1972 "Saptezeci si cinci de ani de la infiintarea invatamintului de arhitectura din Romania." *Arhitectura* 20:35–42.
MAMBRIANI, ALBERTO 1969 *L'Architettura Moderna nei Paesi Balcanici.* Bologna, Italy: Capelli.
MOITRY-BIZARY, RENÉE 1934 "Architecture en Roumainie: Bucarest." *Architecture d'Aujourd'hui* 5, no. 5:55–56.
PATRULIUS, RADU 1973–1974 "Contributii Romanesti in Arhitectura Anilor '30." *Arhitectura* 21, no. 6:44–52; 22, no. 1:53–59.
SASARMAN, GHEORGHE 1972 "Incepturile gindirii teoretice in arhitectura româneasča (1860–1916)." *Arhitectura* 20, no. 6:44–46.

DOLCEBUONO, GIOVANNI GIACOMO

An architect and sculptor, Giovanni Giacomo Dolcebuono (1440–1506) worked mostly as part of teams, and thus he remains a rather mysterious personality of the Lombard Renaissance. His active life forms a bridge between the movement headed by GIOVANNI ANTONIO AMADEO and DONATO BRAMANTE's period of influence. He was building master of Milan Cathedral at least in the 1490s, where earlier he also built the altar of San Giuseppe. He was simultaneously involved with the construction of the octagonal *tiburio* of Santa Maria presso San Celso, and did a project with Bramante for Pavia Cathedral. The *matroneo* of San Maurizio, a striking design employing Serlian motifs, and its vaulting were finished according to his plans. Dolcebuono's activity at the Incoronata Church in Lodi completed his participation in the construction of this illustrious group of Lombard buildings.

MARTHA POLLAK

WORKS

1472, Cathedral (altar of San Giuseppe); 1478–1501, Santa Maria presso San Celso (tiburio); Milan. 1489, Incoronata, Lodi, Italy. 1490–1503, Cathedral (building master); 1503, Maggiore Monastery, San Maurizio; Milan.

BIBLIOGRAPHY

BARONI, CONSTANTINO 1941 Pages 112–114 in *L'architettura lombarda da Bramante a Richini.* Milan: Edizioni de L'arte.
D'ANCONA, PAOLO, and GENGARO, M. L. (1948) 1958 Pages 355, 377, 409 in *Umanesimo e Rinascimento.* 4th ed. Torino, Italy: U.T.E.T.
GRASSI, LILIANA, and PORTALUPPI, PIERO 1961 "Scuola e 'maniera' nell'architettura lombarda del Cinquecento." Pages 225–242 in *Saggi di storia dell'architettura in monore di Vincenzo Fasolo.* Rome: Istituto di storia dell'architettura.

DOMÈNECH I MONTANER, LLUÍS

Lluís Domènech i Montaner (1850–1923) was, together with ANTONÍO GAUDÍ, the most representative architect of *modernismo,* a specifically Catalan version of the artistic movement of the end of the nineteenth and the beginning of the twentieth centuries, whose stylistic and cultural foundations lay in the Art Nouveau movement, the Modern Style, the *Jugendstil,* and the Secession. The extraordinary breadth and quality of *modernismo* has to be understood as a consequence of the factors that brought modern Catalonia into being in the nineteenth century: a social basis growing out of the industrialization in which the new bourgeoisie and the fledgling proletariat felt themselves clearly set apart from the social and economic backwardness of the rest of Spain. This popular base laid claim to its own autonomous nationality, dependent upon the recognition of medieval historical factors—corresponding to the Mediterranean hegemony of the old Catalan nation—as opposed to the unified, French-inspired model of the decadent Spanish state; they became part of the social processes in Europe and, consequently, of its cultural processes. Domènech i Montaner was a prime representative of this movement because he participated significantly in all its aspects: an archeologist dedicated to the discovery of the stylistic founda-

Domènech i Montaner
Café Restaurant de
l'Exposició (now the
Zoological Museum).
Barcelona, Spain.
1887–1888

tions of a specifically Catalan art within the great works of the Romanesque and Gothic periods, a political activist who promoted the great unifying actions of Catalanism, an architect of the most cultivated sector of the industrial bourgeoisie who anticipated the aesthetic of Art Nouveau in the last stages of eclecticism, he emulated the English programs for the renewal of the industrial arts and adhered to an innovative rationalism that, at one and the same time, nurtured itself on the historical reconstructions of EUGÈNE EMMANUEL VIOLLET-LE-DUC—which provided for a new attitude toward technology—, the enthusiasm for new materials, and the deterministic theories of functional and environmental character that started with GOTTFRIED SEMPER.

In 1878, he published an article ("In Search of a National Architecture") which established the foundations for the transition from eclecticism to a modern idiom that would still allow for national

Domènech i Montaner.
Palau de la Música
Catalana.
Barcelona, Spain.
1905–1908

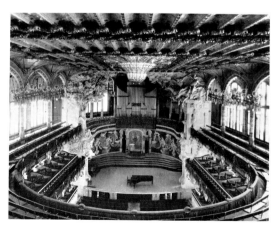

idiosyncrasy; it can be considered as the document that summarizes the origins of *modernismo*. His first works developed in this still eclectic line. At the Publishing House of Montaner i Simón, the allusions to mudejar architecture served to instill a constructive, polemically progressive rationalism and an ornamental touch of the *coup de fouet*. For the Barcelona Universal Exposition of 1888 he built the International Hotel in the record time of eighty-three days—with a modular system based on criteria that anticipated some of the processes of industrialization—and the Café Restaurant (1887–1888), which was the first European structure to reclaim the value of the plane for brick walls organized according to a system of double facades, with a touch of scandalous modernity, despite allusions to formal models of medieval origin.

The Palau de la Música Catalana (1905–1908) and the Hospital de Sant Paul (1902–1910), both in Barcelona, constitute the central period of his work. The first—a concert hall, site of the Orteó Català, a choral institution most representative of the general cultural renaissance of Catalonia—is, without doubt, his masterpiece. It is the first edifice of its kind, built with a structure of interlaced iron, enclosed by a continuous glass façade. This very strict execution is embellished with the richest ceramic ornamentation, rooted in Art Nouveau. The most significantly modern elements of this work are surely the radical structural purity and the intention to represent the façade as a simple glass continuity in the central part of the auditorium. One must add to that the intelligent use of the double façade in the area of the hallways which—as in the Café Restaurant—created some intermediary spaces that resolved, by their own existence, the transition from inner spaces to urban surroundings which were hardly adequate to contain the autonomous monumentality of the edifice.

The Hospital is a complex of great urban importance, occupying four blocks of the Barcelona Extension, which was designed according to the well-known plan of engineer ILDEFONSO CERDÁ in 1859, on the basis of a uniformly square arrangement of streets. The complex interrupts the continuity of the design, and the four blocks, with the streets they cover, become an autonomous monument with an unusual ordering of buildings at a 45° angle. This ordering introduces, in addition, an important typological innovation: the hospital has pavilions isolated among gardens, beneath which is organized, underground, the entire unified operation of the services.

At the same time that he built the Hospital de Sant, Paul Domènech constructed in Reus another

Domènech i Montaner.
Hospital of Saint Paul.
Barcelona, Spain.
1902–1910

great hospital complex, the Institute Pere Mata (1897–1919), with analogous plans. In both, the typological innovation is the fundamental characteristic but, also in both, there appears the same effort to have modernity co-exist with the vestiges of national tradition: the formal inspiration in Gothic architecture as the cultural basis of the old Catalan nationality and the use of the aged, revived crafts, especially in the arched building systems—the Catalan vault—and in the ornamentation.

These central works of Domènech's production establish him as the modernist of rationalist and purist tendency, despite possible confusion occasioned by the superimposition of a great ornamental richness. The latter trait must be interpreted in its proper stylistic limitation. If Gaudí was the leader of an expressionist position within *modernismo* because of the will to subject structure and morphology to symbolic contents and dramatic expression, Domènech was the chief proponent of a strict structural and formal order. His attitude constituted the basis for a later evolution of Catalan architecture along a very definite historical line, which moved through the residues of the Viennese and Munich Secessionists, through the attempts of JOSEF HOFFMANN and AUGUSTE PERRET, and through the risks of Art Deco before reaching the orthodox rationalism that appeared in the thirties with the GATCPAC.

The process toward a definitive formal simplification in the work of Domènech can be encountered in the series of residential groups from the Lleó Morera House (1905) to the Fuster House (1908–1910), both on the Passeig de Gràcia in Barcelona. The Art Nouveau graphic quality of the first, today unfortunately much disfigured, is superimposed on an innovating typology and is used in conjunction with some essentially modern elements. In the second, that graphic quality reaches a simplification in which the traditional elements—columns, capitals, cornices—lose their historic meaning and acquire the value of a simple allusion to established codes, adopting thereby a subversive attitude in regard to tradition and convention.

The entire scope of Domènech's cultural work cannot be understood without stressing his contribution to political and historical themes and his extensive written works. His studies of the vicissitudes of the Catalonian national entity, of the coats of arms of Catalan families, of medieval architecture, of the Monastery of Poblet and the Baptistery of Centcelles are extremely significant and helped to found a school of investigators that was to yield very soon the best fruits of Catalonian culture. Between 1900 and 1919, he was director of the School of Architecture of Barcelona and we owe to him its radical transformation, from a still neoclassical and eclectic mentality to a modernity in which the entire second generation of Catalan modernism was formed.

ORIOL BOHIGAS
Translated from Spanish by
Florette Rechnitz Koffler

WORKS

1880, Editorial Montaner i Simón; 1885–1896, Palau Montaner; Barcelona, Spain. 1887, Casino, Riera Sant Domènec, Canet de Mar, Spain. 1887–1888, Café Restaurant de l'Exposició (now the Zoological Museum); *1888, Hotel Internacional; Barcelona, Spain. 1889–1892, Comillas Seminary (rebuilding and interior decoration); 1890, Marqués de Comillas Monument; Santander, Spain. 1895–1898, Thomas House (later altered by Guàrdia i Vial), 291–293 Carrer Mallorca, Barcelona, Spain. 1897–1919, Pere Mata Institute; 1900, Rull House, 27 Carrer Sant Joan; 1901, Navàs House, 7 Plaça Espanya; Reus, Tarragona, Spain. 1902, Lamadrid House, 113 Carrer Girona; 1902–1903, Espanya Restaurant; 1902–1910, Hospital of Saint Paul (first wing); Barcelona, Spain. 1902–1912?, Gran Hotel (now Institut Nacional de Previsión), Palma de Mallorca, Spain. 1905, Lleó Morera House (later altered), 35 Passeig de Gràcia; 1905–1908, Palau de la Música Catalana; 1908–1910, Fuster House, 132 Passeig de Gràcia; Barcelona, Spain. 1913–1916, Solà House, Firal, Olot, Girona, Spain. 1914, Restaurant, near the Santuario de la Misericordia, Canet de Mar; n.d., Roura House, Riera Sant Domènec, Canet de Mar; Barcelona, Spain.

BIBLIOGRAPHY

BOHIGAS, ORIOL (1967)1973 "Lluís Domènech i Montaner." Pages 71–84 in Nikolaus Pevsner and J. M. Richards (editors), *The Anti-rationalists*. Reprint London: Architectural Press. Originally published as an article in *Architectural Review*.

BOHIGAS, ORIOL 1970 *Reseña y Catálogo de la Arquitectura Modernista*. Barcelona, Spain: Lumen.

BOHIGAS, ORIOL 1976 *Once Arquitectos*. Barcelona, Spain: La Gaya Ciencia.

BORRÀS, MARIA LLUISA 1970 *Lluís Domènech i Montaner*. Barcelona, Spain: Polígrafa.

Cuadernos de Arquitectura. 1963 nos. 52–53: entire issue.

RAFOLS, J. B. 1956 "Lo decorativo en la obra de Doménech i Montaner." *Cuadernos de Arquitectura* 1956:97–102.

SOSTRES MALUQUER, JOSE MARIA 1958 "Luis Domenech y Montaner a través de un edificio cincuentenario." *Revista Nacional de Arquitectura* 202:26–30.

DOMENICO DA CORTONA

Domenico da Cortona, called Boccador (1470?–1549?) was one of several Italian architects who came to France following Charles VIII's 1494 invasion of Italy. Among those who visited France but did not remain were FRA GIOCONDO and Giuliano da Sangallo (see SANGALLO FAMILY), but Domenico da Cortona, who arrived in 1495, remained there until his death. Thought to have been born in Cortona, Italy, Domenico was probably a pupil of Giuliano da Sangallo, and it is believed that he spent time in Naples when his master was in the service of Ferrante of Aragon.

After his arrival in France, Domenico da Cortona's first work was at Amboise; in 1507, he is called *valet de Chambre de la reine*. He then became overseer of the works at Blois for Anne of Brittany. Account books of the reign of Charles VIII speak of him as *faiseur de chasteaux et menuisier*, and he seems to have spent much of his time as a woodcarver and designer of temporary decorations. In 1514, he is referred to for the first time as *maistre des oeuvres de maconnerie du Roy*, and the first architectural project for which he prepared designs was the royal Château of Chambord, begun in 1519 for Francis I.

The building history of Chambord is complicated. Some scholars, including Ludwig Heydenreich, have suggested that LEONARDO DA VINCI provided the ultimate source for the ideas expressed in the building (1952, p. 282), whereas others, among them Anthony Blunt, have remained unconvinced of this thesis (1981, p. 406). Domenico da Cortona was certainly the architect responsible for the wooden model of Chambord, the appearance of which is documented by drawings made in the seventeenth century by ANDRÉ FÉLIBIEN DES AVAUX. Chambord has a Greek-cross plan and reflects Italian prototypes by Giuliano da Sangallo, the Medici Villas at Poggio a Caiano and Poggio Reale in Naples. The division of space into *appartements* at Chambord was to be very influential in France as was the elaborate staircase seen in Domenico da Cortona's model. The ideas of the Italian architect were, however, much altered by the French masons who carried them out.

The only other building which can be assigned to Domenico da Cortona with any certainty is the Hôtel de Ville of Paris which was destroyed in 1871. Domenico is first associated with the project in a 1532 document, and the commemorative stone which adorned the building carried the inscription "DOMINICO CORTONENSI ARCHITECTANTE." Domenico, who had resided in Paris since about 1531, is thought to have died there in 1549.

SHERYL E. REISS

WORKS

Begun 1519, Château of Chambord, France. *Begun 1532, Hôtel de Ville, Paris.

BIBLIOGRAPHY

BELTRAMI, LUCA 1882 "L'Hôtel-de-Ville di Parigi e l'architetto Domenico da Cortona." *Nuovo Antologia* 64:454–475.

BELTRAMI, LUCA 1892 "Nuovi documenti comprovanti Domenico da Cortona come architetto dell'Hôtel-de-Ville di Parigi." *Archivio storico dell'arte* 5:129–133.

BLUNT, ANTHONY (1953)1981 *Art and Architecture in France 1500–1700*. 4th ed. Harmondsworth, England: Penguin.

FABRICZY, C. DE 1889 "Domenico da Cortone, architetto del palazzo municipale di Parigi." *Archivio storico dell'arte* 2:489.

GUILLAUME, JEAN   1968   "Léonard de Vinci, Dominique de Cortone et l'escalier du modèle en bois de Chambord." *Gazette des Beaux-Arts* 71, Feb.:93–108.

HEYDENREICH, LUDWIG H.   1952   "Leonardo da Vinci, Architect of Francis I." *Burlington Magazine* 94:277–285.

LESUEUR, F.   1951   "Les dernières étapes de la construction de Chambord." *Bulletin Monumental* 109:7–39.

LESUEUR, PIERRE   1928   *Dominique de Cortone, dit Le Boccador: Du Château de Chambord a l'Hôtel-de-Ville de Paris.* Paris: Laurens.

LESUEUR, PIERRE   1936   "Nouveau document sur Dominique de Cortone (1510)." *Bulletin de la Société de l'Histoire de l'art français* 1936:30–35.

DOMMEY, ETIENNE THEODORE

Born in Altona, Holstein, of French parents, Etienne Théodore Dommey (1801–1872) returned to France in 1814 and in 1820 enrolled at the Ecole des Beaux-Arts, the pupil of LOUIS HIPPOLYTE LEBAS, for whom he worked also, from 1823, at Notre Dame de Lorette. In 1827 he won the competition for the Palais de Justice at Lille, in 1834 that for the abbattoir at Rouen, but his greatest energies were to be focused on the building of the Palais de Justice in Paris, where he worked with his nephew, LOUIS JOSEPH DUC, from 1840 to 1871.

R. D. MIDDLETON

WORKS

*1835–1837, Palais de Justice et Maison d'arrêt (supervised by Victor Leplus), Lille, France. 1836–1838, Abbattoir, Rouen, France. 1840–1871, Palais de Justice (with Louis Joseph Duc), Paris.

BIBLIOGRAPHY

BALTARD, VICTOR; DUC, LOUIS JOSEPH; and GODEBOEUF, ANTOINE ISIDORE EUGÈNE   1872   "Funérailles de Mr. E. Th. Dommey." *Bulletin mensuel de la Société Centrale des Architectes* 1872:240–246.

DAVID DE PENANRUN, LOUIS THÉRÈSE; ROUX, LOUIS FRANÇOIS; and DELAIRE, EDMOND AUGUSTIN   (1895)1907   *Les architectes élèves de l'Ecole des Beaux-Arts: 1819–1894.* 2d ed. Paris: Chaix.

DONALDSON, THOMAS LEVERTON

Thomas Leverton Donaldson (1795–1885) was born in London and was articled to his father, James Donaldson, a district surveyor. Donaldson toured Greece and Italy from 1818 to 1823; he was elected a member of the Academy of Saint Luke in Rome. He was a prominent founder-member of the Royal Institute of British Architects, of which he was president from 1863 to 1864. From 1842 to 1865, he was professor of construction and architecture at University College, London. From 1844, he was also district surveyor for South Kensington. Doyen of the profession, Donaldson was less notable for his buildings than for his influence as a teacher and writer. He published many works including *Architectural Maxims and Theorems* (1847) and *Architectura Numismatica* (1859).

MARGARET RICHARDSON

WORKS

1826–1829, Holy Trinity; Brompton Road; 1848, Great Hall (interior) and Library, University College; 1848, Doctor William's Library, Gordon Square; *1849–1851, Henry Thomas Hope Mansion (with Pierre-Charles Dusillon), 116 Piccadilly; 1857, Offices, 7–9 Fetter Lane; 1865, German Hospital, Dalston Lane, Hackney; 1877, Royal Scottish Corporation Offices, Crane Court, Fleet Street; London.

BIBLIOGRAPHY

BLUTMAN, SANDRA   1967   "The Father of the Profession." *Journal of the Royal Institute of British Architects* 74:542–544.

DONALDSON, T. L.   1847   *Architectural Maxims and Theorems.* London: Weale.

DONALDSON, T. L.   (1859)1966   *Architectura Numismatica.* Reprint. Chicago: Argonaut.

HITCHCOCK, H. R.   (1954)1972   *Early Victorian Architecture in Britain.* Reprint. New York: Da Capo.

"Obituary."   1886   *Transactions of the Royal Institute of British Architects* New Series 2:1–2, 89–109.

DONTHORN, W. J.

William John Donthorn (1799–1859), born in Swaffham, Norfolk, practiced in London and East Anglia. He was a pupil of Sir JEFFRY WYATTVILLE, whose picturesque planning techniques he adopted. Donthorn was a little employed, but highly original designer of country houses, parsonages, and public buildings of utilitarian, Gothic, Italianate, and Norman styles. His Greek Revival designs were influenced by the austere style of GEORGE DANCE THE YOUNGER, JOHN SOANE, and ROBERT SMIRKE, and he was a friend of the Italianate architect Charles Parker. In Highcliffe Castle, Hampshire (1830–1834), a ruinous, picturesque French flamboyant Gothic structure Donthorn incorporated Louis XV interiors, and medieval fragments and details. The building was criticized by A. W. N. PUGIN. He died in Saint Leonards, Sussex.

RODERICK O'DONNELL

WORKS

1823–?, High House (additions), West Acre; *1824–1830?, Hillington Hall; 1827–1830, Cromer Hall; *1830–?, Elmham Hall; *1830–?, Watlington Hall; Norfolk, England. *1830–1834, Highcliffe Castle; 1830?–1835?, Bure Homage; Hampshire, England. 1842–1850, Leicester Testimonial Column, Holkham, Norfolk, England.

BIBLIOGRAPHY

O'DONNELL, RODERICK 1978 "W. J. Donthorn (1799–1859): Architecture With 'Great Hardness & Decision in the Edges.'" *Architectural History* 21:83–92.

D'ORBAY, FRANÇOIS

François d'Orbay (1634–1697) was born in Paris, the son of a master mason–entrepreneur. His initial training is unknown, but he may have assisted LOUIS LE VAU, the First Architect of the King, at the Château de Vincennes (built 1654–1661). Le Vau sent d'Orbay to study in Rome in 1660, where he produced a design for a stair in front of Santa Trinità dei Monti. Beginning in 1663, d'Orbay worked as Le Vau's chief draftsman in the Royal Building Administration. From 1662 on, he also functioned as an independent architect, providing designs for minor commissions.

Upon the death of Le Vau in 1670, the post of First Architect was left vacant, but d'Orbay continued ongoing activity at the Collège des Quatre Nations and the Louvre in Paris, and at Versailles. He was responsible for the final form of the Ambassadors' Staircase at Versailles, as well as other features of the palace. In 1671, he was appointed a founding member of the Royal Academy of Architecture. In 1678, JULES HARDOUIN MANSART became chief architect at Versailles, and d'Orbay then served as principal draftsman under Mansart, con-

tinuing in this position until his death in 1697. In his last years he produced independent designs for the Theater of the Comédie Française, Paris (1688–1689), the Arc de Triomphe du Peyrou, Montpellier (designed 1690, built 1691–1692), and the cathedral of Montauban (designed 1691, built 1692–1739) with modifications by Mansart and ROBERT DE COTTE.

D'Orbay would be an almost forgotten figure today, were it not for the monograph of Albert Laprade (1960), which maintains that he was the real designer of virtually all the major projects of Le Vau (1660–1670) and Mansart (1678–1697). Most important, Laprade claims that d'Orbay designed both the Louvre Colonnade (begun 1667) and the garden elevations of Versailles (begun 1668), the two most significant manifestoes of French architectural classicism under Louis XIV. Since the Colonnade was officially the work of a committee (Le Vau, Charles LeBrun, CLAUDE PERRAULT), the precise roles of the participants (and their assistants) are difficult to assess (in 1694 d'Orbay claimed that both he and Le Vau were responsible for the Colonnade). In the case of Versailles, Le Vau is the sole putative designer. However, the garden façades are unlike anything in Le Vau's established oeuvre. Either he was capable at the close of his career of a startling stylistic change or he left the design to someone else (that is, his chief assistant). As long as the problems surrounding the authorship of these two royal buildings remain open, the possibility exists that d'Orbay was one of the major creators of French classical style.

ROBERT W. BERGER

D'Orbay.
Project for a stair at Santa Trinità dei Monti.
Rome.
c.1660

WORKS

*1662–1663, Convent of the Prémontrés; *1671, Chapel of the Trinity (façade); Paris. *1674–1680, Ambassadors' Staircase, Château de Versailles, France. *1688–1689, Theater of the Comédie Française, Paris. 1691–1692, Arc de Triomphe du Peyrou, Montpellier, France. 1692–1739, Cathedral of Montauban (with modifications completed by Jules Hardouin Mansart and Robert de Cotte), France.

BIBLIOGRAPHY

HAUTECOEUR, LOUIS 1948 *Le règne de Louis XIV.* 2 vols. Volume 2 in *Histoire de l'architecture classique en France.* Paris: Picard.
HAUTECOEUR, LOUIS 1960 "François d'Orbay." *Journal des savants* April–June:59–66.
HUILLET d'ISTRIA, MADELEINE 1966 "L'art de François d'Orbay révélé par la cathédrale de Montauban." *XVIIIe siècle* 72:3–69.
LAPRADE, ALBERT 1953 "François d'Orbay (1634–1697)." *Bulletin de la Société de l'histoire de l'art français* 1953:85–95.

LAPRADE, ALBERT 1960 *François d'Orbay, architecte de Louis XIV.* Paris: Vincent, Fréal.

DORTSMAN, ADRIAEN

Born in Vlissingen, Netherlands, Adriaen Dortsman (1625–1682) studied mathematics in Leyden and settled in Amsterdam in 1665. He was the first to build blocks of houses in a flat, unadorned style, without pilasters, accented only by entrances, balconies, and attics in harmonious proportions. His best known work, the Lutheran Church (1668–1671), Amsterdam, is the only Dutch Protestant church on a circular groundplan. The imposing exterior has heavy Doric pilasters and a dome. He was fortification engineer for Amsterdam and for the fortress of Naarden and was a controller in the "Hollandse Waterlinie," a line of defense against the enemy, reinforced by inundations.

MARIET J. H. WILLINGE

WORKS

1665–1666, 619 Heerengracht; 1668–1671, Round Lutheran Church (burned in 1822 and rebuilt); 1671, 456 Heerengracht; 1671, 1672–1674, Keizersgracht; 1671, Walloon Orphanage; 1672, 586–596 Heerengracht; 1672, 621–629 Heerengracht/208 Amstel (only 623 Heerengracht is extant); Amsterdam.

BIBLIOGRAPHY

FOCKEMA ANDREAE, S. J.; KUILE, E. H. TER; and HEKKER, R. C. 1957 *De bouwkunst na de Middeleeuwen.* Volume 2 in *Duizend jaar bouwen in Nederland.* Amsterdam: Lange.
KUYPER, WOUTER 1980 *Dutch Classicist Architecture.* Netherlands: Delft University Press.
EEGHEN, I. H. VAN 1970 "Adriaen Dortsman en Jan Six." *Amstelodamum: Maandblad voor de Kennis van Amsterdam* 57:152–159.
ROSENBERG, JAKOB; SLIVE, SEYMOUR; and KUILE, E. H. TER (1966)1972 *Dutch Art and Architecture: 1600–1800.* Rev. ed. Harmondsworth, England: Penguin.
VERMEULEN, FRANS A. J. 1941 Volume 3 in *Handboek tot de geschiedenis der Nederlandsche bouwkunst.* The Hague: Nijhoff.

DOTTI, CARLO FRANCESCO

Carlo Francesco Dotti (1670–1759) was born in Piazza di San Stefano, Como, Italy. He was the third generation in a family of architects and builders. He was self-taught in architecture, geometry, and mechanics. He practiced as builder as well as architect, and often fulfilled both responsibilities for the same building. He was forty when he did his first independent project. Patronized by the

Dotti.
Madonna di San Luca
Sanctuary.
Near Bologna, Italy.
1723

distinguished Monti family through whom he obtained his major projects, Dotti was in competition with Torregiani, who was better placed.

In 1731, Dotti became architect of the Senate, Bologna's governing body. His tenure occurred in a period lacking in urban development. The forty local families alternating in government maintained a traditional environment, intent on preservation. His participation in the two major competitions of the century in Rome, for the façade of San Giovanni in Laterano (1732) and the reinforcement of St. Peter's dome (1743), kept him in touch with events.

Dotti's major works are the pilgrimage church of Madonna di San Luca (1723) and the Arch of Meloncello (1722), both in Bologna. Dotti first presented a design for the Meloncello arch in 1714. This was to be a structure at the beginning of the arcaded portico that led to the pilgrimage site. It was located near Bologna's Saragosa gate. Urbanistically, it served as a hinge between the street and the arcaded exurban "road to Calvary." Dotti's design differed from other competitors' entries: only he proposed to build over the road rather than on it. In 1718, he was invited to submit another design, followed by various elaborations in which the structure whose central tribune was intended for religious ceremonies developed into a double S-curve and became more aulic. The design may have been inspired by the Bonaccorsi Arch by Monti and by the entry arch to the Sacro Monte di Varese. The Meloncello formed the first baroque space in Bologna, resolving its program with rationality, synthesis, and verve.

The portico to which the arch gave access masks the sanctuary until arrival to the top. At the top, the portico becomes the façade of the church which it embraces, forming an enclosed, undulating space in front of it. Originally, the building had stood in a field. When Dotti took over in 1723 he had to face two difficult problems: how to attract pilgrims, and how to both emulate and contrast nature. He resolved both in a masterly way, the former through the Meloncello arch and the latter through the design of the church itself. It was a homogenous, elliptical design on a Greek-cross plan and crowned by a dome. The richly articulated building represented a type, impressively scenographic, that the age was fond of. Its siting showed the control of nature by men in service of God. Already in the eighteenth century, it was compared with the Superga in Turin, but the Madonna di San Luca is closer to the surrounding landscape and to its convent.

The interior is less interesting, using Santi Martina e Luca in Rome as model. By conventionalizing PIETRO BERRETTINI DA CORTONA's dynamic motifs, Dotti drained Cortona's style. Furthermore, Dotti returned to traditional conceptions, emphasized verticality, and gave the building axial direction by reducing the arms. In his use of columns, Dotti is closest to Carlo Rainaldi at Santa Maria in Campitelli. The theme of the free-standing column, a leitmotif of Bolognese architecture, is developed in the design of the interior, and the relationship between the wall and the orders is theatrical rather than sculptural. Dotti's reasons for using Santi Martina e Luca as model may have been prompted by symbolic rather than aesthetic choices, given his association with the Accademia di San Luca in Rome where he exhibited the project for the main altar of the Bologna sanctuary.

Dotti worked with strong restrictions in the rehabilitation of existing buildings of which his practice largely consisted. However, his restoration of San Domenico (1727–1732), adopting the Michelangelesque (see MICHELANGELO) use of the minor order, gave it a unified interior. The double-return staircase of the Palazzo Davia Bargellini is spectacular in the balance between architecture and the luxuriant use of stucco.

MARTHA POLLAK

WORKS

1710, Marsigli Rossi Theater (restoration); 1712, Chapel of the Holy Sacrament, San Maria Maggiore; 1715, Santo Stefano (refectory); 1722, Meloncello; 1723, Madonna di San Luca Sanctuary; 1725–1728, San Sigismundo; 1727–1732, San Domenico (restoration); 1729, Convent of Celestines; Bologna, Italy. 1733–1737, San Giovanni Battista, Minerbio, Italy. 1734, San Maria della Morte (rehabilitation); 1736–1738, Palazzo Monti (rehabilitation); Bologna, Italy. 1739–1741, Savena Bridge, Italy. 1740, Palazzo Agucchi; 1744, San Procolo (rehabilitation); Bologna, Italy. 1745, San Sebastiano, Renazzo, Italy. 1748, San Maria Maggiore (presbytery); Bologna, Italy. 1755, San Mamante (belltower), Medicina, Italy.

BIBLIOGRAPHY

DOTTI, CARLO FRANCESCO 1710 *Ragioni con le quali si dimostra il perche sia inviolabile il quesito famoso delle terre aggravate con inequale proporzione delle pertiche espresso in due dialoghi: e si dimostra le fallaccia delle regole fino ad ora ostentate.* Bologna, Italy: Barbiroli alle Rosa.

DOTTI, CARLO FRANCESCO 1730 *Esame sopra le forze delle catene a braga con che si mostrano le bragature essere inutili per reggere l'urto degli archi e volte e come possa reggere la semplice catena horizzontale, posta nella sommita degli archi senza bragature, come anche tante fabbriche munite con dette catene a braga, che reggonsi fino al giorno d'oggi possano essere un'argomento forte, per dimostrarle valide, come viene creduto da molti.* Bologna, Italy: San Tommaso d'Aquino.

DOTTI, CARLO FRANCESCO n.d. *Scrittura volante sul proposito del nuovo teatro pubblico in difesa del sentimento di CF Dotti e del Torreggiani architetto, contro le opposizioni del sig. Antonio Bibiena inventore e direttore della fabbrica del nuovo pubblico teatro.* Bologna, Italy.

FORATTI, ALLO 1913 "Carlo Francesco Dotti." *L'Arte* 16:401–418.

MATTEUCCI, ANNA MARIA 1969 *Carlo Francesco Dotti e l'architettura bolognese del Settecento.* Bologna, Italy: Alfa.

OECHSLIN, WERNER 1971 "CF Dotti (1670–1759) architekt des frühen Settecento in Bologna." *Zeitschrift für Kunstgeschichte* 34, no. 3:208–239.

DOW, ALDEN B.

Alden B. Dow (1904–), born in Midland, Michigan, was educated at Columbia University and, in 1933, apprenticed to FRANK LLOYD WRIGHT. Dow's sense of composition and appreciation of the decorative effects of natural materials and exposed structures reveal his assimilation of Wright's design principles. His buildings, many of which are located in or near Midland, Michigan, have been critically acclaimed for their careful detailing and studied integration with their sites.

ALFRED WILLIS

WORKS

1932, Townsley House; 1934–1941, Dow House and Studio; 1937, Dow Chemical Company Administration Building; 1943, Midland Hospital; 1970, Midland Center for the Arts; Midland, Mich.

BIBLIOGRAPHY

DOW, ALDEN B. n.d. *A Way of Life.* Mich.: Midland Center for the Arts.

DOW, ALDEN B. 1970 *Reflections.* Midland, Mich.: Northwood Institute.

FLINT INSTITUTE OF ARTS, MICHIGAN 1965 *A Retrospective Exhibition of Architecture by Alden B. Dow.* Flint, Mich.: The institute. Exhibition catalogue.

ROBINSON, S. K. 1974 "Composed Places: Taliesen and Alden Dow's Studio." Unpublished Ph.D. dissertation, University of Michigan, Ann Arbor.

DOWNING, A. J.

Andrew Jackson Downing (1815–1852) or A. J. Downing, as he regularly wrote his name, coined for himself the title "rural architect." The description is accurate insofar as it suggests an interest in country life and a corresponding distrust of the city, but it should not be thought of as implying that more than a handful of buildings were designed by Downing, working alone, and even for these any claim to originality must be qualified.

If Downing changed the face of rural America, as is often said, he did so through his three major books and through his editorials in *The Horticulturist,* the "journal of rural art and rural taste" that he edited for the last six years of his life. Modern architectural critics should perhaps find here the beginnings of their profession in the United States. And Downing's place among horticulturists and landscape architects is even more secure; he was the first native gardener and writer on gardening topics to achieve international recognition; the numerous editions of his *Fruits and Fruit Trees of America* (1845) hastened the emergence of his country as one of the major fruit-growing regions of the world; many consider him the father of the public park in America.

When he was sixteen, Downing left school to help in the nursery at Newburgh, New York, that his elder brother Charles had been managing since their father's death nine years before. In this he probably acted more from choice than from economic necessity; few of Downing's contemporaries attended college, and the English authors in which he was becoming increasingly interested must have been well represented in the libraries of neighboring estates along the Hudson. Any question concerning the young nurseryman's access to such private resources would have been effectively allayed by his marriage in 1838 to Caroline De Windt (De Wint), a young woman from Fishkill Landing (now Beacon) across the river. Mrs. Downing's mother was the granddaughter of John Adams, second president of the United States, and the niece of John Quincy Adams, sixth president to whom Downing dedicated his first book.

Doubtless in preparation for the younger brother's approaching marriage, in 1837 Charles moved to the outskirts of the village and A. J.

began the construction of a substantial stone house adjacent to the nursery, of which he now became sole proprietor. Inspiration for the new "Elizabethan" residence came from a plate in FRANCIS GOODWIN's *Rural Architecture* (1835), and other English authors, especially John Claudius Loudon, were admittedly the sources of most of Downing's ideas on gardening and architectural design. The title of his first book, *A Treatise on the Theory and Practice of Landscape Gardening Adapted to North America* (1841), represented a conscious borrowing from that of a well-known work by HUMPHRY REPTON, the leading English authority on garden design at the turn of the century. Predictably, Downing's later writings also show the influence of JOHN RUSKIN, and he himself edited the American editions of three popular books by English authors: John Lindley's *Theory of Horticulture* (with Asa Gray, 1841); Mrs. Loudon's *Gardening for Ladies* (1846); and George Wightwick's *Hints to Young Architects* (1847). Coming as it did at the end of a long development of English gardening style and theory, Downing's contribution lay not so much in the originality of his ideas as in his ability to combine abstruse theory with practical knowledge. In a series of graceful essays he sought to convince middle-class Americans that taste was not the exclusive property of the rich and that the simplest cottage could be as tasteful as the most pretentious mansion.

While admitting that the classical styles might do well enough for public buildings in the city, Downing believed that the abrupt and often asymmetrical lines of the Gothic suited best the irregular—and therefore especially picturesque—qualities of the rural landscape. For more regular sites nearer the city, he favored the "modern Italian," which characteristically combined classical motifs with a remarkably free plan. Those who found both the rural Gothic and the Italianate too rich for their taste or purse were advised to consider the "Bracketed" style, characterized, as its name implies, by prominent brackets under boldly projecting eaves. This last was as near to producing an "American mode" as Downing ever came, and even here sources could be found in the Swiss or Italian styles, not to mention some of the contemporary designs of ALEXANDER JACKSON DAVIS, a prominent New York architect and one of the most talented draftsmen of his day.

From time to time, Downing might illustrate his remarks with the work of such contemporary architects as JOHN NOTMAN, GERVASE WHEELER, or RICHARD UPJOHN—all British immigrants to America—but it was on Davis that he principally relied. For more than a decade, the Hudson River steamers that plied between Newburgh and New

Downing.
Design for an Ornamental
Farm House.
1842

York carried the young nurseryman's rough sketches for his older and more experienced colleague to redraw on the whitened woodblock, which was then passed along to one of several engravers. Many of the illustrations produced in this way bear the initials "AA," indicating that they were the work of Alexander Anderson, a physician who over a period of many years established himself as America's first wood engraver of note. Considering the respective talents of the three participants, it is easy to understand how this informal collaboration produced the most popular books of their kind ever published; during the 1850s and 1860s they inspired scores of imitators and in the end they completely changed Americans' concept of what an architectural book should be. Whereas earlier guides had contained a variety of details intended principally for the builder, Downing's books regularly showed the dwelling in its appropriate landscape setting and accompanied by an extended text that sought to explain to the reader the philosophical and practical considerations that should underlie the planning of a house.

Those who found such general statements insufficient for their purpose might engage directly the professional services of the author. For a fee of twenty dollars a day, Downing was prepared to go about the eastern seaboard giving advice on the siting of houses and the laying out of gardens. From his cousin's diary we learn that the grounds of Joshua Francis Fisher's estate, begun about 1849 near Philadelphia, was one such commission, and there is a long-standing tradition that the present garden of the George Read House, laid out about 1847 in Newcastle, Delaware, is another, but beyond a few examples of this kind, we have no firm evidence concerning the numerous clients whom

Downing must have served in this way. Presumably, any sketches or written instructions would have been slight and informal at best, and there is of course no way of knowing how much even these might have been modified in execution. In many cases, the purchase of a few plants from Highland Gardens, the Downing nursery at Newburgh, was probably reason enough for the buyer to boast that in planning his grounds he had consulted the acknowledged arbiter of American taste.

From his writings it is clear that Downing shared fully the prevailing nineteenth-century belief that human behavior was largely to be explained by environment and that of all environments a rural one was most to be desired. City dwellers of means usually had a second house in the country to which they could escape, and for those who could not afford this luxury, Downing took the lead in urging the creation of public parks in which the beneficial effects of the rural landscape could be made available to those obliged to live out their lives in the city. According to this view, the soothing effects of rural life could also benefit the insane, whose condition was often attributed to the frantic pace of urban living. Inevitably, America's leading authority on rural design was consulted about the landscape settings for several of the new state hospitals, including one for New Jersey at Trenton (1848). Although he did not live to see established the large New York park for which he had pleaded so eloquently, in 1851 Downing was asked by President Fillmore to develop a plan that would make the Public Grounds (Mall) in the nation's capital into the first urban park in America, as distinct from the colonial square and commons.

For the nineteenth century, with its concern for relating the building to its site, training as a landscape gardener would have been considered ideal preparation for a career in architecture. A discussion of rural architecture forms Section IX of the *Treatise on Landscape Gardening,* and the following year Downing published *Cottage Residences* (1842), a smaller volume devoted specifically to architecture and containing a number of designs that soon gained wide acceptance. Of these, Design IX, An Ornamental Farm House, was the simplest and perhaps for that reason by far the most popular. As its author recognized scores of houses based on it and on other of his designs, his own perception of himself and of his career began to change.

In order to devote his full attention to writing and consultation, in the winter of 1846 Downing sold his nursery to John A. Saul, who had been managing it for a number of years. This move was the more necessary because the previous July he had become editor of a new monthly journal with which the Albany publisher Luther Tucker proposed to capitalize on the growing interest in "rural taste" for which the *Treatise on Landscape Gardening* and *Cottage Residences* were largely responsible. *The Horticulturist* was a success from the outset, and a number of the engravings that illustrated the opening editorials were later republished as part of Downing's third and last book, *The Architecture of Country Houses* (1850).

Recognizing both his own lack of architectural training and his professional debt to A. J. Davis, Downing was at first only too glad to recommend the talents of his friend and informal collaborator to all who sought expert advice about designing a house. By the late 1840s, however, Downing was beginning to think about establishing his own architectural office, one large enough to attract substantial commissions and at the same time to provide space for at least some of the increasing number of persons who sought to become his students. With this in mind, he began to enlarge his house in Newburgh and in 1849 proposed to Davis that they transform their working arrangement into a more formal partnership. When nothing came of this, Downing left for England in the summer of 1850 with the express intention of finding a suitable partner. For this role he chose CALVERT VAUX, a young English architect nine years his junior who had trained in the office of Lewis Nockalls Cottingham, an architect remembered principally for his interest in the medieval structures of England.

On their return to Newburgh in the fall of 1850, the new partners found no scarcity of clients. Their design for a building to house the New York Exposition of 1853 was not chosen, but Matthew Vassar engaged their services in planning *Springside,* his estate on the outskirts of Poughkeepsie, New York, and in fashionable Newport, Rhode Island, Daniel Parish proposed to build a large house in the Renaissance style then coming into fashion. In these, as in other of the firm's commissions later published by Vaux, the hand of the junior partner is clearly in evidence. Most would seem more at home in Victorian England than among the picturesque cottages and farm houses that had first brought Downing to public notice.

Unfortunately, we can do no more than speculate concerning the direction the new firm would have taken or about how it would have fared in a changing America in which architecture was soon to become a recognized profession. While on his way to inspect work in progress at the Washington park and at Mr. Parish's villa, Downing perished in the burning of the Hudson River steamer *Henry Clay.* He was not yet thirty-seven, and his untimely

Downing.
A.J. Downing Residence.
Newburgh, New York.
1838–1839

Downing.
Design and Plan for a
*   Marine Villa for Daniel*
*   Parish.*
Newport, Rhode Island.
1851–1852

death affected those closest to him in a variety of ways. To settle his estate, the Newburgh house had to be sold promptly at auction and at considerably less than its estimated value. Recognizing that its appeal owed much to its popular editor, Luther Tucker lost no time in selling *The Horticulturist,* which never again achieved the popularity of its early years. A. J. Davis tried repeatedly—and always unsuccessfully—to step into the position Downing had left vacant, which it would be hard to believe he had not envied almost from the first. In the end, the Washington park was completed along the general lines its designer had intended, only to be swept away in 1901 when the Park Commission of the United States Senate reconstituted the processional avenue, or mall, envisioned in the original plan prepared by PIERRE CHARLES L'ENFANT.

At least in its earlier phases, Vaux's story proved a happier one. He is remembered most for his association with FREDERICK LAW OLMSTED, the man who had the talent and the will to develop Downing's tentative beginnings into a recognized profession which he was the first to call "landscape architecture." During 1857–1858, Olmsted and Vaux together won the competition to design New York's Central Park, a project for which Downing's writings had prepared the way but which in execution proved more innovative and more influential than anything even he had imagined.

GEORGE B. TATUM

BIBLIOGRAPHY

DAVIS, ALEXANDER JACKSON (1837)1980 *Rural Residences.* Reprint. With a new introduction by Jane B. Davies. New York: Da Capo.

DOWNING, A. J. (1841)1967 *A Treatise on the Theory and Practice of Landscape Gardening Adapted to North America . . . With Remarks on Rural Architecture.* Facsimile edition. New York: Funk.

DOWNING, A. J. (1842)1967 *Cottage Residences.* Reprint. Watkins Glen, N.Y.: Library of Victorian Culture.

DOWNING, A. J. (1850)1968 *The Architecture of Country Houses.* Reprint. With a new introduction by George B. Tatum. New York: Da Capo.

DOWNING, A. J. (1853)1974 *Rural Essays.* Reprint. New York: Da Capo. A collection of many of A. J. Downing's editorials from *The Horticulturist.*

DOWNS, ARTHUR CHANNING 1972 "Downing's Newburgh Villa." *Bulletin of the Association for Preservation Technology* 4:1–113.

KOWSKY, FRANCIS R. 1980 *The Architecture of Frederick Clarke Withers and the Progress of the Gothic Revival after 1850.* Middletown, Conn.: Wesleyan University Press.

SCHUYLER, DAVID 1976 "Rural Values and Urban America: The Social Thought of Andrew Jackson Downing." Unpublished Ph.D. dissertation, University of North Carolina.

SILLIMAN, BENJAMIN, JR., and GOODRICH, C. R. (editors) 1854 *The World of Science, Art, and Industry.* New York: Putnam. Illustrated from examples from the New York Exhibition, 1853–1854.

STEIN, ROGER B. 1967 *John Ruskin and Aesthetic Thought in America, 1840–1900.* Cambridge, Mass.: Harvard University Press.

TATUM, GEORGE B. 1950 "Andrew Jackson Downing, Arbiter of American Taste." Unpublished Ph.D. dissertation, Princeton University, N.J.

VAUX, CALVERT (1857)1970 *Villas and Cottages.* Reprint of 2d ed. New York: Dover.

WAINWRIGHT, NICHOLAS B. (editor) 1967 *A Philadelphia Perspective: The Diary of Sidney George Fisher Covering the Years 1834–1871.* Philadelphia: The Historical Society of Pennsylvania.

WIGHTWICK, GEORGE (1847)1851 *Hints to Young Architects.* 2d ed. New York: Wiley.

DOXIADIS, CONSTANTINOS A.

Constantinos A. Doxiadis (1913–1975) was born in Bulgaria of Greek parentage. He grew up in a Greek community and was educated in Athens. In 1935, he graduated from the National Metsovion Technical University in Athens with a degree in architecture and engineering. Two years later, he received a doctorate in civil engineering from the Charlottenburg Technical University in Berlin. He was particularly interested in town planning, and his thesis on the discovery of the geometric properties used in laying out the public buildings of ancient Greece was highly acclaimed by scholars for its originality. While in Berlin, Doxiadis became more and more interested in large-scale planning using a multidisciplinary approach and philosophy and dealing with built forms as well as systems.

After his studies in Berlin, Doxiadis returned to Greece to work as an architect and city planner. His first post was director of town planning studies in Athens. This position involved town planning for all the municipalities and communities around Athens. In 1939, Doxiadis was instrumental in creating the Office for National, Regional, and Town Planning Studies and Research which studied and later administered large-scale regional planning. This newly formed office continued to grow throughout World War II in spite of the many interruptions caused by the war and Greece's occupation. Through this office, Doxiadis coordinated Greece's first housing census and set up an Archive of Greek Settlements which gathered and catalogued documentation on 11,000 settlements in Greece. Doxiadis understood the importance of research and theory in the development of regional and global planning and used the war years, when site planning was impossible, to develop these areas of thought. Also, throughout the occupation of Greece, Doxiadis led an organization called the Circle of Technologists in which members gave reports on research concerning human settlements and developed the formative ideas of ekistics, the science of human settlements.

Following World War II, Doxiadis was involved in assessing war damage in Greece and outlined plans for the country's redevelopment. This project was followed by his appointment as minister in charge of the entire Greek development program. Throughout the 1940s, Doxiadis represented Greece on many international committees and organizations. In 1946, he attended the international conference in San Francisco on the organization of the United Nations. He represented his country at meetings in the United States, France, and England on the redevelopment of postwar construction and also headed the delegation at the International Conference on Housing, Planning, and Reconstruction held in Brussels. When the Marshall Plan was instituted to aid war-torn European countries, Doxiadis supervised the handling and distribution of American aid to Greece. During this time, Doxiadis formulated and refined his concept of ekistics, and his many international contacts gave him a comprehensiveness of vision and a unique global understanding.

In 1951, Doxiadis's program for implementing the Marshall Plan was nearing a satisfactory completion. However, Greece's Ministry of Coordination, fearing that Doxiadis might have political ambitions, abolished his post, and Doxiadis's formal alliance with the Greek government was terminated. In the same year, he founded Doxiadis Associates, a consulting and engineering firm in Athens. Since its inception, the firm has provided engineering, architectural, and planning consultation in over thirty countries. The firm has been involved in the coastal redevelopment of Greece, the urban and rural renewal of Iraq, and many other planning assignments. In the United States, Doxiadis Associates has developed regional renewal projects for Washington, Cincinnati, Ohio, and Detroit, Michigan. In 1960, the firm was commissioned by the Urban Renewal Program to develop plans for Eastwick involving over 2,500 acres in and around Philadelphia.

Doxiadis's most important contribution to architectural and planning thought was the development of ekistics. Ekistics is the study of human settlements which examines not only built forms but also the interface of time, movements, and systems in the built environment. It is an integrative body of knowledge organized into a cohesive system. Doxiadis saw ekistics as an intellectual approach to balance the convergence of the past, present, and future in human settlements as well as a system for creatively coping with the growth of population, rapid change, and the pressures of large-scale, high-density housing.

Doxiadis founded the Graduate School of Ekistics at the Athens Technological Institute where he taught for many years. He was also president of the Ekistic Center of Athens and sponsored *Ekistics,* a continuing journal on the study and science of human settlements published in Greece and the United States. Doxiadis was a visiting lecturer at many American universities, including Yale, the University of Chicago, Harvard, and Trinity College.

He was the author of many articles on planning and ekistics and wrote a number of books, including *Architecture in Transition* (1963), *Between Dystopia and Utopia* (1966), *Ekistics: Introduction to the Science of Human Settlements* (1968), and *Building Entopia* (1976). Doxiadis died in 1975, a year before the United Nations' Conference on Human Settlements convened in Vancouver, British Columbia. His work and the foundations of ekistics which he developed over four decades helped to focus the issues, ideas, and vocabulary of this conference and of planning in general.

PATRICIA C. PHILLIPS

BIBLIOGRAPHY

"C. A. Doxiadis 1913–75: Pursuit of an Attainable Idea." 1976 *Ekistics* 41, no. 247: special issue.
DEANE, PHILIP 1965 *Constantinos Doxiadis: Master Builder for Free Men.* Dobbs Ferry, N.Y.: Oceana.
DOXIADIS, CONSTANTINOS 1963 *Architecture in Transition.* New York: Oxford University Press.
DOXIADIS, CONSTANTINOS 1966 *Between Dystopia and Utopia.* Hartford, Conn.: Trinity College Press.
RAND, CHRISTOPHER 1963 "Profiles: Constantinos Doxiadis, The Ekistic World." *New Yorker* May 11:49–85.

DOYLE, ALBERT E.

Albert Ernest Doyle (1877–1928) was Oregon's leading architect from 1907 until his untimely death at age fifty. He was born in Santa Cruz, California, but at an early age moved to Portland where his father was a building contractor. He apprenticed with the prominent architectural firm of WHIDDEN AND LEWIS where he stayed for twelve years. In 1903, Doyle went to New York where he pursued design studies at Columbia University and worked in the office of Henry Bacon. With a traveling scholarship he toured Europe during 1906.

Early in 1907, he opened his office in Portland and took on a partner, William B. Patterson, a construction supervisor. Within a year, the firm received its first major commission, the ten-story annex to the Meier and Frank Department Store in downtown Portland. Many major commissions soon followed. Doyle's commercial designs were all in revival styles with emphasis on the Italian Renaissance. In 1912, the engineer J. G. Beach became a partner, and three years later the firm was again reorganized as A. E. Doyle, Architect.

In addition to the eclectic urban work, Doyle designed a series of simple beach cottages on the

Oregon and Washington coast that later became the inspiration for the regional style developed by JOHN YEON, PIETRO BELLUSCHI, and others in the 1930s. Most notable is the 1916 Wentz Studio-Bungalow at Neahkahnie, Oregon.

After Doyle's death the firm was continued as A. E. Doyle and Associate by senior staff members, including Belluschi who had joined the firm in 1925.

GEORGE A. McMATH

WORKS

1908-1909/1915, Meier and Frank Company Store; 1910, Selling Building; 1911, Lipman, Wolfe Company Store; Portland, Ore. 1912, Isom Cottage, Neahkanie, Ore. 1912-1913, Central Library; 1912-1914, Eliot Hall and Dormitory, Reed College; 1913, Benson Hotel; Portland, Ore. 1913, Oregon College of Education, Monmouth. 1914, American Bank Building; 1914, 1923, Pittock Block; Portland, Ore. 1915, A. E. Doyle Cottage; 1916, Wentz Studio and Bungalow; 1916, Crocker Cottage; Neahkanie, Ore. 1917, 1923, United States National Bank; 1918, F. J. Cobbs Residence; 1925, Bank of California; 1925-1926, Pacific Building; 1927-1928, Public Service Building; Portland, Ore.

BIBLIOGRAPHY

CAREY, CHARLES HENRY 1922 *History of Oregon.* 3 vols. Chicago, and Portland, Ore.: Pioneer Historical Publishing.
CHENEY, CHARLES H. 1919 "The Work of Albert E. Doyle, Architect of Portland, Oregon." *Architect and Engineer* 8, no. 1:38-96.
"Obituary." 1928 *Oregonian* Jan. 24.
VAUGHAN, THOMAS, and FERRIDAY, VIRGINIA GUEST (editors) 1974 *Space, Style and Structure.* 2 vols. Portland: Oregon Historical Society.

DOYLE, J. F.

John Francis Doyle (1840-1913) of Liverpool chiefly designed churches and commercial buildings in the Merseyside area of England. His churches are serious essays in late Victorian Gothic but his major work was the Royal Insurance Offices in Liverpool (1896-1903), a swaggering baroque building, which helped to usher in the ornate Edwardian phase of Liverpool's traditionally classic manner of architecture.

ANDREW SAINT

WORKS

1879-1883, Saint Ambrose's Church, Widnes, Lancashire, England. 1896-1903, Royal Insurance Offices; 1898-1901. Saint Luke's Church, Walton; 1900-1914, Saint Barnabas's Church, Mossley Hill; Liverpool, England. 1901-1904, Grand Hotel, Llandudno, Wales.

1910-1911, Saint Nicholas's Church, Wallasey, Cheshire, England.

BIBLIOGRAPHY

"Obituary" 1913 *The Builder* 104, Feb. 21:253.

DRESSER, CHRISTOPHER

Christopher Dresser (1834-1904), designer, theorist, writer, and lecturer, was one of the most original industrial designers of the nineteenth century and one of the earliest proponents of functional design. Born in Glasgow, he studied at the Government School of Design in London, but he first gained a reputation as a botanist, and from an interest in plant geometry, he began developing design theories, resulting in his first treatise, *The Art of Decorative Design* (1862). He was an early admirer of Japanese art and traveled to Japan in 1877 to collect examples and to document manufacturing processes. He was art editor of the *Furniture Gazette* from 1880 to 1881, and directed the short-lived *Art Furnishers' Alliance,* whose London shop sold furnishings of good design from 1880 to 1883. From about 1878 to his death in 1904, he was responsible for a multitude of designs for metalwork, glass, ceramics, textiles, and wallpapers.

BETTY ELZEA

BIBLIOGRAPHY

BURY, SHIRLEY 1962 "The Silver Designs of Dr. Christopher Dresser." *Apollo* 76:766-770.
DENNIS, RICHARD, and JESSE, JOHN 1972 *Christopher Dresser: 1834-1904.* London: Fine Art Society. Exhibition catalogue.
DRESSER, CHRISTOPHER 1862 *The Art of Decorative Design.* London: Day.
DRESSER, CHRISTOPHER 1873 *Principles of Decorative Design.* London: Cassell.
DRESSER, CHRISTOPHER 1882 *Japan: Its Architecture, Art, and Art Manufactures.* London: Longmans, Green.
PEVSNER, NIKOLAUS 1937 "Minor Masters of the XIXth Century: Christopher Dresser." *Architectural Review* 81:183-186.
"The Work of Christopher Dresser." 1898-1899 *Studio* 15:104-114.

DREW, JANE B.

Jane Beverley Drew (1911-) was born in Thornton Heath, Surrey, England. She gained admission to the Architectural Association School, London, in 1928 and after graduating in 1933, worked for Joseph Hill, a London architect, while privately concentrating on architectural competitions with

James T. Alliston whom she had married in her final year as a student and with whom she set up practice in 1934. They had twin daughters. Competition successes included first prize in 1937 for Dawlish Cottage Hospital, Devon, with a compactly planned, formal, and symmetrical entry (never constructed). Her partnership and marriage with J. T. Alliston broke up in 1939, at the outbreak of World War II, the two having built some small houses (Cliftonville, Kent, 1937, and Winchester, Hampshire, 1938) and other small-scale works.

Drew then opened her own independent office and was strongly motivated to employ and encourage women in architecture. She had already become the first woman member of the Architects' Registration Council of the United Kingdom in March 1939 and later was to become the first woman president of the Architectural Association (1969–1970). During the war years her office designed national emergency buildings and an office at Walton-on-Thames, Middlesex (1941). In 1943, she organized the Royal Institute of British Architects "Rebuilding Britain" Exhibition, held at the National Gallery. In the same year, the British Commercial Gas Association appointed her consultant on the design and equipment of kitchens, leading to the Kitchen Planning Exhibition, Dorland Hall, London, in March 1945.

During this wartime period she started to become interested and involved in the architecture of hot climates. In 1942 she worked on a project in Kenya for the Kikuyu tribe and in 1944 she was appointed an Assistant Town Planning Adviser to the British West African colonies with E. MAXWELL FRY, to whom she had been married since 1942. Out of the West African experience came an important small book called *Village Housing in the Tropics* (1947) and, although formally co-authored with Fry, the book was largely her work. This manual provided the basis for two subsequent tropical architecture books by Fry and Drew which were to become standard texts for tropical designers.

In 1945, in reaction to the state of architectural journalism in Britain, Jane Drew founded the Architect's Year Book and with Trevor Dannatt she co-edited the first four of the irregularly published fourteen volumes which were produced up to 1974. The Drew/Dannatt volumes cover the arts, education, planning, design, and housing theory, but they also contain extensive technical presentations. These volumes constituted a critique of the narrowness of architectural journalism while providing a problematic model for imitation.

In 1951, Maxwell Fry and Jane Drew were appointed Senior Architects to the Capital Project

in Chandigarh, India, where they worked with CHARLES E. J. LE CORBUSIER, Pierre Jeanneret, ALBERT MAYER, and others. Jane Drew was centrally involved in the design and construction of housing, schools, health facilities, and the general amenities of the neighborhoods, and during the period of her stay in Chandigarh, between 1951–1953, more than 20,000 people were housed in that city.

The architectural practice of Fry and Drew had been founded by them in 1945, and in 1951 they took into partnership LINDSAY DRAKE and DENYS LASDUN. Jane Drew has acknowledged the influence of Lasdun on her work. Drake and Lasdun left the partnership in 1958, and Frank Knight and Norman Creamer became partners in 1960.

Jane Drew worked actively in the practice until she retired in 1974, and the buildings which she designed or took part in designing are widespread and of many types. Principally, she has worked in Nigeria, Ghana, India, Iran, Kuwait, Ceylon, Mauritius, as well as in Britain, and the building types have included universities, hospitals, schools, housing, offices, exhibition buildings, and art galleries. But the kinds of design problems which have been solved most successfully by her approach have probably been those that demanded an appreciation of a complex social and functional program, such as the School for the Deaf, Herne Hill, London (1966); or Torbay Hospital and Nursing Residence, Torquay, Devon (1966–1970); or The Open University, Milton Keynes (1969–1977). Her design could respond in a formally controlled and precise way, but the environment so created would need to achieve a human and above all friendly atmosphere.

ROYSTON LANDAU

WORKS

1937, Houses (with J. T. Alliston), Cliftonville, Kent, England. 1938, Houses (with Alliston), Saint Giles Mount, Winchester, Hampshire, England. 1941, Walton Yacht Works Office, Walton-on-Thames, Middlesex, England. 1946, Prempeh College (with E. Maxwell Fry), Kumasi, Ghana. 1947, Wesley Girls School, Cape Coast, Ghana. 1949, Tea Centre, Regent Street, London. 1950, Ashanti Secondary School (with Fry), Kumasi, Ghana. 1951, Festival of Britain (Waterloo Bridge Entrance and Restaurant), London. 1951–1956, Capital (with Le Corbusier and Fry), Chandigarh, India. 1953, Whitefoot Lane Flats, Lewisham, London. 1953–1959, University College (with Fry), Ibadan, Nigeria. 1958, Women's Teacher Training College (with Fry), Kano, Nigeria. 1958, Wudil Teacher Training College (with Fry), Nigeria. 1959, Gach Saran New Town, Iran. 1959, Gulf House; 1960, House, Hyver Hill, Hendon; London. 1964, Housing, Hatfield, Hertfordshire, England. 1964, Housing, Mark Hall Neighborhood, Harlow, Essex, England. 1964, Housing, Welwyn, Hertfordshire, England. 1965, Dewint Art Centre, Ceylon. 1965, Olympic Stadium and Pool, Kaduna, Nigeria. 1966, School for the Deaf, Herne Hill, London. 1966–1970, Torbay Hospital and Nurses Residence, Torquay, Devon, England. 1969–1977, Open University, Milton Keyes, Buckinghamshire, England. 1970, Institute of Contemporary Arts, Carlton House Terrace, London. 1976, Gestetner Factory, Stirling, Scotland. 1977, Institute of Education, Reduit, Mauritius.

BIBLIOGRAPHY

BROCKMAN, H. A. N. 1978 *Fry, Drew, Knight, Creamer: Architecture.* London: Lund Humphries.
DREW, JANE B. (editor) 1945–1974 *Architects Yearbook.*
FRY, E. MAXWELL, and DREW, JANE B. (1944)1976 *Architecture and the Environment.* Rev. ed. London: Allen & Unwin. Originally published with the title *Architecture for Children.*
FRY, E. MAXWELL, and DREW, JANE B. 1947 *Village Housing in the Tropics.* In collaboration with Harry L. Ford. London: Lund Humphries.
FRY, E. MAXWELL, and DREW, JANE B. 1956 *Tropical Architecture in the Humid Zone.* London: Batsford.
FRY, E. MAXWELL, and DREW, JANE B. 1964 *Tropical Architecture in the Dry and Humid Zones.* London: Batsford.

DUBAN, FELIX

Born in Paris, the son of a hardware merchant, Félix Louis Jacques Duban (1797–1870) went to the Lycée Napoléon and in 1813 entered the atelier of his brother-in-law, François Debret. The following year, he enrolled at the Ecole des Beaux-Arts, Paris, winning the Grand Prix in 1823. From the first, Duban was associated with HENRI LABROUSTE, LOUIS JOSEPH DUC, and Léon Vaudoyer (see VAUDOYER AND VAUDOYER). They were seeking to reform architecture. His final *envoi,* a Protestant church, was intended as a challenge to the reactionary royalists in the Académie des Beaux-Arts. It was well timed. When Duban returned to Paris in 1829, he was invited to take over ABEL BLOUET's atelier during the latter's absence in Greece. He also took up work with Debret at the Ecole des Beaux-Arts and began to teach in Debret's atelier, but by 1831 he had led off most of Debret's students to an atelier of his own. In the same year, Duban was nominated a member of a commission of inquiry into the teachings of the Ecole des Beaux-Arts.

On July 31, 1832, Duban succeeded Debret as architect to the Ecole des Beaux-Arts. The south wing of the Palais des Etudes was already complete, the west wing was up to first floor level, and the foundations were laid, but Duban managed to change the design considerably. He raised the height of the main façade and used the Arc de Gaillon and other fragments of architecture and sculpture that had survived on the site from Alexandre Lenoir's Musée des Monuments Français to create a processional way from the entrance off the rue Bonaparte to the Salle des Prix at the rear of the building that was both formal and circuitous, classical and local in its celebration of French architectural history. The whole was composed in a deliberately picturesque manner. Duban's reputation was made. Indeed, it had been made in 1833, when he designed the *Fêtes de Juillet* in a similar manner and was acclaimed in a celebrated article in *L'Artiste* as the leader of a new movement in architecture—the Etruscan movement, so called because the young radicals who had explored the newly opened Etruscan tombs in Italy were aiming to infuse something of their primitive strength and bold coloring into their own architecture. They were even compared to CLAUDE NICOLAS LEDOUX. This, though, was not Duban's way. His designs are marked rather by an exquisite and delicate richness of style. His Hôtel Pourtalès is an oversensitive variant of a Renaissance Florentine palazzo. His restoration of the Louvre salons provided an opportunity for a full and gilded display of his decorative talents (an example not lost on CHARLES GARNIER when he began the Opera), although it was this very facility for ornamental elaboration that was to be Duban's downfall at the Louvre. The railings and garden furniture he introduced into the courtyard were thought too fiddly by far; they were ridiculed by General Baraguay d'Hilliers, among others, and he was dismissed.

Italian classicism was certainly at the center of Duban's vision, but his decorative talent was so strong that he could adapt it even to styles for which he had little inclination. His restoration of the thirteenth-century Sainte Chapelle, in which he was aided by J. B. A. LASSUS and EUGÈNE EMMANUEL VIOLLET-LE-DUC, was a dazzling and resplendent tour de force, stirring even A. W. N. PUGIN, who returned to England after visiting it in 1844, determined to make more colorful yet the decorations at Saint Giles, Cheadle. At the Château of Blois, Duban indulged in French Renaissance fantasies, as he did on a lesser scale at the Château of Jozerand. At the Châteaux of Chalay (Loir et Cher) and Sandat (Lot et Garonne), where he is reported to have done work of a similar kind, his contribution is difficult to determine.

Duban left almost no important buildings entirely his own. Only the Salle de Melpomène gives some indication of his ability as an individual creator on a large scale; it shows also that he gained in authority as he grew older. To his contemporaries, he was to remain most famous for his intricate architectural drawing compositions, allegorical studies rather than mere decorative compositions.

R. D. MIDDLETON

WORKS

1833–1867, Ecole des Beaux-Arts (Palais des Etudes [1833–1839]; Cour du Mûrier remodeled; Salle Melpomène [1860–1863]; interior court covered with iron and glass [1861–1867]), rue Bonaparte and Quai Malaquais; 1835–1839, Hôtel Pourtalès (supervised by ANTOINE NICOLAS BAILLY), 7 rue Tronchet; 1840–1849, Sainte Chapelle (restoration with J. B. A. LASSUS and Eugène Emmanuel Viollet-Le-Duc); Paris. 1844–?, Château de Dampierre (interiors, in particular the Salle d'honneur; later called the Salle de la Minerve), Seine et Oise, France. 1845 Château de Jozerand (restoration), Puy de Dôme, France. 1845–1870, Château de Blois, (restoration; continued between 1870 and 1878 by Jules Edouard Potier de la Morandière, then by ANATOLE DE BAUDOT), Loire et Cher, France. 1848, Château de Chantilly (Galerie de Psyche, northeast side of the cour d'honneur), Oise, France. 1849–?, Château de Fontaine-bleau (restoration), Seine et Marne, France. 1849–1854, Louvre (restoration in particular the Galerie d'Apollon, Salle des Sept Cheminées, Salon Carré, Pavillon Lesdiguières, and railings in the courtyard), Paris. 1855–1857, Hôtel Monaco (now Polish Embassy; main stair and interiors), 57 rue Saint-Dominique; n.d., François Arago Tomb; n.d., Delaroche Tomb, Montmartre Cemetery; Paris. n.d., Pierlot Tomb, Bordeaux, Gironde, France.

BIBLIOGRAPHY

BALTARD, VICTOR 1872 "Exposition d'une collection de dessins de Félix Duban." *Bulletin mensuel de la Société Centrale des Architectes* 1872:83–90. See also *Revue Générale de l'Architecture* (1872) 29:22–29.

BEULÉ, CHARLES ERNEST 1872 *Institut de France. Académie des Beaux-Arts: Eloge de Duban.* Paris: Firmin-Didot. Also in *Revue Générale de l'Architecture* (1872) 29:206–217.

BLANC, CHARLES (1872)1876 "Félix Duban: 1797–1870." Pages 1–22 in *Les artistes de mon temps.* Paris: Firmin-Didot. See also *Le Temps,* April 4, 1872, and *Gazette des Architectes et du Bâtiment* (1872) Second Series I:44–46, 53–55, 60–62.

CANAC, PHILIPPE, and MARMOZ, CATHERINE 1979 "L'Ecole nationale des Beaux-Arts." *Monuments historiques* 102:17–32.

COCKERELL, FREDERICK P. 1875–1876 "Biographical Notices of Deceased Foreign Members: Felix Duban." *Sessional Papers of the Royal Institute of British Architects.* 1:209–215.

DELABORDE, HENRI 1872 "Félix Duban: L'exposition de ses dessins à l'Ecole des Beaux-Arts." *Revue des Deux Mondes* 1, Feb.:606–629.

DELABORDE, HENRI; DUC, LOUIS JOSEPH; LABROUSTE, HENRI; VAUDOYER, LÉON; and GUILLAUME, EUGÈNE 1872 *Notice des dessins de Duban exposés à l'Ecole Nationale et Spéciale des Beaux-Arts.* Paris: Laine.

GUILLAUME, EUGÈNE 1894 "Duban." *L'Architecture* 11:390–392.

"*Legs du Madame Veuve Maillot, née Duban.*" 1898 *L'Architecture* 11, 1898:369.

LUCAS, CHARLES 1894–1895 "Inauguration du monument de Félix Duban." *La Construction Moderne* 10:61–63.

MARMOZ, CATHERINE 1982 "The Building of the Ecole des Beaux-Arts." In R. D. Middleton (editor), *The Beaux-Arts and Nineteenth Century French Architecture.* London: Thames & Hudson.

MARSUZI DE AGUIRRE, CAMILLE 1852 "Le Louvre: Les derniers travaux de M. Duban." *Mercure de France* 1852:5–47.

P. B. 1833 "Du mouvement en architecture." *L'Artiste* 6:74–78.

QUESTEL, CHARLES AUGUSTE 1872 *Institut de France. Académie des Beaux-Arts: Notice sur M. Duban.* Paris: Firmin-Didot.

VAN ZANTEN, DAVID 1978 "Félix Duban and the Buildings of the Ecole des Beaux-Arts: 1832–1840." *Journal of the Society of Architectural Historians* 37:161–174.

VAUDOYER, LÉON; BALTARD, VICTOR; DALY, CÉSAR; DONALDSON, THOMAS LEVERTON, ET AL. 1871 "Funérailles de Felix Duban." *Bulletin mensuel de la Société Centrale des Architectes* 1871:137–151. Also published by the *Institut de France, Académie des Beaux-Arts* (1871) and the *Revue Générale de l'Architecture* (1870–1872) 28:199–224; 29:206.

DUC, LOUIS

Joseph-Louis Duc (1802–1879) was architect of the Palais de Justice in Paris (1840–1879), judged by a commission appointed by Napoleon III to be the greatest work of art produced during his reign. A potent blend of romantic, classical, and rationalist architectural ideas, this building appealed equally to the innately conservative taste of the Emperor and to the stringent logic of EUGÈNE EMMANUEL VIOLLET-LE-DUC, while its vigorous three-dimensionality foreshadowed the designs of CHARLES GARNIER.

Contemporaries described Duc as a calm, self-possessed, strong-minded individual. Born in Paris, the son of a maker of decorative sword-cases, he was educated at the Collège Bourbon and entered the Ecole des Beaux-Arts in 1819 as a member of the atelier of André-Marie Chatillon. In 1825, he won the Grand Prix de Rome with a design for a Hôtel de Ville, whose composition was enriched by a progression from a lower to an upper story. In Rome, his artistic future was sealed by a rapidly developed friendship with three other *pensionnaires,* FELIX DUBAN, HENRI LABROUSTE, and LEON VAUDOYER. These four young men were soon known in Paris as a company of romantic

Duc.
Colonne de Juillet.
Paris.
1835–1840

Duc.
Palais de Justice
    (restoration and
    extension).
Paris.
1840–1879

radicals, whose yearly projects elicited the scandalized disapproval of the Académie des Beaux-Arts. Duc's fourth-year project, a magnificent study of the Colosseum, was widely praised. But when he followed it in 1830 with a project consisting of a single sheet of paper on which was drawn a massive, primitively detailed column rising from a three-tiered base of stacked sarcophagi and inscribed, *"Aux victimes de juillet 1830,"* the official reaction was one of horror.

Appropriately, on his return from Rome, Duc was appointed *inspecteur* of the Colonne de Juillet, a monument to the victims of the revolution of 1830. He served in this capacity under JEAN-BAPTISTE-ANTOINE ALAVOINE, who had proposed a simple bronze Doric column rising from the center of the place de la Bastille. On Alavoine's death in 1835, Duc inherited the commission and redesigned the column, for which foundations had already been laid. Inaugurated on July 28, 1840, the monument consists of a pedestal bearing a bas-relief of a lion and four French cocks holding garlands, from which arises a shaft wrapped with the inscribed names of the victims of the revolution and supporting a statue of Victory. The column's capital is its most distinctive feature: a rich, eclectic composition of Egyptian, Greek, Roman, and Renaissance elements which was one of the first

manifestoes of the Romantics' reassessment of the architectural past.

In 1840, Duc received the great government commission which occupied him for the rest of his career: the restoration and extension of the Palais de Justice in Paris. He abandoned a project prepared by his predecessor, JEAN-NICOLAS HUYOT, and proceeded to restore the existing Gothic, Renaissance, and post-Renaissance buildings on the site and to add to them in his own manner. His first concern was for the restoration of the Gothic Tour d'Horloge and Conciergerie and the Salle des Pas Perdus of SALOMON DE BROSSE. But he began projects for new buildings almost immediately, and as early as 1852 he had completed a new façade on the wing of a building lying along the boulevard du Palais. His first entirely original addition was a building for the Police Correctionnelle (1846–1854), which met with immediate critical approval. In 1862, he also took over the design of the Cour de Cassation from LOUIS LENORMAND, completing it in 1865. But Duc's most important work was the building for the Cour des Assises and the Vestibule de Harlay (1857–1869), which lies along the base of the triangular place Dauphine. Duc originally intended to demolish all of the sixteenth-century houses on the place and create a complex of official buildings and colonnades around the tip of the Ile de la Cité. Only the Vestibule de Harlay was erected, but this was his masterwork.

The building's façade is Duc's homage to the orders, which, as he wrote during the 1850s, he believed to be both the unifying element and the poetic essence of architecture. Across a plain façade pierced by segmentally arched windows, Duc drew a screen of engaged columns and a broken entablature of partly Greek, partly Egyptian inspiration. By detaching the order from a structural role, he emphasized its necessarily symbolic position in a work of nineteenth-century architecture. Behind the smooth inner skin of the building's façade lies a heroically vaulted space with deeply articulated walls, in which classical motifs are integrated into a structure that is almost Gothic in its expressiveness. It was Duc's adaptation of vigorous, three-dimensional classical forms to a structure that is essentially romantic rationalist in its principles that made his building such a critical success in its time, as well as an inspiration to a younger generation of architects. It also brought Duc the prize of one hundred thousand francs from Napoleon III in 1869, part of which he used to found a prize administered by the Académie des Beaux-Arts for the creation of a new architectural style.

Duc had several other government and private commissions to his credit. He and Labrouste designed the public funeral ceremonies for the victims of the *attentat de Fieschi* (1834) and the victims of the revolution of 1848 (1848), and Duc also designed temporary structures and decorations for the dedication of the Colonne de Juillet (1840). In 1859, he was given charge of Parisian school buildings and designed the Lycée Michelet in Vanves (1862) and an annex to the Lycée Condorcet in Paris (1864). He won fourth prize in the competition for the Paris Opera in 1861, but withdrew from the second stage of competition. He also designed two tombs, for the sculptor Henri Cahieux (1855) and for his friend Félix Duban (1872–1872). Duc was obliged to rebuild portions of his own Palais de Justice after they were destroyed during the Commune of 1871. But he also devoted his later years to building a rustic villa for himself in the Parisian suburb of Croissy (1864) and another at Biarritz, which remained incomplete at his death.

ANN LORENZ VAN ZANTEN

WORKS

1835–1840, Colonne de Juillet; 1840–1879, Palais de Justice (restoration and extension); Paris. 1862, Lycée Michelet, Vanves, France. 1864, Lycée Condorcet (annex), Paris. 1864, Villa, Croissy, France.

BIBLIOGRAPHY

CERNESSON, L. C. 1880–1882 "Joseph-Louis Duc, membre de l'Institut." *Revue Générale de l'Architecture* 37:75–79, 156–160; 39:124–127, 263–264.
DELABORDE, H. 1879 *Notice sur la vie et les ouvrages de M. Duc.* Paris: Institut de France, Académie des Beaux-Arts.
"Notices of Deceased Members: Joseph Louis Duc, Hon. and Corr. Member (Paris)." 1880 *Transactions of the Royal Institute of British Architects* 12–13: 210–217.
PASCAL, J. L. 1879 "M. Duc et son influence sur le mouvement architectural contemporain." *Gazette des Beaux-Arts* 19:430–443.
QUESTEL, C. 1879 *Discours prononcé . . . aux funérailles de M. Duc.* Paris: Institut de France, Académie des Beaux-Arts.
SÉDILLE, PAUL 1879 "Joseph Louis Duc, architect (1802–1879)." *Encyclopedie d'architecture* Series 2 8:65–74.

DU CERCEAU FAMILY

Jacques Androuet Du Cerceau the Elder was the founder of a dynasty of architects, engravers, and decorators who worked in France during the sixteenth and seventeenth centuries, that is, in the very period that spans the development of French architecture from its early assimilation of the Italian Renaissance to the flowering of a national classical style. Largely as a result of his printed works, the elder Du Cerceau is by far the most renowned member of the family. His magnum opus, *Les plus excellents bastiments de France* (1576–1579), still among the masterpieces of printed books, provides an unparalleled source for our knowledge of the great buildings of sixteenth-century France, since altered or destroyed. But, despite the fact that the legacy of books, engravings, and drawings is enormous, little is known about Du Cerceau's work as an architect and even less about his personal life. Changes in attributions and critical attitudes notwithstanding, H. von Geymüller's monograph, *Les Du Cerceau* (1887), remains the fundamental work on its subject.

Jacques Androuet Du Cerceau the Elder (c.1515?–1585). A map of the county of Maine engraved on a copper plate by "Jacques Androuet, Parisian, called Du Cerceau, and printed at Mans in 1539" is recorded by a contemporary, La Croix du Maine (Berty, 1860, p. 93), who also explains that the surname Du Cerceau derives from the circle that served as a sign for his house. Supposedly born in Paris, Du Cerceau is said to have experienced a turning point in his life when around 1530–1533 he journeyed to Italy, where he studied and drew the ruins of antiquity and newly built Roman edifices. However, the principal evidence for this trip, namely fourteen sheets from a sketchbook discovered in Munich by H. von Geymüller, has been reattributed to PHILIBERT DELORME (Blunt, 1958, pp. 15–16). One, or perhaps two voyages were very likely made to Italy with other architects in the entourage of Georges d'Armagnac, French ambassador to Rome from 1539 to 1544. Upon returning from Italy, Du Cerceau resolved both to disseminate the knowledge of ancient architecture and to propagate the style of the Italian Renaissance in his native country. He began to engrave and etch plates of architecture and ornament in publications destined to serve those who worked in architecture and in the decorated arts and related professions. His aim was to beautify France through the heritage of classical art, to make works accessible without foreign travel, and to provide a practical handbook for designers, craftsmen, architects, painters, cabinetmakers, sculptors, goldsmiths, and jewelers by furnishing all the instruments for their respective tasks.

The earliest work by Du Cerceau, *Exempla Arcuum* (1549), comprises twenty-five imaginary triumphal arches, variations on antique prototypes. A printing atelier at Orleans may be assumed on the basis of at least six known works published there by Du Cerceau in the years 1549–1551. They range from fanciful renderings of ancient monuments actually seen to capricious gro-

Jacques Androuet Du Cerceau the Elder. Engraving from Vues d'Optiques. *1551*

Jacques Androuet Du Cerceau the Elder. Engraving of Montargis. France. 1576–1579

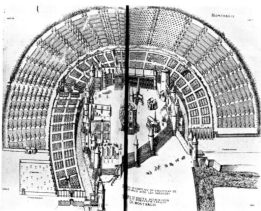

tesques that adopt the Italian design of the School of Raphael to French taste and to the intricate perspectives of his *Vues d'optiques* (1551).

Du Cerceau's major contribution to architectural literature begins with the publication in both Latin and French of the *Premier livre d'architecture* (1559). Dedicated to Henri II, this book marks the start of relationships with the royal family. It sets forth a series of plans and façade elevations of fifty different townhouses, and was perhaps the earliest practical handbook, analogous to SEBASTIANO SERLIO's unpublished "Sixth Book" in circulation at that time. The *Second livre d'architecture* (1561), dedicated to Charles IX, was concerned with architectural details such as mantelpieces and dormers. In 1562, he returned to Montargis and from there in 1572, he dedicated the *Troisième livre d'architecture* to Charles IX, requesting (because of his age and state of health) the means to complete future books on the great buildings of the kingdom now. In the practical genre of the first book, the third provides plans for country houses.

No greater contribution to the history of French Renaissance architecture exists than *Les plus excellents bastiments de France.* Volume I, origi-

nally dedicated to his great friend and benefactress, Renée de France, was rededicated after her death in 1575 to Catherine de' Medici "to contemplate here a part of the most beautiful and excellent buildings with which France today is still enriched." Supplementing field trips and drawings made on the site, Du Cerceau also worked from "presentation" drawings by the architect (*portraits du vif*) or models of the buildings. Each volume is composed of fifteen châteaux, both royal and private. A brief text is followed by a series of engraved plates—plans, elevations, illustrations in perspective, and details such as buildings and gardens in use, animated by figures with French and Latin captions, varying from two to ten plates and not necessarily in accord with the importance of the château. The text begins with the topography of the site, the materials used, the history of construction, the architecture of the building, its environment, and its state of preservation. Much attention is given to the locality as well as to the medieval origins, chronological data, and patronage. The proprietor assumes prime importance; his intentions rather than those of the architect are paramount and explicitly stated. Emphasis in the description is on function and this is most clearly discerned by the plan. The château itself is seen in a larger context, as related to its gardens and landscape, indeed the territory and the "world," as in the view of Montargis. Marked by the precision of the surveyor's drawing, the bird's-eye views convey little of the sites' atmosphere. Although most of the châteaux are drawn with remarkable detail and accuracy, the work is deemed less reliable in regard to the unfinished buildings where the artist's tendency to modify and to complete incompleted works has been noted. Fancy co-exists with fact, especially in the representations of ancient buildings.

Du Cerceau's last work, *Livre des edifices antiques romains* (1584), containing the ordonnances and designs of the most conspicuous and principal buildings in Rome was dedicated to the Duke of Nemours and "to those who are curious about antiquity and still more . . . to masters in architecture . . . to find beautiful features and enrichments to add to their inventory."

Aside from engravings, including certain maps such as the plan of Paris, called the *Plan de Du Cerceau* (c.1560), many collections of drawings are ascribed to the artist. Most significant are those preparatory drawings (116) for *Les . . . Bastiments* in the British Museum and in the Cabinet des Estampes, Bibliothèque Nationale (eleven drawings of Chambord, Madrid, and the Louvre). Other notable collections are the manuscript in the Vatican (Barb. Lat. 4398), comprised of fifty drawings including designs of Madrid, Charleval, Verneuil, and Saint Leger for *Les . . . Bastiments,* and circular plans for a hospital providing isolation by means of a moat. A manuscript in the Pierpont Morgan Library in New York contains plans after ANDREA PALLADIO, thus demonstrating Du Cerceau's knowledge of his *Four Books,* published in 1570 but perhaps in limited circulation earlier. Missing among all these collections are working drawings. We see but ornamental caprices, "paper plans."

Du Cerceau's role as an architect is far more difficult to pinpoint. Although he is referred to as *architecte* in some sixteenth-century sources—the title architect was far more inclusive in the sixteenth century and we cannot be absolutely certain to what the term refers. Du Cerceau's work as an architect is inextricably linked to his Protestantism. As a Huguenot, he was severely limited in his sphere of activity. He found refuge at Montargis, a Huguenot sanctuary, from 1560 until Renée's death where he probably restored the choir of its church in 1545 and may have done other work on the château in the 1560s.

Although documentation is scarce, Du Cerceau's name has been linked to the design of the châteaux of Verneuil (1568) and Charleval (1570) and to the Maison Blanche (1565) in Gaillon because of certain stylistic analogies such as a predilection for the colossal order and use of rustication and highly embellished surfaces. It may be argued, however, that the similarities in question reveal no more than a familiarity with the current anticlassical taste and that the surfeit of ornament is more in keeping with the work of a decorator than that of an architect.

Regarding Verneuil, Du Cerceau's description of the building history, as well as the ten plates devoted to the château in *Les . . . Bastiments,* discloses an intimate knowledge of building details as well as of the intentions of the two proprietors of the château. Moreover, his involvement with Verneuil may have been reinforced by family ties since his daughter Julienne was married to Jehan de Brosse, an architect who settled at Verneuil and probably was in charge of the works. Begun in 1568 for Duke Philippe de Boulainvilliers (in Du Cerceau's words, an "ardent amateur of architecture" who wished to create a "unique work"), this first project was modified in 1576 for the duke's successor, Jacques de Savoie, duke of Nemours (son-in-law of Renée of Ferrara and a benefactor of Du Cerceau in his last years) in order to achieve a more coherent and classical design. The château, virtually demolished in the eighteenth century, is remarkable for its accommodation to the sloping terrain of the site. In the annals of architecture, Verneuil assumes added importance as the place

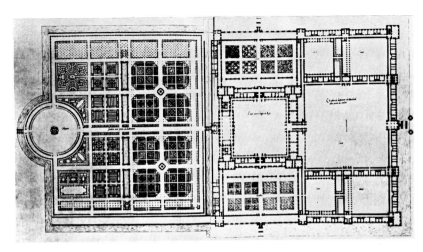

Jacques Androuet Du Cerceau the Elder.
Plan of Château of Charleval.
France.
1570

where SALOMON DE BROSSE was raised, and for the resemblance of its plan to that of Salomon's design for the Luxembourg palace.

Few schemes for unbuilt châteaux are as tantalizing as Du Cerceau's plan of Charleval, the immense château designed for Charles IX in a valley near Rouen. Begun in 1570, work on the building ceased with the death of the king in 1574, only to be resumed by Catherine de' Medici in 1577. The scheme has been compared to that for the enlargement of the Louvre as given in Serlio's Book VI (1541–1546) and to the anonymous Destailleur plan (accepted by Henri II in 1549–1551). To Blunt (*Art and Architecture,* pp. 143–144), the plan rivals Delorme's Tuileries and JEAN BULLANT's Chenonceau; it is certainly indicative of a new grandiose scale coming into prominence. Furthermore, in its symmetry, logic, geometric distribution, garden parterres, and axial perspective, it not only antedates the mature classicism of seventeenth-century France but is also in tune with a number of Du Cerceau's ideal designs. Considering that little of the château was actually built, *Les . . . Bastiments* gives us a remarkable record. A document cited by Adhémar (1961, pp. 243–244) points to an Italian as author of the plan while conceding that Du Cerceau was probably responsible for its décor and execution. One "Jean Gallia, French engineer, said to be from Ferrara" appears to have offered the king a plan of Charleval in 1572 and five months later the king was presented with a wooden model made by two Italian brothers.

Critical opinion about Du Cerceau may be changing. REGINALD BLOMFIELD viewed him as an ornamentalist, a virtuoso surveyor and engraver. Gebelin (1927, pp. 33–34) could note that the Du Cerceau family was part of the decline after the grand masters. Recently, Du Cerceau's oeuvre has been examined as an ensemble rather than as a source of information on French Renaissance châteaux. From this perspective, we see that Du Cerceau was interested in the total patrimony of architecture, the medieval heritage as well as most recent buildings, civic as well as ecclesiastical architecture, and in the symbolic meaning of buildings.

Although Du Cerceau's Protestantism did not preclude dedication of three books to Catherine de' Medici after the Saint Bartholomew's massacre, it did lead him to seek the protection of the duke of Nemours in Geneva or Annecy, where he died. Of his progeny, three of his four sons were architects and, as we have noted, a daughter married Jehan de Brosse, father of Salomon.

Baptiste Androuet Du Cerceau (1544/1547–1590). We are introduced to the oldest son in the *Mémoires du Duc de Nevers,* where he is mentioned as a Huguenot and an architect taken into the service of Henri III in 1575. Prominent in the last decades of the century, Baptiste served under Henri III and was in charge of schemes for the improvement of Paris under Henri IV. He is first cited in a 1577 pension list of Henri III. There he is said to be residing at Charleval, together with his father, though receiving a larger stipend. In 1578, he must have been the leading architect in Paris. Succeeding PIERRE LESCOT as architect of the Louvre, he was responsible for the prolongation of the Grand Gallery (1578); following Bullant, he worked on the Mausoleum of the Valois (1578) in the northern transept of Saint Denis (though Blunt, *Art and Architecture,* p. 98, has stated that "nothing . . . suggests the intervention of Baptiste"). At the same time, Baptiste is recorded as directing the king's works at Saint Denis and Fontainebleau and designing the Pont Neuf in Paris (1578–1604). The latter is his only preserved work, completed after his death in 1603 and altered in 1843–1853 (unedited documents on the building of the Pont Neuf were published by R. de Lasteyrie, 1882).

Baptiste was appointed adviser and architect to Henri III in 1584 and was put in charge of the king's buildings in 1585, the same year in which Baptiste fled Paris because of religious persecutions. Attributed to Baptiste is the Hotel d'Argoulème (1584), but because of its use of colossal order pilasters and the interruption of the entablature by dormers, Blunt has noted that the style is closer to that of Bullant than to that of Baptiste's father. Supposedly Baptiste also worked on the châteaux of Verneuil and d'Ormesson.

Jacques Androuet Du Cerceau II (1550–1614). Together with Baptiste and his father, Jacques II worked at Charleval (1570s). In 1576, he is recorded as being a secretary to the duke of Anjou. A year later, he is named *valet de chambre* and architect of the duke of Alençon. In 1588, he built the Wall in Tours; a resident there, he is referred to as "architect of the king." He became Henri IV's

architect in 1594, and the next year was put in charge of the Louvre and other royal houses. In 1598, he received payment for the king's survey of castles, gardens, and city parks, including the castle and garden of Nérac. Among his important works at the Louvre and the Tuileries was the completion of the second half of the Grand Gallery (1602–1608) which unites the Louvre to the Tuileries. Visible in DANIEL MAROT's engravings and in JACQUES FRANÇOIS BLONDEL's *Architecture française* (1753), this building was demolished by HECTOR M. LEFUEL and others in the nineteenth century. Blondel's judgment is severe: "here are to be found all that is most licentious in architecture . . . piers of unequal width, quoins of different sizes, a solid where there ought to be a void . . . entablatures interrupted by windows . . . extravagant proportions" (Blondel, Vol. IV, 85). Works attributed to Jacques II in Paris include a townhouse in the rue Saint Antoine (1605) based on the Hôtel Carnavalet, and the Hôtel de Bellegarde (Séguier) from 1611–1614. (Jean I may have worked on the latter townhouse at a later date.) In 1606–1609, Jacques II is succeeded by de Brosse, who worked with him as early as 1597 at Montceaux.

Charles Androuet Du Cerceau (?–1606). The third son of Jacques Androuet was *valet de garderobe* to the duke of Anjou, and has been cited as "architect of the king." In 1594, he transferred to Châtellerault where he directed the building of the Hôtel de Roubet and the bridge (both 1594) later completed by his son René, who is recorded as "architect of the king" at Châtellerault until 1640.

Jean Androuet Du Cerceau I (c.1585/90–1649). The first sign of architectural activity appears in a note of 1614 by his cousin, Salomon de Brosse, affirming that he is part of the latter's atelier and that the title "architect of the king" was passed on to him by his uncle, Jacques II. The document asserts that Jean was at that time collaborating with de Brosse on the Luxembourg Palace, then under construction. In 1617, he was appointed architect to Louis XIII.

One of the most popular architects of the day, Jean built many townhouses in Paris, including in all probability the Hôtel Sully on the rue Saint Antoine (1624–1629), the paradigmatic early seventeenth-century Parisian townhouse. Attributed to Jean on the basis of style rather than on firm documentary evidence, the building possesses certain archaisms similar to the work of Jacques II, for example, its elaborate façade decorated with allegorical figures, sculptural friezes, masks, and highly embellished dormers. In 1624, Jean was also called upon to furnish designs for the façade of the new transept of the Cathédrale Sainte-Croix in

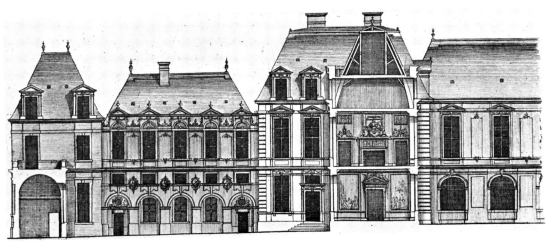

Jean Androuet Du Cerceau I.
Hôtel de Bretonvilliers (completed by Louis Le Vau).
Paris.
1635–1638

Orleans. After suffering a grave illness in 1628, he began a new phase of work around 1630–1631. In 1632, he replaced Delorme's intricate staircase in the Cour du Cheval Blanc at Fontainebleau with an even more forceful and complex design. The same year he joined forces with Charles du Rys and Paul de Brosse on the new fortifications of Paris. In 1633, he worked on the townhouse acquired by Chancelor Séguier in the rue de Grenelle-Saint Honoré, completed in 1635–1636. Attribution for the sumptuous Hôtel de Bretonvilliers (1635–1638) is confirmed by a first set of contracts and specifications relating to the townhouse for M. de Breton, "in the construction and perfection of his grand house on the Ile Notre Dame in Paris." Only the left wing of the court was built, however, and the new design of 1638–1643 is almost surely by LOUIS LE VAU. Destroyed in 1873 and known to us via engravings, this townhouse was remarkable for the richness of the façade's sculptural décor with its busts and ornamental lucarnes.

From 1639 to 1645, Jean worked on a new bridge, the Pont au Change. A sophisticated ensemble of vaulted galleries and arcades, the construction won the admiration of Parisians. Jean is last mentioned in a 1649 document. No innovator but one of the most gifted architects of his generation, Jean prolonged the ideas of Jacques II and Salomon de Brosse, giving them a more modern tone. In a eulogy by the deputy of Sainte-Croix d'Orleans in 1625, he was cited as "in great demand for his ability."

NAOMI MILLER

WORKS
JACQUES ANDROUET DU CERCEAU THE ELDER
(A)1545, Eglise de la Madeleine (choir); (A)1560s, Château of Montargis; France. (A)*c.1565, Maison Blanche, Gaillon, France. (A)*1568–. Château of Verneuil, France. (A)*1570, Château of Charleval (with others), France.

BAPTISTE ANDROUET DU CERCEAU
*1577, Château of Charleval (with others), France. 1578, Grand Gallery (extension), Louvre; 1578, Valois Mausoleum (with others), Saint Denis; 1578–1604, Pont Neuf (later altered); (A)1584, Hôtel d'Angoulème (now Lamoignon); Paris. (A)1580s, Château of Ormesson, France. (A)*1580s, Château of Verneuil, France.

JACQUES ANDROUET DU CERCEAU II
*1570s, Château of Charleval (with others), France. *1588, Wall, Tours, France. 1598, Château of Pau, France. 1598, Château of Nérac, France. *1598, Château of Verneuil, France. *1602–1608, Grand Gallery, Louvre; (A)1605–1613, Hôtel de Mayenne (or d'Ormesson); (A)1611–1614, Hôtel de Bellegarde (Séguier); Paris.

CHARLES ANDROUET DU CERCEAU
1594, Hôtel de Roubet; 1594, Pont Henri IV; Châtellerault, France.

JEAN ANDROUET DU CERCEAU I
1614, Luxembourg Palace (with Salomon de Brosse), Paris. 1624, Cathédrale Sainte-Croix (transept), Orléans, France. 1624–1629, Hôtel Sully, Paris. 1632, Cour de Cheval Blanc (staircase), Fontainebleau, France. *1632, Fortifications (with Charles du Rys and Paul de Brosse); 1633–1635/1636, Hôtel Séguier (Bellegarde); *(A)*1635–1638, Hôtel de Bretonvilliers (completed by Louis Le Vau); 1639–1645, Pont au Change (later rebuilt); Paris.

BIBLIOGRAPHY
ADHÉMAR, JEAN 1961 "Sur le Château de Charleval." *Gazette des Beaux-Arts* Series 6 58:241–244.
BAUCHAL, CHARLES 1887 Pages 12–13 in *Nouveau Dictionnaire biographique et critique des architectes français*. Paris: André, Daly.
BEAULIEU, MICHÈLE 1948–1949 "Jacques I Androuet Du Cerceau." *Pro Arte* 6:166–182.
BERTY, ADOLPHE 1860 Pages 91–115 in *Les Grands Architectes Français de la Renaissance*. Paris: Aubry.
BLOMFIELD, REGINALD (1911)1974 *History of French*

Architecture: 1494-1661. Reprint. New York: Hacker.

BLOMFIELD, REGINALD 1912 *Architectural Drawing and Draughtsmen.* London: Cassell.

BLONDEL, JACQUES FRANÇOIS (1753)1904-1905 Volume 4 in *Réimpression de l'Architecture française.* Reprint. Paris: Lévy.

BLUNT, ANTHONY (1953)1977 *Art and Architecture in France: 1500-1700.* Harmondsworth, England: Penguin.

BLUNT, ANTHONY 1958 *Philibert De L'Orme.* London: Zwemmer.

BOUDON, FRANÇOISE, and COUZY, Hélène 1974 "Les Plus Excellents Bâtiments de France: Une anthologie de châteaux a la fin du XVIᵉ siècle." *L'Information d'Histoire de l'Art* 19, no. 1:8-12; no. 3:103-114.

CHEVALLEY, DENIS A. 1973 *Der grosse Tuilerienentwurf in der Überlieferung Du Cerceaus.* Frankfurt: Land.

CIRPUT, E. J. 1967 "Notes sur un grand architecte parisien: Jean Androuet Ducerceau." *Bulletin de la Société de l'Histoire du Protestantisme français* 113:149-201. Includes sixteen documents from 1625 to 1649.

COOPE, ROSALYS 1962 "History and Architecture of the Château of Verneuil-sur-Oise." *Gazette des Beaux-Arts* Series 6 59:291-318.

DEZALLIER D'ARGENVILLE, A. N. 1787 *Vies des fameux architectes depuis la renaissance des arts.* Paris: Debure l'aîné.

GEBELIN, FRANÇOIS 1927 *Les Châteaux de la Renaissance.* Paris: Les Beaux-Arts.

GEYMÜLLER, H. VON 1887 *Les Du Cerceau: Leur vie et leur oeuvre.* Paris: Rouam.

HAUTECOEUR, LOUIS (1943-1957)1965-1966 Volumes 1, 2, and 3 in *Histoire de l'architecture classique en France.* Paris: Picard.

JAL, AUGUSTE (1867)1872 Pages 339-342 in *Dictionnaire critique de biographie et d'histoire.* Paris: Plon.

JAMES, CHARLES, and THOMSON, DAVID A. n.d. "Jacques et Baptiste Du Cerceau: Recherches sur l'architecture française (1545-1590)." Geneva: Bibliothèque de la Société Française d'Archéologie. Forthcoming publication.

MILLER, NAOMI 1962-1964 "A Volume of Architectural Drawings Ascribed to Jacques Androuet Du Cerceau the Elder, in the Morgan Library, New York." *Marsyas* 11:33-41.

PLANAT, PAUL 1903 Volume 1, pages 148-154 in *Encyclopédie de l'Architecture et de la Construction.* Paris: Aulanier.

ROUSSET-CHARNY, GERARD 1974 "Le Relevé d'architecture chez Jacques Ier Androuet du Cerceau: *Les Plus Excellents Bâtiments de France* (1576-1579)." *L'Information d'Histoire de l'Art* 19, no. 3:114-124.

SEIGNEUR, MAURICE DU 1888-1892 Volume 1, pages 147-154 in Paul Planat (editor), *Encyclopédie de l'Architecture et de la Construction.* Paris: Dujardin.

TAFURI, MANFREDO 1971 "Alle origini del Palladianesimo: Allesandro Farnese, Jacques Androuet Du Cerceau, Inigo Jones." *Storia dell' Arte* 11:149-161.

TOESCA, ILARIA 1956 "Drawings by Jacques Androuet Du Cerceau the Elder in the Vatican Library." *Burlington Magazine* 98:153-157.

WARD, WILLIAM HENRY 1909 *French Châteaux and Gardens in the Sixteenth Century: A Series of Reproductions of Contemporary Drawings Hitherto Unpublished by Jacques Androuet Du Cerceau.* London: Batsford.

WARD, WILLIAM HENRY (1912)1926 *The Architecture of the Renaissance in France.* 2 vols. 2d ed. London: Batsford.

DUDLEY, HENRY

Born and trained in England, Henry Dudley (1813-1894) was first employed by John Hayward of the Exeter Diocesan Architectural Society; he emigrated to New York in 1851 and practiced with FRANK WILLS, a former colleague in Exeter, England, until 1853. Later, Dudley worked in partnership with FREDERIC DIAPER (1864-1869). During his long career in America, Dudley designed 162 churches, half of which were erected in New York State. A principal architect of the New York Ecclesiological Society and the Protestant Episcopal Church, he specialized in the Gothic revival church, designing principally in the traditional early English and early Decorated styles. Dudley was a charter member of the American Institute of Architects and the designer of its original seal.

DENNIS STEADMAN FRANCIS and
JOY M. KESTENBAUM

WORKS

1853-1855, Saint John's Episcopal Church, Troy, N.Y. 1856-1859, Trinity Church, Mount Vernon, N.Y. 1858-1863, Saint Mark's Episcopal Church, Hoosick Falls, N.Y. 1859-1867, Church of the Advent (completed by William Kiddell), Nashville, Tenn. 1860, George M. Tibbits Residence, Hoosick, N.Y. 1861, Warren Family Mortuary Chapel, Oakwood Cemetery, Troy, N.Y. 1863-1865, St. James's Episcopal Church, Bronx, N.Y. 1864-1865, Trenor W. Park House (with Frederic Diaper), North Bennington, Vt. 1865-1866, Grace Episcopal Church, Amherst, Mass. 1868-1870, Saint Peter's Church, Auburn, N.Y. 1871-1874, Church of the Holy Trinity, Middletown, Conn. 1872-1880, Saint Peter's Church, Niagara Falls, N.Y. 1883-1885, Saint Paul's Episcopal Church, Syracuse, N.Y.

BIBLIOGRAPHY

FRANCIS, DENNIS STEADMAN 1980 *Architects in Practice, New York City, 1840-1900.* New York: Committee for the Preservation of Architectural Records.

History and Commerce of New York. 1891 New York: American Publishing and Engraving.

New York's Great Industries. 1885 New York: Historical Publishing Company.

STANTON, PHOEBE B. 1968 *The Gothic Revival and American Church Architecture.* Baltimore: Johns Hopkins University Press.

DUDOK, W. M.

Willem Marinus Dudok (1884–1974) was born in Amsterdam and grew up in a musical family. In 1902, he entered the Royal Military Academy in Breda, Netherlands, where he was trained as a military engineer. Architecture played no role in his education. After finishing his studies, he was engaged in building barracks and forts. In 1915, after working for two years in Leiden, he was appointed director of public works in Hilversum. His tasks included designing the new Town Hall (1928–1930) and drawing up expansion plans. In addition to his work in Hilversum, he became the successor to H. P. Berlage as town planner of expansion projects in The Hague.

It is remarkable that in spite of an enormous body of work (about 240 buildings), Dudok is generally identified only with the Hilversum Town Hall. In the course of his career, Dudok went through a whole architectonic development and did not bind himself to one particular style. In Dudok's early phase (1907–1916), Berlage, and particularly his Amsterdam Stock Exchange (1901), was Dudok's main source of inspiration. Afterward, the predominant influence was the Amsterdam school. An architectural style that was typically Dudok's own can be seen to emerge at the beginning of the 1920s. In the villa at 19 Sevensteyn, The Hague (1920), space is conceived not as a closed cell, but as volumes extending outward from a central point. This notion of space had its roots in the movement *De Stijl*.

With a flawless sense of composition, Dudok gradually refined the size and shape of the volumes. Characteristic elements are recessions and projections of the façade and a dynamic balance between a strong horizontal tendency and vertical accents (often in the form of a tower). The horizontal element is reinforced by use of long, narrow bricks (the Hilversum shape). Because of this stress on the horizontal, Dudok's architecture is often compared with the prairie houses of FRANK LLOYD WRIGHT, even though Dudok always denied Wright's influence. In the 1930s, Dudok strongly simplified his compositions by employing large, uninterrupted façade surfaces. His work grew less recognizable as the elements so typical of his 1920s architecture slowly began to disappear.

Hilversum Town Hall. Dudok began as early as 1915 with the first sketches for the Hilversum Town Hall. These first studies were still clearly influenced by Berlage. In 1924, he completed the definitive design which the Town Council accepted on the recommendation of fifty-five prominent architects who convinced the council that they were "involved with one of the best buildings of contemporary architecture."

Town planning. In 1915, there was a tremendous housing shortage in rapidly growing Hilversum. Dudok's first duty was to draw up an expansion plan which he based on the town planning notions in EBENEZER HOWARD's *Garden Cities of Tomorrow*. This plan was the first in a series which Dudok continued to make until the 1950s. Thus, Dudok was almost single-handedly able to determine the shape that Hilversum took as it grew from a small village to a sizable town.

Dudok's reputation. Dudok is most famous for the work he did in the 1920s and 1930s. In his Town Hall, schools, and public housing projects of that period, he developed a strongly individual (and therefore easily recognizable) style. The formal vocabulary displayed in these works is at the same time modern and traditional.

This period of Dudok's development has been stressed so heavily that his earlier phase is often overlooked and the myth has come into common belief that Dudok developed, without any outside influences, a completely new and individual style which he maintained throughout his career. A look at his work before 1920 proves this to be untrue. His early work was influenced by the prevailing architectural movements in Holland: Berlage and the Amsterdam school. Early on, though, he was recognized by Berlage and by his professor at the academy as a distinguished talent.

There was a duality in his career after World War II. Dudok tended more and more toward traditional architecture as he applied arches, columns, pillars, and seventeenth-century Dutch façades. By the 1950s, his architecture had grown so anonymous that many in the Netherlands questioned whether he was still alive. But if he was forgotten in Holland, there remained great interest in his work abroad. He received commissions in Baghdad (Iraq) and Izmir (Turkey). He was also invited in the early 1950s to lecture in various cities in America. Even in the 1980s, there are differing opinions about Dudok. Many Dutch architects who received their training after World War II and became acquainted with Dudok during his most authoritarian and unsuccessful period are very critical of his character and work. However, a renewed interest in Dudok and his work may restore his place among the foremost Dutch architects of the twentieth century.

MAX CRAMER and HANS VAN GRIEKEN

WORKS

1916, Secondary School, Leiden, Netherlands. 1920, Villa, 19 Sevensteyn, The Hague. 1921, Municipal Baths; 1921, Residential Development, Fourth Municipal Quarter; 1923, Slaughterhouse; 1925, Sports

Ground (manager's office and dressing rooms); 1926, Juliana School; Hilversum, Netherlands. 1927, Van Heutsz Monument, Gambir, Indonesia. 1928–1930, Town Hall; 1929, Noorder Cemetery; 1936, Aquatic Sports Pavilion; Hilversum, Netherlands. 1941, Municipal Theater, Utrecht. 1948, Royal Dutch Steelworks Offices, Velsen, Netherlands. 1953, Park Flats, Bussum, Netherlands.

BIBLIOGRAPHY

CRAMER, MAX, and VAN GRIEKEN, HANS   1981 *W. M. Dudok: 1884–1974.* Amsterdam.
FRIEDHOFF, G.   1930   *W. M. Dudok.* Amsterdam.
MAGNÉE, R. N. H.   1954   *Willem M. Dudok.* Amsterdam: van Saane.
STUIVELING, G.; BAKKER-SCHUT, F. ET AL.   1954 *Willem M. Dudok.* Amsterdam.

DUFOURNY, LEON

Léon Dufourny (1754–1818), a French antiquarian and architect trained by JULIEN DAVID LEROY and Marie Joseph Peyre (see PEYRE FAMILY), lived in Italy (1782–1794) and built the neoclassical Ginnasio in Palermo (1789–1792). Elected to the Institut de France in 1795, he administered the national museum and succeeded Leroy as professor of architecture.

RICHARD CLEARY

WORK

1789–1792, Ginnasio, Orto Botanico, Palermo, Italy.

BIBLIOGRAPHY

DELAROCHE, HIPPOLYTE   1819   *Catalogue des tableaux, dessins et estampes composant l'une des collections de feu M. Léon Dufourny.* Paris: Nouzou.
MEEKS, CARROLL L. V.   1966   *Italian Architecture: 1750–1914.* New Haven: Yale University Press.
QUATREMÈRE DE QUINCY, ANTOINE CHRYSOSTOME (1822)1834   "Notice historique sur la vie et les ouvrages de M. Dufourny architecte." Pages 234–248 in *Recueil de notices historiques lues dans les séances publiques de l'Académie royale de beaux-arts à l'Institut.* Paris: Le Clere.
TOURNEUX, MAURICE   1910   "Mission de Dufourny et de Visconti au château de Richelieu en 1800." *Archives de l'Art Français* New Series 4:351–413.

DUGOURC, JEAN DEMOSTHENE

Brother-in-law of FRANÇOIS JOSEPH BÉLANGER, Jean Demosthène Dugourc (1749–1825) conceived Etruscan-styled decorations and panels of arabesques for such notable clients as the comte d'Artois at Bagatelle. After 1800, he worked in

Madrid, and, returning to France with the Restoration, contributed projects for the Tuileries.

MARIE-NOËLE DE GARY
Translated from French by Richard Cleary

BIBLIOGRAPHY

GUILMARD, DÉSIRÉ   1880–1881   *Les Maitres Ornemanistes.* Paris: Plon.
HARTMANN, SIMONE   1978   "L'Ornemaniste Jean Dugourc." *L'Estampille* 98, June:30–35.
MONTAIGLON, ANATOLE DE   1877   "Autobiographie de Dugourc." *Nouvelles Archives de l'art Français* 1877:367–371.
TRÉVISE, DUC DE   1925   "La Reapparition de Dugourc." *Renaissance de l'art Français* 1925, Feb.:75–84.

DUHART, EMILIO

Best known for the United Nations headquarters (1960–1966) near Santiago, Chile, Emilio Duhart (1917–) was born near Temuco, Chile. He has degrees in architecture from France and Chile in addition to receiving a master's degree from Harvard in 1943 where he studied with WALTER GROPIUS, and a year with LE CORBUSIER working on Chandigarh.

From 1953 to 1960, he was director of city and regional planning for Santiago. Thereafter, he focused on prefab designs appropriate to the Chilean climate. Since 1970, he has been teaching in Paris, but he returned to Chile in 1977 to receive the National Prize for Architecture.

ELIZABETH D. HARRIS

WORKS

1945–1952, Verbo Divino Community High School; 1946, Duhart House; Concepción, Chile. 1955–1960, Jardín del Este Residential Neighborhood, Santiago, Chile. 1958–1969, Universidad de Concepción (Chemistry Institute, Civil Engineering School, Mechanical Technology Institute, Central Library, Main Forum, and Plaza), Chile. 1960–1966, United Nations Building for Latin America; 1962, Carozzi Flour and Pasta Factory; Santiago. 1964, Honsa Hotel, Ancud, Chile. 1969–1970, Ministry of Labor Building, Santiago. 1972–1979, Institut Français de Gestion (business school and offices), Paris.

BIBLIOGRAPHY

BAYÓN, DAMIÁN, and GASPARINI, PAOLO   1977 *Panorámica de la Arquitectura Latino-Americana.* Barcelona, Spain: Editorial Blume.
BULLRICH, FRANCISCO   1969   *A History of Latin American Architecture.* New York: Braziller.
CASTEDO, LEOPOLDO   1969   *A History of Latin American Art and Architecture.* New York: Praeger.

DUIKER, JOHANNES

From the inception the Dutch magazine *de 8 en Opbouw* Johannes Duiker (1890–1935) was editor and a constant contributor (1932–1935), and in fact he vivified parts of the 8's manifesto in his writings. Chief among these were antistyle protests against beauty and a functionalist insistence on following the demands of the educated client's dictation of program.

Duiker was also greatly influenced by his school, the Technische Hogeschool in Delft and by Henri Evers, who had at least two sides—one as a modernist who touted OTTO WAGNER, ADOLF LOOS, and JOSEF HOFFMANN in his classes and the other side as a conservative, as seen in his Beaux-Arts–Italianate City Hall of Rotterdam.

Duiker never considered the Beaux-Arts in any of his work; he relied fairly heavily on FRANK LLOYD WRIGHT for many of his earlier works, and probably the swan song of this early period was his entry design for the Royal Academy of Fine Arts Building (1918) for which he and his partner Bernard Bijvoet won first prize. Wright's Larkin Building and Unity Temple seem to have been direct models, and the general Wrightian tendencies of strong axiality and horizontally oriented fenestration are likewise present and are effected with much verve.

Six of his later buildings really stand out independently as heroic gestures of the Modern movement—the House in Aalsmeer (1924); Zonnestraal Sanitorium (1926–1928); the Open-air School (1929–1930); the Nirvana Flats (1927–1930); the Gooiland Hotel (1934–1936); and, last but best of all, the Cineac Cinema (1934) in Amsterdam. The Aalsmeer House is pure and sharp in the horizontal lines of wood siding with subtle fluctuations of the shingled texture of the cylinder stairwell. From this point on, the material is almost all reinforced concrete—the column and beam variety derived from FRANÇOIS HENNE-BIQUE—with the exception of the Czech tan sheathing tiles of the hotel. The sanitorium's strict symmetry is its most striking feature, but when exploring the building complexes, one notices the asymmetrical parts of the central building, especially the boiler chimney and the cylinder water-tank. The Cineac, a news film theater, is stunning for the architect's astuteness in arranging the forms in a Constructivist manner—the changing of line at the corner, the use of graphics as a major statement in the design. Perhaps the greatest statement Duiker made here was to provide a tightly spaced building in a very confined urban space, a little like LE CORBUSIER was to do at Carpenter Hall in Cambridge, Massachusetts.

Duiker.
Handelsblad-Cineac
Cinema.
Amsterdam.
1934

Despite his use of concrete and steel, Duiker was ultimately a romantic in his strong belief in intuition and his stress on a spiritual content of art to counter the extreme influence of materialism in the capitalist dominance of society.

SUZANNE FRANK

WORKS

1924, Country House, Stommerkade 64, Aalsmeer, Netherlands. 1926–1928, Zonnestraal Sanatorium Complex (with Bernard Bijvoet), Hilversum, Netherlands. 1927–1930, Nirvana Flats (with Wiebenga), Benoordenhoutseweg and Willem Witsenplein, The Hague. 1929–1930, Public School, Cliostraat; 1934, Handelsblad-Cineac Cinema; Amsterdam. 1934–1936, Grand Hotel Gooiland (completed by Bijvoet), Hilversum, Netherlands.

BIBLIOGRAPHY

"Bauten von Johannes Duiker." 1968 *Bauwelt* 59:175–179.
"Duiker." 1971–1972 *Forum* November and January. Special issues.
"Duiker and the 'Zonnestraal'." 1962 *Forum* 16:entire issue.
Duiker, Johannes 1930 *Hoogbouw.* Rotterdam, Holland: Brusse.

Duiker, Johannes   1932–1935   *De 8 en Opbouw.* Several articles.
"Grand Hotel Gooiland te Hilversum."   1936   *Bouwkundig werkblad architectura* 57:529–537.
"Hotel at Hilversum."   1947   *Architectural Review* (London) 102:128–130.
LIONNI, LEO   1935   "Jan Duiker." *Casabella* 8:4–7.
VICKERY, ROBERT   1971   "Bijvoet and Duiker." *Perspecta* 13/14:130–161.

DÜLFER, MARTIN

Born in Breslau, the capital of Prussian Silesia, Martin Dülfer (1859–1942) studied at the Technische Hochschulen in Hannover and Stuttgart. After a brief apprenticeship with Kayser und von Grossheim in Berlin, Dülfer moved on to Munich, where he was briefly associated with FRIEDRICH VON THIERSCH. In private practice in Munich, Dülfer won commissions for a wide range of commercial buildings and began to establish a reputation as an expert in theater design. From 1902, he taught at the Technische Hochschule in Dresden, remaining in Dresden until his death.

Dülfer's architecture was a curious blend of south German historicism, decorative elements drawn from the German *Jugendstil* movement, and overwhelmingly massive forms. His Dortmund Municipal Theater (1903) exemplified this highly personal style: a huge blocky building executed in rough-cut masonry, its weighty appearance ameliorated by vertical and horizontal bands of windows which formed an abstract and decorative pattern, and by a variety of surface ornamentation. Because of its unusual appearance, the Dortmund Theater was regarded by many contemporaries as unique. In actuality, however, Dülfer's work belonged to a broader movement in Germany—to a rather widespread experimentation with massive masonry forms. Others working in a similar vein included PAUL BONATZ, WILHELM KREIS, EDMUND KÜRNER, and OSKAR KAUFMANN. Their architecture was rooted in the neo-Romanesque and in the teachings of Friedrich von Thiersch and THEODOR FISCHER.

BARBARA MILLER LANE

WORKS

1887–1890, Residence and Stores for L. Bernheimer (with Friedrich von Thiersch); 1897–1898, Bruckmann Publishing House; Munich. 1899, Theater, Meran, Germany. 1900–1901, Münchner Allgemeine Zeitung Newspaper Offices, Munich. 1903, Dortmund Municipal Theater, Germany. 1904, Terminus Hotel, Munich. 1904, Becker Family Vault, Jewish Cemetery, Weissensee, Berlin. 1907, Municipal Theater, Lübeck, Germany. 1910–1912, Dresdner Bank, Leipzig. 1912?,

Technische Hochschule, Dresden, Germany. 1929, Theater, Sofia.

BIBLIOGRAPHY

CREUTZ, MAX   1910   "Martin Dülfer." Volume 4 in Hugo Licht (editor), *Die Architektur des XX. Jahrhunderts.* Berlin: Wasmuth.
DÜLFER, MARTIN   1914   *Ausgeführte Bauwerke.* Berlin. "Neuere Grabendenkmäler auf den Friedhofen in und bei Berlin."   1906   *Blätter für Architektur und Kunsthandwerk* 19:27, plate 39.

DULIN, NICOLAS

Nicolas Dulin (1670–1751), also spelled d'Ulin, Dullin, d'Ullin and d'Hullin, was born in Paris. He served as a member of the Royal Academy of Architecture from 1718 to 1734, and was also appointed contrôleur des bâtiments du roi.

Dulin's designs, although strongly influenced by JULES HARDOUIN MANSART and PIERRE LASSURANCE, display elements of originality. This can be seen particularly in his best known building, the Maison Dunoyer (1709), where he emphasized a central, projecting pavilion with a high, sloping roof. The Maison Dunoyer also included, for the first time (according to Louis Hautecoeur), a kitchen located next to the dining room in the corps-de-logis.

Dulin was the teacher of PIERRE CONTANT D'IVRY and the brother of the painter Pierre Dulin.

KATHLEEN RUSSO

WORKS

1704, Hôtel d'Etampes; 1709, Maison Dunoyer; 1709, Hôtel de Nevers (renovation); 1711, Hôtel de Soning; 1721, Hôtel du Plessis-Châtillon (renovation); 1724, Hôtel de Richelieu (renovation); 1730, Hôtel Locmaria; 1730–1732, Château de Crosne (renovation); Paris. n.d., Château de Villegenis, near Massy, France. n.d., Hôtel Jabach (restoration); n.d., Hôtel de Pontferrière; Paris. n.d., Maison Galepin, Auteuil, France.

BIBLIOGRAPHY

BLONDEL, JACQUES FRANÇOIS   (1752–1756)1904–1905   Volumes 1–3 in *L'architecture français.* Reprint. Paris: Lévy.
BRICE, GERMAIN   (1752)1971   Volumes 1–2 in *Nouvelle description de la ville de Paris.* Geneva: Droz; Paris: Minard.
GALLET, MICHEL   1972   *Paris Domestic Architecture of the Eighteenth Century.* London: Barrie & Jenkins.
HAUTECOEUR, LOUIS   1950   *Première moitié du XVIIIᵉ siècle: le style Louis XV.* Volume 3 in *Histoire de l'architecture classique en France.* Paris: Picard.
HERLUISON, HENRI   1873   *Actes d'état civil d'artistes français: Peintres, graveurs, architectes, etc.* Paris: Baur.
KALNEIN, WEND GRAF, and LEVEY, MICHAEL   1972

Art and Architecture of the Eighteenth Century in France. Baltimore: Penguin.

MARIETTE, JEAN   (1727)1927–1929   Volume 1 in *L'architecture français.* Edited by Louis Hautecoeur. Paris and Brussels: Van Oest.

ROCHEGUDE, FELIX, and DUMOLIN, MAURICE   1923 Volume 11 in *Guide pratique à travers le vieux Paris.* Paris: Champion.

DUPERAC, ETIENNE

Architect, painter, engraver, and landscape designer, Etienne Dupérac (c.1525–1604) was born in Paris and was in Italy from 1559–1578. He is primarily known for his representations of ancient Rome (1573–1575), his important archeological reconstructions of the city, and his engravings after MICHELANGELO's architectural projects (1567–1569). In Rome, he was in contact with A. Lafréri, O. Panvinio, and PIRRO LIGORIO, and was architect to the papal conclave in 1572. As painter to the Cardinal of Ferrara, Ippolito d'Este, he engraved the bird's eye view of the Villa d'Este at Tivoli in 1573. Later, as architect to the duke of Aumale, he planned the gardens of Anet. As architect to Henri IV in 1595, he probably designed the terraced gardens of Saint Germain-en-Laye, and was also engaged on works in the Tuileries (c.1600–1603).

NAOMI MILLER

WORKS

*(A)1595, Gardens, Saint Germain-en-Laye, France. *c.1600–1603, Tuileries (additions), Paris.

BIBLIOGRAPHY

CIPRUT, E. J.   1960   "Nouveau documents sur Etienne Dupérac." *Bulletin de la Société de l'Histoire de l'Art français* 1960:161–173.

DE SACY, J. S.   1968   "Dupérac." Volume 12, page 326 in *Dictionnaire de Biographie française.* Paris: Librarie Letouzey et Ané.

DUPÉRAC, ETIENNE   (1575)1973   *I vestigi dell'antichità di Roma.* Reprint. London: Warren.

EHRLE, FRANCESCO   (1577)1908   *Roma prima di Sisto V: La pianta di Roma Du Pérac–Lafréry del 1577.* Rome: Danesi.

LAFRÉRY, ANTOINE   1540–1620   *Speculum Romanae magnificentiae.* Rome. Includes almost all of Dupérac's *Vestigi dell'antichità di Roma* (1575).

ZERNER, H.   1965   "Observations on Dupérac and the *Disegni de la ruine di Roma e come anticamente erono.*" *Art Bulletin* 47, no. 4:507–512.

DURAND, GEORGE

George F. Durand (1850–1889) was southwestern Ontario's most accomplished High Victorian architect. Born in London, Ontario, Durand trained under William B. Robinson, a local engineer and surveyor. From 1870 to 1876, he was employed by THOMAS FULLER as chief assistant for Fuller and Laver's ill-fated New York State Capitol building in Albany. In 1878, Durand returned to London to become a partner in Robinson's architectural firm. For the next eleven years, until his untimely death in 1889, Durand designed many of the region's major High Victorian buildings. His assured designs, which were frequently picturesque and usually imposing, expressed the prosperity of late nineteenth-century southwestern Ontario. Although Durand's designs were derivative, his close attention to siting and his sensitive use of local materials lift his work from the ordinary and mark it with a distinct regional stamp.

LYNNE DELEHANTY DISTEFANO

WORKS

*1880–1881, Masonic Temple; completed 1882, London Club; begun 1833, Charles Goodhue House; *completed 1884, John Labatt House; London, Ontario. 1885–1887, Perth County Courthouse, Stratford, Ontario. 1886–1887, Hensall Presbyterian Church, Ontario. 1886–1888, Infantry School, London, Ontario. *1888–1891, Upper Canada College, Toronto. Completed 1889, Petrolia Town Hall, Ontario.

BIBLIOGRAPHY

DISTEFANO, LYNNE DELEHANTY   1978   *George F. Durand.* Ontario: London Public Libraries and Museums. Exhibition catalogue.

DURAND, J. N. L.

The lectures of Jean Nicolas Louis Durand (1760–1834), an influential teacher, summarized the rationalist thought of the late eighteenth century in France.

Born in Paris, the son of a poor cobbler, Durand was able to attend the Collège de Montaigu through the generosity of wealthy patrons. At first interested in sculpture, he studied architecture with Pierre Panseron, professor at the Ecole Militaire, and JEAN RODOLPHE PERRONET, founder of the Ecole des Ponts et des Chaussées.

At the age of sixteen, Durand entered the office of ETIENNE LOUIS BOULLÉE as a draftsman, earning enough to enroll at the Académie d'Architecture, placing second in the Prix de Rome competitions of 1779 and 1780.

In 1795, Durand was named professor of architecture at the new Ecole Polytechnique and remained there until shortly before his death in 1834. His lectures, published as the *Précis des leçons d'architecture données à l'école polytechnique* (1802–

1805), remained influential through several editions in France and abroad. His audience of students preparing for more specialized training at the various engineering schools and the brief time allotted architecture in the curriculum demanded a straightforward and practical approach, which helps to explain his practice of drawing ground plans on a gridded paper using the square as a module. Already in his *Recueil et parallèle des édifices de tout genre* (1800)—the first historical survey of world architecture organized according to building type and drawn to a common scale—he had simplified many of the illustrations to bring them into conformity with his taste for modular composition.

The neoclassical vocabulary of Durand—including Renaissance and Romanesque elements—had no symbolic or expressive function as it had for Boullée. Rather, it was a convention to be taken for granted in order to concentrate on utilitarian problems. Accepting the classical orders, he rejected any connection with the form and proportions of the human body. Symmetry and simple geometrical forms are to be preferred because they are more economical than irregular and complex forms. He illustrates how the material of JACQUES GERMAIN SOUFFLOT's Panthéon in Paris could enclose a much greater volume if disposed in an hemispherical vault above a circular plan. Aesthetic issues are irrelevant; if a building achieves functionalism and economy it must be beautiful.

Although Durand appeared too early in the industrial revolution to achieve structural systemization, his formal systemization, consisting of the additive repetition of a limited repertory of modular elements, can be seen to anticipate the standardization appropriate to industrial production and prefabrication.

RAND CARTER

WORK

1788, Hôtel Lathuille, rue du Faubourg-Poissonnière, Paris.

BIBLIOGRAPHY

BRAHAM, ALLAN 1980 *The Architecture of the French Enlightenment.* Berkeley and Los Angeles: University of California Press.

COLLINS, PETER 1965 *Changing Ideals in Modern Architecture.* London: Faber.

DURAND, J. N. L. 1800 *Recueil et parallèle des édifices de tout genre, anciens et modernes, remarquables par leur beauté, par leur grandeur ou par leur singularité, et dessinés sur une même échelle.* 2 vols. Paris: The author.

DURAND, J. N. L. 1802–1805 *Précis des leçons d'architecture données à l'école polytechnique.* Paris: The author.

HAUTECOEUR, LOUIS 1953 *Révolution et Empire: 1792–1815.* Volume 5 in *Histoire de l'architecture classique en France.* Paris: Picard.

HITCHCOCK, H. R. (1958)1977 *Architecture: Nineteenth and Twentieth Centuries.* Baltimore: Penguin.

JANINOT, JEAN-FRANCOIS 1792 *Vues pittoresques des principaux édifices de Paris.* Paris. Plates engraved by Janinot after drawings by Durand.

KRAFFT, JEAN CHARLES, and RANSONNETTE, NICOLAS (editors) 1802 *Plans, coupes, élévations des plus belles maisons et des hôtels construits à Paris et dans les environs.* Paris: The editors.

RONDELET, ANTOINE 1835 *Notice historique sur la vie et les ouvrages de J.N.L. Durand.* Paris: Pihan de la Forest.

DU RY FAMILY

The du Ry family of architects, emerging in the beginning of the seventeenth century, originated in Argentan, Normandy, France. The founder, Charles du Ry, brother-in-law and collaborator of SALOMON DE BROSSE, worked for the French court. His son, Mathurin du Ry, was court architect in Paris.

Mathurin's son, Paul du Ry (1640–1714) trained as a pupil of FRANÇOIS BLONDEL, mainly as a military architect. Persecuted as a Protestant, he moved to the Netherlands in 1665 and worked as a fortification architect in Maastricht. He returned to Paris in 1674 and in 1685 again emigrated, traveling via Holland to Kassel, Germany, where he entered the service of Landgrave Karl of Hessen-Kassel as court architect, an office that remained in his family until 1799. Here his most important task was urbanistic. For the Huguenots who settled in Kassel in 1685, he designed and built the Oberneustadt (Upper New City 1638–1714). Beyond the glacis of the baroque fortifications, on the plateau above the river banks of the Auegarten, southwest of the old town, the new quarter rose in a rectangular area crossed by two streets running at right angles to two others. Beginning along the Frankfurter Strasse, which ran from the town gate, Paul du Ry built up the area with simple, well-proportioned two- or three-story middle class houses with mansard gables, plain portals, and balconies. This unified scheme of puritanical but noble and friendly buildings was accentuated by the Karlskirche (1698–1710). Containing an octagonal preaching hall with a hipped dome and lantern, the church was fronted toward the street by a staircase-façade topped by a segmented pediment, the building being placed in such a way as to break the run of a cross-street, thus serving as a *point de vue,* a square having been left free behind it. On the *Bellevue* above the Aue Gardens, he planned a garden palace, and in 1705–1710 he built the Palace of Prince Wilhelm, adapting it to the unified building style. In 1714, he built the Observatory (later Palais Bellevue) and in the Aue itself the Orangerie Castle after plans by Giovanni Francesco Guerniero (1703–1710). When he died on June 21, 1714, he had created "the noblest Huguenot city" (du Colombien, 1956) in a sparse baroque-classicistic style deriving from a Dutch rather than a French tradition. The plans for the Huguenot city of Karlshafen, Hesse—executed between 1699 and 1720 by Colonel Friedrich Conradi—were also his work; with its rectangular blocks of houses grouped around a harbor basin, it is one of the best preserved of the Huguenot towns.

Paul's son, Charles Louis du Ry (1692–1757) took over the office of chief court architect (*Oberhofbaumeister*) and continued the construction of the Oberneustadt in Kassel after the plans of his father, retaining the same type of house. The training he had had from his father was technically solid, but he remained artistically insignificant, unable to free himself from his father's example (Philippsthal Palace, c.1730). Although later, with the help of François Blondel's Maison de Plaisance (1737), he tried to establish a connection with contemporary French architecture, for larger commissions the designs of foreign architects (FRANÇOIS CUVILLIÉS, Michel Léveilly) were preferred over his; only the execution of the building remained to him (for example, the Picture Gallery, 1749–1751). The canalization of the Oberneustadt (1739) was a worthy technical achievement, which was renewed only in the twentieth century.

When Charles Louis died, his son, Simon Louis du Ry (1726–1799) took his place. First trained by his father, Simon Louis studied architecture at state expense with the Swedish court architect Karl Hårleman (see HÅRLEMAN FAMILY) in Stockholm (1746–1748) and at the Academy of JACQUES FRANÇOIS BLONDEL (1748–1752), becoming thoroughly versed in theory and practice. On a study tour to Italy (1753–1756) he saw Venice, Padua, Vicenza, Florence, Rome, Naples, Pompeii, Herculaneum, Bologna, Genoa, and Turin, and trained himself by carefully studying the models of antiquity. Only in 1763, after the Seven Years War had ended, under the new Landgrave Frederick II, whose enlightened attitude was modeled on English and ancient examples, did du Ry begin his extensive building activity. This activity permanently shaped the appearance of Kassel until its destruction in World War II. In 1766, du Ry became professor of architecture at the Collegium Carolinum in Kassel. This was followed by a string of other appointments: court architect (1767), court building counselor (1776), chief building director (1785) and, finally, director of the Academy for Architec-

ture and vice-president and secretary of the Academy of Arts (1795). Together with the painter Johann Heinrich Tischbein the Elder and the sculptor Johann August Nahl, he dominated the artistic life of the city. In 1776–1777, he traveled once more to Italy, this time as the companion of the landgrave.

Simon Louis du Ry's most significant achievement was also urbanistic. Not only did he continue building the Oberneustadt begun by his grandfather, carrying it to completion in 1776—here he constructed the French Hospital (1770–1772), the Town Hall (1771–1775), several palaces for the nobility, as well as middle class houses—but furthermore, after the fortifications were razed in 1767, he also connected the Oberneustadt to the Old Town in such a way as to achieve a unified urbanistic organism. Using the street plan of the Oberneustadt as his starting point, he extended its streets toward the Old Town and designed large connecting squares between the two districts, after the fashion of the *places royales*. The plaza that ties them together is named Königsplatz in memory of Landgrave Frederick I, who was also king of Sweden. From this unified circular plaza, six streets debouch at regular intervals. The length of the entire front of the Oberneustadt facing the Old Town beyond the old glacis—now a tree-lined esplanade—determined the length of the Friedrichsplatz in a relation of two to one. This square, open on its short side toward the landscape, cleverly combined French plaza shapes with English solutions. On the long, representational side, du Ry built the Museum Friedricianum which was combined with an observatory (1769–1779). This was a nineteen-axial two-story, three-wing building with a pedimented Ionic portico in the center and flat colossal pilasters articulating the rest of the building. This façade form is a combination of French examples (JEAN FRANÇOIS DE NEUFFORGE, 1767, vol. 7, p. 462) and English-Palladian (see ANDREA PALLADIO) models (Senate House, Cambridge, by JAMES GIBBS), with its planar wall arrangement, sharp profiles, and balanced proportions in spite of the often criticized lack of a plinth. The interior disposition and furnishing (on the ground floor and in the wings collections of art, instruments, and natural objects, and a library taking up the whole of the upper floor) was a masterly development, based on Georg Mattarnovi's *Kunstkammer* in St. Petersburg (1717–1725), published in 1744, as well as on the library hall of the Palazzo dell'Istituto delle Scienze in Bologna by CARLO FRANCESCO DOTTI (1736–1756). With this first free-standing public museum, du Ry also created—apart from the Schloss Wörlitz—the first Palladian-early classicist secular building in Germany, a building which in shape and style fittingly represented its contents and intellectual purpose. Two palaces, flanking the museum but set off by tree-lined open spaces, were also erected by du Ry: the Palais Jungken (1768–1771) and the Geistliches Haus (1770–1774), each with three-axial pedimented central sections, so that the representative side of the plaza, opening vistas over the Old Town, took on a loosely rhythmical form and the museum stood out as the main building. Within the Geistliches Haus, hidden from the outside, was the Roman Catholic court church of the converted landgrave, a short, barrel-vaulted-built-on-wall-piers church combined with a two-story domed choir rotunda. In the lower story, in its wall articulation and its relation to the side rooms, it suggests a variation on the Pantheon in Rome, while the Corinthian colonnade in the upper story refers to the palace church of Versailles.

For his palace buildings, du Ry liked the U-shaped Palladian arrangement around a courtyard, where the corps-de-logis and side wings are bound together by connecting buildings, the ground-plans of which are quadrant-shaped (Schloss Hüffe, Westphalia, 1775–1784; Schloss Fürstenberg, Westphalia, 1776–1783). The plans, dating from 1786, for Schloss Weissenstein (later Wilhelmshöhe) near Kassel, are also a variant of this arrangement: the side wings which were built first (1786–1792) are set diagonally. With their masterful use of the Ionic columnar orders (with the beautiful motif of curved columned walls on the ends) they reveal the mature early classicism of Du Ry's late work, which merged English with French inspiration (ANGE JACQUES GABRIEL), as does the intentionally loose grouping of the wings to include the surrounding landscape, so typical of du Ry. It was above all in terms of proportion that he criticized the plans of his pupil, HEINRICH CHRISTOPH JUSSOW, for a monumentalized corps-de-logis for the palace—however, without success. During the expansion of Bad Hofgeismar, Hessen, he erected the simple little Palladian country seat Montcheri (1787–1788) and the Ionic monopteron over the mineral spring (1792).

Rooted in the tradition of Huguenot baroque classicism, trained in the noble rationalism of Blondel's Academy, formed by an appropriate understanding of ancient architecture, and always informed on contemporary international architecture, Simon Louis du Ry was able to adapt to existing conditions and, with a sure sense of style (which allowed him, for instance, to prevail over CLAUDE NICOLAS LEDOUX) to complete the urbanistic work of his father and grandfather. Next to Dresden and Potsdam, he made Kassel into one of the most beautiful middle-German court residence cities. He died, the last of his family, on August 23, 1799. His son, Karl, who likewise wanted to become an architect, had died two years earlier in Naples during an Italian study trip.

FRITZ-EUGEN KELLER
Translated from German by
Beverley R. Placzek

WORKS

PAUL DU RY

*1688–1714, Oberneustadt (Upper New City; not completed until later by Charles Louis du Ry and Simon Louis du Ry); *1698–1710, Karlskirche (later rebuilt), Oberneustadt; *1705?–1710?, Palace of Prince Wilhelm; 1714, Observatory (later Bellevue Palace); Kassel, Hesse, Germany.

CHARLES LOUIS DU RY

*1730, Philippsthal Palace; 1739, Canals, Oberneustadt; *1749–1751, Picture Gallery (for Wilhelm VIII; with Michael Leveilly after plans of Francois Cuvilliés); Kassel, Hesse, Germany.

SIMON LOUIS DU RY

*1768–1771, Jungken Palace (later White Palace); *1769–1779, Friedricianum Museum (later rebuilt); *1770–1772, French Hospital; *1770–1774, Geistliches Haus; *1770–1774, Saint Elisabeth's; *1771–1775, Oberneustadt Town Hall; Kassel, Hesse, Germany. 1775–1784, Schloss Hüffe, near Minden; 1776–1783, Schloss Fürstenberg; Westphalia, Germany. 1786–1792, Schloss Weissenstein (later Wilhelmshöhe; side wing), near Kassel, Hesse, Germany. 1787–1788, Schloss Montcheri; 1792, Monopteron (for a mineral spring); Hofgeismar, Hesse, Germany.

BIBLIOGRAPHY

BOEHLKE, HANS-KURT 1958 *Simon Louis du Ry als Stadtbaumeister Landgraf Friedrichs II. von Hessen Kassel.* Kassel, Germany: Bärenreiter.

BOEHLKE, HANS-KURT ET AL. 1979 "Die Städtebauliche Entwicklung Kassels." Pages 60–75, 204–205 in *Aufklärung und Klassizismus in Hessen Kassel unter Landgraf Friedrich II. 1760–1785.* Kassel, Germany: Verein für Publiktionen.

BOTH, WOLF VON, and VOGEL, HANS 1973 *Landgraf Friedrich II von Hessen-Kassel.* Munich: Deutscher Kunstverlag.

COLOMBIER, PIERRE DU 1956 Volume 1, pages 44, 83–87, 226–243 in *L'Architecture française en Allemagne au XVIIIᵉ siècle.* 2 vols. Paris: Presses Universitaires.

GERLAND, OTTO 1895 *Paul, Charles und Simon Louis du Ry. Eine Künstlerfamilie der Barockzeit.* Stuttgart, Germany: Neff.

GUTKIND, E. A. 1964 Pages 387–389 in *Urban Development in Central Europe.* London: Macmillan.

HEMPEL, EBERHARD 1965 Pages 160, 257–258 in *Baroque Art and Architecture in Central Europe.* Baltimore: Penguin.

KELLER, HARALD 1971a Pages 19–26 in *Goethe, Palladio und England.* Munich: Beck in Komm.

KELLER, HARALD 1971*b* Pages 120, 215–216, 218–219, 245–246 in *Die Kunst des 18. Jahrhunderts*. Berlin: Propyläen.

PAETOW, KARL 1929 *Klassizismus und Romantik auf Wilhelmshöhe*. Kassel, Germany: Bärenreiter.

DUTERT, CHARLES LOUIS FERDINAND

Charles Louis Ferdinand Dutert (1845–1906) was born in Douai, France. The architect of the spectacular Galerie des Machines at the Paris International Exhibition of 1889, in collaboration with the engineer VICTOR CONTAMIN, he received a conventional education at the Ecole des Beaux-Arts in Paris. There, he was the pupil of the aging LOUIS HYPPOLITE LEBAS and the more youthful Ginan. In 1869, he won the Grand Prix. Like Labrouste many years before, he subsequently became a renowned teacher at that institution. None of this prepares one for the effect produced by his above-mentioned masterpiece, the Galerie des Machines, whose 115-meter span rivals in its distinctive way the structural heroics of GUSTAVE EIFFEL's nearby tower, likewise a feature at the 1889 event. Its breathtaking dimensions (it was 420 meters in length) and its three-hinged arch structure insured its fame, even though it was torn down in 1905, after it had been reused rather unimaginatively for the 1900 Exposition.

It was the culmination of a species of metal-and-glass construction that had proliferated during the second half of the nineteenth century, its illustrious progenitors including the Palace of Industry, Paris (1855), subsequently the site of numerous *Salons,* and the sheds designed by W. H. BARLOW for Saint Pancras Station, London, built in the 1860s. Significantly, no subsequent fair sought to exceed its dimensions and unified spatial effect. Thus, the Dutert-Contamin Galerie marked, in its fashion, the end of an era in construction, their building a brontosaurus marked for extinction. It is thus ironic if nonetheless appropriate that critics have included this building as a key monument in the history (or prehistory) of modern architecture. This is all the more paradoxical since its vast scale, realizable only through new technical methods, represented in a limited way a belated realization of ETIENNE LOUIS BOULLÉE's gigantesque neoclassic visions of vaulted halls in a different, even antithetical style. Dutert's career was largely centered on this one spectacular achievement, a typical phenomenon in the lives of nineteenth-century French architects, CHARLES GARNIER and his Opéra being an especially famous instance.

The Galerie des Machines was so vast that it was deemed necessary to install a kind of elevated railroad, a *pont roulant,* so that spectators could gain a literal overview of the spectacle before plunging into a detailed examination of the exhibits on the floor. However successful it was as a spacious construction and as a home for its indus-

Dutert.
Galerie des Machines, Paris
International Exhibition.
1889

trial exhibits, Dutert's building seemed to have no further purpose. In 1900, an ornate *salle des fêtes* of vast proportions was improvised within a mere portion of the Galerie! After that it was destined to be scrapped since the relatively modest proportions of the Grand and the Petit Palaces, constructed for the Exhibition of 1900, proved more manageable for quotidian exhibition needs. Inevitably, Dutert's subsequent work was anticlimactic, although the new galleries that he constructed for the Paris Museum of Natural History in 1896 are significant for their exposed metal structure and a decorative system based upon the forms of plants and animals.

JOHN JACOBUS

DUTHOIT, EDMOND

Edmond Duthoit (1837–1889) was a protégé of EUGÈNE EMMANUEL VIOLLET-LE-DUC in whose office he began his career designing neomedieval interiors for châteaux inspired by Napoleon III's Château de Pierrefonds. Early Christian, Byzantine, and even Arab motifs, culled from his 1861 trip to Cyprus, Sicily, and Syria and from Algeria where he headed the Commission des Monuments Historiques from 1872, are united in his major building: the pilgrimage basilica at Albert, France.

BARRY BERGDOLL

WORKS

c.1860–1870, Château de Chamousset, Saint Laurent de Chamousset, Rhône, France. 1862–1865, Church for the *Ophelinat Français;* 1862–1865, Church of the Capuchins; Beirut. 1864–1870, Château of Roquetaillade (continuation of the restoration and interiors begun by Eugène Emmanuel Viollet-Le-Duc), Mazères, Gironde, France. c.1864–1879, Château d'Arragori (d'Abbadia) (begun by Viollet-Le-Duc), Bidassoa, near Hendaye, Basses-Pyrénées, France. c.1867, Fountain, Waddington Estate, Neuilly-Saint-Front, Aisne, France. c.1878, Church, Champeaux, Deux-Sèvres, France. *c.1879, Chapelle des Cathechismes, Saint Jacques Church, Amiens, France. 1880–1884, Church, Bryas; c.1883, Church, Souverain-Moulin; Pas de Calais, France. 1884–1889, Notre Dame-de-Brebières (completed in 1896 by Henri Bernard and Louis Duthoit), Albert, Somme, France.

BIBLIOGRAPHY

BERGDOLL, BARRY 1979 "The Architecture of Edmond-Armand-Marie Duthoit, 1837–1889." Unpublished Ph.D. dissertation, Cambridge University.

BERGDOLL, BARRY 1982 "The Synthesis of All I Have Seen: The Architecture of Edmond Duthoit, 1837–1889." Pages 216–249 in Robin Middleton (editor), *The Beaux-Arts: Architecture and Attitudes.* London: Thames & Hudson.

Edmond Duthoit architecte, 1837–1889. 1890 Amiens, France: Privately printed.

MIDDLETON, ROBIN, and WATKIN, DAVID 1977 *Neoclassical and 19th Century Architecture.* New York: Abrams.

PHILADELPHIA MUSEUM OF ART 1978 *The Second Empire: Art in France under Napoleon III.* Philadelphia: The museum.

VOGÜE, M. DE 1865–1877 *Syrie Centrale: Architecture civile et religieuse; du Ier au VIIe siècle.* 2 vols. Paris: Noblet & Baudry.